THE SLINGS & ARROWS
COMIC GUIDE

THE SLINGS & ARROWS
COMIC GUIDE

Editor: Frank Plowright

AURUM PRESS

First published in Great Britain
1997 by Aurum Press Ltd
25 Bedford Avenue, London WC1B 3AT

Design by Hassan Yusuf

A catalogue record of this book is available from the British Library.

ISBN 1 85410 486 1

2001 2000 1999 1998 1997
10 9 8 7 6 5 4 3 2 1

Printed in Finland
by WSOY

CONTENTS

INTRODUCTION

Comics have been published in the USA since the 1930s, and are considered, alongside jazz, as an indigenous American art form. Once seen as disposable entertainment, they are now, as with anything of sustained cultural appeal, hugely collectable; indeed they can, if only in rare cases, be regarded as investments. The graphic-novel boom and the high profile accorded to projects such as *Maus* and *Dark Knight Returns* (poles apart in style and content) made millions aware that there are comics for adults – though this isn't to deride the titles intended for children. It's an insecure adult reader who can't enjoy *Uncle Scrooge* or *Asterix*. Most large English-speaking cities have at least one shop dedicated to comics and affiliated items. It's odd, then, that the only comic guides available primarily concern themselves with the perceived monetary value of comics, although they do include a great deal of additional information and trivia. The aim of *The Slings and Arrows Comic Guide* is to present the first widespread qualitative guide to comics published for the American market from the 1930s to the present day. It's the hope of the reviewers that everyone who buys this book will be rewarded by discovering at least one excellent series they'd previously overlooked or not heard of.

This volume doesn't review every comic ever printed. There are quite a few reasons for this, not the least being space limitations. Beyond that the comics of the 1930s, 1940s and 1950s were sold to a market that almost exclusively considered them as disposable items. The publishers' policy was to produce a quick read: standards were generally very low. Despite huge print runs, few copies exist today and the cost of those that do is prohibitive; therefore only the better-quality material from that era has been included. Other exclusions are comics produced for pre-teens, the plethora of home-produced black and white titles that flooded the market during the 1980s, collections of single-tier-gag newspaper strips, promotional and give-away material, and adaptations of films and TV series. The exception, in all instances, is if a comic possesses particular artistic merit.

What the guide does include is most comics published by major publishers from the late 1950s onwards, and anything of note from smaller companies. The majority of the titles covered were read and reviewed during 1996 to allow a contemporary perspective. The text encompasses comics up to those cover-dated December 1996, occasionally slipping into early 1997 in cases of short-run series.

Although comics are a world-wide phenomenon, we've chosen to concentrate on English-language comics produced specifically for the American market. There's enough European material to merit a separate volume: let's hope someone gets around to it one day.

Finally, there are going to be errors in this guide. Whether they're typos or mistakes, we hope they've been reduced to a minimum. Wherever possible we've attempted to verify information ourselves, largely through reference to original sources, and this will account for some discrepancies between this and other publications. In cases where we're just plain wrong, though, please let us know care of the publishers' address, so that any future editions can be corrected.

ACKNOWLEDGEMENTS

Thanks are due to the following people for letting us dig into their collections: without them this guide would have been a much poorer book, not to mention incomplete: Simon Baker, Dewi Black, Malcolm Bourne, Lee Brimmicombe-Wood, Mark Buckingham, Phil Clarke, Andy Clow, Mike Conroy, Simon Curran, Allan Harvey, Emma Hull, Niall Gordon, John Freeman, Dave Gibbons, Duncan Lang, John McShane, Ruth Pankhurst, David Pardoe, Peter C. Phillips, Peter Rubinstein, Chris Savva, Andrew Sweeney, Dave Thomas, Dean Whittaker and Win Wiacek. Thanks also to John Higgins, Karen Ings, Sheila Murphy, Michael Paul and Frank Quitely, all of whom have contributed to this book.

Thanks are also due to Chris Bleistein at Kitchen Sink, Ruth Cole at Titan, Charlie Novinskie at Topps, Chris Pape of Slave Labor, and Eric Reynolds at Fantagraphics. They're oases of good sense in a desert of publishers who couldn't give a damn.

Special thanks are due to the following retailers who have been generous enough to lend comics they might have sold while in our hands. They've been unfailingly helpful when asked to search their entire stock for specific comics, or to let us do the same, and in supplying, out of the blue, comics that had been eluding us for months. We can vouch for the wide selection of hard-to-find comics available in these shops; without their assistance and generosity this guide wouldn't have been possible:

Bob Napier of High Impact Comics, Forbidden Planet, 2 Teviot Place, Edinburgh EH1
Peter Root of City Centre Comics, at Forbidden Planet, 168 Buchanan Street, Glasgow G1
Paul Hudson of Comics Showcase, 76 Neal Street, London WC2
Rob Rudderham of 30th Century Comics, 1st Floor Putney Market, Putney Exchange Shopping Centre, Putney High St, London SW15

PUBLICATIONS CONSULTED

Amazing Heroes (assorted issues)
Amazing Heroes Preview Special (assorted issues)
Comic Book Marketplace (assorted issues)
The Comic Book Price Guide, Duncan McAlpine, Titan, various editions
The Comic Reader (assorted issues)
Comics Forum (assorted issues)
Comics International (assorted issues)
The Comics Journal (assorted issues)
DC Archive Editions, DC, various editions
Dictionnaire Mondial de la Bande Dessinée, Patrick Gaumer & Claude Moliterni, Larousse, 1994
The Encyclopedia of Comic Book Heroes, Volume 1 – Batman, Michael L. Fleisher, Collier Books, 1976
Graphic Story Monthly (assorted issues)
A History Of Underground Comics, Mark James Estren, Ronin Press, 1993
Krazy Kat: The Comic Art Of George Herriman, Patrick McDonnell, Karen O'Connell & Georgia Riley de Havenon, Abrams, 1986
The Mad World Of William M. Gaines, Frank Jacob, Lyle Stuart, 1972
The Marvel Comics Indexes, George Olshevsky, 1975–1981
Nemo (assorted issues)
The Overstreet Comic Book Price Guide, Robert Overstreet, various editions
The Panelhouse (assorted issues)
Popeye: The 60th Anniversary Collection, Mike Higgs, Hawk Books, 1989
Speakeasy (assorted issues)
The Steranko History Of Comics Vols 1 & 2, Jim Steranko, 1970 & 1972
Tintin, Harry Thompson, Sceptre 1992
Two Decades Of Comics, Slings & Arrows 1980
Uncle Scrooge: His Life And Times, Carl Barks & Edward Summer, Celestial Arts 1987
Whizzard (assorted issues)
Wizard (assorted issues)
The World Encyclopedia Of Comics, Maurice Horn, NEL 1976
Plus essays and interviews accompanying the EC boxed sets published by Russ Cochran

HOW TO USE THE GUIDE

Definition of entries

It's long been a tradition that comics named after people such as Katy Keene are listed in trade publications under Katy, and we stick with that. There are also cases where the exact title of a comic is uncertain, conflicting versions being on the cover and the first-page indicia. Our solution is simple but effective: the title is the largest lettering on the logo. As always, though, there are exceptions. One is *Marvel Premiere*, the home for dozens of different features, many for no more than a single issue and each with its own logo printed in larger type than the words 'Marvel Premiere'. For cases like this there's an appendix on page 676 advising where to locate assorted one-offs and features from umbrella titles. In cases of one-shot superhero team-ups, the relevant reviews are listed under the first-named character in the title.

Multiple series with the same title and the same feature from the same publisher are covered under one entry, so you'll find all volumes of *Elementals* together. Properties from outside comics are generally only licensed to publishers for a limited period. As each successive publisher has different editorial approaches and creators there are separate entries for such licensed titles – *Tarzan* and *Star Trek*, for instance – each time they change publisher. These are listed in chronological order. Creator-owned properties switching publisher, such as *Madman* or *Cud*, are only allocated the single entry that befits a consistent creative vision. Limited series are generally allocated a separate entry, but if they have a parent title or spawn an ongoing series there'll only be the single entry. Likewise, multiple miniseries featuring the same characters are gathered under the one entry.

Graphic novels are the hardest items to categorise. Those titled after characters already given an entry – such as *She-Hulk* – are covered in that entry. The exceptions are characters such as Batman who star in multiple graphic novels; in these cases a separate entry has been allocated, as it has been for characters best known from an ongoing series of graphic novels such as *Corto Maltese* or *Tintin*. Beyond that, the simplest manner of covering other graphic novels has been to include them in an entry allocated to the publisher's imprint: DC, Catalan, Comcat, Eclipse, Epic, Fantagraphics, Heavy Metal, Kitchen Sink, Knockabout, Marvel, NBM, Piranha Press and Vertigo. The occasional one-off graphic novel from publishers that don't generally deal with such material, like *The Cowboy Wally Show*, is given a separate entry.

Ordering of entries

In cases where a character occupies multiple comics with slight variations of title they're largely to be found in the same general area. The largest lettering on the cover is considered the title portion and capitalised, while for purposes of identification the remainder of the title is in upper and lower case. Entries are ordered according to the capitalised portion of the title, and titles with identical upper-case portions are ordered according to the remaining mixed-case words. *SUPERMAN* therefore precedes *Adventures Of SUPERMAN*, which in turn precedes *SUPERMAN ADVENTURES*. Numeric titles such as *22 Brides* are ordered as if spelled out, and for purposes of easy location acronymic titles such as *M.A.C.H. One* are also treated as if spelled out. Again, for ease of location, titles featuring the contractions 'Dr', 'Mr', or 'St' are filed under 'Doctor', 'Mister' and 'Saint' respectively. Titles with two or more words will precede all single-word titles starting with the same letters, so *Black Hood* will be found before *Blackball*.

Components of entries

Below the title the publisher is listed, followed by the number of issues plus any annuals, specials or giant-size issues, and years of publication. Where the run doesn't start with 1 – which is most commonly due to continuing the numbering of another title or to zero-numbered issues – issue numbers are noted in parentheses: '43 issues (41–83)'. Short gaps in publication are ignored, but a large gap is noted together with the split in issue numbers and range of years: '1–14 (1967–1968), 15–32 (1970–1972)'. In the case of titles ongoing as of December 1996 the number of issues is followed by a '+' sign. If there's no cover date the publication date noted is that printed in the indicia. The text of each review is followed by the initials of the reviewer.

Recommended issues

There's a wealth of recommended comics here, many of which will be filling your local comic shop's discount boxes. The choice of recommended issues will occasionally be controversial, with accepted classics neglected and previous non-contenders reappraised. It amounts to personal choice, although a guiding principle was that this isn't intended to be an élitist selection. In terms of artistic achievement and literary qualities an issue of *Love and Rockets* is clearly a greater work than most *Spider-Man* comics, yet on a different level there's plenty to enjoy in *Spider-Man*, and we therefore recommend issues of both. The criterion for recommendation was to assess how a particular issue had achieved what it set out to do, with only the best being recommended. The best issue of an abysmal run is never listed by default, only if it matches better issues of similar comics. Inversely, with titles of exceptional quality throughout perfectly acceptable issues may not be listed simply because they fail to match the high standards attained by other issues in the run. It's usually only issues containing original material that are recommended. Plenty of comics, often starring Disney characters, have continued by reprinting stories up to four times during the run. We felt it less likely to confuse if just the original received a recommendation, although the reprints will obviously be easier to find. The exceptions are anthology titles gathering reprints from hither and yon, or titles reprinting material almost impossible to obtain in original form, such as *The Spirit* or *Little Nemo*.

Collections

Wherever possible we've attempted to list collected editions of material, which should prove easier to locate than piecing together runs of comics. Not all collections listed are still in print, although a large proportion are. It should also be noted that some collections may not have been available outside the UK, predominantly some material licensed from DC and Marvel and published by Titan and Boxtree respectively.

TERMINOLOGY

The creative process – Comics feature a bewildering array of credits for the creators. Generally a person credited as '**writer**' has conceived and written the story, although until the 1960s it was commonplace for editors to suggest plots and assign them to writers. Since the 1960s it's usual for comics to be produced under what's come to be known as Marvel Style, involving the writer passing a plot to the **pencil artist**, who'll then interpret the plot to fit the required amount of pages. Otherwise a writer will produce a full script – resembling a film script – complete with a precise description of what's to be conveyed in every panel. If the writing is a collaborative process there will often be separate credits for the person who conceived the story (credited for **plot**), and the person who writes the contents of the word balloons (credited for **dialogue**).

The artwork for ongoing titles is generally a collaboration between a **penciller** and an **inker**, born of the necessity to meet a monthly publication deadline. The penciller will decide how to break down each page (if just given a plot), then draw the story in pencil, depicting all necessary elements. The pencilled pages will then be passed to an inker, who will draw over the pencilled artwork in black ink as required for reproduction. Inkers can determine the final look of a page of artwork, and each will interpret a pencilled page in a different fashion. Occasionally an artist with a distinctive style will produce **layouts**, a further shortening of the creative process. These will be rough sketches for the pencil artist to follow.

A **letterer** is the person who actually writes all text in legible style, although it's increasingly common to use specifically developed computer packages today. The same applies to colouring. Traditionally the **colourist** filled copies of the inked pages, but today they're more likely to produce guides for computer colouring. **Designers** are becoming more prevalent as well, particularly with regard to graphic novels and collections, although many comics also have a distinctive design these days. The **editor** oversees the creative process from conception to completion.

Anime – Japanese animation.

Bad Girl Art – A 1990s equivalent of Good Girl Art (q.v.): a plethora of violent scantily-clad females with attitude bursting out all over.

The Comics Code – A self-regulating method of designating comics as wholesome which was introduced in 1954 with the threat of Congressional investigation hanging over the comics industry. The prominent application of the Code stamp on the cover of a comic provided assurance to parents that the contents conformed to a stringent set of guidelines. It was once essential to ensure the distribution of comics, but nowadays only titles from larger companies distributed to news-stands continue to carry the stamp (at about an eighth of its original size).

Continuity – Ongoing plot elements continuing from issue to issue in the manner of TV soap opera. This was introduced to comics in the 1960s; it's now rare to have stories complete in one issue.

Crossover – When a story from one title is continued in another. In recent years four monthly Batman titles and four monthly Superman titles have been essentially used as weekly editions of the same comic. Since the 1980s DC titles feature an annual event affecting all their characters (*Crisis On Infinite Earths*, *Millennium*, *Zero Hour* and *Underworld Unleashed*, to name some).

The Golden Age – Term coined for 1940s superhero comics by 1950s comic fans nostalgically looking back through rose-coloured glasses at material that was largely poorly executed and predictable.

Good Girl Art – Most prevalent in the 1940s and 1950s as artists tended to over-emphasise female attributes and provide provocative poses.

Graphic Novel – Basically a big comic. Usually a self-contained story of forty-eight pages or longer like *Asterix* and *Tintin*, but often also applied to collections of previously serialised material.

Limited Series – Title planned as a self-contained story of pre-determined length – upwards of six issues.

Logo – Artistically distinctive title lettering.

Manga – Name applied to a form of comics in Japan, but generally used as a term for all Japanese comic material outside Japan.

Microseries – Two-issue self-contained story.

Miniseries – Title planned as a self-contained short-run story, usually of three to six issues.

One-shot – Individual issue with self-contained story.

The Silver Age – If the Golden Age was that of the 1940s superhero comics, the natural successor is rather an elastic term that can begin with the arrival of Martian Manhunter in *Detective Comics* in 1955. It's more commonly acknowledged to start with *Showcase*'s revival of The Flash a year later, but can stretch to encompass superhero comics up to the late 1960s.

Underground – The 1960s counterculture found comics a cheaply produced and effective way of communicating ideas, and a medium that had been the exclusive province of the major publishers was suddenly host to a wide variety of new talent and adult topics.

Zero issues – In the early 1990s companies went through a phase of issuing comics numbered 0, often to introduce a new title. DC's reorganisation of their universe in *Zero Hour* was followed by every title reverting to issue 0 and providing an origin story for new readers with their comics cover-dated October 1994.

Imprints and publishers

Several companies have used several imprints, usually to distinguish a selection of titles differing from their traditional output, so the company of origin isn't immediately apparent from the name. Listed below are imprints together with the name most regularly associated with their parent companies. In the case of companies still existing today we're using the current publishing name.

Adventure = Malibu
Aircel = Malibu
Armada = Acclaim
Amaze Ink = Slave Labor
Atlas (pre-1962) = Marvel
Big Bang = Caliber
Bravura = Malibu
CX = Fantagraphics
Epic = Marvel
Eros = Fantagraphics
Eternity = Malibu
Fanny = Knockabout
FX = Eclipse
Gauntlet = Caliber
Hard Boiled = Fantagraphics
Helix = DC
Iconographix = Caliber

!mpact = DC
Krupp = Kitchen Sink
Malibu (post-1994) = Marvel
Mighty Comics = Archie
Monster Comics = Fantagraphics
Next = Mirage
Red Circle = Archie
Star = Marvel
Tekno = Big Entertainment
Timely (became) Marvel
Tome = Caliber
Ultraverse = Malibu
Upshot = Fantagraphics
Valiant = Acclaim
Vertigo = DC
Windjammer = Valiant
Zongo = Bongo

NOTES ON THE CONTRIBUTORS

DWC – Dave Cutler wrote some witty commentaries almost twenty years ago, never considering that they'd one day be resuscitated for professional publication.

FC – Fiona Clements was beyond childhood on discovering comics, but compensated for a lack of previous experience with a thorough immersion. She's co-editor and sometimes publisher of *Comics Forum*.

JC – Jennifer Cole has contributed to several comics-related Amateur Press Alliances, and currently pays for her standing orders at the comic shop by editing a *Star Trek* part-work.

NF – Nigel Fletcher is co-editor of *The Panelhouse*, a highly regarded quarterly comics-related magazine for the reader with broad tastes.

FJ – Fiona Jerome's trenchant commentary has been a feature of comics publications for years, and she currently edits the national magazine *Bizarre*.

WJ – William Jobbie was a freelance music journalist before being a foreign correspondent. Now back in the UK, he's delighted at combining critical writing with his first love, comics.

GK – Gerard Kingdon is a hopeless drunk whose professional involvement in comics amounts to making tea for a couple of pals who used to submit the odd bit to *Deadline*.

AL – Andrew Littlefield has contributed interviews, articles and reviews about comics to numerous publications, including *The Comics Journal*, *FA*, *The Panelhouse* and *Amazing Heroes*.

GL – Guy Lawley is on the board of the Comics Creators Guild, and also co-edits the Guild's magazine *Comics Forum*.

FP – Frank Plowright co-organises the UK Comic Art Convention. He's spent many years masquerading as a writer, including a stint as British correspondent for *The Comics Journal*.

TP – Tim Pilcher once had an editorial position in the British office of DC's adult-oriented comics line Vertigo, but these days applies his editorial talents to educational CD-Roms.

DAR – David Roach has an encyclopaedic appreciation of comics history and trivia, while his meticulous artwork has graced *Batman*, *Judge Dredd* and several lesser-known titles.

APS – Adrian Snowdon is possibly the world's greatest authority on *Spider-Man* comics, but thankfully applies a fine intellect to many topics beyond.

HS – Howard Stangroom is co-editor of *Comics Forum*, the journal of The Comics Creators Guild, an organisation for which he's also served on the board.

SS – Sunil Singhvi is a good decade younger than all other *Guide* contributors, and brings a freshness and enthusiasm lacking in his companions, tired and cynical old hacks all.

SW – Steve Whitaker is a respected colourist, with credits for all major publishers. It's less known that he's also a talented artist and writer, and a repository of recondite information of all kinds.

HY – Hassan Yusuf spent several years at Marvel Comics before a career in magazines. He co-organises Britain's only annual comic convention, the UK Comic Art Convention.

A1
Atomeka Press: *6 issues, 1 Special 1989–1992*
Epic/Atomeka Press: *4 issues 1992–1993*

A1 allowed a lot of class artists to let off steam, sometimes without a writer in tow, and published some corking stories alongside the resultant indulgences, which were always great to look at. Where else will you find Glenn Fabry writing and drawing a modern story of street life ('Bricktop' in 1–6)? Encouraging more mainstream creators to experiment was part of the remit: Barry Windsor-Smith submitted loose black and white strips, and Moebius was notable among other contributors. The first issue started auspiciously with Ted McKeever and Dave Gibbons each writing a story for the other to illustrate, and Pete Milligan and Brendan McCarthy's experimental collage about a child molester sitting next to a wacky Bob Burden Flaming Carrot strip. A similar willingness to mix and match on the part of editors Dave Elliott and Garry Leach prevailed throughout.

The emphasis was on British creators; there are a lot of strips from *Warrior* ('Father Shandor', Warpsmiths, 'Bojeffries Saga') in the first series and *Deadline* (Tank Girl, Cheeky Wee Budgie Boy) in the second. Sexy fantasy stories by Leach and Bolland, particularly in the Bikini Confidential Special, rub shoulders with serious drama, comedy and slice-of-life tales. Although it's lacking in direction at times it's a pleasure to see so many great names in one place, rarely doing what you expect of them. Series one was in black and white, while the Epic volumes were in colour.~FJ
Recommended: Series one 1, 3, Special

A.A.R.G.H.
Mad Love: *One-shot 1988*

A benefit comic intended to raise funds to combat anti-gay legislation. The acronym stands for Artists Against Rampant Government Homophobia, and the list of contributors is stellar – Neil Gaiman, Frank Miller, Alan Moore, Bill Sienkiewicz, Dave Sim and a cast of thousands. Unfortunately the stories tend to be painfully earnest (Moore), or suspectly flippant and dismissive (Miller's 'Robohomophobe'). Still, most readers will find something of interest.~HS

A & D Armed Dangerous
Acclaim: *4-issue miniseries 1996–1997*

'I can do that,' thought Bob Hall after a glance at *Sin City*, and indeed he can. Not as well, though. Charly Donovan is a washed-out drunken ex-gangster who inadvertently becomes involved in a gang war. It prompts some old questions Donovan had previously ignored by finding refuge in a bottle, and resolves itself in suitably violent fashion. Hall marks out similar territory to *Sin City* with the loser forced to fight against his will. There's plenty of variations on that story, so it's a shame that he's elected to draw in an approximation of Frank Miller's stark contrasting black and white style. He lacks Miller's sense of design and dynamics, and while his writing is good enough why buy *A & D* when the real thing is so much better at the same price?~WJ

ABC WARRIORS
Fleetway/Quality: *8 issues 1990–1991*

Atomic, Bacterial and Chemical are the ABC forms of warfare that the robot warriors were able to resist where humans faltered. The team are gathered during the Volgon War, and they're an eccentric bunch, none more so than the mystical Deadlock, combining spells and steel. Originally serialised in five-page episodes in *2000AD*, when collected together the lack of any developing plot is a glaring fault. Luckily, the largely inventive scripts of Pat Mills ensure individual episodes remain memorable, and the first four issues serve as a showcase for almost all the artists working regularly on *2000AD* in the late 1970s. Mike McMahon and Kevin O'Neill shine above the remainder, with McMahon's chunky stylings and O'Neill's more angular work suiting the mood equally well. Other artists of note include Carlos Ezquerra, Dave Gibbons and Brendan McCarthy. By *2000AD*'s third run of ABC Warriors, serialised from the end of 4, Mills plotted the entire story in advance, and the greater cohesiveness and a fixed destination make for a more satisfying read. It features the first comics work of Simon Bisley, although the other artist used, SMS, is generally overlooked and actually better suits the tone. In the end, though, the shoddy printing ensures that everything looks terrible. The Titan volumes reprinting the early stories are the best place to see *ABC Warriors* outside the original issues of *2000AD*.~WJ

Collections: *ABC Warriors* Vol (1–2), Vol 2 (3–4) Vol 3 (5–6), Vol 4 (7–8)

ABOMINATIONS

Marvel: *3-issue miniseries 1996–1997*

Hulk-free sequel to his 'Future Imperfect' microseries by Ivan Velez Jr and Angel Medina. In the wake of the Maestro's departure a decaying Abomination rises to take the tyrant's throne, motivating some of the Outlaws to escape to our present. Inevitably, they face off with the current Abomination. Everyone and his brother has an attitude and it is all too cute for its own good.~APS

ABRAHAM STONE

Platinum: *1 graphic novel 1991*
Epic: *2 issues 1995*

In the graphic novel Abraham Stone leaves his rural homeland to seek his destiny in New York. Since this is the century's second decade his experiences of getting to grips with city life manage to include a fair amount of violence, especially since he's looking for the criminals that killed his family. In doing so he becomes an enforcer for a local mobster, eventually moving closer to the person who ordered his parents' execution.

The Epic volumes are traditional comic size, and see Abraham bedding a rich woman who takes him to Hollywood, where he gets involved in the early days of the movie industry, in 1, and becoming an unwilling part of Pancho Villa's revolution in 2. Abraham looks out for himself first, and is all too easily cajoled into illicit activities, but he retains a nobility and sense of justice that sees him through to the other side. Written and drawn by Joe Kubert, it's well up to standard artistically with Kubert evoking a strong period flavour in all issues, but equally all issues could have used a tighter script.~NF

The ABYSS

Dark Horse: *2-issue miniseries 1989*

Film adaptation notable for Mike Kaluta's art. Unfortunately his usually decorative and well designed pages are muted by the necessity of multiple-talking-heads panels. The special effects endowed the movie with an eerie splendour, and lacking them the script's resemblance to a 1950s B-movie is highlighted.~FP

Collection: *The Abyss* (1–2)

AC ANNUAL

Americomics: *4 issues, 1991–1994*

Expanded adventures of AC's *Femforce* and their supporting heroes and villains. That's all there is to say really. Go on to the next entry. Or look up *Deadbeats*, which is rather good.~HS

ACE

Harrier: *One-shot 1987*

The pick of Eddie Campbell's earliest comic work, done for the fun of it, documenting the adventures of attendees at the Ace Rock And Roll Club, a 1950s revival hang-out in Southend. Stories don't get much more kitchen-sink than 'If Monkeys Could Fly', in which a girl recounts how she may have become pregnant and considers an abortion, and while the art is sometimes rough in places, the writing is among Campbell's best.~FJ

Recommended: 1

ACES HIGH

EC: *5 issues 1955*

Aces High is a comic about the rather limited subject of World War I flying aces which, after only five issues, was clearly running out of creative direction. The artists and writers faced several problems, not least finding ways to introduce American characters to stories set in France. Visually, while there is some stunning artwork, particularly from George Evans, it proved difficult to make the multiple dogfights that comprised the bulk of the action look different from story to story. The issues followed a similar pattern, opening with a visually accurate Evans story with beautiful artwork, followed by a story illustrated by Wally Wood, which usually had less fights and more characterisation. Even so this is obviously not Wood's favourite subject matter and some of the figure work looks rushed. Bernie Krigstein looked most out of place in the line-up, cluttering his art as if trying to ape Evans and Wood's level of intricacy. It doesn't suit him, although the writers have obviously tried to accommodate his strengths and supply him with more character-based stories such as 'Revenge' in 1 and 'The Mascot' in 2. Finally Jack Davis, again drawing in a slightly more detailed style than one associates with him, would round out the issue with a quirky shock story like issue 5's 'Iron Man', about a seemingly invulnerable fighter who doesn't realise he's a ghost. Davis' broader line and robust approach to story-telling added a much-needed vigour.

Although lovely to look at, it's clear Evans would have happily illustrated the same basic story until the cows came home. In 1's lead story, 'The Way It Was', an old man reminisces to his grandchildren about how fine and chivalrous fighting was in the old days, and how the air aces subscribed to a forgotten code of conduct which was transgressed at their peril. It's repeated time and again ('Chivalry!' in 2, 'Footnote' in 3). Evans does get to draw the best story in the run, 'The Green Kids' in 4, in which a squadron leader, sickened by the way young pilots with almost no experience were supplied as aerial cannon fodder, continually harangues his commanding officer, who seems cold and distant. When appointed to replace him he discovers that he had been futilely battling for the same ends. Generally, *Aces High* soft-pedals the 'awfulness of war' angle for which Kurtzman's earlier titles became justly famous, and here the idea is refreshing. Ultimately, beautifully drawn but few stories worth reading.~FJ

Collection: Aces High (1–5)

ACME NOVELTY LIBRARY

Fantagraphics: *7 issues + 1993 to date*

Chris Ware's *Acme Novelty Library* is an astounding publication, presenting comics that engage the intellect, and managing from the first issue to do so in an accessible manner, thus succeeding where *Raw* failed. It's also arguably the first comic to move the medium forward since the undergrounds of the 1960s, yet keeps a clear eye on the past. Ware employs a regular cast including an archaic representation of a robot, an aged superhero archetype (sometimes presented as God), a hapless rural character dominated by his father, and Jimmy Corrigan, the smartest kid on Earth. Seen as child, adult and old man, the appellation is a cruelly capricious label, as Corrigan's strip, described in 5 as 'an attempt to accurately counterfeit the mechanism of mundanity', portrays him as the loneliest and most pitiful person seen in comics. Occupying a spartanly furnished apartment, dreaming of dating his co-workers, his only social interaction is frequent phone calls from his mother. Ware's very dark humour puts his character through the grinder and an optimistic childhood becomes a lonely adult life punctuated by brief bursts of aspiration, always unfulfilled. The very epitome of the person who's always worse off than you are, Corrigan's incessantly depressed existence and hangdog face can't help but induce laughter. Quimby The Mouse is also remarkable, a 1930s-style cartoon mouse going about his business in an enormous series of intricate, minute panels, encompassed within a far larger design. Echoing the tomfoolery of *Krazy Kat*, Quimby's existence is also solitary and troublesome, and is the focus of 2 and 4. This all makes *Acme Novelty Library* sound depressing, when in fact it's riotously funny if you're of a cruel-humoured disposition.

Ware's art is astounding. With what is on the surface a clear and simple line, his ability to portray a full range of emotions within this style is remarkable, and his frequent bleak land- and cityscapes, intended to convey isolation, are surprisingly edifying. His skill as a designer is even more impressive, with each issue meticulously pieced together and living up to the novelty aspect of the title. Only the first resembles the traditional comic format. 2 and 4 are each over a foot high, with 7 standing a full 18 inches, while Jimmy Corrigan's reconciliation with his father in 5 and 6 is presented in two small pocket-sized landscape editions. 3 is a slightly larger portrait variation.

The comics are rounded out with ludicrously formally phrased (and very funny) nonsensical articles and fake ads, and intricately designed cut-out models of the type that might have been presented had there been comics in the Victorian era. This would be mere whimsical window-dressing elsewhere, but the archaic and convoluted language and formality of address bestow a cohesive substance to the entire package. Collections would prove troublesome, and are superfluous when each innovatively designed issue stands alone as a worthy artefact.~FP

Recommended: 1–7

ACTION Comics

DC: *728 issues +, 4 Annuals 1938 to date*

Action Comics 1 is clearly the most important comic ever published, defining the entire future of the American comics industry and creating a new genre in the superpowered crimefighter. Editor Vincent Sullivan made a bold decision in allocating the cover of his new title to a feature rejected by several other comic companies and newspaper syndicates. It was, of course, Superman, created by Jerry Siegel and Joe Shuster. While he may not have been the first skintight-costumed character in comics, he was the first to lift a car over his head and smash it, and his position as an idealised version of what we'd all like to be struck an instant chord. Comics were certainly different in 1938 and for ten cents you got your money's worth. In addition to Superman the first issue included two black and white strips, one a Western strip titled 'Chuck Dawson', the other 'Scoop Scanlon Five Star Reporter'. Additionally in colour there were the adventures of Marco Polo, a cartoon strip, Bernard Bailey's 'Tex Thomson', adventurer, who would have a long run under various names, and 'Pep Morgan', a boxer by Fred Guardineer. 'Zatara The Master Magician' rounded out the issue, again by Guardineer, and probably inspired by Mandrake the Magician, to whom he bore more than a passing resemblance. What differed him, though, was that he would recite his spells backwards! He was later better known as father of Zatanna, who inherited his abilities.

Contrary to current wisdom, the comics of the 1930s weren't all simplistic, and *Action* contained well plotted material. In his first appearance Superman must stop an execution, confront a wife beater, and almost becomes involved in political corruption. Siegel's plotting is tight, and Shuster's art, while perhaps a little crude, is very dramatic, and it's easy to see why this strip was a hit from day one. It contained large portions of the legend that remain today. Lois Lane appears in the first story, admiring Superman, but despising his timid *alter ego* Clark Kent. She's gutsy from the off, and Kent's persona is also well established as he begins working at *The Daily Star* (changed to *The Daily Planet* in 23). By all accounts this was an extremely high-selling comic, but DC didn't appear to realise this was due to Superman, who wasn't cover-featured again until 7, but from 9 either his name or image was presented, and from 19 there was no doubt who was the star of the comic. 6 introduced an office-boy generally thought to be the first appearance of Jimmy Olsen. Superman's career as a journalist sees off Scoop Scanlon from 13, and Lex Luthor débuts in 23, oddly with a shock of red hair, although he does have a bald assistant. He'd not be seen again here until 42.

1940s Superman stories were strictly Earthbound, often initiated by Clark Kent's newspaper career, although his enemies were initially gangsters, then largely humans with a gimmick such as the Prankster and Toyman, introduced in 51 and 64 respectively. The former in particular proved more popular at first than Lex Luthor, and it wasn't until the 1950s that the bald evil genius was beefed up into Superman's pre-eminent foe. Like most other superheroes, Superman played a large part in the war effort, fighting home-front saboteurs and Nazis abroad. The most notoriously jingoistic result of the conflict was 58's cover proclaiming 'You Can Slap A Jap', and Superman putting up posters saying so.

Assorted back-up features replaced those from the first issue over time, with 23, 33, 37, 40 and 42 seeing the débuts of the Black Pirate, Mr America (actually Tex Thomson, who would further become the Americommando in 51), Congo Bill, The Star-Spangled Kid and the Vigilante respectively. Congo Bill lasted well in to the 1950s, eventually as the giant golden gorilla Congorilla, and in lasting to 86 the Star-Spangled Kid turned convention on its head by having an adult sidekick Stripsey. Often drawn by the expressive Mort Meskin, it was the Vigilante who was the quality act, replacing Shelly Moldoff's Black Pirate and

running until 198. Country singer ('Prairie Troubadour') Greg Sanders had a dual career as radio star and crime fighter, masking himself by means of a distinctive red scarf tied around his mouth. The back-up features remained remarkably stable for years, some only dropping out when the page count was reduced. The last significant addition was Tommy Tomorrow in 127, a space-adventure strip set in the 21st century, who would run until 251.

Superman's powers gradually increased over the years, with X-ray vision being introduced in 18, and his strength and speed on an upward curve. Pretty soon he was no longer leaping buildings in a single bound, but flying over them easy as you like. In 60 Lois Lane gains superpowers to become Superwoman, nicely handled for what was then a new idea. It would be recycled many times in the following decades. By this time Superman was established on Earth, although fantastic elements were added to his stories by recurring inept magicians Hocus and Pocus. Seemingly popular in the mid-1940s, they were the nearest Superman came to comedy sidekicks, but their bumbling was soon deemed surplus to requirements, and the jokes were left to the Prankster. There were few glimpses into his Kryptonian background until the late 1940s, and 158 features his own personal album 'The Kid From Krypton', expanding on his origin. This was in the early 1950s, and by this point Superman's stories had become more fantasy oriented. The appearance of aliens was frequent, as were time-travel stories, and Superman saw out the demise of the superheroes that had followed him with ease. This was possibly because as well as being the original article, despite his powers Superman had always offered more than a succession of villains, and the strip was consistently strong, with a distinctive supporting cast. Of course, that there was a Superman radio show throughout the 1940s and TV series running between 1952 and 1957 may have helped.

Although Jerry Siegel was still writing Superman stories, Shuster had long since given way to other artists. The pair maintained a studio from which various artists drew the strip, most notably Fred Ray, Paul Cassidy, Leo Nowak and John Sikela, who would go on to be the pre-eminent *Superboy* artist of the 1950s. Foremost among them, though, and longest lasting was Wayne Boring. His figures were stiff, but there was a dynamism, albeit coupled with a tendency to draw everyone with lockjaw. DC also appointed Jack Burnley to draw some strips.

The mid-1950s Superman is probably the version that most commonly comes to mind for most people. Still at *The Daily Planet*, Clark Kent was now a fully rounded and distinct character, and Luthor was making more of a nuisance of himself with a succession of outlandish schemes. The Kryptonian heritage was being mined to the full, not least with the various forms of Kryptonite, each affecting Superman in a different way, with green the deadliest. Assorted villains from Krypton's past would pop up with increasing frequency, starting with 194, and Lois Lane played a big part in most stories, now often obsessed with the idea of uncovering Superman's other identity. In 206 Superman married Lois Lane, except he didn't, but this teaser, and many others later, were for an event probably ordained from their first appearance. The Superman series was gathering momentum in *Action* by the late 1950s, and additions to his legend were constant, with the origin of Brainiac in 242, in which it was revealed that an entire Kryptonian city had been shrunk and was preserved in a bottle. The miniature inhabitants often later emerged to give Superman a hand when required, and he in turn would regularly shrink himself to visit the city for an adventure, occasionally masquerading with Jimmy Olsen as Kandorian superheroes Nightwing and Flamebird.

252 is a landmark, with the origin and first appearance of Supergirl. She's also a Kryptonian, who escaped the planet's destruction, and was, coincidentally, Superman's cousin. Not a hoax, villain or robot, she was for real, a female counterpart for Superman and a permanent addition to the legend, gaining a back-up strip from 253. Her late arrival on Earth was due to her domed city being detached whole from Krypton's destruction, and her only following Superman into space when a meteorite devastated the city. She lived in an orphanage, adopting the identity of Linda Lee, and secretly shooting out to perform heroic deeds in her Superman-inspired costume, during which a robot Linda Lee would replace her. Some stories focused on her romantic interludes, and she had a particular crush on a fellow orphan, Dick Malvern. Leo Dorfman and Jim Mooney provided constantly well plotted and drawn stories, page-turners each and every one. In 285 Supergirl became known to the world at large, and a good sampler of her back-up years is 295–298, conveniently reprinted as a one-shot special. They put Supergirl through the wringer, but even more so did the same to her friend, Lena Thorul. Hmmm, can't those letters be rearranged? Yes, you've guessed it, Lena was Lex's younger sister, and the family changed their name when Lex went bad. Other samples of classic Supergirl can be found in reprint issues 334, 347, 360 and 373.

By the mid-1960s there'd been an upheaval in the comics industry, but Superman, both here and in his own title, never really stood still. While editor Mort Weisinger had a low regard for the opinions of fans he nonetheless gave them what they wanted with tight continuity and inventive additions to Superman's legend. The regular artists at this time were Al Plastino and Curt Swan, with Swan being the more special of the two. A highlight of his is 'The Death Of Luthor' in 318–319, in which Luthor returns to the planet Lexor, named in his honour after he used his great scientific know-how to save the planet from destruction. Here he's a hero, and lures Superman to the planet and fixes events to seem as if Superman has killed him. 319 is the trial, and even when Luthor's deception is revealed he's so beloved that he's forgiven and Superman banished. Luthor remains, married to the delightful Adora, apparently to live happily ever after. Of course, it never happens. The 1960s was also the heyday of the 'Imaginary Stories', which, unconstrained by continuity, allowed Superman's writers to present some very interesting ideas. 332, for instance, has the wrinkle of Supergirl preceding her cousin's arrival on Earth, and then training him, while 338 and 339 star Superman's descendant. 351–353 are Wayne Boring's finest hour, featuring Zha-Vam, a character obviously inspired by the original Captain Marvel. 357 was Boring's last issue, while the back-up Supergirl strip was drawn by the excellent Kurt Schaffenberger from 359. 363 began a great multi-part story in which Luthor afflicts Superman with a disease turning him into a leper. Not wanting to infect others, he exiles himself into space, and then plans suicide in order to destroy the virus. Before he becomes cosmic dust, though, he's saved by the Bizarros. This strange tale was the work of writer Jim Shooter and artist Ross Andru.

From 377 Supergirl was elevated into *Adventure Comics*, while the previous headliners there, the Legion Of Super-Heroes, occupied her back-up slot. With only a few pages to play around with, Shooter turned in some memorable character-driven stories, particularly 378, which dealt with drug addiction, albeit obliquely, and 381, which revealed Matter Eater Lad, who lived in the poorer section of town, and showed the hardships of other inhabitants. Shooter's last story was 384, and the remainder of the run was continued by E. Nelson Bridwell and Cary Bates in admirable fashion.

Back in the lead feature Cary Bates was also becoming an inventive and popular Superman writer. Try 385–387, where the Man Of Steel is trapped in the future and becomes immortal. The end of an era came with 392 as Mort Weisinger retired, having edited the Superman line for decades. Fittingly his final issue was an imaginary story, a form he pioneered. It was also the death knell for the Legion Of Super-Heroes, not required by new editor Murray Boltinoff, whose preferred back-up feature was 'Tales From The Fortress Of Solitude', introduced in 395 and detailing the history of assorted artefacts kept by Superman in his Arctic hideaway. Boltinoff also introduced credits for creators, and teamed now regular penciller Curt Swan with the magnificent inking of Murphy Anderson for the Superman art team supreme. There was no great change in the substance of the stories, but the team of Swan and Anderson made events look substantially more dynamic. Boltinoff also dropped the idea of 'imaginary' stories, the final one occupying 396–397.

403–413 are all fifty-two pages in length, all containing a nice selection of reprint strips, and a new back-up starts in 413, running until 418. Bob Haney and John Calnan completely fail to capture the quirky flavour of Metamorpho, although Haney did pack a lot of plot into eight pages. 419 introduced a new back-up, The Human Target, an inventive idea from Len Wein later to become a TV movie. Christopher Chance took the place of people marked for murder, using his wits to trap the killer. Carmine Infantino pencilled the first strip, inked by Dick Giordano, who thereafter pencilled as well. The Human Target alternated with Green Arrow (nicely drawn by Sal Amendola and Giordano) and the Atom in the back-up slot.

Throughout a period of revitalisation at DC during the early 1970s, the Superman strip in *Action Comics* had remained largely unmodified, unlike his own title, even when the instigator of those changes Julie Schwartz, became editor. The only changes filtering through were that Clark Kent now worked for Galaxy Broadcasting, facilitating the introduction of Sports Correspondent Steve Lombard to the cast. He was always a practical joker, with Kent his constant target, but the jokes rarely went as planned. It also returned Lana Lang to the strip on a regular basis, now a more mature character able to appreciate Clark Kent a lot more, and eventually a relationship develops. Lucky old Clark. Although the art of Swan and Anderson remained very nice, the stories, now mainly written by Cary Bates and occasionally Elliot Maggin, were only average. The outstanding issues during this run were 437 and 443, both with a lead story written by Maggin, but with an excellent selection of reprints.

484 is another wedding between Superman and Lois Lane, but this time it's not a hoax, a dream or an imaginary story. It's the marriage of the 1940s Superman, whom DC continuity revisions had consigned to an alternate Earth. It's a charming issue giving the fans what they wanted. 488 saw the start of an occasional Air Wave back-up strip. This was an updated version of a 1940s superhero, and while competent was never outstanding, and ran to 535, often teaming with the Atom. 500's 'The Life Story Of Superman' recaps Superman's life from the explosion of Krypton onwards; it's from Martin Pasko and the usual Swan and Anderson art team. It coincided with the release of the *Superman* film, and it also seemed to prompt some outstanding stories. 507–508 offer the miraculous return of Jonathan Kent, a time paradox story involving aliens, but returning a 70-year-old Pa Kent, who hadn't died when Superman was a boy. It was a moment of inspiration from Cary Bates, who was also responsible for the marvellous 510–512, in which Lex Luthor apparently abandons his villainous ways. It's a very well plotted story, and very convincing. Sadly, having hit form, Bates was replaced by an uninspired Marv Wolfman. Combined with Bob Rozakis' determination to retain a 1960s feel to the Air Wave, Aquaman and Atom back-up strips, the early 1980s was far from a golden era for *Action*. This was compounded by Curt Swan's departure with 534, although he returned for 544, the 45th anniversary issue, to draw an excellent Cary Bates-scripted Lex Luthor story, returning him to Lexor. New artist Gil Kane drew some nice issues between 539 and 552, and his contribution to 544 was a Wolfman-written tale transforming the old-style Brainiac into a new, grotesque cybernetic model.

Kane's art was distinctive, but he didn't last: he gave way to Kurt Schaffenberger in 556. Splendid artist though he is, Schaffenberger's style was definitely 1960s, which can't have helped declining sales. 560, 563, 565 featured Keith Giffen's wacky Ambush Bug in the back-up slot, a decidedly welcome breath of fresh air. Giffen also drew the Superman strip in 577–579, the latter a nice Asterix homage written by Jean Marc and Randy L'Officier. It was a welcome change of pace, but the Superman strip was just coasting along with ever poorer plots. Something needed to be done, and soon. It was, with a whole new look for Superman from 584. Before that, though, in 583 there was one of the best Superman stories ever, a nostalgia-drenched imaginary story drawn by the classy team of Curt Swan and Kurt Schaffenberger, and written by Alan Moore. It concluded the story begun in *Superman* 423 featuring all the classic Superman elements. It's magnificent, and no comic fan should deny themselves this story.

584 featured the new Superman in a revised continuity. The strip had reverted to its roots, and Superman's unique nature was emphasised by his being the only Kryptonian to survive the destruction of the planet. Artist and writer John Byrne had full control of the title until 600, and revived the *DC Presents* idea of Superman teaming with different guest stars each issue, kicking off with the popular Teen Titans. The selection of guest stars was engagingly off-beat, as Byrne seemed to be running through his favourites. Jack Kirby-created characters were high on the list with the New Gods, Demon, Big Barda and Mister Miracle appearing in 586, 587, 592 and 593 respectively. He also had a soft spot for the Metal Men, featuring them in 590 and 599, but his most notable story was 591, in which the old Superboy starred in a tale of alternate realities. None of these stories dealt with Superman's personal life apart from 597, which guest-starred the two women in Clark Kent's life, Lana Lang and Lois Lane, sorting out their relationships with Clark. Byrne's run ended in impressive fashion with 600, an anniversary issue, with a number of stories all plotted by Byrne. There's a possible romance with Wonder Woman, drawn by George Perez and featuring Darkseid, and we're also treated to solos for many of Superman's supporting cast, drawn by classic artists. Although a nostalgic look at *Action Comics* it's also decidedly modern.

601 to 642 saw a complete change as *Action* became a weekly publication with episodes of several ongoing strips in each issue. This was innovative for the USA (although an emulation of the traditional British format), and further risks were taken with the choice of strips, few of them headliners. Max Allan Collins and Terry Beatty's Wild Dog was a vigilante-style defender of the suburbs; numerous attempts at popularising Blackhawk had failed since the 1950s; while the espionage strip Secret Six hadn't been seen since their own short-run comic in the 1960s. Mike Baron and Dan Jurgens revived Deadman, later illustrated by Kelley Jones, and Superman was relegated to a two-page centre-spread in newspaper style format. The nominal star of the comic was Gil Kane, returning to former glories in illustrating Green Lantern, but the stories were disappointing. Later highlights included the return of 1940s tease Phantom Lady in a new incarnation from 636, the same issue in which Alan Grant started the restoration of the Demon. The weekly format was a brave experiment, but eventually produced little of note, much of the problem stemming from a generation of writers not used to providing a beginning, middle and

end, or cliffhanger, in an eight-page story every issue. The final weekly issue is notable for a story running through the Deadman, Nightwing, Green Lantern and Superman strips pencilled by a number of veteran artists inked by young Turks. There's some nice combinations, including Carmine Infantino and Kevin Nowlan, Steve Ditko and Art Thibert and Curt Swan and Ty Templeton.

George Perez was at the helm as artist/writer in 643 to 652, producing decent enough stories scripted by Roger Stern, who carries on as writer after Perez' departure, with Brett Breeding taking over the art. A significant story occurs in 660, in which Lex Luthor dies. And we see the body. But who's this person with flowing red hair claiming to be Luthor's long-lost son? Even more significantly, in 662 Superman finally confides in Lois Lane, revealing his Clark Kent identity. It's the end of an era and the beginning of a new one as they decide to get married. Superman's immediately whisked away for two issues as part of the 'Time And Time Again' story crossing over between all the Superman titles. Here he encounters old DC villain Chronos in the Stone Age and moves to the 1940s in 665, featuring a nice cameo from the Justice Society Of America, while the new Luthor Jnr is proving very popular with the citizens of Metropolis. 674 was part of another crossover story 'Panic In The Sky', and introduced the new Supergirl, an artificial creature called Matrix, with shapeshifting abilities among others. She's befriended by the new, genial Luthor. Jackson Guice becomes regular penciller with 476, by which point *Action* had become part of what was to all intents and purposes a weekly *Superman* comic. Stories ran through all the Superman titles, with each having individual sub-plots, and the running order denoted by triangles on the cover. *Action*'s main sub-plot concerned Luthor, a paragon of virtue in public, yet with Supergirl apparently under his thrall. 683–691 are part of three long crossover stories in which Superman is killed by Doomsday, after which four possible versions of Superman appear, with each occupying one of the Superman titles. *Action* concentrates on the Eradicator, most resembling Superman physically, but brutal and vengeful in his actions. The genuine article is back in 692. Despite some faults, the entire idea of killing Superman and subsequent plots were well conceived and marketed, drawing many new fans to the comics, and convincing them that the oldest superhero could still be exciting and worthwhile. It rejuvenated Superman, who now has a higher profile than at any time since the *Superman* movie era.

The plots concerning Supergirl and Luthor

come to a head in 700, which contains a nice sequence involving the wedding of Clark Kent's best childhood friends, Lana Lang and Pete Ross. The main story, though, has Lois Lane's investigations of Luthor bear fruit at last, to the great detriment of Metropolis. David Michelinie writes from 702, and Keiron Dwyer is the artist from 713. A lot of media attention focused on 720 as Lois calls off her engagement to Superman. The tiff didn't last long, though, and Lois and Clark are now happily married, again with much media attention, and tying in to the 1990s TV series. While the weekly frequency sacrifices the individual personality of the *Superman* titles, it makes for stronger *Superman* comics. For the past few years *Action* has been generally well produced with decent suspenseful plots, tight continuity, good art and a soap opera feel. Any single issue sampled at random is likely to be a decent comic, which is what counts.~HY

Recommended: 309, 318, 319, 351–353, 363–366, 378, 380, 381, 384–387, 400, 437, 443, 484, 500, 507, 508, 510–512, 544, 577–179, 583, 591, 597, 600, 700

Collections: see *Adventure, Superman*

ACTION GIRL
Slave Labor: *8 issues + 1994 to date*

Outgrowth of editor Sarah Dyer's *Action Girl* zine, this women-only anthology suffers from the common delusion that excluding men is somehow less wrong than any other form of discrimination. To be fair, though, that's the only male bashing you'll find in this generally fun, upbeat and energetic book. The contributions of Patty Leidy, Chris Tobey, Carolyn Ridsdale and editor Dyer are the front runners. *Action Girl* is a candybox comic, and with the range and diversity on offer you're not going to like everything, but the odds are that you'll love some of it.~HS

ADAM STRANGE
DC: *3-issue miniseries 1990*

His *Mystery In Space* appearances have a nostalgic charm, but Adam Strange has rarely seen the limelight even from a distance since, and his guest appearances have decreased over the years. Instead of letting a character whose time had passed remain a fond memory, DC issued this pointless 1990s revision. Unsavoury aspects of Adam's apparently random trips across the universe to Rann are revealed, and it appears he'll be absent in his adopted planet's greatest hour of need. Despite Adam Kubert art, it's all downhill from there, and by the end of the series few constants remain in Adam Strange's life. The success of the makeover can be measured by Strange's continuing lack of presence in recent years.~WJ

ADOLESCENT RADIOACTIVE BLACK-BELT HAMSTERS
Eclipse: *9 issues 1986–1989*

Don't be tempted by early Sam Kieth art, this is slipshod pre-pubescent derivative rubbish.~FP

ADOLESCENT RADIOACTIVE BLACK-BELT HAMSTERS IN 3-D
Eclipse: *4 issues 1986*

Slipshod pre-pubescent derivative rubbish in 3-D.~FP

ADVANCED DUNGEONS & DRAGONS
DC: *36 issues, 1 Annual 1988–1991*

Surely the joy of role-playing games is participating, affecting the fate of characters yourself, challenging others and relying on your wits and creativity? This seemed to be the opinion of all the writers, who consequently did their utmost to ensure people would stop buying the comics and return to playing the game. There were plenty of writers to start with, as they were rotated every four issues, but it eventually fell to Dan Mishkin to ensure a consistent level of tedium. Jan Duursema's art, though, is rather a surprise. She obviously enjoyed this a whole lot more than other titles she's worked on.~WJ

ADVENTURE Comics
DC: *472 issues (32–503) 1938–1983*

This series actually began life as *New Comics* in 1935, featuring cartoony humour strips, most notably by Sheldon Mayer, but also an adventure strip called 'Federal Men', which ran until 70, from Jerry Siegel and Joe Shuster, yet to create Superman. With 12 the title became *New Adventure Comics*, largely supplanting the humour strips with more adventure material, and with time the comedy was altogether phased out for a bunch of rugged he-men and 'Nadir, Master Magician'. With 32 the title changed to *Adventure Comics* ('still offering 64 pages of thrill-packed action'), and remained that way for forty-five years, although the page count diminished.

The first departure from the norm, representing the gradual sneaking in of superheroes, is 40, with the début of the original Sandman (currently starring in *Sandman Mystery Theatre*). Playboy Wesley Dodds donned cloak, hat and gas mask, and used a gas gun to subdue the criminal element, and was obviously inspired by the pulp-fiction success, *The Shadow*. He quickly became the lead feature and dominated the covers, with stories largely illustrated by Craig Flessel. With superheroes becoming ever more dominant, 48 introduced The Hourman, drawn by Bernard Bailey. Physicist Rex Tyler swallowed a miracle pill to become super strong and agile for an hour. Certainly a popular strip, and even more so when aided by the Minutemen of America, a young kids' gang. A third superhero débuted in 61, Starman, with distinctive art from Jack Burnley. He was powered by a 'cosmic rod' that drew energy from the stars, enabling him to fly and shoot energy bursts. The Shining Knight arrived in 66, a genuine member of King Arthur's Camelot, transported through time with a winged steed. 69 sees the début of Sandy, the Golden Boy, a kid sidekick for Sandman courtesy of writer Bob Kane, in a story giving Sandman a new skintight superhero costume just in time for the arrival of Joe Simon and Jack Kirby on the strip with 72, who produced some truly dramatic stories until 91. In 73–80 the prolific duo offer us the first appearance of Manhunter, a costumed acrobat, having transformed the Paul Kirk strip about a big-game adventurer introduced in 58. Although a short-run obscurity at the time, he'd have considerable impact on DC continuity decades later. Jack Burnley left Starman after 80, and Hourman dropped out from 83, although Sandman was continued by other creators until 102, when he and Starman faded away, ending the first flush of DC superheroes.

A new look and several new features transferred from *More Fun Comics* with 103. That issue introduced Aquaman, underwater adventurer and King of the Seven Seas, speedster Johnny Quick, ace archer Green Arrow, and 'The adventures of Superman as a boy', Superboy. The latter was immediately given cover status, an attempt to add to the popularity of the company's most prominent character by introducing an equivalent around the age of most readers. One of Superboy's most significant adventures was in 128, which featured the first meeting between Superboy and a young Lois Lane. Superboy monopolised the cover and was the main selling point, but oddly enough this may have contributed to the longevity of the Green Arrow and Aquaman strips, which outlasted the demise of superheroes towards the end of the 1940s, surviving all the way to 269 and 284 respectively. Even Johnny Quick survived until 207. Connoisseurs of good art may be interested to know that the Shining Knight was illustrated by a young Frank Frazetta, in 150, 151, and every alternate issue thereafter until 163, in stories later reissued as a *Shining Knight* one-shot. The art, though not spectacular, certainly stands out, and it was the final fling for the character, who departed with 166. By this time Ramona Fradon was drawing a fine Aquaman, and George Papp would become the regular Green Arrow artist, making way for Jack Kirby in 250–256. 262 introduces Speedy, Green Arrow's kid helper, and

Aquaman's young assistant Aqualad makes his first appearance in 269.

Superboy's light-hearted adventure strip continued with few changes in format and substance from the 1940s to the late 1960s, mirroring stories in his own title, and those of his adult counterpart. Typical plots had him travelling into the past, the future, or battling strange beasts. Lana Lang, teenage pal of Clark Kent, was often the catalyst for the stories. In 167 she's transformed into Supergirl, complete with superpowers, the first use of the concept, although it wasn't lasting. 195 is typical, featuring 'Lana's Romance On Mars', with Superboy desperately jealous because she has a date with Mars Boy! Young love, eh? It's all frivolous and enjoyable in small amounts. As Superboy continued, the legend of Superman was slowly being enhanced, never more so than in 210, which introduced Krypto, the superdog, who arrives on Earth in an experimental spaceship fired off by Superman's father as a trial run for that saving his son. Of course, Krypto is a dog with super strength, and would play a major role in succeeding Superboy stories. 217–218 are, for the period, a rarity, being a continued story where Superboy's parents are apparently resurrected. Thereafter a robot teacher prepared by Jor-El to instruct Superboy how to use his powers arrives on Earth, and soon the entire population of Krypton appears to have avoided its destruction as assorted other superpowered beings turn up. The most significant Kryptonians, and an imaginative addition to the myth, were those from The Phantom Zone, a concept introduced here in 283. Kryptonian criminals were transformed into phantoms, unable to materialise but seeing everything, and surviving the destruction of the planet in their ghostly forms.

By far the most significant issue of *Adventure* was 247, which introduced the Legion Of Super-Heroes, a superhero club from the 30th century. Cosmic Boy, Lightning Boy and Saturn Girl (complete with names written on their chests in case of confusion) came back in time to test Superboy's eligibility to join their club. When introduced by Otto Binder and Al Plastino, the Legion were no more than another odd idea to be used for a single issue and forgotten like the earlier Mars Boy, but something about them captured the imagination of the readership, and they returned in 267 (sadly, this time with only symbols on their costumes). Between those appearances Superboy and Lois Lane met again, and he befriends the young Green Arrow in 258.

Giant golden gorilla Congorilla has a run in 271–281, and a Bizarro World back-up runs from 285 to 299, flying in the face of

Bizarro when first introduced as a tragic Frankenstein's monster-like figure. He lives on a square world populated by Bizarro comedy equivalents of the Superman cast of characters. The distinguishing aspect of the Bizarro world was that everything was the opposite of the known world. You stop at green for their traffic lights, and gold is worthless while coal is almost priceless. It can be explained by the Bizarro code, which is 'Us do opposite of all Earthly things. Us hate beauty. Us love ugliness. Is big crime to make anything perfect on Bizarro World'. There you have it. The perfect world was the imperfect world. The strip was written by Superman creator Jerry Siegel with his tongue planted firmly in his cheek, and wonderfully illustrated by John Forte. If you like your stories ludicrous, they don't come more so than Bizarro World. It's the Legion of Super-Heroes who're gradually in the ascendant, though. In addition to slots in *Action, Superboy* and *Superman*, they're back here in 282, 290 and 293, gradually introducing new members. From 300 they have a regular strip, starting as a back-up, but quickly usurping the lead strip, absorbing Superboy into the team.

The Legion were the first teenage super-team, and the longevity of the feature owes a lot to the colourful characters in its ranks, living up to its name when reaching a high of twenty-six members in the late 1960s. Early adventures were usually written by Siegel or Edmond Hamilton, and were illustrated by Forte, and have a certain primitive charm. In some ways, though, the strip was quite progressive, with one character dying in 304, and although he was later resurrected it was at the sacrifice of another character. An early blow for women's rights was struck when Saturn Girl became team leader, but then negated very soon after when she was barred from a mission because it was too dangerous for a girl! Incidents like these only add to the charm and daft nature of the series, as do some of the lesser powered characters such as Matter Eater Lad, who could eat anything, Bouncing Boy (he could bounce), and Triplicate Girl, who could split into three people.

While the Legion's early run was well received, the golden age of the feature began when a young Jim Shooter's first story was published in 346, introducing some new Legionnaires, one of whom he kills off a few issues later. While the action was just as dramatic, Shooter developed the personalities of the team, redefined many relationships and was able to flesh out the minor characters. The majority of Shooter's stories were further improved by the art of Curt Swan and George Klein. Swan was able to give each Legionnaire

a distinctive look, and Shooter provided many milestones. Worth mentioning are the introduction of the Fatal Five in 352–353, who became mainstay adversaries, and one of the best Legion stories to date, 'The Outlaw Legionnaires' in 359–360. Bad guy Universo, introduced by Shooter in 349, takes over the minds of virtually the whole of Metropolis, causing the Legion to be outlawed. Some are arrested and put to work on a chain gang, and others aren't permitted to use their powers. It's pure excitement all the way, and is reprinted in *Superboy And The Legion Of Super-Heroes* 238. 354–355 has Superman travelling to the 30th century to meet the team as adults. It proved awkward in later years as it committed the Legion to a fixed history, but was interesting at the time. 365–366 return the Fatal Five and introduce Shadow Lass, and 367 débuts The Dark Circle, another perennial enemy. Shooter's other great two-parter was 369–370, concentrating on Superboy, Mon-El, Duo Damsel and Shadow Lass and introducing us to the evil magician Mordru. Shooter's work was occasionally interrupted by the stories of E.Nelson Bridwell, who's best is 350–351, featuring almost everyone ever connected with the Legion.

The Legion ended its run in 379. It was thought at the time that they were taking sales away from the *Superboy* comic whenever he appeared prominently on *Adventure*'s cover, so they moved to back-up status in *Action*, with the former occupant of that slot becoming the lead in *Adventure* from 381. The Supergirl stories were much as they had been since the 1950s, with the changing times having little effect. Stories usually involved a romantic interlude for the Maid of Steel, who, it was thought, appealed mainly to female readers. There were two Supergirl stories each issue, one drawn by the magnificent Kurt Schaffenberger, and the other rendered adequately by Win Mortimer. Progressive times finally reached Supergirl in 397 with the appointment of editor/writer/artist Mike Sekowsky, recruited to rejuvenate a staid series. Sekowsky instituted some interesting changes, not the least being continual new costumes, many designs submitted by the readers, but not many of them any good. Supergirl now had a recurring villain in Starfire, and her civilian identity Linda Danvers began employment at a TV station, where one of her colleagues happened to be Nasthalthia, Nasty for short, the evil niece of Lex Luthor. More significantly, Supergirl's powers began to fade, leading to a few interesting moments. Very much up to date, Sekowsky's costumes and scenarios reflected the late 1960s and early 1970s, and while often a stiff artist, his style is quite unique and engaging, and Supergirl has possibly never been better. His departure was certainly felt, his sense of style and wonder leaving with him, although he did return to draw Supergirl's final few issues here 421–424. In the interim Bob Oksner, primarily known for his cartooning, adapted well to a more realistic style, drawing a far more feminine Supergirl, but the stories are forgettable.

From 409 *Adventure* moved back to fifty-two pages, offering a selection of back-up reprints including Animal Man, The Enchantress, Hawkman, The Phantom Stranger and The Shining Knight among others. There were also new strips, including a beautiful Alex Toth Black Canary story in 418–419, and a gorgeous Zatanna story by Len Wein and Gray Morrow in 413–415, while Morrow also drew lovely Vigilante stories in 417 and 422. Zatanna was also well handled by Wein and Dick Giordano in 419.

425–428 showcased a number of features reflecting the title, with only the Alex Toth-drawn Captain Fear in 425 standing out. Black Orchid was in 428–430, and it was a well produced series about a mysterious silent superpowered heroine whose identity and origin were never revealed. Written by Sheldon Mayer with art by Tony DeZuniga, Black Orchid was quite unlike anything else DC were producing at the time, with a nice Gothic mood to the strip. Her origin was revealed many years later in her own miniseries. 431–440 revived 1940s ghost The Spectre. This series was very controversial, not least due to the unusual ways writer Michael Fleisher had the Spectre dispose of villains. One group was turned into wood and run through an electric buzzsaw, another villain cut in half by a giant pair of scissors, all gorily drawn by Jim Aparo. While always a spirit of vengeance, The Spectre had never been quite so extreme. Michael Fleisher was obviously having a whale of a time conceiving ways to kill villains, but the over-the-top nature of the strip led to a hasty cancellation. Luckily for you the entire run plus the stories completed but never previously printed were collected as a four-issue series titled *Wrath Of The Spectre* in 1988. Aquaman was back in 441–452 after successful back-up appearances in 435 and 437 by Paul Levitz and Mike Grell. It was an enjoyable series by David Michelinie and Jim Aparo that led to Aquaman's own title being revived, though 452 did see the pointless death of Aquababy, the son of Aquaman and Mera, included as gratuitous shock. In 449–451 there was a Martian Manhunter strip written by Denny O'Neil, and nicely illustrated by Mike Nasser and Terry Austin, that heralded the return of the character after an absence of many years.

Superboy is back for 453–458, with not a notable moment among them, yet popular enough to promote him back into his own series. With 459 *Adventure* became 64 pages without ads until 466, running a variety of superheroes. The better ones were the Deadman strip written by Len Wein with art by Jim Aparo or José Luis Garcia-Lopez, Gerry Conway and Don Newton continuing the New Gods story and the continuation of the Justice Society Of America strip, recently of *All-Star Comics*. Paul Levitz and Joe Staton continued as the creative team and the most significant event here is 462's death of the original Batman, now consigned to an alternate Earth.

Starman, a new superhero with an old name, appeared in 467–478 from Levitz and Steve Ditko in an interesting space saga. Those issues also featured Plastic Man by Marty Pasko and Joe Staton, who was a natural for the strip and produced his best artwork since *E-Man*. Aquaman, seemingly never able to keep his own series, was back for 475–478 in a story revealing his past before moving over to *Action Comics*. It was clearout time again in 479 as everything was replaced by 'Dial H For Hero', an update on the 1960s *House Of Mystery* strip. This time there were two magic dials transforming the finders into a different superhero each time they dialled the word 'hero'. All the heroes were designed by readers, and largely drawn by Carmine Infantino, with Marv Wolfman scripts. The feature continued in *Superboy*. Cancelled with 490, the title was quickly revived as a 100-page digest comic that reprinted previous glories including The Legion Of Super-Heroes, Sandman, Aquaman, Spectre and Superboy, and occasional issues featured a single new story. This was largely inventory material that had been gathering dust in a drawer, the most notable of which was Shazam drawn by Don Newton.~HY

Recommended: 343, 349–353, 357–360, 365–367, 369–370, 380, 397–408, 428–440, 462

Collections: Legion Of Super-Heroes Archives Vol 1 (247, 267, 282, 290, 293, *Action* 267, 276, 287, 289, *Superboy* 86, 89, 98), Vol 2 (306–317, *Jimmy Olsen* 72), Vol 3 (318–328, *Jimmy Olsen* 76), Vol 4 (329–339, *Superboy* 124, 125), Vol 5 (340–349), Vol 6 (350–358), Vol 7 (359–367, *Jimmy Olsen* 106)

ADVENTURE STRIP DIGEST
WCG: *4 issues + 1994 to date*

Originally produced as a small-press series, this is an appealing attempt to recreate the adventure tradition that is best exemplified by *Terry And The Pirates*, *Steve Canyon* or *Johnny Hazard*. Rob Hanes is a private detective working in a fictional Middle Eastern country threatened by rebels. When he falls for a princess he is thrown into the conflict. Randy Reynolds tries hard and the artwork, heavily influenced by Caniff and Toth, is clean and simple, but somehow he doesn't quite carry it off. This is partly because Hanes looks far too young.~NF

THE ADVENTURERS
Aircel: *2 issues 1986*
Adventure: *11 issues (0–10) 1986–1987*

It's a standard Dungeons and Dragons campaign: the by-the-dice assortment of fighters and magic-users, undertaking an escalating series of quests, in this case, for a set of keys. Nothing startling, but it trots along at a fair pace and the ideas get steadily better. The artwork in Issues 1 and 0 (the origin issue, published out of sequence) is by Peter Hsu, who has a definite talent with architecture that can make a small panel seem like the set of an epic film.~FC

ADVENTURES INTO THE UNKNOWN
ACG: *174 issues 1948–1967*

On its début this became the first continuing horror anthology comic, setting the tone with an adaptation of Horace Walpole's *Castle Of Otranto*. In several issues from 5 there's a continuing strip, 'Spirit Of Frankenstein', although once it finished in 16 no other ongoing feature appeared until Nemesis in the 1960s. 27 is notable for a strip drawn by Al Williamson and Roy Krenkel, but by and large there's very little in the early days that would have anyone demanding the comics. Always professionally produced, the 'shock' endings were nevertheless predictable. The arrival of the Comics Code Authority in the mid-1950s toned the content down considerably, and forced writer/editor Richard E.Hughes to become more inventive, and given the already high standard of art, it's worth sampling at least one issue after 62. Some of John Buscema's early work can be found in 100, 106, 108–110.

Changing with the times, a superhero, Nemesis, was introduced in 154, running until 170. He was returned from the dead in order to avenge himself on his murderers in an origin story clearly inspired by DC's Spectre. The artwork by Pete Costanza and later Chic Stone could hardly compete with DC or Marvel's superheroes. The tongue-in-cheek scripts of Hughes never really clicked. Realising Nemesis was a bit of turkey, he was ousted as the final four issues returned to the anthology format, but by then it was too late for ACG.~SW

THE AGE OF HEROES
Halloween: *2 issues + 1996 to date*

Ye olde comic booke fantasy, written and published by James D. Hudnall and classically illustrated by John Ridgway. Clearly a labour of love for its creators, *Age Of Heroes* boasts an ambitious mythic structure that has so far amounted to little more than typical tales of demons, barbarians and elves.~AL

AGE OF REPTILES
Dark Horse: *4-issue miniseries 1993–1994, 5-issue miniseries 1996*

Each issue contains a well conceived vignette of what life might have been like during the Cretaceous era. Dinosaur fans will be seduced by the excellent, although oddly coloured, art from Ricardo Delgado while everyone else will flick through the comics in a minute.~WJ
Collection: The Age Of Reptiles (Series one 1–4)

AGENT LIBERTY
DC: *One-shot 1994*

The origin of the character who appears in the various Superman titles. The story by long-term *Superman* scribe Dan Jurgens is lack-lustre and Dusty Abell's pencils disappoint.~SS

AGENTS OF LAW
Dark Horse: *6 issues 1995*

An unknown figure called Law arrives at the gates of Golden City carrying the corpse of its ruler Grace. Within weeks he's organised a coup, and Golden City is his. An excellent compact study in the acquisition and maintenance of power from plotter Keith Giffen, scripter Lovern Kindzierski and artists Dan Lawlis and Ian Akin. By focusing largely on the cold-blooded brutality of Law some events are related only in expository dialogue, and others given no explanation in a curtailed series. Additionally, the peremptory dismissal of previously essential Golden City characters with unfulfilled potential is a shame. Otherwise a fine title let down only by an abrupt resolution predicated by poor sales.~FP
Recommended: 1–5

AIR FIGHTERS CLASSICS
Eclipse: *6 issues, 1987–1989*

Facsimile reprints of the 1940s *Air Fighters Comics* (2–7), featuring such heroes as Airboy, Black Angel Flying Dutchman *et al.* Invaluable for Golden Age buffs.~HS

AIR RAIDERS
Marvel: *5 issues 1988*

Insipid toy tie-in featuring – no doubt to his eternal shame – early work by later acclaimed artist Kelley Jones.~HS

AIRBOY
Eclipse: *50 issues 1986–1989*

Tim Truman and Chuck Dixon's revival of the 1940s flyer was a fond homage that captured the spirit of fun and adventure of the original, who appeared in Hillman Periodicals' *Air Fighters Comics* during the 1940s. Colourful and flamboyant, Truman and Dixon's hero, the son of the original, faced a series of pulp-inspired foes including left-over Nazis, zombies and robots, with a supporting cast re-introduced from the 1940s. *Airboy* proved popular enough to spawn numerous spin-offs including a solo series for Valkyrie and The Airmaidens, several one-shots, team-ups (vs The Prowler and Mr Monster) and reprints. Back issues have never descended to bargain box prices, but are relatively cheap for the easy, satisfying read they deliver.~JC

AIRBOY AND MR MONSTER SPECIAL
Eclipse: *One-shot 1987*
Continues the story begun in *Airboy* 28, which teams the two popular Eclipse characters and most of their supporting casts.~JC

AIRBOY MEETS THE PROWLER
Eclipse: *One-shot 1987*
What seemed like a bizarre pairing of the colourful, flamboyant Airboy and the more detective- *noir*-influenced Prowler actually produced an entertaining tale in which the two second-generation heroes take time out from the action to reflect on what it means to live up to their 1940s legends. Especially useful for the complete Eclipse *Airboy* checklist contained in the back.~JC

AIRBOY VS THE AIRMAIDENS
Eclipse: *One-shot 1988*
Under the influence of a brainwashing drug, Valkyrie and the Airmaidens assassinate a drug baron for a rival crimelord. Wondering what the hell his girlfriend's up to, Airboy follows her and – wait for it – her love for him snaps her out of it, where upon the lot of them whup the bad guys and live happily ever after. Actually, it's not (quite) as bad as it sounds.~JC

THE AIRMAIDENS
Eclipse: *One-shot 1987*
Yet another spin-off from the popular *Airboy* comic, the Airmaidens were essentially a team of superheroines led by Valkyrie, Airboy's reformed ex-Nazi girlfriend. Like *Airboy*, the comic was a lot of fun as the girls travelled round the world righting wrongs and generally enjoying themselves. This features the origin of La Lupina. Not the best of the spin-offs, but nonetheless worth picking up from the cheap boxes.~JC

AIRMAN
Malibu: *One-shot 1993*
The Hawkman-alike member of The Protectors has a pointless solo adventure continuing directly into issue 7 of the team title. Reads like

a *Protectors* fill-in that was drawn too badly, so issued as a one-shot to flog it to a few 'must have number ones' diehards.~HS

THE AIRTIGHT GARAGE
Epic: *4-issue miniseries 1993*
Moebius' rambling science fiction epic was originally published in black and white in France's *Metal Hurlant* magazine 1976–1978, then translated into English in *Heavy Metal*. Epic first published this colour edition, also substantially rewritten (since Moebius wasn't happy with the *Heavy Metal* version), as Moebius Graphic Novel 3 in 1987. After two miniseries sequels plotted by Moebius and finished by other hands, *The Elsewhere Prince* and *The Onyx Overlord*, Epic also re-ran *The Airtight Garage* in the same format. The story is hard to follow. Moebius proudly admits that he made it up as he went along. Time Traveller Major Grubert has created a pocket universe with three separate levels of reality, the Garage itself, whose existence is threatened by various competing factions. These include Lewis Carnelian ('Jerry Cornelius' in the original version), a servant of the god-like Nagual, whose technology the Major has stolen to create the Garage. While the art is gorgeous, and the colouring largely sympathetic, the pages were created to be read at magazine size, and it shows. To appreciate the drawing, read the graphic novel. As for the story, many Anglo-American readers noted that it was just as incomprehensible as the original French. Epic's faithful translations reveal that Moebius may rule as an artist, but as a writer, the king has no clothes.~GL
Collection: Moebius 3: *The Airtight Garage*

AIRWAVES
Caliber: *5 issues 1991*
Sadly uncompleted story of a future where corporate power and government are synonymous and the masses are kept docile by pabulum fed through radio programming. Michael Lark's art brings Ted McKeever to mind, and although an expansive use of space restricts the plot it's intriguing enough to investigate.~FP

AKIRA
Epic: *38-issue limited series 1988–1995*
The first thing to make clear about *Akira* is that it's important to the history of comics. It was a huge success in Japan when it first appeared, helping *Young Magazine* achieve a circulation of a million (bi-weekly!). It spawned a state-of-the-art animated movie that broke into the English-speaking mainstream, and created a large market for Japanese animation in the West. Visually, Katsuhiro Otomo set standards and started trends that have had

vast repercussions for Japanese comics and then, in turn, for US and European comics. If the current popularity of Manga in the West can't be laid entirely at Otomo's door he has certainly played the most important role in popularising them. *Akira* is his *magnum opus*.

Akira is set in Neo-Tokyo, 2030AD, a world recovering from World War III. Kaneda and Tetsuo are school friends forever getting into trouble on their motorbikes. While Kay and Ryu, members of an underground resistance organisation, try to rescue an escaped paranormal, child- like figure from the military, Tetsuo is captured by them. They discover he's a latent psychic himself, and when he escapes starts exhibiting dangerous powers and needs large amounts of drugs to stay sane. The military have been looking for a way of controlling Akira, potentially the most powerful psychic of all, who has been imprisoned since birth. When Tetsuo frees Akira a laser canon is fired at them and the city is devastated by the force of Akira's mental response.

Tetsuo and Akira create the Great Tokyo Empire, healing and organising the survivors of Akira's blast. As Tetsuo relives his past and tries to find more psychics, the religious leader Lady Miyako tries to hold together what remains of the resistance with the help of her own psychics and Kay. The Western powers eventually take an interest in what's happening in Japan, sending an assassination squad against Akira and using biochemical weapons. Then things get really weird. After destroying part of the moon, Tetsuo's arm begins to mutate. In the final chapters Akira consumes Tetsuo and then seemingly himself, as Otomo hammers out his message about the necessity for humankind to evolve.

Though action-packed, the strip staggers forward with, sometimes, little sense of direction and there are times when characters disappear and reappear later with no explanation. Otomo seemed to have abandoned *Akira* at one point, there was such a wait before it was completed, and maybe this accounts for the disappointing conclusion. Though the artwork remains of high quality, there is a real sense of retreading old ground towards the end and the metaphysical nonsense of the final revelations sours the memory of the previous issues. With a detailed and labyrinthine plot, the huge scope of *Akira* warrants attention but it's not always all it's cracked up to be.~NF

Recommended: 1–12

Collections: Akira Vol 1 (1–3), Vol 2 (4–6), Vol 3 (7–9), Vol 4 (10–12), Vol 5 (13–15), Vol 6 (16–18), Vol 7 (19–21), Vol 8 (22–24), Vol 9 (25–27), Vol 10 (28–30)

ALARMING ADVENTURES
Harvey: *3 issues 1961–1962*

This title sported intelligent stories by editor Joe Simon and a débuting Archie Goodwin among others with artists of the calibre of Bailey, Crandall, Powell and Williamson adding a touch of class to the package. Sadly Simon's efforts to reprise the quality achieved in 1950s science fiction anthologies seemed ill-advised at a time when everyone else was shutting down science fiction titles or converting them to superhero venues.~SW

ALBEDO
Thoughts & Images: *15 issues (0–14) 1984–1989*
Antarctic Press: *10 issues 1991–1993, Series two 3 issues (1–3) 1994*

Albedo was originally a science fiction anthology, primarily featuring anthropomorphic characters. Steve Gallacci's 'Erma Felma EDF' became the mainstay and *raison d'etre*, a complex, hard-science tale concerning the Extraplanetary Defense Force, which concentrates on the social and political aspects of policing, largely eschewing scenes of conflict. The 'Erma Felma' stories from 1–14 and the first two issues of the Antarctic series are reprinted in four issues *of Command Review* and a 1993 colour special reprints the first story. Stan Sakai's Usagi Yojimbo made his first appearance here (2–4), as did Matt Howarth and D.M.Kister's 'Konny And Czu' (6–14), a humour strip about interplanetary trading featuring aliens who actually look and behave like alternate life forms. Both have since appeared in their own titles. *Albedo* is an ambitious project, but the wordiness of much of the content often gives the impression of an illustrated story.~NF

ALEC
Escape: *3 issues 1984–1986*

Before embarking on his *magnum opus* with *Bacchus*, Eddie Campbell was exploring similar themes of drink and companionship in self-published stories. His thinly disguised *alter ego* Alec MacGarry socialised in the King Canute pub, into which wander sooner or later a rich collection of friends and acquaintances, most notably van driver, pub philosopher and all-round good egg Danny Grey. Warm and knowing, Campbell tells his stories in the manner of a pub raconteur, rolling all around the houses before getting to the point, which is by no means a complaint. Anecdotes in the first issue relate to those in the third, which in turn will have connections to those in the second, so don't expect a linear narrative. MacGarry/ Campbell makes a good observer of life, constantly puzzled by people, continually unable to grasp his opportunities, and always reactive rather than proactive.

Campbell's artwork is as understated as his stories, sketchy characters and backgrounds with endearingly appended patches of letratone. Even at this early stage, though, Campbell's story-telling is excellent, particularly in knowing when to leave a pause for emphasis. Anyone who's enjoyed an active social life ought to be able to see aspects of their friends mythologised by Campbell. A typical story, this from the second issue, has MacGarry and friends awakening on the pub floor after a heavy night, clearing up, being fed breakfast by the landlady, then returning to the bar as the lunchtime crowd arrives and attempting to name the fifty states of the USA between them. It's a recollection, not a plot, but its strength lies in prompting similar recollections and a consequent warm glow in the reader. If it all seems like a pile of self-indulgent wank, then *Alec* is not the comic for you.

The Acme/Eclipse collection publishes previously unseen (outside small press) material comprising 25% of the book, and is, therefore, a more desirable purchase than the individual volumes.~FP
Recommended: *The Complete Alec*
Collection: *The Complete Alec* (1–3 plus extra material)

Nightwing ALFRED'S RETURN
DC: *One-shot 1995*
After the events of 'Knightfall', Alfred has moved to London, where he's been convinced by an old flame that he has a son who's in trouble and needs help. When Nightwing turns up to ask Alfred to return to Gotham, they are both involved in an attempted coup against the British government. The plot's daft but the background on Alfred's past is well handled. Alan Grant and Dick Giordano provide adequate, if uninspired script and pencils.~NF

ALICE COOPER - THE LAST TEMPTATION
Marvel: *3-issue miniseries 1994*
Writer Neil Gaiman's almost unblemished streak of quality comics comes crashing to an end with this half-baked nonsense. Apparently developed as both album and comic, *The Last Temptation* is sorely lacking as the latter. It's the all-too-common seduction-of-the-innocent scenario with Alice playing the role of a manipulative and theatrical tempter. In a world of AIDS and school massacres Alice is as threatening as a gerbil, and if souls or coins of the realm are to be redeemed it should be for the consistently excellent art of Michael Zulli.~FP
Collection: *The Complete Temptation* (1–3)

ALIEN ENCOUNTERS
Eclipse: *14 issues 1985–1987*
Mixing humorous and twist-in-the-tail plots, this science-fiction anthology suffered from the predictability of its stories, and with little space to develop characters it was largely artwork that carried the series. Worth seeking out are Micheluzzi (3, 8), Tim Truman (4), David Lloyd (5), Richard Corben (5), Rick Geary (7), John Bolton (9) and Gray Morrow (10). Later issues tended to use fewer established artists and writers though the overall quality of the strips remained consistent. Sometimes attacked for including unnecessary nude scenes, *Alien Encounters* did largely manage to avoid gratuitous sex and violence.~NF

ALIEN FIRE
Kitchen Sink: *3 issues 1987, One-shot ('Pass In Thunder') 1995*
In the near future Earth has been devastated by nuclear war, but *Alien Fire* is not a dystopian story, it's about the legacy of Earth and a few humans living among alien races. Ed's a crew member aboard the Wooden Bird, which trades in antiques from Earth – jukeboxes, books, anything that survived. When Chia X Hong, a Vietnamese businesswoman, accidentally comes into possession of an ancient artefact, made in Japan, sold in a gumball machine, an item regarded with horror by the Hive Nations, a mystery starts to unravel that threatens the peace on Leyden Frost, the artificial world on which she lives. There's much more going on than this can begin to explain. Writer Anthony F. Smith and artist Eric Vincent have created a wonderfully rich future, populated by imaginatively conceived and designed aliens, reflecting the thought that has clearly gone into the series. It is really unfortunate that *Alien Fire* has never been finished. 'Pass In Thunder' reprints stories from *Dark Horse Presents* and *Plastron Café*, dealing respectively with Ed trying to trade a convertible and an alien's passage through Ed's mind.~NF
Recommended: 1–3, One-shot

ALIEN LEGION
Epic: *Series one 20 issues 1984–1987, series two 18 issues 1987–1990, 3-issue miniseries ('On The Edge') 1990–1991, 2-issue microseries ('Tenants Of Hell'), Grimrod 2-issue microseries 1992, One-shot ('Binary Deep') 1993*
Alien Legion was basically Epic's attempt at straight science fiction. In 'a future age', the TGU is an alliance of three galaxies devoted to achieving and maintaining peace. The Alien Legion is the Foreign Legion idea spread onto a galactic stage: soldiers of fortune getting the dog end of the jobs with no questions asked. The first issue opened on eight pages of

handbookesque text info. It's hardly the best way to immediately snare the reader's attention, especially when it's leading into a fairly clichéd and none too original Marvel-style intra-group bickering and 'oh this terrible war' *angst*. Early issues read as a fast-track immersion course in the Alien Legion's universe, deluging the reader with alien glossaries and text explanations, which could have been introduced more slowly, and less confusingly, in the stories themselves. Back-up stories about the characters' pasts were more entertaining than the main event, and perhaps writer Carl Potts just needed tighter editing to have made what wasn't a bad idea more palatable. The series improves when there's no more info to be dumped on you by the truckload and you can just settle down to reading the story.

Following the regular series, the characters were kept in print through miniseries and one-shots. Of these, *Grimrod*, written by Chuck Dixon with innovative art by Mike McMahon, is the best, achieving the sense of alien weirdness so often striven for and so seldom obtained, as Legionnaire Grimrod sets off for what he thinks is going to be an easy job on a paradise planet, only to find that he's made a terrible mistake. If you sample any *Alien Legion* make this the one and forget the rest.~JC.
Collection: Slaughter World (Series one 1, 7–11)

ALIEN NATION
Adventure: *4-issue miniseries ('The Spartans') 1990, 4-issue miniseries ('A Breed Apart') 1990–1991, 4-issue miniseries ('The Skin Trade') 1991, 4-issue miniseries ('The Firstcomers') 1991, 4-issue miniseries ('Public Enemy') 1992, One-shot ('The Lost Episode') 1992*

After DC's release of a straight-faced unexciting movie adaptation, rights went to Adventure who produced a series of mini-series featuring new stories set in the continuity of the TV show. The first, *The Spartans*, proved unexpectedly successful, to the point that it generated several variants of its first issue (four different colour covers, a gold limited, an embossed with additional art and a regular second printing). None of the hoo-hah could conceal the stories were done with more fannish enthusiasm than skill and interest rapidly died away. 'The Lost Episode' one-shot wraps up all dangling plot-lines from the TV show.~HS
Collection: Alien Nation - The Spartans

ALIEN WORLDS
Pacific: *7 issues 1982–1984*
Eclipse: *2 issues (8–9) 1984*

An attempt to revive the quality of the EC science fiction comics was a laudable editorial decision, and an opening tale from Al Williamson in the first issue reinforced the intent. Sadly, it was an experiment that largely failed. Bruce Jones wrote almost all the material, varying wildly in quality, but instead of enforcing a unity through a stable of regular artistic contributors, the net was stretched far and wide, with only Bo Hampton and Al Williamson drawing more than two stories. The sex and nudity permissible in 1980s comics is largely gratuitous and juvenile, and 30 years after EC too many stories still hinged on the last-panel shock ending. Two better twist-in-the-tail shorts appear in 8, Ken Steacy drawing a story based on *Mars Attacks* bubblegum cards and Al Williamson adapting a wistful William Nolan story. The issue is rounded out with a strange Paul Rivoche-illustrated private-eye tale, and a poor story drawn by Rand Holmes. Other notable contributions amid the rough are the Tim Conrad-illustrated 'Talk To Tedi', which pulls on the heartstrings in 1, some fine John Bolton art in 5, and Bo Hampton's 'The Maiden And The Dragon' in the final issue. Dave Stevens is in 2 and 4, which is a particularly good issue for artists, with Bo Hampton, Jeff Jones, Ken Steacy and Al Williamson all on hand. The latter's contribution is a vintage piece, actually completed in the 1950s, while the Roy Krenkel story in 6 is his last work. Having published the work inherited from Pacific, Eclipse chose to start anew with the similar *Alien Encounters*.~WJ
Recommended: 8

ALIENS
Heavy Metal/Futura: *Graphic novel 1979*
Dark Horse: *6-issue miniseries 1988–1989, 4-issue miniseries ('Aliens II') 1989–1990, 4-issue miniseries ('Earth War') 1990, 4-issue miniseries ('Hive') 1992, 4-issue miniseries ('Genocide') 1992, 3-issue miniseries ('Aliens III') 1992, 2-issue microseries ('Newt's Tale') 1992, One-shot ('Tribes') 1992, 4-issue miniseries ('Rogue') 1993, One-shot ('Sacrifice') 1993, One-shot ('Salvation') 1993, 4-issue miniseries ('Labyrinth') 1993–1994, 10-issue limited series ('Colonial Marines') 1993–1994, 4-issue miniseries ('Stronghold') 1994, One-shot ('Earth Angel') 1994, 4-issue miniseries ('Music Of The Spears') 1994, One-shot ('Mondo Pest') 1995, 6-issue miniseries ('Berserkers') 1995, One-shot ('Mondo Heat') 1996, One-shot ('Lovesick') 1997*

A huge success for Dark Horse, the *Aliens* series have not really inspired much work of note, although many notable writers have worked on one-shots or miniseries and have tried numerous approaches to the central idea up to and including comedy aliens. Artists have done better. Fans of Sam Kieth, Kelley Jones, Mike Mignola or Kevin Nowlan will not be disappointed by their bits of this extended epic.

Aliens, *Aliens II* and 'Earth War' all feature Hicks and Newt from the *Aliens* film (Ripley turns up in 'Earth War') as they continue their own battle on the alien homeworld and then on Earth itself. Mark Verheiden writes all three in competent fashion, concentrating on the madness of corporate greed and the relationship between the three combatants. Artwork by Mark Nelson, Denis Beauvais and Sam Kieth respectively is diverting. Kieth in particular pays homage to EC science fiction but he's not yet fully developed his own skills. Beauvais' painted artwork suffers from over-colouring and, like Nelson, a stiffness of composition. These stories are collected but later editions have changed the names of the characters.

'Hive' is a change of pace. Written by Jerry Prosser, it concerns a bizarre plan to use a robotic alien to steal the alien queen's royal jelly, which is "the most sought after consciousness-altering substance in existence". Drawn by Kelley Jones, who does great aliens but weak faces. 'Newt's Tale' is a basic retelling of the *Aliens* screenplay from her point of view. Mike Richardson and Jim Somerville write and draw it in an uninspired fashion, lacking the pace or atmosphere of the film itself. 'Genocide' has a story by Richardson and script by John Arcudi, picking up on the idea of manufacturing royal jelly if only some can be stolen to synthesise. An expedition to do so is plagued by scientists who want to breed aliens and an alien tribal war. Damon Willis' artwork is very lack-lustre and there's no passion to the story at all. Also lacking zip, although much admired, is 'Tribes', a graphic novel written by Stephen Bisette and drawn by the static Dave Dorman. 'Salvation', by contrast, has gorgeous artwork by Mike Mignola and Kevin Nowlan, and a punchy script by Dave Gibbons.

'Rogue', by Ian Edgington and Will Simpson, and 'Sacrifice', by Pete Milligan and Paul Johnson, are both reprints of stories produced for the UK. 'Colonial Marines' marks a change of emphasis. It concentrates on the troopers sent into battle against the aliens. Also different is 'Labyrinth', the most chilling and intelligent *Aliens* story to date, written by Jim Woodring. A scientist survives for six weeks as a captive of diseased aliens and then dedicates his life to experimenting on them for the government. The Labyrinth refers to the tests he puts the aliens and an enquiring soldier through. The artwork by Kilian Plunkett bears comparison with Art Adams and is clearly also indebted to Moebius, which is no bad thing for this tale of clinical horror.

There are several *Aliens* series which experiment with the established scenario. Set in the 1950s, John Byrne's 'Earth Angel' is yet another angle on the basic premise, while 'Music Of The Spears' is another oddity, in which an alien is trained to produce the right sounds to perform a symphony. What were C.Williamson and T.Hamilton on when they thought of that idea? 'Stronghold' is John Arcudi and Doug Mahnke's attempt at a funny aliens story, featuring a cigar-smoking alien. None of them are outstanding, except for their quirks. And unfortunately John Wagner's 'Berserkers' is equally forgettable, as is 'Mondo Pest', reprinting the story from *Dark Horse Comics* 22–24, and 'Mondo Heat', by Henry Gilroy and Ronnie del Carmen. But none are as avoidable as the adaptation of *Aliens 3*. Bad film, bad comic.

People who liked the films should seek out the 1979 adaptation of the original by Archie Goodwin and Walt Simonson, two creators who know something about creating a tense atmosphere. There are few moments in the entire Dark Horse *Aliens* series that better it.~NF
Recommended: Alien graphic novel, 'Labyrinth' 1–4
Collections: Aliens (1–6), *Aliens II* (1–4), *Earth War* (1–4), *Genocide* (1–4), *Hive* (1–4), *Labyrinth* (1–4), *Rogue* (1–4), *Stronghold* (1–4)

ALIENS VS PREDATOR

Dark Horse: *5-issue miniseries (0–4) 1990, 12-issue limited series ('The Deadliest Of The Species') 1993–1995, 2-issue microseries ('Duel') 1995, One-shot ('War') 1995, 4-issue miniseries ('War') 1995, One-shot ('Booty') 1996*

Dark Horse's decision to pair their two successful licensed properties was another canny commercial move and the results are at least entertaining, if not exactly thought-provoking.The first series has the Predators seeding a planet with Aliens with the intention of returning to hunt them at a later date. Before that return, however, human colonists arrive to provide the Aliens with food and the means of expanding their population to a greater extent than expected. Randy Stradley's script creates a sassy heroine in Machiko and it's really her story that draws you in. Phill Norwood's artwork is rather stiff, particularly on faces, and Chris Warner's final chapter doesn't much improve things. The collection of the series includes the prequels from *Dark Horse Comics* (also collected as issue zero) and the short sequel from the *Dark Horse Presents Fifth Anniversary Special*.

'Deadliest Of The Species' is an ambitious thriller in which Chris Claremont pulls out all the stops with a story featuring his trademarks, strong women and physical transformation, as Aliens, Predators and humans fight for survival against a common foe. It starts with the nightmares of a rich man's wife. Pretty soon she's forced to fight a female Predator, who calls her Ash Parnell, a name that's not familiar until she begins to regain her memory. Mostly drawn by Eduardo Barreto, after the initial issues by Jackson Guice (1–3), the script calls for switches between genres and gives him plenty of room to display his skill. While Guice's pencils aim for the realism of a Paul Gulacy, Barreto's style shows the influence of Joe Kubert and Berni Wrightson and is more complementary to Claremont's tale.

'Duel' is a clichéd tale (from Stradley again) of humans and Predators overcoming their differences against an Alien/Predator hybrid. The artwork by Javier Saltares is all open mouths and snarls, craggy and unattractive. The 'War' one-shot collects the strip originally published in Dark Horse's publicity zine, *The Insider*. 'War', the miniseries, sees the return of Machiko, initially working with the Predators but ultimately having to choose between their code of honour and the lives of the humans threatened by the clashes between Aliens and Predators. Stradley's script has more depth this time around but the artwork by Mark Heike and Ricardo Villagran is what makes this a more enjoyable series. 'Booty', by Barbara Kesel and Ron Randall, is a straightforward adventure story in which a cargo ship becomes the scene for a battle between Predators and Aliens. It's good humoured and well presented but doesn't add anything to the concept.

'Deadliest Of The Species' comes closest to making the series interesting rather than just an enjoyable series of blood-thirsty romps and is almost worth recommending on the strength of the artwork. Claremont's obsessions, however, get in the way of his telling a great story.~NF

Collection: Aliens Vs Predator (0–4), Deadliest Of The Species (1–12)

ALL ACCESS
DC/Marvel: *4-issue miniseries 1996–1997*

The character Access is jointly owned by DC and Marvel, and first appeared during their 1996 crossover. His job is to ensure that the DC and Marvel worlds remain separate, by ensuring there are no rifts in reality. Of course, without them there wouldn't be a story, so when Venom turns up on DC Earth Spider-Man is brought across to help Superman battle him, and other teamings include a reprise meeting for young loverhearts Jubilee and Robin, and Batman meeting Doctor Strange, who has an idea of what's going on. The final issue features a tiff between the X-Men and the JLA, during which the characters merge for a short time, leading to some interesting combinations. All in all it's some nice hokum that passes the time, but is nothing to be taken too seriously.~HY

ALL-AMERICAN MEN OF WAR
DC: *119 issues (127, 128, 2–117) 1952–1966*

This rose from the ashes of *All American Western*, hence the unusual numbering. As with other DC war titles, unconnected short stories are the order of the day throughout the 1950s. Almost from the start the title favoured editor Robert Kanigher's stable of top-light artists, with plenty of work from Russ Heath, Joe Kubert, Jerry Grandinetti, Irv Novick and the team of Ross Andru and Mike Esposito. The first year saw notable additional art contributions from Bernie Krigstein (2, 3, 5) and Gene Colan (3, 4, 6–8), while a little later Wally Wood (29, 30), John Severin (58) and Bill Everett (77) all left their mark. Mort Drucker is worthy of a special mention for his exceptional combination of realism, grit and narrative, and his work can be found in 47, 48, 52, 58, 61, 63, 68, 69, 71, 73, 74 and 77. Kanigher wrote stories, although the likes of Dave Wood, Bob Haney and Bill Finger also made significant contributions. The archetypal 1950s story would use a gimmick or theme of some sort, most infamously in 41's '50-50 War' by Kanigher and Kubert, where a soldier who can't walk teams with one who can't see. The era's best tale, though, was 'Toy Jet' in 78 by Haney and Heath. Atypically set in Korea, it concerned an escape from a prisoner-of-war camp, and was surprisingly convincing. As a rule, almost any issue to 80 will contain at least one good story and some lovely artwork.

Early attempts at series with Gunner And Sarge (67, 68, then quickly transferred to *Our Fighting Forces*) and 'Tank Killer' (69, 71, 72, 76) foundered, but led to the long-lived Kanigher and Novick strip 'Johnny Cloud'. The eponymous hero was a Mustang-flying pilot who also happened to be a Native American – "the Navajo Ace' as the title had it. The writing continually drew parallels between the character's military endeavours and native customs and beliefs, even to the extent that Cloud would habitually thank his 'Brother in the sky', an actual cloud conveniently shaped like a horse-riding brave! Cloud himself was a grim, uncharismatic character, and the strip's most outstanding feature was Novick's stylish art.

One final strip was introduced in the comic's death throes, 'Lt Savage.. The Balloon Buster', a World War I aviation strip that was very much conceived as a counterpoint to the German Enemy Ace. Savage was a sharpshooter very much given to saying 'I'm th'gun' (yes, it was written by Kanigher), and something of a rebel. The strip's brief run in 112, 113, 114 and 116 never really gave it time to (ahem) take off, but Russ Heath's art, particularly on 116, was glorious.~DAR
Recommended: 2, 3, 5, 78, 112–114, 116

ALL-OUT WAR
DC: *6 issues 1979–1980*

War comics were on the decline in the 1980s, so it's not surprising that this oversize comic didn't last. It's main feature was Viking Commando, a true Viking who avoided Valhalla and spent his time helping the Allied cause against the Nazis in the usual Viking way without a uru hammer in sight.~HY

ALL-STAR COMICS
DC: *57 issues 1940–1951, 17 issues (58–74) 1976–1978*

The first two issues resembled any number of other 1940s anthologies with several popular heroes in separate stories under one cover, but with the third issue a revolutionary new concept was introduced. There were, as before, separate stories for each featured hero: The Flash, Hawkman, Green Lantern, Hourman, Atom, Dr Fate, the Spectre, Sandman and Johnny Thunder, but in a framing sequence these heroes met, talked and compared notes on what was happening in the world of 'mystery men'. A fraternity of superheroes, the Justice Society Of America, was introduced to the readers and became the mould for countless other superteams. The heroes would meet in the first and final chapter of each issue, and each JSA member would battle an aspect of the menace featured in that particular issue in his own chapter drawn by that hero's regular creators. This initial formula became compressed by the shrinking page count as the decade progressed, with chapters starring two or three heroes, but remained essentially unchanged until the title's conversion into *All Star Western* with 58. In the intervening decade most of DC's heavy hitters joined the team (with Wonder Woman making her début in 8 in a story unrelated to that issue's JSA tale, before joining in 11), and fought bizarre menaces such as Per Degaton, Brain Wave, Solomon Grundy, The Wizard, the Injustice Gang, and of course Hitler. Along the way they were the first heroes to tackle social issues, with stories on racial prejudice (16), juvenile delinquency (40) and the role of disabled people in society (27).

Roaring across time and space, treating the solar system like a small neighbourhood where it was possible to go to Jupiter, thrash the bad guys and still get back for supper, the scope of these adventures rattles the reader along at a hectic pace. Yet for all their world-conquering power, the JSA were never reluctant to help the common man, as in the memorable 21, where the team travels back in time solely to help a dying man undo his earlier misdeeds and die with a clear conscience.

Falling sales for the entire superhero genre killed *All Star* in 1951, but it lived on in fandom's collective mind, and when the JSA were revived in 1963 as Flash guest stars it was rapidly followed by the first teaming with the Justice League Of America in *JLA* 21, inaugurating an annual tradition continued until the 1980s. A clamour for the revival of All Star began, but it wasn't until 1976 that DC finally revived the title. Even then the JSA connection was downplayed, with the emphasis on three younger characters: Robin, the Star-Spangled Kid and Power Girl as The Super Squad. This bogus ploy was only discarded in 66 when they were accepted as JSA members and the JSA logo was again heavily cover-featured. Possessed of snappy scripts by Paul Levitz, working with Gerry Conway on 58–62, and excellent art from Giffen and Wood, supplanted by Staton and Layton from 66, the new JSA was rapturously received. The old heroes were portrayed realistically as older people still striving to do the right thing, and the newly created Power Girl, a startlingly pneumatic Kryptonian with a major attitude, was a huge hit. Abrasive, rude and arrogant, she proved you don't have to be a nice person to be a good person, and people who've only seen the gutless shell of Power Girl around today don't know what they've missed. Sadly not even her introduction and, later, the Huntress, daughter of Batman and Catwoman, helped the book survive. The JSA stories continued for a while in the extra large *Adventure Comics*, and there's a fine explanation for why the JSA didn't win World War II on their own in *DC Special* 29, but by 1980 they were once again mere guest stars in the DC Universe.~HS

Recommended: 13, 21, 27, 33–38, 58–73

Collections: All Star Archives Vol 1 (3–6), Vol 2 (7–10), Vol 3 (11–14)

ALL-STAR SQUADRON
DC: *67 issues, 3 annuals 1981–1987*

The greatest DC heroes of the 1940s live again in a series of untold World War II adventures recounted by writer Roy Thomas – surely his dream assignment, having been a Justice Society Of America buff since the 1940s. Originally under instruction not to use too many characters with modern counterparts, Thomas had to work with second-stringers as his core team. When the restriction was dropped the title was a JSA series in all but name. Sadly, to the comic's detriment, Thomas proved unable to detach himself from his fanboy roots. Rather than concentrating on entertaining the reader, he worried over explaining and correcting perceived continuity errors. Many issues were excessively wordy and dry, lacking the gung-ho zeal of the 1940s originals. Although often well illustrated (Jerry Ordway's run of 19–26 and Annual 2 being particularly lovely), the series was all too often strictly for ageing nostalgists. A pity.~HS

ALL-STAR WESTERN

DC: *Series one 62 issues (58–119) 1951–1961, series two 11 issues 1970–1972*

As the first era of the superhero came to a close, DC wasted no time in shunting out the Justice Society Of America, and adding the word 'Western' to their title for a seamless overhaul. In contrast to the majority of DC's themed titles of the time, *All Star Western* featured ongoing characters from the off. The Trigger Twins, introduced in 58, ran until 116, often illustrated by Carmine Infantino. Town sheriff Walt was often aided by twin brother Wayne. Gimmick-led from day one, more humour came from Wayne's shop assistant forever holding up Walt as a paragon of virtue and bravery. Simple, yet only charming in small doses, it's astounding the twins lasted so long.

The other features introduced in 58 weren't as long lived. Jeff Graham, the Roving Ranger, joined the Texas Rangers following the American Civil War, and roamed the state apprehending ne'er-do-wells using his sharpshooting skills. It's as stereotyped and unimaginative as it sounds. Slightly more interesting was Don Caballero, *All Star's* Zorro rip-off. He named his fencing sword El Capitan, protected his local community from an odd assortment of villains, and earned his living as a fencing instructor. Luckily the bullet with his name on never came his way. Strong Bow was the only survivor member of the massacre that wiped out his tribe. A sort of Native American ronin (masterless samurai), he wandered a 14th-century USA preaching peace, but perfectly able to defend himself.

All Star Western's other mainstay was an already proven success. Johnny Thunder made his début in *All American* 100, created by Robert Kanigher and Alex Toth. Sadly, Toth didn't follow him to *All Star Western*, where he débuted in 67, but Gil Kane was an acceptable substitute. Were it not for Kanigher, Johnny Thunder would have been your typical lightning-fast sureshot, but Kanigher introduced complexities to the story, with Thunder promising his dying mother he'd become a schoolteacher, thus devastating his Sheriff father, who'd seen Johnny as his successor. Johnny circumvents his emotional conflict by adopting a disguise to fight crime at his father's side. Arch-enemy Silk Black was a regular visiting desperado and Kanigher introduced a further complication in the dying days in Madame .44. She was a glamorous woman driven to ensuring that those who robbed and cheated others faced justice; she ended up marrying Johnny.

The only other notable feature was Super Chief, by Gardner Fox and Carmine Infantino

(whose art can be found in almost every issue), introduced in the title's death throes. Flying Stag is waylaid by rivals *en route* to a contest to see who should be the supreme chief of the Iroquois. Trapped in a pit, the great spirit Manitou answers his prayers, and as long as he carries a mystical stone (a chunk of meteorite) he's a thousand times stronger than the bear, with the leading prowess of the wolf and swifter than the deer. Wearing a rather fetching buffalo head mask, he protects his people.

In 1970 DC revived the idea of the Western anthology comic. Early issues feature a mixed bunch of strips, the best of which are the Gray Morrow-drawn El Diablo stories from 2. Paralysed in a wheelchair by day, by night he was a mystical spirit of justice. It was gruesomely disfigured bounty hunter Jonah Hex, however, who was to prove enduring. In comparison with what was to follow, his first two outings (10 and 11) are relatively tame, although they do set the tone for the series, with people requiring Hex's prodigious gunslinging talents but unwilling to accept his company. With 12 the title was altered to *Weird Western*.~FP

The ALLAGASH INCIDENT

Tundra: *One-shot 1993*

Recounting famous UFO abductions using clumsy computer-generated images. One for Forteans only.~HS

ALLEGRA

Image: *4-issue miniseries 1996*

Allegra leads a corps of warriors whose job it is to defend Midian against the sky colony of Kioram. Both of these societies live above a desolate Earth but Kioram's leader, Dr. Tullus, hopes to return to the surface eventually. Powered by armour invented by Dr. Huber, Allegra has been conditioned to believe that returning to Earth is a crime. Nevertheless she's continually drawn to the all-but-uninhabitable surface world. As Allegra starts to question the nature of her world clues are dropped that the whole is an elaborate virtual-reality creation and, as she remembers another name, that she's the unwilling subject of a weapons experiment. Intriguingly plotted by Steven Seagle, with good art by Scott Clark, it's not a bad mystery tale.~NF

THE ALLIANCE

Image: *4-issue miniseries 1995*

Superhero space opera in a distant galaxy. Not as dire as some other titles from Valentino's portion of the Image franchise, but with the usual tendency for ridiculously (and barely) costumed women. Don't bother unless you've read at least 90% of the other titles reviewed here.~FP

Robert E.Howard's Ironhand of ALMURIC
Dark Horse: *4-issue miniseries 1991*

Amateurishly drawn sword-and-sorcery clichés using Esau Cairn from the Howard novels. Far superior is the one-shot collecting the Roy Thomas and Tim Conrad story originally serialised in *Epic Illustrated*.~WJ

ALPHA FLIGHT
Marvel: *130 issues, 2 Annuals, 1 Special, 1983–1994*

Created by John Byrne and marketed largely on the novelty of being Canada's first superhero team, *Alpha Flight* featured the characters who first appeared in *X-Men* 120 and had already been established as Wolverine's original team-mates. The first dozen or so issues, until Byrne loses interest, are amongst his best solo work, with tight plotting and good characterisation. The death of Guardian, the team's leader, in 12, is particularly well handled although, this being a Marvel comic, it's not all that long before he's back. Unfortunately the title never found a direction without Byrne, lacking any outstanding creators for the rest of a surprisingly long run. The issues around 50, written by Bill Mantlo, are so cringingly bad, and have such ludicrous plots, that they become unintentionally funny. Alpha Flight tended to have a knack for ludicrous plots. In the issues leading up to 50 stories include Sasquatch trapped in a female body and (among other things) trying to get his ex-wife to vouch for him so that he can access his bank account, and the adventures of Beta and Gamma Flight, Alpha Flight's increasingly inept reserves. All this from a team who put their leader's widow in charge because they didn't know what else to do with her – and the real joy is that it's never intentionally a comedy series. 97–100 were also issued as a four-issue miniseries titled *Alpha Flight Special*. The series will, however, be remembered for introducing Marvel's first openly gay character, Northstar. Although the character's sexuality was obvious without being stated from about 30 onwards, it was not until 106, written by Scott Lobdell, that it was set in stone. For those who want to read between the lines, hints start to be dropped around the time Northstar tells the sex-changed Sasquatch that he preferred the old male body, carry on through a (too) long flirtation by team-mate The Purple Girl, and almost cumulated in what was expected to be an AIDS revelation in 50. Except that Marvel wimped out at the last minute in favour of a revelation far too stupid to have been planned (go on – read it yourself, a snip at 10p). An unimpressive *Northstar* miniseries followed, but despite the publicity the 'outing' brought,

the book's days were already numbered. Most issues between 51 and 64 are notable for containing some of Jim Lee's earliest work for Marvel, but the best place to read about Alpha Flight is in the excellent 2-issue *X-Men/Alpha Flight* miniseries by Chris Claremont and Paul Smith.~JC

ALTER EGO
First: *4-issue miniseries 1986*

A young boy is transferred to another dimension where comic book heroes are real, and he joins the heroic fraternity as Alter Ego. The comics and character are named after writer Roy Thomas' fanzine about 1940s comics, and the slightly disguised Golden Age characters who abound will provide diversion for nostalgia buffs.~HS

AMALGAM COMICS
DC/Marvel: *12 one-shots 1996*

Following the events in issue 3 of the *DC Vs. Marvel* crossover, the two superhero universes got 'smooshed' together, and these odd titles, created as if they were part of an ongoing joint universe that had 'always' been that way, were the result. Think of them as issues 3a–3l of the 4-issue parent series. (Ulp!) Some of them work as stand-alone stories, others were deliberately created with references to fake previous and future issues, to enhance the illusion. The twelve, all numbered 1, are *Amazon* (a Storm/Wonder Woman hybrid), by John Byrne; *Assassins* (Catwoman/Elektra teamed with a female Daredevil/Deathstroke), by Chichester and McDaniel; *Bruce Wayne, Agent of S.H.I.E.L.D.* (Batman/Nick Fury), by Dixon and Nord; *Bullets & Bracelets* (Wonder Woman/Punisher), by Ostrander and Frank; *Doctor StrangeFate* (Drs. Strange and Fate), by Marz and Garcia Lopez; *JLX* (Justice League and X-Men), by Waid, Jones and Porter; *Legend of the Dark Claw* (Batman/Wolverine), by Hama and Balent; *Magneto and The Magnetic Men* (X-Men/Metal Men), by Waid and Matsuda; *Speed Demon* (Ghost Rider/Flash), by Mackie, Felder and Larocca; *Spider-Boy* (Spider-Man/Superboy) by Kesel and Wieringo; *Super-Soldier* (Superman/Captain America) by Waid and Gibbons; *X-Patrol* (X-Force/Doom Patrol) by Kesel, Kesel and Cruz). Much to everyone's surprise, the gag worked brilliantly. Some were better than others – *X-Patrol*, *Bullets & Bracelets* and *Dr.StrangeFate* being the wittiest and grittiest, while the pompous *Amazon* and plodding *JLX* were definitely poorest, but all of them were much more fun than the lack-lustre *Marvel Vs. DC* crossover itself.~HS
Recommended: *Bullets & Bracelets, Dr. StrangeFate, Spider-Boy, X-Patrol*
Collections: 2 volumes (all issues)

AMAZING ADULT FANTASY

Marvel: *8 issues (7–14) 1961–1962*

'The Magazine That Respects Your Intelligence'. This mix of science fiction and fantasy stingers continues numbering from the first series of *Amazing Adventures* and differs from Marvel's other anthology titles in that it features stories by Stan Lee and Steve Ditko exclusively. This, plus the illustrated contents page and Marvel's earliest letters page, shows Lee's obvious pride in his story-telling formula. All issues run four or five stories and are of equally classic quality. 'The Icy Fingers Of Fear' in 7, 'The Terror of Tim Boo Ba' in 9, 'For The Rest Of Your Life' and the superb 'Secret Of The Universe' in 11 are all highspots. 'The Man In The Sky' introduces Lee's concept of mutants, with several striking similarities with scenes in *X-Men* 1 a year or so later. The title changed to *Amazing Fantasy* for its famous final issue in which Spider-Man débuted.~SW

Recommended: 7, 11, 14

AMAZING ADVENTURES

Marvel: *Series one 6 issues 1961, series two 39 issues 1970–1976, series three 14 issues 1979–1981, One-shot 1988*

Dr Droom was the feature connecting issues of *Amazing Adventures'* first run. Droom was a bargain-basement mystic seen by some as a putative Dr Strange, being written by Stan Lee and drawn by Jack Kirby and Steve Ditko. Although appearing in every issue, he was never cover-featured, the covers instead depicting one of the standard mystery stories inside. Truth be told, his stories were no better than the surrounding material, but once the cult of Marvel hit full pelt in the 1970s he was revived as the more fortunately named Dr Druid. After six issues Marvel changed the title to *Amazing Adult Fantasy*.

The second series began by splitting the twenty-two pages, and, more eccentrically, the cover between The Inhumans and the Black Widow. Both were perennially popular supporting characters, and neither really took off as a solo feature, with the Inhumans nudging out their co-star to occupy the whole title from 9. The Black Widow's pages were competent but dull throughout, and the highlight of the Inhumans strip was the artwork of Neal Adams on 6–8, particularly excelling on Thor's guest appearance in 8. Roy Thomas tied 9 and 10 in tangentially with his 'Kree/Skrull War' story running in the *Avengers* at the time, and *X-Men* fans might be enticed to sample by Magneto's appearances, but venture in with expectations low. Of even greater interest to *X-Men* fans was the next lead feature – Marvel didn't drop the back-up reprint short strips until the late 20s – The Beast. It's hard to conceive of a time when the

X-Men were considered a sales failure and consigned to limbo, but that was the case in the early 1970s, when none of them had been seen since their title went reprint with 66. New writer Steve Englehart was given the opportunity to flex his muscles, and, tapping into the mode for horror characters at the time, transformed the mutant Hank McCoy into a character more in keeping with his alias. Now possessing the hirsute body of an animal, but retaining his human intellect, Hank McCoy stars in a decent run, well illustrated by Tom Sutton. Sample 13, when some old *X-Men* villains come calling for the Beast. Not a sales success, the Beast was ousted after six issues, and plot-lines were concluded in *Hulk* 161.

Although certainly not obvious from its early appearances, the best strip to appear in *Amazing Adventures* saw the second series to a close. Roy Thomas conceived the idea of extrapolating on H.G. Wells' *War Of The Worlds* and having his Martians return for a second and more successful invasion of Earth in the mid-21st century. Luckily there was the charismatic and effective Killraven on hand to lead a band of rebels against the Martians. Alternating between being cover-featured as *War Of The Worlds* and *Killraven*, its a pedestrian feature until the arrival of Don McGregor. McGregor's 1970s work is now often regarded as pretentious and over-written, but credit must be due for attempting to inject a poetry into Marvel material, and for producing a story propelled as much by the interaction between the cast as by any conflict. He was also able to convey eloquently the horror of a subjugated humanity. The series would probably have remained obscure had McGregor's original artistic collaborators Rich Buckler and Gene Colan continued. Luckily deadline problems introduced P.Craig Russell. Once given the opportunity to ink and colour his pencils, Russell matched McGregor's vision with his own to create stunning illustrations with an almost fragile line, and if his experimental layouts sometimes confused it was a small price to pay.

Killraven's band of freedom fighters attack the Martians and their agents wherever possible, but rarely without cost. A character called Sklar is a proto-Terminator whose head features mouth and ears, but disturbingly and memorably only a gaping hole instead of nose and eyes. The camaraderie between Killraven and best buddy M'Shulla – far too often tweely referred to as 'Mud brother' – is exceptionally well developed, and the surly Hawk, simple but strong Old Skull, and the only woman of the group, although far from a token, Carmilla Frost round out the regular cast. One of them is killed in 34, a rare occurrence in the comics of the time, and it's a testament to McGregor and

Russell that the story remains the highlight of the run. Such was the detail of his work that Russell obviously had difficulty maintaining even a bi-monthly schedule, and fill-ins punctuate the run, but they're also interesting. The Keith Giffen- illustrated 'The 24 Hour Man' is a weird take on an old science fiction concept, and Giffen also illustrates 38, obviously designed to pull in new readers, as it cover-features assorted familiar Marvel heroes. The series finale is a beautifully drawn, but ultimately empty Killraven solo, obviously intended as an interlude issue. Readers had to wait over five years for a conclusion among the first flush of Marvel graphic novels. Russell's art has progressed immensely by this point, and McGregor's florid tendencies have diminished, but it's a muddled and disappointing affair.

The peculiar idea of reprinting the first eight issues of *Uncanny X-Men* over two issues apiece provided the third *Amazing Adventures* series. The stories are reprinted elsewhere with more care and attention. The one-shot was issued to utilise material seemingly commissioned for cancelled titles, particularly *High Adventure*, as many of the stories have a historical bent. On the face of it the lead story should have been the most appealing, combining the creative talents of Chris Claremont and Michael Golden (inked by Terry Austin). Unfortunately, it's nonsense. Anticipating *The Accused*, a woman is raped and afforded the opportunity to revenge herself on her rapists. So far, so good, except to do so she has to be transformed into a space warrior riding a dragon. It's a distressingly trivial and offensive solution to a ghastly experience. Mike Vosburg contributes a decent short about Reilly, Ace Of Spies and 'Mata Hari', and 'The Grail' by DeMatteis and Ridgway also succeeds. In its entirety, though, this is only worth picking out of a bargain box.~FP
Recommended: 29, 31, 34–37

THE AMAZING CYNICALMAN
Eclipse: *One-shot 1987*

Matt Feazell's photocopied minicomics were a revelation. Extremely confident from the off, Feazell's speedy stick-figure style of art and stream-of-consciousness plotting resulted in some very funny moments, the best of which are collected in Caliber's paperback volume *Ert*. Eclipse gave Feazell the opportunity to extend his talents over a complete comic, and despite some very funny moments and pointed comments, 'Cynicalman Sells Out' begins to ramble long before the end. There are several other minicomics creators backing up the lead strip, including one drawn by Bob Burden.~WJ

AMAZING FANTASY
Marvel: *4 issues (15–18), 1962 (15), 1995 –1996 (16–18)*

Stan Lee knew that this series, previously titled *Amazing Adult Fantasy*, was heading for cancellation graveyard. With nothing to lose, he and Steve Ditko introduced a new and different superhero in the final issue. This superhero had real-life problems in his normal identity as shy, unpopular, teenaged Peter Parker. Thus Spider-Man was born. The rest is history.

Thirty-three years later the title was revived. Some concepts do take time to catch on. Kurt Busiek retrospectively conceived the tale linking *Amazing Fantasy* 15 to *Amazing Spider-Man* 1. This will grate on continuity buffs as inconsistencies inevitably result and the difference in sophistication between the 1960s and 1990s narratives is jarring. Nevertheless, his story is sensitively written and Paul Lee supplies moody, painted artwork. Surely no other title will ever undergo a 3192% price rise between consecutive issues.~APS

THE AMAZON
Comico: *3-issue miniseries 1989*

American journalist Malcolm Hilliard becomes obsessed with discovering the truth about rumours concerning missing workers and disruptions at a Brazilian logging camp. The local tribes believe a physical manifestation of the Amazon occurs to protect the land in times of need, and the further Hilliard digs the more he's forced to question his beliefs. A remarkably assured comic début from writer Steven Seagle, and while Tim Sale's early art is less adept this is a rare instance of a series managing to wrap a forceful point in a well paced story.~FP
Recommended: 1–3

AMBUSH BUG
DC: *6-issue miniseries 1985, 6-issue miniseries (Son Of Ambush Bug), 1 Special 1986, One-shot 1992*

Keith Giffen at his best and most original with an irreverent parody of the world of comics and their creators under the guise of a surreal superhero strip. The first series works best, with the joke running a bit dry for the second, titled *Son Of Ambush Bug*. Completists may be interested to know about guest appearances from The Joker in 1986's *Stocking Stuffer* and Aquaman, Lobo, Death and Sandman in the 1992 *Nothing Special*. Then again, maybe they won't.~TP

AMERICA VS THE JUSTICE SOCIETY
DC: *4-issue miniseries 1985*

Set on Earth Two, where DC consigned their 1940s heroes at one stage, Batman's diary posthumously accuses the JSA of murder. Dick

(Robin) Grayson and Helena (Huntress) Wayne are on opposite sides of the judicial fence. Overly talky, inappropriately illustrated, and you know you're onto a loser when the text pages are much more interesting than the story they surround.~HS

The AMERICAN

Dark Horse: *8 issues 1987–1988, 1 Special 1990, 4-issue miniseries ('Lost In America') 1992*

Well loved super-soldier 'The American' is a media darling and hero of the masses, but one determined reporter uncovers a fraud perpetrated over generations of false heroics, which has cost untold lives. He, and his loved ones, suffer the consequences, and despite help along the way, including catastrophic intercession from the former 'Kid American', the hero's sidekick, he stands alone against overwhelming forces. Deft writing from Mark Verheiden keeps the suspense tight, and the, at best, partial victory of the protagonist adds an unexpectedly realistic note of compromise. The second series focuses on the latest American himself, and his attempts to find an identity now that his cherished façade has been stripped away. This leads him to a strange cult – a carefully non-litigious blend of the Moonies and the Scientologists – and a disturbing series of revelations, about himself and the behaviour of the 'Average Man' from which he's been so carefully shielded for most of his life. An interesting sidenote is that the original *American* series was allegedly a proposal for Marvel's *Captain America*, rejected because the then Marvel management didn't want to drastically revamp their hero as a pawn of the government. Considering what they've allowed to happen to him since, it might have been kinder if they'd followed this proposal.~HS

AMERICAN FLAGG!

First: *Series one 50 issues, 1 special 1983–1988, Series two 12 issues 1988–1989*

The world of American Flagg is one of the most intelligently realised dystopian futures ever to appear in comic books. Writer/artist Howard Chaykin had more creative freedom than ever before on this series, and he put it to better use than he ever has since. Three years before *Watchmen* and *The Dark Knight Returns*, Flagg brought thoughtful adult themes to American mainstream comics...wrapped up in plenty of sex and violence.

In 2031, the government of the USA has relocated to Mars, a witty take on the trend for the rich and powerful to isolate themselves in ever more secure enclaves. Earth is beset by all the ills we see around us today, only more so. Chicago is now the Plex, an island of shopping malls and luxury-apartment fortresses, in a sea of poverty and drug addiction. Video screens blast out continual images of sex linked to commerce, and cartoon violence linked to gun sales. The Plex is also the complex of political, military and commercial interests which runs everything behind the scenes. The militaristic police force, The Rangers, is under continued assault by well-armed biker gangs.

Drafted from Mars into the corrupt Rangers comes Reuben Flagg, pampered star of a pornographic TV series, in which he plays a Ranger on the vice squad. 'Life imitates art,' he points out as he greets his new boss, Sheriff Hilton Krieger. No one believes, of course, that Flagg is real Ranger material. But, in 1–3, as Krieger is murdered and a web of intrigue and corruption is revealed, Flagg rises to the occasion, stops the gang rampages and apparently takes control of the Rangers. He also looks ready to root out the forces of corruption, which clearly reach right up to government level. This may sound like a tired futuristic re-run of a thousand Westerns and urban thrillers, but several factors lift it above the mire. Flagg himself, clearly Chaykin's own fantasy alter-ego, is not a fearless fighter; when the violence hits, he's often motivated by sheer terror. Nor is he a hopeless naïf: he knows that even a basically honest Ranger cannot avoid being manipulated, and maybe corrupted, by many vested interests within society. But Flagg personally is not exactly pure of heart. He is often led by his carnal lusts, and part of his appeal to women is his nasty streak. Humour is also important. Luther the dumb robot deputy and Raul the talking cat are integral members of the cast, Raul in particular providing more than just comic relief. The women too are strong characters. Though tending to the tough bitch stereotype so beloved of male writers, they are more complex and interesting than most examples. The sheer bravura of Chaykin's story-telling is another factor in the success of *Flagg*. He pioneered new panel layouts and uses of sound effects which owe a debt to Eisner but are clearly the work of an individual talent; letterer Ken Bruzenak must take some of the credit.

Three-issue story arcs from 4–12 take Flagg to Brasilia, for some cross-racial/trans-gender shenanigans, the US cattle belt, then back to urban Chicago for more action-packed political infighting. 13–14 are fill-ins drawn by lesser lights. Thereafter there are back-up strips and features, to take the pressure off Chaykin, and story arcs run across four issues. Wild West action meets socialism in Canada in 15–18 and 23–26 take Flagg to London to meet 'Mad Dogs and Englishmen'. Chaykin went on to other things after 26, though he continued to have writing or plotting input for a while. Not all the non-Chaykin issues are utterly hopeless.

Alan Moore provided an enjoyable, sex-packed back-up strip in 21–26 which expanded to fill the whole of 27, drawn by Don Lomax. But after that Chaykin and others, including J.M.DeMatteis, Joe Staton and Mark Badger, could only manage to stir the fading embers of the book's original brilliance. The Special is a pointless story which serves only to spin off Chaykin's new strip, *Time Squared*.

The early *American Flagg* is a violent, fast-paced, funny comic which verges on the soft-core pornographic, clearly a commercial product intended to reach a large audience. Yet beneath its lurid, cynical surface is a liberal ethical core. Sadly, the title's promise remains unfulfilled, including the tantalising possibility that Reuben Flagg could actually make a difference to America...or might at least try. The Chaykin issues are like a moderately adult graphic novel with no ending, but maybe he is too lazy a story-teller to confront the deeper issues in a sustained way, and perhaps the lack of a happy (or even nobly tragic) resolution fits with *American Flagg*'s ultimately cynical world-view.~GL
Recommended: 1–27
Collections: Hard Times (Series one 1–3), *Southern Comfort* (Series one 4–6), *State Of The Union* (Series one 7–9)

AMERICAN FREAK, A tale of the Un-Men
Vertigo: *5-issue miniseries 1994*

Army orphan Damien Kane discovers his true lineage as the offspring of procreation experiments between genetically engineered freaks. Discovering he's also mutating, Kane is befriended by the deformed Crassus, who promises a cure for Kane's condition and leads him to a community of others with deformities. Don't be put off by the preposterous covers and their glaring taglines. *American Freak* is a fine study of humanity's reaction to anyone different, and Dave Louapre's poignant script avoids sentimentality or a predictable outcome.~WJ

AMERICAN SPLENDOR
Harvey Pekar: *16 issues 1976–1991*
Dark Horse: *One-shot ('A Step Out Of The Nest') 1994, 2-issue microseries ('Windfall') 1995, One-shot ('Comic-Con Comics') 1996*
Four Walls Eight Windows: *Our Cancer Year 1995*

Harvey Pekar's *American Splendor* is a truly unique creation. Long before the fashion for autobiographical comics Pekar was documenting the trials, tribulations and trivia of being a filing clerk and part-time journalist in Cleveland. In magazine-size issues, illustrated by a host of artists including Frank (Foolbert Sturgeon) Stack, Robert Crumb,

Spain, Garys Zabel and Dumm and Jim Woodring, Pekar lays bare his life, from tiny crises about feeding the cat or meeting a college friend after twenty years to major upsets, like divorce and cancer. Rarely has anyone been willing to open up and show the world all their insecurities, stupid acts, fleeting moments of triumph, petty worries and often pettier hatreds like Pekar, joined in later issues by his current wife Joyce Brabner. Despite this many of his most beautifully scripted strips are about overheard conversations, jokes told to him by co-workers, or bits of local oral history, such as the Crumb-illustrated 'The Maggie' in 7, about Yiddish linoleum salesmen, that frequently top and tail the more dramatic pieces. As the series has developed the shorter pieces become fewer as Pekar settles down to chronicle his fears and worries over illness and old age. He kvetches constantly, whinges and whines and probes his own psyche like a kid unable to stop poking an aching tooth with his tongue. All his worst fears are realised on discovering he has cancer. The impact of his illness, on himself and all around him, is brutally explored in *Our Cancer Year*, an extraordinarily frank graphic novel co-written with Joyce Brabner. Pekar lays bare his deepest fears in this book, loosely but effectively documented by Frank Stack. It's the closest comics get to effective documentary, and is deeply moving.

'A Step Out Of The Nest' concerns a trip to do *The David Letterman Show* for the first time in years. He used to be a regular guest until he and David had a falling out. 'Windfall' is about a trip to Chicago to give a lecture, in which Joyce Brabner allows herself to be portrayed as a pushy, politically annoying woman who analyses her husband's every action. Fascinating. 'Comic-Con Comics' is the least engaging of the specials. The tale of Harvey winding up Matt Groening about only being placed 96 on his list of favourite people strikes a chord (and a nerve) but the rest of the book is a ramble about a tele-salesman stroke cartoonist who tells Harvey more than you want to know about selling knock-off T-shirts.~FJ
Recommended: 2, 3, 7, 12, 15, *Our Cancer Year*, 'Windfall'
Collections: American Splendour (assorted strips from 1–10), *Bob and Harv's Comics* (all Robert Crumb illustrated stories)

AMERICOMICS
AC: *6 issues, 1 Special 1983–1984*

One of publisher Bill Black's first attempts at crossing over from fanzines to small-press comics, this anthology is a very mixed bag indeed. It features several of the pneumatic heroines that would later comprise *Femforce* (Dragonfly, Tara), heroes who would become mainstays of AC continuity (Shade, Captain Freedom), and odd material created under a temporary licence starring discontinued Charlton heroes such as Blue Beetle. Seldom better than fair, *Americomics* showcases the early efforts of several folk who would progress to less embarrassing work, including Jerry Ordway, Will Nyberg and Vic Bridges. The special teamed Blue Beetle, Captain Atom, Nightshade and The Question as *The Sentinels Of Justice*, a titled later co-opted by Black for his own creations.~HS

AMMO ARMAGEDDON
Atomeka: *One-shot 1993*

If some boys haven't got big toys then they'll write about them and draw them. An excellent Geof Darrow cover conceals a largely dull weapon-and-war anthology, although at least Warren Ellis and Phil Winslade have the wit to turn in a story about a mechanised penis.~FP

AMETHYST, Princess Of Gemworld
DC: *Series one 12 issues, 1 annual 1983–1984, series two 16 issues, 1 special 1985–1986, 4-issue miniseries 1987–1988*

On her thirteenth birthday, Amy Winston discovers that she's also the twenty-year-old Princess Amethyst, rightful ruler of Gemworld and its twelve royal houses. She discovers this the hard way when she's abducted by the evil Dark Opal, who wants to dispose of her to make his domination of Gemworld complete. From the title and the covers, this looks all pastel colours and dressing-up-games, a truly girly girls' comic, providing yet another princess fantasy for those girls who are so inclined. But, no. It's a thoroughly intelligent adventure story, where the good characters have to work hard at it, facing some very tough decisions, and where the ultimate outcome owes quite as much to sub-plots among the villains as to our heroes' superior firepower, which makes for a particularly satisfying and logical ending. The writing by Dan Mishkin and Gary Cohn is terrific, with some wonderful characters (the swashbuckling Princess Turquoise striking a chord), and with pace and plot that make the twelve issues fly by. The story would probably have worked even without Ernie Colon's artwork, but with it, it's unforgettable. Goodness, that man can draw!

Maybe it's a testament to how very good the first *Amethyst* series was that DC were back the very next year to maul her beyond recognition. Mishkin and Cohn returned as writers (for the Annual, and Issues 1–8), but this time they have no real story to tell, and they take out their boredom and frustration on the characters, ripping from them all integrity and zest for life. From 9, the writing team starts changing every few issues, and thereafter we

all know that it's just a matter of time. Sad, very sad. And what can one say in favour of the miniseries? It's mercifully short, and the characters are so far from their 1983 versions that the sight of their zombie forms lurching through these pages is less traumatic than it might have been. The story-line is some gibberish about Amethyst returning to Gemworld to sort out a problem with the next generation, while the real problem – the devastating failure of self-esteem that's affected every one of the female characters – goes unacknowledged and unremedied. Hideous.~FC

Recommended: Series one 1–12

AMY PAPUDA
Northstar: *2 issues 1990, One-shot (Amy Papuda Returns) 1992*

As bizarre a series as has been seen in comics, *Amy Papuda* blends the spirit of *Beavis And Butthead* with an incredibly bleak sense of humour. The ugly Amy is the butt of many typical high-school jokes, and is abused by a drunken father, but when she arranges revenge she's jailed for her troubles. Her chief tormentor, jock Doug and his sidekick Wally, are suitably ghastly creations, and moments of triumph for Amy are few and far between. Writer and artist Michael Perlstein's style bears a similarity to that of J.R.Williams (whose 'Bad Boys' strip would seem to be an influence). He's obviously enjoying himself, but the nihilistic approach and casual treatment of deeply upsetting subjects may render *Amy Papuda* thoroughly offensive to some.~WJ

AN ACCIDENTAL DEATH
Fantagraphics: *One shot 1993*

Originally serialised in *Dark Horse Presents* 65–67, artist Eric Shanower and writer Ed Brubaker's quiet but terrible story of teenage death and unspoken codes of secrecy among army brats in the 1970s is brilliantly observed and drawn. The military background is essential to the resonance of the story, particularly the conclusion, and Brubaker's distanced narrative serves to bring the reader closer to the horror.~WJ

Recommended: 1

ANARCHY COMICS
Last Gasp: 3 issues 1978–1981

A mixture of political and social commentaries, plus historical strips about various Anarchist actions, there's still room for poetry, humour and melodrama in this fine series. In the spirit of the title, the first issue of *Anarchy Comics* is numbered 2.

From Spain's excellent 'Blood And Sky' about anarchy during the Spanish Civil War to Melinda Gebbie's ornate story of Estelle

Dufy, and Epistolier and Volny's 'Kronstadt' (reprinted from *L'Echo Des Savanes*), issue one sets a high standard, actually matched by the following issues. It also includes work by editor Jay Kinney, Paul Mavrides, Cliff Harper and Gilbert Shelton. 2 features Kinney and Mavrides' 'Kultur Dokuments', an Archie parody/parable, 'The Black Freighter', adapted by Cliff Harper from Brecht, another terrific history lesson by Spain about Spanish Anarchist leader Durruti (he of Column fame) and more work by Gebbie and Epistolier. 3 is more of the same, augmented by strips from Albo Helm, Gerd Seyfried, early Gary Panter, Sharon Rudahl, Greg Irons and Matt Feazell. Throughout *Anarchy Comics* squarely addressed its theme, prompting creators to produce work of the highest quality, and the inclusion of European material strengthens an already worthwhile package.~NF
Recommended: 1–3

ANGEL AND THE APE
DC: *7 issues, 1968–1969, 4-issue miniseries 1990–1991*

A humour series débuting in *Showcase* 77 and featuring private investigators Angel O'Day and her gorilla partner, Sam Simeon. The cases they took involved them in the usual hairy detection adventures. An interesting sub-plot involved the part-time job Sam had, a comic strip artist for an editor named Stan Bragg, who dressed in a Stars and Stripes costume – and why not? The final 1960s issue was titled *Meet Angel*. Angel and Sam returned in 1990 with a more realistic tone, which revealed that Dumb Bunny from *Inferior Five* was her half-sister and descended from the ancient Amazons. Worth sampling.~HY

ANGEL LOVE
DC: *8 issues, 1 special 1986–1987*

This was an unusual series by Barbara Slate, drawn in cartoon style, but with quite realistic settings involving the life of Angel Love, a young woman coping in modern society. The talking cockroaches in her apartment gave the series a nice kookie feel. This would have made a great TV series, and is worth a look.~ HY

ANGELA
Image: 3-issue miniseries 1994–1995

Neil Gaiman fleshes out the background to the angel Angela in this *Spawn* spin-off. Angela is put on trial after her battle with Spawn and his appearance during the proceedings doesn't do much to restore her to the good graces of the rulers of her angelic homeworld, Elysium. Gaiman has fun with the odd couple's adventure in Hell and sets the stage for Angela to go solo in this enjoyable if lightweight series. Greg Capullo's artwork is, as ever, reminiscent

of McFarlane's but his straightforward story-telling and attention to detail make the whole thing visually attractive.~NF

ANGRYMAN
Iconografix: *3 issues 1992–1993*

Ned's life falls apart as he has dreams letting him view the actions of Angryman. There's a germ of a good idea hiding in *Angryman*, but the comic can't decide if it wants to be superhero parody or semi-autobiographical. The best issue is 2, in which Ned forms a new relationship and there's a well conceived back-up parody of the *Fantastic Four*.~WJ

ANIMA
DC: *15 issues 1994–1995*

Clumsy attempt at a superheroic Tank Girl. Grunge chick gets superpowers and stumbles off into unfocussed, forgettable adventures.~HS

ANIMAL CONFIDENTIAL
Dark Horse: *One-shot 1992*

Peculiar selection of short stories involving animals. Randy Stradley and Eric Vincent retell the legend of the Hartlepool monkeyhangers to hilarious effect, backed up by Rick Geary, Nina Paley, and parody text stories and ads. Spotty, but entertaining.~HS

ANIMAL MAN
DC/Vertigo: *89 issues, 1 Annual, 1988–1995*

Prior to Grant Morrison getting hold of Animal Man, his previous appearance had been in *Action Comics* 552–553, 1984, as part of a group called The Forgotten Heroes, which wasn't far off the mark. Before that he'd been a small-time 1960s superhero from a short run in *Strange Adventures*. His own title will prove more memorable, not least for the superb cover art of Brian Bolland on 1–63. Chas Truog's interiors in 1–32 are markedly less attractive, and strong scripts by Morrison made the comic a success despite Truog rather than helped by him.

1–4 is a tremendously confident opening story, reintroducing Buddy Baker and explaining his power to take on the abilities of any animal in the immediate vicinity. He's relaunching his superhero career, while living with his wife and two kids. This gives the title a lasting family flavour all its own. Another enduring issue is that of animal rights, introduced with the arrival from Africa of an even shorter-lived 1960s hero, B'wana Beast, to free animals from zoos and research labs. Animal Man fights B'wana Beast at first, but then realises he agrees with him. Such attitudes will complicate his relationship with the authorities, and thus his career (another lasting theme). 5 is a poignant tale of a Wile E.Coyote figure who comes from a dimension where animated cartoons are reality. Alternate worlds and the suffering of cartoon characters for our entertainment will be important later. Things really hot up in 10. *Secret Origins* 39 is a prologue to this story, which sees the reappearance of the yellow aliens whose exploding space-ship accidentally gave Buddy his animal powers. Animal Man's naïve 1960s origin is given the now-traditional late 1980s twist – it wasn't an accident, the aliens deliberately linked Buddy into the 'morphogenetic field' generated by all life on earth. But Morrison then goes as far beyond the 'realistic' superhero style of contemporary comics as they are beyond the 1960s, as characters in *Animal Man* start to perceive the comic-book nature of their reality. In 18–19, Buddy takes a peyote trip and sees the readers of his comic staring down at him. In 20–24 the reality of the DC Universe almost breaks down. It's a sequel of sorts to *Crisis On Infinite Earths*, but with built-in satire and comics criticism, aimed at grim'n'gritty modern superheroes. In 25–26's epilogue, Buddy meets his maker, Grant Morrison, and some of Grant's motivations in writing the series are explored. It's been a truly unique experience.

27–32 is Peter Milligan's underrated run, satisfyingly weird, in which the formerly vegetarian Buddy acquires a strong taste for raw meat, and has more alternate reality adventures. With 33 writer Tom Veitch takes over, with Steve Dillon artwork. Veitch brings a more superficially serious tone to the comic, but achieves less than his predecessors did with their apparently lighter-hearted romps. Case in point: Morrison's Native American character is a professor of physics who helps Buddy perceive the nature of reality, i.e. they are living in a comic book. Veitch's Amerindians are Carlos Castaneda-style mystics, the good guys in a struggle against evil corporate America with its arms factories, computers and killer clones. Which is the more radical, and which a case of seen it all before? Veitch gives us the kind of 'realistic' comic that Morrison mocked. Buddy's powers are explored in tedious detail, and the yellow aliens are revealed as a childish rationalisation of Animal Man's true Native American mystical roots. It's a slim story spread out too thin. Not all that bad, just not in the same league as what came before.

In 51 Jamie Delano arrives to prove that 'serious' doesn't have to mean 'dull'. He integrates Veitch's settings and character-isations respectfully, as with Buddy's daughter Maxine's inherited superpowers (climaxing in 1993's annual, crossing over with *The Children's Crusade*). He also develops *Animal Man* into something new, if decidedly gloomy in outlook. Animal Man dies in 51, struggling back to a new form of life via the morphogenetic field in 56. Meanwhile his son Cliff suffers at the hands of the sadistic Uncle Dudley, another well developed Veitch element: no supervillains here, but some very dark human evil. In the urban jungle, wife Ellen is almost raped and joins some lesbian feminists in 57–60. 61–63 introduces the idea that the natural world has had enough of mankind's abuses and is going to fight back. In 71, Buddy mutates into a hideous, gargoyle-like form, remaking himself as Mother Nature's champion. He starts a new natural religion, the Life-Power Church, and gathers around himself an army of the dispossessed – hippies, punks, slackers and grungers. The State, of course, fights back. At 79's huge religious meeting/rock festival/love-in Animal Man commits ritual (and overtly messianic) suicide. He thinks that a martyred dead hero will be better remembered than an embittered one living on. With strong art from Steve Pugh and others, Delano takes elements from Morrison and Veitch, plus some familiar to readers of Moore's *Swamp Thing*, and stirs them into his own potent brew, with confrontation of difficult real-world issues, and refusal to find easy answers. Grim'n'gritty to be sure, but in a unique way, with high quality and a mordant wit. Sadly, Buddy Baker couldn't be allowed the peace of the grave, and once again his connection to the Life Web brings reincarnation. From 80 it's writer Jerry Prosser and artist Fred Harper who take on the thankless task. They have a pretty fair stab at it. The Animal Man experience is looked at from the Shamanistic point of view, and the travails of the Life-Power Church continue. It doesn't really go anywhere, though, and it's all over by 89. Ten issues too late.~GL

Recommended: 1–5, 17–26, 27–32, 51–63, 72–79
Collection: Animal Man (1–9)

ANIMANIACS
DC: *21 issues + 1995 to date*

Wakko, Yakko and Dot are the Warner Brothers (and sister) in this comic adaptation of the cartoon. This series details the adventures of the three Warners as they escape from captivity and cause havoc. The intense wackiness of the cartoon just doesn't translate here, and the visual gags fall flat in the static environment of comic panels.~SS

ANNEX
Marvel: *4-issue miniseries 1994*

It's quite an achievement to write a strip featuring a 1990s state-of-the-art-technology-based superhero with the contemporary sophistication of 1940s comics. Jack C. Harris pulls off this feat with aplomb.~FP

ANOTHER DAY
Raised Brow: *1 issue 1995*

A young man discovers he has telekinetic powers, but spends most of his time trying to prevent his sexist friend from being beaten up by various women he's offended, or avoiding the sex games of an all too sociable couple. Charming, funny, underplayed comic that's keenly observant of relationships. If the title continues it deserves a wider audience.~HS
Recommended: 1

ANT BOY
Steeldragon: *2 issues 1988*

Originally self-published minicomics from creator Matt Feazell, these are drawn in a pleasingly loose style. Ant Boy is a human boy raised by ants, and therefore has a skewed view of humanity, their habits and their artefacts. It's very silly, particularly the battle with the lawnmower in 2. Further stories can be found as back-ups in *Captain Confederacy*.~WJ

ANTHRO
DC: *6 issues 1968–1969*

Not the usual prehistoric/jungle series that it appeared to be. Starting life in *Showcase 74*, *Anthro* was a well written, witty account of a Stone-Age family, the titular character being the eldest son. Howie Post wrote and drew the strip and his wonderful art style suited the setting perfectly. If you want to read something different, try this series, but don't expect *The Flintstones*.~HY
Recommended: 1–6

ANYTHING GOES
Fantagraphics: *6 issues 1986–1987*

Fund-raiser featuring some top talent delivering short stories. Among the contributors are Bob Burden, Eddie Campbell, Mark Martin and Dave Sim. Look out 4 with Gilbert Hernandez contributing a 'Heartbreak Soup' vignette, Peter Bagge and a *Journey* short, and 2 with Jaime Hernandez, a disappointing Jack Kirby and Joe Sinnott *Captain Victory* and Alan Moore and Don Simpson's excellent 'Pictopia'. It's a fondly observed lament about the monopolisation of comics by superheroes with thinly veiled guest appearances.~WJ
Recommended: 2, 4

APE CITY
Adventure: *4-issue miniseries 1990*

Charles Marshall writes a far livelier and more interesting version of the apes in this miniseries than he does in the parent title. Mixing monkey gangsters, ninja apes, heavily armed human killers and a fair amount of humour, Marshall is forced to write with a beginning, middle and end, and does so with aplomb. The thrust of the plot is the chase for a crystal that powers the humans' craft, but also offers unlimited energy for the apes. The artwork, though, deteriorates as the series progresses, becoming slipshod and amateur by the conclusion.~FP

APE NATION
Adventure: *4-issue miniseries 1991*

Mixing the concepts from *Planet Of The Apes* with TV show *Alien Nation* might not seem a sensible idea. They've little to link them beyond both races being subjugated by humans at some stage, and the comic rights for both series being in the hands of Adventure. Featuring the cast from Adventure's regular Planet Of The Apes series, the stories have Tectonese forces landing on the apes' planet and forming an alliance with the renegade General Ollo. Joining forces they march on Ape City, on the way encountering a party of apes led by Heston (!) sent to investigate the strange craft. It's lack-lustre stuff ending in one big battle. There, saved you buying it.~FP

APPLESEED
Eclipse: *Book one 5 issues 1988–1989, book two 5 issues 1989, book three 5 issues 1991, book four 2 issues 1991*

This translates Masamune Shirow's manga epic set in the aftermath of a non-nuclear World War III. The main characters are Deunan Knute, cute girl soldier who's only really happy when inside an exoskeleton, and Briareos, cyborg warrior and Knute's partner and lover. At the beginning of Book 1, the pair are invited to Olympus, a 'utopian' city with ambitious plans for world peace and for the refinement of the human race. Books 1 and 2 concentrate on this 'refinement' plan, and this means a lot of factional meetings and parliamentary debates, conducted throughout in fluent gibberish masquerading as philosophical profundity. Meanwhile, Knute and Briareos join the local police force, so each issue has many pages devoted to frenzied and incomprehensible fight sequences, particularly Books 3 and 4, which take a break from the refinement plan in order to spout gibberish about international relations.

Shirow seems incapable of telling a story in a direct, interesting or believable way. One suspects he doesn't really know what the refinement plan involves or what the nations are intriguing about, and to avoid the effort of working out the details, he just has his characters talking about things in vague and pompous terms. Hellishly dull. To call his cast characters, by the way, is to be generous. You can tell them apart only by gender (i.e. bambi-eyes or scars), or by the make of their cyborg parts, or by whether their nose is drawn badly or really badly. With this shaky foundation, it's not surprising that they have problems conducting conversations along the you-make-a-statement-I-make-a-related-response lines favoured by mentally competent adults. Surely the translators could have helped Shirow out here? A thoroughly unrewarding and irritating read – though if you're mad keen on exoskeletons you may get a buzz from skimming through and looking at the pictures.~FC

Collections: The Promethean Challenge (Book one 1–5), *Prometheus Unbound* (Book two 1–5), *The Scales Of Prometheus* (Book three 1–5), *The Promethean Balance* (Book four 1–2)

Underworld Unleashed
APOKALIPS Dark Uprising
DC: *One-shot 1995*

Tying in with both *Underworld Unleashed* and *New Gods* , Darkseid is, temporarily, among the deceased. This offers arch-tempter Neron the opportunity to set the next tier of the Apokalips hierarchy at each other's throats, promising them all that they're destined to succeed Darkseid. It's all reasonably well produced, but merely tangential to both the series with which it's tied, and not a strong enough story to be worth having for itself.~WJ

Not APRIL HORRORS
Rip Off: *One-shot 1992*

A misleadingly repackaged collection of Doug Wheeler's 'Classics Desecrated' stories from *Negative Burn* and other sources. Kind of, well, a rip-off.~HS

AQUABLUE
Dark Horse: *2 volumes 1990*

Stranded in space as an infant and raised by a robot, Tumu Nao finally locates an inhabitable planet. Consisting largely of water, it's known as Aquablue, and on landing there he faces a whale and survives. The locals see this as part of a prophecy regarding a saviour who will ensure the planet's survival in a time of great threat. Growing up on Aquablue, Nao reaches manhood before encountering anyone else from Earth. Unfortunately a now less than benign Earth government intends to exploit the energies of Aquablue, riding roughshod over the wishes of its inhabitants, seducing the warriors with alcohol. In the second book, titled 'The Blue Planet', Nao returns to Earth to claim his inheritance in order to halt the exploitation of Aquablue, but it doesn't quite go as planned. There's some lovely artwork from Olivier Vatine, and while the parallels aren't exactly subtle, the story's an enjoyable romp, although seemingly incomplete. Full

credit to Dark Horse for publishing in European album format instead of the reduced American comic format.~FP

AQUAMAN
DC: *Series one 63 issues 1962–1971 (1–56), 1977–1978 (57–63), miniseries one 4 issues 1986, One-shot 1988, One-shot 1989, miniseries two 5 issues 1989, series two 13 issues 1991–1992, 4-issue miniseries ('Time And Tide') 1993, series three 27 issues, 1 annual 1994 to date*

Aquaman is one of DC's longest running heroes, making his first appearance in *More Fun Comics* 73 in 1941, created by Mort Weisinger and artist Paul Norris. Throughout the 1940s and 1950s he appeared in *Adventure Comics*, *Detective Comics* and *World's Finest Comics*, and was one of only five DC superheroes to survive the death of such characters in the late 1940s and early 1950s.

Aquaman was Arthur Curry, the product of a human and a princess of the underwater world of Atlantis, and his powers relate to the ocean. To withstand the enormous pressures of the sea he had great strength and speed, and he also had the ability to communicate with all marine life. Despite his long career he was never a member of any of DC's 1940s supergroups, and never tried as a headliner until a four-issue run in *Showcase* 30–33 in 1961. These were written by Jack Miller and Bob Haney, and illustrated by the artist of most 1950s Aquaman strips, Ramona Fradon, who gave him a slight cartoony look. 31, though, had art by Nick Cardy, another artist who would play an important role in developing the character, drawing the new title from its inception. The stories all featured Aquaman's sidekick Aqualad, and introduced a new development as Aquaman became king of Atlantis. The early issues, though, don't really convince in any respect, and there's the feeling that Haney and Miller were still rattling off plots designed for a back-up feature, forgetting this was now an ongoing title. To make matters worse there's the introduction of a 'humorous' water spirit called Quist. One notable issue among the mediocrity is 11, which introduces Mera, an underwater character from another dimension. It's a short courtship when Aquaman and Mera marry in 18. She was no ordinary underwater breather, though, being able to create hard substances from water, an odd talent never fully utilised. Gestation times underwater must be reduced, because Aquababy, that's right, Aquababy, turned up in 23.

When Cardy first began drawing Aquaman he approximated Fradon's cartoony style, but there are noticeable changes over the issues as his art becomes bolder and more fluid: he drew the most luscious lips on any female character!

Another positive side to Aquaman now being a headliner was that he slowly built up a cast of recurring villains, most prominently the Ocean Master, who débuted in 29. He had a particular emotional resonance, being Aquaman's half-brother, Orm, who had always grown up in Arthur's shadow and so became an international marine criminal and scavenger. Tula the Aquagirl was a bit of a wild girl who liked to party, and led Aqualad astray on her first appearance in 33, luring him with her two-piece swimsuit. Or, as Aqualad put it, 'Wowee. I like. You're some chick, Tula. In fact that's what I'm calling you from now on, Aquachick!' Not all stories were as trivial, though, with 37's 'When The Sea Dies' excellent. It begins with an outstanding cover with a rotting seabed and Aquaman holding Mera in his arms. Inside Aquaman battles Ocean Master and the Scavenger, a villain who's slowly polluting the Earth's oceans.

From 40 it's all change as writer Steve Skeates and artist Jim Aparo take over. They produce what remains *Aquaman*'s finest run, starting with a multi-part epic culminating in 48. Mera is kidnapped in 40, and while trying to find her Aquaman encounters assorted underwater civilisations, but with Aquaman away his deputy is planning a permanent succession to the throne of Atlantis, and only Aquagirl is left to thwart him. This was a major departure for DC, who at the time considered an extended story one that occupied two issues. When Aparo began drawing he attempted to emulate Cardy for the sake of continuity, but his unique style shone through rapidly. These days not as detailed, in the late 1960s and early 1970s he was a very impressive artist indeed, dynamic and thoughtful, and there's no better examples than his issues of *Aquaman*. Aparo's art had a superficial similarity to that of Neal Adams, who drew some wonderful Deadman back-ups in 50–52, actually tying in to the Aquaman story. Alas, quality doesn't always equate with sales, and the series was cancelled in 1971.

The character was by no means dead, though. He returned to *Adventure Comics* with 435, and a successful run led to a revived title, in which Aquaman comes to terms with Black Manta's murder of his son in *Adventure* 452. It wasn't a long run, and although competent, produced little of note, with Aparo's art now a shorthand version of his earlier style. Aquaman continued as a supporting character in back-up strips in *Adventure, Action* and *World's Finest*, and was given another solo run in 1986. Neal Pozner wrote and Craig Hamilton worked wonders with a complicated new blue costume intended to camouflage Aquaman in the sea. Atlantis is on the verge of

war with humanity over a stolen Atlantean seal, in what's a well plotted series and very impressive visually. The 1988 special contains nothing of note, and 1989's *The Legend Of Aquaman Special* outlines the revised history of Aquaman, with an expanded origin, and sets up the 1989 miniseries, also written by Keith Giffen and Robert Loren Fleming, and pencilled by Curt Swan, who turns in a wonderfully illustrated series in which Atlantis has been taken over by alien creatures. The aliens are a sideline, though, as the series focuses on the relationship between Aquaman and his estranged wife, with 3 featuring a magnificent battle between them. The series only ranks below the 1960s Skeates and Aparo run in Aquaman's history.

The 1991 ongoing series is a celebration of Aquaman's 50th anniversary, and takes the previous miniseries as a starting point. Politics and ecological problems feature strongly in Shaun McLaughlin's plots as Atlantis is attacked by a composite Scandinavian country, leading to civil unrest. Aquaman confronts the Black Manta and the issue of sea pollution is effectively dealt with in 9 and 10's 'Eco-Wars'. Guest artist Vince Giarrano manages a more action-packed style than regular penciller Ken Hooper, who nevertheless always turns in a decent job. Despite the failure of this series DC refused to give up on the character, and 1993's miniseries is written by fan favourite Peter David, and pencilled by Kirk Javinen, once more recounting Aquaman's origin. By this time he's had about half a dozen origins since the 1940s, but for the time being this is the bona fide version. 1 has him chronicling his first meeting with surface-world heroes in the form of the Flash, and subsequent issues deal with his upbringing, coming of age, first love, stepping up to the throne of Atlantis, meeting Mera and producing the doomed Arthur junior.

'Time And Tide' sets up the 1994 *Aquaman* series. Peter David continues as writer, with Martin Egeland illustrating, and they certainly get to grips with the character. It had slowly been changing since the 1970s, becoming more aggressive, and from the start of this series it's no more Mr Nice Guy. In line with DC's policy of giving their older characters a bit more bite, Aquaman grows his hair and a beard necessary to maintain his body weight, since he loses a hand in the second issue. It's replaced with a form of harpoon, and there's another new costume, this time armoured. David populates the series with some old characters, with Aqualad as expected, plus the return of Dolphin, a mysterious water-breather who appeared in *Showcase* 79, and here becomes Aquaman's love interest. We also meet the product of Aquaman's first love interest when a teenage son turns up. He's a chip off the old block with a chip on his shoulder. David explores the scenario of Atlantis imaginatively, and doesn't run shy of using unlikely guest stars such as Superboy in 3, Lobo in 4, the Deep Six in 6–8. Mera returns in 12, prompting domestic strife, and there's sibling strife with the return of Ocean Master in 19. Older *Aquaman* readers might not appreciate the modernising of the character, but he had to change. Although he blows hot and cold, on better days David keeps the pages turning with inventive plots and new concepts, well illustrated by Egeland, and they should ensure a lengthy run.~HY

Recommended: Series one 37, 40–52, 1989 One-shot, miniseries two 1–5
Collection: Time And Tide (miniseries 1–4)

ARAK, Son Of Thunder
DC: *50 issues, 1 annual 1981–1985*

It was quite a surprise when Roy Thomas, former editor-in-chief and long-time writing mainstay of Marvel Comics, elected for a career and company change with their rivals. DC already had properties in place able to cope with his particular interests – World War II, super teams, tightening up continuity – except for a title to replace *Conan* in his schedule. Not to worry, though, because with a few tweaks and nudges Roy came up with a Native American wandering the globe during the Dark Ages. Unfortunately he'd run through every possible permutation of sword and sorcery while writing two *Conan* titles, and there's nothing to distinguish *Arak* from any other attempt at the genre – not even when the relatively fresh Dann Thomas comes on as co-plotter. It says something for DC's faith in Thomas' ability that they let this meander on for four years, eschewing the neat ending when Arak's heart stops beating in 32. Instead it begins a new sequence with our man now a full shaman. Viking Prince fans may want to investigate his back-up strip in 8–11. Although artist Jan Duursema tries hard to live up to Kubert's version, writer Robert Kanigher certainly holds up his end.~HY

ARCADE
Print Mint: *7 issues 1975–1976*

This was the transition between the often indulgent underground of the 1960s and the idea of producing comics as intelligent material for an adult audience as the class of 1968 grew up. It merged the vitality of the undergrounds with an ambition that far outstrips them and is possibly the finest anthology comic ever produced. Every issue contains work from Bob Armstrong, Robert Crumb, Kim Deitch, Justin Green, the under-rated Willy Murphy, Spain Rodriguez and co-editors Bill Griffith and Art

Spiegelman (at a time when he still used traditional upper-case lettering). More than half also play host to Aline Kominsky, Gilbert Shelton, Robert Williams and S.Clay Wilson. Encouraging the top underground creators to flex their talents beyond what they'd produced before results in startling work like Crumb's 'Modern America' (2) and 'That's Life' (3), Justin Green's Brooklyn adaptation of *The Winter's Tale* casting Karl Malden as Polixenes (1), Griffith's biography of Henri Rousseau (3) and Spain's memorable 'Stalin' (4).

The editorial care taken by Griffiths and Spiegelman is represented not only in the almost impeccable choice of material, but also in the design, with every contents page presenting a new self-portrait from all contributors. The balance is also perfect. Each issue features vital contemporary material and the work of a top cartoonist or illustrator from the early part of the century, a short strips section, and prose fiction from the likes of Burroughs and Bukowski, illustrated by Crumb or Green. *Arcade* matches the mixture indicated by the title with humour, polemic, questioning, introspection and plain lunacy from the top talents of the day. If you feel inclined to sample only a single issue, try 2, but you shouldn't stop there.~FP

Recommended: 1–7

ARCHANGEL
Marvel: *One-shot 1996*

This black and white one shot, written by Peter Milligan and drawn by Leonardo Manco, was an unusual package for a Marvel X-book, and one that didn't really work. Instead of giving the book an air of sophistication, as was presumably the intention, the scratchy art looks amateurish and out of place on a Milligan script which is no better suited to the subject matter. The dialogue is stilted, and the plot about the ghost of a woman whose mutant powers draw birds to her is predictable and contrived. Best avoided.~JC

ARCHER AND ARMSTRONG
Valiant: *27 issues (0–26), 1992–1994*

Archer is an ascetic teenage martial arts expert raised in a Buddhist monastery and Armstrong is a bulky immortal carouser. The well conceived and engagingly mismatched characters make for an entertaining run of comics as Archer is incredulous at Armstrong's indulgent lifestyle, and Armstrong is forever the tempter. The first issue, confusingly numbered 0, introduces the pair along with a centuries-old single-minded religious sect who believe Armstrong to be Satan and seek his death, with 1–2 jumping straight into the *Unity* crossover. Earlier issues are the best, being written and drawn by Barry Windsor-Smith, who stays just the right side of dropping into farce. In 8 (also issue 8 of *Eternal Warrior*, Armstrong's brother) Smith introduces the interesting idea of showing Armstrong's earlier escapades, accompanied by a suitably naïve character in the Archer role. The resulting *Three Musketeers* plot is the best of the run. Mike Baron writes most issues from 13, with Mike Vosburg art from 17. Their run also entertains, but doesn't quite match the Smith issues. The final issue is again combined with *Eternal Warrior*.~FP

Recommended: 0, 3–8, 12

ARCHIE

MLJ/Archie: *460+ issues 1942 to date, plus countless spin-offs, related titles, one-shots, annuals and specials.*

Introduced in MLJ's *Pep Comics* 22 in 1941 as a back-up feature to the tolerably successful superheroes the Shield and the Black Hood, Archie Andrews, a well-meaning but maladroit teenager, was to become a money-spinning juggernaut that, by the end of the 1940s, had ousted all MLJ's superheroes and netted MLJ so much revenue that they renamed the company in his honour. Red-haired, freckle-faced Archie is in love with Betty Cooper, the blonde, virtuous (but spunky) girl down the road. He's also in love with Veronica Lodge, the rich, spoiled (but sweet) brunette who lives in a mansion on the outskirts of Riverdale, USA His best friend is Forsythe P. 'Jughead' Jones, fervent omnivore and woman-hater. Archie's rival for Veronica's and Betty's affections is Reggie Mantle, a braggart and schemer with a well-concealed heart of gold. And that's all you need to know to comprehend virtually any of the thousands of Archie stories published over five decades. Within a year of Archie's début, all these pieces were in place, and the essential dynamic of the series was established. There are many more supporting characters, but these key players have kept an eternal, ageless soap opera spinning for over fifty years. Hairstyles and clothing trends change; a polite nod of recognition is given to whatever fashion, music or media fads are 'in', but nothing really alters. The Archie gang have been secret agents, superheroes, pop idols and actors; they've been recast as tiny tots, as pre-teens, as their own prehistoric ancestors and futuristic descendants, but the relationships remain the same, and at the end of every story, whatever events may have occurred, the *status quo* is lovingly restored. Currently, not only Archie, but Jughead, Betty and Veronica (the latter two together and individually) have their own series, there are two 'ensemble' books – *Archie & Friends* and *World of Archie* – and Cheryl Blossom, a comparatively new (introduced 1981) 'bad girl' character, has just been awarded

her own series; there have also been scads of previous Archie titles. Some of the longer-running ones you may encounter are *Pep*, *Laugh*, *Life With Archie*, *Archie's Pals n' Gals*, *Archie and Me*, *Betty & Me*, *Reggie & Me*, *Reggie*, *Reggie's Wise-Guy Jokes*, *Archie's Joke Book*, *Archie's TV Laugh-Out*, and many, many more, including a line of hugely successful paperback-size Digest Comics that have been busily recycling old material since the early 1980s. Since they all have the same cast and set-up, this review encompasses them all, though a couple of allied but separate titles from this publisher, *Josie* and *Sabrina the Teen-Age Witch*, merit their own entries. The Archie gang are archetypes – some would say stereotypes – whose ageless, unchanging façade is curiously reassuring to those of us who have seen all our childhood heroes mutate into murderous psychopaths. Long may they reign.~HS

Collections: Best of the Forties, Best of the Fifties, Best of the Sixties

AREA 88

Eclipse: *36 issues 1987–1989*
Viz: *6 issues (37–42) 1989*

One of the first Japanese comics to be translated for the American audience, and the choice was a wise one. Kaoru Shintani's story is about Shin, a mercenary fighter pilot who's been tricked into signing a three-year-mission contract to fight as part of a force embroiled in a fictional African nation's civil war. Shin's the best pilot at the base, but tormented by his circumstances. Within a simple structure the stories address complex emotional issues, particularly once the focus expands beyond the airbase and skies from 17. At that point we learn more of Shin's past, his friends and his enemies. The introductory issues tend towards aerial combats, which, while dynamic and varied, don't thrill as they should. 9's story of a war correspondent trapped behind enemy lines is a good starter, and 13 goes a long way to explaining the circumstances of the war and the isolated airbase.~FP

ARGUS

DC: *6 issues 1995*

Another of the heroes created during 'Bloodlines' tries out for a regular series. Argus is an undercover cop in the mob whose childhood links to the underworld have given him a position of power as second-in-command to D'Angelo, a mob leader. With super strength, invisibility and some mysterious visual powers, Argus finds himself fighting to prevent D'Angelo using satellite technology to create his own empire. Mark Wheatley and Allan Gross tell a good story, making Argus' character a pivotal aspect of the plot and showing how it influences his powers. Phil Hester's artwork on 1–4 is stylish and makes excellent use of blacks for atmosphere, but Luke McDonnell's two issues are less adventurous.~NF

ARIANE & BLUEBEARD
Eclipse: *One-shot 1989*

One of P. Craig Russell's series of opera adaptations, in this case Maurice Maeterlinck's allegorical poem and Paul Dukas' music/ stage-play. Russell's ornate artwork is always a delight and he manages to capture both the beauty and the drama of the original work (the colouring doing much to offset the lack of sound).~NF
Recommended: 1

ARIK KHAN
Andromeda: *3 issues 1977–1979*

One of the earliest independent titles, and seemingly a labour of love from creator Franc Reyes. He put a lot of work into creating a real world for his character, which makes it a shame that this is nothing but bog-standard barbarian material. Except the back-ups, which are sub-standard barbarian material.~FP

ARION
DC: *Lord of Atlantis 35 issues, 1 special 1982–1985, 6-issue miniseries (The Immortal) 1992*

Introduced as a back-up in *Warlord* 55–62, the first series is sword-and-sorcery-based, with Arion as Lord High Mage of Atlantis in 45,000 BC, a period of mystical transition as a great civilisation begins a slow decline. Paul Kupperberg and Jan Duursema are responsible for most issues (although Doug Moench donates Arion's origin in 4 & 5), and provide quests, sorcery, dragons and other standard fantasy trappings. If that appeals, look at 12, featuring most of the cast and a fair feel as to the rest of the series despite Arion being temporarily bereft of power. The first series concludes in the 1985 *Arion Special*.

The second series has a very different flavour. The age of magic is long past, but the immortal Arion remains, barely surviving as a card sharp in New York and telling true stories about his past that no one believes. Magic returns, tensions in the Middle East escalate, a familiar foe is back and Arion has to figure how to make a 20-year-old woman love an immortal. The ideas are better, and this series makes for a more satisfying read.~WJ

ARISTOCRATIC XTRATERRESTRIAL TIME-TRAVELLING THIEVES
Comics Interview: *One-shot 1986, 12 issues 1987–1988*

Small alien Fred and human Bianca are the best thieves any time any place, and in their two first issues steal the formula for Coke and

artwork for the *Dazzler*, which indicates the way the series is. Fred and Bianca are likeable, gags abound and entertainment is a priority for creators Henry Vogel and Mark Propst. Quality varies, but no issue is dull. Try 3, in which the pair steal a Mom robot without understanding what it is. Created during the fad for adjective-heavy titles, the joke had worn thin by 7 when the title was contracted to *X-Thieves*.~FP
Collections: Graphic Album 1 (one-shot, 1–2), Graphic Album 2 (3–5), Graphic Album 3 (6–8)

ARMAGEDDON 2001
DC: *2 issues 1991*

DC have been issuing multi-part crossovers since the mid-1980s as clearing house exercises and attempts at boosting sales. These particular issues bookend their 1991 annuals and are by no means the worst examples, but they certainly lack any punch. Matthew Ryder travels back from 2001 to save the DC Universe's superheroes from destruction from the self-styled Monarch, one of their own turned bad. While traversing the decade Ryder becomes, surprise, surprise, a superhero called Waverider, and has to discover the identity of the rogue hero in order to prevent the glum future. The final revelation hardly rocks the DC continuity to the core, and leaves too many threads for the inevitable sequel. While Archie Goodwin's writing succeeds where others might have failed, the art of Dan Jurgens and Dick Giordano is strictly functional.~TP

ARMAGEDDON: ALIEN AGENDA
DC: *4-issue miniseries 1991–1992*

The sad sequel to the above involving the defeated Monarch, Captain Atom and a bunch of aliens in a predictable time-travelling tale involving the destruction of Earth.~TP

ARMAGEDDON INFERNO
DC: *4-issue miniseries 1992*

Determined to flog the dying horse one more time, DC has one more crack at making Waverider an exciting character. Old Wavy yet again groups a bunch of heroes from various times to save the time continuum, this time from a demon called Abraxis. Despite the impressive list of creators including Simonson, Netzer and Ostrander it's very much bread-and -utter work for all of them.~TP

ARMATURE
Olyoptics: *1 issue + 1996 to date*

A strange, self-published fantasy created by colorist Steve Oliff, set in Dark Park and Lightworld, 'the only holographic alternative reality theme park on the planet'. It owes something to Jim Woodring's *Frank* and Sam Kieth's *Maxx* (who makes a guest appearance in the first issue). That said, Armature, a mute, twisted, skeletal figure, looks to be a playful but potentially more serious character. One to watch.~NF

ARMOR
Continuity: *Series one 13 issues 1985–1992, series two 6 issues 1993*

Even amongst a company that prizes artwork as much as Continuity, Armor stands head and shoulders above its companion titles. Pencillers Tom Grindberg (1–4), Sal Velluto (12–13, series two 1, 2 and 4) and particularly the excellent Brian Apthorp (7, 11 and series two 3, 5, 6) all produced some fine work, but it was the superlative inks of Rudy Nebres (2–10, 12, 13, Series two 1, 2) that raised this title to its lofty artistic heights. Sadly the fine art was saddled with Continuity's typically addled stories and English-as-a-second-language dialogue. The title's nadir came with 10's hard-hitting drug exposé 'Kracky The Clown's Krack House', which was every bit as stupid as you'd imagine it to be. The second series is chapters of the company crossover 'Deathwatch 2000', but, as with the first, a comic to savour visually but on no account to be read.~DAR

ARMORINES
Valiant: *13 issues (0–12), 1994–1995*

A bunch of U.S. Marines are equipped with armoured suits and weaponry derived from the X-O Armour, and become pawns of various factions within the government and military. A mostly action series lacking well defined characters, launched when Valiant was in decline, and an early victim of their 1995 cutbacks. 0 was released as a separate premium item, but is more commonly available bound into *X-O Manowar* 25.~HS

ARMY AT WAR
DC: *1 issue 1978*

The 'exciting new idea' proclaimed on the cover banner appears to have been cancelling this ordinary war anthology title after a single issue.~WJ

ARROW
Malibu: *One-shot 1992*

Malbiu's archer type has a chance to rectify a mistake from five years previously in this rather pointless one-shot. Artist Lee Moder was to go on to better things.~FP

ART D'ECCO
Fantagraphics: *4 issues 1990–1992*

Art D'Ecco contains various strips by the Langridge brothers, Andrew and Roger. Andrew 'generally' writes them, and Roger 'generally' draws them, in a variety of angular styles, if the introductions are to be believed. The title character, a Frankenstein's monster lookalike, and his triangular friend Gump engage in various surreal and zany adventures interspersed by short strips. Throughout *Art D'Ecco* is clever and considered and has an extremely good line in visual slapstick. And which other creators would box off congratulatory letters from fellow artists and writers and call it 'Wank Corner'?~FJ

ARTISTIC LICENTIOUSNESS
Starhead: *1 issue 1991*
Comix Bitch: *2 issues (2–3) 1994, 1997*

The original impetus for this, before Roberta Gregory's success with *Naughty Bits*, was to produce a quickie porno comic to make easy money. Gregory took every opportunity to introduce sex between her characters, writer Denise, comic book artist Kevin and all their acquaintances. Despite this it grew into an organic soap opera about which Gregory rapidly became as obsessive as she does about everything else, hence the long gap between issues. Reading a sex comic about human-looking, normal people who don't have perfect chiselled fantasy bods and are as fucked-up as the rest of us still has great appeal even if the original prurient motivation didn't quite come across.~HS

ASH
Event: *6 issues + 1994 to date*

Firefighter Ashley Quinn is massively burned, but makes an inexplicable recovery. Shortly thereafter he morphs into a nine-foot-tall fire-wielding behemoth. Understandably puzzled, he bumbles about having adventures until he meets a powerful entity named Covenant, who claims to have the secret of Ash's origin. The artwork is exquisite, with Quesada and Palmiotti doing their tightest work to date, both dynamic and credible. The story, however, wanders whenever Ash is in his heroic monster form. The scenes with him interacting with his friends, his girl, hell, even his cats, are all much more interesting than the action stuff. Ash is a nice comic, but its mystique surely owes more to it taking a geological epoch between issues.~HS
Collection: *Ash* (1–6)

ASH/22 BRIDES
Event: *2-issue microseries 1996–1997*

Enjoyable enough adventure as the Brides and Ash get drawn into a chase to possess a key to some secret technology (that may or may not be related to Ash's origin). Girl gang the Brides are portrayed in the usual light-hearted way by writer Fabian Nicieza but fireman Ash is more of a cipher. Humberto Ramos provides good, tight pencils which give the work a harder edge, nicely undercutting the comedy-thriller basis of the story.~NF

ASHES
Caliber: *6 issues 1990*

A selection of short stories by John Bergen (with occasional writing assistance), mixing reprints from his arty self-published zine *Brain Dead* and new material. Bergen circles round the same themes like a vulture: religious guilt, vampires, torture and doomed love surface again and again. Amateur psychologists will have a field day counting the number of times a *vagina dentata* (women's bits with teeth) crops up in the artwork. *Ashes* is an angry book that broods on the unfairness of life without becoming tiresome. Some of the stories attain an almost transcendent sense of magic realism; others come over like Hammer horror. It deserves to be read for the inventiveness of Bergen's drawing, from spiky inks to soft charcoal, if nothing else.~FJ

ASKANI'SON
Marvel: *4-issue miniseries 1996*

Following the first series of *The Adventures of Cyclops and Phoenix*, *Askani'son* continues the story of the boy who will one day grow into the man called Cable. Scott Lobdell and Gene Ha once again weave an intricate tale which is part fantasy, part superhero, mixed with liberal dashes of science fiction. As young Nathan continues his journey towards his destiny as the saviour of a desperate world, more of the pieces fall into place, among them the first meetings with his mysterious mentor Blaquesmith and his wife-to-be Alyia. ~JC

ASTERIX
Hodder and Stoughton: *32 volumes 1961 to date*

Created for the weekly French anthology comic *Pilote* in 1959, Asterix has become one of the few globally recognised comic characters through world-wide circulation of the *Asterix* collections. The stories are set in the Roman-occupied Gaul of 50BC. One coastal village remains beyond Caesar's reach due to the magic potion brewed by village druid Getafix. Those drinking the potion are endowed with great strength, speed and invulnerability, the exception being the giant Obelix, who requires no potion, having fallen in the brew as a baby, with lasting consequences. Artist Albert Uderzo's open and expressive cartoon style is ideal for conveying René Goscinny's largely slapstick scripts.

Asterix the Gaul, although primitive by later standards, sets the premise and introduces most of the recurring cast. The best of the early titles is *Asterix the Gladiator* (4), as Asterix and Obelix fight in Caesar's arena to free their village's captured bard Cacofonix. The *Asterix* formula develops early, with most stories involving Asterix on a quest accompanied by Obelix, often in a foreign land, enabling the creators to take easy swipes at national stereotypes. Running gags include a band of inept pirates whose ship invariably sinks on contact with Asterix, the fearsome Roman legionnaires reduced to a bruised mass, and modified speech balloons conveying mood, nationality or character. By *Asterix and Cleopatra* (6) Goscinny and Uderzo are finding their feet, stepping beyond mere farce to address wider concerns, and the series begins to gel as both children's entertainment and social satire. Uderzo's art has become more detailed and researched, and the main characters have solidified into their final forms.

1967's *Asterix the Legionary* (10) begins a golden era, with both creators hitting peak form and inventive plots flowing for the next five years. Obelix volunteers to rescue the boyfriend of a girl he himself yearns after in a story satirising military bureaucracy and inflexibility. It temporarily exhausts the national stereotype jokes, as Asterix and Obelix encounter assorted other foreign legionnaires. It's noticeable that there are only two foreign adventures in the following nine albums, *Asterix in Spain* (14) and the excellent *Asterix in Switzerland* (16), with its hilarious portrayal of a corrupt official.

The problem with an invincible village is that their indomitability works against the strip after a while, requiring Goscinny to conceive ever more inventive ways to circumvent the easy answer of the magic potion (although it invariably saves the day eventually). In *Asterix and the Big Fight* (7) Getafix becomes amnesiac and is unable to brew a potion, and in *Asterix and the Soothsayer* (19) the villagers' own superstitions almost cause their downfall. In the best album of the series, *Asterix and the Roman Agent* (15), Caesar, realising force alone won't prevail, enlists a Roman with a particular talent for sowing discord wherever he travels. His arrival has the villagers at each other's throats, and the book ends with a mass battle involving all local Roman garrisons and the village, masterfully condensed to a single page. Developing the area around the village is Caesar's plan in *The Mansions of the Gods* (17). It's an uncharacteristic tale castigating urban development and promoting conservation: not only is Asterix omitted from the title, but the Gauls only play a small part for much of the story, planting magic acorns to replace trees removed by the Romans.

By 1972 Goscinny appears to have overdosed on *Asterix*. Stories now only appeared on an annual basis, and although always professional, some were more contractual obligation than inspiration. *Asterix and Caesar's Gift* (21), with a challenge to Vitalstatistix's position of Chief, is excellent, but only *Obelix and Co* (23) otherwise displays much spark. Goscinny died after completing *Asterix in Belgium* (24), and Uderzo continues the series alone to this day. His first efforts, *Asterix and the Great Divide* (25) and *Asterix and the Black Gold* (26), were shaky, but by *Asterix and Son* (27) he'd mastered the formula. *Asterix and The Secret Weapon* (30), with the arrival of feminism in the Gaulish village, while tending to deride the central concept, stands alongside the best Asterix stories.

A portion of the credit for the English-language success of Asterix must go to Anthea Bell and Derek Hockridge. Avoiding the cardinal sin of literalism, their sympathetic and inventive translations deftly convey the verbal dexterity and anachronistic references to contemporary culture in the French originals. The back cover running order on Hodder and Stoughton's editions is not the chronology of the series, referred to with the numbering here, and includes illustrated text adaptations of *Asterix* films. The Asterix books are also available as large-format hardcover and softcover editions, and, more recently, as small-size paperbacks.~FP

Recommended: *Asterix and Cleopatra, Asterix and the Big Fight, Asterix the Legionary, Asterix at the Olympic Games (12), Asterix and the Cauldron (13), Asterix in Spain, Asterix and the Roman Agent, Asterix in Switzerland, The Mansions of the Gods, Asterix and the Soothsayer (19), Asterix and Caesar's Gift, Asterix and the Secret Weapon.*

ASTONISHING TALES
Marvel: *36 issues 1970–1976*

Initially featuring two strips per issue, Doctor Doom surrendered the entire title to Ka-Zar with 9. Roy Thomas and Wally Wood handled Doom's first four solos and managed a creditable job on a difficult concept – giving the hero-with-problems treatment to a villain. Larry Lieber and George Tuska's take wasn't as successful, and neither was the Ka-Zar strip as a whole, which never managed to get on even keel, although several issues make for good reading. The best story guest-stars Man-Thing in 12–13 as Ka-Zar temporarily manages to shed his Tarzan-clone character. He graduated to his own title after 20, replaced by It, The Living Colossus, an awful reworking of one of Marvel's many pre-1962 monster strips. Avoid it. Deathlok occupied the remainder of the series. He was an oddity, completely outside the Marvel mould as an army colonel who dies and is rebuilt as a cyborg in the then future of 1990. He revolts against his masters and goes in search of his humanity in a well-portrayed future of intrigue and decay. Rich Buckler (whose concept it was) managed some of his finest art and plotted these stories. When Deathlok was revived in the 1990s these stories were collected as a four-issue series titled *Deathlok Special*.~DWC

The Original ASTRO BOY
Now: *20 issues 1987–1989*

Japan's most famous comic character, Tetsuwan Atom, is known as Astro Boy in the USA and, due to regular screening of his cartoon series, is familiar to most Americans under forty. Ken Steacy provides light children's adventure in 1–16, but our kind-hearted super-strong robot chum suffers with Steacy's departure. Astro Boy's origin is in 8.~FP

Kurt Busiek's ASTRO CITY
Image: *6 issues 1995*
Homage: *3 issues + 1996 to date*

On first appearances this seems to be set in a 1950s-style futuristic city, but Astro City is in fact a modern-day American city inhabited by ordinary and extraordinary people. Following his work on *Marvels*, Kurt Busiek has created a niche for exploring the world of the superhero through the eyes of ordinary people, but *Astro City* offers more. We see the human side of superheroes, with their aims and personalities confidently and intelligently explored, and they're a marvellous set of characters, some with obvious resemblances to the icons of the comics world. The real stars, though, are the city's non-powered inhabitants whose lives are affected by the activities of the superheroes. 4's tale of a secretary whose office becomes a battleground won an industry award for Best Story, and is a fine example of the series. The superpowered characters all seem to be designed by Alex Ross, Busiek's partner for *Marvels*, who also provides the covers, but the interior art is by Brent Anderson. Although, very well drawn, one feels cleaner, crisper linework would be better suited to the look of the series. If you had to live in a world full of superpowered beings you couldn't do better than to move to Astro City, but as you probably don't settle in for a good read instead.~HY

Recommended: Image 1–6, Homage 1–3
Collection: Life In The Big City (Image 1–6)

ASYLUM
Maximum: *10 issues + 1995 to date*

A showcase anthology for Rob Liefeld's Extreme Studios, the one redeeming feature of this series is the occasional appearance of Larry Marder's Tales of The Beanworld. There are new stories, albeit only four pages per issue, in colour in 1–6. Using the anthology as a way of premiering new titles or characters, Liefield gives us the adventures of Starbuck from Battlestar Galactica, Avengelyne, Warchild (drawn by Art Adams in 1), Deathkiss (art by Mike Deodato) and Christian (script by Robert Loren Fleming, art by Pop Mhan). From 7, Megaton Man replaces Tales of the Beanworld and if it's not as interesting, it's better than its companion pieces.~NF

ATARI FORCE

DC: *20 issues 1984–1985, 1 special 1986*

Space adventure that's far better than it had any right to be considering it originated as a corporate promotion for Atari, which in the comic stands for Advanced Technology and Research Institute. Engaging characters and compelling plots from Gerry Conway and never less than excellent art from José Luis Garcia-Lopez, inked by Ricardo Villigran and Bob Smith, ensure that the first thirteen issues are a roller-coaster ride. 1–5 introduce and unite the Atari Force under Martin Champion, leader of a previous incarnation, in order to battle a being calling himself the Dark Destroyer. Despite the stupid name, he's a threat that lasts until 13, after which Mike Baron and Eduardo Barreto take over and keep the quality up for the remainder of the run. Light-hearted back-up stories from 13 focus on individual members of Atari Force, but the 1986 special with none of the regular creators didn't pave the way for a revival as hoped.~FP

Recommended: 1–3, 8, 11, 14, 15, 19, 20

ATLANTIS CHRONICLES

DC: *7-issue limited series 1990*

Current *Aquaman* scripter Peter David cut his teeth on undersea legends a few years beforehand by detailing the fables and history of the lost continent of Atlantis, or at least the DC history thereof. This seemed a labour of love for him, but to most readers it may just seem a bit laboured. At forty-eight pages for seven issues it's stretched too far to keep the interest up. David fleshes out the characteristics of all the major players in recording the history of the turbulent continent, beginning before it sank, featuring Arion, up to the present day and Aquaman. In brief, there are two warring factions, the humanoid water-breathers who come to occupy Poseidonis and the mer-people living in Tritonis, and along the way there's plenty of intrigue and treachery. Esteban Maroto's fluid art is well suited to the period pieces. Each issue can be read independently, and anyone wanting to sample it should try 3, a well-paced story combining much wit and violence.~HY

Recommended: 3

ATLAS

Dark Horse: *4-issue miniseries 1994*

Writer and artist Bruce Zick has a fair turn at producing a Jack Kirby homage. Zick's art strives for the Kirby grandeur, and there are plenty of interesting ideas packed alongside Kirby-style themes, but there's also the often terrible Kirby-style dialogue as well. This distracts from what would otherwise be a good miniseries.~FP

The ATOM

DC: *Series one 38 issues 1962–1968, series two 18 issues 1988–1989, 2 specials 1993–1995*

Using a white-dwarf star fragment, scientist Ray Palmer developed a method of shrinking himself down from six foot to sub-microscopic size. This was another case of DC recycling the name from one of their 1940s superheroes, and the new Atom was another successful graduate of try-out title *Showcase* (34–36). Editor Julius Schwartz was always interested in imparting scientific knowledge as part of his comics, and The Atom was particularly science-heavy, with most of his adventures being science-fiction based with an emphasis on detection and characterisation. Unusually, very few supervillains turned up, the most notable among them being nutty botanist Jason Woodrue, who would later be beefed up as the Floronic Man in *Swamp Thing*, and the time-obsessed Chronos. He was a ludicrous figure in black and white striped tights, and yellow cape, gloves and boots, yet, when unmasked, drawn by Gil Kane to resemble Richard Nixon! The most noteworthy of the earlier issues involved the Time Pool, through which the Atom was able to meet historical figures such as Jules Verne and Edgar Allan Poe.

With the exception of the final issue, the first series was written by Gardner Fox and drawn by Gil Kane, so there's no complaints about artistic quality here. And with Sid Greene inking Kane's pencils the Mighty Mite was a six-inch powerhouse of pure muscle. A perfectly acceptable standard was maintained throughout, but few issues jump out as particularly noteworthy until the end of the run. Then the comic became more action-oriented, with the issues starring the 1940s Atom, 29 and 36, standing out. Hawkman dropped by for a guest slot in 31, foreshadowing the future of the title, which became *Atom And Hawkman* with 39.

When that run ended the Atom spent fifteen years as a little-used cog in *Justice League Of America* before returning in the radically different *Sword Of The Atom* (dealt with as a separate entry). He returned in a straight superhero series titled *Power Of The Atom*, originally written by Roger Stern. A good sample issue is the John Byrne-drawn 6, which beefs up Chronos considerably. The most persistent and mysterious of the villains introduced, though, is Humbug, who débuts in 11 and becomes a particular thorn in Atom's side. The CIA are background players throughout the series, and the final three issues tie up all plots, including some left over from *Sword Of The Atom*. Never spectacular, but always solid, Graham Nolan draws most issues. The first of two specials is a worthy effort by Tom Peyer and Steve Dillon featuring recurring baddie Chronos. The second focuses on his coping with being seventeen again (don't ask) and he's currently a core member of the latest *Teen Titans* incarnation.~HY

Recommended: 29, 36, special 1

THE ATOM AND HAWKMAN
DC: *7 issues (39–45) 1968–1969*

Editor Julius Schwartz's idea of making the eponymous heroes here best buddies (like the Flash and Green Lantern) seems to have led to the merging of their titles (continuing *Atom's* numbering) at a time when split books were all but extinct. Both crossover and solo stories were featured. Unusual but distinguished artwork and some interesting stories by Bob Kanigher, Denny O'Neil and Gardner Fox characterise this curious, doomed title. High points are Fox's 'Panic Button' stories in 40–41 drawn by Joe Kubert, a memorable villain in 43's spectral 18th- century highwayman The Gentleman Ghost, and Kubert's superb covers.~SW

Recommended: 40, 41

THE ATOMIC AGE
Epic: *4-issue miniseries 1990*

A renegade alien called Nimbus appears in this retro look at the 1950s, which contrasts the fears of the age (alien invasions, communism) with mom's-apple-pie rose-tinted nostalgia. More aliens arrive and it all becomes rather silly.~WJ

ATOMIC CITY TALES
Black Eye: *3 issues, 1 special 1994–1995*
Kitchen Sink: *3 issues +1996 to date*

Jay Stephens' Atomic City is a strange and wonderful place to visit, populated by a vast selection of imaginative superpowered characters who behave as most real folk would if they had abilities beyond the levels of everyone else. They go about their business as usual, living, loving and holding parties, except that every now and then there's a planet to save, a robbery to carry out or a score to settle. Stephens even incorporates himself into the strips as official cartoonist to Big Bang, near omnipotent, but also shallow and self-centred. The disjointed aspects of Stephens' *Sin Comics* have been discarded, but, in the manner of a Ronnie Corbett monologue, don't expect a strictly linear structure. Stephens weaves all over the place, creating the impression of a stream-of-consciousness comic with wit and artifice, at times knowing and at times seemingly naïve.~WJ

Recommended: Black Eye 1–3, Special, Kitchen Sink 1–3

AUTUMN
Caliber: *3-issue miniseries 1995*

This is an unusual World War II serial killer story, written by Chris Dows and Colin Clayton, and illustrated by Horus in a rather lumpen but striking black and white style. The emphasis is on a young boy who becomes obsessed with a killer who only strikes during the autumn, and only murders in the London Underground, rather than on police procedure and tracking him down. However, by the end of 2 it's turned into a historical version of the *X-Files*, with the boy, grown up, donning a costume to track down the inhuman creature he thinks has been living down the sewers. In the final issue, although it's atmospherically drawn by Horus, things go further astray as the serial killer is revealed. After a effectively short and unspectacular struggle, and a great deal of emotional language, there's a neat and poetic end to an interesting but rather wavering story-line.~FJ

A-V IN 3-D
Aadvark-Vanaheim: *One-shot 1984*

If you were looking for the best independent anthology in the world you might well feel that one that included *Cerebus*, *Journey* and *Flaming Carrot* would be hard to beat. That this sampler of A-V's comics line also includes *Neil The Horse*, *Ms Tree* and *Normalman* ought to be the spur that has you rushing to find a copy. This is certainly the best of the mid-1980s 3-D comics fad, partly, at least, because all creators were drawing for 3-D and incorporated special scenes to take advantage of it, while retaining the integrity of the stories.~NF

Recommended: 1

AVALON
Harrier: *14 issues 1986–1988*

Cheap and cheesy mainstream anthology full of sub-standard artwork. The occasional one- or two-page gem fails to make this grim array of bargain-basement superheroes and reprinted fan strips worth a look.~FJ

AVATAR
DC: *3-issue miniseries 1990–1991*

TSR role-playing game spin-off. At 96 pages extra thick! More absorbent! Well meaning but stodgy stories with some nice art.~HS

AVENGELYNE
Maximum: *3-issue miniseries 1995. One-shot ('Avengelyne/Glory')1995, Avengelyne Swimsuit Edition 1 issue 1995, 3-issue miniseries ('Power') 1995–1996*

An angel is sent to Earth, as punishment for her sins, to help redeem mankind, seemingly by striking appallingly drawn cheesecake poses and carrying a big sword. Total drivel.~HS

AVENGELYNE/WARRIOR NUN AREALA

Maximum: *1 issue 1996*

Maximum Press's half of this crossover (though each is a separate story) is co-plotted by Rob Liefeld and Robert Napton, scripted by Napton and drawn by Dan Fraga and Michael Chang (leaving aside the two inkers); shaping up to be another Extreme comic by committee. It's a big fight as the angel and nun team up against the demon Sojourn but it's so much by the numbers that there's just no heart to it at all.~NF

THE AVENGERS

Marvel Comics: *Series one 402 issues, 23 Annuals, 5 Giant-Size, 1 Graphic Novel 1963–1996, Series two 2 issues + 1996 to date*

Initially conceived of as a way of uniting most superheroes in the then nascent Marvel comics line, *The Avengers* has grown to incorporate almost every major Marvel superhero and plenty of minor ones besides. Astonishingly for a comic about to celebrate its 25th anniversary, a mere seven writers have handled the bulk of the 400+ issues.

The combination of writer Stan Lee and pencil artist Jack Kirby created the title, teaming Iron Man, Thor, Giant Man, the Wasp and the Hulk in the first issue, and reviving 1940s character Captain America in issue 4. Although entertaining enough, it lacked the inspiration of other early Marvel comics. 8, the best of the Lee/Kirby run, introduced recurring time-travelling villain Kang the Conqueror and was Kirby's swansong (although he returned as layout artist for 14–16). Replacement artist Don Heck never approached Kirby's dynamism, but, with inker Dick Ayers maintaining the house style, turned out adequately rendered action until 36.

The first indication that the Avengers were anything other than superheroes by numbers came with the brave decision to replace the founding cast with three characters from the Marvel school of well-intentioned but misunderstood villains. Hawkeye, Quicksilver and the Scarlet Witch arrived in 16, establishing a long tradition of membership changes (although everyone returns sooner or later). Lee relinquished the writing to Roy Thomas with 34, and Thomas established a tradition of Avengers writers taking a year or so to settle. Joined by pencil artist John Buscema with 37, Thomas gradually became more adept and imaginative and gave a hint of what was to come with issues in the mid-50s introducing another recurring adversary, Ultron. Of particular note were 57/58, introducing the android Vision, the first character created specifically for the title. From issue 69 onwards Thomas crafted stories that

stand among the best *Avengers* issues to date. He introduced a take on DC's *Justice League of America* in both evil (70/71) and benign (85/86) versions, and dealt with topics such as race-hate groups (73/74) and land rights and corporate greed (77, 80/81). It's best to look on his feminism issue (83) as well meant but misguided, although it's an entertaining superhero comic. Sal Buscema took over the pencilling from brother John until 92, and many regard the space opera of the Kree/Skrull war, illustrated by Neal Adams in 93–97, as Thomas' finest moment. It was reprinted as a miniseries in 1983, but the story drags and suffers from a *deus ex machina* ending implausible even for superhero comics. Far superior were 98–100, drawn by Barry Windsor-Smith, dealing again with the fermentation of hate groups.

Steve Englehart took over with issue 105. Struggling initially, and suffering throughout his run from changing art teams, he became the best writer the title's had. His forte was mixing and matching characters to provide the thrust of the plot, and then throwing in adversaries to complicate matters. Englehart's first big story was the *Avengers/Defenders War* in 115–118, a portent of the multi-title crossovers to follow fifteen years later, but then a noteworthy event. He made logical use of the time-travelling Kang, who would attack the team, retire defeated and return next issue to fight the exhausted Avengers, having rested for ten years. Kang's attempt to kidnap an Avenger destined to become the all-powerful Celestial Madonna formed the linchpin of issues 129–132, and incorporated *Giant Size Avengers* 2 (featuring the genuinely touching death of a team member) and 3 (reviving assorted 'dead' characters). The story concluded in 133–135 and the appallingly drawn *Giant Size* 4 (an unwelcome return for Don Heck). Having dealt with the future, Englehart changed the cast again and sent the Avengers into the past and an alternate world to meet Marvel's cowboy characters and the Squadron Supreme in 141–144 and 147–148. George Perez débuted as artist in 141, and was to be the longest-running artist since the Buscema days, but Englehart left with issue 152, having revived another Avengers mainstay, Wonder Man, believed dead since issue 9.

The next writer, Jim Shooter, with Perez, and later John Byrne, turned out a succession of fast-moving stories, mixing Thomas' flair for superheroes with Englehart's deft characterisation. The battle against a superstrong Count Nefaria (164–166) is highly entertaining, but his peak was 'The Korvac Saga', in which almost every Avenger to date combats a being determined to impose a peaceful autocracy on the planet (167,168, 170–177). Also of note is

Avengers Annual 7, concluding Jim Starlin's laudable *Warlock* series.

David Michelinie adhered to the *Avengers* template, producing solid stories that fell short of previous quality, with 194–196 the exception. A highspot during this run was the tenth *Avengers* annual by the team of Chris Claremont and Michael Golden, introducing future X-Person Rogue. Sadly, the subsequent return of Jim Shooter (both alone and collaborating with Michelinie) was less successful. The continuing plot-line saw the gradual mental dissolution of founder-member Hank Pym, once Giant Man, now Yellowjacket. His marriage dissolves and he's later framed and jailed. It has fine moments (particularly the single issue 224 and the finale 229–230), but lacks the dynamic artwork that graced previous *Avengers* epics.

Roger Stern, from 231 onwards, was also hamstrung by lack-lustre art throughout the early part of his run, but didn't lack for ideas. He bowed to popular demand by inducting Spider-Man (232), had the Vision attempt to take over the world (253/254), and returned Kang in fine fashion (267–269), by which time the old art team of John Buscema and Tom Palmer were back on board. His best story took the obvious idea that the villains always failed against the Avengers singly or in pairs, but an army should succeed (274–277).

Stern's departure heralds a dismal period during which no writer managed to stamp any personality on the title, despite consistently fine art from the Buscema/Palmer team. The situation lasts until the emergence of Bob Harras in 343. In the company of highly regarded pencil artists Steve Epting and Mike Deodato, Harras was adept at creating new adversaries, sustaining mystery and the soap-opera aspects of the title, but also at stretching a single issue of plot over five issues. Initially he wrote the most entertaining *Avengers* comics in years, his best being the one-issue examination of the Vision in 348, but his conclusions to multi-part stories consistently fail to deliver the pay-off. Longer plots see alternate-reality counterparts of the Avengers emerging to kill Sersi (255–275), and in 'The Crossing' (391–395, plus one-shot *The Crossing*) Tony Stark near-enough destroys the team and a long-gone former Avenger returns with a vengeance. An unwelcome development is that to follow individual stories one's had to buy assorted issues of other titles and one-shots, and almost all the oversize anniversary issues are disappointing. By the conclusion drastic surgery was required, although if he'd been allocated more than three issues new writer Mark Waid might have rectified matters.

The relaunched issues are risible. Given both the necessity and the opportunity to revise *The*

Avengers, we're served average plots, dialogue reading as if it's been pulled straight from 1960s issues, and the artistic distortions of Chap Yaep, who's not lacking in basic talent, but chooses instead to present pin-ups and misproportioned figures. The graphic novel 'Death Trap: The Vault' is a pedestrian affair as the Avengers team with Freedom Force to prevent the escape of dozens of supervillains.~FP

Recommended: 57, 58, 71, 73–82, 85,86, 98–100, 116–122, 129–132, 139, 141–144, 147, 148, 160–168, 170–177, 254, 267–269, 274–277, 348, Annuals 2, 7, 10, Giant Size 2–3.

Collections: Bloodties (368, 369, *Avengers West Coast* 101, *Uncanny X-Men* 307, *X-Men* 26), *Marvel Masterworks* Vol 4 (1–10), *Marvel Masterworks* Vol 9 (11–20), *Marvel Masterworks* Vol 27 (21–30),*The Korvac Saga* (167,168,170–177)

AVENGERS Miniseries and one-shots

Marvel: *The Terminatrix Objective 4-issue miniseries 1993, Avengers/Ultraforce 2-issue microseries 1995, 'The Crossing' one-shot 1995, 'Timeslide' one-shot 1995, The Last Avengers Story 2-issue microseries 1995, 'The Legend' one-shot 1996*

For one of Marvel's flagship titles, *The Avengers* have been somewhat neglected in the miniseries stakes. Two of the above, 'Timeslide' and 'The Crossing', tied into story arcs from the regular series and were little more than an excuse to justify a more expensive format, while 'The Legend' is more of a guidebook than a comic, charting the Avengers' history for new readers about to jump on board. Of the others, none are particularly memorable. The prestige format *The Last Avengers Story*, by Peter David and Ariel Olivetti, is another dark and dismal Marvel future full of in-jokes and extremely dodgy continuity; *The Terminatrix Objective* has three second-division Avengers transported into the future to fight old enemy Kang, where they meet up with their first-division team-mates, then jump about in a couple of other time periods before going home; and *Avengers/Ultraforce* is a run-of-the-mill crossover between the Avengers and the Malibu flagship team, into which Malibu put far more effort than Marvel. Better than all of them is *X-Men Vs Avengers* (see *X-Men Miniseries* entry).~JC

Collection: The Last Avengers Story (1–2)

AVENGERS SPOTLIGHT

Marvel: *20 issues (21–40) 1989–1991*

Having previously been *Solo Avengers Starring Hawkeye*, this title faced a considerable problem when that run ended. The title began to be used as a try-out feature for new writers and artists, and although many later worked on regular Marvel titles, to begin with they weren't up to a lot. The blight continued here, with the editors believing the popularity of the characters would see them through the succession of appalling material. Dwayne's McDuffie and Turner earn an honourable exemption for their 'Acts Of Vengeance' tie-ins in 26–28, which show some wit and spark.

Howard Mackie continues to write the Hawkeye strip, but with little wit or imagination, until 30, which institutes some changes. The Hawkeye strip is expanded to occupy two-thirds of the comic, and Steve Gerber becomes writer. This is nowhere near his best work, but he immediately throws in one resolutely logical plot element, the unlikelihood of Hawkeye surviving a shooting. This leads to a beefed-up costume, and a vendetta against drug gangs concluded in shocking fashion in 36. The Al Milgrom and Don Heck art is adequate, but no more. The other change instituted from 30 is continuing back-ups with USAgent in 31–34, and Gilgamesh throughout 35, although only the staunchest of fans – if there is such a thing as a Gilgamesh fan – are advised to seek them out.

'Avengers Reborn' is the tagline for 37–40, with Hawkeye ousted as each issue spotlights a neglected character and returns them for new use. Doctor Druid, Tigra, the Black Knight and the Vision are the chosen ones, and the stories by Roy and Dann Thomas are universally slapdash. The best of them is the Greg Capullo-drawn Black Knight in 39.~WJ

AVENGERS UNLEASHED
Marvel: *6 issues 1995–1996*

An editorial decision seems to have been made that as this title was selling for a third less than the regular *Avengers* comic there was little point in bothering about such standards as coherency, plot or basic artistic knowledge. Absolutely worthless.~FP

AVENGING WORLD
Bruce Henderson: *One-shot 1973*

Avenging World was the best of the four mid-1970s Ditko solo titles. As with *Mr A* and *Wha..!?* the point of the title was to get across his right-wing views. Less of a strip than an illustrated essay narrated by the world himself, this contains some of Ditko's most startling imagery and fevered philosophy. In fact, as the comic progresses the text becomes ever heavier until we're left almost solely with Ditko's incessant ranting. Mad, but compelling.~DAR
Recommended: 1

AVENUE D
Fantagraphics: *One-shot 1991*

A collection of Glenn Head's previously self-published strips showing the sordid underbelly of New York. An excellent cartoonist, Head portrays sadly true-to-life seedy characters with brutal lives and no hope.~FP
Recommended: 1

The Man Called A-X
Bravura: *6-issue limited series (0–5) 1994–1995*

A heavily armed behemoth of a man is rampaging through Bedlam City, wiping out the gangsters infesting the place. Apparently indestructible, the survivor of numerous deathtraps, and able to regenerate to an extent, his major concern is that he's unaware of who he is and why he's killing gangsters. Meanwhile, the local gangsters have to club together to stand any chance of dealing with him, and a newspaper reporter is on his trail. In his introduction writer Marv Wolfman compares *A-X* to a Hong Kong action movie, and it's certainly got that fast-paced, relentless, over-the-top feel, but Wolfman is also canny enough to avoid presenting the clichéd big bloke with bigger guns. The gangsters are colourful, and artist Shawn McManus, usually known for subtler projects, proves very adaptable indeed. The zero issue starts to offer the explanation as to what A-X is, and slots in between 3 and 4, rather than starting the series.~WJ
Recommended: 0–5

AXEL PRESSBUTTON
Eclipse: *6 issues 1984–1985*

Classic reprints from *Warrior* in (unnecessary) colour. Shining examples of Steve Dillon and Garry Leach's early artwork accompany Pedro Henry's witty, sexy and savage script. Axel is a florist turned psychopath assassin after having three-quarters of his body eaten by a sentient plant, leaving him with a pathological hatred of vegetables. Attached to a huge metal body complete with meat cleaver and button for sexual stimulation he teams with a beautiful cloned hitwoman for adventures across the galaxy. It's every bit as silly and fun as it sounds, with the perverse antics of the bizarre, featureless alien Zirk standing out and glistening like a... ahem. Back-up strips, also culled from *Warrior*, include work by Jim Baikie, Brian Bolland, Hunt Emerson, Dave Gibbons and Cam Kennedy, a veritable Who's Who of top British comic creators.~TP
Recommended: 1–6

AZRAEL
DC: *24 issues +, 2 annuals 1995 to date*

Jean Paul Valley is the avenging angel Azrael, defender and chief assassin of the ancient order of Saint Dumas. Conditioned from birth by the System, Jean Paul does not really know who or what he is. This series picks up where the Batman 'Knights End' story left off, with Jean Paul living on the streets of Gotham, unsure of anything. The first story-line (1–4) gives him some companions, the drunken ex-psychiatrist Brian and Sister Lilhy, who has rejected the teachings of Saint Dumas. Ras Al Ghul aids the fugitives (5,6) because his own organisation is a rival to that of Saint Dumas. Before returning to Gotham Jean Paul discovers more about his past and that he was born in a laboratory (7–9). 10–14 see Jean Paul nearly catatonic except while, as Azrael, he struggles to come to terms with what he's learned. He finds himself protector to Sandra (Shondra) Kinsolving (Bruce Wayne's ex-doctor) and target of Simon LeHah, who killed his father.

Seeking a cure for his condition, Jean Paul comes between two brothers, a cultist and a scientist (17–20), and the monsters they create. 'Angel In Hiding' (21–23) is a prelude to 'Angel At War' (24–26), in which Jean Paul takes the battle to Saint Dumas. The 1995 Annual explains the events leading up to Valley's introduction in the miniseries *Sword of Azrael*, and the 1996 Annual is a tale of a future Azrael. Written by Denny O'Neil and drawn by Barry Kitson, this is an average superhero title, however much O'Neil tries to provide a psychological undercurrent to show it's more than that.~NF

AZTEC ACE
Eclipse: *15 issues 1984–1985*

Doug Moench, long-running writer on Marvel's occasionally inspired *Master Of Kung Fu*, seemed to lose all sense of proportion when granted a greater degree of editorial freedom by Eclipse for this series. *Aztec Ace* is an impossibly prolix time-travel yarn full of such hippy dippy philosophizing as this load of old tosh from issue one: 'The whole thing was a symbolic realization of time, space, history's mystery, and that which could unravel the whole ball of yarn, an onion with five layers and a nasty center – or five apples sharing the same worm-riddled core.' Like wow, man. No wonder the letters page is full of people recommending Grateful Dead albums...

Moench throws away an interesting mix of time travel, alternate worlds, mythology, history and the occult on a series of hideously complicated and pretentious story-lines. They're full of distracting cameos from the likes of Benjamin Franklin, Humphrey Bogart and Charlie Parker, which require great concentration for very little reward. By 13 even Moench's resolve was weakening, as our Aztec hero wearily donned a superhero costume to become imaginary 1940s hero The Crimson Comet. The passable artwork of Mike Hernandez (1, 2) and Dan Day (3–15) plays second fiddle to writer Moench's text-heavy scripts.~AL

AZTEK: The Ultimate Man
DC: *10 issues 1996–1997*

Grant Morrison and Mark Millar teamed up to provide a new hero for the end of the century: naïve and unworldly (he's been brought up in a Tibetan monastery), inexperienced but nevertheless bred to battle the Shadow God. While he's waiting for the latter to show up, he has to find a place for himself in Vanity, an ugly city. In 1 he's involved in the death of the city's resident superhero, Bloodtype, and from then on he becomes a target of the city's various ganglords, who don't want a superhero around. A team-up with Batman (6–7) against the Joker sets him firmly within the DC Universe. This is followed by a closer look at the Q Society that trained him. The Society is revealed to have connections to Lex Luthor when Aztek is given a new past so that he can continue to live in Vanity.

The artwork by N.Steven Harris and Keith Champagne, neither of which sound like real names, is pretty good, with clean lines and clever use of shadows (though the faces out of costume need work). Perhaps Morrison and Millar took too long to get to the point, although the title's humour and the lack of their familiar psychobabble was refreshing. With *Aztek*'s cancellation, it looks as though Aztek's future will be played out in the JLA.~NF

BABE

Dark Horse: *4-issue miniseries 1994, 2-issue microseries 1995*

An unscrupulous agent – showbiz, not secret – almost runs down a naked lady one rainy night. She's seven feet tall, amnesiac, and phenomenally strong. He decides to search for her true identity, but not too hard, since there's money to be made in the meantime. The first series is lightweight, but an amiable read, polluted by the sickeningly cutesy 'Proto-Tykes' back-up. The second is so pointless and perfunctory one wonders why John Byrne bothered. Presumably the hugely successful talking pig movie of the same name will preclude a third attempt.~HS

BABYLON 5

DC: *11 issues 1995*

Adapted from the TV show, this series is possibly unique in the annals of comic adaptations in attempting to complement then current events in the show's continuity. With previous base commander Jeffrey Sinclair having left the programme, in the story it's revealed he's become Earth ambassador to Minbari. 1–4 focus on him there coping with being framed for murder. It's very well connected with the TV show, and plotted by series creator Jan Straczynski, who also writes the first issue. Thereafter it's written by Mark Morretti, and drawn by Mike Netzer and Carlos Carzon, who are better at capturing likenesses than John Ridgway, who draws the following story arc. 5–8 are set prior to the arrival of The Shadows in the TV series, and have Garibaldi discovering a Shadow base in a story also detailing his first meeting and adventure with Sinclair. It's a decent story by Tim DeHaas that doesn't quite match its predecessor. DeHaas and Ridgway return for a psi-ops story in 11. 9 and 10, written by David Gerrold, although competent, don't match the remainder of the run.~WJ

Recommended: 1–4

Collections: Babylon 5 (1–4), Shadows Past And Present (5–8)

Eddie Campbell's BACCHUS

Harrier: *2 issues 1988*
Eddie Campbell: *20 issues + 1995 to date*
Dark Horse: *1 special 1995*

Bacchus was originally begun as a companion title to Campbell's *Deadface* series, which starred Bacchus but was much more adventure-oriented than the eponymous book, or at least as active as Eddie Campbell stories get. It begins as a vehicle for retelling whichever Greek myths catch Campbell's magpie eye, with a certain joyous irreverence. The narrator is the 4000-years-old god on history's longest bender: 'It's all a bit of a blur after I invented wine.' The scripting perfectly captures the simultaneously wise and rambling nature of pub conversations, and yet there is always a certain threat. The Harrier story shows us the old rascal in Rome laughing at the roly-poly version of himself the Romans dreamt up. He remains firmly the anarchic god whose followers ripped people apart in their god-sent, wine-fuelled frenzy.

Eddie Campbell's self-published issues feature a combination of reprint material from *Deadface*, the previous *Bacchus* series and the many titles which carried Bacchus material and new stories. 1 kicks off with a disappointing Cerebus jam but 2 starts a new story, 'King Bacchus', in which his local pub secedes from UK rule. All would be well if Delirium Tremens and his Screaming Habdabs weren't on Bacchus' trail, forcing him to take refuge in a nearby painting. As Bacchus is chased through a world of artworks the cleverest people in the pub bring in Neil Gaiman to re-write the story for a 90s superhero version of Bacchus. Even Alan Moore turns up in 13 as the keeper of demons. The story's among the most inventive in the series, but there's rather too much art assistance from Pete Mullins, who smoothes out Campbell's rough and scratchy edges, and doesn't have his feel for line quality – apart from being a poor draughtsman – which is a great pity. The Dark Horse colour special is painted by Teddy Kristiansen, and is a slight but poignant tale of Bacchus' attempt to stop a dilettante from opening a bottle of his 400-year-old wine. Bacchus is an intensely civilised comic book, whose charms may

bypass many readers. Lovers of raconteurs and good wines will adore it, however.~FJ
Recommended: Harrier 1–2, Eddie Campbell 4–13

BACKLASH
Image: *26 issues + 1994 to date*
Backlash is Marc Slayton, an ex-member of Team 7. As the series starts, Slayton has been employed as a teacher by Stormwatch, but when his girlfriend Diane LaSalle is put into a coma by a daemonite he is forced to become a renegade in order to find a cure. He breaks Taboo, a member of the Cabal, out of jail in the hope that her inside knowledge will help him. From this premise the series concentrates on Slayton's place in the scheme of things, introducing a daughter, Crimson, and a rivalry between the cured Diane and Taboo. His hitherto unknown Kherubim ancestry comes out. As a result he loses his Team 7 powers, but he and Taboo are pardoned and hired by the government's Psi Department. His relationship with Team 7 continues to cause friction, however, in the Wildstorm crossovers 'Wildstorm Rising' (8) and 'Fire From Heaven' (19, 20). Written by Sean Ruffner and drawn by Brett Booth and later Juvaun Kirby, *Backlash* is a better than average superhero series, strong on characterisation and always seeming to be going in a definite direction.~NF

BACKLASH/SPIDER-MAN
Image: *2-issue microseries 1996*
While conforming to most of the rules about inter-company crossovers (namely 'for every one of yours you'd better include one of mine'), Sean Ruffner and Brett Booth manage to produce a pretty good story about Venom being misled by Pike into believing that Taboo is somehow related to his symbiote and therefore drawing himself into conflict with Spider-Man and Backlash when he kidnaps her. The story ties in more to Backlash's than Spider-Man's continuity but is frankly all the better for avoiding any clone nonsense, and Brett Booth's artwork is excellent. Not good enough to recommend, perhaps, but well worth a look.~NF
Collection: Backlash/Spider-Man 1–2

The BAD EGGS
Armada: *4-issue miniseries 1996*
Dinosaurs as sitcom? Hasn't this been done before? Yes, and considerably better than this, although there are funny moments in this story of dinosaur tearaways, particularly in the final issue, when no dinosaur other than the leads will believe the local volcano is going to blow. All in all, though, stick to the TV series.~WJ

BADE BIKER AND ORSON
Mirage: *4-issue miniseries 1987*
Bade and Orson decide to go on a motorcycle trip across America. During the trip they are joined by another rider who happens to be on the run from the devil. Decent cartooning and a fast-paced plot are present and correct. The only problem is that we have no idea what Orson is. He looks like two olives on matchsticks.~SS

BADGER
Capital: *4 issues 1983–1984*
First: 66 issues (5–70), 1 Graphic Novel 1984–1991, 4-issue miniseries ('Badger Goes Berserk') 1989, One-shot ('Bedlam') 1991
Dark Horse: 4-issue miniseries ('Shattered Mirror') 1994, 2-issue microseries ('Zen Pop Funny Animal Version') 1994

This remarkably long-running series was written for all but a few issues in early mid-50s by creator Mike Baron, working with a string of artists who were mostly below the standard you'd expect of a mainstream book. Bill Reinhold and Ron Lim had the longest runs. The series opens in Wales, 412AD, where the angry population are calling for the blood of the child-murdering weather wizard. Deciding that the best way to do him in is to toss him off the edge of the world, a boat sets sail… and the scene changes to the 1980s. The weather wizard from the first scene is in a Wisconsin mental hospital, in a ward next to a man who calls himself the Badger, though his real name is Norbert Sykes. Norbert thinks he's a superhero; everyone else thinks he's nuts. All the same, when he and the weather wizard, Ham, leave the asylum Badger sets about beating up muggers, while Ham plans to sort out the world's weather. Aiding and abetting them is Daisy Fields, who, despite being a psychiatrist, doesn't seem to doubt for one moment that these two lunatics are on the level, although she does want to observe them (after all, it's not every day you get to psychoanalyse a real 5th-century Druid). *Badger* is meant to be funny, although it's sometimes hard to tell whether the stupidity is deliberate or just down to ineptitude. In other words, it's not funny enough to pull it off.

The move to First doesn't improve matters. Badger is a psychotic martial arts expert who can talk to animals, Ham is only interested in the weather, and you'd be better off reading another comic. The 'joke' of Badger being generally nuts just becomes disturbing after the issues dealing with the abused childhood that led to the trauma (5–7), especially when it's all interspersed with attempted laughs and slightly dodgy political messages. Mostly, Badger and Ham fight against pretty dull street thugs and magical demons, with one or another of Badger's split personalities taking over to (allegedly) spice things up. Now and again, Baron tries to throw in an animal rights story to show us how Badger is the animals' pal. Almost always, these come out reading as if they're written by a man who thinks that showing that his hero is into animal rights is another way of reminding us that he's totally wacko, because anyone who's into animal rights must have at least a few screws loose, right? And Badger's black sidekick, Riley, has dialogue meant to be hip and cool, but ends up as caricature.

In 45, Badger wakes up next to Mavis Davis (oh my poor aching sides), whom he met and married the night before in Las Vegas. Mavis is oriental, and switches from perfectly normal dialogue in her first few appearances to 'Honorable Husband' etc from 49 onwards, after which she seems to alternate between the two for no apparent reason. Overall, there's surprisingly little to say about a series which ran for so long. There are no running sub-plots, no character development to speak of, and it leaves a nasty taste from Baron's portrayal of racial minorities. The regular series ends with Badger playing Santa Claus. First also published a graphic novel, 'Hexbreaker', which told the story of Badger and Mavis's first meeting. The first Dark Horse issues, 'Shattered Mirror', take the continuity back to square one for the benefit of new readers, and try to play the character a bit straighter, which isn't altogether a good idea. On the plus side, it does seem that Baron's more unsavoury political views were being kept in check, either by himself or the editor, though they do occasionally slip through. Unfortunately, by the bizarrely named 'Zen Pop Funny Animal Version', which is none of those things, it's back to the same old offensive rubbish as before. It's hard to believe this stuff is from the same man responsible for the superb Nexus, and if the difference is down to Steve Rude's influence then the latter is a saint.~JC

BADLANDS
Dark Horse: *6-issue miniseries 1991–1992*

It's 1963 and small-time crook and full-time patsy Connie Bremen is contacted by a former cellmate on release from jail with an offer of work. He's moved to Texas and given a job guarding the promiscuous daughter of a local businessman. It gradually dawns on Bremen he's there for a reason. Yup, it's Kennedy shooting time in Dallas. Considering the assassination shaped the American psyche, astonishingly few comic stories have used it, even as a touchstone for the times. Steven Grant and Vince Giarrano weave a compelling story around a man no longer in

control of his destiny, but about to change the destiny of a nation.~WJ
Recommended: 1–6
Collection: Badlands (1–6)

BADROCK & COMPANY
Image: *6-issue miniseries 1994–1995*

Youngblood's rocky adolescent giant worked his way through a series of guest stars in this light, entertaining series. The plot involved him desperately trying to become older heroes' sidekick until they finally told him to go away and never come back, a joke that just about lasted the six issues and into the spin-off *Grifter & Badrock* miniseries that followed.~JC
Recommended: 3 (Mighty Man), 5 (Grifter)

BAKER STREET
Caliber: *10 issues 1988–1992*

Former police inspector and current punk Sharon investigates in an alternate London setting experiencing a resurgence of Victorianism amid the prevalence of rival punk gangs. The allusions to Sherlock Holmes and his world form an intriguing setting, but they're secondary to a well portrayed cast and well plotted mysteries, which would work with any window dressing. 'Honour Among Punks' occupies the first five issues, a tale of forgeries and gang wars from Gary Reed and co-plotter and artist Guy Davis, whose art is detailed, expressive, confident and far removed from his amateur efforts on *The Realm*. We're in Jack The Ripper territory for 'Children Of The Night' (6–10). It's even better, with Davis now solo and managing to surprise with the identity of his killer. There's far more to *Baker Street* than mystery, though. Sharon and Susan, her straight American counterfoil, are endearingly portrayed, having a warmth never present in Holmes and Watson, and if you want more there's a short in *Caliber Presents 9*.~FP
Recommended: 1–10
Collection: Children Of The Night (6–10), *Honour Among Punks* (1–5)

BALDER THE BRAVE
Marvel: *4-issue miniseries, 1985–1986*

This ties in with *Thor* 353–362, where Balder is established as a hero who has a special ability to communicate with birds. Here he's involved with the sorcerer Karnilla, the Queen of Norn, but has to leave on a rescue mission to Hel, and while he is gone the Frost Giants attack Norn and abduct Karnilla. Poor Balder, two rescue missions in the space of a single issue, with not even time between for a change of underwear. Actually, it's not a bad story, and stands on its own quite happily after a slow, Thor-burdened start. Walter Simonson keeps it zipping along, with plenty of twists and turns, with some unusual dark aspects. Sal Buscema's artwork works well, and the scenes in the giants' castle are particularly enjoyable. It's above average, but it's not essential reading.~FC

BALLISTIC
Image: *3-issue miniseries 1995*

Kracus, the mad-god leader of the Ethreal (a race of vampire/werewolf hybrids), pursues *Cyberforce*'s Ballistic to force her to become his queen. With the help of some of the *Wetworks* team and Kracus' sister, Ballistic must use the combination of her cybernetic powers and newly acquired vampire abilities to overcome Kracus' destructive urges. This is an excellent example of how to handle crossovers between different universes. Brian Haberlin connects Mother One from *Wetworks'* origin to the Cyberdata corporation that created Ballistic, and it's Cyberdata's search for alien technology that brings them into contact with the Ethreal from the Wildstorm universe. Despite annoying tendencies to distort the human figure for the sake of a good pose, Michael Turner's artwork is very pleasing. Haberlin's script avoids a lot of the superhero clichés but fails to make much use of the *Wetworks* characters other than Mother One.~NF

BANZAI
Kitchen Sink: *One-shot 1978*

Banzai was a nice collection of three underground artists – Kim Deitch, Joel Beck and Roger Brand – all of whom were on top form. Brand's 'More Innocent Times' was a typically autobiographical piece about a drug bust, whilst the best of Beck's efforts was 'The Great Comic Book Conspiracy', which featured the Mafia robbing a comic shop. Better than either, however, was Kim Deitch, whose 'Anthropomorphism' centrespread was an astonishing feat of anthropomorphism gone mad.~DAR
Recommended: 1

BAOH
Viz: *8-issue limited series 1990*

Given licence to continue their bacteriological experiments after World War II, the Judas Laboratory also takes an interest in humans with paranormal abilities. One such is Baoh, who's biologically engineered to be the perfect organic weapon. Once he's freed from the clutches of Judas by a nine-year-old precognitive girl, the pair want to make their own way in the world, but the ruthless Judas aren't about to let their investments disappear. From there it's one long chase scene punctuated by occasional conflicts. *Baoh* is certainly competent and romps along at a fair clip unencumbered by what seems to be a far

too literal translation, but ultimately there's nothing to distinguish the series or render it memorable.~FP
Collections: Baoh vol 1 (1–4), vol 2 (5–8)

BAR SINISTER
Windjammer: *3 issue miniseries 1995*

The Bar Sinister team are a group of genetically engineered Human/Animal half-breeds originally introduced in *Shaman's Tears*. This is the story of their battle against the humans who have branded them freaks. Mike Grell's script is clichéd while the art by Rick Hoberg is rushed and boring.~SS

BARB WIRE
Dark Horse: *9 issues 1994–1995, one-shot 1996, 4-issue miniseries ('Ace Of Spades') 1996*

The *Barb Wire* movie might be an all-time turkey, although the one-shot adaptation achieves the miracle of making it seem okay, but the regular issues are of a high standard throughout. Operating out of a bar in the run-down industrial city Steel Harbour, Barb is a bounty hunter, albeit a particularly glamorous one prone to displaying acres of flesh. Despite her aversion to superpowered types they just can't avoid her. Luckily more off-beat paranormals Motorhead and the Machine are also on hand when matters escalate. John Arcudi writes a solid superhero comic, and artists Paul Gulacy (in the *Comics Greatest Word* issue), Dan Lawlis and Mike Manley match the scripts. Barb Wire was created by Chris Warner, but the 1996 miniseries is actually the first time he's worked on the character, and he does a fine job. In a story set a while after the conclusion of the first series, the fickle finger of fashion has made Barb's club a jumping hotspot, and there's another more ruthless female bounty hunter in town. She's adopted the identity of an old villain and is killing off Steel Harbour's thugs with the aim of deliberately setting off a gang war. As everyone has her fingered as Barb there's one person with a vested interest in stopping her… ~FP
Recommended: 1–9, Miniseries 1–4
Collection: Barb Wire (1–7)

The BARBARIANS
Atlas: *1 issue 1975*

Contents: one below-par *Iron Jaw* story, and one duff German reprint. You could surely better spend even the pittance this would cost from back-issue boxes.~ WJ

BARBIE
Marvel: *63 issues 1991–1995*

The famous fashion doll saunters through innocuous adventures. One of the earlier *Barbie* writers, Trina Robbins, commented on the difficulty of scripting these stories since Mattel wouldn't allow any character to have any negative traits, even minor 'friendly rival' ones like a Veronica Lodge or Chili Storm, so no real conflict could be created. Having said that, the series and its companion title *Barbie Fashion* (55 issues 1991–1995) had a loyal following. They were only cancelled due to Marvel withdrawing from the licensing agreement, not because of a lack of sales, and they regularly featured talented creators. One can't help feeling the likes of Robbins, Anna-Maria Cool, Amanda Conner, Barbara Slate and Lisa Trusiani were ghettoised because of their gender into working only on the *Barbie* comics. If you have to check out a *Barbie* try 63, the 'Flying Hero Barbie' special. Trippy.~HS

The BARBI TWINS ADVENTURES
Topps: *1 issue 1995*

Science-fiction adventure starring real life *Playboy* models the Barbi Twins. It gave writer Robert Conte the opportunity to meet the girls, and he certainly looks happy in the photograph, but one can't imagine too many purchasers were pleased with this daft and nonsensical piece of exploitation. Topps followed it up with a Barbi Twins Calendar.~FP

BAREFOOTZ
Kitchen Sink: *3 issues, 1975–1977*
Renegade: *One-shot 1986*

The first three issues reprint many of Howard Cruse's earlier 'Barefootz' strips from various underground comix and papers, with some new stories. Barefootz is an eternal optimist living in the strange and sinful city. His closest friends are the stressed-out artist Headrack and the voracious, man-hungry Dolly, both engaging and well developed characters. The stars of the strip, though, are the myriad cockroaches who run free through his apartment, cultivated by him as friends, but usually obsessed by their own affairs, and Glory, the thing under the bed who 'makes frogs' at people she doesn't like. The cutesy style leads a lot of people to underestimate *Barefootz* – a fact Howard Cruse himself took a swing at on the back cover of issue 3, a 'traditional' underground pastiche cramming as many sexual, violent, and drug-related references as possible onto one page – but it's a witty, understated strip with great charm and imagination. The Renegade one-shot reprints the previously uncollected 'Barefootz' strips from the 1970s *Comix Book*.~HS
Recommended: 1–3, one-shot

BARTMAN
Bongo: *6 issues 1993–1995*

Spinning off from the *Simpsons* TV show and comic, this stars Bart's superheroic incarnation as he battles injustice in Springfield. One of the most successful TV-to-comic adaptations ever, this is just as funny as the real thing.~HS
Recommended: 1–6
Collection: Simpsons Comics featuring Bartman (1–3, *Simpsons* 5, *Itchy & Scratchy* 3)

BASEBALL Comics
Kitchen Sink: *2 issues 1991–1992*

Will Eisner's attempted introduction of a baseball-themed comic in 1949 failed, and the first issue reprints the original, featuring Eisner and Tex Blaisdell's hick from the sticks; it makes a good story. 2 reprints a tale of more recent vintage from *Death Rattle*, and a very average *Spirit* effort. There's no issue 3, proving that forty years hadn't increased the market for baseball-themed comics.~WJ

BASEBALL GREATS
Dark Horse: *3 issues 1992*

Never materialising into the planned ongoing series, this presents biographies of Jimmy Piersall, a very good, if eccentric outfielder, driven pitcher Bob Gibson, and power hitter Harmon Killibrew. Triple A rather than major league, but a grand slam better than similar titles from Revolutionary.~WJ

BASTARD BUNNY
That Rabbit: *9 issues + 1993 to date*

A bloody great skinhead rabbit in braces and docs is not yer average comics character, and he's the star of some great T-shirts. Unfortunately, when it comes to the comics the idea wasn't as funny, with writer Dave Anderson extending silly jokes and slapstick routines beyond the cause of duty. With 5 things start to improve, not least because there are finally some people able to draw working with Anderson's scripts, which are improving with every issue. David Jukes and John Moore are particularly talented artists, and there's a decent supporting character in Toot Toucan. Any issue after 6 will while away those few minutes waiting at the bar, or elsewhere.~FP

BAT LASH
DC: *7 issues 1968–1969*

Premiered in *Showcase* 76, Bat Lash was a fast gun with an eye for the women and an appreciation of the finer things in life. Created by Sergio Aragonés, who wrote the feature with Denny O'Neil, and beautifully drawn by Nick Cardy, the combination of humour and action is a winner. Ironically, in a fine run the best issue is 6, revealing Lash's past, at odds with other stories by being played straight. Despite high quality throughout, the feature was never fully appreciated at home, but proved very successful in Europe, particularly in Italy, where collections are

easily found. Bat Lash was to return in the *Jonah Hex Spectacular* and as a back-up in *Jonah Hex* 49, 51 and 52.~FP
Recommended: 1–7

BATGIRL Special
DC: *One-shot 1988*
The story of Batgirl's final case before being crippled in *Batman: The Killing Joke*. This shows her coming to terms with the villain who had injured and terrorised her, now himself the target of a criminal who kills abusers of women. There's a neat resolution of moral dilemmas that refreshingly avoids a twist ending.~HS

BATMAN
DC: *537 issues + 19 annuals, 1 special, 1 spectacular 1940 to date*
Batman is one of the few American comic characters to have passed beyond the comics world into common public recognition. A large percentage of the population would be able to relate his origin. Wealthy Bruce Wayne is inspired by a bat flying through his window to adopt that identity as his manner of fighting crime, having trained since childhood, when his parents were murdered in front of his eyes. Created by Bob Kane with help from Bill Finger, the dark and brooding result was instantly successful, and a year after his début in *Detective Comics* Batman was awarded his own title. It begins by adding two major pieces of the myth as Catwoman débuts minus costume, which she'll get in 3, as The Cat, and also the first appearance of the Joker, indisputably created by Robinson.

Belied by the colourful covers, often of a patriotic nature as the USA entered World War II, *Batman's* early issues contained dark and gritty detective-oriented stories, with the odd colourful villain thrown in. The Joker was instantly popular, and 11's cover is a classic, with Batman and Robin punching him out surrounded by giant playing cards (although that issue is noted for the début of the Penguin). Kane's art quickly developed from being quite crude to sophistication, and Jerry Robinson, also a very fine artist, and with a better eye for design, drew many of the early tales. Very simple by today's standards, plots were nonetheless emphasized over all other story elements, and there's an admirable quirky quality to them. In 25 the Joker and the Penguin team up (for the first time), drawing up a deed of partnership, but each at first falls prey to his attempts to swindle the other. With Batman captured and trussed, he outwits the pair by appealing to their vanity. Other early landmarks included the first solo story of Alfred the butler in 32; and look for a very detailed origin of Batman in 47. Wacky villains

and crime stories weren't enough for the fans, though, and Batman and Robin occasionally travelled into the past, such as 24's trip to ancient Rome, 32's meeting with the Three Musketeers, and a journey to King Arthur's court in 36. And, like all good superheroes, Earth wasn't their only battleground. In 41 they became interplanetary policemen battling green-skinned aliens, and 59 offered us 'Batman Of The Future', in which the bat-signal was projected onto the moon! The Joker, Catwoman (with an origin in 62), Penguin, Two Face and Killer Moth remained popular villains. Many of these stories were written by Bill Finger, and Gardner Fox, Otto Binder, Bill Woolfolk and Jack Schiff also contributed, but as they were uncredited attributing writers is far more difficult than artists. By the early 1950s Robinson was sometimes still drawing *Batman*, with Kane only occasionally turning in a story, and the bulk of the art was being handled by Sheldon Moldoff and Dick Sprang. It was the latter's angular style and penchant for setting fight scenes on giant props that made him come to be associated with Batman more than any other artist until the 1970s.

Noting the popularity of Lois Lane in the Superman titles, Batman was given his own prying female journalist in the form of Vicki Vale, who débuted in 45, returning in 49 along with villain The Mad Hatter. She would never achieve the popularity of Lois Lane, and attempts at transforming her into a romantic interest for Batman were half-hearted, as if even among aliens and time travel this was a preposterous concept. An oddity occupied 78, with Roh Kar, the manhunter from Mars. The first Martian lawman to visit Earth was perhaps an inspiration for the début of the Martian Manhunter four years later. The story personified the increasing fantasy elements around which Batman comics were based from the early 1950s, seemingly attempting to emulate the style of the very successful Superman comics of the time. Batman's darker persona was completely eroded as everything became light-hearted, and the franchise was milked for all it was worth, a mood sealed with the arrival of Ace, the Bat-Hound, complete with mask (!) in 92. Batwoman in a bright yellow outfit in 105 was only slightly better, given a young companion, Bat-Girl, in 139. The costumed villains were gradually phased out, with only the Joker recurring regularly, and not as frequently as in the 1940s. As ever, the stories were competently produced, unique in their own way, offering decent entertainment, but far removed from the original Batman.

Readers at the time seemed to agree, and sales began a gradual decline. By the early 1960s the comic was in trouble, with Bat-Mite – an imp from another dimension who wanted to help Batman – indicative of how far Batman had strayed from his roots. In an attempt to jump start a change, Julie Schwartz was appointed editor of the *Batman* titles, having successfully revived the superhero genre from the mid-1950s at DC. He introduced a new look to Batman from 164. While Bob Kane continued drawing the interiors, co-artist Carmine Infantino gave the title a new look, most significantly adding a yellow oval around Batman's chest emblem. Alfred the Butler was killed, only to be revived because he was a major part of the *Batman* TV show. Batman's stories now reverted to the old detective format, but this style didn't last with the arrival of the TV show in 1966, at which point Batman's colourful adversaries were restored to the series. While certainly pepped up, Batman's stories weren't as overtly comic as the TV episodes, though they occasionally verge on farce. These were hot sellers, but with the waning of interest in the TV show sales dropped back down again.

DC redefined many of their comics in the late 1960s, and *Batman* was no exception. The first sign of change came with 200's cover from Neal Adams, a man who was to become very important to the series. First, though, Bob Kane had to leave, and was paid a lump sum to do so. While accepting the injustice of in effect sacking the man who'd created Batman and therefore earned DC millions of dollars, from a purely creative point of view Kane was burned out, and, it's suspected, farming out the work to others despite his name being credited. The contrast between his final issues and those of his successors – writer Frank Robbins and artists Irv Novick and Joe Giella – was immense. Robbins' Batman was certainly more dramatic, the artists had a cleaner style, and when Dick Giordano began inking Novick's pencils with 219 the new look had been clearly established. Although Robbins didn't write the more noted stories of the era, he was consistent and imaginative, and all his Batman stories are polished.

Things improved still further when writer Denny O'Neil joined the team and Neal Adams began contributing artwork. Adams' image of Batman remains a definitive version, modern, stylish and dynamic, and when combined with O'Neil and Giordano you have a classic Batman creative team. A conscious decision was made to divest Batman of almost all fantasy trappings. He now operated largely at night, only rarely with Robin, and his detective skills were emphasized as he dealt as often as not with the type of criminals infesting the real world. The sight of Batman swooping from the rooftops was once again striking fear into the hearts of cowardly criminals. A new arch-villain was introduced in 232, Ra's Al

Ghul, along with alluring daughter Talia, both of whom would play a considerable part in the years to come. 237's 'The Night Of The Reaper' is a classic of the time from O'Neil, Adams and Giordano, with Berni Wrightson and Harlan Ellison also contributing to a story concerning revenge on a Nazi butcher. The back-up is also noteworthy, reprinting Batman's last solo adventure pre-Robin from *Detective* 37. 234 is another triumph from the same creative trio, returning Two-Face, 'twice as evil, twice as dangerous', as the cover tells us. If that wasn't enough, 243–245 had a classic Ra's Al Ghul story, again by Adams, O'Neil and Giordano, and 251, with Adams inking his own pencils, is the first modern-day appearance of the definitive Joker: mad, bad and decidedly very dangerous to know. This was also a growing-up period for Robin, who left for college in 217 and a back-up strip keeping readers abreast of his adventures and college life. 234–242 were forty-eight pages long, with a new Batman story leading off, followed by the Robin strip and a reprint of a classic Batman tale in the back, with 238 a hundred pages with assorted reprints. All are excellent packages for Batman fans.

Fans of the pulp hero The Shadow should look for 253 and 259, in which he guested. His influence on Batman's creation in reality is nicely mirrored by an admission in the stories that Batman modelled himself on the character. 254–261 were all a hundred pages, with a new Batman story in the front and classic 1940s, 1950s and 1960s reprints filling the remainder. The standout story of this period was again drawn by Adams, his finale in 255, a werewolf tale written by Len Wein. Novick also left, to be replaced by Ernie Chua with 262, who portrayed Batman more as a superhero than a creature of the night, and O'Neil went with 269, initially replaced by David Reed.

This wasn't a banner period for Batman. Although what consensus has as the correct mood for the comic had been restored, successive short-run creators turned out adequate Batman stories, but ones which altogether lacked any extra spark, with the contemporary Batman strips in *Detective* definitely the star turn. The highlights during the late 1970s are all artistic. The peculiar combination of Rich Buckler inked by Berni Wrightson can be found in 286, Mike Grell illustrates his only Batman stories in 287–290, Michael Golden draws 295 and 303, and the vastly underrated Sal Amendola illustrates 296. 300 was a special issue: 'The Last Batman Story' by Reed, illustrated by Walt Simonson and Dick Giordano. Again, art apart, it was merely adequate, with an older Batman and adult Robin. Simonson was back in 312. 321 was an oasis, with Wein and Simonson turning in a very nice Joker caper. By that time Wein was writing most Batman issues, and he played a significant part in reviving Catwoman, with Selina Kyle attempting to go straight in 322–324.

A significant change occurred with 327 (until 354) as Dick Giordano became editor, bringing Gerry Conway along with him as writer. Giordano is a rare editor able to bring out the best in the most unlikely creators, and this certainly worked with Conway, whose writing was a considerable improvement on the previous several years. It was Marv Wolfman, Irv Novick and Frank McLaughlin in 332–335 who provided the era's most significant story, 'The Lazarus Affair', involving Ra's Al Ghul, Talia and Catwoman in a mystery and action-packed adventure. 332 also contained the first solo Catwoman story. In order to stimulate sales of both titles throughout the early 1980s, *Batman* often crossed over with *Detective*, where, of course, Batman also starred. Gene Colan drew 343–351, and one might imagine that if ever there was an artist suited to Batman it was Colan, with his flowing, moody artwork and distinctive night scenes. The other regular penciller was Don Newton, who drew 354 and 356, a very good Gerry Conway story crossing over into *Detective* 520, featuring Hugo Strange once again usurping Batman's identity. It's Conway's final fling as Doug Moench becomes writer, and by this time Vicki Vale is back, now having a far more convincing romance with Bruce Wayne. Except he's also developing strong feelings for Selina Kyle, and the pallid and mysterious Nocturna. Oh woe! How did he find the time to fight crime? It all comes to a head in messy fashion in 391.

368 is significant in introducing a new Robin. The previous version had now outgrown the role, and was then a mainstay of the Teen Titans as Nightwing. Jason Todd, the new incumbent, was several years younger, and lost his parents in a story told in 408–410. Editorial judgement for once was misplaced, and the revival of an adolescent Robin didn't prove as popular as expected with the readership. Letters demanding Robin's removal began arriving soon after his introduction, and their frequency and quantity increased to the point where DC agreed to let the readers decide. 'A Death In The Family' began in 426, and rather innovatively DC ran a poll in which readers could vote as to the ending in 429. It was a close call for Jason Todd, but he was murdered by the Joker, the series being written by Jim Starlin and drawn by Jim Aparo.

In issues leading up to 400 Catwoman is a regular co-star, almost completely reformed, and slobby Gotham police detective Bullock is also playing a larger part, often as comic relief.

Paul Gulacy draws 393 and 394, but Tom Mandrake is now the regular penciller, never outstanding, but more solid here than elsewhere. 400 is a longer than usual anniversary issue in which all of Batman's major villains escape confinement, and in a series of short chapters illustrated by a stellar line-up he has to recapture them all. There's lovely art from Bill Sienkiewicz, Joe Kubert, Steve Leialoha, George Perez, Brian Bolland and many more. Although 400's art is deservedly remembered, the art of Trevor Von Eeden in 401 is equally memorable, giving Batman a fine Gothic look. Von Eeden was equally good on the 1992 annual (15). 404–407 is 'Batman: Year One', by Frank Miller and David Mazzucchelli. Miller returned to Batman's past to write an impressive story dealing with his early career. It also covers the past of Selina Kyle and Commissioner Gordon, who arrives in Gotham at the same time as Batman first appears, and a long-lived relationship begins. Mazzucchelli's art superbly evokes the period and the action for a must-have four issues. Jim Starlin began contributing both art and stories to *Batman* in 1987, writing 414–425, and for a man known more for his cosmic and mystical series his Batman scripts were satisfactorily down to Earth. His best was 'Ten Nights Of The Beast' in 417–420, drawn by Jim Aparo, and introducing the KGBeast, a Russian stalking victims in Gotham.

433–435 have now regular artist Jim Aparo drawing a John Byrne story 'The Many Deaths Of Batman', in which everyone who had a hand in training Batman is being murdered. Look who's introduced in 436, only seven issues after Robin's death: here comes Tim Drake, who would become Robin. This was in the first part of 'Batman: Year Three', Marv Wolfman's début as regular writer, with art by Pat Broderick, the last and weakest of the early-days four-parters ('Year Two' had been in *Detective* 575–578). It details Batman meeting Dick Grayson and training him as Robin. 'A Lonely Place Of Dying' in 440–442 is an improvement, with Aparo returning as artist and the restoration of Robin, who first appears in costume in 442. By now Batman is once again crossing over with *Detective* on a regular basis, and the best of the crossovers is plotted with *Detective* writer Alan Grant, and features the Penguin in 448 and 449. The creative teams of *Batman* and *Detective* swap with 455 as Grant becomes the regular writer, bringing dynamic artist Norm Breyfogle with him. Grant's stories maintain the action, mystery and suspense, and add a welcome touch of British humour, an example being 475, with the return of Scarface, the mad ventriloquist dummy and the most successful addition to Batman's enemies in recent years. With one exception: Bane.

492–500 are chapters of the 'Knightfall' saga by Moench and Breyfogle, a massive story running through both main *Batman* titles in which all Batman's enemies are freed by Bane, and he becomes more and more exhausted in his attempts to recapture them. At his weakest Batman is confronted by Bane, a drug-powered powerhouse, who cripples him in 497. Bane is defeated, but by Jean Paul Vallelly, Azrael, introduced in the *Sword Of Azrael* miniseries. Also raised to combat crime, he takes over as Batman, but significantly modifies the costume, incorporating armour and weaponry. The attendant publicity for the series boosted sales, and Bruce Wayne's recovery was strung out for almost two years during the 'Knightquest' (501–508) and 'Knightsend' (509–510) stories, crossing over into *Shadow Of The Bat* as well as *Detective*. Azrael as Batman becomes increasingly more violent, to the point where he oversteps the boundaries between wrong and right, and, as we always knew he would, the real Batman returns.

The more notable of the annuals and specials are 1984's special with Michael Golden art, the 1987 annual (11), which has an Alan Moore and George Freeman Clayface story, and the 1989 annual by Mike Barr and Jerry Ordway.

The publishers having seen proof that committee-conceived blockbuster story-lines crossing over between all Batman titles pull in the readers, there's been a policy to introduce more of them. 'Contagion' (529–530) and 'Legacy' (533–535) are interspersed with stories incorporating elements pertaining to DC's annual cross-company event. This may boost sales, but leaves little room for the quiet change of pace or human-interest story that regularly appeared during the 1970s and 1980s, or for an individual interpretation of the character, now consigned to *Legends Of The Dark Knight*. There's no denying, though, that these well-marketed stories have maintained an interest in the character during a period of decline in the comics industry, keeping Batman fans happy and the character going strong into the next century.

Fans wanting a cheap method of looking at early Batman stories are referred to the reprints. Alas, the giant-sized annuals 1–7 now also fetch premium prices, as do the earliest reprint issues in the run (176, 182, 187, 193, 198, and every issue ending in 3 or 8 until the 240s). There's a good selection in *The Greatest Batman Stories Ever Told* (DC/Titan), and in the 100-page issues 238 and 254–261. There were also two un-numbered 100-page Batman reprint titles issued in the early 1970s, which also reprinted other features.~HY

Recommended: 232, 234, 237, 242–244, 251, 255, 300, 321, 323, 324, 332–335, 355, 390, 391, 400, 404–407, 475

Collections: *Batman: Year One* (404–407), *Dark Knight Archives* Vol 1 (1–4), vol 2 (5–8), *A Death In The Family* (426–429), *The Demon Awakes* (232, 237, 242–245), *The Greatest Batman Stories Ever Told* Vol 1 (1, 25, 47, 61, 156, 234, 250, 312), Vol 2 (62, 76, 169, 190, 197, 257, 345, 346, 355, annual 11), *The Greatest Joker Stories Ever Told* (1, 4, 63, 73, 74, 110, 159, 163, 251, 321), *Knightsend* (509, 510), *Knightfall* Vol 1 (492–495), Vol 2 (496–500), *A Lonely Place Of Dying* (440–442), *Prodigal* (512–514), *The Many Deaths Of Batman* (433–435), *Tales Of The Demon* (485, 489, 490), *Ten Nights Of The Beast* (417–420)

BATMAN ADVENTURES
DC: *36 issues, 2 Annuals, 2 Specials 1992–1995*

The stylised animated *Batman* TV series of the early 1990s is arguably the best ever TV depiction of a character originating in comics. For the comic Kelley Puckett and vastly underrated artists Mike Parobeck and Rick Burchett adopt the TV formula of simple continuity-free stories paying attention to detail and character with equally impressive results. Most issues by the regular creative team are excellent, but for samples try the début of Batgirl in 12 or three villains hijacking the title in 30. This isn't to say issues by people other than the regulars are substandard, they're just fall a little short unless the TV series writer and artist Paul Dini and Bruce Timm drop by. Their *Mad Love Special* focuses on the Joker's sidekick Harley Quinn, and the attraction she has for a lunatic criminal mastermind, and was one of the best comics published anywhere in 1994. Dini and Timm return for the Holiday Special along with other animators from the TV show, and it's another treat.~FP

Recommended: 1–3, 6–10, 12–16, 18, 20, 25–28, 30, 33–36, *Mad Love Special*, *Holiday Special*, *Annual 1*

Collections: *Batman: The Collected Adventures* 1 (1–6), *Batman: The Collected Adventures* 2 (7–12)

BATMAN AND ROBIN ADVENTURES
DC: *14 issues, 1 annual 1995 to date*

As the TV show changed title to accommodate the increased participation of Robin, DC took the opportunity to restart their *Batman Adventures* title. Paul Dini writes 1–3 (and the annual), drawn by Ty Templeton, who then writes the following issues. Oddly enough for a man whose art displays fine humorous technique, Templeton's scripts so far have been largely played straight, and the missing ingredient shows. Brandon Kruse is an excellent and under-acknowledged penciller, and there's not been a dud issue, but nothing so far matches the best of the previous series.~WJ

Recommended: 1–3, 6, 8, 11

BATMAN AND THE OUTSIDERS
DC: *46 issues 1983–1987, 2 annuals*

At a time when Batman was moving back to his darker, more serious roots, this spin-off team title allowed a lighter feel to the Dark Knight, albeit away from his own comic. With the help of some perennial second-stringers and equally uninspired new creations, Batman escapes the clutches of Nazi-sympathiser Baron Bedlam and restores the rightful ruler to the throne of Markovia, a fictional Bavarian state. The new king's superpowered brother heads back to the US with Batman and his new pals, and together the team engage in a series of pedestrian, but generally entertaining, adventures under the creative team of Mike Barr and Jim Aparo. When Batman bowed out and left the others to their own devices, the book was retitled *Adventures Of The Outsiders* from 33, but survived less than a year, indicating that perhaps his presence was the only thing that had kept it going as long as it did. 'Nuclear Fear' (39–41) is worth a look if you like stories so-bad-they're-almost-good, but overall the series pretty much deserves the cheap-box obscurity that has become its fate.~JC

BATMAN BLACK AND WHITE
DC: *4-issue miniseries 1996*

In over fifty years Batman's stories had always been in colour, so the concept of black and white short stories was an unlikely innovation. The format also allowed creators to produce a limited number of pages, thus attracting a stellar line-up of artists. While it's nice to see Brian Bolland once again drawing a strip (4), or Batman by Richard Corben (2), Joe Kubert (1), Libatore (3), José Muñoz (1) and Otomo (4), this is very much the artists' showcase and few of the stories offer anything new, with Otomo's being particularly abstruse. Credit to Neil Gaiman and Simon Bisley for attempting something different in 2, but overall more novelty than treat.~FP

Collection: Batman Black and White (1–4)

BATMAN CHRONICLES
DC: *7 issues + 1995 to date*

48-page quarterly Batman comic focusing on his friends, allies and environment, and his interaction with them. At least one, usually two or three, self-contained stories complete in each issue should appeal to the more casual reader wanting to pick up the occasional *Batman* comic without having to cope with a multi-part story arc. Never less than

competent and readable, watch out for 4's Hitman crossover and the 'Oracle: Year One' story in 5, which is a bloody good read.~HS

Recommended: 5

BATMAN FAMILY
DC: *20 issues 1975–1978*

Initially a Robin and Batgirl team-up title backed up with 1940s and 1950s Batman reprints, from 11 it's all new material, with Robin and Batgirl solo strips that remain bland throughout. The Man-Bat strip débuting in 11, though, is a creditable treatment of the character graced with some particularly fine artists, including Chaykin, Golden and the team of Rogers and Austin. With 17 the title became a dollar comic, and although the Man-Bat stories declined, the Batman stories are all very good. 18–20 all contain Michael Golden strips, and some good work from writers Denny O'Neil and David V. Reed. The title was cancelled when *Detective* adopted the role with 481.~DWC

Recommended: 18–20

BATMAN Graphic Novels and One-Shots

Batman graphic novels and one-shots cover a vast territory, with the most common prompt seemingly giving creators the opportunity to work on a 20th-century cultural icon without being bogged down by the monthly deadlines of the regular titles. Perhaps the obvious place to begin is with adaptations of the films. *Batman* is by Denny O'Neil and Jerry Ordway, covering Batman's origin and first encounters with a Jack Nicholson-style Joker. Visually, Ordway captures the look of the film and its actors, but O'Neil doesn't really have any scope to do more than plough through the plot. *Batman Returns* presents exactly the same problem for O'Neil, though there's a lot more plot to play with (and with Catwoman, Penguin and Max Shreck there's even a choice of villains). Steve Erwin and José Luis Garcia-Lopez go through the motions, but there's no sign of inspiration in the artwork. O'Neil sticks to the formula for *Batman Forever*, but Michael Dutkiewicz, despite some good background work, is a very stiff figure artist.

In connection with the second and third Batman films, DC released single issues spotlighting their villains. *Penguin Triumphant* by John Ostrander and Joe Staton sees the Penguin apparently going straight and living the high life in Wayne Manor, while he plots the downfall of his childhood tormentors. Not particularly interesting either in story or artwork. *Batman: Two Face* suffers from J.M. DeMatteitis, but Scott McDaniel, a successful artistic cross between Frank Miller and Matt Wagner, gives the dreary psychobabble lots of visual impact. *Batman: Riddler – The Riddle Factory* is the best of them, written by Matt Wagner. Wagner weaves characterisation and good detection around the story of The Riddler's search for an old gangster's hidden stash. Dave Taylor's artwork is attractive. Even if he doesn't really stamp his own personality on the character, he's well enough versed in the trademarks of Miller, Toth and Adams, coupled with the modern feel of Wagner himself.

By far the most frequent form of Batman graphic novels is Elseworlds tales, which resent Batman as he might have been if born in different times or different circumstances – otherwise known as 'imaginary' stories. *Gotham By Gaslight* set the trend (and predates the Elseworlds tag), merging the Batman's origin with the story of Jack The Ripper in 1880s Gotham. Brian Augustyn overwrites a little, but this doesn't undermine the strength of Mike Mignola and P. Craig Russell's atmospheric artwork, which makes the book. Augustyn's sequel, *Master Of The Future*, had a better script and some of Eduardo Barreto's best artwork. As a madman threatens to destroy Gotham before it can open an exposition to celebrate the dawn of the 20th century, Bruce Wayne must decide whether to put on the costume again. *Batman/Houdini: The Devil's Workshop* returns to the idea of *Gotham By Gaslight*, this time, as the title suggests, teaming Batman with Houdini against the Joker and a vampire, Baron Montenegro. Written by Howard Chaykin and John Francis Moore, and painted by Mark Chiarello, the artwork lets down the script, being far too static and forced. Chaykin also wrote and drew *Dark Allegiances*, set just before World War II. It employs many of Chaykin's usual touches, including a sordid atmosphere and racial politicking, as Bruce Wayne and Catwoman try to prevent the assassinations of Roosevelt and Hitler. It's not exactly charming but Chaykin's flair pulls it off.

The Blue, The Grey and the Bat is a disappointing foray into the Wild West, incorporating real-life characters like the Batman/Houdini book. It's set during the American Civil War: Colonel Bruce Wayne disguises himself as Batman in order to flush out murderous gold thieves with the aid of an Indian called Redbird. Elliot S.Maggin's plot is chaotic while Alan Weiss (even inked by José Luis Garcia-Lopez) seems completely ill-suited to the project. A much more interesting mix with real history is Max Allan Collins' *Scar Of The Bat*, in which Eliot Ness puts on a cape and cowl in his fight against the Chicago mobs. With Eduardo Barreto providing an excellent period feel this is definitely one of the most original Elseworlds tales.

Holy Terror is an alternative history tale. It postulates that Oliver Cromwell didn't die in 1658 but lived to spread his Commonwealth to the New World. As a result America is a fiercely religious country where agitators like Bruce Wayne's parents are executed by the state, covertly or otherwise. Alan Brennert sets the whole thing up neatly and has Batman at first seeking revenge, then coming to understand the need to change the system itself. With appearances from other DC characters this is more an alternative version of the DC universe than a simple Batman What If? They're used to good effect without detracting from the main thrust of the story. Artist Norm Breyfogle is too much like a 1990s Neal Adams and despite the background there are too many superheroics for this to be more than a good Batman yarn. Jack C. Harris' *Castle of the Bat* is a classic horror story, setting Bruce Wayne on the path of Dr Frankenstein while a rival of his father's conducts his own hellish experiments on passing travellers. Bo Hampton's painted artwork is rather washed-out for this gloomy tale, and fails to match the intensity of the plot.

The mysterious side of Batman's character lends itself to horror plots, and therefore a Dracula story comes as no surprise. *Batman & Dracula: Red Rain* sees Batman aided in his fight against the vampire by the convenient Tanya, whose gift to him is exactly the power he needs to overcome Dracula. In the sequel, *Bloodstorm,* a lycanthropic Selina Kyle helps the now vampiric Batman against a serial-killer Joker. Doug Moench's Gothic ideas are perfectly realised by Kelley Jones (whose artwork here shows touches of Berni Wrightson and Paul Gulacy). These are grim fairy tales, enhanced by Moench's obvious feel for the character and surrounding mythology. It's therefore a disappointment to find that the same team don't quite hack it on the oddly titled *Dark Joker – The Wild*. It's a dark fantasy about sorcerers, flying islands and a man who turns into a bat in order to fight the evil Joker's magic. It's okay if you like that sort of fantasy but lacks sparkle.

Brotherhood of the Bat is a traditional imaginary story. Batman is dead and Ra's Al Ghul has succeeded in killing millions in his absence. Taking over the Batcave, Ra's costumes his assassins as Batman and sends them out to make a ruined Gotham his. His daughter Talia, however, has borne Batman's son and guides him along the path that will restore a true Batman to the city. Doug Moench tells a good tale but there's too much plot and not enough characterisation, while the use of eight different artists distracts rather than pleases. Jim Aparo gets the largest chunk and does a good job but overall it lacks spirit. *In*

Darkest Night picks up another old favourite among imaginary tales: what if Bruce Wayne had been given Abin Sur's power ring and become a Green Lantern? Little more than a mishmash of both origins, it's of no particular interest despite the attempts of Mike Barr and Jerry Bingham.

Mite-Fall is a real curiosity, featuring the return of Bat-Mite, the impish creature out to have fun at Batman's expense. Drawn by Kevin O'Neill, it at least looks good, but the humour is way past its sell-by date and not even Alan Grant can raise a smile out of the tired old jokes.

Finally, *The Last Angel* is the first graphic novel by Eric Van Lustbader, illustrated by Lee Moder in a clean, sensuous style. Though not categorised as an Elseworlds tale, the death of Rupert Thorne and the distinctly different version of Selina Kyle (Catwoman) seem to indicate that it should be. In any event, it's a well-told story involving the Joker, Catwoman and an ancient mask with evil powers.

There are some Batman one-shots, sometimes originally released as hardcovers, sometimes just deluxe editions, and sometimes just labelled 'specials', that take place within accepted Batman continuity. They may be referred to or continue from the regular comics. One of the earliest graphic novels incorporated into continuity was the controversial *The Killing Joke*, the infamous clash between Batman and The Joker in which Barbara Gordon (Batgirl) is crippled and Commissioner Gordon tortured. Alan Moore tells this grim tale alongside an origin of The Joker, contrasting his madness with that of The Batman, but reportedly was reined in by editors at DC. Brian Bolland's lovingly detailed artwork (which delayed the book for many months) stays just the right side of glamorous. *Arkham Asylum* suffered similar interference. Long anticipated, when it arrived it turned out to be an overwritten, pretentious exercise by Grant Morrison and Dave McKean. The Joker has taken over the asylum, and Batman must journey through the heart of madness to recapture him. This is wrapped up in the memoirs of the builder of the asylum, too clever for its own good by half. Dave McKean paints in his usual, multi-layered style, full of montages and bits of photos. DC may have interfered with the original script but the unhappy results must still be laid at the creators' door.

Full Circle reunites Mike W.Barr and Alan Davis for a sequel to 'Batman: Year Two' (*Detective* 575–578) in which The Reaper seemingly returns from the dead for revenge. Barr produces good mysteries and Alan Davis' artwork is bold and distinctive, while there are lots of elements from Batman's past sprinkled throughout the story for nostalgia fans. There was a 1995 tie-in to the *Underworld Unleashed* crossover series, *Devil's Asylum*, in which Batman is tempted by the poisoner Kryppen, who's sold his soul to the devil. Alan Grant writes and Brian Stelfreeze 'story-tells' (whatever the difference is) while Rick Burchett does the artwork. It's a bit better than many crossovers but retreads a lot of old ground as far as Arkham Asylum is concerned.

Vengeance of Bane Special introduced Bane, the character that would eventually break the Batman's back in the 'Knightfall' story-line. Graham Nolan and Eduardo Barreto do a reasonable job on the art, and Chuck Dixon's script gets all the information over succinctly, but this remains a pretty heartless tale that reads like the scene-setter it obviously is. It was followed in 1995 by *The Vengeance of Bane II* by the same creative team. It's a better tale, making use of the past, freeing Bane from his drug dependency and getting him out of prison. After facing Batman at the end, Bane gets to walk away to pursue his own personal demons. Chuck Dixon creates another simplistic story in *Blackgate*. Batman has to infiltrate Blackgate prison to prevent an escape by one of the inmates. When it goes wrong the prisoners start killing anyone they suspect of being Batman. Joe Staton and James A. Hodgkins make a good art team but the story drags *Blackgate* down.

Seduction Of The Gun was much praised on its release because of its stance on the question of gun ownership and use. John Ostrander manages to avoid preachiness but the issue itself impairs any real plot. Vince Giarrano's artwork shows occasional flashes of inspiration but overall the quality is patchy. *Night Cries* is another issue-based story, this time by Archie Goodwin with painted artwork by Scott Hampton. Goodwin handles child abuse sensibly, but once again there's no escaping the lack of a decent plot. Commissioner Gordon's family problems are added to the mix to bulk up the story, as Batman seeks out an ex-army doctor who can still hear the cries of murdered children. Hampton's artwork isn't completely unattractive but it's far too static most of the time. Perhaps inspired by the success of other issue-based Batman strips, DC had author Neal Barrett Jr adapt Andrew Vachss' novel *Batman: The Ultimate Evil* (2 issues, 1995), which concerns child prostitution, inventing a past crusade of Martha Wayne's to draw Batman into a nation at war, where children are offered to tourists as a way of financing a repressive regime. Denys Cowan's artwork doesn't really help the sensitive subject. The final graphic novel in which concern outweighs plot is *Death Of Innocents*, written by

Denny O'Neil. Despite its rather gloomy ending it has a rather stupid plot about landmines, although why Batman should be considered the ideal vehicle for a story about such an issue is odd. The art is another matter. Joe Staton inked by Bill Sienkiewicz is an unlikely marriage made in heaven. They're wasted on this, but hopefully it will prompt them to work together again.

The Joker: Devil's Advocate finally has The Joker sentenced to death for his crimes, but there's a catch. He's not guilty of the particular deed for which he was tried and it's up to Batman to prove his innocence before he's executed. It's a rather obvious moral dilemma and certainly not worth paying for in hardback, even if you're a Batman completist. Chuck Dixon and Graham Nolan should have stayed in bed that morning. *Digital Justice* is another failure, full of high-tech babble and hideous computer-generated artwork by Pepe Moreno. As you might expect, the Batman 3-D graphic novel is in 3-D. John Byrne produces an unexciting adventure that pits The Batman against The Joker, Two-Face, The Riddler and The Penguin, who are now trying to outdo each other in the murder of a millionaire. It reads too much like a history lesson to be very entertaining and certainly offers no new insights into any of the characters, but the 3-D effects do make it a fun read. There are also 3-D pin-ups and a reprint of a rare, but poor, Batman story that was first produced during the original 3-D craze in 1953.

There's a sequence of graphic novels concerning Batman's relationship with Ra's Al Ghul, The Demon. *Son Of The Demon* and *Bride Of The Demon* are both written by Mike W. Barr and take up the idea, from an earlier, non-continuity special, that Batman and Ra's daughter Talia are lovers. Both have plenty of action as Batman spoils Ra's Al Ghul's plan to recreate the world in his own image. The first ends with the birth of Batman and Talia's child, and the second with the conception of Ra's' own offspring. Jerry Bingham has never bettered his art on *Son of the Demon*. Tom Grindberg on *Bride Of The Demon*, by contrast, does a bad Neal Adams and gets the look completely wrong, as he does so often. *Birth Of The Demon* is by The Demon's creator Denny O'Neil, and concerns the character's origin. The story should probably not be considered part of continuity since it involves a dying Batman being revived by Ra's Al Ghul's Lazarus Pit, which is what has kept him alive for centuries. Nevertheless it's not a bad tale and has the advantage of Norm Breyfogle's best artwork on Batman.

Perhaps unsurprisingly, the best Batman team-ups have generally been with characters from other companies, notably Judge Dredd and Grendel. See also entries for Spider-Man one-shots and *Judgement On Gotham*. Starting with DC team-ups, *Batman/Demon* by Alan Grant and David Roach, sees the pair joining forces to battle a devil worshipper and the devil he's trying to bring to Gotham. It's a facile excuse for taking Batman to hell, complete with guilty vision of the dead (his parents, Robin). It's not unentertaining, just a waste of time. *Batman And The Incredible Hulk* is an undemanding crossover that has the usual origin recaps and set-ups but overall avoids the clichés common to company crossovers. The Hulk and Batman battle The Shaper Of Worlds and The Joker (who, given the power to bring his dreams to life and on the verge of victory, is actually defeated by the rather awful cop-out 'I never dreamed…'). The artwork by José Luis Garcia-Lopez is smooth and flowing but the whole is uninvolving. *The Poison Tomorrow* teams Batman with Green Arrow, and is Denny O'Neil at his most moralistic as Poison Ivy plans to poison the world to save it (shades of Ra's Al Ghul). While the Black Canary lies dying Green Arrow teams up with Batman to track Ivy down via a businessman whose motives are obscure but who is financing her. Michael Netzer's art is too reminiscent of Neal Adams, but not as good, ensuring that the entire affair is missable. *Batman/Captain America*, by John Byrne, is better, if only because it's set during World War II. The Red Skull has tricked the Joker into helping him steal atomic weapons and the plot's going swimmingly until the characters are called upon to outfly a nuclear blast. Still, there are some good touches for nostalgia buffs. *Batman/Punisher* and *Punisher/Batman* form a two-part story that sees The Punisher visit Gotham in search of Jigsaw and run into first the Azrael-Batman and then the real Batman. In the meantime Jigsaw has teamed with the Joker. Denny O'Neil on the first half is restrained but Chuck Dixon goes for big gun battles and has the Batman release the Joker rather than have The Punisher kill him. Sorry, but no way. On the art front, Barry Kitson and James Pascoe do creditable work on O'Neil's script but John Romita Jr and Klaus Janson make a very unappealing meal of Dixon's. Overall an oddity not worth seeking out unless you're a completist. *Batman/Spawn: War Devil* and *Spawn/Batman* aren't related, and you know you're in trouble when one of them needs three writers. Doug Moench, Chuck Dixon and Alan Grant stick their collective oars in for a fiasco that involves Gotham being the site for the return of the dead. Yes, all of them and, yes, again. Klaus Janson's art is suited neither to Batman nor to Spawn. Todd McFarlane has the sense to get Frank Miller to script for him and the Image issue is much more successful as far as it goes. Unfortunately, since most of the issue consists of Spawn and Batman fighting each other (understandable in context, although a bit of a cliché), it's not exactly a long read. In both portions too much space is given over to how the characters react on meeting, leaving little space for a good story.~NF

Recommended: *Bloodstorm, Gotham By Gaslight, The Killing Joke, The Last Angel, Master of the Future, Red Rain, Son Of The Demon*

BATMAN/GRENDEL

DC/Dark Horse: *2-issue microseries 'Devil's Riddle' 1993, 2-issue microseries 'Devil's Bones'/'Devil's Dance' 1996*

In 'Devil's Riddle' the original Grendel, Hunter Rose, visits Gotham City while planning an elaborate stunt involving an Egyptian artefact, purely for his own aggrandisement. Since the artefact is being shipped by Wayne Enterprises, Bruce Wayne gets involved. 'Devil's Bones'/ 'Devil's Dance' sees the accidental appearance of the robotic Grendel Prime in Gotham during a demonstration against the museum exhibition of Hunter Rose's skull. Displaced in time, Grendel Prime wants the skull to help him to return himself to the future. Reminiscent in style of Miller or Toth, Matt Wagner nevertheless brings his own distinctive viewpoint to well-written, playful tales that avoid the normal cross-company team-up clichés.~NF

Recommended: 'Devil's Riddle' 1–2, 'Devil's Bones' 1–2

BATMAN: JAZZ

DC: *3 -issue miniseries 1995*

Written by Gerard Jones and drawn by Mark Badger, this is an unusual Batman story. Taking as a starting point the possible reappearance of old jazz musician Blue Byrd, long thought dead, Jones weaves a story that though personal somehow characterises a lost age (much as Clint Eastwood's *Bird* tried to do). Though Batman participates in some fighting it's his detective skills that draw out the mystery surrounding Byrd's past. A cut above most Batman stories of the last ten years.~NF

Recommended: 1–3

BATMAN/JUDGE DREDD

DC/Fleetway: *Judgement On Gotham 1 issue 1991, Vendetta In Gotham 1 issue 1993, The Ultimate Riddle 1 issue 1995*

In *Judgement On Gotham*, writers Alan Grant and John Wagner let Judge Death and the Mean Machine loose in Gotham while Batman tries to avoid doing hard time in Mega-City One. In one of a series of good jokes, Dredd takes exception to Batman's utility-belt arsenal and wants to lock him up. Only Judge Anderson can return Batman to Gotham, where Death has teamed up with the

Scarecrow to attack people at a rock concert. The script's witty and knowing considering these are two of the most serious characters in comics. Seeing Judge Death perform *Sympathy For The Devil* as a prelude to his killing spree has to be some sort of highlight. Simon Bisley's distorted painted art isn't to everyone's taste, but in this case the script's so good the excesses of the artwork are minimised, and he produces an exceptional Judge Anderson on page 18.

Vendetta In Gotham is much less satisfying as it involves a drawn-out fight between Batman and Judge Dredd as Dredd tries to keep him from being somewhere fatal. Its villain is Scarface but it's just not as funny or interesting, although Cam Kennedy's attempt to draw like Mike McMahon is surprising. *The Ultimate Riddle* is another more serious tale, albeit with a good smattering of Dredd one-liners, but the reason for Dredd and Batman meeting is flimsiest here and the artwork, by Carl Critchlow and Dermot Power, is painted and mostly free of background and inspiration.~NF

Recommended: *Judgement On Gotham*

BATMAN: THE LONG HALLOWEEN

DC: *4 issues + 1996 to date*

A planned 13-issue series, building on the success of the *Legends of the Dark Knight* Halloween Specials, this is by the regular team for those specials, Jeph Loeb and Tim Sale. Set during Batman's early career, the issues actually cover different holidays (Christmas with The Joker, Valentine's Day with Catwoman), starting off with Batman and Catwoman getting caught in the middle of a Mob family wedding. Sale's artwork has come on by leaps and bounds, and with its references to Miller and Toth seems perfectly suited to the Batman.~NF

Recommended: 1–4

BATMAN: SHADOW OF THE BAT

DC: *57 issues +, 3 Annuals 1992 to date*

Written by Alan Grant, this series focuses on the darker, psychological side of Batman's adventures, starting with 'The Last Arkham' (1–4), in which Batman is committed as part of a plan to catch a serial killer, Zsasz. Leavened with a characteristic black humour, Grant's stories often seem rather too tongue-in-cheek, as in 'The Misfits' (7–9), in which Catman, Killer Moth and Calendar Man team up to break their losing streak. 'The Nobody' (13) deals with Batman's motivations when his secret identity is threatened, 'The God Of Fear' (16–18) is a 'Knightfall' tie-in featuring The Scarecrow, while 19–31 are part of the 'Knightquest' (19–25) and 'Knightsend' (30,31) crossovers in which Azrael is Batman and Bruce Wayne must recover his confidence, 21–23 also being part of the Shondra

Kinsolving story-line. 31 is a comedy *Zero Hour* tie-in in which an alternate-world Alfred (the fat one with a desire to be a detective) turns up to keep house, which eloquently expresses Grant's feelings about such tie-ins.

35 is part two of 'Troika' (the return of the KGBeast, featuring Batman's new costume) and then Black Canary (36), The Joker (37–38) and Solomon Grundy (39) guest before Grant brings back his favourite anarchist Anarky, a disillusioned, bored youth whose motives seem pure but whose actions are criminal. 43 and 44 are part of a crossover with *Catwoman* 26 as the pair face Catman in 'The Secret Of The Universe'. The pace changes for 45, a murder mystery set in Wayne Manor after a skeleton is found in the cellar and proves to belong to Joshua Wayne, who was involved in helping slaves escape from the South during the American Civil War. New villain Narcosis is introduced in issue 50–52, and 56–58 is an anti-drugs tale featuring Poison Ivy and the Fluoronic Man. The 'Contagion' crossover takes up 48 and 49, and its sequel, 'Legacy', is covered in 53 and 54.

Artwork for the series starts well with Norm Breyfogle (1–5,13) but swiftly becomes inconsistent as different artists guest. Exceptions include Tim Sale (7–9), Kevin Walker (39), John Paul Leon (40–41) and Barry Kitson (43–44 in a departure from his normal style). Most other issues are drawn by Vince Giarrano or Bret Blevins but with 51 a semi-regular was finally introduced, giving the title the consistency it's lacked. Dave Taylor's supple figures and detailed backgrounds are sometimes let down by his stiff faces, but his work is promising and counterpoints Grant's edgy scripts well.

An issue 0 (1994) follows *Zero Hour*, and there have been four annuals, all written by Grant. 1993's is part of the 'Bloodlines' crossover, introducing Joe Public, not seen since, and the 1994 annual is an Elseworlds story where Bruce Wayne controls Gotham and Anarky helps free the city from his tyranny. An excellent recap of Poison Ivy's first year as a criminal is drawn by Brian Apthorp for the 1995 annual and 1996's is one of the 'Legends of the Dead Earth', featuring the legacy of Batman.~NF

Recommended: 7–9, 39, 43–44, Annual 3

BATMAN VERSUS PREDATOR

DC/Dark Horse: *3-issue miniseries 1991–1992, 4-issue miniseries ('Bloodmatch')1994*

The first Batman/Predator miniseries, written by Dave Gibbons and drawn by Andy and Adam Kubert, is very much within the parameters established by the *Predator* films. A predator kills Gotham's leading powers (whether boxers, criminals or politicians) and

forces Batman into hiding after badly wounding him. Whilst the city lives in fear and the police are incapable of finding the alien, Batman recuperates and plans a showdown in the caves under Wayne Manor. In the sequel Batman faces a rogue Predator, its alien pursuers, and several human assassins who've been set on him by a drug lord. Fortunately, this time he has the help of the Huntress, despite not wanting it. Doug Moench and Paul Gulacy have always worked well together, and Moench's understanding of the Batman's character is what makes this more than just another novelty crossover.

Whilst the Batman has never been at his best in such overtly science-fiction story-lines, both Gibbons and Moench, in their different ways, emphasise that it is the Batman's human abilities that make him a hero. Moench, in particular, creates a series full of characters rather than stereotypes, including the main Predator.~NF

BATTLE

Atlas/Marvel: *70 issues 1951–1960*

A general war anthology title that featured 'Buck Private O'Toole' in early issues. The anthology format means there are contributions from some excellent artists, including EC stalwarts Bernie Krigstein in 21 and 23, Jack Davis (49), John Severin (28, 32, 34) and Al Williamson (55, 67, and 68, inking Jack Kirby). Others to be found include Russ Heath (6), Joe Maneely (4), Angelo Torres (59) and plenty of Kirby in the late issues. Combat Kelly and Combat Casey were briefly featured in 60–62. Although it survived Marvel's great bout of cancellations in 1957, the greater need for *My Girl Pearl* in 1960 killed Marvel's only remaining war title.~SW

BATTLE ANGEL ALITA

Viz: *Book One 9 issues 1992–1993, Book Two 7 issues 1993, Book Three 13 issues 1994–1995, Book Four 7 issues 1995, Book Five 7 issues 1995–1996, Book Six 8 issues 1996, Book Seven 8 issues 1996–1997*

Alita is a cyborg with little memory except for her knowledge of the Panzer Kunst, a very powerful fighting technique. In the world of the Scrapyard, Alita is reconstructed by Ido, a refugee from the floating city of Tiphares – everyone wants to go there but it's fiercely protected. There's plenty of opportunity in the early series for Alita to show off her fighting abilities, whether against rogue cyborgs or in the Motorball arena. After the death of her boyfriend Hugo at the end of Book Two she seeks her own death in this arena, where the most powerful cyborgs work in teams to race around a circuit. Book Three contains this story-line but is also the story of the champion

Jashugan, whose victories come with a higher and higher cost to his health. Book Four features the return of Zapan, the rogue cyborg from Book One, determined to destroy Alita and the whole of the Scrapyard if it won't surrender her to him. Book Five sees a new direction as, searching for Ido, who's been taken prisoner by an old colleague, Alita becomes a member of an élite force in service to Tiphares. She's a bodyguard on a nuclear-powered train until it's attacked and destroyed. Book Six continues the search, with Alita now accompanied by her new friend Figure.

Yukito Kishiro's artwork is what draws you to this tale, although as the series progresses his characterisation and story-telling grow in depth, increasing our understanding of the whole situation but politicising and adding emotion where it had been lacking. Book Four shows a growing maturity, being mostly a big fight but containing seeds of emotional and physical rebirth. The scripts have a lighter touch too, as Kishiro's confidence increases and touches of humour are allowed to shine through.~NF

Recommended: Book Four 1–7, Book Five 1–7

BATTLE CLASSICS
DC: *1 issue 1978*

An attempt by DC to earn a bit of extra pocket money by reprinting some of their vast library of war stories. It teams their main World War II characters – Sgt Rock, Mlle Marie, Johnny Cloud and Jeb Stuart – and was intended to initiate an ongoing series. As it débuted, though, swingeing cuts were being applied to DC's entire line and there was only ever the one issue.~HY

BATTLE TIDE
Marvel UK: *Miniseries one 4 issues 1993, Miniseries two 4 issues 1993*

'Tag Team Wrestling Inter-Galactic Style!' screams the cover blurb, and that's about all you need to know. Death's Head II and Killpower co-star, Psylocke and Sabretooth guest star. Series two is more of the same, but with only the Hulk getting between Killpower and Death's Head.~HS

BATTLESTAR GALACTICA
Marvel: *23 issues 1979–1981*

Based on the post-*Star Wars* TV series, *Battlestar Galactica* was launched in *Marvel Super Special* 8, with the TV pilot adapted by Ernie Colon. The subsequent ongoing title was a cut above your average tie-in comic, thanks mainly to Walt Simonson's regular appearances as penciller. Although his blocky style didn't produce the greatest likenesses he was well suited to drawing the dog-fights, and there were plenty of them in issues 4, 5, 11–13, 15–20 and 23. The

last remnants of space-faring humanity are fleeing across galaxies, hotly pursued by the evil robot-like Cylons. Their mission: to find the legendary home of mankind without leading the Cylons there to massacre whoever they may find. Their motley fleet of small craft is protected by the Galactica, which is crewed by the usual bunch of white-toothed young people, crusty old blokes, cute kids with pageboy haircuts and comedy aliens. Louise Simonson's scripts brought a heart-warming touch to the book without getting as mawkish as the series itself. She developed the characters well. As in the TV series most adventures centred around staid but sexy pilot Apollo (who just happened to be the son of Adama, the Battlestar's commander), his spunky sister Athena and his devil-may-care best buddy, Starbuck, a gambling womanizer with a cheeky grin. There was more space to develop the struggle for power between the military Battlestar and the secular Grand Council, although this was used chiefly to generate plot ideas.~FJ

BATTLESTAR GALACTICA
Maximum: *4-issue miniseries 1995, 3-issue miniseries ('The Enemy Within') 1995–1996, 3-issue miniseries ('Starbuck') 1995–1996, 3-issue miniseries ('Apollo's Journey')1996, one-shot ('Journey's End')1996*

Having liked the TV series as a kid, Rob Liefeld decided to revive the comic using various Maximum Press regulars to flesh out his concepts. He concludes the search for earth and kills off Adama, leaving Apollo in charge. However, there's no sign of the thirteenth tribe of Israel (yes, there is a grand design behind all these escapades) so Apollo *et al.* have to find them. The best of the miniseries focuses on Starbuck, predictably the most popular character.~FJ

BATTRON
NEC: *2 issues 1992*

A series that surely sank without trace on the appalling and unrepresentative covers. Anyone purchasing 1 on the basis of the (poorly depicted) naked woman draped behind a sheet would surely be put off by Wayne Vansant's tale of a French Foreign Legionnaire named Battron during World War II. Despite featuring a travelling brothel, it's sober fare, extremely well drawn in Vansant's nigh-photo-realist style, but very dry and slow-paced in the telling.~WJ

Bobby Benson's B-BAR-B RIDERS
Magazine Enterprises: *20 issues 1950–1953*

Based on the radio show of the same name, this concerned adventures on a modern-day ranch. Owner Bobby Benson is a kid, and most of the ranch work is done by the foreman Tex Mason, conveniently leaving Bobby and his friends Harka, Irish, Waco and Windy Wales free to get into scrapes. When Tex has finished running the ranch he's usually called upon to get them out of trouble as well. As if this wasn't enough, he also finds time to star as the *Lemonade Kid* in the back-up strip, an FBI Agent pitted against would-be world-conquerors and the like. Other back-up strips included Ghost Rider and Red Hawk. While fighting bank robbers and rustlers for the most part, Bobby also managed to get involved with Fifth Columnists and evil scientists from time to time. The first thirteen issues were drawn by Bob Powell; Dick Ayers continued *Bobby Benson* and drew the first Ghost Rider episodes.

14 has a famous horror cover featuring shrunken heads, marking the series' move away from straight Western stories to compete with the rising number of crime and horror titles. The B-Bar-B riders also featured in *Model Fun* and *Best of the West* (Magazine Enterprises 1951–1953). In 1990 AC Comics published a black and white one-off reprinting three of Powell's *B-Bar-B* stories and one *Red Hawk* back-up strip.~NF

B.E.A.S.T.I.E.S.
Axis: *1 issue 1994*

Artist Javier Saltares comes a cropper with this travesty revolving around a new superhero team, organized by a secret society. The layouts are ridiculous, the colours worse and anatomy appalling. This is, believe it or not, a poor man's *Youngblood*.~SS

BEAUTY AND THE BEAST
First: *2 issues 1989–1990*

Spin-offs from the mid-80s TV show about the unlikely romance between a crusading social worker and a bestial subterranean whose deformed exterior hides a noble spirit. Okay, they're 'girlie' comics: pretty, soft-focus, soft-centred and sentimental, but they're lovingly illustrated by Wendy Pini and more satisfying and coherent than the irrational show that generated them.~HS

BEAUTY AND THE BEAST
Innovation: *9 issues 1993*

The soppy romantic TV series gets another run through comics, this time adapting episodes, beginning with the pilot stretched over the first three issues. Mike Deodato produces decent likenesses among the adept but static artwork. The stories are taken from the original scripts, so there's some scenes that weren't in the screened versions to attract fans of the series. Those who aren't already fans are likely to find this saccharine and ridiculous.~FP

Stan Shaw's BEAUTY AND THE BEAST
Dark Horse: *One-shot 1993*

There's no beauty in this art-wank adaptation of the traditional fairy tale.~FP

THE BEAUTY AND THE BEAST
Marvel: *4-issue miniseries 1985*

Not to be confused with the TV series or Disney movie, this was one of the earlier miniseries spun off from *The X-Men*. Dazzler and Dr Hank McCoy, aka the Beast, team up to take on the evil machinations of Dr Doom. Basic stuff with some nice Bill Sienkiewicz covers.~TP

BEAVIS AND BUTTHEAD
Marvel: *28 issues 1994–1996*

The nerds from hell leap from the screens of MTV to star in an ongoing series of gross-out adventures. As is the case with the TV series, the actual adventures aren't as good as the dismal duo's commentary on the pop culture, in this case Marvel's superhero comics. The likes of Mark Beacham, Ron Frenz, Rick Leonardi, Gene Ha, Fred Hembeck, John Romita Snr and Ron Lim supply the muscle-bound art, and you're best sampling either 3 or 8. The observations range from 'If I was Spider-Man I'd, like, do it hanging from the ceiling' to 'How come superhero chicks have such big thingies?' Indeed. This comics, like, rocks!~TP

BECK & CAUL Investigations
Gauntlet: *4 issues, 1 annual 1994*
Caliber: *2 issues (5–6) 1995*

Jonas Beck, a centuries-old werewolf, and 'Caul' Guillane, a young Cajun psychic, form an uneasy partnership to fight evil when they're both involved in trailing a succubus serial killer to the Underside. Reginald Chaney manages some neat twists on established ideas of supernatural beings, but his dialogue is plodding and expository, and the plot over-dramatic. In 3 they go up against a child-killing witch and then Caul reinvestigates the mysterious disappearance of her brother. There are some nice touches, but ultimately Paul Kowalski's overblown art, which looks like a bad 1970s Neal Adams rip-off, is enough to put anyone off, with its distorted faces, hackneyed poses and gimmicky panel arrangements. A 1994 special reprinted the first two issues.~FJ

BEER NUTZ
Tundra: *3 issues 1991–1992*

Picture three versions of *Cheers'* Cliff Claven and you've hit on Bink, Humphrey and Luther, three sad cases who substitute boastful bar conversation for friendship. This isn't subtle, but Wayno's observations are very funny,

especially the illustrated synonyms for defecation in 1. Issue 3 spotlights another loser, social retard Howie, also seen in 1, and his comic collection.~FP
Recommended: 1–3

BEOWULF
DC: *6 issues 1975–1976*

Another of the mid-1970s DC barbarian strips. Despite writer Mike Uslan's credible plotting it's hard to read American idioms such as 'I owe him one' or 'In a pig's eye it is!' coming from the mouth of a character from popular European folklore. Ricardo Villamonte's artistry is similarly inconsistent, but on the whole passable. Result: forgettable.~SW

BERLIN
Black Eye: *2 issues + 1996 to date*

On a train journey into 1930s Berlin artist Marthe Müller is befriended by unorthodox journalist Kurt Severing, investigating the Nazis. Attending the art college she meets several people who begin to change her view of life. Jason Lutes is slowly unwinding a character-driven story about a city on the cusp of enormous and inconceivable changes. So far it's every bit as compelling as his *Jar Of Fools*, and should be well worth following.~WJ
Recommended: 1, 2

BERNI WRIGHTSON, MASTER OF THE MACABRE
Pacific: *4 issues 1983–84.*
Eclipse: *1 issue (5) 1984*

A collection of Wrightson's work for Warren black and white magazines, *Creepy*, *Eerie* and *Vampirella*, the first three issues contain the better material, with some spirited versions of Poe's *Black Cat* and Lovecraft's *Cool Air*. The final issue is very badly coloured and Wrightson's detailed artwork and beautiful rendering are done no favours throughout the series. Steve Oliff does his best on the first three issues but the considerable reduction in size of the artwork hampers him; colouring the strips is ultimately a misjudged decision and seriously mars the quality of these books.~NF

BERZERKERS
Image: *4-issue miniseries 1995*

On the basis of his artwork herein one has to assume that Dan Fraga has spent his life devoid of any contact with other human beings, mirrors, or any film, TV show or book depicting humans. Given his sheltered existence and that he's obviously drawn this entire series with only verbal instructions on how a human being looks, one has to

commend Fraga on his achievement. Beyond that it's assembly-line superheroes in a ridiculous plot.~FP

BEWARE
Marvel: *8 issues 1973–1974*

This all-reprint title contains weird horror shorts from the 1950's. The title changed to *Tomb of Darkness* from issue 9.~APS

BEYOND THE GRAVE
Charlton: *6 issues 1975–1976*

Can you imagine the person so starved of even the most basic forms of entertainment in the 1970s that they might resort to buying a Charlton mystery title? Universally unimaginative and poorly drawn (even by Steve Ditko, who features in every issue), there's a thrill rating of absolute zero here. Back to the original poser, though. Back covers feature adverts inviting readers to train for a career in law enforcement, border patrols or broadcasting. The successful applicants will by now be running your local police and immigration services or be heads of programming somewhere. Now you know why they're so humourless and lacking in imagination.~WJ

THE BIBLE
DC: *One-shot 1975*

This tabloid-sized comic adapted the Book of Genesis from creation to Sodom and Gomorrah, and was intended as the first of a series that sadly never materialised. Sheldon Mayer's script very concisely reduces the stories down to the bare essentials, and uses quite contemporary and straightforward writing so that the comics would be accessible to a young audience. To an older readership it may be too simplistic to be wholly engaging, but the emphasis on the Bible's panoramic scale is an enormous compensation, thanks to Nestor Redondo's spectacular artwork. Redondo, working from editor Joe Kubert's layouts, excelled himself in providing page after page of detailed, almost baroquely intricate tableaux, making full use of the comic's large format. Almost inevitably, there's nothing ground-breaking here, but for fans of great art this is an absolute must.~DAR
Recommended: 1

BICENTENNIAL GROSS-OUTS
Yentzer & Gonif: *1 issue 1976*

Despite its title few of the contents have anything to do with America's bicentennial, the real meat of the comic being two strips by William Stout, the hard-hitting 'Filipino Massacre' and the libellous Disney spoof 'Realityland'. The other strips are largely inconsequential.~DAR

BIG APPLE COMIX
Big Apple: *One-shot 1975*

A group of New York-based comic professionals step away from the mainstream to produce an underground comic with the Big Apple as a theme. Revelling in the freedom bestowed by retreat from superheroes, everyone's work is top notch, so selecting the best strip is difficult. 'Over and Under' sees Neal Adams portraying the city's high life while the team of Larry Hama and Ralph Reese contrast on the opposite side of the page, and Wally Wood parodies his own highly regarded 'My World'. Other contributors include Archie Goodwin, Mike Ploog and Al Williamson. A must-have double-bag item.~FP
Recommended: 1

BIG ASS COMICS
Rip Off/Last Gasp: *2 issues 1969–1971*

When the politically correct critics have the knives out for Robert Crumb, *Big Ass Comics* provides prime ammunition. 'Weird sex fantasies with the behind in mind' runs the coverline to the first issue, and it doesn't lie, but neglects to mention the racist caricatures. The odd thing is, it's all such absurd nonsense, drawn by Crumb in his early-period cartoony style. As part of his canon *Big Ass Comics* is a trivial footnote. Kept in print since the original publication, the most recent editions were published in the 1991 by Last Gasp~WJ

BIG BANG
Caliber: *5 issues (0–4) 1994–1995*
Image: *6 issues + 1995 to date*

'Comics haven't been this fun for fifty years!' exclaims *Big Bang* 1's cover, and, guardedly, one can agree. An affectionate homage to the comics of the 1940s to the 1960s, Big Bang introduces lookalike versions of archetypal heroes, mimicking all the old styles. Caliber's 1–2, the Golden Age tributes, were very successful, 3's Silver Age homage less so with the artists simply lacking the fluidity of Sekowsky and Sachs, whom they were imitating in this JLA-style salute. 4 ill-advisedly takes the heroes to modern times, with distorted anatomy and moronic dialogue, but 0 is back to the Golden Age and apparently impressed Image's Erik Larsen sufficiently that he offered to relaunch the comic as an ongoing series. It adds retro versions of Image heroes to the line-up. Of the various contributors, Billy Fugate stands out as an artist who combines a nostalgic feel with exquisite skill.~HS
Recommended: Series one 0–2, Series two 1, 3, 4

BIG BLOWN BABY
Dark Horse: *4 issues 1996*

Picking up where its appearances in *Dark Horse Presents* left off, this broad superhero parody (DC and Marvel both come in for some spectacularly scatological attacks) from the twisted minds of Bill Wray (ideas and art) and Robert Loren Fleming (script) is the kind of comic it's easy to dismiss as juvenile and disgusting. It also happens to be rather funny, in a tasteless way. When you get used to it, Fleming's script, which at first appears overwritten, begins to crack you up, especially when teamed with Wray's manic drawings. All this and jokes about Stan Lee's wig and Vinnie Colletta's death too. Told you it was tasteless.~FJ

THE BIG BOOK OF...
Paradox Press: *8 volumes 1994 to date*

Paradox Press' *Big Books* are an important attempt to bring comics to a wider audience. Always concerned with the weird side of life, they build upon people's enjoyment of odd stories. 'Did you know about the person who...?' is their stock in trade.

The first volume, *Urban Legends*, was based on the many books of folklorist Jan Harold Brunvand. Writers Robert Loren Fleming and Robert Boyd Jr misguidedly tried to make each story fit a single-page format, with the result that many are rushed, while there are simultaneously stories without punchlines that are really one-sentence funnies. After that the format was relaxed, and stories of up to eight pages were occasionally included, especially in Doug Moench's *Conspiracies* volume, which does a creditable job of rounding up a very difficult subject, introduced by a Mr A-type figure, but has trouble adapting it successfully to a comic book format – complex conspiracies are better explained in prose.

Early volumes tended to rely on a single writer/editor. Carl Posey, for *Weirdos*, provides an interesting selection from a very rich and diverse field of ridiculous human endeavour, Bronwyn Carlton, for *deaths!*, comes up with some very dull ideas, like illustrated tours of famous cemeteries, and Gahan Wilson, on *Freaks*, approaches his subject with the right mix of prurience and understanding. *Little Criminals* benefits from the input of several writers (George Hagenauer, Carl Sifakis, Joel Rose, Tom Peyer, Lou Stathis and Judy Maguire) and is probably the most rounded volume to date, although the name is a misnomer. In the mix of well-known criminals and obscure but interesting stories are a number of rather inept thieves, fakers and murderers. Carl Sifakis gets to edit *Hoaxes*, with help from several regular contributors to the series. Unfortunately the subject is repetitive: there are only so many forgers you can get interested in. The latest offering, *Thugs*, edited by Joel Rose, suffers from the same problem. After an introductory strip explaining the derivation of the word from the Hindi *thuggee* the editor, for some unknowable reason, limits himself to American gangsters and gang leaders, mostly from 1850–1930. Although packed with info, the many scripts about New York street gangs and Wild West outlaws often don't have stories to tell, just facts to recount, rather drily.

Part of the joy of reading these volumes is the wide range of artists who illustrate the tales, from mainstream to underground, old pros alongside talented newcomers. Frank Quitely rubs shoulders with Russ Heath, Drew Friedman shares space with Bryan Talbot. Something for everybody's taste, provided it's a little twisted. Selected offerings from Paradox's highly successful Big Books have been repackaged in magazine format as *100% True*.~FJ

Recommended: *Freaks, Little Criminals*

BIG DOG FUNNIES
Rip Off: *One-shot 1992*

Collects a selection from five years' worth of utterly feeble humour one-pagers. Lead character M. Littlechief Bigdog is a hippy Native American fount of philosophical aphorisms, and his meditations on life and TV, seemingly intended as satire, make one scream for all the comforts of the straight life. Creator D.M. Pitts' 'jokes' are on a level with those found on Garfield mugs. He'd probably be appalled at the comparison. Good.~WJ

THE BIG GUY AND RUSTY THE ROBOT
Dark Horse: *2-issue microseries 1995*

This delightful oversized comic, written by Frank Miller with beautiful artwork from Geof Darrow, is a treat for lovers of big-robot comics everywhere. The story is a mix of pure whimsy and comic genius, following the adventures of Rusty, a cute lil' two-foot high robot boy created to save Japan from the threat of big monsters. He wants nothing more than to be a success so that the army will build others like him and stop him being so lonely. But, sadly, Rusty's pretty crap as robots go and the monster kicks his butt, meaning that Japan has to take advantage of a gift from America in the form of a huge robot called the Big Guy. Big Guy sees off the monsters and, in gratitude, Japan gives him Rusty to be his kid sidekick. The Big Guy is not impressed. Will Rusty be able to prove himself worthy? Or is he really just too – sob – small? Let's just hope that

Miller and Darrow continue this wonderful series so we find out either way. A real joy.~JC
Recommended: 1–2
Collection: *The Big Guy And Rusty The Robot* (1–2)

BIG NUMBERS
Mad Love: *2 issues 1990*

Big Numbers united Alan Moore and Bill Sienkiewicz, two creators at the height of their powers and popularity. Their combined clout enabled them to convince distributors that twelve issues of a square, oversize comic about seemingly unconnected events in the lives of inhabitants of a grey home counties town (not unlike Moore's native Northampton, England) was the biggest thing since *Watchmen*. Although critically acclaimed, *Big Numbers'* complexity, oblique story-telling techniques and lack of conventional 'action' left some fans of Moore's earlier mainstream work bewildered. Moore explores the mechanics of modern society through the device of a writer returning to the places and people she outgrew ten years earlier. The story is aggressively multi-cultural and plays upon our perceptions of the British class system. Of particular note is Moore's ear for dialogue and speech rhythms, which the dialogue attempts to spell out for the benefits of American readers. Sienkiewicz matches the 'kitchen sink' story-line with evocative, detailed imagery that often dissolves into pencil lines or brush strokes, emphasising the transience of the characters' existence. He puts a wealth of techniques to the service of the story, using extensive photo reference.

This ambitious series began falling apart before issue 2 was even printed, with the artist continually delaying delivery of artwork. Plans to replace Sienkiewicz with Dave McKean or Al Columbia, who at the time was drawing in a very similar style, never came to fruition, and the story remains becalmed after two tantalising, morally-pointed issues.~FJ
Recommended: 1–2

The BIG PRIZE
Eternity: *1 issue*

The peculiarly named Willis Austerlitz dreams of the gentler days of the 1930s, when, he feels, everything was somehow more decent. He's then given the opportunity to live his dreams courtesy of the big prize, the winning ticket in a planet-wide lottery of the future that's somehow materialised in 1988. The thin plot contrivance can be forgiven in context, as the remainder of the issue compensates. Austerlitz is wearing rose-coloured glasses, of course, and, able to travel to 1934, he finds it's not what he anticipated. Gerard Jones writes in an intriguing and wistful manner, and although the art of Bryon Carson and Mike Roberts is somewhat static it's not enough to detract from the whole. Disappointingly, the story remains incomplete, but what there is is worth investigating.~FP

Colin Upton's BIG THING
Ed Varney: *1 issue 1990*
Fantagraphics: *4 issues 1991–1992*
Starhead: *1 issue 1994*
Aeon: *1 issue 1994*

Stop sniggering. Contrary to what you might expect, *Big Thing* is an autobiographical title. There's an occasional excess of self-pity and whining about the day-to-day annoyances of life, but it's balanced by plenty of observations and telling asides that ensure each issue contains something worthwhile. In the opening issue 'Looneys' is the standout strip, contrasting the mixed feelings Upton has about a local eccentric with his own mental traumas. All too often, though, there are recollections that are obviously important to Upton, yet fail to engage the readership as intended. This is largely due to Upton's drawing style, which, while functional, is very limited and cluttered, and unable to convey the full emotional range of his stories. This is most vividly brought home in the second Fantagraphics issue, an over-extended story of the problems occurring when Upton crossed from Canada into the USA to see an art performance group. Ironically the strongest issue is 4, in which there's an angry response to hearing about *Big Thing*'s impending cancellation, 'Fuck'. It rails against superficial sweeteners in comics while bemoaning that *Big Thing*'s more intelligent content is sadly uncommercial. There's also a good selection of shorter stories, closing with another 'Famous Bus Rides' strip. A carry-over from Upton's minicomics days, there's one strip in most issues, all of them short, sharp and wry.

Bizarrely, the Starhead issue, titled *Big Black Thing*, is a response to a fake issue of *Big Thing* circulated with blank black pages. Initially despondent, Upton pasted in several of his minicomics, and a strange story about Hotxha The Albanian. The Aeon issue, officially *Aeon Focus 2*, is the strongest issue overall. There's a brutal and hard-hitting honesty transcending the still limited art with strips Upton had completed with no idea of where they'd see print. 'I'm Not Angry Anymore' is a visceral depiction of the bouts of despair and low self-esteem Upton experiences, and 'Chris' encompasses narrow-minded feminism and positive discrimination. Bleak and thought-provoking, the only page-filler is a strange humorous attempt at depicting the life of St Anthony. The Ed Varney issue and first

Fantagraphics issue are magazine-sized, but the remaining issues are all in standard comic format.~FP
Recommended: Aeon Press 1

BIJOU FUNNIES
Bijou/Kitchen Sink: *8 issues 1968–1973*

One of the first and best underground anthologies, edited by Skip Williamson and Jay Lynch. Both were excellent cartoonists in their own right and the comic featured Williamson's Snappy Sammy Smoot and Lynch's Nard'n'Pat in a series of skits that mixed counterculture politics, knockabout humour and surrealism to great effect. Other artists included Robert Crumb, Justin Green and Art Spiegelman, making *Bijou* an essential buy. The final issue was an all-colour *Mad*-style spoof, which featured almost all the main underground artists drawing each others characters and is a big favourite among some collectors despite lacking the bite of the previous seven.~DAR
Recommended: 1–8
Collections: The Best of Bijou Funnies, Apex Treasury: Best of Bijou

BILL & TED'S Excellent Comic Book
Marvel: *One-shot 1991, 12 issues 1991–1992*

Magnificent, although anyone who's not a fan of the *Bill & Ted* films should stay away. Writer and artist Even Dorkin populates the comic with all the characters from both films and more, consistently delivering hilarity based on the dumb characters. As with the films, the plots are thin, but Dorkin packs a full complement of silly jokes in, and, this being a comic, there's the added bonus of all sorts of visual asides. He doesn't skimp on his backgrounds either, so pity poor inkers Stephen DeStefano (1–3) and Marie Severin (4–12) having to ink page after page of crowd scenes. There's Bill and Ted's wedding party in 1, while 4 introduces Fight Man, later to star in his own one-shot, and in 10 Bill and Ted enter his world. It's obvious Dorkin's favourite cast member is Death, who is humiliated in assorted hilarious ways each issue, with 9 being the best as Death has to find a job to pay his rent and is replaced by Death Jnr. In 2 he goes on vacation with most egregious consequences, and the funniest issue is 11. Bill and Ted discover their friend Abraham Lincoln is to be assassinated and vow to prevent his death. Prior to this series Dorkin produced the comic adaptation of *Bill & Ted's Bogus Journey*, which, as the cover promises, is most excellent. Be warned, though, to stay well clear of issue 8, produced by altogether heinous and non-righteous less talented individuals, dude.~FP
Recommended: 2, 5–7, 9–11, *Bill & Ted's Bogus Journey*

BILL THE CLOWN Comedy Isn't Pretty

Slave Labor: *One-shot 1992*

Poor old Bill, the time of the clown is past. He's yesterday's unsophisticated laughter- maker without a future ahead. Discovering a pile of discarded toy clown heads in a junkyard is the final straw, sending Bill on a righteous rampage. Silly satire on the testosterone breed of anti-heroes populating comics, drawn in appropriate Lobo style by Troy Nixey from a Dan Vado script. There's plenty of worse comics to buy, but there's plenty better as well.~WJ

BILLI 99

Dark Horse: *4-issue miniseries 1991*

In the year 1999 America is falling apart; police forces need corporate funds to fight crime; there's mass unemployment. Billi's father, a cross between Batman and Zorro, is killed and she is framed by her uncle, who's a serial killer. Billi runs her father's company but can't inherit until she's cleared of his murder. Only her Mob boyfriend and a rogue honest cop can help her. *Billi 99* is a rather grim political thriller written by Sarah Byam and drawn by Tim Sale. It's one of Sale's earliest published works and the first issue shows some rough edges. By the end of the series, however, his confident, European style has firmly established the pessimistic tone of Byam's story. The politics sit a little uneasily with the favourable portrayal of organised crime, but overall the script is intelligent, with strong characterisation driving the story along.~NF

BINKY

DC: *82 issues 1948–1958 (1–60), 1968©1971 (61–81), 1977 (82)*

An imitation of *Archie*, Binky's teenage adventures ran for a decade, even more innocuous and dated to the contemporary eye than their inspiration, particularly the bizarre Lord Fauntleroy outfit affected by his kid brother Allergy. Revived following a successful try-out in *Showcase* 70 in 1967, a new, 'groovy' version had limited success – spawning a spin-off title, *Binky's Buddies*, which ran for twelve issues in 1969/1970 – but couldn't crack the Archie monopoly long-term. For no known reason, issue 82 unexpectedly dribbled out in 1977, six years after the title's cancellation.~HS

BINKY BROWN Meets the Holy VIRGIN MARY

Last Gasp: *1 issue 1972*

Underground artist Justin Green's Binky Brown single-handedly invented the autobiographical comic, and it remains to this day one of the finest strips ever drawn. It's a frenzied tale of Catholic and sexual guilt that keeps the reader riveted to the page in admiration and sometimes disbelief. Some may find the art initially crude, but it's perfectly suited to the story. Quite possibly the finest comic ever made, and recently reissued in book form by Kitchen Sink as *The Binky Brown Sampler*.~DAR
Recommended: 1

BIO-BOOSTER ARMOR GUYVER

Viz: *Part one 12 issues 1993–1994, part two 6 issues 1994–1995, part three 7 issues 1995*

Written and drawn by Yoshiki Takaya, this lengthy slice of robot Manga is unremarkable, and similar to hundreds of other Japanese comic strips. Here, high-school student Sho is possessed by the Guyver, a alien life-form which turns our hero into an armoured superhero – Guyver meaning 'beyond the norm', incidentally. Sho soon finds himself in a drawn-out conflict with secret organisation Chronos, developers of the Guyver technology, who despatch vicious mutated humans the Hyper-Zoanoids to reclaim their deadly biological weapon. The by now formulaic combination of teen-*angst* soap opera and extended sci-fi fight sequences gives *Bio-Booster Armor Guyver* a curiously impersonal air. Takaya's identikit artwork, obviously the product of several artists of varying ability, reinforces the impression that this strip will appeal only to the most undemanding of Manga enthusiasts.~AL
Collections: Bio Booster Armor Guyver (series one 1–12), *Revenge Of Chronos* (series two 1–6)

THE BIOLOGIC SHOW

Fantagraphics: *2 issues (0–1) 1994–1995*

Surreal, visceral caprice from the mind and pen of Al Columbia. Almost every strip in this anthology is gratuitously unpleasant with mutilation, a recurring theme. Al obviously needs to get something out of his system, and the sooner he does so the better, because he can draw like a demon.~FP

BIRDLAND

Eros: *3-issue miniseries 1990–1991, One-shot 1994*

This frivolous black and white series by writer-artist Gilbert Hernandez is dominated by hard-core sex scenes, with forays into alien encounters and psychiatry. It baffled fans of his *Love And Rockets* stories, with their serious characterisation and social/political content, although two of the characters were later incorporated into *Love And Rockets*. The large cast and their intertwined sex lives are pretty baffling too, especially in the one-shot's wordless dream/fantasy story-line. It's beautifully drawn, however, and though the

frenetic pace of the story-telling largely works against eroticism, when it slows down a bit there are some very sexy moments indeed.~GL
Collection: *The Complete Birdland* (1–3, one-shot plus some new pages)

BIRDS OF PREY: MANHUNT
DC: *4-issue miniseries 1996*

Following the success of the *Black Canary/Oracle; Birds Of Prey* one-shot, DC decided to keep the team going in a series of miniseries and specials under the umbrella title, *Birds Of Prey*. The first of these, *Manhunt*, teams the Black Canary – and, unwittingly, Oracle – with rogue vigilante Huntress and bad girl Catwoman, when the latter two and the Canary discover something unexpected in common: they've all been screwed – fiscally, or... otherwise – by the same man, and are hot for revenge. It's *Thelma and Louise* with spandex, as the girls go on the road, and across the world, to get their own back. Slick, fast, punchy, and the relationship between the travellers is handled with humour and sympathy by writer Chuck Dixon. Matt Haley turns in gorgeous art, and the deadline-crunching addition of Sal Buscema in 4 works surprisingly well.~HS
Recommended: 1–4

BISHOP
Marvel: *4-issue miniseries 1994–1995*

A later addition to the X-Men, Bishop was given his own miniseries relatively soon after arrival. Slick, stylised art by Carlos Pacheco and Cam Smith accompanying John Ostrander's script makes this the equivalent of the latest Schwarzenegger film. An evil mutant, Mountjoy, has escaped from the future into the past, and Bishop makes it his business to track him down. Basically, this is one long chase stretched out too thin with some character *angst* thrown in. Pretty to look at, but switch your brain off.~TP
Collection: The Mountjoy Crisis (1–4)

BIZARRE ADVENTURES
Marvel: *10 issues (25–34) 1981–1983*

The title *Bizarre Adventures*, to encompass more than one lead feature in *Marvel Preview* 20 and 23, must have boosted sales considerably, because it switched to that title with 25. The magazine format remains the same, though, with more adult-oriented stories and concepts in black and white, largely offering solo slots that wouldn't fit elsewhere in the Marvel line. Consistently good cover paintings entice for often average interior material. The best story of the run is Walt Simonson's adaptation of *The Lawnmower Man* in 29, a glorious bacchanalian celebration of excess worth the cost of the issue alone, although the other features disappoint.

John Bolton's art on Kull in 26 is magnificent and overcomes a standard sword-and-sorcery story, and he's back in the otherwise meagre 32. *X-Men* fans might want to look out 27, with serviceable solos for Iceman and Nightcrawler and a daft Phoenix story, and 28's list of talent includes Frank Miller, Neal Adams and Michael Golden, none of them at their best. Miller's on far better form in 31, the best overall issue in the run. Seemingly cobbled together from inventory material with the theme of violence applied as an afterthought, the sheer contrast and variety works. Miller's followed by the over-the-top cartooning of Larry Hama before the styling of Bill Sienkiewicz, and there's also the solid old-fashioned art of Herb Trimpe, the disturbing Steve Bissette, and the excellent Mark Armstrong. The horror theme in 33 never gels, nor does 34's Christmas issue, also published in a standard colour comic format.~WJ
Recommended: 26, 29, 31

BIZARRE SEX
Kitchen Sink: *10 issues 1972–1982*

Bizarre Sex more than lives up to its name – animals, aliens, robots, they all got 'em off and got it on in Kitchen Sink's ground-breaking underground anthology. Right until the end it retained a home-made quality that was by turns annoying and appealing. A typical issue mixed goofy comic strips drawn in cartoony styles with po-faced drama featuring stiff-figured, over-inked artwork. Issue 9 featured a full-length *Omaha The Cat Dancer* story, far and away the most sophisticated strip in the entire run. There's also a short follow-up tale in 10, with the story continued in *Omaha The Cat Dancer* 1. The only other work of note is Howard Cruse's *Barefootz*.~FJ

BLAB!
Monte Comix: *2 issues 1986–1987*
Kitchen Sink: *6 issues + (3–8) 1988 to date*

Blab! began as a professionally produced EC fanzine; the comic content in the first two issues is minimal, and restricted to reprinted panels in 1 and four pages apiece by Dan Clowes and Kim Deitch in 2. The remainder of these paperback-sized publications is devoted to assorted comic creators recounting their memories of EC comics, along with an interview concerning the influential Mars Attacks bubblegum cards. In 2 there's also the first appearance of the Blab Dating Depot, assorted illustrations of Wolverton-style deformed humans by XNO. Both make excellent reading and have been reprinted by Kitchen Sink, who assumed the publishers' role with 3, issuing a square-bound package. Increased comic content was the order of the day, with strips by Richard Sala, Clowes and

Spain along with Deitch and Joe Coleman illustrating text pieces, and a recollection section on the 1960s undergrounds. The comic content increased again in 4 (Clowes, Sala, Spain alongside Doug Allen, Drew Friedman, Jay Lynch and Gary Whitney, and Skip Williamson) and 5 (the same line-up, but replacing Lynch and Whitney with Lloyd Dangle).

With 6 the balance had shifted almost 180 degrees, with the comics all but edging out the features and interviews. Gary Lieb, Mary Fleener and Frank Stack join the regulars with that issue, and it's Stack who single-handedly raises the quality threshold of *Blab!*'s comics quota. Whereas almost all the contributors seem to have seen *Blab!* as a home for dashed-off shorts or hollow whimsy (with the possible exception of Sala, who produces nothing but), Stack takes the infrequent publications schedule to produce noteworthy material. All his strips have a historical context, with the best in 7 concerning Shakespeare's deliberations about being asked by King James to postpone writing plays until he's rewritten the Bible. 7 also contains good work from Mary Fleener, Terry LaBan and the startling Chris Ware's Jimmy Corrigan, under an excellent Clowes cover that bears close examination. 8 is a squarebound 10" x 10" package with a colour section featuring the brilliantly depressing Ware and Peter Kuper, and another excellent Frank Stack strip, this time about the excesses of Caravaggio. There are also several Drew Friedman illustrations and accompanying interview, and it's nice to see publisher Denis Kitchen drawing once again.~FP
Recommended: 1, 2, 7, 8

BLACK & WHITE
Image: 3-issue miniseries 1994, one-shot 1996

A cross between superheroics and James Bond-style adventures, *Black & White* is the story of Whitney Samsung and Reed Blackett, hired to defend Whitney and thereafter cast into the role of bodyguard/guardian as she refuses to listen to reason and throws herself headlong into trouble. She's seeking vengeance against the company that killed her father. Creators Art and Pamela Thibert produce competent scripts, while Art Thibert's drawing is better than average, with some attention to detail. However, the series didn't catch on and was never finished, despite an attempt to relaunch it in 1996.~NF

BLACK AXE
Marvel UK: *7 issues 1993*

10,000-year-old assassin Black Axe is revived in modern-day Japan, where he uses his big black axe against ninjas, giant robots,

Japanese Marvel hero Sunfire and fellow Marvel UK hero Death's Head 2. The idiosyncratic artwork of Ed Perryman may be something of an acquired taste, but it remains the most distinctive thing about this otherwise uninvolving series.~AL

BLACK CANARY
DC: *4-issue miniseries 1991–1992, 12 issues 1993*

After years of neglect and misrepresentation in *Green Arrow*, Dinah Lance, the Black Canary, was given a try-out miniseries. No one seems to have been more surprised at its success than DC, who'd been content with her third-class citizenship. Nevertheless, a tough, uncompromising script from Sarah Byam and striking visuals by the team of Trevor Von Eeden and Dick Giordano made 'New Wings' the sleeper hit of 1992. Without Giordano's sharp ink line on the regular series Von Eeden's art was too often blurred and confusing. Too many panels require squinting to figure what was going on. Although Byam's scripts remained thoughtful and interesting, too many social and political issues were brought forward too rapidly and a disastrous misjudgement was made when Black Canary ditched her traditional hell's-angel-cum-cocktail-waitress look for a 1990s punk outfit of cropped hair, boots, fishnets, a basque and a leather jacket. Contrary to editorial expectations this didn't make her look 'street', it just seemed she'd omitted an entire layer of clothing. This is the single action that probably ended Black Canary's solo flight. A pity, because until the rather schlocky final issue the stories remained strong.~HS
Recommended: Miniseries 1–4

BLACK CANARY/ORACLE: Birds Of Prey
DC: *One-shot 1996*

Since being crippled, Barbara Gordon, the former Batgirl, is forced to fight evil by proxy. Using her computer skills, photographic memory and contact network she develops the persona of Oracle, supplying information to support other heroes. Enlisting the unemployed Black Canary for a one-off case, she senses a rapport between them and the two form a friendship and partnership despite never meeting face to face. Sleek, stylish and gorgeously illustrated by Gary Frank, and sharply written by Chuck Dixon, this reads like a superior action movie with a brain behind it. Highly enjoyable, and, thank goodness, sufficiently successful to lead to a series of one-shots and miniseries under the title *Birds Of Prey*.~HS
Recommended: 1

BLACK CAT

Harvey: *65 issues 1946©1958 (1–62), 1962–1963 (63–65)*
Recollections: *2 issues 1988*
Lorne Harvey: *9 issues (3–11) 1990–1992, One-shot 1995*

'Linda Turner, Hollywood Star and America's Sweetheart, becomes bored with her ultra-sophisticated life of movie make-believe and takes to crime-fighting in her most dramatic role of all as... The Black Cat!' Phew. This blurb ran in most 1940s stories of our eponymous heroine, and aptly evokes the breathless pace of the series. A successful alumna of Harvey's *Speed Comics* anthology, the Cat was drawn by Joe Kubert in her first two issues, after which Lee Elias took over, and made the Cat a sophisticated Hollywood lady, as opposed to Kubert's busty virago. One of the few heroines of the 1940s who didn't start her career as a sidekick or a team member, the Cat was popular with both male and female readers. The girls liked the Hollywood setting, the cool toughness of the heroine, and Elias' carefully detailed clothing and fashions, while the boys liked the action scenes, and the way the Cat fitted into her low-cut satin costume.

By 1951's issue 30, things were changing, and the cover of that issue was the last we saw of the Cat herself for a while, as the title switched to horror and mystery stories, several of them among the most gruesome recorded in comics. Most of the stories, though derivative from the EC twist-ending formula, were beautifully illustrated, with Meskin, Nostrand, Powell and equally gifted artists taking the helm. The Cat came back for issues 54–56, inventory material pulled in to keep the magazine regular while Harvey rewrote and redrew stories in the wake of the Comics Code Authority and their new standards, which must have puzzled the hell out of regular readers. Jack Kirby contributed some really off-the-wall work for issues 58–60, but, faced with declining sales, Harvey folded the title in 1958. Four years later, in the wake of the superheroic revival, 63–65 were published as reprint compilations of the Black Cat, in the hope that she'd catch on. Sadly, it didn't take, but the character was affectionately remembered, and was the subject of two later revivals. The first, entitled *The Original Black Cat* to distinguish her from Marvel's impostor, ran eleven issues from 1988 to 1992, reprinting the Kubert and Elias work with occasional new covers. The 1995 revival, dubbed *Alfred Harvey's Black Cat*, featured a new short story by Mark Evanier and Murphy Anderson in which an actress and stuntwoman, working on a biopic of the original Black Cat, finds herself recast as the heroine in life as well as on film. More Lee

Elias reprints and some inferior new material filled out the issue, which was announced as a two-part miniseries, but which never – as far as anyone can tell – concluded.~HS

Felicia Hardy, the BLACK CAT

Marvel: *4-issue miniseries 1994*

Marvel's imitation Black Cat, a former lover of Spider-Man, flies solo in what was promised in advance solicitations as a light-hearted, fun series. What emerged was a leaden, plodding battle with cyborgs, so one can only assume plans were altered.~HS

BLACK CONDOR

DC: *12 issues 1992–1993*

A Native American develops the power of flight as the result of strange experiments, and is reluctantly drawn into the heroic life, guided, or haunted, by what appears to be the ghost of the 1940s Black Condor. Nice artwork by Rags Morales doesn't compensate for wilfully obtuse scripting.~HS

BLACK CROSS Special

Dark Horse: *One-shot 1988*

Collecting the first two episodes of Chris Warner's series originally published in *Dark Horse Presents* 1 and 3, this includes a new prequel establishing more background to the death squad from which Black Cross rebels. Set in a near-future totalitarian America, this is pretty much the comics equivalent of a spaghetti Western. Warner's script doesn't really offer any surprises but his detailed black and white artwork is very effective.~NF

BLACK DIAMOND

AC Comics: *5 issues 1983–1984*

The lead character is a female James Bond fighting the hoards of QUANSA. The comic's based on a projected B movie to be followed by a projected TV series starring Sybil Danning. Needless to say, neither materialised. The back-up strip features Colt, Weapons Mistress, and might be of marginally more interest to fans of *FemForce*. The Paul Gulacy covers and pin-ups are the best thing about the title since neither strip really manages to rise above its fannish origins.~NF

Morningstar Book One: BLACK DOG

Trident: *1 issue 1990*

Better-than-average fantasy story written and drawn in his distinctive blocky style by Nige Kitching, with the last eight pages inked by Nigel Dobbyn. Kitching takes a traditional British legend (of ghostly black dogs which appear near water, harbingers of doom) and brings it up to date for his magical hero Morningstar to fight.~FJ

BLACK DOGS
Fantagraphics: *One-shot 1993*

Ho Che Anderson's response to the 1993 Los Angeles riots is a confused and fence-sitting tale detailing an ongoing discussion between a black couple as to the merits of the action filtered through the thoughts of black leaders. Part polemic, part soap opera, it's an uneasy mix. Anderson's art is an appealing and curious fusion of Kyle Baker and Bill Sienkiewicz, well worth a glance if you're unfamiliar, but at a miserly fourteen pages plus promo material, this isn't the place.~WJ

THE BLACK DRAGON
Epic: *6-issue miniseries 1985*

Chris Claremont is to be commended for taking a risk at the peak of his popularity as *X-Men* writer to pen this tale of 12th-century sorcery, although there's places where it creaks under his excess verbiage. *The Black Dragon* doesn't succeed as the classical tragedy it appears to be intended as, with Claremont's aptitude for characterisation all but deserting him, but it's never predictable and there's enough action to keep the pages turning. John Bolton, though, is on stunning form, with his art looking far better in the current black and white collected edition than in the muddy original colour comics.~FP
Collection: The Black Dragon (1–6)

BLACK FLAG
Image: *1 issue 1994*

Prelude to an ongoing series that never materialised, *Black Flag* features three distinct episodes with some kids, a talking gorilla and a muscular hero called Sniper, but the only thing that ties them all together is violence. Not worth getting out of bed for.~NF

BLACK GOLIATH
Marvel: *5 issues 1976*

A miniseries before such things were conceived. Stark technician Bill Foster taking a serum to become giant-sized seemed a good bet in a boom period. It was duff throughout, though. Come a recession this patronising title was cancelled, and Bill joined *The Champions* with White Angel, White Black Widow, White Hercules, White Iceman and Pallid Skeletal With A Fiery Halo Ghost Rider.~FP

BLACK HOLE
Kitchen Sink: *3 issues + 1995 to date*

Charles Burns is the master of presenting, deep, disturbing fantasy wrapped in simple thick-lined art. *Black Hole* is an ambitious project, and certainly his longest to date, the spur to the story being a disturbing sexually transmitted virus. The virus only affects teenagers, but causes irreversible mutation, ranging from lesser afflictions like webbed fingers to full-blown plague-of-boils deformity. Burns combines the horrors of the virus with the nightmares of high-school social interaction to weave an unsettling story. So far, given the content, he's also been remarkably restrained in drawing the obvious analogy. It might be said that content is slim and price is high, but the mood of the story requires a leisurely pace. Confusingly, issues aren't numbered on the cover, so those wanting to start should look for the cover illustration of shed human skin with a gaping hole in the chest.~FP
Recommended: 1–3

BLACK HOOD
Red Circle: *3 issues 1983*

Since his 1960s incarnation mincing about and cracking wise in the pages of *Mighty Comics Presents*, the Black Hood had been partially rehabilitated by Neal Adams, Al McWilliams and Gray Morrow-illustrated stories in the otherwise reprint *Archie Superhero Comics Digest Magazine*. The digest introduces policeman Kip Burland as a less flamboyant Black Hood, with the hood the only concession to crimefighting costume. Riding a motorcycle modified by fellow hero The Comet, Burland stars in a series of atmospheric short stories drawn by excellent old-school artists like Pat Boyette, Gray Morrow, Dan Spiegle and Doug Wildey. Alex Toth draws three excellent covers, and illustrates 2's back-up strip starring The Fox. It's not his best art, but there's little Toth that's poor. All in all an unpretentious and extremely well drawn series worth investigating.~WJ
Recommended: 1–3

The BLACK HOOD
!mpact: *12 issues, 1 Annual 1991–1992*

As with other former Archie superheroes, there's an inventive !mpact twist on Black Hood: the hood empowers the wearer. The first issue is a Punisher-style parody at the end of which the character (who is introduced only after several guest appearances in other titles, in which he met all the other !mpact characters) is slain. The story really begins in 2 as 17-year-old Nate Cray inherits the distinctive hood. It enables him to become an athletic hero, but he's unsure why. Mark Wheatley and Rick Burchett (usually) weave an appealing story, and that the title is consciously aimed at younger readers matters not a jot. Cray is later the focal point for *Crucible*, tying up the !mpact line.~FP

BLACK KISS
Vortex: *12 issues 1988–1989*

Howard Chaykin's noirish sex tale *Black Kiss* came in for a lot of flak when first published. Although set in Reagan's America, from the look, sound and action of it it could well have slunk in from the 1930s or 1940s. Cass Pollack, a small-time crook, finds his hated wife and kid murdered and himself in the frame for the shootings. In order to have the famous actress who happened to be giving him a blow-job on the motorway while the triggers were being pulled to alibi him he has to do a small service for her: retrieve from a mystery woman a film that will ruin her career. Some of Chaykin's end-of-issue revelations are rather predictable, but on the whole the scripting is fast and stylish. His black and white art looks rather crowded, packing a great deal into each panel and using detail to build up the sense of a coherent world inhabited by the characters. Right at the start it's established that they're all pretty unpleasant; it's also clear that they like to play sexual roles, which is what prompted a lot of the criticisms. No one who enjoyed *American Flagg!*, which is littered with moments of violent sex, should really complain that the fucking and sucking in *Black Kiss* oversteps the boundaries. It's definitely pornographic, but hardly harmful. Originally published in short segments, prior to being issued as a collection it was republished as three issues titled *Big Black Kiss*.~FJ
Collection: Thick Black Kiss (1–12)

BLACK KNIGHT
Atlas: *5 issues 1955–1956*
Marvel: *4-issue miniseries 1990*

Stan Lee wrote the 1950s series, ably illustrated by Joe Maneely, most of which was reprinted in *Fantasy Masterpieces* and the first series of *Marvel Super-Heroes*. It's set in the court of King Arthur. Sir Percy was unable to oppose the machinations of Mordred and Morgan Le Fay openly, so adopted the identity of the Black Knight. The ebony blade he used was cursed with repercussions for his descendant Dane Whitman centuries later, rendering him less mobile every time it drew blood. By the start of the 1990 series he's a statue. Roy and Dann Thomas condense the histories of the assorted Black Knights admirably in the first issue, there are plenty of guest stars, and Mordred and Morgan Le Fay are up to their old tricks, but Tony DeZuniga and Rich Buckler's uninspired art torpedoes their efforts.~WJ

THE BLACK LAMB
Helix: *6-issue limited series 1996–1997*

Much as you may like Tim Truman, this tale of a vampire avenger is terribly hackneyed. The Black Lamb visits vengeance on those who kill vampires, whoever they may be, and as such is a sort of bogeyman to human and vampire alike. As concepts go it's a dead end, with a vaguely futuristic setting to qualify it as part of the Helix science-fiction line.~NF

BLACK LIGHTNING
DC: *Series one 11 issues 1977–1978, Series two 13 issues 1995–1996*

The man with the electric force field was DC's attempt to portray a modern black superhero in the 1970s. Created by Tony Isabella, the series had Black Lightning battling the 100, a criminal organisation run by the aptly named Tobias Whale. The last issue had a back-up starring Golden Age character The Ray, but that didn't save the series from cancellation. Tony Isabella revived his creation in 1995 and fared a bit better than the original, with somewhat grittier stories. There was certainly a decent urban feel to them, but not much seemed to have changed over the decades.~HY

BLACK MAGIC
DC: *9 issues 1973–1975*

A reprint series that featured pre-comics-code horror stories by Joe Simon and Jack Kirby. High quality as you would expect from these two (one of the industry's most successful team-ups), especially the eerie art style. A lot better than most new mystery/horror comics during the 1970s.~HY

BLACK MAGIC
Eclipse: *4-issue miniseries 1990*

There is much that is good about Masamune Shirow's work, and much that is bad. That it emanates from a largely alien culture exacerbates the often annoying differences in plot-structure and pacing you experience when reading *Appleseed*. *Black Magic* reprints his earliest series, a rather obvious (but nonetheless complicated) re-telling of the Greek creation myths set in a far future were a genetically-engineered mankind lives on Venus, ruled over by a bioroid called Zeus and closely watched by the Nemesis computer. Nemesis has created another bioroid to challenge Zeus' supremacy and hidden her among the ordinary populace until it's time to fight him. Shirow tells the story of Typhon the bioroid with the mixture of pomp, charm and humour peculiar to his work. The trappings are rather too grand for such a simple story and the development of character is jerky, as huge amounts of space have to be found for battles. Interesting for fans of his work, but not the place to start exploring Manga.~FJ

BLACK ORCHID

DC: *3-issue miniseries 1988–1989*
Vertigo: *22 issues, 1 Annual 1993–1995*

The Black Orchid débuted in 1973 in *Adventure Comics* 428, a flying, superstrong mystery woman whose true identity and origin were never revealed. After a few stories, she fizzled out into such obscurity that writer Neil Gaiman, on proposing a revival of the character to DC, was allegedly greeted with blank looks and one puzzled question: 'Blackhawk Kid? Was he in the Legion of Super-Heroes?' Fortunately, Gaiman persisted, and the three-issue series gave us a new take on the Orchid, solving some mysteries while generating others, in a suspenseful and haunting tale that established the Orchid as a major player on the darker side of the DC Universe. Superbly illustrated by Dave McKean at a time when he still bothered to draw, it's a thoroughly satisfying read. Somewhat after the event, DC decided to add an ongoing Black Orchid series to their new Vertigo line, and Dick Foreman initially set her in an urban environment, where she worked surprisingly well. Rather too soon, the action switched to the rainforest, and things began to ramble rather, despite the ironic humour that characterised Foreman's work. Coupled with the replacement of opening artist Jill Thompson by less talented hands, it all added up to an impression that some heroes don't stand up to being explained, analysed, or even portrayed in too much detail. The annual ties in to the 'Children's Crusade' crossover.~HS
Recommended: Miniseries 1–3.
Collection: Black Orchid (miniseries 1–3)

BLACK PANTHER

Marvel: *15 issues 1977–1979, 4-issue miniseries 1988, 4-issue miniseries ('Panther's Prey') 1991*

The Black Panther, aka King T'Challa of the hidden African nation of Wakanda, first appeared in *Fantastic Four* 52, His strength, agility and heightened senses come from the ancient rituals and sacred herbs of his tribe's Panther Cult, and his costume is the cult's sacred garb. The Wakandans also own the only known deposits of an alien metal called vibranium, which has unique and powerful properties. As a result, Wakanda has developed into a futuristic city-state within the jungle.

In 1976, the Panther got his own title for the first time. Writer/penciller Jack Kirby chose to utterly ignore dangling plot-lines from the Panther's run in *Jungle Action* and do it his way, with a jarring switch back to tales of Rider-Haggardian derring-do. In 1–7, T'Challa falls in with a disparate group of international jetsetters who manipulate him into helping them find King Solomon's Frog (it's a

disguised time machine) and various other legendary items like the Yeti and the Elixir Of Life. Set in exotic locations around the world, with much shooting, swordplay, shouting and running about, it's silly but much fun. However, fans who had come to love Don McGregor's 'serious issue' stories in *Jungle Action* were appalled.

In 8–10, T'Challa's half-brother deliberately turns himself into a monster by exposure to vibranium radiation, and a posse of Panther cousins are recalled to Wakanda to deal with the situation. They are a doctor, a racing car driver, a financier and… er… a woman. Well, not just any woman. 'A woman who has grown too fat,' as T'Challa's wise vizier puts it. With the Panther stranded thousands of miles away, can these 'Four Musketeers', as they call themselves, save Wakanda, and indeed the world, from the vibranium monster? Here Kirby, mired in the adventure genres of the past, was in his own way spinning yarns about heroism and the responsibilities of kings, and moral fables about greed and the lust for power (as McGregor had been before). And his artwork, with inks by Mike Royer, achieves in places a unique grandeur that is perhaps the peak of his mighty career in terms of style, if not in substance of the stories.

If 8–10 were a decline in quality, 11–12 were worse. The Panther gratuitously gains telepathic powers, and there's a generic mad scientist who lives in a mountain and steals people's life forces. It's weak stuff, and Kirby left in mid-story. Ed Hannigan and Jerry Bingham feebly wrap it up in 13, and return the Panther to the USA to meet both the Avengers and the villain from *FF* 52, Klaw the Master of Sound. The travails of Wakanda as an emerging African nation were also being explored, but the title folded with 15.

The 1988 miniseries finds writer Peter B. Gillis in serious mood, and penciller Denys Cowan showing more than an echo of *Jungle Action*'s popular Buckler/Janson art style. The Panther Spirit which has empowered T'Challa all these years leaves him, summoned to the aid of a political prisoner from Wakanda being tortured in nearby Azania, a thinly fictionalised South Africa. The Panther Spirit starts an animalistic reign of terror and murder in Azania, a nice metaphor for the anger so many felt about the pre-reform Apartheid regime. But T'Challa, as king of a neighbouring nation, also respects the need for diplomacy, and sees the terror that will stem from open revolution. The story tries hard to reflect the complexity of the issues, and is far more successful than McGregor's overwritten efforts.

McGregor returned to the Panther in 1988, in *Marvel Comics Presents*, sending him to the real

South Africa to find his long-lost mother, and also wrote 'Panther's Prey' in 1991. Harking strongly back to 'Panther's Rage' in *Jungle Action* 6–18, this includes the return of T'Challa's old girlfriend Monica Lynn. The baddies are a minor *Jungle Action* villainess, and her lover, who's given himself superpowers through the application of mad science. When they fail to take over Wakanda by introducing crack cocaine to its streets, they try to blow up the Vibranium mound. Themes of kingship, love, heroism, tradition versus Westernisation etc. are flying around as before (as are some winged dinosaurs) in a rambling story that lacks any sense of thematic unity. And it's heavily weighed down with purple prose. Dwayne Turner can draw when he tries, but putting four oversized issues together stretches his talent too thin. Avoid like the plague.~GL
Recommended: 1–7

The BLACK PEARL
Dark Horse: *5-issue limited series 1996–1997*

Appearing in so many films and TV shows since his break in *Star Wars* has obviously given Mark Hamill an appreciation of the elements, resulting in a decent script, and here he combines with Eric Johnson to produce just that. The theme concerns just what would prompt someone to don a costume and fight crime in the real world. The mantle falls on court clerk Luther, part-time voyeur whose object of desire is abducted in his presence. Lashing out, he kills one of the kidnappers, but can't prevent her kidnap. His escape is filmed, and the film stolen by a talk-show host on the slide, doctored and screened to show a hero dubbed the Black Pearl escaping. Luther subsequently adopts the identity, tracking the remaining kidnappers down and killing them. Public reaction veers from gung-ho endorsement to concerns about civil rights via opinions between, with the talk-show host reviving his career via extensive Black Pearl promotion. This comic has some interesting points to make, and enough fine touches displaying the care applied to the scripts, such as Luther having to bolt to stop his answerphone message from activating during a public broadcast. The art team of H.M. Baker and Bruce Patterson provide clean, detailed and appealing visuals conveying the necessary small details very well, making for a solid adventure thriller.~FP
Recommended: 1–5

THE BLACK TERROR
Eclipse: *3-issue miniseries 1989–1990*

In a world where a Capone is Governor of Illinois, Ryan Delvecchio appears to be just another Mob enforcer. At night, however, he becomes the Black Terror, a masked vigilante trying to bring down the Capones' criminal empire. Allison Capone has her own plans, that involve displacing her father and destroying the world's financial centres. Frankie Dio, Ryan's partner in crime, has his own hidden backers who would be as happy to grab the power for themselves as bring down the Capones. This moody, noir thriller is written by Beau Smith and Chuck Dixon in an efficient, hardboiled manner but it's Daniel Brereton's artwork that raises the story from the humdrum. The images of Allison, in particular, always catch the hint of her true nature. Overall, it's a good read. Brereton's not reached his best yet but there's plenty to enjoy.~NF

Gene Day's BLACK ZEPPELIN
Renegade: *5 issues 1985–1986*

An anthology title created in the late 1970s, featuring work by Gene Day, his brothers Dan and David, and various creative friends, including a young Dave Sim. Day's busy schedule never allowed him time to publish, and after his untimely death friends and family dusted off the old pages and finished it. Most stories are horror and fantasy tales by young enthusiasts, which show promise but are immature, thus more interesting as history than entertainment. The first issue encapsulates the balance of the series as a whole, with scripts by Day, illustrated by himself and brother Dan, plus strips from Charles Vess and Sim.~NF

BLACKBALL COMICS
Blackball: *1 issue 1994*

Short-lived anthology series (and company) bringing together Kevin O'Neill, Keith Giffen, Simon Bisley and others to little effect. O'Neill's 'John Pain' retreads some of the ground of Marshall Law, while Keith Giffen's Trencher is more unreadable, expressionistic experimentation.~NF

BLACKHAWK
DC: *Series one 166 issues (108–273): 1957–1968 (108–243), 1976–1977 (244–250), 1982–1984 (251–273), 3-issue miniseries 1988, Series two 16 issues, 1 Annual 1989–1990, 1 Special 1992*

Created by Will Eisner and Chuck Cuidera and originally published by Quality Comics, Blackhawk leads the team of fighter pilots named after him. Formed during World War II, their original *raison d'être* was as refugees from occupied countries fighting Nazis. At the time of their acquisition by DC they were a tired bunch, having spent a decade seeing off Nazis, then assorted Communist-sponsored threats. Keeping the solid Dick Dillin as artist, DC dispensed with the Commies, introducing more science fiction and supervillains, the most frequently recurring of whom was former Nazi Killer Shark. They also returned Lady Blackhawk, an adventuress who often accompanied the team, and made a positive step in transforming Chinese racial caricature Chop Chop into a more rounded human being. That said, the comics were unremarkable, with little to differentiate the Blackhawks from similar adventure titles published concurrently. All applied a simple formula of an attention-grabbing cover featuring an astounding situation, all too often explained away by ridiculous contrivance inside, two to three short gimmick-plot-based stories per issue and little characterisation. What made the Blackhawks unique was their ability as pilots, and a long career as combat adventurers, yet this was of little relevance to most stories.

Gaudier uniforms débuted in 197 and Bob Haney become writer with 202. He gave the cast and stories some individuality, starting with an origin and motivation for Chop Chop in 203. The back-ups were formalised into series, with the individual tales of the team members in 'Detached Service Diary' the best. The changes obviously did little for sales, however, and from 228, during the height of the Batman TV show's success, the all-time misguided editorial judgement transformed the Blackhawks into the most preposterous superheroes imaginable. Each team member assumed an identity conforming to a particular skill, with the most embarrassing being radio operator Chuck, now clad in blue pyjamas spattered with pink ears and rechristened The Listener. Only Blackhawk himself retained a modicum of dignity amid this sorry camp bunch, and it was the kiss of death for a title that had lasted over twenty years, a last-itch attempt to restore honour in 242–243 coming too late. Cancellation could be ascribed to mercy killing.

The 1970s revival was uninspired, but correctly restored the team to Blackhawk Island as a respected mercenary and security force. Mark Evanier and Dan Spiegle are the creative spark for the next revival, and, recognising that the Blackhawks have the greatest impact in World War II, their contribution is set in 1940, combining the frequent appearances of Hitler common to comics of the time with strong stories and characterisation. For the first time the entire squad have characters transcending national stereotypes, although Blackhawk himself is still rather the brave blank slate. Evanier also restores the 'Detached Service Diary' in the company of a stunning selection of artists (260 and 268 are nothing but). Producing the best Blackhawk stories to date wasn't manifested in sales, though, and the first *Blackhawk* series finally died an honourable death.

A Howard Chaykin shock-tactic makeover finally gave Blackhawk a character. Unfortunately it wasn't a particularly pleasant one, with him designated the callous libertine, previously the exclusive province of the French André. The miniseries proved popular enough, though, to warrant another stab at a regular series in *Action* 601–635 before a second and ongoing title. It moves the team forward to 1947, with Blackhawk operating an air charter service acting as a front for CIA-sponsored activities. The more distasteful aspects of the miniseries are tempered by Martin Pasko and Rick Burchett, who deal largely with the murky consequences of an association with the CIA and the anti-communist paranoia that fuelled the era. From 4 those in power who consider the Blackhawks a liability take action, and from that point the title is very good, second only to the Evanier and Spiegle run. It tinkers with the Blackhawks personnel for the first time in fifty years, and is solid adventure with interesting narratives and imaginative plot twists. Sadly, once again, this wasn't enough to attract an audience able to sustain the title. Doug Moench concludes things, rapidly finishing Pasko's plots and starting his own, which, although adequate, don't match preceding issues.~WJ

Recommended: Series one 259, 264–267, 269–271, Series two 6–10

BLACKMASK
DC: *3 issues 1993*

Jim Baikie's moody, noir style gives this retro pulp thriller atmosphere, but Brian Augustyn's script lacks depth and suspense. Harking back to Hollywood's preoccupation with organised crime, Augustyn updates the setting to the 50s and his script reflects the nihilistic overtones of the classic 1960s thriller (by the likes of Donald Westlake and Lawrence Block). His main character is a shellshocked Korean veteran, but unfortunately neither he nor any of the bit players engage your sympathy. Comes over as a bit of a technical exercise.~NF

BLACKOPS
Image: *5-issue miniseries 1996*

A hi-tech spy story throwing a team of government agents against a would-be world ruler specialising in the construction of robots and high-power battle suits. It's all very Cold War, and laughable when authenticity is conveyed by the use of dozens of military acronyms, each of which has to be explained with a footnote. That said, there's enough action and deception to keep up the interest, and it's encouraging to see spy novels as an influence in the place of old comics.~FP

Collection: Blackops (1–5)

BLACKWULF
Marvel: *10 issues 1994–1995*

If the pages-long fight scenes had been trimmed a little there might have been something interesting going on. As it is there are about twenty new superpowered characters involved in an interstellar plot about genetic manipulation stretching back centuries that all comes to a premature end after the sales figures have been scanned.~FP

BLADE The Vampire Hunter
Marvel: *10 issues 1994–1995*

Streetwise dude clichés left over from the days of Blaxploitation movies abound as our hero, a leftover supporting character from *Tomb of Dracula*, stalks the undead. The whole lacklustre premise should have remained in the 1970s, but if you need more check out *Nightstalkers*.~HS

BLADE OF THE IMMORTAL
Dark Horse: *1 Special, 6 issues + 1996 to date*

Hirokai Samura, the man behind this extraordinary Modernist re-interpretation of the classic Samurai revenge comic, is probably the most important creator to be introduced to Western audiences in the 1990s. Drawing upon a long tradition of carefully observed action artwork, he brings a tightness of line and breadth of technique to his black and white work that is quite stunning, frequently using pastel effect and pencil work alongside tight inking to give an immediacy. The sensitivity of his line is immensely pleasurable and the design of his splash pages, usually carried out in soft pencil, despite the extreme violence they portray, is at once beautiful and terrifying.

Dark Horse published a special introducing his scruffy but arrogant twelve-bladed hero Manji, cursed to live until he's killed a thousand bad men. He was cursed because he killed his lord once he realised that the man he was willing to kill and die for was a thief himself, and now he has trouble seeing the world in the black and white terms demanded of honourable samurai. The themes of honour and correct behaviour are further explored in the next three-issue story, 'Conquest'. A young girl seeks his help to revenge the death of her father, leader of a fighting school, cut down by renegade warriors who wish to destroy all the myriad forms of swordsmanship in Japan and unite all fighters within their school.

Samura's use of language is startling, and may not please some purists. He switches from formularised utterances to street slang within the same word balloon, has his characters speak in poetry then swear at each other. This gives a startling modernity and vitality to the period setting. The other difficulty with the series is that Samura did not want his artwork

'mirrored' (the flipping of pages so they read from left to right prevalent in Manga translation). Wherever possible the panels are cut and re-pasted, but at times you'll find you have to read from right to left to make sense of the action!~FJ
Recommended: Special, 1–6

BLAKE AND MORTIMER
Editions B&M: *6 volumes 1986–1988*
Comcat: *2 volumes 1989–1990*

Robust English adventurers Captain Francis Blake and Professor Philip Mortimer made their début in the September 26th 1946 edition of the Belgian children's anthology *Tintin*. Written and drawn by baritone opera singer and former Hergé assistant Edgar P. Jacobs, from the start the strip was distinguished by the author's obsessive attention to detail, as well as a 'clear line' drawing style that showcased his formidable design skills. Inspired by the works of H.G. Wells and Jules Verne, Blake and Mortimer's exotic science-fiction adventures are amongst the most revered of all European strip classics, 'juvenile' comic albums still capable of engaging adult imaginations.

When the outbreak of World War II put an end to Jacobs' promising operatic career he resumed his first calling, as an artist contributing illustrations and cartoons to a variety of publications. From the mid-1940s Jacobs worked as an assistant to Hergé, re-formatting old Tintin pages, adding glorious colour to black and white stories, working on the strip's authentic backgrounds and décor (most notably for *King Ottokar's Sceptre*) and making an appearance on the front of *Cigars Of The Pharaoh* as mummified Professor 'E.P. Jacobini'. Encouraged by Hergé, Jacobs began work on the first Blake and Mortimer adventure 'The Secret Of The Swordfish' in 1946, a vast narrative eventually collected into three albums, which were published between 1950 and 1953. This futuristic war story introduced many of the strip's defining motifs: Jacobs' love of technology and archaeology at the expense of human feeling, huge chunks of expository dialogue, recurring villain Orlik, and a peerless story-telling technique. Marred by its racist depiction of 'The Yellow Peril', the three volumes of 'Swordfish' nevertheless chart the maturation of Jacobs' style. By the following story-line, the two-volume adventure 'The Secret Of The Great Pyramid' (1954–1955), the marriage between style and content was complete, with Jacobs immersing himself in the world of Ancient Egypt to produce a mesmerising story about the hidden tomb of heretic pharaoh Akhnaton. Next was Jacobs' undisputed masterpiece, the single-volume adventure 'The Yellow Mark' (1956).

Set in fog-bound London, this moody mind-control mystery pits Blake and Mortimer against a seemingly superhuman burglar who marks his crimes with the letter M, the yellow mark of the title. Using his own extensive photographic reference collection, Jacobs created a love-letter to England's capital, his inherent conservatism clearly enraptured by London's dark history, timeless monuments and respectable institutions.

After 'The Yellow Mark' Jacobs completed only four more forty-four-page albums: 'S.O.S Meteors' (1959), a French-based noir with Orlik as advance guard for a Soviet invasion, 'The Time Trap' (1962), an almost solo Mortimer time-travel romp, 'The Queen's Necklace' (1965), a fairly straightforward detective adventure, and the first volume of 'The Three Formulae Of Professor Sato' (1972). The second volume of Sato remained uncompleted after Jacobs' death, and was eventually finished by former Hergé assistant Bob De Moor in 1990. Whilst Jacobs' work lacks the sharp character humour of Hergé's Tintin – Blake and Mortimer remain little more than functional stereotypes, the dotty Prof and stiff-upper-lipped military man – its imaginative scope and passionate verisimilitude continue to inspire and seduce readers and creators.

Despite Blake And Mortimer's European pre-eminence, Jacobs' *oeuvre* remains largely unknown in America and Britain. In the mid-1980s Jacobs' estate established Blake And Mortimer Editions and finally produced English editions of 'Swordfish', 'Pyramid' and 'The Yellow Mark' (as 'The Yellow M', for some reason). Despite their attractive size and faithful reproduction these volumes were poorly publicised, ineptly translated and are now out of print. Also hard to come by are the two volumes issued by Catalan, through their children's imprint Comcat Comics. Despite their smaller size, these versions of 'Atlantis Mystery' and 'Time Trap' boast far better translations, and are well worth seeking out.~AL

Recommended: *Atlantis Mystery, The Time Trap, The Yellow M*

BLANCHE GOES TO HOLLYWOOD
Dark Horse: *One-shot 1993*

The whimsy and nostalgia forming the strongest threads of Rick Geary's works are united in this tale of a new arrival in 1915 Hollywood. Blanche has come to assemble an orchestra for scoring movies, and her story is told as an illustrated letters home. By emphasising the expanse of Los Angeles, the general naïvety, and the head of the film studio attempting to impart wholesome entertainment with a moral message, Geary implicitly contrasts them with today's

equivalents in a wistful fashion. There's an edge to the story, though, with agitation concerning the poor working conditions in the early picture industry, but for Geary it's more a occurrence for Blanche to witness than any comment. It's all drawn in his gloriously simple, yet detailed style, and the conclusion hints at an era floating away. Magnificent.~WJ

Recommended: 1

BLASTERS Special
DC: *One-shot 1989*

Writer Peter David performs a minor miracle by taking a bunch of feeble throwaway characters created by DC's *Invasion* crossover and combining them with the Justice League's old mascot Snapper Carr to forge the most eccentric superteam yet. Finding that none of the genetically altered humans can find a purpose on Earth, they hook up with a spacefaring cat-woman and head off for adventures in the outer galaxy. The Blasters won't be to everyone's taste with lots of in-jokes, comedy clichés and breaking of the fourth wall, but the light tone of the comic is a pleasant bubblegum read. Fry and Campanella's art remains just the right side of cartoonishness to retain its appeal.~HS

BLAZE
Marvel: *4-issue miniseries 1993–1994, 12 issues 1994–1995*

Johnny Blaze, the original demon biker at Marvel, stars in limp supernatural encounters in the hope of mounting the then lucrative *Ghost Rider* bandwagon. Happily, the anticipated demand was of short duration, and within eighteen months he was back to a supporting role in his successor's comic.~HS

BLAZING BATTLE TALES
Atlas: 1 issue 1975

In common with other Atlas titles you got more graphically portrayed violence for your buck, but otherwise an ordinary war title.~FP

BLAZING COMBAT
Warren: *4 issues 1965–1966*

This was packaged like a standard bloodthirsty war comic: 'Exciting Battle and Adventure', it says on the cover, and 'Illustrated Excitement in War'. I wonder how many outraged letters were sent along the lines of: 'What kind of war comic do you call this? You must be a bunch of pinkos, making out that the Germans and even the gooks are human beings, and never showing our boys but to have them fighting each other or running scared.' They didn't print such letters if they arrived – maybe the potential critics were overawed by the quality of the work. It's not too hard to imagine such a reaction, since this is an astonishing comic. Almost all the stories are written by Archie Goodwin, also the editor, and they're mature, intelligent, sobering and always readable. Add to this a generous seven stories per issues and stunning black and white artwork from people such as Alex Toth, John Severin, Reed Crandall, Joe Orlando, Wally Wood, Gene Colan, Russ Heath, Gray Morrow and Angelo Torres, and it truly is breathtaking. Everyone should read this comic. There's barely a weak story in the four issues, but some deserve special mention: 'Cantigny' (1) for Reed Crandall's fine pen and ink work; 'Enemy!' (1) for John Severin and a story of one American disturbed by another's brutality; 'Holding Action' (2) for John Severin and a depiction of the long-term mental effects of combat; 'Foragers' (3) for Reed Crandall's wash work and the reality of enforcing a scorched-earth strategy; 'U-Boat' (3) for Gene Colan and an exceptionally strong story of confused loyalties; 'Survival' (3) for Alex Toth and a grim post-World War III story; 'Souvenirs' (3) for John Severin and a gruesome moral tale; and 'Give and Take' (4) for Russ Heath's perfect artwork. Surely the best comic Warren ever produced.~FC

Recommended: 1–4

Collection: Blazing Combat (selected stories from 1–4)

BLAZING COMBAT

Apple: *2 issues ('Vietnam And Korea') 1993, 2 issues ('World War I and World War II') 1994*

As the subtitle suggests, the first series reprints the Vietnam and Korean war stories from the Warren comics, and the second the World War stories. Alongside the first series, though, there's material from Don Lomax reprinted from the *Vietnam Journal* collections, and featuring his reporter from that series. It's equally sympathetic and hard-hitting, and the remaining material has already been canonised. As the cheapest way of obtaining otherwise expensive masterpieces these series are indispensable.~WJ

Recommended: 'Vietnam And Korea' 1, 2, 'World War I and World War II' 1, 2

BLEAT

Slave Labor: *1 issue 1995*

Often screamingly funny odds and sods from the hearteningly demented mind and pen of Basilio Amaro. In this one issue you've got several condensed comics ('Good Cop, Bad Cop' is the best), wine reviews, a guide to the people who use communication forums on the Internet, a great introduction, a brilliant downbeat back cover, and wonderful cartooning. In a parallel universe Amaro lives in a luxury penthouse apartment, hosts his

own talk show, and his inside-back-cover comments are true. More, more, more, please.~FP

Recommended: 1

Peter Kuper's BLEEDING HEART

Fantagraphics: *4 issues 1992–1993*

Kuper is a true original, adopting a stark, fast style, often scratched onto black board, sometimes stencilled. His art is unique and instantly recognisable among comic artists, yet he's more appreciated as an illustrator. *Bleeding Heart* has autobiographical recollections alongside quirky nonsense, dream recollections, travelogues and the political commentary for which he's best known. This is useful in collecting Kuper strips that have previously appeared elsewhere (most frequently in *World War 3* and *Heavy Metal*), but the consequent lack of unity damages the magazine as a whole, and only the fourth issue contains a significant proportion of new material. That said, there's at least one essential strip in each issue, and such is Kuper's adaptability that they're completely different in tone and style. 'Gorillas' in 1 recounts a trip to Tanzania and the difficulty associated with a trip to see mountain gorillas, while 2's caustic premonition about New York, 'The Wall', is an all too believable fantasy. 'The Jungle' in 3 is a ghastly tale of urban 'renewal', and 4's tales of relationships and masturbation are frank and funny.~FP

Recommended: 1–4

BLITZKREIG

DC: *5 issues 1976*

An attempt to show World War II through the enemy's eyes, which never really lived up to expectations. DC's top war story writer, Robert Kanigher, scripted and Ric Estrada's artwork, though not exceptional, suited the series. While DC made an attempt to be unbiased, we must nevertheless remind ourselves that the Germans did actually lose the war. Both of them, in fact.~HY

THE BLONDE

Eros Comics: *3-issue miniseries ('Double Cross') 1991, 5-issue miniseries ('Bondage Palace') 5 issues 1993–1994, 3-issue miniseries ('Phoebus III') 1995*

Translations of the adventures of Italian foot-fetishist Franco Saudelli's extremely popular supercriminal *The Blonde*. Saudelli manages to incorporate bare feet, high heels and foot bondage at every opportunity as The Blonde shows off her rope tricks in these light-hearted tales. His style is smooth but naturalistic, and his love of the female form shines through. Although he regularly draws from life and uses photos to work unusual angles and compositions into his strips,

unlike many artists his end result looks neither stiff nor disjointed.~FJ
Recommended: 1–3
Collections: Double Cross (1–3), *Bondage Palace* (1–5)

BLOOD: A Tale
Epic: *4-issue miniseries 1988*
Vertigo: *4-issue miniseries 1996*
Laboured, tedious necroporn about the trials of a young vampire man, with incestuous overtones and something to offend everybody, if they can force their way past J.M. DeMatteis' purple prose and the wispy, arty semi-nudity. Not PC, and sadly not VG either, despite a superficial overripe prettiness courtesy of Kent Williams' art. A cop-out reincarnation non-ending destroys whatever shreds of patience remain. The Vertigo issues reprint the four Epic issues, with new covers but, sadly, no added coherence.~HS
Collection: Blood (1–4)

BLOOD AND SHADOWS
Vertigo: *4-issue miniseries 1996*
Another tale of the walking (and frankly rather tedious) undead from the pen of Joe Lansdale. Chet Daly is hired to find a missing person and ends up trekking through realities as he fights The God of the Razor, a terrifying monster that slaughters its victims and wears parts of their skin, never able to completely destroy it. Unappealingly drawn by Mark Nelson, there are some grotesque elements that qualify this as a modern horror story but ultimately it's too derivative to be at all compelling.~NF

BLOOD IS THE HARVEST
Eclipse: *4-issue miniseries 1992*
Marylynne Joseph's journalist brother is killed while investigating Lavia International. When she begins asking questions the company is revealed as a front for corporate vampires, but luckily she's saved by two vampire killers. This doesn't take itself seriously, thank goodness, but even a tongue-in-cheek approach doesn't compensate for minimal plot and unattractive art (which a change of artists fails to rectify).~WJ

BLOOD OF DRACULA
Apple: *Series one 19 issues 1987–1990, Series two 2 issues 1991*
Three takes on Dracula are combined in the one title. The lead story in most issues occurs in 19th-century Bukovia and has the stale smell of Hammer Horror about it. 'Death Dreams Of Dracula' is an abstract feature allowing for stories involving Drac only peripherally and at any time. Most segments are very slight, seemingly no more than an opportunity to engage a guest artist, with the best being Pat

Boyette's Milton Caniff tribute in 7. This slim idea was later extended to a four-issue miniseries. Most interesting of the three is 'Dracula 2199'. Revived in a technologically advanced age that refuses to concede his existence, Dracula strives to reclaim his world. 15 comes with a flexi-disc, and 16–19 replace 'Death Dreams' with Berni Wrightson's Frankenstein illustrations. Ultimately the three-features format is an unsatisfactory mix, never allowing enough space in any issue for writer Rickey Shanklin to develop ideas. The second series is titled *Big Bad Blood of Dracula*, and actually features very little Dracula.~FP

BLOOD OF THE INNOCENT
WaRP: *4-issue miniseries 1986*
Interesting and well researched telling of the Jack the Ripper story rather let down by shoehorning Dracula into the mix.~FP

BLOOD PACK
DC: *4-issue miniseries 1995*
An ill-conceived and ill-executed mess which concerns the soporific all-fighting antics of a group of what one hesitates to call characters who are recruited for a 'real world' type TV show by some naughty 'Producers' who are, surprise, out to control the world. Some of them look like X-persons and some of them look like toys. They all look awful.~GK

BLOOD SYNDICATE
Milestone: *35 issues 1993–1996*
The experimental 'tear gas' used by the authorities to disperse the 'Big Bang', a huge gang battle, killed almost every gang member present. Those who survived gained strange, often disfiguring, powers, and banded together to establish themselves as Dakota City's toughest gang ever. As you can surmise from the premise, the Blood Syndicate are not nice people. They finance themselves by violence and theft, admittedly against other criminals, but still illegal, and don't hold back from maiming or killing opponents. They include crack addicts, racists, sexists, homophobes and other unpleasant types amongst their members. But being assembled from several fragmented gangs, which included women, gay men and various races, they are forced to get along, to mutually exploit each other's power. From this forced alliance a sense of family arises, of clan, which is intriguing to watch develop.

Blood Syndicate isn't a 'Big Event' title. The characters don't stagger from one crisis to another. Rather, the tension, in between the fight scenes, of which there are many, lies with the questions that arise between the protagonists. Will Brickhouse and Third Rail consummate their burgeoning relationship?

Can they, since she now seems to be made entirely of stone? Will Fade blurt out the truth about Masquerade's gender before Masq reveals the truth about Fade's gender preference? Is DMZ really a 'brother from another planet'? It's these, and other questions, the human questions, that keep you coming back for more. Ivan Velez Jr, who writes thirty-two of the thirty-five issues, tugs on the heartstrings intelligently and deftly, creating an engrossing and poignant narrative that avoids overt sentimentality. Criss Cross, the regular artist for most of the run until 30 (after a début issue drawn by Trevor Van Eeden), handles both drama and the bitter, bleak comedy of the characters well. Where the series is let down is by the colouring – and this is a criticism levelled, without exception, at the entire Milestone line. Much fuss was made of their 'Milestone 100' colouring process, but all it seems to do is enable them to colour in a hundred shades of grey, beige and mud. It makes their comics look dull and uninviting, which is a shame, as they're a generally well written line with much to offer.~HS
Recommended: 1–10

BLOODLINES
Vortex: *7 issues 1986–1988*

A complicated thriller with symbolic undertones, written and drawn in a clipped, hard-to-follow style by writer and artist Rob Walton, assisted by Rick Taylor. Rival leather gangs battle for control of the streets and the drug trade that goes with them. This, however, masks 'a full scale war of undisclosed divine importance', to quote Walton. Deborah Judges, an enforcer for one of the gangs, and fellow member Church Boy, face a crisis of conscience over the deaths their work involves. With cast members such as the horse-like Manasseh, Treblinka and police officers Maxine Daley and Thomas Pilate, you're left in little doubt as to each character's metaphorical function. Sadly 7's summing up seems to be a desertion before the plot has run its course, presumably not Walton's choice.~SW

BLOODSCENT
Comico: *One-shot 1988*

Utterly pointless and predictable horror tale about a serial killer who in turn finds himself stalked. Dean Allen Schreck's captioned prose is accompanied by Gene Colan artwork reproduced from his pencilling, and although long adept at depicting moody horror, here he's given little to do beyond illustrating what's already in the captions. A more successful combination is provided by the prose back-up strip with Bernie Mirault illustrations, but the story is as dull as dishwater, an apt metaphor in this particular instance.~FP

BLOODSEED
Marvel UK: *2 issues 1993*

A mighty-thewed barbarian roams the frozen wastes, and, courtesy of artist Liam Sharp, encounters an equally startlingly endowed woman following the usual fantasy rule of 'The colder it is, the less you wear'. One of Marvel UK's Vertigo wannabe Frontier line, this takes advantage of the 'Mature Readers' to present nudity and implicit nomping, but otherwise remains barbarians by numbers.~HS

BLOODSHOT
Valiant: *52 issues (0–51) 1993–1996*

A Mafia hitman is set-up, disgraced, jailed, abducted, has his blood replaced by nanites and is left amnesiac. Some days it isn't worth getting up, is it? It's not all bad news, though. The nanites are able to repair body tissue almost instantly and they allow Bloodshot to control machinery. With that and armed to the max he's able to work for the British secret service as James Bond played by Rambo. He comes, he sees, he blows away, unless he's suckered, in which case he sees and blows away. 1–28 are dull, but with more challenging adversaries and better art matters improve slightly with 29. So what does it take to make Bloodshot a decent comic? Simple really: Kevin Van Hook's replacement as writer by Mark Moretti. Already-in-place artist Sean Chen produces dynamic action art, and Moretti's interesting plots and crisp dialogue make 40–48 worth a glance.~WJ

BLOODSTRYKE
Image: *25 issues + 1993 to date*

A team of dead characters is quite a novelty, but you wouldn't know it from the appalling first few issues, where they're indistinguishable from any other Rob Liefeld creations. *Bloodstryke* has large splash pages, fight scenes, all kinds of misproportioned superheroes, more fight scenes, characters almost crushed by badly placed word balloons filled with expository dialogue, and some more fight scenes. When they're not beating villains up, they're beating each other up. With all that in each and every issue it would be simply churlish to request a plot as well. Replacing one set of crazy guys with a bunch of new characters, one of whom inherits the title's name, doesn't change anything. Did I mention the fight scenes?~FP

BLOODWULF
Image: *4-issue miniseries, 1 Special 1995*

One of Rob Liefeld's, let's be polite, 'derivative' characters unexpectedly comes up trumps in the hands of writer Andy Mangels and artist Daerick Gross. On a quest to find his kidnapped mother, Image's Lobo clone proves much funnier than his spiritual parent ever was, in a pot-pourri of atrocious puns, sight gags, gratuitous violence (but funny gratuitous violence!) and wholesome family life. Lightweight, but great fun. The special is by a different creative team, and dismissable.~HS

BLOODY MARY
Helix: *4-issue miniseries 1996*

Written by Garth Ennis and beautifully drawn by Carlos Eszquerra, this is the story of a world at war, not so very far in the future, with Britain and the US fighting mainland Europe. Bloody Mary is the middle-aged survivor of a crack fighting team who must find and kill her old commander before he sells a secret to the Europeans that will ensure their victory. A very dark satire on the UK's current failing relationship with the rest of the world, Ennis' script is brutal but witty, and though the plot is nothing new it's well executed and redeemed by its humour.~NF

BLUE BEETLE
Charlton: *Series one 10 issues (1–5, 50–55) 1964–1966, series two 5 issues 1967–1968*

After a long and largely undistinguished career at Fox Comics throughout the 1940s, Blue Beetle was acquired by Charlton for a very poor four-issue run in 1955. Mind you, the 1964 series was no better: with infantile stories (one, embarrassingly, by a young Roy Thomas) and breath-takingly inept art from basement hacks Bill Fraccio and Tony Tallarico the comic struggled to reach the dizzy heights of mediocrity. Still, with 'great' villains such as Mr Thunderbolt and Praying Mantis Man, and a hero whose physique resembled the Pillsbury doughboy, there's sniggers aplenty to be had here. The peculiar numbering, by the way, was unique to Charlton, who wouldn't think twice about cancelling a recently introduced series to continue the numbering of a completely unrelated title. In this instance it was mediocre horror comic *Ghostly Tales*.

Charlton's last attempt at reviving the character was a different kettle of fish entirely. It premiered as the back-up strip in *Captain Atom* 83–86: archaeologist Dan Garrett was gone, and in his place was scientist Ted Kord, with a new costume, a nifty flying vehicle, the bug, and a new artist, Steve Ditko. The new series had all the action and excitement of the strip Ditko had just left, *Amazing Spider-Man*, but lacked Stan Lee's ear for dialogue. Still, two particularly notable issues are 2 and 3. The first told how a dying Dan Garrett passed on the mantle of the Blue Beetle to Kord, and the latter featured outlandish villains The Madmen, surely prototypes for Ditko's DC creation The Creeper.

Another Ditko creation, The Question, ran as a back-up strip in each issue, contrasting with the light-hearted Blue Beetle strip. The Question was Vic Sage, a somewhat acerbic and sanctimonious TV newsman, whose Question *alter ego* (basically Sage with a blank mask covering his face) was frighteningly uncompromising. Scripts on both series were credited to D.C. Glanzman, a pseudonym for co-writers Ditko and Sam Glanzman. Certainly the comic's best issue reeks of Ditko, as both strips feature stories mercilessly attacking modern art and liberal values. The feverish intensity is breathtaking, though it's doubtful anyone will actually agree with his seething invective. A sixth issue, drawn by Ditko, wasn't printed at the time, but its Blue Beetle strip appeared in the difficult-to-find *Charlton Portfolio*. The Question strip, a continued story intended to run over four parts, and almost completed at the time of cancellation, was later published as *Mysterious Suspense*.~DAR

Recommended: Series two 1–5

BLUE BEETLE
DC: *24 issues 1986–1988*

The first issue could be the template for the traditional superhero comic. Blue Beetle comes out of retirement to kick the issue off, and his *alter ego* millionaire chemist Ted Kord is on top of the world, in demand and popular, with an efficient secretary, cute lab-researcher girlfriend and an Asian-American former college buddy. In addition to the firestarting villain, though, there's the foreshadowing: a lab assistant up to no good, a surly type rummaging around an island tying in to the Beetle's origin and the police about to re-open the investigation into the death of his predecessor. Len Wein and Paris Cullins follow through with all plots for a pleasingly good natured, if unsophisticated, superhero series. Early villains include a welcome return for the Madmen in 3 from Blue Beetle's Charlton days, followed by a bunch of DC's more colourful old villains such as Dr Alchemy, Chronos and the Calculator. The latter's appearance in 8 is the best sampler, telling a complete story in the one issue. The Question guest-stars in 5–7, the Teen Titans grace 11–13, Ross Andru pencils from 15 and everything comes to a satisfactory conclusion with the final issue. What more could you want?~FP

BLUE DEVIL
DC: *31 issues, 1 Annual 1984–1986*

Stuntman Dan Cassidy encounters an escaped demon and finds himself merged with his B-movie stunt suit, leaving him big and blue with horns. Cassidy comes to terms with his new identity, moves into a house connected with other dimensions, and also appears to act as a 'weirdness magnet'. With a CV like that Blue Devil was never going to be gut-wrenching melodrama, and fun is the watchword for writers Gary Cohn and Dan Mishkin. Unfortunately they straddle a thin line, resulting in slapstick comics some of the time, albeit slapstick comics drawn by Paris Cullins and Gary Martin and later Alan Kupperberg and Rick Magyar (then Bill Collins) in an excellent flowing style. Sometimes, though, the silliest ideas work well, as with the introduction of Kid Devil in 14. For a flavour try the annual, guest-starring a selection of DC's stranger heroes, or 25, the St Patrick's Day special.~WJ

Recommended: 7–9, 14, 19, 22, 25, Annual 1

BLUE LILY
Dark Horse: *2 issues 1993*

An Angus McKie creation based on Dave Weir's short story. Rusty Spade – metallic, semi-sentient, cigar-smoking, philosophising, robotic private dick – is hired on an ostensible missing-persons case that subsequently proves to be the tip of an iceberg. This dense read is lovingly littered with complex and subtle puns, but the relentless, metaphysical dialogue turns from fresh and challenging to overbearing. The non-publication of the final two issues of this projected four-issue miniseries delivers unfulfilment.~APS

BLUE RIBBON COMICS
Red Circle: *4 issues 1983–1984*
Archie: *10 issues (5–14) 1984*

A showcase series to support Red Circle's re-introduction of Golden Age characters as stars of their own books during the early 1980s. On the whole *Blue Ribbon Comics* suffered from changes in editorship and direction but did produce some interesting material. Two issues (1 & 10) reprint Fly material by Joe Simon and Jack Kirby and Al Williamson and there's more Kirby in 5, which contains reprints of *Lancelot Strong: The Shield*. New stories feature the following characters: Mr Justice (2); The Fox (6,7); Black Hood (11), Agents of Atlantis (9); Jaguar and The Web (14).

There are two worthwhile pieces: the Steel Sterling story in 3, a delirious romp through themes that have always motivated scripter Robert Kanigher's characters (in which a cute puppy bears the same relationship to Steel as 'my brother' the wolf does to Enemy Ace); and issue 8, a Black Hood special featuring stories drawn by Gray Morrow, Al McWilliams and Neal Adams with Dick Giordano on inks. And a Toth pin-up. Classic stuff.~NF

Recommended: 3, 8

BLUEBEARD
Slave Labor: 3-issue miniseries 1992

A dark and disturbing story about a man who adds to his wealth by marrying and murdering lonely rich women. Interesting story-telling from James Robinson, using a different character as the narrative voice for each chapter, and artwork from Phil Elliott, successfully adapting his open, clean style to a darker mood to match the tale.~FP

Recommended: 1–3
Collection: Bluebeard (1–3)

BLUEBERRY
Epic/Titan: *5 graphic novels 1989–1990, 'Lieutenant Blueberry' 3 graphic novels 1991, 'Marshal Blueberry' 1 graphic novel 1991*

Charlier and Giraud's *Blueberry* is one of the best-loved and best-received Western series in the history of comics, running to some twenty-three volumes (plus several *Young Blueberry* volumes) following the career of Mike Blueberry during the most turbulent years of America's history, from the Civil War and the building of the railroads and destruction of the Indian Nations to the onset of 'civilisation' which killed off the life of soldiering, tracking and hunting that Blueberry and his friends enjoyed.

Epic begin their reprints towards the end of the saga, with one of the most complex and harrowing series of graphic novels reprinted in five colour volumes. The mature Blueberry, in the army and on patrol near the turbulent Mexican border, intercepts a message for President Grant from El Cuchillo, one of the top US secret agents, concerning a shipment of half a million dollars worth of Confederate gold that went missing in the final days of the War. Blueberry is sent to look for it, but to give him cover government agents arrange for him to be courtmartialled and escape with a price on his head. When he finds that the gold has disappeared from its hiding place he becomes a wanted man in earnest. The Blueberry graphic novels, starting with *Chihuahua Pearl*, see the hero imprisoned, embroiled in a plot to assassinate the President, hiding out with the Apaches during *The Long March* and facing a Mexican firing squad. Everyone and his brother wants that gold, and most of them believe Blueberry knows where it is.

The three, slimmer *Lieutenant Blueberry* volumes and single *Marshal Blueberry* volume come from an earlier period, around the time of the construction of the Atlantic-to-Pacific railroad, when two companies were vying to see who would get furthest into the American heartland (claiming land rights as they went). Charlier's scripts are particularly good at interweaving history and fiction, with Blueberry playing an interesting, but not significant, role in many historical events. The art, by Jean Giraud (better known as Moebius), is realistic but splendidly wrought, full of vibrant detail but very smoothly paced and fast-moving, despite quite a wordy script. Excellent throughout.~FJ

Recommended: *Blueberry* 1–5, *Lieutenant Blueberry* 1–2, *Marshall Blueberry* 1

BOB THE GALACTIC BUM

DC: *4-issue miniseries 1995*

John Wagner and Alan Grant treat the American comic-reading public to the sort of inventive whimsical and humorous science-fiction series they've written so adeptly in the pages of *2000AD* over the years, accompanied by long-time cohort artist Carlos Ezquerra. Or at least that was the idea. Bob is transparently W.C.Fields attempting to finangle favour with the idiot heir to five galaxies stranded in space with him. Lobo, heavily cover-featured for commercial purposes, limits his contributions throughout, and overall there are not enough jokes packed in to compensate for a paucity of plot. The repeated jokes about the blind axemen consistently raise a smile, though.~FP

Star Wars: BOBA FETT

Dark Horse: *One-shot ('Bounty On The Bar-Kooda') 1995, one-shot ('When The Fat Lady Sings') 1996, one-shot ('Twin Engines Of Destruction') 1996*

The character of bounty hunter Boba Fett was well conceived in the Star Wars films, able to communicate, yet choosing to do so in no more than grunts. He was surly, cold and emotionless. These one-shots choose to ignore this, and present a positively verbose gun-toting hunter, and all three are rubbish. The first story has Fett as a messenger (how exciting!), and the second continues the story of Fett trying to organise a marriage, remaining as lame as the first in all aspects. The equally mediocre last one-shot has an impostor pretending to be Boba Fett. A meaningless cash-in. Please, Dark Horse, no more.~SS

BODY BAGS

Dark Horse/Blanc Noir: *2 issues + 1996 to date*

Mack is giant of a man who wears a satanic smiley-face mask when he goes about his business, which is bounty-hunting. The last thing he needs is for his cocky and resourceful 14-year-old daughter Panda to turn up. Cute and stacked, she can also handle herself. Writer and artist Jason Pearson has set this a few years in the future, and has put a lot of thought into realising a convincing society with some amusing throwaway extrapolations on today. The seemingly over-the-top nature of Mack's behaviour, particularly when

confronting a drug dealer in the first issue, will possibly outrage some readers. Suitably warned, however, delight in the imaginative characters and settings and hope that the concluding issues of this miniseries are as good as the first.~FP

Recommended: 1, 2

BOGEYMAN

San Francisco: *2 issues 1969–1970*
Company and Sons: *1 issue (3) 1970*

Rory Hayes was a deeply troubled artist whose crude, childlike style had a powerful intensity. Bogeyman was his horror title, and its material was uniformly disturbing, primarily for the insight it appeared to give into Hayes' psyche. It's also of great historical importance as one of the first underground horror comics, and by the second issue it had attracted a number of underground stars. Jay Lynch (2, 3), Jim Osbourne (2) and Greg Irons (3) are among those weighing in with significant contributions, but it remained very much Hayes' title.~DAR

The BOGIE MAN

Fat Man Press: *4-issue miniseries 1989–1990*
Tundra: *1 issue 1992*
Atomeka: *4-issue miniseries ('Chinatoon') 1993*

Francis Clunie is possessed of a personality disorder through which he's convinced he's Humphrey Bogart in *Maltese Falcon* mode. The first series has him causing chaos in Glasgow, and comes complete with a glossary. John Wagner and Alan Grant's hilarious scripts are adroitly rendered in totally deadpan fashion by Robin Smith, making them even funnier. Removing Clunie to the USA for the one-shot results in a diluted Bogie Man, although not without funny moments. That the concept withstands a repeat performance is demonstrated by Clunie's return to Glasgow and to form for *Chinatoon*, the Atomeka series.~FP

Recommended: Fat Man Press 1–4, Atomeka 1–4

Collection: *The Bogie Man* (Fat Man Press 1–4)

BOLD ADVENTURE

Pacific: *3 issues 1983–1984*

A showcase for the scripts of Bill Dubay, *Bold Adventure* featured an eclectic mix of SF/Fantasy and adventure serials. 'Time Force' (1–3), illustrated by Rudy Nebres, is about how good Armageddon will be. 'The Weirdling' (1–2), drawn by Trevor Von Eeden, features an amnesiac who seems to be able to turn into a shadow. Alex Nino illustrates a story about mercenaries (2–3) and John Severin draws the first part of 'Spitfire' (3). Though all four artists mentioned are generally worth a look, these stories don't inspire their best work.~NF

BOMBA The Jungle Boy
DC: *7 issues 1967–1968*

Based on a TV series, this was a worthy try at the jungle hero theme. Following a poor start the series steadily improved under the talents of Denny O'Neil and Jack Sparling. But nothing really to beat your chest about.~HY

BONE
Cartoon Books: *20 issues 1992–1995*
Image: *10 issues + (21–30) 1995 to date*

Three cousins of indeterminate species, Fone, Phoney and Smiley Bone, are run out of their community by outraged townspeople, and become separated and lost in the desert. By different circuitous routes, they find their way to a forested valley, and are forced to rebuild their lives amongst wonderful and terrifying creatures, not the least of which are the human townspeople. Although owing more than a slight debt to Walt Kelly's *Pogo* strip, *Bone*'s creator, Jeff Smith, has successfully created a charming and intricate fantasy world, with memorable characters (the quiche-eating rat creatures), and occasional hilariously surreal moments (The Great Cow race), which means that his revelation about his heroine Thorn's past fell particularly flat, given his previous level of imagination. Not intending to divulge a major plot twist, if I say, 'Oldest fantasy cliché about a character's parentage', you'll have probably worked it out. Yawn. I mean Y*A*W*N. This misjudgement irritated people to the point of giving up the series in disgust. However, Smith's endearing characters have rallied from this error on their creator's part, and the book, while a tad whimsical for some people's tastes, remains a solid, meticulously crafted read.~HS
Collections: The Complete Bone Adventures Vol.1 (1–6), *The Great Cow Race* (7–12), Vol.3 (13–18)

BOOF
Image: *6 issues 1994*

The only positive thing that can be said about this is that the cast was designed by Todd McFarlane. The title character is an alien who arrives on Earth, befriends a young boy, and accompanies him on adventures, usually ending in disaster. Rumour has it that this is a humour title, yet the only remotely funny aspect is that someone was paid to produce such utter junk. John Cleary's art is spirited, but it does little to improve the plots. For masochists there's also a second *Boof* title. Look under *Bruise Crew*.~SS

BOOK OF BALLADS AND SAGAS
Green Man Press: *2 issues + 1996 to date*

Fey, self-published title from Charles Vess, who prettily illustrates traditional folk tales interpreted by his writer mates, including the ever-popular Neil Gaiman and, strangely, the acidly-observant detective novelist Sharyn McCrumb. Some original ideas from the writers are balanced by Vess' traditional approach to illustration. Issue one gets off to a bad start with two reprints, and although Vess reprints the ballads and discusses folk literature his strips are pretty insubstantial as commentary; they illustrate, for those lacking in imagination, but that's all. Pretty package. Pretty insubstantial, too.~FJ

Charles Vess' BOOK OF NIGHT
Dark Horse: *3-issue miniseries 1987*

Mostly a series collecting Charles Vess' work for *Epic Illustrated*, it also contains some early and obscure pieces that hadn't seen print before. In this latter category are 'Bug Tales' (1), 'Morrigan's Tale' (1) and 'Priest' (2). 'Legend' (2) and 'Spirit' (3) are short self-contained fantasy pieces while 'Jack Tales' (2, 3) are two magical adventures of a young man whose companions are small flying robots. The longest piece is 'Children Of The Stars' (1–3, from *Epic Illustrated* 8–10), which is another fantasy piece about a young woman's quest to destroy the demon lord who wiped out the People of the Stars, leaving her and her brother the only survivors. 'Legend' and 'Spirit' are both written by Laurie Sutton but the rest of the material is all by Vess. His delicate, sinewy and detailed pen and ink work is always a pleasure to read despite the often light and insubstantial stories.~NF

The BOOKS OF MAGIC
Vertigo: *4-issue miniseries 1990–1991, One-shot ('Arcana Annual') 1994, 25+ issues, 1 annual 1994 to date*

Thirteen-year-old Tim Hunter is the designated heir to the power of magic in the DC Universe, and four supernatural experts – the Phantom Stranger, John Constantine, Dr Occult, and Mr E – must determine whether he can be allowed to attain that power, or whether he must be destroyed to save humanity. Neil Gaiman writes the miniseries, with four different artists, respectively John Bolton, Scott Hampton, Charles Vess and Paul Johnson, each sumptuously illustrating one of the episodes. The star turn is Vess' lavish and intricate portrayal of the Realm of Faerie in 3. Following the success of the prestige-format miniseries, the one-off *Arcana Annual* formed part of the *Children's Crusade* crossover, and reintroduced Tim to the comics world, setting him up for his own title. The *Books Of Magic* ongoing series, written by John Ney Rieber and drawn, mostly, by Peter Snejbjerg, follows young Tim as he struggles through adolescence, a tricky enough minefield for anyone, let alone someone of his potential power. Compared to the epic and dazzling miniseries, a lot of people find the ongoing *Books Of Magic* a tad subdued, but it's merely working with a subtler canvas. Aware of the monster that he may still become in the future, searching for the truth behind his parentage, and coping with hormonal barrages, Tim keeps his perspective through all these upheavals with a hard core of common sense and a refreshingly mordant sense of humour which is a pleasure to behold. Better read in complete story arcs than in monthly instalments, *Books Of Magic* is a quiet treasure.~HS

Recommended: Miniseries 1–4, Ongoing 1–25
Collections: Bindings (1–4), *Books of Magic* (miniseries 1–4), *Reckonings* (14–20), *Summonings* (5–13)

BOOSTER GOLD
DC: *25 issues 1986–1988*

Dan Jurgens' creation was perhaps the least altruistic hero ever to hold down a mainstream title. Michael Jon 'Booster' Carter was a promising 25th-century sportsman who threw away the chance of a stellar career by fixing games for a quick buck. Ruined by the allegations, he ended up a cleaner in a superhero museum, where it occurred to him that if he nicked a time-machine he could travel back to the past with future technology that would give him relative superpowers. And a quick check on the late 20th-century movements of the stock exchange could net him a small fortune while he was at it. While this could have made for an unsympathetic character, Jurgens made him a lovable rogue, throwing in numerous red herrings and sly hints about his mysterious background before the full truth came out in 6. Surprisingly, the revelation did harm sales – leading to an interesting letters-page debate – and Booster was soon packed off (along with his strong supporting cast) back to the future to suffer a little for his crimes, before it was revealed that everything he'd done had been leading to a destiny which had to be fulfilled. He returned to the present A Better Person, but the series never really found its way again, lost in guest stars and crossovers until it petered out in the middle of the cross-company multi-parter, *Millennium*. The character moved into, and remains with, various incarnations of the *Justice League*. Issue 6 is notable for the first appearance of the post-crisis Superman.~JC

Recommended: 1–9, 13–15

BOP
Kitchen Sink: *1 issue 1982*

A great John Pound cover depicting dancing jukeboxes gives a false impression of a largely disappointing attempt to merge music and comics. That the articles outshine most of the strips sings volumes. Page after page of dull

material is finally vindicated by the brilliant Alex Toth, managing to convey more life and rhythm in five pages than in the entirety of the previous forty-nine.~FP

BORDERWORLDS
Kitchen Sink: *7 issues 1986–1987, One-shot ('Marooned') 1990*

Intelligent science-fiction series written and drawn by Don Simpson. On a deteriorating artificial world, political renegades and pirates cross paths and try to avoid the attention of the authorities. Strong characterisation and a willingness to develop the situation slowly mean that the individual issues never seem to have a great deal of action but everything suggests that this would have been a classic if it had ever been completed.~NF

Recommended: 1–7, 'Marooned'

BORIS' ADVENTURE MAGAZINE
Nicotat: *1 issue 1988, 2 issues + (2–3) 1996 to date*

The 1988 issue was a rather pointless Rocketeer parody issued alongside the regular comic when it would have fitted there just as well. The 1996 continuation is an altogether different beast. The cute, cuddly Boris still occupies the lead strip with comic parodies (Punisher in 1, Captain America in 2), but there are also two back-ups. Bikini Beach Patrol is a parody of *Baywatch* style tit'n'arse TV and there's an un-named science-fiction strip with even more cute cuddly animals. All very nicely drawn, but following a well trodden path.~FP

BORIS KARLOFF TALES OF MYSTERY
Gold Key: *97 issues 1962–1980*

Titled *Boris Karloff Thriller* for the first two issues (which were 80-page giants), this was the first Gold Key anthology title, and the early issues contain some fine artwork. You can't go wrong with the likes of Crandall, McWilliams, Orlando, Torres, Williamson, Wood and Jeff Jones (in 21). The stories are initially competent too, if uncredited. After the first twenty or so issues the quality dropped and the later trend for Filipino artists at Gold Key meant that if you've seen one 1970s issue you've seen them all, although McWilliams still appears occasionally.~SW

BORIS THE BEAR
Dark Horse: *12 issues 1986–1987*
Nicotat: *22 issues (13–34) 1987–1992*

Starting as a parody with a cute robot teddy bear beating up characters starring in other titles, creator James Dean Smith moved beyond to social humour as he began self-publishing with 13. Smith's appealing artwork is a strongpoint of the title, which otherwise has largely one-dimensional characters and repeated jokes. This works for *Groo*, but Smith and collaborator Steve Mattson aren't quite up to making recurring encounters with the neighbour's cat funny. The series isn't without charm, though, and typical of the run are 9 and 10's defection of G.I. Joseph or 15's day in the life of Boris. If you like them you'll probably enjoy the others. 32 and 33 are different, stepping out from the fiction into 'reality'. 1–3 were reprinted in colour by Dark Horse *as Boris' Instant Color Classics*, and Boris returns in *Dark Horse Presents* 64, then in *Boris' Adventure Magazine*.~WJ

BORN TO BE WILD
Eclipse: *One-shot 1991*

Benefit book for PETA (People For The Ethical Treatment of Animals). Worthy and sporting many big names like McFarlane, Moebius, Morrison and Starlin, but with the exception of the Neil Gaiman story not very interesting.~HS

BOY COMMANDOS
DC: *2 issues 1973*

One of DC's short-lived experiments with a reprint line, these two comics re-present some classic Joe Simon and Jack Kirby stories from the 1940s, in which four boys – from America, France, the Netherlands and Britain – take on the Axis in World War II. A silly premise, but hugely popular in its day, and Simon and Kirby's work still crackles with energy over the decades. Further reprints also graced *Mister Miracle* 4–8.~HS

THE BOZZ CHRONICLES
Epic: *6-issue miniseries 1985–1986*

I say, I say, I say, what do you get if you cross a big yellow blancmange with Sherlock Holmes? A very poor series attempting to put a twist on the *ET* theme by having a blubbery alien investigating mysteries in Victorian England. Unfortunately, not a joke.~FJ

BRAIN BOY
Dell: *6 issues 1962–1963*

The adventures of teenager Matt Price, who has potent mental powers including telepathy, telekinesis and auto-suggestion. Matt is used as an agent by a government undercover agency and wages a secret war on other, less moral, ESP-ers. The first issue is drawn by Gil Kane, although the inker does his best to disguise the fact. An interesting idea, but a lack-lustre series.~SW

BRAIN CAPERS
Fantagraphics: *1 issue 1993*

Mario Hernandez is a decent loose illustrator with a sympathetic eye for a story, and this collection pulls assorted work from

anthologies between the covers of one comic. Looking at relationships is a favourite topic, but while not dull neither do his strips spark. There's also a Richard Sala parody, and the best of the bunch, a selection of 'Fake Foreign Funnies', which are just what the title indicates, with odd goings-on accompanied by indecipherable word balloons.~FP

BRASS
Image: *3-issue miniseries 1996*

A janitor finds out he has cancer, becomes a murder suspect and, when chased by the police into the New York sewers, is infected by the Brass virus, which mutates his body into that of a metallic fighting machine. Though scripted by Aron Wiesenfeld, this is really Richard Bennett's book. It's a showcase for his Manga-influenced, incredibly detailed artwork. The use of zippatone gives it an edge and there are some good dramatic panels, but there's also too much reliance on odd panel shapes which have a tendency to make the story over-dynamic. An oversize version of the first issue in black and white has also been published. Don't expect too much new work from Bennett (this has been in the works since 1993) but, with time, expectations of quality should be high.~NF

BRAT PACK
Tundra: *5-issue miniseries 1990–1991.*

In the wake of the Maximortal's disappearance, the city of Slumburg has fallen into the hands of a new breed of 'protectors': venal, psychotic, dissipated, they exacerbate the city's troubles. Even though these brutal 'heroes' need no help, they all keep a young 'assistant' in their stable, and, when these sidekicks perish in the line of duty, make seeking out a replacement their first priority. What's the hidden agenda? Rick Veitch, fresh from his ejection from *Swamp Thing*, gives the old kid-sidekick cliché a new twist with this savage and repulsive, but horribly compelling, exploration of why grown men and women would run around the rooftops with spandex-clad teenagers. And yes, in at least one case, it is exactly what you're thinking, but there's a great deal more to it than that. If you can find the collection, read that rather than the miniseries, since it has new material, better editing and proofreading, and a rewritten ending that's much more coherent than the original.~HS
Collection: Brat Pack (1–4)

BRATS BIZARRE
Epic: *4-issue miniseries 1994*

Superpowered juvenile delinquents rebel against a repressive future regime. After three issues of pointless fighting, the 'good' paranormals (agents of said regime) are converted to the Brats' side and everyone settles down to partying, crude sex and terrorising normals. Sadly less interesting than it sounds.~HS

The BRAVE and the BOLD

DC: *200 issues, 1 Special 1955–1983, 6-issue miniseries 1991–1992*

The Brave and the Bold began, as the title suggests, as a historical adventure comic, and the Robert Kanigher and Joe Kubert Viking Prince strips (1–24) are still fondly recalled today, while the Silent Knight (medieval mystery man who fought crime without speaking so no one would recognise his voice in 1–22) doesn't quite have the same appeal, having the disadvantage of not being drawn by Kubert. The Golden Gladiator in the first half dozen issues isn't remembered at all, with good reason.

25 introduced a second editorial phase, a series of three-issue try-out runs for prospective new titles. While not quite as influential as its companion title *Showcase* in introducing lasting new concepts to DC's line, *The Brave and the Bold* certainly had its share of successes, hitting gold with its second feature, The Justice League Of America (28–30). Superhero team-ups were much the novelty in the early 1960s, and the JLA moved almost directly into their own title. The *Mission Impossible* style escapades of Suicide Squad (25–27, 37–39) and spelunker Cave Carson (31–33, 40, 41) didn't catch on, although the former's title prompted a decent quality run for another idea in the 1980s. The other success of the try-out period was Hawkman. This was elegantly drawn by Joe Kubert in the 1940s, and the artist returned to illustrate a new Hawkman in 34–36 and 42–44, this time an alien. Strange Sports Stories, while drawn impeccably by Carmine Infantino in 45–49, failed to find an audience as a solo feature, although they were similar to material that had been appearing in DC's science-fiction comics in smaller doses for years.

It was with 50 that *The Brave and the Bold* premiered the idea that would, with a few modifications, see out the remainder of the run: team-ups. The first was a nice attempt featuring two of the Justice League's lesser lights, the Martian Manhunter and Green Arrow. Assorted odd teamings continued until 65 (including a memorable teaming of Flash and Atom illustrated by Alex Toth in 53), but spliced by two further features that would porgies to greater success. The conception of the Teen Titans was 54, with the teen sidekicks uniting to defeat the diabolical Mr Twister, the first of a succession of inane villains to plague the 1960s Titans. They

returned in 60, while 57 and 58 introduced Metamorpho, a wacky concept who teamed with other oddball heroes The Metal Men in 66 before moving into his own title. 61 and 62 return two further 1940s superheroes, Starman and Black Canary, in a pair of decent stories by Gardner Fox, beautifully illustrated by Murphy Anderson.

In 67 Batman teamed with the Flash, and remained a fixture of the title until cancellation. He'd already appeared in 59 and 64, and for years had teamed with Superman in *World's Finest*, but in the mid-1960s, with a TV series running, there was no doubt which of the pair was the more popular. Having Batman star in another title made perfect sense. His early run of team-ups was workmanlike, but undistinguished, and it took the arrival of artist Neal Adams to breathe some life into the title from 79's teaming with Deadman. Drawing the title regularly until 86, then 93's trip into the House Of Mystery, and contributions to 100 and 102, his remained the best art seen on the series. His most notable issue is 85, which beefed up Green Arrow considerably, introducing his new look. The writer of the title by this point was Bob Haney. Although never a favourite with the hard-core, continuity-obsessed fans, Haney was consistently inventive, delivering suspenseful plots, intriguing mysteries and generally packing a lot of story into a single issue. His run is also distinguished for its selection of co-stars, with far from obvious selections such as Metal Men, Plastic Man and Sgt Rock recurring. Post-Adams Nick Cardy, and more commonly Jim Aparo, at his peak, were the regular artists for a run of entertaining and tightly plotted stories, and most issues between 86 and 110 are decent material. 100 in particular stands out, with a poisoned Batman sending Robin, Green Arrow and Black Canary on a desperate search for an antidote. 112–117 were 100-page issues, offering an odd selection of reprints in addition to the lead feature, which by this time had begun to stultify. With the exception of 124's spirited and odd teaming of Batman and Sgt Rock the title was in a slow decline.

There was never really a recovery. Haney struggled on, never matching former glories, until 157, at which point an editorial decision was made to run with stories from an assortment of writers, most frequently Mike Barr. Aparo remained to draw most issues, with the occasional break, his looser style no longer showing a hint of Adams. Marv Wolfman and Dave Cockrum teaming Batman with ace flyers the Blackhawks during World War II in 167 was interesting, Martin Pasko had a trial run for his revival of

Swamp Thing in 176, and the Metal Men finally discover what happened to one of their number, Nameless, in 187. The best writer of the later issues was Alan Brennert. His contributions were limited, but each is memorable. 181 returns Hawk and Dove, giving them some historical context as 1960s throwbacks, 182 teams Batman with the twenty-something Robin of an alternate Earth, and 197 has the older Batman of that Earth marrying Catwoman. The latter, drawn by Joe Staton and George Freeman, is a gem. Also of note is the back-up series running between 167 and 193's full-length teaming with Batman: Cary Burkett and Dan Spiegle provide generally imaginative stories of Nemesis, a master of disguise. The series finale in 200 is written by Mike Barr and illustrated by Dave Gibbons, teaming Batman with his alternate Earth counterpart. It was a nice epitaph to both an era and a series, *The Brave and the Bold* having been cast aside to release Barr and Aparo for *Batman And The Outsiders*.

A 6-issue miniseries titled *The Best Of The Brave and the Bold* represented the Neal Adams-drawn classics from 80–83, 85 and 93, along with a Viking Prince strip in each issue. The title returned for a miniseries in 1991 featuring Green Arrow, the Question and the Butcher in a convoluted plot involving IRA gun-runners and Native Americans. Somewhere there's a message about ecology. But writers Mike Grell and Mike Baron fail to impress or keep the interest up, while artist Shea Anton Pensa needed a lot more practice on his story-telling. Its success can be judged by the fact that there's been no repeat.~HY

Recommended: 28–30, 34–36, 42–44, 57, 58, 61, 62, 65, 79–86, 100, 102, 181, 182, 197
Collection: Hawkman (34–36, 42–44)

BREAK-THRU
Malibu: *2 issues 1993–1994*

A flashy Ultraverse title, efficiently illustrated by George Perez, book-ending an arc through eleven different regular series. The first issue is bitty as it has to set up stories told elsewhere about the many members of the enormous cast, but 2 is a pretty good high-blood-pressure all-in bout in space fit to excite any bred-in-the-bone superhero buff.~GK

BREAKNECK BLVD
MotioN Comics: *3 issues (0–2)1994*
Slave Labor: *6 issues 1995–1997*

When Frank Dunkard tries to escape from the humiliations of his family and his dull job, he heads for the bars and clubs of Breakneck Boulevard, in downtown September City. Conned out of some possessions, he's befriended by Scarlett Dee, exotic dancer, and

Pall Blighter, writer. Pall helps Frank recover his goods but they earn the enmity of Blu-J, prostitute and con-artist. Frank gains the street name Urban Angst and continues to visit the Boulevard. In the Slave Labor issues, Frank is nearly killed by Blu-J's old gang, the Jailbait Jills, and then becomes involved with Chaz, with deadly consequences. Written and drawn by Timothy Markin, this is a downbeat series that makes good use of its mean-streets setting. The stories tell of harsh lives, and though Frank stays alive he and his friends seem to step from one near-death experience to another, whether it be a simple mugging or a paranoid drug-dealer taking exception to Frank's being armed. Through it all, Frank comes to learn that his self-image isn't enough – cool and sophisticated is more likely to get him killed than get him the girl. Only let down by the rough, stiff artwork (which is getting looser and more natural), *Breakneck Blvd* is a series worth trying.~NF

BREATHTAKER
DC: *4-issue miniseries 1990*

An outstanding tale by writer Mark Wheatley and artist Marc Hempel. This modern-day version of the succubus myth features a strong female lead, Chase Darrow, a genetically engineered beauty who prematurely ages her infatuated lovers, including government superhero The Man. Hempel's deceptively simple style captures the necro-kinkiness of Wheatley's surreal script, which neatly balances humour and pathos. The rather unsatisfying ending was revised for the graphic novel collection.~AL

Recommended: Collected Edition
Collection: Breathtaker (1–4)

BREED/BREED II
Bravura: *Miniseries one 6 issues 1994, miniseries two 6 issues 1994–1995*

Jim Starlin back on familiar territory writing and drawing this sci-fi/horror series about intergalactic demons with big swords. Plenty of guts'n'gore for them that like it. Certainly not Starlin at his best.~TP

Collection: *Book Of Genesis* (miniseries one 1–6)

BRICKMAN
Harrier: *1 issue 1986*

Batman parodies are commonplace, but it's rare to find one that's actually funny. *Brickman* is. With its protagonist driving around in his brickmobile, throwing brickarangs (bricks) at criminals like the Man-Brick, and having a clockwork Houdini in his utility belt to help him escape deathtraps, Lew Stringer's *Brickman* is very silly laugh-a-panel stuff, and his cartooning is excellent.~FP

BRIGADE
Image: *4-issue miniseries 1993, 27 issues + 1993 to date*

This was introduced as a sister title to *Youngblood*, and is unfortunately an embarrassing sibling. The characters of this superteam are all one-dimensional and fail to hold the attention for more than a few issues. In common with other Rob Liefeld-instigated titles, instead of existing characters being worked on, new ones are introduced every time a new personality trait is required, and most of them look like the more popular X-Men.

The miniseries sets the scene and tone with a four-issue fight (how unique). The ongoing series has Battlestone trying to keep his fractious team together to fight various costumed foes. The first story arc revolves around an underwater city and Brigade's attempts to save it. Issue 8 is part of the 'Extreme Prejudice' crossover, which has a host of characters fighting a powerful opponent who seeks to destroy mankind. 11–12 guest-star the WildC.A.T.S. as the two teams have to work together to recover an orb of power. Issues 25–26 are chapters of the 'Images of Tomorrow' crossover and present a future image of the team. *Brigade* suffers from weak characters, dull scripting from Eric Stephenson and, to add insult, appalling art from Marat Mychaels.~SS

BROOKLYN DREAMS
Paradox: *4-issue miniseries*

There have seemingly always been autobiographical insertions into the work of J.M. DeMatteis, and they've seemingly always been weighed down by the desire or necessity to tell a story unconnected with those events. Here there's no such wall, and although they hide behind a created identity, the rambling recollections have the ring of authenticity. Narrated with knowing hindsight, the bulk of the story told concerns adolescent experiences of Brooklyn in the early 1970s, with detours back through a childhood punctuated by explosive parental disagreements and forward to parental communication and judgement as an adult. There's none of the woolly mysticism which often renders DeMatteis' writing unpalatable, and plenty of the humour he rarely injects into serious material.

To hang the success of the project entirely on DeMatteis, though, is to undervalue the contribution of artist Glenn Barr. He switches effortlessly, and effectively, from skimpy cartooning, through glorious wash work and into detailed pen and ink sketches, conveying every necessary mood and nuance. A less talented and adaptable artist would

have made a right hash of the imaginative exaggerations that characterise the story, and he stamps his own personality on *Brooklyn Dreams* as much as DeMatteis does.

In four paperback-size volumes *Brooklyn Dreams* puts the work of the majority of the autobiographical comics creators in the shade. It's great.~FP
Recommended: 1–4

BROTHERS OF THE SPEAR
Gold Key: *17 issues 1972–1976*
Whitman: *1 issue (18) 1982*

The strip created by Gaylord DuBois had been the back-up in *Tarzan* for twenty years drawn by Jesse Marsh and Russ Manning. It finally moved into its own title when Gold Key lost the rights to publish *Tarzan*. Unfortunately the adventures of the two young primitives, one black, one white, were drawn by Jesse Santos' Filipino studio, who did nothing other than prove they were back-up material through and through. The Whitman issue reprints the second Gold Key story.~SW

The Twisted Tales Of BRUCE JONES
Eclipse: *4-issue miniseries 1986*

Bruce Jones can be talented both as writer and artist, but you'd be hard pressed to realise it from these feeble twist-ending horror and science-fiction stories. Largely reprinted from late 1960s and early 1970s Warren magazines, they do Jones no favours, and I would suspect earned few royalties, despite the excess, and gratuitous, female nudity.~WJ

Boof and the BRUISE CREW
Image: *6 issues 1994*

Spun-off from Boof's own title, clear and amusing cartooning from Tim Harkins is a plus for this comedy of errors about a greedy homunculus and his space-hopping idiot chums. Particularly well coloured, but the script is full of in-jokes and not funny enough.~GK

THE BRUTE
Atlas: *3 issues 1975*

A frozen giant caveman was defrosted in 1975, and, *quelle surprise!*, was prone to mindless rampages through civilisation. Poorly written and poorly drawn.~FP

BRUTE FORCE
Marvel: *4-issue miniseries 1990*

Odd eco-themed comic developed in the hope of attracting TV cartoon interest. Members of endangered species put on exo-skeletons to become avengers of the environment. Routine stuff.~HS

BUBBLEGUM CRISIS
Dark Horse: *4-issue miniseries*

Big global company. Evil, bad, nasty. But, hey, lighten up, don't worry, because the Knight Saber can save MegaTokyo. Who're they? Four ineffably cute women. But don't get the idea they're bimbos. Oh no. One of them runs a lingerie shop, and another is a rock star. *Bubblegum Crisis* is every bit as daft as sounds, and presumably intentionally so. Adam Warren has obviously watched way too many Japanese animations, and successfully subsumes any elements of his own art style to make this seem genuine Manga. One could ask why, when there's plenty of similar material already out there, not least *Dirty Pair*, which Warren also drew.~FP
Collection: *Grand Mal* (1–4)

BUCK GODOT: Zap Gun For Hire
Donning/Starblaze: *2 graphic novels 1986–1987*
Palliard: *6 issues 1993–1995*

Phil Foglio and Barb Kaalberg's pleasant, cartoony artwork might lead you to conclude that *Buck Godot* is a comedy science-fiction strip about a 'zany' private eye. In fact it's an extremely convoluted space opera with hardly a chuckle in sight. Creator and writer Foglio overcrowds his story-line with alien religions, interplanetary alliances and cosmos-threatening conspiracies, while neglecting to develop his rather one-dimensional title character. The story remained incomplete, but there hasn't been a new issue for over a year.~AL

BUCKY O'HARE
Continuity: *1 issue 1986*

This is a 49-page graphic novel written by Larry Hama and drawn by Michael Golden. The Toad Empire is plundering the universe right, left and centre, and the United Animals Security Council has responded by setting up a defensive fleet: three used frigates and one combination orbital dry-dock and snack bar. Bucky O'Hare is the captain of one of the frigates (the 'Righteous Indignation') and the UASC paperwork is something brutal. It's a very funny comic, with great dialogue and no cuteness. Well, apart from the Toads, who are endearing villains with their compulsive honesty about their fear of Betelguesian Berserker Baboons (they even mention it in their battle song). Read and enjoy, and forget about the cutesy cartoon series that followed.~FC
Recommended: 1

BUGS BUNNY
DC: *3 issues 1990*

Reasonable Chuck Fiala artwork fails to lift this from the ranks of third-rate parody. A quest for magical busts of Elmer Fudd sends Bugs and Daffy Duck around the world. *En route* they meet most of the major Warner Bros stars, throwing in references to recent movies or other studios' characters along the way. Nowhere near enough of the anarchic surrealism that illuminates the best cartoons; and nowhere near enough of Bugs Bunny himself.~NF

BURGLAR BILL
Trident: *1 issue 1990*

Why Paul Grist hasn't been elevated to the ranks of cartooning greats is an unexplained mystery to be brought to the attention of Arthur C.Clarke. All the elements characterising his work are present and correct in this early piece. The simple, clear and adaptable art is delightful, and the writing well observed and insightful. Burglar Bill's appearance is merely a cameo in a story concentrating on how the childhood fantasies of first-week-on-the-beat policeman Stephen Hill contrast with reality. A gem.~FP
Recommended: 1

BURIED TREASURE
Pure Imagination: *3 issues 1986–1987*
Caliber: *5 issues 1990*

Interesting selection of lovingly reconstructed 1940s stories from Greg Theakston's Pure Imagination studio. Western, funny animal, supernatural, romance and 'true life' stories sit side by side, making an odd mixture, but with many stellar names from comics' earliest days represented (Kirby, Simon, Cole, Frazetta, Kubert, Wood, Toth, Briefer, Williamson) they packed a lot into eight issues.~HS

BUTCHER
DC: *5 issues 1990*

Butcher than who, exactly? Oh well. This tale of an eco-terrorist occupies an odd position in DC's continuity, being set firmly in the DC Universe but still being creator-owned. It set a precedent for later series such as *Sovereign Seven*, for which no one thanks it, but has little intrinsic interest.~HS

BUTT BISCUIT
Fantagraphics: *3 issues 1992–1993*

File under 'experimental to the point of nauseating'. Dean Williams and Ted Couldron pool their talents to produce this series of stories about a cripple being mistreated. I think it's likely that many people will find this offensive for one reason or another, which doesn't mean you shouldn't try it.~FJ

BUTTERSCOTCH
Eros: *3 issues 1991*

Originally released in English as an NBM collection, Manara's *Butterscotch* short stories are uneasily voyeuristic pieces about an

invisible man who is in love with another woman, who persecutes a young woman, stripping and arousing her in public, making her look like a whore. How the situation comes about is not explained, but there are flashes of Manara working towards the kind of meta-fictional relationship between reader and creator he explores at great length in his *Guiseppe Bergman* series of graphic novels.~FJ
Collection: *Butterscotch* (1–3)

BUZZ
Kitchen Sink: *3 issues 1990–91*

Twisted anthology of top-notch material, edited by Mark Landman, who contributes computer-generated strips of his own including the demented *Fetal Elvis* in issue 3. Although short-lived the title featured work by Richard Sala, Charles Burns, Daniel Clowes, Jim Woodring and Jeremy Eaton. Issue 2 reprints a Basil Wolverton story, 'Supersonic Sammy'. Highlights include Charles Burns' *Naked Snack* in 2 & 3 and Mack White's *The Mutant Book Of The Dead* in 3.~NF

Joe Lansdale's BY BIZARRE HANDS
Dark Horse: *3-issue miniseries 1994*

Adaptations of Joe Landsdale's short stories that, frankly, weren't all that good in the first place. Often disgusting and gross, seldom disturbing.~HS

BY THE TIME I GET TO WAGGA WAGGA
Harrier: *One-shot 1987*

Good on Harrier for recognising Eddie Campbell's talent and pumping out one-shots and series in the late 1980s, despite sales figures rarely looking promising. *By The Time…*'s rationale is provided by a six-page Campbell/Trevs Phoenix strip contrasting travel now and in the future, a thin concept at best. Much better is the 'In The Days Of The Ace Rock And Roll Club' reprint, some of Campbell's earliest work, where the crudeness of the drawing, especially of figures, is more than balanced by the astute observation, both of body language and of human behaviour.~FJ

CABLE

Marvel: *2-issue microseries ('Blood and Metal')* *1992, 38 issues +, 1993 to date*

Cable, who first appeared in *New Mutants* 87, is the quintessential Rob Liefeld big-gun-toting character, who, despite having immense telekinetic powers, would rather shoot people. And yet it's not always as bad as it sounds. In amongst the ultra-violence, the convoluted *X-Men* continuity (Cable is the son of Cyclops and Madelyne Prior, sent to the future to become the ultimate warrior, then returned to the past to...never mind), blood and bullets there are some decent plots. Cable has a vulnerable side: he might have a destiny to save the world from Apocalypse, but that doesn't mean he has to like it. He has a difficult relationship with his father, due to the problems they both have forming relationships and expressing their feelings. His entire life has been filled with suffering, pain and the death of anyone who he lets get close to him. He's more violent than the X-Men but, along with his partner/lover Domino and his protégé's X-Force, he also gets the job done – the job being making sure the Apocalyptic future he grew up in never occurs.

The original miniseries and first ten issues of the ongoing title, written by Fabian Nicieza, and the subsequent issues by Glenn Helding, are readable (provided you've acquired a taste for the big-guns genre), but the series really takes off with the arrival of Jeph Loeb. Starting out, in 15, with a night-on-the-town date for Cable and Domino, Loeb strikes a good balance between soap, action and future-mythology which manages to pull together the mixed aspects of Cable's character, aided by lovely Ian Churchill art from 20 onwards. Cable is 100% a 1990s comic, certainly not for those stuck in the simplicity of 1960s comics, but for those who aren't, it's one of the best of its kind.~JC

Recommended: 15, 20, 36

CADILLACS AND DINOSAURS

Topps: *9 issues 1994*

Since *Xenozoic Tales* creator Mark Schultz was having difficulty putting out issues in the early 1990s he licensed the concept to Topps to produce a trio of three-issue stories in colour.

They continue the adventures of 26th-century mechanic Jack Tenrec and his co-adventuress and love interest, the feisty Hannah Dundee, in a far future where dinosaurs roam and small tribes of human survivors face a harsh fight for survival – although the way the two of them romp around relishing their run-ins with sundry scaly monsters you'd be hard pressed to sympathise.

Roy Thomas writes all three stories competently, bringing in plenty of new, commercial characters, although the accompanying artwork is variable, and the colour rather harsh. Dick Giordano draws the first story in a bit of a hurry, in which someone seems to be trying to take control of the City In The Sea's governing council, with back-ups by Rich Buckler. Jean-Claude St Aubin handles the art on the second, and has obviously tried to study the same sources as Schultz (Wood, Wood again, and maybe a pinch of Williamson). The final tale, in which Jack encounters a rapacious motorbike girl, 'Wild Ones', is disastrously drawn by Esteban Maroto, who tightens up his loose, open style but still looks extremely unsuited to the title. Overall, *Cadillacs And Dinosaurs* only serves to emphasise how reliant on the quality of Schultz' art the success of the concept is. There was also a six- issue Epic miniseries under the same title reprinting Schultz' *Xenozoic Tales* stories in colour.~FJ

CAFFEINE

Slave Labor: *3 issues + 1996 to date*

Nihilism as entertainment with poorly conceived characters and anecdote as plot. Sadly, one also gets the impression that creator Jim Hill considers his cast cool. He's a talented cartoonist, but will look back on this with embarrassment.~FP

CAGE

Marvel: *20 issues 1992–1993*

Marvel's hero with attitude returns without Iron Fist (who does turn up in 12) as Luke Cage moves to Chicago and becomes associated with a campaigning newspaper and Dakota North, private detective, and star of her own failed series. Cage trusts no one and is now merely out to earn a living supporting causes he approves of. When persuaded that Dakota knows something about his supposedly dead father he sticks around to help her against villains like The Untouchables (Kick-Back, Nitro and Tombstone, 2–4). Guests are used to help boost the title's profile right from the start, Punisher in 3–4, West Coast Avengers in 5–8 and the Hulk in 9–10. The main story-line, however, up to 14, concerns Cage's past and his attempts to prove himself innocent of all the crimes he's been charged with over the years. A six-part crossover with the *Silver Sable* and *Terror Inc.* titles (15–16) is followed by an *Infinity Crusade* tie-in before the final story creates Dark Cage. Written by Marc McLaurin throughout, it's all hard-nosed superheroics with no room for subtlety or anything beyond the bare minimum of characterisation. Dwayne Turner's artwork is dynamic but ragged and unattractive (1–10). Scott Benefiel (from 15) has a more open, flowing style but is stifled by the colouring. Unless you're a researcher into the smallest minutiae of the Marvel Universe you won't ever have reason to read this.~NF

CAGES
Tundra: *10 issues 1991–1993*

Cages is the series by which you will judge whether Dave McKean is a gifted creator of comics or a painter who happens to have wandered into the world of the cartoon. Gone are all the scratchy overlays, multiple layers, photographs and collages, but *Cages* remains a work that examines the role of the artist and the function of art as a creative process. Just as many artists exhibit work in progress and preparatory material alongside their finished creations, so McKean begins the series with several pages called 'Scaffolding' in which he displays his initial thoughts and explains his purpose. He launches into accounts of *ur*-myths of creation and death which are a bit embarrassing in their simplicity. They're best skipped: after all, artists don't stand by their paintings telling you what they think they're doing on the canvas, do they? The unkind may decide that *Cages*, with its obsessions with art and jazz, is actually about McKean and his own creative process. However self-centred, though, the construction of the comic remains interesting.

Creation comes up again and again in the series of grey, thematically interlinked plot-lines in which nothing much happens, but which contain a lot of thinking and saying. The protagonist arrives at a house, already inhabited by several artists, particularly Sabarsky, the painter looking for inspiration in solitude, and Angel, the jazz pianist. McKean gradually gathers them together, examining their lives, and reveals his greater purpose,

although less patient readers will tire of the wait. The opening to the first chapter spends several pages observing a cat (beautifully, admittedly). It's pretty much the *Magnificent Ambersons* of comics story-telling. His artwork is extraordinarily restrained at the start but soon degenerates into bursts of different styles, rather showily laid out for us, although along the way there are some wonderful, loose character studies.

The story in *Cages* becomes much more interesting when McKean turns away from the artistic inhabitants of the house, having delivered his messages about himself as creator, and puts the spotlight on more ordinary characters, such as Mrs Featherskill in 6. The whole issue, a careful unpeeling of the layers of her life, told via her ramblings and dreams, is McKean at his best.~FJ
Recommended: 1, 6

CAIN
Harris: *4-issue miniseries 1993*

The central character looks very similar to Rogue Trooper, but unfortunately is nowhere near as interesting. Cain is a private law enforcer who is known for hi-tech weaponry and killing people for no reason. The tedious story revolves around violence, disregarding any notion of characterisation or plot. Cain himself is well drawn but at the expense of any other characters or background.~SS

CALIBER PRESENTS
Caliber: *23 issues 1989–1992*

Caliber's original showcase title is the curious *mélange* of all such beasts, offering few delights, but numerous different perspectives and a very catholic editorial policy. For all that, there have been very few successful graduates from the title, the best known being James O'Barr, whose Crow strip first appears in 1. Always more about mood than talent, it's basic stuff, as is Tim Vigil's appalling slash-and-sex *alter ego* strip in most issues to 8. If the size of the character and his weapon is inverse proportion to the creator and his, Tim Vigil is a midget lacking a penis. More respectable in the early issues is 'Faerie Tails', a funny-animal fantasy by Dave McKinnon and James Dean Smith, drawn in Smith's appealing open style, but 5 is the best of the first flush. For starters there's no Vigil, with the overriding theme being maternal and tragic love, but there is a poignant tale of an old lady being robbed, and a decent prose piece from Mark Perry. Many issues contain illustrated prose, but it's largely mundane. Another feature of the earlier issues is previews of the more popular Caliber titles such as *Deadworld* (2, 9), *The Realm* (3), *Fringe* (8) and most effectively *Baker Street* in 4, with an original 'Baker Street' story in 9. That issue, the best overall, also features a 'Jazz Age Chronicles' short, and two very different, well written stories from Rafael Nieves. The cover claims it introduces 'Street Shadows', which has to wait an issue, but it's a generally fine selection of stories concerning life in the city, with 20's 'The Caretakers', about garbage collectors, and 12's tale of a retiring diner-owner standouts.

Of other semi-regular strips, the meandering and tedious 'Orlak' was somehow popular enough to warrant two comics collecting his escapades, while the far superior 'Taken Under' was also collected. By Debra Rodia and Michael Lark, it's an odd and mood-driven story about a guy whose father ran a funeral parlour and sold his soul to the devil. 'Mack The Knife' is almost underground cartoony, while there are too many strips seemingly progressing without a conclusion in mind, 'The Fugitive' foremost among them. Originally a novel idea of a killer being chased through various TV dramas and comedies, the joke is stretched way too far. 'Eyes Of The Hero' takes the innovative (for comics) idea of depicting exactly what the crimefighter is seeing for every panel, and departs with a decent conclusion after three instalments. Beyond the fact that there's a decent 'Silencers' short in the final issue and O'Barr returns in 5, there's little else worth noting. The missing extra ingredient ensuring the greater popularity of the similarly conceived *Negative Burn* was the addition of more personal works by already highly regarded creators.~FP
Recommended: 9

CALIFORNIA COMICS
Bob Sidebottom: *3 issues 1974–1977*
Largely trivial sex-and-trips material is occasionally redeemed by the appealing cartooning of Ed Watson, although Scott Shaw and Will Meugniot are also on display in the first issue. Of perhaps more lasting interest is the comprehensive A-Z listing of underground comix begun in 2, and sadly never finished.~FP

CALIFORNIA GIRLS
Eclipse: *8 issues 1987–1988*
Trina Robbins writes and draws the adventures of Max and Mo, twin sisters and teenage models. Light, fluffy, fun and with some surprising high-profile names among the 'guest fashion designers'.~HS

CAMELOT 3000
DC: *12-issue limited series 1982–1985*
Brought back from centuries of slumber to fight evil alien invaders, King Arthur, Merlin and the rest of the Round Table make for an unlikely superhero team in Mike W. Barr and Brian Bolland's popular *Camelot 3000*. Writer

Barr – 'continuing legends chronicled by Sir Thomas Malory', apparently – wastes no time in reviving the love triangle between Arthur, Queen Guinevere and Lancelot, reincarnates Sir Tristan as a woman, turns Sir Perceval into a monstrous 'Neo-Man' and has Arthur's wicked half-sister Morgan LeFay leading the baddies. Bolland's typically refined pencils occasionally suffer at the hands of inkers Bruce Patterson, Dick Giordano and even Terry Austin, but this remains a highly professional piece of enjoyable old tosh.~AL
Collection: Camelot 3000 (1–12)

CANCERMAN
Edge: *1 issue 1994*
'In a market glutted with costumed heroes, a new face can get lost in the crowd! But not this face!' Sadly, it seems to have done. Some excellent Kurtzmanesque cartooning on the part of the mysterious 'Sherm' provides value throughout. His first strip considers the real effects of radiation on the creation of superheroes as Irwin Meek, at first delighted with his new X-ray vision, develops a bloated, tumour-riddled body. A tame attempt at a newspaper gag strip precedes the preposterous Wotta Woman, whose breasts grow to massive proportions, stopping criminals in their tracks. There's definite promise here, and further issues wouldn't go amiss.~WJ

CANNIBAL ROMANCE
Last Gasp: *One-shot 1986*
A late underground anthology that celebrates all forms of flesh digestion, *Cannibal Romance* includes the work of Kristine Kryttre, Carol Lay, Paul Mavides, Dori Seda and Japanese cartoonist 'Mr Tero'. The highlight is a deliciously obscene collaboration between Lydia Lunch and the late Mike Matthews entitled 'Portrait of an American Princess', featuring the finest head-up-an-arse moment in all comics history.~AL

CANNON
Wallace Wood: *4 issues 1979–1980*
Eros: *8-issue limited series*
The original publications were lavish oversized black and white collections of Wally Wood's armed-forces newspaper strips. *Cannon* was a heady mix of brutal violence, cold war rhetoric and copious nudity that most right-thinking people will find enormously offensive. On the other hand, it was also a lot of fun, and Wood's art is always a pleasure to look at, even if saddled to some very dubious writing. The Eros series reprints the series in traditional comic size, but is faithful to the artwork by spreading each oversize page over two comic pages.~DAR

CAP'N QUICK AND A FOOZLE
Eclipse: *3 issues 1984–1985*

Thinks it's cute, but it isn't. Cap'n Quick is a child of deliberately indeterminate gender wearing a flying helmet and goggles for a mask, and a towel tied round his (or her?) head for a cape. She (or he) invents a pair of dimension-hopping sneakers, as kids do, and gets into scrapes among comedy aliens with new pal, the Foozle. The Foozle is an ugly, big, black talking bird. Plotted and drawn by former fan favourite and ex-architecture student Marshall Rogers, the book suffers from his inability to draw convincing human beings, aliens, big black birds etc. Good building and furniture art, though. 1–2 continue the story from *Eclipse Monthly* (the color comic). The covers say 'A Funny Fantasy' but someone seems to have removed all the jokes. 3 is titled The Foozle, and Cap'n Quick doesn't appear, as it reprints the original Foozle story from *Eclipse* (the black and white magazine) which Steve Englehart rewrote from a rejected Superman and Creeper script. Have fun figuring out who's who! It's a very readable story, in which the Creeper/Foozle questions the superhero's air of absolute authority, but loses a lot of its bite in this form. If you're still burning to know after all these years, a source close to the comic assures us that The Cap'n was in fact female.~GL

CAPTAIN ACTION
DC: *5 issues 1968–1969*

DC beat Marvel by a decade in adapting an action-toy into a comic, when Captain Action briefly became embedded in the DC Universe. Archaeologist Prof. Clive Arno found ancient coins which, when held, gave the holder the power of the god portrayed on the coin. Arno became Captain Action, and his son, Action Boy. Creative talents included Jim Shooter, Wally Wood, and especially Gil Kane, who produced some of his best-ever material, story and art by his own reckoning. The only letdown was the awful costume. A peaked officer's hat and skintight costume made the good Captain a natural to sing with the Village People. Still, a well produced series that deserved a longer run.~HY
Recommended: 1–5

CAPTAIN AMERICA
Marvel: *Series one 355 issues (100–454), 13 Annuals, 1 Giant-Size 1968–1996, series two 2 issues + 1996 to date*

Not seen since his commie-baiting run during the 1950s, the iconic Captain America was revived into the then relatively new Marvel Universe in *Avengers* 4. The 1950s run conveniently forgotten, it was explained he'd been frozen in a block of ice since the 1940s,

having fallen into the sea during an attempt to foil a plan of his arch enemy, the Nazi Red Skull. His sidekick Bucky wasn't quite as lucky, and died. The emotional guilt and leftover Nazis under the Red Skull's control have provided the springboard for numerous stories since, the other recurring theme of the run being explorations of what a hero costumed in the US flag means to the nation he represents. His *Avengers* appearances led to a series occupying *Tales Of Suspense* with Iron Man from 59, and when Marvel's shared titles split into solo affairs, Cap's title continued *Suspense*'s numbering.

Initially the expanded page-count was the only difference, the stories being as bland as ever despite Jack Kirby artwork, although there's the first of countless tinkerings with the origin story in 109. Jim Steranko stepped in for 110–111 and 113, a story later reprinted as two issues of *Captain America Special Edition*. Certainly a welcome breath of fresh air artistically, the battles against Hydra and the Hulk are only marginally better than the run-of-the-mill material appearing regularly. The only real item of note in 100–150 is the introduction of the Falcon (in 117) and his subsequent co-star status. In retrospect seemingly tokenism, an issue later addressed in the comic, the Falcon was only Marvel's second black superhero when introduced in 1969 (and remained so for the following three years). A social worker attempting to improve conditions in the ghetto, he was encumbered with a militant character and preposterous costume. Like Captain America he was a trained athlete, and was accompanied by a trained falcon he used in fighting crime! The positive aspect of the Falcon was that he was able to introduce the topic of social conditions into story-lines, and the title became *Captain America And The Falcon* between 134 and 216

With the title so far in the mire that it seemingly mattered not a jot who was responsible, Steve Englehart became the writer, joining the already-in-place art team of Sal Buscema and John Verpoorten. With nothing to lose, Engelhart introduced a greater element of continuity and began an ambitious tinkering with Cap's origin, in the process explaining away the 1950s Captain America and Bucky (153–156). It was the beginning of the over-riding theme of Englehart's writing on *Captain America*: that the title character was more than another costumed crimefighter, he was a living symbol of America. With the seeds already planted for a story examining the idea, the events of Watergate provided a conclusion (172–175). Feeling he could no longer represent a country whose president had betrayed everything he stood for, Steve Rogers first renounced his other identity, then adopted another as Nomad. It didn't last, and neither did Englehart, who departed with 185, having written the first decent run of Captain America stories in thirty years. Assorted undistinguished short runs followed, with the next substantial run of issues being put together by Cap's co-creator Jack Kirby, who returned with 193.

As was the case when he returned to another of his old creations, the Panther, Kirby wasn't interested in continuing anyone else's story or style, thus alienating readers who'd greatly enjoyed Englehart's approach. Stuck with the Falcon, he grudgingly incorporated him into the stories as little more than a substitute Bucky, but alongside mad scientists, Texan cowboys and an eight-part story about the Madbomb (193–200), a thin allegory concerning the fragility of world peace. Kirby also produced the *Captain America's Bicentennial Battles* in 1976. The oversized format showcased his all-action art magnificently, but the plot left a lot to be desired. The best story Kirby produced during his run was atypical. While containing all the dynamism and action associated with his work, 206–208 were a pointed attack on brutal South American dictatorships, something Kirby had avoided in the past, preferring to lampoon his targets. The final chapter is rather a let-down, but it's a powerful story overall. Kirby's art also deserves mention. Powerful, blocky and exciting, this was a Kirby who'd developed considerably since his first stint on the title. The sheer individuality and exuberance of his art here hasn't been matched since.

Kirby left after 214, and beyond that there's little creative consistency for over two dozen issues, with everyone and their mother seemingly having a try at the title, each speedily dumping what had gone before. The Falcon is quickly discarded post-Kirby, and his name removed from the masthead. By 1978 he was somewhat of an anachronism, no longer the token black guy, but lacking any real character or purpose. He's not seen again until 272 (also the début of popular villain Vermin), and then runs in a back-up series as Sam Wilson running for Congress in 276–278. Peter Gillis writes a decent one-shot returning obscure Spider-Man villain A Guy Named Joe in 246, but this tends to be overshadowed by the arrival of Roger Stern and John Byrne to produce 247–255. Their run is an oasis among the general mediocrity. They dispense with the obligatory personification of the American ideal story in a single issue, 250, in which Cap is nominated for the presidency, and noticeably sharpen up the relationships between Steve Rogers and his friends. There are intriguing plots, good art and unpredictable superhero fights, although they

don't dominate, and the all- too-short run concludes with an expanded retelling of Captain America's origin and continuation of the story during World War II.

J.M. DeMatteis and Mike Zeck put together a lengthy run on *Captain America* from 261. While they never knocked out masterpieces, there's an admirable consistency to their work in producing decent adventure stories, and their issues stand head and shoulders above the majority of *Captain America* comics. Zeck has a fluid, engaging art style, and the humanity DeMatteis brings to his work was welcome on a title where, his immediate predecessors excepted, characterisation had been a low priority for some years. 264 is a fine story involving the warping of reality by assorted conflicting minds, and in 270 Steve Rogers meets a boyhood friend whose reacquaintance will have serious consequences in 275–279. That story returns Cap's wartime nemesis Baron Zemo (previously seen in another identity in 168) for a solid tale with long-term repercussions. Another Nomad turns up in 282, also having been in suspended animation, apart from a brief release in 153–156 as the surrogate Bucky. He's written in as another sidekick, but soon develops from that role and into his own title. Team America, introduced in 269, also achieved their own title. 292 has Paul Neary installed as regular penciller, and DeMatteis begins his swansong, a long and rambling epic involving all the major supporting characters in the series to date. There's the requisite action and suspense, but in the end it amounts to so much steam, with the exception of 298, in which the Red Skull relates his background.

Mike Carlin enjoyed himself writing a fight with the French villain Batroc in 302, and with 307 Mark Gruenwald became the writer and went on to accumulate the longest run seen on the title, only relinquishing the reins after 137 issues. Gruenwald significantly altered the atmosphere of *Captain America*, making it a lighter title packed with supervillains. His plots are strong on continuity and consistently inventive, but the execution is generally mundane, with dialogue and expository thought balloons being occasionally woeful. One is sometimes put in mind of a group of pre-teens acting out the adventures of Captain America and villains with models, particularly midway through Gruenwald's tenure, when Cap begins an unlikely flirtatious relationship with Serpent Squad member Diamondback. Gruenwald's obsession for uniting characters with similarities leads to such ridiculous concepts as The Serpent Squad, a recurring group of villains similar only in having taken their aliases from snakes. There's also all wolf types together (402–407), and, most preposterously, a cruise liner occupied by seemingly every Marvel female villain (387–392 – they even have a costume parade!). At a time when the comics medium was straining to produce material of appeal to adults, Gruenwald ensured the age level of the average *Captain America* reader dropped several years, and anyone aged under 13 will probably still enjoy what he wrote here.

314 ties in to Gruenwald's *Squadron Supreme* limited series, although isn't an essential part of it. From 332 Steve Rogers is forbidden to be Captain America, the reason being that as government funding financed the supersoldier experiments that transformed him he should work for the government. When he refuses, a new Captain America, Jack Walker, later to become the USAgent, takes his place and he resorts to a another new alias, the Captain.

It marks another turning point for the title, which becomes a team comic as the Captain is accompanied by Nomad, the Falcon and the preposterous D-Man (introduced in 228) as he tours the country. By this point the novice Captain America and his assistant are far more interesting, lacking the necessary experience and generally giving the costumes a bad name, and from 345 the focus gradually shifts to Walker. It's spoiling no big surprise to reveal that from 351 it's the original Captain America back in control. A representative sample of Gruenwald's run is 'The Bloodstone Hunt' in 358–363, which combines his love of tying up loose plot-ends from other Marvel stories with the recurring Baron Zemo, and Batroc with his phoneticised French accent. By this time Keiron Dwyer's been pencilling the title for over twenty issues as a confident action artist, and if you can tolerate Diamondback here you may want to investigate further Gruenwald issues. 358–363 also have a USAgent back-up, and thereafter there's usually a short feature at the rear of the comic. Others with a solo slot include Cobra, Battlestar (formerly Bucky II) and Diamondback. 369 sees the unwelcome replacement of Dwyer as penciller by Ron Lim, a man who wouldn't know dynamic art or decent figurework if it jumped up and slapped him round the cheeks. By the time chapters of the multi-title crossover 'Operation Galactic Storm' roll around in 398–401 he's been replaced by Rik Levins, who's only a marginal improvement.

'Fighting Chance' is the title of the stories presented in 425–437. It's a quartet of trilogies forming a year-long exploration of what Captain America is as he endures a debilitating illness, and how he relates to the contemporary trends in superhero comics. It's obvious where Gruenwald's sympathies lie, as he contrasts Captain America with an ever more daft selection, starting with the revived Super-Patriot. He's followed by a heavily armed caricature enforcer called the Americop, a scantily clad product of genetic experimentation on a college girl, and the preposterous Jack Flag complete with power boom box. Dave Hoover's pencils are the most expressive seen on the title for some considerable while, but his fondness for pin-up poses for female characters is laughable as he's unable to execute them properly. The conclusion is astonishingly downbeat, and there's the inevitable Serpent Squad before the end, but for the first time in years there was a spark of interest in the title. It was too little, too late, though, and from 444 there's a new team of creators consisting of writer Mark Waid and penciller Ron Garney.

Their style provided a much-needed metaphorical new broom. Over their initial five issues Waid and Garney restored the character and title to prominence. Particularly noteworthy is the conclusion in 448, in which a ludicrous all-powerful device provides the means for examining what Captain America means. Waid also employs a light touch in his writing, but his characterisation is such that he engages the reader in a manner that Gruenwald couldn't, and his dialogue is much sharper. He also convincingly returns a character long believed dead (and not the obvious one). Garney's art meanwhile is expansive and stylised, and provides the first really distinctive look for *Captain America* since Kirby. Waid and Garney continued in fine style until the marketing people decided that instead of sticking with the best creative team on *Captain America* in over a decade, more sales might result from relaunching the title with the enthusiastic but inept Rob Liefeld in control. The result is risible. Jeph Loeb, elsewhere a decent writer, struggles with Liefeld's clichéd plots, and Liefeld's art is truly appalling, lacking any basic sense of perspective or anatomy.

In addition to the regular title there was a one-shot titled 'The Medusa Effect' issued in 1994. While no masterpiece, it's a decent enough story from Roy Thomas, set during World War II, with Captain America partnered by Bucky. Rich Buckler and M.C. Wyman's art is crisp and appealing, conveying the largely post-sunset setting of the story very well indeed. The giant-size issue is reprints of Kirby material, as are the first two annuals. The remainder of the annuals are universally unmemorable, although there's Kirby's distinctive art on 3 and 4 (along with his distinctive dialogue).~WJ

Recommended: 155, 156, 159, 180, 206, 207, 250–255, 264, 270, 298, 448, 450–454
Collection: Operation Rebirth (445–448)

The Adventures of
CAPTAIN AMERICA
Marvel: *4-issue miniseries 1991*

Writer Fabian Nicieza and the art team of Kevin Maguire and Terry Austin all seem to be having a good time with this enjoyable look at the early career of Steve Rogers, injected with the supersoldier serum to become Captain America. There's the first Shield, the emergence of a Nazi villain seen many times since, and the appearance of kid sidekick Bucky, as all the i's are dotted and t's crossed concerning Captain America's origin.~WJ

CAPTAIN AMERICA COMICS
Timely: *75 issues 1941–1950, 3 issues (76–78) 1954*

Not the first patriotic hero, being predated by The Shield, but certainly the best. Steve Rogers, otherwise too puny to serve his country during wartime, volunteers for a dangerous experiment to become a prototype supersoldier. The experiment succeeds, but enemy saboteurs ensure Rogers is the first and last of his kind. Donning the star-spangled garb of Captain America, he sets out to embody the ideals of liberty, gaining a sidekick Bucky when his army camp's teen mascot discovers his identity and, well, blackmails Rogers into letting him tag along! Gee, that's not very American.

Created by the legendary team of Jack Kirby and Joe Simon, the superpatriot smashed through Nazis, home-front saboteurs and plain exotic villains with equal verve and gusto, in dynamic and atmospheric stories that redefined the limits of the comics page. The founding creators left after 10, but the momentum of their legacy, including Cap's nemesis the Red Skull, one of comics' most vivid villains, carried the title through the post-war years in less talented hands. Sales only began to drop in the late 1940s, when reader interest in superheroes was fading and the entire medium was coming under attack by various groups of concerned mothers. Bucky was replaced by the strip's Lois Lane-alike Betty Ross, who became Golden Girl in 66, and story focus moved to either true crime or human interest, then to an increasing emphasis on horror. These tactics failed to stem the tide of departing readers, and the series ended with the ignominiously titled *Captain America's Weird Tales*, a horror anthology in which Cap himself didn't appear. The 1954 revival was risibly subtitled 'Commie Smasher'. Although it featured some nice art, including work by a fledgling John Romita, the resulting simple-minded stories hooked no one and Cap and Bucky fell back into limbo until the 1960s.~HS
Recommended: 1–10

Collection: Captain America: The Classic Years (1–10)

CAPTAIN ATOM
Charlton: *12 issues (78–89) 1965–1967*

The triumphant return of Charlton's space-age hero in his own title, after three issues of reprints in *Strange Suspense Stories*, from which the numbering continued, had signalled the demand for new material. US test pilot Captain Adam is trapped inside a test-detonated nuclear missile, but instead of dying manages to reintegrate his body by sheer force of will. Given a costume to inhibit the harmful radiation he now emits, he functions as the guardian of Earth and the enemy of Cold War communism. 78–83 feature the original Captain Atom in all his nuclear-powered splendour, then, in 84, his powers are drastically reduced and his costume altered in order that he more readily fit the Charlton 'Action Heroes' line. In the meantime a female sidekick, Nightshade, and an arch villain, the Ghost, joined flight engineer Gunner Goslin as the regular supporting cast. Dave Kaler's scripts have a bizarre mixture of camp inventiveness and inexperience that rarely totally satisfy. Art was from the inimitable Steve Ditko, who also handled the superb Blue Beetle back-up strip in 83–86. Nightshade had her own strip drawn by Jim Aparo in 87–89. A story left unpublished when the title was cancelled was eventually printed in the 1970s *Charlton Bullseye* 1 and 2.~SW

CAPTAIN ATOM
DC: *57 issues, 2 Annuals 1987–1991*

On obtaining the rights to Captain Atom, DC decided to reinvent the character, starting back at the beginning and introducing him into their mainstream. The series starts with the Captain's origin, courtesy of Cary Bates and Pat Broderick. Framed for a crime he didn't commit, he volunteers to participate in a government experiment. Apparently destroyed, he reforms in 1986. His military background and gung-ho attitude made him a fan favourite, and Captain Atom soon became a member of DC's premier superteam Justice League International. The series is largely simple fare, though: a villain appears and transgresses, at which point Captain Atom flies off to have a fight with him. For that sort of material DC have far better characters along the same lines. It would be unfair, however, to write *Captain Atom* off as a complete waste of time. The supporting cast were strong, especially the violently unstable Major Force, who was introduced in the first annual and became one of the Captain's most frequent headaches. 26–28 have the revelation of Captain Atom's true origin, which is even less pleasant than the false one. The highlight of the series was the 'Janus Directive' crossover in 30, linking with issues of *Suicide Squad* and

Checkmate. This story was full of intrigue and offered more than repetitive superhero action. The replacement of writers Cary Bates and Greg Weisman by John Ostrander with 50 couldn't reverse the poor sales that eventually killed the title. At one point it was intended that Captain Atom be the hero who would turn bad in the future, thus prompting the *Armageddon* crossovers. Premature revelation in the fan press forced an alternative solution, and Captain Atom departed with a whimper, next to be seen in the *Armageddon* series and in *Extreme Justice*.~SS

CAPTAIN CANUCK
Comely: *3 issues 1975–1976, 11 issues (4–14), 1 Special 1979–1981*

Early issues were the solo work of Richard Comely and rather painful to read. With the arrival of George Freeman as artist Canada's flag-clad superhero began to improve, although the Canadian chauvinism was marked. The back-up strips were interesting, particularly *Beyond* in 9–12 and 14.~DWC

CAPTAIN CARROT and his Amazing Zoo Crew
DC: *20 issues 1982–1983*

The Zoo Crew was a funny animal superteam written by Roy Thomas, with excellent cartooning from Scott Shaw. Led by a rabbit powered up from eating a radioactive carrot, and returning old DC funny animal character Peter Porkchops in the guise of Pig Iron, it's amusing in places, though Thomas concentrates too much on lampooning contemporary comics and films for this to have much to offer readers in the 1990s. Those wanting a complete collection shouldn't miss the début in *New Teen Titans* 16, or Changeling from the Titans dropping by in 20 to close the series out. Captain Carrot and friends later returned for the surreal *Oz-Wonderland War*.~FP

CAPTAIN CONFEDERACY
Steeldragon: *12 issues 1986–1987*
Epic: *4-issue miniseries 1991–1992*

With the first twelve self-published issues writer Will Shetterley set up a carefully crafted alternate universe in which the Confederacy seceded and the USA never came to pass. Although one of the changes he envisions is that the South would have more readily renounced slavery of their own choice, the Confederate States Of America is a nation where the races are far from equal.

Jeremy Gray, a superserum-enhanced WASP actor of little talent and intellect to match, is Captain Confederacy, the star of propaganda films presented to the public as reality in which he fights Blacksnake, a black villain. According to his superiors this sets a good example as the Captain is a role model for whites while it teaches black kids that crime doesn't pay. When the black actors question their roles the authorities kill them. The remainder of the series presents a complex and engaging political plot as Gray becomes a valuable pawn to all parties, and has to make his own decisions about whether to keep quiet, go public or fight the system from the inside. By the end of the series Gray's wife Kate has taken over the mantle.

Unfortunately the miniseries forgoes much of the politics in favour of a more colourful, but less intelligent international superhero conference, with the world's powers plotting how best to manipulate the North American nations. Although more polished, the Epic issues lack the edge of the originals, and are noteworthy mainly for Kate spending the entire run eight months pregnant. Like the original run, the series has long and engaging letters pages in which fans swap their ideas of what an alternate world should be like, and detailed biographies of Confederate alternate-world characters.~JC

CAPTAIN HARLOCK
Eternity: *13 issues, 1 Special 1989–1990*

Captain Harlock is the creation of Leiji Matsumoto, and he originally appeared in the animated film *My Youth In Arcadia* (the English-language adaptation is the more prosaic *Vengeance Of The Space Pirate*). The story is set in the 30th century, with Earth defeated and enslaved by the alien Illumidas, and Harlock and the crew of his space galleon are the last hope for freedom. Written by Robert Gibson and drawn by Ben Dunn, the comic is set two years after the action of the film. Nothing happens. And it keeps on not happening. OK, there are fights and mechanical breakdowns and reunions and infatuations but none in service of an actual story-line. This world is a cosy place to hang out, but otherwise there's no point.~FC

The Adventures of CAPTAIN JACK
Fantagraphics: *12 issues 1986–1989, 1 Special 1991*

Mike Kazaleh attempts to marry the slapstick story-lines of a *Tom & Jerry* cartoon with outer-space romance. Captain Jack, his crew Adam the Android and Herman Feldman (and Herman's unruly personal devil, Beelzebub), try to earn a living shipping freight from one star system to another but end up penniless after each trip. 5 introduces Herman's girl-friend Janet, and their developing relationship is the backdrop for the rest of the story. Captain Jack quickly outgrew its funny animal, science-fiction setting and showed potential to reach the emotional sophistication of *Omaha The Cat Dancer*. The *A*K*Q*J* special retold Herman and Janet's romance in the form of a fairy story.~NF

CAPTAIN JOHNER & THE ALIENS
Gold Key: *One-shot 1967*
Valiant: *1 issue 1995*

This series was created by Russ Manning as a series of four-page strips to back-up his *Magnus Robot Fighter* stories. Running in 1–28 of that title, the Valiant issue collects the first seven episodes while the earlier Gold Key reprint omits the second and fifth chapters, but includes episodes eight, nine and ten. It matters little, as a sample is all you really need. The story begins with an Earth spaceship encountering a matched alien vessel. Each unable to outmatch the other, it's agreed both will return home carrying fifty percent of the other's crew. Incidents along the way slow their returns. Manning's art is, as always, impeccable, while his plots are thoughtful and intelligent, presenting a generally optimistic view of the future.~FP

CAPTAIN JUSTICE
Marvel: *2 issues 1988*

The popularity of comic hero Captain Justice is fading. Luckily, blessed with extra-dimensional awareness, he realises it's due to lack of inspiration on the part of his creator, and travels to the real world to resolve the situation. Along the way he turns a lad from a life of crime and Philip Marlowe comes along to save the kid's mother from a lifetime of local-newspaper drudgery. Adapting the TV pilot *Once A Hero*, this is sentimental tosh, but deftly handled sentimental tosh can push the right buttons, and this does so.~FP

CAPTAIN MARVEL
MF Enterprises: *4 issues 1966*

A little-known all-time camp classic. The copyright on the instantly recognisable name of a once popular comics character had lapsed, so in stepped MF with a humanoid robot whose bodily parts flew in all directions when he shouted 'Split'. The series is every bit as ludicrous as the premise. Apparent success prompted a companion title *Captain Marvel Presents The Terrible 5*, which differs little from the parent (the Terrible 5 referring to the number of daft villains in the comics) and lasted two issues. Quoting the villain in one story as he returns to Earth conveys the prevailing quality far better than any review: 'Wahoo! Am I happy I failed to destroy [Earth]. Now I've a place to rest, even though I can't see too well inside the Earth's atmosphere without my glasses.' Quite.~FP

CAPTAIN MARVEL
Marvel: *62 issues, 1 Giant-Size 1968–1979, Graphic Novel 1982*

Captain Marvel's first two appearances in *Marvel Super-Heroes* 12–13 swiftly led to his own title. Early issues saw this Kree alien-with-a-conscience concoct unconvincing ruses to disobey his superiors' orders to perform lethal experiments on us earthlings. A better-designed red and blue costume was introduced in 17, and writer Roy Thomas couldn't resist a homage to the original 1940s Captain Marvel (see *Shazam*) by merging his Kree successor with the company's all-purpose teenager Rick Jones. Henceforth the Kree Captain Mar-Vell hung about in limbo until summoned by Jones clashing his 'Nega-bands' together. After two brief cancellations, a shaky restart was swept aside by the glorious 'Thanos War' in 25–33, all plotted and drawn by Jim Starlin. This run defined 'cosmic' and displayed considerably more mood and awe than his later regurgitations of the same concept. It was later reprinted as a series called *The Life of Captain Marvel*. Steve Englehart and Al Milgrom maintained a high standard in succeeding issues. Notably, 36–39 portrayed the Watcher's trial by his own race for interference in affairs on Earth and the oft-times hallucinogenic 41–46 revealed the Kree Supreme Intelligence's long-dormant scheme against our planet. This latter story-line explained some of the inconsistencies and contradictions of earlier issues. A new direction spluttered from 47 until Doug Moench and Pat Broderick provided a pickup with their Titan plot-lines in 58–62. This story concluded in *Marvel Spotlight* (second series) 1 and 2.

After sporadic guest appearances following his *Marvel Spotlight* run, Jim Starlin finally closed the book on the Kree warrior's adventures in the first Marvel graphic novel, *The Death of Captain Marvel*. There is no death at the hands of some arch-enemy for Mar-Vell. He succumbs to cancer caused by the toxic nerve gas to which he was exposed in 34. There are no battles of any consequence in this book, aside from the efforts to cure his affliction. The serenity of his passing conveys a staggering emotional impact as the story deftly treads the fine line between the trivial and the over-dramatised. Expressive pencils and inks by Starlin at his peak contribute to one of the finest comic books ever produced.~APS
Recommended: 25–33, Graphic Novel
Collection: *Captain Marvel* (25–34)

CAPTAIN MARVEL
Marvel: *One-shot 1989, one-shot ('Speaking Without Concern')1994*

These star Monica Rambeau, the second Captain Marvel at Marvel. She was very popular during her tenure in *The Avengers*, and one of Marvel's potentially most powerful characters, possessing the ability to transform into any form of energy, limited only by her understanding and imagination. Needless to say, the House of Sexist Ideas couldn't handle that. The first inept, barely articulate one-shot was seemingly created solely to reduce and downgrade her powers to a more manageable level. Bet they don't do that to the Silver Surfer. The second one-shot has the black Captain Marvel speaking out about prejudice in a heavy-handed but well-intentioned story. Unfortunately one of Marvel's more likeable recent creations has been shoved aside in favour of Legacy aka Captain Mar-Vell Jnr. Sigh.~HS

CAPTAIN MARVEL
Marvel: *6 issues 1995–1996*

It appears that the Kree version of Captain Marvel fathered a son. He's now a teenager with cosmic powers who feels he has to live up to his father's reputation. Why is never explained. As he's been subjected to accelerated growth and given memory implants it shouldn't matter, but matter it does and he stomps about the universe alternately mouthing off or wringing his hands in despair. Mind you, he's got good cause, having been tricked into activating a bomb that killed 2000 people. Once he's dealt with the manipulator (and guess what, it's the son of his father's greatest enemy) in 4 matters improve, but it's too late by then. It would seem the copyright on the series title was up for renewal, and God forbid it should return to DC and the first and most famous character to bear the name.~WJ

CAPTAIN NICE
Gold Key: *1 issue 1967*

Alleged superhero parody based on the short-run TV show. The worst of four uncredited stories features a villain called The Rooster, cursed with a compulsion to crow about his crimes as the sun rose, and captured when a spotlight is shone on him in darkness.~FP

CAPTAIN OBLIVION
Harrier: *1 issue*

Odd mixture of hokey old science fiction (giant ants in the moon) and a superhero with a waning relationship. All very enjoyable if you're not expecting straight superhero action from Glenn Dakin. Captain Oblivion, or at least Abe Rat, his civilian counterpart, was also a regular in *Gag*.~WJ

CAPTAIN PARAGON
AC: *4 issues 1993*

Returned to life after 30 years in suspended animation, an old hero searches for information about his past and meaning in his present. It's all a bit predictable and run-of-the-mill, though.~HS

CAPTAIN PLANET
Marvel: *12 issues 1991–1992*

Uninspired adaptation of the briefly faddy TV cartoon about an environmentally friendly superhero and his kid sidekicks.~HS

CAPTAIN SAVAGE
Marvel: *19 issues 1968–1970*

Very similar to Sgt Fury, but lacking the well-defined characters of the original. Gary Friedrich wrote, with art by Dick Ayers and John Severin, and although they were competent the title was never anything but a pale imitation of *Sgt Fury and his Howling Commandos*. The best samples are 2–4, featuring the origin of Hydra in an attempt at continuity.~DWC

Bernie Wrightson's CAPTAIN STERNN Running Out Of Time
Kitchen Sink: *5-issue miniseries 1993–1994*

Captain Sternn is Wrightson's large, square-jawed rogue, and the series begins with him escaping from jail for crimes committed when last seen in *Heavy Metal*. He's soon back on the track of a vast amount of money he stole from Fillmore Coffers, head of Cosmic Coola Industries. It's been taken back into pre-history by his partner Hanover Fist, conveniently able to transform into a giant brute of a man to deal with the indigenous saurian life. Back in the present, or Sternn's future, to be precise, the population are gradually transforming into shambling zombies for some reason. Wrightson's reputation is as a fine illustrator of horror material, but this denies an obvious talent for comedy. While not as detailed or shadowy as his more familiar style, this appears to be one of the few projects he's cared about in recent years. He deftly manipulates his comedic cast, provides plenty of twists to his plot, and throws in some excellent jokes. All in all very satisfactory.~WJ
Recommended: *1–5*

CAPTAIN STORM
DC: *18 issues 1964–1967*

'Skipper, your leg's being blasted,' cries out one of the marines on the cover of the first issue. 'It's only wood,' replies the title's namesake; 'I'll get another.' Real teeth-clenched action characterises Captain Storm, a PT-boat skipper with a wooden leg! Average war stories, based in the Pacific fighting the Japanese. Captain Storm eventually turned up with The Losers (in *Our Fighting Forces*), once the rot set in and his title was cancelled.~HY

CAPTAIN THUNDER and BLUE BOLT
Hero: *10 issues 1987–1988*

The eponymous Captain and his son perform heroic deeds with an electrical bias. One of the few Hero titles that didn't strongly emphasise the tits-and-ass angle, having no recurring female characters, and consequently one of the shortest-lived of that line. After all, nobody bought Hero comics for the story.~HS

CAPTAIN VICTORY and the Galactic Rangers
Pacific: 14 issues 1981–1984

Written and pencilled by Jack Kirby. They patrol the galaxy, saving us from the Insectons and Paranex the Fighting Fetus, and uttering lines such as 'He's reacting to monumental surges of anti-death!' and 'Finarkin kills with a devious brain!!' Utterly stupid and a barrel of laughs, but sampling an issue or two at random is probably quite enough for most of us. That is unless you're a Kirby completist, since later issues drop hints as to how Kirby would have concluded *New Gods* had he been allowed to let it run a natural course.~FC

CAR WARRIORS
Epic: *4-issue miniseries 1991*

Adapting a role-playing game to comics was never likely to stimulate the creative juices, and the resulting mess merges *Wacky Races* with *Mad Max*. Scripting by Chuck Dixon on autopilot is only occasionally redeemed by the unusual art team of Steve Dillon and Phil Winslade.~FP

CARAVAN KIDD
Dark Horse: *Series one, 10 issues 1992–1993, Special 1993, Series two 10 issues 1993–1994, Series three 8 issues 1994*

Science-fiction comedy epic from Johji Manabe, translated from the Japanese by Dana Lewis and Toren Smith. Mian Toris has a mission to single-handedly destroy the expansionist ambitions of the Helgebard Empire. She is accompanied by two black marketeers, the dim but lovable Wataru and the venal Babo. Babo is of the Akogi race, whose only interest is profit. Wataru provides the romantic interest for Mian though they spend most of the series fighting each other as well as the Empire. However, nothing is what it seems in Manabe's clever script, which pulls the rug out from under the reader with each new revelation about Mian's origins and the history of the 'Empire' against which she's supposed to be rebelling. Manabe's artwork is extremely well-paced, particularly suited to telling a story combining humour with adventure, but it's the twists and turns of plot and character that will keep you reading the series.~NF

Collection: Caravan Kidd (Series one 1–10, plus special)

Where in the world is CARMEN SANDIEGO?
DC: *4 issues + 1996 to date*

Carmen Sandiego is the master criminal in a computer game, where the object is to trap her. The same scenario is transferred to comics with a games champion being brought in to do the job. Aimed squarely at the younger end of the market with appealing cartoony artwork, and wacky scripts echoing the game, it entertains and informs.~WJ

CARNAGE
Marvel: *One-shot ('Mind Bomb') 1996, one-shot ('It's A Wonderful Life') 1996*

There's a decent, if resolutely unpleasant, story in 'Mind Bomb', with writer Warren Ellis taking a pointed jibe at the slim nature of previous Carnage appearances. Safely jailed, Carnage is visited by a ghastly egocentric psychiatrist for a revelations session. Kyle Hotz conveys the claustrophobic and gloomy surroundings of the containment facility excellently, having obviously studied his Berni Wrightson, most likely via Kelley Jones. He's back for the dismal second one-shot. Here writer David Quinn passes off a surreal trip into Carnage's mind as a plot, keeping the punters happy with a gore overdose. It's crap.~WJ

CARNOSAUR CARNAGE
Atomeka: *One-shot 1993*

Anthology with dinosaurs as a theme. The best of a good bunch is lead strip 'Skin Of The Hadrosaurs', gorgeously painted by Kev Walker, and also worth noting is 'Gomra', in which a Godzilla-like monster has to renegotiate his film contract. Both are written by Dan Abnett, and there's also a wacky cavemen vs dinosaurs strip by Nick Abadzis and John McCrea.~FP

Larry Gonick's CARTOON HISTORY OF THE UNIVERSE
Rip Off: *13 issues 1978–1994*

Everyone thinks it's a joke title. The cartoon history of the universe? Who would want it, and how would you go about doing it? The answer to the latter question is 'Exactly like any editor would if asked to write a single-volume history of anything, even such a big topic as this, by carefully paring down facts and then working out how to present them in a clear and appealing fashion'. As to who would want it: anyone with a sense of humour, of course. underground veteran Gonick, whose approach to factual comics with a sense of humour is reminiscent of Hunt Emerson, creates a work that is inventive and informative, witty and wryly observed throughout. He's also responsible for a similar-quality one-off 380-page volume detailing *The Cartoon History Of The United States*, published by Doubleday.~FJ

Recommended: 1–13

Collections: The Cartoon History Of The Universe (1–7), The Cartoon History Of The Universe II (8–13)

CASUAL HEROES

Image: *1 issue 1996*

Intended to be the first of a continued series, only one issue of *Casual Heroes* has so far seen the light of day. Behind a beautiful Steve Rude cover, the comic, about a group of slightly off-beat hedonistic young superheroes, has a naïve charm, looking more like a glossy colour fanzine than an Image comic. Writer/artist Kevin McCarthy has an unpolished skill which, while far from being mainstream professional, promises much for the future. It would be a shame if this is all we ever see.~JC

Claws of the CAT

Marvel: *4 issues 1972–1973*

Young widow Greer Nelson becomes the research assistant of Dr Tumolo, who uses her knowledge to raise Greer's physical and psychic abilities to their fullest potential. Linda Fite's script combines a solid, traditional Marvel origin with simple but sound feminist ideas in a sincere attempt to put a new spin on superheroics. The first issue also had glorious Marie Severin and Wally Wood art. Unfortunately, Marvel's 1970s women's comics line wasn't given much creative support or time to prove itself, and the strip became an ordinary superhero series with the very next issue. Increasingly lame matches against Marvel villains coupled with slapdash and inappropriate art killed the comic very swiftly. Shame. One can't help but feel that Marvel had something, but pissed it away. The character mutated into Tigra the Were-Woman and forged a third-banana career in various *Avengers* titles.~HS

Recommended: 1

CAT AND MOUSE

Aircel: *18 issues 1990–1991*

A well-conceived series that established the writing skills of Roland Mann. Artist Mitch Byrd was considerably better by the end of the run, but retains a consistent look throughout, despite having a different inker on practically every issue. The story concerns a policeman who puts on a mask to become Cat, an ex-con who becomes his partner, Mouse, and a vet called Keith who happens to be a dog-like demon. Fortunately there's not much by the way of supernatural happenings (apart from a sub-plot about an evil cult); instead the plot centres on the gangland battle for control of the

city between the Yakuza and the Mafia. While Cat and Mouse struggle to clear themselves of a murder charge the Yakuza send their own costumed fighters to kill policemen who're on the Mafia payroll. A sub-plot featuring the romance between Mouse and Keith rounds out a decent adventure thriller.~NF

Collection: Cat And Mouse (1–4)

CAT CLAW

Eternity: *9 issues 1990–1991*

Translated from the Serbo-Croat, Bane Kerac's sexy superheroine fights monsters, mad scientists and supervillains with names like The Caterminator. The series is mostly played for laughs, with lots of knowing references to other strips and movies. Cat Claw usually manages to lose what is already a very skimpy costume in the course of each adventure. Very much an 'adult', European take on superheroes, similar to *XXX-Women*, Cat Claw is undemanding fun if not exactly politically correct.~NF

CATALAN Graphic Novels

Catalan Communications specialised in translating European graphic novels, primarily from France and Italy, for the American market and as such their list revolved around the work of several accessible illustrators like Milo Manara, Vittorio Giardino and Enki Bilal, and around lighthearted erotica. When Catalan ceased trading in 1993 NBM picked up many of their sex titles and a handful of other books.

Generally the work reprinted wasn't particularly challenging, although a number of individual volumes are intellectually stimulating. *The Magician's Wife* (1988), by American crime writer Jerome Charyn and French artist François Boucq, is a complex fabulation about the obsessive relationship between a young girl and her ageing mother's lover, a magician, who is the eldest son in the creepy, fantasy-filled house where her mother works as a maid. They run away and gradually the girl supplants her mother both as his assistant in a magic act and in his bed. *Billy Budd, KGB* (1991), by Charyn and Boucq, is about a loner who's recruited by the KGB and sent to the USA as a spy. Charyn examines the idea of belonging through Budd, who feels out of place in his native Ukraine from the start, using a film noir plot to continue the sense of alienation. Of less interest is *Pioneers Of The Human Adventure* (1989), a collection of solo stories by Boucq centred around peculiar juxtapositions and out-of-place objects, where the art runs away with the story. Boucq's complex, layered style, full of shifting outlines and soft, pastel lines, is particularly suited to depicting fantastic elements in everyday settings.

Lorenzo Mattotti's *Fires* (1989) is a richly

painted fable relying heavily on the art to tell the story. Equally art-heavy is *Bell's Theorem* (3 vols, 1989) which, despite a brave translation by Bernard Metz, remains an impenetrable metaphorical tale largely driven by writer/artist Matthias Schultheiss' artwork. *Hurricane* (*Stella Norris* vol 1, 1991), by Canossa and Baldazzini, is also dominated by its striking art. Baldazzini's style is reminiscent of a stiff Charles Burns, telling the story of a group of people, all with something to hide, stranded in a small-town hotel in America by an impending hurricane. As the winds get more violent so does the mood inside, in a story reminiscent of a Douglas Sirk melodrama.

Catalan published two volumes by Philippe Paringaux and Jacques de Loustal: *Love Shots*, a collection of pointed shorts, and *Hearts Of Sand*, a carefully constructed examination of the dynamics of relationships which brings together French Legionnaires and mysterious women in North Africa in the 20s. Loustal illustrates with curiously flat but effective, haunting images of people who are all trying to hide something. If these appeal to you you'll also like Max Cabanes' *Heartthrobs*, an award-winning series of stories about the pangs of growing up, drawn in a broad, pastel style that shows the influence of both Loustal and Prado.

Also important is the first part of François Bourgeon's *Companions Of The Dusk* series set in Medieval France. In the *Spell Of The Misty Forest* magic mixes with history as two children are led into a sinister forest by a faceless knight and are taken over by goblins. Bourgeon's strange fantasy is not only immaculately researched, it's beautifully drawn in the detailed but flowing style peculiar to European history comics.

Finally, some quality oddments that don't really fit in. We can thank them for proving that Guido Crepax draws something other than S&M and Gothic horror: *The Man From Harlem* (1987) is an aching evocation of the post-World-War-II jazz scene, strangely coloured as though the pages are bruised. Less successful is his *Dr Jekyll And Mr Hyde* (1988), a frankly dull version of the Stevenson classic with extraneous dirty bits added, which do nothing to illuminate the original. Another oddity in their line-up was *Joe's Bar* by Muñoz and Sampayo, which features many of the characters from their *Sinner* series. A series of connected short stories, about the regulars at a run-down New York bar, it's beautifully drawn in Muñoz' trademark heavy black style, the tales effortlessly dovetailed together by Sampayo. Also by Sampayo, this time with artist F. Solano Lopez, better known for his period erotica, is the corruption thriller *Deep City*. Lopez's art is a little heavy-handed, but looks effectively threatening.

And finally in the oddments section, *Goodbye And Other Stories* by Yoshihiro Tatsumi. It's a pity it didn't sell well, as it could have popularised some of the different approaches found in Japanese comics with US audiences at a time when action/adventure Manga were only just getting a grip on the market. *Goodbye* is a series of *gekiga* ('realistic stories') about the loneliness and isolation of life in post-war Japan. They centre on troubled relationships and social pressures and visually are a far cry from the slickly-drawn, wide-eyed image we have of Japanese comics.

Quite where the work of Mattioli fits into all this is anyone's guess. He draws like a Disney animator on crack, creating vicious parodies of famous cartoon characters in *Superwest* (1987).

One of Catalan's earliest graphic novels, Nazario's *Anarcoma* (1983), is an ugly but sharply observed story about a streetwise transvestite detective reprinted from *El Vibora*. The over-detailed but naïve art has a very underground feel, with packed pages that don't worry much about the conventions of story-telling. *Anarcoma*'s no less violent than the *Torpedo 1936* series by Sanchez Abuli and Jordi Bernet. Visually highly stylised, though in a pared-down manner, the brutal tales of a 30s assassin for hire proved popular and seven volumes were published, including prose stories as well as strips. They also published Bernet and Abuli's *Dark Tales*, a series of murderous but sexy stories. Later Catalan also published Bernet's collaboration with Trillo, *Light And Bold*, a peculiar love story between a woman who's been conditioned to feel no pain and a huge thug who keeps accidentally hurting her. There's something not quite right about the way violence towards women is excused in the story but it's very attractively drawn by Bernet in his 'Betty Page' style.

Catalan's other early success was *Click!* by Milo Manara (1985), the story of a man who falls in love with his friend's frigid wife and implants her with a device that will allow him to 'turn her on' at any time. It was considerably more explicit than an English reading market was used to and was a breakthrough in getting dirty, if beautifully rendered, comics on the shelves. It was quickly followed by his other sexy romps such as *Butterscotch* (1987), about an invisible man who chases a young woman, *Hidden Camera* (1990), about a film crew trying to persuade women to show their pussies in public who film something they shouldn't and decide to investigate, and *Shorts* (1989), a series of light, voyeuristic meditations. Catalan also translated the first three volumes of Manara's more heavyweight series about Guiseppe Bergman and his mentor, HP. Based on Manara and his old friend Hugo Pratt, *The Great Adventure* (1988), *An Author In Search Of Six*

Characters (1989) and *Dies Irae* (1990) are meandering adventure stories in which symbol and reality blend. This continually plays with our expectations, with characters addressing the readers and haranguing them about what should happen next. In a similar vein is *Trip To Tulum*, Manara's collaboration with Italian cinematic *auteur* Federico Fellini, the cement on a late friendship that began when Manara created a series of drawings based around Fellini's most famous films. Although many considered Fellini a spent creative force by this stage in his career, the collaboration is of interest.

Other Manara translations are his comedy Western, *The Paper Man* (1986), a reprint of the *Heavy Metal* translation of *The Ape*, written by Silverio Pisu, a version of Wu Ch'en Eng's Monkey legends adapted to become a political satire about Communism, and *The Snow Man*, written by Castelli, about an explorer who discovers a race of transcendent monks (probably the only Manara not to feature a naked woman of some sort, although he gets a couple of naked men in there). However, the best work by Manara that Catalan brought us was *Indian Summer*, written by Hugo Pratt, a huge, sumptuous reworking of *The Scarlet Letter*. Immaculately researched, beautifully drawn, the only thing spoiling this tale of human viciousness among the early American settlers was the translation, which, in common with that of much of Manara's *oeuvre*, erred on the casual side.

Another impressive creator whose back catalogue Catalan raided was Enki Bilal. They published his solo series about strange, animal-headed 'gods' returning to a near-future earth and the impact their return has on everyone from governments to the individuals they choose to use as their agents (*Gods In Chaos* 1988, *The Woman Trap* 1989). Beautifully drawn and coloured in almost iridescent fashion, they are complicated and playful science fiction. Rather more challenging is the *Modern Legends* series that Bilal produced from Pierre Christin's scripts. Catalan published two of the four books, the urban fantasy *The Town That Didn't Exist* (1989) and *Ranks Of The Black Order* (1989), an excellent examination of how people mature in the form of a mystery surrounding a phalanx of freedom fighters who, in old age, find their past is coming back to haunt them. Frank Wynne's translation of a conceptual and wordy work must be commended. A pity he didn't get his hands on the final Christin/Bilal collaboration, *The Hunting Party* (1990), although Elizabeth Bell does a dependable job. Set in 1983, it has a similar theme and structure to *Ranks*. High-ranking Communist officials are taking a hunting trip together, during which they will

remember many moments, acts and betrayals that shaped not only their own lives but the history of their country. Christin mixes a taut thriller plot with a haunting sense of nostalgia. Catalan also published another Bilal collaboration, *Exterminator 17*, a futuristic adventure written by Jean Paul Dionnet, better known as an artist in his own right (1988). There are also British editions of most Bilal volumes available from Titan Books.

The other creator who proved popular with Catalan's audiences was Vittorio Giardino, who draws in a very measured style using even lines and putting in lots of detail. Again, easily accessible art and story formats characterised the earliest translations, two substantial but sophisticated detective stories set in the 30s, *Hungarian Rhapsody* (1986) and *Orient Gateway* (1987), both featuring his calm and collected detective Max Friedman. They were followed by the harder-edged *Sam Pezzo PI* (1987), a more violent, noirish story, and then two volumes of erotica, the whimsical but not very horny *Little Ego* (1989), a Winsor McCay parody, and *Deadly Dalliance* (1991), a series of interlinked tales in which couples seeking thrills via holiday affairs often find they end up looking down the barrel of a gun. Nicely done, but again, not very sexy.

More thrilling, in every sense of the word, was Alex Varenne's *Erma Jaguar* (2 vols). Varenne is one of the classiest pornographers Europe has to offer, creating clever, referential tableaux with succinct lines. Erma Jaguar has an unusually coherent story about a rapacious sexual adventuress on the road, who sucks passers-by into her highly-charged world. *Black Squares On White Pieces* is more typical, a collection of stories featuring dream women in a variety of situations. Varenne's work has a distinct fifties feel about it, even going back to great *femme fatale* artists like Milt Caniff. Similarly referential, although much more European in look, is Daniel Torres' work. His *Rocco Vargas* series – *Triton*, 1986 (reprinting the *Heavy Metal* translation), *The Whisper Mystery*, 1990, and *Saxon*, 1991 – feature a slick interplanetary investigator up against a galaxy-wide drug network.

Catalan printed a lot of prettily drawn, mild erotica, about the best of which is Silvio Cadelo's *The Romantic Flower*, a piece of nonsense about a gardener who gives his pubescent daughter a mysterious seed for her birthday which turns out to be a nymphomaniac plant from outer space. Two-tendrilled action all the way. Also by Cadelo is *Mark Of The Dog*, a rather more ambitious collection of four stories about a mysterious masked man who drifts through a futuristic Paris uncovering murders, which is reminiscent of the atmosphere of early Christin and Bilal collaborations. *The Love Machine*, drawn in soft detail by Altuna to Trillo's uninspired script, is one of those erotic what-ifs: what if the 'women' in a video machine came to life? At least it's attractively drawn, which is more than you can say for *Dom Girls*, by Galiano, Marta and Pons, a piece of fluff that has no redeeming features.

Similarly futuristic are Serpieri's *Morbus Gravis*, the first two volumes in a long-running series about Druuna, a large-chested woman living in a world overrun by a disease that turns people into C'thulu-type monsters unless they keep injecting themselves with a mystery serum. There are a few panels edited out of the second volume, showing violent anal sex, but generally the use of extremely large word balloons and edited text gets round the differences between US and European obscenity laws. The art's very detailed but softly pencilled, with lots of pencil hatching and rounded forms. Paul Gillon is a straightforward artist and story-teller in the same vein. His *Survivor* series (2 vols) concerns a pretty young woman who survives a nuclear apocalypse that had wiped out mankind by getting stuck in a cave while deep-sea diving. Making her way to Paris she finds the robotic remains of civilisation as much a hindrance as a help in finding other survivors, and that the few remaining officials who sheltered in nuclear bunkers have turned into flesh-eating zombies.

They also printed erotic work by Guido Crepax, much of it taken over by NBM when Catalan ceased trading (see NBM listing for full details of series that they completed). *Venus In Furs*, Crepax' adaptation of Leopold von Sacher-Masoch's ground-breaking masochistic novel about Severin, a man who becomes obsessed with the beautiful but uncaring Wanda, is easily the classiest and most interesting piece of erotica they reprinted. Crepax, unusually, adds little to the plot, drawing in a large-panelled, open way with body shapes and page layouts echoing the movement of a whip. They also finally got around to releasing his version of *Justine* (1 vol), by de Sade. Again there's little addition (in fact Crepax goes through the original text like a scythe, pruning out a lot of interesting discourse but keeping the heart of the book's argument, as well as the plot). His by now fine-lined, scratchy style fits the mood of de Sade's satirical reflection of the moralistic novels of his day. Readers looking for sexy stuff should be warned that Crepax's *Justine* is just as unerotic as the novel it's based on. Just because it's about sex doesn't mean it's sexy.

The closest Catalan got to the bone was *Necron* (3 vols, 1989, 1990 and 1991), a black comedy about a female scientist who can only get it on with corpses. Consequently she creates a sex-mad android using odd body parts including, naturally, a gigantic dong. Much hilarity ensues, if you like that sort of thing. Magnus' jokes aren't up to much, but his bold, blocky linework is appealing. His *Specialist* series, about a hitman, didn't go down so well, and only one volume (*Full Moon In Dendera*) was published. Much more surprising, though, is *Peter Pank*, a punk re-working of the J.M. Barrie kids' story drawn in a highly stylised manner by Spanish cartoonist Max. The sex is rough but funny and the line work beautifully executed. Equally stylised, although reminiscent of woodcuts and Russian workers' art, is Igort's *Dulled Feelings*.

Straightforward adventure books are rare in the Catalan line-up. Ortiz and Segura's *Burton and Cyb* is the exception that proves the rule, a futuristic shoot-'em-up that's well drawn in a style reminiscent of a more traditional Liberatore (they published his collection of colour shorts, *Video Clips*, but it's nowhere near as exciting as *RanXerox* or its sequel). Fantasy was represented by two volumes of Frank Thorne's wide-eyed barbarienne *Ghita Of Alizarr*, and by Loisel and Le Tendre's *Roxanna* series (4 vols). The plot's not so bad but the pouty-faced child-woman heroine is annoying with her band of cute helpers. Fernando Fernandez' dire *Zora And The Hibernauts* is an over-coloured adventure with plenty of cheesy t&a and little else. And speaking of t&a, there's plenty in Richard Corben's *The Bodyssey*, yet another interplanetary romance story full of rippling muscles.

Rod Kierkegaard Jr's *Shooting Stars* features stiff but accurate drawings of famous popsters (some, like Madonna, still enduring, others, like Boy George, largely forgotten). Rather poor. But not as tedious as John Findley's *Tex Arcana*, or Paul Kirchner's *Realms*. Whimsy at its worst. Notably all of these rather dull offerings are culled from the pages of *Heavy Metal*.

Humour is equally lightly represented. Ralf Konig's *The Killer Condom*, subtitled 'Just when you thought it was safe to have sex', is a madcap and rather bloody murder comedy which looks like it's been drawn by Wicked Willy creator Gray Joliffe. Baciliero's *The Talking Head*, even more predictably, is about the (mis)adventures of a man who, to his horror, finds his dick talking back to him one day.~FJ

Recommended: *Click!, The Great Adventure, Gods In Chaos, Goodbye And Other Stories, Heartthrobs, The Hunting Party, Indian Summer, Joe's Bar, The Magician's Wife, The Man From Harlem, Peter Pank, The Ranks Of The Black Order, The Spell Of The Misty Forest, Super West*

CATALYST: Agents of Change
Dark Horse: *7 issues 1994–1995*

Introduced in *Comics Greatest World*, Catalyst is the band of superheroes controlled by Amazing Grace, benign autocratic ruler of Golden City. Events stemming from her decision to secede from the USA occupy 1–3, and the aftermath of *Will To Power* takes up the final two issues. 5 is a giant gorilla story, leaving 4 as the best of a slightly above average bunch as Grace has to take on Titan, the most powerful member of her team. Plots continue in *Agents of Law*.~WJ

CATFIGHT
Dog Soup: *1 issue 1995*

This is a collection of short strips by Paty Leidy starring two young women apparently prepared for newspaper syndication. The quality varies widely from the funny to the mediocre, and some strips are printed too closely together, making them hard to read.~SS

CATWOMAN
DC: *4-issue miniseries 1989, Graphic Novel 1992, 41 issues + (0–40), 3 Annuals 1993 to date*

Mindy Newell and J.J. Birch's miniseries chronicles Catwoman's origin, a dark, bitter affair of her sister nun, her pimp and her early life as a prostitute. Her motivations for donning the cat costume are all too self-evident and the Stygian artwork complements the mood perfectly. The story intertwines shrewdly with Miller's 'Batman Year One' tale in *Batman* 404–407.

Over fifty years after her first appearance, Batman's *femme fatale* finally earned her own ongoing series after scattered outings in her miniseries, the *Catwoman Defiant* graphic novel and *Showcase '93*. Villains have frequently fared poorly in their own titles but Mary Jo Duffy gave Catwoman a flying start by defining her supporting characters, morals and life outside her skin. However, to load readers on board, a plague of Bat crossovers (6, 7, 12, 13) cursed the first year and sadly stunted her development. 14 is a delightful, carefree *Zero Hour* tie-in which laughs at the concept's pomposity. Chuck Dixon assumed plotting from 15 and whilst main story-lines are adequate, he threw away Selina Kyle's personal life, continuing supporting cast and sub-plots, much to the title's loss. Not until 28–30 did some desperately needed character interaction finally surface. Recently, an infestation of multi-title crossovers (26, 27, 31–36) has weakened the series' stature – needlessly so since this villainess has now proved quite capable of landing on her own four feet.

Issues 0 (childhood), Annual 2 ('Year One') and 38–40 ('Year Two') catalogue a reworked origin of Catwoman inconsistent with Newell's vision. Arguments as to the merits of these versions have raged through the letters pages, but despite the bleak, sordid nature of the earlier tale, there is little doubt that it lends a far more powerful and convincing motivation for Selina assuming the mantle of the cat than Moench and Gorfinkel's watered-down retake.

The Great Catwoman Breast Debate has reached the fan press, letters pages and Internet as the preposterous pair of massive mammaries receives silicon injections by the issue. This submission to the current Bad Girl art fad lends little credibility to her acrobatic exploits and unfortunately detracts from the series' most superlative feature: the artwork. Jim Balent has drawn every issue bar Annuals 1 and 3, both imaginary stories. No little credit should go to colourist Buzz Setzer. A temporary blip in quality occurred for a few issues from 21, when DC switched to slicker paper stock before coming to terms with the artistic techniques it demanded. Many issues are worth the admission price for Balent's covers alone (10, 15, 18, 29, 36), and his clean lines, attention to detail, facial expressions (e.g. issue 20 page 13) and good humour (dig the squirrel in the oxygen mask in 30) have produced a near faultless performance.~APS

Recommended: Miniseries 1–4, 1–4, 14, 28–30
Collections: Catfile (15–19), Her Sister's Keeper (miniseries 1–4)

CAULDRON
Real: *1 issue 1995*

Considering a Shakespearean quote begins this tale of witchcraft, elves and ogres, the choice of dialogue for the witch Ulna is questionable, 'holy spit' or 'knob cheese' seeming out of place. The cauldron opens a portal from a fantasy land to New York City, and when this is discovered by the evil lord Vile, Ulna has to escape to New York. Steve Brown's artwork is fully painted but was scanned through a computer, which leaves the colours looking dull and the edges of characters lacking definition. A workable story with interesting characters, it's a shame there was never a second issue.~SS

CECIL KUNKLE
Renegade: *One-shot 1986, 2 issues, 1 Special 1987–1988*

Continuation of a comic strip that ran interminably and to no purpose in *The Comics Buyer's Guide*, a feeble domestic comedy with occasional comics references, execrably drawn. Why this was given four issues, let alone one, is inexplicable.~HS

CELESTINE
Image: *2 issues 1996*

Continuing the story of the angel Celestine from the pages of *Violator/Badrock*, in which she had her heart torn out, died and went to Hell. Chronologically this story takes place before the *Angela/Glory* series as a scientist tries to resurrect her, hindered by a demon and some angels who don't want her back. Blackly amusing tale by Warren Ellis (the Devil is a woman, Celestine is a murderer), drawn with some panache by Patrick Lee (though the inking on 2 is poor). As entertaining as Liefeld's obsession with angels and demons is likely to get.~NF

CENTRIFUGAL BUMBLEPUPPY
Fantagraphics: *8 issues 1987–1988*

Why did Fantagraphics follow the not particularly successful *Honk!* with an even more obtuse humour anthology? Joe Sacco edits, but doesn't induce the best from contributors, many of whose names will be familiar. J.R. Williams delivers, and the Calahan strip that kicks off issue 2 is worth seeking out, but by and large the standard is disappointing. Several name artists, including Beto Hernandez, tread water, and too many strips suffer from amateur execution or lack of pacing. Still others suffer from humour so obscure it's virtually non-existent.~FJ

CENTURIONS
DC: *4-issue miniseries 1987*

Boy, did the DC licensing execs see these folk coming. If you had a TV cartoon series and toy line to promote would you demand to have Bob Rozakis and Don Heck producing your comic? Perhaps by that stage this cartoon-by-numbers was already beyond redemption.~FP

CENTURY Distant Sons
Marvel: *One-shot 1996*

Origin for Marvel's mysterious alien who became popular in the pages of *Force Works*. Sadly, Century's mystery is his only real attraction and this comic neither enhances our understanding of his abilities and personality, nor tells a particularly interesting story. It's nicely drawn by J. Calafiore and P.L. Palmiotti, but that's not really enough.~NF

THE CEREAL KILLINGS
Fantagraphics: *8-issue limited series 1992–1995*

From a good pun, James Sturm weaves a haunting mystery about the disappearance of former cereal box icons. The narrative switches between their heyday, when the frog, rabbit, elephant and chimp all had long contracts and endorsements aplenty for sugary cereals, and the present, when they're washed up, and often bitter. Carbunkle, their agent, is

experiencing apparitions involving dead colleagues, but has plans to launch a new cereal based on a short-run 1950s product represented by a scarecrow. Attempts to contact him lead to recollections of his behaviour questioning the ethics of what he represented, and revelations about the past of the other cereal celebrities. Giving reality to cheery cartoon icons has a disturbing effect, but the seemingly rushed and wishy-washy conclusion is a disappointment. 8 is cover blurbed 'chapter nine' (which indeed it is).~FP

CEREBUS The Aardvark
Aardvark-Vanaheim: *213 issues + 1977 to date*

When writer/artist Dave Sim began *Cerebus* in 1977 his was one of only a handful of titles whose creators had rejected (or been rejected by) mainstream publishing but felt confident enough in their creations to publish them themselves. *First Kingdom* and *Elfquest* are other examples from the period. *Cerebus* started out as a parody of *Conan The Barbarian*, down to Sim's appropriation of Barry Windsor-Smith's art style and his Howardesque definition of Cerebus' world, both geographically (it wasn't long before a map became a staple of the text page) and politically. The latter was the far more wide-reaching element of the stories. It would be a couple of years before Sim announced that he had Cerebus' story mapped out to issue 300. No longer a simple monthly fix, the title now demanded a staying power never before attempted by a comic creator nor demanded from an audience.

Cerebus initially and temperamentally is a barbarian, albeit one of only three aardvarks in this world, wandering around the world using his sword to get what he wants. At the heart of the series is the humour, and Sim's parodies are an important aspect of his story-telling. He hurls them at the reader in the early issues but they're built upon throughout, or new targets are found. The level of humour depends on the target, from homage (Groucho Marx) to cruel (Margaret Thatcher). The subjects are taken from many sources: other comics (Red Sophia, the various guises of The Roach); books (Elrod The Albino); film (Lord Julius/Groucho); music (Mick and Keef) or politics (Mrs Thatcher). The humour drives and predominates throughout 1–25, but with the introduction of Lord Julius in 'The Walls Of Palnu' there's a real sense that Sim has a plan for the characters and that rather than just one-off parodies, we are actually reading a story that just happens to have had a funny start. Lord Julius is Groucho Marx, mad bureaucrat and arch-politician, whose ministers are given completely misleading titles in an effort to keep everyone off balance. These twenty-five issues introduce almost all the major characters who will be the stars of the next 125 including Sophia, Elrod, Julius, Jaka (6, Cerebus' true love) and Weisshaupt, master-conspirator. The Roach is variously the Cockroach, Captain Cockroach and, in later issues, Moon-Roach and WolveRoach amongst others. Bran Mak Muffin (5) is leader of the Pigts, who worship a statue that looks remarkably like Cerebus, the explanation for which would come almost 200 issues later. A parody of the film *The Beguiled*, leading into a meeting between Woman-Thing and Sump-Thing (parodies of Marvel and DC's swamp characters), concludes the first phase of the narrative.

'High Society' begins in 26 and marks a real turning-point for the series. Cerebus arrives in the city of Iest, puts up at the Regency Hotel and finds himself an important guest due to his past employment by Lord Julius. The latter's ex-wife, Astoria, shows up with the Moon-Roach and manages Cerebus' candidacy for the post of Prime Minister. Despite Lord Julius putting up a goat against him, Cerebus wins, and promptly tries to enrich himself by invading his neighbours. It all goes terribly wrong, however, when the Eastern and Western Churches unite to force him out of office and out of Iest. In 'High Society', almost every character from the previous issues is revealed as part of the bigger picture, though their true roles may not be explained for a long time. Cerebus is manipulated by his social and intellectual superiors but ultimately they can't control him; he doesn't understand anything but personal gain.

52 starts 'Church and State', to date the longest story, running to 111 and concentrating thematically on the effects of faith and power. Weisshaupt engineers Cerebus' return to Iest as Prime Minister (having tricked him into marriage with Sophia) but his political and religious enemies undermine his control over Cerebus by electing him Pope. Unfortunately for everyone, Cerebus decides that, as Pope, he can do anything he wants, and demands that all true believers hand over all their money. The plotting behind his back comes to naught when it is Cerebus who ascends to what he expects to be godhood but which instead turns out to be a history lesson on the Moon. Sim here intimates, as did R.E. Howard, that this fictional world is merely Earth's distant past. He returns to Earth to find that the religious leader Cirin (also an aardvark) has conquered Iest and taken all his wealth. 'Jaka's Story' in 114–136 is the best and most well-rounded part of the continuing novel so far. Oscar Wilde writes a book about Jaka's childhood as told to him by her husband, Rick. Jaka is earning the household's money by dancing in a local tavern whose owner, Pud, is in love/lust with

her. Cerebus is given refuge by Jaka and Rick, and is convinced she can be persuaded to leave with him. Jaka's story itself is told in illustrated prose alongside the contemporary narrative. To the Cirinists, women are the most important people and amongst them the mothers have the greatest respect, but men are second-class citizens, tolerated purely for their part in the child-bearing process. Whilst this is a love story, it's also about the nature of art, whether it be dancing or writing, both of which are done for their own sake, both of which are illegal in Cirinist society.

In 'Melmoth' (139–150), Cerebus is even more of a bystander. He's in shock after the arrest of Jaka, incapable of speech as he sits outside a bar holding a child's rag-doll while a waitress serves him and talks at him. The real story here is Sim's depiction of the death of Oscar Wilde. Seemingly out of place within the narrative framework, it pursues the themes of liberty, death and art as displayed in the life of the great outsider/artist/criminal, finally ground down by society. These themes are integral to the process by which Cerebus' personality is expanded again in 'Reads'.

'Mother and Daughters' begins with the battle between Cirin and Astoria and their different philosophies. It comes down to which of them is strong enough to ascend to godhood, if Cerebus doesn't beat them to it. It draws many of the long-standing plot threads together and paves the way for a new direction in 201. Along the way Sim himself becomes more intrusive into the story, particularly in the chapters collected as 'Reads' (175–186), in which artists speak out against publishers and the nature of editorial decisions. More controversially, there's also an extended diatribe on the nature of the relationship between men and women in which feminism takes a battering – woman is the Void, opposite of Light. 'Guys' (201–219) is something of a return to the humour of the first issues with plenty of drinking and male bonding as Cerebus tries to find oblivion after the revelations at the conclusion of 'Mother and Daughters'. There are new characters (including one based on Marty Feldman) and even guest appearances by other self-publishers and their characters.

Artistically, from the primitive but witty Windsor-Smith copies, Sim developed quickly with a highly individual style that retained a lot of Windsor-Smith's attention to detail but added a smoother, more rounded finish. Throughout the series he's continued to experiment with his story-telling techniques – printing sideways, including prose sections, writing himself into the story. His use of language and literary pretensions have grown as the scope of the series has grown. Since early issues of 'Church And State' he's been more than ably assisted by Gerhard, responsible for the backgrounds, often elaborate and always entirely in keeping with Sim's own contributions.

Sim has continued to champion the cause of the self-publisher both by providing space in *Cerebus* for previews of other titles and by offering to print 'single-pages' in the Bi-Weekly reprint series. His work has been compromised in some eyes because of his views (on women in particular) but *Cerebus* is an evolving (and involving) series that defies instant judgement. With ninety issues still to come, it's nevertheless shaping up to be a significant achievement in the comics medium. Its scope, ambition and complexity make sampling difficult. It's designed as a massive novel, and although it's not quite fully developed, readers wanting to sample are best advised to begin with one of the later *Swords Of Cerebus* collections.

The *Cerebus Bi-Weekly* (followed by *High Society* and *Church And State*) series reprinted issues in order from 1 with additional (non-Cerebus-related) material in the form of single pages by a wide variety of creators. *Swords of Cerebus* reprinted the series in four-issue batches with new short stories by the likes of Marshall Rogers and Barry Windsor-Smith. These shorts were themselves collected in *Cerebus World Tour Book '95*. *Cerebus Zero* (1993) reprints the issues between books that are missing from the collections.~NF

Recommended: Cerebus 5, 6, 26–213

Collections: Cerebus (1–25), *Church And State* Vol. 1 (52–81), Vol. 2 (82–111), *High Society* (26–50), *Jaka's Story* 114–136), *Melmoth* (139–150), *Mother And Daughters* Vol. 1 *Flight* (151–162), Vol. 2 *Women* (163–174), Vol. 3 *Reads* (175–186), Vol. 4 *Mind Games* (187–200), *Swords Of Cerebus* Vol. 1 (1–4), Vol. 2 (5–8), Vol. 3 (9–12), Vol. 4 (13–16), Vol. 5 (17–20), Vol. 6 (21–24)

CEREBUS JAM
Aardvark-Vanaheim: *One-shot 1985*

The first of a projected irregular series, *Cerebus Jam* was the result of Dave Sim's search for back-up strips for his first reprint series, *Swords of Cerebus*. An excellent cover by Bill Sienkiewicz precedes four stories by the usual team of Sim and Gerhard, with contributions of varying degrees from Scott and Bo Hampton, Murphy Anderson, Terry Austin and Will Eisner, who variously pencil and ink different parts. The strips themselves are designed to fit into Cerebus' continuity as part of Sim's 'Young Cerebus' series. Perhaps too much of a novelty to be really indispensable, but each strip is interesting, especially Terry Austin's *Popeye* homage and Eisner's Spirit tale.~NF

CHAIN GANG WAR
DC: *12 issues 1993–1994*

This certainly was one of the oddest ideas to have hit mainstream comics in some while, and one can imagine writer John Wagner chuckling all the way through it. Starting with the viewpoint that wealth enables too many criminals to evade justice, those criminals are abducted to be kept in dungeons for an indefinite period. The perpetrators come to be known as the Chain Gang. Action is prioritised, and the tension in the title comes from their abductions, the threat of discovery, holding a DC celebrity from 5, the ill-advised escape attempt and Batman dropping by (11). Occasionally the eccentric elements intrude too far into what's been established as a gritty title – the street gang that talks in rhyme – but overall it's a better than average read.~FP

CHALLENGERS OF THE UNKNOWN
DC: *87 issues 1958–1971 (1–77), 1973 (78–80), 1977–1978 (81–87), 8-issue limited series 1991*

After four try-outs in *Showcase* (6, 7, 11, 12), Jack Kirby's first 1950s group were promoted into their own title. The Challengers were four men: 'Ace' Morgan, pilot and astronaut, 'Prof.' Haley, a playboy scientist, 'Red' Ryan, adventurer and acrobat, and 'Rocky' Davis, an ex-Olympic wrestler. All had survived terrible accidents and saw themselves as living on borrowed time, so banded together to fight injustice in whatever guise it appeared.

This was Kirby's last major series before co-creating the *Fantastic Four*, and with the wonderful Wally Wood inking his pencils you can see Kirby's Marvel style emerging. Aliens ('Prisoners of Robot Planet' in 8), sorcery ('The Sorcerers of Forbidden Valley!' in 6), time-travel ('The Wizard of Time!' in 4) and the like were all strongly featured in 1–8. Kirby really was in his element here, as the concept gave his prodigious imagination full scope with a wide range of genres in which to set his stories, but alas, his destiny lay elsewhere. The artist most associated with the Challengers was his replacement, the much underrated Bob Brown, who drew skilful, action-packed stories. The writing chores went to Arnold Drake and France Heron, and later to Bill Finger, all of whom forgot about the adventure origins and tried to have the Challengers compete with the superhero titles. The 1960s were the heyday of the Challengers. They were given new, brighter costumes, a supporting cast (including Cosmo, their space-pet!) and a bunch of recurring villains. It was these silly-looking villains that actually probably anchored the series in its second-rate position. There was Multi-Man, a pint-sized adversary with pointed ears and an enlarged head; his creation Multi-Woman, a giant female robot;

Kra, an alien robot; and Volcano Man, a tower of living lava. Yes, well, definitely different. These and others comprised the League of Challenger-Haters, and were usually imprisoned in the Challengers' own jail, with the team making supply trips once a month! So much for human rights! Given the superhero direction, the success of such series largely depends on imaginative adversaries (where would the Batman TV series be without those colourful characters?), and unbelievably the Challengers foes became even worse. Along came Villo, Brainex and the Sponge-Man, all among the worst DC had to offer. Sadly, they all fitted well within the context of the stories. Of a poor bunch Drake wrote the best of the post-Kirby adventures, particularly a crossover with the Doom Patrol (*Challengers* 48, *Doom Patrol* 102).

Towards the end of the 1960s mystery comics were slowly increasing in popularity, and with falling sales the Challengers were quick to change tack: from 70 they dealt mainly with the occult. Artist Jack Sparling gave the series a nice eerie touch, occasionally assisted by Neal Adams, and veteran Robert Kanigher took over the scripts, soon to be replaced by Denny O'Neil, while Sparling was soon replaced by George Tuska. Even a Neal Adams- drawn Deadman guest appearance in 74 couldn't save the first run, though. The final three issues reprinted Jack Kirby material, as did the 1973 revival. Seek these out as they're much cheaper than the originals.

A successful revival in *Super-Team Family* 8–10 returned the Challengers to their title. The mystery and superhero adventures of the later issues of the original series were ignored, as the Challengers went back to their roots for a decent revival, with Steve Skeates and Gerry Conway producing interesting plots. There was nice artwork too, from Mike Nasser and Joe Rubinstein (reminiscent of Neal Adams' stint on the title), later replaced by the young Keith Giffen. This run only lasted seven issues, but managed to squeeze in guest appearances from Swamp Thing (82–87), Deadman (84–87), and even Rip Hunter, Time Master (86), tying up lots of loose ends.

You can't keep a good idea down, however, and the 1991 miniseries was very impressive. It took the angle that Challengers folklore was now a money-spinning venture. The Challengers lived in their headquarters in Challengers Mountain (introduced in the early 1960s) and a whole town, Challengerville, had been built nearby as a tourist attraction. Their quiet lives are shattered by one of Prof's experiments apparently gone disastrously wrong, exploding the mountain, killing Prof and his companion of many years, June Robbins, and half the town with them. The surviving Challengers go their separate ways. Ace becomes a mystical guru and journeys to the Amazon to seek a forgotten tribe; Red develops a blood thirst, becoming a vigilante and then a mercenary; while Rocky becomes a movie star and an alcoholic to boot. Their lives are still intricately connected, though, and the catalysts for their reuniting are a reporter, Harold Moffet, and a supernatural presence unleashing itself into the world, causing horrific acts. You can't help feeling a bit disappointed when the culprit turns out to be another ho-hum demon, but Loeb handled the character with much skill and humour. What makes this series outstanding, though, are the personalities Loeb gives the Challengers. While they always had distinctive characteristics, Loeb makes them very human and believable, which was no mean feat. Artist Tim Sale is also to be credited for giving each of the Challengers an individual look, whereas previously they all resembled muscle-bound heroes. A follow-up to this series from the same creative team was promised, but never materialised. Pity.~HY

Recommended: 1–8, 48, 74, 81–87 Limited series 1–8

CHAMBER OF CHILLS
Marvel: *25 issues 1972–1976*

Beginning with originated material, most notably 'Brak the Barbarian', by 8 this had become yet another home for 1950s reprint shorts well past their sell-by date.~FP

CHAMBER OF DARKNESS
Marvel: *8 issues 1969–1970*

Instead of shunting out their 1950s reprints, Marvel commissioned new stories in the same style from their then current freelancers, with often interesting results. Roy Thomas and Barry Smith's 'Sword and Sorcerers' in 4 was the first Marvel *Conan* strip in all but name, and you'll find Neal Adams writing for Marie Severin in 2. Reprints started creeping in with 6, and 8 only contained one new story. The title switched to *Monsters on the Prowl* with 9.~WJ

CHAMPION SPORTS
DC: *3 issues 1973–1974*

An obvious attempt to make a fast buck out of the sporty holiday seasons. Was it really worth the effort? A waste of Joe Simon and Jerry Grandenetti's abilities. Read *Prez* instead.~HY

CHAMPIONS
Marvel: *17 issues 1975–1978*

The somewhat unlikely union of Angel, Iceman, Ghost Rider, Hercules and Black Widow was formed after they foiled one of Pluto's more obscure schemes, attacking the University of California in Los Angeles to capture Venus and Hercules. Marvel's first

West Coast supergroup was established, in theory, as 'The super-team to help the common man'. In practice this rarely transpired. Tony Isabella's insipid seven-issue stint was overturned by Bill Mantlo on the scripting reins from 8 and John Byrne on pencils from 11. Their solid superhero fare was rudely interrupted by cancellation with 17. The dissolution of the Champions was tidied up in *Spectacular Spider-Man* 17–18.~APS

CHAMPIONS
Eclipse: *6 issues 1986©1987*

Taken from the role-playing game of the same name, this simple-minded superhero adventure is more interesting for two ancillary points than for anything actually contained in the story. Firstly it introduced the work of Carol Lay to a mainstream audience, and secondly Marvel initiated a lawsuit against the publishers for use of the term 'Champions', which they eventually lost.~HS

THE CHAOS EFFECT
Valiant: *4-issue miniseries 1994–1995*

A peculiar numbering system provides issues signified by alpha and omega symbols, which are the bookends to this Valiant Universe crossover. It begins when Solar starts to fade away and only Dr Mirage can restore his power before villains Master Darque or Caldone and Noir can take it for themselves. The two issues designated Epilogue 1 and 2 concern a Magnus lost in time attempting to find his mother, who's in hiding from the Harbinger foundation. Appalling drivel.~NF

CHAPEL
Image: *2-issue microseries 1995, 6 issues 1995–1996*

Those expecting a pious Presbyterian character are liable to be disappointed by this big brute, as are those expecting any attempt at a plot. A rambunctious type, Chapel has been returned from the dead to bash heads, and does so incessantly. The microseries relates how Chapel was the first Spawn, but don't be fooled, both that and Spawn's guest appearances in 5–6 are dreadful.~WJ

CHARLEMAGNE
Defiant: *8 issues 1994*

In 1973, 13-year-old Charlie Smith hitch-hikes to Vietnam to search for his older brother, who is missing in action. Two years later, against all odds, he finds him, but as a tragic after-effect of their meeting, Charlie spends eighteen years in a coma, and awakens in 1993 with strength beyond that of mortal men. Ignoring the silly origin and the religious overtones, there's little to commend this series beyond some early Adam Pollina artwork.~HS

CHARLEY'S WAR
Titan: *2 Volumes 1983, 1986*

Given the brief of creating a World War I strip for British adventure comic *Battle*, Pat Mills wanted it reality-based, but without relying on officers' accounts, feeling they were too distanced from the horrors experienced by the ordinary soldier. Researching the idea he only found four memoirs written by troops who'd survived the trenches, and based *Charley's War* on these. In doing so he created the most evocative anti-war strip ever seen in British comics, more used to over-the-top Jerry-bashers. Artist Joe Colquhoun was very much from the old school, providing clear, detailed, expressive and well researched art in three-page segments. Charley begins as a naïve teenager arriving on the Somme, and Mills' chosen method of narration is the trivialities of his cheery correspondence to and from home – hoping the garden fence will be fixed – contrasted with illustrations of his day-to-day existence. It's a horrific coupling as the genial Charley gradually becomes aware of the realities of trench warfare, yet disguises the ghastly events he witnesses from his parents. In the hands of lesser creators this could all be very worthy but dull, but Mills writes involving stories, and Charley's personality is very engaging. It's a shame the remainder of the strip, with an older and wiser Charley experiencing World War II, is uncollected, as subversive history lessons have rarely been so well produced.~FP
Recommended: 1, 2

The Legion Of CHARLIES
Last Gasp: *1 issue 1971*

One of the most demented comics of all time, Tom Veitch and Greg Irons' powerful mix of the My Lai massacre and the Manson Family killings was extreme, even by underground standards. The spirit of Charles Manson takes over the minds of Vietnam vets, who become cannibals and eventually take over the world, digesting the likes of Spiro Agnew, Chairman Mao, the Pope and George Harrison along the way. Any comic that ends with Richard Nixon trying to eat the head Charlie deserves a place in any collection, although it should go without saying that some may be offended.~DAR
Recommended: 1

CHARLTON BULLSEYE
Charlton: *Series one 5 issues 1975–1976, series two 10 issues 1981–1982*

The first incarnation of *Charlton Bullseye* was a black and white house magazine, which featured news and articles about Charlton's comics, as well as unpublished strips from their archives. Other than an average kung-fu strip in 3 there were terrific Captain Atom stories by Steve Ditko in 1 and 2, a Jeff Jones short in 1, John Byrne's 'Doomsday + 1' in 4 and 5, E-Man in 4, and, best of all, 'The Question' by Alex Toth in 5.

The second series was a catch-all anthology title that ran everything from superheroes (1) and funny animals (2, 6) to horror and sword-and-sorcery. The twist was that these were by and large drawn by fans for no money, so the quality was enormously variable. Of the run, the fantasy/science fiction-themed 3 is the best, its highlight being a strip by the largely unknown Ian Carr. The only features to move on to greater success were Neil The Horse (2) and Thunderbunny (6, 10).~DAR
Recommended: Series one 1, 2, 4, 5

CHARLTON PREMIERE
Charlton: 4 issues 1967–1968

Charlton were without a doubt the most conservative comic publishing company of the 1950s and 1960s, chugging along on their almost identikit romance, war, mystery and hot-rod titles. When it came to new ideas for their try-out title, however, they were far more imaginative than anything from other companies, except in 4. The Steve Ditko-drawn 'Unlikely Tales' could have slotted into any of the Charlton mystery comics. 1 introduces two new heroes and a kid gang, the Tyro Team, who were very ordinary indeed. Far better was The Shape by Grass Green, off-the-wall humour capturing the spirit of the original Plastic Man more convincingly than DC's 1960s series. The issue is rounded out with Pat Boyette's Spookman, in which a moonstone transforms archaeologist Aaron Piper into a vengeful puritan time-traveller. It's mad. 3's Sinestro, Boy Fiend is even nuttier, a satanic child who battles Charlton headliners Blue Beetle and the Peacemaker. The standout issue, though, is 2's 'Children Of Doom'. Through circumstances detailed in the letters page Denny O'Neil (as Sergius O'Shaughnessy) wrote the story against a really short deadline, and came up with an inventive tale of a doomsday device constructed to trigger and destroy Earth on detecting atomic power. It's intended to hold the planet to ransom and deliver a new age of peace, but conventional warfare instead devastates the planet, transforming humanity. Pat Boyette is again the artist, using a startlingly effective mixture of toned black and white art and colour for some sequences, again a process determined by the short deadline. Disjointed and rushed, it's nonetheless a fascinating story with a point to make, which holds up after thirty years.~FP
Recommended: 2

CHASSIS
Millennium: 2 issues + 1996 to date

The promise of artist William O'Neil is the standout in this retro-science-fiction look at the career of rocket-car racer Chassis. It's difficult to convey the excitement of a car race in comics, and that problem's not overcome here, but this is a spirited enough mirror image of *Speed Racer*, with off-track complications as big a problem as the races themselves.~WJ

CHECKMATE
DC: 33 issues 1988–1990

Much underrated spy/superhero title spinning out from the *Action Comics'* bi-weekly run. This secret government agency was based on a chess set, with Knights (costumed characters) as field operatives, pawns as back-up teams and bishops as the central control. The enjoyable aspect of the series was that everyone was expendable, and Knights died or left frequently. The plots are complex, with lots of political intrigue, and the bizarre choice of Gotham City Police Department's slobbiest detective Harvey Bullock as one of the company chiefs. Despite Gil Kane covers and tight script-writing it never caught the fans' attention until it limped into retirement two years later. Perhaps *Checkmate* never took off due to the weak art or lack of superhero fights, although there's a surprising amount of gunplay and bloodshed to compensate. 1–6 give a fair flavour of what to expect, and considering most issues fill the really cheap boxes in the comic shops they're well worth a browse. Look out for 15–18, the 'Janus Directive' crossover issues with the *Suicide Squad* (another under-appreciated title), but avoid later issues. From 28 the title becomes very superheroey in a last-ditch attempt to boost sales.~TP

The Complete CHEECH WIZARD
Rip-off: 4 issues 1986–1987

To some people Vaughn Bodé was the misunderstood genius of the underground comics scene, using gentle humour to point out the evils of the world. To others he was that spaced-out cartoonist most notable for auto-asphyxiating himself while pulling on his pork. If you like his squat, truncated anatomy and doe-eyed women you'll probably want to get your hands on these druggy collections reprinting the original *National Lampoon* strips and collecting various underground newspaper appearances and colour strips, plus some new material. Cheech Wizard looks like a mage's hat on legs who, assisted by his bumbling and easily tricked toad apprentice, dedicates his life to doing nothing much. If you don't find his cutesy characters appealing you may be less enthusiastic.~FJ

THE CHEQUE, MATE
Fantagraphics: *One-shot 1992*

Collection of out-and-out funny stuff from Eddie Campbell, drawn in a wonderfully loose way, with thick lines and bold scribbles. Highlights include Professor Bean's attempts to demonstrate the principles of comedy to a loutish audience and the 'Great Wasters From History Not Counting Dave Sim' series of one-pagers.~FJ
Recommended: 1

CHERRY
Last Gasp: *18 issues + 1987 to date*

Titled *Cherry Poptart* for its first two issues until an injunction from Kelloggs dissuaded writer/artist Larry Welz, this title is deliberately drawn in a style imitating the innocuous *Archie* comics line. Don't be fooled. *Cherry* is a very different kettle of flesh altogether. Eternally 'just 18', her voracious sexual appetites – and those of her divorcee mother and various nubile friends – are explicitly depicted in numerous encounters from the mildly salacious to the outright bizarre. While an isolated issue of *Cherry* is fun – it is, after all, kind of a head-trip to see what appears to be the squeaky-clean *Archie* gang having it off in various ways – its perky bone-headedness becomes irritating after a while, and reading multiple issues will make your brains dribble out of your ears. A companion title, *Cherry's Jubilee*, was launched in the late 1980s and is very much more of the same, except largely by creators other than Welz.~HS

CHEVAL NOIR
Dark Horse: *50 issues 1989–1994*

Long-running black and white anthology that was instrumental in introducing several important European creators to an English-speaking audience. *Cheval Noir* mixed familiar names such as Moebius ('Man From Ciguri' 26–37) with unknown stylists like Didier Comes ('Tree Heart', a symbolic folk-tale-like narrative illustrated in a cursive style relying on heavy blacks and decorative mark-making, 24–31). The stories were run in chapters, with up to seven different narratives in the early issues, although later on the book switched to larger chunks of three or even two. *Cheval Noir* travelled far from *Heavy Metal*'s science-fiction and adventure remit, and included detective, fantasy and, for want of a better term, mainstream stories.

Important creators who received exposure include: Matthias Schuiten (on his own for Fever in 'Urbicand' in 1–6 and with long-time collaborator Peeters on the extraordinary, visionary architectural tale 'The Tower' in 9–14); Jacques Tardi, with his blunt-lined detective tales staring the single-minded Adele Blanc-Sec ('Adele And The Beast' 1–4, 'Demon of the Eiffel Tower' 5–8, 'The Mad Scientist' 14–18, 'Mummies On Parade' 19–23 and 'Adieu Brindavoine' 24–27), plus his superb evocation of New York, 'The Roach Killer' (10–12); and Cosey, whose complex 'Voyage To Italy' appeared in 13–27, followed by 'In Search Of Peter Pan' in 31–39. Although compromised by the quality of the paper and the squashing and stretching necessary to reproduce the artwork on comic-book-sized pages, *Cheval Noir* features much fine work.~FJ
Recommended: 1, 10–12, 24–31

CHEYENNE KID
Charlton: *92 issues (8–99) 1957–1973*

The first seven issues went under the title *Wild Frontier*, and despite the Al Williamson art in some very early issues and John Severin (at his most unimaginative), this was a wholly undistinguished title. The one notable feature was the 'Wander' back-up strip in 66–87. It featured a galactic merchant from Sirius 5 stranded in Earth's Wild West. It was written by Denny 'Sergius O'Shaughnessy' O'Neil and drawn by Jim Aparo, who both had their tongues firmly planted in their cheeks. It's the best Western satire this side of *Bat Lash*.~SW

CHIAROSCURO
Vertigo: *10-issue limited series 1995–1996*

A beautiful but duplicitous artist's model, Salai, vamps his way through Renaissance Italy ruining the lives of Leonardo DaVinci, Isabella D'Este and sundry others. Tawdry but readable series reduces the life of one of the greatest artists to the level of a made-for-TV movie, but it's the guys who have the pouty lips and big hair.~HS

CHILD'S PLAY
Innovation: *3-issue miniseries 1990, 3-issue miniseries (Child's Play II) 1991, 3-issue miniseries (Child's Play III) 1991, 5-issue miniseries (Child's Play: The Series) 1991–1992*

Uninventive and inattentive adaptations of the controversial movies starring Chuckie, everyone's favourite killer doll. The fourth series is original (using the term pretty damn loosely) horror tales. Gore galore, but little imagination.~HS
Collections: Child's Play (1–3) *Child's Play II* (1–3), *Child's Play III* (1–3)

CHILDREN OF FIRE
Fantagor: *3-issue miniseries 1988*

An odd science-fiction tale from Richard Corben that ties in to his Den universe eventually but which is not representative of Corben at his best. For completists only.~NF

The CHILDREN'S CRUSADE
Vertigo: *2 issues 1993*

The children of the village of Flaxdown have gone missing, and Rowland and Paine, dead schoolboy detectives, are hired by the sister of one of the missing children. Writer Neil Gaiman weaves in the historical Children's Crusade, the legends of the Pied Piper, and an intriguing pot-pourri of myths, legends and nursery rhymes to lead us into Vertigo's first and only Annual crossover. Succeeding chapters take place in *Black Orchid Annual* 1, *Animal Man Annual* 1, *Swamp Thing Annual* 7, *Doom Patrol Annual* 2, and *Arcana Annual* 1, featuring the young heroes or supporting characters of those titles, as they discover the Free Country, where children rule, before concluding in *Children's Crusade* 2. Chris Bachalo and Mike Barreiro provide lavish detailed opening-chapter artwork, and the opening scenes in Flaxdown convey a fine sense of unease. Unfortunately, the inferior quality of some of the in-between chapters means the whole crossover cannot be recommended.~HS

CHILI
Marvel: *26 issues, 1 Annual 1969–1973*

Millie The Model's redhead rival gets her own title, which looks eerily like Millie's – not surprisingly, since the stories were pulled from the same inventory. Early issues show off Ms Storm at her motor-mouthed bitchy best and are quite fun, but the comic rapidly becomes all reprint from 12.~HS

Giant-Size CHILLERS
Marvel: *3 issues 1975*

The first series was retitled *Giant-Size Dracula* from 2 onwards. This second series mainly reprints 1950s horror shorts. Issue 3 has more recent reprints with art by Barry Smith and Berni Wrightson.~APS

CHOICES
Angry Isis: *One-shot 1990*

Pro-choice benefit book intended to combat anti-abortion legislation in the USA. Over fifty contributors, including Howard Cruse, Roberta Gregory, Ramona Fradon, Waller and Worley. Considering the stories are largely one or two pages there are very few misfires and a high number of powerful, intelligent tales.~HS
Recommended: 1

The New Adventures of CHOLLY AND FLYTRAP
Epic: *3-issue miniseries 1990–1991*

Cholly is a humanoid of indistinct persuasion behind his airman goggles and jacket, and Flytrap is a giant, mute, obese albino of enormous strength. They roam a rough fantasy world and do what they must to survive. This series has the pair caught between two warring mobs, one of whom has captured Flytrap for training as a boxer. Arthur Suydam's art has progressed since the *Epic Illustrated* shorts that introduced the pair (and which are collected in graphic novel form). Sadly it isn't good enough to recommend what is basically one long shaggy dog story with inventive visual asides.~WJ

CHOPPER Earth, Wind & Fire
Fleetway/Quality: *2-issue microseries 1991*

The skysurfer Chopper was popular enough in Judge Dredd tales to spin off into a solo series, presented here by Dredd (and Chopper) creator John Wagner and artist John McCrea. Now living in Australia, Chopper's peaceful existence is threatened by large-company shenanigans. Wagner has some fun parodying the laid-back Australian attitude to life, and McCrea's painted art is a far cry from his Hitman style, although equally good. It all adds up to a diverting read, with the benefit of sharp reproduction.~FP
Recommended: 1–2

Walt Disney's CHRISTMAS PARADE
Gladstone: *2 issues 1988–1989*

Dell commissioned Christmas stories for a series of specials starring Disney characters published annually between 1949 and 1958, with Gold Key continuing the tradition in the 1960s with slimmer or reprint volumes. When Gladstone acquired the Disney licence they revived the Christmas specials, populating these 100-pagers with the best from previous volumes and other stories with a Yuletide theme (*Uncle Scrooge* 47 in 2). Both contain meaty chunks of Carl Barks material, but there's plenty to recommend them beyond that, with Al Hubbard's *Three Little Kittens* in 1 and Paul Murry's strips in 2 particularly delightful.~FP
Recommended: 1, 2

CHRISTMAS WITH THE SUPER HEROES
DC: *2 issues, 1988–1989*

The first issue reprints a selection of special Christmas-themed stories from years ago. It proved such a hit that the following year DC issued all new stories, with an all-star line-up of creators and characters. There's Batman by Dave Gibbons and Gray Morrow, Superman by Paul Chadwick, Wonder Woman by Eric Shanower, Enemy Ace (he's a superhero?) by John Byrne, the 1960s Flash and Green Lantern teamed up by Bill Loebs and Colleen Doran, and Deadman by Alan Brennert and Dick Giordano. An Olympic-class medley of festive sentimentality, with not a turkey in the lot!~HS
Recommended: 2

CHROME
Hot: *3 issues 1986–1987*

This is a tantalisingly solid start to an unfinished series, written by Peter Gillis and pencilled by Kelley Jones. Two astronauts, one American and one Russian, are the guinea-pigs for a new technology intended to replace bulky spacesuits. They were completely covered in a flexible metal coating that blocked off their normal senses but conducted electrical signals so they could 'see' via video cameras, etc. Their shuttle crashed on re-entry, and there was only one survivor – but the coating won't come off, and no one's sure which man it is, and each side is insisting on their claim to him. It's original, intriguing and intelligent, as you'd expect from Gillis. Any chance of an ending?~FC
Recommended: 1–3

CHRONOWAR
Dark Horse: *9-issue limited series 1996–1997*

When a communications satellite falls on a Tokyo apartment block, the lives of three people are transformed by what appear to be alien lifeforms. They attach themselves to a housewife, detective and murder suspect, who all begin to move a hundred thousand times faster than normal. While it's still unfolding, it's difficult to tell what may come of Kazumasa Takayama's science-fiction thriller. His artwork's reminiscent of Otomo's but his blending of flesh and machine is heading into Giger territory.~NF

CINDER AND ASHE
DC: *4-issue miniseries 1988*

A superior action page-turner by Gerry Conway and José Luis Garcia-Lopez, rather lost in the shuffle when originally published. Certainly out of step with the contemporary DC line, there was no Vertigo imprint to see it reached the audience it deserves. Ashe is a Cajun vet complete with irritating accent, and Cinder is the result of a mixed marriage in Vietnam. They're now partners in a New Orleans problem-solving agency. Garcia-Lopez, rarely less than excellent, is at his peak for *Cinder And Ashe*. The art is warm and meticulous, and his flawless story-telling, flow and anatomy are a joy to see when distorted figures and pin-up pages are considered state of the art. The transitions between past and present are masterful and no matter what he's called on to illustrate, he does so in convincing fashion. Conway's also on top form, presenting intriguing characters and proceeding to fill them out and reveal their pasts during an investigation into pressure being placed on a local farmer. Lurking in the background there's the deadly and manipulative presence of a man believed dead for over a decade, and with a grudge against Cinder and Ashe. Excellent.~WJ
Recommended: 1–4

CLANDESTINE
Marvel: *12 issues 1994–1995*

A sadly truncated superhero epic created, written and pencilled by Alan Davis, *ClanDestine* tells the story of the Destine family, a centuries-old clan of superbeings who are forced to emerge from hiding after a number of their members are mysteriously murdered. Despite some occasionally clunky dialogue, Davis' wit, invention and meticulous artwork make this a pleasingly old-fashioned read. He sets up numerous tantalising sub-plots, introduces a number of well defined new heroes and villains, and slyly insinuates *ClanDestine* within the Marvel Universe. After 'creative differences' caused Davis to quit the series with 8, new writer Glenn Dakin and artist Bryan Hitch totally lost the plot. Davis returned to tie up some of the loose ends in a rather ho-hum two-issue team-up with the X-Men in 1996.~AL
Recommended: 1–8

CLASH
DC: *3-issue miniseries 1991*

Uncovering a machine that endows him with an ancient power, Joe McLash goes rampaging through a politically unstable Middle Eastern state, and when the superpowers sit up and take notice he ensures there'll be no further remonstrations. It's another of Tom Veitch's treatises on the corrupting consequences of absolute power, very nicely drawn by Adam Kubert, but saying very little in a loud voice.~WJ

CLASSIC STAR WARS
Dark Horse: *20 issues 1992–1994, One-shot 1995*

This reprints the *Star Wars* newspaper strips from the late 1970s, corresponding with the original release of the movies. Despite top-notch creators in Archie Goodwin and Al Williamson, the stories don't make the transition from strips to comics well, remaining disjointed, and the 'retouched' colours are dubious in places. Full marks, though, for not just adapting the film. Most stories are short adventures of the film's main characters, and have them fighting the Empire; some are Luke's solo adventures before joining the fight. The one-shot subtitled 'The Vandelheim Mission' reprints Marvel's *Star Wars* 95 by the same creative team.~SS
Collections: Classic Star Wars vol 1 (1–7), vol 2 (8–14)

CLASSIC X-MEN
Marvel: *110 issues 1986–1995*

Reprints of the enormously popular *Uncanny X-Men* from (an edited version of) *Giant Size X-Men* 1 (the first appearance of the new team) to 206. Short back-ups, which develop characters or throw a new perspective on events featured in the main story, ran until 44, after which the title reduced to reprints only, and the title changed to *X-Men Classics* with 46. Much cheaper than buying the 'real thing'.~JC

CLASSICS ILLUSTRATED
Berkley/First: *27 issues 1990–1991*

Following the format of the highly regarded but long out of print Dell *Classics Illustrated*, the idea is simple: adapt literary classics for comics. It's editorially acknowledged these aren't substitutes for reading originals, particularly as a shortened text is required in most cases. The poems of Poe illustrated by Gahan Wilson, the short stories of O. Henry and Ambrose Bierce and *The Rime Of The Ancient Mariner* survive relatively unedited. It's with the hefty out-of-copyright 19th-century novels that there are problems. With no fluctuation from the uniform 44 pages, some works are more sympathetically abridged than others, and attempts to remain faithful to the source mean that many artists do little more than illustrate a text caption. Visual impressions being paramount, *Classics Illustrated* stand or fall largely on the quality of the art, and artists are generally well matched with their subject matter. Particular triumphs are Rick Geary's portrayal of Victorian England for *Great Expectations* and *Wuthering Heights*, and Peter Kuper's depiction of the industrial turmoil and tragedy of Upton Sinclair's *The Jungle*. Mike Ploog's rendition of *Tom Sawyer* is superb. Given the restrictions, most adaptations are of a reasonable standard, and some much better than could be expected. An appallingly drawn *Hamlet* and lacklustre *Rip Van Winkle* are to be avoided, and while Bill Sienkiewicz's stunning art conveys the density of *Moby Dick*, it's not very accessible, surely contradicting an intention of the series.

First ceasing publication scuppered the project. Already completed adaptations of *Last Of The Mohicans* and *20,000 Leagues Under The Sea* were published as *Dark Horse Classics* in 1992, but the advertised *Kidnapped* and *Around The World In 80 Days* never appeared. Although numbered in solicitations, there's no numbering on the covers of *Classics Illustrated*, hence recommended issues are listed by title.~FP

Recommended: *A Christmas Carol, The Fall Of The House Of Usher, The Gift Of The Magi, Great Expectations, The Jungle, Through The Looking Glass, Tom Sawyer, 20,000 Leagues Under The Sea, Wuthering Heights*

CLAW The Unconquered
DC: *12 issues 1975–1978*

Like his contemporary *Iron Jaw*, DC's *Conan* wannabe had a gimmick to distinguish him from the numerous other beetle-browed barbarians littering the publishing schedules of the time, in this case a demon hand which, like Elric's runesword Stormbringer, acts to protect its owner whether he likes it or not. Otherwise Claw is an identikit character inhabiting a world that looks and feels just like Conan's, which is unsurprising with practised *Conan* artist Ernie Chua working on issues 1–7. Writer David Micheline trots out all manner of monsters for Claw to conquer and throws in some eye-watering self-mutilation scenes for good measure, but the series remains undistinguished.~FJ

CLOAK AND DAGGER
Marvel: *4-issue miniseries 1983–1984, series one 11 issues, 2 Graphic Novels 1985–1987, series two 19 issues 1988–1991*

She's white, he's black, and they were runaways in New York when snatched from the street to be test subjects for narcotic substances. The pair escape, but they are oddly changed: he has acquired an enveloping, madness-inducing darkness (hence 'Cloak'), and she can emit cleansing, dazzling white light, and throw light-knives (hence 'Dagger'). Starting a mission to protect other runaways attracts the attention of Detective Bridget O'Reilly, who has no time for vigilantes. Her arguments cause them moments of doubt, while their successes are troubling to her certainty. And through all this, Cloak is very unhappy with aspects of his new powers and the way they make him dependent on Dagger. The miniseries makes for an interesting depiction of the early stages of a team: 'Are our goals and methods the right ones?', 'Do I really want to be tied to you indefinitely?' The characterisation is too thin to allow for any sustained or consistent arguments but writer Bill Mantlo gives it a good try. The artwork by Rick Leonardi and Terry Austin tells the story well, and supports the script in making the detective the most convincing and vibrant character.

The ongoing title picks up immediately after the miniseries, and the pair still have teething troubles. The priest they've taken shelter with wants Dagger away from the 'evil' Cloak and back to her normal life as a poor little rich girl, the detective comes across corruption in the police force but has a radical change of personality (5), C&D meet Spider-Man (3), lose their powers for a while (4), and there's barely a runaway child in sight. No, Cloak and Dagger have elected to help runaways indirectly, by fighting the drug trade, which means they never have to meet the brats, and they travel the world from 7 onwards. This change of direction takes away most of the comic's character, and without the soul-searching, the nagging detective and the sense of mission, *Cloak And Dagger* rapidly hops to the shelf marked 'Superhero Team (Generic)'. Bill Mantlo writes and Terry Austin inks throughout. Rick Leonardi pencils most of the early issues (1–6), but thereafter it's a different penciller every issue, including Mike Mignola (8) and Art Adams (9), who is a good choice for the story in that issue.

Bridging their first and second ongoing series, Cloak and Dagger starred in *Strange Tales*, where it was revealed that they owed their powers to their mutant natures, and they were thus able to join in all manner of mutant hijinks. The new series has the title *The Mutant Misadventures Of Cloak and Dagger*, and jumps into the middle of a story-line from *Strange Tales*, with Dagger on the side of the bad guys. 1–13 issues are written by Terry Austin and show a greater sense of humour than previously, and many of the story-lines seem to be played solely for laughs – which contrasts strangely with some traumatic events in the lives of the characters, such as Dagger's struggle with the disability she acquires at the end of Issue 1. Austin's writing does make it a more entertaining read, but the characters are now very far removed from those two runaways, and surely the shelf marked 'Mutant Superheroes (Generic)' is crowded enough already? Marvel must have been asking the same question, since 14 brought an abrupt change of direction. The cover reads "The misadventures are over! Now the terror begins', and the first page starts with a statement of their 'sworn' mission to protect others. Detective O'Reilly is back (almost) as before, investigating grisly deaths among runaways which seem to be linked to neo-Nazis. It's a relief to be back on track, thanks to writing from Steve Gerber and Terry Kavanagh, though by 17 the story is derailed and wildly out of control (goodbye, runaways – hello, demons). The final issue is a reinterpretation of Cloak and Dagger's origin story, which actually works rather well, adding nuances rather than rubbishing the original. There were many changes of art team throughout the series. The longest runs were Mike Vosburg in various capacities (3–11), and Rick Leonardi as penciller (12–16). There's nothing remarkable, but it works well enough. That sums up *Cloak and Dagger* overall, really: not a great series, but it could have been worse.~FC

COBALT BLUE
Innovation: *One-shot 1989*

An old prospector uncovers a long-buried alien city containing the last survivor of an alien race. On the other side of town another city rises containing the last survivor of another alien race, mortal enemy of the first; and events take their course. For a story Mike Gustovich claims he waited ten years to tell, it's all rather silly and pointless.~WJ

COBALT 60
Tundra: *4 issues 1992*

Vaughn Bodé created endearing stories about a cartoon character wandering a post-atomic wasteland and having to fight for his survival at every turn. Twenty years later Vaughn's son Mark and Larry Todd continue the story, adding a complexity absent from the original. As the original stories are reprinted alongside it makes for an uneasy mixture.~FP

COBRA
Viz: *12 issues 1990–1991*

Cigar-smoking, superpowered outlaw Cobra criss-crosses the galaxy in search of a legendary treasure that turns out to be the ultimate weapon. The action never stops as Cobra is pursued by agents of The Guild, eager to claim this new weapon for themselves. Buichi Terasawa's original Manga (translated by Marv Wolfman!) is a lot of fun but never really transcends its space-opera conventions.~NF

CODENAME: DANGER
Lodestone: *4 issues 1985–1986*

There are some interesting creators involved in this superhero/spy series but it's not their best work by any stretch of the imagination. Kyle Baker (2), Paul Smith (3) and Paul Gulacy (4) never really manage to raise any sparks from the scripts, dialogue at least being provided by Robert Loren Fleming in all issues.~NF

CODENAME: STRYKEFORCE
Image: *15 issues (0–14) 1994–1995*

Taking their name from their leader, Stryker, who was also a member of Cyberforce for the duration of this series, Strykeforce was a team of mercenaries that also included Kill Razor, Black Anvil, Bloodbow and Tempest. Created and written by Marc Silvestri and drawn by Brandon Peterson, the first two story-lines provide the team with a base in an ex-Russian nuclear submarine and see them join Stormwatch in battle against invading aliens, the Shu'rii. The series takes an unusual turn here as Bloodbow is killed and replaced by one of the aliens, who betrays her own kind to help the team. It is the revelation of this secret that precipitates the break-up of the group in *Cyberforce, Strykeforce: Opposing Forces*.

The creative team is a little unsettled after 8, but 10 sees Steve Gerber take over the scripts and Billy Tan Mung Khoy the artwork. With well-thought-out stories that were really just beginning to explore the characters, *Strykeforce* never quite got things right. The series wavered between humour and seriousness but was always entertaining. 0, the team's origin, actually appeared after 14.~NF

COLLIER'S

Fantagraphics: *3 issues 1991–1994*

With limited cartooning skills, David Collier provides extended slice-of-life stories that largely fail to engage or stimulate. His best issue is the third, recounting the life of Native American chief Grey Owl, who has a more complicated history than at first seems to be the case.~FP

COLOR

Print Mint: *1 issue 1971*

Conceived as storyboards for an unmade film, this has the distinction of being the first colour underground comic. As one would expect from noted psychedelic poster artist Victor Moscoso, this digest-sized comic looks ravishing, but is rarely troubled by anything approaching a story.~DAR

COLORS IN BLACK

Dark Horse: *4 issues 1995*

An agreement with film-maker Spike Lee resulted in this affirmative-action title giving new comic creators the chance to reach a wider audience. Resolutely uncommercial covers and the odd title probably dissuaded many people from sampling this anthology on publication, which is a shame as there's plenty of good material within. Each issue is loosely themed, with 3's examination of crime being the best, and if the writing occasionally hammers a point home in obvious fashion, there's also depth, subtlety and warmth. Sarah Byam and Gil Ashby's 'Larry Can't Wash It Off' in 2 is a fine, understated exploration of personal identity, and one has to wonder why Ashby's engaging watercoloured pencils and artists of the calibre of Greg Simanson haven't been seen before.~FP
Recommended: 2, 3

COMBAT KELLY

Marvel: *9 issues 1972–1973*

A Second-World-War platoon of ex-cons, one female, led by the Combat Kelly of the title. It doesn't get any more interesting than that except for the final issue, in which Marvel, giving a nod to the realism of combat, killed the lot of them.~WJ

COMCAT Graphic Novels

Although they were intended as the junior arm of Catalan Communications graphic-novel enterprises, many adult readers will find some Comcat graphic novels of interest. Their output consisted of four series – *Young Blueberry, Code XIII, Yoko, Vic And Bob*, and *The Magic Crystal*, plus the first volume in an intended series, *Kogaratsu*.

The three *Young Blueberry* graphic novels ('Blueberry's Secret', 'A Yankee Named Blueberry' and 'The Blue Coats') were produced in 1969 and 1970 by Charlier and Giraud at great speed while working on the regular Blueberry strips, and tell the story of how Blueberry became a hard-bitten sergeant in the army. A certain simplicity in plotting and use of open pen work (as opposed to the usual brush detail Giraud employed for the regular strip) gives them a hurried feel. If you like *Blueberry* you'll get something out of these, although they're appallingly coloured.

Code XIII is a series of thrillers by J. Van Hamme and W. Vance which show no sign of being produced for children. The first volume sets the tone for the later pair: a man is washed up half-dead, unable to remember who he is or how he got there. Befriended by a young couple, he has to flee when people start trying to kill him. With no clues to his identity but a tattoo on his shoulder reading 13 and the address on the back of a photo he doesn't recognise, he sets off to discover his identity. Whoever he is he knows a lot about killing, as evinced by the way he polishes off various agents of the mysterious Mongoose. The art's extremely tight and detailed, and the scripts are highly competent thrillers.

The three-volume *Magic Crystal* saga ('The Magic Crystal', 'Island of the Unicorn' and 'Aurelys' Secret') by Moebius and Marc Bati is a fantasy based on philosophical principles shared by the two creators, and drawn in a simplified version of their styles. Another series that was actually created for children is the adventures of *Yoko, Vic And Bob* by Roger Leloup. Two volumes appeared, 'Vulcan's Forge' and 'Three Suns Of Vina', both cheerful juvenile adventures in the Jules Verne mould. The first features a mysterious undersea race and 'Three Suns' sees them battling an evil scientist and his robots on a distant planet.

Finally *Kogaratsu: The Bloody Lotus* (1990) is a historical drama set in feudal Japan, written by Bosmans and drawn in a cod-Japanese print style by Michetz. Real Manga, fresh and dynamic, made the series rather pointless and it was not picked up when Catalan stopped publishing.~FJ

COME OUT COMIX

Portland Women's Resource Centre: *1 issue 1974*

As the title suggests, this is an autobiographical comic about coming out by Mary Wings. While the art is undeniably crude, the story remains gripping and eminently readable.~DAR
Recommended: 1

The COMET

!mpact: *18 issues 1991–1992*

This Mark Waid-scripted revival of the silly old *Mighty Comics* superhero started off with jolly stories about carefree orphan Rob Connors'

youthful attempts to fit the novelty of superheroics in with his journalist girlfriend and his ambition to make a career in baseball, which is all rather reminiscent of early Spider-Man stories. The series gradually became more serious as it revealed that the Comet's corny 'electrical charge' origin wasn't true and hid a nasty tale of alien experimentation. Unusually, the story has a very firm conclusion in the last issue and makes some curious moral points on the way about blood ties, selfishness versus selflessness, and corrupt sex-partners. The Comet is also a focus of *Crucible*, the series tying up all loose ends of the !mpact titles.~GK
Recommended: 7

COMET MAN
Marvel: *6-issue miniseries 1987*

An astronaut is destroyed by a comet, but reincarnated with amazing powers. Returning to Earth he faces the duplicity of his best friend, the abduction of his son and the death of his wife. Graced with striking Bill Sienkiewicz covers and strikingly bad interior art by a neophyte Kelley Jones, this was the attempt of actors Bill Mumy and Miguel Ferrer to add to the Marvel Universe. Never mind.~HS

Spümco COMIC BOOK
Marvel: *1 issue*
Dark Horse: *2 issues + 1996 to date*

There's always a problem with John Kricfalusi's animated shows, the most famous being *Ren And Stimpy*. While magnificently designed and animated, some are gut-bustingly funny, while others leave one scratching one's head going 'Wha..?'. If the latter permit the former the ratio is high enough that it's fair exchange, and so it is with the *Spümco Comic Book*. The comic uses the same contrasts as Kricfalusi's animation, switching from line drawings to painted panels for effect, and with madcap illustration from Kricfalusi, Mike Fontanelli and Jim Smith on the oversize format (12" x 9") it looks great. The main characters are Jimmy The Idiot, a slavering retard, and the redneck good ol' boy George, a man's man; the best place to start is with Jimmy's gut-busting chase for an elusive quarter in the second Dark Horse issue. Rarely is the spirit of animation so successfully transferred to comics. While the portrayal of Jimmy is bound to offend some, others will find the depiction of bodily functions gross, so be warned. In a fine show of moral hypocrisy, Marvel, the company that publishes superheroes willing to eviscerate or kill on a monthly basis, apparently decided Kricfalusi's work was too distasteful, prompting the move to Dark Horse. It appears to have worked out better for all concerned, with a $1 reduction in cover price and better paper to boot.~WJ
Recommended: Marvel 1, Dark Horse 1–2

COMICO CHRISTMAS SPECIAL
Comico: *One-shot 1988*

Doug Wheeler supplies a selection of unashamedly heartwarming off-beat stories with Christmas as the uniting theme. Contributing artists Ken Holewczynski, Bernie Mirault, Tim Sale, and the teams of Steve Rude and Al Williamson, and Bill Willingham and Chris Warner, all excel, and you'd have to be a humbug of enormous proportions not to be charmed by this sentimental selection.~FP
Recommended: 1

Tex Avery's COMICS AND STORIES
Dark Horse: *4-issue miniseries 1996*

One of four Dark Horse titles featuring Tex Avery characters, *Comics and Stories* has writers like Scott Shaw and Mark Martin, but neither seem to be inspired by the antics of Bad Luck Blackie or Meathead and Screwball Squirrel. Jay Stephens comes closest to matching the appearance of the cartoons (see, for example, 'Son Of King Size Canary' in 3) but overall the title's nowhere near as interesting as a video of the cartoons themselves.~NF

COMICS GREATEST WORLD
Dark Horse: *12 issues 1993*

Dark Horse introduce a new line of superheroes in this action-packed tour guide to four areas of their new world. Steel Harbour is the best observed, a run-down industrial city home to Barb Wire, The Machine and Motorhead, all of whom graduated into their own series (and Wolf Pack, who didn't). Golden City is clean and safe the way cities used to be, run by Amazing Grace and her team of superpowered agents including Mecha, Rebel and Titan. Arcadia's administration is corrupt to the core and home to X, Ghost and the lesser known Pit Bulls and Monster. Aliens observe in each four-issue arc (one per location) before homing in on the desert area of Cinnibar Flats, finding Division 13, humans who've been mutated through exposure to something emanating from The Vortex. It's the Vortex that's the crux of the slim plot uniting the stories, and *Out Of The Vortex* continues the mystery. There's some excellent artwork, particularly Chris Warner on *X*, Adam Hughes on *Ghost* and Paul Chadwick's *King Tiger*.~WJ

COMIX BOOK
Curtis: *3 issues 1974–1975*
Kitchen Sink: *2 issues (4–5) 1975*

A bizarre idea. Superhero publishers Marvel note the popularity of underground comix five years after everyone else, so decide to produce one of their own. But hey, just in case those crazy underground cartoonists include sex and drug use in their work why not put it out under another imprint? Despite the warped logic of

wanting to absorb something successful, but only if it can conform to their corporate standards, *Comix Book* manages to entice a fair number of the underground greats over five issues. It's a patchy anthology, though, with only Howard Cruse, John Pound, Sharon Rudahl and Skip Williamson consistently approaching top form, although Art Spiegelman previews *Maus* in 2. The marriage between Marvel and the underground appears to have ended over the matter of creators' rights, so Kitchen Sink published material already commissioned for the following issues. Ironically and entirely coincidentally they're the best of the run, with 5 a real quality package. In addition to Cruse, Pound, Rudahl and Williamson there's good stuff from Bob Armstrong, Leslie Cabarga, Gary Hallgren, Richards and Murphy; and Justin Green finishes the very odd 'We Fellow Travellers' started in the first issue.~FP
Recommended: 5

COMIX INTERNATIONAL
Warren: *5 issues, 1974–1977*

These are collections of the colour stories from Warren's regular horror titles (*Creepy, Eerie, Vampirella, Spirit*). In 1 all the artwork is by Rich Corben, whose style and colours are lush to the point of claustrophobia and can induce queasiness with the most innocuous scene, let alone when he's depicting a face pecked raw by gulls (grisly photorealism in 5). From 2 onwards, there's a mixture of artists, and the variety is welcome. The writing is always competent, and the artwork well above average, but few of the stories really stick in the mind. The best is Berni Wrightson's 'Muck Monster' from 2. It's yet another version of *Frankenstein*, but beautifully done.~FC
Recommended: 2

COMMIES FROM MARS
Last Gasp: *6 issues 1982–1987*

Largely second-rate underground title produced periodically by Tim Boxell. The name comes from a repeated satirical strand in which Martians have invaded earth and are trying to spread their Communist ideals among an unwitting populace. Each issue also had a separate theme (passion and romance in 4, crime in 5). Later issues contain excellent work by Hunt Emerson and Peter Kuper.~NF

CONAN The Adventurer
Marvel: *14 issues 1994–1995*

A short-lived Conan title, set in his youth, to tie in with the animated TV series of the same name. Roy Thomas churned out reliable but slight single-issue stories, drawn by Rafael Kayanan, who seemed to have picked up on a

lot of superficial rendering schticks from Barry Smith's work on the character in the 1970s. Sadly this is without the necessary accompanying design and story-telling skills.~GK

CONAN The Barbarian
Marvel: *294 issues, 12 annuals, 5 Giant-size 1970–1993*

For many years almost any issue of *Conan* provided reliable entertainment, but it never quite matched its enormous early promise and certainly hobbled along in a horribly drawn-out decline during most of its final decade. Conan was created in 1932 by pulp-magazine writer Robert E. Howard and is the most famous sword-and-sorcery character, a genre almost unknown in the comic format before this successful attempt. The genre consists, very basically, of simple heroes wandering about primitive civilisations battling supernatural enemies such as monsters and wizards, usually winning through using a combination of brute strength, bloody violence and dumb luck.

The character presented in comics by Roy Thomas and the young British artist Barry Smith (now Windsor-Smith) didn't match one's idea of a typical barbarian. With his nice long hair and clean bare chest the lithe young Conan looked like no one so much as Jim Morrison of The Doors before his dissipation. The art on the first half-dozen issues, like all Smith's early comics, is notable only for its huge debt to Jack Kirby's work, but he soon began to experiment with sets of congruent frames in which each picture differed only slightly from the last. This quasi-cinematic technique, often emphasised by the absence of word balloons or captions, is derived from the work of the EC artist Bernard Krigstein, probably, in Smith's case, via Jim Steranko's 1960s Marvel work. Simultaneously, Smith, aping his favourite painters, started packing his panels with ornate detail. Thomas, who is rarely less than competent, responded with increasingly ambitious prose, and even some of Howard's atrocious poetry. Such obviously carefully crafted dramatic comics had not appeared in the USA since the heyday of EC in the early 1950s.

Smith drew 1–24 (apart from 17–18, by Gil Kane). Many won industry awards and are widely regarded as classics. 11's 'Rogues In The House' is a good representative story. Conan is jailed thanks to his treacherous girlfriend Jenna. He swaps his freedom, stopping only to do something quite appalling to Jenna, for a hit job on a corrupt priest whose house has been taken over by his King Kong-like friend. Ultraviolence ensues. 'The Song Of Red Sonja' in 24 shows the style taken right over the top. All inquisitive readers will want to try these early Conans, though they may find Smith's figures stiff and over-decorated and Thomas's captions florid and pompous, if not unfaithful to Howard. The team's best work on the character was the 'Red Nails' sequence, originally published in black and white magazines but reissued in colour in the 1980s *Conan Special Edition* and, to great advantage, at very large size in *Marvel Treasury Edition* 4 (1975), which also includes 'Rogues In The House'.

Thomas decided from the start that each year of the comic would cover a year in Conan's life, which caused the comic, while he was writing it, to be sometimes crammed with decent stories, as in the first twenty issues, and at other times rather short of them. There were some good ideas for filling gaps Howard had left, such as teaming Conan with Michael Moorcock's Elric of Melnibone in 14–15. Unable to use Howard's often superior stories of the older Conan and lacking the rights to the books written by other authors, Thomas later resorted to adapting *Kothar The Barbarian* novellas by Gardner Fox, who was better suited to science fiction.

John Buscema took over the art from 25. He'd been the original choice of artist, but Marvel were unwilling to match his page rate on an untried title where extra expenditure was already being incurred in paying for rights. Once aboard, though, he drew most of the next 165 issues. His Conan was much brawnier than Smith's, looking for the first time as though he really could lift and swing the heavy swords and axes he needed so often. Buscema was consistently good, usually inked by the reliable Filipino artist Ernie Chua (later known as Chan), though he couldn't help looking rather plain after Smith's baroque excesses. Most issues from 25 to 56 are unexceptional, though 37, gruesomely violent in places, is a good Howard adaptation by Gil Kane and Neal Adams, reprinted from the black and white magazine *Savage Sword of Conan*. Conan's only interests are sex and violence and he doesn't much like conversation, so the stories require good supporting characters other than the procession of cruel kings, mad wizards, grasping merchants and treacherous whores. They don't often get them, though. The introduction of Red Sonja in 23, lifted and rejigged by Thomas from one of Howard's non-Conan stories, was popular. She persistently refuses Conan's advances, reflecting the early 1970s atmosphere of female liberation. Tara, the tomboy acrobat who appears in 52–57, is also not a bad character. These issues reintroduce 11's crooked nobleman Murilo, now turned mercenary. 57 is beautifully drawn, in his slightly cute style, by Mike Ploog, and events therein force Conan to

leave the comforts of the city for a while.

58–100 are among the most interesting of the run. Derived, remarkably, from a single Howard short story, they cover the three years Conan spent in what was, for him, a relatively mature relationship with Belit, Queen Of The Black Coast, leader of the Black Corsair pirates. These issues differ from most others in having a long running supporting character, and in deviating from the usual Western-derived Conan settings of dusty plain, wooded riverside and tavern in the town, by being largely set on sailing ships. Belit is a much more convincing cast member than the silly Red Sonja (who, for contrast, also appears), and issues from this period are a refreshing read. Buscema continued to draw most, inked at first by the excellent Steve Gan, and from 70, by Ernie Chan again.

The 'Black Coast' story was marred by many fill-ins, though the two stories reprinted from *Savage Sword* (in 78 & 87) are good. The first is a classic pairing with Red Sonja, notable for some of Buscema's best art. Beware 79–81, drawn by a young Howard Chaykin. There are some curious things in later chapters, such as big blue lions and men riding on eagles, but the conclusion in the double-sized 100 is touching and quite eerie. Thomas was unable to match this standard before leaving with 115 in 1981. J.M. DeMatteis took over the writing, introducing a couple of clownish kid sidekicks, which doesn't make for good reading. Gil Kane was back as artist from 127, a sad tale that he also inked, notably, as in the remainder of his issues to 134 he's saddled with poor inkers and Bruce Jones' scripts are riddled with inappropriate wise-cracking dialogue. Buscema returned to the art with 135, but seemed to have lost interest unless able to ink his pencils himself. The stories became formulaic and there was no overall direction.

146 is a pleasant exception, written by Mary Jo Duffy. A drunken Conan is teamed up with three young wizardesses with personalities like Josie & The Pussycats. Reader reaction was polarised. Michael Fleisher, who wrote from 150, simply rehashed old single-issue story ideas, though everything improved for 155–159 as John Buscema plotted the comic, endowing a flavour of the Thomas years. Fleisher then reverted to the formula of having Conan, riding alone, perhaps talking to his horse, alerted by cries and rescuing a string of witless female characters from various gangs of evildoers. In 172 Jim Owsley introduced Tetra, a new, and continuing, resourceful female character who turned out to be a witch-queen, and she seemed to inspire Buscema's drawing. Owsley wrote a good story full of twists and political intrigue, and some

excellent dialogue, some of which was about Conan not saying certain things. Buscema's final issue was 190, and he was replaced by Val Semeiks, who tried initially a little too hard to be like Barry Smith. The now multi-charactered story climaxed well in 200. After Owsley's departure *Conan* became chaotic in the hands of various old hacks until 232, which, with a cover pastiching that of the first issue, returned to Conan's youth in the frozen north. The nine issues set there look very rough by contrast with the first few from 1970.

Roy Thomas returned with 241 and wrote off all the stories since he'd left as a busy but inconsequential couple of years for Conan. The rapidly improving, and soon superb, Mike Docherty was the most expressive artist since Buscema, and, with a Falstaffian foil for Conan called Hobb providing light relief, the comic was an above-average read until cancellation. A great many of the first ten years' Conan stories were reprinted in ninety-eight issues of the excellent black and white magazine *Conan Saga*, with annotations and some new Smith covers, published from 1987 onwards.~GK

Recommended: 11–13, 16, 19–24, 57, 70–72, 100, 127, 'Red Nails'

CONAN THE KING

Marvel: *55 issues 1980–1989*

Known as *King Conan* for 1–19, this double-length comic delineated the mighty barbarian's late middle age after he had become King of Aquilonia and taken the harem girl Zenobia as his bride, a period not covered by his creator, Robert E. Howard. Their son, Prince Conn, was showcased, either behaving recklessly, requiring rescue action from Dad, or inquisitively requesting from old buffers tales of his father's past bold strokes.

1–4 adapt L. Sprague de Camp and Lin Carter's *Conan Of Aquilonia* stories and 5–8 Sprague de Camp and Bjorn Nyberg's novel *Conan The Avenger*. These eight, by Roy Thomas and John Buscema, are all good, if a little dense. Other seemingly less interested creators, including writers Doug Moench and Don Kraar and artists Mike Docherty (not doing his best work) and Geof Isherwood, slogged on but there is not an interesting issue in the rest of the run. This is not the place to start with this character. Try *Conan The Barbarian* instead.~GK

CONAN THE SAVAGE

Marvel: *10 issues 1995–1996*

Marvel cancelled *Savage Sword Of Conan* and swiftly replaced it with this, also a black and white magazine, featuring rather similar stories to those that would have appeared in its forerunner. It includes contributions from the likes of Roy Thomas and John Buscema, although the work of both seems rather weary after so many years producing Conan stories, Chuck Dixon and Rudy Nebres. There doesn't seem to be any discernible difference between the two titles. So, if you liked *Savage Sword Of Conan*...~FJ

CONCRETE

Dark Horse: *10 issues, 1 special 1987–1989, One-shot ('Earth Day Special') 1990, 4-issue miniseries ('Fragile Creature') 1991–1992, 2-issue microseries ('Eclectica') 1993, 4-issue miniseries ('Killer Smile') 1994, 6-issue miniseries ('Think Like A Mountain')1996*

Paul Chadwick is hardly the world's most prolific cartoonist, but each one of his Concrete stories is well thought out, gripping, and has a point. Although some may find the eco-sensitivity of his later books annoying, he is always careful to point out both sides of the argument and present enough information to allow readers to make their own minds up, in an action-packed format. His artwork is precise but flowing, centred around meticulous hatching and modulated use of heavy and fine line. His occasional weakness for cosmic splash pages is more than balanced by the simple but expressive way he draws his central character, who has all the visual charm of a boulder.

Having débuted in early issues of *Dark Horse Presents*, by the solo series Concrete had evolved into a comic about character. Its first thought is: How does Ron Lithgow, his brain transplanted into a huge, alien cyborg, feel about being near-invulnerable but trapped in a body he doesn't understand, unable to touch, unable to have sex, but capable of walking along the sea bed for an hour or climbing Everest unaided? Throughout the series Concrete is finding out more about himself both in terms of physiognomy and emotionally. Scientist Maureen Vonnegut, who's been assigned to carry out continual testing on his body and whom he soon falls in love with, is key to both channels of exploration.

Concrete sets out both to earn a living and to do things ordinary men cannot. In the 1989 colour special he is hoaxed by two artists into thinking the aliens who created him have returned. In 'Fragile Creature' he takes a job on a fantasy film to defray the increasing costs of being a huge rock monster living in a fragile world. 'Killer Smile' is a change of pace as Larry Monroe, his aide-de-camp, is kidnapped by a couple of psychotic teenagers on the run. Chadwick's answer to *Natural Born Killers*, it's both funny and insightful, getting behind the romance of killing. The 'Earth Day Special' introduces a number of devices Chadwick will routinely employ in later series, such as drawing landscapes showing what's beneath the ground as well as above it. His stories are more monologues on preserving the earth, while Charles Vess contributes some illustrations to random selections of Thoreau and Moebius turns in a long, wordless tale of two explorers encountering a new, alien civilisation. In 'Think Like A Mountain' Concrete is involved with an Earth First! expedition to save virgin forests in Washington State, at first as an observer and then, comically, as a fake Bigfoot. Each 'Eclectica' contains a couple of short, humorous strips and a series of watercolour paintings, done as commissions, in which the influence of Moebius shows strongly.~FJ

Recommended: 1–6, 'Fragile Creature' 1–4
Collections: The Complete Concrete (1–10), *Fragile Creature* (1–4), *Killer Smile* (1–4), *Land And Sea* (1, 2), *A New Life* (3, 4), *Odd Jobs* (5, 6)

CONGO BILL
DC: *7 issues 1954–1955*

Various stories, typically two or three per issue, featuring 'ace adventurer' Congo Bill and his sidekick Janu the Jungle Boy. It's a shame they're such boring, pompous characters since work has clearly gone into this comic. The Nick Cardy art is clean and attractive, and the stories involve plots rather than just a succession of fight scenes. Admittedly, they're not compelling plots and they usually hinge on some piece of jungle lore that Congo Bill reveals only at the end, and in that smug, plonking way that makes you want to thump him. The most interesting aspect of the comic is probably the large number of stories involving film-making. They appear in nearly every issue and make it clear that *Congo Bill* grew out of the Saturday serials. Was the comic consciously trying to convince people that *Tarzan* was shot in the Congo and not in California?~FC

CONGORILLA
DC: *4-issue miniseries 1992–1993*

Starting in *Action* from 248 in the late 1950s, Congorilla was a means of attracting interest to the near moribund Congo Bill strip. Jungle explorer Bill acquired the ability to transfer his consciousness into a giant golden gorilla, while being tied tightly to a tree by a scantily clad jungle boy. The latter part was essential to the ritual as the gorilla transferred its consciousness into Bill, leading to much hijinks and boffo yocks. This fine concept was revived in *Swamp Thing* Annual 3's guest appearance, handled there with as straight a face as possible. Sadly thereafter the Golden Ape of the Jungle was revived for a grim'n'gritty miniseries. Incoherent where it wasn't merely stupid: the resultant mess proves that not every old character can be successfully-spin doctored.~HS

CONQUEROR
Harrier: *9 issues, 1984–1985, Special 1987*

Initially a gag twist-ending strip in the fanzine *Bem, Conqueror* was extended to a full-length strip as Harrier Comics spun-off from *Bem*. After an initially favourable response, the suspiciously familiar adventures of the spaceship 'Conqueror' and her motley crew had a certain musty charm, helped considerably by the sedate artwork of Dave Harwood, whose renderings gave a very 1950s, *Boy's Own Paper* look to the series. There was also one issue of a companion title, *Conqueror Universe*, which was stretching the idea a little too thin.~HS

CONQUEROR OF THE BARREN EARTH
DC: *4-issue miniseries 1985*

Once humanity has colonised the universe attentions are turned back to the home planet. By this time Earth is a ravaged wasteland populated by assorted human mutations. Cadet Jinal is assigned to recover the planet wearing folded down thigh boots and a nice blue short skirt in an ordinary sword-and-sorcery romp with a dubious moral subtext. The series débuted in *Warlord* 63.~FP

Marvel Superhero CONTEST OF CHAMPIONS
Marvel: *3-issue miniseries 1982*

Two mix-and-match squads of twelve superheroes must locate hidden quarters of a golden globe. The Collector will be returned to life should Grand Master's team win the game. They don't, but luckily neither the editor nor any of the omnipotents present notices and it's welcome back, Collector. Average precursor to the crossover titles that were to strangle Marvel Comics.~WJ

COOCHY COOTY Men's Comics
Print Mint: *1 issue 1970*

To date this is still the only solo title by *Zap* regular Robert Williams, and it contains some of the most obsessively detailed artwork and truly bizarre subject-matter ever seen on the printed page. The fact that the lead story is titled 'Coochy Cooty and the Gorilla Women of the Third Reich' speaks volumes. This is not a comic for everyone, but for a certain type of reader it's an absolutely essential purchase.~DAR

Recommended: 1

COPS
DC: *15 issues 1988–1989*

Doug Moench does his best to instill some sort of sophistication into a comic developed to showcase yet another toy at a time when, in place of the bar code, comics sold through comic shops got 'DC Comics aren't just for kids!'. The Central Organization of Police Specialists consists of different law-enforcement stereotypes with big guns fighting against villains with names like The Big Boss, Dr Badvibes, Buttons McBoomboom and 'Junior' Berserko. Pat Broderick's unrealistic style doesn't help much. The Bart Sears issues (3 and 4) are a better attempt at humanising the plastic policemen.~NF

COPYBOOK TALES
Slave Labor: *3 issues + 1996 to date*

'Portrait of the artist as a Fanboy' runs the header to this, apparently, semi-autobiographical tale of daydreaming young comics fans and the ambitious young adults they become. It flips back and forth between the two eras in a somewhat disconcerting manner. Continued from a popular mini-comic, the stories are underplayed and engaging.~HS

CORMAC MAC ART
Dark Horse: *4-issue miniseries 1990*

Uninspired Roy Thomas adaptation of four of Robert E. Howard's *Cormac MacArt* stories. Tying them into one story-line may have seemed like a good idea to avoid repetition but there's too much plot to get a decent feel for the character. E.R. Cruz's artwork is static and lacks any real sense of atmosphere. If you must know, the late 5th-century warrior fights druids, Picts, monsters and gods when hired to find the kidnapped daughter of a British chieftain.~NF

CORN FED Comics
Cartoonists Co-Op: *2 issues 1972–1973*

An early solo title from the inimitable Kim Deitch, *Corn Fed* features his 'usual' mixture of midgets, aliens and 'America's favourite psychic detective' Miles Mycroft. The stories frequently revolve around a nostalgia for the 1920s and 1930s and old entertainers of various sorts. Deitch was to go on to greater things, but there's certainly much to enjoy here.~DAR
Recommended: 2

CORPORATE CRIME COMICS
Kitchen Sink: *2 issues 1977, 1979*

A good mixture of contemporary and historical corporate-sponsored injustices, union-bashing, swindling and tragic lack of concern for basic employee safety. Some, like the case of Karen Silkwood, have since become well publicised, others have been forgotten. Sadly, the message conveyed is that those with enough money can get away with anything.~FP

CORTO MALTESE
NBM: *8 volumes 1986–1990*

Hugo Pratt's *Corto Maltese* books, originally published in Europe, are among the most gripping adventure yarns ever told in the comic-book format. They're the adventures of a mysterious Maltese sailor who seems to wash up wherever history is being made in the early years of this century, from the Easter Rising in Ireland to the Russian Revolution. What distinguishes them from even the best American adventure strips like *Terry And The Pirates* is a philosophical depth and a sense of creative exploration. Corto exists in a world full of fantastic possibilities, and doesn't question meeting Oberon and his fairies in Ireland or having mystical experiences among the cabbalistic courtyards of old Venice. But while *A Midwinter Morning's Dream* has its whimsical fairies, it also successfully explores a difficult issue like the founding of Sinn Fein in a way rarely seen in popular literature.

Corto also exists very much in a 'real' world, full of accurate detail, meeting historical characters in books like *Corto In Africa*, a complex exploration of the breakdown of empire in North Africa, full of Lawrence-like agitators, foreign spies, hard-pressed British soldiers and independence-minded natives. By propelling Corto into the centre of the conflict Pratt can explore the various viewpoints using significant characters such as the mercurial young warrior Cush. Hugo Pratt was a great traveller, and based many of the details of his stories around his own experiences, producing hundreds of sketches on his journeys that would later bring his strips to life, commenting sagaciously on the cultures he was presenting in his introductions (sadly omitted from the NBM editions). Corto travels the world in the last possible days of true adventure, before World War II destroyed the glamour. Pratt never explains him, never reveals all the secrets. His agenda is often inexplicable, selfless heroism followed by self-seeking machinations. Is he hero or anti-hero? His behaviour is generally better than the extraordinary cast of characters he becomes involved with, but that's not saying much.

Throughout the series, from which there are a lot of longer stories still untranslated, Pratt is refining his cartooning style in the same way that Toth pared his down over the years – from pretty basic to complete minimalism. Influenced by the broad brushwork of Caniff and Roy Crane, among many others, there is a rough edge to Pratt's artwork even at its most polished. By *Corto In Siberia*, a long and extremely rewarding chase across Russia by train in search of a hoard of smuggled gold, there is a vast gulf between the foreground figures, drawn by Pratt, and the background details (cars and trains) by his assistants, which almost look as though they've been cut out of a book and pasted in. *Fable Of Venice* is the first Corto story in his mature style, expressionistic, ornately patterned, with form often reduced to vague shapes. It also reflects a change in approach to plotting in which actions become even more oblique and the exploration of ideas comes to the fore rather than sitting within a plot-driven structure. But it's also a cracking Masonic mystery in which Pratt draws upon childhood memories of visiting Venice's Jewish quarter to conjure up atmospheric alleyways, hidden gateways guarded by magical symbols and secret societies within societies.

Read *Corto Maltese* and you're reading the work of a master story-teller, magnificent in his confidence.~FJ

Recommended: *Banana Congo, The Brazilian Eagle, Corto In Africa, Corto In Siberia, Fable Of Venice, A Midwinter Morning's Dream, The Early Years, Voodoo For President*

Michael Moorcock's The Chronicles of CORUM
First: *12-issue limited series 1987–1988*

Corum is one aspect of Michael Moorcock's 'Eternal Champion' series: the sole survivor of an elder race, he doesn't escape his encounter with the Mabden unscathed. Luckily, he's given a replacement eye able to see into other dimensions, and a replacement demon's hand, which prove both boon and curse. Adapting *The Knight Of The Swords* and its two successors at four issues apiece, Mike Baron's scripts never really humanise Corum in any fashion, and the feeling is that those who've not read the original novels might be left scratching their heads. It doesn't stand in the way of a good story, though. The highlight of the run is the magnificent Mike Mignola artwork, particularly as inked by Kelley Jones in 3–6. Although Jones remains to ink succeeding pencillers Jackson Guice, Ken Hooper and Jill Thompson, none match the elegance of Mignola's finely rendered pages.~WJ
Recommended: 3–6

COSMIC BOY
DC: *4-issue miniseries 1986–1987*

Legion of Super-Heroes co-founder Cosmic Boy and his significant other Night Girl become trapped in the twentieth century. They have an inconclusive scuffle with the Time Trapper, and find their way home with the plot continued in *Legion Of Super-Heroes*. Cos comes across as an amazingly liberated guy who's not threatened by his girlfriend's vastly superior strength, but that's the sole, and accidental, interesting aspect.~HS

COSMIC ODYSSEY
DC: *4-issue miniseries 1988–1989*

Complete gobbledygook in terms of what's meant to be happening, but Jim Starlin's characterisation makes for a surprisingly

successful read, and Mike Mignola's artwork (after early reminders of Walt Simonson) is splendidly appropriate. The Anti-Life Equation is discovered to have sentience and a desire to return to the universe that contains Earth, New Genesis and Apokolips. Darkseid and High Father decide to recruit a band of superheroes to battle the four aspects of the Equation that are threatening four planets – Earth, Rann, Thangor and Xanshi – the destruction of any two of which will cause a cosmic upheaval which will destroy the galaxy. Why this will happen is nonsense, and Starlin willfully disregards what is already known about Jack Kirby's Fourth World, let alone facts about characters as diverse as The Demon, Dr Fate, Orion and John Stewart. Mignola's efforts deserved better.~NF
Collection: *Cosmic Odyssey* (1–4)

COSMIC POWERS
Marvel: *6-issue limited series 1994*

Oddly structured limited series essentially comprising solo tales of various cosmic entities. A framing sequence dictated by Thanos links all the stories and takes centre stage in the first and last issues as he pulls strings around Terrax, Jack of Hearts, Ganymede, Legacy, Morg and Tyrant. Ron Marz writes and Various Artists pencil forty pages of story per issue with as much substance and reading-time as a regular twenty-page comic, owing to the profusion of double-page spreads and single-page panels. Exceptional artwork would merit the format. This doesn't. Plots go through the motions. 4 starring Legacy, the 1990s Captain Marvel, is the pick.~APS

COSMIC POWERS UNLIMITED
starring Silver Surfer
Marvel: *5 issues 1995–1996*

Thick, glossy, sixty-four-page mothers weighing in at a hundred grams apiece.
Each issue anthologises two or three cosmic tales, many spotlighting the newer generation of cosmic heroes: Kismet, Sundragon, Ganymede and Xenith. More established entities such as Silver Surfer, Quasar and Beta Ray Bill ensure a blue-chip feel. The largely unconnected stories are scripted by Many Writers and pencilled by Even More Artists.

It is a sad reflection on the series that the traditional Silver Surfer, Thanos and Captain Marvel openers in 1 stand head and shoulders above the subsequent newer concepts. Describing these as ordinary would be unwarranted flattery and the Lunatik short in 3 leaps out as an appallingly blatant *Hitch-Hiker's Guide To The Galaxy* rip-off.~APS

THE COUGAR
Atlas: *2 issues 1975*

Dull genre title about a stuntman who sees off a vampire, then a werewolf. The blurb for issue 3 promised 'the most devastatingly different superhero of all time', and for once there might have been truth to the claim since the Cougar broke his spine in 2. Alas, the third issue was never published.~FP

COUNTER-PARTS
Tundra: *3-issue miniseries 1993*

A wealth of interesting concepts and a surfeit of alliterative dialogue characterise this strange story about a future where personalities can be switched and replaced. When composite body parts from an experiment gone wrong assume their own agenda, allying themselves with rebels, the social structure begins to collapse. Obviously not to be taken seriously, there are amusing moments but by and large *Counter-Parts* is too clever for its own good, sacrificing coherency and structure for each opportunity to include another pun or whimsical thought.~FP

A COUPLE OF WINOS
Fantagraphics: *One-shot 1991*

Adapted from one of the autobiographical short stories collected in *South Of No North*, Charles Bukowski's low-key slice of dirty realism really is about a couple of winos – two unnamed drifters who get work laying railway tracks, before blowing their meagre wages on whores and booze. The Moebius-influenced line-style of German artist Mathias Schultheiss perfectly captures Bukowski's bleak view of human nature.~AL
Recommended: 1

COUTOO
Dark Horse: *One-shot 1994*

Collected from its appearances in *Cheval Noir* (8–11), *Coutoo* is a strange thriller about a murderer who's been killed but whose spirit keeps moving on. A detective whose father killed Coutoo (meaning 'knife') is assigned to the latest slayings and begins to find odd clues to the real nature of the killer and his father's recent illness. Illustrated and written by Andreas in a style that's looser and more experimental than his Rork stories, this is atmospheric and nicely done but, in the end, lacks depth.~NF

COVENTRY
Fantagraphics: *1 issue + 1996 to date*

A great cover of a small frog heralds Bill Willingham's new series. The title, which is the only other item on the cover, refers to an American state very similar to Oregon, except that it's also a nexus for magic, with assorted supernatural visitations and occurrences affecting day-to-day life. Claudia Nevermore is the person to call when you want something sorted out. The first issue gives little away, but introduces several eccentric characters and lots of frogs, all extremely nicely drawn by Willingham. One to watch.~FP

COVER-UP LOWDOWN
Rip Off: *1 issue 1977*

Flip-book pocket-sized compendium of every conspiracy theory going from Jay Kinney and Paul Mavrides. Amongst other pieces it includes such gems as 'Lee Harvey Oswald: Robot Or Rastafarian?' and 'You Killed Kennedy And Here's The Proof!', but the undoubted highlight is an inspired self-assemble moebius-strip flow-chart of conspiracies, linking the Vatican to Will Eisner and the Beach Boys to Satan.~DAR

COVERED IN GLORY The 26th North Carolina At Gettysburg
Heritage Collection: One-shot 1996

The second in Heritage Collection's series of comics imparting the history of the American Civil War. This is far more successful than its predecessor, *Shiloh*, in its presentation of a decisive battle, working because it doesn't attempt to show the entire battle from numerous aspects. Wayne Vansant's art is excellent, and his approach of humanising the conflict by focusing on ordinary troops as well as the top ranks makes for an enjoyable history lesson.~FP

THE COWBOY WALLY SHOW
Dolphin Books/Doubleday: *Graphic Novel 1988*

A hilarious satire on the American media, especially television. An obnoxious and rather dense TV star is interviewed about his career: cue flashbacks and behind-the-scenes revelations. Will particularly impress anyone who has ever thought how bad American TV is, especially cable and local programming, but funny enough to entertain all comers. Kyle Baker had impressed many as a top-notch superhero artist, mostly inker. His genuine talent as a writer of humour came as some surprise.~GL
Recommended

COYOTE
Epic: *16 issues 1983–1986*

Returning from a self-imposed exile from mainstream comics, hot 1970s writer Steve Englehart, with artist Marshall Rogers, originally presented Coyote in 2–8 of the black and white *Eclipse* anthology title. At Epic Englehart and new artist Steve Leialoha continued the story of Sly Santangelo, shape-changing superhero educated in 'the ways of the were-world'. For purely personal reasons Sly, as Coyote, is waging a war against 'an international conclave of unknown dimensions, dedicated to toppling the North American Governments', called The Shadow Cabinet. Leialoha's fine artwork on 1–2, beautifully coloured by the artist and Steve Oliff, is ideally suited to Englehart's ambitious combination of South American mysticism, Arab/Israeli conflict and security-service conspiracy. Sadly deadline problems forced Leialoha off the title.

He was replaced by the inexperienced Chas Truog, whose slapdash pencils brought the flaws in Englehart's scripting into sharper relief. His headstrong, arrogant central character was difficult to warm to, the sub-Castaneda waffle quickly became tiresome, and the conflict between Coyote and The Shadow Cabinet mutated into a mundane alien-invasion plot. Finding an inker for the crude, and apparently unpopular, Truog also proved problematic. Bob Wiacek, Richard Howell and Frank Springer all tried their hand, with varying degrees of success. 7–10 also featured back-up strip 'The Djinn', an entertaining Middle Eastern adventure written by Englehart and drawn by Steve Ditko, one of this legendary creator's most satisfying late works. The first part, inked by Steve Leialoha, is especially fine, and shows how good artwork brings out the best in Englehart's writing.~AL
Recommended: 7–10

CRAP
Fantagraphics: *7 issues 1993–1995*

J.R. Williams, who writes and draws *Crap*, is a very funny and accomplished underground cartoonist. His 'Bad Boys' strips (collected by Fantagraphics as *Completely Bad Boys*) are packed with hilarious incident depicted in tiny, simple but characterful drawings. Much of his early work, including brilliantly inventive and anarchic wordless minicomics such as *Mr. Artistic And Mr. Badd*, entirely in silhouette, is collected in *Fun House* (published by Starhead in 1993).

Crap presents more conventional, albeit mature, work. Most of the lead strips concern the tribulations of an old Williams character, Milt the Mutation, his socially inept housemates, and their various addictive behaviours. Sadly, Williams' drawing style seems to have relaxed too much and there are fewer panels, and they're larger and more repetitive. It's all a little lame and predictable, rather like a television sitcom. The characters, a cowardly aspiring writer who drinks too much, a fragile recovering bulimic, an extreme feminist, a jock and a nerd, are too like real boring and pathetic people to be very funny. The dry, perhaps would-be educational tone is

maintained in autobiographical work such as 'My Bad Trip' in 6.

It's not all disappointing, though. 'Milt The Mutation Goes To Heaven' in 7 is marvellously bleak, as is 'The Junkeez', a violent fantasy about consumerism gone wrong, and 'Sheep', in 5, is a self-mocking piece about non-conformist ranting. Williams remains an interesting talent well worth investigating.~GK

CRASH RYAN
Epic: *4-issue miniseries 1984–1985*

Writer and artist Ron Harris revives the classic adventure strip with 1930s flyer Crash Ryan having to face a pulp villain called The Doom. Sadly, talent doesn't match ambition, and while the plot is fine adventure, Harris' artwork falls short of the folk he's trying to emulate, particularly in a rushed issue 4. Crash re-appears in *Dark Horse Presents* 44–46.~WJ

CRAZY
Marvel: *94 issues, 1 special 1973–1983*

Crazy was one of many shameless rip-offs of *Mad*, and it's only surprising feature was its longevity. Like *Mad* it was a mixture of film and TV spoofs, text, and, in this case borrowing from *National Lampoon*, photo strips. Sadly, what it lacked was a sense of humour. In its favour the first few issues boasted some top-flight artists: Mike Ploog (1, 4, 7), Neal Adams (2) and Ralph Reese (2, 3) in addition to the inevitable Marie Severin. The magazine soon became dominated by lesser talents, though, many of them shameless Mort Drucker clones, and most issues have little of interest. Towards the end of its run *Crazy* revived Howard The Duck for a number of very poor short strips and introduced the world to the wretched Obnoxio The Clown. Avoid.~DAR

CRAZYMAN
Continuity: *Series one 3 issues 1992, series two 4 issues 1993–1994*

Typical for a Continuity production, *Crazyman* mixed decent artwork with absolutely unintelligible writing, in this case applied to one of comics' most repellent characters. Despite principal artist Dan Barry's best efforts the title is more likely to be remembered for the stupid gimmick of the second-series première: yes, each and every one of the pages is cut in the shape of Crazyman's head. Under no circumstances should this be considered a recommendation, however.~DAR

CREATURES OF THE ID
Caliber Press: *1 issue 1990*

A beautiful black and white anthology, this forerunner to *Graphique Musique/Grafik Musik* contains the first appearance of Michael Allred's Frank Einstein, the character who

will eventually become Madman, in a real gem of a tale. The other two stories, both illustrated by Allred, are written by Jeffrey Lang.~JC
Recommended: 1

CREATURES on the LOOSE
Marvel: *28 issues (10–37) 1971–1975*

Numeration continues from *Tower of Shadows*. 10 features Marvel's first *King Kull* strip. 11–15 reprint weird/horror short stories. Gulliver Jones and Thongor occupy 16–21 and 22–29 respectively. The former is an early version of John Carter, concerning a man teleported to Mars to engage in heroic fantasy battles. Created by Lin Carter, Thongor is a Conan clone in all respects bar quality, which is abominable.

In *Amazing Spider-Man* 124–125, J.J. Jameson's astronaut son John was revealed to have discovered a weird gem on the moon which embodied the essence of an alien intelligence and transformed him into a werewolf at night. Man Wolf won his own series from issue 30, limply scripted by Tony Isabella until Dave Kraft and George Perez evolved his story-line into a gem of a tale from 33. Perez's first full published stories in comics were cancelled in a most intriguing situation which eventually saw conclusion three years later in *Marvel Premiere* 45–46.~APS
Recommended: 33–37

The CREEPER
DC: *6 issues 1968–1969*

Newscaster Jack Ryder attended a costume party in a garish green wig and yellow body make-up. While there he discovered an imprisoned professor who injected him with a serum infusing him with extra strength and stamina; he also implanted a device that enabled him to transform himself instantly back to Jack Ryder. This was Steve Ditko's major contribution to DC's 1960s renaissance. An appearance in *Showcase* 73 led to the Creeper's own title. The main body of this comic's all too brief run is linked together by a continuing plot thread, although Denny (Sergius O'Shaughnessy) O'Neil's clever co-plotting with Ditko makes each issue self-contained. The epic is marred by Ditko's departure during the last issue, leaving them stuck for an appropriate artist to finish it off. Each issue is great, but check out 4 for a *tour de force*. The Creeper soloed again in *First Issue Special* 7, *Flash* 318–323 with Dave Gibbons art, and *World's Finest* 249–255, written and drawn by Ditko, but has otherwise been a perennially popular guest star.~SW
Recommended: 1–4

CREEPY
Warren: *145 issues, 5 Yearbooks 1965–1985*
Harris: *1 issue 1985*

Spawning a host of imitators over twenty years, *Creepy* was a black and white magazine-sized anthology title in the tradition of EC's horror comics. As with any anthology the contents were inevitably variable in both subject-matter and quality, but *Creepy* was blessed with two periods of consistent excellence.

For the earlier issues publisher Jim Warren managed to reassemble almost all the major EC horror artists, and in editor/writer Archie Goodwin he had the ideal man to bring out the best in them. Artists like Reed Crandall, Angelo Torres, Alex Toth, Gray Morrow and Johnny Craig were all on top of their form and produced far too many notable stories to list in detail here. A few, however, deserve particular mention, like 'Werewolf' in 1, regular cover painter Frank Frazetta's last comic strip; 'Success Story', also in 1, by Al Williamson, in which a conniving cartoonist is killed by his assistants (ironically reflecting the much-assisted Williamson's own work patterns); and 'Collector's Edition', by Steve Ditko, in 10. Perhaps the best art of this period was to be found in 14's glorious 'Curse Of The Vampire' by the young Neal Adams. Sadly, by 17 almost all the Warren artists and, vitally, Goodwin had suddenly left.

Between 17 and 34 *Creepy* was a sorry mixture of reprints and dross, only occasionally enlivened by the odd Tom Sutton strip. With the exception of 32, containing the Harlan Ellison and Neal Adams collaboration 'Rock God', these issues are best avoided, and it was only with the return of Archie Goodwin in 35 that things improved. *Creepy* briefly became a showcase for fresh talent, introducing the likes of Richard Corben (36), Frank Brunner (39), Dave Cockrum (39), Don McGregor (40) and Bruce Jones (41) to a wider audience. Goodwin also enticed Wally Wood back for two memorable science-fiction and fantasy epics in 38 and 40. More significant, however, was the discovery of Spanish artists, first featured in 42, who came to dominate the title. An early triumph was Lynn Marron's 'Spellbound', breath-takingly illustrated by José Luis Garcia-Lopez, though strips by the likes of Felix Mas, Esteban Maroto and José Bea were also highly impressive. The Spaniards brought a unique illustrative flair to their work and were technically far in advance of their American counterparts.

Creepy's second golden age began with 50 and the appointment of Bill Dubay as editor. Whereas Goodwin's stories had been largely sting-in-the-tail material, Dubay's stable of writers (Jim Stenstrum, Budd Lewis, Steve

Skeates, Jack Butterworth, Gerry Boudreau and Rich Margopoulos) favoured more psychological subjects and denser scripts. *Creepy* was soon crammed with excellent stories and there's something of interest in every issue between 50 and 90. Along with top-flight Spaniards like José Ortiz and Luis Bermejo, Dubay enticed back Alex Toth (75–80) and John Severin while Richard Corben was a regular (54, 56–64, 66–70, 73, 77, 83, 84). The best artist of the period was Berni Wrightson, who produced a number of memorable strips in 62, 63, 87 and 95, often with Warren's top writer Bruce Jones. Other stories of note from this period are 'Creeps', by Goodwin, Wood and Severin, and 'Unreal', a silent-movie tribute by Alex Toth, both in 78, and the horrifying shark story 'In Deep' by Jones and Corben in 83. Undoubtedly the best story in this or any other Warren comic was 'Thrillkill' in 75, by Jim Stenstrum and Neal Adams, a deeply troubling story of a rooftop sniper, which epitomises the literate approach of the Dubay era.

Dubay also introduced the notion of theme issues, an idea continued under his successor, from 79, Louise Jones. Notable themes were Edgar Allan Poe (69, 70), sports (84, 93), monsters (85), Mars (87) and sharks (101). Early Jones issues were largely indistinguishable from Dubay's, but as time went on she increasingly turned to American artists instead of Spaniards, built up her own stable of writers and played down the sex and violence that had begun to creep into the comic. Highlights of her editorship were the strips by Russ Heath (79, 83, 92, 100, 105) and Alex Nino (94, 96, 97, 100, 101, 104, 105, 108, 112). Issues after 100 are far less consistent than earlier ones and, although not without merit, many later issues lack the inspiration of the comic's glory years, a situation the returning Bill Dubay in 117 failed to rectify. The last few years saw increasing gore and reprints. On the plus side Dubay did bring back his favourite writers and Spanish artists, although the best art of the period came from little-known Filipinos Anton Caravana (125, 126) and Noly Panaligan (127, 128, 131). It was clear, however, that the comic had lost direction and it was no surprise when *Creepy* was cancelled.

The early *Creepy Yearbooks* reprinted the best of the magazine's strips and when they ceased the tradition was continued in the regular title (48, 55, 65, 74, 82, 91 103), with later issues concentrating on the work of a particular artist. Wrightson (113), Nino (119), Severin (121), Corben (132), Williamson (137), Toth (139) and Torres (142) were collected, and for casual readers would be the ideal introduction. In 1985 Harris published a low-print-run issue consisting of some new material and choice reprints, but a series failed to materialise and copies are now almost impossible to find.~DAR

Recommended: 1–16, 38, 41, 46, 50–90, 95, 100, 112

Collection: Creepy (Assorted stories from the entire run)

CREEPY
Harris: *4-issue miniseries 1992*

Although using the same logo and host, this bears little relation to the Warren title. On a dark and stormy night eight people arrive at a mysterious house to be confronted with their past and the consequences thereof. Main writer Peter David toys with familiar clichés, but is adept enough to sidestep them while keeping the reader interested to the end. A selection of fine artists including Dave Cockrum, Gene Colan, Carmine Infantino, Jim Mooney and Tom Sutton contribute.~WJ

The CRIME CLINIC
Slave Labor: *2 issues + 1995 to date*

Dylan Williams is single-handedly trying to revive the crime-comics genre all but killed off by the Comics Code Authority in the mid-1950s. Beginning with a hilarious and possibly slanderous exposé of Charlton Comics, Williams also relates the biographies of mobsters Kid Sly Fox (in 1) and Dillinger (in 2). It's real two-barrelled action with a blackly humorous narrative voice.~WJ

CRIME SUSPENSTORIES
EC: *27 issues 1950–1955*
Russ Cochran: *17 issues 1993 to date*

By the beginning of the 1950s William M.Gaines had transformed his ailing company Educational Comics – publishers of such bland fare as *Animal Fables* and *Fat And Slat* – into the much racier Entertaining Comics, responsible for the legendary anthology titles *Tales From The Crypt*, *Frontline Combat* and *Weird Science*. Gaines and his talented roster of artists, editors and writers, quickly broke free of the polite restraints crippling the American newsstand comic by offering 'a new trend in magazines'. Using such commercial genres as horror, science fiction and crime, EC comics mixed beautiful artwork from the likes of Harvey Kurtzman, Wally Wood, Bernie Krigstein and Al Williamson with florid, literate scripts inspired by radio shows, B-movies, pulp fiction and the whole atmosphere of 1950s USA. The proudly paternalistic Gaines showcased his artists, allowed his creators a great deal of freedom (within the admittedly constraining limits of the EC 'twist ending' formula) and developed brand loyalty through witty editorials appealing to 'EC Fan-Addicts'.

Soon notorious for their extreme gore and dark black humour, EC titles also contained a fair measure of socio-political satire, liberal sermonising and cultural critique, more than enough to offend 'the powers that be'. Latching onto Dr Fredric Wertham's bizarre 'exposé' of the link between comics and juvenile crime (*Seduction Of The Innocent* in 1954), Senator Estes Kefauver convened outraged Congressional hearings with a flippant, benzedrine-fuelled Gaines as chief victim. In the wake of falling sales and outraged public opinion, many of the major comic-book companies formed the Comics Code Authority, a voluntary body designed to reassure anxious distributors and parents that any titles with the Code seal on had met 'the high standards of morality and decency required'. It also effectively put Gaines out of business, although salvation was at hand in the shape of the phenomenal *Mad Magazine*, created by Kurtzman for EC in 1952.

Crime Suspenstories was the fourth 'New Trend' title launched by Entertaining Comics, and followed on from their 'Pre-Trend' crime titles *Crime Patrol* and *War Against Crime*. Before *Crime Suspenstories*, comics in this genre, like Lev Gleason's best-selling *Crime Does Not Pay* (1942–1955), revolved around the victory of law and order over vicious gangster killers. Now Gaines and editor Al Feldstein turned away from detective heroes, and concentrated instead on 'ordinary' men and women caught up in tawdry crimes of passion.

Early, rather uncertain issues of *Crime* featured such inappropriate artists as Kurtzman (in numbers 1 and 3) and Graham 'Ghastly' Ingels, but soon settled down to the inspired roster of George Evans, Reed Crandall, Jack Kamen, Jack Davis and the perpetually underrated Johnny Craig. A painfully slow writer and artist, Craig drew the vast majority of *Crime*'s shatteringly lurid covers and provided the lead strip for most of its run. His sweating, hysterical, atmospheric artwork, reminiscent of Will Eisner and Milton Caniff, defined *Crime*'s obsession with human corruption and despair, marking it out as the comic-strip equivalent of film noir, or the work of writer James M. Cain. In stories like 21's superb 'Understudies' or 'When The Cat's Away...' (15), Craig's adulterous lovers plot to bump off unwanted spouses, their murderous desires motivated as much by money or power as by love or lust, their fates inevitably tragic and absurd. Other highlights include three exquisitely experimental strips from Bernie Krigstein: 'Monotony', 'More Blessed To Give...' and 'Key Chain' in 22, 24 and 25 respectively.

Although the strips in *Crime* were required to end on ludicrous plot twists that often made nonsense of the establishing narrative, read in small doses many of the stories still offer a pleasingly sick blend of dark social realism and over-the-top revenge fantasies. As with all anthology titles, individual issues are highly variable, and although towards the end of the run one senses a certain tiredness and timidity setting in, *Crime Suspenstories* remains one of EC's most consistent and entertaining achievements. The Russ Cochran-published editions are facsimiles of the originals.~AL
Recommended: 5, 15–17, 21–25
Collection: Crime SuspenStories (1–27)

CRIMSON AVENGER
DC: *4-issue miniseries 1988.*

The oldest DC costumed adventurer, predating Batman, the Avenger premiered in *Detective Comics* 20, in 1938. Originally a masked vigilante similar to the pulps' *Shadow*, he later switched to red tights and enjoyed a second career as a superhero. This series by Roy Thomas and artist Greg Brooks takes him back to his thirties roots, in an amiable, if unexceptional, B-movieish tale of love and death.~HS

CRISIS On Infinite Earths
DC: *12-issue limited series 1985–1986*

In the late 1950s DC started creating new superheroes based on 1940s characters, such as Flash, Green Lantern and Hawkman. Eventually it was decided to reintroduce the 1940s versions, explaining that they existed in a parallel dimension, christened Earth Two, while the newer heroes lived on Earth One. Over the years more other-dimensional Earths arrived, housing various *doppelgängers* (On Earth Three, the Earth One superhero counterparts were villains, and Earth C housed DC's funny animal creations). The DC worlds expanded to the point where it was deemed that all these parallel universes with similar characters were confusing readers. Nonsense, of course, it was this multiverse that made the DC's universe such an interesting tapestry. If a ten-year-old could understand the dual universes of Earth One and Earth Two during the 1960s, why should a ten-year-old in the 1980s find it confusing? Nevertheless, it was decided to merge all parallel universes into one new definite DC Universe.

Over twelve issues, writer Marv Wolfman, with artists George Perez, Dick Giordano and Jerry Ordway, expertly wove an intricate plot featuring virtually every DC hero from the Stone Age to the far future. Earths started to disappear and characters were displaced through time by an entity known as the Anti-Monitor who was slowly destroying the multiverse. After an inter-dimensional struggle, the heroes manage to destroy the Anti-Monitor, but not until the surviving Earths, One and Two, are merged. Characters in action during both the Golden and the Silver Age (such as Superman, Wonder Woman and Robin), and thus existing as two versions, had their older incarnation removed. New characters were created (female versions of Dr Light and Wildcat), and many minor (Aquagirl, the Dove, Immortal – apparently not – Man) and major characters were killed. In 7 Supergirl dies gallantly to save the life of her cousin Superman, still able to bring a lump to the throat, while 8 contains the final fate of the Silver Age Flash.

As a series, *Crisis* was a magnificent effort and a true delight for any DC fan, but ultimately the exercise failed. The whole point was to clean up the DC Universe, but over the years in fact it complicated matters more. *The Crisis* was used an a excuse to reboot features (sometimes years after the event) such as Superman and Hawkman, thereby contradicting the series. Only in recent times has the DC Universe settled into a consistent timeline. Still, that shouldn't stop you enjoying this fine effort, which shows what a varied and wonderful place the DC Universe is, or was.~HY
Recommended: 1–12

CRITICAL ERROR
Dark Horse: *One-shot 1995*

One begins to wonder just how many times John Byrne can recycle this simple wordless story of an astronaut crash-landing on an idyllic world. Run in the back of his *Art Of John Byrne* book and in *Epic Illustrated*, it's now coloured, with the naked female's pubes neatly airbrushed out for the prudish 1990s audience. Any kids who want to know how babies are made should pick this up, but otherwise inessential.~WJ

CRITICAL MASS, A Shadowline Saga
Epic: *7-issue limited series 1989–1990*

This squarebound series concludes the plots from Epic's cancelled superhero titles *Doctor Zero, Powerline* and *Saint George* in fine fashion. Good plots from Dan Chichester and Margaret Clark are allied to decent artwork from the likes of Gray Morrow, Kev O'Neill, Jorge Zaffino and pre-Image and appallingly coloured Jim Lee (in 4). The thread running through two stories per issue is the coming apocalypse organised by Henry Clerk, who's so grateful for the restoration of his memory that he intends to set off nuclear explosions

across the USA as thanks. As he plans, Doctor Zero continues to manipulate everyone, the Order of St George want Zero brought down and Powerline need him as an ally.~FP

CRITTERS
Fantagraphics: *50 issues, 1 special 1986–1990*

There are very few anthologies that leave one feeling that every strip deserves its place. *Critters* almost manages it in that, even if there are some strips that you don't enjoy, Kim Thompson's editorial selection is of a consistently high quality so that you can admire the craft if not the result.

Critters proved to be a valuable showcase for both new and established creators, though only Stan Sakai's and Cathy Hill's creations continue to be published in the U.S. Funny animal strips had seen a resurgence of interest in the mid 1980s (with *Omaha, Albedo* and *Neil The Horse* leading the way alongside the longer established *Cerebus* and *Maus*), and Thompson provides space for practically everyone of note in the field, including Sam Kieth (7, 11, 12, 23), Ty Templeton (8, 11, 23 – including a song on the free flexi-disc – and 50), Mark Armstrong (7, 8, 11, 13, 23), Steve Lafler (9,11), Holland and Wilber (11, 17, 19, 21, 23, 24, 29, 31, 32), Jim Engel (18, 50), Steve Purcell (19, 50), Mark Martin (30, 50), Stephen De Stefano (32, 38, 50), Donna Barr (38), Arn Saba (50), Tim Fuller (15, 18, 22, 28, 31, 34, 38, 44, 50), Cathy Hill (50), Doug Gray (50), Joshua Quagmire (1, 50) and Sergio Aragonés (50).

Stan Sakai's excellent samurai tale 'Usagi Yojimbo' appears in 1, 3, 6, 7, 10, 11, 14, 23, 38 and 50, while the Groo-like 'Adventures of Nilson Groundthumper and Hermy' features in 5, 16, 27 and the whole of the *Critters Special* (1988). From the same source (*Albedo*), Steve Gallacci's 'Birthright' is a furtherance of the science-fiction series 'Erma Felda', which began in that title (1–6, 12–17 and 47–49).

Translated from the Danish by Thompson himself, 'Family Gnuff' by Freddy Milton is the heavily Barks-influenced story of a family of dragons. Light-hearted and good-humoured, the strength of this strip serves as the cornerstone for much of the title's run (2–5, 7, 9–11, 13–16, 19–26, 30–34, 40). 2 contains a preview of the just-released *Captain Jack* series by Mike Kazelah, who contributed a number of other strips to *Critters*, though his best work remains that on *Captain Jack* (42, 50). J.P.Morgan's 'Fission Chicken' and Tom Stazer's 'Lionheart' are both parody strips, the former of superheroes, the latter of hard-boiled detectives. Well presented, they only occasionally hit all the right points but are generally good fun.

William Van Horn's 'Ambrose' and 'Angst' series, however, are definitely worth looking out for. The former is a Krazy Kat-inspired frog (22, 25, 26, 30, 33, 38), the latter has a couple of small-time crooks waxing philosophical about their lot (20, 45, 50). Another series inspired by a great newspaper strip is Kyle Rothweiler's Duck 'Bill' Platypus. Taking *Pogo* as a starting point, this is much more manic and surreal (34–37, 41).

From 39, each issue contained a single character in hopes of improving sales but the series ended with 50, on a high, though, with an 84-page issue. Cathy Hill's 'Raccoons' strip had previously appeared in *The Dreamery* while Doug Gray's *The Eye of Mongombo* was a short-lived but excellent title about an intrepid explorer who was turned into a duck. Reed Waller and Kate Worley's 'Speakingstone' (12, 20) was unfortunately never finished.~NF

Recommended: 1–3, 6, 7, 10, 11, 14, 20, 22, 23, 25, 26, 33, 38, 42, 45, 50

CROMWELL STONE
Dark Horse: *One-shot 1992*

Presented in comic size, rather than the traditional European graphic novel format, Andreas' Lovecraftian mystery tale was published without fanfare or explanation, though Dark Horse were printing his Rork series in *Cheval Noir* at the same time. Beautifully rendered in black and white, Andreas' artwork is too clinical for some but he combines the influence of Gustave Doré and Escher to create stunning pages. The story's much what you'd expect: strange buildings, weird 'dreams', hidden worlds and a limp hero who stumbles around, just managing to keep one step ahead of whatever dark lump is after him.~NF

Andrew Vachss' CROSS
Dark Horse: 6-issue limited series 1995–1996

Despite the prominence of his name on the cover, crime-fiction writer Andrew Vachss only appears to have co-plotted these stories. They're uncompromising material, featuring the former inmate of a Chicago young offenders institution during the 1960s, Marlon Cross. Already tough on arrival, the years there hardened him, and supplied him with his lifelong companions. In the present day they're a respected, if off-beat, crew who'll move beyond the law to kill for a price. The proviso is that it's a case Cross wants to take, and he has no qualms about turning down pleas from close friends. After the first issue's background run-through Cross targets a particularly unsavoury gang distributing videos they film of brutal assaults and rapes. The narrative captions are disjointed and often superfluous, and the cast is sometimes just too contrived, but if you're looking for a well-drawn, fast-paced thriller there's plenty worse than this.~FP

CROSSFIRE
Eclipse: *26 issues 1984–1988*
Antarctic: *1 issue 1994*

A textbook example of how to produce an entertaining mainstream comic. First pretend it's not a detective comic by having the lead costumed, then situate in Hollywood and populate with has-beens, wannabes, never-wills, sleazy execs and celebs all clawing for that golden opportunity. Mark Evanier's witty scripts ensure *Crossfire* reads like a superior TV drama, matched by great artwork from the adaptable and woefully underrated Dan Spiegle.

Bail bondsman Jay Endicott inherits the trademark costume of now deceased industrial spy and burglar Crossfire. He trades on Crossfire's reputation and contacts to appease his sense of right by helping those who can't afford any other justice. Fallible and generous, Endicott's a likeable soft-boiled detective, and a further strength is the detail afforded supporting characters, even if they're only present for a single issue. Endicott's relationship with the DNAgents' Rainbow means she often features, with her superpowers sometimes providing all-too-convenient get-out-of-jail-free solutions to seemingly insurmountable problems. A temporary hiatus in publication between 17 and 18 is filled by the four-part *Crossfire and Rainbow* series, stories that would have occupied *Crossfire* 18–21. From 18 the title becomes black and white, although not to its detriment, and 24 concludes the *Whodunnit* series, which starred Endicott sans costume.

Promoting an already excellent package to higher level are the text pages, in which Evanier recounts experiences as a TV writer, a sort of *Adventures In The Small Screen Trade*. There's not a bad issue in the run, with 15, featuring Howard Hughes and both Crossfires, a good sampler. The putative revival in 1994 didn't come about, although in addition to Crossfire and the DNAgents the package includes another excellent essay, about attempting to develop the latter as a TV series.~FP

Recommended: 5–7, 10–13, 15–22, *Crossfire and Rainbow* 3, 4

CROSSROADS
First: *5-issue miniseries 1988*

First's attempt at unifying all its titles into one coherent universe in the manner of Marvel and DC was the first time this had been tried by an independent company. Five individual stories bring American Flagg, Badger, Dreadstar, Nexus, Sable and Whisper together, written by Mike Baron, Roger Salick and Steve Grant, with artists including Shawn McManus and Luke McDonnell. Gorgeous

Steve Rude paintings adorn the covers. The stories are all relatively self-contained, but nothing stands out, so unless you're a fanatical follower of the above characters it's safe to miss this one out.~TP

THE CROW
Caliber: *4 issues 1989*
Tundra: 3-issue miniseries (1–3) 1992, 3-issue miniseries ('Dead Time') 1996, 3-issue miniseries ('City Of Angels') 1996, 3-issue miniseries ('Flesh And Blood') 1996, 3-issue miniseries ('Wild Justice') 1996

Débuting in *Caliber Presents* 1, James O'Barr's bleak vigilante thriller does have a sort of poetry to its vision of violent city streets contrasted with the beauty of love. Eric Draven and his girlfriend are killed by thugs, high on drugs, when their car breaks down in a bad area. Resurrected as a spirit of vengeance, Eric becomes The Crow, who wreaks bloody revenge on those responsible, plus anyone else in the criminal chain that leads back to the drug lords. O'Barr's artwork is influenced by Will Eisner, among others, but changes wildly according to the prevailing emotional winds. It becomes more accomplished as the series progresses, but faces remain a weakness throughout.

The Tundra series begins by reprinting the Caliber issues before continuing the story of Draven's quest. For 'Dead Time' O'Barr hands over to John Wagner and Alexander Maleev for a story about a different Crow. This one is a farmer, murdered with his family during the American Civil War and resurrected in the present to exact revenge on the reincarnations of his killers. Wagner returns for the adaptation of the second film, *City Of Angels*, illustrated by Dean Ormston. It's very much a re-run of the original, even down to the villain managing to find a way to make the Crow mortal for the final showdown. Ormston's artwork owes much to Ted McKeever but doesn't really impress. 'Flesh And Blood' features the first female Crow. James Vance introduces an environmental plot-line and tries to heighten the emotional tension by playing off her unborn (now dead) child with the villain's large family. Maleev's artwork is promising but too reliant on illustration and lacking basic story-telling abilities.

'Wild Justice' returns to the original premise as the Crow resurrects Michael Korby, killed with his wife by car thieves. Charlie Adlard's artwork is suitably dark in his scratchy and impressionistic style, but Jerry Prosser's story doesn't manage to work new life out of the old plot.~NF

CRUCIAL FICTION
Fantagraphics: *3 issues 1992*

The off-kilter strips of Julian Lawrence tackle a variety of strange topics without particularly illuminating or offering a new insight. There's some nice cartooning, but 2's story of Pope Joan is as good as this gets.~WJ

CRUCIBLE
!mpact: *6-issue miniseries 1993*

Tying up all the loose ends from DC's failed *!mpact* line of titles, *Crucible* works well independently. A group of would-be global rulers have a device offering glimpses of the future, showing that Nate Cray (Black Hood) is somehow an important part of what is to come. Attempts to capture Cray are complicated by the return of the Comet, and by the story's end most Impact characters are back. Fast-paced scripts from Brian Augustyn and Mark Waid and complementary art from Quesada, Wojtkiewicz and Palmiotti make for an engaging series.~FP

THE CRUSADERS
Jack Chick: *17 issues 1974–1980*

Originally produced during the 1970s, *The Crusaders* is still available in speciality religious-themed bookshops, along with the equally amusing (and well drawn) smaller pamphlets from the same organisation. The series begins relatively well, with the wholesome Jim and Tim as church troubleshooters sorting out problems around the world. Whether performing an exorcism in India or inducing vomiting in some devil-worshipping Druids at home, a few prayers will do the trick. This is a world where God always comes through. If money is needed for a flight to India there'll be a mysterious donation. If a potential teenage suicide requires some convincing life's worth living, a few biblical quotations and a lightshow are just the answer, and she's turned on to God quicker than you can say Sodom and Gomorrah. Generally well plotted, 1–8 are a desperate attempt to appeal to the kids with contemporary fashions and hip language. There's no specific creator credit, although it seems likely Jess Jodlman is the artist, or perhaps it's God. With 9, though, the comic becomes completely mad, promoting text-heavy conspiracy mania pertaining to the Vatican's alleged manipulation of the world through the centuries, and its agenda to subvert the word of God and promote Satan. 13 has some particularly graphically rendered Spanish Inquisition tortures. Each comic has a different title, with the series name appearing in the top right corner. Narrow-minded in their version of the One True Way, and appallingly intolerant: just remember that if there were a God there'd never have been a *Birdie Song*.~FP

CRUSADERS
!mpact: *8 issues 1992*

Following the *!mpact Winter Special*, which saw these heroes team for the first time, a crossover story running through all !mpact titles resulted in this ongoing team comic. Named for The American Crusaders, an earlier group of heroes who disappeared, these five set out to discover what happened to their predecessors, only to be distracted along the way by various and sundry menaces. Light, boppy, fun superheroics, abruptly terminated by the collapse of !mpact following disappointing sales results. The ultimate fate of the Crusaders was revealed in the final !mpact series, *Crucible*.~HS

THE CRUSH
Image: *5-issue miniseries 1996*

Psychiatrist turned judge, jury and executioner struggles manfully against the all-pervading clichés. There's no current trend or street language too ridiculous for inclusion here. Funny now, expect it to be hilarious in ten years, particularly the Irish gang in 4.~WJ

CRY FOR DAWN
CFD: *9 issues 1989–1992*

An anthology considered synonymous with gratuitous gore actually has plenty of redeeming features, not least the constantly improving black and white wash artwork of Joseph Michael Linsner. Linsner and writing partner Joe Monks appear to have been damned by their first issue, featuring stories associating sex with violence and an ill-advised examination of abortion. Both Monks and Linsner are prone to florid prose, but they can also write genuinely bleak and shocking stories like 'Birthmarks' in issue 2 or 'Dropping Anchor' in 6. Sadly, Frank Forte excepted, other contributing artists are a shoddy bunch.~FP
Collection: Angry Christ Comics (Linsner's solo work)

CRYING FREEMAN
Viz: *Series one 8 issues 1989–1990, Series two 9 issues 1990–1991, Series three 10 issues 1991–1992, Series four 8 issues 1992, Series five 11 issues 1992–1993*

Despite its frequent and explosive violence, *Crying Freeman* has a lot to recommend it to female readers. Its violence is almost balletic, its plot quasi-mythical, its story-line centred around romance: the central characters' love for each other, and the reader's infatuation with beautiful gangsters. The origin in series one immediately confronts us with the duality of the title. Crying Freeman is a sensitive potter forced to become an assassin, who kills impassively but with tears streaming down his face. The first story concerns the young artist Emu, who will eventually become his wife, who

witnesses him in action, and is convinced he will return to kill her. Everyone accepts what happens to them as though it were fated. Freeman becomes leader of one of the most powerful and ancient secret societies and proceeds to defend his position against genetic mutations, Amazons and supersoldiers as a matter of honour. Emu unquestioningly marries him, and starts to learn the art of fighting, eventually receiving a magical sword; they swan around in a submarine tricked out to look like a dragon and have adventures that are halfway between *James Bond* and the Twelve Labours of Hercules in their romantic inevitability.

Ryochi Ikegami's delicate linework and dry-brush shading produce images of extraordinary impact and elegance. The pace of the story allows for lots of splash pages, long, loving delineations of exceptionally violent fights, and really very beautiful sex scenes. Exciting but simplistic, *Crying Freeman's* heady blend of martial arts, steamy sex, blood, doomed criminals and tattoos is an addictive mix.~FJ
Recommended: first series 1–8
Collections: Books 1–5 (Series 1–5)

CRYPT of SHADOWS
Marvel: *21 issues 1973–1975*

Reprints 1950s weird and horror shorts, with a Basil Wolverton strip in the first issue of note.~APS

CRYPT OF TERROR
EC: *3 issues (17–19) 1950*

Continuing the numbering from *Crime Patrol*, *Crypt of Terror* was the first EC horror comic, and the template for all that was to follow. The formula and artwork haven't hit their peak here, but there's a curiosity in seeing Harvey Kurtzman illustrate the typical O. Henry-style horror tale and future successful science-fiction author Harry Harrison also trying his hand. With 20 the title changed to *Tales From the Crypt*, and immortality was assured.~FP

The Saga of CRYSTAR Crystal Warrior
Marvel: *11 issues 1983–1985*

Fantasy by numbers, created by committee, with wizards, feuding sibling princes, half-naked women, dragons, prophecies and pacts, but without any real heart. As if acknowledging the creative redundancy, Marvel superheroes begin appearing from 3.~WJ

CUD Comics
Fantagraphics: *8 issues 1992–1994*
Dark Horse: *6 issues + 1995 to date*

Written and drawn by Terry LaBan, *Cud* eschews the confessional mode of many 'alternative' comics in favour of broad, adult, character-driven satire. LaBan is confident and accomplished enough to get laughs whatever the genre or situation, be it exotic adventure (with occasional character Muktuk Wolfsbreath, Hard-Boiled Shaman), rude Archie parody, 'The Primitives', or a Jewish parable, 'Ben Dordia's Confession' – respectively in the fourth issues of the first and second series.

Each issue of the Fantagraphics *Cud* features 'You Can't Spank The Monkey If He's On Your Back', a strip about the rise and fall of absurd performance artist Bob Cudd, one of the stars of LaBan's previous comic, *Unsupervised Existence*. Although he's a vaguely sympathetic lead, Bob is also a terrible phoney, and LaBan uses this extended storyline to take some hilarious, if rather easy, potshots at numerous 'radical' lifestyles. The Dark Horse series features archetypal slacker couple Eno and Plum, in a series of inventive, raunchy domestic vignettes bound to appeal to readers of Peter Bagge's *Hate*. 2's story 'Virtual Anxiety', where Eno dons a Virtual Reality headset and lands up in a brutal prison, is a particularly effective example of LaBan's ability to sidestep the often limiting realism of many strips bound up with grunge culture. In the superbly smutty porn fantasy 'Class Action' (series one, 2) LaBan calls himself 'Just another lame "alternative" cartoonist with a ponytail', which, as with his other satirical observations, is a harsh but not wholly inaccurate judgement. LaBan always draws 'The Author' as a spindly, thirty-something hippy, and one often gets the impression that *Cud*'s creator is a detached, bemused observer rather than a fully fledged participant hangin' with The Kids. *Cud*'s superb, broad-brush artwork reinforces the sense of deceptive professionalism and personal detachment that further characterises all of LaBan's non-mainstream work.~AL
Recommended: Series one 1–8, series two 2

CUIRASS
Harrier: *1 issue 1988*

It's hard to credit that anything as piss-poor as Harrier's indescribably unerotic bondage fantasy *Barbarienne* could warrant a cash-in; however, the evidence is before us, sadly.~FJ

Batman: THE CULT
DC: *4-issue miniseries 1988*

Despite the big star names, Jim Starlin and Berni Wrightson, this was a best-selling disaster. After Frank Miller's *Dark Knight Returns* DC were obviously looking for another critical and commercial success. Starlin, despite having done little of note since leaving Marvel several years previously, still had a good reputation that promised much, and

tempting Wrightson back to comics was another coup for DC. Neither creator was up to the task, though. Wrightson's artwork was far too loose for the ponderous script. Starlin's premise that Bruce Wayne's motivation for becoming The Batman was fear and the much-flaunted 'first time Batman is broken' storyline are entirely unconvincing. The series is representative of the failure of DC to understand how to handle Bruce Wayne, pretty much ignoring his character in favour of an emotionless Batman who's only allowed to interact with Robin and Alfred.~NF
Collection: The Cult (1-4)

CURSE OF THE MOLEMEN
Kitchen Sink: *One-shot 1991*

Charles Burns combines domestic brutality, childish curiosity and a smidgen of the inexplicable in 1960s-TV small-town USA. Originally issued by *Raw* in black and white, it's simple stuff given atmosphere by Burns' expressive and disturbing art.~FP

CURSE OF THE WEIRD
Marvel: *4 issues 1993–1994*

Together with *Monster Menace*, an attempt by Marvel to revive its mystery line by reprinting classic stories lovingly selected and presented. *Curse Of The Weird* was definitely the more fun of the two, focusing on the loopier side of things with disembodied brains, floating eyeballs, amnesiac ghosts and literal roadhogs! Very *mondo bizarro*. In their native 1950s these demented ideas were the result of too many benzedrine-soaked nights trying to grind out fodder for the company's two dozen mystery titles; now they can be appreciated for the nostalgic trash classics they are.~HS
Recommended: 1–4

Army Surplus Comics Featuring CUTEY BUNNY
Army Surplus: *7 issues 1982–1986*

Rather poor *risqué* anthropomorphic title, written and drawn by Joshua Quagmire, whose rough and ready approach to inking squeezed out what little eroticism there might have been in the unlovely original pencils. Comes over as vulgar and adolescent, rather than as a spirited and irreverent underground, which I suppose is what it was aiming to be.~FJ

CYBER CRUSH Robots In Revolt
Fleetway/Quality: *14 issues 1990–1991*

Reprints of early *2000AD* stories with covers bearing no relation to the contents. Ironically for a comic selling itself on the idea of robots, it's the humanity of the robots within that makes the strips work. 'Ro-Busters' is a *Thunderbirds*-style rescue squad wherein the team revolt against their masters. There's nice Mike McMahon on some chapters, but little worth noting otherwise until 14, which has an Alan Moore and Steve Dillon tale. Better by far are the earliest Robo-Hunter stories, finally reproduced sympathetically in colour. John Wagner (under the alias of T.B. Grover) and Alan Grant write hilarious scripts, matched by Ian Gibson's whimsical, detailed art. 1–8 have Sam Slade accompanied by a foul-mouthed, cigar-chomping pilot regressed to childhood on a planet where robots are eliminating humans, and the even funnier 'Day Of The Droids' in 9–14 has all of the city's leaders replaced by robot duplicates.~WJ

Shuhoi Tahashi's CYBER 7
Eclipse: *Miniseries one 8 issues 1989, miniseries two 10 issues 1989–1990*

Two teens become aware, as you do, that they're extra-dimensional aliens who've been exiled on Earth, although they're the rightful heirs to the throne of a faraway world. There are, naturally, those who want to prevent their return, among them a giant rabbit called Cunningham. Luckily, they have allies in the form of the Cyber 7, a mixture of sprite and miniature robot. Excellent art and considerable charm combine for a decent first run, set on Earth as the strange events unfold. The second series, sub-titled 'Rockland', is more fantasy-oriented as our crew start travelling home through the dimensions with their path blocked by enemies.~FP

CYBERAD
Continuity: *Series one 7 issues 1991–1992, series two 3 issues 1993*

Unique among Continuity titles for keeping the same creative team (Peter Stone and Richard Bennett) for its entire run, *Cyberad* was best known for its inspired enhancements, from holograms to stickers and gatefold pages. Artistically Bennett's pages were a strange mixture of Neal Adams figurework and obsessive Manga-esque detail, but ultimately the frantic pace and muddled story adds up to little. The second series was three chapters of the cross-company 'Deathwatch 2000' story.~DAR

CYBERELLA
Helix: *5 issues + 1996 to date*

Howard Chaykin, who's always had a retro love affair with the future, joins forces with animator Don Cameron to give us a boldly drawn, info-heavy version of the future. The Karoshi-Macrocorp run just about everything, thanks to their Cyberella system, personified as a cute virtual woman. Our heroine, Sunny Winston, is being questioned by computer because she's beginning to question the system

when, due to a power surge, she's sucked into Cyberella itself. As ever Chaykin's grasp of recent social history adds interest, and saves the series from being just another cyberpunk comic.~FJ

CYBERFORCE
Image: *5-issue miniseries (0–4) 1992–1993, 27 issues + 1993 to date*

Yet another made-to-measure superhero team. In an already tired format *Cyberforce* has some good characters and a greater sophistication than the majority of Image titles. The miniseries gives us the origin of the team, which amounts to a group of mutants set up to look after each other and fight the anti-mutant organisation Cyberdata. The ongoing series continues this plot. The story-lines are filled with intrigue and conspiracy, which add to the book's action-packed themes. 2–3's 'Killer Instinct' links it with *WildC.A.T.S*, and 8 is drawn by Todd McFarlane as part of Image's X month, for which the top artists switched titles for one month only. Eric Silverstri does a good job of giving his characters depth while his brother Marc produces the best artwork of his career.~SS
Collection: *Cyberforce (1–4)*

CYBERFORCE, STRYKEFORCE: Opposing Forces
Image: *2-issue microseries 1995*

Following *Codename: Strykeforce* 14, this series sees Cyberforce and Strykeforce joining forces against the return of the Shu'rii, out to kill Sh'rrunn/Bloodbow for betraying her race. Leaving the future of the characters pretty much up in the air, Steve Gerber tells an engaging tale that wraps up most of the Strykeforce plot-liness.~NF

CYBERFROG
Harris: *4-issue miniseries 1996*

Part frog, part machine, little explanation, Cyberfrog is out there maiming, mutilating and murdering ne'er-do-wells. As ideas go there are far worse, and with that concept it's hardly going to be *angst*-ridden soul-searching all the way. While the dubious morality and celebration of gratuitous violence may offend some there's an equal crowd to be attracted by Ethan Van Sciver's appealing art and often very funny dialogue. Van Sciver's obviously having a ball, but drop the smug and irritating captions, mate.~WJ

CYBERNARY
Image: *5 issues 1995–1996*

Cybernary is the fusion of a freedom fighter and the daughter of Kaizen Gamorra, ruler of Gamorra Island. His head scientist Vandaua, trying to please his master, decides to improve his daughter, but neither she nor Kaizen is exactly overjoyed by the end result, especially when the freedom-fighter part of her wants to join the rebels in their attempts to free Gamorra from her father's rule. Written by Steve Gerber and drawn by Jeff Rebner, this is an entertaining series, shedding light on a particular aspect of the Wildstorm Universe, which partially sets the scene for *Fire From Heaven*.~NF

CYBERPUNKS
Innovation: *One-shot 1989*

A lesson that should have filtered through to Innovation very early in their existence was that painted art doesn't necessarily mean good art. Here we have shocking anatomy placed on blurred backgrounds in a rescue story about teens jacked into cyberspace via neck implants. Good ideas, weak story, bad art.~FP

CYBERPUNX
Image: *3-issue miniseries 1996*

It's heartbreaking to see Robert Loren Fleming, the man who wrote the magnificent *Thriller*, eking out a living by scripting nonsense like this for Rob Liefeld, even if he does manage to insert a few digs about the concept into the script. Computers control the world, and the remaining humans can be digitised and transferred about the place. That's not enough, though, and the Cyberlords want to eradicate humanity. It's not a bad idea, but unfortunately, having conceived it, Rob's more interested in people duffing each other up.~WJ

CYBLADE/SHI
Image/Crusade: *2-issue microseries 1995*

Steamin' babe-on-babe action from comics' hottest heroines. Nah, only kidding. It's actually a pompous allegory about creative little guys fighting against a huge evil out to destroy their individuality and, with it, the land of wonder. The creators' hearts were in the right place, but the whole thing's a terrible mish-mash, written by William Tucci and Gary Cohn and drawn by Tucci, Nelson Asencio and Jimmy Palmiotti. Shi and Cyblade don't even do much. Along the way Cerebus, Fone Bone, Mr Spook and a host of other characters from better independent comics turn up.~FJ

The Adventures of CYCLOPS AND PHOENIX
Marvel: *4-issue miniseries, 1995, 4-issue miniseries two 1996*

Just to further complicate the already impenetrable *X-Men* continuity, Cyclops and Phoenix are snatched from their honeymoon and thrust into the dark, distant future. They're tasked with raising the child who will be Cable, doing all they can to ensure that a prophecy about the future stays on-line despite knowing the pain and anguish the future will hold for all of them. The artwork, by Gene Ha, is finely detailed and has almost fairy-tale qualities amid the usual big guns and helicopters of the X-Books house style, while Scott Lobdell's story puts flesh on the bones of a future mythology which has been hinted at but never before fully explored. The second series, written by Peter Milligan, has them thrust into the past of Victorian England to witness the origin of their arch-nemesis, Mr Sinister. Essential for *X-Men* aficionados but be warned: the complicated continuity may well be incomprehensible to the casual reader.~JC

CYCOPS
Comics Interview: *3 issues 1988*

Cybernetically enhanced policemen strive to uncover an assassination plot. Notable for the début of artist Brian Stelfreeze, it's nonetheless very ordinary science fiction.~WJ

DAGAR The Invincible
Gold Key: *18 issues 1972–1976*
Whitman: *1 issue (19) 1982*

Gold Key's slide from grace was precipitous during the early 1970s. While rarely reaching great heights, their titles had always attained a level of professional competence, and their distinguishing painted covers (repeated as pin-ups on the back cover without logo and cover text) were always a treat. This is almost plotless sword-and-sorcery anonymously hacked out. Why on earth Whitman (who dropped the Gold Key imprint in the early 1980s) would imagine a reprint might revive an interest is beyond all speculation.~WJ

DAILY BUGLE
Marvel: *3-issue miniseries 1996–1997*

Gritty Paul Grist story accompanied by gritty Karl Kerschl black and white artwork of the life and times of New York City's premier newspaper. Corrupt landlords and money-laundering rear ugly heads as this Spider-Man institution fails to have everything its own way. The gritty script is fine. The gritty pencils spurn the opportunity to depict a single recognisable character.~APS

DAKOTA NORTH Investigations
Marvel: *5 issues 1986–1987*

Nominally a thriller featuring spies on the Orient Express and corporate double-dealing in the world of high fashion. In reality, a piece of soft porn through which Ms North struts in stilettos and tight black leather, displaying her delectable rear as often as possible. This is more often in Issue 1 than in any other, but the story doesn't improve to compensate for the loss, and it's a relief to discover at the end of Issue 5 that there will be no more.~FC

DALGODA
Fantagraphics: *8 issues 1984–1986*

Dalgoda's a classic science-fiction tale set in a war-ravaged future where spending on space development means Earth technology is no more advanced than in the 1950s. Earth has made contact with one spacefaring race, the dog-like Canidans; both are threatened by a mysterious race of destructive spacefarers called The Nimp. Writer Jan Strnad builds a believable background of political manoeuvering against which his lead characters struggle to survive: Dalgoda, a Canidan spaceman sent to Earth when his own planet is about to be destroyed; Posy, a disgraced ex-Spacer who's on hand when Dalgoda's ship crashes; and Hathaway, Posy's ballsy sometime-lover, a mechanic with the space fleet.

It is in the development of characters that *Dalgoda* distinguishes itself as an adult story. By the end of the series you'll care about their futures so thoroughly that the ending will both shock and touch you. It's pretty inconclusive, however, clearly cobbled together when the series was curtailed early. Dennis Fujitake's art mixes equal parts Moebius and Manga to give a gorgeous, rounded, clear-line style. In later issues the colouring (subtly suggesting a different future in its use of purple, orange and green where primary colours would normally be employed) suffered due to the downgrading of paper stock.

Dalgoda was also blessed with a superb back-up strip in issues 2–6. Written by Strnad, atmospherically illustrated by Kevin Nowlan, 'Grimwood's Daughter' is a tart antidote to sugary elf comics with its surly, often frightening heroes who are preparing for their final battle with man. As in the main strip he resists writing an easy, happy ending.~FJ
Recommended: 5, 8

DAMAGE
DC: *21 issues (0–20) 1994–1996*

When the villain Mentallo crashes into a school classroom he activates the metagenes of the teenage Grant, who then becomes a reluctant superhero. This extremely basic series only had the one limp twist, that Grant couldn't fully control his new powers, thus creating wholesale real-estate destruction. It's not surprising that after several bog-standard punch-ups poor old Damage was retired, destined to spend the remainder of his days lurking in the bargain boxes of comic shops everywhere.~TP

DAMAGE CONTROL

Marvel: *4-issue miniseries 1988–1989, 4-issue miniseries 1989–1990, 4-issue miniseries 1991*

What to do when the Masters Of Evil trash downtown Manhattan in an all-out, no-holds-barred battle with the Avengers, for the third time this week and it's only Tuesday? Send for Damage Control! A massive repairs and renovations business, they specialise in cleaning up the mess after superbattles. A charming and logical idea, handled with a sense of humour by writer Dwayne McDuffie and penciller Ernie Colon, but sufficiently serious that it integrates smoothly into the Marvel Universe. For a while, we were treated to *Damage Control* miniseries on an annual basis, and it looked like it was going to become a regular feature. No such luck, which is a pity. Series one features a tie-in with the *X-Men's* 'Inferno' story-line, series two are all 'Acts of Vengeance' crossovers, but with enough story that they can be read independently. Series three goes cosmic with the Silver Surfer. Guest appearances by the Marvel heroes and villains abound.~HS

Recommended: Miniseries one 1–4, miniseries two 1–4, miniseries three 1–4

DAN O'NEILL'S COMICS AND STORIES

Company and Sons: *3 issues 1971*
Comics and Comix: *2 issues 1975*

O'Neill's 'Odd Bodkins' newspaper strip was collected from the underground paper *The Chronicle*. Visually O'Neill manages a beautifully loose evocation of the turn-of-the-century cartoonists, which is what one would expect from the founder of the Air Pirates group, whose style was based on the pioneers. Unfortunately the writing is completely mad, featuring characters like Billie The Giant Space Bunny, Micky Mouse and Jabberwocky. It sounds great, of course, but is frankly unreadable. Far, far too many drugs... ~DAR

DANCES WITH DEMONS

Marvel UK: *4-issue miniseries 1993*

A Native American college student finds out his dying grandfather is the Ghost Dancer, a guardian of the gateway to the spirit worlds. He is put through a series of deadly tests to see if he is worthy to inherit the ancient power (and a rather fabby costume to go with it) while demonic enemies beset his path. Although the plot is hardly original, it's more than competently told by newcomer Simon Jowett and artist Charlie Adlard. The use of ideas and characters from American Indian myth livens it up considerably, especially visually, and particularly on the covers, where Adlard brings Ed Perryman's character designs strikingly to life.~GL

DANCING WITH YOUR EYES CLOSED

Iconografix: *One-shot 1992*

A lonely guy in a new city joins an improvisational dance group that opens him to alternative ideas, but he eventually finds them as hidebound as conventional acquaintances. An admirable attempt to try something different, to be filed under 'worthy but dull'.~WJ

DANGER TRAIL

DC: *5 issues 1950–1951, 4-issue miniseries 1993*

The 1950s issues feature superspy King Faraday in adventures with agents of the Iron Curtain. Lovely art by Alex Toth and Sy Barry doesn't disguise the fact that they're unexceptional espionage tales, sought after today only because of their rarity. The 1993 miniseries, garnished with Paul Gulacy covers, sets Faraday and the lovely Natalia against the agents of Kobra. Written by Len Wein, drawn by Carmine Infantino, it's even duller than the originals.~HS

DANGER UNLIMITED

Dark Horse: *4-issue miniseries 1994*

Depending on your point of view, this is either a homage, pastiche or bare-faced rip-off of Marvel's long-running *Fantastic Four*. Written and drawn by John Byrne (who enjoyed a long, critically acclaimed, run on the FF during the 1980s), the story deals with the experiences of Calvin Carson, aka Thermal, who wakes up after seventy-five years of suspended animation to learn that his team-mates and family are dead and that the Earth is ruled by alien invaders. Events yo-yo between flashbacks to the original team and the formation of a new one in Calvin's present, giving us precious little of either before the series ends. All four issues have back-up stories featuring the Torch of Liberty, a character owing as much of a debt to Captain America as Danger Unlimited do to the FF. So far, sadly, the further adventures promised at the end of issue 4 have not materialised.~JC

DANGLE

Cat Head: *1 issue 1991*
Drawn and Quarterly: *4 issues + 1993 to date*

Lloyd Dangle's strips, broadly speaking, fall into the category of autobiographical comics, and as such he has substantially less of interest to relate than many others, and takes a long time to tell it, particularly with a strip about domestic conflict in 3. His scratchy style of cartooning often appears unformed, and the gag effects he attempts just don't really have the power they should. The Cat Head issue is reprinted as the first Drawn and Quarterly comic.~WJ

DARE: The Controversial Memoir of Dan Dare

Monster: *4-issue miniseries 1991–1992*

It's a mystery why *Dare*, reprinted from British anthology *Revolver*, was issued under Fantagraphics' short-lived Monster Comics banner. Grant Morrison and Rian Hughes' radical re-think of the Pilot of the Future probably upset a lot of fans as a prime example of what happens when the desire to make all superheroes 'adult' runs riot. The future is once again grim, with food riots, Space Fleet HQ being turned into yuppie flats, and a crippled Dan Dare returning from retirement as a propaganda tool for the unpopular right-wing government. Rian Hughes draws in an ironic *Jetsons* style as Dare begins to smell a rat while investigating Jocelyn Peabody's supposed suicide. Morrison relies on simplistic politicking to give the strip an edge, alongside shock revelations about Dare's previous behaviour. Involving, but leaves a nasty taste in the mouth.~FJ

Collection: Dare (1–4)

DARE The Impossible

Fleetway/Quality: *15 issues 1990–1991*

Reprinting the Dan Dare stories from British science-fiction anthology comic *2000AD*, *Dare the Impossible* introduced American audiences to some of the earliest work produced by artist Dave Gibbons, who made his name on the other side of the Atlantic with *Watchmen*. Reviving the old Eagle comic character in little more than name, the Dan Dare of the title was a descendant of the original, and has his adventures in the further-flung future. Often violent, but always fast-paced and entertaining, with clones, big monsters, aliens and, of course, the Mekon, it's worth picking up from the cheap boxes if you can find it.~JC

DAREDEVIL

Marvel: *359 issues +, 10 Annuals, 1 Giant-Size, 1 Graphic Novel 1964 to date*

Daredevil was not the first blind superhero in comics. DC's Dr Midnite beat him by about twenty years. Nor was he the first hero to bear the name. Lev Gleason published the first Daredevil, who had a very successful career from 1940 to 1956, but was not linked to the character who made his début in 1964. The first cover and splash page bear a drawing pencilled by the uncredited Jack Kirby, who probably designed the costume at least. Stan Lee scripts the title, and veteran artist Bill Everett draws 1, in which we learn DD's origin. As a boy, Matt Murdock is blinded by radioactive waste, but it develops his remaining senses to an amazing degree, and endows him with a new radar sense. By working out in the gym, Matt turns himself into a costumed hero, firstly to avenge his father's death, then to fight crime in general. Old pulp character The Black Bat (secret identity: blind lawyer) and Batman himself must have both been influences. Matt's dad is at the opposite end of the social spectrum to millionaire Bruce Wayne's, though. He's a boxer, victimised by a crime cartel, who pushes his son into law studies so the boy can escape his father's sleazy lifestyle. The adult Matt thus works as a lawyer, and his secretary Karen Page and partner Foggy Nelson provide much of the soap-opera ambience of the comic.

With 2 Joe Orlando and Vince Colletta start providing undistinguished art. 5 introduces star artist Wally Wood, who gives DD a new costume in 7, ditching the complex red and yellow original for an all-red number that has lasted more than three decades. Wood also scripts 10. Plenty of durable villains are introduced during this enjoyable run, the romantic triangle is developed, and 7 is a minor masterpiece, with DD fighting the vastly more powerful Sub-Mariner. With 12–14, competent John Romita arrives on pencil art, for a solid story developing Ka-Zar, Lord of the Jungle, and giving him an origin. 15 is a genuinely touching tale of the Ox, a supervillain from the Wood issues, given a chance to redeem himself, and 16–17 guest-star Spider-Man, who is either pencilled by Ditko or swiped in several of 16's early panels, until Romita starts to develop his own version. By 20, Romita was drawing Spidey in his own comic, and was replaced on *Daredevil* by Gene Colan, who, like Romita, had been drawing romance strips for years. Both men were well suited to continue the soap-opera elements of *Daredevil*. Colan, though, was a more original stylist, and brought a shadowy, quasi-photographic look to Marvel that was miles from the dominant Kirby style, but no less dynamic. Frank Giacoia's slick inking worked even better on Colan than Romita, and helped smooth the transition. As befitted a hero with no superstrength and an origin linked to the New York underworld, Daredevil's adventures had thus far leaned heavily on a gangster milieu, but supervillains dominated more and more during the next phase. In 25, with his secret identity in peril, Matt masquerades as his own twin brother, Mike, who is supposedly DD's real identity. This gets really stupid. Matt and Mike can never be seen together, but Foggy and Karen are still fooled. In 31, having lost his supersenses, DD has to convince his friends that Mike Murdock has now also become blind! And they believe it! Old Thor villains the Cobra and Mister Hyde are beautifully rendered by Colan in this story (30 – 32). Annual 1, 1967, is a Lee/Colan funfest, with five baddies ganging up on DD in a typical no-brainer plot, but beautifully done. A humorous back-up, showing Stan and Gene working on a story, reveals that Colan did most of the plotting. 35–38 is an enjoyable tale involving Doctor Doom and crossing over into *Fantastic Four* 73. In 41 the ludicrous Mike Murdock identity is finally killed off. 42's new villain, the Jester, transparently rips off of Batman's Joker. 43 guest-stars Captain America, and 44–46 is an enjoyable Jester epic, after which he should have been pensioned off. He wasn't. 45 has one of Marvel's most effective photo covers of the period, with Colan's battling figures on a Statue of Liberty background, and 46 begins a memorable run on inks by DC alumnus George Klein. 47's 'Brother, Take My Hand' is a little gem, in which both Matt Murdock and Daredevil help a blinded Vietnam veteran in trouble with the Mob. That the victim is black is typical Lee, starting to bring liberal themes into his comics, and also points up both the strengths and the weaknesses of his approach. It could be read as patronising and tokenistic, but this was 1968, and Lee really was breaking new ground.

48 and 49 have stunning Colan/Klein covers, but from 50 the barely competent, Kirby-worshipping young Barry Smith pencils three issues guest-starring the Black Panther. Roy Thomas takes over the writing from 51 and introduces Starr Saxon, a camp, film-obsessed mad scientist, later claimed to have been the first gay character in comics, though it's not very overt. Colan and Klein are back on 53, for a beautiful origin and career recap issue, with another fabulous cover. Syd Shores arrives on inks with 55. An era of artistic excellence is over, but Thomas's scripts intelligently develop the Stan Lee mode. In what is probably a superhero first, Matt reveals his secret identity to Karen in 57. It's the beginning of the end for their relationship, as she can't stand the strain of sharing his secret, and starts a new career as a Hollywood actress in 63. Roy Thomas bows out with a liberal bang in 70–71's story of student protests. From 72 the mediocre Gerry Conway is the writer, and the only saving grace of the next twenty-five issues is the arrival of inker Tom Palmer with 76. At least the title looks good again, though Colan is past his peak. 77, guest-starring Spider-Man and Sub-Mariner, is distinguished only by a caption on page 17 which gave a cult rock group from Liverpool their name – The Teardrop Explodes. In 81, former Soviet spy turned heroine the Black Widow enters Daredevil's life, taking the romantic reins from Karen Page in 86. From 87 the action shifts to San Francisco, and 92–107 are titled *Daredevil And The Black Widow*. From 95 there is no more Tom Palmer, and a game of 'musical artists' sets in, until the dull Bob Brown takes residence from 107. Steve Gerber's arrival on scripts in 98 prevents a total decline, but only temporarily. Conway had taken *Daredevil* away from its gangsterish roots and New York setting, and firmly into science-fiction/supervillain territory. Gerber continued this, but with far more wit and inventiveness – 101's villain gets his powers from LSD. In 109 jungle heroine Shanna The She-Devil starts a longish guest run, and 113 introduces a lasting new villain, Death-Stalker. After 117 there's no more Gerber, but Daredevil's back in New York, and in 124 inker Klaus Janson arrives and the Black Widow leaves. 131 sees the arrival of the new Bullseye, a bad guy who will be back later in a big way, but these are mostly second-hand plots by second-rate creators, except for Janson, who leaves after 132. Jim Shooter starts scripting with 144, but only when he links up with penciller/plotter Gil Kane from 146, and Janson returns in 147, do things start to pick up. From 152 Roger McKenzie scripts, and it's good solid stuff until talented young penciller Frank Miller joins in 158, which also reveals Death-Stalker's origin at last (not worth the wait!).

Miller's run on *Daredevil* is legendary, and rightly so. Obviously influenced by the drawing styles of Gil Kane and Neal Adams, plus the story-telling of Will Eisner, he found his own look very quickly. Credited as co-plotter with McKenzie from 165, he starts scripting from 168, which introduces Elektra. This female assassin has an origin story which pays homage to Eisner, and links back to DD's earlier life. She is a major new love interest, incorporated through Miller's retrofitting of Daredevil's origins. A lowlife Zen master called Stick is brought in to give Matt's early years a kung-fu flavour, and in the present day DD needs Stick's help as he gets into deep water with Elektra and her nasty oriental pals, the Triad-like Hand. Gang boss the Kingpin, predominantly a Spider-Man villain before this, and Bullseye are the main bad guys of Miller's extended story-line, which takes DD back to his street crime roots in a big way. The grim and gritty New York street scenes in *Daredevil* were a major influence on mainstream US comics for years to come. Elektra is killed by Bullseye in the historically good 181, following which Miller does increasingly thin layouts for Janson to finish. The stories remain first-rate. Into the potent mix of superheroics, mysticism and street life comes the new look Black Widow from 188. In 190's double-sized finale, all Miller's plots come to a rousing conclusion. 191 manages to top it with an epilogue in which DD plays Russian roulette with the helpless Bullseye. In this issue, Miller gives us one of the most powerful stories ever told about the pros and cons of superheroes, as bringers of justice, role models for the young and violent vigilante figures. Miller's revolutionary Batman story,

The Dark Knight Returns, is foreshadowed here.

After a couple of fill-ins, Denny O'Neil starts a long run from 194. His scripts are thoughtful, but increasingly less exciting as he works his way up to 200's showdown with the revived Bullseye. DD has been having traumas of guilt ever since he failed to kill Bullseye, and it's no secret that Miller wanted his hero to end the life of this contemptible villain. In 200 O'Neil turns this about, and would have us believe that DD's guilt trip is all because he dared to harbour wicked thoughts of killing. Ho hum. O'Neil thinks he can take superheroes a step back into such naïve comforts as this, but the 1986 revolution is coming fast! Janson bows out with 197 and the art plummets in quality, making the book virtually unreadable despite O'Neil's solid stories, which include a recurring villain, the Gael, who is an Irish Republican. Penciller David Mazzucchelli starts in 206, and gets into gear around 209. He has a strong Gene Colan influence, with Milleresque touches, but he is given terrible inking, until he takes on the job himself. 219 is a street-tough fill-in written by Frank Miller, drawn by John Buscema. 227–233 see the return of Miller on script, and Mazzucchelli is energised to produce astonishingly good artwork, his Miller influence given free rein. This is another tough tale of the Kingpin, who comes close to destroying Daredevil after learning his secret identity from the forgotten Karen Page, now a fading porn starlet and desperate heroin addict. As if this triumphant return wasn't enough, Miller also writes one of the best- ever Captain America stories in 232–233, and Cap's only the guest star.

233 leaves Matt Murdoch, true to his roots, providing legal services for the poor of a New York slum, Hell's Kitchen, and 234 is an amusing Gruenwald/Ditko/Janson filler. Ann Nocenti's long and well-respected run starts with 236, a fill-in drawn by Barry Smith, who's improved a bit since 52! Nocenti's stories have themes which ought to be interesting, but are often clumsily handled, with an excess of sentiment. 244 is a good example: Karen is once again stressed-out by Matt's violent *alter ego*, but comes to admit she loves his violent side too, after it saves her life. And just what are we supposed to make of Karen's reference to Matt's 'loving fist'? Dubious sexual practices are suggested, but Nocenti really means his 'loving hand'. Some clunky scripting and some very mixed messages. In 245 the Black Panther thinks a defeated villain should be allowed to commit suicide. DD thinks he can be cured of his lowlife ways and, amidst many tears, he gets a legit job and is reunited with his wife and son. This is story-telling which aspires to the dizzyingly high standards of daytime TV. Still, once Nocenti hooks up with penciller John

Romita Jnr (yes, the son of 12–19's artist) and inker Al Williamson (the third EC veteran to make a major contribution to *Daredevil*) from 248, there's no denying that things look good again, and the stories do improve. Typhoid Mary, Nocenti's most enduring character, débuts in 254. A tough-bitch assassin with a split personality, she's hired by the Kingpin to seduce and then kill Daredevil. There is undoubtedly power in many of the scenes which follow, especially in Typhoid's confrontations with the Kingpin, but the story has an unresolved dénouement in 261 which shades uneasily into the silly 'Inferno' crossover of 262–265. Nocenti next brings DD up against a redesigned Mephisto, Marvel's bargain-basement Satan. Karen has rejected Matt after finding out about Typhoid, and DD is close to despair. Mephisto in 266 thinks the hero is nearly ready to be plucked from the path of righteousness. In 267 DD goes to church, and his first confession in many years, which doesn't help, because he's started to enjoy hurting criminals, as developed in 268.

Nocenti's greatest epic is 270–282, and characteristically the ending muddles its themes and poisons them with sentimentality, though it has excellent moments along the way. Daredevil, Gorgon and Karnak of the Inhumans, and various others, end up in Mephisto's Hell. Though there are heavy hints that God is on their side, our heroes essentially beat all Mephisto's ploys by learning the following lessons: Self-knowledge is power. Whatever does not kill me makes me strong. The strong will attain victory. All these are overtly Nietzschean doctrines, yet Nietzsche was the first major writer to proclaim openly the Death Of God. After all this, Mephisto is all set to fry Daredevil and company anyway, when the Silver Surfer flies in out of nowhere to save their bacon! Talk about mixed messages!

After these philosophical excesses, 283 signals a return to superheroics by guest-starring Captain America again, in a blue-collar but sentimental tale of what it means to be an American. Compared to Miller's 232–233, this is like a 1950s story. Then it's back to New York City for more Kingpin, as DD's wild mood swings take him from the steely determination he showed against Mephisto back to despair, and the brink of madness. 288–290 has Bullseye in a Daredevil costume fighting DD in a Bullseye suit, and the dubious conclusion that 'We turned out to be the same man.' The art on this run is by Lee Weeks, who operates in the territory between Mazzucchelli and Romita Jnr., which is good stuff. Nocenti leaves, and D.G.Chichester writes an epic tale of the Kingpin, Typhoid Mary and the Hand from 294. In 297–300's 'Fall Of The Kingpin', Matt

Murdock plots the downfall of the crime boss, with help from Nick Fury and Hydra, as thoroughly as the Kingpin destroyed Matt's life in 227. It's intelligent material, but Chichester diffuses the power of the ending, when the Kingpin bounces back too quickly. The next run is undistinguished fare, treading water.

Chichester's 'Fall From Grace' in 319–325 brings Image-style art from Scott McDaniel, and a tough, armoured new costume in red and grey. This is an attempt to do a 30th-anniversary Dark Knight renewal on DD. It's not too bad, the art capturing some of Miller's surface flair, though with poor story-telling clarity. Among a complex set of plot elements, Elektra is forced to return from her peaceful spiritual retreat, reviving her marketability as an ongoing character. The creators stayed until 332, then left for an *Elektra* miniseries. Lesser hands continued the tough, grim new DD until readers voted with their wallets, and writer J.M. DeMatteis was given the task of bringing back a kinder, gentler version. 343–347 sees three different Daredevils apparently running around (original costume, red costume, new costume) and Matt Murdock once again losing his shaky grip on sanity. In 348–350 he seeks help from Stick and his long-lost mother (revealed as a nun by Miller in 229) in getting himself back together. This paves the way for 353's return to courtroom dramas, the red costume and 1960s-style heroics. Karl Kesel writes, Cary Nord and Matt Ryan draw, and it all looks very nice. Matt Murdock returns from the dead, Foggy Nelson figures out his secret identity, and after thirty-three years, Matt finally asks Karen Page what colour her eyes are. Many readers love this, but others speculate on how long the retreading of old ground can last.

The 1986 graphic novel, 'Love and War', is written by Frank Miller and drawn by Bill Sienkiewicz in a variety of media and styles. Some individual panels are stunning, but there's a mismatch between the arty look and the superheroic sequences. The story also has psychological elements, with the Kingpin desperate to find a cure for his beloved wife Vanessa, left in a vegetative state after *Daredevil* 180. Intelligently handled for the most part, but with a well-meant but disastrously non-credible scene in which a blind kidnap victim fights back.~GL

Recommended: 7, 12–14, 20–24, 35–38, 42, 44–48, 53, 147, 151, 161, 163, 164, 174, 175, 178–182, 187–191, 227–233, 254–261, 270–272

Collections: Born Again (226–229), Daredevil /Punisher: Child's Play (182–184), Fall From Grace (319–325), Fall Of The Kingpin (297–300), Gang War (169–172, 180), Love And War (230–233), Marvel Masterworks Vol.17 (1–11), Marked for Death (159–161, 163, 164)

DARK DOMINION
Defiant: *10 issues, 1993–1994*

Michael Alexander has learned how to shift to the 'Quantum Field', where he fights demons that feed off the fear that permeates New York. An idea with potential, and a good evocation of urban paranoia, but the rules governing the Field and the demons are never spelled out, reducing the fights to random splatterings. Sometimes the demons are used well as metaphors for madness or interior struggle, but too often they're treated as entirely external, so that Alexander can make someone happier simply by shooing off their anxiety-demon, and this makes a nonsense of any characterisation.~FC
Recommended: 5–6

DARK GUARD
Marvel UK: *3-issue miniseries 1993*

The more popular of Marvel UK's early 90s superheroes are pulled out of time and united to fight a threat to the future. Death's Head, Killpower, Motormouth and Dark Guard all feature, but apart from the occasional piece of nice art from Carlos Pacheco it's poor stuff.~FP

DARK HORSE COMICS
Dark Horse: *25 issues 1992–1994*

This anthology title from Dark Horse contains serialised tales of licensed properties alongside features owned by Dark Horse. *Robocop, Predator, Indiana Jones, Aliens, Star Wars* and *James Bond* share the pages with the lack-lustre *Time Cop* (1–3), the introduction of *X* (and consequently *Comics Greatest World*) in 8–10, and other Dark Horse heroes.

Predator and *Aliens* features come to dominate the title; best of the *Aliens* tales is 'Horror Show' by Sarah Byam and David Roach in 3–5. The Predators generally come off better, switching times and locations. A group of paintballers get theirs in the prelude to *Bad Blood* in 12–14, there's a good Chuck Dixon and Alcatena tale in 10–12 and Howard Cobb's art in 21–22 is excellent. From 19–24 there are segments of *Comics Greatest World* characters each issue. Reducing from four to three features per issue with 12 is an improvement, but there's still a real feeling of inconsequential filler material throughout. From 20 it's two features per issue, but the final issues are the worst of the run, with a very poor *Mecha* effort, an over-the-top cartoon-style *Aliens* and a daft *James Bond* story.~WJ

DARK HORSE PRESENTS
Dark Horse: *121 issues (5 x 100) + 1 Special 1986 to date*

Randy Stradley, editor until issue 87, worked hard to create an anthology that was both willing to be experimental but also capable of drawing on the work of established creators.

At the beginning it was a place to preview new series like Boris the Bear or Trekker (though the only real success of this period was Concrete) or publish an eclectic mix of series that were unlikely to fit elsewhere (Mindwalk, by Stradley himself, 1–4, 20, Roma by John Workman, 5, 6, 8, 9, 11, and The Masque by Mark Badger, 10–15, 18–21). Later previews include Aliens (24, 34, 42, 43, 56, 101, 102), Predator (35, 46, 67–69), Aliens vs Predator (36), Next Men (54–57), Monkeyman and O'Brien (80, 100–5), Hellboy (88–91,100–102), Too Much Coffee Man (92–95) and Cud's Eno and Plum (93–95). Homeless creations too (Roachmill, 17, 28, Kings In Disguise, 42, Crash Ryan, 44–46, Mr. Monster, 14, 20, 28, 33 and Alien Fire, 57–59) were given the opportunity to gain a new audience when their own titles failed.

Throughout, Stradley tried to match known quantities with more difficult or less populist work such as that of Rick Geary (19, 20, 22–24, 44, 53, 56, 57, 59, 60, 82, 87, 92, 100–104, 109), Leopoldo Duranona's 'Race of Scorpions' (23–27, 30–34), Gary Davis' 'Paleolove' (16, 20, 21, 25, 26, 32, 36–39, 43, 68–70, 77–79, 88), Matt Wagner's 'Aerialist' (40, 45), Jodorowsky and Moebius' 'Madwoman of the Sacred Heart' (70–76), Robert Boyd and F. Solano Lopez' 'Buoy' (77, 81–84), Harvey Pekar and Joe Sacco (99, 100–1, 100–3, 100–4, 101,102, 104) and Ivan Brunetti (100–3).

Though the concentration was primarily on writer/artists, teams of creators weren't unknown, whether on the licensed material (Predator, Aliens), John Arcudi's Homicide and Creep (which employed a number of artists including Gray Morrow, 53–55), Stefano Gaudiano's artwork on Harlequin (48–51) and Here and Now (96–98), Jo Duffy's Manga-influenced 'Nestrobber' with Maya Sakamoto (67–69) or the sublimely detailed artwork of Frank Quitely (91–93).

Several longer-running series deserve special mention, whether confined to the title, continuations of other series or preludes to greater things. 'Bob The Alien' by Rich Rice (18–20, 29–32, 39, 40) is a delightfully downbeat series of episodes of an alien adapting himself to big-city life. Eddie Campbell's brilliant Bacchus, now self-published, proved itself to a US audience here (32, 37, 40, 44, 46, 52, 57, 71, 76–84: 'Hermes vs The Eyeball Kid', 94–99: 'Picture of Doreen Grey' and 66–70 and 100–2 gave space to his semi-autobiographical Alec). Frank Miller's noir 'Sin City' first appeared in the Fifth Anniversary special and continued in 50–61, with 62 being devoted to it entirely. Paul Pope's quirky science-fiction saga 'The One-Trick Rip-Off' (101–112) is the latest example of the title's urge to promote newer talent and its

willingness to give it plenty of space.

With Bob Schreck taking over the editorial role with 88, there has been, perhaps, a higher proportion of less well known creators: Jim Alexander and Robert McCallum's 'Baden' (93–95), Dave Cooper (98, 106), Renée French (100-1, 107–112), Jon Lewis (100–1), Robert Loren Fleming and Bill Wray's 'Big Blown Baby' (106), Jack Pollock (100–2, 107–109), mixed in with only slightly better known ones with their own titles (Roberta Gregory, Shannon Wheeler, Terry LaBan, Evan Dorkin).

Issues 20, 32 and 56 are sixty-four page Annuals, while the Fifth Anniversary Special was over a hundred pages of Give Me Liberty, Concrete, Aliens, The American, Roachmill, Black Cross, The Aerialist and Sin City amongst others. So much material was gathered for Issue 100 that it spread over five issues, numbered 100–1 on. Few anthologies have lasted this long, fewer still can boast such a large proportion of high-quality creators. Long may it continue.~NF

Recommended: 1–6, 20, 32, 51–62, 76–84, 91–93
Collection: Sin City (Sin City from 51–62)

THE DARK KNIGHT RETURNS
DC: 4-issue miniseries 1986

Now an acknowledged classic, and responsible for several key developments in American comics, at the time DC were taking a bit of a flyer. Although lauded for his work on Daredevil, Frank Miller's succeeding project Ronin had received a lukewarm reception. It took a confident editor (Denny O'Neil) to say 'Okay then' when given a proposal for a wholesale and uncharacteristic reworking of the company's most popular character in a pricey and untested format. Miller repaid the faith by turning in what remains a career peak. From the well-considered title pun to the extraordinary subtle, unusual and effective colouring of Lynn Varley, The Dark Knight Returns is stunning. And it's Miller throughout.

It's set ten years after Batman has last been sighted in public. Commissioner Gordon is due for retirement and Gotham is plagued by the marauding Mutant gangs pillaging at will. Batman's old enemy Two-Face has been released back into the community, seemingly a reformed man, and certainly a repaired one thanks to plastic surgery, and immediately picks up his former career. Events have reached a point where Batman can no longer remain a bystander, but this is a different Batman. He's in tune with the times, realising that at his age he requires extreme measures to deal with society's ills. That alone is interesting, but Miller counterpoints the re-emergence of Batman and his actions with incessant flashes of public opinion and commentary through TV (a narrative technique pioneered by Howard Chaykin in *American Flagg*), making for an extremely dense read. The use of numerous small panels on each page jumping to a full-page illustration only serves to emphasise the iconic effect of the character, and when fellow-icons Superman and The Joker turn up for the second half of the series they receive similar resonant treatment. Miller explores all kinds of opinions pertaining to the concept of the vigilante without reaching a real conclusion, but still providing food for thought a decade on. Plot, dialogue and art are all well considered, effective and top notch.

It's astonishingly rare that a legitimate claim can be made that anyone has changed the face of their artform, but consider what followed in the wake of *The Dark Knight Returns*. There was a plethora of 'radical' reworkings of established characters, some more successful than others. The miniseries had been popularised and *Dark Knight* had proved that there was a market for a well-produced package. Designers became key personnel at leading publishers, more talented creators were given greater freedom with regard to individual interpretations of characters and concepts, and the *Dark Knight* collected edition seeped into public consciousness beyond the comic market. Most important was the return of respect for the creator. Tangentially it also wiped away the final vestiges of the Batman TV show, re-establishing the property as a desirable licensing option. That all of these can be attributed to a single series is remarkable, and that there was a serious and rapid dilution of its strengths and influence shouldn't detract from the achievement. None of the above could ever have been foreseen by Miller, though, who set out to produce a thought-provoking superhero story and succeeded beyond his wildest dreams.~WJ

Recommended: 1–4
Collection: The Dark Knight Returns (1–4)

Batman: Legends of the DARK KNIGHT

DC: *89 issues +, 1 Special, 6 Annuals 1989 to date*

This was conceived as a vehicle for Batman stories without creators having to compromise by adherence to the continuity of regular Batman comics. It's since also become a home for individual artistic interpretation of the character. It's impossible to conceive Mike McMahon's brilliant, almost cubist, styling in 55–57 gracing a regular title, yet that it appeared one issue after Arthur Ranson's near-photo-realism speaks volumes for editorial catholicism.

1–20 comprise four stories of five chapters apiece set early in Batman's career. Opening with the type of decent but unmemorable

Batman story Denny O'Neil can probably write in his sleep, the best of the early quartet is by Grant Morrison and Klaus Janson. More than fulfilling its title, 'Gothic' (6–10) is a disturbing brew of public-school brutality, mad monks and compacts with the devil, showing the début of the bat-signal along the way. 'Venom', in 16–20, initially portrays a Batman out of control, having sampled powerful steroids, but the conclusion doesn't live up to the premise. Since 20 no story has run beyond four issues, and the first single instalment was 27, establishing a look for Gotham City based on stunning illustrations by Anton Furst (included). Denny O'Neil, Chris Sprouse and Bruce Patterson's story crosses over into *Detective* 641.

'Faces' by Matt Wagner in 28–30 is a dense, complex tale of freaks, freedom and finance, and among the best stories to have appeared here. Other contenders are James Robinson and Tim Sale's 'Blades' (32–34), introducing a new defender for Gotham, and 'Masks', written and drawn by Bryan Talbot in 39–40, with an utterly convincing portrayal of Bruce Wayne as a deluded alcoholic with a costumed fantasy life. By contrast 'Turf', by Steven Grant and Shawn McManus, in 44–45 falls just short, yet is still a compelling story, taking the video footage of Rodney King as inspiration. Grant and Mike Zeck's 'Criminals' in 69–70 is another fine effort.

There have been few really duff issues of *Legends of the Dark Knight*, and plenty of artistic legends worked on well crafted stories, including Gil Kane (24–26), P. Craig Russell (42–43), Russ Heath (46–49), Mike Mignola (54) and Scott Hampton (76–78). The best of the single episodes are 'Mercy' (37) by Dan Abnett, Andy Lanning and Colin MacNeil, Alan Grant and Kev O'Neill's hallucinogenic return of Bat-Mite in 38, 'Storm' by Graham Brand, Andrew Donkin and John Higgins (58), and Chris Bachalo and Mark Pennington illustrating Jamie Delano's bleak 'Terminus' in 64 (although it's not as terminally depressing as 'Engines' by Ted McKeever in 74–75). Best annuals are 2, with Commissioner Gordon's unconventional wedding, and the 'Elseworlds' (alternate out-of-continuity version of Batman) story in 4, with remarkable art from the team of Joe Staton and Horacio Ottolini. Staton also illustrates the J.M. DeMatteis look into the Joker's psyche, 'Going Sane' in 65–68. Believing he's killed Batman, the Joker's mental problems retreat as he settles into an ordinary life and relationship.

The best of the more recent stories is James Vance's deftly plotted 'Idols' in 80–82, with good action art from Dougie Braithwaite and Sean Hardy. Set early in Batman's career, a serial killer arrives in Gotham at the same time as a Batman fad hits the city; an intense FBI agent is also on hand to complicate the nascent relationship between Commissioner Gordon and Batman. Generally better writers Warren Ellis and James Robinson are on autopilot for 83–85, but Quique Alcatena's art on 'Clay', the origin of Clayface, is the best seen in the title for some considerable time.~FP

Recommended: 6–10, 27–30, 37–40, 52, 53, 55–58, 66, 80–82, Annual 4

Collections: Collected Legends of the Dark Knight (32–34, 38, 42–43), *Dark Legends* (39, 40, 50, 52–54), *Faces* (28–30), *Gothic* (6–10), *Prey* (11–15), *Shaman* (1–5), *Venom* (16–20)

DARK MANSION OF FORBIDDEN LOVE
DC: *4 issues 1971–1972*

One of several experiments with Gothic romance comics, this featured lengthy stories best remembered for their artwork. Typically the writing, by the likes of Dorothy Manning and Jack Oleck, leant more heavily on the romance than the mystery, with the horror element usually confined to creepy-looking houses. Artistically, Tony DeZuniga excelled in the first two issues, with 3 and 4 pencilled less impressively by Don Heck. In some respects, though, the comic's visual highpoint was its beautiful painted covers. From 5 the comic was renamed *Forbidden Tales Of Dark Mansion.*~DAR

DARK SHADOWS
Gold Key: *35 issues 1969–1976*

The arcane atmosphere of the cult TV series is reduced to trite soap opera and supernatural clichés at the hands of journeymen creators. The saving grace is the occasional nice cover painting.~FP

DARK SHADOWS
Innovation: *Miniseries one 4 issues 1992–1993, Miniseries two 4 issues 1993, One-shot 1993*

Based on the 1991 TV series, itself a spin-off from the long-running 60s series, *Dark Shadows* is primarily the story of the vampire Barnabas Collins and his relationship with Victoria Winters. More psychological than physical horror, the painted artwork, heavily photo-referenced, makes the whole thing seem very wooden and lifeless.~NF

The Pirates Of DARK WATER
Marvel: *6-issue miniseries 1991–1992*

Dwight Zimmerman, Bruce Zick and Rick Magyar produce creditable adaptations from the children's fantasy-cartoon adventure series. Elf-like Ren has to locate the thirteen treasures of Rule, but it wouldn't be any kind of quest if he could pick them up in Tesco, would it? So pirate king Bloth is there to complicate matters.~WJ

DARKHAWK
Marvel: *50 issues 1991–1995*

Sticking religiously to the Marvel template of a teenager unexpectedly receiving mysterious superpowers that constantly complicate their social life, *Darkhawk* confirms the principles of diminishing returns. Acknowledging creative redundancy, Marvel pump guest appearances by Spider-Man, Daredevil, Captain America and the Punisher into the first nine issues, but even characters with a following can't transform this into anything above mediocre. Ironically, issues where Darkhawk carries the comic on his own are marginally better. The mystery behind the power amulet found in the first issue is strung out to 25, and 42 makes a good sample with Chris Powell intending to reveal his other identity to his parents.~FP

DARKHOLD
Marvel: *16 issues 1992–1993*

Individual pages from The Darkhold, an ancient book of incredible evil, are offered to people who, once they read the mystic incantations thereon, set off demonic forces beyond their control. A group calling themselves The Redeemers seek to put matters right. Old hero/villain Mordred is a regular and guest-stars aplenty seek to boost sales, but serve only to further confuse already muddled plots. Much was made of one of the characters being lesbian. Of course, she's a male fantasy figure. If you must read more, *Marvel Comics Presents* 146 concludes their story.~WJ

DARKLON The Mystic
Pacific: *One-shot 1983*

Sword-and-sorcery by Jim Starlin reprinted from *Eerie*. A peculiar tale, almost deliberately handicapped by the choice of claustrophobic small panels and the decision to relate most of the story as first-person flashback narrative. It all seems an experiment, and doesn't gel at all, with the supposedly mystical Darklon manifesting little in the way of arcane talent.~FP

THE DARKNESS
Top Cow: *2 issues + 1996 to date*

Creator Marc Silvestri says he's been pondering the idea behind *The Darkness* for months, years even, which tells you something about the quality of his thought processes. Fortunately he's bought in Garth Ennis to 'flesh out' the characters. A bit. Jackie's a pretty young *mafioso* who discovers, on his twenty-first birthday, that he's the heir to The Darkness, an all-consuming force that allows him to do nasty things to people. As he's involved in a gang war one suspects this will prove useful in the future. Meanwhile Angelus has been waiting for his first transformation to kill The Darkness at its weakest. A dozen assassins prove unequal to this task. Of course, there's a price to be paid for this sort of power. If you can get over Silvestri's slimy art it could be fun. Ennis isn't exactly stretching himself, but it's reasonably sharp mind candy and it certainly wastes no time getting going.~FJ

DARKSTARS
DC: *39 issues (0–38) 1992–1996*

A better-than-average spin-off from *Green Lantern*, as the Darkstars take over as Galactic Guardians after the dismantling of the Green Lantern Corps. The constantly rotating cast prevents boredom setting in, and there's an almost hi-tech Western feel, with a Texas base setting and the assistant Darkstars known as deputies. Jan Michael Friedman's writing is tight and Travis Charest's highly detailed art is pleasing to the eye, although his run is sadly restricted to 4–11. John Stewart, former Green Lantern, and Donna Troy, former Wonder Girl, both join the team to provide familiar faces, but later issues become more cosmic, moving away from the idea of alien intervention on Earth.~TP
Recommended: 1–8

DART
Image: *3-issue miniseries 1996*

In a prequel story to her *Savage Dragon* and *Freak Force* appearances, our novice heroine meets the appalling Kill-Cat for the first time and gets embroiled with rogue toy manufacturers who try to steal her likeness for commercial exploitation, and their superpowered minions. A peculiar tale with some interesting plot elements, dreadful script, and weird art by Joseph Szekeres, who from the evidence here has the desire, but not the skill, to be a fetish artist when he grows up.~HS

DATE WITH DEBBI
DC: *18 issues 1969–1972.*

This freckle-faced, red-haired teenage klutz looks even more like a female clone of Archie than Archie's own distaff counterpart Josie did. Stories inevitably revolved around love-hungry Debbi's social and physical clumsiness ruining her chances for happiness, with allegedly hilarious results. Briefly popular, a spin-off, *Debbi's Dates*, ran for eleven issues from 1969 to 1971.~HS

DAWN
Sirius: *3 issues + 1995 to date*

In an alternative New York Darrian Ashoka meets an enigmatic woman during the regular Times Square Battle To The Death. An aspect of the Goddess of Death and Rebirth, she involves him in her quest to steal Lucifer's halo. It's a gift from God, which, after a lover's spat, God wants back. Artist and writer Joseph Michael Linsner has something going on here.

It's all very wispy and irritatingly mysterious, and there are certainly too many panels of our resident goddess strutting and posing in lingerie, but there's still a creeping suspicion that there's an actual plot somewhere. And it's awful pretty to look at. Solicited as a six-issue miniseries, it's now running a year or two behind schedule. If you're reasonably fit, though, and under forty, there's every reason to hope you may live to see the conclusion. It had better be worth the wait.~HS

DAYS OF DARKNESS
Apple: *6-issue miniseries 1992–1993*

Wayne Vansant tells the story of the extended Cahill family and their involvement in aspects of World War II, beginning with the Japanese bombing of Pearl Harbour. It's an odd comic, attempt to merge TV-style generational fiction sagas with war action. Although meticulously researched and drawn, it falls short because Vansant is seemingly far more interested in the battles than the family. Characterisation has never been Vansant's strongpoint, but here it matters for once, and there's little point in introducing a large cast only to sideline most of them. That said, there are portions of the series that are powerful and affecting, particularly the first half of issue 5. It depicts the brutality of the Japanese towards captured Filipinos (ironically duplicating American behaviour forty-five years previously) and the conditions endured by captured Americans. If you like pages of authentic-looking, lovingly depicted air and naval battles, they don't come better than *Days Of Darkness*, but for a story try elsewhere.~FP

DAYS OF WRATH
Apple: *4 issues 1993–1994*

Wayne Vansant continues his saga of the Cahill family during World War II, showing battles through the eyes of ordinary American conscripts. Always excellent art from Vansant can't compensate for his very dry story-telling methods. It was planned as a six-issue series, but the final two issues were never published.~WJ

DAZZLER
Marvel: *42 issues 1981–1986, Graphic novel 1984*

Originally conceived as *The Disco Dazzler*, a rapid re-think was in order as the disco backlash hit with full force. Instead of scrapping the idea of a mutant disco singer able to generate light blasts as too late to cash in on a passing fad, Marvel flew in the face of fashion to publish a total turkey listing no less than eleven people in the credits of the first issue. That enough people bought this to keep it going over three years is astounding. Ironically, cancellation came as then writer Archie Goodwin was actually injecting some life into issues drawn, probably to his eternal shame, by Paul Chadwick, who was to go on to better things. Dazzler later ended up in *X-Men* (where she'd made her début in 130).~FP

DC CHALLENGE
DC: *12-issue limited series 1985–1986*

A mystery starring dozens of characters was set up in the first issue, and had to be solved and concluded in the last. Each issue had a different set of creators, who ended their segment on a cliffhanger for the next creative team to solve. A nice idea, with lots of good creators and characters, but proving to be a fundamentally flawed, fortuitous, fussy fable that festered and failed to impress with force-fed plots. The whole thing turned into a feeble mess – a flamboyant fraud that flaked at the seams. Fundamentally, a farce. The finale was a godsend. A fatwa on the instigator! So are there any more words beginning with 'f' to describe this series? Why, yes… ~HY

DC COMICS PRESENTS
DC: *97 issues, 4 Annuals 1978–1986*

Well, Batman had a monthly team-up title introduced when he was DC's most popular hero in the 1960s, so with the Superman films having elevated him to that position in the late 1970s it was only fair he also got a team-up title. As one might expect, there's a lot of average stuff punctuating the occasional good issues, but the series began well with José Luis Garcia-Lopez drawing 1–4, teaming Superman with Flash, Adam Strange and the Metal Men. The next story that really stands out is in 26–29: Len Wein with Jim Starlin art featuring team-ups with Martian Manhunter, Supergirl and the Spectre in a connected story introducing Mongul, who'd later play a devastating part in Green Lantern's history. 26 is also of note for a free insert introducing DC's hit of the early 1980s, *New Teen Titans*. Roy Thomas returned the unlikely Hoppy The Marvel Bunny from limbo in 33–34, teaming Superman with Captain Marvel and his extended family, and in 36 Paul Levitz concluded the Starman feature that had been running in *Adventure*, again with Jim Starlin art. Martin Pasko and Joe Staton offered a very unusual Plastic Man team-up in 39, and 41 contained the first sighting of Roy Thomas' 1982 revising of Wonder Woman. 1982's first annual featured the unlikely teaming of Superman and Superman (from an alternate Earth) combatting their evil counterpart from yet another Earth.

Paul Levitz and Keith Giffen produced two very stylised team-ups featuring the Doom Patrol in 52, and the Legion Of Substitute Heroes in 59. The latter failed to take the second string Legionnaires seriously at all, and launched a period of ridicule for them as foul-ups in the Legion is a charming, q type DC once ducing the long-s conceived by Elliot fourth annual, ni Barreto, but repetiti are notable for their a Morrow drawing a M Joe Kubert illustrating …nd the classic 1960s Superman …un of Curt Swan and Murphy Anderson drawing a teaming with Santa Claus!

77's 'Forgotten Heroes' revives and teams a number of obscurities, of whom Animal Man went on to greater glories, and 78's 'Forgotten Villains' brings back even more recondite characters. Keith Giffen returns for a quirky Ambush Bug story in 81, and 85 has Alan Moore delivering a Swamp Thing team-up. It's a highlight of the run, but doesn't match Moore's work on Swamp Thing's own title, but then he was writing for a different audience. 87 is the interesting idea of Superman arriving as a baby on our Earth, and growing to adolescence as the only superhero on the planet. If that sounds creatively redundant, it towers over the final few issues, by which point the title was cancelled to make way for John Byrne's revision of Superman.

A back-up feature asking 'Whatever Happened To…' débuted in 26, and continued in most issues until 42, the best of them spotlighting Star Hawkins (33), Rex The Wonder Dog (drawn by Gil Kane in 35) and The Crimson Avenger (38).~HY

Recommended: 26–29, 37, 39, 52, 59, 66, 85, annual 2

DC Graphic Novels

DC have published about twenty titles as Graphic Novels, and these can be divided into four categories: stories based on established comics characters; good science-fiction stories; bad or indifferent science-fiction stories; and *Tell Me Dark*.

None of the stories dealing with established comics characters are truly bad, but none are compulsive reading either. In approximate order of increasing merit: *Viking Glory* is about the problems and adventures that the young Viking Prince has when he leaves his clan to be married. It could have been interesting but the delivery is deadening. *Hunger Dogs* concludes Jack Kirby's *New Gods*, written and pencilled by Kirby ten years on. The panels seem to be taken from ten different stories, mixed at random – not so much bad, as baffling. *Ganthet's Tale* is a Green Lantern story about a threat to the fabric of space and time, and lively enough to entertain even if you know nothing about the GL character. George Pratt's

War Idyll has a Vietnam veteran
about the old German WWI pilot
... he is haunted by what he learned
about himself and the ruthlessness of his will
to survive. The story makes its points clear, but
it's rather hard to believe that these two men
would actually be talking like this. *Lex Luthor:
the Unauthorised Biography* has a journalist
taking on the task of writing a biography of
Lex Luthor from the team of James Hudnall
and Eduardo Barreto. There are no surprises in
what happens to him, but there's a certain
fascination in watching the inevitable.

On to the good science-fiction stories. *Frost
and Fire* is an adaptation of a Ray Bradbury
story about the survivors of a crash on a planet
with a brutal, quickly-changing climate. Their
metabolism is accelerated so that they
managed to survive, but their lifecycle was
reduced to eight days. Sim is convinced that he
can win himself enough time to escape.
Fascinating, and beautifully done. *Merchants of
Venus* is a good, old-fashioned prospectors'
yarn, but with a setting of Venus instead of
Alaska. The ending is weak, but it's still worth
a look. The Robert Silverberg adaptation
Nightwings is set in a future society that has
reverted to a medieval technology and social
structure. The narrator is a member of the
Guild of Watchers, who scan the skies to give
warning of the predicted alien invasion. A rich,
absorbing story, with exceptionally complex
characterisation, and not even the perfunctory
artwork can break the mood. *Space Clusters* has
the art-lover on the run as a murder suspect,
pursued for a hundred years by the art-censor
turned cop. A refreshingly tongue-in-cheek
start, and then the two of them fall into a black
hole and it's non-stop psychedelia right to the
end. A romp. Finally, *Warlords*, in which
Dwayne, the resourceful troll, becomes
embroiled in the conflicts between four
Warlord brothers. Told with a light touch, and
with careful, affectionate artwork.

The bad or indifferent science-fiction stories
make for a longer list. *Demon With A Glass
Hand* features Trent, who appeared in the city
ten days previously devoid of memories, and
wonders who he is, and why all these men are
trying to kill him – very ordinary. *Generation
Zero* is set after a nuclear war, and Juan Falcon
and two friends are given a mission: to fly
around the world and contact other groups of
survivors. The ideas just aren't there, and the
writing is leaden. *Hell on Earth* concerns a
horror writer who is involved in an experiment
to summon the devil, and it becomes
grindingly predictable within pages. *The Magic
Goes Away* is set in a sword-and-sorcery world
in which the magic is nearly exhausted, with a
group on a last-chance mission to replenish the
supply. Memorable for incoherent story-telling

that leaves you flicking back and forth
wondering if the pages are in the wrong order.
Me and Joe Priest is set in a future where all men
have become sterile, yet one man (who
happens to be a priest, and the son of a priest)
is on a divine mission to reseed the planet. It's
witless. *The Medusa Chain*... well, who knows
what Ernie Colon thought he was producing
here? Space-going prison drama, or romance,
or corporate conspiracy, or war story? It's a
mess. *Metalzoic* is an African wildlife
documentary with fearsomely-armed robots
instead of animals, and with the traditional
struggle for leadership of the tribe. Great
imagination from both writer Pat Mills and
artist Kevin O'Neill in the details and
atmosphere of the machine-based ecology, but
with some clumsy dialogue and near-
incomprehensible fight scenes. *Sandkings* is an
adaptation of George R.R. Martin's simple but
powerful morality tale, and you'd do better to
read the non-graphic version since the
illustrator here seems to have missed the point
of the story completely. Last and least, *Star
Raiders*, which has a bunch of freedom fighters
up against the Zylon hive-mind – many flashes
and bangs and funny kid-animals, and not a
story in sight.

In a category of its own is *Tell Me Dark*.
According to the jacket-blurb, the genre is
Femme Fatale Story, and as such the words
and the painted artwork combine for an
unusually good example of the genre. But need
the story be taken literally? Is it actually about
a man having a nervous breakdown far from
home? Or about the torment of being
emotionally involved with someone who's far
from sane? Or simply about the end of an
affair? The story (maybe despite itself?) allows
all of these readings, and more.~FC

Recommended: *Frost and Fire, Nightwings,
Space Clusters, Tell Me Dark*

DC SPECIAL

DC: *29 issues 1968–1971 (1–15), 1975–1977
(16–29)*

This began life as an oversized reprint title and
over the course of the second run gradually
switched to all new material. Archivists will be
interested in 3's Black Canary and Wonder
Woman stories, produced in the 1940s, but
never previously published, and other
highlights of the initial run were entire issues
devoted to the art of Carmine Infantino (1) and
Joe Kubert (5). Towering above the run, though,
is issue 15, offering one of the few relatively
cheap opportunities to sample the comedic
genius of Jack Cole's Plastic Man strips. They're
so off the wall that the term 'wacky' doesn't
begin to do them justice: Cole was way ahead of
his time with this stretchable superhero. Despite
nicely drawn Gil Kane Green Lantern reprints

in 20, the second run is largely lack-lustre, with the only standout being the final issue. In 29 Paul Levitz and Joe Staton construct a marvellous story explaining exactly why the Justice Society Of America were unable to win World War II on their own.~HY
Recommended: 1, 5, 15, 29

DC SUPER-STAR HOLIDAY SPECIAL
DC: *One-shot 1980*
This Christmas issue of the DC Special Series contains five stories from across DC's range of titles. A *House of Mystery* story features all the DC horror-title hosts of the period but is otherwise inconsequential. The *Legion of Superheroes* tale has the advantage of José Luis Garcia-Lopez pencils inked by Dick Giordano, but is a hopelessly sentimental tale of alien races working in harmony. Robert Kanigher's *Sgt Rock* is completely typical of the series, a simple parable in which the horror of war is contrasted with the hopefulness of little children, but Dick Ayers and Romeo Tanghal art does it no favours. They also illustrate the Michael Fleisher-penned Jonah Hex story in which Hex, out of character, helps a poor family find food for Christmas Day – his reasons are explained in a flashback to his childhood. Finally Denny O'Neil provides a (by now) traditional Christmas Batman story, drawn by Frank Miller (with distinct nods to Neal Adams' version). An attractive package, overall, which Miller completists will probably want to track down.~NF

DC SUPERSTARS
DC: *18 issues 1976–1978*
1–11 are reprints, largely from the 1960s, and largely unmemorable, although there's Infantino Flash in 5, and Legion of Super-Heroes in 3. From 12, though, it's all new material, starting with Superboy. Sergio Aragonés providing a wealth of short strips is the focus of 13, then not as well known to comic readers in general, but none the less talented for that. The Star Hunters débuted in 16 before moving into their own title, and Paul Levitz and Joe Staton supply the origin of the Huntress in her first appearance in 17, an issue also reprinting Green Arrow's origin and the first recorded case of the Legion of Super-Heroes. The series bows out with a teaming of Deadman and the Phantom Stranger.~HY
Recommended: 13, 17

DC versus MARVEL/
MARVEL versus DC
DC/Marvel: *4-issue miniseries 1996*
The involved collaboration uniting the Marvel and DC superheroes is inevitably contrived and cosmically scaled, yet is still superior to previous crossovers. This time, rationale for the meeting of their universes is supplied as dozens of cross-company heroes and villains clash. The *Green Lantern/Silver Surfer: Unholy Alliances* one-shot serves as a prequel (not required reading) and the Amalgam universe spins off from the conclusion. Light, tender moments of character development preserve us from an endless barrage of brain battering and although no lasting effects on each universe linger, genuine suspense is generated by having five major battles decided by readers' votes. Thus one company wins. Writers Ron Marz and Peter David are to be commended for their handiwork considering the daunting constraints; Claudio Castellini and Dan Jurgens ably assist on pencils. A great series if you're 14.~APS

DEAD IN THE WEST
Dark Horse: *2-issue miniseries 1994*
Joe R. Lansdale, best known for horror fiction, almost single-handedly reinvented the Western comic with this and his work on *Jonah Hex*. Whether that's a good thing or not depends on your appreciation of what is, in effect, a zombie story in a Western setting. Adapted by Neal Barrett Jr from Lansdale's novel, *Dead In The West* is the story of a dying man's curse on the town that killed him. With an incestuous preacher as a hero and the sense that the townspeople only get what they deserve, there's more than a nod to *Pale Rider* and *High Plains Drifter*. With artwork by Jack Jackson (Jaxon) and covers by Tim Truman, Dark Horse managed to bring together the best of the new Western creators for this story.~NF

THE DEAD MUSE
Fantagraphics: *One-shot 1990*
Don't read this book when you're feeling down. Ostensibly a collection, edited by Eddie Campbell, of various Australian comic talents, it's actually a series of annoying short stories that interrupt Campbell's gripping account of one of the most depressing periods in his life, interspersed with how he met various of the contributors. Actually the stories aren't that bad – Phil Bentley and M. Pena adapt an amusing episode from 'The Wilder Shores Of Love', and Kupe's piece is rough but charming – only they become less memorable when faced with the editorial itself, tragic yet funny, brooding dolefully on the short life of the Tenth Muse, the muse of comics.~FJ

DEAD OF NIGHT
Marvel: *11 issues 1973–1975*
Staple reprint diet of 1950's weird/horror shorts. 11 contains the only original feature, the first appearance of the supernatural Scarecrow by Scott Edelman. The subject of a painting forming a gateway to a demonical dimension,

Scarecrow came to life to combat demon worshippers on Earth. Uninspired, as were subsequent roles in *Marvel Spotlight* (first series) 26 and *Marvel Two-In-One* 18.~APS

DEADBEATS
Claypool: *25 issues + 1993 to date*

Four centuries old, but seemingly youthful, vampires terrorise a small American town. Opposing them are a rag-tag-and-bobtail bunch of townies and, separately, a local youth whom the self-styled Deadbeats converted to vampirism and set up as a puppet leader. Now with an agenda of his own, he's their deadliest enemy. Decadence, an underlying perverse sensuality and loquaciousness are the keynotes of the title. All of writer/artist Richard Howell's characters, good or evil, are oratorical to a degree seldom seen in today's comics, and that's not a complaint. A particularly pleasing aspect is that moral values – of the genuine sort, not the twisted and bigoted evangelical type – are presented in a positive and affirming way. It's ironic that this eerie and horrific merger of grand opera and soap opera also presents virtually the only cool and sane Christians ever seen in comics! Sexy, spooky and able to keep the reader genuinely off balance and disturbed.~HS
Recommended: 1–25

DEADFACE
Harrier: *8 issues 1987–1988*
Dark Horse: *3-issue miniseries ('Doing The Islands With Bacchus') 1991, 4-issue miniseries ('Earth, Water, Air And Fire') 1992*

If you were 4000 years old and suffering from a lifetime of dissolution, wine, women and song, mightn't you look a bit battered? The Greek god Bacchus now spends his time in bars spinning tales of the old days, accompanied by faithful companion Simpson, and a few dog-eared Maenads. Joe Theseus, however, has reason to fear Bacchus and sends a hitman after him, but finds himself pursued by The Eyeball Kid, who stole his father Zeus' thunderbolt and killed most of the gods of Olympus. The Kid wants to know the whereabouts of Poseidon's skull, which grants longevity. Together Theseus and the Kid return to pick up the pieces of Joe's criminal empire but find themselves the target of some other mythological throwbacks, Chalcon, Chryson and Argyson, the Telchines. The Eyeball Kid's powers are sucked away by the Stygian Leech and although Theseus saves him they are forced to retreat. This is the plot in simple terms, but Eddie Campbell's strip is much more than a simple adventure fantasy. His carefully researched retelling of myths complements the action and his artwork, rough and scratchy but always expressive and textural, is full of life and imagination.

Doing The Islands With Bacchus is actually a collection of sixteen short stories that appeared in a number of different anthologies for a variety of publishers. Bacchus strikes out from the *Deadface* story-line to wander around the Aegean Islands, telling a different, suitable story on each. These issues are pure Campbell magic, thoughtful, playful scripts that aren't afraid of the darker side of mythology, and are matched by delicate artwork. In *Earth, Water, Air And Fire*, Theseus is tempted back into human affairs with a bargain that would gain him The Eye Of Fate which once belonged to the Eyeball Kid. Seduced by his own daughter, he finds himself in the middle of a Mob war and his troubles are compounded when the Kid comes looking for his lost orb. All this and police violence too. Though there's humour in Campbell's stories there's also an understanding of the nature of mythology and oral story-telling patterns.~NF
Recommended: *Doing The Islands* 1–3
Collection: *Immortality Isn't Forever* (Harrier 1–8)

DEADLINE U.S.A.
Dark Horse: *Series one 3 issues 1991–1992, Series two 8 issues 1992–1993*

British anthology comic *Deadline* was a late 80s success story, combining irreverent self-indulgence with genuine innovation and talent. The most successful graduate was Jamie Hewlett and Alan Martin's *Tank Girl*, but it wasn't the only good strip. The mistake at Dark Horse was adding new strips by off-beat American creators like Richard Sala and Alec Stevens, whose po-faced introspection misses the point entirely. Still, there's enough good reprints from the British editions to make every issue worth a look. The likes of Philip Bond's 'Wired World' (*Love and Rockets* in Clapham), Pete Milligan and Brett Ewins' hard-boiled *Johnny Nemo*, Evan Dorkin's *Milk And Cheese*, and *Beryl the Bitch* from Julie Hollings shine, and a fine supporting line-up includes strips from Nick Abadzis, Rachael Ball and D'Israeli.

Series two halves the page-count to forty-eight, without Tank Girl (moved to her own title), and gets better as it progresses, phasing out Sala and Stevens with new US contributors Dave Cooper and Scott Musgrove mixing more easily. There's always some utter tosh in *Deadline*, but there's always some essential reading as well.~FP
Recommended: Series two 8

DEADPOOL
Marvel: *Miniseries one ('The Circle Chase') 4 issues 1993, miniseries two 4 issues 1994*

The mouthy mercenary was introduced in *X-Force*, and it seems the vague *X-Men* connections worked in his favour, bestowing a greater level of popularity than similar mercenary types introduced elsewhere, most notably Paladin. The first series has a group of superpowered freelance types in search of a dead man's will, which of course means there's plenty of fights between them. Far from lightening the deadly dull stuff Deadpool's constant wisecracking, a toughened-up version of old Spider-Man quips, quickly becomes irritating. The second series is much better. As Deadpool's defining characteristic is his motormouth, it made sense to have a writer with a facility for dialogue, hence Mark Waid, and penciller Ian Churchill provides exciting action-packed pages. This time old X-Men villain Black Tom Cassidy needs Deadpool's regenerative abilities to save himself. Deadpool also has to face Tom's cousin, Banshee, and his mate, the unstoppable Juggernaut. Banshee's daughter Siryn tags along for the ride. An ongoing *Deadpool* series began in 1997.~FP

THE DEADLY DUO

Image: *Miniseries one 4 issues 1994, Miniseries two 4 issues 1995*

Comedy superheroics from Eric Larsen's universe. A thick time-traveller, Kid Avenger, teams up with Kill Cat and the two get into some scrapes, usually involving lots of fighting. Don't expect subtlety but it is better amusement than most parody titles. Issue 3 of the second series features a guest appearance by Grunge of Gen13.~NF

DEADLY HANDS OF KUNG FU

Marvel: *33 issues 1974–1977*

Marvel put a lot of effort into its black and white magazines in the seventies. Unfortunately they didn't always have the talent to go with it. *Deadly Hands* sells itself as a general martial arts magazine with articles on Bruce Lee, the *Kung Fu* TV series and the many martial arts. The two regular comic strips suffered from fluctuating standards in artwork (usually the inking). The Shang-Chi strip runs parallel to his own series and has the advantage of Doug Moench scripts, but Mike Vosberg (inked by Al Milgrom and Jack Abel) is seriously unsuited to an action strip of this kind, while Rudy Nebres' artwork is fluid during the fights but terribly stiff otherwise. 'The Sons Of The Tiger', running throughout the series, is a deadly dull story, though Bill Mantlo does try to redeem it with characters like The White Tiger and Jack of Hearts. Iron Fist replaced Shang-Chi for 19–24, bringing with him his regular writer Chris Claremont, with artwork again by Nebres. A multi-part story-line featuring all of the above ran from 29–31 after a Bruce Lee special in 28. For completists only.~NF

DEADMAN

DC: *Miniseries 4 issues 1985–1986, Microseries one (Love After Death) 2 issues 1989, Microseries two (Exorcism) 2 issues 1992*

Introduced in the 1970s with runs in *Strange Adventures* and *The Brave and The Bold* (reprinted as a seven-issue series in the 1980s), Boston Brand is Deadman, sent back to Earth as a ghost able to temporarily possess the bodies of others. Andy Helfer and José Luis Garcia-Lopez's miniseries attempts to redefine the character after a number of guest appearances and short stories since the ending of the run in *Strange Adventures*. Tying up the loose ends of the original story-line that saw Boston's killer still head of the League of Assassins, Helfer kills off a few characters and sets Deadman up as a hero with a mission within the DC Universe. Lopez's artwork bears similarities to Adams, or Ross Andru, but has a 'European' influence that keeps it fresh and a delight to read. Mike Baron presents a more traditional horror story in *Love After Death*, as Boston meets an undead circus troupe. Kelley Jones, a knobbly Berni Wrightson, provides suitably atmospheric artwork but the whole is a rather characterless affair. The sequel, *Exorcism*, sees Baron and Jones pursuing this horror line as Boston goes insane and confronts various denizens of hell, aided by the Phantom Stranger. Whilst tying in with DC's attempt to create a more 'mature' set of horror characters, the shifts in personality and behaviour seem forced.~NF

DEADSHOT

DC: *4-issue miniseries 1988–1989*

Batman foe Deadshot was a core member of Suicide Squad, and has been diagnosed as a hitman with a death wish. While Floyd Lawton is on a mission to locate his kidnapped son, his therapist, now harbouring feelings for Lawton, checks into his past. It's a gloomy, depressing story of a fractured family from the *Suicide Squad* team of John Ostrander, Kim Yale and artist Luke McDonnell, but excellently plotted and executed. Deadshot's fatalism and the desperate optimism of therapist Marnie Herrs are well contrasted, particularly in an epilogue scene. Not a laugh to be had, and all the better for it.~FP
Recommended: 1–4

DEADWORLD

Arrow: *9 issues 1986–1988*
Caliber: *Series one 17 issues (10–26) 1988–1992, Series two 15 issues 1993–1995*

Off-putting, gratuitously gory covers disguise this initially quite enjoyable Troma-style romp (although Arrow wised up and provided retailer-friendly alternative covers from 6). A black-magic ceremony gone wrong turns almost the entire population into zombies. The few survivors, initially a group of typical Troma teenagers, struggle in a world gone very wrong. Stuart Kerr and Vincent Locke produced the original issues (reprinted in the collections and as *Deadworld Archives* 1–3), and after they left it all began to go pear-shaped. The humour disappeared and grim and gory was the order of the day. A Punisher-style character called Deadkiller is introduced in 19, and that and the two succeeding issues are also available as a reprint one-shot titled *Deadkiller*.

A miniseries titled *To Kill A King* separates the first and second Caliber series. Dead Killer decides it's time to finish King Zombie, who's able to unite the otherwise mindless dead under his control. By series two the cast had grown to massive proportions, and there are myriad sub-plots, but they're competently handled, which makes it a shame the artwork is never more than mediocre, with 6–11 appalling. 12 and 13 are flip-books doubling up as *The Realm* 9 and *Beck and Caul* 6 respectively. Story-lines conclude in disappointing fashion with 15, as further issues are promised.~FP

Collections: *Deadworld* book 1 (1–7), *Deadworld* book 2 (8–16)

DEAR JULIA
Black Eye: *2 issues + 1996 to date*

Boyd Soloman stands on a window ledge about to throw himself off in an attempt to fly. It appears to be a metaphor for Boyd also teetering on the edge of sanity. The story unfolds in a letter sent to Julia, reviewing past events as a means of explaining his present situation. The first impression of *Dear Julia* is unsettling, with Brian Biggs' art imparting loneliness and isolation, and although the pace is occasionally only a notch above static there's enough atmosphere to compensate. Biggs is also balancing on the edge, though, and his Lynchian quirks may yet fall apart. One hopes not.~WJ

DEATH
Vertigo: *3-issue miniseries ('The High Cost Of Living') 1993, 3-issue miniseries ('The Time Of Your Life') 1996*

As introduced in *Sandman* 8, Death is personified as a pallid young woman in a black vest and tight black trousers, certainly a more attractive manifestation than the traditional hooded and caped skeleton with scythe. Although largely sympathetic and somewhat capricious, Death was never particularly strongly characterised in *Sandman*, and her popularity would seem to lie in her appealing appearance to the *Sandman* audience, a group writer Neil Gaiman plays to particularly well.

For her miniseries Death remains somewhat the cipher, tossing out Zen remarks and reacting to those around her instead of instigating events. 'The High Cost Of Living' takes as its premise that once every century Death becomes human for a single day in order to retain a feeling for humanity. In 1993 she appears in New York to alter the life of Sexton Furnival, precocious, self-absorbed and self-pitying teenager, unwittingly involving him in a search for a missing heart and an encounter with a dangerous demon. Gaiman's writing skills carry this slim plot over three issues. It works as Furnival's perceptions of life are subtly altered through experience, and Death holding up a mirror to him, and Gaiman's particularly good ear for naturalistic dialogue and skilful small humorous touches go a long way. There's the odd twee moment, particularly the song lyrics in 2 (pandering to a perceived audience, one hopes), but overall 'The High Cost Of Living' is a triumph.

'The Time Of Your Life' is even better, with Death's participation minimal and enigmatic, as the story concentrates on lesbian couple Foxglove and Hazel. Since their début in *Sandman* 32 (and cameo in the previous *Death* series) they have a child and Foxglove has become a successful singer on a global scale. All is well, so it would seem, but that's not the case. By the end of the third issue both have learned something about themselves on a journey that's had plenty of surprises along the way.

Of course, good writing in comics is forever jeopardised by unsympathetic artists, but penciller Chris Bachalo is distinguished at conveying small moments of characterisation, while smart enough to ensure dialogue-heavy sequences remain visually interesting. When he departs midway through the second issue of the second series, former inker Mark Buckingham seamlessly continues the series, proving equally adept at conveying the emotion necessary to the story. The irritating fantasy stylings that occasionally prompt groans of disbelief in *Sandman* are largely missing here, and those who find that title too mannered should still enjoy the Death stories. Those who love *Sandman* will enjoy them anyway, and those who've never read either ought to sample.~WJ

Recommended: *The High Cost Of Living* 1–3, *The Time Of Your Life* 1–3

Collection: *The High Cost Of Living* (1–3), *The Time Of Your Life* (1–3)

DEATH BY CHOCOLATE
Sleeping Giant: *2 issues 1996*

Very silly for the first few pages of the first issue, as a chocolate-shop owner is transformed into living chocolate by an alien enslaved in a chocolate factory. David Yurkovich's captions are a tortured first-person narrative, heightening the ridiculous situation, and his pages are drawn in deadpan, starkly contrasting black and white with no hint of parody, giving the entire comic a *Twilight Zone* feel. Unfortunately, Yurkovich doesn't know when to stop, and what would have been an excellent short story is dragged on through a standard mad-scientist plot. The second issue, subtitled 'The Metabolators', sees our man return to his home town and transform everything and everyone into chocolate. Luckily the authorities have the Metabolators on hand. If he learns how not to flog an idea to death Yurkovich will be worth looking out for.~FP

DEATH METAL Vs GENETIX
Marvel UK: *4-issue miniseries 1993*

Robotic psycho-killer desperate to end murderous sprees tries to dupe superteens into offing him. A bit more plot than most Marvel UK stuff.~HS

DEATH RACE 2020
Cosmic: *8 issues 1995–1996*

It's always nice to see Pat Mills and Kev O'Neill working together, even if the script does have a 'helping hand' from the less talented Tony Skinner. 1–3, if not completely satisfying, are an enjoyable and bloody romp. Based on the cult movie *Death Race 2000*, the strip continues the story of Frankenstein, the genetically altered driver who becomes President of the US after killing the incumbent during the violent cross-continental race. In the early issues Frankenstein, who's banned the Death Race, despairs of a populace who've made death into a religion and calls a free election. When he loses he returns to the race and the strip becomes nothing but a formulaic carnage, which coincides with O'Neill bowing out and handing the art chores to Trevor Goring. Goring does his best, but the less angular, less exciting art, and the predictability of the plot, make the rest of the series lacklustre.~FJ

DEATH RATTLE
Kitchen Sink: *Series one 18 issues 1985–1988, Series two 6 issues + 1995 to date*

The freshest thing about *Death Rattle* is its experimental covers. Many don't work, but at least it shows there's a spark of life in the old corpse yet. It's the comic-book equivalent of *Friday The 13th*, a vaguely competent horror anthology tending towards figurative art and straightforward narrative, frequently in the EC mould but told with less economy. Don't look to this title for subtlety because you'll be sorely disappointed. A number of good people have turned up in its pages (Mark Schultz's popular *Xenozoic Tales* previewed in 8, and indeed he produced the lead story for the second-series

opener), but rarely at their best. Jaxon fans will delight in *Bulto*, his long-winded tale of morally-soured monks vs Indians and squidgy Cuthulu-type monsters in 17th-century Central America; the rest of us will find it interminable and be forced to skip large chunks of issues where it constitutes the main attraction.

If you don't like predictable gore, look at issue 18. Behind a pedestrian Frank Miller cover is a neat Gerard Jones-scripted story, probably the most clever piece of writing the title's ever seen. 'When I Grow Up', illustrated by Doug Potter, concerns a little girl who, out playing with her friends, wishes she could find out what becomes of them. They proceed to act out all the everyday traumas and tragedies of adulthood. Potter's drawings of pre-pubescent children kissing, getting pissed, rowing etc. make particularly unsettling images. Also of note are a couple of early Charles Burns stories and some Basil Wolverton reprints.~FJ
Recommended: Series one 18

DEATH'S HEAD
Marvel UK: *10 issues 1989*

An eccentric cyborg starts a career as a 'freelance peacekeeper'. The peculiarly homemade look of the title character gives the strip a certain visual charm, but the joke quickly wears thin. If you must sample go for the Dr Who guest appearance in 8, which was quite fun. With the popularity of Death's Head's successor this series was reprinted and completed as *The Incomplete Death's Head* in 1993.~HS

DEATH'S HEAD II
Marvel UK: *4-issue miniseries 1992, 16 issues 1992–1994*

This is new, improved, sleekly redesigned version of the original Death's Head, complete with a multi-morphing weapons arm. This was fleetingly popular in the early 1990s, and served as springboard for artist Liam Sharp to more lucrative gigs. His art aside, it's all carnage by numbers, and he left after issue 4 of the ongoing series, which then rapidly followed the usual Marvel UK path of decline into rotating creators and pointless mutant guest stars.~HS

DEATH'S HEAD II & The Origin of Die Cut
Marvel UK: *2-issue miniseries 1993*

Well now, it's the origin of Die Cut and it's got Death's Head II in it. John Royle's art is quite nice. That's all.~HS

DEATHBLOW
Image: *30 issues (0–29) 1993–1996*

The title character is an agent working for the US government as a trained killer. Deathblow is a weapons expert and a superb hand-to-hand fighter, but more interesting, in the beginning at least, is that he is a man dying of an incurable disease. This adds humanity to an otherwise cold and callous operator.

1–2 set the scene well and Jim Lee provides some strong visuals, with the stark contrasting art very similar to that used by Frank Miller on *Sin City*. From 3 Lee only plots, turning in a fast-paced three-part story about an attack on an Iraqi base for Tim Sale to draw. Although Sale is competent, his art lacks Lee's dynamism. The next story-line is an improvement, with Deathblow becoming caught up in a religious battle between rival cults. Action-packed, suspenseful, it also features guest appearances from Grifter and the WetWorks team. That story concludes Deathblow's relations with the government, and he takes a private contract from a Hollywood bimbo with conspiracy theories. The story quickly draws in the supernatural with the appearance of Werewolves, but those aspects divert from the reality-based plots that make the other issues superior. From this point *Deathblow* never regains the previous quality as action scenes supplant all other aspects, although the possibility of a cure for Deathblow's condition remains an issue. 20–21 guest-star Gen-13.~SS.
Recommended: 1, 2
Collection: The Black Angel Saga

DEATHBLOW AND WOLVERINE
Image/Marvel: *2-issue microseries 1996–1997*

Absolutely stunning. With crossovers teaming characters from different companies all the rage in 1996, most, predictably, were little more than beat-'em-ups, and with two of the more violent types in their respective universes paired one couldn't have expected anything more. Step forward then, Aron Wiesenfeld and Richard Bennett. They've obviously studied Geof Darrow, but that doesn't make the detailed art and clean line any easier, and it's all the more gorgeous for the subtle pastel tones used by colourist Monica Bennett. Weisenfeld also writes, and provides an intriguing connection between Deathblow and Wolverine, found in San Francisco's Chinatown in 1982. It's a simple story well told, but it's the art that this pairing will be remembered for.~FP
Recommended: 1–2

DEATHLOK
Marvel: *4-issue miniseries 1990, 34 issues, 2 Annuals 1991–1994*

Despite appearances, this doesn't follow on from the cybernetic psychopath's mid-1970s adventures in *Astonishing Tales*. Instead of soldier Luther Manning, the new Deathlok is a pacifist scientist who believed he was working on developing cybernetic limbs for the disabled but was in fact creating a killing machine, into which his brain is placed and programmed to kill. Oh, the *angst* and irony. Writer Dwayne McDuffie takes him through cyborg conspiracy adventures and team-ups with everyone from Misty Knight to Doctor Doom a little too often for the series' own good. In between all the guest stars there's not quite enough space left for Deathlok himself, although overall it's not too bad a read. 31–34 try to tie up the continuity between the 1970s series and the later ones, which pretty much boils down to alternate worlds and time paradoxes that could have been left to the simple explanation of 'it's a new series, it doesn't have to be the same guy'. Then, to make it even more complicated, the original Deathlok turns up in a Captain America short story in the first issue of the 1996 *Marvel Fanfare* (having hung around with him in the late 280s of his own comic) and it seems as if the Dwayne McDuffie issues have been forgotten completely. Even if it is all explained somewhere, you don't really want to know.~JC

DEATHMATE
Image/Valiant: *6-issue miniseries (prologue, red, black, blue, yellow, epilogue) 1993–1994*

The summer of 1993 saw the two biggest independent comic companies producing a fan's dream. *Deathmate* told the story of Void (Image) and Solar (Valiant) meeting and creating a joint universe. What could have been an impressive project is limited by a drab story-line. The most interesting thing in the end is the contrast between Valiant's complex, interesting characters and Image's flat, clichéd characters.~SS

DEATHSTROKE THE TERMINATOR
DC: *60 issues, 4 Annuals 1991–1995*

Marv Wolfman created this villain, a mildly interesting assassin with a conscience, for his successful *New Teen Titans* revival in the early 1980s. In the aftermath of the *Punisher* phenomenon, there was clearly potential in a *Deathstroke* comic, and Wolfman started shoehorning Slade Wilson into the *Titans* at every opportunity, as antagonist, as reluctant ally, and most conspicuously as father of Jericho. DC were eventually bludgeoned into publishing a *Deathstroke* title, but almost from day one it was a serious misfire, oscillating between espionage plot-lines, superhero stories and 'Men's Sweat' adventure tales, while uneasy in all genres. 10 introduced the new female holder of the Vigilante title, a rehash of a similar character Wolfman had already spun off from *Titans*, who became a semi-regular supporting cast member and

romantic interest. 13 is the second half of a crossover from *Superman* 68, and 14–16 tie in with the 'Total Chaos' story in *New Titans* and *Team Titans*. The series kept trying to break away from guest appearances and stand on its own, but clearly sales flagged every time, and the bulk of the readers, one suspects, were simply *Titans* completists who bought the title grudgingly. It eventually staggered to a close a year or so before Wolfman finally wore out his welcome on *Titans* itself.~HS
Collection: *Full Cycle* (1–5)

DEATHWISH
Milestone: *4-issue miniseries 1995*

A series of murders with transsexuals the victims is investigated by a detective who is herself transsexual. This oddball premise could have been interesting, but strayed and rambled, eventually stuttering to the inevitable halt.~HS

A DECADE OF DARK HORSE
Dark Horse: *4-issue miniseries 1996*

A something-for-everyone collection of ten years of Dark Horse comics, with new material from their most successful publications. The best is rather obvious but consists of Frank Miller's 'Sin City' (1), Matt Wagner's Grendel (1), Eric Luke and Scott Benefiel on Ghost (2), Mike Baron and Steve Rude's Nexus (3), Paul Chadwick's Concrete (4) and Masamune Shirow's 'Exon Depot' (4). The other features are either good examples of the series – *Predator* (1) by Henry Gilroy and Igor Kordey, *Trekker* (2) by Ron Randall and Chris Warner's 'Black Cross' (3) – or competent if unappealing – Star Wars (2), *Aliens* (3), Outlanders sketches (3), *The Mask* (3), *Godzilla* (4).~NF
Recommended: 1, 4

DEFCON 4
Image: *4-issue miniseries 1996*

The Patron has sent four assassins back through time to prevent his past self from creating the technology that he now feels has ruined the future. Unfortunately for his plans, the assassins choose to complete their mission by killing him. The four assassins have not been transported through time physically but in essence, into bodies chosen to match their abilities. Well written and drawn by Matt Broome and Jeff Mariotte, this is a fast-paced science-fiction story that creates an intriguing situation but spends too much time on fight scenes instead of exploring either the Patron's future or his present. Intended to be ongoing, the first part ends with the assassins free but having to regroup after failing in their first attempt to kill the Patron. There's no indication when it will restart.~NF

DEFENDERS
Marvel: *152 issues, 1 Annual, 5 Giant-Size 1972–1986*

The Defenders first appeared as a try-out in *Marvel Feature* 1–3. Their *raison d'être*, in contrast to the Avengers, was a loosely knit band of heroes with no permanent members and no formal structure who rallied when necessary. They were often referred to as a 'non-team' in view of their reluctant, uneasy bonding. The team experienced two distinct incarnations, separated by issue 125. During the first phase the most lasting participants were Dr Strange, Sub-Mariner, Hulk, Valkyrie, Nighthawk and Hellcat. Lesser roles were played by Silver Surfer, Son of Satan, Gargoyle and Beast. *The Defenders* never found a comfortable niche. Dr Strange fitted poorly with the more conventional heroes owing to his ability to whisk rabbits out of hats whenever the plot was stuck for a device.

Steve Englehart, Len Wein and Sal Buscema crafted a respectable nineteen issues' with 8–11 chronicling half of the 'Avengers-Defenders War'. Steve Gerber's reign to 41 produced the most consistently excellent run of the book, with his Headmen saga (31–40, Annual 1) wonderfully bizarre, yet contrasting with the touchingly realistic sub-plot detailing Valkyrie's quest to discover the past of her human host, Barbara Norriss. See also Giant-Size 4 for a delightful single-issue story sporting some fine Don Heck art.

Dave Kraft took over and soon hit form with the 'Who Remembers Scorpio?' tale in 46–51. His character study of this morose, introspective villain recommends these issues to any collection. Keith Giffen aided and abetted with quality pencilling in a title admittedly well short of artistic highlights. Kraft maintained solidity until 61, but fell into a decline, which was accelerated by Ed Hannigan until J.M. DeMatteis assumed penmanship from 92. Don Perlin ousted the musical artists and pencilled on to the final issue. DeMatteis' frustrating run comprised interesting, well-knitted plots encompassed in patchily written stories. His most notable issue is 111, delving into Hellcat's past.

The Defenders' second incarnation manifests in 124–125, pivotal issues in which the Beast reforms the team as himself, Angel, Iceman, Valkyrie, Gargoyle, Moondragon and Cloud (from 127). They gain a recognised structure and headquarters in Angel's Rocky Mountain retreat. These issues also resolve the sub-plot of the enigmatic Elf, who first appeared a hundred issues earlier, and supply a lame rationale as to why the old Defenders had to disband. 125 also heralds the title change to *New Defenders* and classy covers abound through to 152.

Peter Gillis' scripts from 131 mainly revolve

around Moondragon's battles against the limits on her powers imposed by Odin. Inevitably, she is thrown into conflict with most of the rest of the team. In an inappropriate cosmic finale, she contests a nebulous entity, The Dragon of the Moon. All the Defenders bar the ex-X-Men apparently die, with Angel, Iceman and Beast subsequently forming X-Factor.~APS

Recommended: 31–40, 46–51, Annual 1, Giant-Size 4

DELERIUM

Metro: *2 issues 1987*

Mixed bag anthology title with Keith Giffen and Robert Loren Fleming's alternate Ambush Bug March Hare in 2 being the standout. There's also nice art from the undersung Chuck Roblin in 1, but otherwise ordinary is the watchword.~FP

The DEMON

DC: *Series one 16 issues 1972–1974, 4-issue miniseries 1987, series two 58 issues, 2 Annuals 1990–1995*

Jack Kirby's New Gods saga was cancelled, and his Demon on first appearance seemed like a poor replacement. But Kirby came though, taking the legend of Camelot one stage further. The opening pages of *Demon* 1 resemble nothing so much as a space battle set in medieval Britain. Merlin summons up Etrigan the Demon to do his bidding and protect the fabled city from the clutches of the evil Morgaine Le Fey, but to no avail. After the fall of Camelot, Etrigan is given human form, and is left to wander the world for aeons. The scene changes to modern-day Gotham City, where we're introduced to Jason Blood, Demonologist, who is unaware that he's the human guise of the demon. Not for long, though, as the ageing Morgaine Le Fey drops by looking for Merlin and the scene is set for supernatural encounters in true Kirby spirit. The supporting cast played a major role in the series. There was Randu Singh, a turbanned telepathic UN delegate, the cigar-smoking advertising executive Harry Mathews, and the lovely Glenda Mark, Jason's romantic interest. The Demon and pals encountered many unusual adversaries, the most endearing being Klarion the Witch Boy, a young fugitive sorcerer from another dimension, who was up to lot of mischief in 7, and caused even more havoc in 14–15, accompanied by his cat Teekl, who could turn into a beautiful female. Overall, *The Demon* isn't Kirby's greatest achievement, with a few stories stretched beyond interest, but his imagery was flawless.

The character survived as a guest star in various titles, particularly *Swamp Thing*, which inspired the second series by Matt Wagner. This four-parter has a very positive role for Glenda Mark trying to cure Jason Blood of the curse of the Demon. This saga is steeped in rituals and mysticism rather than superheroics, and we also encounter Etrigan's father and learn more about his relationship to Merlin. The series is well executed, but Wagner tries to stress the eldritch mood of the series too strongly, which makes for laborious reading at times, particularly as Etrigan's speech patterns all rhyme.

The fate of Harry Mathews, only hinted at in the Wagner series, sets the mood for the next ongoing series, written by Alan Grant. Mathews is now a seat cushion. His face is there, but he lacks a soul. Tongue firmly in cheek best describes the mood, very well illustrated by Val Semeiks. All the regular cast are back, with the Demon now more a character of mirth and mischief. Demonesque imaginary dominates the series, where Hell's a horrible place (not surprising) with some really outrageous scenes of black humour, well conceived by Grant. When not set in hell, the series is still set in Gotham, so a few Batman appearances were to be expected, but it's guest stars galore in the multiparter 'Apocalypse Now' saga in 9–15. It involves Klarion the witch boy, who's out to destroy Etrigan, the Phantom Stranger and Lobo, the intergalactic psychopathic hitman hired to drop a nuclear bomb. It's a frantic tale nicely produced. 19 offers the secret origin of Etrigan (and a free Lobo poster), while Matt Wagner returns to write and illustrate 22. The Kirby villain the Howler returns in 23–24, also starring Batman and Robin with a gruesome ending initiated by the usually passive Glenda. Superman takes on Etrigan in 'Political Asylum' (26–29), in which the Demon runs for President. 'The Eternity Quest' in 31–37 has a janitor finding Merlin's long-lost Eternity Book, with unusual consequences. Lots of fun and games again with Wonder Woman and Lobo, whom Grant can't keep away from this title. The Demon was a fine character and particularly apt for Grant's warped imagination, and his successor was no less suited. Garth Ennis took over with 40, along with ace illustrator John McCrea. Ennis's Etrigan was just as mischievous, but more brutal. 41 offers a one-off special by Kevin Altieri, a director of the Batman animated series, in a tale about the Crusades, and 42–45 features Hitman (introduced in Annual 2) in 'Hell's Hitman' as Etrigan hires the assassin to see off fellow-demon Asteroth. Meanwhile Jason and Glenda are going through bad patch, even though she's carrying his child. 50 is an extra-long, amusing pirate tale, but there's nothing funny about issue 0, where Jason Blood's memory of the last thousand years is restored. It seems he's not the innocent he thought he was, which leads well into the story of Glenda giving birth and Etrigan kidnapping the child. Appalled by his past, Jason Blood hires Hitman to finally destroy Etrigan and be rid of his curse. Overall this run is a thoroughly entertaining series that does justice to the Kirby character. if you like your humour silly or black, you can't go wrong. There were two annuals, both well done. The first had Klarion the witch boy being possessed by the evil Eclipso, while 2 introduces Hitman, the most successful character to come from the 'Bloodlines' annuals introducing new heroes that year.~HY

Recommended: Series one 1, 2, 7, 14–16, series two 0, 9–15, 19, 23, 24, 40–44, Annual 2

DEMON DREAMS OF DOCTOR DREW

Horror House: *1 issue 1994*

Reprints of Jerry Grandenetti's 1950s strips. Lovely Eisner-style artwork, but the stories have a disregard for logic and consistency to rival the dumbest porn 'plot'.~FC

DEMON HUNTER

Atlas: *1 issue 1975*

Rich Buckler turned out one of the better Atlas comics with his story of Demon Hunter preventing the birth of a demon race on Earth. Buckler later re-named the character Devil Slayer and the story was concluded at Marvel in *Defenders* 58-60.~FP

DEN

Fantagor: *10 issues 1988–1989*

Richard Corben's first two Den stories, 'Neverwhere' and 'Muvovum', appeared in *Heavy Metal*. Den is an Earthman who finds himself stranded on a barbaric fantasy world full of monsters and wizards. This self-published series presents part three of the *Den* saga, which runs through to 7. In it Den searches for his missing lover, Kath, meeting characters from the previous stories in a tale which also encompasses a parallel quest for magical stones of power owned by an evil wizard. There's an almost photographic feel to Corben's drawing, which is strangely at odds with the grotesques that populate his strips. The strong colouring and lettering styles play an important role, producing an unsettling overall effect on the artwork. His scripts, however, often fail to impress. In addition to the 'Den' story there is usually at least one back-up, including interesting examples of Corben's early work, short horror strips by Bruce Jones (6–8) and two collaborations between Jan Strnad and Alex Nino (9, 10).~NF

Doug Potter's DENIZENS Of Deep City

Kitchen Sink: *8 issues 1988–1990*

A spotlight shone on the citizens of Deep City, spread over all levels of the community. The first issue, with its obsessions about the trivialities of life, paints rather a false picture of the series, although the full regular quotient of charm and despair is present. Later issues encase the capricious aspects more fully in a rounded story, but all suffer somewhat from being bitty, due in part to the ambitious scope of the series, and occasionally difficult to follow. Doug Potter's art is consistently appealing in an Eisneresque fashion, and when he successfully combines the whimsy with a strong narrative the effect is heartwarming. The best sampler is 5, which recaps the characters featured to date, focuses on the kid gang, and ends with a reclusive figure once able to be anywhere just by wishing it so.~WJ

The DESERT PEACH

Thoughts & Images/MU/Aeon: *1988–present, 25 issues to date*

Donna Barr's most famous creation owes his existence to a chance remark made by one of her former fellow-employees following the repainting of a file room. According to Barr, 'The all-female staff... unnerved by the nameless, effeminate colour, try to identify it: "It's not really pink, is it?" "No, sort of a peachy orange tan." "Desert tan." "Desert Peach?" The obvious pun on 'Desert Fox', Erwin Rommel, World War II's famous Field-Marshal, blooms full-blown from Barr's root-bound mind. The Desert Fox's (fictitious) gay younger brother, Pfirsich Rommel, commands the 469th Support and Grave-digging Battalion, a rag-tag-and-bobtail accumulation of dregs and misfits unsuitable for combat, in Africa during World War II. Initially a one-note joke character, and never without humour, the Peach and his associates – long-suffering batman Udo Schmidt, Pfirsich's dashing but shallow fiancé Rosen Kavalier, and the battalion – swiftly evolved into multifaceted and often disturbing characters. Politically astute, and gleefully politically incorrect, Barr's work is characterised by a delight in shaking the reader's complacency and a splendid indifference to 'what the neigh-bours will think'. Most issues are good self-contained introductions to the series, though the first three, concentrating mainly on the comedy aspects, aren't a true taste of the title's sweet-and-sour sharpness. In addition to the collections there are also volumes entitled *Ersatz Peach*, featuring stories by creators other than Barr.~HS

Recommended: 4, 6–17, 19

Collections: Beginnings (1–3), *Politics, Pilots And Puppies* (4–6), *Foreign Relations* (7–9) *Baby Games* (10–12), *Belief Systems* (13–15), *Marriage And Mayhem* (16,17 & 19), *Peach Slices* ('guest' and unpublished stories)

DESERT STORM JOURNAL
Apple: *8 issues 1991–1992*

Scott 'Journal' Neithammer, the journalist hero of Don Lomax's previous war comic *Vietnam Journal*, here emerges from retirement to cover the Gulf War, after learning that his estranged daughter is living in a threatened Israeli kibbutz. This is a curiously schizophrenic series, perhaps foreshadowed by the variant covers to the first issue, one featuring Norman Schwarzkopf, the other Saddam Hussein. The action divides between thoughtful human interludes, where mouthpiece characters 'explain' some of the background to the conflict, and page after page of military hardware fetishism. Tellingly, Vietnam vet Lomax is better at drawing tanks than he is at human beings, and although he's honest enough to admit that 'EVERYTHING in the Middle East has to do with oil' his sympathies obviously belong with the American military – the 82nd Airborne are 'the best of the best', while anti-war protesters 'recycle tired slogans'. Dismayingly, the comics themselves are full of ads for books and videos called things like 'Battles and Weapons of War!' and 'Vietnam Home Movies'.~AL

DESPAIR
Print Mint: *1 issue 1969*

As the cover legend has it, 'Plunge into the depths of despair' with R. Crumb at his inventive best. The lead strip, 'It's Really Too Bad', is a nihilistic masterpiece and about as far from the hippy idealism of Crumb's earlier material as you could get.~DAR
Recommended: 1

DESTROY!
Eclipse: *One-shot 1986*

Scott McCloud produces a giant-size one-shot featuring two musclebound superheroes beating the crap out of each other and inadvertently invents Extreme Studios comics six years early. *Destroy!* was created with tongue positively glued to cheek (there's a route map of the destruction in the back), and the artwork is great.~FP
Recommended: 1

THE DESTROYER
Marvel: *Series one 10 issues 1989–1990, One-shot 1991*

The series adapts the best-selling stories of Remo Williams, the ironically named Destroyer who's a reluctant extra-legal problem solver for a top-secret government department. The real star character, though, is Williams' irascible Korean teacher Chiun, master of the ancient bodily ideal of sinanju. Mainly written by Will Murray, the stories capture the tongue-in-cheek flavour of the

novels. The first series is a black and white magazine, while the one-shot is a traditional comic.~WJ
Collection: *The Destroyer* (Series one 1–3)

DESTROYER DUCK
Pacific: *7 issues 1982–1984*

Begun as a benefit comic to raise funds for Steve Gerber's court case against Marvel concerning ownership of Howard The Duck, the polemic soon becomes tiresome, but Gerber mistakenly believed there was life beyond a one-shot for this G.I. Duck. Illustrated for three issues by Jack Kirby, also with a legitimate axe to grind concerning Marvel, there's a great irony in that the first issue's back-up feature became more successful than either fowl. Groo began his wandering here.~FP

THE DESTRUCTOR
Atlas: *4 issues 1975*

Writer Archie Goodwin is working from the Spider-Man template of teenager suddenly acquiring powers beyond his dreams, so it helps to have Steve Ditko aboard as pencil artist (inked by Wally Wood in 1 & 2, and inking himself in 3). The twist is that teenager Jay Hunter was a budding gangster before seeing the error of his ways. Not a masterpiece, but certainly one of the better Atlas titles.~WJ

DETECTIVE COMICS
DC: *704 issues, 9 Annuals + 1937 to date*

The second-longest-running ongoing comic and the title from which DC takes its name, early issues are almost impossible to find and command prices concomitant with their rarity. An anthology with a theme, it featured characters called Slam Bradley, Speed Saunders and Larry Steele, hard men with hard names, and it can be taken for granted that the early content is as crude as most of its contemporaries. The Crimson Avenger, a strongly pulp-influenced hero, débuted in 20, and is now seen as DC's oldest superhero, despite not actually putting on a costume until 44. *Detective* would probably be long dead by now had it not been for the 1939 début of Batman in 27. Showcased amid the company of Cosmo, Phantom Of Disguise and Slam Bradley and his ilk, it's small surprise he captured the reading public's imagination in a way only Superman had before. A grim and silent crimebuster, the visual impact of the character is there from the beginning, and it took just over a year for Batman to edge all other features off the cover.

By today's standards the initial Batman stories are crudely illustrated and written, by Bob Kane and Bill Finger. Jerry Robinson's gradual elevation from assistant to pencil artist over the first three years instituted greater fluidity in the art, and after the first year Batman is developing a personality, albeit a slim one. The emphasis of the early strips is detection, with most adversaries meeting a brutal demise. Robin's arrival in 38 initiates a lighter tone, but he's often merely a convenient infiltrator of groups playboy Bruce Wayne is too prominent to join. An early landmark is 43, when Batman combats his first 'dealer of habit forming drugs'. By this point plots are acquiring a veneer of sophistication, and colourful foes are escaping to plague Batman another day. The Penguin débuts in 58, and with Clayface (40), Hugo Strange (36) and most importantly the Joker (*Batman* 1) already introduced, exotic recurring villains become the norm. Despite his appearance the Joker was originally merely a gang boss and thief, his characterisation as a madman developing in the 1970s. His *Detective* début is 45, and he's a frequent foe throughout the 1940s, with his best appearance being 64, when he's actually electrocuted in gruesome fashion. He's not given an origin, though, until 168. Two-Face débuts in 66, and returns in 68 for an uncharacteristically touching story as he attempts to repair his relationship.

Batman saw out World War II in good shape, with nary a nod to the Nazis. Pulp writer Don Cameron was the best of the regular writing staff, submitting scripts a cut above the norm, with decent gimmicks, and from 84 artist Dick Sprang began developing a distinctive look for Batman. His became the definitive style for almost two decades, but it coincided with the humanising of Batman. By the 1950s the once grim and feared dark knight had been reduced to an all-round genial guy who starred in largely light-hearted adventures and fought on giant typewriters. And that was the good stuff. There were also ill-advised science-fiction elements, encounters with robots and a plethora of inane Bat-associates and accessories. The 1950s were not classic years for Batman either here or in his own title.

Oddly, given the success of Batman, *Detective* remained relatively free of other costumed types populating the back-up features, although they certainly proliferated elsewhere. Slam Bradley, created by a pre-Superman Siegel and Shuster, had an astonishing longevity, only surrendering his slot in 152 to dull TV detective Roy Raymond (often nicely illustrated by Ruben Moreira). Air Wave had a long and ordinary run between 60 and 137 before being replaced by the only slightly more engaging Robotman, a human brain in a robot body. Both he and Native American detective Pow Wow Smith (patronising name but nice Infantino art) bowed out with 202. The best early back-up was Boy Commandos from 64, a multinational

kid gang overseen by Captain Rip Carter. They foiled a remarkable amount of Nazi plots in occupied Europe, and lasted way beyond the end of World War II both in their own title and here, with 150 their final issue (although creators Simon and Kirby left with 83). The Martian Manhunter débuted in 225, accidentally transported from Mars with a startling array of abilities largely subsumed by his assumed identity as a police officer. He lasted until 326, his demise hastened by the addition of irritating alien companion Zook. The back-ups decreased in number as the page-count shrank, with Batman remaining consistent at twelve pages from the mid-1940s. It wasn't until the 1970s that he evicted all other tenants, and even then they often sneaked back in.

327 is a landmark. The rot was unmistakably established, and Batman was revamped, marking the change by the addition of a yellow oval surrounding the bat emblem on his chest. The previous Batman was ascribed to an alternate Earth and destined to become a slate on which stories unsuitable for the hidebound, now 'proper' Batman were written. The new art team of Carmine Infantino and Sid Greene (later Joe Giella) signalled a clean step away from the past, and writer Gardner Fox introduced shock and suspense, beginning with the apparent death of Wayne's butler Alfred and a recurring new villain called the Outsider. The same team also produced the light and fun Elongated Man back-ups. The revamp was partially successful, although gimmickry still abounded, but the Batman TV show was in the works, drawing on the sillier aspects of the previous incarnation. When it hit, the camp humour transferred back to comics, bringing Batgirl with it in 359, emblematic of the era. It wasn't until the end of the 1960s that a gradual change introduced a far more realistic Batman. He once again became the brooding creature of the night, and mysteries supplanted the costumed villains, making their rare appearances special. Although sometimes straining too hard to be contemporary, and no masterpieces, these are the earliest *Detective* Batman stories to withstand a modicum of critical scrutiny as anything other than curiosities, but don't be suckered in by the generally excellent covers. The writing of Denny O'Neil and Frank Robbins has a greater sophistication than previous plots, and the artwork is well suited to the tone of the character, particularly the illustrative commercial style of Neal Adams (although his greatest triumphs were in *Batman*). In 400 Robbins and Adams introduce Man-Bat.

A feature of the 1970s *Detective* was numerous attempts to return to an extended format. 414–424 feature Batgirl back-ups

alongside reprinted detective fillers, and
438–445, at a hundred pages, are uniformly
excellent. Editor Archie Goodwin wrote a fine
selection of Batman tales, drawn by artists new
to the character, with a spirited Howard
Chaykin job in 441 and Alex Toth's 'Death Flies
The Haunted Skies' in 442 a standout. In 439
Steve Englehart, a writer who'd have a later
impact on *Detective*, turned in his first Batman
story. Goodwin filled the remainder of the
hundred pages with an oddball, varied
selection of reprint material, largely from the
1940s, and another strip of his, *Manhunter*,
which débuted in 437. Illustrated by the then
unknown Walt Simonson, it's a fascinating
blend of mystery, martial arts and action with
ties back to the previous DC Manhunter, varied
story-telling, and complete over six short
episodes and one longer concluding team-up
with Batman in 443. By far the best back-up
feature to see print here, *Manhunter* has been
reprinted both as a one-shot in 1984 and as a
black and white book. The next attempt at an
oversize title, between 481 and 495, consisted of
all new material, having absorbed the oversize
Batman Family. The Batman stories apart,
mediocrity was prevalent, but look for some
nice Michael Golden art in 482.

Goodwin was to return with a fine story
about obligation in annual 3, but when he
stopped editing *Detective* it slipped back, if not
into mediocrity, then into mundanity, with only
the gradual return of the costumed villains
noteworthy. The best of the period is Denny
O'Neil's sentimental addition to Batman's
origin in 457. It took Steve Englehart and the art
team of Marshall Rogers and Terry Austin to
breathe life back into the comic, and they did so
in spectacular fashion between 471 and 476,
producing arguably the best run of stories seen
in the title. In six issues Englehart returned
Hugo Strange and Deadshot as credible foes,
delivered memorable encounters with the
Penguin, and particularly The Joker, introduced
crooked councilman Rupert Thorne, set up the
only believable relationship Bruce Wayne's ever
had with a woman, and brought continuity to
the title. Rogers' art was stylish and thoughtful,
and both drew on the mood of the 1940s
Batman, reflecting it with a distinctly
contemporary outlook. Reissued as the five-part
Shadow Of The Batman, it also included material
drawn by Rogers after Englehart's departure,
serviceable without ever thrilling.

Englehart and Rogers had upped the quality
considerably, and since then there's never been
a prolonged dip back into mediocrity, although
crossover stories have, at times, tried the
patience. Artists like Don Newton, Gene Colan
and Norm Breyfogle maintained Batman as the
mysterious figure of the night, while plots
have been varied. For a sample of Newton see

497's *Spirit* homage, and Colan's rendition is
consistently good. The 1980s also introduced
the concept of the anniversary issue, with any
excuse serving to increase the page-count and
celebrate. Initially this resulted in fine material,
with the oversize 500 a real nostalgia-seeped
bonanza. Batman has an opportunity to prevent
his parents' murder on an alternative Earth, and
there's also an intriguing story of Batman at
death's door, a Hawkman tale drawn in his
father's style by Adam Kubert and a teaming of
the assorted non-costumed detectives to have
appeared in *Detective* over the years. 526's
celebration of Batman's 500th appearance in
Detective takes a different tack, as Batman and
allies, in a single night, have to face all his major
foes and a threatening new introduction in
Killer Croc. It also has a new Robin in costume
for the first time, but he doesn't become Robin
until 535. 572's fiftieth anniversary of the title is
disappointing apart from the Alan Davis art,
but 600 is outstanding, the best of the
anniversary issues. Sam Hamm's screenwriting
experience and Denys Cowan's cinematic
layouts contribute to 'Blind Justice' (598–600)
being an excellent page-turner. Focusing on
Bruce Wayne more than Batman, it involves
morally repugnant experiments and a
seemingly unbreakable set-up for which Wayne
will take the fall. At 144 pages *Blind Justice* is
never padded or slow, and contains some
insightful, almost throwaway observations
about Batman and his milieu. 627's reworking
of Batman's first appearance falls way short in
comparison; an interesting idea, albeit used
previously in 387. 700 is very ordinary.

A characteristic of early to mid-1980s
Detective is the constant crossing over with
Batman, creating in effect a two-weekly Batman
comic. A tight continuity was maintained, and
there are no really bad stories, but none that
stand out either. The creative team of Mike
Barr, Alan Davis and Paul Neary transfer from
Batman and the Outsiders in 569. Davis and
Neary quit a chapter into 'Batman: Year Two'
(575–578), leaving Todd McFarlane to finish
the story. It's a pointless exercise and very
ordinary in comparison with 'Year One'
(*Batman* 404–407). With 583 John Wagner and
Alan Grant join in place pencil artist Norm
Breyfogle to start the final run of really good
Batman stories here to date. Starting strongly
with the début of gang boss The Ventriloquist
and his psychotic dummy Scarface, they rely
on bizarre and interesting new adversaries,
and infuse a macabre humour to lighten the
increasingly grim tone of the title without
returning it to the stupidity of the 1950s. Grant
eventually becomes the sole writer until 621.
He unites all four Clayfaces in 604–607,
touching and fun, but stretched thin over four
issues. The following Anarky two-parter is

better, and the Penguin story in 610 and 611 the highspot of Grant's solo run.

The otherwise excellent and innovative Peter Milligan disappoints here between 629 and 643, and succeeding writer Chuck Dixon takes until chapters of 'Knightfall' in 658–666 to settle in. As a title 'Knightfall' stretches a sobriquet too far, but having Batman beaten and replaced in a story crossing between all the Bat titles generated controversy and acres of print and boosted sales enormously, making the DC accountants very happy indeed. Sadly, it prompted only a minor upswing in quality. Many chapters were dull and padded to extend the story beyond its natural lifespan, but one aspect in its favour was the sense of uncertainty. For the first time ever Batman wasn't guaranteed an eventual victory. 'Knightquest', with the former Azrael in Batman's costume, provided for better comics, with 670's eerie Mr Freeze story being the best, and 'Knightsend' (676–677), in which Batman goes over the top and is dealt with, is an improvement, and all the better for its brevity.

Bruce Wayne reclaims the Batman costume in 682, and it's been largely Dixon and Graham Nolan since. Improved production has resulted in a better-looking package, but it's a deceptive step forward. With frequent crossovers, a leisurely pace, and larger illustrations meaning fewer panels, a story once told in twelve pages now takes two issues. Sales are healthy, though, and sadly that's all the seems to matter.~FP

Recommended: 437–443, 471–476, 500, 584, 591–593, 598–600, 608–611, 613, Annual 3
Collections: Batman Chronicles Vol 1 (27–50), Vol 2 (51–70), Vol 3 (71–86), *Batman: Year Two* (575–578), *Blind Justice* (598–600), *Challenge Of The Man-Bat* (395, 397, 400, 402), *The Greatest Batman Stories Ever Told* Vol 1(31, 32, 211, 235, 345, 404, 429, 437, 442, 457, 574, 482, 500), Vol 2 (203, 473, 568), *The Greatest Joker Stories Ever Told* (168, 475, 476), *Knightsend* (676–677), *Knightfall* Vol 1 (659–663), Vol 2 (664–666), *Manhunter* (*Manhunter* stories from 437–443), *Tales Of The Demon* (411, 485, 489, 490)

The DETECTIVES
Alpha: *One-shot 1993*

Anthology commemorating seventy years of the private eye. Best stories feature *The Maze Agency* and Michael Mauser, both better in their own titles.~WJ

DETECTIVES INC.
Eclipse: *Graphic Novel 1980, 2-issue microseries 1985, 3-issue miniseries 1987*

Detectives Inc was among the earliest graphic novels published for the American market, and a favourite with older comic readers throughout the late 1970s. Don McGregor's

writing had always tackled adult subjects, and artist Marshall Rogers was fresh from the most acclaimed run of Batman stories for several years. Titled 'A Remembrance Of Threatening Green', the title gives a clue to writer Don McGregor's prose style, which gets whole huge typeset panels to itself among Marshall Rogers's once-fashionable heavily zipatoned drawings with their bizarrely extruded human figures. McGregor celebrated the idea of being able to produce a big comic for adults by including just about everything that he wasn't previously allowed to use that would fit into the contemporary private eye genre he'd chosen. So you see explicit sex (hetero and lesbian only – the male gayness is all in the relationship between the two detectives and well repressed, of course), children as killers and as victims of terrible violence, and references to sado-masochistic prostitution. The real emotional content is at the Mary Tyler Moore TV level so it's nice to see comics finally aspiring to something so elevated, if you can stand reading 'memories and fantasies' likened to 'Siamese twins' or 42nd St to a 'neon dinosaur'. The 1985 microseries reprints the graphic novel. The follow-up series from 1987 is the one to try. McGregor restrains himself a bit and gets on with a good little mystery story, brilliantly illustrated by Gene Colan in pencil printed in sepia.~GK

DEVIANT SLICE
Print Mint: *2 issues 1972–1973*

For once a comic that absolutely lives up to its title, as this Greg Irons/Tom Veitch masterpiece is about as deviant as they come. There's gore aplenty to be sure, but it's conceived by a keen sense of moral outrage at the establishment's shortcomings. It remains one of the most chillingly perceptive documents of the death of the *Age of Aquarius*.~DAR
Recommended: 1, 2

DEVIL CHEF
Dark Horse: *One-shot 1994*

In small doses, amid the eclectica of *Deadline USA* (in strips reprinted here), Devil Chef raised a smile or two. It's a caricature of the temperamental and tyrannical French chef, prone to towering rages, but twenty-eight unrelenting pages spread the paté far too thin. If you really can't get enough of our satanic gastronome, he's back in *Dark Horse Presents* 107–109.~WJ

DEVIL DINOSAUR
Marvel: *9 issues 1978*

One of many titles written and drawn by Jack Kirby – in a hurry, one suspects – where the grandiose concept and promise of an astounding universe was never fulfilled by the rather clichéd characters that peopled it. The misleading title doesn't help. Devil Dinosaur is, in fact, a singularly intelligent member of his species, telepathically controlled by a rather advanced cave youth called Moon Boy. The Devil doesn't come into it and Devil Dinosaur does nothing demonic except batter a few villains with his tail. Moon Boy communicates in odd bursts of purple prose, which gives the title an undeniably batty charm lacked by many later Kirby offerings. Certainly the maddest of many rather peculiar Jack Kirby creations.~FJ

DEVILINA
Atlas: *2 issues 1975*

Alias the sister of Satan, our behootered nominal heroine struggled to overcome her evil heritage while wearing a variety of skimpy fetishistic outfits. A patent Vampirella rip-off, she was backed up in this black and white magazine-sized comic by horror stories which, the ads boasted, 'focused on fabulous females!', i.e. had a bit of badly drawn gratuitous nudity. Pathetic.~HS

DEVLIN WAUGH
Fleetway/Quality: *One-shot 1992*

The stylish and refined bodybuilder Devlin Waugh also happens to be the papal envoy and a freelance exorcist. When an underwater prison becomes infested with vampires, Devlin is the only man able to break the survivors out. He's just a little too glib and idealised to work properly in what is otherwise a gory thriller, but there's some excellent art from the under-rated Sean Phillips.~WJ

DICK TRACY Monthly
Blackthorne: *25 issues 1986–1988*

Published as a companion title to Blackthorne's 'Reuben Award Series' of Dick Tracy reprints, Blackthorne's monthly was edited by Shel Dorf. Though Dorf's love of the strip is clear, the decision to cut and paste the newspaper strip to fit a comic page was seen as heresy by purists. In fact, it is the change in panel size that does the most disservice to the strip. 14, containing the marriage of Tracy to Tess Trueheart, has the oddest printing, with two panels to a page instead of the usual nine of the daily pages. Chester Gould's Dick Tracy is a classic whose violence and conservatism has perhaps put it out of favour with today's comics readership. The series begins with reprints from 1940 but switches to 1949 with number 10. Lacking any information about the strip, the comic is nevertheless a noble attempt to bring Dick Tracy to a new audience.~NF

The Original DICK TRACY
Gladstone: *5 issues 1990–1991*

Even more heretically than Blackthorne, Gladstone's Dick Tracy comic (again, a comic to accompany a series of graphic novels) actually edited strips to avoid repetition, cut and pasted everything to fit a nine-panel page and coloured the originals. Published in no particular order (but all from the mid-1940s) each issue did contain a complete story-line, including the wedding of B.O. Plenty and Gravel Gertie in 5. Whatever purists might say, Gladstone's high production values made this an excellent showcase for Gould's artwork. Tracy himself is rather characterless but Gould's story-telling abilities make *Dick Tracy* an important part of newspaper strip history.~NF

DICK TRACY
Disney: *3 issues 1990*

John Moore and Kyle Baker turn in a witty and vividly coloured version of Dick Tracy, not at all harmed by having to include Warren Beatty's likeness as Tracy throughout. The first two issues act as a prequel to the 1990 movie, introducing Madonna's character Breathless Mahoney, and featuring several of Chester Gould's classic villains, including Flat Top and Prune-Face. Gripping, amusing and well plotted, they're the best Dick Tracy seen since Gould himself. Of course, Kyle Baker's sketchy and fluid art couldn't be further from Gould, but works nonetheless in conveying Dick Tracy's world. There's some doubt as to whether the third issue, containing the movie adaptation, was actually published. It is to be found, though, in the collection. Writer Len Wein was a little restricted by the film's less than sparkling script, but works wonders with it, and Baker is also present for consistency's sake.~WJ
Collection: True Hearts And Tommy Guns (1–3)

DIE CUT
Marvel UK: *4-issue miniseries 1993–1994*

Blade-handed anti-hero hacks his way through scratchily illustrated fights with the X-Men's Beast. Dismissable.~HS

DIFFERENT BEAT COMICS
Fantagraphics: *One-shot 1994*

Effectively a Fantagraphics sampler, it's a pity that *Different Beat* shows so few of their star creators to advantage. The blurb calls them rarities, but you're better off thinking of it as odds and sods by Joe Sacco, Los Bros Hernandez, Robert Crumb, Peter Bagge, Roberta Gregory and the other usual suspects behind a striking Dan Clowes cover. The best piece is the colour back cover by Chris Ware, an unsettling Jimmy Corrigan strip about going to a burger bar.~FJ

DIGITEK
Marvel UK: *4-issue miniseries 1992–1993*

One of the more interesting concepts thrown up during Marvel UK's expansion period, Digitek is a warrior combination of deceased computer technician and advanced computer intelligence, able to move through electric conduits. The story never moves beyond battles with less benign counterparts, but there was potential here.~FP

DINO ISLAND
Mirage: *2-issue microseries 1993*

Stunningly simple and gorgeous line art from Jim Lawson, with every illustration a postcard, sadly accompanies a stunningly simple and not so gorgeous story from Jim Lawson. Okay, there are dinosaurs, but they're not what we're used to, and even Amelia Earhart and a solution to the Bermuda Triangle mystery don't liven things up.~WJ

DINO RIDERS
Marvel: *3-issue miniseries 1989*

Everyone starts their career somewhere. Later fan-favourite Kelley Jones artist probably neglects to list this early work on his CV. A dull toy tie-in with a lame plot about opposing warring forces harnessing the power of dinosaurs after arriving in prehistoric Earth.~WJ

DINOSAUR REX
Upshot Graphics: *3-issue miniseries 1987*

Upshot was an imprint of Fantagraphics, primarily publishing the work of Jan Strnad. *Dinosaur Rex* is a pulp adventure story written in a style that owes a great deal to P.G. Wodehouse. It's more homage than pastiche; the characters are well-drawn and the script adapts well to the search for a dinosaur graveyard. Henry Mayo's artwork is smooth (in a similar way to Sam Kieth's), but though he's obviously inspired by such greats as Roy Krenkel and Burne Hogarth, he manages a distinctive style of his own. A back-up strip by Bill Messner-Loebs and Dennis Fujitake is light-hearted science fiction that deals with the question of racism without ramming its politics down the readers' throats.~NF

DINOSAURS, A Celebration
Marvel: *4-issue miniseries 1992*

Half of each issue is illustrated factual text, which is suitable for intelligent children or adult general readers. This is broken up by short strips about imagined everyday episodes in the lives of individual dinosaurs of the various orders. These are painted by star UK artists such as John McCrea and Liam Sharp. There's no dialogue, of course, and the stories inevitably tend to focus on the threat of gory

death, but it's all intelligently and enjoyably done.~GK
Recommended: 1–4

DINOSAURS ATTACK
Eclipse: *1 issue 1991*

The fondly remembered *Mars Attacks* bubblegum card series spawned a successful imitator years later in *Dinosaurs Attack*. It's much the same plot told over a series of cards, but substitutes saurians for Martians committing atrocities the globe over. The comic tells the same story with additional scenes, or at least begins to do so, as the proposed second and third issues never materialised. Despite this Earl Norem's painted art is worth seeing, but in contrast the pages pencilled by Herb Trimpe and inked by George Freeman come off distinctly second best.~FP

DINOSAURS FOR HIRE
Eternity: *9 issues 1988–1989*
Malibu: *13 issues 1993–1994*

Prevented from running a strip called *Elvis For Hire*, featuring clones of Elvis working for the FBI, Tom Mason switched the central characters to dinosaurs and publication ensued just in time to catch the crest of the *Teenage Mutant Ninja Turtles* craze. This is one of the better cash-ins, with a strong sense of irony and more than a sly poke at the comics industry. Archie (tyrannosaurus), Lorenzo (triceratops), Reese (stegosaurus) and Cyrano (pterodactyl) are US government agents loaded with guns and gags and out to fight criminals. The original black and white series is a little shaky in places, relying on too many knock-back jokes from *TMNT* and weak art, but the run really kicks in with the second series. With added colour and new artists, Mason gets very silly. 6 has a nice *Jurassic Park* parody, and in 8 the team are split up when Lorenzo disappears, having to be located before he's sliced and diced by a bunch of sicko gourmets. 8–13 have the fun lovin' foursome hopping through the dimensions accompanied by their beautiful blonde professor team-mate, but sadly they were all driven into extinction with 13. One hopes they'll be back.~TP
Recommended: Series two 6, 8–13
Collection: Guns'n'Lizards (Series one 1–3), Dinosaurs Rule (Series one 4–6)

The DIRTY DUCK Book
Company and Sons: *1 issue 1971*

Not a book at all, the title notwithstanding, but a comic collecting Bobby London's 'Dirty Duck' strips. London was one of the 'Air Pirates', a group of counterculture cartoonists who based their art styles on early comics pioneers. London's influence was very clearly George Herriman and his *Krazy Kat* feature.

The first half of the comic contains typical underground humour, applied to animals, but by the second half London had grown confident enough to almost totally abandon dialogue, and his similarity to Herriman is astonishing.~DAR
Recommended: 1

DIRTY LAUNDRY
Cartoonists Co-Op: *1 issue 1974*
Last Gasp: *1 issue (2) 1977*
The first couple of an underground comics team to reveal all about their life together. Individually both Robert Crumb and Aline Kominsky had produced some of the finest comics of their time, so the combination of the two should have been terrific. Sadly, it just doesn't work. For one thing the combination of their styles was simply too jarring. On her own Kominsky's art works because of the power of her stories, but when put next to Crumb's draughtsmanship it simply comes across as crude. Thematically, too, their stories are either misguided (the science-fiction segment in 1, for instance), repetitive (far too many stories of the pair 'doing it') or simply too domestic.~DAR

DIRTY PAIR
Eclipse: *4-issue miniseries 1988–1989, 4-issue miniseries ('Dangerous Acquaintance') 1989–1990, 5-issue miniseries ('A Plague Of Angels') 1990–1991, 4-issue miniseries ('Sim Hell') 1993*
Viz: *5-issue miniseries 1994–1995*
Dark Horse: *4-issue miniseries ('Fatal But Not Serious') 1995*
Yuri and Kei think of themselves as The Lovely Angels. Trouble-shooters for the WWWA (Worlds-Wide Welfare Association), they visit whichever of the three-thousand-plus inhabited planets in the known universe has a problem and sort it out. At least, that's what they're supposed to do. Comedy action comic featuring a sexy and violent duo more prone to lose their tempers and solve a poser with an Uzi than an argument, *Dirty Pair* is unusual in being developed in America by Adam Warren and Toren Smith at Studio Proteus, then sold back to Japan, where it was made into a successful anime. The Viz series is based on the animation cells for the anime, and is smoothly drawn in full colour, as opposed to the slightly scratchy, semi-Westernised art of the originals.~FJ
Collections: *Biohazards* (Miniseries one 1–4), *Dangerous Acquaintance* (1–4), *A Plague Of Angels* (1–5), *Sim Hell* (1–4)

DIRTY PLOTTE
Drawn & Quarterly: *9 issues + 1990 to date*
Julie Doucet is one of the best, and probably laziest, cartoonists to come out of the Canadian scene this decade. Confrontational and abrupt,

her strips about such unacceptable topics as cutting yourself with a razor blade shimmer with real anger and frustration. There's something iconic about the way she draws, with rough, broad lines, filling in the page with pattern around her large-headed, somehow helpless characters. Although the quantity of her output is minimal, with various friends helping out on the art in later issues, *Dirty Plotte* is well worth seeking out, if only for vicarious thrills. The wittily titled collection also includes hard-to-find work from Doucet's earlier mini-comics.~FJ
Collection: *Lève ta jambe, mon poisson est mort* (1–5)

The Mundane Adventures of DISHMAN
Eclipse: *1 issue 1988*
Paul Mahler discovers he has the ability to wave his hands over dirty dishes and they're instantly cleaned and put away. Of course, he designs a costume and goes out to change the world. A very funny superhero comic pastiche that works well because it's treated in a totally deadpan manner. *Dishman* appropriates the look of superhero titles with no hint of artistic exaggeration, and accurately represents the shorthand emotional conflict so commonly passing as characterisation. May John MacLeod never have to wash his own dishes.~FP
Recommended: 1

A DISTANT SOIL
WaRP: *9 issues 1983–1985*
Donning/Starblaze: *2 Volumes 1987–1988*
Aria Press: *14 issues 1991–1996*
Image: *2 issues + (15–17) 1996 to date*
Superficially, this looks like a schlock fantasy comic: big eyes, pretty pictures, knights in armour, faery types and aliens for *Elfquest* meets *Star Wars*. While there is a grain of truth in that evaluation, it doesn't do the series justice, by any means. Our heroes are a young girl, Liana, and her brother Jason, both possessed of immense psychic powers. For several years, they've been held in a government institute, following the deaths of their parents in suspicious circumstances, while scientists attempt to duplicate their powers. On escaping, they immediately find themselves caught in another conflict as the Ovanan rulers seek out Liana, who has the powers of the Avatar – Ovanan's hereditary ruler – in sufficient degree to prevent the current Avatar from using his abilities. Liana is rescued by two men from Ovanan's resistance faction, the enigmatic Rieken, and his lover and protector D'Mer, but Jason falls into the hands of the Ovanan rulers, notably the lovely but evil Lady Sere. Meanwhile, Rieken and

D'Mer assemble a bunch of warriors from human volunteers (including a conveniently time-lost Sir Galahad) and one Ovanan exile, the formidable shapechanger Bast. The battle lines are drawn.

Yes, the plot is nothing particularly original, and some of the events are forced. We simply have to accept creator Colleen Doran's word that everything will, eventually, tie together. Doran has a fine ear for natural, unstilted dialogue and good delivery of emotional lines. These are people that one quickly comes to care about. Her art is striking, with influences of Mucha and Beardsley visible, but also homages to various Japanese comics creators in the use of apparently irrelevant background images to denote strong emotion. The beauty of her work also conceals a cold, hard edge to events. You marvel at a lovely picture, then realize that what you are admiring is an illustration of a pile of children's corpses. The contrast between the cruelty of events and their lovingly rendered depiction creates a sense of unease that suits the story admirably. Despite appearances to the contrary, this is no soft, fluffy comic.

A copyright dispute and litigation resulted in *A Distant Soil* leaving WaRP after 9, although there were solicitations for several non-existent issues afterwards. The graphic novels, in full colour, retell the events of the WaRP issues, but manage to take the story a little further, ending with events that would become the conclusion of the Aria Press run's issue 11. With the Aria Press self-published series, substantial portions of the story were redrawn and revised, with much new material added. Every issue to 11 has some previously unseen work, and from 12 upwards, it's all new. Doran regards this as the definitive version of her story, though comparing and contrasting between the two incarnations is an interesting exercise. 14 was an all-sketchbook issue, and 15 saw Aria Press joining Image, for better distribution and solicitation. Now that all issues are more widely available, you've really got no excuse for not trying it.~HS

Recommended: Aria 1–17
Collections: Immigrant's Sacong (Aria 1–5), *Knights Of The Angel* (6–10)

DIVISION 13
Dark Horse: *One-shot 1993, 4 issues 1994–1995*

Introduced as part of *Comics Greatest World*, Division 13 was a military complex housing and testing superpowered and mutated humans. A break-in by escapees isn't entirely successful, but by the end of the introductory one-shot the facility has been breached and the internees are loose. The ongoing series concentrates on the previously introduced cast, which is a shame, as the imposing presence of

fellow-prisoner Law is far more interesting. It's a decidedly average title, with Law coming into his own in the course of the far superior *Agents Of Law.*~WJ

DJANGO & ANGEL
Caliber: *5 issues 1990*

Donne Avenell is better known as the writer of *Axa*, the popular European sword-and-sorcery newspaper strip. *Django & Angel* is a little-known thriller originally printed in Sweden. The premise is this: each issue Django, an ex-FBI agent working for Interpol, and Angel, an English private detective, solve a self-contained mystery, although they spend very little time in the same room together. Of minor interest to *Axa* groupies (if such sad beings exist).~NF

DNAGENTS
Eclipse: *Series one 24 issues 1983–1985, Series two (The New DNAGENTS) 17 issues, 1985–1987*
Antarctic: *1 issue 1994*

As ever, Mark Evanier turns out an entertaining and well-crafted superhero tale, which just about manages to rise above the clichés on which it is built. The mad-scientist-infested Matrix Corporation discovers a formula by which to make creatures as near to human as you ever need to get, but who are capable of being programmed to obey. As a bunch of totally subservient superheroes wouldn't be much fun to read, the DNAgents soon manage to think for themselves, and spend the rest of the series at loggerheads with their (mostly) immoral Matrix bosses while they try to explore and discover their own identities. Despite the unoriginality of the basic concept and the high level of *angst*, probably influenced by contemporary *X-Men* stories, the title had its moments, not least of which were due to Evanier's strong characterisation ensuring that the artificial humans weren't always in agreement on how much, or in what way, they wanted to mix with the real world. The soap-opera elements of the series always outdid the action sequences. The final issue, which does its best to tie-up all the plot threads, finishes on one of the best cliffhangers you're ever likely to come across. Also noteworthy is the early Erik Larsen art in second series 13–17. A planned revival from Antarctic never worked out.~JC

D.O.A. COMICS
Jim Osbourne: *1 issue 1976*

Jim Osbourne was an undeservedly obscure underground artist with a fine eye for the grotesque, and this comic collects much of his best material. While his early work was a little crude, he quickly developed into a fine artist, and strips like 'The Suicide Of Lupe Velez' are beautifully detailed, and written with some

elegance. However, his subject matter was almost universally demented, and casual readers should be prepared to be offended.~DAR
Recommended: 1

DOC CHAOS
Escape: *2 issues 1984–1985*
Hooligan Press: *1 issue 1988*

The Escape issues are an expanded, magazine version of four comics published by Hydra/Anti-Matter, establishing the humorous premise of a near future in which politics are still conservative and the dangers of biotechnology (now, strangely, very relevant) have begun to exhibit themselves in random mutations throughout the population. While burger-giants are still experimenting to find the perfect burger, a group of anarchists hire detective Tito Livio to find Doc Chaos (a radical scientific genius who may or may not exist) so that they can persuade him to kickstart the revolution. This looks like being a difficult task since no one knows what he looks like and he can move from one body to another, anyway.

Dave Thorpe and Lawrence Gray take a leisurely approach to story-telling but there's a lot of plot and you can never be sure about the significance of the various events. Apart from an idea-packed script, the series also has the advantage of Phil Elliott's artwork. At once clearly European in style (heavily indebted to Hergé), it has a roughness that suits the sometimes outrageous characters and retains a distinctive feel. Well worth a look.~NF

DOC SAMSON
Marvel: *4-issue miniseries 1996*

Relying heavily on the cover-featured guest stars to sell the title, Marvel, one supposes, thought a series starring a superstrong psychologist wasn't exactly a winner, particularly with the relatively unknown creative team of Dan Slott and Ken Lashley. Lashley's gone halfway through 2, which is just as well since he's from the school of artists equating the number of lines used with quality, but spends so long over-elaborating his figures there's no time for backgrounds. It takes three artists to replace him at obviously short notice. Slott, meanwhile, throws every psychologist cliché (and plenty of others besides) into the brew, hoping to meld them into a plot. What story there is takes its cue from Peter David's extrapolation in the Hulk that exposure to gamma radiation results in a superstrong version of a previously repressed character facet. We therefore have a gamma-irradiated serial killer attempting to piece together the perfect woman. Other than She-Hulk, the guest appearances are forced, and new gamma-superpowered character Geiger is irritating in the extreme.~FP

DOC SAVAGE
Gold Key: *1 issue 1966*

Pulp novel adventurer Doc Savage has been licensed from comic publisher to comic publisher, most of whom have treated him rather shabbily. The first to do so were Gold Key in this lack-lustre adaptation of 'Thousand-Headed Man'.~FP

DOC SAVAGE
Marvel: *Series one 8 issues 1972–1974, series two 8 issues, 1 Giant-Size 1975–1977*

Relatively faithful to the all-action, convoluted adventures of the pulps, this short-lived series consists of two-issue adaptations of four original *Doc Savage* novels: 'The Man Of Bronze', 'Death In Silver', 'The Monsters', 'Brand Of The Werewolf'. Written by Steve Englehart, then Gardner Fox, and finally Tony Isabella, the comics are all plot, with most 'characterisation' taking place around the rivalry between Monk and Ham, two of Doc Savage's five aides. As a result the stories seem hurried but manage to retain something of the atmosphere and mystery of the originals. Ross Andru's artwork is not entirely inappropriate and is significantly improved by Tom Palmer's inking, but unfortunately with five different inkers in eight issues there's not much by way of a consistent look. Originally planning to bring Doc Savage into the 1970s, Marvel changed their plans and kept the adventures in the 1930s, but decided that other quirky period elements (such as Monk's pet pig) should be dropped.

Given more space to work with in the magazine-sized second series, Doug Moench wrote new Doc Savage stories, making good use of foreign locales, and gave him a chance to make greater use of Doc's companions and his cousin, Pat. Though several issues were drawn by others (John Buscema, 1 and 3, Val Mayerick 7), only the final issue, drawn entirely by Ernie Chan, doesn't bear the mark of Tony De Zuniga. Whether providing pencils and inks or just inking, his distinctive look provides a consistency that enhances the action-packed scripts. Not great, but faithful to the pulps and very entertaining.~NF

DOC SAVAGE
DC: *4-issue miniseries 1987–1988, 24 issues, 1 Annual 1988–1990*

DC tested the waters for a Doc Savage revival with a miniseries by Dennis O'Neil, drawn by the Kubert brothers, Adam and Andy, who then went on to produce a satisfying two-year run. It's a clever series, probing the origins of the Doc Savage 'myth', reintroducing the characters but updating them by providing Savage with a grandson and bringing Savage himself into the present. Though purists might dislike some elements of the story it does no disservice to the legend. Continuing from the miniseries, Denny O'Neil pits the Savages against creatures from the moon in 1–6. Mike Barr takes over the scripting with 7, which reintroduces Pat Savage, while 17 and 18 cross over with *The Shadow*. From 19 the series reverts briefly to the 30s before a final story-line that ties up the stories from both eras. Drawn by Rod Whigham and Steve Montano, there's a blockiness and stiffness to the artwork that really dulls Barr's scripts. The highlights of the series are the covers by the Kubert brothers. The annual contains the first meeting of Doc and his companions in a story that takes them to the 1936 Olympic games.~NF

DOC SAVAGE: CURSE OF THE FIRE GOD
Dark Horse: *4-issue miniseries 1995*

Steve Vance has a good idea of what makes a cracking Doc Savage story, including the prominent use of his cousin, Pat. Pat Broderick's artwork doesn't suit the characters or the setting. Gary Gianni's eye-catching covers are a definite plus and the whole thing's a reasonable approximation of a pulp adventure.~NF

DR FATE
DC: *3-issue miniseries 1985, 4-issue miniseries 1987, 41 issues 1988–1992*

The first miniseries reprints the Walt Simonson story from *First Issue Special* 9, and back-up stories from *Flash* 306–313. The second miniseries moved the goalposts. Previously archaeologist Kent Nelson, aloof and nigh-omnipotent master of magic, Dr Fate was now the mystically aged former ten-year-old Eric Strauss merged with his stepmother Linda. When not being Dr Fate they separated, and were monitored by Nelson's mentor, the immortal Nabu the Wise, now occupying Nelson's aged body. Writer J.M. DeMatteis stuck around for the ongoing title, added some humour absent from the miniseries, introduced a varied supporting cast, and produced a solid enough run in the company of ever-improving artist Shawn McManus. For the best of the bunch try 7's pastiche of *Romeo and Juliet* with Yiddish demons in New York (honestly). There's a death in issue 12, and the tone of *Dr Fate* becomes markedly darker. DeMatteis starts exploring the nature of fate and spirituality, ground he's positively stamped to death elsewhere, and the series isn't the better for it.

A change of the title logo to read *Doctor Fate* with 25 is as good an indication as any that a new broom is in town, and writer William Messner-Loebs makes sweeping changes. It's farewell to the previous supporting cast, and,

indeed, to the previous Dr Fate, as a youthful Kent Nelson returns in the company of his wife Inza. Unpredictably, it's Inza who is now Fate. Rather than occupy herself with cosmic matters she works on an altogether more human level, deciding that her destiny is to improve the lot of her immediate New York neighbourhood, making some interesting moral decisions along the way. Engaging supporting characters abound, not least a surly Lord of Order trapped in Kent Nelson's old body. Once Messner-Loebs hits his stride with 28 almost every issue is worth a look, and things improve further as Scot Eaton and Peter Gross take over the artwork with 33. A good sample issue is 35, by which time Inza has re-shaped the neighbourhood and the authorities are starting to take an interest. The stories published as *Scarab* were initially intended for this title (doubtless in very different form) and the next try is as *Fate*.~FP
Recommended: 28–32, 34, 35, 39, 40

DOCTOR GORPON
Eternity: *2 issues 1991*

Created by Marc Hansen, Doctor Gorpon combines elements of cartoonist Ed 'Big Daddy' Roth's manic monsters-in-dragsters style of art with Michael Gilbert's Mr Monster character. No originality in conception or art then, what about plot? Ummm, actually not much cop there either. It's slapstick cartoon violence with Gorpon going about dispatching monsters with glee and relish, while his former assistant wants revenge for poor treatment at Doc's hands. Announced as a three-issue miniseries, the final issue doesn't appear to have been published.~FP

The Second Life of DOCTOR MIRAGE
Valiant: *18 issues, 1993–1995*

Destroyed by the evil entity Master Darque, parapsychologist Hwen Mirage is brought back from the beyond by the love of his wife, Carmen Ruiz. Unfortunately, his 'second life' is as an intangible spirit with supernatural powers. The supernatural powers are fine, but the intangible bit causes Hwen and Carmen certain… romantic problems. How they solve them, and how their relationship survives this crisis, is the charm of this witty and likeable series. Most readers, one suspects, picked up the title to see how Hwen and Carm were getting along, rather than to see the spook-of-the-month action (though there was that too, for them as liked it). Bob Layton and Bernard Chang created two leads whose relationship was a partnership of genuine equals, with a refreshing lack of the power struggle that characterises so many comic relationships. It's also indicative of Valiant's willingness to take risks that there wasn't a major Caucasian character in the series, and interesting that most folks don't actually notice this until it's pointed out. While some people found the fact that our heroes were genuinely passionate about each other a little stifling, the series' strong romantic bias made it an unexpected hit with female readers – of whom, sadly, there weren't enough to give the title a long run. Cancelled mid-plot (19 was advertised, but never appeared), Carm and Hwen languish in limbo, mercifully untarnished by any of Valiant/Acclaim's attempted relaunches to date.~HS

DOCTOR SOLAR Man Of The Atom
Gold Key: *27 issues 1962–1969*
Whitman: *4 issues (28–31) 1981–1982*

When scientist Doctor Solar is exposed to a lethal dose of atomic radiation his body is transformed into a walking reactor, giving him various atom-related powers. Eventually assuming the masked identity of the Man Of The Atom in 5, Solar uses his miraculous abilities to counter the plotting of his arch enemy Nuro. 1–4 feature Solar before he donned his costume, and are drawn by Bob Fujitani. Most of the remaining issues are written by Paul Newman, with Frank Bolle drawing the bulk of the run. Al McWilliams produced some splendid art on 20–23's experiment with a continuing story-line before handing the art chores to José Delbo. The best individual issue is 15, wherein the Man Of The Atom has to relive his origin, but don't bother with the shoddy Whitman revival, where they dub the scientist Ray Solar... I mean, please!~SW
Recommended: 1–5, 15, 20–23

The Occult Files of DR SPEKTOR
Gold Key: *24 issues 1973–1977*

Basically an ordinary anthology title, this is different in that Dr Spektor is brought into the 1970s Gold Key universe with 7, revealing a blood link between him, Dagar and Tragg. There were guest appearances by Dr Solar in 14 and 23, and the artwork is mainly by the Filipino artists Gold Key used at the time.~SW

DOCTOR STRANGE
Marvel: *Series one 15 issues (169–183) 1968–1969, Series two 81 issues, 1 Annual, 1 Giant-Size, 1 Graphic Novel 1974–1987, series three 90 issues, 3 Annuals (2–4) 1988–1996*

The first series was an enigmatic little number that owed more to its breath-taking Colan and Palmer artwork and wild panel layouts than to the scripting. Plots improved from those in *Strange Tales*, from which the publication and numbering continued directly, but Roy Thomas' ideas somehow failed to gel. 174–177 and 180–183 are a cut above the rest in both story and art departments. Plot-lines concluded in *Sub-Mariner* 22 and *Incredible Hulk* 126, wherein Doctor Strange renounced his use of magic and abandoned his role as a sorcerer. He returned in *Marvel Feature* 1 and *Marvel Premiere* from 3 onwards.

The second series continued directly from his spell in *Marvel Premiere*. Ever since 1973, the character of Doctor Strange has been almost unrecognisable from that of the man portrayed in the 1960s *Strange Tales* stories. Whereas he was once little more than a superhero functioning in magical dimensions, he graduated into a truly eldritch and universal occultist. Steve Englehart and Frank Brunner finally broke through to concepts and abstract plots that could have flourished in very few other titles. Witness the story line in 10–13 wherein Earth is annihilated, then recreated instants later. Many issues are cerebral but the absence of limits on the writers' scope does not endear the title to every reader. Four of their early issues are reprinted as *Doctor Strange Special Edition*.

Later issues, mostly written by Roger Stern, are a touch more conventional, but quality is high from 48 on. A foothold on this planet is maintained through new supporting characters, particularly Morgana Blessing, who adds spice to Strange's static love life. Blessed by mouth-watering pencils from Marshall Rogers, Dan Green and Paul Smith, the second-half highlights capture a delightful time-travel tale in 49–53 (epilogue in 55) and an astonishingly powerful fable in 58–62, wherein Earth is rid of vampirism. The Doctor's adventures continued back into a new series of *Strange Tales*. The graphic novel *Into Shamballa* by J.M. DeMatteis and Dan Green accommodates lavish, abstract artwork but the grandiose presentation fails to disguise the pretentious story.

Doctor Strange is back in his own title for a third series after *Strange Tales*, but it's difficult to believe that good sales were responsible. Peter B. Gillis' Doctor Strange has lost one eye and nearly all his mystical talismans, and is now a shadow of his former self. Mind you, it's almost worth buying for the Kevin Nowlan cover on the first issue. When Roy and Dann Thomas take over the scripting, they promptly revert everything back to the way it was before Gillis mucked it up ('The Faust Gambit', 5–8), reintroducing lots of old characters while they're at it. If Jackson Guice isn't particularly appropriate as penciller, his artwork's not that bad. With 6 a back-up strip was introduced, 'The Book Of The Vishanti', written by Roy Thomas and R.J.M. L'Officier, which serves as a history of magic. With excellent, moody artwork from Tom Sutton (6–8), suddenly the title was worth reading again, particularly as the back-up moved on to the history of the Darkhold, the legendary book of evil.

10 introduces Strange's brother, Vic, and establishes a relationship with scientifically created vampire Morbius which is then explored throughout the series. Thomas also takes the opportunity to restore vampires to the Marvel Universe's plot-line in 'The Vampire Verses' (14–18), with guest appearances by Brother Voodoo and Morbius. The next major plot-line (21–24) has a big fight between Strange, Baron Mordo, Dormammu, Clea and Umar, and things start getting sticky from there in. Chris Marrinan takes over the pencils with 27, and the title becomes dogged with crossover issues. The interminable *Infinity Gauntlet* issues (31–36) are enough to make anyone give up the title. With 37 Geof Isherwood becomes regular penciller and it looks like the Thomases have once more got their act together, first with a Frankenstein story and then the three-part 'Great Fear' story-line in 38–40, featuring Nightmare, D'Spayre and Dweller In Darkness. A Daredevil guest appearance still suggests a lack of confidence in the character's ability to generate sales on his own, as does Wolverine popping up in 41 before six *Infinity War* crossover issues (42–47). After this Roy bales out (Dann having left with 40), leaving Len Kaminski holding the baby. Of course, this means a whole new 'new' direction for Doctor Strange as he decides, after all these years, that he's fed up with all these gods that he has to keep calling on for help. Therefore he decides in 50 to call on other heroes instead, leading to the formation of *The Secret Defenders*.

By 53 another change in direction is being announced, but not before the *Infinity Crusade* has taken up issues 54–56. Roy Thomas returns as co-plotter with Isherwood, who writes and draws the whole comic, instituting a fantasy direction led by Isherwood's introduction of Kyllian, a Celtic mystic, in Annual 3 (1993). His story is concluded in 59. The 'Midnight Sons' banner now starts to have its effect on *Doctor Strange* (essentially a line of characters including Ghost Rider, Blaze, Morbius and other 'horror' titles). The 'Siege Of Darkness' crossover affects 60 and 61, written by David Quinn and pencilled by Melvin Rubi, after which the good Doctor is a different person with new powers. This 'new' Strange lasts until 75 (in 76 he gets a new costume), with a series of stories in which guest appearances are used to keep reader interest, with Morbius, Polaris and The Hulk all turning up. Warren Ellis writes 80–83, followed by J.M. DeMatteis. Mark Buckingham and Kev Sutherland took over the artwork with 80 but, good as the pairing is (despite some rather odd facial expressions), they're wasted on some very poor scripts. DeMatteis' characteristic 'let's take a look at the human being in this character' ploy may have been necessary after a long period when writers didn't know what to do with him, but it's just an excuse to go over old ground.

After what seems like years of indifference, having large chunks of crossover continuity dumped into its story-lines, and a stream of half-hearted revamps of the character, none of which are allowed time to fully develop, it's no surprise that *Doctor Strange* was cancelled again.~APS/NF

Recommended: Series two 6–13, 15–16, 49–53, 55, 58–62, 71–73

DR WEIRD
Big Bang: *1 issue 1994*

Those with an interest in unearthing the earliest works of writers and artists are directed to Dr Weird, which features not only the fanzine-style art of Jim Starlin, but the fan writing of science-fiction author George R. Martin. It's utter tosh. Dr Weird is based on 1940s mystical superhero Mr Justice, himself based on The Spectre, and runs through assorted poorly drawn and written genre material. Curiosity won't pay off.~WJ

DOCTOR WHO
Marvel: *23 issues, 1 Graphic Novel 1984–1986*

Colour reprints of the mainly Dave Gibbons-drawn stories for Britain's *Doctor Who Magazine*. Largely concentrating on the Tom Baker version of the Doctor, if you've not seen his quirky and eccentric portrayal his persona in the comics quickly becomes irritating. Unlike the TV show, there's no respite from a supporting cast as Marvel's contract only covered likenesses of the Doctor. The Peter Davison version of the Doctor is featured from 16, illustrated by other artists, and the Doctor can also be found in a trial run for this series in *Marvel Premiere* 58–60. The stories are generally well crafted and faithful, but lack the vital spark. The graphic novel, titled 'Voyager', is a further collection of stories reprinted from *Dr Who Magazine* (88–99), this time enveloping the Tom Baker incarnation in a battle of wits against an ancient time-lord. Steve Parkhouse and John Ridgway combine well for an imaginative romp introducing a new helper.~FP

DR WIRTHAM'S COMIX AND STORIES
Clifford Neal: *6 issues (1–4, 5/6, 7/8) 1976–1981*

After a solo first effort by Cliff Neal (or Oisif Egaux, as he prefers), this became a very patchy underground anthology. Steve Bissette and Rick Veitch contributed some obviously very early work to 2 and 4, while other artists included Will Meugniot (2) and Gene Day (3). Neal himself had a beautifully detailed style, and each issue featured a number of illustrations and 'stories' by him, though story-telling was obviously not an interest of his. The final two issues are double-numbered and a great improvement, with nice work from a greatly improved Bissette and Veitch, Jay Kinney, the great Greg Irons (in 5/6) and Peter Bagge and Mike Matthews In 7/8.~DAR

DOCTOR ZERO
Epic: *8 issues 1988–1989*

Doctor Zero is the nemesis of the characters comprising the remainder of Epic's 'Shadowline' saga, but through top-quality promotional work has set himself up as Earth's ultimate saviour. Unknown to the mere mortals, he has a sinister and Machiavellian scheme involving the evolution of the human race, and he's not going to be stopped. Almost all-powerful and certainly amoral, he's not above killing anyone who messes with his plan, including Powerline and St George. While the premise sounds interesting, the scripts of Dan Chichester and Margaret Clark are sadly overwritten, and contain far too many fight scenes for the older Epic audience (a clash with a genie in 5 being particularly stupid). The story concluded in *Critical Mass*. Stick with the other Shadowline titles and have this quack struck off.~TP

DOG BOY
Fantagraphics: *10 issues 1987–1988*

Be careful not to mistake the title, written and drawn by Steve Lafler, with Charles Burns' book of the same name. Lafler's opus is a humorous anthropomorphic tale, and while both get humour out of contrasting dog and human behaviour, Lafler's jokes are very much more obvious. Lafler's art is up to conveying what's going on, but little more than that. The inking is heavy-handed and the characters visually unsympathetic.~FJ

DOGS OF WAR
Defiant: *8 issues 1994*

Another bow-wow from Jim Shooter's short-lived Defiant comics. The Dogs Of War are Shooter and Mouse, two supersoldiers introduced in the unreadable *Warriors Of Plasm*. Presumably not based on the editor, Shooter is a hair-triggered psychotic with the power to turn invisible while Mouse, a gentle soul, quickly becomes horrified by his friend's single-minded viciousness. Returned to Earth and unemployed, this odd couple decide to become vigilantes, taking on child pornographers, tobacco barons, gun smugglers and general scum-of-the-earth. Drawing liberally from Steve Ditko's *The Hawk And The Dove* and numerous

buddy movies, writer Art Holcomb obviously believes that virulent misogyny and mindless violence are the stuff of gritty realism. However, the rest of the comic is so laughably unreal that these calculated moments of political incorrectness only serve to underline *Dogs Of War's* general mediocrity.~AL

DOLL
Rip Off: *8 issues 1988–1991*

Guy Colwell's *Doll* is a sensitive erotic story of a hideously deformed man who approaches a hyper-realist sculptor to create a truly realistic sex doll, since no living woman will consent to have sex with him. The plot is complicated when a porn magazine editor who agrees to bankroll the projects wants to keep Doll for himself. There's plenty of tension and exploration of how men relate to women sexually in the book, but very little sex. The occasional penis sighting validates the 'adults only' label on the cover, but the actual encounters are more like asides.~FJ
Collections: Doll 1 (1–3), *Doll* 2 (5–8)

DOMINION
Eclipse: *6-issue miniseries 1989–1990*
Dark Horse: *one-shot 1994, 6-issue miniseries ('Conflict 1') 1996*

It's a future where the Earth's atmosphere is poisonous and direct contact with the air can be deadly. The Tank Police are a force created to deal with the threat of a single criminal, Buaku, whose gang has been proving very difficult to stop. The heroic Leona, despite being very fond of her tank (named Bonaparte), can't seem to stop Buaku, even though she and her pilot, Al, do keep coming close. The first series introduces the Tank Police and its world, culminating in Buaku's plan to leave Earth on a space shuttle, involving a truckload of hostage babies and lots of mayhem. In case you hadn't guessed, this is a comedy. Normal citizens fear the Tank Police more than they fear Buaku, and certainly more than Buaku fears the Police. The Chief's constantly on the verge of a nervous breakdown, incompetency runs rife and the citizens keep withdrawing funds.

After that, 'Conflict 1' seems to be a completely different series. The Tank Police still exist but are just another department of a large police force and the poisonous air has somehow been cleansed. Leona now leads a team (without Al) and finds herself nursemaid to Anna and Uni, mayhem-prone androids that once worked for Buaku. There's still an overall story-line but it's almost redundant given the interest shown in the background to the series and the many social and political conflicts within the force. 'Conflict 1' is certainly a maturer work, though the humour

remains, including Masamune Shirow's trademark footnotes and occasional 'to the reader' comments. There is a density to Shirow's later work that can be off-putting, especially his tendency to tell you more than you need to know, but it repays careful reading, and the comedy is always there to counterpoint the political machinations.~NF
Recommended: Dark Horse 1–6
Collection: No More Noise (Dark Horse 1–6)

DOMU: A Child's Dream
Dark Horse: *3-issue miniseries 1995*

A translation of Katsuhiro Otomo's Manga novel. A housing estate has had twenty-five mysterious deaths in three years. The police investigate, but how likely are they to get to the truth: that a spiteful, senile old man is using his psychic powers to drive people to suicide or murder? And their job is made no easier when a young girl with matching powers moves into the estate and within days the conflict turns to open war. A superb piece of work. If you've been avoiding Manga because you think it's all bambi eyes and huge robots, have a look at *Domu*. The story is exciting, intriguing and truly frightening, given an excellent translation here. The psychic conflict is handled particularly well, with both fighters staying in character throughout, so you can recognise the emotions and tactics from playground skirmishes. The artwork is beautiful: the characters are all individuals, not a stereotype in sight, and the domestic details of the estate are rendered with a degree of loving care which serves to make the violence that much more real and horrifying. Read this comic. You owe it to yourself.~FC
Recommended: 1–3
Collection: Domu (1–3)

DON ROSA'S COMICS AND STORIES
CX: *2 issues 1983*

College professor and adventurer Lance Pertwillably becomes involved in a quest for lost Nazi treasure at the South Pole and the problems caused by a universal solvent. Don Rosa's now considered the best creator to work on Disney's ducks since Carl Barks; these 1970s stories contain all the hallmarks of a classic Uncle Scrooge adventure tale. Difficult to find, but worth the effort.~WJ
Recommended: 1, 2

Walt Disney's DONALD AND MICKEY
Disney: *18 issues 1991–1993*
Gladstone: *Series one 12 issues (19–30) 1993–1994, series two 8 issues + 1995 to date*

Despite the title, only 26 by Paul Murry actually features Donald and Mickey in the same story (versus the Phantom Blot). Carl

Barks' ten-page Donald stories from *Walt Disney's Comics And Stories* feature in all but that issue, while apart from odd stories, the rest of the strips are produced by Jaime Diaz and the Disney studios. Diaz' strips in 23–25 and 28–30 are extended stories featuring Mickey and Goofy in Egyptian and Arthurian adventures respectively, and although nicely drawn, they're too reliant on dumb one-liners (and Goofy being goofy) to be satisfactory. The Disney studios (19, 21, 22) produced an oddity in Mickey Mouse's adventures with The Sleuth, a Sherlock Holmes type, only dumb and reliant on Mickey to do the real detective work. They're not great, but they're mildly entertaining. Issue 20 has the added attraction of a few Floyd Gottfreidson Sunday pages from the Mickey Mouse newspaper strip.

Renaming the title *Donald Duck and Mickey Mouse*, Gladstone started to publish ten-page Donald Duck stories by Barks coupled with Mickey and Goofy adventures. The latter include 'The Arabian Adventure' (1–3) by Disney and Jaime Diaz studios, 'The Treasure Of Shark Reef' and 'The Trojan Horse', both by The Egmont Group.~NF
Recommended: Series one 20, series two 4, 6ac

Walt Disney's DONALD DUCK
Dell: *85 issues 1952–1962*
Gold Key: *121 issues (86–216) 1962–1981*
Whitman: *29 issues (217–245) 1981–1986*
Gladstone: *34 issues (246-279) 1986–1990, 30 issues + (280–299) 1993 to date*

It's assumed readers will know who Donald Duck is, and that he has a girlfriend Daisy, three nephews, Huey, Dewey and Louie, and an uncle, Scrooge McDuck. Making his screen début in June 1934, it was only a few months before he was also appearing in a 'Silly Symphony' comic strip. Not until 1940, however, did Donald star in a comic, reprinting the newspaper strips drawn by Al Taliaferro in issue 4 of the original *Four Color* series. His first new story was notable also for being Carl Barks' first comic-book work. *Four Color* 9, 'Donald Duck Finds Pirate Gold' (reprinted in 250), was the first of twenty-nine *Four Color* issues before he started his own title with 26. Someone at Dell obviously failed their maths.

Until 1966, Carl Barks produced the best of the Donald Duck stories both in this title and elsewhere, and his characterisation was the one other writers and artists – such as Paul Murry and Bob Gregory – tried to emulate. Donald is generally short of money and either struggling at work or else at the top of his chosen profession (of that month) until something goes wrong (and it always does). Sometimes Donald does get the better of his nephews or his cousin Gladstone (whose luck is near supernatural), but he's just as likely to be picking a fight with his neighbour Jones as getting anything done. Donald's irascibility is his greatest weakness and though he's perfectly happy playing pranks on other people, particularly his clever nephews, they almost always backfire. Apart from the short stories about life, love (Daisy's a little fickle and quite happy to date Gladstone) and getting ahead in Duckburg, there are longer adventure stories such as 'Secret Of Hondorica' (46), 'The Lost Peg-Leg Mine' (52), the search for wasps in 'The Forbidden Valley' (54, 248) or 'The Titanic Ants' (60). Other Disney characters, including Goofy and Chip and Dale, appeared in short back-ups or in single-page gag strips, but after 163 the title became increasingly a reprint comic.

In 1986, Gladstone restarted publication of the Disney material and, naturally, made the basis of their titles the reprinting of the work of Carl Barks. Since 246, only 283 hasn't contained a Carl Barks strip, and that had the first new Donald strip since 236, written and drawn by Don Rosa, a man widely regarded as Barks' natural successor. Gladstone didn't stop with Barks, though. Determined to attract new readers, they reprinted European material not previously seen in the US. As the popularity of the Disney characters in Europe has not diminished as it has in their homeland, and Disney magazines have been published since the 1930s, there was plenty of material to choose from. Volker Reiche (247, 249, 251, 260), Fred Milton (258, 277), Romano Scarpa (279) and Frederico Pedrocchi (286) are the named artists but many issues contain work by the Danish Gutenburghus and Dutch Oberon Studios. Rosa himself produced work for the Europeans (278) before getting the opportunity to create new stories for Gladstone. His main rival for Barks' crown is William Van Horn (263–265, 268, 269, 271, 272, 286), whose artwork is quite similar to that of Barks but more rounded and uniform in line, while Rosa's ornate, more detailed style has fewer dramatic angles than that of Barks.

Donald Duck's first strip artist was Al Taliafero, whose short strips can be found in 247, 258, 259, 262–265, 267–276 and whose work on the Donald newspaper strip, written by Bob Karp, features in 280–285, 287–299). Taliafero's smooth, long-necked Donald is one of the highlights of American newspaper strip history. Of note also in the Gladstone series is Walt Kelly's version of Donald in 275 and Floyd Gottfredson's in 286, co-starring with Mickey Mouse. The break in publishing between 1990 and 1993 was caused by Disney's decision to publish the characters under its own imprint though, strangely, they didn't continue Donald's title but launched *Donald Duck Adventures* in its place.

Though Barks didn't actually provide much of the material for issues 27–163, his influence can be seen in practically every story in the series. The Barks reprints in the Gladstone issues are mostly from *Walt Disney's Comics and Stories* but those that aren't are often from the many one-shots and specials that have been published since the 1940s (*Vacation Parade* in 257 or *Firestone's Christmas Special* in 251). In addition to the collections listed below, there are Donald Duck collections from Gladstone, reprinting Carl Barks' work from *Walt Disney's Comics And Stories*.~NF

Recommended: 246–299

Collections: The Complete Donald Duck Adventures 1–25 (Four Color 9, 29, 62, 108, 147, 159, 178, 189, 199, 203, 223, 238, 256, 263, 275, 282, 291, 300, 308, 318, 328, 367, 408, 422, Donald Duck 26, 46, 52, 54, 60 + Barks stories from Walt Disney's Comics And Stories), Gladstone Album 5 (Four Color 199), 10 (Four Color 275), 13 (Four Color 408), 16 (Four Color 238), 23 (Four Color 26), 25 (Four Color 367), Gladstone Giant Album 1 (Four Color 9), 5 (Four Color 282, 422, Donald Duck 46)

DONALD DUCK ADVENTURES

Gladstone: *20 issues 1987–1990*
Disney: *38 issues 1990–1993*
Gladstone: *21 issues + (21–42) 1993 to date*

Primarily a vehicle for the longer Donald Duck stories, starting with reprints of the *Four Color* stories by Carl Barks, later issues have included more European and non-Barks material, including that by William Van Horn, Ron Fernandez, Pat Block and Daniel Branca. Of note are the new stories by Don Rosa ('The Crocodile Collector', 8 and 'Return To Plain Awful', 12), Marco Rota's Viking adventure 'Andold Wild Duck' (23) and the two stories written by Barks but drawn by Daan Jippes ('Traitor In The Ranks', 31 and 'Storm Dancers', 32) both from Huey, Dewey and Louis Junior Woodchucks in the early 70s.

Barks' own stories are masterpieces of story-telling, where the additional story length provided full scope for his detailed backgrounds and exotic locales. His scripts extend from the satirical 'Dangerous Disguise' (2), which spoofs Cold-War spy stories as Donald matches wits with 'Madame Triple-X', to the slapstick 'The Pixilated Parrot' (22) and the adventure of The Golden Helmet (32). Others of particular note are 'Lost In The Andes' (3), 'Mystery Of The Swamp' (7), 'Ghost Of The Grotto' (9) and 'Sheriff of Bullet Valley' (28).

Disney decided to publish their own comics in 1990, and showed a greater willingness to publish the work of writers and artists other than Carl Barks, though they mostly maintained the principle of using reprints from

Europe previously unseen in the USA rather than commissioning new work. Vicar is represented most frequently (all issues except 1, 9, 10, 24, 26, 29, 33, 35–38), but the series also introduces Don Rosa (1, 22, 24, 34, 37), William Van Horn (2–8, 10, 13, 15, 16, 19, 20, 27, 37, 38), Daniel Branca (12, 24, 25, 26, 32, 33), Fernandez (19), Scarpa (22, 28), Santanach (1, 25) and Jippes (26). Rosa and Van Horn, spiritual heirs to Barks, consistently account for the most diverting material.

Barks is represented in almost half the Disney issues, more so towards the end of the series (2, 4, 9, 17, 18, 21, 23, 26–29, 31, 33, 35, 37,38), but these issues do include the first Uncle Scrooge story ('Christmas On Bear Mountain', 9), 'The Golden Christmas Tree' (21), 'The Lost Peg Leg Mine' (23), 'In Darkest Africa' (29) and the 'Titanic Ants' (36).~NF

Recommended: Gladstone 1–23, 26, 28, 30–33, Disney 1–10, 13, 15, 16, 19, 20–24, 27, 29, 34, 36–38

DONNA MATRIX
Reactor: *1 issue 1993*

A pleasure android goes bad. With all the editorial bluster about the advantages of computer graphics the folk at Reactor forgot a story's also desirable. Dreadful.~FP

DOOM FORCE
DC/ *One-shot 1993*

Shortly after Image Comics launched, Grant Morrison and assorted artists came up with this hilarious pastiche of what was then their house style. Daft superheroes with dafter names (all with trademark notification appended) were drawn in misproportioned fashion with an excess of lines and on as many preposterous pin-up pages as could be managed. All women had globular breasts and buttocks, all men were impossibly muscled, and the characters argued among themselves throughout. The writing is staccato and ludicrously dramatic, but at fifty-six pages the joke is stretched too far, and probably won't appeal if picked up cold.~WJ

DOOM PATROL
DC/Vertigo: *Series one 39 issues 1964–1978 (86–121), 1973 (122–124), series two 87 issues, 2 Annuals 1987–1995*

The 1960s series is a largely undiscovered treasure. Introduced in *My Greatest Adventure* 80, the 'World's Strangest Heroes' proved so popular that the title became *Doom Patrol* with 86. The team consisted of a wheelchair-bound genius, Niles Caulder, The Chief, who brought together three outcasts: Hollywood actress Rita Farr, the Elasti-Girl, inhaled strange volcanic fumes that enabled her to expand or reduce her body; Larry Trainor was a pilot exposed to

solar rays that made him radioactive, and enabled him to release Negative Man, a radio-energy being; and adventurer Cliff Steele's body was destroyed in an accident, but his brain was saved by the Chief to be placed in a cybernetic body, creating Robotman. He was an updated version of a character who'd had a long run in DC back-up strips from the mid-1940s. If a team of outcasts led by a wheelchair-bound character sounds familiar, it should be noted that the Doom Patrol débuted at the same time as *X-Men*. Stretching the coincidence, while the X-Men fought the Brotherhood of Evil Mutants, the first Doom Patrol tale introduced the Brotherhood of Evil. Furthermore, scripter Arnold Drake was the only contemporary DC writer to predict the later popularity of Marvel. His writing upheld DC's high standards of plotting, but was also heavy on characterisation, and the excellent interaction between the characters created a wonderful soap-opera feel. It separated *Doom Patrol* from its 1960s DC counterparts, although Bruno Permiani's artwork, wonderful as it was, maintained the more subtle DC look.

The creation of many strange adversaries ensured Doom Patrol lived up to its 'World's Strangest Heroes' subtitle. The most notable were the Brotherhood of Evil. Their leader, the Brain, was an evil genius whose body died, but who lived on as dismembered brain. He used his intellect to advance the IQ of a gorilla to genius level, and named him Monsieur Mallah. They were joined by Madam Rouge, who could remould and stretch her features. That she was French was another unusual touch. The recurring Brotherhood of Evil gave the series a nice sense of continuity, and their appearances were eventful. 91 introduced Mento, the wealthy and clever Steve Dayton, who created a helmet giving him telekinetic powers. His interest in the Doom Patrol was purely Elasti-Girl, with whom he was madly in love.

The mid-1960s issues contain lots of wisecracking jokes or situations, particularly 104, where Mento and Elasti-Girl wed, with Robotman and Negative Man trying to stop the event. These were momentary lapses of concentration, because on the whole the series was well handled. Another landmark was 99, introducing Gar Logan, the green-skinned youngster, Beast Boy, who could change into any kind of creature. In due course he was adopted by Mento and Elasti-Girl. The most exciting soap-opera theme running through the series was the development of Madam Rouge, who fell in love with the Chief, but was always under the influence of the Brain. The weirdness returned with a vengeance in 115–116, featuring three grotesque creatures, perhaps a precursor to things to come in the 1980s. One had an eye for a head, another had eyes only on his palms, and the last was headless with his face on his torso. This continuing strangeness probably contributed to the falling sales, but given its general nature the surprise is that *Doom Patrol* lasted so long. Editor Murray Boltinoff and artist Premiani guest-starred in the final issue, asking the readers to keep buying the title to keep it going. If so, the Doom Patrol would return. The plea didn't work, and the Doom Patrol, who sacrificed their lives to save a small community, remained dead for many years.

Three reprint issues arrived in 1973, but nothing was heard of the Doom Patrol until the 1980s *Teen Titans*, which featured Gar Logan as the Changeling. Robotman also returned there, apparently a survivor of the explosion that killed his comrades. He was joined by three new characters – Celsius, who claimed to be the widow of the Chief, Tempest, and Negative Woman – to form the new Doom Patrol as introduced in *Showcase* 94–96, written by Paul Kupperberg. This new team stepped into their own title in 1987. Although there was nothing outstanding, Paul Kupperberg produced an entertaining series that centred more on superheroics than weirdness. He wasted no time in introducing new outcasts and reintroduced the not-so-dead Larry Trainor – now lacking his negative-being, which to his dismay was inhabiting Negative Woman instead. This caused a lot of tension, as did the fact that Celsius believed her husband to be alive. She was the only one, but readers were kept guessing for quite a while before The Chief revealed himself to his old comrades in 15, meaning that everyone but poor Elasti-Girl survived their apparent death. Kupperberg ended his run in good form, tying in with the company-wide *Invasion* crossover (17–18), with dire consequences for a few members. His stories were helped by some nice artwork. Steve Lightle brought a smooth look to 1–5, while Erik Larsen provided a more dramatic line in 6–15, when he was replaced by Graham Nolan.

It was all change with 19. British writer Grant Morrison, with artist Richard Case, took the original concept of the Doom Patrol being the world's strangest heroes to a new level of weirdness and originality. Joining the Chief, Tempest and Robotman are Rebis, a new radioactive hermaphrodite composed of Larry Trainor and physician Eleanor Poole, and Crazy Jane, with sixty-four separate personalities, each possessing a super power. 'Crawling From The Wreckage' in 19–22 magnificently establishes Morrison's version of the Doom Patrol, introducing the Scissor Men, creatures who can literally cut people out of reality, and come from a plane of existence created by a bunch of philosophers. The weirdness continues with a sort of spirit of Jack

the Ripper who's out to marry the comatose Doom Patrol member Rhea Jones (from Paul Kupperberg's run). The story introduces Dorothy Spinner, a young girl with an ape-like face who gives life to characters from her imagination – not always a pleasant experience. Morrison excelled himself with the creation of Mr Nobody and the Brotherhood of Dada (26–29), who transfer themselves into a painting that then swallows Paris. While there's certainly an element of style over content, Morrison is so imaginative that this is acceptable, and when he incorporates potentially touchy topics, such as Crazy Jane's childhood abuse in 30, it's sensitively handled. 31–33 is another gem, featuring the obnoxious Willoughby Kipling, a Knight Templar who brings word to the Doom Patrol that the world is going to be destroyed. The story-line features the Book of the Unwritten Verse and the men from N.O.W.H.E.R.E, who all speak in anagrams. Hours of fun for all. Bit by bit, the universe starts to disappear. But luckily not for long, otherwise fans of the original Doom Patrol would've missed the appearance of the Brain and Monsieur Mallah in 34. Some will wish they had, as it's a great black comedy, but with little respect for the original characters.

35 introduced one of the most bizarre comic characters ever invented, Danny The Street, a sentient transvestite street with the ability to teleport itself anywhere, named for Danny La Rue, Britain's most famous female impersonator! The issue begins a plot-line involving the Doom Patrol in intergalactic conflict, but of course nothing is as straightforward as that, and the story-line offers the final fate of Rhea Jones. It also leads into the origin of the wonderful Flex Mentallo in 42. Originally a wimp who's had too much sand kicked in his face, Flex gains mastery of all his powerful muscles and investigates just why the Pentagon is five-sided. Facial hair haters will love 45's Beard Hunter, who kills people with beards and shaves them, and he's now after the red-bearded Chief. Mr Nobody and his new Brotherhood of Dada return in 49–52, where he runs for the Presidency of the US. Well, why not? There have been worse candidates. By this time Morrison is becoming a victim of his own success. The genuine weirdness that had been so startling originally is becoming stale with repetition, and even change-of-pace issues such as 53's Marvel pastiche, with the Doom Patrol in the Fantastic Four role, lack bite.

Events starting in 55 attempt to play with the readers' preconceptions. Dire consequences are in store for the Chief and Cliff Steele with the emergence of the Candlemaker in a story-line ending in 61. Morrison leaves with 63, chronicling the final tale of his marvellous

Crazy Jane character. In a text page new scripter Rachel Pollack asks how she follows genius. Well, you don't. Obviously, you try to do your own thing. Perhaps editorial pressure resulted in her pale attempts to emulate Morrison's style, but she would have been better off making the series her own and introducing an entirely different direction. 64 is the first Vertigo issue, and while Pollack's run produced some good efforts, on the whole it didn't work, a particular drawback being the continuing exposure for Dorothy Spinner's countless manifestations. Her better ideas included George and Marion, 67's Sexually Remaindered Spirits, who like shopping. Then there's 70's villain the Codpiece, a none too well endowed, penis-size-obsessed character who builds a powerful mechanical codpiece with many abilities (the fantasies are endless). That issue also introduces a young woman who's had a sex change, calls herself Coagula and has the ability to dissolve things. Not her penis, by the way, but the Codpiece wasn't so lucky. Pollack makes good use of her own creations and the Chief, and her best moment is 'The Teiresias Wars' in 75–79. An ancient conflict between the Builders and the shapeshifting Teiresae involved the creation of the Tower of Babel inside the Pentagon. The story is helped by the unique and refreshing artwork of Ted McKeever, whose stark stylings added to the weird nature. Pollack and McKeever end the series on a relatively high note with 'Imagine Aris Friends' in 84–87, a story with Biblical overtones about a renegade Hassidic miracle-worker trying to stop a cult of messianic magicians from destroying the world. Doom Patrol to the rescue. But not in time to save the series.

Overall you have a title in three parts. If you like solid 1960s-style superheroics with a subtle sense of wonder, then the original series is for you. If, however, you like lots of superheroics with colourful characters, powers and personalities, then the Kupperberg/Lightle/Larsen issues are for you. And if you're a budding pseudo-intellectual then the Morrison/Pollack issues are for you. Lots of hours to ponder the relevance of surrealism.~HY

Recommended: Series one 86, 87, 90, 91, 93, 96, 97, 99, 100, 104, 107, 108, 110–113, 115–119, 121, series two 19–34, 42, 45, 57, 70, 75–79
Collection: Crawling From The Wreckage (19–25)

DOOM 2099
Marvel: *44 issues 1992–1996*

Although it's faint praise, under John Francis Moore and Pat Broderick the initial issues of *Doom 2099* are the best of the 2099 line's first flush. With Latveria crushed under the heel of a brutal tyrant, an armoured figure claiming to be Dr Doom appears, and 1–4 see him oust the incumbent and assume control. Although a

technological genius, is he really the 20th-century Doom beloved of the Latverian population? 6–10 have Doom in cyberspace, which wears thin long before the end, following which there's a global tour of 2099. All stories run to a formula in which Doom gets his armoured butt kicked, but returns to triumph over adversity. It's a relief when 25 resolves the question of who Doom is and how he came to be in 2099. From 26 Warren Ellis portrays a more vindictive and brutal Doom, and is handed a plot that sees him assuming control of the USA. This spills over to other 2099 titles, but it's soon all change again, with Doom on the run and hunted. Then he's in 1996 to encounter current Marvel superheroes. The problem with *Doom 2099* throughout is that continually changing circumstances prevent any sense of cohesiveness. New readers never have time to adjust before the desperation to appeal to a larger audience overturns everything. The final issues have extraordinary but totally out of place pencil art from Jeff Lafferty, perhaps more suited to parody than a straight superhero title.~FP

DOOM'S IV
Image: *4-issue miniseries 1994*

Grimm, Slyder, Burn and Brick (which might give you some idea of the level of creativity Rob Liefeld brought to the creation of this mess) are a team of superheroes who are in conflict with Doom's Corporation, which has the nasty habit of sending armed robots to kill them. Co-scripted by Kurt Hathaway and penciller Mark Pacella, it's not very good, although well placed as a contender for the most stupid character ever in villain Dr Lychee, whose head is an enlarged lychee. A freebie issue 1/2 was offered via *Wizard*, also by Pacella.~NF

DOOMSDAY + 1
Charlton: *6 issues 1975–1976, 6 issues (7–12) 1978–1979*

Early John Byrne art applied to the time-honoured cliché of astronauts returning to a post-nuclear-devastated Earth and fighting assorted mutants, monsters and aliens. Joe Gill wrote the early issues, with Byrne taking over later. 7–12 reprint the original series, and new story can be found in 4–5 of the Charlton house fanzine *Bullseye*.~DWC

DOOMSDAY SQUAD
Fantagraphics: *7 issues 1986–1987*

A retitled reprint of *Doomsday + 1* including the *Charlton Bullseye* strip, but of interest really only as a curiosity. Far more appealing are the short back-ups promoting the published Fantagraphics strips. Dalgoda and Usagi

Yojimbo in 1 and 3 are fine, but the standout is Daniel Clowes' *Lloyd Llewelyn* in 2, a commentary on the fuss surrounding John Byrne's 1986 reworking of Superman.~WJ

DOORWAY TO NIGHTMARE
DC: *5 issues 1978*

DC fiddled with their house mystery format, extending stories over the entire issue, but the lovely Mike Kaluta covers are the only recommendation for this otherwise ordinary title.~FP

DOPE Comix
Kitchen Sink: *5 issues 1978–1984*

A very odd concept indeed. Almost five years after underground comics had largely given up the ghost one of the few publishers to survive and thrive from the era decided to publish a series of stories about drugs. It's not quite as narrow in scope as the title might suggest, with all sorts of illicit substances covered. Predictably enough, there's a fair amount of contributors deciding to detail hallucinogenic experiences, boring bastards one and all, and most of 1–3 are extremely self-indulgent, with little of note. The standout strip is Howard Cruse's 'The Guide' in 3, in which a group experimenting with LSD appoint one of their number to ensure there are no accidents during their trip.

By contrast 4 is vastly improved. Of the previous regulars only Dan Steffan and Steve Stiles remain, both among the better artists. The new contributors include Valentino, Greg Irons, Aline Kominsky-Crumb and Michael Gilbert, whose touching tale of an acid casualty is a salutary reminder of the possible payback among the general celebration. Steffan and Stiles are back for 5, but it's probably the Reed Waller Omaha short that's of most interest in an issue title that had run out of puff.~WJ
Collection: All American Hippie Comics (1–5)

DOPIN' DAN
Last Gasp: *3 issues 1972–1973*

Ted Richards gives us Beetle Bailey with dope. A few chuckles, but don't go out of your way.~WJ

DOUBLE DARE ADVENTURES
Harvey: *2 issues 1966–1967*

A misguided attempt to introduce light-hearted superheroes in the wake of the *Batman* TV show. Cover feature B-Man is stung by alien bees, develops wings, increases his strength by ingesting a honey concentrate, and turns criminal. 'What sheer irony... Barry E. Eames, whose very initials spell BEE, is about to reap a harvest of riches because I almost am one,' he proclaims. We're not talking high

concept here. Nor is that a path followed by companion feature The Glowing Gladiator, although Magicman at least aspires to competency. Better by far are the short reprints by Jack Kirby in 1, and Reed Crandall and Al Williamson in 2.~FP

DOUBLE DRAGON
Marvel: *6-issue miniseries 1991*

Insipid adaptation of a video game starring a duo of martial artists. The sole redeeming feature is an Art Adams cover for the second issue.~HS

DOUBLE EDGE
Marvel: *2-issue microseries 1995*

These issues partition the Punisher's old titles and a new one, and bookend his rampage through *Ghost Rider* 65, *Daredevil* 344, *Hulk* 433, and *Dr Strange* 81. In the first issue (un-numbered, but designated 'alpha') he's captured by S.H.I.E.L.D, and while under hypnosis is convinced that S.H.I.E.L.D. head honcho Nick Fury is responsible for the death of the Castle family, thus starting the Punisher's career. A chase ensues through the above titles, before a conclusion of sorts in the 'omega' issue. The second issue's better than the first, revealing the machinations of a factor within the law enforcement agency which used Castle as a pawn, with tragic consequences. Strangely, though, the ending appears rushed.~WJ

Dark Horse DOWN UNDER
Dark Horse: *3-issue miniseries 1994*

Perhaps inspired by Fantagraphics' attempt to introduce Australian cartoonists to the US in *Fox Comics*, Dark Horse launched this unsuccessful anthology, featuring material of mixed quality. Rather than feeling like a showcase, there's an air of ghettoisation about the book. Far better to have included the strips in *Dark Horse Presents*. Gary Chaloner and Ashley Wood's *The Undertaker* is the only constant across the three issues, a dark but comic story of a serial killer and his stuffed dog. The scratchy, heavily inked artwork shows promise in the style of Dave McKean and Bill Sienkiewicz. The highlight of the series is the episode of Bacchus in 1. Eddie Campbell tells the tale of 'That Crafty Bastard Sisyphus' in his fine, irreverent style.~NF

DP7
Marvel: *32 issues, 1 Annual, 1986–1989*

Following a celestial phenomenon known as the 'White Event', people all over the world start spontaneously developing powers beyond those of mortal men, though often with a painful or disfiguring cost. Desperate for help and advice, an elderly schoolteacher, a suburban housewife, an overworked doctor and several others travel to a clinic that offers assistance in coming to terms with these 'parabilities'. The clinic has its own plans for them, though, and when they come to light, seven of the 'Displaced Paranormals' – our DP7 of the title – flee the clinic, hotly pursued by its agents. An intelligent, enjoyable read, with likeable protagonists who are refreshingly capable of being selfish and indecisive, rather than the infallible paragons favoured by most comics. Mark Gruenwald turns in the second best writing job of his career (*Squadron Supreme* being the best), and Paul Ryan's realistic, low-key art enhances the human scale of the drama admirably.~HS

DRACULA
Dell: *7 issues 1962 (1), 1966-1967 (2–4), 1972–1973 (6–8)*

The success of the sixties *Batman* TV show encouraged numerous new superhero comics from publishers who hadn't a clue about irony, believing stupidity to be the essential ingredient for success. Dell don't disguise the fact, producing a wholesome superhero Dracula attempting to redeem the tarnished family name. He adopts the transparent alias of Al U. Card and was able to transform himself into a bat, only ever drawn as a black outline by appalling artist Tony Tallarico. He (Dracula, not Tallarico, although the latter might have been better value) appeared in plots so dumb even 1960s school kids could pick out flaws. The nadir is 4, in which Al deals with a guy who stands on chairs wearing a sheet to scare old women into donating their savings. 1 adapted the classic 30s *Dracula* film, there was never an issue 5, and 6–8 reprint 2–4, presumably in a misguided attempt to sucker in readers enjoying the contemporaneous sophistication of *Tomb Of Dracula*.~FP

DRACULA CHRONICLES
Topps: *3-issue miniseries 1995*

The history of Dracula is retold in this comic adaptation. Roy Thomas' script is captivating and the strong character of Dracula comes across well. The artwork by Esteban Maroto is a real let-down, with the dark Gothic feel of the story submerged in an appalling colour scheme that makes Dracula look like a circus clown.~SS

DRACULA LIVES
Marvel Comics: *13 issues, 1 annual 1973–1975*

A companion title to *Tomb Of Dracula*, this black and white magazine mixes stories of Dracula's adventures in the past with contemporary stories and articles on *Dracula* films. Roy Thomas and Dick Giordano adapted the Bram Stoker original (5–9), while a whole collection of artists and writers had a go

at depicting the dread Count, including Wolfman and Adams (2) telling the story of Dracula's origin, Thomas and Colan, Mike Friedrich and George Evans (7), Tony Isabella and Colan (5), and Doug Moench and Tony DeZuniga (8). *Dracula Lives* lacks any real gems and the number of different creative teams means that there's no real consistency of approach. The 1975 annual reprints material from the regular series.~NF

DRACULA VERSUS ZORRO
Topps: *2-issue microseries 1993*

Returning by ship from Europe, where he's picked up a near-mystical sword, Zorro tries to defend a fellow-passenger from the attentions of Dracula, who's looking for a new bride to keep him company during the journey. Jousting over the beautiful Carmelita, Zorro and Dracula learn a healthy respect for each other before a final showdown in Notre Dame Cathedral. Don McGregor's writing is as sparse as he gets and becomes a treatise on the nature of love and loyalty. Tom Yeates' artwork beautifully complements the script. All together, a well-characterised, suspenseful package.~NF
Recommended: 1, 2

THE DRAFT
Marvel: *One-shot 1998*

This is set in Marvel's 'New Universe', one populated by just dozens of superpowered characters, not the usual thousands. A massive explosion has destroyed Pittsburgh. Not knowing who's responsible, the government's response is to start a massive military programme to test the entire population aged under forty-five for possible superpowers in case of a war. Nightmask, prominently cover-featured, is largely redundant inside, where half a dozen new superheroes are introduced and there's a surprise about Ronnie Reagan. It's entirely unremarkable stuff. The continuation can be found in *The War*.~FP

DRAGON: BLOOD & GUTS
Image: *3-issue miniseries 1995*

Jason Pearson writes and draws this miniseries, relating the trials and tribulations of a childhood friend of Savage Dragon's cop buddy, Alex, as she decides to testify against her husband, a superpowered evil maniac. The art is classy and confident, but the characters struggle to achieve one-dimensional status. There is less to this than meets the eye.~HS

DRAGON CHIANG
Eclipse: *One-shot 1991*

In many respects a straightforward action adventure, Tim Truman's *Dragon Chiang* gets its edge from its black humour and grim political background. Told in a cold, detached manner, it's the tale of a truck journey from China to San Francisco via a bridge across the Bering Straits. Violent and brutal, it's everything you want and expect from Truman, in fact.~NF

DRAGON LINES
Epic: *4-issue miniseries 1993, 2-issue microseries ('The Way Of The Warrior') 1993–1994*

Blending ancient Chinese fables and mysticism with a plot concerning taking over the world thirty years hence is just window-dressing concealing your basic superhero punch-'em-up. The second series is marginally better, probably by virtue of being shorter.~WJ

DRAGONFLIGHT
Eclipse: *3-issue miniseries 1991*

Painted graphic novel adaptation by Brynne Stephens and Lela Dowling. The inevitably abridged nature of the comic-book version expurgates much of the explanation behind the story in Anne McCaffrey's original book. Avoid if unfamiliar with the novel. Flat, wooden dialogue flows like a pile of bricks.~APS
Collection: *Dragonflight* (1–3)

DRAGONFLY
AC: *8 issues 1986–1987*

Nancy Arazello interrupts her boyfriend Ken in the middle of a deal. Unfortunately the deal is with a demon, and Nancy, blundering in, obtains the powers Ken wanted. The demon, being a petty sort, collects Ken's soul anyway. It's an oddball opening to a series that quickly became a routine, if not badly done, superheroine feature. After the demise of the title, with poor old Ken now a rampaging cyborg, Dragonfly could still be seen as a member of Femforce.~HS
Collection: *Cycle Of Fire* (1–2)

DRAGONLANCE Comics
DC: *34 issues, 1 annual 1988–1991*

Based on a role-playing game, *à la* Dungeons and Dragons, *Dragonlance* is a fantasy adventure that makes the characters 'real', therefore negating the whole point of being able to become them in the game. Mostly drawn by Ron Randall, there's really nothing good to be said about it.~NF

Tandra: The DRAGONROK Saga
Hanthercraft: *10 issues + 1993 to date*

After spending twenty years on *Tandra*, relating the life story of an Earthman transported to a sword-and-sorcery world, creator Hanther switched to a comic-size publication. He retains the text and accompanying illustration format, and for the first two issues it's life as normal on Tandra, but thereafter the story switches to Earth. The

glamorous Tremaine and General Kargor arrive attempting to locate a sword, deliberately drawing attention to themselves with a high-profile campaign establishing them as the first aliens to visit Earth. There are some good jibes at the possible reaction to extraterrestrial life, and 7's superhero parody is well handled, but without the unique background of Tandra to sustain them, Hanther's characters lose their way somewhat, and the constant nudity appears exploitative. This isn't to say the series is bad. It's very good, if lacking the title character, but so far doesn't live up to what came before. 10, however, is essential for explaining most of what Tandra was and is.~FP
Recommended: 2, 4, 5, 7, 10

DRAGON'S CLAWS
Marvel UK: *10 issues 1988–1989*

Written by Simon Furman, drawn by Geoff Senior, and clearly influenced by movies like *Rollerball, Death Race 2000, Star Wars* and *Mad Max*. Set in 'Greater Britain' in 8162, Dragon's Claws are Mercy, Scavenger, Digit, Steel, and leader Dragon, ex-Champions of 'The Game', a murderous free-for-all now outlawed by the World Development Council. After being 'reactivated' by an embittered Agent named Dellar, Dragon's Claws begin new careers as unwilling Government Operatives, paving the way for routine encounters with villains like The Evil Dead (2), or the first version of robot bounty-hunter Death's Head (5). Competent enough stuff, but lacking any of the imagination or sadism that made the UK *Action* future-sport strip 'Death Game 1999' such a guilty pleasure.~AL

DRAWN AND QUARTERLY
Drawn and Quarterly: *Series one, 9 issues 1990–1992, Series two 5 issues + 1994 to date*

The personal vision of editor and publisher Chris Oliveros shines through this anthology. Although primarily a black and white publication in its first incarnation, the rotated use of the few colour pages among regular contributors works well, and the contributor line-up is impressive on paper. Unfortunately, in early issues, the contributions are slight in content, seemingly pages that had been lying around the studio for a while. Only Joe Matt's one-pagers (a selection every issue) and Julie Doucet consistently shine. By the later issues the good material far outweighs the bad, with Maurice Vellekoop's vignettes on gay culture and the likes of Mary Fleener (3–7), Roberta Gregory (7,8), David Mazzucchelli (9) and Michael Dougan (6–9) all impressing. Issues 8 and 9 gave an indication of the direction the title was to head with translations of Spanish artist Marti's work.

The first issues of the second volume showed yet further improvement, with longer strips giving the contributors a chance to shine. Jacques Tardi's stories of ordinary folk caught in the madness and squalor of World War One's trench warfare are magnificent, Vellekoop continues to impress while Carol Tyler and Avril and Petit Roulet make the first relaunched issue outstanding. Baru's story of an Algerian boxer in France unwillingly caught in his homeland's struggle for independence in 4–6 is also of note.

Drawn and Quarterly has developed into an excellent anthology, mixing North American cartoonists with well chosen European material appearing in English for the first time. Despite a penchant for material that's worthy but dull, every issue contains something worthwhile.~WJ

Recommended: Series one 5, 7, 9, Series two 1, 3, 5

DREADLANDS

Epic: *4-issue miniseries 1993*

Fleeing from scavenging mercenaries in an ecologically apocalyptic future, a band of soldiers and scientists end up in what they believe is Earth's distant past. Then the aliens arrive... An uneasy blend of popular science-fiction movie influences (*Aliens*, *Predator*, *Terminator*), this never quite gels.~HS

DREADSTAR

Eclipse: *1 Gaphic Novel ('The Price') 1981*
Epic: *26 issues, 1 Graphic Novel, 1 Annual 1982–1986*
First: *38 issues (27–64) 1986–1991*

Jim Starlin's *magnum opus* began in the pages of *Epic Illustrated*, switched to Eclipse for the magazine *The Price* (reprinted by Epic as the *Dreadstar* annual), moved back to Marvel for another graphic novel, then into the pages of a regular series. You can start with the ongoing comics, as everything necessary to understanding events is précised there. Set in a galaxy far, far away, the saga of Vance Dreadstar certainly tips the hat more than once to *Star Wars*. Dreadstar is caught between two opposing forces, The Church Of Instrumentality and The Monarchy, reprising the ages-old conflict of church and state in a war that's lasted two centuries. Dreadstar decides to end the war once and for all, and gathers a small group of rebels, including Odei the cat man, a blind telepath, Willow, ex-smuggler Skeevo, and deformed mystic Darklock. The latter is a piece of caprice as Starlin revives a version of his old *Eerie* character. Dreadstar struggles at making alliances, but is adept at making enemies, with the Lord High Papal a particular nemesis determined to crush the rebels. Early key issues include 2's very moving 'Willow's

Story', detailing her origin, and 6, where Dreadstar reveals his plan to save the galaxy from utter destruction, the mysterious plan M. 1–6 are conveniently reprinted as *Dreadstar And Co*, giving the best introduction to what became a sprawling saga.

Where *Dreadstar* succeeds best is in the frailty of its characters, with even the evil Lord High Papal portrayed as the victim of a cruel and inhuman system in 11. Dreadstar eventually acquires superhuman abilities, and when plan M fails, numerous friends and allies die in subsequent attacks. The inevitable final confrontation between Dreadstar and the Lord High Papal takes place in 26, as they slug it out in a savage head-to-head. Dreadstar wins, but at a very high price, the least of which is losing two years of his life spent in a coma. When he came to he discovered a very different galaxy, and, in fact, a different universe as Starlin left Epic and took the series to First.

A new empire, the Empirical Galaxy, has been set up by soulless technocrats. There initially seems no place for Dreadstar in this new order, but he's reunited with his surviving team mates, and they're hired by the government to track down former members of the church as war criminals. The strain begins to show when one of Dreadstar's associates commits suicide in 36, after which Willow merges with the Empire's main computer, effectively staging a bloodless coup, but at a cost. There's a further price to be paid in 39 as Darklock's long-term enemies the Twelve Gods come to call. It's all too much for Dreadstar, who starts to drink heavily (what appears to be toilet ducks!), and realising he can't adapt to the new system departs for a new galaxy and new adventures with his remaining buddies. This was issue 40, and Starlin's last.

The authorship passed to Peter David with a clear path ahead, Angel Medina taking over the art. While their issues aren't bad, they rely too much on David rehashing old plots, pulling the team back into another intergalactic war with the chief villain being one Lord Palafox. 50 is their best, with a full complement of space fights, and certainly not offering the predictable ending, but beyond that, without Starlin's hand, the series limps to an inevitable cancellation.~TP

DREAMERY

Eclipse: *14 issues 1986–1989*

This fantasy anthology is probably best remembered for carrying the earlier appearances of Donna Barr's gentleman centaur, 'Stinz', but the other features, Cathy Hill's 'Mad Raccoons' and Lela Dowling's 'Alice In Wonderland', are also charming and eminently readable.~HS

THE DREAMING
Vertigo: *7 issues + 1996 to date*

After the conclusion to *The Sandman*, DC began this title using various characters and concepts that had been established or reintroduced in that series. The title is taken from the Sandman's kingdom and the series is intended to feature various-length stories by different creative teams. It begins with a three-issue tale by Terry LaBan and Peter Snejbjerg about Goldie, the pet Gargoyle belonging to Abel from the House of Mystery. Confused by Abel's inability to defend himself against Cain, Goldie leaves home but gets tempted back to Eden while Cain and Abel try to discover why the golden gargoyles are so special. LaBan shows a keen understanding of the characters while Snejbjerg's artwork is a pleasure. The story succeeds because momentous events hinge upon such otherwise minor characters. Peter Hogan and Steve Parkhouse serve up 'The Lost Boy' in 4–7, about a young man who meets some fairies in 1956 and wakes up in 1996. Mad Hettie has given him a key which she needs in 1996 in order to keep an appointment with Destiny. It's good-humoured and rather charming though not warranting four issues.~NF

Star Wars: DROIDS
Dark Horse: *6-issue miniseries 1994, 10 issues + 1995 to date*

This is the embarrassment of Dark Horse's usually decent quality *Star Wars* titles. The two droids who were merely supporting characters in the films fail to hold the reader's attention as headliners, a problem exacerbated by Artoo's only being able to communicate in a series of electronic bleeps. The cartoony art by Bill Hughes is motionless, and the droids look terrible. Dan Thorsland's script for the miniseries is dire, a boring story involving the droids saving a group of refugees from intergalactic pirates. The ongoing series continues with the same sort of rubbish as the two badly drawn droids become involved in bland space adventures. The comic can't even claim to be aimed at younger readers, as even kids should see through this travesty.~SS

Tex Avery's DROOPY
Dark Horse: *3 issues 1995*

Another failed attempt to bring cartoons to life in comics. Droopy's appeal is in no small part due to the fixed hangdog expression and drone of a voice. The latter's absence reduces the impact of these already weak strips. The back-ups featuring other Avery creations similarly fail to live up to cinema cartoons.~WJ

DRUID
Marvel: *4 issues 1995*

Doctor Druid was a dated mystic dredged out of Marvel's 1950s mystery titles in the early 1980s, eventually graduating to membership of the Avengers in a desperate attempt to popularise him. Always a third-stringer, there was plenty of scope for revamping. Warren Ellis turns in a tattooed, misanthropic sociopath in an ill-advised attempt to deliver the first New-Age horror comic. A total yawner.~HS

DUCK TALES
Gladstone: *12 issues 1988–1990*
Disney: *19 issues 1990–1991*

How comics fold back on themselves. Carl Barks' *Uncle Scrooge* stories inspired a TV cartoon christened *Duck Tales*, which in turn ends up as a comic. 1–2 have the Disney TV animation studio adapting episodes of the show, although they turn their hands to original material after that, and Barks reprints feature throughout. The better issues are those concentrating on Scrooge, Huey, Dewey and Louie, and avoiding the characters created for the TV show. The well intentioned but inept pilot Launchpad McQuack grates, as does the saccharine Webbigail, although matronly housekeeper Mrs Beakly has charm. William Van Horn either writes or draws most issues from 5, and does a fine job. With Disney temporarily deciding to publish their own comics, *Duck Tales* becomes the first title to run continued stories with Disney characters (although each episode is complete in itself). The initial 7 part encounter to retrieve Scrooge's number one dime from Magica De Spell is followed by shorter continued tales, and the reprints are cut. As with the Gladstone issues, the stories are fine, but fall far short of the Barks material that inspired them.~WJ

DUCKMAN
Topps: *3-issue miniseries 1994–1995, 6 issues (0–5) 1995*

This looks like early *Simpsons* cartoons, but badly thought out. Making his début in *Dark Horse Presents* 22, Duckman went on to become a popular off-beat cartoon series. He's an irritable and abusive private detective who accepts cases which are meant to be funny, but consistently fail to hit the mark. Factor in the scratchy art, and there are no redeeming features. Roasting would be too good for this poor excuse for humour.~SS

David Greenberger's DUPLEX PLANET Illustrated
Fantagraphics: *15 issues + 1991 to date*

David Greenberger, toiler in a retirement home, gets residents to tell him stories or answer questions. Transcribing the responses, since 1979 he's been publishing an infrequent magazine featuring their comments and anecdotes. A cult item, the poems of one resident have been set to music by various artists, and this title has Greenberger's transcriptions illustrated by various comic artists. Notable contributors include Chris Ware (2, 15), Jason Lutes (3, 4), Peter Kuper (4, 6), Mark Martin (5, 8, 11), J.R. Williams (2, 3, 5, 7, 10, 12) and Wayno in almost every issue. The comments are occasionally surprisingly moving, but more often just wandering and pointless.~HS

DV8
Image: *3 issues + 1996 to date*

Designed to be an antidote to the feel-good nature of *Gen13*, DV8 are similarly a team of young gen-actives led by Ivana Baiul, who was part of the operation that originally tried to enslave Gen13 and exploit their powers for government ends. Now they're out on their own, Ivana plans to use the 'Deviants' as a spoiler force against other intelligence agencies, though just what this means in practice is unclear. They're a nasty bunch on the evidence so far and it's difficult to see how long Warren Ellis can keep this up without thoroughly alienating all reader sympathy. Humberto Ramos' artwork is its usual Manga-influenced self, except that those wide eyes are anything but innocent, so Moral Majority and born-again Christians should stay away. Could be interesting but unless these kids grow up real fast it won't have many friends.~NF

DYKE'S DELIGHT
Fanny: *2 issues 1993–1995*

Collection of lesbian cartoonists, edited by Kate Charlesworth and fronted by her amazing Auntie Studs character. Other contributors include Roberta Gregory, Griselda Grislingham, Jeremy Dennis and Lucy Byatt. Funny, wry and occasionally heart-rending, but sadly currently on hiatus. It's hoped further issues are in the pipeline.~HS
Recommended: 1, 2

DYNAMITE DAMSELS
Solo: *One-shot 1976*

Not quite Roberta Gregory's début, but her first major impact on the underground comics scene, and the first documented one-woman comic. The majority of the comic concerns Freida Phelps' struggle to attain her own identity and purpose, wrestling with issues of gender politics and sexuality. Far from being didactic, however, these strips are tender, wry and moving, with Freida's self-questioning confusion being oddly endearing. The stories at the front and back of the issue are fantasies: 'Superdyke' and 'Liberatia', one a naïve power

trip, the other a bitter-sweet fable about a separationist nation of women.~HS
Recommended

DYNAMO
Tower: *4 issues 1966–1967*

A spin-off title from *T.H.U.N.D.E.R, Agents* featuring the hero with the power belt and back-ups starring his team-mates. Art is by such notables as Reed Crandall, Steve Ditko and Wally Wood and it's good reading throughout.~DWC
Recommended: 1–4

DYNAMO JOE
First: *15 issues, 1 special 1986–1988*

Dynamo Joe débuted as a back-up strip in *Mars* 10–12, reprinted in the *Dynamo Joe Special*, and then shared *First Adventures* before moving into his own title. It's set in the future, when humans are one of three races peacefully cohabiting in the universe. The peace is shattered by the arrival of a seemingly invincible new race destroying all in their path, and they're only temporarily halted by the construction of the seventy-foot-tall Dynamo battle suits. These suits are humanoid in shape for maximum mobility for the two occupants, and have a number of potent weapons. Yup, this is the American equivalent of the Japanese robot comic. There's a well conceived political backdrop to the ongoing conflict, and there's a definite similarity to plots later used in *Babylon 5*. Often surprisingly unpredictable, but the comic sticks closely enough to the restrictions of its genre to ensure it'll only appeal to those already hungry for giant robot titles.~WJ

E-MAN
Charlton: *10 issues 1973–1975*
First: *25 issues 1983–1985*
Comico: *One-shot 1989, 3 issues 1990*
Alpha: *1 issue 1994*

E-Man is a sentient energy mass who adopts human form on arriving on Earth, where he's accompanied by full-time student and part-time exotic dancer Nova Kane. Written and drawn with a comic lightness by Nicola Cuti and Joe Staton respectively, the Charlton series is a lot of fun. E-Man being able to transform into any object sentient or otherwise gives Staton the opportunity for plenty of visual asides, and Cuti packs a lot into sixteen pages, sometimes achieving an unexpected poignancy in what is an off-beat superhero strip. Michael Mauser, private eye, who gives the term 'seedy' a bad name, is introduced in 3. He proved popular enough to run in a series of back-ups (also by Cuti and Staton) in the otherwise banal *Vengeance Squad*, and an Apple Comics one-shot in 1991. The cast is completed by Teddy Q, an intelligent koala introduced in 8 as piece of whimsy. In that issue Nova is also transformed into sentient energy, making her an equal partner rather than the admittedly spunky female who nonetheless ends up abducted too often. After cancellation E-Man continues to appear in *Charlton Bullseye*. The Charlton series also contains some notable back-up strips. Steve Ditko's obviously enjoying himself lampooning liberal ideas by way of excessive exaggeration in the hilarious 'Killjoy' (2 and 4), and Rog 2000 (6, 7, 9, 10) was also popular. Created by a John Byrne then at the start of his career, Rog is a robot cab driver who interacts with the world as if he's human. As scripted by Cuti, there's the same whimsical nature that characterised the lead strip, and the series was later gathered as a collection by Pacific. The first six issues were coupled with the Mauser strips by First for a series titled *The Original E-Man and Michael Mauser* in the mid-1980s.

Fan fondness for *E-Man* made the title a welcome sight from the then fledgling First line, but sadly the editorial designation was misguided. *E-Man* was quite flexible enough to cope with being a monthly title parodying other comics, and the joshing of the new X-Men in 2–3 was among the earliest and best of such stories,

but the idea wore thin after a while, and neither Staton nor new writer Martin Pasko seemed to have much enthusiasm for it. Furthermore Nova's superpowers disappeared in 3, and she was back to her previous role. Matters improved when Staton also began writing the title with 11. The parody element diminished, and his was a more sympathetic touch, but a succession of lack-lustre issues had taken their toll. There was a demotion to bi-monthly publication and cancellation beckoned. 24 saw the return of Nic Cuti as writer. He'd always been the first choice for the revival, but other commitments prevented his appointment. His début is the one outstanding issue of the First run. Dying from gunshot wounds, Mauser relates the story of his early, and defining, years, his character cemented in Vietnam. It's a masterful character study from Cuti, and it's to Staton's credit that drawing the story in the familiar *E-Man* cartoon style doesn't detract in the slightest from the tragic events. Cuti also writes the final First issue, which isn't as good, but tops most of the run and introduces E-Man's sister – in as much as sentient energy can have a sister – Vamfire. She's his opposite in all respects, but mischievous as opposed to dastardly.

The Comico one-shot reintroduces all the characters in a surreal story, and restores Nova's powers, but the highlight is the Mauser back-up strip concerning a missing child. The following three issues can be read independently, but contain a continuing plot about E-Man's search for his mother. They're a return to the light-hearted tales of the Charlton series, but Vamfire is unnecessary, and the longer page-count seems to make the story drag. The Alpha productions issue is more of the same. There may have been further issues published by Alpha, but we've been unable to verify this.~FP
Recommended: Charlton 3, 7, First 24

EARTH 4
Continuity: *Series one 3 issues 1993, series two 4 issues 1994*

A bizarre numbering system barely hides the fact that *Earth 4* is in fact *Urth 4*, although someone clearly learned how to spell in the interim. As before, the writing is barely readable, but tragically the art from Walter

McDaniels (and a cast of thousands on inks) owes more to Image than to Neal Adams. Lamentable stuff, with the first series being part of the company-wide 'Deathwatch 2000' crossover.~DAR

EATING RAOUL
Mercury Film Distribution: *One-shot 1982*

This oddity was distributed through cinemas accompanying Paul Bartel's decidedly off-beat, riotous independent film *Eating Raoul*. Uptight Paul and Mary Brand dream of opening a restaurant, but their dream seems to be fading until a chance encounter with a swingers party in a neighbouring apartment. Realising there's money to be made from sex, they lure prospective clients to their place and murder them. Their nest-egg is accumulating nicely when the scheme is rumbled by crooked lockfitter Raoul, at which point things become complex. The sexual themes apart, Bartel's script could almost be a classic Hepburn and Stewart movie. It's hilarious, and this excellent adaptation by Kim Deitch is one of the rare instances where a comic of his doesn't connect to his intricately contrived and interlinking stories.~FP
Recommended: 1

ECHO OF FUTUREPAST
Continuity: *9 issues 1984–1986*

Ambitious if flawed attempt to create a *Heavy Metal*-style comic. Starting with the artistic line-up of Mike Golden, Neal Adams and Arthur Suydam on 'Bucky O'Hare' (1–6), 'Frankenstein' (1–5) and 'Mudwogs' (1–5) respectively, the title seemed likely to attract a following even if Jean Teule's 'Virus' (1, 3, 4, 6, 7) and Farley and Mitchell's 'Tippie Toe Jones' (1, 5–9) were less inspiring. 'AE-35' (6–9) by the little-known Tim Ryan and William Jungkuntz, a science-fiction thriller, showed promise. The real bravery of the title was in including non-US material, but deciding to colour it, presumably for commercial reasons, now seems a mistake. Though creditable, the colours hide too much of the subtlety of Toth and Bernet's work on 'Torpedo' (8, 9) and Giminez' work on 'The Damned City' (7–9). Apart from 'Torpedo', the real strength of the title is in its artists, and the mix of science fiction, fantasy and thrillers should have provided the variety that keeps as many readers as possible coming back for more. However, it ceased publication with 9, leaving all the stories unfinished.~NF

ECLIPSE Graphic Novels

Early on, Eclipse were innovators in seeing the idea of stand-alone works for a more mature audience, and also in bringing a number of classics to the attention of a new audience.

Their graphic novel line, though, was a real hodge-podge of reprints (both of their own and other companies work from the 1940s to present day), translations and original material, produced in a number of formats that we might not easily recognise as graphic novels today. For titles also having their own series, look under that entry.

Among the most important reprint collections are *Zorro* (2 vols), collecting Alex Toth's superb work on the Dell series, *Zorro In Old California*, more swashbuckling adventures by Nedaud and Marcello, translated from the French, and *Real Love*, a collection of Simon and Kirby romance strips from the 1950s. *Fast Fiction* reprints a rather poor version of Rider Haggard's *She* by Vincent Napoli which originally appeared in the Fast Fiction series *Famous Authors Illustrated*.

The rest of the originated material is of very mixed quality. Worth a look is *Brought To Light*, a hard-hitting political book containing two stories about American atrocities in Central America, one written by Alan Moore and the other by Joyce Brabner. The desire to instruct occasionally gets the better of the pacing, but Bill Sienkiewicz's elliptical art on Moore's script gives it subtlety. *Floyd Farland*, by a then nineteen-year-old Chris Ware, reworks his newspaper strips from *The Daily Texan*. In an Orwell-style dictatorship, Floyd is so conformist that the authorities think he's involved with a new, subversive movement, but he's immune to their brainwashing techniques because he already believes. A curiosity in light of his extraordinary later work. *Stewart The Rat* is Steve Gerber's rather unsuccessful attempt to recreate the satirical appeal of *Howard The Duck*, drawn by Gene Colan. *Sisterhood of Steel*, by Christy Marx and Peter Ledger, continues their story from *Epic Illustrated* about an island of female mercenaries and is pappy stuff, if prettily drawn. *Samurai, Son of Death* is a US/Japanese collaboration. Sherman DiVono (writer) and Hiroshi Hirata (artist) base their tale on 16th-century Japanese history for a story about a samurai who seems to have returned from the dead.

Finally, there are two real curiosities. *Pigeons From Hell* is Scott Hampton's adaptation of Robert E. Howard's quite awful epic poem (poetry was the very least of Howard's accomplishments, way down the list below shooting, mother-fixating and self-pitying) and *XYR* is a choose-your-own-plot fantasy story. It's rather like a role-playing game book, where you read different bits in different orders depending on what you feel like.~NF
Recommended: *Heartbreak Comics*, *Real Love*, *Zorro* Vols 1 & 2

ECLIPSE Monthly
Eclipse: *Series one 8 issues 1981–1983, Series two (comic size) 10 issues 1983–1984*

High-quality mainstream anthology, with good production values and an adventure-based remit. *Eclipse Monthly* mixed superheroes and Westerns, moral tales and thrillers, and featured a star-studded line-up. Steve Ditko's 'Static', while not the work of a creator at the peak of his powers, is still a thing of wonder (series two 1–3), and Doug Wildey's complex Western, Rio (1–4, 9–10), equals Clint Eastwood's finest efforts in the genre. Steve Englehart and Marshall Rogers' Coyote appeared in series one 2–8 before spinning off into its own Epic title, and Don McGregor and Gene Colan's 'Ragamuffins' was a far-sighted attempt – with its pencil-only artwork and reflective insight into the terrors and pressures of childhood – to expand what was an acceptable topic for a comic story. Although not to everyone's taste, Trina Robbins' stylised adaptation of a neglected and rather *risqué* Sax Rohmer pulp, *Dope*, is sympathetically executed. Although relying on a backbone of superhero adventures (such as B.C. Boyer's Spirit homage The Masked Man and Mark Evanier and Mike Sekowsky's Nightingale), *Eclipse Monthly* got the best out of its contributors and is a lasting monument to the publishing company. The first series is a black and white magazine with occasional colour pages, but the second is traditional comic format.~FJ
Recommended: Series one 2, series two 1–3, 10

ECLIPSO
DC: *2-issue microseries ('The Darkness Within') 1992, 18 issues 1992–1994*

The first two issues start and finish DC's 1992 big crossover in which Eclipso, an evil, god-like creature, takes over the bodies of various superheroes in order to destroy the Earth. Like all good characters he has a major fatal flaw: light. Bruce Gordon, the scientist who unleashed Eclipso, secretly puts together a group of superheroes to fight him, while a separate team under Hawkman is infiltrated by a possessed Starman. It all ends badly for Starman and nothing is really resolved (as if we expected it to be) because Eclipso's own series was due in a few months. Not bad, as crossovers go, written by Keith Giffen and Robert Loren Fleming, drawn by Bart Sears, but equally as disappointing as they tend to be, promising much but changing little.

For the ongoing title Eclipso takes over the South American country of Parador, killing a lot of people in the process. Bruce Gordon puts together another Eclipso SWAT team, including The Creeper, Cave Carson and Amanda Waller (from *Suicide Squad*). Darkseid turns up to emphasise how big a bad guy Eclipso is in the

DC Universe and in 11 additional heroes turn up to continue the fight against him, including Commander Steel, Dr Midnight, Major Victory, Manhunter, Nemesis, Peacemaker and Wildcat. The series tries hard to be different – Eclipso is both villain and host – but in the end it becomes another team book because Eclipso's evil is too downbeat and serious for him to carry the narrative by himself. By far the best issues are 7 and 8, Eclipso vs Sherlock Holmes, by regular writer Robert Loren Fleming and guest penciller Ted McKeever. An unlikely recipe, but it works.~NF
Recommended: 7, 8

ECTOKID
Marvel: *9 issues, 1 Special 1993–1994*

The result of a union between ghost and human, Dex Mungo is able to walk the Ectosphere, where the deceased exist. An interesting idea, initially well handled, soon descends into a standard human-battles-demons title. The special, titled *Ectokid Unleashed*, is an improvement and ties up loose ends from the series.~FP

EDGE
Bravura: *3 issues 1994*

After almost six decades it's difficult to present a totally new take on superheroes, but Steven Grant and Gil Kane begin with a decent attempt concerning the ages-old idea that absolute power corrupts. Intended as the harbingers of a new and better age for mankind, a group of genetically created superheroes in a world otherwise largely lacking in superpowered individuals gradually decide that might justifies their interpretation of right and wrong. The son of their creator returns in the guise of one of their dead comrades, determined to end their oppression. It's a shame the ethical motivations are swept under the carpet after the first issue, because although *Edge* is a decidedly superior superhero series it's nowhere near the comic it might have been. It is a treat, though, to see Gil Kane illustrating an out-and-out super-hero strip. The concluding issue was never published.~WJ

Over The EDGE
Marvel: *10 issues 1995–1996*

What a strange concept. In 1995 Marvel recompartmentalised their titles, cleaving off a bunch of them to be labelled 'Marvel Edge', the idea being that those darker and more violent characters would henceforth have their own more closely linked editorial structure. That being the case, it's very odd, to say the least, that this title appeared at low price (signified by some issues being subtitled 'And Under A Buck') designed to attract younger readers to what was ostensibly the more mature section of the Marvel line. Daredevil is the star of 1, 6 and 10, Ghost Rider occupies 4 and 9, and there's The Hulk in 3, the Punisher in 5 and Elektra in 8. The majority of issues don't stray above average, the exception being Dr Strange's appearance in 7 (he's also in 2), which is the highlight of the run. It's a suspenseful and intelligent story, also featuring Nightmare, drawn by Stephen Jones, who shares the pencilling duties on the series with Robert Brown. Both provide dynamic layouts, with Brown from the school of artists whose linear over-indulgence fails to hide a multitude of defects. Jones needs to sharpen up his anatomy and liven his action shots, but is the better of the pair and a name to watch out for.~FP

Recommended: 7

EDGE OF CHAOS
Pacific: *3-issue miniseries 1983–1984*

Gray Morrow's personal view of the Gods of Olympus seen through the eyes of his latter-day Hercules, Eric Cleese. Having been set his own quest to fulfil, Eric gets the chance to meet numerous interpretations of mythical deities and creatures, all drawn in the inimitable Morrow style. The licence to depict semi-naked nymphs and goddesses must have been something of a dream come true for Morrow. His scripting, while entertaining, reads as rather corny, which doesn't detract from the sword-and-sorcery feel of the title one whit. The format and paper stock changed from issue to issue, ruining any feeling of consistency. Indeed, the colour does the title few favours.~SW

EERIE
Warren: *139 issues, 3 yearbooks 1965–1983*

Like its sister publication *Creepy*, *Eerie* was a black and white horror magazine that differed from most Warren publications by eventually featuring serials rather than solely short stories. Unusually, the first issue was a short-press-run collection of inventory and reprint material to secure copyright on the name, so to all intents and purposes 2 was the first proper issue. The first twelve issues of Eerie were predominantly drawn by former EC artists, so they're full of the likes of Al Williamson, Reed Crandall and Joe Orlando. While EC alumni Johnny Craig (2, 6, 7, 11, 12, 16) and Angelo Torres (2, 3, 5, 6) excelled themselves, it was the moody wash work of Gene Colan (2–11) and Steve Ditko (3–10) that impressed the most. Of writer and editor Archie Goodwin's many fine scripts the finest was 3's 'Monument', the tale of a murderous architect, rendered in a suitably elegant and sophisticated style by Alex Toth. Dan Adkins' breathtaking work on 'The Day After Doomsday' (8), and early strips by Neal Adams (9, 10) and Jeff Jones

(11, 12, 15), round out this exceptional early period.

Sadly, as with other Warren titles, the late 1960s saw a calamitous drop in quality, and from 13 to 28 the comic was a sorry mixture of reprints and mediocre new material. Issues after 29 saw a gradual improvement due to an influx of new talent such as writers Gerry Conway, Marv Wolfman and Steve Skeates, and artists Pat Boyette, Tom Sutton and Billy Graham. More significantly, however, from 34 *Eerie* increasingly featured work from the more technically accomplished Spanish artists such as Victor De La Fuente (35), Luis Garcia-Lopez (41) and Ramon Torrents (50). Amidst the European tide American artists were still very much in evidence, more so here than in Warren's other magazines, notably Mike Ploog (35, 40), Frank Brunner (35) and Neal Adams (53).

Eerie's first series ran in most issues from 39 to 52. Esteban Maroto's beautifully drawn sword-and-sorcery epic 'Dax The Warrior' proved popular enough despite its frankly bonkers story-line, to inspire a flood of serials. Early efforts 'Dracula', 'Werewolf' and 'The Mummy' were patchy at best, but 52–57's post-apocalyptic 'Hunter', by Rich Margopoulos and Paul Neary, heralded a golden age of continued stories. A typical Warren serial ended with the hero's death, so sequels were rare, but Neary followed up his 'Hunter' story with the equally well drawn series 'Exterminator One' in 60, 63 and 64, written by Bill Dubay, and 'Hunter II' (67, 68, 70–73), written by Budd Lewis. Other notable stories were the Sherlock Holmes pastiche 'Dr Archeus' (54–58, 60, 61) by Gerry Boudreau and Isidoro Mones, the similarly Victorian set 'Hacker' by Steve Skeates, Tom Sutton (57) and Alex Toth (65, 67) and the Greg Potter and Richard Corben collaboration 'Child', a poignant and moving exploration of the Frankenstein myth.

52–72 are overflowing with fine strips, not all of them serials, and both Berni Wrightson (58, 60, 62, 68) and Wally Wood (60, 61) produced some of the finest work of their careers here. 54 and 55 featured beautifully coloured reprints of Will Eisner's 1940s strip 'The Spirit', which proved popular enough to lead Warren to begin publishing a *Spirit* magazine. Two of this era's finest stories were Bill Dubay's superb 'Daddy And The Pie' in 64, which predated *E.T.* by a decade and boasted typically fine Alex Toth artwork, and Budd Lewis' 'Godeye', drawn by Leopoldo Sanchez in 68, a deliciously acerbic debunking of fantasy clichés. No-one typified the era more than the veteran Spanish artist José Ortiz, whose gloriously dark and textured drawings graced a number of continued tales. Most notable were Bruce Bezaire's violent *Dr Jekyll And Mr Hyde*-inspired 'Jackass' in 60, 63–65, Budd Lewis' grisly Western 'Coffin' (61,

67, 68, 70) and his masterpiece 'Apocalypse', also scripted by Lewis, in 62–65. Following editor Bill Dubay's departure with 73 the comic took a significant dip in quality, from which it never recovered.

The post-Dubay period also saw a significant move away from horror to science fiction, fantasy and even the occasional superhero strip, but though it never achieved its earlier consistency the magazine could still come up with the occasional flashes of brilliance. The team of Bruce Jones and Richard Corben produced a fine time-travel story in 'Within You, Without You' (77, 79, 87 and later to prove an inspiration for the comic *Rip In Time*), and also contributed a nice story to 90. Jim Starlin's suitably cosmic 'Darklon The Mystic' (76, 79, 80, 84, 100) boasted both fine artwork and Starlin himself committing suicide, and was later collected for a one-shot comic published by Pacific. 81 was a themed issue based around a Frank Frazetta cover, featuring contributions from Corben, Torrents and Carmine Infantino among others. More significantly, the following issue saw the first appearance of Bill Dubay and Luis Bermejo's time-travelling cowboy The Rook, which quickly came to dominate the comic. Although rarely exceptional, The Rook was at least well crafted, and while its pre-eminence robbed *Eerie* of some of its diversity, following its departure to its own title in 105 the parent magazine became badly directionless.

With the exception of the odd Russ Heath (98) and Alex Nino (87, 92, 93, 95) efforts, the Rook era's finest hours were provided by Paul Gulacy, whose 'Trespasser', written by Don McGregor in 103–105, and 'Blood On Black Satin', written by Doug Moench for 109–111, were career highpoints. More typical, sadly, were the likes of Pablo Marcos' brainless 'Beastworld' (104, 105, 107–110) and the breathtakingly blatant *Star Wars* clone 'Mac Tavish' by Bill Dubay and Pepe Moreno (95, 96, 105, 107, 109, 111). *Eerie*'s last few years were, if anything, less appealing, with half-baked space opera becoming its staple ingredient. The sole exceptions to this were Victor De La Fuente's 'Haxtur And Haggarth' stories, which ran in most issues from 11 to the comic's demise. Even here, though, the fine art was sometimes scant compensation for the poor writing. With ever-increasing numbers of reprint issues, the magazine's days were clearly numbered, though the last few issues contain a few nice surprises. There's the return of the Rook in 132, a lovely Howard Chaykin strip in 127, and, best of all, the first English translation of Paul Gillon's masterful 'Les Naufrages Du Temps' (129, 132, 134, 136).

Between 1970 and 1972 Warren issued annual reprint anthologies, which they transferred to the parent title with 42. Subsequent reprint issues collected some of the comic's most popular serials: 'Dax' (59), 'Hunter' (69), 'The Mummy' (78), 'Within You, Without You' (97), José Ortiz' 'Hard John' (106), Leopoldo Sanchez' 'Spook' (112) and 'Jackass' (115). Other reprint issues concentrate on specific artists, with Richard Corben (86), Neal Adams (125), Wally Wood (131), Ramon Torrents (133) and Steve Ditko (135) those featured. For the more casual readers any of these would provide an excellent starting point for the comic.~DAR

Recommended: 2–12, 35, 44, 50, 52–73, 76–81, 84, 87, 90, 103–105, 109–111, 127, 129, 132, 134, 136

EGYPT
Vertigo: *7-issue limited series 1995–1996*

Pure filth. Incest, human excrement, zombies, murder, torture, sex, foul language, missing penises, and even more human excrement – have comics ever seen such depravity? Well, the more the better, because Peter Milligan has conceived an excellent series.

One Vincent Me, selfish, self-obsessed, miserable cretin, is murdered by a group of nutters experimenting with near-death experiences, influenced by the ancient pharaohs of Egypt. Poor Vince doesn't survive the experience, but is reincarnated in ancient Egypt. And that's when all the fun starts. After taking revenge on his murderers, he's back to Egypt to become involved in various battles between gods and the like. Milligan's plot is masterful, centring on rebirth and love, and his dialogue is exceptional. He also fleshes out the personality of our protagonist with great skill, especially the references to his incestuous thoughts regarding his sister. Milligan has really excelled himself here, while the ancient Egypt of artists Glyn Dillon, Roberto Corona and Phil Gascoine is a captivating place. You can believe the brutality and depravity as the underbelly of the advanced Egyptian culture. And just when you think you've figured everything out there's a surprise revelation about Egypt. The only letdown is the Hollywoodish ending, where our antihero sails off into the sunset with his lover. Then again the poor lad did atone for his past (or future) misdoings. After all, who of us is perfect?~HY

Recommended: 1–7

EIGHTBALL
Fantagraphics: *18 issues + 1989 to date*

The late 1980s were a golden age for quirky but intelligent cartoonists, with Chester Brown, Peter Bagge and a host of others creating funny but scary series characterised by individual world-views and killer artwork. Chief among them was Daniel Clowes. *Eightball* is, in Clowes' own words, 'An orgy of spite, vengeance, hopelessness, despair and sexual perversion'. What a pity he didn't select the title *Hate*, later used by Fantagraphics stablemate Bagge, which would have suited Clowes' glowering persona, ranting diatribes and black sense of humour, always tipping over into despair, to a tee.

Clowes' drawing style lends itself to the loving depiction of the grotesque and deformed: the American heartland has rarely looked uglier than in his 'Like A Velvet Glove Cast In Iron' (1–10). Preceding *Twin Peaks*, it shares the same sense of visceral whimsy. A young man becomes obsessed with an S&M film, and in trying to track down its origins he becomes drawn into a world of mysterious symbols, crackerjack wisdom, mutant fishwomen and bizarre coincidences. It's deeply disturbing stuff, as are Clowes' violently expressed narrative dialogues. He's forever finding the unnerving in the ordinary, even when illustrating the amusing non sequiturs of old people giving their opinion on various topics in a series of strips reminiscent of Pekar's observational humour. Even his seemingly straightforward parody of Marvel Comics, the wickedly funny Dan Pussey series, soon turns into a bile-driven lash out at the whole of the comic industry, from Stan Lee to *The Comics Journal*, taking in everything in between.

Some readers have complained that 'Ghost World, 'Velvet Glove''s replacement, the suburban adventures of two anti-fashion girls, is much too ordinary. It's not: it's superbly observed, and shot through with bitterness. Clowes manages to make juvenile cynicism fresh all over again.

Brave stuff for stylish readers. Bring your own neuroses.~FJ

Recommended: Issues 1–10, 18

Collections: Like A Velvet Glove Cast In Iron ('Velvet Glove' from 1–10), *Lout Rampage* (misc), *Orgy Bound* (misc), *Pussey* (all Dan Pussey stories)

80 PG GIANT
DC: *15 issues 1964–1965*

DC's first attempt at mining their then almost thirty years of material. Every issue contains a sympathetically selected parade of reprints, generally from the 1950s, that represented tremendous value at the time of publication. Sadly these are no longer cheap ways of obtaining classic old stories, having a rarity value themselves through their desirability and novelty at the time. Superman stars in 1, 6 and 11, with his pals Jimmy Olsen (2, 13) and Lois Lane (3, 14) also having their own editions, along with Superboy (10) and Superman's teamings with Batman from World's Finest (15). Batman inhabits 5, celebrating twenty-five years, and 12, with the Flash in 4 and 9 and Sgt Rock's Battle Tales in 7. The best issue is the

'Secret Origins' selection in 8, reprinting *Justice League Of America* 9, and backing it up with the origins of Aquaman, Atom, Robin and an expanded Superman origin story. Having confirmed the popularity of the package, DC continued to use the title for reprint selections incorporated in the runs of their more popular titles, for some reason continuing the *80 pg Giant* numbering in the logo, even when the page-count dropped to 64 pages. *JLA* 39, 48, 58, 67, 76, 85 and 93, for instance, are all labelled 80 pg or 64 pg Giants.~WJ

EL DIABLO
DC: *16 issues 1989–1990*

The title took the name of the former *All-Star Western* character; its main themes were social issues and ethnic problems. A young Mexican councilman, disgusted at the soaring crime rate, decides to take matters into his own hands and clean up the barrio in a US/Mexican border town. This was one of DC's most realistic attempts at a superhero comic, with the protagonist being a regular José in a mask. El Diablo had no powers whatsoever, and, beyond fighting, Gerard Jones' scripts dealt with alcoholism, economics and racism. It was probably the lack of escapism that ensured cancellation, but the series is worth a look with its slightly Western feel, akin to a combination of the old *Vigilante* series and *Love And Rockets*. 'The River' in 13–15 sticks out, a discussion of the problems of illegal immigrants entering the USA.~TP

Recommended: 13–15

ELECTRIC UNDERTOW
Marvel: *5-issue miniseries 1989–1990*

A prestige format miniseries spun off from *Strikeforce Morituri*, set ten years after the original series. It doesn't deserve the format, length or the time spent reviewing it other than to note bad script, worse art.~TP

ELECTRIC WARRIOR
DC: *18 issues, 1986–1987*

The rich live in the top layers of the city and have various means to keep the bottom-dwelling poor in line: from the sprinklers that spray acid to the cyborg enforcers known as Electric Warriors. This story depicts what happens when one of the Electric Warriors starts to develop self-awareness, swiftly followed by a conscience – and it's a stronger conscience than any of the humans here display. There's something bad on the way (although it's a long time before we find out what), and the city's leaders take desperate and brutal measures to defend themselves. Doug Moench has written an absorbing story, where the ideas are powerful enough to move it steadily forward, even where the issue-by-

issue plotting loses focus and the dialogue creaks loudly enough to wake the whole house. The style of the artwork is set by Jim Baikie, who pencils throughout and inks 1–7. While not striking, it establishes the atmosphere and tells the story well. All in all, a sturdy piece of craftsmanship.~FC
Recommended: 1–18

ELEKTRA
Marvel: *4 issues + 1996 to date*
In his premise for an ongoing *Elektra* series, Pete Milligan manages to turn one of the strongest and most unique characters in the Marvel universe into just another hyper-violent babe. Mike Deodato Jr gives her the big, globular tits, scowl and frizzy perm of your average bad girl *arriviste*. Having briefly skittered around her death and apotheosis at the hands of Miller for the benefit of newcomers, Milligan begins an uninteresting plot in which Elektra must work out her inner demons while seeking out the mysterious, fire-starting Architect, who's drawing the world's top assassins to NY for his own nefarious purpose. Frankly poor, especially when you think what Milligan's capable of when he tries.~FJ

ELEKTRA ASSASSIN
Epic: *8-issue limited series 1986–1987*
There are certain characters you don't want to know about or see too much, and Elektra is one. Matt Murdock's mysterious ninja ex-lover from the pages of *Daredevil* was such a good character precisely because she was never explained. During his first run on *Daredevil*, and especially in *Elektra Lives Again*, writer/artist Frank Miller dealt with Elektra on an almost mythical level. Contrariwise, in *Elektra Assassin* – where the slow-starting plot mixes real-life conspiracy theory with eastern mystical societies – the impression left after you brush aside all the ninja jiggery-pokery is that this is actually a comic about disturbed minds.

Miller asks questions about perception and reality, having Elektra mentally dominating a number of other characters, bouncing consciousnesses from body to body. She's partnered with Garrett, a half-cyborg criminal turned agent of S.H.I.E.L.D. with a recorder implanted in his head, who embodies the concept of nothing being as it seems. Miller gets excited about using various narrative voices to give multiple versions of 'the truth', employing showy techniques that may annoy some as much as the multiple visual styles Bill Sienkiewicz uses will annoy others. Sienkiewicz produces some stunning single images, but his experimental approach to panel layout and order often hinders the flow of the story rather than reflecting its rhythms as intended. Nonetheless it's a brave try. If you can get

through the inclination of both creators to show off, this series offers plenty of action linked to intelligent concepts.~FJ
Recommended: 3–8

THE ELEKTRA SAGA
Marvel: *4-issue miniseries 1984*
The episodes of Frank Miller's first run on *Daredevil*, featuring the return of Matt Murdock's previously unglimpsed college sweetheart as a ninja assassin, were among the most resonant of his ground-breaking tenure on the title. Despite the hoary premise, in Elektra Miller created a mysterious and dangerous figure. If you only want to read this portion of his excellent revamping of the title, Marvel conveniently collected it as a miniseries, chopping pages out of issues, with a few new sequences and some cracking new Miller covers.~FJ

ELEMENTALS
Comico: *Series one 29 issues, 1 special 1984–1988, Special 1989, series two 26 issues 1989–1992, Sex Specials 4 issues 1991–1992, one-shot ('Oblivion War Special') 1992, one-shot ('Ghost Of A Chance') 1995, 3-issue miniseries ('Birth Of A Supernation') 1995–1996, 4-issue miniseries ('How The War Was Won') 1996, 4-issue miniseries ('The Vampires Revenge') 1996*

Through a long publishing history there's a rule of thumb easily applied to *Elementals*: if creator Bill Willingham has something to do with the issue it stands the chance of being a decent read. Otherwise it's not really worth bothering with. The concept was first seen in the back of the *Justice Machine Annual*, in which four ordinary humans are chosen by ancient forces to be beneficiaries of the ancient elemental powers of air, earth, fire and water. Thus, respectively, Vortex, Monolith, Morningstar and Fathom are killed, then returned to life with the new abilities. 1–22 of the first series are sprightly superhero comics, relying as much on characterisation as supervillains, although the first special, looking at child abuse, is weak. Willingham's art develops from not quite the finished article, with skimpy backgrounds, to a very accomplished story-telling with an appealing style. He's helped on scripts by Jack Herman (from 6), who will later write most of the issues Willingham doesn't. For a good character piece try 14 from the first series, or 9's going-public issue, or for a decent battle 17 has some serious damage. After 22 Willingham's involvement is zero, and the only decent issue is 24's off-beat tale of the team being summoned to help Peruvian revolutionaries, written by Laurence Schick, and drawn by Jill Thompson.

The second series is launched with the second special written and drawn by Willingham, who then lets Mike Leeke and Mike Chen provide most of the art. They start off a little shakily, but develop quickly (although 12 is notable for Adam Hughes filling in). Willingham's outspoken editorials in early issues are largely spot-on, and his stories the same character-led sagas as previously, with former enemy Ratman now almost part of the team. There's a major surprise in 6 concerning old villain Shapeshifter, and 11 is an odd experiment in rhyme. Most issues from 10 are leading towards 'The Oblivion War', with 15's Elementals Inc board-meeting a highlight. 16 introduces Strike Force America, but Willingham once again leaves before he completes his story, and under Herman the title wanders all over the place into cancellation. Those wanting a conclusion to the story will find it in 1996's miniseries 'How The War Was Won'. Tony Daniel art notwithstanding, it's lack lustre stuff, as are the remaining 1996 series. Willingham returns to write 'The Vampires' Revenge', hinging on the events of issue 9 from the second series, as a vampire council convenes to try the Elementals. In no small part a Ratman solo, it lacks the spark of his earlier writing.

There are a number of unique and commendable aspects to *Elementals*, the first being that the characters have aged and changed since their introduction, particularly Monolith, who starts the series aged fifteen. Secondly, although his characters are in many ways superhero archetypes and there's a core of supervillains, Willingham moves the cast through a variety of tales, with fantasy and reality-based stories. He's not afraid to acknowledge that his characters have a sex life either. None of the sex specials are essential reading, but effort is made to see that beyond the bonking they tie into the ongoing continuity. Don't expect much in the way of a story in most, although Willingham rather comes up trumps in the first issue.~WJ

Recommended: Series one 14, 24, series two 6, 15
Collection: The Natural Order (series one 1–5)

ELF-THING
Eclipse: *1 issue 1987*

It's odd to imagine that this lame humour/parody title induced such laughter among the Eclipse staff that they were compelled to publish. Perhaps blackmail was involved. Oddly enough there was no glorious career in comics ahead for the creators.~FP

ELF WARRIOR
Adventure: *3 issues 1987–1988*
Quadrant: *1 issue (4) 1989*

Half-witted fantasy, with the only item lacking being a checklist to ensure all the genre clichés have been included. Peter Hsu's artwork draws lavish praise from letter-column scribes, though one wonders why when he's unable to trace a pose from a wank mag accurately.~FP

ELFLORD
Aircel: *Series one 6 issues 1986, series two 30 issues 1987–1989*

Touched by controversy, as was almost everything Barry Blair went near, *Elflord* was either a substandard *Elfquest* rip-off or child pornography. Whatever its intentions, it was fairly dull and uninteresting unless you're into elfy quests enough to read any old rubbish or like to see half-naked pre-pubescents. Enough readers were, it seems – as well as the relative longevity of the original, the series was reprinted as *Elflord Chronicles* (8 issues, 1990–1991) and new material was presented in a string of *Elflore* miniseries between 1992 and 1994.~JC

ELFQUEST
WaRP Graphics: *21 issues 1978–1985, 2-issue microseries ('Elfquest Gatherum') 1985*
Apple: *8-issue limited series ('Siege At Blue Mountain') 1987–1988*
WaRP Graphics: *9-issue limited series ('Kings Of The Broken Wheel') 1990–1992, 20-issue limited series ('Blood Of Ten Chiefs') 1993–1995, 6-issue miniseries ('Wavedancers') 1993–1994, 12-issue limited series ('The Rebels') 1994–1996, 12-issue limited series ('Jink') 1994–1996, 16-issue limited series ('Shards') 1994–1996, 6-issue miniseries ('Kahvi') 1995–1996, 5-issue miniseries ('Two Spear') 1995–1996, one-shot ('Metamorphosis') 1996*

ELFQUEST: NEW BLOOD
WaRP Graphics: *35 issues 1992–1996*

ELFQUEST: THE HIDDEN YEARS
WaRP Graphics: *29 issues 1992–1996*

However far it's wandered from the original premise, and however much the strand of fantasy that it popularised has become debased, the original *Elfquest* series is still worth a look. Wendy Pini's story of a group of elves searching for the High Ones, their legendary ancestors, features strong characterisation and a number of sharp plot twists, even though the story itself seems to sprawl towards the latter quarter of the initial epic, never mind the innumerable spin-offs. However, against this creativity you must weigh the sad sight of pudding-faced eighteen-year-olds with painted denim jackets and characters tattooed in the place where their bicep is supposed to be.

In Cutter, the brave but youthfully indecisive elf chief, and Skywise, his older but more daring best friend, Pini created a classic buddy team, and worked hard throughout the first ten or so issues to breath life into their many tribesfolk, as foolish humans burnt their forest home and drove them across the desert to the discovery of a group of sun-loving elves.

In the early issues Pini was obviously feeling her way, with occasional single-issue stories and at least one plot element wound up in each chapter, rather than the longer tales more typical of the later issues, when Cutter and his wolfriders discover first a group of less devolved elves under the influence of the evil sorceress Winnowill, who believe themselves the equals of the High Ones, and finally snow elves The Go-Backs, who're engaged in a continual battle with trolls for the mountain inside which the original elves' palace is supposed to be hidden. Throughout, the development of relationships is kept in balance with the having of adventures. By the end of twenty issues Wendy Pini has become an accomplished heart-string plucker.

Later series create an extremely complex continuity as Pini and numerous other writers and artists initially continue the story of the discovery of the palace, but then start filling in gaps, telling stories about the wolfriders' chiefs in 'Blood of Ten Chiefs', starting with Timmoran, a high elf who turned herself into a wolf and mated with one to produce a tribe of wild elves, denying these wolfriders the longevity of other elves. To make up for their short lifespans some of the riders take to spending long periods 'wrapped' by the preservers, annoying little fairy creatures who serve the High Ones by 'preserving' their ways, which means that they can pop up during 10,000 years of elf history for various story-lines about the Sun Folk. Some stories appear entirely unconnected with the main characters, in which case Winnowill will almost certainly be the missing link (as in the 'Wavedancers' miniseries about underwater elves). By dividing the original wolfpack into several questing groups, the Pinis can have an awful lot of stories going at once. Cutter's daughter Ember leads some of the riders to find a new home after the destruction of the palace in 'The Hidden Years' series, the adventures of Cutter's old rival, the magician Rayek, are explored in 'Rogue's Story', and 'New Blood' offers a selection of stories from creators new to the Elfquest universe at first, but with 11 turns into a major story-line about the war between the snow elves (or Go-Backs) and the sun elves, leading into the Forevergreen stories, in which Cutter's son leads the elves to a promised paradise, only to find he's been tricked by an ageing elf kept prisoner by humans who worship him. The main problem with 'New Blood' is you never know if you're going to get a comedy or a tragedy. The main problem with all of this is that it makes it difficult for readers to penetrate the story without starting at the beginning, making Elfquest more of a fantasy phenomenon than a comics one.

There are some other problems with the

original Pini creation. Although she periodically pulls her readership up sharply and reminds them that elves are fierce, despite their doe eyes, diminutive stature and long hair, she allows there to be altogether too much cuteness in the series for any but the most hardened lover of ditsy fantasy. From plucking at your heart-string in early issues, she soon moves to playing showy arpeggios, and, let's face it, the orgy scene in Elfquest 17, although hilarious, was a big mistake. If you are a fantasy fan who can, with equanimity, sit in a convention hotel bedroom at one in the morning singing about Dorsai to the tune of 'My Bonnie Lies Over The Ocean' then this is probably the best comic you'll ever read. If you'd rather cut your tongue out and cauterise the stump with your zippo than do any such thing, you probably won't be able to stomach more than a few issues, in which case the earlier the better. If you're undecided into which camp you fall and would like to try pretending to be a wolf-riding warrior in the privacy of your own bedroom, there are plenty of poems and 'filk' songs reprinted in the two gatherums (21 of the first series is also a scrapbook with poetry). Oh, and a book of bedtime stories 'for young cubs, with an Elfquest twist'. Oh, please.

Wendy Pini's art, however, is great: clean, clear, bold of outline, making good use of patterns and styles to distinguish between the different cultures the elves encounter. Within two or three issues she's firmed up her style and continues to influence the many artists who now draw Elfquest books. Most are even more fantasy/illustration-influenced that she is, except for Barry Blair. Although his elves still look like they've come from paedophile heaven, at least he knows how to get a story moving, which is more than can be said for the likes of Gary Kato, whose elves look like close relations of Yoda, or Jozef Szekeres, whose work on 'Wavedancers' is all twiddly illustration without drama or pacing.

Elfquest is surprisingly good, particularly given its reputation. Like all good things, the more hands involved, the more watered down it gets. Little of any lasting importance happens in strips not written by Wendy Pini, which is a useful guide to which of the innumerable spin-offs to read, but one can't help but feel that twenty great issues (reprinted by Epic over thirty-two issues) and then a nice, long rest would have produced better results than this sprawling epic.~FJ

Recommended: Elfquest 4–6, 8–13, 17 (for the orgy!)

Collections: Elfquest Book 1 (1–5), Book 2 (6–10), Book 3 (11–15), Book 4 (16–20), The Hidden Years (Hidden Years 1–5), New Blood (New Blood 1–5), Rogue's Challenge (Hidden Years 6–9), Siege At Blue Mountain (Siege At Blue Mountain 1–8)

ELIMINATOR
Malibu: *4 issues (0–3) 1995*

Written by Hank Kanalz and Roland Mann and drawn by Mike Zeck, this is a meandering series about a manhunter/assassin who becomes involved with the Ultraverse's secret government organisation, Aladdin. Very dull – probably most of note because Siren's first appearance is in 1.~NF

ELONGATED MAN
DC: *4-issue miniseries 1991–1992*

After many years of back-ups in *Flash* and *Detective*, Ralph Dibny aka the Elongated Man finally receives his own title. After taking time away from Justice League Europe, Ralph and his wife Sue become involved with a bunch of international supervillains, leading to a wonderful romp across Europe. The cartoony art matches the fun script perfectly, and watch out for the Italian villain, Calamari, who's a bloke in a giant squid outfit!~TP
Recommended: 1–4

Michael Moorcock's ELRIC
Marvel: *Graphic Novel ('The Dreaming City')1982*
Pacific: *6 issues 1983–1984*
First: *Sailor On The Seas Of Fate 7 issues 1985–1986, Weird Of The White Wolf 5 issues 1986–1987, The Vanishing Tower 6 issues 1987–1988, The Bane Of The Black Sword 6 issues 1988–1989*

Michael Moorcock's albino warrior has proved an enduring fantasy-fiction character, and even diluted by adaptation it's easy to see why. He's a striking and unique figure, with the weakness that he's beset by illness and initially sustained only by a mixture of magic and drugs. The combination of frailty and regal poise is exceptionally illustrated by P. Craig Russell in the graphic novel, and the team of Russell and Michael Gilbert for the Pacific series is also appealing, if somewhat muted initially by unsympathetic reproduction. That series adapts the first Elric novel, scripted, as are all the sequels, by Roy Thomas. It might be assumed that Thomas carries baggage with him from years of handling a diametrically opposed fantasy character, Conan, but his scripts here are faithful and dramatic, conveying Elric's questioning and tormented nature.

Michael Gilbert teams with George Freeman as artists for *Sailor On The Seas Of Fate* and *Weird Of The White Wolf,* but their art, while very good, doesn't quite match the delicacy of Russell's illustration. *Sailor* unites Elric with other Moorcock heroes and introduces the idea of The Eternal Champion, but it's not the strongest *Elric* story. The same team adapt *Weird Of The White Wolf,* a chapter of which formed the Marvel graphic novel. It's summarised by Russell, and the series also includes a chapter originally published in *Epic Illustrated.* By the end of the story Elric is without a kingdom and despised by his former subjects. *The Vanishing Tower* has Elric wandering the lower kingdoms, eventually ties back in with other Moorcock stories and is well and truly scuppered by Jan Duursema's art falling sadly short of previous standards. In *The Bane Of The Black Sword* it seems as if Elric has actually made amends of sorts and found peace and happiness, but what's the point of a tragic hero if into his life a little tragedy does not fall, eh? Initially the art of Mark Pacella and Nicholas Koenig vastly improves on the previous series, but is very rushed by the end.~FP
Recommended: *Elric 3–6*
Collections: *Elric (1–6), Sailor On The Seas Of Fate (1–7)*

Moebius' Airtight Garage: THE ELSEWHERE PRINCE
Epic: *6 issues 1990*

Moebius plots an engaging fantasy story with science-fiction overtones, returning Major Grubert from his *Airtight Garage* project. The major's more of an observer here, with an un-named artist the focus of the story saving the princess in true fairy-tale style. Excellent art from Eric Shanower.~FP

ELVEN
Malibu: *5 issues (0–4) 1994–1995*

Elven is a female Prime, though her powers have a magical as well as a scientific basis. She spends most of her time angry at men, while Prime or Primevil turn up in most issues to fight her. Len Strazewski practically clubs readers with his moralising and there's really no indication that the series had any kind of direction. Very poor.~NF

ELVIRA, Mistress Of The Dark
Claypool: *40 issues + 1993 to date*

Licensed from the B-movie actress of the same persona, Elvira recounts the adventures of a TV horror-show hostess with minor mystic gifts, who becomes involved in one supernatural calamity after another. Despite her simple desires for home, hearth and fabulous wealth, she's constantly forced to battle to make the world safe for bad moviegoers! Unlike her DC incarnation, Claypool gets our heroine firmly into the thick of the action, with no monster so menacing that she can't send them packing with a blue-tinged retort. Occasional infelicitous art teams render an unqualified recommendation impossible, but it's seldom less than amusing, and frequently riotous.~HS
Recommended: 1, 10, 17, 22, 26
Collection: *Mistress Of The Dark* (selections from 1–10)

ELVIRA'S HOUSE OF MYSTERY
DC: *12 issues, 1 Special 1986*

Although some very striking covers were produced to exploit the pneumatic assets of B-movie queen Cassandra Petersen aka Elvira, they were insufficient to disguise the fact that this was mainly stale inventory material from *House of Mystery's* previous incarnation. Delivered much less than it promises.~HS

THE ELVIS MANDIBLE
Piranha: *One-shot 1990*

Starting with the preposterous proposition that Elvis Presley's allure derived from his jawbone, said mandible disappears when he's buried at Graceland. It falls into the hands of a market analyst, and the remainder is one seemingly endless, seemingly stream-of-consciousness shaggy dog story. Unfortunately it's more the shaggy dog's arse than the shaggy dog's bollocks.~WJ

EMERALD DAWN
DC: *6-issue miniseries 1989–1990, 6-issue miniseries 1991*

Of all the late 80s DC revamps, Green Lantern initially got one of the better deals. Rather than riding wholesale over his past history, these two miniseries are more a 'Year One' and 'Year Two' for the character, bringing his origin up to date without doing anything to upset long-term fans too much. Apart from his being given a drink problem, Hal Jordan's origin remains largely unchanged. The second series has more of its own story to tell. Hal is behind bars for drink-driving, but that doesn't stop him using the power ring to slip out whenever he feels he's needed, which turns out to be mostly when Sinestro (not yet a recognised villain) comes calling, looking for help in controlling the society he has bullied into worshipping him. The last issue, featuring the trial of Sinestro, poses some interesting questions on the Guardians' self-appointed right to interfere with the Universe.~JC
Collection: Emerald Dawn (miniseries one 1–6)

EMPIRE LANES
Northern Lights: *4 issues 1986–1987*
Comico: *1 issue 1989*

A group of stock fantasy characters, including the princess, the dwarf, the knight and the priest, transport themselves to Earth, arriving in the Empire Lanes bowling alley. They're an engaging bunch, but the innovative setting remains largely unexplored beyond a few skirmishes with the local gangs, and even then they're possessed by other-worldly demons. Writer and artist Peter Gross seemed to be pacing his story as a novel, but it was never concluded.~FP
Collection: Arrival (1–4)

EMPTY LOVE STORIES
Slave Labor: *2 issues + 1994 to date*

A hilarious, skilfully crafted parody of the old DC style of romance stories with dilemmas only slightly more ridiculous than those found in the originals. How can a socialite beauty and a zombie find happiness together? How can you make a comatose trauma victim fall in love with you? Steve Darnall's stories, effortlessly invoking the spirit of the originals, are lovingly illustrated by Rob Walton, Scott Beaderstadt, Hilary Barta and other classy illustrators. With covers by Alex Ross and Mike Allred it's a quirky, engrossing read.~HS
Recommended: 1–2

ENCHANTER
Eclipse: *3 issues 1987*

Intended to be an eight-part series, Don Chin and Mike Dringenberg's fantasy tale had a lot of promise. Minimal dialogue and beautifully rendered black and white artwork make it hard to understand why the story has never been finished. On the strength of these issues it looked likely to create the sort of following that *Elfquest* had.~NF

Steven Grant's ENEMY
Dark Horse: *5-issue miniseries 1994*

Well-constructed thriller encompassing the FBI, covert government agency shenanigans and a man led to killers by the ghosts of those they've killed.~FP

ENIGMA
Vertigo: *8-issue limited series 1993*

When he's on form there's no contemporary writer working in mainstream comics to challenge Peter Milligan. He brings a knowing and erudite accumulation of popular culture and literary appreciation and an often-concealed sense of humour to almost every title he handles. He's also a rarity in being far superior when conceiving and following through his own projects, tending to quickly lose interest when handling other people's characters, and appears to have no fear of tackling topics likely to engender controversy. Admirably, the hallmark of political correctness is of no concern in tempering his ideas. This, naturally, leads to some controversy, in the case of *Enigma* from his handling of the homosexual propensities or otherwise of his lead character Michael Smith. With *Enigma* he has the wit and imagination to present an innovative take on superheroes, another rarity.

Michael Smith orders his life to such an extent it's stultifying, but a near-death experience during which he glimpses The Enigma, the hero of a fondly recalled comic from childhood, transforms him. Villains from the comic have also begun terrorising reality, and Michael searches out the writer of *The Enigma*, who can make no further sense of events than he. The most persistent and troublesome of the comic villains is The Truth, and the key to the entire series, although seemingly a throwaway line in the third issue, is when the comic's writer says, 'I always figured The Enigma would have trouble with The Truth.' Smith somehow feels drawn into and connected with the events playing themselves out, and indeed he is, although exactly how is a mystery only resolved at the death.

Enigma also charts the artistic growth of Duncan Fegredo. His first major work in pen and ink, it was begun in a somewhat cluttered and scratchy fashion, hiding a lack of confidence previously secreted behind painted pages under a multitude of lines. By the concluding issues he's becoming confident enough to dispense with un-needed embellishments, which isn't to say the art here is substandard. Fegredo is an expressive artist who's a natural at conveying emotion and movement, and is ideal for the heady brew offered here. The final touch elevating *Enigma* to greatness is the cynical voice whose captions tell the entire story. Consistently transcending standard comic captions, they offer an extra layer of commentary, providing a fully rounded graphic novel. The identity of the narrator is unknown until the final pages and will surprise every reader. Intelligent, seductive and compelling, *Enigma* is a must read for anyone drawn to adult-oriented comics.~WJ

Recommended: 1–8
Collection: Enigma (1–8)

EPIC
Epic: *4 issues 1992*
This was an attempt by Marvel to relaunch several series that had lost their own titles, including *Alien Legion* (3), *Stalkers* (1–4), *Wild Cards* (1–3) and *Nightbreed* (1, 2), and, perhaps, to test the waters for a new regular anthology. Using primarily British artists for these strips (Dougie Braithwaite, Mark Farmer, D'Israeli, David Roach, Steve Whitaker and Woodrow Phoenix), it did them no harm but cannot have been considered a particularly commercial decision, especially given that there was a very good reason for the original failure of these titles. Of special interest is a *Cholly And Flytrap* two-parter (3, 4), drawn by Arthur Suydam but written by Bob Burden in his usual surreal style.~NF

EPIC Graphic Novels and One-Shots
Even though this book deals with the *Groo* graphic novels under that character's entry, Marvel's creator-owned graphic novels and one-shots collectively make for strange

bedfellows. Starting at the bottom of the quality rankings, in 1993 Epic launched a number of new titles under the collective promotional tagline of 'Heavy Hitters', publishing the *Heavy Hitters Annual* as a one-shot sampler. There's a story apiece of Alien Legion, Feud, Lawdog, Lester Girls and Spyke. The best is Feud (despite two pages printed out of order), and it's a meaningless codicil to the series, so don't bother unless a complete set is essential. Acclaimed science-fiction author William Gibson's *Neuromancer* is adapted with very static airbrushed art by Bruce Jensen. Or at least the first part is. Epic don't have the consideration for the people who bought that to complete the story, so it's not much use now unless you're a major Bruce Jensen fan. And how many can say, hand on heart, that they are? There's more static painted art, this time from John Pierard, adapting Steven Brust's fantasy novel *Jhereg*. It's a slight story about an assassin with a difficult hit, but at least complete in itself.

Harvey Kurtzman's Strange Adventures isn't technically a graphic novel, rather a collection. In the 1950s and 1960s Kurtzman was an innovator and the master comics satirist of his generation. Sadly, his day had passed by the time he plotted and laid out these disappointing, limp genre parodies. A stellar line-up of artists including Sergio Aragonés, Dave Gibbons and Rick Geary faithfully follow the layouts, but respect outweighs inspiration here. The best strip is Robert Crumb's two pages concerning Kurtzman's influence on his life and career, and yet how difficult he found it conforming to Kurtzman's exacting standards. The production department deserves full credit for designing an appealing and reverential hardback tome that also finds space to publish Kurtzman's story layouts.

It's a shame the in-house staff weren't as respectful when it came to *67 Seconds*, which manages to mis-spell artist Steve Yeowell's name on both the cover and the credit page (in two different ways). To add insult to injury, the editors responsible then have their names up front when you open the book, leaving the creative team anonymous until the following page. *67 Seconds* is excellent. James Robinson weaves a rivetting adventure, told in flashbacks as a man contemplates his past and circumstances while he risks his life leaping for a flailing rope. Rich characterisation, a compelling mystery, a well-realised fascist retro-future and top art combine for a sadly ignored story deserving the assignation of graphic novel. *Someplace Strange*, though, garnered plenty of interest on release. The stunning John Bolton illustrations are immediately captivating on just flicking the book open, and were enough to send plenty of folk into enthusiasm overdrive. One suspects they didn't actually attempt to read this surrealistic modern-day fairy tale. While living up to the title, Ann Nocenti's script does little more than string together a succession of quirky happenings for an entirely unsatisfying read. But, oh, that glorious art! *Last Of The Dragons* can also boast fine art, from writer Carl Potts inked by Terry Austin. Originally serialised in *Epic Illustrated*, there's a greater cohesiveness to the collected edition of this tale of 19th-century guardians of ancient Japanese dragons bringing them to the USA. Slightly awkward at times, it's off-beat, involving and under-rated.

The comic-sized *Seven Block* has rushed Jorge Zaffino art with plenty of ill-advised crosshatching that often turns to complete mud despite the well-selected and limited palate of colourist Julie Michel. What makes this all the more distressing is that the story is a career benchmark for writer Chuck Dixon. It's a disturbing tale of medical experimentation on volunteer prisoners that inevitably goes disastrously wrong. Despite the predictability, *Seven Block* works, as it's about mood, atmosphere and perception, but the artistic shortcomings from a generally superior creator preclude recommendation.~WJ
Recommended: *67 Seconds*

EPIC Illustrated
Epic: *34 issues 1980–1986*

Marvel's attempt to emulate the success of *Heavy Metal*, *Epic Illustrated* had far fewer nods to the world of European cartooning. Using pretty much the same formula of serials and short stories, *Epic* relied heavily on established creators, including some whose work had appeared in *Heavy Metal*, including Paul Kirchner and Bob Wakelin.

There are some strong stories to be found: Delany and Chaykin's 'Seven Moons' Light Casts Complex Shadows' (2), Roy Thomas and P. Craig Russell's *Elric* adaptations (3, 4, 14, 15), Ken Maclin's funny Dr Watchstop (10, 14, 17, 21, 29, 33, 34), Dave Sim's Cerebus colour strips (26, 28, 30), plus work by Trina Robbins (8, 16), Alan Moore (34) and Sergio Aragonés (a Groo story in 27). It's the artwork that most people will remember, however, whether the black and white linework of Mike Kaluta (17, 21, 24, 26), Charles Vess (5, 8–10, 16, 21, 22, 24, 27) and Tim Conrad (on 'Toadswart' in 25–28, 30–33), or the richly coloured artwork by Kent Williams which adorns 18–21, 29–31 and 33, while Arthur Suydam turns up in 1, 8, 10, 13, 14 and 34, and John Bolton has work in 7 and 15. He also illustrates Marada The She-Wolf (10–12) in black and white, then in colour (22, 23). Interesting artwork carried a lot of so-so short stories, but on continued stories the series was weak. They included Jim Starlin's indulgent prelude to

Dreadstar, 'Metamorphosis Odyssey' (1–9), Thomas and Conrad's clunky Almuric (2–5), Rick Veitch's interminable 'Abraxas And The Earthman' – a sort of Moby Dick in space (10–17) – plus science-fiction shorts in 4–6, 19, 25, 28 and 29), Archie Goodwin and Pepe Moreno's post-holocaust 'Generation Zero' and the utterly tedious 'Last Galactus Story' by John Byrne in 26–34, still unfinished when the title was cancelled.

Slightly more interesting, but still only average, were Vaughn Bodé's Cobalt 60 (27–31), Doug Moench and John Buscema's Weirdworld (9, 11–13) and Dean Motter and Ken Steacy's Catholicism-vs-pure-evil-in-outer-space epic 'The Sacred And The Profane'. Of the European reprints, only Zoran Vanjaka made more than a couple of visits, including various appearances by his science-fiction detective Gideon Plexus (12, 15, 23, 28, 29, 31). Leo Duranona was in 1 and 11, Mirko Ilic in 1 and 5, and Paulo Serpieri in 34.

Alongside strips, *Epic* included portfolio pages and interesting articles on various aspects of comics. Of note are Maurice Horn on fantasy in European comics in 2, the Barry Windsor-Smith interview in 7 and a Basil Wolverton retrospective by Ron Goulart in 12. *Heavy Metal* wasn't great during this period, but it still outshone *Epic Illustrated*.~NF
Collected: *Generation Zero, Last Of The Dragons, Marada The She-Wolf* (10–12), *The Sacred And The Profane* (20–26)

EPIC LITE
Epic: *1 issue 1991*

Patchy humour anthology. On the plus side there's Evan Dorkin's TV sitcom parody 'The Murder Family', Scott Saavedra's satire on macho rednecks and some nice art from Hilary Barta. Kyle Baker's on autopilot for a lesson in comics economics, and Jim Valentino returns Normalman in order to get some venom about TV companies off his chest. Richard Rice's *Bob The Alien* is simple stuff and Mike Kazeleh occupies eight pages to no good effect.~WJ

EPICURUS THE SAGE
Piranha Press: *2 graphic novels 1989 & 1991*

Bill Messner-Loebs takes a whimsical look at the heyday of ancient Greek philosophy. It's an unlikely subject, with an unlikely hero, the moderate and reasonable Epicurus, who despairs of the rhetoric and weird notions flying among his fellows. Let's not forget that Plato thought everything existed in a big cave, and that our 'reality' was just a reflection of that cave. In volume 1 Epicurus sorts out the dispute between Demeter and Pluto over his kidnapping of Demeter's daughter, Persephone, hindered by the young Alexander the Great, and in vol 2 he tackles Zeus' various peccadilloes. The historically minded among you will

already have noticed that Messner-Loebs plays fast and loose with history and mythology to create a rich fantasy Athens in which philosophers act like *Tom & Jerry* characters, as well as taking clever pops at each other's ideas. Unfortunately if you haven't had the benefit of a classical education many of these are too obtuse to be funny, which is a problem when addressing a twentysomething audience. Sam Kieth illustrates the whole slickly, drawing mythological monsters with great dash, and throws in lots of visual jokes to keep the story moving, but ultimately *Epicurus The Sage*, like *Deadface*, can only be fully appreciated by a limited audience.~FJ
Recommended: Vol 1

ERADICATOR

DC: *3-issue miniseries 1996*

One of the four pretenders to Superman's throne during that gentleman's temporary demise, the Eradicator is a Kryptonian personality overwritten on a dead human psyche. This series explores the conflict between his two aspects, and is sensitively written by Ivan Velez Jr, with pleasant, if static, art by Roger Robinson. It's thoughtful, but ultimately a bit solipsistic for your average reader.~HS

The EROTIC Worlds Of Frank Thorne

Eros: *6 issues 1990–1991*

Good old Frank Thorne, never afraid to dress up in a silly costume to get his picture taken with a large-breasted fan. Many (including Wendy 'Elfquest' Pini) flocked in chainmail bikinis to impersonate Frank's heroines and are shown here. 1 contains two *Ghita of Alizarr* adventures; the language is colourful – 'Out of my way, Bumhole, or I'll pry loose your junks with this nutpick' – but the pictures rarely match what's being said, making it read like a bad translation. The art's much more carefully composed than the loose line suggests and you'll either like his pouty-mouthed, wide-eyed women or not. 2 and 3 feature *Moonshine McJuggs: Li'l Abner* with added incest, hick stupidity and carnal knowledge of cows. For 4 it's strap on your oxygen helmet (and not much else) for a continuation of the sci-fi graphic novel *Lann*, while 5 reprints the *Danger Rangerette* strips he did with Ted Mann and 6 features *Red Sonja*. Several worlds, pretty much the same character.~FJ

ESCAPE

Escape: *9 issues 1983–1986*
Titan: *10 issues (10–19) 1986–1989*

The British self-publishing scene of the early 1980s was healthy and vibrant, and *Escape* began as an attempt to present the best of that material to a wider audience. Eddie Campbell, Glenn Dakin, Phil Elliott, Hunt Emerson, Myra

Hancock and Rian Hughes are all well represented in the first seven digest-sized issues, which are a 50/50 combination of text and strip. The interviews with the likes of Leo Baxendale and Raymond Briggs are illuminating and the articles, largely on the work of European comic creators, are informed, but the bite-sized pieces of comics are unsatisfying. This changes when the title switches to magazine size with 8 and broadens its remit to include longer strips, more eccentric North American contributors, and translated work from respected European creators such as Baudoin (15), Mattotti (11), Muñoz (10), and Varenne (18). Phil Elliott and Paul Grist's 'Absent Friends' in the uncharacteristically sub-par issue 11 exemplifies the charm of *Escape*. A guy bumps into the nutter who used to live on the roof above his flat two years after they'd last met, and attempts to explain to his girlfriend the mixture of threat and allure he exuded. In this eloquent and well-observed story tension, wit and a twist in the tale are combined by two top-notch creators whose work is sadly under-appreciated.

The glorious eclecticism of *Escape* permits the publication of such astonishingly diverse and uncharacteristic material as Brian Bolland's introspective and questioning 'Mr Mamoulian' (11–19), Simon Bisley's fashion illustrations (15), and Howard Chaykin's biography of Lester Young (18). The Pleece Brothers' hilarious pastiche '70s Cop' is in 19, as is the prologue to the graphic novel *London's Dark*. The title is a reference to the blackouts observed to confuse enemy bombers during World War II, and James Robinson and Paul Johnson weave a tale of romance and dirty dealings amid a convincingly portrayed 1940s. The creators might handle aspects differently with more experience, but it's an assured début for both. The same can be said of *Violent Cases*, by Neil Gaiman and Dave McKean. It's a recollection of a childhood encounter with Al Capone's osteopath, and in turn the osteopath's recollections of Capone, in which a child's puzzled acceptance of the world is vividly evoked.~FP
Recommended: 7–10, 13, 14–16, 18, *Violent Cases*

ESPERS

Eclipse: *5 issues 1986–1987*
Halloween: *4 issues + 1996 to date*

A pan-continental group with paranormal abilities are gathered independent of any official organisation to rescue people held hostage by a Beirut-based terrorist organisation. Writer James Hudnall concentrates on personalities more than powers, with the Espers remaining in civvies throughout, and artist David Lloyd proves very able at conveying emotion through posture. The first four Eclipse issues form a good self-contained thriller very much tied to the real world, but the proposed second story is still-born, with 5 notable for being the only American comic drawn by British master artist John M. Burns. It's eventually told in *Interface*, which bridges the first and second series of *Espers*. By the Halloween issues the characters introduced in the first series are a more confident and experienced outfit, and the focus is largely back on them, but as seen through the eyes of a new teenage esper. New artist Greg Horn is very good, and his technique of avoiding the inking process works surprisingly well.~WJ

Recommended: Eclipse 1–4
Collection: Espers (Eclipse 1–4)

ETC
Piranha: *5-issue limited series 1989*

Tedious pseudo-sci-fi female Frankenstein story that looks half-drawn with broken ballpoints and painted with old bath sponges by a commercial artist having his first go at comics. Writer Tim Conrad's sub-Anthony Burgess or William Burroughs attempts at future language and science are laughable.~GK

ETERNAL WARRIOR
Valiant: *50 issues 1992–1996*

Gilad Abrams is an immortal driven by a constant need to wage war against injustice, and finds himself drawn to scenes of conflict, aided by Geomancers through the centuries. These Geomancers are the eyes and ears of the Earth to Gilad's fist and steel, and guide him on his pretty much undefined mission. Unluckily for the Geomancers, they aren't immortal, and tend to drop dead with alarming frequency. Each issue begins with a nice flashback to one of Gilad's earlier adventures in feudal Japan, the Wild West or another era. The initial concept is intriguing and relatively well written, but the series is let down throughout by substandard artwork, although 1–8 are worth checking out. 8 is a joint issue with *Archer and Armstrong* 8, Armstrong being Gilad's brother, and 25 repeats the idea with Mikes Baron and Vosburg creating a fun story involving the pair in the Crusades. By the time John Ostrander gets his teeth into the series with 27, pretty much all the interesting stories have been told, and the series begins to repeat itself. 33–35 have Gilad fighting one of his many children, now turned into a sociopath, a problem afflicting all his offspring, creating at one point the rather unlikely Jill The Ripper. Add to this a secret Nazi werewolf cabal and a body-jumping immortal evil spirit and you can see where the series is going…. going… gone.~TP
Recommended: 1–8, 25

ETERNALS
Marvel: *19 issues, 1 Annual 1976–1978, 12-issue limited series 1986–1987, one-shot 1991*

When Jack Kirby returned to Marvel Comics in the mid-1970s expectations were high. He was, after all, co-creator of a cast of characters that had seen Marvel very nicely through fifteen years and was just coming off what many felt to be a career peak with *New Gods* at DC. *The Eternals* was the highspot of what was an unhappy return. It concerns itself with familiar Kirby themes. Two races who've lived among humanity since the dawn of time are the god-like beings who've inspired myths of the Greek deities, and the ugly Deviants living beneath the planet's surface. The impending arrival of the Celestials, creators of mankind, to sit in judgement on humanity draws the immortal beings into open conflict. Unfortunately, great plots, wonderful ideas and expansive artwork are monumentally flawed by Kirby's often terrible dialogue. The best samplers of the original series are 11, in which the Soviets attempt to topple a Celestial while the Eternals gather to communicate, and the annual. Stay away from the saga of the cosmic-powered Hulk in 13–16, though. It's a stinker. Dangling plotlines from the prematurely cancelled first series were resolved in *Thor*.

For the revival writers Peter Gillis and Walt Simonson and pencil artists Sal Buscema and Paul Ryan wisely opt not to imitate Kirby, and settle on political intrigue and the pursuit and responsibilities of power as themes. Although very different from the original, it's initially okay, but drags over twelve issues. The 1991 special, 'The Herod Factor', is plain daft. Among other plot holes you could drive a bulldozer through, everything hinges on the deceit of someone who had no way of knowing the information that sets events in motion, there's silly expository dialogue throughout, and Mark Texeira's figurework is very lax.~FP

ETERNITY SMITH
Renegade: *5 issues 1986–1987*
Hero: *10 issues 1987–1988*

Sent back from the future to the 1980s, Smith has to prevent the future that spawned him, but there are already those in place whose task it is to ensure that his mission fails. Smith is helped by future technology, but there's no way he'll be returning, and a previous visit to the 1960s produced a daughter, now a renowned rock star and reunited with her father. That's the premise of the Renegade series, which is concluded in the first Hero issue. It's a well-conceived science-fiction romp, but whenever matters begin to become absorbing there's a tedious, intrusive fight scene. Once the initial plot is concluded, the series meanders for a horror story set, for some strange reason, in the Antarctic, and dull back-ups spotlighting the supporting cast.~WJ

THE EUDAEMON
Dark Horse: *3-issue miniseries 1993*

Mark Nelson is an excellent action artist. Unfortunately Nelson's talent as a writer is ordinary, and this tale of the renewal of an age-old battle between demons is only noteworthy for the art.~FP

EVANGELINE
Comico: *2 issues 1984*
Lodestone: *1 special 1986*
First: *12 issues 1987–1989*

The concept of a sexy killer vigilante nun neatly encompasses a variety of comic archetypes in a single package, and should, therefore, have been enormously successful. The scripts from Charles (more recently Chuck) Dixon show he's studied his action movies, and Judith Hunt's art, if a little static at times, moves the Comico issues along nicely despite the shoddy colouring. They're reprinted with additional codas as the Lodestone special, and the First series picks up from the conclusion. Evangeline's background is presented in 2 and 8. She's a nun working for the Vatican, distressingly still wielding power and influence in the 23rd century. The period is never particularly well evoked, and with Evangeline back on Earth for most of the series one is left with the feeling it might have carried more punch with a contemporary setting. Dixon's plots hold up throughout, but Evangeline, despite her background of inherent contradictions, rarely transcends a blank slate. Hunt leaves with 7 and the spirit of the title departs with her. Never previously exploitatively handled, the final issues by inferior artists have plenty of gratuitous poses. As an undemanding action/adventure title this is better than many.~WJ

THE EVERYMAN
Epic: *One-shot 1991*

The only work (so far) for Marvel from Bernie Mirault and *Madman* creator Michael Allred featured familiar themes of death and rebirth. A murdered witch is resurrected as a hermaphrodite and given the chance to avenge her death. When the job is done, her personality recedes, allowing other restless souls to take over the body. As yet, their stories remain untold.~JC

EVIL ERNIE
Eternity: *5 issues 1991–1992*
Chaos: *4-issue miniseries ('The Resurrection')* *1993, 4-issue miniseries ('Revenge') 1994–1995, one-shot ('Evil Ernie Vs The Super Heroes') 1995, 5-issue miniseries ('Straight To Hell')1995–1996*

Despite the claims of writer Brian Pulido that he's created something different, other than a slapdash attempt to explain his murderous personality as the result of childhood abuse, *Evil Ernie* is identical to the horror movies it's inspired by. So, in the same spirit... the Eternity series has one guy ripped in half, two eyeballs poked out, the pneumatic personification of death in a bikini, a swimming pool of blood, the storming of the White House by killer zombies, dozens of corpses, ten ribs, a nutty-dream reading machine, graveyard-fu, zombie biker-fu and square-jawed psychiatrist pushed too far-fu. Heads roll, eyeballs roll, truckers roll. Half a breast, no beasts unless you count Ernie, no dwarves. The Chaos series are much the same, except in colour with four fewer ribs, and there's an Adventure Comics reprint of the first Eternity issue.~WJ
Collections: The Resurrection (1–4), *Youth Gone Wild* (Eternity 1–5)

EXCALIBUR
Marvel: *104 issues +, 4 Specials, 1 Annual 1988 to date*

Following a successful introductory special that is *Excalibur* progressed to a regular series that is still going strong almost a decade later. Initially written by Chris Claremont with art and more than a little creative input from Alan Davis, *Excalibur* essentially continues the characters and situations from Marvel UK's *Captain Britain*. Joining the Captain, his shape-shifting girlfriend Meggan and his already strong supporting cast are former X-Men Nightcrawler, Shadowcat and Rachel Summers to make the comic more familiar to the American market. The team take on a succession of villains familiar to all characters' long-term readers. Although this is essentially a British-cum-European branch of the X-Men, links with the parent book are rarely overdone and early issues, brimming with Davis' enthusiasm, are light-hearted to the verge of comedy, with beautiful art and entertaining plots. Unfortunately, as was the case with many of the humorous books popular at this time, the joke soon wears thin, and was particularly tedious in most of 'The Cross-Time Caper', which saw the team visit a succession of alternate Earths throughout the series' teens. Around the same time, Davis' involvement becomes less regular, leading to a number of fill-in issues, most drawn by Ron Lim, which aim to play the comic straight and are best avoided.

Things improve with Davis' return to regular writing and pencilling in 42, which echoes the feel of the earlier issues, expanding the cast with a series of weird and wacky characters such as Kylun the Barbarian. The quality stays high until he leaves again, with his swansong in 66 and 67 (continuing the 'Days of Future Past' story-line from *X-Men* 142–143) worth a mention. After Davis's departure, the quality drops off again until the arrival of Warren Ellis with 88. Immediately imposing a style more reminiscent of 2000AD/Vertigo on the series, Ellis' style is darker than Davis', infused with a humour somewhere between black comedy and sick sarcasm. He focuses attention on Kitty Pryde and Pete Wisdom in the 'Dream Nails' trilogy, running from 88–90. Establishing both a professional and a romantic partnership between them, he is later to give the duo more exposure in the three-issue *Pryde And Wisdom* miniseries, and he departs with 103. 104, by John Arcudi and Alan Davis draw-alike Bryan Hitch, appears to be taking *Excalibur* back to its roots as a light, fun superhero comic. If Ellis isn't going to stay around for the ride it's perhaps the best we can hope for.~JC

Recommended: 1–7, 66–67, 88–92

EXILES

Malibu: *4-issue miniseries 1993*

The Exiles are a group of superpowered youths whose abilities have been triggered by the Theta Virus. Corporation head Malcolm Kost is planning to use the virus to create an army and the Exiles are out to stop him. Unfortunately they haven't the experience and after recruiting Amber Hunt most of them are killed in an accident caused by her reckless attempt to activate her powers. Written by Steve Gerber, *Exiles* is rather frantic, and after a promising start with Paul Pelletier drawing the first issue, Rob Phipps' work looks rather clunky. The series serves as a prelude to *Break Thru*, which begins to explain the origin of the ultrapowers in the Ultraverse. Ghoul survived this title to become a member of Ultraforce.~NF

The All New EXILES

Malibu: *11 issues 1995–1996*

After Marvel's absorption of Malibu's Ultraverse, The Exiles name is re-allocated to the group of characters from both companies' universes lost and thrown together on an alien world. The new line-up is Juggernaut, Reaper, Siren, Blaze, Shuriken, Amber Hunt and Warstrike (renamed just Strike). As with pretty much all the Ultraverse material since the Marvel takeover, it's really not worth the effort.~NF

EXIT

Taxi: *8 issues 1992–1994*
Caliber: *5-issue miniseries 1996*

A triumph of design over content, this highly acclaimed series by Nabiel Kanan is possibly one of the most oblique comics ever. The introductory issue is the most impenetrable, with captions and dialogue balloons sprinkled almost randomly over the pages. It's a story of people discovering the lies they've told to and

about each other, with a backdrop of one young man's obsessive quest to get to America, and the sudden outbreak of war.

Granted, any series which opens a couple of issues with sophomoric poetry deserves a degree of condemnation, but nevertheless there is much to commend here. From 2, while the story-telling is as deliberately ambiguous, the art is much stronger, with striking and lovely images grabbing your attention. Nevertheless, virtually the entire series is talking heads or conversational set-pieces, with an elegant avoidance of anything actually happening that isn't related to conversation. Just when you think this is the only way Kanan can tell a story, an unconnected little tale, 'Accident; The Recovery Room', appears in 4, and is clear, concise and punchy. So all this floaty, woolly stuff must be a deliberate choice, then. Ah, well. Later issues are told with single horizontals over double-page spreads, which enhances the already considerable visual appeal. The Caliber series exaggerates the faults of the first, with Karl and Louise returning. There's a continual feeling of being short-changed as admittedly nicely drawn static illustrations accompany blocks of text. The conclusion is even worse for having hardly any text, and very little story.~HS

EX-MUTANTS

Eternity: *Series one 8 issues 1986–1987, series two 15 issues, 1 special 1988–1989, series three 18 issues 1992–1994*

Ron Lim's first comics work was this daftly titled idea of a bunch of genetically created humans being the only non-mutates in an otherwise devastated world. Don't bother. The second series was subtitled 'Shattered Earth Chronicles', and revives all the characters for another go round. It's no better. The third series was a relaunch as part of Malibu's superhero line, with the fantasy and horror aspects toned down. There's some cross-pollination with *The Protectors* in later issues, but this remains undistinguished in every respect.~WJ

Collection: *The Saga Begins* (Series one 1–3)

EXQUISITE CORPSE

Dark Horse: *3-issue miniseries 1990*

An exploration of the psychology of a sex-murderer. Designed so the issues can be read in any order, it has the feel of an eastern European experimental film: clarity and resolution not a priority, but it leaves something behind in your head.~FC

EXTRA!

EC: *5 issues 1955*

When EC could no longer publish tales of zombies and ghoulish revenge they cast around for fresh, action-packed genres and came up with the glamorous and dangerous world of news reporting. *Extra!* was largely created under the aegis of Johnny Craig, who drew the lead story in each issue and edited. In his hands the stories owe more to newspaper adventure strips than traditional EC fare, with no tendency for shock/suspense endings or ghostly goings-on creeping in. Unfortunately they're also among the dullest stuff EC ever produced.

Unlike most ECs, *Extra!* established a regular set of strips. Craig's 'Dateline' featured fearless newshound Keith Michaels (oh for the days when Keith was a heroic name!) travelling the world with his assistant Vicki to follow up rumours of secret conspiracies and hidden Nazi treasures. It should have offered plenty of variety, but many of the stories are pedestrian; but they're nowhere near as contrived as the adventures of Slick (later wisely changed to Steve) Rampart, photographer, who always seems to be bumping into assassins disguised as snappers (1) or taking pictures of things he shouldn't (2). John Severin's artwork was bold and assured, if a bit roughly inked, especially when compared to Reed Crandall's super-smooth efforts on the third regular, 'Geri Hamilton'. Being a woman was pretty much Geri's only gimmick; inevitably as well as having Far East adventures she ended up investigating sob stories, as in 3's eponymous tale of a young hood who's convinced his dead father must have been someone important. It's dire, but not as bad as 1's 'Holiday For MacDuff', in which a Scottish reporter stumbles upon a scientist hidden from enemy nasties on a tiny Scandinavian island. Much 'hoots, mon'-ing and 'wee while'-ing ensues.~FJ
Collection: Extra! (1–5)

EXTREME JUSTICE
DC: *16 issues 1995–1996*

This spin-off series from the *Justice League* has Captain Atom, Booster Gold, Blue Beetle, Maxima, Amazing Man and Firestorm splitting off to form their own group after dissatisfaction over the League's association with the UN. Pretty pointless and basic superhero stuff, lacking the wit and humour that made its parent title a hit. Don't bother.~TP

THE EXTREMIST
Vertigo: *4-issue miniseries 1993*

Peter Milligan wrote an interesting story, which jumps back and forth in time, concerning hidden desires and frankness in sexual relationships, vigilante killings, racism, seduction, corruption and hairdressing. Probably a little too much was attempted in such a short run, and the whole may seem slight because of it, but it's very readable indeed, not unprovocative. Additionally, Ted McKeever produced throughout some of the best of his blotched, smeared and scratchy (to great effect)

high-contrast art. It's an all-too-rare serious piece of work, and Patrick/Pierre, the memorably sarcastic, campy, manipulative, bisexual (at least), Marquis-de-Sade-quoting, immoralist, cigarette-holdered presiding villain, is more self-consciously extreme than any of the soppy characters who wear the Extremist bondage uniform. That might be the point of it, or part of the point of it. Interesting.~GK

THE EYE OF MONGOMBO
Fantagraphics: *7 issues 1989–1991*

Imagine if you will Indiana Jones played by Donald Duck. That's the thrust of *The Eye Of Mongombo*, played strictly for laughs by Doug Gray. Renowned archaeologist Cliff Carlson pisses off the wrong witch-doctor and is transformed into a talking duck. Before searching for a way out of his situation he decides to follow an unscrupulous colleague who's stolen a map purporting to reveal the location of the legendary eye of Mongombo. It's deep in the Amazon jungle, so that's where our cast head. When each issue's recap and page-numbering systems are a delight in themselves, you know you're on to a good thing. Unfortunately, Gray was obviously tempted away by the thought of earning money somewhere, and leaves the story incomplete. What there is, though, is consistently and astonishingly funny in a slapstick and wisecracking fashion.~FP
Recommended: 1–7

THE EYEBALL KID
Dark Horse: *3-issue miniseries 1997*

Ed 'Ilya' Hillyer illustrates an action-packed story that spins off from Eddie Campbell's *Deadface*. Written by Campbell, it originally appeared in *Dark Horse Presents* and stars the multiple-eyed grandson of Argus, who stole Zeus' power and slew all the Greek gods except for Bacchus and Hermes. This series takes up the story after a particularly nasty group of mythical brothers, the Telchines (rendered in Campbell's updating as corporate nasties), have in turn stolen the power, using the Stygian Leech. After a whistle-stop tour of the Eyeball Kid's origin, there's a madcap, knockdown fight between Hermes and his Big Hand (don't ask) and the Telchines for possession of the leech. Ilya does a good Eddie Campbell take-off on the art, and the script is amusing if slight.~FJ

FABULOUS BABES
Drawn & Quarterly: *1 issue 1995*
Anthology title by Rozanna Bikadoroff, Fiona Smyth and Maurice Vellekoop that seriously lacks direction. It has the feel and contents of a fanzine behind a deluxe colour cover, and trots out some very tired ideas (fake ads in which Charles Atlas becomes Charlene Atlas, for instance). There are more illustrations than strips, and while Fiona Smyth's work is very pleasing on the eye, it doesn't tell a story.~FJ

THE FABULOUS FURRY FREAK BROTHERS
Rip Off/Knockabout: *12 issues 1976 to date*
Certainly the world's most popular underground comic, Gilbert Shelton's The Fabulous Furry Freak Brothers first appeared in a 1967 issue of *The LA Free Press.* They continue to star in their own comics, each edition kept constantly in print throughout Europe and America. The Freak Brothers still appeal to nostalgic hippies, pot-smoking ravers, and a huge general readership, uninterested in superheroes but in love with Shelton's wild humour and accomplished story-telling.

Exemplars of the long-hair lifestyle, The Freak Brothers are Fat Freddy, Phineas and Freewheelin' Franklin, three shiftless roommates whose constant craving for dope forms the basis for many of Shelton's funniest strips. Born in Texas in 1940, Shelton was a teenage EC-addict with a particular fondness for the work of *Mad* creator Harvey Kurtzman. In *Blab* 1 Shelton wrote that 'Kurtzman's style was my favorite. It was strong, full of action, and well-suited to a story-teller's style.' (Kurtzman once returned the compliment, describing Shelton as the 'true pro' of the underground.) Inspired by the first manifestations of flower power, Shelton's early Freak Brothers strips were drug-guzzling, cop-baiting, free-loving farces that both epitomised and satirised the counterculture scene. Whilst Shelton's drawings were often extremely crude, his well-defined characters and meticulously constructed scenarios sustained a series of thigh-slapping one- and two-pagers, collected in the first four issues of the comic. He also began a series of strips devoted to Fat Freddy's Cat, a flea-ridden ginger tom who proved

almost as popular as the Brothers. By issue 5, longer stories like 'Grass Roots' or 'Come Down' allowed Shelton to stray from the basic formula of failed dope deals and run-ins with Norbert The Narc, leading to the epic 'Idiots Abroad' story-line in 8–10, which remains Shelton's finest work to date. The Freaks decide to travel to Bogotá to buy cheap weed 'from the source', only to be separated at the airport. They are soon caught up in a series of misadventures. Franklin is captured by pirates, Freddy travels through Europe (stopping in Amsterdam, natch) and Phineas becomes the ruler of a powerful Middle Eastern country. Produced in collaboration with Paul Mavrides, gloriously coloured by Mavrides and Guy Colwell, this globetrotting romp also enabled Shelton to abandon the hard-core drug humour which had previously alienated potential readers.

The popularity of The Freak Brothers enables Shelton to work at a leisurely pace and exercise a great deal of quality control over his best-loved characters. Never fully embraced by either the mainstream or 'serious' comics pundits, the static Freak Brothers world often strikes non-believers as anachronistic or tired, a stale joke. However, devotees understand that while the hippy dream may well be dead, Shelton's comics transcend their historical moment. They remain constantly amusing and endlessly re-readable, and how many other comics can you say that about?~AL
Recommended: 1–10
Collection: The Idiots Abroad (8–10)

FACTOR-X
Marvel: *4 issues 1995*
X-Factor became *Factor-X* for the four months of 'Age of Apocalypse', which thrust the X-characters into an alternate Earth where their enemy ruled supreme. Probably the best of the Apocalypse books, the root of the story here is the jealousy between Alex Summers and Scott, the brother whose shadow he can never hope to escape. It's easy to see the characters we know in these darker versions of themselves, a tribute to the skill of John Francis Moore and Steve Eptig, at the time the 'real' X-Factor's regular creative team.~JC
Recommended: 1–4

FAFHRD AND THE GRAY MOUSER
Epic: *4-issue miniseries 1990–1991*

Howard Chaykin might not have been the obvious choice to adapt veteran fantasy writer Fritz Leiber's light-hearted sword-and-sorcery stories, but his scripting is deft, witty and faithful to the source material. 1 adapts *Ill Met In Lankhmar*, explaining how the sophisticated barbarian Fafhrd and dapper cutpurse The Gray Mouser come to be partners. Thereafter each issue contains two stylish stories of swordsmanship, thievery and magic. Mike Mignola, inked by the great Al Williamson, does an excellent job of capturing the decadent atmosphere of Lankhmar and the nightmarish, almost surreal quality of the magic permeating every scene. Credit should also go to Sherilyn Van Valkenburgh, whose colouring ensures that the look of the work as a whole is richly rounded. A fine example of how to get adaptations right.~NF

FALCON
Marvel: *4-issue miniseries 1983–1984*

A politically correct superhero comic for the 1980s starring Captain America's former partner. The series shows the Falcon as the champion of the ghetto, but the subject itself is only touched briefly. The most humorous sequence is in the last issue, where three ghetto kids tell Ronald Reagan about their troubles. Standard superhero fare very similar to *Captain America*.~SS

FALLEN ANGELS
Marvel: *8-issue limited series 1987*

This is a *New Mutants* spin-off. Roberto da Costa attacks a friend in a moment of anger, decides instantly that he must be an evil person just like his father, and runs away to New York to make a start on his life of crime. The mutant group Fallen Angels invite him to join them, and despite themselves they end up teaching him about friendship and loyalty and stuff like that. The series is probably intended as humour (what else can one make of the lobsters that are part of the group?) but there aren't nearly enough jokes and the few that there are should never have been stretched over eight issues. Highpoint: the origin stories for the lobsters from issue 3, pencilled by Marie Severin.~FC
Recommended: 3

FALLING IN LOVE
DC: *143 issues 1955–1973*

Another long-running DC romance title, *Falling In Love* had the usual stable of consummate craftsmen working on the stories: Sekowsky, Pike, Colan, Romita, Rosenberger *et al*. One odd thing, though, is the bizarre medical fetish present from the early 1960s onwards. This title could hardly claim sole licence on the trick, of course, but it does seem that *Falling In Love* had a particular fondness for stories depicting a crippled/blind/disfigured heroine tearfully confronting or fleeing from the man she loved! The Editor-in-Chief must have spent a lot of time in hospitals about then. Dying in dignity in 1973, without reaching the frantic hysteria that its sisters attained trying to keep an audience in more permissive times, *Falling In Love* is remembered by those who remember it at all as a solid, craftsmanlike title with many exquisitely illustrated stories.~HS

FAMILY MAN
Paradox: *3-issue miniseries 1995*

The second of Paradox's series of mystery novels, *Family Man* is written by noted thriller-writer Jerome Charyn and drawn by Joe Staton. It's set in the near future, when New York is a ruined city, the police are out of control and the Mafia families have all been wiped out. The Family Man is Alonzo, haunted by the murder of his wife and children. His brother Charles is the leader of the police force and is coming ever closer to total power in the city. When Charles orders a round-up of all 'criminal' elements into a makeshift prison camp, the various plots start to come apart and only Alonzo can save the city. Charyn is a good writer and this is some of Staton's best work. The result is not perhaps the best thriller ever written, but it's certainly worth a look.~NF

FAMILY TREE
Diva: *One-shot 1994*

Collection of a gay comic strip sequence with a 'pretend family' of friends visiting the Gay Games. Amusingly written and roughly but appealingly drawn, this was planned to launch an ongoing title that never materialised.~HS

FANNY
Knockabout: *4 issues + 1991 to date*

The flagship title of the British Women's Comic Collective, each issue has a different theme. *Ceasefire* dealt with women and war, mostly the then current Gulf conflict, and the topic of *Voyeuse* was sex. *Dissenting Women* covered religions, and 4's *Night Fruits* related women's experiences with dreams, prophesies and the general supernature. The title got off to a slow start, and was originally something one bought to be seen to be doing the right thing rather than with expectation of enjoyment; nevertheless there were always one or two good pieces. By 4 *Fanny* had become a solid, thought-provoking read. Although it's temporarily run aground, plans are afoot to publish 5's *Angry Women* soon.~HS

FANTAGOR
Last Gasp: *4 issues 1970–1972*

An underground anthology put together by Richard Corben, whose own contributions are by far the highlights. All issues feature beautiful and occasionally fully painted Corben art, but it's only 4's 'Space Jacked' that has a memorable story.~DAR

Recommended: 4

FANTAGRAPHICS Graphic Novels and Collections

Looking over Fantagraphics' output of graphic novels it becomes apparent that editors Gary Groth and Kim Thompson have chosen each carefully. Their line shows no inclination to jump on bandwagons and it is clear that, given the limited financial options available to them, they have tried consistently to introduce new reading experiences to a comics-reading audience. Initially the output was intermittent, beginning with a reprint of Gil Kane's violent *Savage*. There were early anomalies like *Children Of The Night*, a volume containing two black and white fairy stories, both written by Jan Strnad. His long-time collaborator Dennis Fujitake drew the first strip, about Winston, a bored dragon, and Tim Solliday illustrated 'Goblin Child' entirely in pencils. Both are competent but unexciting.

Ignoring the many collections of comics already published by the company, from the first year or so three distinct strands to Fantagraphics' graphic-novel output become obvious. The first is the production of collections of material by single creators, largely underground cartoonists, collecting strips from obscure sources accompanied by bibliographical material and strong introductions. The most notable of these is *The Complete Crumb* series (eleven volumes to date), which starts with Crumb's earliest attempts at anthropomorphic strips and chronologically prints every strip and published piece of artwork since. Equally wonderful is *Love That Bunch* by Aline Kominsky-Crumb, his wife. Her autobiographical strips about growing up fat and Jewish are no less brutally honest than her husband's more famous work. As the cover says, there's something for everyone: 'Sex, food, death, pain and romantic adventure.' Three Kim Deitch collections, *All Waldo Comics*, *A Shroud For Waldo* and *Beyond The Pale*, offer a broad sampling of his work. *All Waldo* collects the early strips about his eponymous cat hero plus appearances in *RAW* and *Weirdo*, while *A Shroud* collects weekly strips from the *LA Reader*, and *Beyond The Pale* selects material from two decades of cartooning, again offering a fascinating insight into Deitch's creative development from a rough, sub-Crumb style to his smooth, doll-like images today.

Deitch is a painstaking stylist, but few artists approach the obsessional attention to detail evident in the work of the Friedman Brothers, who comment on modern life via the iconography of trash culture. They're not afraid to show their teeth either, lampooning everyone from Bob Hope to Tor Johnson in two collections, *Warts And All* and *Any Similarity To Persons Living Or Dead*.

The collection of Spain Rodriguez's Trashman strips, *Trashman Lives!*, is less successful because Spain's work hasn't really moved over the twenty years covered in the collection. It depends on whether or not you're interested in his dystopian politicking in a series of stories set in a grim future where America has divided up into self-governing states. The compilation volume, *My True Story*, is a mix of autobiography and historical accounts of key political movements such as the Paris Commune. *Optimism Of Youth* collects Jack Jackson's often horror-inspired underground work, including the infamous Leather Nun stories, and *Housebound With Rick Geary* sees Geary examining the minutiae of everyday life. Great if you like his *lumpen* illustrative style. Less exciting is Howard Cruse's *Early Barefoots*, a collection of old underground work which features all the standards – sex, drugs, rock'n'roll – but lacks the smooth sophistication of his later work. Basil Wolverton was an inspiration for the underground cartoonists, and there are also two bits of Wolverton material from the 1950s and 1960s: *Wolvertoons*, a mind-boggling selection of grotesques, and *Powerhouse Pepper*, collecting strips about the dumb but kind-hearted strongman.

The second strand is the publication of lesser-known creators, many of whom have not produced regular comics, being editorial cartoonists or illustrators instead. Fantagraphics introduced the comics-reading public to Peter Kuper with *New York, New York*, a series of meditations on life in the big city drawn in a variety of styles à la Spiegelman, and published *World War 3 Illustrated*, collected writings and drawings from the magazine of the same name he edited from 1980 to 1988. Carol Tyler's *The Job Thing* is barely long enough to qualify as a graphic novel, but it's a fun collection of 'stories about shitty jobs', including various cartoonists' recollections of spectacularly awful ones. They also publish the *RAW*-inspired Kaz (*Buzzbomb, Underworld, Sidetrack City & Other Tales*), whose sophisticated but simple style illustrates skull-headed creatures, tales of Satan and such uplifting stories as 'Demis-O, The Clown Of Death'.

Alongside his erotic work, Fantagraphics

also published two graphic novels by Ho Che Anderson. *King*, the first of a series that never appeared, is an attempt to humanise the lionised black leader. It begins with contemporary reminiscences, followed by a series of incidents displaying racism in America today, before plunging into the story of Martin Luther King's early life, especially his eye for the girls. It's an uneven structure but an interesting experiment. Much more compelling is the later *Young Hoods In Love*, a series of tales about young black people in the city. It starts with a superb story in which a young couple are bickering about whether to take their baby to work with them. As the story progresses you realise they're about to rob somewhere.

Less successful efforts at expanding our appreciation of comics include Richard Lupoff and Steve Stiles' *Professor Thintwhistle*, a take-off of Jules Verne, and *A Sleepyhead Tale* by Jeremy Eaton, which uses dreams to satirise America. Ralph Steadman's *America*, by contrast, is a sharp-road trip of observation by the great British satirical cartoonist, whose work stands squarely beside the two volumes of Jules Feiffer's Collected Works, also put out by Fantagraphics. Recently they also published *Clover Honey* by Rich Tommaso, a rising comic star. In the mould of Paradox Press' hard-boiled detective series, it's a comic thriller about Abigail, an aspiring hitwoman, who has to track down her old mentor who's absconded with Family funds, drawn in an expressive sub-Hernandez style. *Daddie's Girl* by Debbie Dreschler will be remembered longer. It's a harrowing series of vignettes about growing up with sexual abuse. Far funnier than you'd think possible, it's also deeply moving.

The other early thrust of their graphic-novel line was the translation of outstanding European graphic novels from outside the adventure and erotic traditions favoured by most American publishers. This function now seems to have been taken over by NBM's Comics Lit line of books. The first was *Barney & The Blue Note*, Philippe Paringaux's extraordinarily haunting account of the life of a fictitious jazz genius told in flashback, as pieced together by an admirer, drawn in a flat, blocky style by Jacques de Loustal. It was followed by Muñoz and Sampayo's *Billie Holiday*, again about a jazz great, again written from the point of view of someone looking back. One big problem with a number of translations is the difficulty of translating idiomatic or linguistic devices in the original language into contemporary English. By using three translators who're clearly as familiar with the language of comics as they are with the source language (Katy MacRea, Robert Boyd and Kim Thompson), *Billie Holiday* has a fresh, lively voice.

Fog Over Tolbiac Bridge, an early attempt to popularise Jacques Tardi (which cause would later be taken up by *Cheval Noir*), is a difficult, stimulating thriller featuring his observant turn-of-the-century detective, Adele Blanc-Sec. They also published Tardi's collaboration with French thriller-writer Leo Malet, *Nestor Burma*, featuring his eponymous iconoclast detective. *Lea* is a morality play about under-age sex, wordy but clever. Christian Rossi creates rounded, modern characters and Serge LeTendre's lanky artwork suits the world of self-satisfied, arty folk in which the story's set. And finally *Ana* (1991), the story of a young woman caught up in a violent political struggle against a fascist state. Writer Gabriel Solano Lopez systematically tramples his characters' idealistic notions into the mud, while his son F. Solano Lopez, better known for his soft porn, draws the ugliness in grim detail.

Finally, two must-have collections that don't really fit in anywhere else. Fantagraphics have always put their money where their mouth is when it comes to publishing cutting-edge comics. In *The Best Comics Of The Decade* (2 vols, 1990), editors Gary Groth and Kim Thompson were also willing to make enemies as well as friends by selecting the best creators. And there's very little to disagree with in their choices, from huge commercial successes like Matt Groening to near-forgotten scribblers of genius like Dori Seda.~FJ

Recommended: *Any Similarity To Persons Living Or Dead…, Barney And The Blue Note, The Best Comics Of The Decade* Vols 1 & 2, *Beyond The Pale, Billie Holiday, The Complete Robert Crumb* 5, 6, 9, 10, *Daddy's Girl, Love That Bunch, New York, New York*

FANTASCI
WaRP: *5 issues 1986–1987*
Apple: *3 issues (6–8) 1987–1988*

Terrible title for a terrible black and white anthology that unimaginatively mixes fantasy and science fiction. For the record, *Fantasci* contains three continuing features. There's Don Lomax's tiresome superhero skit Captain Obese (big fat bloke becomes a costumed do-gooder for 'the common man' and, er, that's it), a laugh-free dwarf comedy 'A Hero Named Harold', by Kevin Davies and Steve Stirling, and an atrocious science-fiction adventure from Mark Stadler and Dave Hoover entitled 'Hunter XX'. The good news is that the latter is gone from 7.~AL

FANTASTIC FORCE
Marvel: *18 issues 1994–1996*

This *Fantastic Four* spin-off title joined the adult team's teenaged son Franklin Richards with another two superpowered youths and an other-dimensional warrior who claimed somewhat dubiously to be his aunt. The comic never really raised itself above being just another teen hero book, and despite later additions of more established and more popular heroes from the mother book – both the Human Torch and She-Hulk were members at one time – it suffered badly from clichéd dialogue and uninspired plots. It's not until the last issue that any depth is given to the characters. As Franklin reflects on mistakes which have led to the break-up of his team and the pressure he is under to live up to his parents' legend there's a hint that perhaps, underneath everything, this book did have a story to tell. Unfortunately, by then it was too late.~JC

FANTASTIC FOUR

Marvel: *Series one 416 issues, 27 Annuals, 6 Giant-Size 1961–1996, series two 3 issues + 1996 to date*

Hot on the heels of the DC (then National Periodicals) superhero revival, Stan Lee and Jack Kirby launched the *Fantastic Four*. A more mature approach to comics, with strong characterisation and soap-opera plots to counterbalance the action, the comic revived the flagging fortunes of the company which had, until then, been Atlas but with *FF* 1 was renamed Marvel. The exact history of that first issue has been lost in apocrypha and legend. Debate rages on how much creative input came from Lee and how much from Kirby, and on the (still uncertain) identity of the uncredited inker, but what is certain is that *Fantastic Four* changed the face of the industry, and presented the 1960s comic reader with sophisticated stories that have given the comics themselves a remarkable endurance.

1 tells the story of brilliant scientist Reed Richards who, determined to beat the Commies into space, blasts off ahead of them. This is despite warnings from his best friend and pilot, Ben Grimm, that the effect cosmic rays may have on their rocket has not been sufficiently researched. Grimm's caution is vindicated: the rocket hits a cosmic ray storm and crashes back to Earth, giving its crew (Richards, Grimm, Richards' fiancée Sue Storm and her brother Johnny) fantastic powers. As all upstanding citizens do, they soon agree to use these powers to fight evil and save the world. Early issues have a look and feel reminiscent of the monster comics which were popular at the time and on which Lee and Kirby had both worked. It is not until the distinctive blue costumes are introduced in 3 that the title becomes unmistakably a superhero comic. *Fantastic Four* 1 and 2 mark an evolution between these and the superhero comics DC had started to revive. It's speculated this was a deliberate attempt not to compete obviously with the superhero titles of National Periodicals, on whom Marvel then relied for distribution.

Kirby and Lee's remarkable 102-issue run is unparalleled in comics, both for the scope of characters and situations introduced and for the sheer quality of the art and writing. Almost all of the villains who will reappear over the next four decades are introduced in the first twenty issues, creating a formula few writers have tampered with since. The Thing vs The Hulk battle (25–26) is considered to be the classic slugfest by readers who like that sort of thing. It is around the mid-30s, however, that Kirby and Lee really hit their stride, and by 44, the first appearance of Gorgon of the Inhumans, the comic is in a golden age. The Inhumans story-line leads straight into the 'Galactus Saga', arguably the title's greatest moment. Kirby and Lee keep the quality high throughout the next twenty issues, and even when the partnership begins to run out of steam the quality is still above average, such as the *Prisoner*-inspired issues 84–87.

Without Kirby's creative input after 102, Stan Lee's scripts were never enough to carry the comic alone and 103–125 are best avoided. Once Lee had left, an unimpressive run by Archie Goodwin was followed by strong stories from Gerry Conway, and Roy Thomas lifted the comic over the following fifty issues, with notable high points being the alternate-world tale in 160–163, The Thing vs The Hulk battle in 167 and the George Perez/Joe Sinnott art on most issues between 164 and 192. By this time, however, the quality of the stories was already starting to drop and rarely climbs above mediocre again until the arrival of John Byrne, sporadically from 209 and permanently in 232–293. Byrne brought back much of the classic feel of the 'old' *Fantastic Four* and his run is generally considered to be a second golden age. It's worth noting that Byrne was one of the first writers to tamper with established Marvel continuity, changing the Fantastic Four to suit his own vision even when this didn't necessarily fit in with what the creators between him and Lee/Kirby had done. While not as drastic as the effect Frank Miller had on *Daredevil*, Byrne's tampering nevertheless changed the book and ensured its success into the 1980s. The Byrne stories are amongst the most popular in the comic's long history. Those around 250, packed with guest-stars such as the X-Men and the Avengers, are worth mentioning, as is the plot concerning the death of Galactus in 244, 257 and 261–262. Not afraid to challenge the *status quo*, Byrne replaced The Thing with the She-Hulk (for whom he had always had a particular fondness), and proceeded to have the character's long-time girl-friend, Alicia

Masters, fall for and marry the Human Torch. The soap-opera implications of this added a new undercurrent to the title under Byrne and his successors, and it is almost a snub to Byrne that Marvel eventually decided to reveal that it was not the real Alicia but a Skrull impostor whom the Torch had married. Other major changes he made to the series were to seriously upgrade the Invisible Girl's powers (and change her name to the Invisible Woman), and alter the team's costumes for the first and only time, albeit mildly. Byrne's last issue comes halfway through a story-line finished admirably by Roger Stern and Jerry Ordway, 293–295.

After the following twenty-fifth-anniversary issue, the FF enters what must be the nadir of its run, suffering often ludicrous plots and competent but uninspired art from issue 297 for pretty much the next hundred issues. The only notable exceptions are 334–350, written and sometimes drawn by Walt Simonson, which at least attempted to try something new, although the off-beat direction doesn't always hit the mark and some issues are incomprehensible. Around the late 380s, the regular creative team of Tom DeFalco and Paul Ryan start to get well enough acquainted with their cast to produce stories which, while by no means classics, are at least good fun, and more readable than most of the previous runs had been. The 'Nobody Gets Out Alive' story-line in 387–392 is the closest this period gets to a highlight.

By the time Marvel decided to turn to flavour-of-the-nineties writer-artist Jim Lee for a revamp and continuity overhaul, the *Fantastic Four* was in dire need of a new direction. Marvel's flagship title had, it seemed, never really recovered from Jack Kirby's departure, with subsequent creators building on old glories but never able to move on nor bring much originality to the series. It remains to be seen exactly how much of a difference Jim Lee can make to a series which, had it not been the comic which saved Marvel and ushered in a new age for comics, would probably have died a natural death long ago. The few issues that have appeared so far indicate faithful adherence to the old continuity, infused with the enthusiasm and energy Lee previously brought to the *Uncanny X-Men* and his own creations at Image, appealing to both old and new fans alike. It will be interesting to see what he manages when he's worked through enough of the old order to start off plots and concepts of his own. Early issues show him sticking tightly to the old continuity while updating the stories for a more demanding 1990s audience. For instance, Richards now takes his fiancée and her teenaged brother with him because the rocket is owned by their father and they are needed to initiate its launch sequence, not just because he thinks it's a good idea. Whatever he does with the book, it would appear that Lee is a much-needed breath of fresh air.

The first of the 1974–1975 giant-size issues was actually titled *Giant-Size Superstars*, and there have been numerous reprint packages of the classic Kirby & Lee FFs over the years, most notably in *Marvel Collectors Item Classics* (which became *Marvel's Greatest Comics* with 23), which ran ninety-six issues from 1965 to 1981, and the hardback volumes of *Marvel Masterworks*, which reprint the first 50.~JC

Recommended: 1–6, 10, 19, 25, 26, 38–51, 84–87, 150, 160–163, 234, 239, 261–262, 267, 285, 292–295

Collected: Greatest Villains Of The Fantastic Four, Nobody Gets Out Alive (387–392), *Marvel Masterworks* Vol 2 (1–10), Vol 6 (11–20), Vol 13 (21–30, Annual 1), Vol 21 (31–40, Annual 2), Vol 25 (41–50, Annual 3), *Monsters Unleashed* (347–349), *Trial of Galactus* (244, 257, 261–262 plus pages edited in from other issues)

FANTASTIC FOUR ROAST
Marvel: *One-shot 1982*

One-shot issue to mark the Fantastic Four's twentieth anniversary, written by Fred Hembeck with art by, amongst others, Hembeck, Frank Miller, Bill Siekiewicz, Sal Buscema, Marshall Rogers, John Byrne and Terry Austin. Intended to be funny, it unfortunately more often misses the mark.~JC

FANTASTIC FOUR 2099
Marvel: *8 issues 1996*

The best of the *2099* revamps of familiar characters, this is a title where the accent is on fun. The post-Art Adamas-style art by Matt Ryan, Al Williamson, Pascual Ferry and others is pleasing to the eye, and the scripts by Joe Kelly and Ben Raab evoke the early Lee/Kirby days of the FF. Big fight sequences executed with panache, evil Atlanteans taking over the world, the Negative Zone and the expected appearances of Doctors Strange and Doom make this well worth a look. The best the funky four have been for a long time.~TP

FANTASTIC FOUR UNLIMITED
Marvel: *16 issues 1993–1996*

Quarterly specials focusing on one character and/or telling a self-contained story. Started at a time when the monthly title was at its most tired and formulaic for years, these 'extra' stories have been no better and the series is best avoided. If you're an Ant-Man fan there's big changes in 9.~JC

FANTASTIC FOUR UNPLUGGED
Marvel: *6 issues 1995–1996*

Unbelievably poor low-price, lower-quality FF stories from new (and mostly never to be heard of again) creators. Most issues are self-contained, all are best avoided. If you really have to sample, issue 4 – which sees the Human Torch's estranged shapechanger wife disguise herself, chat him up and then get pissed off when he uses the same chat-up lines he lavished on her first time round – is so ludicrous it's funny, and reminds you that here are two characters so stupid they deserve each other. Or maybe don't bother.~JC

FANTASTIC FOUR VS THE X-MEN
Marvel: *4-issue miniseries 1987*

At the time this was published industry rumours suggested that Chris Claremont wanted the *FF* full-time but wasn't allowed to move off the immensely popular *X-Men*. Whether there was any truth in this or not, he turned out a piece of writing far above concurrent *X-Men* story-lines, on which signs of boredom were already apparent.

Aided by the clear, whimsical art of Jon Bogdanove, Claremont scripts an engaging and thoughtful tale. The FF are sent a diary allegedly kept by their leader insinuating that Reed Richards knew the risks of the rocket trip that caused their powers, but was prepared to take them for the sake of scientific advancement. This transforms the Fantastic Four's origin from an accident to a calculated scientific experiment into the effect of cosmic rays on the human body. As the relationships between the team try to survive this revelation, the X-Men ask for help in stabilising Shadowcat, whose out-of-control phasing powers are threatening to kill her. With other things to think about, Richards denies them his aid and thrusts them instead into the arms of Doctor Doom, a last hope they are prepared to accept no matter what the cost. The trademark Claremont *angst* runs through the story, but in-depth characterisation produces some wonderfully touching moments. This came as a timely reminder of what the writer was, at his best, capable of producing and if it only touched on the ideas he had for the FF it's a great loss that we were never allowed to see more.~JC
Recommended: 1–4
Collection: Fantastic Four vs X-Men (1–4)

FANTASTIC GIANTS
Charlton: *1 issue (24) 1966*

This is a giant-rampaging-monsters comic, formerly *Konga*, which only ran for one issue in this incarnation. All four stories are drawn by Steve Ditko: there's Konga (huge gorilla in London), Hogar (alien robot in South Africa), Gorgo (sea-reptile in London again), and 'The Mountain Monster' (hooded creature in central Europe). They're all off-the-shelf stories, but he does bring a lot of character to Gorgo.~FC

FANTASY MASTERPIECES
Marvel: *Series one 11 issues 1966–1967, series two 14 issues 1979–1981*

The first series is an odd selection of reprints largely unavailable elsewhere which are useful as samplers of otherwise expensive material from the 1940s and 1950s, although it's monster stories in 1 and 2. The Sub-Mariner and Human Torch clash – regarded as a 1940s highlight – is in 8, and the original Human Torch's origin is in 9. Captain America occupies 3–6, and the Black Knight reprints in 11 have some fine Joe Maneely artwork. The 1940s Marvel team the All-Winners Squad is in 10, and the remaining issues star Sub-Mariner. The reprints continued backing up a new story as the title changed to *Marvel Superheroes* with 12. Series two reprints the first fourteen issues of the 1960s *Silver Surfer* series and, from 8, Warlock's appearances in *Strange Tales* 178–181 and 9–11 of his own title. The reproduction is shoddy and you're better advised to seek out *Marvel Masterworks* volumes for the Silver Surfer stories and the later 1980s reprint for *Warlock*.~WJ

FAREWELL TO WEAPONS
Epic: *One-shot 1992*

Akira creator Katsuhrio Otomo story about cyberwarriors of the future being slaughtered by an automated combat drone. A neatly written, beautifully illustrated parable on the futility of war.~HS
Recommended: 1

FASHION IN ACTION
Eclipse: *One-shot 1986, one-shot 1987*

Spinning off from back-ups in early issues of *Scout*, *Fashion In Action*'s 1986 appearance was subtitled a summer special, and the 1987 version was a winter special. John K. Snyder's strip is more typical of European adventure strips than American, concerning a team of women acting as celebrity protection agents. The second is better than the first, focusing on team leader Frances Knight, as she recalls an episode of US 'special forces' having been involved in an African state in the past , while having to deal with another plan of arch-enemy Dr Cruel in the present. There are some nice original touches in both – Dr Cruel's sympathetic henchman in the Winter Special for one – but overall the characterisation of the leads isn't good enough to engage reader sympathy.~WJ

FAST FORWARD
Piranha: *3 issues 1992–1993*

According to a first-issue text page, *Fast Forward* is 'a free-form forum' for 'today's brightest talents'. More accurately, it's a hotch-potch anthology, each issue loosely assembled

around a different theme. 1 is Phobias, and leads with a long strip entitled 'A Glass Of Water', by Grant Morrison and Dave McKean. A lengthy monologue from a spinster librarian only threatens to become interesting. McKean's sinister artwork is a technically impressive mixture of treated photos, photomontage and linework, but often feels inappropriate when accompanying Morrison's resolutely ordinary script. There are also some minor fillers from Andy Helfer and Glenn Barr, David Quinn and Gil Ashby, Alec ('overrated') Stevens, and Russell Braun. The Family-themed 2 leads with a peach of a strip by Kyle ('underrated') Baker. 'Lester Fenton And The Walking Dead' is an inventive, funny zombie farce, rendered in Baker's beautifully offhand style. Lester's father returns from the dead, and proceeds to mess with his son's teen love-life. Baker now seems to have pretty much abandoned comics for TV – a real shame. Average work from Bob Rozakis and Stephen De Stefano, Dean Motter, Douglas Michael, Mark Williams and Brian Stelfreeze, and John Figueroa and Kirk Etienne rounds up the rest of the issue. The third number, Storytellers, is dominated by two lousy short stories with a few illustrations, a pointless rip-off for something sold as a comic book. William Messner-Loebs and Sam Kieth slightly redeem things with one of their entertaining yarns featuring philosopher Epicurus the Sage, but Steve Purcell inexplicably wins the cover slot for his overly cute fantasy 'Toybox'. ~AL
Recommended: 2

FAT DOG Mendoza
Dark Horse: *1 issue 1992*

Scott Musgrove's *Fat Dog Mendoza* is a completely off-the-wall slice of whimsy that will have any right-minded person falling off the chair with laughter. Some, of course, won't get it. Plot is minimal, but jokes are plentiful as Fat Dog roams about impersonating the Pope and being trapped under a tree. It's a joy to see fellow *Loose Teeth* alumni The Fruitheads return, and Musgrove also introduces a new character, overweight superhero The Whoosh, who leads The Squad Patrol. In the latter assemblage are some of the most preposterous supertypes ever conceived, complete with listings of superpowers and exploits. If you ever see Ol' Pops Pimple run for it. Fat Dog returns in *Dark Horse Presents* 116.~FP
Recommended: 1

FAT FREDDY'S CAT
Rip Off/Knockabout: *7 issues + 1978 to date.*

Frederick Freekowski, Esq, the nutritionally unchallenged member of the *Fabulous Furry Freak Brothers*, gives his feline companion free rein in these short stories, which show the feline species at its finest: puking, crapping, lazy, vicious hairballs. Mostly half-pagers culled from various underground newspapers, the longer stories which front each issue add occasional surreal touches (the Cockroach Wars in 5 for example), but it's the short strips which are the funniest, when our hero is behaving most like a cat and least like a human Everyman. The 'Just wait till he puts on his stereo headphones' gag is still a classic.~HS
Collection: The War Of The Cockroaches (5)

FATALE
Broadway: *8 issues + 1995 to date*

Introduced in *Powers That Be* and *Shadow State*, Broadway's leading lady rapidly spun off into her own title. Reminiscent of the X-Men's Rogue in that she leeches strength and knowledge from others on skin contact, she significantly differs in that she can choose to 'drain' others or not, and as a consequence revels in her power. The product of experiments by a sinister organisation called The Brotherhood, Fatale spends most of her time fleeing from the organisation's various warring factions. Attempts have been made to cast her as a superpowered Modesty Blaise, complete with eccentric supporting cast and at least two romantic interests. The blatantly voyeuristic nature of the art, held in check in the early issues, becomes increasingly creepy as the series progresses, robbing the strip of its initial appeal.~HS

FATE
DC: *17 issues 1994–1995*

The disembodied power was formerly affiliated with Dr Fate, but the events of *Zero Hour* rendered this relationship redundant, and it seeks a new host. Unaccountably it selects a chain-smoking thing with guns and an attitude. This series tramples the ideals of Dr Fate into the ground for no good purpose, as, the questionable association aside, this is to all intents and purposes a new character. Worse, it does so incompetently. It's worth a look at almost anything rather than this.~HS

FATHER AND SON
Kitchen Sink: *4 issues 1995–1996*

Inept and cynical grunge cash-in from writer/artist Jeff Nicholson. Uptight straight Richard Schultz is perpetually at war with his slacking son Christopher. Dad (there is no Mom) believes in hard work, talent and integrity, while Son is an idle moron who sponges off his hard-working old man. In almost every strip, Dad is shown to be more sophisticated than his couch-potato offspring, a curiously reactionary message from a comic clearly trying to grab some of that 'alternative' Seattle action (five years too late, but never mind). Perhaps it's all highly sophisticated parody, and Nicholson is a fierce satirist baiting his intended audience. However, none of the characters, situations or locations are especially well observed, the humour is strictly sitcom fare and the drawing amateurish.~AL

FATHOM
Comico: *Miniseries one 3 issues 1987, miniseries two 3 issues 1992–1993*

Two dull miniseries spun-off from the briefly popular *Elementals*. In the first, slightly superior, instalment, writer Lawrence Shick ponderously recaps our aquatic superheroine's origin – sailing accident leads to Rebecca Golden's reincarnation as 'Wet! Wild! Webbed!' Fathom, acolyte of watery deity Aqua – before sending her to a strange underwater city where she's literally treated like a Princess. Future *Sandman* artist Jill Thompson here blandly mimics the work of mediocre series creator Bill Willingham. In the 1990s story Fathom is summoned by Aqua to battle the dreaded Dera Aeshma, 'despoiler of the world's pure waters', a turgid eco-thriller from David DeVries and Tim Eldred.~AL

FATMAN THE HUMAN FLYING SAUCER
Lightning: *3 issues 1967*

The creators of the original Shazam Captain Marvel reunite twenty years on with this strange series aimed at the younger end of the market. Rotund Van Crawford is a superhero called Fatman who can also transform himself into a flying saucer in times of need, but with a tendency to be distracted by any food. Lacking the charm of *Captain Marvel*, it proves lightning doesn't strike twice.~FP

FAUST
Northstar/Rebel: *10 issues 1989–1995*

An inordinately violent psychopath with apparent multiple-personality disorder assumes a costumed identity with metal claws, eviscerating to quench an uncontrollable bloodlust. There's more to the series, but the central theme is an exploration of what occurs when the rage inside everybody bursts loose. *Faust* certainly attempts to justify the high sex-and-gore content with a credible, if confusing, plot, but is ultimately unrewarding on any level other than as vicarious gratification.~FP

FAX FROM SARAJEVO
Dark Horse: *1 volume 1996*

Since the term 'graphic novel' was introduced very few publications have achieved anything particularly meriting the term in a literal sense. It's bandied about for double-length superhero stories that, by and large, could have occupied two issues of a regular comic, and applied to works of greater merit, but still tapering off at 48, 64, or 72 pages. *Fax From Sarajevo* weighs in at 165 pages, and while length is hardly a factor ensuring literary merit, it's encouraging to see someone with the ambition to create a work living up to its appellation. That Joe Kubert already has five decades of accomplishments behind him (as has Will Eisner, the only consistent American creator of graphic novels), and therefore might be expected to be resting upon his well-earned laurels, and furthermore is tackling a subject of political intensity, makes *Fax From Sarajevo* all the more astounding. So that's the credentials of worthiness and achievement established, and given the topic it would count for nothing without a responsible hand. Kubert approaches an emotive subject the only way he can, through personal involvement.

As the war in what was Yugoslavia bloated ever outwards, Kubert's European art agent Ervin Rustermagic was stranded (along with tens of thousands of others) in his home town, the Bosnian city of Sarajevo. Once a beautiful resort, from March 1992 it was shelled incessantly by Serbian forces, whose snipers fired at civilians, and whose troops surrounded the city. Under siege with no apparent escape, Rustermagic's only contact with the outside world was the desperate faxes he sent and received from his clients. These faxes form the basis of the graphic novel, detailing Rustermagic's life from an initial terror and escalating hardship and discomfort to increasingly desperate attempts to find a way out for his family. The faxes also relate his continuing puzzlement at the inaction of United Nation forces, seemingly permitting the Serbs to plunder and attack at will. Conversely, *Fax From Sarajevo* charts the impotence his friends experience as they encounter an army themselves, the implacable forces of bureaucracy standing in the way of humanitarian solutions.

Kubert certainly brings a lot of baggage to this project. For years the artist of largely fictitious DC war stories, there was the danger that the effectiveness of his approach to a current event would be trivialised by his previous work. Thankfully that's not the case. His skill at telling the story is such that everything but the desperate existence of the Rustermagic family is forgotten. Although the story focuses on the Rustermagics, various acquaintances of theirs drift in and out of it, with no hint of their fate thereafter, which draws the reader's thoughts towards the wider picture of what was going on in Sarajevo.

Alongside only *Palestine*, *Fax From Sarajevo* is comic journalism, and, unlike *Palestine*, by concentrating on one family the strength of the narrative partially relies on suspense

concerning the eventual resolution of their circumstances. It's to trivialise a harrowing year for the Rustermagic family, but better that's the case than that their story remains untold. *Fax From Sarajevo* is an emotionally draining and intelligent work, and without doubt the best American graphic novel of the 1990s. It should be considered essential reading way beyond the comic market when a more affordable paperback edition is released.~WJ
Recommended

FAZE 1 FAZERS
AC: *4-issue miniseries 1986*

Artist and writer Vic Bridges introduces the Fazers, a collection of superhumans with the most unlikely names in the history of comics (Non-Man and Girl-Bot being favourites). Drawn very much in John Byrne's style, they're kidnapped by aliens for no good reason. 4 features early Erik Larsen fill-in art and a splendidly bitchy publishorial about Bridges' deadline problems.~HS

F.B.I.
Dell: *One-shot 1965*

One of the many one-off title produced by Dell in the 1960s, this is a little dated, but has some nice art by Joe Sinnott. It's probably the last comic he pencilled before becoming the definitive inker on the *Fantastic Four*.~SW

Adventure into FEAR
Marvel: *31 issues 1970–1975*

The first nine issues reprint 1950's weird/horror short stories, then Man-Thing became the cover feature running to 19. Marvel's muck monster was created by a combination of a defective supersoldier serum and the magical affinity of the Florida swamps. Captain America should be thankful. A foul, seven-foot-tall mass of rotting vegetation with no mind to speak of, Man-Thing reacts involuntarily to the emotions of those around him, fear causing him the most distress. Following his initial appearance in *Savage Tales* (first series) 1 and a handful of guest appearances, he graduated to his own strip under the masterful touch of Steve Gerber and Val Mayerik. Most issues are above par, with the outstanding 18 summarising the nature of the human race in nineteen pages. 19 introduces Howard the Duck in a slightly substandard story which concludes in *Man-Thing* 1.

In 20 Marvel jumped on the vampire vogue by starring Morbius in two concurrent series (see *Vampire Tales*). Neither lasted. In *Amazing Spider-Man* 101, Michael Morbius developed a serum from bat enzyme to cure his rare blood disease. It worked but endowed him with selected vampiric symptoms as a side-effect. Marvel's 'scientific' vampire experienced revulsion at his blood-sucking antics but was powerless to break his habit. This directionless series does science fiction, fantasy, horror, detective, mystery, supernatural, and singing crabs (in 29), and does them all badly – especially the singing crabs. Four writers and seven pencillers in twelve issues provides explanation for the awful standard. Paul Gulacy's art saves issue 20, but it is hard to find a single redeeming script feature. 31's 'She bit me! On the neck! What'll I tell Joey if it leaves a mark??' is the best that can be mustered. Unbelievably, some of these stories were reprinted in 1993 as *Morbius Revisited* during the heyday of the *Midnight Sons*. The first issue is cover-blurbed 'Classic Tales of the Living Vampire'. Were Marvel to be less disingenuous it might read 'Ropey old reissues for a fast buck'.~APS
Recommended: 18

Bissette & Veitch's FEAR BOOK
Eclipse: *One-shot 1986*

Eight very short horror stories, being early professional work done while the excellent artists Steve Bissette and Rick Veitch were at Joe Kubert's Comic Art school, and originally published in educational magazines. They're silly fun.~GK

FEDS'N'HEDS
Print Mint: *1 issue 1968*

This effervescent collection of counterculture humour by Gilbert Shelton was one of the first important underground comics. It featured early appearances by both of Shelton's much-loved family favourite strips Freak Brothers and Wonder Warthog, as well as songs, poems, posters and the legendary Oat Willie. Consistently funny, the humour has a universality that easily overcomes its hippy origins.~DAR
Recommended: 1

FEM FORCE
AC: *100 issues +, 1 special, 7 one-shots 1985 to date*

An all-woman team of superheroes, the Fem Force was assembled from the characters that AC founder Bill Black had been publishing in fanzines since the late 1960s. Having survived uneven distribution, retailer indifference and almost universal critical disdain, they've achieved their hundredth issue, a feat very few independent titles can equal.

Core members of the team include the ultra-patriotic Ms Victory, the feral She-Cat, the mystic Nightveil, intergalactic adventuress Stardust, and my personal favourite Synn, the Girl from LSD, a burned-out acid casualty ex-stripper whose hallucinogenic powers ensure that when she trips out everybody trips out. The implausibly costumed and impossibly stacked protagonists are very much in the cheesecake good-girl art tradition, and as such attract a negative response from the po-faced comics establishment. However, if you manage to set the enormous breasts aside – and those puppies take a lot of setting, it has to be admitted – what you're left with is a very traditional and moral superhero title. Tragedies occur occasionally, but virtue is generally rewarded, evil is thwarted and there's a clear distinction between the bad guys and the good guys, or good gals in this instance. As such, it's a welcome contrast to the plethora of twisted, psychopathic, murderous 'heroes'. *Fem Force* is very much a curate's egg. There are a few real stinkers, particularly a run in the late 1980s drawn by Dick Ayers, who not only can't draw gorgeous women but can't manage humans, but most issues are an undemanding fun read.~HS

FERRET
Malibu: *One-shot 1992, 10 issues 1993–1994*

Spin-off from The Protectors team starring their token feral misanthrope. Mostly competent, with a few glimpses of potential, but sunk by the hopelessly derivative nature of the character. The first issue, however, has a gimmick so dumb it should be in any collection of esoterica – the cover is trimmed to match the shape of our hero's head!~HS

FEUD
Epic: *4-issue miniseries 1993*

In an otherworldly scenario four races co-exist: the Stokers are engineers, the Grunts are a hardy working race, the Kites are flying artists and the amphibious Skids are fishermen by trade. Their uneasy alliance is shattered when the heir to the Skids' throne is abducted by Kites, leaving clues implicating Stokers. With the co-dependency of the races, this is merely the old game of paper/stone/scissors transferred to comics, but it's well conceived by Mike Baron, well illustrated by Mark Nelson and hideously coloured by Ray Murtaugh.~WJ

FIGHT MAN
Marvel: *One-shot 1993*

What does Fight Man do? He fights. Evan Dorkin turns out a very funny super-hero pastiche starring the dimbulb crusader so beloved of Bill and Ted. With the merchandising, the alimony, sidekicks dying all the time and public protests, Fight Man's having a hard time of it. What's the solution? To fight, of course.~FP
Recommended: 1

FIGHT THE ENEMY
Tower: *3 issues 1966*

Oh dear, oh dear. Tower's comics usually looked quite good, and so does this, with the occasional art by Mike Sekowsky, Al

McWilliams and Dick Giordano amongst others, but these war and espionage stories (featuring the macho Mike Manly) leave a lot to be desired. For every story with a poignant statement, there's a matching one that's pure jingoism. There's an early Boris Vallejo story in 2, but by and large the adverts offer more enjoyment. Especially the 'Man-Oh-Man! How Slim You'll look Wearing the New New Commander Abdominal Supporter Belt'. If only. Wonder if they're still on sale… ?~HY

FIGHTIN' 5
Charlton: *14 issues 1964–1967 (28–41), 7 issues (42–48) 1981–1982*

Hank Hennesey and his World War II espionage task force do little to distinguish themselves in any of their lame adventures by writer Joe Gill and artists Montes and Bache. Far more interesting are the first Peacemaker strips by Pat Boyette in 40 and 41. The title continued the numbering from *Space War* and the 1980s issues are reprints.~SW

FIGHTING AMERICAN
Headline: *7 issues 1954–1955*
Harvey: *1 issue 1966*

When crippled war hero Johnny Flagg is killed by Communist agents, his timid younger brother Nelson promises to bring his murderers to justice. Military superscience transfers Nelson's consciousness into his brother's rebuilt and fortified body. With the aid of kid sidekick Speedboy the freshly minted Fighting American sets out to defeat a ludicrous array of Bolshevik villains, including Rhode Island Red, Count Yuscha Liffso, Poison Ivan and Hotsky Trotski. After creating Captain America in the 1940s, top team Joe Simon and Jack Kirby revived their patriotic superhero concept at the height of 1950s Communist baiting. Although Fighting American was a sincere Cold War warrior, Simon and Kirby's decision to play things mainly for laughs ensures this comic remains a good fun read some forty years after it was first published. The Harvey issue reprints selections from the 1950s run, and many copies of the Marvel hardback collection were misprinted, so *caveat emptor*.~AL
Recommended: 3, 4
Collection: Fighting American (1–7)

FIGHTING AMERICAN
DC: *6-issue miniseries 1994*

This is an updating of the 1950s Fighting American. A government research team combines the 'fortified' dead body of Johnny Flagg with the mind of his brother Nelson, with the aim of producing a superhero to fight communism. But by the time Fighting American emerges from the vat, the USSR is no more, and the enemies confronting our hero are all 100% American. There's the Media Circus (a 'performance art mercenary terrorist troupe'), the Gross National Product (pure, guzzling greed), and the Phoroptor (whose rose-coloured lenses produce paralysing rays of nostalgia). Obviously, you're in for a few panels of lecturing with each issue, but the touch is generally light, and the priority is entertainment.~FC

Recommended: 1, 5

THE FINAL NIGHT
DC: *4-issue miniseries 1996*

The year's big crossover, suspensefully written by Karl Kesel and smoothly drawn by Stuart Immonen. After destroying New Tamaran, home of Starfire, the Sun-Eater heads for earth and puts out its sun. With Superman's powers soon depleted by lack of solar energy, the rest of Earth's heroes race against time to cope with the panicked population and try to devise a means of restarting the sun. Green Lantern, Parallax, Lex Luthor, Superman, Briniac 5 and Ferro are the major players in what is a better-than-usual annual get-together for DC's heroes. The effects spill over into most of DC's regular superhero titles and leave Superman powerless in his own titles for several issues.~NF

FIREARM
Malibu: *18 issues 1993–1995*

Despite writer James Robinson's heavy-handed literary references and occasionally clichéd writing, this is a surprisingly enjoyable comic. Alexander Swan, the protagonist, is a British ex-government agent turned private investigator who deals in cases involving ultras (Malibu's equivalent of superheroes). Swan is frequently beaten up, and Robinson has a good crack at hard-boiled writing, only to let himself down by constantly referring to Chandler *et al.* The art, however, is desperately inconsistent, with a new team almost every other issue, and by 10 what could have been a nice private-dick comic with a twist is yet another average title in a sprawling superhero universe. A sad waste of a good idea.~TP

FIREBRAND
DC: *7 issues 1996*

Drawn by Sal Velluto, *Firebrand* has a distinctive and appealing visual style not matched by the lacklustre sub-*Knight Rider* story-line. An ex-cop was blown up hunting child abusers and has returned as an enhanced vigilante thanks to a wealthy benefactor. Brian Augustyn's script doesn't work hard enough to make the full story any more readable than it sounds in thumbnail form.~NF

FIRESTAR
Marvel: *4-issue miniseries 1986*

This is an *X-Men* and *New Mutants* limited series. At thirteen, Angelica Jones starts to exhibit her high-temperature mutant power. She is immediately recruited by the evil White Queen, who spends the next few years working to make the unsuspecting Angelica into her best weapon against the X-Men. The story could have been interesting, but the delivery is plodding and repetitive – it would have been twice as good at half the length.~FC

FIRESTORM The Nuclear Man
DC: *Series one 5 issues 1978, series two 100 issues, 5 Annuals 1982–1990*

Following a long career writing for Marvel, including a stint as Editor-in-Chief, Gerry Conway had begun writing for DC in the mid-1970s, although he never seemed entirely at ease following the house style. Firestorm, though, was his own creation, and the best title he produced for them. This was partially because he followed the Marvel template in creating the character and his world. In the usual implausible comic way, high-school student Ronnie Raymond attends an anti-nuclear demo and is caught when a bomb detonates near a nuclear pile. His personality is fused with the creator of the reactor, a Professor Martin Stein, and together they become the atomic-energy being Firestorm. Raymond controlled Firestorm's body, but was directed by Stein, and he was also able to separate their bodies and return them to normal. Whenever trouble was at hand Raymond would concentrate, and no matter how far apart they were, the bodies would merge to become Firestorm. For a long while Stein had no memory of what had occurred once they separated. You couldn't go wrong with a red-and-yellow costumed hero throwing atomic fireballs from his hands, and there was double the soap-opera content with the teenage Raymond and the disoriented Stein. Firestorm was light superhero action drawn by Al Milgrom, but was cancelled before it really had a chance to take off, along with a large proportion of DC's line in 1978.

Conway realised Firestorm was a decent idea, and kept him in the comic public's eye through a back-up strip in Flash 289–304 and membership of the Justice League. In 1982 he was given a second shot at a solo title, this time called *The Fury Of Firestorm*. Solidly written by Conway and well illustrated by Pat Broderick, the formula was much the same as before, with an early plot concentrating on Professor Stein's increasing instability regarding his memory blackouts. Ronnie doesn't escape on the mental-anguish front either, as his journalist father apparently has some very shifty friends, and dies in 16. Never mind, though, because the next issue introduces Firehawk, a female counterpart to Firestorm, who'd become very popular. She was a bit less popular with Ronnie, who'd been dating her as Lorraine Reilly. Still, making the best of a bad thing Firestorm and Firehawk start dating instead. How nice it is to have a girl-friend with similar interests. Ronnie was now conveniently attending the same college at which Stein was teaching, making transformations a little less traumatic for him, although the knowledge of what was going on also helped. 19 sees the début of Rafael Kayanan as penciller, and Blue Devil débuted in 24's insert (and for those who really care, 6 had an insert featuring The Masters Of The Universe).

By this stage it's apparent that Conway is still producing what is in essence a Marvel-style comic with a DC bullet on the cover. There's the emphasis on soap-opera characterisation, light superheroics and the occasional bombshell, generally resolved within five issues. The Phantom Stranger drops by in 32 for an unusual teaming of light and dark. Ronnie's college nemesis, as introduced in the first series, was Cliff Carmichael, a continuing irritating presence for our young hero. This leads to a confrontation in 40, alienating his friends. Joe Brozowksi takes over the art in 43 and there's a happy moment in 50 when Ronnie's father marries again. Just as well he didn't really die in 16 after all. Those who feel a need to know can find a run-through of the Raymond family history in the first annual. Conway ends his long run in 57, by which time, although never poor, Firestorm's light tone had become very familiar and slightly stale. It required a good jolt, and that's what occurred with new writer John Ostrander.

Ostrander was a far grittier writer, and started introducing more character-based plot elements, although he continued Conway's plot for the unlucky Professor Stein, diagnosed with a brain tumour. Wanting to do something useful before he dies, he and Ronnie use Firestorm to destroy the world's nuclear weapons, which doesn't sit too kindly with the Soviet Union. In annual 5 they despatch Pozhar to deal with him, and just to make sure, detonate a nuclear missile on the pair of them. As Firestorm and Pozhar are in contact during the detonation their matrixes merge and transform, leading to the creation of a new Firestorm. This one, though, has a personality independent of his constituent parts, and can form spontaneously, making life difficult for both, but more so for Mikhail, formerly Pozhar. During his absence his family has been arrested by the KGB, and in a disturbing and stressful plot he's reliant on a group of superpowered teenagers called Soyuz to pull his fat out of the fire (Firestorm being unavailable). It all comes to a head in 73.

As the series continues Firestorm grows as an entity, and resents being used only in combat. His powers are almost limitless, and he wants to have a greater influence on the good of the world than merely fighting supervillains. 77–79 form 'The Eden Trilogy', in which Firestorm's solution to famine in Africa is to replenish the soil, creating a new garden of Eden. It may seem a glib answer to a real world tragedy, but Ostrander handles the plot with sensitivity, making it more than just an excuse for a superhero adventure. Tom Grindberg brings his Neal Adams stylings to Firestorm from 81, but is soon replaced by Tom Mandrake with 86. Having been tinkering with Firestorm and who can form him since his début on the title, Ostrander's revelation in 85 that the character is actually a fire elemental still comes out of left field. Unfortunately the idea is taken one step too far as a battle ensues in 90–93 between Firestorm and the planet's other elemental entities Swamp Thing, Red Tornado and the freshly created water elemental Naiad. 100 concludes the series in satisfying fashion with still more revelations concerning Firestorm's origin.

Ostrander's issues are more inventive than Conway's, but not necessarily any better. Both were well served by their respective pencillers, and both turn in solid superhero stories. As subplots tend to continue unresolved from issue to issue, noting sample issues is difficult, but the first and fifth annuals adequately showcase the differing approaches of each writer. Anyone enjoying them is likely to enjoy most issues of Firestorm.~HY

FIRKIN
Knockabout: 7 issues, 1989–1993

These are collections of two-page strips that originally appeared in the soft porn magazine Fiesta, written by Tym Manley and drawn by Hunt Emerson. Firkin is a cat, and he provides a robust commentary on human sexual behaviour. The first few strips are rather down-to-earth, in the style of observational comedy ('Hey, lads, you know what it's like when you…'), but they steadily become more and more fantastical and extravagant, as you'd expect with Hunt Emerson involved. Throughout, the attitude to sex is well-balanced. It recognises that women as well as men have sexual fantasies, and that life feels no obligation to fulfil the fantasies of either side. This is very refreshing given the sadly misogynist track record of sex comics. Not that every strip is a gem: there's a persistent weakness in the endings, and an over reliance on fart and constipation jokes (though if that pushes your buttons…). Still, there are nice touches every few panels, regardless of the story. The best issues are 4 for the Dan Dare spoof and the part

of the time-travelling urinal saga that takes place in the Garden of Eden, and 7 for the sexual problems of various comics heroes, the survey of methods of penis-enhancement, and the little footballers in 'Words of Fear'. You will doubtless find your own favourites.~FC
Recommended: 4, 7
Collection: Firkin (1–4)

FIRST ADVENTURES
First: *5 issues 1985–1986*

Anthology featuring Blaze Barlow (comedy detective), Whisper (Steven Grant's tale of espionage, a precursor to the Bad Girls trend) and Dynamo Joe (a Manga-influenced giant robot adventure series). Whisper and Dynamo Joe made it to their own series.~NF

FIRST ISSUE SPECIAL
DC: *13 issues 1975–1976*

As an updated version of *Showcase*, this try-out title wasn't a great success. Only Mike Grell's Warlord (8) and a revived New Gods (13) graduated to their own titles, and neither was particularly interesting. Other issues also featured revived characters, and while Metamorpho (3) and The Creeper (drawn by his creator Steve Ditko in 7) were pleasant enough, Dr Fate (9) by Martin Pasko and Walt Simonson was absolutely outstanding. Jack Kirby updated his old Manhunter feature in 5, and also produced two new strips, the mythological Atlas (1) and the kid gang Dingbats (6). None of them neared his finest work, but all were entertaining. So were two efforts by Kirby's old partner Joe Simon, The Green Team (2) and the Outsiders (10). Both were drawn by Jerry Grandenetti and Craig Flessel, both were kid gang strips of a sort, and both were completely mad. The remaining issues starred Code Name: Assassin (11) and a new Starman (12), though neither was of any note.~DAR
Recommended: 9

THE FIRST KINGDOM
Comics and Comix: *3 issues 1974–1975*
Bud Plant: *21 issues (4–24) 1976–1986*

Written and drawn in black and white by Jack Katz, this was one of the first independent comics. The earth was laid waste by war, and many generations later, the survivors are still at the Stone Age level, hunting giant lizards and fleeing man-eating ogres, clad only in ragged loincloths. But some of the gods who live on the high towers want to see change, and they have chosen the great hunter Darkenmoor to build the first city. That is to say, it's utterly standard heroic fantasy, until 4, when some utterly standard space opera gets mixed in too. The problem is that Katz cares too much. It's perfectly perfunctory hackwork, but he finds every detail of his world fascinating, and, of

course, utterly necessary to the story he's telling. If only he'd had a ruthless, soulless, commercial editor to say, 'This sequence is completely irrelevant', or 'This is the third time you've had Fara sold into slavery', or 'These panels are so crammed with detail, I can't figure out what I'm supposed to be looking at', or 'I can't tell any of your women characters apart. If you won't put clothes on them, at least show some difference in the shape of their breasts'. Pruned to six issues, the ideas (and they are there) would retain their vigour, and the virtues of Katz's art would not stale with repetition. He has a striking way with landscape and monumental architecture, and with eerie rituals, such as the sequence in 1 where a god is banished to hell. The sequence turns out to be irrelevant, but it casts a spell.~FC

FIRST SIX PACK
First: *2 issues 1987*

Bite-sized snippet previews of First's regular publications, excerpting a maximum of five pages from each title and providing text page with background information. There's a decent Dave Dorman cover painting on the first issue, but there's no other conceivable reason for buying this now.~WJ

FISH POLICE
Fishwrap: *11 issues 1985–1987*
Comico: *1 special 1987, 13 issues (5–17), 1988–1989, 1 issue (0) 1991*
Apple: *9 issues (18–26) 1989–1990*
Epic: *6 issues 1992–1993*

Everyone has their fifteen minutes of fame, and for a while it looked like *Fish Police* would stretch theirs to several hours. Steve Moncuse's easygoing funny fish comic is exactly what the title suggests, a pleasant soap opera about crime and love set in a world of talking fish, centring around the adventures of Inspector Gill. The quirk is that Gill may be a real policeman reliving his life as a fish in his dreams. The characters are pleasing, there are plenty of quirky humorous touches and it's drawn in a clean, open style with neither too much nor too little detail. But something doesn't smell right. It's just too smooth around the edges, like a glossy dramatisation of a blockbuster, specially designed not to be too upsetting or too taxing.

Fish Police had more chances at becoming a hot title than anything else that comes to mind. Originally printed under creator Steve Moncuse's own imprint in black and white, it was picked up first by Comico, who preceded their tenure by collecting the first four stories in colour as the graphic novel *Hairballs*. They then continued reprinting the previous series in colour from 5, picking up with new stories from 12. Comico also printed a 0 issue, originally designed as a pilot issue set earlier in *Fish Police* continuity. Under Apple the series reverted to new black and white stories, and after a two-year hiatus Marvel took it up on the basis of the cartoon series' popularity, and started reprinting from the original issue 1, in colour. So if you want it, it's not hard to find the start of the story.~FJ

Collection: *Hairballs* (1–4)

FISH SCHTICKS

Apple: *6 issues 1992–1993*

This is an offshoot of the *Fish Police* comics, and is written by *Fish Police* creator Steve Moncuse with art by Steve Hauk. It's a world much like ours, except funnier, and with everyone turned into a fish or other aquatic lifeform. The action centres around Inspector Gill, the local bar, and the reporters at the Fishwrap newspaper. The stories are quietly surreal, but the star is the dialogue: fresh, funny and wonderfully human.~FC

Recommended: 1–6

FISSION CHICKEN

Fantagraphics: *4 issues 1990*
Mu Press: *1 issue 1994*

Spewed from the pages of *Critters*, J.P. Morgan's superhero chicken stories are primarily a vehicle for parodies of everything from other superheroes through H.P. Lovecraft and *Nightmare On Elm Street* to weird UFO conspiracy theories. How on earth Fantagraphics thought the character strong enough to carry its own title is anyone's guess, although some people have a sneaking fondness for the sheer daftness of it all. The back-up strip, *Duck "Bill" Platypus* by Kyle Rothweiler, is much more interesting. An anarchic cross between *Pogo* and *Krazy Kat*, it's full of puns, visual and literal, political satire and surreal plots. The 'Chicken of Wrath' returns for a long adventure in the one-shot *Plan Nine From Vortox!*, fighting old enemies the Vortoxians, 'marketing experts from beyond!' The usual targets are hit about quite a bit, particularly commercialism and media manipulation.~NF

FIST OF THE NORTH STAR

Viz: *Part one 8 issues 1989–1990, part two 8 issues 1995–1996, part three 5 issues 1996*

Kenshiro, the Fist of the North Star and all-round paragon of virtue, wanders a post-apocalyptic world duffing up *Mad Max* extras and military clichés. Gory deaths aplenty, but otherwise as dull as Mr Dull from Dull City, Dullland. And it goes on, and on, and on and on.~FP

FIVE STAR SUPERHERO SPECTACULAR

DC: *One-shot 1977*

No false modesty at DC when it came to titling this anthology, but honesty in calling it *Two Star Superhero Average* probably wouldn't have helped sales. There are rather pointless solo spots for Atom, Aquaman, Green Lantern and Flash. The Batman story is the best, concluding the plots from *Kobra*.~WJ

FLAMING CARROT

Killian Barracks: *One-shot 1981*
Aardvark-Vanaheim: *6 issues 1984–1985*
Renegade: *11 issues (7–17) 1985–1987*
Dark Horse: *14 issues (18–31) 1988–1994*

The Flaming Carrot is an ordinary young man, brain-damaged after reading five thousand comics in one sitting. Putting on a giant carrot mask he patrols Iron City (his favoured mode of travel is a pogo stick), protecting it from villains like the Artless Dodger and Gonzaga. There is an element of whimsy and wish-fulfilment to all of this: when Death turns up, he and the Carrot go out for a night on the town; The Bikini Teens (superpowered bimbos) seem to exist for no other reason than to hang out with the Carrot. His friends include Uncle Billy, whose Jungle Woman story is told in 18, Death and Dr Heller.

The early issues chronicle adventures from his early days as a crimefighter (2, 3). The following issues take him from the bender to end all benders (and a miraculous recovery courtesy of Dr. Heller) to a dastardly Communist Revolution, engineered by Gonzaga, who has perfected a superexplosive made from the cellulite of pampered American women (5–11).

Of course there are a few other heroes around, too. As a member of the Mystery Men (Screwball, The Shoveler, Captain Attack, Jumpin' Jehoshaphat, Red Rover, Mr Furious, Jackpot and Bondo-Man) the Carrot helps defeat the Vile Brotherhood's clones of Hitler's feet (16–17). It's Screwball's pet shoelace that saves the day when Flaming Carrot teams up with the Teenage Mutant Ninja Turtles against Frankenstein's head (25–27), and the Bikini Teens are helpful when the Carrot must defeat Don Wiskerando and his flying dead dog, who has tricked Dr Who and Star Trek fans into helping an alien invasion (19–24). And when Iron City secedes from the Union and becomes a Communist state, it is a hunted Carrot who must restore order and democracy.

Burden himself describes the Carrot as a 'second-string, cut-rate hero of marginal glamour and dubious powers'. His powers are actually non-existent, though he has a catchphrase: 'Ut!' The Flaming Carrot is only vaguely sane and if, in Iron City, the extraordinary seems ordinary, the Carrot's adventures are still a constant surprise. Bob Burden's *Flaming Carrot* is one of those odd creations that may not appeal to everyone but

whose wit and inventiveness will endear itself to those who like a touch of surrealism in their comics.~NF
Recommended: 5–11, 16, 17, 19–24, 30

FLARE

Hero: *Series one 4 issues 1985–1986, series two 17 issues, 1990–1993*
Heroic Publishing: *5 issues 1992*
Hero: *17 issues 1992–1993*

Like almost all of Hero Graphics' output, the comics listed above were good-girl art superhero titles, generally using scantily clad, impossibly proportioned heroines to make up for the lack of artistic and writing quality. At least *Flare* was more honest about its intentions than some of the other Hero titles which tried to pass their protagonists off as straight superheroes; there was never any suggestion that it was intended as anything other than soft porn. The last incarnation was as a flip book with one of Hero's other long-running series, the dull and forgettable *Champions*.~JC

FLASH

DC: *Series one 246 issues (105–350), 1 Annual, 1 Spectacular 1959–1985, series two 120 issues +, 9 Annuals, 2 Specials 1987 to date*

The Flash of series one is Barry Allen, actually the second Flash. His comic continues the numbering of the 1940s *Flash Comics*, which starred the first Flash, who we'll get to later. As written by Robert Kanigher, then John Broome, and drawn by the team of Carmine Infantino and Joe Giella, Flash proved his popularity in try-outs in *Showcase* 4, 8, 13 and 14. By his own title a formula is already established. It involves a gimmicky villain, superspeed thrills, the odd scientific fact thrown in, and Barry Allen being late meeting his girlfriend (and future wife) Iris West, who often refers to him as the slowest man in the world, not realising his other identity (ho ho). Variations included time travel, 'inescapable' traps, visiting other Earths and bizarre transformations. Flash's foes later became known as The Rogues Gallery (holding meetings as such) and are an essential part of the formula, devising ingenious heists and deathtraps, and almost acting out conflicts instead of actually getting stuck into them. There's little effort made to explain their abilities, nor, indeed, to explain Flash's superspeed. That he was bathed in chemicals when struck by lightning suffices, as it should. For ten years *Flash* was light-hearted superheroics with excellent art, and very enjoyable as such, although a little dated now. Anyone enjoying one issue pre-175 is likely to enjoy most of them, so try one of the fine reprint giants, 160, 169, 178, 187, 196, 205 or excellent hundred-page 214 and the unnumbered hundred-page Super Spectacular. Particular

mention should be made of 'Flash Of Two Worlds' in 123. As a story it's no better or worse than average, but its importance lies in the reintroduction of the 1940s Flash, now established as living on Earth Two, a dimension separated from Earth One and accessible to the Flash if he vibrated at a certain frequency. Outstanding at the time, the irony is it began the alleged complication of the worlds occupied by DC's superheroes, precipitating *Crisis On Infinite Earths*, in which Barry Allen was killed.

The late 1960s and early 1970s were not happy times for *Flash*. There's a bizarre revisionist origin tale in 167, and with 174 Infantino departed, to be replaced by Ross Andru, who, while technically fine, lacks Infantino's style and individuality. Irv Novick from 200 is more suitable. He was initially paired with Robert Kanigher, whose human-interest stories were too great a contrast to what had come before, eschewing the popular villains in favour of one-off challenges. For his best see 206, in which two people are given a second chance at life.

Cary Bates became permanent writer with 210, having contributed a bizarre story in 179. He went on to be the longest-running creator on a title noteworthy for people having long runs. Bates reverted to old-style Flash stories with the accent on superspeed action and cleverly plotted battles of wits between Flash and his foes, with characterisation an afterthought. He was soon managing this as well as, if not better than Broome, and with few exceptions this remained the pattern until 275. 254–256 is a good sample of the Bates/Novick issues, with plenty of villains and a good plot. The landmark Green Lantern and Green Arrow pairing is concluded in 217–219, with GL remaining as back-up feature until 246. Firestorm occupied the back-up slot in 289–304, Dr Fate was there in 305–313, and The Creeper was in 318–323, meaning that Flash was rarely allocated the full page-count in his own title. 275 is a pivotal issue as The Reverse Flash (also known as Professor Zoom!) murders Iris Allen. The story injected a dose of realism into the Flash's world, and Cary Bates proved himself as adept with the introduction of continuity as he had been with simpler stuff. Don Heck's pencils are surprisingly good, tiding the series through until the return of Infantino with 296, on a fine off-beat story. The excellent 300 has a paralysed Barry Allen convinced his career is a delusional fantasy, but despite the death of Iris *Flash* remained essentially light-hearted. That changed with 324, in which the Reverse Flash returns, and in order to stop him from murdering again Flash has to kill him. Arrested for manslaughter, he has to lose his civilian identity, and there's little respite from a depressing story-line working its way to series one's final issue. Although successful in maintaining suspense, the story is too long, but nearing the conclusion with Flash's trial from 340 it improves, with an extraordinary amount of well-conceived twists and red herrings, including the return of a character believed dead, but, credit to Bates, not the obvious selection. Bates, the old sap, gives everyone a better ending than could have been hoped for, which is just as well, because in *Crisis* 7 Flash dies.

With Barry Allen dead, his mantle was inherited by Wally West. Beginning the second series, writer Mike Baron had a difficult task. Flash had been surplus to requirements as out of step with the times, yet his successor was the long-time kid sidekick wearing the same costume. Baron has a brave stab at differentiating them. Reasoning that superspeed burns calories and energy at an excessive rate, they obviously had to be replaced at an equally excessive rate, therefore Flash needed vast amounts of sleep and food. Never mind the cost, though, because he also won the lottery. And whereas Allen almost introduced the term Mr Nice Guy, West is a selfish dilettante and nowhere near as fast. Baron doesn't resort to using the old supervillains either, but it's all just window-dressing because once West is costumed there's little difference between the new *Flash* and the old. The best samples are 9–11, introducing the intriguing Chunk and the transition between pencillers Jackson Guice and Mike Collins.

By the time *Flash* became a TV series William Messner-Loebs had been writing the comic for almost two years, arriving with penciller Greg LaRoque on 15. It's a smooth changeover. Loebs emphasises West's individuality and confidently returns the Rogues Gallery in a very funny 19. That's followed by a heavy-handed but right-minded story about the destitute involving a rogue missing from 19, and an encounter with Fidel Castro in 21 and 22. The diversity sums up Loebs' tenure. He turns out consistently grabbing stories, but they could be about anyone. His only interest in superspeed is abstract, exemplified by 30's cinema assassination attempt or 54's story of how it can be used to escape a plane. For a sample try 53, with a guest appearance from Superman, an interesting revelation from reformed villain Pied Piper, and Wally at his foot-in-mouth best.

62 starts a four-part story scrutinising Wally's first year as a superhero. It also premieres Mark Waid as writer. Waid has a fine ear for dialogue and a sense of humour which serves him well, but his greatest professional asset is an ability to keep readers turning the pages. On top form he's currently unsurpassed at concocting plots over several issues where you really want to know how things turn out. What's more, he

does so by combining the simplicity and superspeed tricks of the previous Flash with a 1990s sensibility. Waid's initial issues are all good, but with 73 Barry Allen returns and the pages start turning as if Flash was reading the comic himself. Dragging the circumstances and mystery out to 79, Waid pulls strings like a puppet master, and comes through with a well planned pay-off. That's the final issue for penciller Greg LaRoque, not everyone's favourite but, like Novick on the first series, always solid and reliable. A succession of pencillers have arrived and departed since.

If Waid excels with multi-issue mysteries, his one- and two-parters are no better or worse than those of his predecessors, although his cynical spirit-of-Christmas story in 87 stands out. It's not really until 'Terminal Velocity' in 95–100 that he hits his peak again. With West haunted by not being able to deal with two crises in three seconds, Waid begins investigating the intricacies of speed, why Barry Allen was faster and more controlled than Wally West and where other speedsters fit in. Impulse débuts in 92, and Max Mercury, who'd been introduced/revived during the Barry Allen story, also plays a large part, as Flash discovers there's a nebulous energy known as the speed force that they all tap into, some with greater control than others. This is taken further in 'Dead Heat'(108–111 and *Impulse* 10–11) as someone less benevolent taps into the speed force. Beyond that Flash becomes lost in the future as the 27th-century Flash (introduced in the 1990 spectacular) replaces him in the 20th century. While Wally is fighting his way back through different eras John Fox is making time with his girl-friend and generally not proving up to the task of being Flash. 118's conclusion is masterful.

Over the years, in both incarnations, *Flash* has been a very good superhero title. The small quantity of recommended issues is testament to the consistency achieved, with few issues managing to stand out above the general run. Of the various annuals, specials and spectaculars, annual 3 sees William Messner-Loebs having fun with Chunk, 5 is of note for the artwork of Travis Charest, while 7 provides the best story, giving Flash a problem he can't outrun.~FP

Recommended: Series one 214, 219, 296, 300, 308, 309, 314–320, 345–350, series two 19, 22, 30, 33, 53, 74, 76, 78, 79, 87, 90, 91, 97, 108, 110–112, 118, 120–121

Collections: *The Flash Archives* (series one 105–108 + *Showcase* 4, 8, 13, 14), *The Greatest Flash Stories Ever Told* (*Flash Comics* 1, 66, 86, *Showcase* 4, series one 107, 113, 119, 124, 125, 137, 143, 148, 179, series two 2), *The Return of Barry Allen* (series two 74–80), *Terminal Velocity* (0, 95–100)

FLASH GORDON

King: *11 issues 1966–1967*
Charlton: *7 issues (12–18) 1969–1970*
Gold Key: *9 issues (19–27) 1978–1980*
Whitman: *10 issues (28–37) 1980–1982*

Created by the great Alex Raymond as a newspaper feature in the 1930s, Flash's 1960s chronicles were initiated by Archie Goodwin and Al Williamson, and the three issues (1, 4, 5) by the team are among the finest comics produced in the 1960s. After their departure Larry Ivie and Reed Crandall continued until King folded. The Charlton issues are poor. 12 and 13 have good art from Crandall and Jeff Jones respectively, drawn for King in 1967. A back-up, also drawn for King, by Mike Kaluta appears in 18. The Gold Key revival featured solid scripting from John Warner, and nice art from Carlos Garzon to begin with, and there's a seamless transition after the change of company name. 31–33 had Bruce Jones and Al Williamson adapt the 1980 Dino De Laurentiis movie admirably, but subsequent issues were drab in comparison.~SW
Recommended: 1, 4–6, 8, 11, 31–33

FLASH GORDON

DC: *9 issues 1988–1989*

This is a retelling of the veteran science-fiction story of football star Flash Gordon versus Ming the Merciless. At four issues, it might just have worked, at least as nostalgia, but there's no justification for dragging it out to nine. The only tiny spark of interest is the fact that this Flash Gordon is in his forties, and has moments of bitterness as he looks back at his sporting career. This idea is used well at the end, but not well enough to repay the effort of reading.~FC

FLASH GORDON

Marvel: *2 issues 1995*

One of the medium's finest draughtsmen, Al Williamson, is near the top of his form on the character created by Alex Raymond, who was so influential on Williamson's romantic style. Mark Schultz wrote traditional characterisations of all the leading players in this classic space opera, such as Emperor Ming and Dr Zarkov. It's well coloured and exceptionally well printed, too. An old-fashioned bit of escapism, perhaps, but of top-drawer quality. It's a treasure not to be overlooked.~GK
Recommended: 1–2

FLEENER

Zongo: *2 issues + 1996 to date*

Mary Fleener moves from the slice-of-life, adults-only emphasis of her previous series, *Slutburger*, to more whimsical subjects in this general-audience series. Animated tiki gods and sentient canapés (who, disturbingly, run a restaurant) are the stars of the two issues to date, still drawn in Fleener's distinctive, frenzied pseudo-cubism.~HS

FLESH AND BONES featuring Dalgoda

Fantagraphics: *4-issue miniseries 1986*

Flesh & Bones continues where *Dalgoda*'s hastily truncated story-line ends, with the cute canine spacer of the title on his way towards the wreckage of his home planet in a fleet that's been hastily cobbled together by an Earth government not completely convinced they should help their doggy allies out, even if it increases the chance that they won't suffer the same fate at the hands of the mysterious and violent Nimp. The action comes thick and fast, punctuated by lovely character touches, as Dal fights to keep his leadership and his sanity. Highly recommended if you're more interested in reading about people (albeit some with bushy tails and wet noses) than the costumes they wear.~FJ
Recommended: 1–4

FLESH CRAWLERS

Kitchen Sink: *3-issue miniseries 1993–1995*

An alien-attacks-small-town script that would have been rejected by 1950s B-movie makers as too pedestrian combined with fanzine quality art doesn't make for the usual Kitchen Sink quality package. All the more remarkably, there was a seventeen-month gap between first and second issues, yet the series was still completed. One can only assume that pressure was brought to bear.~FP

FLEX MENTALLO

Vertigo: *4-issue miniseries 1996*

Flex Mentallo has all the hallmarks of a classic Grant Morrison script: a slightly ludicrous hero, lots of referential bits and a soupçon of surrealism. As part of his new, uncynical take on superheroes he makes Flex a big-hearted muscleman slightly (and amusingly) out of his depth in a world of nasty villains. Morrison effectively contrasts his character's happy-go-lucky attitude to life and adventuring with the realisation that there are problems a good right hook can't solve. The series is notable for bringing Frank Quitely (think about it) to a wider US audience. Not only is his artwork breathtakingly detailed, it's also beautifully composed – his handling of perspective in crowd scenes makes you want to weep. Rarely do you see action story-telling and such beautiful drawing so effectively balanced.~FJ
Recommended: 1–4

FLOATERS
Dark Horse: *5-issue miniseries 1993–1994*

There are a lot of interesting ideas concerning a future society where use of narcotics is commonplace and legal. Both script and art leave a lot to be desired, however, which is odd as this was originally conceived as a Spike Lee screenplay.~WJ

FLOOD RELIEF
Malibu: *One-shot 1994*

Fund-raiser that perhaps rather tastelessly has the Ultraverse heroes fighting a flood that actually occurred, but ascribing it to a supervillain, thereby trivialising very real problems. Buying it now won't pass money to a good cause, so don't.~FP

THE FLY
Archie: *30 issues 1959–1964*

Teenager Thomas Troy was given a ring by a representative of a race of fly people from another dimension. This ring enabled him to become The Fly, a winged superhero, once every twenty-four hours. 1–2 were by Joe Simon and Jack Kirby, with the following two issues being thrown together by associates such as Jack Davis, Bernard Bailey and Bob Powell. As might be expected, they were good, solid adventure stories that still make enjoyable reading. With Simon and Kirby's departure the title began a decline into lunatic plots, inane scripts by Jerry Siegel and bland art from John Giunta and John Rosenberger. With 31 the title changed to *Fly Man*.~SW

THE FLY
Red Circle: *9 issues 1983–1984*

A grown-up Thomas Troy is called upon by the mystic Turan to take up once more the mantle of the Fly, as crime hasn't gone away and nor have the Fly's old villains. The first issue gets off to a good start artistically with work by James Sherman on the Fly and Trevor Von Eeden on the back-up Mr Justice, but the scripts, by Jack C. Harris and Chris Adams respectively, seem clichéd, if enthusiastic. Sherman's gone by 2 but one of his replacements is Steve Ditko so that's all right, even inked by Rich Buckler. It is strange, however, that Harris doesn't get to conclude his first story, instead writing the second while Buckler adds Flygirl to the Fly's adventure against the Spider. Flygirl remains a major part of the stories in 3 (both drawn by Ditko) but then goes missing. By 5 Ditko is plotting the Fly strips as well as drawing them and Vicatan is illustrating Chas Ward's version of the Jaguar. Ditko's work is always interesting but in this short-lived series he's not given enough time to expand the nature

of the strip, nor its main characters. The back-ups are no better than average and the initial enthusiasm of the editorial team seems to evaporate quickly.~NF
Recommended: 3

THE FLY
!mpact: *17 issues, 1 Annual 1991–1993*

The Fly sums up the whole !mpact range, simple superhero comics. Retaining the 1950s origin, a young boy finds an amulet that gives him all the abilities of a fly (later used more prominently for Spider-Man). The comic deals with the problems of being both a teenager and a superhero. Len Strazewski's plots are lightweight reading without real depth, and the cartoon-style art suits the feel of the book. The Fly also becomes a member of a *Justice League*-style superteam, the Crusaders, during the crossover 'Coming Of The Crusaders' in issue 13. The title interests for a few issues, after which it becomes tired and bland, although the Mike Parobeck art throughout is of note.~SS

FLY MAN
Mighty: *8 issues (31–39) 1965–1966*

Noting the success of the more jocular and realistic style of superheroes being published at Marvel, Archie reinvented themselves as Mighty Comics, remodelling their existing superheroes in the process. Thus *The Fly* became *Fly Man*, and Jerry Siegel's plots became even sillier than they'd been for the previous incarnation. Attempting to mimic Marvel, Siegel picked up on the idea of guest stars, the sometimes corny humour and the bombastic dialogue, but didn't appear to understand how it slotted in alongside other elements to make readable titles. And instead of having Jack Kirby to draw his comics he had Paul Reinman, a man who hadn't let an inability to master a single basic artistic technique deter him from a career as an artist. Not bothering with trivialities such as perspective or anatomy, Reinman had plenty of time left to draw Siegel-written back-ups featuring other revamped Archie superheroes. Their skewed Marvel imitation is bizarre, and best sampled in small doses only by those already submerged in kitsch. With 40 the title was changed again, and, unbelievably, *Mighty Comics Presents* was a further plunge down into the chasm of ineptitude.~FP

FOG CITY COMICS
Stampart: *3 issues 1977–1979*

This wonderful Canadian underground comic started life as a funny-animal anthology and grew into a varied collection. Contributors of the funny-animal strips in 1 include Norm Drew, Mark Newgarden and the scatologically-

minded Rand Holmes, but the highpoint was George Metzger's wonderfully evocative reminiscence 'Comic Book Addict'. The remaining two issues again featured Metzger and Holmes in fine form on more traditional science-fiction material, but the comic's real star was the little known Brent Boates. From the anthropomorphic issue 1 to the stunningly drawn science fiction in 2, Boates excelled astonishingly, making his lack of strips elsewhere very regrettable.~DAR
Recommended: 1–3

FOOD FOR THOUGHT
Gary Millidge: *One-shot 1985*
It doesn't really matter what a famine-relief comic contains, although the fewer politically naïve, heavy-handed satires the better. This UK effort brings together specially created strips with oddments that were clearly not done for the anthology. As you'd expect there are some highlights and some stinkers. Best contribution is Alan Moore and Bryan Talbot's 'Cold Snap', a slick tale of anthropomorphic dinosaurs that starts 'It was early evening in the late Cretaceous…' The point's not new but the broad parody of US consumerism will make you smile anyway. Most of *2000AD*'s stars of the time (Gibbons, Gibson, Mills, O'Neill) make respectable contributions and Grant Morrison completists will need to find it for the Gideon Stargrave two-pager, the art for which makes you appreciate Morrison's writing skills in a whole new way.~FJ

FOOLKILLER
Marvel: *10 issues 1990–1991*
Introduced in Steve Gerber's *Man-Thing*, the Foolkiller executes those he deems to be fools. Depressed over his father's murder, bank employee Kurt Gerhardt loses his job, wife and home, and settles for work in a burger joint when other attempts to find employment fail. Seeing the previous Foolkiller on TV he begins a correspondence and assumes the identity, starting by killing local muggers and drug dealers. Pencil artist J.J. Birch is unspectacular throughout, making this very much Gerber's title. He uses the series as a treatise on the acceptance and fear of violence in society and to study what transforms someone into a vigilante and how far the obsession can progress. Gerhardt's rite of passage in 4 is truly frightening. Why this works so much better than *The Punisher* in exploring similar territory is that *Foolkiller* concentrates on Gerhardt's entire life, not just his costumed escapades. The series overruns in making its point, but has a satisfactory conclusion.~WJ
Recommended: 4, 5

THE FOOT SOLDIERS
Dark Horse: *4 issues 1996*
Once again, the future's a dismal, oppressive time with all the heroes gone. They've left their accessories, though, to be found by three teenage runaways kicking against the pricks. The trio acquire useful relics, and proceed to battle the odds and inspire a downtrodden population. Writer Jim Kreuger's put a lot of thought into the concept and packs the comic with innovative ideas, and his enthusiasm and proselytising in the editorial pages are heartwarming. He's managed to concoct a rarity, a superhero comic that for all its strained allegory and referential material aims for the stars and makes quite a distance. Michael Avon Oeming and Jason Martin's artwork adequately portrays the grim future, and they draw a nice set of big boots. Kreuger's to be commended for aspiring to more than superheroes by numbers, and is a name to remember. Following the conclusion the team make a short stopover in the showcase title *Asylum*.~FP
Recommended: 1–4

FORBIDDEN KNOWLEDGE
Last Gasp: *2 issues 1975, 1978*
As the title suggested, this was a compendium of facts too shocking to be common knowledge. Amongst the contents were such shockers as 'The True Story Of The Hellfire Club' and 'The Castrators Of Russia' in 1, and 'The Man They Couldn't Hang'. This is in addition to a number of more unmentionable subjects. Creatively, only the three pages by Brent Boates in 1 stand out, making this a fun read, but not an essential one.~DAR

Dark Mansion of FORBIDDEN LOVE
DC: *4 issues 1971–1972*
Despite mystery comics being popular with many females, this mainly well-produced Gothic romance series never hit the mark, though issue 1 does contain some spectacular Tony DeZuniga artwork in a full-length story. The title changed to the more asexually appealing *Forbidden Tales of Dark Mansion* with issue 5.~HY

FORBIDDEN TALES OF DARK MANSION
DC: *11 issues (5–15) 1972–1974*
After a patchy first few issues continuing from *Dark Mansion Of Forbidden Love*, this settled down to become one of DC's better mystery titles. 5 contained a Gothic romance story left over from the previous incarnation, memorable only for the heroine's uncanny resemblance to Wonder Woman in her white catsuit period. 6 contained inventory material, including a decent Jack Kirby story left over

from his *Spirit World* magazine From 7 on the comic contained new mystery stories written by Jack Oleck, Robert Kanigher and Michael Fleisher, and predominantly drawn by Filipino artists. Highlights were provided by Alfredo Alcala (9–11, 13), the little known, but highly talented Ernie Santiago (8), and, best of all, Alex Nino (8, 12, 14) and Nestor Redondo (14). American artists Howard Chaykin (7), Gil Kane (13), George Evans (14) and a young Dan Green (14, 15) also contributed. While none of the stories were ground-breaking they were often raised to greater heights by exceptionally fine art. This was never more so than the case of the title's masterpiece, Oleck's vampiric 'They Walk By Night', graced with the astonishing artwork of Bill Payne in 8.~DAR
Recommended: 8, 10, 12, 14, 15

FORBIDDEN WORLDS
ACG: *145 issues 1951–1967*

Suspense anthology that has a plethora of vampires, ghosts, witches, werewolves and even a were-spider populating the early issues and 'Exploring the Supernatural' as a tagline. The advent of the Comics Code in 1954 put a stop to the staple fare of *Forbidden Worlds*, and a temporary hiatus saw the comic renovated from 35 with a new tagline of 'Strange Adventure'. It might not have seemed so at the time, but this was for the best, forcing writer and editor Richard E. Hughes to stretch himself a little, resulting in a stronger comic. He operated under numerous aliases, even to the extent of conceiving fake biographies for the likes of 'Zev Zimmer'. Artist Ogden Whitney began appearing from 35, and there's even a strip by Leonard Starr in 37. Al Williamson is an occasional contributor and other regular artists like John Forte and the mysterious John R, probably John Rosenberger, were suited to the material supplied. The popularity of superheroes sees the introduction of the mundane Magicman as lead feature in 125, but he's dropped for the final five issues. While never matching the contemporary EC titles on which it was originally based, *Forbidden Worlds* has far more to offer than most other similar titles, ranking far above similar Marvel product, for instance. Richard E. Hughes was a fine, imaginative writer of science-fiction suspense, and had a good eye for contributing artists, making this a decent read more often than not. 75 is a good sample. John Buscema débuts with a story about a clock foretelling the future, John Forte draws an ironic commentary on modern furnishing, the magnificent Ogden Whitney's contribution has a man attempting to break a speed record, but managing much more, and there's also Paul Reinman, but you can't have everything. *Forbidden Worlds* is also the place where Herbie

first came to life in 73. He's an obese, bespectacled, semi-comatose child able to do anything or converse with anything, including going back through time when powered with special lollipops. It's insane stuff by Hughes and Whitney, and would recur in 94, but really hits its stride with 110, 114 and 116, at which point Herbie graduates to his own title.~WJ
Recommended: 110, 114, 116

FORCE WORKS
Marvel: *22 issues 1994–1996*

Created after the dissolution of *Avengers West Coast*, Iron Man's new team is intended to act 'proactively, in the interests of defense and security', which translates as 'getting our retaliation in first.' It's consistent for the USAgent to go for that line, but the other founders – Spider-Woman, the Scarlet Witch, and, fleetingly, Wonder Man – seem badly chosen for such an aggressive policy. Not that it really matters, as writers Dan Abnett and Andy Lanning never really pursue said policy, treating the team as just another bunch of people in tights and armour, and Tom Tenney's impenetrable artwork means you wouldn't really be able to tell if they did! Wonder Man's replacement with the enigmatic alien warrior Century creates a not very interesting mystery that occupied much of the title's run. Other diversions along the way include a deeply embarrassing run-in with an aboriginal superhero, and a tedious crossover with *War Machine*. The title folded before it reached a quarter of the run of the comic it replaced, and was largely unmourned.~HS

FOREVER PEOPLE
DC: *11 issues 1971–1972, 6-issue miniseries 1988*

Part of Jack Kirby's highly acclaimed *Fourth World Saga*, the original series dealt with the adventures of five young, idealistic New Genesis Gods – Mark Moonrider, Serifan, Big Bear, Vykin the Black and Beautiful Dreamer – during and immediately after their attempt to rescue the kidnapped Beautiful Dreamer from Darkseid. Filled with many moments of Kirby genius with ties to *New Gods*, the Apokolips/New Genesis war often seems little more than a game to the youthful team, whose ability to combine themselves into the single entity they call the Infinity Man might well have made them major players had they taken things more seriously. Amidst the inevitability of war and constant struggle apparent in *The New Gods* and *Mister Miracle*, *Forever People* offered a taste of the carefree paradise and idealism of New Genesis at its best. 4–9 also included reprints of Kirby's 1940s *Sandman* stories.

If Kirby's intention had been to suggest that the Forever People were too young to be cynical and too innocent to be affected by the war, in the 1980s revival J.M. DeMatteis saw to it that their passage into adulthood was not so smooth, using them as allegory for the 'Me Decade' of the 1980s against the idealism of the 1960s. Kirby's series left them stranded in the otherworldly paradise Adon, and DeMatteis picks up perhaps a decade later when they've grown up and apart, until circumstances force them to take a long hard look at what they've become and how that compares to what they should have been.~JC

Recommended: Series one 1–11

FORGOTTEN REALMS
DC: *25 issues 1989–1991*

Forgotten Realms adapts the characters and settings from the TSR novels and role-playing games. If you enjoy the original source material you'll probably enjoy these light fantasy comics as well. If you don't... well, there's some nice Rags Morales and Dave Simons art in the first 15 issues.~FP

FOUR STAR BATTLE TALES
DC: *5 issues 1973*

Reprints of 1950s war stories from the DC archives, mixing examples of series like 'The War That Time Forgot' (set on an island where dinosaurs still live, by Andru and Esposito) and Johnny Cloud by Irv Novick with one-off war tales by the likes of Berni Krigstein (5), Mort Drucker, Russ Heath and Joe Kubert.~NF

Recommended: 5

FOUR STAR SPECTACULAR
DC: *6 issues 1976–1977*

Wholly undistinguished reprint title, the highlights of which are a Flash story written in the 1940s and redrawn for publication in the first issue, the original art deemed too shoddy, and a 1940s Blackhawk story in the final issue.~HY

FOX AND THE CROW
DC: *108 issues 1951–1968*

This was originally a series of Columbia Pictures (1941–1947) and then United Productions of America (1948–1950) cartoons. DC published the characters in the 1940s in *Real Screen Comics* before giving them their own title in December 1951. Fauntleroy Fox is constantly having to protect himself from Crawford Crow's chiselling nature, and there's no saying which one of them will come off best in these short (4-6 page) stories. Mostly written by Cecil Beard (whose animation credits include *Bambi* and *Fantasia*) and drawn by Jim Davis, the series is good-humoured, and made more interesting by having neither character be the constant victor. Back-up strips such as 'Flippity and Flop' and 'The Hound And The Hare' gave way eventually to all Fox And

Crow issues before, in the mid-60s, DC started to introduce some new concepts, such as 'The Brat Finks' ('rock-n-rollicking rascals') and the very popular Stanley And His Monster (95–108), which took over the title completely with 109. Lisping Stanley believes his monster is a 3000-year-old dog, and they have adventures such as meeting Napoleon's ghost and discovering that the reason for his keeping his hand inside his coat is to keep his socks up. A good series, if not outstanding.~NF

Recommended: 95

FOX Comics
Fox: *23 issues 1984–1989*
Fantagraphics: *5 issues (24–28) 1989–1991*

Beginning as home-made offshoot of an Australian comics fanzine, by its final issue *Fox* had progressed into a fine anthology showing the best of contemporary Australian comics creators. Taking their lead from the self-published comics appearing in Britain in the early 1980s, 1–11 are A5-sized photocopied zines. Enthusiasm outstrips talent, but Martin Trengrove's 'Roscoe The Dawg', a private-eye strip, features polished cartooning from the off. By 3 British small-press creators are incorporated, though often with strips already seen in Britain. Eddie Campbell's 'The Pajama Girl', about an odd Australian murder case, in 5 is the standout of the early issues, and Ed Pinsent and Phil Elliott also submit decent strips. Meanwhile Fil Barlow and Greg Gates are developing very quickly, and Paul Harris' two-page masturbation strip in 7 is an excellent study of facial expressions.

With 11 Fox, by now being printed instead of photocopied, began running colour covers, and the final small-size issue, 13, is a decent all-round read with a theme of EC comics. Ed Pinsent analyses them, several artists attempt to emulate them, and David Bird and Stuart Mann turn in a pastiche of 'My World'. By far the most notable aspect of a generally decent issue, though, is the outstanding art of Darrel Merritt, submitting both a pencilled study of trench warfare and a cartoony strip of childhood fears. Tragically, 16's cover apart, his only recurrence is a disappointing three pages in 18. Considering the better production in magazine size, 14 is a disappointingly trivial issue, with only David Hodson's Rick Geary-like observational whimsy being of note. It's a momentary blip in the steady progress, though, and more British contributors (Glenn Dakin, Chris Flewitt, Steve Way, John Bagnall) mix with the ever-improving Dillon, Ian Eddy and Tony Thorne, a contributor from the start. The fault of issues in the mid-teens is an over-reliance on stilted whimsy, with only Hodson consistently entertaining with the form.

18 introduces the idea of serials to Fox,

although the first, 'Lifestyles Of The Small And Insignificant', is more a series of episodes under a collective title. It's written by Lazarus Dobelsky and drawn by Ian Eddy and begins as poignant tales about life's embarrassing moments, gradually moving beyond into presumably autobiographical recollections. Eddy's cartooning is very expressive, and it's very funny. If only the same could be said of 'Sex' (20–23), which is the least salacious and most tedious musing on the topic you'll ever read. Far more successful is 'Tattoo Man' in 24–28. After being beaten up at a carnival, a man awakens to find his body covered in tattoos. David Hodson's scripts are well matched by the moody art of Greg Gates for a diverting and mysterious idea.

19 has a landmark with the début of the utterly mad Linzee Arnold, who's in most issues thereafter. Considerably older than most of the other contributors, his stories are of adolescence in 1950s Tasmania. His crowded cartooning, complete with labelling, instinctive story-telling and very funny anecdotes are an instant highlight, contrasting with the introspection of several other strips. 'Sex' runs from 19 to 24 but it's matched by a succession of Eddie Campbell strips from 20 onwards, now creating material specifically for *Fox*. The first Fantagraphics issue increases the page-count to good effect, and it's ironic that, still under David Vodicka's editorship, *Fox* instantly betters any Fantagraphics anthology title before or since. All the Fantagraphics issues have at least two excellent strips, with Phil Elliott and Paul Grist's story detailing a singer's rise to success in 27 a standout.~FP
Recommended: 13, 18, 20, 22, 24–28

FRANCIS Brother Of The Universe
Marvel: *One-shot 1980*

If you've been yearning to read the life-story of the first Franciscan monk in comic form, look no further. Taking great care to conform to the approved Catholic version, there's very little of the Dr Doolittle stuff and plenty of handwringing doubt. The interesting artistic combination of John Buscema and Marie Severin is sympathetic, but Buscema carries his baggage with him, and when Francis receives Jesus' stigmata it could be a scene from *Thor*.~WJ

FRANK
Nemesis: *4-issue miniseries 1994*

Dan Chichester (not very many words) and Denys Cowan (extremely sketchy pencils) come together to update Frankenstein so that the monster can have lots of particularly violent fights with the world that doesn't understand him. Ahhhh. The word 'predictable' comes to mind.~FJ

FRANK
Fantagraphics: *1 issue + 1996 to date*

Jim Woodring's surreal hero surfaces once more in his own comic-sized series. In a hallucinatory world just one step to the side of nightmare Frank struggles to make sense of the baffling events and changing environment around him. As straightforward as an innocent child's dream, full of symbols and bizarre creatures, and as frightening as your worst nightmare, *Frank* communicates on a wordless but profound level. For more Frank adventures see *Tantalising Stories*.~FJ

FRANKENSTEIN
Dell: *4 issues 1964 (1), 1966–1967 (2–4)*

The first issue adapts the classic Boris Karloff-led 1930s horror film, and manages a very creditable job of it. The remainder, well, they were part of Dell's superhero triumvirate based on old horror characters, not necessarily a bad idea in principle, but in practice... Frankie has a skintight red costume and a white crew cut, although this is sometimes open to question, as the art throughout is by Tony Tallarico. On seeing this you'd question if Tallarico knew which end of the pencil he should be drawing with. The writer wisely selected anonymity as the preferable option.~WJ

The FRANKENSTEIN Monster
Marvel: *18 issues 1973–1975*

Considering that the success of Marvel Comics is founded on bombast and in-your-face artwork, it's surprising to realise that many of their early- to mid-1970s titles were deliberately understated. Such was initially the case with *Frankenstein*, which gave notice of its intent by adapting Mary Shelley's original novel in the first two issues, rather than any of the film versions. Gary Friedrich's script is workable, and the subtle and expressive artwork of Mike Ploog creates a very nice mood. The series continues in the 19th century, but Friedrich couldn't maintain the quality, and once Ploog left with 6 the artwork was never more than adequate. Doug Moench becomes writer with 12, and sets his stories in the present day, but his work was sloppy, and matched by the art. 1–6 are worth a glance for Ploog's work, but stay well away from the rest.~WJ

FREAK FORCE
Image: *18 issues, 1993–1995*

Following build-up, back-ups and hype in Erik Larsen's *Savage Dragon*, the early issues of Freak Force lived up to expectations. Old-timer Super Patriot and the experienced Dart team up with Mighty Man, Rapture, Ricochet, Barbaric and Horridus. They're five of Chicago's younger and mostly incompetent superheroes, providing a light-hearted romp reminiscent of early Giffen and DeMatteis *Justice Leagues*. Giffen's plots (although the script was Larsen's) no doubt played a large factor in this.

In amongst the jokes Larsen and Giffen nonetheless manage to weave some entertaining and clever plots. A well-executed mystery over Mighty Man's true identity, swimming with red herrings, which reaches a conclusion only obvious in retrospect, provides the most entertainment. While early issues received much critical acclaim, sales were less encouraging, and an inevitable round of team-ups attempting to boost sales in 8–12 leads into to a tedious alien-invasion story-line, after which the series never quite regains its way. Attempts to take itself more seriously by becoming grim and gritty only served to drive away the fans who had enjoyed the fun of the earlier issues. It ground to a halt with issue 18 and the characters went back to their old jobs as Savage Dragon's supporting cast.~JC
Recommended: 1–7, 10

FREAK SHOW
Dark Horse: *One-shot 1992*

The Residents are a difficult band to describe to newcomers. They're four musicians who keep their identities a secret behind giant eyeball masks. Their music is always adventurous and very uncommercial. *Freak Show* is a concept album with each song telling the story of a different freak. Some friends were asked to interpret these songs as strips and this is the result. Given its origins, it was never going to be entirely coherent: the disparate styles work against any sense of coherence and Dave McKean's 'Lillie', in particular, disrupts the visual identity of the book. That said, there are some interesting pieces by the likes of Kyle Baker and Savage Pencil. Particularly worth reading are Brian Bolland's 'Harry The Head', Matt Howarth's 'Jello Jack The Boneless Boy' and Richard Sala's 'Herman the Human Mole'.~NF

FREAKS
Monster: *4 issues 1992–1993*

A bit late in the day for an adaptation of Tod Browning's infamous film about a gold-digger who marries a sideshow freak for his money only to have a horrible revenge visited upon her when his deformed carnival buddies find out what she's up to. Jim Woodring's script is bought to life by F. Solano Lopez's clear pencilling, although Lopez's tidiness doesn't serve the story well during its muddy, rain-drenched climax. Woodring does his best to bring the characters to life, and though flaws in the original film stop the script being truly great, it remains worth reading.~NF

FREAKS AMOUR
Dark Horse: *3-issue miniseries 1993*

Following a nuclear incident known as 'Caliban's Night', 77,000 people are irradiated and mutated to form an ostracised underclass. A harrowing social commentary deftly adapted from the Tom DeHaven novel, it succeeds both as a modern tragedy and a horror story.~HS
Recommended: 1–3

FREEDOM FIGHTERS
DC: *15 issues 1977–1978*

Appallingly sloppy and featuring staggeringly inane villains, Bob Rozakis scripts were a standard feature of DC's second- and third-string titles during the mid- to late 1970s. Here, however, he redeems himself with a well-considered, scintillating revival of a group of 1940s characters. Only joking. It's all rubbish apart from 12, in which the mustard is just about cut. Rozakis did later redeem himself, though, with *'Mazing Man*.~FP

FREEX
Malibu: *18 issues, 1 Special 1993–1994*

Freex was Gerard Jones' attempt at a realistic teen superhero team. They're a bunch of babies injected with a drug/computer virus by the enigmatic nurse Wetware Mary: when they reach their teens their latent powers are unleashed. The team includes a strong guy, a plasma-firing street kid and the all-too-obligatory-these-days computer hacker and surfer, all on the run to hunt down the nurse and those responsible for transforming them into 'Freex'. While the origin stories are different, the overall plot wanes. It's all adolescent *angst*: 'Who are we?', 'What have we become?', 'Why does the world hate us?' etc. It's all far too reminiscent of Marvel's X-comics. There's decent art in the early issues, with 13 giving a huge nod (more of a headbang, really) to Jack Kirby both in the script and the art, supplied by Scott Kolins and Jonathan Holdredge. 17 has a pointless guest appearance from Rune.~TP

FRENCH ICE
Renegade: *13 issues 1987–1988*

French Ice offered readers two classic French humour characters not previously translated into English: Lelong's cantankerous old woman Carmen Cru and Binet's smart-arse dog, Kador. Most readers passed, and they're not entirely to be blamed. While Lelong's cartooning is a delight, his stories of irascible bull-headedness rely to a great extent on a knowledge of French life and an acquaintance with little French peasant women. Carmen Cru, around whom the earlier issues are built, may be a national treasure but she doesn't travel well. Kador, on the other hand, fits in with a long tradition of animal-joke crackers *à la* Garfield, with the added humour of his owner's continual marital problems, and by the last issue Kador dominated the book.~FJ

FRENCH TICKLERS
Kitchen Sink: *3 issues 1989–1990*

Continued from Renegade's *French Ice*, Kitchen Sink wisely added more elements to the staple diet of Lelong and Binet, relying less on the dubious charms of Carmen Cru and more on the selling power of known names such as Moebius and Franquin. Even so it only managed to limp along for three issues. Humour is obviously not as universal as we'd like to think.~FJ

FRESCAZIZIS
Last Gasp: *One-shot 1977*

Best described as a hallucinatory journey through the artist's subconscious, *Frescazizis* was Melinda Gebbie's solo title. Typical of Gebbie's early work, the art has a wonderfully sensuous, almost art nouveau line, and a cavalier disregard for artistic convention. Those looking for a coherent story-line would be best advised to look elsewhere, as the many, frequently sexual short stories on offer here are very short on conventional narrative.~DAR

FRIENDS
Renegade: *3 issues 1987*

Attempting to ape Winsor McKay art is no bad thing, and Bill Dinardi's managed the delicate line characterising McKay's work. He's managed little else, though. While attempting the whimsy of McKay's strips he falls woefully short with twee tales of bonding between Will and his humanoid alien buddy, and the stunning and innovative layouts of McKay elude him entirely. This results in page after page of static talking heads with nothing of interest to say.~WJ

FRIGHT
Atlas: *1 issue 1975*

By the time Atlas began publishing comics Dracula was towards the end of a slow slide from icon of terror to staple of spoofs, but even that doesn't excuse a strip titled 'Son Of Dracula' in which the protagonist assumes the identity of Mr A. Lucard. For once Frank Thorne isn't drawing busty babes, but the story is total cack.~WJ

FRINGE
Caliber: *8 issues 1990–1991*

Nutty telekinetic architect animates superball and is hunted by bald nun. Sounds interesting, no? Sadly muddled and confused, it's very much an amateur effort, notable only for early art from Philip Hester.~WJ
Collection: Fringe (1–4)

The FROGMEN
Dell: *12 issues 1962–1965*

One of small group of 1960s sub-aqua comics. Compared with Dell's usual offerings of the period this title is noteworthy for some surprisingly good artwork from George Evans and Mike Sekowsky among others, and particularly Alex Toth in 5. The back-up strip 'Boy Of The Pacific' was occasionally drawn by Frank Thorne.~SW

FROM BEYOND THE UNKNOWN
DC: *25 issues 1969–1973*

DC's rich legacy of well-drawn science-fiction stories from the 1950s provided adequate material for twenty-five issues of reprints. The actual plots are generally pretty silly, the covers and splash-page teasers being the best thing about them, but artists of note include Murphy Anderson and Carmine Infantino in most issues and 'Al' Toth in 2. 7–17 are forty-eight or sixty-four pages, and the new material by Denny O'Neil and Murphy Anderson in 7 and 8 is neither's best work.~FP

FROM HELL
Tundra: *3 issues 1991–1993*
Kitchen Sink: *7 issues (4–10) 1994–1996*

Alan Moore and Eddie Campbell's *From Hell* concerns the Jack The Ripper murders that occurred in London in the late 1880s, probably the most famous serial killings ever. The perpetrator was never caught. Moore has them committed by the Queen's physician, Sir William Gull, with Victoria's knowledge, to protect her son from a blackmail attempt by a group of prostitutes, one of whom has acted as nursemaid to an illegitimate grand-daughter, the child of Prince 'Eddy' and a shopgirl. Gull is also impelled by his Masonic duty to the crown. As the killings progress he becomes deranged by what he has seen and done, seeking the ultimate, emblematic meaning for his hideous acts in Masonic lore and ritual.

Moore takes the huge body of Ripper scholarship – some of it far from scholarly in tone – and threads through it until he has the means to develop the moral and metaphysical points at the heart of the story. His version of Jack the Ripper starts off as an awful, human tragedy, a monster conjured up by a group of weak people who, once an idea that will get them off the hook has been planted in their brains, cannot forget it. It ends up in an extraordinary vision of evil down the ages. People who object that he's taken his theory from *The Ripper And The Royals*, one of many books on the subject, are missing the point. The point is that the particular and extraordinary circumstances surrounding the Jack The Ripper murders allow the writer to examine certain facets of human nature. They also, of course, ignore the many elements drawn from other sources, all carefully detailed in the appendices for intrigued readers, along with information on which scenes are factual and which have been invented.

Eddie Campbell, illustrating a story which moves from the hideous poverty of the East End of London right through to visionary dreams of Blakean stature, draws extensively on his knowledge of Victorian satirists and illustrators. He adopts an extremely dense, etched style, involving intricate open cross-hatching and the use of very fine lines that you usually associate with printmaking. This is balanced by occasional heavy use of ink, and the many scenes set at night. Occasionally the art unravels at the edges to express extreme emotions. Both he and Moore have researched the project carefully, and it shows, in everything from the correct label on a cocoa tin to the architectural detail of London during the period. There is a tightness and rigidity, echoed in the regular use of page grids, which is juxtaposed by the way certain panels fade out, and the way certain characters are never quite in focus, diffusing into a mass of lines.

From Hell is an extraordinary piece of 'faction', carefully dramatising events, including contradictory evidence, yet also making exciting leaps of the imagination. Moore, as you would expect, brings in all sorts of intriguing odds and ends of Ripperology, from Buffalo Bill Cody to the Mad Monk of Mitre Square and the interest Ian Brady took in the case, while building an overall picture of a time of social unrest, class struggle, racial tension and terrible deprivation. It is beautifully rendered, each panel oozing atmosphere and quietly but firmly supporting the dismal, depressing mood of each of the chapters. In *From Hell* there are no heroes and villains. Judgement is withheld. We are all to be pitied.~FJ
Recommended: 1–10

FROM THE PIT
Fantagor: *1 issue 1994*

Intended as a seven-issue series, this Richard Corben magazine is now merely a tantalising glimpse at what could have been a great horror comic. The art is some of Corben's best of the 1990s, and a nice H.P. Lovecraft-adapted back-up (reprinted from *Slow Death*) only adds to the disappointment of the title's untimely demise.~DAR

FRONTLINE COMBAT
EC: *15 issues 1951–1953*
Russ Cochran: *6 issues 1995 to date*

The immediate success of *Two-Fisted Tales* led to this companion title. Editor Harvey Kurtzman used *Two-Fisted*'s stable of artists to draw stories from his plots and layouts, but *Frontline Combat*

was initially distinct, with more stories focusing on the hardware enabling effective warfare, exemplified by 'War Machines' in 5. Later issues featured a large selection of plane-based tales. The artwork was stunning throughout from the likes of Wally Wood, Jack Davis, Kurtzman in early issues and George Evans from 9, and the team of John Severin and Will Elder. Wood highlights are the heart-rending 'A Baby' in 10, 'The Charge Of The Light Brigade' in 4 and a tale contrasting the nobility of Rommel with the atrocities of the Nazis in 3, while Davis' speciality was evoking the dirt and grime of war in almost every issue. Alex Toth contributes two airplane masterpieces in 8 and 12.

An ambitious and never completed project encompassing both EC's war titles and intending to tell the entire story of the US Civil War began in 9. Opening with a biography of Abraham Lincoln and the attack on Fort Sumpter, it's the only Civil War special to appear in *Frontline Combat*. There are other theme issues, though, an excellent detailing of the Iwo Jima campaign in 7, and an Air Force special in 12. Notable biographies include Julius Caesar in 8, Stonewall Jackson (5), Immelman (14) and both Geronimo and Napoleon in 10. Despite lacking the variety of *Two-Fisted Tales*, as a run *Frontline Combat* is of higher quality. It's also without that title's initial fumblings, and it was cancelled before there could be a misguided change of direction. Issues are currently being reprinted in the original format.~FP
Recommended: 2, 3, 5–10, 14
Collection: Frontline Combat (boxed set of 1–15)

FUN BOYS Spring Special
Tundra: *One-shot 1991*

Fondly remembered days of childhood friendship and comic collecting are deftly contrasted with the disturbing experiences that children accept. Jeff Bonivert's subtlety and illustrative cartooning is a joy. A short back-up strip contrasts the main story with the characters now as cynical teenagers.~FP
Recommended

FUNNY ANIMALS
Apex Novelties: *One-shot 1972*

An anti-vivisection benefit comic edited by future *Crumb* documentary maker Terry Zwigoff, featuring a number of top under-ground cartoonists. For some reason many, including principal artist R. Crumb, somewhat missed the point, and a lot of the stories feature violence against animals as entertainment. It's redeemed, however, by Art Spiegelman's devastatingly poignant *Maus* strip, which still retains its power to shock today.~DAR
Recommended

FURY

Marvel: *One-shot 1994*

Giant one-shot telling the background and origin of Nick Fury and S.H.I.E.L.D. It clarifies inconsistencies and, somewhat unconvincingly, 'corrects' certain events in S.H.I.E.L.D.'s previously revealed history. For completists only.~APS

FURY of S.H.I.E.L.D.

Marvel: *4-issue miniseries 1995*

Great little number with Howard Chaykin on script and slick Corky Lehmkuhl pencils. Plenty of intrigue and double-cross as the heads of S.H.I.E.L.D. and HYDRA team up. Any comic featuring Nick Fury at a Smokestoppers Anonymous meeting must be worth the entrance fee. The decoder supplied with issue 4 is one of the better-comic book gimmicks.~APS

Recommended: 1–3

FUSION

Eclipse: *17 issues 1987–1989*

Fusion is a space opera that follows the adventures of the cargo ship Tsunami, crewed by a mixture of humans (Indio, Dow Cook) and animalistic aliens (Haven, a bird, Tan, a squirrel, Alshain, a cat, Herrick, a flightless bird and Carz, a lion). 'The Soulstar Commission' in 1–5 sets the tone for the whole series: conflict, tragedy and betrayal as the Tsunami becomes caught in a war over a Royal House. Thereafter the stories concentrate as much as possible on characterisation, losing the plot to an extent that isn't helped by the almost constant shifting of writers from issue 6. Originally written by Steve Barnes (1–5), the following twelve issues credit no less than six different writers, including Steve Gallacci (7–9, 16–17) and Christy Marx (14–15). Most of the artwork's by Gallacci and Lela Dowling, neither of whose work is particularly bold or dynamic. Better than the lead feature are Ken Macklin's clever back-ups Dr Watchstop in 1–5 and 7–8, and The Weasel Patrol (5–17). The latter is a deliciously frenzied comedy shoot-'em-up featuring armed and dangerous, but mostly stupid anthropomorphic characters. Check *Fusion* out for the back-ups.~NF

FUTURAMA

Slave Labor: *3 issues 1989*

Art Deco science fiction *à la Metropolis*, or the far superior Hernandez brothers comic *Mister X*. Set in generic future city Kronos, Christopher Klein's silly script has rival night club owners Frank Dekker and baddie Karl Von Horst fighting over beautiful singer Zarah Heiberg. Zarah is engaged to Frank, and exclusively contracted to his establishment, The Egyptian. The singers at Karl's Club Dementia are all robots, so he sets in motion a wicked scheme to convince Zhara that she's actually an android named Zara. In addition to satisfying his own depraved appetites, Karl hopes that Zhara/Zara's drugged, robotic performances at Dementia will cause Frank to forget all about his business, leaving The Egyptian ripe for takeover... Although *Futurama* tries far too hard for it to be really 'cool', the sexy, streamlined artwork of Ken Holewcyznski is worth a mention. While clearly influenced by the 'clear line' style of Spanish artist Daniel Torres, Holewcysnski's gift for retro design still deserves a better showcase than this instantly forgettable piece of fluff.~AL

THE FUTURIANS

Marvel: *Graphic Novel, 1983*
Lodestone: *3 issues 1985–1986*
Eternity: *1 issue 1987*

The graphic novel tells the origin story for this group of superheroes, and it's a complicated one, involving two warring factions from Earth's future who come back to the 1980s to fight their last battle. The villains have arrived with a full warfleet, but the white hats were only able to send one representative. This representative gathers a group of people with various talents and tricks them into undergoing a process that turns them into superheroes, complete with helmets and costumes, and immediately sends them into battle. The other issues, which are published as a collection in the Eternity book, are set in the aftermath of the battle.

Even though many elements of the story-lines have been seen elsewhere, and more than once, Dave Cockrum (as writer) has put in a lot of imagination where it counts, making the comic a fresh read, with solid characters and plots. True, the characters aren't particularly striking as individuals, but Cockrum handles them well as a team, and the tension of their forced origin is always simmering quietly in the background. Cockrum's pencilled artwork doesn't call attention to itself, but tells the story very clearly, and it's a story that deserves to be continued.~FC

Recommended: Marvel Graphic Novel, Eternity collection

G-8 AND HIS BATTLE ACES
Blazing: *1 issue 1991*

Strange attempt to revive G-8, the pulp fighter ace from World War I, in which the green monstrosity Grun hogs the limelight, happily killing Allies and Hun alike. On the flip side of the comic is 'The Spider's Web' (by the same creative team of Chuck Dixon and Sam Glanzman), which explains what happens between a couple of panels in the G-8 story when Grun passes through a time portal and meets another pulp hero, the Web-Man. Nothing more than a curiosity.~NF

GABRIEL
Caliber: *One-shot 1995*

Extrapolating an interesting alternate papal-controlled Glasgow, *Gabriel* ultimately comes down to an all-too-easily resolved God vs Satan conflict. The muddied story-telling obscures what could have been a far better tale, but David Hill's black and white artwork is excellent, echoing the disciplined standards of 1960s British adventure comics.~FP

GAG
Harrier: *7 issues 1987–1989*

Good old Harrier, not just there to fill the shelves with substandard sexist-fan crap, they also picked up on the 1980s British small press, and there are some excellent creators in this anthology. Eddie Campbell is the most successful graduate, and there are plenty of his slices of life, but Glenn Dakin's contributions are consistently better. Both are below par, though, in the best overall issue, 5, with Phil Elliott, Paul Grist, Ed Pinsent and Steve Way carrying the day. Nothing in *Gag* changes the world, and it rarely lives up to the title, but there's a gem in every issue, with John Bagnall's tale of backwoods religious repression in 6 particularly memorable. 1–3 are standard comic size, with the remainder magazine format.~FP
Recommended: *5–7*

GALACTIC GUARDIANS
Marvel: *4-issue miniseries 1994*

Dull and pointless *Guardians of the Galaxy* spin-off. Biff, Bang, Pow all the way.~FP

Super Villain Classics: GALACTUS, THE ORIGIN
Marvel: *One-shot 1983*

Origin of Galactus using panels from Lee/Kirby *Thor* issues, heavily edited with new bridging text by Mark Gruenwald.~APS

GAMBIT
Marvel: *4-issue miniseries 1993–1994*

Spin-off from the *X-Men*, this Creole mutant (with the power to charge playing cards with energy that transforms them into deadly weapons) is embroiled in a bitter feud between his thief clan and the Clan of Assassins in his hometown of New Orleans. It starts promisingly with lots of dark atmosphere, but is soon spoiled by the all-too-familiar expositional dialogue during over-extended fight sequences. One laughable scene has Gambit at his wife's bedside as she lies in a coma. In burst the baddies, who proceed to destroy the bedroom around her in a frenzied fight. She, of course, is unaffected by all this. Accompanied by lots of dodgy accents – 'Vite, vite boys! Let's be gettin' this over' – makes it one for true fans only.~TP

GAMBIT AND THE XTERNALS
Marvel: *4-issue miniseries 1995*

One of the miniseries in Marvel's 'Age of Apocalypse', which placed the X-Men characters in an alternate world where their enemy rules the Earth. *Gambit and the Xternals* was probably the least interesting of the series, pitting the Cajun card-thrower and the immortal Externals against nothing very interesting as they attempt to steal the M'Kraan crystal and restore normality to a fractured universe. It's more cosmic than the other 'Age of Apocalypse' books, but lacks the character-driven analysis which made the best ones worth the effort, leaving a story that would be dull no matter what world it was set on.~JC

GAMERA
Dark Horse: *4-issue miniseries 1996*

Those outside *Godzilla* fandom will be unaware that Gamera is a giant-flying-turtle equivalent of the Big G, and the guardian of the universe to boot. He's summoned via an amulet by a psychic teenager, and called forth initially to fight a genetically engineered giant pterodactyl. *Gamera* is competent without ever being outstanding, but should appeal to all enthusiasts of big monster movies.~WJ

GAMMARAUDERS
DC: *10 issues 1989*

Based on the role-playing game, this reads and looks like an inventive TV cartoon show. The story focuses on Jok Tadsworth, handler of a bioborg (a giant combination of beast and technology), and his well-characterised fellow-handlers. Martin King and Dave Cooper's artwork (most issues) is delightful, and Peter Gillis' scripts are light and witty.~WJ

GANG BUSTERS
DC: *67 issues 1947–1958*

Based on the popular US radio show (1936–1957) in which true crime stories were broadcast and the FBI offered descriptions of wanted criminals, *Gang Busters* began as a fifty-two-page comic (1–23) with four stories and a 'Case Book Mystery' in which the reader was given the opportunity to spot where the criminal had slipped up before the strip ended. This feature became 'You Be The Detective' before being dropped in 1956. With artwork generally above average, the stories, as varied as possible, attempt to pick out the more interesting cases (catching criminals with a police badge, the criminal in the line-up accusing the eyewitness of the crime etc). Artists include Dan Barry, Ruben Moreira and Mort Meskin, with occasional strips by John Buscema, Frank Frazetta and Jack Kirby.~NF

THE GARGOYLE
Marvel: *4-issue miniseries 1985*

As introduced in *The Defenders*, the Gargoyle was a rare interesting idea sinking in a sea of mediocrity. Already in his eighties, Isaac Christians didn't want to become older and die, and was granted his wish by a demon at the cost of being trapped in the body of a gargoyle and therefore shunned by all who knew him. In this series Christians learns the Gargoyle was a malevolent living entity who was transferred into his old body. In parts charming and wistful, particularly when dealing with Christians' past and lost love, and offering some interesting theological theories, the whole never quite gels. It's because the Gargoyle's a superhero and therefore he has to fight, but J.M. DeMatteis and Mark Badger aren't very interested in that concept.~FP

GASP
ACG: *4 issues 1967*

A horror anthology title with nothing outstanding, but with the odd flash of originality in each issue. For instance, in 'The Devil's A Businessman' (1) we see time-and-motion studies being applied in hell, in 'The Fourth Wish' (2) there's a nice spin on the genie-in-a-bottle yarn, and 'You've Got The Wrong Ghosts'(3) is unusual for dealing with cowardice in war. Even in the best stories, the endings fall flat, but you can tell that they're trying.~FC

GAY COMIX
Kitchen Sink: *5 issues 1983–1984*
Bob Ross: *18 issues + (6–23), 1 Special 1985 to date*

Initially an annual collection of comics by or about gay people, edited by Howard Cruse (1–4) and then Robert Triptow (5–13), with issue 6 Bob Ross, publisher of San Francisco's *Bay Area Reporter*, took over and announced a quarterly schedule. Though the contributors didn't have to be gay or lesbian themselves, the content of the stories was always predominantly about homosexual experience. Generally, this meant a light-hearted approach, but harder-edged tales also found their way in and even with the comedy, the difficulties and politics of gay life were never far from the surface. Kitchen Sink's issues contain stories from such notables as Lee Marrs (1–4), Roberta Gregory (1–5), Howard Cruse (1–5), Jerry Mills (4, 5) and Tim Barela (5). Mills' 'Poppers' stories and Barela's 'Leonard And Larry' strips would become firm favourites with the readership, the former a clean, bright comedy about sexy, dumb boys with big muscles, the latter a soap opera about a mature gay couple. 9 is an all 'Poppers' issue, and 'Leonard And Larry' featured in the 1992 special.

The change in publisher didn't affect the series' style or direction to any great degree, although Cruse was a less common contributor (*Wendel* débuted in 6, but the only other Cruse strips are in 10 and 14). There was some effort to give the book an international flavour, with Patrick Marcel's funny animal strip 'Night Of The Hunter' and other contributions from 3–12, Theo Bogart in 2, and Brits Howard Stangroom and Steve Lowther in most issues from 11 onwards. Their 'Ride The Wild Surf' in 14 is an effective *Archie* and Romance parody rolled into one. With 14 Andy Mangels became editor and has generally tried to include shorter strips from a wider range of contributors, some more successful than others. Ivan Velez Jr, Roberta Gregory, Donna Barr, Jennifer Camper and Ralf Konig became regulars. Of the newer contributors, Catherine Doherty (23) looks most promising. 19 was an Alison Bechdel special and 22 was a funny-animal special with Waller and Worley's *Omaha*, plus contributions from Leanne Franson, Diane Di Massa and Joan Hilty.

As an anthology, *Gay Comix* has suffered from a lack of depth to the story-telling, the

special issues being the only place where a consistent quality of contribution has been apparent. Too many issues seem to have earnest but dull contributions, or more of the same old jokes about gay life. Mangels has attempted to address this with the themed or single-contributor issues and, to be fair, there is something in each issue to make it worth reading.~NF
Recommended: 1–6, 14, 15, 19, 22

Brother Power, The GEEK
DC: *2 issues, 1968*
Vertigo: *One-shot 1993*

Well, where shall we begin? This series was ridiculed for decades, and only in recent years has DC owned up to it. 'Here is the real-life scene of the dangers in Hippie-Land!' exclaims the first cover. As you may have gathered, *The Geek* is a period piece set in the heyday of flower power from ageing hippy Joe Simon, the man who gave us Captain America and instigated various comic-book genres. Brother Power is a tailor's dummy who's brought to life by a bolt of lightning and given superstrength (hey, this is comics, remember). Befriended by hippies he helps them further the cause of peace, love and flower power, beats up a bunch of Hell's Angels, goes to school, gets kidnapped by the Psychedelic Circus (oh yes) and forced to appear in their freak show, escapes and naturally runs for Congress, is hounded by the police and eventually drowns. And this is only the first issue. The second is just as, er… inventive. The Geek is actually an original, well-crafted, enjoyable, if indulgent, tale that every comic reader should really experience. Just wear a flower in your hair to get you in the mood, though.

Of course in some ways *The Geek* could be seen as the forerunner to DC's mature imprint, Vertigo, who published the 1993 special (just titled *The Geek*). Scripter Rachel Pollack brings back some elements from the original series – the circus freak, corruption in corporate America and a good dose of Nazis – but updates the character to a sort of 'toy spirit'. Disjointed in places, there seems to be a need to legitimise the character to lessen the absurdity. Why bother? Anyway the art by Michael Allred more than makes up for any shortcomings. *Brother Power, The Geek*: cool or crap – you decide!~HY
Recommended: 1–2

GEMINI BLOOD
Helix: 8 issues 1996–1997
Science-fiction novelist Christopher Hinz adapts his own books about a chaotic future America where genetically engineered people with 'gemini blood' have two bodies, controlled by the same consciousness.

Threatened by a gemini assassin, a large corporation hires a team of misfit mercenaries to protect itself. Hinz's world is full of fascinating detail, but his characters lack life. He falls back on every cliché in the book – gentle giant, genius leader, traumatised veteran – hey, it's *The A-Team*! Tommy Lee Edwards' heavy, blocky artwork suits the action-packed nature of the comic but doesn't seem particularly suited to portraying emotion. Which is fine because there isn't much. Average shoot-'em-up that could have been much better.~FJ

GEN 13
Image: *Series one 6 issues (0–5) 1994, series two 15 issues + 1995 to date.*

The original miniseries told a competent tale of teenagers co-opted against their will into Project Genesis, an attempt to unleash the powers inherited from their fathers, the government-created super-soldiers of Team 7. The first series also dealt with the group's escape from the shady government operation but it is with the second series that the title really comes into its own, as Jim Lee, Brandon Choi and Scott Campbell settle down to have real fun with their characters. Unlike most teen groups, the kids of Gen 13 are irreverent, badly behaved and far from the clean-cut Teen Titans or even New Mutants who have gone before. They defeat villains by distracting them with bad guitar playing, sneak out in the night when their mentor tells them not to, smoke, fart and generally act like real teenagers (with superpowers). Their adventure on an island of half-naked nympho (possibly) lesbian amazons is the creative team at their tongue in cheek best (3–5). Several issues have variant covers, issue 13 is split into three one-third size mini-issues numbered 13a, b and c.~JC
Recommended: Series two 3–5
Collections: Gen 13 (series one), *Lost in Paradise* (series two 3–5)

GEN 13 BOOTLEG
Image: *2 issues + 1996 to date*

This spin-off *Gen 13* series presents one- or two-issue stories from a variety of creators not usually associated with the series. The first two issues are finely crafted by Alan Davis and Mark Farmer, with many other big names and fan favourites promised for the future.~JC

GEN 13 Miniseries and One-Shots
The enormous popularity of Image's teen heroes has led, unsurprisingly, to a rapid succession of spin-off one-shots and miniseries. The bulk of these have been a chance for big-name creators to present their take on the characters, starting with the incomprehensible surrealist nonsense of the

Messner-Loebs/Coker team-up with the Maxx. The next offerings see an upturn in quality, first with the Mike Heisler/Humberto Ramos one-shot *Gen 13: Unreal World*, in which the heroes are trapped in a dream state by the villain Cull, followed by *Gen 13: Ordinary Heroes*. The latter is a two-part series, beautifully drawn and written by Adam Hughes, which suggests that he may be as talented a scripter as he is an artist. The latest offering, *Gen 13 Zine*, is a weak attempt to produce a fake fanzine and answer readers' questions about Fairchild's bra size. ~JC
Recommended: *Ordinary Heroes* 1, 2

GENE DOGS
Marvel UK: *3 issues 1993*

A team of counter-terrorists are saved from death by a secret weapon that rewrites their DNA in combination with the genetic material of various animals, including a dinosaur. The resulting hero-type creatures battle superfoes engaged in a war between rival conglomerates. Bold story-telling can't hide the lack of originality in the premise or the characters.~NF

GENERATION X
Marvel: *22 issues +, 1 Special 1994 to date*

As part of the ever-increasing mutant family of titles, *Generation X* fills the void left by the evolution of *New Mutants* into *X-Force*, re-establishing the idea of teenage mutants being schooled in the use of their abilities. 1–4 set the scene, introducing a whole cast of previously unseen and generally well conceived characters, with the more established Banshee and the White Queen acting as supervisors, trainers and teachers. Writer Scott Lobdell brings a light-hearted touch and witty dialogue and artist Chris Bachalo draws eye-catching layouts that still convey the story, and his dynamic figures remain within the bounds of acceptable exaggeration. Unfortunately, after four issues the story is interrupted in order to cram in a transformation into *Generation Next*, while all the *X-Men*-related titles creak under the weight of accommodating the sprawling 'Age Of Apocalypse' plot. The alternative version of the team in a different world hardly has much impact when the characters have only just been introduced.

7 reveals more about the team leader Banshee, but is also the first issue that Bachalo does not draw, and it's only when he returns with 17 that the title picks up again. That issue is part of another *X-Men* crossover, 'Onslaught', which works better if only for the tension it creates across the various titles encompassed. In the strangest issue, 1970s wisecracking waterfowl Howard the Duck appears in 21, an odd story but well handled. By and large *Generation X* remains the best of the X-Men line

due to consistent scripting and great art and by concentrating on a small, well-developed cast.~SS
Recommended: 1–2, 17–18, 21
Collection: Generation X (1–4), see also *Uncanny X-Men*

The GENERIC COMIC BOOK
Marvel: *One-shot 1984*

My, what a jest in 1984 as Marvel turned out a generic comic by generic creators with a generic superhero, a generic origin and a generic fight. Had it been released five years later it would have put the rest of the line to shame.~FP

Codename GENETIX
Marvel UK: *6 issues 1993*

A team of mutants unsure of its origins battles against one of the evil corporations that also turn up in *Gene Dogs*. Heavily dependent on the dynamics of other, well-established Marvel teams (they have a Danger Room), their membership consists of token stereotypes and they don't even warrant new villains. Dull.~NF

GENOCYBER
Viz: *6-issue miniseries 1993*

The peculiar Japanese blend of innocence and ultra-violence strikes again as a teenage girl's natural psychic talents are accelerated by machine and combined with a battlesuit. This series is an origin story, but the character hasn't been seen since in English translation.~FP

GEOMANCER
Valiant: *8 issues 1994–1995*

Clay McHenry, blind cop on the take, is the unlikely choice as Geomancer, Guardian of the Earth. This tradition, established before recorded history began, chooses one individual every generation to reaffirm humanity's link with the mother planet. The superheroics are competent, but writer Maurice Fontenot's efforts are insufficient to distinguish the title from the rest of the pack. Geomancer's mystically-imbued powers exhibit too many shades of Daredevil, and the slate would have been better filled by examining the roles and responsibilities of the Geomancer, as opposed to parading a string of bad guys for bicep-flexing fodder.~APS

GHOST
Dark Horse: *17 issues +, 1 Special 1995 to date*

Introduced in *Comics Greatest World*, reporter Elisa Cameron is killed by some gangsters and becomes… well, a ghost. Toting some semi-automatics to augment her ghostly powers, she seeks revenge on her killers while trying to keep her lascivious sister Margo on the straight and narrow. Plenty of cheesecake from Adam Hughes, Karl Story and the like, but after them the art suffers and from 10 onwards it's substandard work. The story also falters, and an interesting premise falls into all the usual traps, which is a pity. If you like big babes with guns and are in the mood for an inexplicable *Predator* crossover (5) this is the title for you.~TP

Collection: *Ghost (Comics Greatest Word* story + Special)

Tales of GHOST CASTLE

DC: *3 issues 1975*

A couple of Robert Kanigher-penned tales don't stop this representing DC's horror line at its most mediocre. The predictable stories all have EC format 'shock' endings, with retribution from beyond the grave and ironic dénouements predominating. Lucien the Librarian makes his first comic appearance as host of Ghost Castle, so being a *Sandman* completist is probably the only reason for bothering with the title now.~NF

GHOST IN THE SHELL

Dark Horse: *8-issue limited series 1995*

Deceptively straightforward action adventure series for the first six issues, becoming a treatise on artificial intelligence and the nature of life in the final two. In the near future, a vast computer network covers the planet and a crack team of covert operatives exists to combat terrorism of all kinds. The field leader of this team is the beautiful but deadly Major Kusanagi, an android with a 'ghost' (a sort of artificial soul). Each issue leads the team into deeper and deeper political waters until in 7 Kusanagi undergoes a transformation requiring the assistance of an Artificial Intelligence in the network. Masamune Shirow doesn't provide much in the way of characterisation beyond the hard-headedness of Kusanagi but his technology-heavy stories are still very readable. His artwork is detailed if not particularly elegant while his people can tend towards caricatures, but the action is fluid and the overall effect is unique.~NF

Recommended: 1–8

Collection: Ghost In The Shell (1–8)

GHOST MANOR

Charlton: *Series one 19 issues 1968–1971, series two 77 issues 1971–1984*

Charlton's third 1960s mystery anthology was hosted by a blue skinned, green haired hippy in a mini-skirt and sunglasses, Wanda The Witch. Despite occasional stories from the likes of Joe Gill and Steve Skeates, and the odd bit of drawing from Jim Aparo, Steve Ditko and Pat Boyette, the title suffered from Charlton's late 1960s mediocrity (which is really too complimentary a term for the general standard here). The title became *Ghostly Haunts* in 1971, with Wanda renamed Winnie. Do we detect

some disapproval from Marvel, whose Scarlet Witch was also named Wanda?

Three months after the title was changed, *Ghost Manor* was back with a new host, a ghostly undertake called Mr Bones. Now typical of mid 1970s Charlton mystery anthologies, there's nothing of note. Writing was by Joe Gill, Mike Pellowsky and Nick Cuti, and art by Ditko, Joe Staton, Don Newton, Tom Sutton, Pete Morisi (PAM), and Wayne Howard. From the late 1970s there were also innumerable stories by very poor (especially on Charlton rates) South American artists and the dreadful Korean artist Sanho Kim. Many of the covers from 20 to 32 were painted, and issues from 33 on are all reprint, sometimes dredging as far back as the 1950s.~SW

GHOST RIDER

Marvel: *7 issues 1967*

Ghost Rider mark one was a mundane Dick Ayers-drawn Western character, who coated his clothing and horse with 'a phosphorescent substance' to give the appearance of coming from beyond. One presumes his demise was from a particularly hideous form of cancer. Six of his issues were reprinted as *Night Rider* when the 1970s Ghost Rider was popular, and he went on to star in *Western Gunfighters*.~FP

GHOST RIDER

Marvel: *Series one 81 issues 1973–1983, series two 80 issues +, 2 Annuals 1990 to date*

The second incarnation of the Ghost Rider is one of the most visually striking characters created by Marvel. A flaming skeleton clad in leather biker's gear that leaves only the skull visible sits atop a flaming motorcycle. Carnival stunt-rider Johnny Blaze makes a deal with the devil (later modified to Mephisto in more conservative times), and comes out possessed by the spirit of a demon. This all occurs in *Marvel Spotlight* 5–11, and has been reprinted in the wake of the 1990s version's popularity as a series titled *The Original Ghost Rider*. It's unlikely that any other title as shoddy as the 1970s *Ghost Rider* has lasted half the length. It's difficult to find any redeeming features in the first sixty-eight issues, although Jim Starlin's tale of a cross-country race against death (35) stands out by default among the assorted demons and other half-assed satanic clichés. Perhaps in desperation, then newcomer Roger Stern was appointed writer (68), and something astounding occurred: he raised the title above the mediocrity line. *Freaks* (70), despite appropriating ideas from DC's early *Swamp Thing*, was touching, and the return of very silly villains the Circus of Crime (72, 73) was also enjoyable. By that time, though, the damage had been done, and the series was adequately concluded by the team of

J.M. DeMatteis and Bob Budiansky as Blaze separated from his demonic other half. These later stories were reprinted as seven issues titled *The Original Ghost Rider Rides Again*, and those desperate to see Johnny Blaze again should look for *Spirits of Vengeance* and *Blaze*.

The second series begins well. This time teenager Danny Ketch is drawn to the Ghost Rider's motorcycle in a graveyard, and his transformation enables him to save lives. Far more an obvious force for good than Johnny Blaze in his possessed identity, he also has some other abilities, a particularly inventive one being that when he stares into a villain's eyes said villain is confronted with all the pain they've caused others. The first dozen issues are written by Howard Mackie with the art team of Javier Saltares and Mark Texiera, and they produce a body count so high it's a wonder anyone's left living in Marvel's version of New York. Despite the inevitable return of Johnny Blaze (14) and a nifty glow-in-the-dark cover on 15, the title is a long time recovering from the loss of Saltares after 12. It drags from fight scene to *angst*-ridden soul searching as Mackie tantalises with hints of the Ghost Rider's origin and past. Ironically, it's only once this is revealed (41–43 and *Spirits of Vengeance* 14 & 15) that things begin to improve. An interesting new Ghost Rider takes over the title for 46–50, and the arrival of Salvador Larroca as penciller from 52 finally drags the art back up and beyond the originally established standard. With 66 the Ghost Rider is given a harder edge, becoming the spirit of vengeance the original character was, and that issue has a shock value long absent from the title, but it doesn't last. Despite Larroca improving all the while, the series is dragged down by the dull scripts of Ivan Velez Jr.

At the height of Ghost Rider's renewed popularity three one-shots were issued. *Fear* teamed Ghost Rider with Captain America and the *Ghost Rider Special* reprinted the Ghost Rider and Cable teaming from *Marvel Comics Presents* 90–98. They're both very ordinary. *Hearts Of Darkness* is not, sadly, in this instance a terrifying look into the bleakness and torment of humanity under stress, but a crap team-up of Ghost Rider, Wolverine and Punisher.~FP

Collections: *Resurrection* (series two 1–7), *Midnight Sons* (series two 28, 31 + *Darkhold* 1, *Morbius* 1, *Nightstalkers* 1 and *Spirits of Vengeance* 1)

GHOST RIDER 2099
Marvel: *25 issues 1994–1996*

Marvel's 2099 update of the demon biker portrays a character using technology, instead of the original hellfire incarnation. By far the darkest and most realistic of the 2099 line, this contains a strong computer theme, which led to the birth of the series' own dialect. Although atmospheric, it made the series less accessible to new readers. Chris Bachalo pencilled 1–4, giving the book a crisp, fresh superhero look lost on his departure. The final story arc, (22–25) pencilled by the unknown Ashley Wood, succeeded in giving the title a new Gothic lease of life, but by this point the storyline, with its underground conspiracies and secret societies, had strayed too far from the superhero feel of the 2099 range, resulting in its cancellation.~SS

Recommended: 1, 22–25

Filmation's GHOSTBUSTERS
First: *6 issues 1987*

Oh, the superior knowledge of TV executives. The *Ghostbusters* movie had been a global hit, and the cartoon rights fell to Filmation, who decided that with a little tweaking they could improve matters. 'Who needs the original characters?' they reasoned. 'Let's have their descendants. And a giant talking ape, a ghost-possessed car and a flying vampire bat/pig.' Apathy from the kids was resounding, so much so that a new cartoon was speedily conceived stressing it was the *Real Ghostbusters*. That said, given the duff ideas, Hilarie Staton came up with just the right level of fantasy and humour in the comics to appeal to young children (although not beyond), integrating puzzle and activity pages into the stories. The plots are basic, but have a charm and artifice altogether lacking in Now's comic based on the succeeding cartoon show.~WJ

GHOSTDANCING
Vertigo: *6-issue miniseries 1995*

An apocalyptic tale featuring drumming, revelatory drugs, rock concerts, and a few Native American spirit gods. It sounds desperately worthy, but no – it's fun! The enthusiasm in Jamie Delano's writing is infectious, and the treatment is refreshingly matter-of-fact, as if you've known this story all along, and don't need any lectures. Richard Case's vibrant and direct artwork brings out the best of this approach and it all makes for a great read.~FC

Recommended: 1–6

GHOSTLY HAUNTS
Charlton: *39 issues (20–58) 1971–1978*

Formerly titled *Ghost Manor*, this mystery anthology was typical of 1970s horror fare. Hosted by Winnie, formerly Wanda, the Witch, a mini-skirted, blue-skinned hippy narrator, there's little inspiration. Stories by Joe Gill (whose many pen names included Jack Daniels and Tom Tuna), Mike Pellowksy and Nick Cuti are illustrated by the usual roll call of 1970s Charlton artists: Ditko, Boyette, Staton,

Howard, Newton, Sutton. Work by Mike Zeck and Rich Larson is accompanied in the later issues by art from South American and Korean studios of the most execrable quality. In 1975 Charlton started running painted covers, and issues from 54 onwards are almost exclusively reprint.~SW

GHOSTLY TALES
Charlton: *104 issues (55–169), 1966–1976 (55–124), 1977–1984 (125–169)*

As was often the case with Charlton comics, the numbering was inherited from a completely unrelated title, in this case the *Blue Beetle* series. This was Charlton's first new mystery anthology of the 1960s, and featured their horror host Doctor Graves, who occasionally involved himself in the stories he told. Under editor Dick Giordano there were several interesting artists, although most of the scripts are appalling, the better ones being by Steve Skeates (as Norm DiPlume), Denny O'Neil (as Sergius O'Shaughnessy), Joe Gill and Dave Kaler. Stories drawn by Pat Boyette, Steve Ditko and Jim Aparo are the exception rather than the rule.

Dr Graves moved into his own title, and was replaced here by Mr Lazarus Dedd from 71. When Giordano departed to DC most of his better contributors went with him, leading to an appalling slump in the late 1960s. By the mid-1970s, though, newer talents like Don Newton, Tom Sutton, Joe Staton, and later Mike Zeck and Rich Larson, joined Boyette and Ditko. Writers included Gill (under assorted pseudonyms), Mike Pellowsky and Nicola Cuti. From the 1977 revival the comic is exclusively reprint.~SW

GHOSTS
DC: *112 issues 1971–1982*

The cover proclaims that this horror anthology featured 'True tales of the weird and supernatural'. Despite this, the content was typical of DC's mystery books. One notable feature was that for the first fifty issues almost all the stories were written by Leo Dorfman, which contributed to the lack of highpoints. The stories weren't bad, simply uninspired, with the exception of 22's camp classic 'The Last Shrill Laugh Of The Phantom', wherein Benito Mussolini was haunted by the ghost of Julius Caesar!

Throughout its run *Ghosts* seemed cursed with more than its fair share of John Calnan and Jerry Grandenetti art, though the first five issues did at least have a smattering of choice 50s reprints. Issues in the teens and twenties have a higher proportion of quality art by the likes of Alfredo Alcala, Gerry Talaoc and Rico Rival, with a Nestor Redondo strip in 13 being particularly nice. Undoubtedly the title's best-

ever story was the Bayou shocker 'Blood on The Moon' (31), illustrated in riveting style by forgotten comics genius Bill Payne. Later issues are less impressive, although an occasional decent art job would surface, such as the nice Michael Golden strip in 88. A three-part Spectre story in 97–99 failed to raise much interest, probably due to its total lack of inspiration, and the last few years are best left to collectors who simply can't get enough of Ruben Yandoc's 'unique etchings'. A number of the best early strips were reprinted in 40, a hard-to-come-by sixty-eight-page giant.~DAR
Recommended: 13, 31, 88

G.I. COMBAT
DC: *245 issues (44–288) 1957–1987*

Continuing the numbering after DC purchased the title from Quality, early issues consisted of short unrelated war stories written by the likes of Bob Haney, Bill Finger and editor Robert Kanigher. Though eminently readable, they suffer from an over-reliance on gimmicks and were hamstrung by The Comics Code and DC's reluctance to explore the darker side of war. Almost all early issues feature art by Joe Kubert, Russ Heath, Jerry Grandenetti and Ross Andru, though particularly notable were a number of strips by Mort Drucker (48, 61–64, 66, 71, 72, 76, 78). 87 introduced Kanigher's Haunted Tank strip, which ran almost unbroken until the comic's demise. Jeb Stuart, whose tank was also rather confusingly called *Jeb Stuart*, was haunted by the ghost of his idol, Confederate cavalry leader (you've guessed it) Jeb Stuart. The ghost would pop up periodically to give Jeb advice, but in all other respects it was a straightforward war strip, with the most surprising aspect being how Kanigher kept coming up with fresh ideas, although he unerringly did. The likes of Kubert (99, 100, 102–113), Andru (134–136) and Irv Novick (89, 116, 118–120, 122, 127) all took their turns at the strip, but it belonged to its first artist Russ Heath, a man seemingly incapable of drawing badly. The Kanigher/Heath team so consistently turned out quality work that it's hard to pick out particular highpoints, though 121, 125, 126, 141 and 142 are at least spectacularly well drawn. 138 introduced another long-running strip, The Losers, later to gain their own series in *Our Fighting Forces*.

After a Doug Wildey fill-in on Haunted Tank in 153, veteran war artist Sam Glanzman took over, drawing it in one form or another until its demise. Some later issues contain Glanzman inks over Dick Ayers pencils, but the difference is barely noticeable. More significant was the departure of Kanigher, replaced by writer/editor Archie Goodwin (159–173), who gave the strip a higher emphasis on characterisation and continuity.

Symptomatic of this was the death of long-time crew member Aron Asher in 162, and though Kanigher's stories were always well crafted, Goodwin's tenure was the book's best period. Kanigher returned with 174 and the rest of the run remains readable, if rarely inspired. 201 saw *G.I. Combat* transformed into a dollar comic with a vastly increased page-count and included 'O.S.S.' (by Kanigher and E.R. Cruz) and a number of short stories in addition to three Haunted Tank stories each issue. 242 introduced *The Mercenaries*, by Kanigher and Vic Catan, which, with 282, eventually supplanted the Haunted Tank as cover feature, but this couldn't save the comic from cancellation. 128, 140, 144–154 and 169 are all or part reprint.~DAR
Recommended: 48, 61–64, 66, 71, 72, 76, 78, 121, 125, 126, 141, 142, 159–168, 170–173

G.I. JOE
Marvel: *155 issues, 4 Yearbooks 1982–1994*

Based on an ever-increasing line of action figures, initial issues feature substandard art and uninspired scripts coupled with the most ridiculous character names until Image dredged the barrel still deeper. Breaker, Clutch, Zap, Rock'n'Roll... there's even an Eskimo named Kwinn in issue 2. Appalling quality notwithstanding, there was a rabid market out there. *G.I. Joe* was enormously successful, spawning numerous spin-offs and two reprint titles. The digest-sized *G.I. Joe Comics Magazine* ran for thirteen issues, reprinting 1–37, and *Tales of G.I. Joe* reprinted 1–15, all of them wretched. 1 is also reprinted as a treasury edition and in the first yearbook, and there's a 1995 *G.I. Joe Special* reprinting the Todd McFarlane-pencilled 60.

Described as an élite counter-terrorist strike force, G.I. Joe's target is Cobra, an organisation dedicated to the principle of divide and rule. After the awful early issues, generally drawn by Don Perlin or Herb Trimpe, writer Larry Hama's multi-issue missions develop a greater complexity. He turns the title into an action soap opera with a massive cast (new characters are constantly added, although names didn't improve, with Quick-Kick, Crazylegs, Payload and Snow-Job among them). Letters make comparisons with *Hill Street Blues*, although *Burun Murchstansangar* would be as close, and the title is increasingly hamstrung by having to incorporate more characters and vehicles from the toy line and cartoon show. For a strike force, there's an astonishingly low mortality rate for the first hundred issues, but immediately thereafter the cast is reduced considerably, adding a new edge to the title. Beyond the first twenty-five or so issues *G.I. Joe* is an undemanding and generally reasonably produced action comic, albeit one with the

pernicious subtext of glorifying war and violence in a real-world setting. A representative issue encompassing the spirit of the title is 82, in which Hama has a bit of fun with the new recruit programme before delivering a short mission. The best of the yearbooks is 2, with the uncredited lead story drawn by Mike Golden.~FP

G.I. JOE
Dark Horse: *4-issue miniseries 1996, 4 issues + 1996 to date*

The miniseries is split into two stories, the first being the adventures of the current team, while the second shows the origins of the G.I. Joe characters. Plots are interesting and fast-paced and Tatsuya Ishida's art is consistently excellent. The ongoing series is a let-down, with repetitive plots concentrating on battles against the team's arch-enemy Iron Klaw.~SS

G.I. JOE AND THE TRANSFORMERS
Marvel: *4-issue miniseries 1987*

Teaming of giant mutating robots and all-American heroes to protect a military project from the evil Decipticons and Cobra. A magnificent sermon on the concept of predestination as experienced by a rich and varied cast, and infused with the clash of the instinctive and the intellectual. No, hang on, that's *War And Peace*. This is rubbish.~WJ
Collection: G.I. Joe and the Transformers (1–4)

G.I. JOE SPECIAL MISSIONS
Marvel: 28 issues 1986–1989

'The missions we couldn't talk about until now' proclaims the cover of the first issue. Can't figure why, since there's little difference between this and the regular title right down to the creative team of Larry Hama and Herb Trimpe. The only notable distinguishing feature is that most of the stories here are self-contained.~FP

G.I. WAR Tales
DC: *4 issues 1973*

Reprints of solid but unspectacularly written war stories drawn by a stellar selection of artists. Over four issues there's Neal Adams, Mort Drucker, Russ Heath, Joe Kubert and, most astonishingly, Bernie Krigstein in 4.~WJ

GIANT-SIZE CHILLERS
Marvel: *1 issue 1974*

Marv Wolfman and Gene Colan are responsible for a story that slots between *Tomb of Dracula* 22 and 23. Restoring Dracula's daughter Lilith to life and introducing the tragic Sheila Whittier, this is an issue of Dracula's own title in all but name, and bears the same quality. Dracula-related reprints from Marvel's 50s monster titles round out the issue.~FP
Recommended: 1

GIANT-SIZE MINI COMICS
Eclipse: *4 issues 1986*

The minicomics phenomenon was particularly invigorating and satisfying. There's much dispute as to when the idea started (with a case to be made for the 1920s 'Tijuana Bibles' sex comics), but the principle was that the creator, operating under nothing but personal constraints, wrote and drew and self-produced comics that were photocopied, stapled and distributed, usually in smaller-than-pocket-size format. This series attempted to feature the best of them. Very wisely, four separate editors were each given an issue to present their selection of the best. The greatest variety is in 4, so that's the place to start, but the most biting cartoon of the entire run is Ron Hauge's 'The Known World' in 3, encompassing the US's feelings of paranoia and xenophobia.~WJ

GIANT-SIZE SUPER-HEROES
Marvel: 1 issue 1974

Very ordinary extra-length three way battle between Spider-Man, Man-Wolf and Morbius.~FP

THE GIFT
First: *One-shot 1990*

Basically a sampler for First comics, *The Gift* was a squarebound-format 'Holiday Special' for Christmas 1990, featuring short stories about the major First characters, including Nexus, Grimjack and Badger. Some have a festive theme, all lead into a framing sequence by John Ostrander and Ian Gibson. Incidentally, it wasn't a gift at all. The package cost $5.95, and the name referred to the gift of life needed to save a child's life.~JC

GILGAMESH II
DC: *4-issue miniseries 1989*

The epic poem Gilgamesh is one of the oldest stories known to man, and in his reworking Jim Starlin delivers all his usual trappings. There are bizarre characters, high-tech sci-fi, deep philosophical questions and an extremely weak ending. This brave attempt falls flat on its face due to poor, nay, non-existent, characterisation and jarring set-pieces. It's Starlin writing by numbers, and it shows. Still, his artwork is pleasant, and expertly coloured by Steve Oliff, but that still isn't enough to justify the expensive prestige format. Read the original.~TP

GINGER FOX
Comico: *Graphic Novel 1986, 4-issue miniseries 1988*

Mike Baron scripts in his usual cool, witty, somewhat uninvolving way, and Mitch O'Connell draws the graphic novel like the illustrator he is, i.e. excellent photo-based art style with some neat graphic tricks, but the layout and story-telling lack drama and dynamism. The story: Ms Fox, beautiful, resourceful chief exec of struggling Hollywood film studio, turns detective, to find out why her potential hit kung fu movie is being sabotaged by persons unknown, while romancing its star. Lots of guns, knives, kung fu action and unthreatening satire on life in LA. Insubstantial, but certainly looks classy. The miniseries is more of the same, only this time it's a horror movie at the centre of the plot. Here the ugly, sometimes cubist art of the Pander Brothers makes Tinseltown people look utterly horrible themselves... which is rather appealing.~GL

GIRL
Vertigo: *3-issue miniseries 1996*

Teenage rebellion *par excellence* from Pete Milligan and Duncan Fergredo. Simone's awful family live in a high-rise block where the local boys hang out in her lift counting whether there are more used condoms than syringes in there today. When she breaks the TV and blames it on her dog, her father throws him out the window. Milligan parody of modern Britain is at once funny and hideous. Simone's fumbling attempts to get laid, her daydream of watching her gas-bloated corpse explode all over her family's winning lottery ticket; the make-believe bravura with which she confronts school bullies with a breadknife: Fergredo illustrates all in a brash, over-coloured style full of knock-kneed adolescents and over-made-up tarts. It's not a very deep story. When we discover a lot of what Simone tells us is actually fantasy it comes as no surprise, and the blithe ending rather negates any social criticism, probably in the name of irony. But it is fun, and if you're a mixed-up fourteen-year-old it probably reads very sympathetically.~FJ

GIRL CRAZY
Dark Horse: *3-issue miniseries 1996*

Gaby, Maribel and Kitten are friends whose sixteenth birthdays are fast approaching. One's a lawyer in the Fifties, one's a jungle heroine and the last's a collection agent for the I.R.S., who now control everything. Kitten takes a day off to meet up with her friends to celebrate and they decide to break Una out of prison (she's another friend about to turn sixteen). It's not going to be easy, though, with the I.R.S.'s robot Gaby out to stop them. This odd fantasy series by Gilbert Hernandez is at once a superhero satire and an attempt to explain what growing up is really all about. Humorous for the most part, there's an underlying sadness at the loss of innocence necessitated by age.~NF
Recommended: 1–3

GIRL'S LOVE STORIES

DC: *180 issues 1949–1973*

After the success of Jack Kirby and Joe Simon's pioneering romance titles *Young Love* and *Young Romance*, every comics publisher jumped on the moonlight-and-roses bandwagon in the late 1940s. Most successful of the imitators was DC, who produced very creditable facsimiles using top-notch talent, and created a six-pack of romance titles that lasted until the 1970s. *Girl's Love Stories* was the career-girl variant, a significant number of tales involving the heroine's enforced choice between her career (always in a suitably girly profession such as actress or model. No lady engineers on view!) and The Man. Guess who invariably won. There's some superb art by many distinguished names, among them Colan, Jay Scott Pike and John Romita, a staple of DC's romance line for many years before moving to Marvel.~HS

GIRL'S ROMANCES

DC: *160 issues 1950–1971*

A clone of DC's successful *Girl's Love Stories* released a year later in the hope of repeating its sister's success, which for two decades it did. There's Alex Toth art in some early issues, and a Neal Adams cover and splash in 134, but otherwise the mixture's as before: lovely elegant artwork gracing outstandingly sappy and naïve stories.~HS

GIVE ME LIBERTY

Rip-Off: *One-shot 1976*

Years before Miller and Gibbons, Patrick Henry's quote was used to title a bicentennial special in which Gilbert Shelton, Ted Richards, Garry Hallgren and Willy Murphy apply the wit of the underground to the events of the War of Independence. Basically an educational title, the humorous cartoon style employed minimises dry historical detail while covering all the salient points, making learning a pleasure. Sadly long out of print, this is memorable and incisive and should have been a standard text in US schools during 1976.~FP
Recommended: 1

GIVE ME LIBERTY

Dark Horse: *4-issue miniseries 1990–1991*

Frank Miller's scripts for what are essentially war stories play to Dave Gibbons' strengths: the ability to draw amazing landscapes believably; fast changes of pacing from explosive action to moments of reflection; using heroic poses and angles without irony or pomposity. In near-future Chicago Martha Washington, an angry young black woman who's been brought up in a fenced-in ghetto where the poor are imprisoned, is desperate to get out into the world. Her skills with computers and the encouragement of a liberal teacher seem to point the way until he is murdered and she goes after the killer. Traumatised by her action, she's sent to a mental facility, where she stumbles on an illegal government experiment to use schizophrenic psychics to control computers.

Thrown out of the mental home she ends up joining PAX, America's 'peace keeping' force, and makes a name for herself protecting the Amazon rainforest against rebel fast-food corporations. Although Martha begins fighting solely for her own survival, political change is taking place and she finds herself agreeing with the idealistic new President. She makes an enemy of her superior when she observes him betraying his men. They are the only two survivors of the action and, knowing she won't be believed, Martha keeps quiet about his duplicity, an action which brings trouble on her head for the rest of the story. She meets up with one of the schizophrenics from the mental hospital when sent to stop a gay, right-wing extremist organization from nuking Washington, and together they set out to do the right thing, even when government and generals are deceiving everyone. Miller's political satire doesn't exactly stretch the reader, but it's lushly illustrated by Gibbons and, compared to your average Marvel comic, a masterpiece of insight. Her story continues in the *Martha Washington* miniseries.~FJ

GIZMO

Chance: *1 issue 1985*
Mirage: *Series one 5 issues 1986–1987, Series two 2 issues 1989*

Feeble humour comic about a metal man and his giant koala companion. For the second Mirage series the Fugitoid gets equal billing, and Michael Dooley's artwork has improved immensely.~WJ

GLORY

Image: *16 issues, 3 Specials 1995–1996*
Maximum: *1 issue + (17) 1996 to date*

When she was just a supporting character in Rob Liefeld's Extreme Studios titles for Image, Glory merely seemed heavily derivative of Wonder Woman. When she gained her own title, it became clear she was an entire rip-off, from the Amazonian heritage and matriarchal island home down to the bracelets and lasso accessories. Mary Jo Duffy, scripter, has Glory occasionally say things like 'Don't treat me like a bimbo!', a particularly laughable assertion since the art is screaming 'BIMBO CITY! OVER HERE! ONLY TWO DOLLARS FIFTY A PEEP!' The art, by sundry Brazilians, obsesses on inflato-bint 'anatomy' to the exclusion of any attempt at characterisation, story-telling or even the most basic narrative. They're all crowded out to make way for more tits and ass. The

Bikini Fest special doesn't even pretend to deliver a story, but instead just thrusts page after page of inept tacky pin-ups at the helpless viewer.~HS
Collection: Glory (1–4)

GLORY/CELESTINE: Dark Angel
Image: *2 issues 1996*
Maximum: *1 issue + (3) 1996 to date*

Another crossover for Liefeld's Glory, this time with Celestine and Maximage as they must combat the Talisman of Doom. Written by Jo Duffy and drawn by Pat Lee, there's just really nothing remarkable about it (except perhaps the appearance of Dr Strange rip-off Dr Daedelus).~NF

GLYPH
Labor Of Love: *2 issues + 1996 to date*

A Mike Kaluta cover welcomes a very promising black and white anthology magazine with the only remotely familiar interior contributor being Sarah Byam. There's a wealth of talent accompanying her, from the brutal almost *Raw*-style art of Pia Guerra to the unpredictable heart-tugging writing of Daniel Rivers, both sadly absent from 2. The standout work comes from David Lee Ingersoll. His seemingly unconnected vignettes under the collective title of 'Bonecage Graffiti' are charming little slices that drop into a finely dialogued story and drop right back out again. His toned art is gorgeously expressive and he's a star in the making. Of the other contributors, David Lasky appears to be aping the work of the wonderful Jonathan Edwards in the British *Deadline* with a madcap Neil Young strip, and Michael and Brian O'Connell provide a somewhat ordinary, but distinctly promising leprechaun story in 1. A negative aspect is the few pages given over to prose, dull stuff to the final word, and you're better off ignoring Fred Burke's wanky editorial to 2. That issue overall doesn't quite match the first, but still rewards the time spent reading it.~WJ
Recommended: 1

GNATRAT
Prelude: *One-shot (The Dark Gnat Returns) 1986*
Dimension: *One-shot (Happy Birthday Gnatrat) 1986*
Mighty Pumpkin: *One shot (Darerat) 1987*
Innovation: *One-shot (Gnatrat: The Movie) 1990*

Although the first one-shot is seemingly merely yet another parody of *The Dark Knight Returns*, writer/artist Mark Martin scores on two counts. Firstly that it's not, it merely appropriates the plot in the loosest sense, and the art style, and secondly because it's actually good. A tirade about the endless slew of substandard comics festering in the wake of *Teenage Mutant Ninja Turtles* is combined with

Martin's excellent cartooning and unpredictable sense of humour to produce a very funny and impassioned début. *Happy Birthday Gnatrat* parodies a *Batman* anniversary cover and casts the net far wider, lampooning early Batman, Bill Sienkiewicz, Truman Capote, old ads in comics, Rose O'Neill's Kewpies and more besides. A series of gags rather than a sustained plot, it points the way towards Martin's later extraordinary *20 Nude Dancers 20*. The third comic is an ill-advised and very thin take on Miller's Daredevil and Elektra stories, in which the more obvious focus seems more an exercise in selling comics than anything heartfelt. The same applies to the *Batman* movie parody, although the cartooning remains nice.~FP
Recommended: *The Dark Gnat Returns, Happy Birthday Gnatrat*
Collection: *The Complete Gnat-Rat* (all four one-shots)

THE GOBLIN
Warren: *3 issues 1982*

Although the Goblin first appeared in *Eerie* 71, this particular strip continues from the last issues of *The Rook*, and is typical of Warren's final years. The Goblin strip and its co-features Tin Man, Troll Patrol and the Micro Buccaneers were meant to appeal to superhero fans and horror fans, but end up falling between both camps, satisfying neither. There's lots of nice art on hand, though, from the likes of Lee Elias and Rudy Nebres, but particular mention should be made of Alex Nino's strip in the third issue, which is spectacular even by his standards and needs to be seen to be believed.~DAR
Recommended: 3

GOD NOSE
Rip Off: *1 issue 1969*

This early Jack Jackson strip was originally self-published in 1964, giving it some claim to being the first underground comic, though the humour is more beatnik than counterculture. As a historical artefact *God Nose*, literally the adventures of God, is highly significant, though to a contemporary audience it may seem little more than a dated curio with contents typical of the college humour of the period. It features such things as Jesus becoming a folk singer and God advising a young couple on birth control. Certainly Jackson was to go on to far better things.~DAR

GODDESS
Vertigo: *8-issue limited series 1995–1996*

Rosie Nolan suddenly finds herself manifesting extraordinary and uncontrollable powers at a level at which she accidentally severs Scotland from the British mainland. This kind of behaviour attracts the attention of both a mad CIA agent and a misanthropic British bobby and his brutal Neanderthal henchmen. It's just as well Rosie has a more down-to-earth eco-terrorist companion, enabling her to stay a step ahead of her pursuers. Garth Ennis depicts almost the entire cast as levels of caricature, and Phil Windslade draws up a storm, and a missile attack, a plane crash, an ocean-liner crash... Don't expect anything more than a fast-paced romp with some terrific art and you'll enjoy *Goddess*.~FP

GODWHEEL
Malibu: *4-issue (0–3) miniseries 1995*
Ancient God Argus is a tad distressed to discover that the artefacts required to replenish his strength have been spirited away. Unable to expend the energy required to retrieve them himself, he summons the good and the bad from Malibu's Ultraverse to locate and return the artefacts. Predictably enough, the remainder of the series is good guys vs bad. The slim plot is stretched beyond belief, and beyond the capacity of some nice artwork to redeem it. Don't be suckered in by Thor's appearance in the cover box or prominence on the cover of the collection. He only turns up in the final five pages of the final issue.~FP
Collection: Wheel Of Thunder (0–3)

GODZILLA
Marvel: *24 issues 1977–1979*
Doug Moench wrote this attempt at the 'King of Monsters', but never developed the title beyond its 'Who's Godzilla gonna stomp this issue?' idea. There was a large supporting cast, including most of Marvel's law-enforcement agency S.H.I.E.L.D., but the aimless plots make for juvenile reading, although that might have been intentional. Increasingly desperate attempts to attract a wider audience saw superhero guest-shots aplenty in the final issues.~DWC

GODZILLA, King Of The Monsters
Dark Horse: *One-shot 1987, 6-issue miniseries 1988–1989, One-shot 1992, one-shot ('Godzilla vs Barkley') 1993, 16 issues 1995–1996*
The 1987 special was a horror story told from the point of view of a little girl traumatised during the reawakening of Godzilla and his fellow Disaster Monsters. Inagos, the Locust King, is particularly frightening. Steve Bissette worked excellently on the story and art and the issue also includes some smashing pin-ups by Paul Chadwick, Rick Geary, and Keith Giffen as well as an interesting article by Bissette that lists all the Godzilla films.
The miniseries was a translation, in black and white, of the Japanese adaptation of the

film *Gojira 1984*. It's a very ordinary story, with art to match by Kazuhisa Iwata. The 1992 *Godzilla Color Special*, superbly drawn, and co-written by Arthur Adams, is a grand story about a huge stone statue coming to life when the island it stands on is threatened by Godzilla. The less said about 'Godzilla vs Barkley' the better.
The brightly coloured 1995 series is a surprise treat. Brandon McKinney's art is the best the character has ever had in US comics, and Kevin Maguire's witty script, acknowledging that characters sometimes have more than one motive each, has some ironic plot twists and surprisingly black humour. This gets broader when Arthur Adams takes over on issue 5. The subsequent art by Tatsuya Ishida, and Adams (who drew most of the excellent covers), is exciting on the monster action and adequate elsewhere. McKinney later returned to the comic with scripts by Ryder Windham. This team's work is worth reading, though not as sophisticated as the early issues. The last issue features Godzilla in the days of the dinosaurs. What more do you want?~GK
Recommended: Color Special, 1–4
Collection: Godzilla (miniseries 1–6)

GOLD KEY SPOTLIGHT
Gold Key: *11 issues 1976–1978*
Funny-animal and comedy strips from the Gold Key stable like *Tom, Dick and Harriet* and *The Wacky Adventures Of Cracky* occupy most issues. The exceptions are a new *Dagar* story in 6, more from the *Occult Files Of Dr Spector* in 8 and *Tragg And The Sky Gods* in 9, all every bit as dull as in their regular titles.~SW

THE GOLDEN AGE
DC: *4-issue miniseries 1993*
World War II has ended and many of DC's 1940s superheroes no longer seem to have a purpose in the post-atomic society. Most fall back into civilian life, but Tex Thompson parlays wartime acclaim as the Americommando into a fast-track political career. As America drifts from the golden age of post-war optimism towards McCarthyism a different threat manifests itself, and the retired heroes find themselves back in action as a new decade begins. James Robinson and Paul Smith produce a fond and nostalgic look at some second-string heroes barely given any kind of personality in almost fifty years. The fourth issue's big revelation comes straight from dopey pulp fiction, but the portrayal of the cast throughout the series is so well conceived that what might be a major flaw elsewhere can be forgiven.~WJ
Recommended: 1–4
Collection: The Golden Age (1–4)

GOLDEN AGE GREATS
AC/Paragon Publications: *10 issues + 1994 to date*

These are eighty- to a hundred-page volumes of material from the golden age of comics (1939–1955), culled from a wide variety of smaller, less well-known publishers of the time. That's not to say that these comics don't have their share of good stories and art, though. Otto Binder and Gardner Fox, for example, produced hundreds of stories for Fawcett Comics and Magazine Enterprises respectively. There were plenty of good artists around, too, whether freelancers or members of one of the 'shops' such as the Jerry Iger/Will Eisner or the Harry 'A' Chesler studios. Bill Black, as editor, has been on a crusade for over twenty years to represent and preserve the best work from the period, and although in black and white, this is an excellent project that will provide something for anyone interested in the history of the medium.

There is some attempt to present the different styles in a complementary manner. Each issue has a theme and comes with historical articles and checklists. 1 features the Green Lama (two stories by Mac Raboy), Catman (Bob Fujitani), Rocketman and Miss Victory. 2 is dedicated solely to Matt Baker's work on Phantom Lady while 3 contains work by the Iger/Eisner studio – The Flame (Lou Fine), Espionage: Black X (Eisner) and The Black Terror and Fighting Yank (both by Jerry Robinson and Mort Meskin). The Fawcett Heroes are featured in 4 – Spy Smasher (Alex Blum), Minuteman (Phil Bard), Mr Scarlet (Jack Binder), Bulletman (Fujitani), plus Ibis the Invincible by Mac Raboy. 5 is a Crimebuster vs Ironjaw story from *Boy Comics* 60–62, written by Charles Biro and drawn by William Overgard, Fred Kida and Norman Maurer. 6 and 8 are both fighting-females issues with examples of The Black Cat, Yankee Girl, Miss Masque, Phantom Lady, Blonde Phantom, Mysta of the Moon, Lorna, Jungle Queen, Miss Victory (different stories illustrated by Charles M. Quinlan, Nina Albright and L.B. Cole), Rulah, Senorita Rio (Nick Cardy) and Lady Luck (Klaus Nordling). The splicing issue, 7, although called 'Best Of The West', only features Western strips from Magazine Enterprises, including 'Trail Colt' and 'Dan Brand And Tipi' by Frank Frazetta, Durango Kid, Tim Holt, The Lemonade Kid (Bob Powell), Straight Arrow (Fred Meagher) and the Calico Kid, The (original) Ghost Rider and The Presto Kid, all by Dick Ayers. 9 offers a selection of Fiction House fighting females (Sheena, Mysta by Ruben Moreira, more Senorita Rio, Firehair and Camilla, both by Bob Lubbers, Tyger Girl, Sky Girl and Glory Forbes, all by Matt Baker, Kaanga by Maurice

Whitman and Futura by Walter Palais). 10 collects stories that feature heroes fighting their arch-foes. There are several reappearances (Cat-Man, Crimebuster and Ibis) but also new faces, including Captain Flash (lovely work by Mike Sekowsky), The Avenger (Bob Powell), Frankenstein (Dick Briefer), Don Winslow of the Navy (Carl Pfuefer and John Jordan), Daredevil (Jack Cole) and, uh, Supermouse.

All in all a rewarding series that will have to do in the absence of any systematic reprinting of these characters.~NF
Recommended: 3, 8, 10

GOLDEN AGE MEN OF MYSTERY
AC Comics: *2 issues + 1996 to date*

Golden age reprints featuring costumed crimefighters, rather than superheroes *per se*. Although a few people may still be able to enjoy the scripts taken at face value, most readers will perceive them ironically and get momentary fun out of silly names and period features like Commando Yank's Red Indian buddy writing to him in pidgin: 'Heap bad trubble' etc. There's some interesting art (rough and ready from a young Mike Sekowsky) and some very fine drawing indeed from people like Jerry Robinson, Mort Meskin and Ruben Moreira. However there's not enough good stuff in each issue to make them must-have items.~FJ

GON
Paradox: *4-issue miniseries 1996*

Outstanding work from Masashi Tanaka, whose black and white landscapes and depictions of nature are stunning. Throw in an anomaly in the form of a voracious mini-dinosaur, Gon, and you have a masterpiece. There's no natural predator that Gon won't attack to assuage his all-consuming appetite. Lions, bears, sharks and eagles all fall prey in these very funny strips. Each issue is a variation on the same theme, three to an issue, but the stunning detail of the artwork more than compensates. These paperbacks are essential reading.~WJ
Recommended: 1–4
Collection: Gon (1–4)

GOOD GIRLS
Fantagraphics: *5 issues 1987–1990*
Rip Off: *1 issue 1991*

Carol Lay's solo showcase, this features two series, each drawn in a more realistic style than her later work. 'Ms. Lonelyhearts' describes the adventures of a columnist for a trash paper, as she gets involved with sundry weirdos and psychos. The ongoing saga of lost heiress Irene Van Der Kamp tells of her struggle to find love and acceptance in the modern world, even though her African tribal foster-parents ritually disfigured her to conform to their standards of beauty. Flip, insouciant, good fun. An anomaly is 4's 'The Visitation', in which, mid-story, Lay draws herself as giving up, uninspired. Cue a visit from her muse, who proceeds to gleefully trash her apartment. This is the first evidence of the looser, more manic style that would show up in her later strips.~HS

THE GOOD GUYS
Defiant: *9 issues 1993–1994*

The 'unique selling point' of this woeful series is that the lead characters are all based on real Defiant readers. Quite why creative genius Jim Shooter thought this would make the comic more interesting is hard to fathom, as the adventures of The Good Guys are no more 'realistic' than those of any other superhero team. Full of self-conscious references to popular comics – Rob Liefeld even makes a 'special guest appearance' in issue one – *The Good Guys* gain their powers after they're exposed to a magical 'wish box' which turns them into the hero of their dreams. Much of the action seems to take place in comic shops frequented by Shooter and his cronies. Bet they didn't sell many of this turkey… ~AL

Batman GORDON'S LAW
DC: *4-issue miniseries 1996–1997*

A first solo fling for long-standing Batman ally Gotham Police Commissioner Gordon. A robbery goes wrong, but the perpetrators still escape, and after six months there are still few clues as to their identity. Gordon discovers, however, that the likely culprits are Gotham police officers, and has to root them out without tipping them off. Klaus Janson's art is moody and complementary to the tale, and it's a surprisingly impressive story from Chuck Dixon, better known for action adventure than characterisation.~FP
Recommended: 1, 2

GORGO
Charlton: *23 issues 1961–1965*

Gorgo was a *Godzilla*-style British movie and the first issue of the comic is an adaptation of the film; thereafter, they made it up as they went along. Gorgo is a huge reptile who's captured and exhibited at Battersea Park, but all too soon his mum comes to rescue him and tramples much of London in the process. Since they are both totally indestructible, further tramplings were inevitable, though the action moves from London after 1. However, in 10 the two save Earth from a Venusian invasion, and in 22 Gorgo chomps on Communist China, so they're not totally lacking in community spirit. It's standard

giant-monster nonsense. Steve Ditko drew 1 and 2 and gave the monsters presence, but thereafter the art was generally uncredited and certainly unremarkable, from the likes of Ernie Bache, Vince Colletta and Bill Montes. There was a back-up 'strange fantasy' story in most issues, presumably to make the Gorgo story look good.~FC

Batman: GOTHAM NIGHTS
DC: *4-issue miniseries 1992, 4-issue miniseries 1995*

The first series is about a number of troubled couples whose problems cause them to converge on a particular area of Gotham when a lonely woman decides to attract the Batman's attention by shooting at people from a high tower. It's a nicely told tale by John Ostrander which heads towards sentimentality at the end but which perfectly encapsulates the Batman's feelings for his city. The artwork by Mary Mitchell is quietly effective and Eduardo Barreto provides some evocative covers. After this, the second series is disappointing. It sees Ostrander and Mitchell back with a story revolving around the people who inhabit or work on Little Paris, a floating theme park in Gotham Bay, but it takes rather predictable paths and Dick Giordano's inks overpower the pencils, removing many of the subtleties of Mitchell's landscapes.~NF

THE GRACKLE
Acclaim: *2 issues + 1997 to date*

The big surprise about this book is how much Paul Gulacy's art has developed recently. Although he's still enamoured of zipatone special effects, most of the stiffness and fiddling around with fancy page layouts has disappeared, leaving a gorgeous, realistic but relaxed fine-line style behind. Pity the story's not up to much. Mike Baron has extracted a number of hoary plot devices from various hard-boiled concepts to give us Cross, an ex-policeman who, on the skids, was rescued by the mysterious Colonel. In return the Colonel uses Cross, and a number of other agents world-wide, for his own ends. In the first story-line we find Cross guarding a Chinese Triad boss from usurping Vietnamese gang members who're trying to muscle in on the trade in Firefly, a designer drug that turns users who OD into human torches. The plot is very complicated, but Baron doesn't seem to realise that complicated doesn't equal complex, or indeed good. Reading *The Grackle* you can't help but feel he's crammed a load of favourite things into one comic, rather uneasily. Would have gone down a storm in 1984, but now seems rather dated wish fulfilment stuff.~FJ

GRAFIK MUSIK
Caliber: *4 issues 1990–1991*

Michael Allred comes into his own with this showcase title. It continues 'It Was' from *Graphique Musique* and runs 'Citizen Nocturne' into 'Goulash'. The latter, bringing in the Frank Einstein character from *Creatures of the Id*, is the strip that will soon become *Madman*, once Allred realised that a costume and codename was more commercial. Both strips provide a taste of Allred at his enthusiastic, least constrained best.~JC

GRAPHIC STORY MONTHLY
Fantagraphics: *7 issues 1990–1991*

Once again Fantagraphics rolled up their sleeves and prepared to give the American public a mostly humorous, intelligent, cultivated anthology of cartoons and illustrated stories. Once again the title folded just as it was getting interesting.

The first issues contained *Prime Cuts* leftovers, including Douglas Michael's 'Adventure Ohio' series and Rick Geary's illustrated version of Flaubert's *Dictionary of Received Ideas*, which is almost finished! 1–5 contain Jacques Tardi's adaptation of the Nestor Burma mystery, 'Fog Over Tolbiac Bridge', from the book by Leo Malet. It's faithful to the original, with its 1950s setting and atmospheric detail, as, typically, Burma receives a mysterious note from an old friend who abruptly dies, which draws him into the shady world of anarchist activists. The other translated material is Franquin's 'Gomer Goof', one page of which appears in all issues.

The other regular strips include yet another Jaxon horror tale set among missionaries and Indians in Mexico (4–6, dull as usual) and Craig Maynard's stories of childhood, which communicate mostly by what they don't say or show (1, 4, 5). There are also regular chunks of Disney producer Ward Kimball's car humour in 'Asinine Alley', a collection of observations and single-panel cartoons.

The Tardi is well worth having, but is available in a collected edition, and there's precious little else of a 'must-have' nature in *Graphic Story Monthly*. Plenty of things raise the odd smile, such as Jim Siergey's 'America', written by Tom Roberts, in which artist Siergey takes a Bill Brysonesque role to praise burger culture and motel comforts in humorously overwrought language in 5, or Roger Langridge's 'Professor Cucumber and his Stereotyped Assistants' in 6. There's little consistency, though. 7 was a cartoonists-on-cartoonists special, ignoring regular strips, and was blessed with a great cover and series of pages by Joe Matt. There's also a sharp parody in the form of Dennis Pimple and T. Motley's 'I Was A Self-Confessional Cartoonist', and Brian

Sendelbach's absurdist 'Billy Mathers' strips which, rather in the manner of *Ernie Pook's Comeek*, ramble childishly on about dead dogs and haircuts.~FJ
Recommended: 7

GRAPHIQUE MUSIQUE
Slave Labor: *3 issues 1990*

This Michael Allred showcase contains two strips, 'It Was…' and 'Citizen Nocturne'. The former is a surreal adventure through the daydreams and subconscious of Calvin Lennox, a child who sees himself as an adult. The latter is a bizarre vampire love story. Allred's style is still in need of a little polish here as he finds his feet with the medium and plays around with the luxury of time to develop the stories, but his promise is already apparent and both strips are valuable to the later continuity of the characters depicted.~JC

GRATEFUL DEAD COMIX
Kitchen Sink: *Series one 7 issues 1991–1993, series two 2 issues 1993–1994*

Grateful Dead songs visually interpreted in underground style by a variety of artists (most notably Tim Truman) with little but song lyrics as text. Occasionally, experiences at live concerts are transcribed. Deadheads will lap this up. For the uninitiated, there is little point.~APS

GRAVEDIGGERS
Acclaim: *4-issue miniseries 1996–1997*

Complex whodunnit from Acclaim's crime-fiction line by Mark Moretti and Rodney Ramos. The title refers to a government department that handles long-unsolved cases. Well constructed with vivid backgrounds but it would be better served without the petty, snide asides at the comics industry giants.~APS

GRAVESTONE
Malibu: *7 issues 1993–1994*

A gravestone marks the location of something deceased and mouldering, and so it is with this poor superhero/horror title.~WJ

GREASEMONKEY
Kitchen Sink: *3 issues + 1995 to date*

Although the title is commonly applied to mechanics, in this case the Greasemonkey is actually a gorilla, living in the 21st century on an almost destroyed Earth. Following the devastation, with sixty per cent of humanity destroyed, some kindly aliens bestow intelligence on some other species. Mac Gimbensky, the gorilla in question, is a star mechanic looking after his all-female squadron, the Barbarians, and given a young human assistant. Written, illustrated and excellently coloured by Tim Eldred, who produces great human-interest stories drawn in a clean, crisp style. It's a lot of fun, and can you really go wrong with a talking ape?~HY

Recommended: 1–3

GREEN ARROW

DC: *4-issue miniseries 1983, 115 issues +, 7 Annuals 1988 to date, 4-issue miniseries ('The Wonder Year') 1993*

Created in 1941, DC's ace archer and his bag of trick arrows survived the death of superheroes in the late 1940s, and was still around as a back-up feature for their revival a decade later. Previously Oliver Queen, independently wealthy adventurer, his character was redefined in the early 1970s in *Green Lantern* 76–89, to become a socially aware crusader without fortune. Finally Green Arrow was given his own miniseries in 1983. It's basically a murder mystery adventure, written by Mike W. Barr, with an old flame of Oliver Queen's leaving him her company to run, much to the displeasure of the other relatives. Predictably enough he's soon a murder target. It's not the sort of story you would expect for an action-oriented character like Green Arrow, but the art by Trevor Von Eeden and Dick Giordano is nice.

The ongoing series began from where *The Longbow Hunters* left off. It's written by Mike Grell and illustrated by Ed Hannigan and Dick Giordano. All are on top form, as the relationship between Green Arrow and his partner Black Canary is fully explored. They're now based in Seattle, and their adventures have a greater human-interest angle, concentrating more on down-to-earth criminal activities as opposed to superpowered villains. The series is suggested for mature readers, and with good reason, as sex and violence play a major role in many stories. Although the violence is never glorified there's sometimes the feeling that Grell is setting out to shock, although sanitised violence passes on the wrong message. The problems of gay-bashing and local gang warfare are highlighted in 5–6, while 17–18 feature the sadistic 'Horseman', who butchers a stripper. Fans of Grell's Jon Sable title may want to check 15 and 16.

The mysterious Japanese warrior woman, Shado, from the Longbow series makes another appearance in 9–12. It's an important story-line that has Shado on the run from her previous employers, Japanese gangsters the Yakuza. She holds the key to hidden treasure in the Philippines, and the US government force Green Arrow to hunt her down in order to maintain good relations and stability with the Philippine government. Or so it seems. This story introduces Eddie Fyres, a sort of free agent who works for various organisations, and will be a catalyst for many plot-lines to come. Shado nearly kills Green Arrow in the course of the story, but something happens while he's recuperating, something he doesn't remember. It's strongly suggested, in her next appearance, that she bears his child, which is kidnapped by her former employers the Yakuza, who now blackmail her to assassinate a famous politician. This is told in 21–24, when Dan Jurgens has taken over the pencilling. Grell and Jurgens also worked on *Warlord*, and that character makes an appearance in 27–28, as everyone is getting the two bearded characters confused.

Besides dealing with the nitty-gritty world, the series explores the problems of environmental pollution, as in 29–30. Green Arrow does some soul-searching in 33, after being tortured in the previous issue and rescued by Black Canary. He thinks back to the time when he killed the man torturing Black Canary. He could've stopped him without killing him, but decided not to. This was a major departure from the old Green Arrow, who was practically comatose when he first killed a villain in the early 1970s. The 'Black Arrow' saga begins in 35, involving Eddie Fyres, whom Green Arrow has to hunt down, or be labelled a traitor. Black Canary becomes involved and enlists the aid of Shado, and the conclusion reveals that Green Arrow was set up for a fall by the authorities. This revelation prompts a journey to find his inner self, beginning in 39. The series is now illustrated by Denys Cowan, who supplies a harsher mood. For the next few issues Green Arrow, on his travels, stumbles across IRA gun smuggling, has an adventure in Wales, and in 46–48 he tackles the problems of animal poaching in Africa. Fulfilling his spiritual quest, he's back home with Black Canary in 50 and shows he can be quite nimble in bed for a man of forty-seven years. Hope for us all then.

59–60 explores the significance of a killer who's released from prison and wants revenge. Rick Hoberg has taken over the pencilling from 53. 'The Hunt For The Red Dragon' saga is told in 63–66, again featuring Shado, whom Green Arrow is hired to find to repay a debt. Of course nothing is as clear-cut as it seems. Grell leaves the series with 80, but his swansong is splitting up the Green Arrow/Black Canary relationship, a DC fixture for over twenty years. The new creative team consists of writer Kevin Dooley, replaced by Chuck Dixon from 83, with art by Jim Aparo, whose work looks wonderful under the inks of Gerry Fernandez. They tell a multi-part saga that ends with the *Zero Hour* crossover in 90. Green Arrow's on the move again as he reaches a 'crossroads' in his life, but the series now seemed be immersed firmly within the DC Universe, with guest appearances from

Catwoman in 86 and the JLA in 88, to name just two. Issue 0 between 90–91 has Green Arrow in a monastery re-evaluating his life as he gives up killing and playing Green Arrow. But he's befriended by a young monk, Connor Hawke, who, strangely, is old enough to be his son. Connor accompanies Queen when he leaves the monastery and the youngster dons the Green Arrow outfit, being a top archer and fan of Green Arrow. It's not before long that Eddie Fyres turns up to involve the archers in another espionage caper. 96–100 is part of the 'Where Angels Fear To Tread' story-line involving Hal Jordan, the old Green Lantern character, and Arsenal, who used to be Speedy, Green Arrow's sidekick. Queen becomes involved in a eco-terrorist group, which apparently results in a plane exploding with Queen on board.

The series carries on with young Green Arrow as he searches for his estranged mother. There's a blast from the past with 110–111 crossing over with Green Lantern 76–77, where the two youngsters, who are searching for Green Lantern's father (there are lots of displaced parents in the DC Universe), head for a town called Desolation. This is where the older Green Lantern and Green Arrow travelled to as part of the relevance era in the early 1970s. The young Green Arrow certainly appears to be a chip off the old block, and with Eddie Fyres along as a good supporting character there's lots of scope for action-oriented adventures. And with Black Canary and Shado guest-starring in 115–116's 'Iron Death', the legend of Green Arrow firmly continues, with Chuck Dixon carrying on the good Grell tradition. Artistically the feature is in the capable hands of rising star Rodolfo Damaggio.

With Gray Morrow art work, Grell also produced Green Arrow: The Wonder Year, which recounts Green Arrow's origin as he's marooned on a desert island. Once back in civilisation he begins his Green Arrow career and meets up with a old girl-friend, who's not all she appears. Despite being yet another excuse for trotting out Green Arrow's origin it's a decently produced series, nicely drawn by Morrow. The origin is retold again in annual 7, bearing little resemblance to the Grell version. Of the other annuals 1–3 all guest-star the Question, and are written by Denny O'Neil, so make for good reading, with 2 the best of them.~HY

Recommended: 5–6, 9–12, 17–19, 21–24, 59–60, 100–101, Annual 2

GREEN CANDLES
Paradox: *3-issue miniseries 1995*

Fourth in a series of crime novels from Paradox released in three digest-sized instalments. Whether regular crime readers will take to getting their story in such instalments (and

paying through the nose for it) only time will tell. Written by novelist Tom De Haven, *Green Candles* revolves around the idea of recovered memory. Under the care of her psychotherapist, Grace Penny has been remembering ritual satanic abuse and is now receiving a series of photos each showing a candle that's getting closer to burning out. Convinced that she's become a target of her abuser, she hires a private detective. He's not good enough to save her, but can he track down her killer? It's a reasonable, if predictable tale, ably if unimpressively drawn by Robin Smith.~NF

Collection: Green Candles (1–3)

GREEN GOBLIN
Marvel: 13 issues 1995–1996

Thirty-one years and three deaths (allegedly) since his first appearance, long-time Spider-Man villain the Goblin finally gets his own title. Teenager Philip Urich, nephew of the veteran *Daily Bugle* reporter, stumbles across one of the Green Goblin's infinite secret hideaways whilst investigating a Norman Osborn warehouse. Startled by a rat, he trips into a vat of Goblin creation chemicals, with predictable consequences. The tone is set for the rest of the series as Tom DeFalco attempts to mimic the teenage *angst* of Peter Parker's early days with sledgehammer subtlety, assisted by Scott McDaniel's Lego-brick artwork. Kudos goes to Philip's attitude (he just wants some kicks from the costume and glider, never mind the hero shtick) and the realistic conclusion. But hey, like, DeFalco's rad dialogue imparted to the gnarley dude is, like, so incredibly mega cool, man, it really psyches you out and, like, leaves you totally kicking. Pass the barf bag.~APS

The GREEN HORNET
Gold Key: *3 issues 1967*

Expository dialogue and wafer-thin plots characterise this pedestrian attempt at transferring the Green Hornet from the small screen to comics. Look out for the third issue's cameo appearance of TV football commentator Jimmy 'the chin' Hill.~FP

The GREEN HORNET
Now: *Series one 14 issues 1989–1991, series two 39 issues, 3 annuals 1991–1994*

Series one establishes a family legacy of Green Hornets and Katos in accounting for the original pulp incarnation of the 30s and the TV version of the 60s. Both take their share in the spotlight as Ron Fortier and Jeff Butler run through the family history in 1–7 and set up an inexperienced Green Hornet and female Kato for the 1990s. Series two sees Mishi Kato replaced by her brother in a more traditional pairing for comics distributed beyond comic shops, and has Chuck Dixon's more action-based scripts until 12, when Fortier returns. Later issues are written by Joan Weis, and changing artists are a feature of the title. Remaining light adventure throughout, there's not a bad issue in either series, nor is there an excellent one. For a sample of the first series issue 1 is as good as any, and 33–34 of series two feature a recurring villain and spotlight Green Hornet's romantic life.~WJ

Tales of the GREEN HORNET

Now: *2-issue microseries 1990, 4-issue miniseries 1992, 3-issue miniseries 1992, One-shot 1992*

Wanting to flog their Green Hornet licence for all it was worth, Now had created rather a sticky wicket for themselves by updating the concept to the 1990s in the regular title. Never mind, how about some miniseries of the 'classic' 1940s and 1960s versions? 1960s TV Green Hornet Van Williams plotted the first series, but it's nothing special, and inappropriate, foggy art from Del Barras rather scuppers the project. The following two series are dull. Avoid.~FP

GREEN LANTERN

DC: *Series one: 224 issues, 3 Annuals 1960–1972 (1–89), 1976–1988 (90–224), series two 81 issues + 5 Annuals 1990 to date*

'In brightest day, in darkest night no evil shall escape my sight. Let those who worship evil's might beware my power: Green Lantern's light.' With that oath Earthman Hal Jordan recharges his power ring, a device that enables him to do anything provided his willpower is up to the task. This was the concept as introduced in *Showcase* 22, when a red-skinned alien crashed on Earth, summoning test pilot Jordan, whom he's selected to succeed him in his role as an intergalactic protector. Given the power ring, Jordan must recharge it once every twenty-four hours from a power battery, which resembles a green lantern, the name Jordan adopts as his crimefighting guise.

The concept actually updated a 1940s character, although beyond the idea of the ring Jordan bore little similarity to his predecessor, whose background was more mystical. Editor Julius Schwartz, writer John Broome and illustrator Gil Kane were the initial creators. Broome's plotting was science-fiction-based, but was also adept at characterisation, and Kane was noted for his action-packed style: his layouts were very distinctive and dramatic, although he was sometimes let down by inker Joe Giella. The first issue reveals that Jordan isn't the only Green Lantern, and in fact he's part of a corps under the Guardians Of The Universe, little blue men sworn to protect the universe and operating 3600 Green Lanterns. Jordan's personal life was a constant counterpoint to the superhero action. He was employed by Ferris Aircraft and had romantic intentions towards Carol Ferris, her father's choice of company M.D. She attempted to distance herself from Jordan while lusting after Green Lantern, which made Jordan determined to make her love him for himself. The other supporting character was a young Eskimo grease-monkey called Pieface, although his real name was Thomas Kalmaku. Despite the patronising nickname, he was actually a decently portrayed non-white character. Villains included the belligerent Weaponeers of Qward introduced in 2, the giant intellect of Hector Hammond, Sonar master of magnetism, and, in 7, the renegade Green Lantern Sinestro. The red-skinned, dome-headed Sinestro had been expelled from the Green Lantern Corps, but obtained a yellow power ring, yellow being the one weakness of the Green Lanterns, due to an impurity in the power source. His threat would be the most frequent over the years. Second on that list was actually Carol Ferris, who in 16 was transformed into Star Sapphire by a race of warrior women. It wasn't permanent, but did recur, mostly without her knowledge, thus presenting an extra dilemma when she fought Green Lantern. Their relationship was developed in a back-up strip concentrating on Hal Jordan's civilian life, from 22 the exclusive territory for Broome, who was replaced as writer on the lead feature by Gardner Fox.

13 was the first teaming of Flash and Green Lantern, a partnership successfully repeated many times over the next twenty years. By now Kane's art was looking even better due to the occasional inking of Murphy Anderson, to be followed by Sid Greene, whose delicate feathering style was very suited to dynamic superheroics. Broome was back as the writer for 40. It gave the Guardians of the Universe an origin and featured the 1940s Green Lantern, Alan Scott. He would make occasional appearances over the next few years, and there was always a nice feel to the issues in which the two characters got together. The mid-1960s saw some changes for Jordan, and after his relationship with Carol Ferris collapsed he quit his job to become an adventurer. It should be noted, by the way, that the Guardians' code forbade the use of the power ring for personal gain. The art improved still further when Kane began inking as well, cementing the dynamic, forceful look for the character. 59 introduced Guy Gardner in an 'imaginary' story positing what might have occurred had the power ring initially been given to the second-choice Gardner, then a teacher and a very different character from the one who would later become popular.

There were assorted creative changes from 61, with Mike Friedrich and Denny O'Neil contributing stories, and Kane's spectacular return in 68 after a short absence, now inking his own pencils. The big change, though, came with 76, now renowned, but at the time a desperate attempt to save a dying title. The title now co-credited Green Arrow, Oliver Queen, who'd been given a personality refit in *The Brave And The Bold* 85, and was now a socially aware crusader, and one of the first of the grittier superheroes. His teaming with Green Lantern led them to explore the social issues of the time in 76–89, marvellously written by Denny O'Neil and lavishly pencilled by Neal Adams, inked by Dick Giordano. The Guardians of the Universe had one of their number accompany the pair as they explored into America to learn more about humanity. There was a far greater sophistication than in any other superhero comic to that date, and topics covered included corrupt slumlords, pollution, the treatment of Native Americans, small-town mentality, religious sects and overpopulation. O'Neil never forgets the superhero soap-opera elements, and the reappearance of Carol Ferris in 84 is particularly touching.

85–86 are the most famous issues from this run, shining the spotlight on the drug problem as personified by Green Arrow's former partner Speedy, Roy Harper. Commendably, it offers no easy solutions, but an understanding of how anyone can become hooked. There's also some fine characterisation as Green Arrow, knowing and self-righteous throughout the run, is faced with his own shortcomings. 87 introduces John Stewart, in a story focusing on racial prejudice. Stewart is the Guardians' choice of replacement for Jordan should he be unable to fulfil his duties, and will become an increasingly important character over the years. In the Green Arrow back-up titled 'What Can One Man Do?' a riot ends in tragedy, resulting in Oliver Queen deciding to run for mayor. The run ends with a powerful story counterbalancing ecological needs with employment needs, but despite winning numerous industry awards, the series wasn't popular enough with the readership to ward off cancellation. From that point the back-up strip in *Flash* was Green Lantern's home for the next few years. The O'Neil/Adams stories were later reprinted as a seven-issue series (including their final tale from *Flash* 217–219) titled *Green Lantern/Green Arrow*.

Green Arrow was still part of the title when *Green Lantern* was revived in 1976, and O'Neil, in the company of artist Mike Grell, concentrated on human-interest stories without the overt social issues, but with a nice superhero feel. The best of his early issues was a pseudo-medieval setting with Sinestro in 92. 100 introduced a new Air Wave, Hal Jordan's cousin, an introduction made when someone noticed the 1940s Air Wave was named Larry Jordan, so, of course, they had to be related! Alex Saviuk was now the unspectacular artist. John Stewart and Green Arrow's partner Black Canary were featured supporting characters until Green Lantern flew solo again with 122, and 116 returned Guy Gardner, now a Green Lantern for the first time. O'Neil's issues to 131 gradually define his more aggressive and objectionable character.

123 introduced the artwork of Joe Staton, and the next writer was Marv Wolfman, who introduced Bruce Gordon, Eclipso, to the cast, along with a greater soap-opera feel, dropping subplots here, there and everywhere. Wolfman also began featuring other Green Lanterns, many of them aliens introduced in the *Tales Of The Green Lantern Corps* miniseries, and 148 began a back-up strip with the same title, replacing the uneventful Adam Strange series, which had been in place from 132. Wolfman introduced the Omega Men, later to have their own title, in the undistinguished 141–144, but his best idea was his swansong, exiling Green Lantern from Earth for a year, in 152–171. While giving a needed change to the title, these attempts to emulate the old-style DC science-fiction stories didn't work, with a 1980s audience expecting a contemporary comic, not one rehashing old stories. Mike Barr's wonderfully titled 'Rotten To The Corps' in 154–156 was the best of the run, extrapolating the cultural differences between various Green Lanterns, with 156 drawn by Gil Kane. Keith Pollard replaced Staton from 157, and was far more suited to the space stories, and 171 is notable for the art of Alex Toth, inked by Terry Austin.

It was all change with 172 as a vast improvement was instituted by the new creative team of writer Len Wein and artist Dave Gibbons, who'd drawn a few of the back-up strips previously. Gibbons was by far and away the best artist to work on the revived strip, with an appealing style and excellent story-telling skills. Hal Jordan was returned to Earth and to Ferris Aircraft, where company problems result in an ultimatum from Carol Ferris that sees Jordan resigning from the Green Lantern Corps, to be replaced by John Stewart. With 186, though, Wein and Gibbons left to allow for Steve Englehart and the unfortunate return of Joe Staton. Stewart remained as Green Lantern, becoming romantically involved with red-skinned humanoid Green Lantern Katma Tui. Star Sapphire was also back in 192, and 194–198 involve the entire Green Lantern Corps, the renegade Sinestro, and a battle between Guy Gardner and John Stewart. Hal Jordan returns as Green Lantern with 199, and with 201 the title changes to *The Green Lantern Corps* in order to accommodate the proliferation of Green Lanterns, although the series remains set on Earth. The unfortunately named Killowog becomes a popular character, and 208–210 see him enlisted by the Soviet Union. Not caring for the politically divisive nature of Earth politics, he's happy to develop battle armour for the Soviets, resulting in the Rocket Reds. The story is badly let down by an appalling 'oh, the Commies are bad after all' ending, painting Mikhail Gorbachev, the man revolutionising the Soviet Union, as a deceiver and murderer. The confrontational attitude of Guy Gardner also proves a problem. There are further changes to the cast, including the novel introduction of a dead Green Lantern in 218, but by now the fragmentation has left the series too diluted from its essence. The original idea of one man with a ring able to do anything has no meaning when he's surrounded by a team of similarly endowed people, and, endearing though some of the characters were, the series limped to a close.

The first and the second series were bridged by *Emerald Dawn*, recounting Hal Jordan's background prior to becoming Green Lantern. The first issues of the new series, by Gerard Jones and Pat Broderick, reduce the cast to Jordan, Gardner and Stewart, with none of them predominating. Jones is very much a hot-and-cold writer, and his tenure is very hit-and-miss, although a sense of humour serves well for stories starring the doglike Green Lantern G'Nort (9–12). 14–17 introduce the idea of Mosaic, battles between cities on the Guardians' home planet, and John Stewart is cleaved off into a solo series with that title. 19 was the fiftieth anniversary of the character, and features the original article in a story drawn by his creator Martin Nodell. 30–31 cross over with *Flash* 69–70 for Jones to have some fun with the 'Gorilla Warfare' story, co-starring two more than averagely intelligent animals, Detective Chimp and Rex The Wonder Dog. Apart from nostalgic interludes, though, there was little occurring to grab anyone's attention.

46, however, plays a big role in the advancement of Hal Jordan's character. His home city is destroyed in 46, and 48 begins the 'Emerald Twilight' series written by Ron Marz. Jordan attempts to resurrect Coast City and all its inhabitants, apparently contravening the personal-gain clause of the Guardians' code. The Guardians demand the surrender of his ring and at the same time devastate the restored city, thus driving Hal Jordan to insanity. By the time the plot concludes in 50 (under a glow-in-the-dark cover) pretty much everything has been changed, and when the power ring is passed to the younger Kyle Raynor in 51 there's only one other Green

Lantern, Guy Gardner having been changed. There was obviously a need to revitalise Green Lantern, both title and character. The manner of doing so, though, ran roughshod over previous characterisation, with no consideration for the staunch fans sticking with the title, being crass and callous.

With a new Green Lantern in place, though, the same old themes prevailed, the only difference being the aspect of someone learning on the job. Hal Jordan is still around, now known as Parallax, and meets his successor in 55, while Guy Gardner drops by in 60. 71–73 are titled 'The Hero Quest', as Green Lantern tries to discover just what it is to be a hero, encountering guest stars aplenty, each with a different idea. He's also been romancing Donna Tory, of the Darkstars, the organisation replacing the Green Lantern Corps as protectors of the universe. 76 and 77 shadow those issues from the first series, guest-starring the new Green Arrow. Writer Ron Marz and artist Darryl Banks aren't up to the O'Neil and Adams standard, but they maintain a decent balance of superheroic battles and human interludes. Their best so far is 81, in which Hal Jordan is laid to rest in a very nice homage, with many guest appearances highlighting his heroic past, and enabling Kyle Raynor to fly free of any previous associations.~HY

Recommended: Series one 40, 52, 63, 76–87, 89, series two 81

Collection: Green Lantern Archives (Showcase 22–24, series one 1–5), The Road Back (series two 1–8)

GREEN LANTERN CORPS QUARTERLY
DC: *8 issues 1992–1994*

Spinning off from Green Lantern's own title, this explores various aspects of the intergalactic peace-keeping force, headed by the Guardians of the Universe. Each of the 3600 members protects a sector of the universe; they're limited only by their will in what their power rings enable them to do. Additionally, the series concentrates on Alan Scott, the original 1940s Green Lantern, and a man with no connection to the Corps. His stories are a bit of a treat for fans of the Justice Society of America, as various members guest-star, nicely told by Roger Stern. The story in 3 is a sad occasion, as it concerns the death of the original Black Canary.

The Green Lantern Corps are certainly a mixed bunch. In 1, we're introduced to Jack T. Chance, who's a bad as they come. He's from a long line of lovable rogues and is clearly inspired by that mean-son-of-a-bitch intergalactic hitman, Lobo, and it's no surprise that they meet in 8. The other regular feature

stars G'Nort, a canine Green Lantern, who isn't very good at what he does and is played for laughs. Lots of choice creators contribute to some decent short stories, one of the best being in 6 by Mike Baron and Chas Truog, featuring a middle-aged female alien looking after a community based very much on the old West. She's the local sheriff, but tries not to use her power ring too often, and doesn't like flying because it makes her sick. Others to look out for include Doug Moench/Paul Gulacy collaborations in 1 and 2, a nicely drawn story by Dave Cockrum in 3, and fan favourite Travis Charest contributing to a tale in 6. There should be something here for everyone.~HY
Recommended: 3, 6

THE GREEN PLANET
Charlton: *1 issue 1962*

This contains three science-fiction stories, the longest and most entertaining of which is 'The Green Planet', which deserves a special award for the lack of realism in its depiction of political exile on an uncolonised planet. The other two stories are just as ridiculous, but with no laughs.~FC

GREENHOUSE WARRIORS
Tundra: *1 issue 1992*
Phil Elliott Publishing: *3 issues + 1993 to date*

Phil Elliott's plant-based superheroes are a great deal less politically correct than the concept may suggest. In fact they're a lot of fun, despite fighting eco-villains and occasionally coming on like public-service announcements. Elliott's art is extremely pared down for this title, giving it the feel of a comic for very young children, but his gentle humour and complex characterisation are certainly for adults. Six issues are planned in the series.~FJ

GREGORY
Piranha: *4 issues 1989–1993*

Gregory conclusively proves that Marc Hempel is one of America's most consistently underappreciated comic illustrators. Almost every page in this series contains some delightfully designed drawing, a moment of inventive continuity or a piece of sly visual humour. Gregory is a virtually mute little boy who lives in a lunatic asylum. Although he's offered the chance of freedom, Gregory understandably prefers the comfort of his cell to the terrors of the outside world. His best friend is Herman Vermin, a wisecracking rodent who becomes a little bit tiresome when given the spotlight in *Gregory* 2. In fact, after the self-contained pleasures of the first and longest volume, the following three instalments all seem slightly superfluous, just rehashing the same scenes and situations found in issue one. 4 is particularly disappointing, as Hempel

descends into bathos with a story about a dysfunctional family who adopt Gregory and are healed by his innocent goodness. However, for most of the run Hempel's craft and compassion ensure that *Gregory* is never less than an off-beat, pleasantly gentle read, one which should interest readers bored by the standard brutalities of most mainstream comics.~AL
Recommended: 1

GRENDEL
Comico: *Series one 3 issues 1983–1984, series two 40 issues 1986–1990*
Dark Horse: *10-issue limited series ('War Child') 1992–1993, One-shot ('Devil By The Deed') 1993, One-shot ('Cycle') 1995*

After first appearing in *Comico Primer* 2, Matt Wagner's *Grendel* enjoyed cult success in black and white. Wagner's early artwork showed promise but lacked finish, and these early strips remain more of a curiosity than an essential part of what would become a significant tale. Wagner's commercial potential was fulfilled with *Mage*, which, from issue 6, contained the story of Grendel as its back-up. Christine Spar's novel, 'Devil By The Deed' (reprinted by Dark Horse), is beautifully designed and rendered by Wagner, falling somewhere between comic strip and illustrated story. It's the story of the original Grendel, Hunter Rose, and his downfall at the hands of the wolf Argent. Christine is the daughter of Stacy, adopted daughter of Hunter Rose, who was his heir. From then on the role of Grendel, a masked assassin who carries a deadly, dual-bladed spear, evolves into something more.

The second Comico series is a number of separate tales of various lengths in which the nature of the Grendel persona changes, moving on from one person to the next. 1–12 tell the story of how Christine Spar becomes Grendel after the kidnapping of her son by the vampire Tujiro. Though she can't kill Tujiro she forces him into hiding but can't relinquish the mask and eventually dies at the hands of Argent, though not without taking his life in turn. It's very stylishly drawn by Arnold and Jacob Pander. Christine's boy-friend Brian Li Sung becomes the next Grendel (13–15), illustrated by Bernie Mireault. This is followed in 16–19 with tales of Hunter Rose as told by Captain Albert Wiggins, a policeman who had known him but who would eventually go mad, illustrated in an experimental manner by Wagner himself.

The next four issues leap into the future and examine the way that Grendel moves from physical villain to archetype, the devil, illustrated by Hannibal King and Tim Sale. This is only the precursor to 'God And The

Devil' (24–33), in which a dominant Christian Church has become despotic under the leadership of Pope Innocent XLII (actually the ageless Tujiro). Tujiro plans to build a tower in Denver containing a nuclear-powered gun meant to eradicate the Sun. He is opposed by an idiot-savant Grendel, Eppy Thatcher, a terrorist, and politician Orion Assante. 'Devil's Reign' (34–40) sees the return of Tim Sale as Orion forges a world-wide empire in the aftermath of the sungun's destruction. Orion's troops begin to refer to themselves as Grendels and following his code of ethics, and he becomes the first Grendel-Khan with the destruction of Japan.

War Child picks up the story when, on his death, Orion's wife tries to assume power. The cyborg Grendel Prime kidnaps Orion's heir, Jupiter. After nearly being killed fighting the remnants of the vampires and his mother's troops, Jupiter becomes the second Grendel-Khan, in a series illustrated by Patrick McEown with inks by Wagner. Cycle is a history of the title and character with a timeline and primer illustrated by Wagner. 'Devil's Vagary' (1987) was a special story done for the Comico Collection, written by Wagner and illustrated by Dean Motter. Devil's Quest is a single-issue reprinting of the Grendel Prime back-up story from Grendel Tales. Grendel is an intelligent and ambitious series that thwarts expectations. It can be read simply as an adventure strip (albeit one with a long and complex plot), but it's also an examination of the nature of evil and a satire on the relationship between society and religion, politics and the media.~NF

Recommended: Series two 16–40, Devil By The Deed, Warchild 1–10

Collections: The Devil Inside (13–15), The Devil's Legacy (1–12), Grendel Classics (16–19)

GRENDEL TALES

Dark Horse: *6-issue miniseries ('Four Devils, One Hell') 1993–1994, 3-issue miniseries ('The Devil's Hammer') 1994, 5-issue miniseries ('The Devil In Our Midst') 1994, 2-issue microseries ('Devils And Deaths') 1994, 3-issue miniseries ('Homecoming') 1994–1995, 4-issue miniseries ('Devil's Choices') 1995, 6-issue miniseries ('The Devil May Care') 1995–1996*

Grendel Tales is the vehicle by which writers other than creator Matt Wagner can have a go at Grendel stories. Set in the world following War Child, these concern individual Grendel soldiers, the people they protect (or not) and the clan societies into which the Grendels have fallen.

James Robinson and Teddy Kristiansen get the series off to a good start with 'Four Devils, One Hell', starting as a character-based view of people in a Grendel-run society, and descending into a battle for the throne of France, climaxing in a violent New Orleans Mardi Gras. In 'Devil's Hammer' Rob Walton and Bernie Mireault have a young man, the lone survivor of a village destroyed by Grendels, who becomes one himself for revenge, but is unable to release the power of Grendel once that revenge has been taken. 'The Devil In Our Midst' has a Grendel seeking redemption at an Ice Station in Antarctica but there's a mysterious virus killing the crew and he comes under suspicion as the cause of the disease. This is a fine thriller by Steve Seagle, with excellent artwork by Paul Grist. Darko Macan and Edvin Biukovic's 'Devils And Deaths' seems like another straightforward tale of rivalry amongst Grendels, but blends deception, despair and heroism into a grim little tale about the need to belong.

Grendel Susan returns home to her lover Avril, who has become a whore to the local Grendel clan, in 'Homecoming', by Patrick McEown and Dave Cooper. When Avril tries to leave, she is killed and Susan exacts a bloody revenge. Similarly emotional, though not so violent, is Terry LaBan and Peter Doherty's 'The Devil May Care', a love story, albeit a doomed one. LaBan's script is complemented by Doherty's Moebius-like artwork. Macan and Biukovic return for 'Devil's Choices', which is about clan rivalries and an attempt by several of the Grendels to escape what they see as a life with no future.

Obviously lacking the direction that gave the Grendel series its coherence, Grendel Tales are generally of a high quality, enriching the Grendel world set up by Wagner as the creators stamp their individual visions onto the overall structure. 'Devil Quest', reprinted as a single issue, runs as a back-up by Wagner from 'The Devil's Hammer' to the first issue of 'Devil's Choices'.~NF

Recommended: 'The Devil In Our Midst', 'The Devil May Care', 'Devils and Deaths', 'Four Devils, One Hell', 'Homecoming'

GREY

Viz: *9 issues 1988–1989*

The only way the exotically named Grey Death can escape the grim reality of life in the future is to join The Troopers and work his way through the ranks to Class A, at which point he'll be granted status as a citizen, and afforded a comfortable existence. The odds against this are 33 to 1. Grey's progress is phenomenal, but then he begins caring, and to learn more of the world he inhabits. Long, albeit spectacularly drawn, battle-action sequences give the feel of watching someone play a computer game, and the payoff is predictable once issue 6 reveals the background to Grey's world. Warning: don't read Harlan Ellison's first issue introduction as it rather gives the game away.~FP

GREY LEGACY

Fragile Elite: *1 issue 1994*

The genial Les begins his university career by becoming starstruck in the presence of the glamorous Taija. His constant paeans of praise are a source of distraction and irritation to his room-mate, the studious Grey, who's apparently going to develop into someone who'll change the universe. This collects the first two issues, which were originally self-published, which accounts for the abrupt change of pace halfway through as Les befriends a small alien kept as a class specimen. There's an endearing charm and innocence to this story that might almost date it from the 1950s, but the dialogue is sharper than most 1950s material, and the excellent cartooning comes via Jaime Hernandez and Phil Foglio. Wayne Wise and Fred Wheaton are listed as creators, and it's a great shame there was apparently no second issue.~WJ

GREYLORE

Sirius: *5 issues 1985–1986*

Heroic fantasy saga of two linked worlds, one technological, the other medieval, and rogue hero Greylore, who forms the nexus between them. Meddling wizards steer his actions to ensure that 'destiny is fulfilled'. Bat-like familiar Pox provides the better moments of comic relief. Production problems plague Bo Hampton's artwork and the absence of issue 6 in a six-issue limited series – advertised but never published – renders the whole affair irrelevant.~APS

THE GRIFFIN

Slave Labor: *3 issues 1988*
DC: *6-issue limited series 1991–1992*

In 1967 Matt Williams is recruited by an alien race called the Acacians and transformed into a super-solider. Homesick twenty years on, Williams returns to Earth, causing complications all round. Family and friends have assumed him dead for two decades, and the Acacians believe him to have deserted and are prepared to destroy the planet to ensure his return. By concentrating on the emotions prompted by the scenario, and the political machinations on Earth and Acacia, Dan Vado and Norman Felchle construct a compelling story. Not the least of their triumphs is the transformation of Williams from boy hero with stunted emotional growth to possible planetary saviour. Fine artwork from Felchle and inker Mark McKenna rounds off an excellent title. The Slave Labor issues are re-drawn as the first book and a half of the DC series.~FP
Recommended: 1–6

GRIFFITH OBSERVATORY

Rip Off: *1 issue 1979*
Fantagraphics: *1 issue 1993*

By far Bill Griffith's most accessible work, *Griffith Observatory* is also a career peak, the success of *Zippy The Pinhead* notwithstanding. Collecting one-page syndicated strips, Griffith exposes the foibles, obsessions and trivialities of late-1970s culture with a venomous yet considered eye. Always interesting, by turns it's also wistful, heartfelt, angry and informative. Where else could one learn under one cover about Mansard roofs, that people collect barbed wire, and that Jimmy Durante once played a violin duet with Albert Einstein? And one of his predictions for the 1980s is distressingly true for the 1990s. Griffith would later mine similar territory in more abstruse fashion through Zippy, although never as pleasingly. The Rip Off edition appeared while the strip was still in syndication, so the still available Fantagraphics collection reprinting the entirety along with sixteen new pages is the better purchase.~WJ
Recommended: Fantagraphics 1

GRIFTER

Image: *Series one 10 issues 1995–1996, Series two 14 issues 1996–1997*

WildStorm's favourite tough-guy-with-a-heart gets his own series, and the opportunity to delve a little deeper into his past, motivations and psyche. Flashbacks to childhood abuse and his complicated relationship with Zealot flesh out the action, the continuing theme of which is that no matter how hard Grifter tries to live a quiet life, trouble always finds him. The series loses its way a little in the middle, due more to inconsistent artwork (between 4 and 10 there are five changes of penciller) than to Stephen Seagle's relentlessly action-packed scripts. The last issue finds our hero in a depressed and contemplative mood for a conclusion rounding off the series more logically and sensitively than you might expect. The second series, by Stephen Grant, Mel Rubi and Richard Friend, tells single-issue stand-alone stories which fill in more information on the character's background and motivations. Issue 3 is outstanding.~JC
Recommended: Series one 2–6, 10, series two 3

GRIFTER/SHI

Image/Crusade: *2-issue microseries 1996*

WildStorm's favourite gunslinger and Crusade's ninja babe team up to stop a Korean nuclear bomb from devastating Japan. It's prettily put together by members of both characters' regular creative teams, including some lovely pencil work by Travis Charest; the writing is adequate though nothing special. The 'story so far' at the start of issue 2 takes a whole page of text and tells you a good couple of hundred years of Japanese history, in case you ever wanted to know where to find it in a comic.~JC

Collection: Grifter/Shi (1–2)

THE GRIM GHOST
Atlas: *3 issues 1975*

Satan offers a 17th-century highwayman the opportunity to return to 20th-century USA equipped with a flying horse and assorted superpowers. His purpose is to ensure a steady supply of evil souls flowing to hell. No classic, but readable, with nice art from Ernie Colon.~FP

GRIMJACK
First: *81 issues 1983–1991*

Grimjack should have been First's best title. It's set in the city of Cynosure, where the wily, grizzled bruiser John Gaunt initially showed great potential. Writer John Ostrander set up a peach of a situation, a Cynosure the place where all realities met. This let *Grimjack* have all sorts of adventures, from hard-boiled detective stories to dimension-spanning epics, from *Cat-And-The-Canary*-suspects-trapped-in-a big-house horror tales to Western shoot-'em-ups. Grimjack himself is a classic anti-hero with a sob-story background and a tough reputation redeemed by random acts of kindness. And Ostrander is clever enough to underpin the series with a titanic struggle between Grimjack and the bunch of winning outsiders he has drawn around him, and an array of human and demonic villains, mostly from Grimjack's unpleasant past.

The title started life as a back-up in *Starslayer* 10–18, a pleasing mixture of sudden action and whimsy (particularly reflected in its own back-up strip, *Munden's Bar*, which attracted all sorts of guest writers and artists and its own special). Although Tim Truman was clearly still learning, he picked things up fast and the initial awkwardness of action is largely gone by the third or fourth issue. 1–12 are well worth reading for a satisfying mix of ongoing plotting and terse story-telling, as Ostrander fleshes out the mysterious city and his broody protagonist's many acquaintances. The *Starslayer* shorts and 1–4 are reprinted as *Grimjack Casefiles*. Soon afterwards, however, things get a bit too complicated for their own good. The balance between ongoing mega-plot and satisfactory short sub-plots shifts and suddenly there are so many things to explain that there's barely time to allow existing characters to grow. Ostrander solves this by introducing more and more bad guys from Grimjack's murky past, who pop up whenever the bodycount's getting too low. The other great problem is the characterisation of

Grimjack himself. He's a pawn of the situation, changing from understanding old bouncer to killing machine to tortured soul depending on the needs of the month's plot. However, up until 19, when Truman left the title, there was enough going for it to keep it readable.

Replacement artist Tom Sutton did a competent job as plots nose-dived towards magic and demon wars. When Tom Mandrake took on the art chores with 31 (and he drew like it was a chore), the title was firmly in decline. Grimjack was about to be killed and re-born younger, one page relishing death, the next swearing to come back for revenge. Conveniently, his re-birth allowed him to develop psychic and mystical powers. Having faced up to his past for the umpteenth time, Grimjack mark two bit the dust in 54 after meeting his far-future self, and 55 saw the character re-born yet again, 200 years into the future. At which point most sensible people sighed and gave up, if only because in Flint Henry First found an artist even less capable than Mandrake. Maybe Ostrander fancied a bit more science fiction, a bit more *American Flagg*-style cleverness? Who knows, or indeed wants to know? Anyone who can enjoy the series beyond 50 is to be saluted.~FJ

Recommended: 1–12

GRIT BATH
Fantagraphics: *2 issues 1993–1994*

Deliberately provocative mixture of scatological black humour and child sexuality from writer/artist Renée French. Her crude, naïve art-style makes this a deeply unsettling comic, one likely to offend a great many readers. Certainly unique, but difficult to recommend.~AL

GROO The Wanderer
Pacific: *8 issues 1982–1984*
Eclipse: *One-shot 1984*
Epic: *120 issues, 2 Graphic Novels 1985–1995*
Image: *12 issues 1995–1996*

Groo the Wanderer is an expert fighter whose sword is for hire to whomsoever will pay him or feed him. He's quite possibly the greatest warrior in his fantasy world (whatever you might hear from that blond braggart Arcadio). It has to be said, however, that Groo is a bit (okay, a lot) short on cunning and intelligence. Oh, and he's accident-prone. And he doesn't bathe. In fact he's so fond of a fray that he's as likely to rush in and kill everyone as work out first which side he's supposed to be fighting for. And whatever you do, don't invite him to build anything for you; or demolish anything, for that matter. And especially, don't let him anywhere near your fleet – he can sink a ship just by looking at it. Groo has a sister, Grooella, who is always embarrassed by him. And he has a dog, Rufferto, whose devotion to his master is surpassed only by his willing blindness to Groo's stupidity. Groo's world is further populated by The Sage (a wise man who acts as occasional narrator, and is almost as accident-prone as Groo), The Minstrel, Taranto (Groo's former mercenary buddy who's usually trying to kill him), the witches Arba and Dakarba, who would like to get revenge on Groo, and Pal and Drumm, the one a promoter, the other a dumb fighter who can't believe that Groo's better than him. Not forgetting the beautiful Chakall, skilled she-warrior with whom Groo fancies himself in love.

Driven by a desire for cheese dip, a hatred of being called a mendicant and the inability to hold down a job for longer than it takes to ruin whatever semblance of civilisation he finds himself in, Groo somehow manages to survive, and, even if he doesn't come out on top, ends each adventure in a better state than the unfortunates he's been fighting (or, for that matter, helping). Created, written and drawn by Sergio Aragonés (with scripting assistance from Mark Evanier, lettering by Stan Sakai and colouring by Tom Luth), Groo can be achingly funny but usually it's merely hilarious. The running joke is that every Groo story is the same, although you'll find you appreciate it more the more you read. Aragonés is a genius cartoonist whose densely peopled panels are full of detail, interest and incidental humour.

Six issues of The Groo Chronicles reprint the Pacific and Eclipse issues. The Death Of Groo graphic novel has Groo trying to play St George, but rumours of his death, greeted with some jubilation, are exaggerated. The Life Of Groo covers his birth and youthful adventures, and is available in a standard-comic-sized issue – extremely difficult to find – and the Graphitti Designs book-sized package.~NF
Recommended: pick a dozen, any dozen
Collections: The Groo Adventurer (Epic 1–4), *The Groo Bazaar* (Epic 5–8), *The Groo Carnival* (9–12), *The Groo Dynasty* (13–16), *The Groo Expose* (17–20), *The Groo Festival* (21–24), *The Groo Garden* (25–28)

GROOVY
Marvel: 3 *issues 1968*

Not a comic *per se*, but a comic-shaped collection of gag cartoon panels from cheap men's magazines. Terrible stuff, badly reproduced.~HS

Mike Baron's THE GROUP LARUE
Innovation: 3-issue miniseries 1989

The strained title-pun apart (the French for werewolf is *loup-garue* – geddit?), there's little of note in this inane fantasy title, where a group of gamers actually get to live out their fantasies, one of them being transformed into a man-wolf, hence the title.~FP

GUARDIANS OF METROPOLIS
DC: 4-issue miniseries, 1994–1995

Kirby's Guardian and Newsboy Legion get their own series courtesy of Karl Kesel and Keiron Dwyer. A dopey but entertaining romp through Project Cadmus and the big city as the boys aim to 'rescue' their mentor's great-niece from the clutches of Granny Goodness. Not the most intelligent comic of the decade, but great fun.~JC

GUARDIANS OF THE GALAXY
Marvel: 62 issues, 4 Annuals 1990–1995

The previous run of the Guardians in the pages of *Marvel Presents* had been a quirky little gem, but besides frequent guest status no one expected to see their title again, let alone expected a surprise hit. Although Jim Valentino's art is bog-standard his writing is an interesting twist on the *Blake's Seven* scenario. Charlie 27, Martinex, Nikki, Yondu, Vance Astro and Starhawk are survivors of a vast interstellar war, almost the last of their race, who band together and safeguard the Milky Way (as one does). The interesting twist on the series is that it occurs in the 31st century of the Marvel Universe. This is a galaxy where the legend of Captain America still lives as the ultimate hero, leading the team to name their spacecraft after him. 1–6 start well with a quest for Captain America's shield. We soon start to see future versions of classic Marvel characters such as Iron Man (as Overkill in 11 and 12), and Ghost Rider, in 13. Interesting initially, the novelty wears off as the series progresses and it becomes clear that every present-day Marvel character is likely to pop up in a future guise. A new direction began with 17, in which Vance Astro acquires a new costume and name, Major Victory, to fit his role as Captain America's successor. 21–29 have a huge battle set in the twentieth century between the Guardians and a motley crew led by Doctor Octopus for possession of the Avengers' mansion, the Avengers being away at the time. Much of the actions drifts away from the core team to focus on the machinations of the dull villains. Back in the 31st century plotting between Dr Doom and Rancor, a female future version of Wolverine first seen in 9, comes to a head with a huge fallout in 39, in which Doc uses the long-deceased original Wolverine's adamantium skeleton as armour! Thereafter it's all filling time until a bumper 50, in which the Guardians discover the truth about themselves, a process which continued in *The Galactic Guardians* miniseries and annual 4. Things settle down again until the 30th-century Galactus and Silver Surfer, last seen in 25, pop up again in 60 to cause more trouble. Overall *Guardians Of The Galaxy* isn't bad. The writing is consistent and the art is functional, but there's far better comics out there to be reading.~TP

Collection: *Guardians Of The Galaxy* (1–6)

GUERILLA GROUNDHOG

Eclipse: *2 issues 1987*

Chuck Wagner's mutant groundhog fights his own political war. The title is full of ridiculous ideas, like communism coming from the red spot on Jupiter and a groundhog promoted to a job in the US government. Very poorly written, not very funny and with nothing positive going for it.~SS

GUMBY'S FUN SPECIALS

Comico: *2 issues 1987–1988*

Gumby's Summer Fun Special is a lot of fun. Really. Despite being based on the green clay US children's character. Gumby and Pokey, his orange horse chum, some children and a baby-sitting werewolf get mixed up with hysterical aliens (bad guys) and space bears (good guys), a group of nice pirates and a crazy town where it's permanently Halloween. Bob Burden's script is minimal and funny, with the plot always on the brink of coming apart at the seams The fact that he manages to keep all the plates in the air makes for manic fun, while Art Adams' detailed artwork is always a joy.

The *Winter Fun Special*, scripted by Steve Purcell, doesn't have the same effortless quality that makes the first special so good. Gumby and Pokey have an underground adventure with Mole Men, the Devil and Santa Claus in which the plot's stretched thin and the lunacy is forced in places, especially the satirical references. The joy of *Gumby* is that it is simplistic, pure entertainment. Not that the Winter Special doesn't have some good scenes, which, coupled with Art Adams' intricate, carefully-balanced artwork, make it worth seeking out.~NF

GUN RUNNER

Marvel UK: *3-issue miniseries 1993*

Fast-paced but incredibly predictable series, featuring an alien warrior with no memory who's befriended by an independent-minded female. He saves her from danger and they're attacked by other aliens. The appearance of Blaze and Ghost Rider just gives less room to develop any individuality the strip might have had. Impressive inks from Adolfo Buylla almost make this worthwhile, though.~NF

Mobile Suit GUNDAM 0083

Viz: *13 issues 1994–1995*

Earth begins colonising space in the future, but far from being a solution to problems, it creates worse ones, particularly increasing conflict between the space dwellers and the home planet. Balancing the power of both sides are 18-foot-tall battle robots, known as Gundam. Enormously successful in Japan, where the saga is an animated film, the comic takes its artwork directly from animation cels, and dialogue directly from the film. It's sometimes an awkward procedure, despite similarities between the two media, and as much of the film is action-based there's a distinct lack of excitement in the comic. After much to-ing and fro-ing everything amounts to an unremarkable series of battles in space. And you've never seen any less convincing military types than our two flighty leads Kou and Nina, who're more like two children playing at being soldier and pilot.~WJ

GUNFIRE

DC: *14 issues (0–13) 1994–1995*

Introduced in *Deathstroke* annual 2, Gunfire can agitate the molecules of solid objects. Simply put, it enables him to fire bullets from anything he picks up. If there were a template for the bog-standard superhero comic, *Gunfire* would be it. It's superheroics by numbers for the first few issues, but from 6 the art of Ed Benes transforms Gunfire into a distorted and crippled figure and the title from a 1980s template to a 1990s template. There's thousands of comics to read before you even think of sampling this.~FP

GUNHAWKS

Marvel: *7 issues 1972–1973*

Any comic starring Reno Jones and Kid Cassidy isn't going to be the subtlest of plagiarisms; this one is of interest only for featuring a black Western character.~FP

GUNHED

Viz: *3-issue miniseries 1990*

This is adapted from a Japanese movie: a giant robot has to be re-programmed to destroy a computer intent on taking over the world. Crash! Bang! Wallop! Oh, it's over.~WJ

GUNSMITH CATS

Dark Horse: *Series one 10 issues 1995–1996, series two 7 issues 1996–1997*

Kenichi Sonoda's Manga is the inspiring tale of Rally Vincent and Minnie-May Hopkins, two young women sharing a love of guns, cars and bombs. It's set in Chicago, where Rally is a gunshop owner who makes most of her money as a bounty hunter. Minnie-May is her business partner, ex-Mob, ex-prostitute, current bomb-maker. Together they run up against a sadistic Bonnie and her brother Clyde, Minnie-May's boy-friend, who taught her all she knows about bombs, and a mystery burglar with a machine gun. The second series is an extended story-line in which the girls search for Minnie-May's lover, Ken. *Gunsmith*

Cats is fast-paced and not very politically correct, but Sonoda knows how to make his action work on the page and there are some excellent set pieces that owe much to Hong Kong cinema.~NF

GUY GARDNER

DC: *3-issue miniseries (Guy Gardner Reborn) 1992, 43 issues, 2 Annuals 1992–1996*

Originally chosen as an emergency replacement Green Lantern by the Guardians of the Universe in *Green Lantern* 59, Guy Gardner was originally a one-shot character. Revived years later and given a character makeover, he had a bad attitude and violent temper, and was constantly at loggerheads with Hal Jordan, the first Green Lantern. While this made him unpopular with his fellow heroes, fans of *Green Lantern* and *Justice League* loved him, and it was only a matter of time before he was given his own series. *Reborn* introduced a defeated Guy, kicked out of the GL Corps and powerless. He embarks on a quest with Lobo to find Sinestro's yellow power ring, the only item strong enough to defeat Green Lantern. The series never warranted the expensive format, Joe Staton's pencils don't cut the mustard, and the whole affair would have served better as the first issues of the ongoing series.

That series took off shakily, with Gerard Jones churning out formula stories and familiar faces, and it isn't until 17 that anything of major interest occurred. In that issue Guy adds the suffix Warrior to his title after drinking the waters of the warrior, which kick in dormant genes permitting him to fashion any weapon from his body. It's a radically altered Guy Gardner from this point: bereft of his pudding-bowl haircut, stripped to the waist and covered in war paint, he's out to kick butt. After Gardner's transformation into a sub-Lobo character, his comic surprisingly picks up, with improved art and sassy scripts. 'The Way Of The Warrior' in 32–34 crosses over with *JLA* 101 and 102 and is particularly violent, with Gardner and allies taking on an entire alien species in a complete massacre. Of necessity calmed down after that, Gardner returned to Earth to open a sports bar in New York and gathered together his own team, albeit of has-beens like Wildcat and Lady Blackhawk. The final issues have a lighter tone, with scripting by Beau Smith.~TP

Recommended: 41, Annual 2

The HACKER FILES
DC: *12 issues 1992–1993*

Science-fiction writer Lewis Shiner's first foray into the world of comics is a sad affair. Picking up a little late on the computer and Internet craze, he's created a hacker version of *Hellblazer*'s John Constantine in the shape of Jack Marshall. It's a humdrum story of the little guy versus the evil global corporation, Digitronix, and never creates enough tension or paranoia to suit the concept. Marshall's ability to enter computers and reprogram them is tediously depicted with dull pseudo-computer graphics, and it only points out the difficulties in dramatising the high action of a bloke sitting at a keyboard. Mark Buckingham's inks lack the finesse he would later develop, and the whole package seems rather misconceived. No surprise, then, when it was cancelled after a year.~TP

John Bolton's HALLS OF HORROR
Eclipse/Quality: *2 issues 1985*

John Bolton's understairs cupboard more likely; a ragbag of English reprints. Polished enough artwork, but the monster-club framing sequence can't explain away why the majority of the second issue is devoted to a 2000 Years BC caveman adventure.~FJ

The Ballad Of HALO JONES
Quality: *12-issue limited series 1987–1988*

Reprint of Alan Moore and Ian Gibson's futuristic coming-of-age tale that originally appeared in *2000AD*. Although limited by the need to provide a climax every six pages or so, Moore manages to create a cohesive overall story which attracted many female readers. Ian Gibson, frequently overrated, produces some of his best-ever artwork. The lack of 'prettiness' in his open-lined forms and stubby blocks of ink suits the unromantic tone of the stories perfectly. The stories were planned as individual books, each occupying four issues.

Halo Jones begins with the heroine living in a violent future of floating cities and follows her attempts to escape from the numbing boredom of Earth. She has a naïve vision of what space travel will be like, and in the third book (9–12) is forced to join the galactic army

when down on her luck. Each of the three stories has its own mood. In the first, incredibly, she and her friends strap on grenade-launchers and machine-guns and attempt to go shopping, as Moore gently takes the piss out of ultra-violent science fiction. It ends on a poignant note as, with a job on a space cruiser, she (and we) realise that none of her friends will make the same huge leap. 5–8 are a collection of largely stand-alone stories, including beautifully crafted shorts such as 'I'll Never Forget Whatsisname?', about a stowaway who's become so good at hiding that everyone forgets him seconds after meeting him (an idea Neil Gaiman would develop in his *Neverwhere* TV series). The third book is an unsophisticated, but very moving, diatribe against war. As excellent a way to introduce young girls to the delights of comics as you could wish, but by turns entertaining and moving for the rest of us, too.~FJ

Recommended: 5–12

Collections: The Ballad Of Halo Jones Vol 1 (1–4), Vol 2 (5–8), Vol 3 (9–12), *The Complete Halo Jones* (1–12)

HAMMER OF GOD
First: *4-issue miniseries 1990*

The first in a string of miniseries focusing on The Hammer of God - aka Judah Maccabee, an alien weapons-master and warrior who, as a child, was raised by Hassidic Jews in one of comics' more bizarre origins. The popular Nexus supporting character's first adventure saw him standing for President of the Assassins Guild in an attempt to counteract the Guild's corruption. There was one later miniseries from First, two from Dark Horse between 1991 and 1994.~JC

HAMMERLOCKE
DC: *9 issues 1992–1993*

'Tomorrow's superhumans are here!' it says on the cover of Issue 1. They may well be, but it's hard to spot them among all the talk about corporate politics and the astral railway, which isn't nearly as exciting as it sounds. Boring beyond belief. One point of interest: all the women have lips like sink plungers.~FC

HAMSTER VICE
Blackthorne: *9 issues 1986–1987*
Eternity: *2 issues 1989*

Puerile and appallingly drawn anthropomorphic humour comic about police hamsters. Creator Dwayne Ferguson won Marvel's try-out contest, but on the basis of this the other entries must have been unmentionable. Blackthorne also published two 3-D issues, the second reprinting the first issue of the regular series.~FP

HAND OF FATE
Eclipse: *3-issue miniseries 1988*

It's unusual to find Bruce Jones writing a series about a hard-boiled detective. Of course there's plenty of fantasy, science-fiction and horror elements to the story: what else do you expect when the hero's called Artemus Fate, with a psychic girl-friend and a pet raven? The down at heel Artemus investigates unusual cases, from haunted lighthouses to a woman more spider than human, to killer pussy cats. Gerald Forton's artwork gives the whole thing a 1950s feel and his story-telling's good, although the overall look of the strip isn't particularly pleasing on the eye. A bit of a curiosity.~NF

HANDS OF THE DRAGON
Atlas: *1 issue 1975*

Kung-Fu comics by numbers. Got that checklist ready? Tibetan monastery? Yup. Mystical medallion? Yup. Aged mentor? Yup. Years of training? Yup. Typically dull Atlas shot at bandwagon jumping? Yup.~FP

HARBINGER
Valiant: *42 issues (0–41), 2 Yearbooks 1992–1995*

In Valiant's universe, 'Harbinger' is the term applied to those who'd be mutants at Marvel, teenagers with inherent natural superpowers who're harbingers of humanity's future, hence the name. It also applies to the Harbinger Foundation, run by Japanese businessman Toyo Harada, who collects and trains Harbingers, allegedly in their best interests, thereby enabling them a degree of control over their abilities. This doesn't sit well with one Peter Stanchek, a teenager with prodigious mental abilities, who rebels. 1–7, and the supplemental zero issue, are very much plot- and character-led by writer Jim Shooter and artist David Lapham. Nice touches include that the rotund Zephyr is a major comic fan delighted at becoming a superhero, and that Stanchek has been mentally manipulating his team-mates, one in a particularly despicable fashion. The conflict between two female members of the team over Stanchek comes over as puerile wish-fulfilment, but otherwise 1–7 are the only issues necessary to follow the plots until 25.

8 and 9 are part of Valiant's company-wide 'Unity' crossover, including an unlikely revelation for Kris, while Lapham writes and pencils from 11–13. Most other issues to 25 are one round of skirmishes after another between Stanchek's team and Harada's agents, but 21 is a nicely handled story of Stanchek returning home to meet his father for the first time since he fully manifested his powers. It's the by then regular team of Maurice Fontenot and Howard Simpson, a much underrated artist. 25 is the final conflict between Stanchek and Harada, and has more than a few surprises along the way. 26 begins a new direction entirely, and introduces Sean Chen as penciller, but it's an era of high-school superpowered soap operatics along with plenty of crossovers, most notably with *H.A.R.D. Corps* in 30 and 31. By 34's 'Chaos Effect' chapter *Harbinger* is almost without focus, and has deteriorated into mediocrity. Succeeding issues are an improvement, as some students realise the true nature of the Harbinger Foundation and become renegades, returning the title to more or less its original premise. An abrupt cancellation means there's no real ending.~WJ
Collections: Harbinger vol 1 (1–4), vol 2 (6, 7, 10, 11)

HARD BOILED
Dark Horse: *3-issue miniseries 1990–1992*

Brash, ultra-violent, completely amoral. Is this what Frank Miller thought he needed to do to reinvent himself for the 1990s? *Hard Boiled* is a slick, magazine-size short story of a corporate robot whom renegade robots are trying to recruit. It's the blackest of black comedies, drawn by Geof Darrow, whose panels are crammed with detail and oddly disquieting. Many people rave about the detail in Darrow's pages, but his draughtsmanship and story-telling is merely average. Ultimately the series is a triumph of style over content, the violent excesses highlighting over and over Miller's message of the hopelessness of lost humanity.~NF
Collection: Hard Boiled (1–3)

The H.A.R.D. CORPS
Valiant: *30 issues 1992–1995*

Using implants and satellites, the H.A.R.D. Corps are given a variety of abilities, including flight, power blasts and the projection of protective shields. The snag is they're only able to use one at a time, though can switch instantly by calling base. Teamwork is imperative to ensure maximum efficiency. Ostensibly an interesting concept, for most of the run it's never developed beyond the ordinary, with one-dimensional characters, as exemplified by the best issue being a fill-in starring a one-shot character in 24. Mike Baron improves matters as the team discover they've been manipulated in 26, but by then it's too little, too late.~WJ

HARD LOOKS
Dark Horse: *10 issues 1992–1993*

Hard Looks adapts Andrew Vachss' seriously mean short stories, with one new prose piece each issue. With artists like James O'Barr, George Pratt, Warren Pleece, David Lloyd, Dave Gibbons and Gary Gianni the visual interpretation is as dark as the original prose, and sticking to black and white artwork is very effective. The villains have usually committed sexual crimes of one kind or another and the heroes are often just looking for revenge, but these are powerful stories that steer clear of relying on a twist ending for suspense.~NF
Collection: (assorted from 1–10)

HARDCASE
Malibu: *26 issues 1993–1995*

An average tale about a tougher than average superhero. No valiant deeds, here just lots of power-crazed manics beating the hell out of each other on the moon, at sea and in cities. Jim Hudnall's scripts are perfunctory but the pencils, supplied by Scott Benefiel, are nice to look at.~TP

HARDWARE
Milestone: *50 issues 1993–1997*

In hero mode, Hardware is essentially a black version of Iron Man, but far more effectively so than Marvel's surrogate. Out of his gear he's Curtis Metcalf, scientific genius employed by ostensibly philanthropic business man Edwin Alva, who in reality has his finger in any number of criminal pies. Instead of wiping him out straight off, Metcalf figures it's more satisfying to bring down the criminal activities one by one, with Alva, although beyond the reach of the law, powerless to stop a vengeful armoured warrior. It's a satisfying blend of action and personality that's provided by Dwayne McDuffie and Denys Cowan for the initial issues. In 14 Alva discovers the obvious, but the plot isn't resolved in the way everyone might expect. 17 and 18 are part of the 'Worlds Collide' crossover, in which the Milestone heroes meet some of their DC counterparts. It's also the end for McDuffie and Cowan (for whom several other artists had already filled in), and the start of a forgettable run.

It's all change again from 32 as Metcalf forms his own company, taking several of his colleagues along, while continuing his fight for justice. An appealing aspect to *Hardware*, and indeed most Milestone titles, is that there's a strong editorial control. Different creators work on the title, and sometimes the change of artistic style can be jarring, but overall plot-lines are continued through to conclusion, and there's no new direction with every change of writer. Towards the end of the series Dan Chichester is in charge, and pulls elements of his stories straight from the real world, with

government-sponsored covert-action teams, organ harvesting, and a retired general hawking his autobiography. These issues are deliberately more upfront with action and wisecracking, and there's a far higher percentage of guns than previously. Despite being the first and last of the Milestone imprint, *Hardware* is one of the weaker titles throughout. While never bad, almost any of the others are worth investigating before this.~WJ

HARLAN ELLISON'S DREAM CORRIDOR
Dark Horse: *One-shot 1995, 5 issues 1995*

Not, as you might expect from the title, the infamous science-fiction writer and self-styled gadfly of the establishment rhapsodising about his ideal hallway, but a rather dreary anthology title featuring well-known cartoonists adapting Ellison's short stories. Ellison completists should note that he co-edits and writes new short prose fiction based on the cover illos and framing sequences (drawn by Eric Shanower) between the adaptations. As entertaining as Ellison's bluster and self-promotion can be, and despite nice packaging and a talented roster of contributors such as Peter David, John Byrne, Doug Wildey, Michael T. Gilbert, Jan Strnad, Skip Williamson and Mike Deodato, the stories are lack-lustre. If Ellison's your cup of tea you'd be better off with his collections of short stories.~JC

HAROLD HEDD in Hitler's Cocaine
Kitchen Sink: *2-issue miniseries 1984*

In a manner reminiscent of Carl Barks' *Uncle Scrooge* epics, Harold Hedd and his cousin Elmo set off in search of a cache of cocaine lost during World War II on its way to Hitler. With a parrot, a shark, a treasure map and two other groups after the loot, there's plenty of slapstick action. Rand Holmes' earlier Harold Hedd adventures, reprinted from the same Canadian newspaper that would later début David Boswell's Reid Fleming, were also published in two issues by Last Gasp.~NF

Clive Barker's The HARROWERS, Raiders Of The Abyss
Epic: *6 issues 1993–1994*

Tying into *Hellraiser*, the Harrowers are basically non-costumed superheroes with a mission to save souls from hell, run by the Cenobites. Considering their status as immortal demons the Cenobites are an unimaginative and dull bunch, not improved by Gene Colan pencilling as if he didn't give a damn. The best effort is 'Devil's Pawn' in 5 and 6, wherein the Harrowers have rescued the wrong soul and unwittingly returned a murderer to Earth, but their best story is the Alex Ross-painted début in *Hellraiser* 17.~FP

HATE

Fantagraphics: *25 issues + 1990 to date*

Long before the term 'slacker' was first applied to a lost generation, Peter Bagge was producing stories about suburban teenager Buddy Bradley and his dysfunctional family in *Neat Stuff*. Given a new title, the misanthropic Buddy aged five years to became the focus. Initially sharing a Seattle flat with the disgusting Stinky and the anal-retentive paranoid George, Buddy stumbles from couch to fridge in a life defined by drink, sex and avoiding responsibility. 16 is a turning point. *Hate* goes to colour as Jim Blanchard starts as inker, and given that the slacker culture is itself unknowing self-referential parody, Bagge was smart enough to move Buddy and girlfriend Lisa back to New Jersey, as Seattle went global in the real world. The vicious satire of earlier issues is muted somewhat by a return to the suburbs, but Bagge compensates by proving an adroit writer of domestic sit-com.

Bagge's cartoon style is extraordinary. There's a lineage back to Big Daddy Roth, but he's an original, able to convey a startling array of attitudes with a simple style. He's particularly expressive during moments of great stress for his characters. Eyes bulge, mouths rend agape with tongues elongated into spasm, limbs stretch, and bodies contort to comic effect, yet somehow there's a cohesiveness to the whole effect.

At its best, which is most issues, *Hate* is a vitriolic dissection of blue-collar culture. Bagge's not unique in exploring suburban indignity and stereotypes, but only *The Simpsons* (to which he must have been an inspiration) hit the target as often, and he can descend to levels not permitted by network TV. Any issue can be read without reference to others, and they're all highly recommended.~FP

Recommended: 1–25

Collections: Hey Buddy (1–5), *Buddy The Dreamer* (6–10), *Fun With Buddy and Lisa* (11–15)

THE HAUNT OF FEAR

EC: *28 issues (15–17, 4–28) 1950–1954*
Gladstone: *2 issues 1991*
Russ Cochran: *Series one 5 issues 1991–1992, series two 18 issues + 1992 to date*

Published as *Gunfighter* for the first fourteen issues, the comic was retitled *Haunt Of Fear* with 15, but the eighteenth issue started numbering from 4, so there are two 15–17s, distinguished from their later counterparts by Johnny Craig covers. As with the other EC horror titles, there was some initial fumbling. The stories were categorised into four styles: a psychological study, an adventure in horror, a journey into the supernatural, and a scientific SuspenStory. As was the EC style, each story ends on a twist, usually quite predictable.

There was of course the occasional early gem, such as Johnny Craig's 'Nightmare' in the first 17, where a certain 'John Severin' (a little in-joke on his fellow EC artist) allows himself to be immersed in concrete thinking it's just a nightmare. Craig was the most versatile artist on the early issues, and brought a certain film noir look to his stories before departing to edit *The Vault Of Horror*. The other mainstays were luminaries such as Graham Ingels, who conveyed a great sense of grotesqueness (no wonder he signed himself 'Ghastly'), Jack Kamen, who couldn't draw anything looking horrible, Jack Davis, whose art had a slightly humorous tendency (and he'd later be a *Mad* regular), and George Evans, who produced a nice polished look. When they were joined by the likes of Reed Crandall, Al Feldstein, Bernie Krigstein, Harvey Kurtzman, Joe Orlando and Wally Wood to name a few, there are no artistic complaints.

Within a few issues, the EC terror-tellers (the GhouLantics), the Old Witch, the Vault Keeper and the Crypt Keeper were introducing all the stories, the latter two always advertising their own magazines. Perhaps that's why this title initially seemed the poor relation. Nevertheless, once it picked up stride, it equalled the others in quality. EC was the first major publisher to highlight their creators, featuring biographies of their top professionals. All appear to be happily married with families, which is why it's surprising that so many stories centre on marital unbliss. These *Haunt Of Fear* stories prove the statistics claiming that most murders are committed by family members on each other. 'Take Your Pick' in 14 is a good example, as is Jack Davis' 'Garden Party' in 17, highlighting his rather macabre sense of humour. Of course stories that predicted undying love also had their place. In fact 22's 'Wish You Were Here' was adapted for the 1972 *Tales From The Crypt* film. That issue also features a witty take on the Snow White fable. The grisly reworking (or perhaps reclamation) of fairy tales was a regular feature of EC horror titles, but its primary home was *Haunt Of Fear* under the banner of 'The Old Witch's Grim Fairy Tale'.

The majority of *Haunt Of Fear* was written by Bill Gaines and Al Feldstein (although Carl Wessler and others contributed to later issues), and they were caught out lifting plots from Ray Bradbury short stories. Far from being litigious, though, he enjoyed the comics and allowed the adaptations to continue, with the proviso that he was credited. Two of his stories do particularly stand out, 'The Coffin' in 16, and especially 'The Black Ferris', a time-travelling story in 18. Overall, after a shaky start, this became an entertaining title. After you've read a few the stories become predictable, but that won't stop you from enjoying them. If however you like a lot of gore in your reading, you may be disappointed. It's a myth that the EC horror tales consisted of many ghastly acts of vileness illustrated in detail. The vast majority of the horrific acts were either told off-panel, hinted at, or rendered in a shadowy silhouette – and rightly so – after all, it's up to your sick imagination, dear reader, to fill in the gaps... blood, guts, warts and all!

The Gladstone and Russ Cochran-published issues are reprints, with the second Russ Cochran series exact facsimiles of the original comics, published in chronological order.~HY
Recommended: 13, 14, 16, 18, 21, 22
Collection: The Haunt Of Fear (15–17, 4–28)

HAUNT OF HORROR

Marvel: *Series one 2 issues 1973, series two 5 issues 1974–1975*

Series one was digest reprints of text stories. Fans might be interested in illos by Frank Brunner and Mike Ploog among others, but they're for completists only. Series two was a late entry in Marvel's black and white magazine line, but never achieved the coherency of its companions. The first issue contains text material planned for the unpublished third digest, although it featured two of the best strips of the run: 'In The Shadow Of The City', a psychological shocker by Steve Gerber and Vincente Alcazar, and the beautifully drawn 'Rats' by Gerry Conway and Ralph Reese. The remaining issues were dominated by two continuing strips, 'Gabriel The Devil Hunter' and 'Satanna', the devil's daughter. Though neither was particularly inspired, the latter at least had nice artwork by Romero. The strips continued in *Monsters Unleashed* and *Marvel Preview* respectively.~DAR
Recommended: Series two 1

HAUNTED

Charlton: *75 issues 1971–1976 (1–30), 1977–1984 (31–75)*

Another Charlton mystery anthology hosted by a little white ghost occasionally referred to as Poltergeist. There's very little of note in the first thirty issues, with the same pool of contributors that wrote and drew for *Ghost Manor* and *Ghostly Tales* also submitting here. With 21 the title changed to *Baron Weirwulf's Haunted Library*, and the little poltergeist was evicted on the first page of Don Newton's introductory story. The Baron had a run in all of Charlton's mystery titles in a series of one-pagers by Newton called 'Baron Weirwulf's Library', and his popularity earned him this venue. Some of Newton's painted covers are memorable, but financial problems at Charlton resulted first in cancellation, then in revival as *Haunted*, now an all-reprint affair.~SW

HAUNTED LOVE

Charlton: *11 issues 1973–1975*

One of a couple of Gothic romance comics, this was a decent if largely uninspired title mixing lengthy lead strips with short horror back-ups. Tom Sutton and Joe Staton were among those drawing the comic, and Joe Gill was the principal writer.~DAR

THE HAWK AND THE DOVE

DC: *Series one 6 issues 1968–1969, 5-issue miniseries 1988–1989, series two 28 issues, 2 Annuals, 1989–1991*

Teenage brothers Hank and Don Hall were granted magnified athletic prowess and costumes that appeared by magic. This was courtesy of a mysterious voice in *Showcase* 75, where they débuted. Hank's belligerent temperament and Don's fervent pacifism determined their transformations into the Hawk and the Dove. The Hall brothers' constant arguing for or against violence and their subsequent styles of crimefighting provided the dramatic tension. Their father's career as a judge and their life at college in the late 1960s provided the criminals and crazies they fought. Created by Steve Ditko with scripts by Steve Skeates, the balance of allegory and drama didn't survive when Gil Kane took over the art with 3. It's interesting to note that the hippie killed at the beginning of 4, Warren Savin, bore Steve Skeates' pen-name from his days at Tower and Charlton. Perhaps this suicide signalled Kane's takeover of the writing with 5.

After the demise of his brother in *Crisis On Infinite Earths*, Hawk lost his sense of moral balance, and roamed around as an increasingly unstable and violent loose cannon. In the 1988 miniseries, admirably illustrated by Rob Liefeld back when he still could draw, Karl and Barbara Kesel rectified this by providing a new Dove, a female representative of the force of Order, to counterbalance him. Three potential candidates for Dove's identity were offered, and one of the fun aspects in a fairly grim story-line is trying to follow the clues to determine who the new Dove is. An unexpected hit, the miniseries was followed by an ongoing title. Still written by the Kesels, now illustrated mainly by Greg Guler, the new title had very much the same style: flashes of humour, warmth and human concern, set against some quite grisly crimes. An ill-advised foray into mysticism (15–17) revealed the true relationship of Hawk and Dove to the forces of Chaos & Order, and gave them some new aspects to their powers. Guest appearances by the Creeper (18–19) and the Female Furies of Apokolips (21) were the highspot, fun, frenzied and flippant. Shortly thereafter, the title lost its way, and, in what most readers remain convinced was a last-minute notion, the events of 1991's *Armageddon 2001* crossover closed the book on this series in a singularly inappropriate and dismissive manner.~SW/HS

Recommended: Series one 2, miniseries 1–5, series two 18–20

Collection: Hawk And The Dove (miniseries 1–5)

HAWKEYE

Marvel: *4-issue miniseries 1983, 4-issue miniseries 1994*

Writer Mark Gruenwald stretches out on a rare yet very acceptable pencilling outing. Hawkeye takes a break from the Avengers in this competent superhero fare, which is slightly degraded by an oddball assortment of antagonists. Check out the last page of the final issue for a genuine surprise ending. Between the first and second series Hawkeye had a long run in *Solo Avengers* (later *Avengers Spotlight*). The second series, by Chuck Dixon and Scott Kolins, embroils the ace archer in a rites-of-passage drama as he struggles to come to terms with a singularly tragic occurrence. The pacing is questionable. Writing off supporting characters built up by issue 2 is an unwelcome lurch in a four-issue series. Inferior to the first take.~APS

Collection: Hawkeye (Miniseries one 1–4)

HAWKMAN

DC: *Series one 27 issues 1964–1968, series two 17 issues, 1 Special 1986–1987, series three 33 issues 1993–1996, 2 Annuals*

Following their reworking from the 1940s characters in *The Brave And The Bold* 34–36 and 42–44, and continuing in a bizarre stint sharing *Mystery In Space* 87–90 with Adam Strange, Katar Hol and his wife were finally given their own title in 1964. Winged police officers of the planet Thanagar, they continued their fight against crime on Earth, posing as Carter and Shayera Hall, curators of the Midway City Museum. The collection of ancient weapons there proved very useful for their style of law enforcement.

High points of the first run include the début of Zatanna, itinerant female magician, in 4, the return of the Shadow Thief in 5, the flying gorillas of 6, Ira Quimby and his I.Q. gang in 7, the Viking Queen in 13 and the criminal organisation C.A.W. in 14. Fans of the editorial team of Gardner Fox (writer), Murphy Anderson (artist) and editor Julie Schwartz will be delighted by the first sixteen issues. Anderson's meticulous art style and Fox's obvious enjoyment of scripting a married crimefighting duo only started to tail off when the size of the original artwork was altered in 1967. This resulted in a lower panels-per-page count and continued stories, something that

didn't suit Fox's style at all. The art and story in 22–27 was ugly and feeble. The title was merged with *Atom* from 39 of that series to become *Atom and Hawkman*.

The second series continued from the *Shadow War Of Hawkman* miniseries. Hawkman and Hawkwoman are still fighting their fellow Thanagarians, who seek to take over the Earth, and this remains an ongoing plot for the rest of the series. The relationship between the Hawks is interesting, detailed and quite realistic. Many of the stars of the original *Hawkman* series make welcome returns, in particular the villainous Shadow Thief and the Gentleman Ghost, who becomes a companion to the Hawks. The 'Shadow War' finally climaxes in 10 with the aid of Superman. The best issues of this brief run are 16–17, concentrating on the relationship between the Hawks and the final fate of the Gentleman Ghost.

The successful revisionist *Hawkworld* bridged the second and third series, and the first issues follow closely from the conclusion of that series. It's also written by John Ostrander (until 7), who keeps readers guessing as to the identity of the character's latest incarnation. Once this has been established, Hawkman begins investigating what happened to Hawkwoman. Both plots are intriguing and keep up the suspense. 9–13 feature the 'Godspawn' storyline, the centrepiece of which is a well-choreographed battle, in 11 and 12, between Hawkman and his predecessor. By this time William Messner-Loebs has become writer, and he establishes Hawkman as the recipient of ancient abilities relating to animal gods, and plots numerous encounters with other such beneficiaries, stretching the idea too far. The most effective episode has Hawkman combating a lion-based individual in 24 and 25. Many other superheroes drop by, particularly in 'Eyes Of The Hawk' (14–17), with Wonder Woman and Aquaman, and 22–23, chapters of 'Way Of The Warrior', crossing over with Guy Gardner and the Justice League. Steve Lieber pencils most issues, but his art is rarely dynamic, and he has a bit of a problem with faces. With both Loebs and Lieber departing with 27, the series limps to cancellation under diverse hands. The best of the later issues is the concluding story in 31–33, 'Hunter, Hunted, Prey!', which is simple and effective, fast-moving superhero action.~SW/SS

Recommended: Series one 4–6, 12–14, series two 16–17

HAWKWORLD

DC: *3-issue miniseries 1989, 32 issues, 3 Annuals 1990–1993*

The miniseries is a drastic retelling of Hawkman's origin that has Katar Hol fall victim to an imperialistic, racist government and commit patricide and murder (albeit during a period of drug detoxification); it includes two Shayera Thals. Tim Truman's script is terse, but full of outrage at the treatment of races conquered by Thanagar, forced to live as slaves or outcasts while the Thanagarians themselves live off their labours. His artwork's harder edges are muted by Alcatena and there is a clear debt (acknowledged) to Joe Kubert.

The regular series, written by Truman and John Ostrander and pencilled by Graham Nolan, picks up from the miniseries with Shayera and Katar on Earth to assist the Thanagarian Ambassador mount an exhibit at a Chicago museum. There they must face the plots of Byth, whom Katar has forced into exile at the end of the miniseries. Shayera has an affair with a Chicago cop and struggles to keep up with Katar's increasingly liberal views. Their seemingly irreconcilable differences do much to keep the title interesting, as each has so much to learn about the other. With Byth captured (9), Truman departs and Shayera spends time back on Thanagar and learns about her past, getting involved again in the injustices still being perpetrated by the government (10–14), while Katar is courted by Mavis Trent. 15 and 16 are 'War Of The Gods' crossovers, while 17–19 feature Attila, the vengeful robotic creation of a race destroyed by Thanagar. 'Escape From Thanagar' in 21–25 sees Katar and Shayera aid refugees from Thanagar seeking sanctuary on Earth. In helping them, they are themselves exiled. The final story-line, 'Flight's End', is in two parts. The first, drawn by Jan Duursema, ends in a battle with the original Hawkman, while Tim Truman pencils the final half, which sees the Thanagarian refugees established in their own Netherworld in Chicago but under the influence of Viper, who has apparently killed both Katar and Shayera. This story concludes in the disappointing 1993 *Hawkman* series. The 1990 annual is a continuity implant featuring two Flashes and revealing how there was a Hawkman on Earth during the 1940s, and Attila returns for the second annual. The third, in 1992, is an 'Eclipso: The Darkness Within' crossover. Overall, a better version of Hawkman than any since and certainly a better idea than the preceding 'Shadow War' story-line.~NF
Recommended: Miniseries 1–3, 1–4

HAYWIRE
DC: *13 issues 1988–1989*

If you're into action, mayhem, blood and guts, double identities, betrayal, Y-fronts and kinky villains look no further than this underrated series from writer Michael

Fleisher and penciller Vince Giarrano. As the title implies, this was an all-action affair, involving super-psionic armour that gave its unknowing owner many powers. Originally corporate-controlled, Haywire breaks loose and subsequently has to fight agents of his former employers and those of rival organisations with an interest in the armour. They include a beautiful ninja character, White Lotus, who provides the love interest, and Nightlash, a leather-clad S&M villainess who provides…er…something else, especially with her all-powerful whip (be still, your beating heart). Fleisher keeps the readers coming back for more and Giarrano displays a fine artistic talent. It's a shame there's been no follow-up. We never did find out what happened to Nightlash… ~HY
Recommended: 1–13

HAZARD
Image: *7 issues 1996–1997*

Hazard's an enhanced human pumped full of nanotechs (that's little tiny machines that do the work of cells, to you and me) that give him superhuman powers. Unfortunately, without a computer to control them they'll also start reproducing at an alarming rate. A bounty hunter by trade, Hazard is souped up by the villainous Dr D'Oro, who wants him to assassinate Stormwatch's Weatherman 1. He escapes, but has just two weeks to find Dr D'Oro before his body starts eating itself up. Jeff Mariotte's plot is certainly contemporary. Roy Allan Martinez's angular, sub-Miller art has colour slimed all over it by computer, but is robust enough to stand this treatment. Entirely average chase book, hastily concluded in issue 7 after Hazard finds out he's not actually going to explode when the nanotechs inside him go haywire, and sets off to find out why.~FJ

HEADLIGHTS
Personality: *1 issue 1992*

When among the earliest lines in a comic you get 'Someone wanted her for a superpowered lackey. They kidnapped her and installed headlights on her breasts' you've every right to expect a laugh-fest. Sadly, though, beyond the hilarious initial concept this runs out of steam quickly and even begins taking itself seriously. Very disappointing.~FP

THE HEAP
Skywald: *1 issue 1971*

A test pilot is turned into a man-thing after falling into the usual chemical vat. Tom Sutton turned out an excellent story that compares favourably with similar Marvel and DC concepts, capturing well the man-as-monster notion that abounded in the early 1970s.~DWC

HEART THROBS
Quality: *47 issues 1949–1957*
DC: *99 issues (48–146) 1957–1972*

One of the handful of titles DC continued publishing when they bought the defunct Quality line in 1957. The Quality issues are distinguished by very verbose scripts and a tendency to focus on marital or near-marital misunderstandings, with an emphasis on 'good girl' art as supplied by Bill Ward and Gill Fox or their imitators. With 48, the first under the DC banner, the title was retained, but the emphasis changed to conform with DC romance style. The heroines were younger, and stories focused on first loves, dating triangles and so on. This continued until 1972, with only hairstyles and homeliness indicating the passing of time. 102–123 feature a serial, 'Three Girls – Their Lives And Loves', obviously intended to ensure a continuing readership *à la* TV soaps. The title changed to *Love Stories* with 147.~HS

HEARTBREAK COMICS
Eclipse: *One-shot 1988*

The nominal star of this book is Laszlo, the great Slavic lover, but it's his affair with Lena Fleming, wife of Reid Fleming, that provides the plot and slapstick action as Laszlo winds up in jail with the maniacal milkman. The original strip appeared in the Vancouver underground paper *The Georgia Straight*. David Boswell re-drew the stories in 1984 and they were published in magazine format by Last Gasp. The Eclipse edition is on better paper as part of their graphic album series. Though Reid Fleming doesn't play a great part in *Heartbreak Comics*, it is his sociopathic behaviour, compared and contrasted with Laszlo's, that provides most of the story's humour. David Boswell is one of the most under-appreciated of all cartoonists and it's easy to see from the detail in his work why so little has been published. *Heartbreak Comics* is a seminal work which all lovers of the medium should read.~NF
Recommended: 1

HEARTBREAKERS
Dark Horse: *4-issue miniseries 1996*

There's a complex back-story to *Heartbreakers*, resulting from previous appearances in *Dark Horse Presents* (50–52, 100), but don't let that bother you and step right into the shoot-out starting the first issue. The lead characters are two clones of a now dead bio-geneticist, each reflecting aspects of her personality. Vector has the scientific mind and Queenie is aggressive and adaptable, which is just as well since there's a corporation on their tails wanting to study the remnants of their creator's work. There's also a growing movement to remove the second-class status accorded clones on

Earth. Anina Bennett and Paul Guinan weave a tautly plotted and absorbing tale, while Guinan's art is extremely appealing. His story-telling is compact, expressively portraying the characters without resorting to exploitation or exaggeration, and such is the dominance of his style that Lenin Delsol pencilling the final two issues from layouts meshes seamlessly. Fast-paced and engaging, shame on Dark Horse for letting this sit on the shelf for years.~FP
Recommended: 1–4

HEAVY Tragi COMICS
Print Mint: *1 issue 1969*

An early graphic-oriented offering from the great Greg Irons. Always pretty to look at, if occasionally brutal, this is a little short on narrative for most contemporary tastes.~DAR

HEAVY METAL
HM Communications: *137 issues 1977–1992*
Metal Mammoth: *27 + 1992 to date*

Heavy Metal came into being when the editors of *National Lampoon* chanced upon *Metal Hurlant*, the flagship magazine of a group of radical French cartoonists calling themselves Les Humanoides Associés (Druillet, Dionnet, Moebius and Farkas). Initially, under founder editors Sean Kelly and Valerie Marchant, the magazine was content to translate French strips, and since *Metal Hurlant* had begun in 1975 there was a body of work to fall back on. Home-grown product was gradually added. The magazine started as a glossy monthly and its 'adult' persona was defined from the beginning by a choice of contributors whose science-fiction and fantasy strips offered plenty of sex and violence. Though it was rarely particularly explicit, a large number of topless and naked women in the title appear to have been a priority, whatever the editorial incarnation.

For the first three years the editorial policy was to offer a mixture of short episodes of long stories, short, stand-alone pieces and illustrated text stories. The best strips from this period are the French translations: Moebius' 'Arzach', 'The Long Tomorrow' and 'The Airtight Garage of Jerry Cornelius' (the latter in two-page episodes from 1–37); Lob and Pichard's 'Ulysses'; Jean-Claude Forest's 'Barbarella'; Bilal shorts and 'Exterminator 17'; and Serge Clerc's 'Captain Future' (unusually all fifty-two pages were printed in 27, setting a trend). There was almost an embarrassment of riches. Translations of Druillet's extraordinary space stories (mostly shorts but also 'Gael') appeared alongside Dionnet and Gal's 'Conquering Armies' (1–10), Picaret and Tardi's 'Polonius' (5–8) and single pages by the politically-minded Chantal Montellier.

Meanwhile American contributors were being encouraged. *Heavy Metal* became a home for Richard Corben ('Den', 1–13, 'The New Adventures of the Arabian Nights', 15–28, written by Jan Strnad, then 'Rowlff', 'The Beast Of Wolfton', 'Bloodstar' and 'Den II', taking us up to issue 72). Other regular US contributors in the early years include Vaughn Bodé, E.E. Davis (whose Frazetta-ish barbarian tale 'Worlds Apart' appeared in 3–8), Gray Morrow ('Orion' and 'Amora'), Angus McKie ('So Beautiful And So Dangerous', collected), plus Trina Robbins and the young Steve Bissette and Rick Veitch. Howard Chaykin did some of his most experimental work here, making a brave if failed stab at adapting Samuel Delany's complex novella about the power of communications, 'Empire', into comics form, and having more success with Theodore Sturgeon's seminal 'The Stars My Destination'. So did Walt Simonson, illustrating Archie Goodwin's adaptation of 'Alien'. Oddities worth mentioning are Alex Nino's spot illos for Doug Moench's version of Sturgeon's 'More Than Human' (collected) and the amazing psychedelia of Marshall Rogers drawing Mark Arnold's sexy script for 'Entropics' (26).

With issue 35 (Jan 1980) Ted White became editor and introduced the idea of regular columns on comics, science fiction, music and film. While neither long nor particularly good, they added to the magazine's reputation as more of a gentleman's read than a mere comic, the same trick Playboy had pulled in the 1970s. A year later Leonard Mogel took over and replaced the named columns with 'Dossier' (in 51), a freeform arts column that also included interviews. Finally Julie Simmons-Lynch became editor in December 1981 and settled in for an eleven-year stretch.

Initially, Heavy Metal under Ted White changed little. There was still prose (by the likes of Norman Spinrad, Arthur Byron Cover, Harlan Ellison and Stephen King) and the usual mix of American and European strips, with new translated creators filtering in providing a high-quality backbone to the magazine. These included short stories by Dick Matena (35, 36, 45, 60, 74, 82), the Schuiten Brothers (36, 39, 45), Caza, Trillo and Breccia's 'Mr Valdemar' in 67, Magnus (48), Gillon (58) and Paringaux and Loustal (58). Alongside these were longer pieces: 'Cymbiola' by the Schuitten Brothers (56–64) paving the way for their 'Hidden Cities' sagas; the excellent if rather poorly translated Christin and Bilal strips 'Progress' (40–44), 'The Voyage Of Those Forgotten' (62–68), 'The City That Didn't Exist' (72–78) and 'The Hunting Party' (87–96) – all collected – as well as Bilal's own 'Gods In Chaos' (as 'The Immortals' Party' (50–57) and Christin's popular collaboration with Mézières, 'Valerian: Ambassador of the Shadows' (46–49). Heavy Metal also introduced the work of Crepax to America ('Valentina:

Reflections' in 45–51) and serialised his moody jazz drama 'The Man From Harlem', as well as continuing to print work by the original founders of Metal Hurlant. Druillet's 'Salammbo' (41,42,47,48) and 'Salammbo II: Carthage' (83–90) appeared along with his 'Yragael' (61–70). Moebius' mindbending collaboration with avant-garde film-maker Jodorowsky, 'The Incal', appeared in 59–65 and 82–87.

Reading the above anyone may wonder why Heavy Metal isn't the best regarded comic in the world. This is because readers also had to put up with a number of tedious, long-running series like Godard and Ribera's 'Alchemist Supreme' and 'What Is Reality, Papa?', and Fernando Fernandez' 'Zora', which seemed to go on forever but actually only lasted two years (59–78). And then there were the innumerable contributions from Jeronaton. Technically better but also interminable was Segrelles' 'Mercenary' series (55–62) and Barriero and Gimenez' 'Good-bye Soldier' (49). Also there were few great works by American contributors in this period. Matt Howarth makes an appearance in 35 before beginning his science-fiction epic 'Changes' (which introduced Those Annoying Post Brothers) in 36. There are odd bursts of creativity – Berni Wrightson's comic 'Captain Sternn' in 39, Jeff Jones' 'Yesterday's Lily', Chaykin's 'Cody Starbuck', Arthur Suydam's 'Mudwogs' and Bruce Jones and Wrightson's 'Freak Show' (65–70) – but these have to be weighed up against incredibly long-running duds like Rod Kierkegaard Jr's 'Rock Opera' (34–105) and John Findley's grotesque Western 'Tex Arcana' (48–105, with odd issue gaps), which together with Steranko's dire 'Outland' (51–58) ties for stiffest load of nonsense in the entire run. Fortunately Elaine Lee and Mike Kaluta's ground-breaking 'Starstruck' (68–76) and 'Robot Love' from Charles Burns (70) do suggest that there's a new generation of creators to come.

76 was the start of an attempt to free the title from a rut, with the serialisation of Tamburini and Liberatore's 'RanXerox'. Just as Metal Hurlant had been produced by a radical movement in French cartooning, now Italy's Young Turks were ready to inject some life into the genre. With its high quotient of sex and violence, and a disregard for morality, 'RanXerox' was youthful and rebellious, unlike the rather tired hippy values of many of the strips. Charles Burns' weird wrestling detective 'El Borbah' (77, 84–87, 94–99) and Drew Friedman's irreverent cinema strips completed the reformation. By 1984 Heavy Metal was attracting interviews with the likes of Roger Corman, John Sayles, John Waters and Federico Fellini.

The Schuiten brothers were among the old

guard still translated, while 77–81 had Arno and Jodorowsky, Crepax was in 80–85, and Manara's 'An Author In Search Of Six Characters' featured in 93–99, but they were supplemented by Liberatore (76–86, 94), Pepe Moreno's bold, violent 'Rebel', and stylists like Yves Chaland ('Atomax' in 91 and the excellent 'Elephant Cemetery' in 99–104). Daniel Torres ('Triton' in 92–95 and 'The Whisper Mystery' in 98–102) and the master of clear line, Joost Swarte (81, 92, 93, 101), were also notable among the new blood.

As issue 100 approached the title was in trouble again. From 99 it was no longer printed on glossy paper, and with 106 its frequency was reduced to quarterly, at which point issue numbers no longer appeared, and publication cover dates are used for identification. Citing reader frustration over the length of time it took to complete some stories' serialisation (and on a quarterly schedule this time would be even longer), a new editorial direction promised all-new stories, complete in each issue. With minor variations, this policy has been pursued ever since, one long story backed up by a greater or smaller number of shorts. With the change in schedule, however, all non-story pages were dropped, as was the long-running surreal cartoon series 'The Bus' by Paul Kirchner, which had been appearing in an editorial capacity since 30. However, the changes were also the nail in 'Rock Opera's' coffin, proving that every cloud has a silver lining. The quarterly schedule continued until March 1989, when an upturn in sales enabled the title to return to a bi-monthly schedule with no change in format.

Over the next six and a half years, before Metal Mammoth took over publication, *Heavy Metal* published a lot of excellent material, maintaining the principle of running European strips in translation, and although many of the full-length stories do not warrant individual recommendation it was a good period for the magazine. The big stars of the show, however, were: Hugo Pratt (Winter 1986), Sampayo and Solano-Lopez (Spring 1986), Prado, Bilal ('The Woman Trap', Fall 1986), Yves Chaland ('Freddy Lombard' in Fall 1987), Torres, Manara, Pellejero and Zentner (Summer 1988), Crepax (Fall 1988), Peeters and Schuiten ('Utopias', Winter 1989) plus the Schuiten Brothers ('The Hollow Planet', May 1989, and 'Nogegon', July 1991), Hermann ('Revenge', September 1989, and 'The Towers of Bois-Maury', July 1990), Tronchet and Gelli (January 1992) and Milan Trenc ('Morocco', March 1992). In addition there was Adamov and Cothias' epic five-graphic-novel adventure, 'The Waters of Dead Moon' (May 1990, September 1990, May 1991, September 1991, September 1992).

The new format suited a series of short graphic novels such as 'Hombre' by Segura and Ortiz (set in a post-holocaust world similar to Hermann's 'Survivors' series), 'Druuna' by Eleuteri Serpieri (big-breasted sci-fi epic, very well drawn), 'Burton And Cyb', also by Segura and Ortiz, a comedy science-fiction series, and 'Dieter Lumpen' by Pellejero and Zentner, an excellent Hugo Pratt-inspired hard-boiled detective strip. Look out particularly for the Summer 1988 issue, all about censorship and civil rights, after the previous issue had been seized by Canadian customs officials because of the 'Druuna' story. With work from Breccia, Segura and Ortiz, Manara, a Serpieri Western, Prado, Ruben, Zentner, Will Eisner and Yves Chaland, it has a well-drawn and nicely written something for everyone.

When *Heavy Metal* was acquired by Metal Mammoth there were immediate changes, including the addition of the Striptease slot, a collection of single-page strips by the likes of Mark Martin, Peter Kuper, Kaz, Scott Cunningham, Eric Drooker and Jim Woodring. It's not entirely out of place but the cartoonists chosen owe more to the underground than to *Heavy Metal's* science-fiction and fantasy background. New owner Kevin Eastman waited until January 1993 before taking on the reins of editorship himself, and started introducing new creators. While some of the material is worth unearthing (Ian Edginton and Matt Brooker's 'Kingdom of The Wicked' springs to mind) most of it isn't.

1993 saw more 'Hombre' stories and lots of Prado shorts, a late, episodic reprinting of Vittorio Giardino's 'Little Ego' in the March 1993 issue (already published by Catalan for several years, and distinctly unsexy) plus the return of Den. There are oddities like Turf and Joel Mouclier's 'Ramparts Of Spray', in which the softness of Art Suydam meets the rotund cuteness of Mike Ploog for a strange fantasy in a Mark Twain riverboat setting. May 1993 has Antonio Segura and Ana Mirallés' 'Eva Medusa', a stylish noir tale set on a steamy supernatural plantation in South America, and in July 1993 there was Duranona's atypical 'Hiding', set in 1930s America, about a shoot-out between police and a family of gangsters. Remembering the appeal of Liberatore, and figuring that his work's still rebel-rousing, *Heavy Metal* began printing creators of strips in a similar vein (Vince's 'Eden' in November 1993, Siro's 'Master Volume' in March 1994 and 1995, and Gess' 'Teddy Bear' in January 1995). There was better material from Alfonso Azpiri, Matthias Schultheiss and Font (especially his hard-boiled 'For Private Eyes' in the November issue). Burton and Cyb returned in 94, and Tronchet and Gelli contributed a Raoul Fleetfoot story, 'Killer Death', to the January issue. Highlights of the year, though, were Baudoin's 'The 11.23 Bus', and Fernando de Felipe's 'The Man Who Laughs', which looks like Jack Davis meets Berni Wrightson.

The same formula has been carried on ever since, with regular contributions from Prado, Azpiri, Manara, Ortiz and Segura, six episodes of de Felipe's 'Museum', and the latest Druuna book 'Mandragore' (albeit censored). While the short material continues to please, fewer of the main stories are of note, suggesting that it's time for another shake-up on the editorial front, rather than relying on European science-fiction/fantasy stories, which are still based on the then fresh ideas of those mid-1970s creators who started the whole thing in the first place. The magazine's commitment to European material has been consistent throughout, and without *Heavy Metal* there might never have been European reprints, even if the magazine shied away from many of the more extreme experimental strips printed in *Metal Hurlant*, as well as the less futuristic strips it serialised over the years. It's still a cheap way to discover new artists and, with the recent cancellation of the French magazine *A Suivre*, is one of the few adult mainstream anthologies left in the West. Many stories have been collected, most prominently by Catalan and NBM, or by Heavy Metal themselves in the early 1990s (see below).

There have been a number of special editions, some containing new material, others reprints. In the latter category fall *One Step Beyond*, *Greatest Hits*, *Best Of Heavy Metal* (2 vols) and *Fifteen Years of Heavy Metal*. *Son Of*, *Bride Of* and *Even Heavier Metal* all date from the early 1980s and feature a good cross-section of the usual suspects – Crepax, Giminez, Brecchia, Azpiri, Moebius, Gillon and Loustal. *War Machine* contains lots of material commissioned by the defunct Tundra, the best of which is material by Garry Leach and Dave Gibbons. *Software* has 'Druuna: Carnivore' to titillate, *Special Edition* has the multimedia computer-generated Sinkha and *Overdrive* contains Charyn and Frezzato's Margot. Pin Up and Havoc both star Jodorowsky and Bess' 'Hannibal 5', while *The Venus Interface* is a single, hallucinogenic storyline by Lou Stathis and a host of artists including Rick Geary, Peter Kuper and Arthur Suydam.~NF

Recommended: 26, 27, 45–51, 65, 67, 73–85, 99–104, Winter, Spring, Summer & Fall 1986, Fall 1987, Spring, Summer, Fall 1988, May 1989, September 1989, January, March, May 1990, November 1991, March 1992, May, July, November 1993, January, July 1994, May, September, November 1995, May, November 1996

HEAVY METAL Graphic Novels

Early in *Heavy Metal*'s run several stories serialised in the magazine were collected, most notably Archie Goodwin and Walt Simonson's adaptation of the *Alien* movie. Thoroughly entertaining, it remains the best of the home-grown material. Other collections included Angus McKie's *So Beautiful And So Dangerous* and Howard Chaykin's *The Stars My Destination*, but this flurry of late-1970s activity came to an abrupt halt, and no further *Heavy Metal* graphic novels appeared until the 1990s.

Published first in conjunction with Tundra, and later Kitchen Sink, the editorial aim of the 1990s selection was to present the best European graphic albums in an equivalent hardbound format at an affordable price. Published monthly for almost two years, many of the titles initially saw English-language print in the pages of *Heavy Metal*, so those wanting cheaper-format versions punctuated by ads and strangely separated by other strips are referred to the cover dates of *Heavy Metal* bracketed by titles.

There's a high percentage of decent material over the entire line, but overall the level of writing lags way behind the quality of artwork, never more demonstrably so than in the first release, *Margot In Badtown*. Reading as if every third page is missing, the attractive Margot is a naïf in the big city, but Charyn's plot never goes anywhere, while Frezzato's art is gorgeous. Equally well drawn in a gloomier style is *Ramparts* (March 1993). Joel Mouclier's exceptionally well conceived primitive mechanical world is engagingly designed, but Turf's accompanying script is a woolly tale of doomed love and a disease without cure. A big-breasted babe is Serpieri's forte, and a topic popular with *Heavy Metal* readers from the start. His heroine Druuna appears in no fewer than five albums: *Morbus Gravis* (Summer 1986), *Morbus Gravis II* (Spring 1988), *Creatura* (November 1992), *Carnivora* (July 1993) and *Mandragore* (September 1995). Druuna loves getting her kit off for the lads, and Serpieri loves drawing her doing it, but if you're wanting a story, steer clear. Vince's *Eden* (November 1993) is another step down, with big-breasted babes and gruesome mutants mixing it up in a bog-standard to-be-continued thriller, that never was. More distressingly, neither was Adamov's *Dayak: Ghetto 9* (September 1994), a well-drawn *ligne claire* thriller set in a future where whites are almost extinct, but one of the few remaining has a date with destiny. Adamov's also on hand to draw the samurai tale *Wind Of The Gods*, incorporating a particularly detailed and stomach-churning depiction of *seppuku*, but otherwise ordinary. The only total stinker in the entire selection is *The Man Who Laughs* (July 1994). We're back in doomed-love territory, with a mutilated man the heir to a throne, but Fernando de Felipe's art is so monotonous, gloomy and ugly and his story so trite your money's better spent elsewhere. Like on *Eva Medusa* (May 1993), which displays how dark and gloomy and tragic love can be handled with dexterity. It begins with the awakening of a teenage girl in Brazil, who realises she's inherited her mother's charm, beauty and eldritch abilities. Segura's excellent story combines voodoo, desire and degradation, with the subtle colouring of Ana Mirallés adding significantly to her already accomplished art. *Apocalypse* (July 1993) tells of a Vietnamese teenager able to make objects and people explode just by looking at them. There's the germ of a movie, but the story is strangely paced and with no great pay-off.

The two volumes of Regis Loisel's Peter Pan, *London* and *Neverland*, are puzzlers. Presenting the life of Peter Pan in the days before Barrie's novel, they could almost be children's books were it not for the unsubtle insertion of unrequired adult scenes in each. It's as if Loisel was somehow ashamed to produce children's books. His art is gorgeous, very expressive and able to evoke the squalor of Victorian London in the first book equally as well as the fantasies of Neverland in the second. They're an oddly contrasting pair, with the more upbeat *Neverland* more in tune with the children's adventure of the novel. The Julien Boisvert stories of Dieter and Plessix also stretch over two volumes. *Neekibo* is an excellent statement about colonialism and exploitation in Africa, and a coming-of-age story as junior Foreign Office official Julien Boisvert is prompted to uproot against his inclination by the return of his domineering mother. The unpleasant lesson he learns in the ways of the world carries him through the succeeding story *Grisnoir*, concerning an apparently kidnapped child. Plessix's *ligne claire* art is stunning – expressive, subtle and humorous. Of particular note is the manner in which Boisvert has perceptibly aged between the stories.

Scott Hampton's *The Upturned Stone* (September 1993) is the only originated *Heavy Metal* graphic novel. It's a pre-teenage bonding story in the manner of *Stand By Me*, but with far more sinister overtones. Deftly told and atmospherically painted, *The Upturned Stone*'s tale of ghostly retribution should be saved for a dark and stormy night. Oddly enough, over the past four decades the American Western strip has been far more popular in Europe than at home, and *Adios Palomita* (January 1993) is a fine example of the genre. Sumptuously drawn by Fabrice Lamy,

it's a tale told equally by flashback and contemporary occurrences, its central characters live and breathe, and it surprises with every plot twist. It concerns a love triangle and the consequences of a bungled bank robbery five years previously, but with great verve and imagination. *Desperadoes* is also set in the American West. Although appealingly drawn in typical European cartoon style and with charm and whimsy, the comedy adventure about a trio of female outlaws never quite takes off. The silhouette cartoons at the bottom of each page are a nice touch, though.~FP

Recommended: *Adios Palomita, Eva Medusa, Grisnoir, Neekibo, Peter Pan: Neverland, The Upturned Stone*

THE HECKLER
DC: *6 issues 1992–1993*

Stu runs a small diner in a big city, but sometimes he has no choice but to don his Heckler costume and cut some trouble-maker down to size. There are nice ideas – like the Generic Man and his plot to reduce everything to his own faceless uniformity – and there's lots of humour in the details of the city and in street-level incidents, but far too much of the comic is given over to the fights, and unfortunately these aren't funny and don't make sense as action. *The Heckler* would be great as an eight-page strip, but it drowns in twenty-two pages, and it's not surprising to find the following in the last two panels of issue 6:

Heckler: Hey, don't worry, kids… It'll take a lot more than that to kill the Heckler.

Caption: Yeah, it'll take crummy sales figures.

Heckler: … Well, true, that would do it, all right…

The most tightly told story is in 4, with the Heckler out on patrol with an assassin in pursuit, which has the spirit of a good *Roadrunner* cartoon. It would be nice to enthuse about all six issues because the artwork's great (Keith Giffen and Malcolm Jones III) and there's no problem with the ideas (Keith Giffen, plot) or the script (Tom and Mary Bierbaum), but those superfluous fourteen pages per issue are just too much to demand of a reader's goodwill.~FC

Recommended: 4

HELL RIDER
Skywald: *2 issues 1971*

A dreadful magazine attempting to attract the audiences flocking to see the lame biker movies made in the wake of *Easy Rider*'s success. A Vietnam vet is injected with 'Serum Q47', which gives him superstrength. Being named Brick Reese, he sensibly opts for the alias Hell Rider, but it's about the only sensible decision he makes in two issues, both of which have predictable endings. There's good bikers vs bad bikers in 'The Wild Bunch', a sort of grown-up Archie gang, and The Butterfly is soul singer Marion Michaels, who takes almost all her clothes off, attaches a rocket pack and flies off to deal with ne'er-do-wells. 2's Ku Klux Klan story is particularly daft. It's all intended as vaguely titillating, with skimpy costumes and the odd glimpse of breast, but it's dreadful throughout. If the creators wish to remain anonymous in the next edition of this book they should each send $500 care of the publisher's address.~FP

HELLBLAZER

DC/Vertigo: *108 issues + 1 Annual, 1 Special, 1988 to date*

Nobody ever actually calls John Constantine 'Hellblazer' but it made for a catchy title for his own comic. He was a regular guest star in *Swamp Thing* from 37 onwards, a mysterious Englishman with international contacts in the world of the occult. Not entirely a nice guy, Alan Moore and Rick Veitch's Constantine is prepared to manipulate others mercilessly in order to achieve his own ends. An unlikely hero, perhaps, but his realism seemed to strike a chord with readers. Moore has variously claimed that he wanted to write a realistic, non-superpowered character, and that his art team (who co-plotted with him) simply wanted to draw a character who looked like Sting. Others find strong echoes of Michael Moorcock's Jerry Cornelius in John Constantine, which Moore accepts. (And Jack Carter, played by Michael Caine in the film *Get Carter*, may well have suggested more than just the Newcastle connection.)

In his own comic, Constantine had to be fleshed out in more detail, and Jamie Delano was well up to the task. Constantine is seen to feel more guilt for his misdemeanours than was earlier revealed. Indeed he is haunted by the ghosts of dead friends, and comes close to suicide in 9. He remains committed to looking after number one, and 5 was controversial for his lack of action in the face of a platoon of Vietnam vet ghosts razing a middle American town. He still wasn't enough of a hero for many readers, though this was surely the point. Many of the earlier stories follow Moore's lead in using a 'horror' comic to reflect real social ills: drug addiction in 1 & 2, child abuse in 4, neo-Nazism in 6, pollution and eco-disaster in 13. Even Thatcherism is seen to have roots in occult evil in 3. 6 begins the first major story arc. A sinister cult is trying to create a new messiah, and a badly injured Constantine must accept a transfusion of demon blood in order to stop them. 9–10 cross over with *Swamp Thing* 76. Hints from the

Moore days about a past disaster during Constantine's life in Newcastle are fully explained in 11 and 12, as he confronts his first major demon in flashback and again in the present day. 14–22 is another long story arc, 'The Fear Machine'. Delano really hits his stride here, as Constantine's idyllic life with Britain's neo-pagan travellers is shattered by a Masonic conspiracy combining science and magic. There is a genuine State Of The Nation feel in this story, featuring various elements of England's alternative culture. Annual 1 has more paganism, as Constantine's ancestry is explored in the days when Christianity was taking over Britain from the Old Gods. Grant Morrison and David Lloyd guest to good effect on 25–26, and 27 is an excellent Neil Gaiman and Dave McKean one-off. 24 and 28–31 explore the psychology of a serial killer, and Constantine's disturbed relationship with his own father. In 34–36 he meets up with some old traveller friends who help him to confront the dark side of his own soul in the past, present and future. 39 begins Delano's swansong as Constantine meets his twin brother, who died in child-birth, but lives on in an alternate reality. In a true *tour de force*, 40 brings us Delano and Dave McKean's farewell to the John Constantine we know, as he literally cancels out his own existence in the original reality of the DC Universe. A fitting end for a character who had come so close to despair and self-hatred. Hereafter all tales of John Constantine must be about another character in a different timestream, though DC's editors and future writers didn't seem to grasp this.

Belfast's Garth Ennis was the next writer to take on *Hellblazer*, and he really piled on the gore and nastiness, which made the comic more successful. Constantine seems to take on some of his writers' own characteristics, and he now picks up a real taste for drink. Indeed, 42 sees a bit of very un-Hellblazerish magic, as holy water is turned into Guinness and back again just in time to kill off the Devil and save a friend's soul. This Devil seems to contradict the versions of Hell on offer in other DC comics, but no one seems to care. In 41–46, Constantine gets lung cancer from all those cigarettes, and plays a very complex game with the forces of Hell to save his life. 47–48 is about a haunted pub. 49 is artist Steve Dillon's first guest issue, in which Constantine goes to the pub with the Lord Of The Dance, the embodiment of the drunken revel. Ennis himself revels in the drinking story, but constant trips to the pub turned off many a reader. Dillon will pencil and ink from 57 on, forging a lasting partnership with Ennis. Regular penciller Will Simpson is back for 50, wherein Constantine outwits the King Of The Vampires. 51 is a fill-in by John Smith and Sean

Phillips, and 52–55 is a crude go at the Royal Family and their hangers-on. If Delano mistrusts the institutions of the British state, and sees complex conspiracy theories all over, Ennis simply seems to hate the whole Establishment with a passion. He likes to show them all as devil-worshipping sexual perverts, if not actual vampires, demons or fallen angels. Whereas Delano mixed real-life elements with his fantasy and made socio-political points, Ennis once said that he saw political or social background as just another way to 'bring on the vampires'. He may have been exaggerating for effect. Among his best stories are 64–66, about some utterly nasty National Front fascists, 72–75's American story, debunking the myth of John F. Kennedy among other things, and 'Rake At The Gates Of Hell' from 78 onwards, which sees the Devil cooking up all sorts of social unrest on the streets of London. Ennis reserves particular venom for the priesthood. The Special is about a Catholic priest, a very nasty story, with elements which were read as homophobic. Finally, romantic interest: 46 brings an old girlfriend called Kit back into Constantine's life, and she'll be around until 67. When she walks out on him, John is devastated and goes down and out on the streets.

After Ennis and Dillon left for the highly successful *Preacher*, Scot Eddie Campbell took over, but only lasted from 85–88. It's a clever tale of manipulative ghosts, and takes Constantine off round the world, ending up in New Guinea. Not used to working with editors who wanted constant script revisions, Campbell was succeeded by Englishman Paul Jenkins, while Sean Phillips stayed on as regular artist. Phillips is very different from Dillon, but an equally distinctive stylist and solid story-teller who has benefited the book greatly. Campbell's plot-line was wrapped up in 89–90 as Constantine helps out some Australian Aborigines, then Jenkins was free to pursue his own interests in British pagan stories and folky magic, along with a gang of supporting characters drawn from the crusty end of post-punk alternative culture. It's tempting to see the contrast between Delano and Ennis as a John Lennon approach being followed by Shane MacGowan of the Pogues (flashes of talent occasionally surfacing through the alcoholic haze), whose lyrics Ennis loves to quote. This makes Paul Jenkins something like festival favourites the Levellers – choosing politically correct subject matter, desperate to prove crusty credentials at all times, but frankly not all that good. The comic seems to be holding its own through a period of grave difficulty in the market, so Jenkins must be doing something right, but his stories are weak and dull, though Sean Phillips always comes through, especially with his

angry Green Man figures in 99 and 108. Overall *Hellblazer* seems to be continuing a stepwise decline from its glory days.~GL

Recommended: 1–23, Annual 1, 27, 36, 39, 40, 72–75, 85–88

Collections: Dangerous Habits (41–46), *Fear And Loathing* (62–67), *Hellblazer* Vol 1 (1–4), vol 2 (5–8), vol 3 (9–12), vol 4 (13–16), *Original Sins* (1–9)

HELLBOY

Dark Horse: *4-issue miniseries ('Seed Of Destruction') 1994, one-shot ('Wolves Of St August') 1995, one-shot ('The Corpse and The Iron Shoes') 1996, 5-issue miniseries ('Wake The Devil') 1996*

'Seed of Destruction' starts in 1944. A group of parapsychologists has gathered in East Bromwich, England, convinced that this is the night on which the Nazis will attempt some horrific contact with the spirit world. The Nazis are on a Scottish island, but their effect is indeed felt in East Bromwich, where a juvenile demon materialises. The team name him Hellboy and one of them brings the child up, treating him as a son. Thirty-five years later, the adult demon, still called Hellboy, is a paranormal investigator and definitely one of the good guys despite the off-putting bright red skin, stubs of horns, cloven feet and long tail. His adoptive father is killed, and he's drawn into a struggle with giant frogs, an evil wizard and an elder god. The story has little logic determining the action or resolution, but it doesn't matter, since we're really here for Mike Mignola's artwork. The artwork is stunning: bold and dramatic, and with colours by Mark Chiarello that make each panel glow like a stained-glass window. The back-up strip, 'Monkeyman and O'Brien', by Art Adams, is about a young heiress and an intelligent ape from another dimension. It's extremely pretty to look at, but if there's a point to the story, it hasn't emerged by the end of the series, after which the story moved to its own title.

'The Wolves of Saint August' is a werewolf story set in Eastern Europe. It's another weak story with lovely artwork, though James Sinclair's colours don't cast quite the same spell as Chiarello's. 'The Corpse and The Iron Shoes' has two tales, of which 'The Corpse' is the longer story and has Hellboy in Ireland doing a deal with the fairy folk in exchange for a baby that they abducted. It's funny and spooky and has the atmosphere and strange reasoning of dreams and folk tales. A faultless piece of work, from the story and art by Mignola to the colours by Matthew Hollingsworth. 'The Iron Shoes' is another Irish tale – a short and simple fight with a goblin.

'Wake the Devil' sees the return of the Nazis from the first miniseries, with plans involving vampires as well as those elder gods. The same weakness, the same strength. The back-up story is 'Silent as the Grave', a Monster Men story by Gary Gianni, which is pretty but not compelling. You can pick up any Hellboy story and thoroughly enjoy it: he's an appealing character in a gruff private-eye style, and the artwork will suck you right in. However, because the story-lines are... well... porridge, you'll probably feel on the second or third that you've seen all this before and would get the same effect just re-reading the first one.~FC

Recommended: *Seed Of Destruction* 1–4, *The Corpse And The Iron Shoes*
Collection: *Seed Of Destruction* (1–4)

HELLHOUND

Epic: *4-issue miniseries 1993*

A gunman and a guitarman (a thinly disguised Robert Johnson) are sent up from hell to stop a woman who is healing the sick and raising the dead. They meet the Angel Gabriel, sent down to do the same as 'the balance must be protected'. By no means the mindless bloodfest implied by the covers, though there's certainly enough violence for them as likes it. John Miller's story evokes sympathy for the plight of virtually every character, a very skilful trick indeed, and Floyd Hughes' daring experiment in switching style and technique to suit the scene hits the mark far more than it misses. Flawed, yes, but one to watch out for.~HS

HELLHOUNDS: Panzer Cops

Dark Horse: *6-issue limited series 1994*

Long, wordless would-be cinematic action sequences are the highlights of this otherwise dull police politics and terrorism Manga thriller translation.~GK
Collection: *Hellhounds: Panzer Corps* (1–6)

Clive Barker's HELLRAISER

Marvel: *20 issues, 4 Specials 1990–1994*

A horror anthology nominally featuring the Cenobites from the *Hellraiser* films. In reality their appearance is forced in earlier issues, so 7–16 feature chapters of a series titled 'The Devil's Brigade'. The lives of six humans are divined to have a lasting effect on the realm of the Cenobites, so they must ensure that the humans follow the paths of order. Serving to introduce a recurring cast, chapters can be read as individual stories.

Many creators of note (John Bolton, Denys Cowan, Dave Dorman, Neil Gaiman, Sam Kieth, Dave McKean, Mike McMahon) contribute alongside relative unknowns to produce an eclectic, although unremittingly gloomy, mixture. Mark Kneece, Scott Hampton and John Van Fleet's 'The Tontine' in 9 is the best story of the run, depicting the claustrophobia, hope and despair involved in an annual game of Russian roulette, without moral commentary or resorting to gratuitously illustrated violence. 17 introduces 'The Harrowers', a story prefaced in 16 and sumptuously drawn by Alex Ross. To all intents and purposes they're a group of non-costumed superheroes empowered to combat the Cenobites. The best of four specials is the Christmas-themed *Dark Holiday Special*.~WJ
Recommended: 9, 15, 17
Collection: *Hellraiser* (stories from 1–4)

HELLSHOCK

Image: *4-issue miniseries 1994*

The story begins with a shooting in a church and follows a detective sent to investigate, who ends up finding more than he expected. This is a very interesting project. On the one hand Jae Lee's art is fantastic and the plot is intriguing. On the other, there's an average of twelve pages of story per issue, with the rest filled with adverts for other Image titles. This means the story is rushed, and several opportunities are missed in the process. The idea is good but its poor execution leaves the reader feeling cheated.~SS

HELLSTORM

Marvel: *21 issues, 1993–1994*

In a feeble attempt to do a Vertigo-style horror comic, Marvel took down the Son of Satan from the shelf – admittedly not an A-List character by anyone's definition – and turned him from ridiculous to merely repulsive and tedious, an irritating, amoral and enigmatic poseur. Warren Ellis' intervention on the scripts from 16 merely turned up the squalor. The title has a cult following, but then, so does *On The Buses*.~HS

HELL'S ANGEL

Marvel UK: *16 issues 1992–1994*

Shvaughn Haldane adapts future science for her own ends to avenge her dead father and battle the evil Mys-Tech Corporation. Bizarre attempt to create a New Age hi-tech superheroine, riddled through with pointless guest appearances by sundry X-Men. Following a lawsuit by the international organisation of Hell's Angels (!), the character's name was changed to *Dark Angel* with issue 6, at which point the series was promptly sued again by an independent publisher who had previously issued a title of that name. All this helped the book not one iota, and it eventually staggered to cancellation, weighed down by its own pretentions.~HS

HELYUN

Slave Labor: *One-shot ('A Simple People') 1990, 1 issue ('Bones Of The Backwoods') 1991*

Helyun is from the American south and he believes himself to be a changeling, something that came from the wild to take the place of a

human boy. He lived as a human until he finished school, never quite knowing how to fit in, and soon returned to the wilderness, though he found it impossible to avoid humans altogether. Chas Berlin handles the changeling idea and other fantasy elements well, but the comic is mostly about an outsider's view of disgraceful human behaviour, and this is fascinating and unsettling, with artwork that is appropriately grotesque. 'A Simple People' contains four stories, including a lynching in small-town Arkansas, and Helyun's origin, but the best is 'High School Helyun', which makes some very perceptive comments on the various tribal groupings. 'Bones Of The Backwoods' is the first issue of a longer story which features Helyun going back to his home town and the brewing of a powerful local cider, but it doesn't stand well on its own, and was never completed.~FC
Recommended: 'A Simple People'

HEMBECK
Fantaco: *7 issues 1980–1983*
Marvel: *One-shot ('Fred Hembeck Destroys The Marvel Universe') 1989, one-shot ('Fred Hembeck Sells The Marvel Universe')1990*
Any comic reader should find some pleasure in the Fantaco run, which collects a series of one- and two-page strips Hembeck produced in the late 1970s and early 1980s. Using an appealing cartoon style, he vacillates between interviewing his comic guest stars as the host of a printed chat show, or nostalgia-drenched strips that are in turns wistful and enthusiastic, but always very very funny. Hembeck clearly has a fantastic knowledge of not only the comic characters but the whole medium, and being unaffiliated to any company at the time, he was able to ridicule the more absurd characters and poke fun at then current story-lines. Despite an often right-up-to-the minute commentary, the Fantaco issues have aged well, and even though the stories are history now fans will still find some truly hilarious moments. No one escapes Hembeck's witty scripts and satirical nature.

A talent this good shouldn't be wasted, and while his cartooning was unsuitable for Marvel's mainstream titles, he was ideal for producing an updated version of his previous strip for Marvel's promotional magazine *Marvel Age*. Restricted by editorial guidelines, although still occasionally funny, these strips are far less outrageous than his previous work, and are collected in *Fred Hembeck Sells The Marvel Universe*. In *Fred Hembeck Destroys The Marvel Universe*, he does just that, but in doing so proves that his individual approach can't happily stretch over twenty-four pages.~SS
Recommended: Fantaco 1–7

HEMP FOR VICTORY
Starhead: *1 issue 1993*
In 1943 the US Department of Agriculture produced a documentary encouraging American farmers to grow marijuana and extolling its use in the war effort. This adaptation of that film by Art Penn is both educational and propagandist, as its final pages detail statistics about hemp and explain more of the history of its persecution. Interesting, but more of an illustrated pamphlet than a comic book.~NF

HEPCATS
Double Diamond Press: *12 issues 1989–1994*
Antarctic Press: *1 issue + (0) 1996 to date*
By the time *Hepcats* appeared 'serious' funny-animal comics were two-a-penny, following the success of books like *Omaha The Cat Dancer* and *Cerebus*. Although well-liked by fans of this particular genre, *Hepcats* lacks the deftness of touch to break through to a wider audience.

Creator Martin Wagner's art is serviceable if not particularly eye-catching. The scripting, however, is laden down with concerns and good intentions. His nice but whiney college buddies act out a soap-opera plot, complete with dark secrets and sudden returns of unmentioned spouses/relatives, which tries to pass itself off as meaningful drama. The reader swiftly gets the feeling that Wagner loves his creations to bits, getting so involved with them that he cannot be objective, to the detriment of the book. The cumulative effect can be both dull and irritating.~FJ

HERBIE
ACG: *23 issues 1964–1967*
Dark Horse: *2 issues 1992*
ACG: *1 issue + 1996 to date*
In thirty years nothing has approached the surreal whimsy of *Herbie*, although *Flaming Carrot* is a spiritual cousin. Débuting in *Forbidden Worlds* 73, and returning in 94, 110, 114 and 116, Herbie Popnecker is presented without an origin. He's a near-somnambulant little fat kid with coke-bottle-bottom glasses who can do anything and is known the world over by human and animal alike except to his parents, from whom he hides his abilities, turning the other cheek when referred to as 'a little fat nothing' by his father. For variety, Herbie is also an occasional superhero, The Fat Fury, with a sink plunger on his head and a threat of 'Bop you with this here lollipop'. Without the comic before you it sounds pathetic, but conceive attempting to describe the humour of *Monty Python* to an alien. It can't be done, it has to be experienced, and so it is with *Herbie*. It's the non-existent immaculate 1950s TV suburban life twisted 180 degrees and ironically produced at the birth of drug culture by two men already well into middle

age. Writer Shane O'Shea (one of many aliases used by ACG editor Richard Hughes) and artist Ogden Whitney concoct bizarre fantasies in which Mao Tse Tung is fed worms and uniformed animals aid George Washington in defeating the English. It's all presented in totally po-faced fashion, with Whitney excelling at realistically proportioned art which extends the joke. A generation will testify to the appeal of *Herbie*, so while recent reprints have sunk without trace, a collection is surely more practical. The Dark Horse issues provide cheap samplers of the original material and let John Byrne have a shot at approximating it, which he does with aplomb. The ACG which publishes the 1996 issue bears no relation to the original publishers, and their first issue has a new story (originally prepared for Dark Horse) with astoundingly shoddy Dan Day art.~FP
Recommended: 1–23

HERCULES
Charlton: *13 issues 1967–1970*

A late addition to the Charlton line of Action Heroes, Hercules was the only title to survive their 1968 cancellation. Written by Joe Gill and drawn by comics evergreen Sam Glanzman, the young demi-god's earthly adventures got more and more psychedelic before cancellation in 1970. Steve Skeates and Jim Aparo produce the 'Thane Of Bagarth' back-up strip in the early issues. Issue 1 was reprinted as a one-shot black and white magazine in 1968.~SW

HERCULES
Marvel: *Miniseries one 4 issues 1982, miniseries two 4 issues 1984, Graphic Novel 1985*

Hercules had been knocking around Marvel's superhero titles for fifteen years with but one ordinary solo appearance in *Marvel Premiere 26* before writer and artist Bob Layton propelled him into his own miniseries. Hercules is banished from Olympus until he learns humility. He acquires a robotic being, The Recorder, whose task is to record the exploits of Hercules as they carouse around the galaxy. The first series is consistently funny, and generated a second, in which the jokes about a vain, yet genial, muscle-bound clod begin to wear a little thin (although there are still many amusing moments). By the time a graphic novel followed the idea had been bludgeoned to death.~FP
Recommended: Miniseries one 1–4, Miniseries two 1
Collection: Hercules, Prince of Power (Miniseries one)

HERCULES Unbound
DC: *12 issues 1975–1977*

The appealing combination of José Luis Garcia-Lopez and Wally Wood draw the first six issues, taking the Hercules of mythology into an alternate Earth dying through nuclear warfare in 1986. Hercules has good reason to be peeved, having been chained to a rock for a thousand years, and his mood darkens on learning that his old enemy Ares is behind the war. With 7 the series is used to tie up a few loose ends in DC continuity as Hercules and companions roam the devastated planet; it's ably illustrated by Walt Simonson. Every issue is better than average, with the encounter with the Atomic Knights in 10 and 11 a good sample. Commendably, the series was actually properly concluded when the sales dried up.~WJ

HERO
Marvel: *6-issue miniseries 1990*

Coby Pace, self-centred 1980s business courier, is transported to a fantasy world to become a hero despite himself. Occasionally amusing, but by and large no better than the fantasy it parodies.~FP

HERO ALLIANCE
Sirius: *2 issues 1985–1986*
Wonder: *1 issue 1987*
Innovation: *Series one 18 issues 1989–1991, series two 4 issues, 1 Special 1991–1992*

Despite the needlessly gratuitous good-girl art which always formed a major part of the series, *Hero Alliance* generally presented a solid superhero yarn with entertaining soap-opera overtones in a number of sub-plots which often outdid the main action and probably accounted for the series' surprising longevity.~JC

Luke Cage HERO FOR HIRE
Marvel: *16 issues 1973–1974*

Consciously introduced as Marvel's first ongoing title featuring a black superhero, it didn't get off to a good start with Luke Cage introduced as a petty criminal who's framed and imprisoned. He participates in cell-regeneration experiments in exchange for parole, and they leave him with bullet-proof skin and vastly increased strength, which he uses to set up as a hero for hire. The ill-judged background aside, Archie Goodwin and George Tuska provide an acceptable origin story over two issues, but the remainder of the run under lesser hands is laughable. Consistent use of 1970s street slang and fashion make this read like a poor blaxploitation movie. The title changed to *Power Man* with 17.~FP

HERO HOTLINE
DC: *6-issue miniseries 1989*

Released at the height of *Justice League America*'s popularity. It provides a new slant on the superhero convention by showing a team clocking in and out of a nine-to-five superhero job. Generally silly lighthearted fun.~SS

HERO SANDWICH
Slave Labor: *9 issues 1988–1991*

The Hero Sandwich detective agency is a collection of oddballs. There's an elastic man named Richard, an ordinary human who bears the weird name of Silver Scorpion, a gentleman named Lee with a head that is a dark circle, a crazed female commando named Allison, and Rachel, who runs the agency. The origins of the group's appearances, powers and psychoses remain unrevealed, as we join them bang in the middle of the first story, and things never slow down enough for explanations. In 1–4, the agency is hired by a vampire to track down a murderous vampire wannabe who is, allegedly, giving the species a bad name. Dan Vado's script is skilful and witty, and Chuck Austen's art fluid and appealing. The second story, in which the team has to confront ghosts from their pasts, is less interesting, though sequences of character interaction are still well presented.~HS
Collections: *Nobody Lives Forever* (1–4), *The Works* (1–4, 6–9)

HERO ZERO
Dark Horse: *One-shot 1995*

This is a rather pointless comic, starring as it does another size-changing superhero but offering no new insights into anything at all. The artwork's not bad, crisp and sharp in style, but overall the book lacks its own personality.~NF

HEROES
Blackbird: *6 issues 1986–1988*

Sadly overlooked mutant team title. On the writing side John Nordland II has some intriguing ideas, not the least of which is personalised narrators who also interact with the cast, and artist John Nordland's grey tones work extremely well, looking like nothing seen in comics before or since. The characters take precedence, and the intriguing foreshadowing and the scenarios set up make the premature demise a shame, but that shouldn't discourage sampling of what was published. The first three issues were magazine format.~FP
Collection: Heroes (1–3)

HEROES
Milestone: *6-issue miniseries 1996*

Following the dissolution of the covert Shadow Cabinet, six of its members – Iota, Payback, Donner and Blitzen, Starlight, and the part-timer Static – decide to 'go public' as the first high-visibility superhero group of the Milestone Universe. Establishing a head-quarters in New York's Chrysler Building, they set off adventuring, but find that the path to international celebrity doesn't run smoothly. Their 900 number 'Hero Hotline' keeps getting tied up with crank calls, discarded spouses turn up as Lords of the Innerverse (don't you just hate it when that happens?), and the public doesn't take kindly to Donner's cheery media acknowledgement of her and Blitzen's lesbian relationship. A cheerful, high-spirited miniseries by Matt Wayne and illustrator Chris Cross.~HS

HEROES AGAINST HUNGER
DC: *One-shot 1986*

A forty-eight-page benefit comic starring Superman and Batman, directly inspired by Bob Geldof's *Live Aid*. Jim Starlin and Berni Wrightson, also associated with Marvel's earlier *X-Men: Heroes For Hope*, persuaded DC to produce their version, and all profits went to hunger relief projects in Africa. Their plot doesn't pretend there are any easy answers to famine, and it is beyond this comic's own self-imposed limitations to consider the alternative solution of superbeings actually trying to change the way the world works. Script and art, in two-page segments, by more than seventy creators from Alfredo Alcala to Berni Wrightson, by way of Cary Bates, Dave Gibbons, Jack Kirby, Jerry Ordway, Walt Simonson etc.~GL

HEROES INC presents CANNON
Armed Forces Dist: *1 issue 1969*
CPL Gang: *1 issue 1976*

Although containing broadly the same strips, these two comics had quite different origins. The first was a regular-sized colour comic created for the armed forces, while the second was a black and white magazine aimed at the comic fan market. Both featured editor Wally Wood's 'Misfits' strips and the hard-boiled spy Cannon, pencilled in each issue by Steve Ditko. Wood's art is terrific throughout, but the stories rather let things down. Rounding out each issue were another Wood strip, the humorous 'Dragonella', and Mike Vosburg's humdrum superheroine The Black Angel in 2.~DAR

HEX
DC: *18 issues 1985–1987*

In the year 2050, five years after a world-ravaging nuclear holocaust, Reinhold Borsten provides entertainment for high-ranking members of the Conglomerate that controls the life-saving soames (used to purify irradiated water). Using a time-machine, he brings specimens of warriors from different eras and keeps them drugged before staging private battles. For a Western gunfight he collects Jonah Hex and so unleashes a one-man army on this future world. Hex quickly adapts to the new technology and succeeds in destroying the time-machine and Borsten's operation. Teaming up with Borsten's daughter, Hex sets out to investigate the new era, while looking for a way back to his own time.

Michael Fleisher claims that low sales on *Jonah Hex* weren't the primary reason for creating this series, that he'd always wanted to do something 'about a bleak, war-torn world where civilised moral values were dead', something without superheroes. It didn't take long before they began to appear, though. A future Batman popped up in 11 and there's The Dogs of War in 13. With 15 Keith Giffen took over as artist and the story involved Hex in an alien invasion. Giffen's impressionistic artwork was entirely inappropriate for the hard-hitting action. Having Hex meet his own stuffed and mounted corpse at the end of 18 was a sad end to Fleisher's vision for one of DC's great Western characters.~NF

HIGH ADVENTURE
Kitchen Sink: *1 issue 1973*

A very odd comic to have come from Kitchen Sink at the time. While the remainder of their titles featured the best and worst of the counterculture, this, nudity apart, could have been stories from Warren or Marvel's contemporary black and white magazines. There's some early art from the team of Steve Leialoha and John Pound, Mike Royer proving he can pencil as well as ink, and two stories from Mark Evanier, who would certainly progress to better things. Only now of interest as a curiosity.~FP

Amazing HIGH ADVENTURE
Marvel: *5 issues 1984–1986*

It's shameful that there's only been one mainstream historical adventure title in the past thirty years. This is an obvious attempt to emulate the later issues *of Two-Fisted Tales*, with four stories to each issue, and the art from the likes of John Bolton, Mike Mignola and EC veteran John Severin is largely excellent. Sadly, the writing doesn't generally reach the standards of the artwork. The best all-round issue is 3, but there's at least one excellent story every issue. Standouts include Steve Englehart and Severin's tale of Cromwell (1) and Mike Baron and John Ridgway's 'Skyhook' (5).~WJ
Recommended: 3

HIGH SHINING BRASS
Apple: *4-issue miniseries 1991*

Vietnam specialist Don Lomax relates the story of Robert Durand, who's part of a team co-ordinating raids, ambushes and agitation from within North Vietnamese territory, and covertly into neighbouring countries. He gradually becomes aware that he's surplus to requirements and that his superior officer has ordered him and his squad to be disposed of. It's the likely interference in the war and manipulation of Durand by the CIA that's the

central point of his story, and this really only comes to the fore in the final issue. 1–3, while decent war comics, could be three issues of any of Lomax's other titles. The sometimes heavy-handed inking of Rose Lomax renders this a little less desirable, though.~WJ

HILLY ROSE
Astro: *6 issues + 1995 to date*

Hilly Rose is B.C. Boyer's return to comics seven years after the cancellation of *The Masked Man*. It's a science-fiction adventure with a strong humour element that is used to undercut an otherwise hard-boiled tale. Hilly is a reporter who owes her job to her father's influence. He's a rich crimelord who's been humouring her and is therefore surprised and horrified when she's offered a higher-profile off-world job. As Hilly's investigations into a series of bombings lead her inexorably towards her father, he employs increasingly vicious methods to put her off. *Hilly Rose* is interesting and funny in places, but lacks a coherent voice. The story's serious side is sometimes lost among the pastiche elements and jokes.~NF

HISTORY OF THE DC UNIVERSE
DC: *2-issue microseries 1986*

George Perez beautifully renders Marv Wolfman's tale, in text form, of DC's Universe, from the beginning of time to the far-flung future. The entirety demonstrates what a splendid heritage DC has in terms of characters and scenarios. We see the birth of the Guardians of the Universe, and progress through encounters with, just to name a few, the cave boy Anthro, the Amazons of Paradise Island, the Viking Prince, the Wild West with Jonah Hex, Enemy Ace in World War I, the Justice Society of America and Sgt Rock during World War II, Superman, the New Gods, Teen Titans, and into the future with Star Hawkins and the Legion of Super-Heroes, before ending with the Time Trapper. Perez had always been noted for a good sense of design, and, freed from the tight restrictions of having to tell a story, he really pulls out the stops in providing impressive collages and frescos. Later continuity adjustments made some of the events in this series redundant, but DC buffs will nevertheless find it a useful reference guide.~HY
Recommended: 1–2
Collection: History Of The DC Universe (1–2)

HITCH HIKER'S GUIDE to the GALAXY
DC: *3-issue miniseries 1993*

Prestige-format comic-book version of the first four radio fits or first book, inevitably abridged. It is thus consistent with the myriad other *Hitch Hiker* adaptations in so far as they are all completely inconsistent with each other. DC had one supremely important decision to make for this series and got it right. They chose a British writer, John Carnell, to create this transcription. The metaphysical imagery of Steve Leialoha's whimsical pencils, particularly on the out-of-phase Guide narrations, is really particularly effective. Continues in *Restaurant at the End of the Universe*.~APS

HITMAN
DC: *8 issues + 1996 to date*

Why settle for *Preacher*-lite, when you can have the real thing, same writer (Garth Ennis) and everything? Like one of those poly-unsaturated, low-fat margarines, *Hitman* is like the original, it just has less of everything: less swearing, less violence, less fun. It also has fewer good lines, fewer strong characters and fewer clever plot twists, although the central premise – a contract killer who takes out superbeings, good or bad – is fresh.~FJ
Collection: Hitman (1–3, Demon Annual 2, Batman Chronicles 4)

Wonder Warthog: HOG OF STEEL
Rip Off: *4 issues + 1995 to date*

Reprint of various strips starring Gilbert Shelton's popular early-underground creation. Some of the material dates from as early as 1962, and much of the humour is broad digs at the Establishment. Collaborators Tony Bell and Joe E. Brown Jr add polish to Shelton's artwork on several strips. The series begins with the Warthog of Steel's origin, a Superman parody that can still raise a smile, as his adoptive parents try and cook him but, discovering he's invulnerable, decide to raise him instead. The reprints are rather disorganised, jumping all over the place in Warthog chronology, but there's some interesting older material mixed in with the more familiar, polished work.~FJ

HOKUM AND HEX
Marvel: *9 issues 1993–1994*

This is a Clive Barker-created superhero title, although beyond the initial spurt of imagination he has nothing to do with it, leaving the writing to Frank Lovece. Trip Munore is a failed magician, but his life takes a turn for the better as he's infused with superpowers in order to protect humanity. The stories are quite funny, with Trip learning to cope with his new-found powers, having previously spent his whole life as a failure, and the artwork by Anthony Williams matches the mood of the comic well. Overall an amusing read while it lasted.~SS

HOLIDAY OUT
Renegade: *4 issues 1987*

Feeble local-newspaper humour strips accompany feeble humour-comic strips. Avoid.~WJ

HOLLYWOOD SUPERSTARS
Epic: 5-issue miniseries 1990–1991

Mark Evanier brings his screenwriting background to a series about a down-at-heel private-detective agency. The series is well written and well drawn, by Dan Spiegle, but the anecdotes incorporated into the stories are far more interesting than the stories themselves or the cast. The real highlights, though, are Evanier's rambling end-of-issue text pages, mixing gossip, jokes and a constant incredulity at the stupidity of Hollywood.~WJ

My Name Is HOLOCAUST
Milestone: *5-issue limited series 1995*

Introduced in *Blood Syndicate*, Holocaust is a dreadlocked pyrotechnic who decides the time has come for him to have a larger slice of the underworld action in Dakota. This becomes awkward for the top-ranking suited criminals, who manoeuvre the legitimate law-enforcement agencies against him. Hot-tempered and often brutal, Holocaust has to learn the art of compromise in the face of insurmountable odds. The meshing of power and politics in a well constructed and conceived plot from Ivan Velez is combined with a decent supporting cast and acceptable art from Tommy Lee Edwards, and at the end of the series Holocaust is a different man.~FP

HOLY CROSS
Fantagraphics: *3 issues + 1994 to date*

Malachy Coney's stories are set in Northern Ireland, where the constant background of distrust and fear affects everyone. By turns poignant, poetic and amusing, the most readily accessible issue is 3, in which a child retreats from parental abuse into comic fantasies. Don't be deterred by the wildly different art styles of Davy Francis, Chris Hogg and Paul Holden, as each conveys the necessary emotion.~FP
Recommended: 1–3

HOMICIDE
Dark Horse: *One-shot 1990*

Before *The Mask* the team of John Arcudi and Doug Mahnke were turning out good stories about hard-boiled police detective Ford. This one-shot special is a grim tale of religious superstition and human sacrifice. Further stories can be found in *Dark Horse Presents* 25–27, 48–49 and 53–55.~WJ

HONK!
Fantagraphics: *5 issues 1987–1988*

Generally excellent off-beat humour anthology title combining the best material from British and American cartoonists then self-publishing. Every issue has work by Eddie Campbell, Phil Elliott, David Miller and J.R. Williams. Bob Boze Bell, John Callaghan and Glenn Dakin are

in most, and there's plenty of other good material, including Marc Hempel's forerunner to *Gregory* in 2 and rare translated Gotlib in 4 and 5.~FP
Recommended: 1–3, 5

HONKYTONK SUE
Bob Boze Bell: *4 issues 1979–1980*
Apparently collected from a regional newspaper strip and published by the cartoonist himself, the adventures of the 'Queen of Country Swing' are bizarre, but hugely enjoyable. Sue is a goddess of the American Mid-West, mistress of every situation. Whether she's dancing the crap out of Mr Disco, getting abducted by aliens and teaching them to line-dance, road-testing all comers to find the world's Most Mediocre Lover, or reuniting the Beatles and converting them to country swing (hey, they were all alive then, okay?), Sue takes charge and kicks ass, backstopped by her loyal, if insecure, 'nutritionally unchallenged' buddy Donna-Jean. Closest in spirit to the 'street-level' comics of the mid-1970's, more mature than the mainstream but not as gross as most undergrounds, these stories are only dated by the odd contemporary reference. Being in a setting totally alien to most comics readers anyway, the freshness of the character remains unimpaired. In the late 1980s, there were rumours of Eclipse doing a new *Honkytonk Sue* graphic novel, 'The Man Canyon', but sadly no copies have surfaced.~HS
Recommended: 1–4

HOOK
Marvel: *4-issue miniseries 1991*
Adaptation that transcends a lack-lustre film script by virtue of excellent artwork from the likes of Craig Hamilton, Gray Morrow, John Ridgway, Dennis Rodier and Charles Vess (who also adapted the film script).~WJ
Collection: Hook (1–4)

HOROBI
Viz: *Series one 8 issues 1990, series two 7 issues 1990–1991*
Shuichi and Zen, two friends with the same birthday, find themselves and their mutual friends in the middle of a mystery as students are murdered in horrific ways. To make matters worse, Zen has been dreaming of the murders before they happen and begins to hear voices in the dreams. A series of huge monsters start to appear, causing a great deal of damage before just disappearing, leaving the authorities with no clue to their creation. As the tale unfolds we discover that the deaths and monsters foretell the coming of Horobi, god of destruction, and that the two friends' families (as part of rival political and financial

organisations) have been secretly grooming them, one to represent God, the other the Devil, in a final epic battle that will decide the fate of the world. As the friends try to understand the reasons for the events that are happening around them, they find themselves struggling to cope with the demands of their separate romantic and familial relationships. Yoshihisa Tagami's complex story-telling and stylised artwork make this an absorbing read, which slowly builds to a devastating finale. The philosophical observations that underlie the climactic battle are unconvincing but the series is well worth investigation.~NF

THE HORRORIST
Vertigo: *2-issue microseries 1995*
The Horrorist is a delicately-painted, meandering John Constantine special, in which Constantine, burnt out by all the horrors he's seen, tracks down a young woman who causes catastrophe wherever she goes, from famine to crashes to suicides. The highly symbolic Jamie Delano story comes over as a little pompous, although the dry humour he brings to Constantine is appealing. David Lloyd provides bleak-coloured, loose artwork, full of subtle lines, particularly impressive for its use of underdrawing and coloured linework. Worth a look for the art alone.~FJ

HOT STUF'
SQP: *8 issues 1974–1978*
One of several comics serving as a kind of halfway house between the underground and the mainstream scenes, *Hot Stuf'* was a black and white anthology that never quite established a distinctive personality. Typically, many of the strips were science-fiction or fantasy-oriented, by far the best being by Richard Corben (1–3, 5) and Gray Morrow reviving his 'Orion' strip in 2 and 4, and of particular note was a lovely 1930s detective strip from the great Alex Toth in 4. The comic's most interesting artist, however, was Bill Maher, whose work ran the gamut from bigfoot cartoons and slick dystopian science fiction to rough-hewn autobiography and Manga pastiches. Most issues contained his work, with 7 and 8 being his best. Peculiarly, he doesn't appear to have cropped up in any other publications and that's very much our loss.~DAR
Recommended: 4, 7, 8

HOT WHEELS
DC: *6 issues 1970–1971*
A tie-in with a line of racing car toys, and aimed at boys of about twelve. Jack Wheeler is the son of a retired racing driver, and he and his friends are the 'good', law-abiding teen drivers in town. Dexter Carter is the son of a

millionaire, and he and his henchboys, Dexter's Demons, are giving teen drivers a bad name. With lots of whizzing around race-tracks, attempts at sabotage, and virtue winning through, it's perfectly likeable, helped by artwork by Alex Toth. Worth reading for the shining transparency of the pre-adolescent fantasy – such as the story in which the Chief of Police allows Jack and his friends to soup up four police cars and run their own stakeout on a gang of armed bank-robbers. Ah, innocent times.~FC
Recommended: 3–4

HOTEL HARBOR VIEW
Viz: *One volume 1990*
Two terse and extremely disturbing stories by Natsuo Sekikawa and artist Jiroh Taniguchi. The reader is shown in intimate detail the events leading up to two assassinations. The assassins are both women. The book has a distinctly dark, misogynist feel, but to be fair, this is hardly an unusual quality in the hard-boiled detective fiction and film noir that inspired these pieces. The identification of sex with death and of the female as an agent of betrayal could offend. Manga's tendency to give the impression of slow-motion action sequences is unexpectedly magnified to good effect here. The moment of death is spread over several pages where the victims seem to be watching the fatal bullets glide toward them. The slightly stilted art is drawn in a realistic style that nevertheless conveys both stories' sense of place perfectly.~SW
Recommended

HOTSPUR
Eclipse: *3-issue miniseries 1987*
Swashbuckling fantasy as a stage-fight choreographer is transported to another dimension where he's able to live the life he idealises about for real instead of vicariously, adopting the alias Hotspur. Rather more successful than DC's role-playing game titles, there's still a feeling of them as Hotspur encounters demons, trolls and the like. He's actually been summoned for A Higher Purpose, but by the third issue you don't really care anymore.~WJ

HOUSE OF HAMMER
Top Sellers/Quality: *30 issues 1976–1978 (1–23), 1982–1984 (24–30)*
This magazine was a strange amalgam of horror reviews and strip adaptations of Hammer films. Despite the format's inevitable shortcomings, it featured some good work from the cream of British comics talent. Writer Steve Moore (among others) performed miracles condensing full-length film scripts into twenty pages (or less), but inevitably it

was the art that provided the principal interest. British talents like Paul Neary (1, 5), Brian Bolland (13 with Trev Goring, 17) and David Lloyd (23) acquitted themselves well, as did the magazine's big discovery John Bolton (6, 10, 14). His first adaptation, of *Dracula*, spawned the spin-off strip 'Father Shandor', again by Moore and Bolton, in 8, 16 and 22, which far surpassed its source and eventually led to a lengthier run in *Warrior*. Another semi-original strip predated Shandor: 'Kronos, Vampire Hunter' by Moore and Ian Gibson in 1–3, later to be drawn by Steve Parkhouse. The EC-esque back-up 'Van Helsing's Terror Tales' boasted some fine art by Bolton (4), Dave Gibbons (7, 15, 23), Jim Baikie (9) and Pat Wright (16, 20). The comic's highpoint, however, was consistently provided by the veteran Brian Lewis. Whether painting covers (most issues), adapting films (4, 8, 9, 19), or drawing 'Terror Tales' (2, 6, 11, 13), he produced gloriously vibrant, vital strips that deserve to reach a wider audience. The revived magazine was retitled *Halls Of Horror*, and was almost exclusively text-based, its sole strip being a *Monster Club* adaptation by editor Dez Skinn and artists Bolton and Lloyd in 25 and 26 (reprinting a promo booklet drawn a few years earlier): this was Lewis' final strip. It was intended for the original, never printed, version of 24 and finally appeared in 29.~DAR

HOUSE OF MYSTERY
DC: *321 issues 1951–1983*
Conceived by editor Jack Schiff as a mystery anthology, the title went through a brief superhero phase in the 1960s before returning to its horror roots for a final fifteen years. The 1950s market was dominated by horror titles, and DC cashed in on the craze, though, typical of the company, its stories were hopelessly compromised by their own timidity. These competent, though uninspired, tales were at least well served artistically by the likes of Mort Meskin, Ruben Moreira and Nick Cardy. Jack Kirby surfaced briefly in the late 1950s, but the era's real gems were provided by Alex Toth in 109, 120 and 149.

With 143 the comic changed direction abruptly as the Martian Manhunter transferred from back-up status in *Detective*, but Jack Miller's scripts and Joe Certa's art never manages to rise above mediocre. More fondly remembered was a second superhero strip, 'Robby Reed – Dial H For Hero', by Dave Wood and Jim Mooney, with Robby's ever-changing super-*alter ego*. Neither strip had much staying power, and when Joe Orlando became editor with 174 he wasted no time in booting the pair out.

Orlando redesigned the comics in the mould of EC's infamous horror line, to which he'd contributed, complete with its own 'horror host', Cain. By 178 he had dispensed with reprints and began to feature work by the best writers and artists in the field, cleverly mixing old and new writers. The likes of Robert Kanigher and Jack Oleck were combined with neophyte scripters Gerry Conway, Len Wein and Marv Wolfman, but it was artistically that the comic really shone. Of particular note are strips by Neal Adams (178, 179, 186, 228), Wally Wood (180, 183, 184, 199), Berni Wrightson (179–181, 183, 186, 188, 191, 195, 201, 204, 221) and Alex Toth (182, 184, 187, 190, 194). Indeed, it was a Toth strip written by Kanigher that was the highlight of this period, 187's anti-hunting shocker 'Mask of the Red Fox'. Other talented artists such as Gil Kane, Ralph Reese, Gray Morrow and Al Williamson crop up with regularity in 180–200, the latter containing a particularly nice Mike Kaluta job.

Filipino artists like Tony DeZuniga had been introduced as early as 190, and as the comic passed 200 they came to dominate it. With artists of the quality of Alfredo Alcala and Alex Nino (204, 212, 213, 220, 224, 225, 245, 250) this was no bad thing, and consequently any issue between 210 and 230 is worth a look. By far the most technically accomplished Filipino artist was Nestor Redondo and he was on particularly fine form on this title, so any of his strips are worth a look (194, 195, 197, 202, 203, 211, 214, 217, 219, 226, 227, 229, 235, 241). One non-Filipino highlight was the criminally overlooked Canadian artist Bill Payne, who drew two outstanding strips in 206 and 207. 224–229 were hundred-page spectaculars featuring a nice mix of old and new material. Of particular interest was 'Nightmare Castle' in 229, a thirty-six-page Gothic epic by Kanigher and Redondo that climaxes with the heroine giving birth to Satan!

While the title was artistically impeccable, the writers on House of Mystery were rarely as inspired, with the notable exception of Michael Fleisher, whose stories always had a bit more bite. Probably his peak was the controversial killer-clown story 'Pingo' (221), drawn with gusto by Frank Thorne. Fleisher aside, 230–250 fell into a curious rut, with only the Oleck/Paul Kirchner and Neal Adams story 'Deep Sleep' in 236 worthy of mention. It took a change of format to bring the comic to life again.

251–259 were dollar comics boasting a full eighty pages of new material, which ensured that each issue had at least a few gems. In addition to the likes of Wood (251), Morrow (255) and Marshall Rogers (254), almost every issue has an Alex Nino masterpiece and 253 featured an all-too-rare Sandy Plunkett art job. 259 and 260 carried gorgeous art by Noly Panaligan, but the last few years of the comic

saw new American talent supplant the regular Filipinos, occasionally to the title's detriment. Early discoveries were Arthur Suydam (256, 257, 261) and Michael Golden (257, 259), though it was new writer J.M. DeMatteis who was to have the biggest impact here. His best stories were 'Hellpark', with Rogers, and the ultimate fan-boy exposé 'Collector' (270), beautifully drawn by Jim Sherman and Joe Rubinstein. He also created House Of Mystery's last continuing strip, 'I Vampire' (with art from Tom Sutton), which mixed Gothic ambience with his trademark intelligence. It ran from 291–319, and two issues later the comic, and effectively DC's entire horror line, ended, leaving a rich heritage for the discerning reader to discover.~DAR

Recommended: 109, 120, 149, 178–195, 200, 204, 206, 207, 219, 221, 224–229, 251–261, 270, 274

HOUSE OF SECRETS

DC: 154 issues 1956–1966 (1–80), 1969–1978 (81–154)

Like its sister title House of Mystery this comic went through an early period of short twist-in-the-tail stories followed by a flirtation with superheroes and finally an EC-styled horror anthology. Following a largely uneventful first few years, House of Secrets 23 presented the first regular feature: Mark Merlin, 'sleuth of the supernatural'. These proved to be universally banal adventures, not helped by some very tired Mort Meskin artwork. Far better was Eclipso, from 61, by Bob Haney and Lee Elias. Whenever top scientist Bruce Gordon is exposed to an eclipse he turns into...Eclipso, the twist being that Eclipso was a villain. The first few stories, particularly those drawn by Alex Toth (63–67) were quite inventive, but the idea wore thin, not helped by some lamentable Jack Sparling art. With 73 Mark Merlin became Prince Ra-Man and 80 saw Eclipso pitted against Prince Ra-Man in mortal combat. Not surprisingly, cancellation beckoned.

House of Secrets was revived as an addition to DC's growing horror line with the portly Abel, Cain's brother, as host. Though patchier than House of Mystery it had its share of top artists like Toth (83), Morrow (89, 90), Wood (91) and Adams (82, 90) and the same mixture of old and new writers. Particularly notable strips were a Gil Kane/Neal Adams sword-and-sorcery epic in 85, a Mike Kaluta insect-fest in 98 and, probably Jack Oleck's best story, the poignant Monster, drawn in the finest EC style by Wally Wood in 96. More importantly, 92 introduced Len Wein and Berni Wrightson's Swamp Thing in a story that remains affecting and well worth searching out in DC's classic reprint series.

Despite this, there's too much Jack Sparling and Bill Draut artwork for comfort, and consequently the issues dominated by Filipino artists (99–130) provide the comic's most consistently entertaining period.

Amongst the typically high-quality artwork by Alfredo Alcala and Gerry Talaoc and Co. it's an intricately etched vampire strip by Jess Jodloman in 108 that stands out. Alex Nino provided an number of hallucogenically compelling masterpieces (101, 103, 106, 115, 117, 126, 128, 131, 147, 153), with 109 demanding a place in any serious collection. It was Nestor Redondo, though, who proved the most compelling draughtsman: his strips in 95, 113 and 134 stand comparison with any of the era's more lauded artists. The best stories of the period were generally written by Steve Skeates, though he never quite reached the inventive heights of Michael Fleisher's 'A Connecticut Ice Cream Salesman In King Arthur's Court', drawn by Alex Toth in 123.

Issues after 130 were a mixed bag, with highpoints being a number of strips by Leo Duranona, a short medieval strip by José Luis Garcia-Lopez (154) and 140's strip featuring the Patchwork Man by Gerry Conway and Nestor Redondo. Arthur Suydam's unique and disturbing art had cropped up in 119 and 131, but found its best expression in the Cary Burkett-scripted 'Love Me… Love My Demon' in 151. That issue also features a lovely Michael Golden strip so it's well worth searching out, though generally later issues are for completists only. For readers wanting a taste of earlier material 93–98 are all fifty-two pages and reprint a fair number of 50s stories, many by the ubiquitous Toth.~DAR

Recommended: 63–67, 83, 85, 92, 95, 96, 98, 99, 108, 109, 113, 123, 134, 151.

HOUSE OF SECRETS
Vertigo: *3 issues + 1996 to date*

Bearing no relation to the previous series, the house is a place occupied by ancient supernatural beings who judge their visitors by reference to events previously concealed. There are no secrets from the Juris, though, and those failing their trial are consigned to hell. The Juris is a daft name for a start. Get through that and there's some nice art from Teddy Kristiansen, particularly in the testimony sequences, but so far *House Of Secrets* fails to engage and it's the fault of writer Stephen Seagle. The idea of all-powerful otherworldly supernatural beings has been mined to death, the lead character, teenage runaway Rain, is glib and irritating, and while the fate of the guilty is nasty their stories don't occupy enough space to engage the reader's sympathy. Must do better.~WJ
Collection: Foundation (1–5)

HOUSE OF YANG
Charlton: *6 issues 1975*

Joe Gill scripted this *Yang* spin-off title featuring more adventures of Charlton's Chinese kung fu character. The idea was more interesting than the result, but it's an indication of Charlton's willingness to experiment. Neither the stories nor Sanho Kim's art were up to much.~DWC

HOWARD THE DUCK
Marvel: *Series one 33 issues, 1 annual, 1 Treasury Edition 1976–1986, Series two 9 issues 1979–1981*

Howard the Duck looks a heck of a lot like Disney's more famous Donald. He arrived in *Fear* 19's Man-Thing strip in a story partially reprinted in the Treasury Edition. In Howard's universe, ducks had evolved into the dominant species, and he calls humans 'talking apes'. He started life as a brief anti-Disney spoof, implicitly critical of Disney's sentimental, childish and authoritarian world. What if Donald Duck smoked a cheap cigar, and acted like an adult with a fundamentally cynical world view? Neophyte writer Steve Gerber was at his peak with an early burst of brilliance that threw off ideas such as Howard-like individual sparks from a high-flying firework. The Howard spark should have sputtered and died in the very next issue, *Man-Thing* 1, but reader demand returned him, first in back-up strips in *Giant-Size Man-Thing* 4 and 5 (also reprinted in the Treasury Edition), then in his own comic, where the satirical train of thought that originally brought us Howard started to pick up steam.

1 has an accountant-magician trying to rule the universe with a cosmic calculator, and does Howard as Conan The Barbarian. In 2 Gerber mocks the heroic ideals and purple prose of fellow-comic-scripter Don McGregor. Kung fu, the art world, wrestling and horror movies come under Gerber's satirical attack in 3–6, but by 7 he's clearly decided that spoofing individual media fads has limited potential, and begins cooking with gas. Gerber's real subject is life in modern America, so Howard runs for President in 7 and 8. After politics comes nothing less than The Human(-ish) Condition itself; Howard has an existential crisis in 10 and ends up in psychiatric hospital in 12–14, whee he meets Marvel's exorcist hero The Son Of Satan and rock band Kiss. *The Island of Dr Moreau*, *1001 Arabian Nights* (in the annual) and *Star Wars* are all worked over before Gerber's last regular issue, 27. He's particularly good on the Moral Majority/Religious Right in 20 and 21. Early art by fan faves Frank Brunner and Jim Starlin kicked off the title well, but from 4 on it's nearly all Gene Colan. He'll be remembered as the definitive Howard artist, and Howard will be remembered as one of the

peaks of Colan's career, his excellent, realistic artwork suiting the book well. Sal Buscema and Klaus Janson provide suitably superheroic art for the new material in the Treasury Edition, in which Howard meets Dr Strange and the Defenders. The parody here is reserved for some very silly supervillains. 16 is a controversial deadline-doom fill-in issue. A text piece with illustrations of variable quality, it's much loved by some Gerber fans for its humour and insights into his eccentric mind. Others consider it self-indulgent nonsense and the issue should have been the traditional reprint.

This comic remains a unique triumph. Where else in the world of fiction, let alone comics, is there such a mixture of social, media and psychological satire, with a talking duck as its Everyman figure? Where else but in a comic would it work so well? It's the birth of a new genre, the serious funny-animal comic. A duck in a world of talking apes is a ready-made stand-in for readers feeling alienated from modern society, and there were enough to ensure Howard's success. It spun off a newspaper strip (not bad, while Gerber was at the helm), a movie (legendarily awful) and, sadly, a court case as Gerber tried to gain some ownership of his creation from Marvel.

From 28 on it's fill-in issue purgatory, weak guest-appearance limbo and a three-issue movie tie-in hell for Howard, with revival as an 'adult' black and white magazine worst of all. It meant Howard's girlfriend could show her naked breasts (one panel only, in 1, if you're interested) but the humour became childish. Potent satire became limp parody: Duck-Man, Playduck etc. Colan and Mike Golden drew some lovely big monochrome pages, but unfunny writer Bill Mantlo's big idea was to send Howard back to his home, Duckworld, which sounds like a theme park and is almost as grim to visit. The back-story was never the point with Howard. The point was, he was one of us all along.~GL
Recommended: 7–15, 17–27, Treasury Edition

H.P.'S ROCK CITY
Dark Horse: *One-shot 1996*

Reprints of several of Moebius' short stories, mostly with a science-fiction theme. The title story is wordless, set in a world where everyone is subservient to the media and a rock star dreams of escape from the constant attention. Apart from this, of particular interest are 'White Nightmare', a brutal tale of racism, 'The Long Tomorrow', a hard-boiled science-fiction detective story written by Dan O'Bannon, and 'Is Man Good?' This is a tidy colour edition, nearer paperback than comic,

and though the artwork has been reduced in size, the print quality is excellent. Though none of these strips can be described as major, Moebius' imagination and the beautiful artwork are as captivating as ever.~NF

HUGO
Fantagraphics: *One-shot 1983, 3 issues 1984–1985*

Sub-titled 'Fairy Tales For Adults' and infused with the sensibilities of 1930s cartoons, *Hugo* is a rare funny-animal book that's actually funny. Hugo is the spirited and confident court jester hopelessly in love with the glamorous and selfish Princess Trish, daughter of the downhome King Adolph the Eleventeenth. Hugo vies for the affections of the Princess with the vain and egotistical Sir Loin De Beef, and all regulars take a turn in the spotlight. The one-shot is magazine-sized.~WJ
Recommended: One-shot, series two 1–3

Incredible HULK
Marvel: *Series one 6 issues 1962–1963, series two 347 issues + (102–448), 20 Annuals, 1 Giant-Size 1968 to date*

The Lee/Kirby first series is now quite rightly revered for its nostalgic, pioneering, collectible status. But by any detached, critical assessment it has dated badly. Artless plots are riddled with *non sequiturs* and a ridiculous array of villains. Of most interest is the Hulk's formative relationship with Rick Jones. Modern progress has not provided all the answers, though. The Hulk's origin is encapsulated in the first few pages of issue 1. Nowadays, a plough through the first hundred issues of a new title would unearth a mere handful of circumstantial clues to the protagonist's origin. For those who don't know, scientist Bruce Banner is caught in a gamma bomb blast, and thereafter becomes the enormously powerful Hulk when enraged (although the transformation was originally during the more traditional hours of darkness).

Second-series numbering and publication continues from *Tales to Astonish*. The underlying thread running throughout this book involves the military's attempts to cure or kill the Incredible Hulk, and therein lies the predicament. Were they ever to succeed, cancellation would surely follow. This dilemma, alongside the Hulk's normal state of mind, which limits his vocabulary to 'Hulk smash', makes this a very difficult title to write successfully. Most writers have proved the point with long sequences of desperately dull scripts. Efforts to relieve the tedium usually revolve around changes in his condition (green Hulks, grey Hulks, intelligent Hulks) but this cycle has now been exhausted repeatedly.

The title provided a vehicle for two of

Marvel's stalwart pencillers to exercise extended runs. Herb Trimpe pencilled almost every issue numbered one hundred and something and Sal Buscema did likewise in the two hundreds. Early writers Gary Friedrich and Stan Lee to 120, Roy Thomas (121–147) and Archie Goodwin (148–157) churned out routine tales cementing Hulk's stable of villains, rather too many of whom were aliens. Military attempts were personified by General 'Thunderbolt' Ross, whose zeal gradually developed into an obsessive, personal vendetta against a tragic, misunderstood figure searching for peace yet forever hounded by mankind. Steve Englehart finally showed a little flair in 159–171 with a sub-plot describing Major Glenn Talbot's abduction by Commies and replacement by an impostor. Running alongside, Ross' daughter Betty suffered one of many nervous breakdowns and transformed into the Harpy. Len Wein's stint in 179–222 follows the normal modest standards – a glowing exception is the touching 182, a story sadly submerged by that issue's notability for an early Wolverine cameo. 189 maintains a similar heart-warming theme. Wolverine's first cameo (180) and first full appearance (181) are reprinted in the 1986 one-shot *Incredible Hulk and Wolverine*.

Roger Stern's run (225–242) coincided with the prominence of the Hulk TV series and, in sympathy with these episodes, Stern's scripts contrived a minimal use of supervillains. A very tame product resulted. Bill Mantlo sustained mind-numbing mediocrity from 245–313. Of marginal interest is the Hulk's spell of full intelligence from 271–296. In 278–281 he is granted a full Presidential Pardon for the billions of dollars of property damage his havoc has wrought. The story goes way over the top as at least six spoons of sugar are loaded into the coffee. Shortly thereafter, the alien Bereet from *Rampaging Hulk* emerges to controversially declare that all the stories in that black and white magazine run are fictional within the Marvel Universe, being the result of her film-making exploits on the planet Krylor. Hulk's intellect goes full circle in 297 as Nightmare turns him completely mindless and inarticulate. In an effort to restrain property-insurance premiums below astronomical levels, Doctor Strange exiles Hulk off Earth in 300 and he embarks on a dire sequence of stories under the 'Crossroads' banner until finally re-emerging on Earth in 313. Mantlo's penultimate issue, 312, is his finest, as we are treated to the history of Bruce Banner's birth, childhood and adolescence. John Byrne kickstarts the title's rehabilitation in 314–319 as Hulk and Bruce Banner are split into separate entities and Bruce and Betty Ross finally wed in 319, some 195 issues after their first attempt was aborted at the altar. Al Milgrom preserves

respectability (320–330), initiating new variations on a theme: a Rick Jones Hulk and a grey Banner Hulk, the latter not seen since 1. Milgrom deals the next scripter-elect a favour by disposing of the tiresome General Ross, now well past his shelf life, in his last issue.

From 1987, Peter David has been at the scripting helm, writing every issue regularly from 331, bar two fill-ins (360, 389). He has achieved what many thought impossible on the Hulk: a well written comic book infused with sardonic humour and avoidance of the cliché traps of the past. David crafts the finest Leader story ever in 342–346, strongly enhanced by the patient sub-plot building to it during preceding issues. The follow-up Leader stories in 364–367 and 397–400 are also of high quality. David has been blessed by many fine pencillers during his run: Todd McFarlane 330–346, Jeff Purves 347–366, Dale Keown 367–398 and Gary Frank 403–425 (bar fill-ins). He joined McFarlane during one of his best, if somewhat warty, artistic periods, prior to attainment of mega-stardom.

One of the secrets of David's success is his serious shake-up of locales, supporting characters and plot elements before staleness sets in. In 347 the Hulk goes into hiding, adopts the pseudonym Mr Fixit, and is employed as a bouncer in a Las Vegas casino. He even gets a girl. Marlo Chandler is one of the best comic-book supporting characters introduced in the last ten years. As her flatmate puts it in 348, '… every guy you meet is intimidated by you, just 'cause you're over six foot and built. Now you finally get lucky…' She has proved a marvellous foil for other characters to play off, not to mention for David's sly wit. Later she dates Rick Jones and eventually becomes Mrs Rick Jones in 418. The underrated Jeff Purves has been unfortunate to live in McFarlane's shadow. His expressive pencils are never better exemplified than in Marlo's reaction to 'a good time' last night with Mr Fixit in 347 and Bruce Banner's realisation that he has lost three months of his life (spent in *alter ego* form) in 353.

David continued in hot form. 354's vignette of a gambling frenzy on the outcome of an impromptu fist fight involving Mr Fixit is outstandingly funny. Hulk joins the Pantheon from 382–425, a centuries-old *Thunderbirds* outfit stuffed full with a crew of new superheroes all ripe for the couch. Rick/Marlo's bachelor/hen nights cause rolling in the aisles in 417, yet David shows his versatility with the sobering, sensitive AIDS issue (420). More recently, high-class issues are sparser as David shows signs of straining for new inventiveness, and the Sharp and Medina artistic stints have delivered much flash but little thunder. However, Mike Deodato Jr's début in 447 shows promise and the overall standard of this comic still considerably outstrips the average superhero output of today's industry.~APS

Recommended: 163–170, 176–178, 182, 312, 319, 330–334, 336–348, 353–354, 361–362, 372–377, 397–400, 406, 417–418, 420, Annual 7
Collections: *Ground Zero* (340–346), *Marvel Masterworks* Vol 8 (1–6), *Transformations* (3, 6, 272, 315, 324, 347, 377)

Rampaging HULK
Marvel: *27 issues, 1977–1981*

This is a large-format, sixty-four-page anthology comic, with three distinct phases. 1–9 were all black and white, with a continuing Hulk story written by Doug Moench, with artists including Alfredo Alcala and Walt Simonson. The plot involved alien invaders and giant robots and was well-nigh unreadable. A continuity implant set in the early days of the Hulk's career, the stories offered him the chance of encounters with the likes of the original X-Men (2), but were later wisely written off as a dream. 1–8 also have a back-up story involving the tedious Bloodstone (10,000-year-old hunter, last seen in the first issues of *Marvel Presents*), with a respite in 7 for a bizarre Man-Thing tale.

10–23 correspond with the screening of the Hulk TV series, and from 10 the title became *The Hulk!*, all strips graduated to colour, and the story-lines (still mostly by Moench) changed in line with the budget of the TV series. Out went the alien invaders, and centre stage was occupied instead by Bruce Banner's plight as an outcast and troubled soul. The result was a much better read, with something of merit in almost every issue and some entertainingly outrageous displays of the Hulk's strength – such as uprooting an entire island and towing it ashore! Highlights for the Hulk are the plane crash (13), the desert island idyll (18), Roy Thomas' mirage story (19), and the controversial story in which Banner is the subject of an attempted rape (23). With 10, Ron Wilson took over the art, but it was Alcala's return with 15 that gave the comic some bite, especially the Ditko homage in 20. The first back-up strip during this period was Moonknight (10–18, 20), a caped-hero story written by Doug Moench, with art by Bill Sienkiewicz from 12 on. It improved steadily, with a clever pair of stories in 15 that turn out to be a crossover with the Hulk, and with a solid murder story in its last three issues. The second back-up strip was the gangster story 'Dominic Fortune', starting in 21: never mind the plot, just drink in the Howard Chaykin art.

The Hulk story returned to black and white in 24–27, though Dominic Fortune remained in colour (finishing in 25), and

Moench disappeared from the writing credits. The main writer for these last issues was Lora Byrne, who produced some satisfying, well-rounded stories, particularly in 26. Also of interest: the letters column in 25, dominated by reactions to the attempted rape story in 23. There's nothing here that counts as a masterpiece, but for an hour's entertainment, you could do a lot worse.~FC
Recommended: 13, 15, 18, 19, 23, 26

The Incredible HULK Miniseries and One-Shots

Writer Peter David and artist George Perez offer up the first Hulk microseries, 'Future Imperfect', basically a Hulk take on the dark and depressing future that seems to be in store for all Marvel's hapless characters. The Hulk finds himself transported to a post-nuclear future where his self-to-be is an evil dictator and his modern-day self is the only person who can stand against him. Not a terribly original plot and the execution is equally pedestrian, although as usual with Peter David scripts there are enough comic and movie in-jokes to provide distractions if you're easily impressed by that sort of thing. *Savage Hulk* is essentially a showcase of short stories, held together by a framing sequence of the Hulk on trial. The Dave Gibbons section is by far the best, although Scott Lobdell and Humberto Ramos' old-style fisticuffs between the Hulk and Thor also deserves an honourable mention. *Hulk and Hercules*, on the other hand, is a dull battle between, then teaming of, the title characters by writer Peter David and artist Mike Deodato, and is best avoided. ~JC
Collection: Future Imperfect (1–2)

HULK 2099
Marvel: *10 issues 1994–1995*

Making his début in *2099 Unlimited*, the Hulk of the future is John Eisenhart, accidental recipient of the gamma rays designed by the descendants of Bruce Banner to create another Hulk. He's big, he's green, he's scary, he retains his intelligence and he's got a long, wobbly, protruding red tongue. The art and technobabble serve to obfuscate rather dull stories, most of which concern the Hulk's attempts to protect the film studio he and colleagues run.~FP

The HUMAN FLY
Marvel: *19 issues 1977–1979*

Considering trying this series about a real-life costumed stuntman? Why? Your oven needs cleaning, doesn't it? And that collapsed bookshelf needs fixing. Haven't you been meaning to write to the council about the dog shit on the pavement? What about the pile of ironing, calling your granny, or oiling that squeaky door? Any one of these activities will make you feel you've achieved something. I've read these so you don't have to. And you should see the dust under my microwave, the mud on my football boots and the state of my garden.~FP

HUMAN TARGET Special
DC: *One-shot 1991*

Originally a back-up strip in *Action Comics*, created by Len Wein, the Human Target is Christopher Chance, master of disguise and self-defence. He makes his living by taking the place of people whose lives have been threatened in order to catch their prospective killers before they can actually do any killing. This one-shot was produced to tie in with a TV film and adds a group of associates to the cast, but otherwise retains the original premise of the strip. Unfortunately it's got a derivative plot about druglords trying to kill the cop who's trying to get them extradited, courtesy of writer Mark Verheiden including the usual twists about just who the bad guy really is. The artwork by Rick Burchett and Dick Giordano (who had had a hand in all of the Human Target's previous appearances) is rushed and unappealing.~NF

HUMAN TORCH
Marvel: *8 issues 1974–1975*

If you're desperate to sample the light fluff that was the Human Torch strip in *Strange Tales*, or short back-ups featuring the 1940s character, this is the place for you.~WJ

HUMAN TORCH COMICS
Timely: *34 issues (2–35) 1940–1949, 3 issues (36–38) 1954*

Of Marvel's big three of the 1940s it's the Human Torch who never seems to have had the breaks. His creator, Carl Burgos, was simply nowhere near as gifted as Captain America's Simon and Kirby or Sub-Mariner's Bill Everett, and his origin was ludicrous even by comic standards. Created as an android servant, he spontaneously combusts when exposed to oxygen, and later acquires a kid sidekick when proximity to a circus fire-eater causes the latter to also burst into flame! And while the concept of a man made of fire would seem to beg for exciting and dramatic visuals, few of the original run of artists provided them, with the styles usually employed being either staid or cartoony. Still, the Torch and his little pal Toro plodded on with the occasional burst of imagination, the clashes with Sub-Mariner in 8 and 10 being notable.

In 1948 the Torch, like all of Timely's headlines, responded to certain allegations being made by anti-comics crusader Dr Fredric Wertham: in his case he jettisoned his kid sidekick and adopted a female one. Toro's replacement by Sun Girl assured readers and parents of the Torch's 'normality', but she did little other than shine her 'Sun Ray' (a fancied-up wrist torch) on HT's activities. Right, a man made out of fire really needs a spotlight.

He was the first of the Timely stars to wane; a brief and unimaginative revival failed to catch fire in 1954 and he faded out completely. His name was later borrowed by the Fantastic Four's junior member, but the original returned in *Fantastic Four* Annual 4 and, decades later, in *West Coast Avengers*.~HS

HUMMINGBIRD
Slave Labor: *One-shot 1996*

There's much to admire in this decidedly odd story of a tempestuous few days in a young girl's life. When her mother starts eating the cat, you know it's not an ordinary comic, and Gregory Benton's cartoony art has touches of Ted McKeever about it. Unfortunately his writing isn't as polished, and whimsical detours and Hummingbird's oddly ineffective passivity through an appalling series of events disengage the reader.~FP

HUNTRESS
DC: *19 issues 1989–1990, 4-issue miniseries 1994*

The Huntress was introduced in *All-Star Comics* in the 1970s as the daughter of the Batman and Catwoman of a parallel world. When DC expunged all its parallel worlds in 1985, they were left with a popular character whose history had been declared 'never happened'. Thus, Helena Wayne became Helena Bertinelli, daughter of a criminal family, who, after sundry childhood traumas, turned to fighting crime under the mantle of the Huntress. Much underestimated, the first series featured hard-hitting street-crime stories, Joey Cavalieri presenting Helena as an admirable, though screwed-up, character, and an oddball change of style and tone by artist Joe Staton that suited the series well. It was also different in that the new Huntress wasn't a stereotypical comic babe. She was attractive, but looked wiry and tough, with a lean face and a comparatively sensible costume. Dangling plot threads from the first series were wound up in *Justice League International Special* 2. In the mid-1990s, concerted attempts were made to tie in the Huntress with the *Batman* supporting cast, with numerous guest appearances, resulting in a makeover for the character. Her hair got fuller, her bustline bigger, and her costume developed mysterious cleavage-revealing gaps. This 'bad girl' version was tried out in a miniseries that owed one huge debt to Frank Miller's work, but what was intended to be gritty and noirish ended up merely confusing and ugly.~HS

HUP
Last Gasp: *4 issues 1987–1992*

Let there be no doubt that Robert Crumb is an incredibly accomplished artist. His writing, however, should perhaps come under closer scrutiny. He's at his best when adapting, delivering tirades or with his cringingly open autobiographical pieces. When it comes to turning his hand to fiction, though, the result is deeply unsatisfying and often little more than an embarrassing rendition of sexual fantasy. That's fine and dandy for those sharing the dream of dominating big-assed women but bores everyone else. *Hup* is all Crumb and every work of genius – like 1's 'My Troubles With Women Part II'(part 1 was in *Zap* 10) – is balanced by misogynistic fantasy. The return of Mr Natural and Flakey Foont explores this territory to tedious extreme in 2–4. Everyone should see the great Crumb, but to do so here you also have to endure the banal.~FP
Recommended: 1, 3, 4

HYBRIDS
Continuity: *Series one 5 issues 1992–1993, series two 4 issues (0–3) 1993, one-shot 1994*

One of the most confusing (in both content and publishing history) of Continuity's titles. The first few issues of *Hybrids* were actually titled *Revengers Special*, and in fact half of the first issue was reprinted from *Revengers* 6. The second series was chapters of the 'Deathwatch 2000' crossover, and the one-shot a chapter of the 'Rise Of Magic' crossover. The Hybrids themselves were an extraordinarily unprepossessing bunch of genetically altered people (don't ask) who revelled in confusing fights with a confusing array of dragons, demons and such-like. Artistically it rarely reached the heights of other Continuity comics, exceptions being the zero issue and the 'Rise Of Magic' one-shot, both drawn by Mike Deodato before his descent into Image-inspired hackdom.~DAR

HYDROGEN BOMB Funnies
RipOff: *1 issue 1970*

While the strips in this underground anthology title only occasionally deal with the bomb, it nonetheless contains some excellent material. Of the anti-war strips Greg Irons' brutal 'Raw War Comics' is the standout, though Fred Schrier and Foolbert Sturgeon acquit themselves with honour. Other highpoints include a beautifully drawn Dadaist piece by Robert Williams, and a typically imaginative strip by Kim Deitch. The bulk of the comic, however, is given over to Gilbert Shelton, who weighs in with a couple of Freak Brothers strips as well as the lengthy 'Wonder Warthog And The Pigs From Uranus'. Contributions from Robert Crumb, S. Clay Wilson and Dave Sheridan round out a terrific package.~DAR
Recommended: 1

HYENA
Tundra: *3 issues 1992–1993*

In *Hyena*'s brief existence it managed to offend practically every sensibility known to man, and it did so with style. Each issue of the magazine was packed with talented alternative cartoonists. Regular artists included Roy Tompkins ('Harvey The Hillbilly Bastard' in 1 and 2), Jim Woodring (1, 2), Mac White (1, 3) and Hunt Emerson (1, 3). The first issue was the most consistently good, and highlights were unquestionably the indescribable 'Pee Dog' (by Jocko 'Levant' Brainiac 5 and Eddie Nukes) and 'Jeff And Monty', the rudest funny-animal strip of all time, by Jeff Holcombe. The other issues were patchier, but notable strips included 'Woodfield', a strip about planks of wood by Art Baxter, and some lovely art from 'Pic' in 2 and 3.~DAR
Recommended: 1–3

HYPERKIND
Marvel/Razorline: *9 issues, 1 special 1993–1994*

Clive Barker-created superhero team that survives a dull origin in 1 and 2, to develop some interesting ideas. Best issue is 5, which gives some background to the series, with the team captured by a man who's managed to re-write history.~FP

I AM LEGEND
Eclipse: *4-issue miniseries 1991*

Prestige-format adaptation of the Richard Matheson story about the last man alive trying to survive in a world of vampires. Adequate if perhaps a bit over-reverent.~HS

I BEFORE E
Fantagraphics: *2 issues 1991–1992*

I Before E collects Sam Kieth's strips from places as diverse as *Critters, Stig's Inferno* and *Death Rattle*. Lovingly put together with a few previously unpublished short stories and portfolio material, this is a fine introduction to the work of an artist probably better known for *Sandman, Wolverine* or *The Maxx*. Kieth's style, with lots of Wrightson and Suydam influences, quickly became distinctive and individual and though many of the stories here are slight there's plenty to enjoy.~NF

Isaac Asimov's I-BOTS
Tekno: *5 issues 1995 to date*

Based on an Isaac Asimov premise, this lack-lustre series is the story of a bunch of robotic superheroes created to protect mankind. Less interesting than it sounds: neither the scripts by Steven Grant, then Cliff Biggers, nor Pat Broderick's pencils progress beyond mediocre.~TP

I, LUSIPHUR
Mulehide: *7 issues 1991–1992*

A hard-drinking elf immune to poison, as indeed are all elves in this canon, Lusiphur is almost crushed by blocks of text on several occasions. This is half-baked and poorly illustrated fantasy, although much in demand as the earliest incarnation of the popular *Poison Elves,* to which the title changed with 8. Enthusiasm propels creator Drew Hayes through, but he's still distinctly feeling his way with these magazine-sized issues. The collection includes text précis only of 1 and 2, Hayes feeling they weren't of the standard he later attained. He was right.~WJ
Collection: Requiem For An Elf (3–5)

I SAW IT
Educomics: *One-shot 1982*

As a young child creator Keiji Nakazawa survived the world's first atomic bomb explosion in Hiroshima. This recollection is harrowing, and features many disturbing images. Instead of the overtly cartoon style having a distancing effect, the horrors of Hiroshima are all the more acute for intruding into a familiar and comforting environment. The autobiographical elements extend beyond 1945 to the present day, with the explosion a permanent reminder to Nakazawa of the futility of war. He later expanded on his life in Hiroshima before and after the bombing as *Barefoot Gen,* available and highly recommended as two graphic novels from Penguin.~FP
Recommended

I WANNA BE YOUR DOG
Eros: *5-issue miniseries 1990–1991*

Lengthy, dense, erotic thriller that exudes seediness, more a slice of sado-masochistic life than a piece of titillation. Writer/artist Ho Che Anderson is full of interesting observations on power in relationships, sexual or otherwise, once you get past his highly stylised artwork. At times, though, it can be hard to work out what's going on as his everyday people fight and fuck.~FJ

ICEMAN
Marvel: *4-issue miniseries 1984–1985*

Iceman, former X-Man and current member of the Defenders at the time of this story, is visiting his home for a family occasion, and discovers just how much his parents get on his nerves. To escape, he chats up the girl who's just moved in next door and thus gets involved in temporal paradoxes and cosmic battles, and it all teaches him about family and love and his mission in life and other good stuff. It's outrageously far-fetched and is propelled largely by the power of syrupy sentimentality. The artwork by Alan Kupperberg and Mike Gustovich is fine for the fantasy scenes, but fails badly at normal life. Most of the women look like a fifty-year-old Nancy Reagan, and that's just plain scary when the woman in question is supposed to be seventeen. Strictly for dedicated fans of Iceman.~FC

ICON
Milestone: *42 issues 1993–1997*

An alien exile to Earth takes the form of the first human he meets in the year 1839. Since the first person he meets is black, that causes him some problems in years to come. Immortal, he lives unchanged through wars and revolution, taking no active part in the world despite his vast power, until a chance encounter with fifteen-year-old Racquel Ervin. She's one of a gang of youths who attempt to burgle his mansion in 1993, and goads him out of his complacency. She persuades 'Augustus Freeman IV', against his better judgement, to become a hero to the desperately needy city of Dakota, and manages to haggle a sidekick's gig for herself into the bargain. As Icon and Rocket, they set out to right wrongs, but things don't quite go as planned, with the police officers on their first case assuming they're the criminals! Just as their rocky relationship with the law is being sorted out, Racquel gets another surprise. Her jerkwater boyfriend, Noble, is responsible for more than trying to lure her into a life of crime. She's pregnant, and even with the powers Icon's alien technology can give her, she risks her life, and the baby's, by adventuring.

Although Icon is the nominal star of the comic, Racquel/Rocket is the emotional lynchpin for the readers. Smart, lively and gutsy, she sets the fires under everybody else's butts to get the action going, but she's not so tough that you don't empathise with her when she faces agonising decisions, such as whether to keep her baby, and, she fears, abandon her dreams of a life of her own. But she proves more resourceful than she suspects. During the latter stages of her pregnancy, she finds a substitute for Rocket in the shape of her pal Darnice, and enlists 'Buck Wild, Mercenary Man' (introduced in 13 as a hilarious parody of *Luke Cage, Hero for Hire*, who nevertheless is invested with a dignity of his own) as a replacement Icon when in the 'Mothership Connection'(17–21) he finds a way back to his homeworld. Ultimately, both the replacements, though well-intentioned, prove inadequate, and the originals are forced to step in. Perhaps the strangest issue is 30, in which a memorial service is conducted for a cast member. Poignant, yet achingly funny, it's quite a skilful piece of story-telling. After Rocket travels to Icon's home, the Collective, and saves Earth (31–36), things seem a bit anticlimactic, but writer Dwayne McDuffie and artist Mark Bright continue to deliver sound and entertaining work to the conclusion.~HS

Recommended: 18, 13, 22–25, 30–36
Collection: A Hero's Welcome (1–8)

IDOL
Epic: *3-issue miniseries 1992*

A B-movie being filmed in an almost deserted undersea military base is plagued by power surges and mysterious disappearances. And the base was once used for secret research. Uh oh, could be trouble ahoy. Actually far more entertaining than the formulaic plot would suggest.~FP

ILLUMINATOR
Marvel: *2 issues, 1993*

Illuminator is Andy Prentiss, high-school student and Christian superhero. It's moderately entertaining, with more respect for the act of story-telling than you find in most comics with an overt religious mission. There's always a sermon, but it's tacked on at the end and can easily be ignored.~FC

ILLUMINATUS!
Eye 'n' Apple Productions: *One-shot 1987, 3-issue miniseries 1989–1991*

Anarchic underground adaptation of early books in Robert Anton Wilson and Robert Shea's *Illuminatus!* sequence. Issue 1 (second series) reprints the original issue 1 with retouched artwork. The Illuminati is a secret society bent on world conquest by assassination, intrigue and abduction. Any discussion of them is, of course, extremely dangerous because… ~APS

Ray Bradbury's THE ILLUSTRATED MAN
Topps: *One-shot 1993*

Ray Bradbury's haunting concept of people seeing their fates in the tattoos of The Illustrated Man is well illustrated by Guy Davis. His segments sandwich what appears to be an EC reprint, drawn by Jack Kamen, and a story beautifully drawn and coloured by P. Craig Russell titled 'The Visitor'. It's decent science fiction, well produced.~FP

IMAGINE
Star*Reach: *6 issues 1978–1979, 1 special 1987*

Spin-off from *Star*Reach*, featuring many of the same contributors but offering a broader selection of material than *Star*Reach's* science-fiction/fantasy remit. With creators like Dave Sim (1, 4), Marshall Rogers (1), Gene Day (2) and Michael T. Gilbert (2–5) there ought to be something of interest in every issue, but much of the material is early and unpolished. Much better is P. Craig Russell's beautiful colour artwork in 2 and 3 and Lee Marrs' homage to Moebius (3), or Steve Ditko's illustration of Paul Levitz's 'The Summoning'.~NF

IMMORTALIS
Marvel UK: *4-issue miniseries 1993*

Mortigan Goth, the Immortal Man, becomes involved with an old family friend, Jacqueline Falsworth, formerly Spitfire of the Invaders, and a powerless Dr Strange, as they struggle to free her cousin from a vampiric curse. Flashbacks to Goth's origin, and a side trip to Mephisto's Hell, provide the opportunity for rather more theological discussion than is customary in a Marvel comic, but writer Nick Vince makes it all palatable, and Mark Buckingham's illustrations are appealing.~HS

IMPACT
EC: *5 issues 1955*

The stated policy of *Impact* when introduced was to present twist-ending stories, as if they weren't well enough represented in the remainder of the EC line. A rather substandard first issue storywise (despite Reed Crandall, George Evans and Graham Ingels art) is elevated to greatness by possibly the single best-known EC story. 'Master Race' is unrelenting horror, definitely not for the squeamish, and an adult story in the best sense of the term years before its time. Artist Bernie Krigstein takes Al Feldstein's already powerful script about an escaped Nazi haunted by his past and a fear of retribution, and doesn't hold back with the truth. Packed with memorable images and excellent story-telling, it's deservedly known as a masterpiece. Krigstein returns in 5 with a less noteworthy, but nonetheless very good, tale of envy. Given the limiting factor of the twist ending and its high predictability ratio in the horror and science-fiction titles, it's pleasant to note some genuine surprises in *Impact*. Beyond the ending, the stories are able to range over the full breadth of imagination, spanning the likes of the Graham Ingels-drawn, overtly sentimental story of a young girl selling lemonade in front of a crusty shop-owner's premises in 3 to 4's overwritten but well-meaning polemic hitting out against attitudes towards Jews, still unenlightened in the 1950s USA. Generally a decent read, and occasionally excellent, but beware some howlers. 2 has all-too-simple solutions to the threat of a divorce – its parent/child relations grate – and 3's story about an ugly woman's inability to form a relationship is particularly ludicrous as drawn by Jack Kamen, seemingly incapable of illustrating a plain woman.~WJ
Recommended: 1, 3, 5
Collection: Impact (1–5)

The IMPOSSIBLE MAN Summer Vacation Special
Marvel: *2 issues 1990–1991*

The Impossible Man is a fun-loving, pointy-headed green and purple alien able to transform himself into a green and purple version of anything or one. As a piece of whimsy in the early *Fantastic Four* he was bearable. As a surprise revival fifteen years on he was a few laughs. Ever since he's been a tedious excuse for feeble humour and lame parody. These two specials are a repository for visual puns as he plagues assorted Marvel superheroes.~FP

IMPULSE
DC: *20 issues +, 1 Annual to date*

Written by Mark Waid, drawn primarily by Humberto Ramos, this story of a hyperkinetic, inattentive teenager with zero attention-span and superspeed is mostly a roaring comedy. Bart Allen, grandson of the famous Barry (aka Flash), is the poster child for the judgement-impaired. He was born with a disastrous metabolic condition that caused him to age super-fast; his grandmother sent him back from the 30th century to the 20th, where he could learn to control his metabolism, and his other speed powers, before they killed him. Trouble is, because Bart was brought up in a virtual reality world the conventional one is slow-motion to him, and he hasn't yet caught on that real-life dangers don't have a 'reset' button that gives you another turn! Now, living in the southern town of Manchester, Alabama with Max Mercury, the 'Zen master of speed', he's being forced to approximate a normal life and fit in with other people. The edgy Impulse (Bart's code name) and the phlegmatic Max Mercury work against each other in... well, the closest parallel to the relationship is that of *Calvin and Hobbes*! Skilfully, however, Waid avoids total comedy, and interjects moments of horror and pathos, contrasting admirably with the strip's lighter tone. Particularly notable in a fine run are 6, a shocking but non-clichéd look at child abuse, and 16, where ghosts of Max's past are brought to light. By contrast, the Zatanna guest appearance in 17 is full-throttle comedy, but a classic issue. Ramos' kinetic, bigfoot artwork, a sort of more frenzied Mike McMahon, is the perfect vehicle for these stories, and the occasional fill-in, most notably Nick Gnazzo in 7, keeps up the high artistic standard. 8 is an *Underworld Unleashed* crossover that can nevertheless be read and enjoyed separately. Issues 9–11 team Bart with his future cousin Jenni (XS of the Legion of Super-Heroes) in a multi-part crossover with the *Flash*'s 'Dead Heat' story, and the annual is an odd future version of Impulse easily missed.~HS
Recommended: 1–13, 16, 17, 19
Collection: Reckless Youth (1–6)

IN THE DAYS OF THE MOB
DC: *1 issue 1971*

In a companion magazine to *Spirit World*, Jack Kirby adapts violent tales of America's gangsters during the 1930s in his usual

unsubtle style. Is there no end to the man's versatility? Ma Barker and Al Capone are among those to receive the full Kirby treatment, and even Vince Colletta's inks suited this wonderful period piece. The true crime, of course, was that this only lasted one issue. An advert for the unseen second issue promised 'The colorful, beautiful, pragmatic, inscrutable Ladies of the Gang!' We were robbed! Robbed!~HY
Recommended: 1

IN THIN AIR
Tome: *One-shot 1991*

Famed female pilot Amelia Earhart disappeared in mid-flight somewhere over the Pacific Ocean in 1937. No-one knows for certain what happened, although there have been several postulations. For rather more improbable versions in comics see *Dino Island* and *Lost Planet*. Basic art and a basic run-through of Earhart's career accompany a transcript of her final radio transmissions. Tome Press issued two versions of the comic, each offering a different solution to her disappearance.~FP

THE INCAL
Epic/Titan: *3 volumes 1988*

Subtitled 'The Adventures of John DiFool', the Incal series of graphic novels, with visionary scripts by film-maker Jodorowsky and art by Moebius, are among the most perplexing but haunting comics to come out of Europe. Jodorowsky's scripts have the discipline that many Moebius stories lack, without losing the psychedelic qualities of most of his best writing. John DiFool is an 'R' Class Investigator who thinks he won't amount to much. Possessed by the Incal, a kind of cosmic force which occasionally helps him out of difficulties, he sets out on a quest across a strange world ruled by dilettantes, by the end of which he will have been accidentally caught up in a rebellion led by a dog-headed man, met the androgynous son he never knew he had, and attained something akin to a state of grace. His purpose, indeed his life's purpose although he doesn't know it, is to unite his Incal with its dark counterpart, held by Anime, the rat Princess who lives under a lake of acid in a world of garbage. See, it's visionary and complicated. Unfortunately it's also unfinished. The good news is you can enjoy it without the aid of illicit substances. Moebius' art is clean, wonderfully open, with occasional points of detail contrasting with the narrow-lined landscapes. He creates a series of amazing settings to flesh out Jodorowsky's elaborate fantasy. Inspired stuff.~FJ
Recommended: 13

INCREDIBLE SCIENCE FICTION
EC: *4 issues (3033) 19551956*

After the establishment of The Comics Code, EC were forced to change the title of *Weird Science Fantasy*, and *Incredible Science Fiction* was the result. Title changes aside, the comic featured the same intelligent Al Feldstein writing and high-quality artwork from Wally Wood, Joe Orlando and Bernie Krigstein as its previous incarnation, though perhaps without the same level of inspiration. New boy Jack Davis added some welcome vigour with his energetic covers and strips (30, 31, and 33), but the comic's highpoint was undoubtedly Al Williamson and Roy Krenkel's beautiful 'Food For Thought' in 32. It's worth the price of admission for the stunning splash page alone.~DAR
Recommended: 32

The Further Adventures Of INDIANA JONES
Marvel: *34 issues, 1983–1986, Raiders of the Lost Ark, 3-issue miniseries, 1981, Indiana Jones and the Temple of Doom, 3-issue miniseries 1984, Indiana Jones and the Last Crusade, 4-issue miniseries 1989*

Back in the days before Dark Horse had a monopoly of film franchises, it used to be Marvel's job to take movie heroes beyond their cinema incarnations. With Spielberg and Lucas's 1930s archaeologist/adventurer Indiana Jones, they managed to cover all three films and thirty-four issues of *Further Adventures* with original stories. The creative teams on the latter included John Byrne and Terry Austin on the first two issues, as well as Chaykin, Simonson and Ditko (so heavily inked he's hardly recognisable) on later ones. David Micheline and Herb Trimpe were the most regular creative team, however, and, as you might expect, the majority of issues were nothing special, aspiring to the high-adventure feel of the movies but always falling quite a way short.~JC

INDIANA JONES
Dark Horse: *4-issue miniseries ('Indiana Jones and the Fate of Atlantis') 1991, 6-issue miniseries ('Thunder In The Orient') 1993–1994, 4-issue miniseries ('The Arms Of Gold') 1994, 2-issue microseries ('The Golden Fleece') 1994, One-shot ('The Shrine Of The Sea Devil') 1994, 4-issue miniseries ('The Iron Phoenix') 1994–1995, 4-issue miniseries ('The Spear of Destiny') 1995, 4-issue miniseries ('The Sargasso Pirates') 1995–1996*

Dark Horse's efforts at presenting original Indiana Jones material are slightly better than Marvel's. Presented as self-contained series, some are adapted from the *Indiana Jones* books, some from role-playing games, others are original. The short miniseries approach seems to suit the subject-matter better, allowing a feel of the films to creep back into the narrative, but even so it's unlikely the comics will appeal much to anyone but the most ardent Indiana Jones fan. Do yourself a favour and hire out the videos instead.~JC

INDUSTRIAL GOTHIC
Vertigo: *5-issue limited series 1995–1996*

In a mystery city in a strange and broken-down world, the ugly and imperfect are imprisoned in a huge house. Pencil has been there throughout the thirty-five years of his life, the child of unacceptable parents. Nickel, his lover, who has no arms or legs, once passed for normal with artificial limbs. The two escape from their prison only to find that getting out is much easier than living with freedom. In search of a semi-mythical tower where rebels are welcomed, they meet all sorts of characters on the road, including violent rednecks and a gang of marauding women, as their relationship is reshaped by their new life. *Industrial Gothic* is one of McKeever's most straightforward stories, a comic road movie in which the various events are secondary to the development of the two lead characters, providing action and moving the story along. What makes the story especially good is the complete lack of moralising or explanation. McKeever's art is dense and textural, deep and dull colours overlaying each other. A feast: action-packed, weighty without being pretentious, endlessly intriguing.~FJ
Recommended: 1–5

INFERIOR FIVE
DC: *10 issues 1967–1968, 2 issues (11–12) 1972*

Inferior in name, but certainly not in content, DC's humorous superhero group débuted in *Showcase* 62, 63 and 65. The five seemed to parody the 1960s *Teen Titans*, sidekicks to DC's longer-serving heroes. The membership comprised Merryman, the brains of the gang, though a bit of a wimp; White Feather, a cowardly archer who always missed (unless it was a coincidence); Dumb Bunny, whose image was based on the Playboy bunny, the ultimate bimbo with no brains but plenty of brawn (and, ahem... breasts); The Blimp, an overweight character who could float slowly; and Awkwardman, a clumsy oaf with superstrength and aquatic powers. The characters, with their little quirks, were expertly handled by scripter E. Nelson Bridwell who wrote some first-class stories lampooning the likes of *The Justice League of America*, Tarzan, *Man From U.N.C.L.E.* and, naturally, various Marvel superheroes. While the humour waned near the end of the run, the earlier issues (and the *Showcase* stories, two of

which were reprinted in 11–12 when the title was briefly revived in 1972) should definitely amuse you. Unless of course you're a boring old fart.~HY
Recommended: 1–6

INFERNO
Caliber: *2 issues 1995*

Intriguing title written by Mike Carey with unusual, scratchy art by Michael Gaydos, who uses a lot of lines without making the pages look overwrought, although his figure work is sometimes stiff. A man is killed in a mugging and finds himself in a strange 'historic' land of the undead, where he's hailed as a familiar figure, attacked, hunted, aided. Except he knows nothing about what's going on, why he's there, even where he is. Carey builds character quickly, including a rich cast of sorcerers and immortals, and for a long time it's hard to work out who the good guys are. Fans of Neil Gaiman will probably enjoy taking a look at this.~FJ

INFINITY CRUSADE
Marvel: *6-issue miniseries 1993*

Third, and thankfully last, in the Starlin/Lim *Infinity* sagas, this differs from its predecessors in having an actual concept behind it. A tasteless and grotesque concept, to be sure, but at least they're trying. Adam Warlock's good side, inexplicably incarnated as a woman – The Goddess – recruits the more devout of Earth's heroes to enforce order and bliss upon the cosmos. And it's heathens to the rescue as the remainder go into that 'There is no freedom in Utopia' riff, resulting in many crossovers replete with two-fisted action and theological debate... not a serendipitous combination. Oh, and the Universe is destroyed and recreated. Again. Time was when heroes just had to fight to save individual lives, or their city, or very occasionally their country. Now, everybody has to be saving Everything There Is all the bleeding time, and this overkill numbs the reader. Still, at least this series is equal-opportunity offensive. Both devout and irreligious people will find something to heartily despise within its pages.~HS

INFINITY GAUNTLET
Marvel: *6-issue miniseries 1991*

This multi-crossover series was dubbed *Secret Wars III* at the time of its release by most critics, but Marvel clearly hoped that Jim Starlin's script and George Perez's art would give it some credibility. Nice try. Thanos acquires the Infinity Gauntlet, most powerful weapon in existence, and tries to impress his main squeeze, Mistress Death, by wiping out 50% of All That Is. Worlds live, worlds die, nothing will ever be the same again... you know, the usual. This calls for all Marvel's heroes to band together, in this title and in carefully signposted issues of their own titles, to overcome the menace. Perez's dexterity with cosmic flash and glitter almost fools you into thinking there's something to this, but when over-commitment (he was making a double turkey sandwich, working on this and *War Of The Gods* at the same time!) forces him off the comic, to be replaced by Ron Lim, the scales fall off our eyes and you realise what a load of tat it is.~HS

Collection: Infinity Gauntlet (1–6)

INFINITY INC

DC: *53 issues, 2 Annuals, 1 Special, 1983–1988*

Infinity Inc was another of Roy Thomas's love affairs with the 1940s superheroes. The first issue (drawn by Thomas's co-creators Jerry Ordway and Mike Machlan) saw a number of young heroes, most of whom were children of older members, attempting to join the Justice Society of America. When rejected, they decide to form a team of their own, and are joined by some of the younger JSAers. By 10, Ordway and Machlan's last, they've saved the world from the evil schemes of the Ultrahumantie and have proved their worth to their elders. Following a series of fill-in artists, Todd McFarlane takes over with issue 14, producing some of his earliest professional work between then and 37. Unfortunately, the stories during this period are not as tightly crafted as 1–10, introducing a series of dull villains, including Chroma and the genetic freaks called the Helix, who become the team's main enemies for the rest of the run. One of their members, Mr Bones, eventually joins the good guys. Tie-ins with *Crisis On Infinite Earths* dog the title during issues 19–24, following which many of the stories are (by necessity) taken up with retelling characters' origins in line with revised continuity – if you don't know what *Crisis* is, find out before attempting these issues, as they'll make very little sense if you don't. 27, which tells the first of several flashback stories to when many of the members knew each other as children, is good fun. Most of the new continuity problems have been worked through by issue 31, following which the group embark on an adventure with the Global Guardians, another set of ill-conceived and boring characters. After McFarlane's departure, there's little to recommend in the final issues. Vince Argondezzi takes over the art from 41, in one of the series' most character-driven plots as the team search for missing member the Silver Scarab. The later issues, however, remain largely unremarkable. 45 guest-stars the Teen Titans in a crossover continuing from *Teen Titans* 38, while the final four issues of the series are drawn by Michael Bair.~JC

INFINITY WAR

Marvel: *6-issue miniseries 1992*

Thanos is now on the side of the good guys following *Infinity Gauntlet*, and thus is one of the first to warn the assembled Marvel superheroes of the plan by the Magus (the evil side of Warlock) to replace them all with evil duplicates. One of the most tired and cynical efforts seen even in the money-grubbing crossover stakes. An ideal marketing opportunity for everyone to fight their evil counterpart in their own titles – sometimes for several issues, during which very little else happens. Yawn.~HS

THE INHUMANS

Marvel: *12 issues 1975–1977, one-shot 1990, Graphic Novel 1991, one-shot 1995*

Always popular guest stars, the hidden race of genetically altered beings are perennially dismal when given solo outings, despite art by Neal Adams in their *Amazing Adventures* series and George Perez and Gil Kane in their first comic. The problem is that the plot is always the same. Ruler Black Bolt is possessed of a voice able to shatter mountains, and must therefore remain mute, but his half-brother Maximus has designs on Black Bolt's throne, and you can bet your copies of *Fantastic Four* 44–48 (in which the Inhumans débuted) that he's behind any devilry. Would you trust someone known to his face as Maximus The Mad? The Inhumans do time and again, and always pay. Ironically their origin is divulged in another title familiar with repetition of plot, *Thor* 146–152. By the graphic novel the Inhumans have moved from the Himalayas to the moon, but who's that stirring things? Aw, you've guessed. For a change of pace the 1990 one-shot has Maximus attempting to take over the throne, but the twist is that it's an untold tale from the past! Brilliant! He's not around for the 1995 one-shot, but it's so bad you wish he were.~FP

INSANE

Dark Horse: *2 issues 1988*

With the title tipping the hat to *Mad*, *Insane* lives up to the parody tradition. The first issue is best, with Hilary Barta's Grimjack pastiche packed with inspired lunacy, and the Godzilla story good as well. Sadly, it's the poor *X-Men* story that's cover-featured. 2 is only slightly worse, with Lone Wolf and Cub and Concrete as targets.~WJ

INSECT FEAR

Print Mint: *3 issues 1970–1972*

One of a number of underground horror comics, *Insect Fear* was an uneven collection of strips, and is best remembered for its inspired name. The first two issues contained work by Justin Green, Kim Deitch, Rory Hayes and Jim

Osbourne, but at this early date they were far from their best. By 3 Deitch in particular was experienced enough to come up with the inspired 'Born Again', in which a criminal is reincarnated as a potato, and 3 has an unusually focused and powerful S. Clay Wilson strip as well as some very gory material from Roger Brand and Charles Dallas. The comic's most consistent artist was Spain Rodriguez, whose strip in 3 was beautifully drawn, as were all his covers.~DAR
Recommended: 3

INSTANT PIANO
Dark Horse: *4 issues 1994–1995*

An excellent humour anthology featuring the work of Mark Badger, Kyle Baker, Robbie Busch, Stephen DeStefano and Evan Dorkin. There are few people able to match the observational dissections of Baker or Dorkin's manic intensity, and *Instant Piano* has the best of both: Baker with chapters of a work in progress, and Dorkin with a very funny selection of three-panel throwaways and knowing satires about the obsessions of collectors. Mark Badger's strip about relationships loses out to Baker's hilarious and more concise musings on the same topic, but he's far better with other material, and Robbie Busch seems out of place, the little brother you've got to take with you. Stephen DeStefano is an enigma, with a fine adaptable art style that varies from Don Martin to 1930s cartoon strips: on top form he's every bit as good as Baker and Dorkin. Better with Sunday-lunch-table recollections than with Marx Brothers-style lunacy, he's the quiet heart of the book reflecting the rest. Also great is each cartoonist's page of things that make life worth living.~FP
Recommended: 1–4

INTERVIEW WITH THE VAMPIRE
Innovation: *11 issues 1991–1994*

Undoubtedly the best thing about this title is the eerie John Bolton covers on the first two issues, which capture the urbanity and allure of Anne Rice's famous vampire, Lestat. A young reporter sits down to interview Louis, a man claiming to be a vampire, who obligingly tells the tale of how he was 'created' by the mysterious Lestat in early 19th-century Louisiana. Although widely lauded, Rice's homo-erotic ramble, shot through with moments of extreme violence, is nothing new, and this adaptation lacks even the unintentional humour of the lead characters' incessant bickering.~FJ

INTERFACE
Epic: *8 issues 1989–1991*

This continues the tale of the characters introduced in Eclipse's *Espers* series. Like *Espers*, James Hundall provides a well-plotted thriller concentrating on people not powers, but unlike *Espers* it's bogged down by detail. The necessary précis of its precursor occupies much of the first issue, but the cast, so well introduced originally, is thereafter largely reduced to bit players as all sorts of secondary characters are focused on at their expense until the fourth issue. Also detracting from the premise is the revelation of many others with superhuman abilities. This isn't a bad series, but disappoints in comparison with what had gone before. Issues 1–6, well painted by Paul Johnson, form a self-contained story, and are far better than 7's shoddy story-telling from Bill Koeb and 8's early Dan Brereton. The characters reappear in 1996, once again titled *Espers*.~FP

INVADERS
Marvel: *41 issues, 1 Annual, 1 Giant-Size 1975–1979, 4-issue miniseries 1993*

This was Roy Thomas' wonderful project to revive Marvel's big three 1940s superheroes, Captain America the supersoldier, the original Human Torch Jim Hammond (in fact an android) and Namor the Sub-Mariner, along with their kid sidekicks. The tales were of their adventures during World War Two, but written and drawn in 1970s style. Thomas set himself the task of rationalising some of the uncoordinated events of the 1940s comics, and reintroducing, and partially revamping, some obscure old characters and inventing a few new ones in the old mould.

The regular artist was the extremely underrated Frank Robbins, a former Depression-era child prodigy muralist, highly successful newspaper strip artist (on *Scorchy Smith* and *Johnny Hazard*), and writer/sometime artist for DC in the late 1960s. He was still producing superb work for several Marvel titles late in his career, but *The Invaders* seems to have been his favourite. He clearly loved to draw the tanks, planes, submarines and other hardware of the period in accurate high-contrast detail, but never stinted with his extraordinarily dynamic and expressive figures and faces.

The only giant-size issue contains excellent recaps of the major characters' origins and a good story about a Nazi plot against Winston Churchill, but 1–4 were disappointing, concentrating on boring fights with Teutonic deities. Things picked up with 5–6, crossing over with *Marvel Premiere* 29–30, which débuted The Liberty Legion, a septet of more obscure 1940s supercharacters. 6 is essential for Robbins' definitive portrayal of the maniacal Nazi villain The Red Skull. 7–9 introduced the team to an English aristocratic family, one of whom was a World War I superhero, another the vampire Baron Blood. The intense drama of these issues, largely set in darkness, was not matched again. Thomas moved the action to the Warsaw Ghetto, where The Invaders teamed with a traditional Golem (Robbins excelling himself in 12–13), then too soon unveiled another superteam, The Crusaders. 16–22 raised the standard again with a wild story, set in Germany, featuring captures, escapes, recaptures, Hitler, two hilarious post-modern Nazi supersoldiers, and the near-execution of The Invaders in Berlin. 26–28 are outstanding: Captain America's young pal Bucky Barnes stumbles upon the scandal of US concentration camps interning Japanese Americans. Of course, he founds a new multiracial teen superhero group, The Kid Commandos.

The splendid 1977 annual featured the regular creative team alongside new work from artists who had drawn the characters in the 1940s. Alex Schomburg's Human Torch episode is particularly thrilling. Thomas neatly and entertainingly tied up some inconsistencies between *The Invaders* and *Avengers* 71, where he'd had them guest-star eight years before. *What If?* 4, from the same year, drawn throughout by Robbins, does a similarly great job of clarifying the characters' actions immediately after the war. Giant-Size 1, 10, 20 (the 1939 origin of the Sub-Mariner), 21 and 24 are, incidentally, cheap ways to acquire otherwise prohibitively expensive important 1940s stories. The last dozen regular issues, after Robbins left, were unfit to go under the same name as the others. Don Glut scripted with no sign of interest, although Thomas managed a risible two-parter (32–33) in which The Invaders fought Thor, who conveniently believed everything Hitler told him. The artists need not be named.

In the 1993 miniseries The Invaders returned to New York and battled American Nazi villains. Thomas's lively story unearthed a few old characters that might have been better left alone, rather than drawn in bizarrely revealing costumes by Dave Hoover. Slick inking by Brian Garvey saved it.~GK
Recommended: Giant-Size 1, 5–9, 16–22, 26–28, Annual 1

INVADERS FROM HOME
Piranha: *6-issue miniseries 1990*

Bobby Boomer is approaching a mid-life crisis when his wife tells him she's pregnant. Bobby's inability to come to terms with his new role constitutes most of the plot, which is really an excuse to ask all sorts of stupid questions and get back all sorts of stupid answers. Populated by talking ducks, aliens and bickering household appliances, it's a very witty look at life. Written and illustrated by John Blair Moore, this is Piranha's best and most accessible series.~NF
Recommended: 16

INVASION!
DC: *3-issue miniseries 1988*

One of DC's less remembered company-wide crossover series, but certainly one of the more entertaining. Earth is invaded by various alien races under the control of The Dominators, who want to know why Earth is home to so many superpowered beings. They discover it's due to the meta-gene, which, when subjected to a great deal of stress, mutates the human body, bestowing a special ability. Before you try anything at home, you should know it doesn't work with everyone! The Dominators then decide to live up to their name and enslave Earth by sending in the assorted aliens. Naturally enough, the entire pantheon of DC heroes turns out to stop them. It would have been all too easy for this to become a confusing farce, but scripters Bill Mantlo (in a rare outing at DC) and Keith Giffen, one of the most inventive creators working in comics, turn out a well-paced adventure in three eighty-page issues. Giffen also provides the art breakdowns, but other fan favourite artists who worked on the series include Todd McFarlane, Bart Sears and P. Craig Russell. A marvellously exciting slugfest.~HY
Recommended: 1–3

THE INVISIBLES
DC: *25 issues 1994–1996*

Writer Grant Morrison's avowed intent with this comic is to cram in all the major concerns of his generation, as he sees them, as we approach the Millennium. Its heroes are one 'cell' of The Invisibles, a loose-knit, world-wide group of anarchists, which may make them sound more like villains by the usual standards. However, the villains of the piece are really the forces of law and order; any element in society which seeks to control the masses or deny the potential of individuals. This all sounds very 1960s, and the comic's title and its very logo design are meant to refer back to 1960s TV shows like *The Avengers*, *The Fugitive* and *The Invaders*. It actually reeks more strongly of the 1970s, when real-life 'revolutionaries' like the Baader-Meinhof gang, and Michael Moorcock's fictional assassin Jerry Cornelius, became heroes to many youngsters of Morrison's generation.

The story arc in 1–4, 'Dead Beatles', introduces key characters and themes, including the ghost of John Lennon. Rebellious Liverpool schoolboy Dane McGowan is sent to a correctional facility which is run by one of the Archons, Lovecraftian demonic beings from another dimension. With their various earthly agents, the Archons are the series' major-league bad guys. Dane is rescued by King Mob (alias Gideon Stargrave), head of a British Invisibles cell. Dane is then introduced to the many mystical levels of reality within the city of London, and to the other members of the cell: Lord Fanny, a transsexual mystic from Brazil, Boy (a streetwise young woman from New York) and Ragged Robin, who is made up like a clown and claims to be insane. Hints are dropped about Dane's latent mystic powers, and he is invited to join the Invisibles. In the second, very complex story arc, 'Arcadia', the Invisibles do some time-travelling, Byron and Shelley debate the meaning of freedom, and the Marquis de Sade is observed pushing the boundaries of sexual liberty... among other things. 'Arcadia' is by no means an easy read, but 9–12 are simpler single-issue stories. 10 introduces voodoo-Invisible Jim Crow, and 12's 'Best Man Fall' gives an unusually detailed look back over the life of a minor character, an ordinary soldier who is killed by KIng Mob when rescuing Dane in 1. 13–15 is the origin of Lord Fanny, merging past, present and future in the tale of his/her personal and magical transformation. 16 shows Dane on the run both from the Invisibles and from their enemies, and learning more about his powers. This story-line continues in 21, in which the missing member of the Invisibles cell, Mr Six, re-appears and Dane finally decides to join the group. In 16–19's excellent 'Entropy In The UK', KIng Mob is tortured by one of the Archons' earthly followers, the evil Sir Miles, and mentally retreats into a medley of memory and fantasy in an attempt to resist his mind-probes. Gideon Stargrave's original incarnation in the late 1970s, as young Grant Morrison's Jerry Cornelius clone in Scottish science-fiction comic *Near Myths*, is acknowledged and developed in this story. 20 is the story of how Boy became an Invisible, and 22–24 has Dane and Jim Crow playing key roles in saving the whole team from a direct attack by the Archons. 25 wraps up series one with a tale of Mr Six, who appears as a Jason King/1970s TV cop parody. The 'next issue' trailer in 24 promises that Mr Six will 'explain everything'. Of course, he doesn't; this is another important 1960s reference, to the last episode of *The Prisoner* TV programme, similarly trailed and similarly mysterious.

What mainly brings the comic into the 1990s is its emphasis on alien forces lurking behind the scenes. Whitley Strieber-style space people crop up all the time. Their precise role is unclear as yet, but they appear to oppose the Archons. Morrison's core ideas about personal freedom vs social control can be difficult to fathom in his complex and unconventional story structures, and are further obscured by layers of black magic, drugs, mysticism and The Truth Is Out There twaddle. Still, it's definitely worth a bit of effort following the story. Artwise, varying teams make for inconsistency, but no issue is less than competently drawn. Steve Yeowell on 1–4, Steve Parkhouse on 12, Chris Weston on 10 and the Phil Jimenez/John Stokes team on 17–19 get special praise.~GL
Recommended: 1–4, 10, 12, 17–19
Collection: Say You Want A Revolution (18)

IRON FIST
Marvel: *15 issues 1975–1977, 2-issue microseries 1996*

Martial artist Danny Rand acquires the mystical power of the Iron Fist in the remote Himalayan monastery of K'un Lun. The first series is a classic Claremont/Byrne production: intelligent dialogue, thoughtful artwork, layers of sub-plot and lovely cameos of Marvel staffers and heroes in civilian ID. There is no failure to shirk controversial issues, as the sympathetic portrayal of reformed IRA terrorist Alan Cavenaugh enhances a fine supporting cast. Claremont's final three issues of the *Marvel Premiere* run (23–25), these fifteen issues and the resolution in *Marvel Team-Up* 63–64 all read seamlessly into a continuing narrative. 1–7 suffer from some slightly convoluted side-tracking, but 8 onwards are tops, with 14 featuring the introduction of Sabretooth and 15 a warm, homely X-Men guest appearance.

James Felder's second-series script harkens back to Iron Fist's *Marvel Premiere* tales as Danny Rand returns to K'un Lun. Unfortunately, Robert Brown's scratchy pencils fail to depict a single recognisable character from that era.~APS
Recommended: 8–15

IRON-JAW
Atlas Comics: *4 issues 1975*

Michael Fleisher's metal-mouthed barbarian hero made Conan seem like a New Man. Between threatening to kill children, *de rigueur* monster-slaying and the attempted rape of his sister, Ironjaw tries to claim his rightful kingdom from some Central Casting tyrants. Artist Pablo Marcos decorates said kingdom with numerous scantily clad lovelies ripe for ravishing. Pretty enough to look at, but some of the dialogue is so deliberately provocative it becomes funny. Most likely to say: 'I like a woman with spirit. For the wilder the filly, the better the ride.' Least likely to say: 'Can I have another piece of quiche?'~FJ

IRON MAN
Marvel: *Series one 332 issues, 15 Annuals, 1 Giant-Size 1968–1996, series two 2 issues + 1996 to date*

Mortally wounded in Vietnam, industrialist Tony Stark designs a metal chestplate capable of sustaining a weak heart. This becomes the basis for a gizmo-heavy armoured suit, with the resulting crimefighter, Iron Man, being officially explained away as Stark's bodyguard.

The first 110 issues are characterised by

almost incessant mediocrity. 1–50 have constant coronary scares, secret-identity crises and pedestrian art throughout. You'd have to be mad to want any of them except, perhaps, Barry Windsor-Smith's re-telling of Iron Man's origin in 47 (there's also some great Smith art on a dull story in 232). 50–110 are little better, but do have the odd bright spot. Jim Starlin is obviously making an effort in 55, introducing Thanos, and Steve Gerber's 57–58 are acceptable, but his strange Annual 3, with a young girl controlling the Molecule Man's all-powerful transmutation wand, is unusual and worth a glance. The much-interrupted supervillains war in 73–81 has its moments, but a terrible ending, and the spark Bill Mantlo's scripts from 103 possess is mercilessly extinguished by poor artwork. No sooner has the art improved than Mantlo departs.

116 sees writers David Michelinie and Bob Layton (who also inks) join the previous issue's new penciller John Romita Jr. Michelinie and Layton actually convince you that Tony Stark is an internationally renowned industrial genius, playboy and inventor, and that Iron Man really is a technology-based superhero, while Romita Jr and Layton's artwork gives Iron Man a polish hitherto unseen. There's an immediate quantum leap in quality, although the really good issues only begin with the first indications that Stark has an alcohol problem. 123–128 resolve that problem amid well-conceived supervillainy, corporate shiftiness and a well-rounded supporting cast. 131–132 have an excellent Hulk story, industrial espionage rears its head in 137–141, and there's an off-beat battle with Dr Doom in 149–150 (reprised a hundred issues later). Micheline and Layton conclude their plots by 154, and they're gone by 158, at which point Iron Man once again becomes very ordinary, with an interminable story from Denny O'Neil, Luke McDonnell and Steve Mitchell. Stark loses his business to Obidiah Stane, slips back into the bottle, and long-time confidant James Rhodes takes over as Iron Man. 182 sees Stark conquer the bottle, followed by another tedious plot as Rhodes goes nuts. Everything concludes in 200 with Stark in charge of a new company and new armour.

215 has Michelinie and Layton back, in the company of penciller Mark Bright, who'd made some of the later O'Neil issues tolerable. Could they turn Iron Man around again? They land Tony Stark with a preposterous pimp's hairstyle in 223, but in the same issue he discovers that many of Marvel's armoured characters are using technology stolen from him, and vows to destroy them all. The Armour Wars story to

231 is a 100% return to form, and all issues to 250 are good superhero comics. A failed assassination leaves Stark paraplegic from 243, and although 248's speedy resolution is cheating (as was the quick conclusion to the initial bout with alcohol), better that than interminably repeated scenes of self-pity. 251–257 are largely fill-ins to be avoided (although 253 is acceptable), but welcome back John Romita Jr as penciller with 256 just in time for Armour Wars 2 in 258–266. The title is a misnomer, this having nothing to do with its predecessor, or any other armoured being, John Byrne writing a story about control of Tony Stark. There's a good mystery behind the plot, but it's stretched far too thin, as is the succeeding story with old foe the Mandarin, drawn by Paul Ryan and Bob Wiacek to 275, the result being uncharacteristically dull comics for titles with John Byrne's name on them.

Len Kaminski and Kev Hopgood are in charge from 280, and their run presents some interesting ideas swamped by dull execution. There's the introduction of War Machine in 282, the death and resurrection of Tony Stark, Iron Man becoming nothing more than a remote-controlled shell, and the use of computer capabilities as a recurring feature. Their best is Hopgood's last 'Crash And Burn', a corporate disaster for Stark in 301–306, with plenty of guest stars. Tom Morgan pencils until the end of Kaminski's run with 318, concluding a sometimes touching (and ultimately silly) story about Tony Stark's mentor.

Terry Kavanagh stands as the writer who managed what countless foes hadn't: to kill Tony Stark and Iron Man. From 321 to 325 Iron Man, Force Works and the Avengers tell chapters of the same story. It's a stupid one, relying on shock instead of plot. Tony Stark is revealed to have been under the control of Avengers enemy Kang for years, and actively working to destroy the team. Although he redeems himself in the end, the Avengers win by pulling a young Tony Stark from an alternate time-stream to save the day, and the star of 325 issues of his own title dies. A one-shot titled The Age of Innocence re-caps the original's career and foreshadows what's to come as the younger Stark is set up as star of Iron Man with a virtually clean slate in 326. It all seems to have been prepared with the knowledge that the new series would set things right by starting at the beginning once again. And it does, showing more spark and imagination than the title's seen in years. The first issues have Stark a more convincing egotistical playboy than ever seen before, and intertwine the Hulk's origin with that of Iron Man. The Iron Man graphic novel 'Crash', has computer-generated art and is so dull the script was probably also computer-generated.~FP

Recommended: 123–128, 131–133, 137-141, 149–153, 223–231, 235, 236, 239, 240, 246, Annual 3, 9, series two 1

Collections: The Power of Iron Man (120–128), *Armour Wars* (225–232), *The Many Armours of Iron Man* (47, 122, 142–144, 152, 153, 200, 218), *Iron Man vs Dr Doom* (149–150, 249–250)

IRON MAN AND SUB-MARINER
Marvel: *1 issue 1968*

For some reason, instead of promoting the title characters directly from *Tales of Suspense* and *Tales To Astonish* respectively into their own titles, Marvel issued this combination title. They'd seen sense two months later. Dull content for completists only.~DWC

IRONWOLF
DC: *One-shot 1986, Graphic Novel 1992*

The one-shot reprints Howard Chaykin's classic 1973 Ironwolf story from *Weird Worlds*. Combining elements of fantasy, science fiction and good old rebel-rousing, Ironwulf causes much destruction to the ruling empire and is a great nuisance to its Empress. It's one of Chaykin's earliest published stories, and remains among his best, with a great sense of adventure, great characters and a lovely raw appeal to his artwork. Almost twenty years after the original story there's a graphic novel follow up titled 'Fires Of The Revolution'. This time Chaykin is joined by co-writer John Francis Moore, and the novel is drawn by the art team of Mike Mignola and P. Craig Russell. It's a worthy successor. Ironwolf survives seeming death, but lies comatose for eight years. Now awakened, he's once again pitted against the evil Empress and her Blood Legion. Victory, deceit and political manoeuvring are all part of this excellent story, while Mignola and Russell's imagery rivals that of the original series. Perhaps it lacks the cutting edge of the original – it's always difficult to go back home again – but fans of the original series should be satisfied.~HY

Recommended: One-shot, Graphic Novel

IRONWOOD
Eros: *11 issues 1991–1995*

Writer/artist Bill Willingham, who'd already attracted attention for his sexy, sinuous superhero drawings on *The Elementals*, is one of the few creators who took his work for Eros seriously. His fantasy world is packed with the kind of interesting sexual encounters only possible with a cast of centaurs, magicians and four-armed Amazons in flying yachts. His wise-cracking,

cocky young hero gets himself in all sorts of trouble, including a mystical quest, in a story that has a structure, pacing and a genuinely engaging plot, rather than being an excuse for a load of bonking. *Ironwood* is probably the horniest 'straight' Eros book, equating sex with fun, rather than the rather lamentable violence found in the likes of *Ramba*.~FJ

Collection: Ironwood (1–5)

ISIS
DC: *8 issues 1976–1978*

Professor Andrea Thomas, with the aid of a magic parchment, transforms herself into the Egyptian goddess Isis, nemesis of evil. Based on a TV series, this is an entirely forgettable comic with cardboard scripts from Jack C. Harris and art to match from Ric Estrada and Mike Vosburg.~SW

IT AIN'T ME BABE
Last Gasp: *1 issue 1970*

Frustrated by the misogyny and sexism that permeated underground comix quite as much as it did the mainstream, a group of San Francisco-based women cartoonists formed a collective to publish their own comic. Taking its title from a feminist newspaper, which presumably appropriated it from the Dylan song, *It Ain't Me Babe* is an odd but interesting combination of trippy fantasies and slice-of-life comics, with contributions from Trina Robbins, Michele Brand, Meredith Kurtzman, Lisa Lyons and others. Two strips stand out from the crowd. Brand's 'Monday' is a tale of the workaday fantasies of a wage slave, and the jam strip 'Breaking Out' features comics icons Betty & Veronica, Little Lulu, Juliet Jones, Petunia Pig and Supergirl escaping the confines of their respective series and forming a consciousness-raising collective! The success of this one-shot led to the establishment of the Wimmen's Comix Collective and the still-published *Wimmen's Comix* anthology, and thereby kickstarted many women's careers in cartooning.~HS

ITCHY AND SCRATCHY
Bongo: *3-issue miniseries, 1 Special 1994*

Owing much to *Squeak The Mouse*, this ultra-violent version of *Tom and Jerry*, gleefully presented in snippets during *The Simpsons*, translates astoundingly well to comics. The first issue is an exceptional example, with the pacing, timing and gags brilliantly achieved on the printed page. Every bit as carnage-crammed as the cover claims, it's not for the squeamish. Succeeding issues fall short, but are worth a look.~WJ

Recommended: 1

ITCHY PLANET
Fantagraphics: *3 issues 1988–1989*

This series looks at political and social issues in comic strip form. 1 has a nuclear theme, issue 2 deals with politics, and 3 covers elections. Well-meaning but dry, with Joyce Farmer and Lyn Chyvely's story of their trials and tribulations in launching *Tits & Clits*, in 2, being the best entertainment to be had.~HS

IT'S DARK IN LONDON
Serpent's Tail/Mask Noir: *Graphic Novel 1996*

The Mask Noir series consists largely of young, radical thriller writers. Walter Moseley is their star turn. This anthology, which unites various of their authors, such as Stella Duffy and Graham Gordon, with cartoonists, is intended as a portrait of the city, generally seen from the underside. There are few identifiable thrillers or detective stories as such. Mostly it's meditations, and sometimes it's a load of wank.

Woodrow Phoenix' series of negative, four-panel pages with wordless views of more and less famous sites sets the tone. The story will appeal more to those recognising the iconography than those who've never been to London, though. Some of the stories happen to be set in London but don't need to be, like Neil Gaiman and Warren Pleece's haunting tale of a beautiful boy from a mysterious race, sold to a gangster with a predilection for beautiful youths. Others, like 'Frozen', by Chris Webster and Carl Flint, in which an artist's model takes revenge on the woman who's carved him out of his own piss, have a tokenistic view of the city in the first panel to justify their inclusion. Only Iain Sinclair and Alan Moore actually address the nature of London with any success, though both their pieces are oblique in approach. There's some good work in *It's Dark In London* but as a collection it lacks consistency and direction. There's too much cleverness on display and too many writers unfamiliar with the medium fumbling for effect.~FJ

IT'S SCIENCE with Dr Radium
Slave Labor: *7 issues, 2 Specials 1986–1992*

In the perfect world of tomorrow Dr Radium practises science (in the abstract), usually on his long-suffering assistant Roy. This is school educational films gone mad, as Dr Radium has to deal with the Elvi and a group of time-travellers from 1954 visiting the future. The first special is bit of a mish-mash, but the second, titled 'The Gizmos Of Boola-Boola', is hilarious. This is very funny material crying out to be adapted as cartoon shorts.~FP

Recommended: 1–3, 5–7, 'The Gizmos Of Boola Boola'

Collection: *Dr Radium's Big Book* (1–7)

JAB
Adhesive: *36 issues 1992–1995*
A comic whose response to the proliferation of gimmick covers from major companies is to shoot bullets of varying calibre through their entire print run is to be cherished. Sadly, the contents of this Texas anthology don't always live up to that idea. The most successful graduate is the introspective lunacy of Shannon Wheeler's Too Much Coffee Man, wearing a giant cup of Java on his head for those occasions when an instant full-caffeinated pick-me-up is required. Tom King's 'Teen Squad' also has a few laughs, and both King and Wheeler incorporate the bullet hole into their third-issue stories.~FP

Star Wars: JABBA THE HUTT
Dark Horse: *One-shot ('The Gaar Suppoon Hit') 1995, one-shot ('The Dynasty Trap') 1995, one-shot ('The Hunger of Princess Nampi') 1995, one-shot ('Betrayal') 1996*
All four issues are chronologically placed before Jabba's appearances in the *Star Wars* movies and they all have the same plot. Jabba is attacked by a rival gangster and escapes death. The character is very flat and bland, but the redeeming feature is humour. Some of the villains meet the most hilarious deaths ever seen in comics. One gangster eats his head henchman, who is unfortunately carrying a bomb. The results are very funny. The question must be asked whether the humour is intentional, as the stories are not humour-based but merely hint at it. Art Wetherell's art is sloppy and fails to save this cash-in.~SS

JACK of HEARTS
Marvel: *4-issue miniseries 1984*
Intriguing supporting character given his own miniseries, which turns him cosmic with a *deus ex machina* origin revealing him to be a human-alien hybrid. Bill Mantlo's story limps under fluctuating character motives but George Freeman's all-too-infrequently-seen artwork just manages to save the series.~APS

The JACKAROO
Eternity: *3 issues 1990*
A Jackaroo is the Australian equivalent of a cowboy, and in this case that's Jack Keegan, good bloke in a fight, and not the type to let some bludger make off with his $5000 winnings therefrom. The obvious comparison to Keegan is Crocodile Dundee, but as written by Will Eisner. It isn't written by Eisner, though, it's written and drawn, very nicely as it happens, by Gary Chaloner. A forgotten gem of an adventure series that deserves a far wider audience.~WJ

THE JAGUAR
!mpact: *14 issues, 1 Annual 1991–1992*
Completely dispensing with the ludicrous Archie character, !mpact retain only the name and vague background details for this teenage feral female. William Messner-Loebs and the initial art team of David Williams and José Marzan turn out a fine combination of college *angst* and superheroics, as Brazilian Maria deGuzman attempts to come to terms with not only university life in a new country but also her genetic inheritance of the Jaguar powers. The supporting cast is well conceived, particularly spoiled teenage prom queen Tracy Dickerson, sadly tempered in later issues. David Williams' pencils in 1–6 are extraordinarily confident for a newcomer (although deadline pressures seem to be affecting him towards the end of his run), and his should be a name to look out for. His successors were adequate, but fail in comparison. The improbabilities of plot convenience are the major flaws in an otherwise consistently entertaining series. It could have done without a covert lab beneath the college, for instance, unsubtle expository dialogue and thought balloons, and the occasionally woefully pedestrian diary entries as narrative. On the plus side, Loebs has a fine time prodding at political correctness and insulting comedians, among other more prosaic topics.~FP

Adventures Of The JAGUAR
Archie: *15 issues 1961–1963*
Following the moderate success of *The Adventures Of The Fly*, Archie launched this companion title, in which zoologist Ralph Hardy discovers a magic Jaguar belt in an ancient temple. It grants him the power of flight (via belt jets – pretty sophis, these ancient Incans), incredible strength and control over all

animals. It also, inexplicably, gives him a snazzy red jumpsuit and rips off his moustache (ouch!) whenever he uses it to sally forth and fight crime as The Jaguar. Art for most of the series was by John Rosenberger, benign but bland, and the writers remain anonymous, but were almost certainly moonlighting *Superman* staffers, as the similarities between the two series were marked. Sample 7, in which the Jag's three girlfriends – immortal goddess Cat Girl, 'sea Circe' Kree-Nal and secretary Jill Ross – join forces as the 'Jaguar Rescue Team' to fill in during his absence. Lightweight, silly fun.~HS

THE JAM Urban Adventure

Matrix: *1 issue 1987*
Comico: *1 Special 1988*
Slave Labor: *5 issues 1989–1991*
Dark Horse: *3 issues (6–8) 1993–1995*
Caliber: *5 issues + (9–13) 1995 to date*

This is almost sit-com, and the Matrix, Comico and Slave Labor issues are magnificent. Bernie Mirault is a one-man-band producing these stories of Gordon Kirby, an ordinary guy who likes to dress up in tracksuit and hood to roam the streets performing good deeds as The Jammer. He encounters bizarre situations, and a rabid and preposterous terrorist group, and serves as a test case for the Devil to ruin his cosy and contented domesticity: this isn't your everyday superhero title. The delightful whimsy begins to fade a little with the Dark Horse issues, in which Kirby is psychoanalysed, and non-Mirault material begins creeping in. At Caliber *The Jam* coasts into navel-gazing and becomes prone to meaningless padding and interludes; while it still contains good ideas, they're stretched very thin indeed. Worse still, issues are packed with wilfully self-indulgent and plain bad strips from other creators. Many guides list the existence of a second Matrix issue, which was never actually published, and portions of the Matrix comic were reprinted in the first Slave Labor issue.~WJ
Recommended: Matrix 1 Comico Special, 1–7

JAMES BOND

Acme/Eclipse: *2-issue microseries ('Permission To Die') 1989, one-shot ('Licence To Kill') 1989*
Dark Horse: *3-issue miniseries ('Serpent's Tooth') 1992, 2 issues ('A Silent Armageddon') 1993, 2 issues ('Shattered Helix') 1995, 3-issue miniseries ('The Quasimodo Gambit') 1995*

Mike Grell started off the James Bond revivals hoping to revert from the gimmick-ridden format of the later films back to the suave, rather sadistic mood of Ian Fleming's originals. Bond is dispatched to Hungary to smuggle out the daughter of a scientist who's developed a cheap method of space travel and is offering it to the West if she can be delivered to the US safely. There are some nice touches, and Grell

carefully limits the villains, who're flamboyant, but not ridiculously superheroic characters. Of course, nothing is what it seems, as Bond finds out when he delivers the girl. Grell also worked on a bog-standard movie adaptation of *Licensed To Kill*, written by Richard Ashford, and also featuring the art of Chuck Austen, Tom Yeates and Stan Woch.

Doug Moench's take on the quintessentially British superspy in 'Serpent's Tooth' relies much more on our familiarity with films, taking from them its pacing and its reliance on a pretty woman popping up with a vital piece of info whenever the plot starts to droop. Moench attempts some of the trademark one-liners, which, never exactly side-splitting on screen, fall even flatter on paper. A standard-issue mad villain (who's experimented on himself with some lizard genes and become a serpentine hybrid) plans to use stolen nuclear missiles to set off earthquakes that will destroy 83% of the Earth's population and allow him to remake the earth in his own image. Bond discovers his secret base, stocked with beautiful women and dinosaurs created from fossilised DNA. Gripping it isn't, and it's not helped by Paul Gulacy's stiff, badly painted artwork that looks like a relic from the 1970s. He'd have been much better off drawing a crimplene safari-suited Moore than a slick, narrow-trousered Connery. Poor show all round in 'Serpent's Tooth'.

John Burns restores some dignity, drawing Simon Jowett's scripts for 'A Silent Armageddon', and drags our hero kicking and screaming into the computer age with Cerberus, one of many evil organisations in the Bond universe, trying to infiltrate the new global computer network using a child prodigy, Terri, and a 'worm' (that's virus to you and me) accidentally 'discovered' by a junkie hacker, that can break through the security of any system. Bond is assigned to protect her, but soon discovers that the beautiful cyberneticist who's befriended Terri is actually an agent of Cerberus. If this all sounds rather specious, Jowett doesn't write like he knows what he's talking about in cyberspace, either. Jowett's Bond doesn't grate, but neither does he shine, and Burns' art is the real star of the show. For some reason only two parts of the advertised four were ever published.

This was also the case with 'Shattered Helix', although Dark Horse had more cautiously only promoted a three-issue run. Jowett's back, with David Jackson pencilling, offering another threat from Cerberus. For their own best reasons they attack a biosphere research project and kidnap one of the scientists, who had previously created an uncontrollable mutagen for the CIA. My biology's much less up to date than my hacking, so I haven't the foggiest how silly this plot is. It doesn't have many twists, though. Bond and a floosie race Cerberus to the CIA's old Antarctic hang-out, which Bond must destroy.

Finally there's Don McGregor's stab at Bond. His characters traditionally have plenty of flair, but here he saves most of it for the villains. Larger-than-life characters are right up his street and the deadly warrior Maximilian 'Quasimodo' Steele could have stepped straight out of an issue of *Sabre*. The plot, such as it is, is an excuse for a face-off between the two that has Bond tracking Quasimodo and other bizarre disciples of the 'Heavenly Way' through the Georgia swamps.~FJ
Collection: Serpent's Tooth (1–3)

JAR OF FOOLS
Black Eye: *2 volumes 1995*
Ernie Weiss is a destitute magician obsessed with his brother's suicide and mourning over a relationship break-up when he encounters a conman and his daughter. The conman wants Weiss to teach his daughter magic, and the trio are accompanied by Al Flosso, former master of the prestidigitatory arts, now nursing-home escapee. Esther, Ernie's former lover, is facing a dead-end working in a coffee bar. All have problems to face and resolve, and over 140 pages creator Jason Lutes skilfully weaves a compelling plot. The warmth and humanity of the cast shine through the pages, and Lutes' assured story-telling is all the more amazing for this being his début. The first part is also available as a self-published volume.~FP
Recommended: 1, 2

JASON GOES TO HELL - The Final Friday
Topps: *3-issue miniseries 1993*
A lack-lustre adaptation of the final *Friday The 13th* film with Jason jumping from body to body in an attempt to be reborn.~WJ

JAZZ AGE CHRONICLES
EF Graphics: *3 issues 1989*
Caliber: *5 issues 1990–1991*
Well-researched and engrossing stories set largely in Boston, 1926. The EF series is a very competent début for creator Ted Slampyak, a decent story about a vampire on the loose and a mysterious baroness. It introduces private eye Al Mifflin, uncouth and inventive as should be the case, and Harvard archaeologist Clifford Jennings, cultured, refined and deliberately conceived to play off Mifflin. Many elements of the first Caliber story (1–2) stem from the Boston police strike and rioting of 1919, most pertinently revealing Mifflin's former career, and it's the highlight of the series. While not original, Slampyak has the

private-eye routine down well, and if there's a few too many talking-head shots, those interested in detective stories will find the tale compelling enough to overlook them. The final story, 'The Flowers Of San Pedro', is the weakest *Jazz Age Chronicles* tale, very much in Indiana Jones territory, with a remote Arizona town falling prey to evil machinations, and two new female characters, one introduced as no more than the irritating bimbo whose part in the plot is to be captured.~FP
Recommended: Caliber 1–2
Collection: Jazz Age Chronicles (EF Graphics 1–3)

JEMM, SON OF SATURN
DC: *12-issue limited series 1984–1985*
This is basically DC's version of *E.T.* Jemm is a displaced prince of Saturn – obviously the rightful ruler since he was born with the pulsating jewel embedded in his forehead that allows him to see into people's souls. Luther Mannkin is an orphaned boy living in Harlem, whose elder brother is mixed up with some very nasty people. Jemm and Luther meet, and it's love at first sight. But there are baddies demanding their attention on Earth and on Saturn: gangster bosses with artificial eyes, and Saturnian warrior women with high-heeled boots and whips. In its favour, it's downbeat in unexpected areas, but it seems to go on forever, and the plot (writer, Greg Potter) and story-telling (artists, Gene Colan and Klaus Janson) are very confused. You'd need a heart as big as a house to care a jot about any of the participants, and the last two pages should carry a health warning.~FC

JEREMIAH
Adventure: *2-issue micro series ('Birds Of Prey') 1991, 2-issue microseries ('A Fistful Of Sand') 1991, 2-issue microseries ('The Heirs') 1991*
Catalan: *Graphic Novel ('Strike') 1990*
This black and white series contains just three of revered Belgian artist/writer Hermann's *Jeremiah* graphic novels, now numbering seventeen in European editions. Each album is split into two comics. Set in violent and lawless post-apocalyptic America, the series chronicles the adventures of two young drifters, Jeremiah, the young, trusting Everyman, and Kurdy, his worldly-wise partner, as they attempt to survive in a violent and lawless world. 'Birds Of Prey' tells how they meet after Jeremiah's farm compound is destroyed by outlaws.

Like *Judge Dredd*, *Jeremiah* works in many timely icons and fads such as bowling, commenting on current society as it goes. Many of the stories revolve around Western scenarios. 'Fistful Of Sand' finds our heroes lost in the desert, trapped between a bunch of thieves and a local militia band, both trying to find and steal a stash of gold. It could just as well be a *Blueberry* strip. The third graphic novel, 'The Heirs', concerns the now infirm but still tyrannical community ruler whose son is a drunken wastrel and whose daughter is scheming to inherit his position. Jeremiah's arrival changes everything.

The reprints are inferior to the colour graphic novel translations as the wider, European-size pages are shrunk considerably to fit the US comic format, and while Hermann's artwork is detailed, but loose and full of energy, the ochres and oranges of coloured versions add greatly to the spaghetti Western atmosphere. One further graphic novel, the thirteenth, has been published by Catalan. Combining the pleasures of bowling with recruitment for a shady religious cult, it works its way to a facetious, if unpredictable ending.~FJ

Recommended: Birds Of Prey 1–2
Collections: Talons Of Blood ('Birds Of Prey' 1–2), *Fistful Of Sand* (1–2)

JERRY LEWIS
DC: *84 issues (41–124) 1957–1971*

This was originally *Dean Martin and Jerry Lewis;* the alleged comedian inherited the title when the pair severed their professional relationship, so the 'début' issue of *Jerry* is 41. Mostly, these are innocuous, if irritating, slapstick routines, with little to commend them apart from the sterling work of DC's comedy stable of artists: Bob Oksner, Win Mortimer *et al.* Hard-core fanatics of one persuasion or another might want to pick up some later issues for one shaky reason or another. 92 has a Superman cameo, 97 a guest-shot by Batman, Robin and Joker, 101–104 are alleged to feature Neal Adams art, though because of the high stylisation in humour comics, picking out styles is tricky. 105 features a full Superman guest appearance, 112 co-stars the Flash, and 117 the non-superpowered version of Wonder Woman.~HS

JEZEBEL JADE
Comico: *3-issue miniseries 1988*

Spinning off from *Jonny Quest*, this miniseries spotlights Race Bannon and Hong Kong's best thief, Jezebel Jade, in a fast-moving thriller. The Quests' old foe Dr Zin has kidnapped an American scientist who's working on a formula to prolong life, and it's up to Jade and Bannon to rescue him. Strongly plotted by William Messner-Loebs, with plenty of action and surprises, the illustration by Adam Kubert is excellent. Don't be put off if you haven't read Comico's *Jonny Quest* (although you should): this is superior adventure material.~FP

Recommended: 1–3

JIGSAW
Harvey: *2 issues 1966*

Astronaut Gary Jason's body is reassembled by aliens after they have unwittingly injured him. He discovers his limbs now stretch just like Mr Fantastic's and Plastic Man's. A very silly comic.~SW

JIM
Fantagraphics: *4 issues 1987–1990, 6 issues + 1993 to date*

Jim Woodring's first magazine-sized series contains some of a character called Jim's Dreams and Daydreams, the introduction of the cat Big Red, whose gruesome feeding habits are explored, and Pulque (in 4), a frog-shaped vegetable that smells terrible. Woodring packs text stories and pages of novelty items in as well to make for a delightful comic. The dream stories are full of surreal images and *non sequiturs*, usually involving some sort of artistic endeavour but also as simple as getting drunk before going to the public baths and coming across a one-legged man. These strips remain rooted in an everyday world that proves to have hidden depths of suffering if you know where to look. Some of the greatest pieces in these issues, however, are the covers and single-page images, from the skeleton leaning against a gate-post to the horse's head with a cigarette between its teeth.

The second series continues in much the same vein with a mix of stories centring around the above characters but now, significantly, adding Woodring's best-known character, Frank, to the roster. The colour Frank stories are beautiful, wordless reflections on voyeurism, godhood and, as usual, suffering, especially in the plight of the Manhog, usually coming off the worse in his encounters with Frank or the other strange denizens of Jim's fantastic landscape. Woodring's tales of insecurity are simply told, often deceptively so, but whether you feel that there's any real meaning here or not, they're an extraordinary read.~NF

Recommended: Series one 1–4, series two 1–6

JIMBO
Zongo: *6 issues + 1996 to date*

Anyone who has seen Gary Panter's primitive cartooning in *Raw* will not find it easy to forget. In this series Panter brings back a number of familiar characters, most notably his dense, punk Everyman Jimbo, for a series of oblique adventures and encounters. Initial issues are structured as one-page strips, drawn in Panter's distinctive, child-like style. It is almost impossible to explain the quality of his work if you don't see it immediately; if you're put off by the wavering lines and crude panels, and think the dialogue pointless don't bother with this. However if you like it, *Jimbo*'s a feast,

giving Panter room to regularly experiment, producing extraordinary comics pages like the 'Bogstage' sequence in 5, where he uses a combination of scratchy line and minute hatching alongside crudely outlined negative image drawings in a circular panel framework, drawing deranged, multi-armed rock star monsters and picturing Godzilla, straddling the Empire State Building, strumming away. One of the great iconographers of our times having fun. Read it.~FJ
Recommended: 1–6

Superman's Pal JIMMY OLSEN
DC: *163 issues 1954–1974*

Introduced very soon after Superman (in *Action* 6), Jimmy Olsen is the red-haired cub reporter at the *Daily Planet*. Always striving to better himself or obtain that elusive scoop, he'll don any disguise no matter how preposterous, indulge in any ruse no matter how ridiculous, or undergo any transformation no matter how astounding. The structure of the strip is very basic, and almost any issue until 133 will feature the same rudimentary elements. Jimmy dates Lois Lane's younger sister Lucy (from 36), and due to his propensity for stumbling into unfortunate circumstances he's got a signal watch, which when activated attracts Superman to bail him out of trouble.

The early issues are generally light-hearted, but not as preposterous as what would come afterwards, with following news leads high on the agenda. From the mid 1950s, though, the title became ever more daft. The news angle was forgotten in favour of densely plotted gimmick stories, sometimes three eight-pagers to an issue. The writers, perhaps advisedly, remained anonymous, but the artists were those regularly used on other Superman titles, usually Curt Swan, with the occasional John Forte, Al Plastino or Kurt Schaffenberger strip. Popular transformations for Jimmy included a rampaging giant turtle man, the superhero Elastic Lad, a wolfman, a human octopus and a human porcupine. All of these and more can be found in 105. Elastic Lad was particularly popular, débuting in 31, and as that character Jimmy would regularly meet the 30th-century Legion Of Super-Heroes. Jimmy often went undercover, using myriad disguises, with a particular fondness for cross-dressing, and he's masqueraded as a hitman, an oil millionaire, a robot, a witch doctor and many more.

Quite honestly, any story selected at random gives an indication of the series as a whole, so here's 'The Menace of Insect Island' from 79, 1964. Jimmy and Lucy see a film about giant ants, and journey back to Metropolis in the *Daily Planet* helicopter. Jimmy is overcome by a 'strange mental compulsion' and heads out to sea to land on a remote island. There he and

Lucy are greeted by a strange race of... wait for it, ant people! He pricks his finger on the local thorny plants. So far, by the way, this is packed into eight panels. The ant people are an advanced civilisation transformed when a vengeful scientist infects their water supply with a potion. 'Incredible! I took a drink a while ago. Now I'm shrinking into an ant-like creature,' says one remarkably detached individual. 'Me too!' replies his equally sanguine chum. 'And I can detect your thoughts with these antennae which are growing out of my head!' Some red ants escape a war with black ants to land on Earth, but on noting that their side won the war they want to return. They require Superman's help to recharge their craft, and so have lured Jimmy to signal him. But Superman's away in space, and won't be back until the next day. And we're still only halfway through the story. The following morning Jimmy wakes to see white protoplasmic blobs edging their way towards the ant people, engulfing those they catch. Jimmy is given an anti-gravity ray, with which he propels himself to the top of a cliff, cutting his finger again as he lands. Shining the anti-gravity ray on the blood produces dozens of little Pillsbury dough-boy creatures that chase the white blobs into the ocean. At that point Jimmy realises he could have signalled Superman for help, and does so. Superman refuels the craft, the aliens return home and, back in Metropolis, Jimmy realises the white blobs and red dough-boys were actually enlarged corpuscles from his dripped blood! That's eight pages and a contracted synopsis from an issue that also includes the equally nutty 'Red-Headed Beatle of 1000 BC', as Jimmy, thrown back in time, earns a living selling Beatle wigs!

There's hundreds of Jimmy Olsen stories every bit as insanely enjoyable, and anyone with a sense of humour should sample at least one. The best way to do so is via the oversize reprint issues 95, 104, 113, 122, 131, 140, each chock-a-block with silliness. This light touch made the series the most enjoyable of the Superman titles on a regular basis (although individual issues topped it), but by the late 1960s these stories were beginning to lose their charm. A particular duffer is 'Planet of the Capes' in 117, which features a tale about... er... capes. Pete Constanza was the main artist by now, and his cartoony style combatted any seriousness, but 127's more serious 'The Secret Slumlord of Metropolis' drew more letters than any previous DC comic.

Readers of the series must have had a shock when 133 turned up. 'Kirby is here!' exclaimed the cover. Not half! Kirby introduces the new Newsboy Legion, children of the 1940s kids gang he co-created with Joe Simon, and their super-vehicle the Whiz Wagon. With Jimmy they become involved with a motor-bike gang and the mysterious Hairies (it's still hippie season in 1970), strange inhabitants of a place called the Wild Area. Kirby seemed ahead of his time in revealing that The Hairies are actually clones bred by a secret government organisation called The Project. The Golden Guardian, the Newsboys' mentor, makes a reappearance as a clone in 135, while current Superboy supporting character Dubbilex makes his first appearance in 136. Kirby firmly places the series within his *New Gods* saga, as Darkseid's minions are also tampering with DNA in a rival project aiming to develop a creature powerful enough to destroy Superman. 139 introduces Goody Rickles, a comic double of American comedian Don Rickles, in an amusing story stretching through 140's reprint to 141 and displaying the diversity of Kirby's writing. There's another change in 142–143 with a Count Dracula lookalike, but afterwards Kirby returned to the events surrounding the Project. Kirby certainly ended his run a high note in 147–148, as Jimmy and the Newsboys get involved with a megalomaniac Victor Volcanum who wants to rule the world. Of course Jimmy Olsen almost became a supporting character in his own title, but Kirby's great plots compensate. His artwork was stunning. Even the inking of Vince Colletta didn't do much damage, though the issues inked by Mike Royer (146–147) do stand out. 141–148 also offered 1940s reprints of the Newsboy Legion by Kirby and Simon. Could you ask for anything more?

After Kirby everything had to be downhill, and so it proved. His initial replacements were John Albano and José Delbo, providing mundane adventure stories, with the Newsboy Legion cast back into limbo, although 149–150 are worth picking up for the Jack Cole Plastic Man reprints. It was a return to the 1960s when writers Leo Dorfman and Cary Bates took over thereafter and tried to revive the past with those loveable stories, but it was actually the 1970s, and having Jimmy imagine he's Olsen the Red set in Viking times is a bit much to bear. Even Kurt Schaffenberger's lovely art was subdued by Vince Colletta. The series was transformed into *Superman Family* with 164, featuring stories also starring Lois Lane and Supergirl. It couldn't have come too soon.~WJ/HY
Recommended: 127, 133–148
Collected: see *Adventure*

Scott Russo's JIZZ
Fantagraphics: *10 issues 1991–1993*
The product of a seriously disturbed mind, this is part cut-and-paste fanzine and part comic, guaranteed to offend everyone somewhere along the way. Stories range from encounters with celebrities through self-loathing and racial diatribes to autobiographical vignettes.

Jizz won't be to everyone's taste, but there's plenty of funny content. The best starting point is 9, drawn more traditionally by Jeff Wong and detailing the events following a crank assassination letter sent to George Bush signed in Russo's name. Wong also illustrates decent (and disgusting) parodies of the work of Canadian cartoonists in 10.~WJ
Recommended: 9

Cops: THE JOB
Marvel: *4-issue miniseries 1992*
Admirably realistic attempt at recording the day-to-day life of two New York policemen. Larry Hama and former cop turned artist Joe Jusko handle the writing and there's good art from the team of Mike Harris and Jimmy Palmiotti. The breakneck pace of the comics conveys the fast life, where one wrong move can mean death, and dialogue and social interaction are deftly handled. An excellent package, from the Mike Golden covers to the experiences of real cops on the text page.~FP
Recommended: 1–4

JOHN CARTER OF MARS
Gold Key: *3 issues, 1952–1953*
Soldier John Carter is injured in battle on Earth, and finds himself walking away from his body, and then, paces later, realises he's on Mars. Yes, that's all there is to it. He's captured by warlike lizard creatures, escapes, is recaptured, rescues a human-like princess, etc, etc. Hopelessly confused and boring. Were people really that desperate for entertainment in 1952 that they'd sit through three issues of this? Read this and you'll never complain about TV again. These Jesse Marsh-drawn issues are reprinted by Gold Key in the 1960s.~FC

JOHN CARTER, Warlord of Mars
Marvel: *24 issues, 3 Annuals 1977–1979*
Unlike Edgar Rice Burroughs' more famous creation, Tarzan, John Carter has never been well known outside the field of fantasy. However Burroughs' early stories of a Virginian gentleman transported when near to death from an Indian-besieged cave to the violent and barbaric world of Barsoom (Mars) were immensely influential in the heroic-fantasy genre. Unlike Conan, John Carter represents the forceful necessities of civilisation, championing the Martian race, who looked most like him, against the numerous funny-shaped, multi-coloured barbarians at the gate and marrying its princess, Dejah Thoris, who promptly laid an egg to establish the Carter dynasty. The comic version is loosely based on the series of novels, many of which feature ludicrous plots, as Carter engages in much sword-swinging to defeat the devilish intentions of wizards,

mad scientists and marauding tribes. Marv Wolfman's initial scripts were no more than average, although he was allocated some talented guest pencillers on their off days (Gil Kane, Carmine Infantino and Walt Simonson, for instance). Sadly, few of them lasted long, even when Chris Claremont, a long-time fan of the stories, took over. Unsurprisingly, he made Dejah Thoris into a sword-toting adventurer alongside her husband, and played up the power of their relationship. Unless you particularly like sword-and-sorcery with a remarkably silly slant, *John Carter* is only of note because a young Frank Miller pencilled issue 18.~FJ

JOHN LAW Detective
Eclipse: *1 issue 1981*

In his attempts to work up a successful newspaper strip in the 1930s, Will Eisner created John Law, hard-boiled detective. The preparatory pages were produced, but no one picked up on the idea, and the stories were later reworked for the successful *Spirit*. Although there's some nice early Will Eisner artwork, this is nothing more than a curiosity for those wanting a complete collection of Eisner's work.~WJ

JOHNNY The Homicidal Maniac
Slave Labor: *6 issues + 1995 to date*

This is the archetype from stalk-and-slash movies taken to logical extremes without the requirement to conform to any parental guidance system. For the more acceptable pieces, gratuitous and explicit violence is served up as the answer to life's trivial annoyances. The less pleasant delve into sordid brutality that creator Jhonen Vasquez seeks to mitigate with blocks of ponderous self-analysis for his lead. It's deliberately unpleasant without any leavening humour, thus all in all very unsatisfactory. As your parents always told you, it's not big, it's not clever, and in this case it's not good either.~FP

JOHNNY DYNAMITE
Dark Horse: *4-issue miniseries*

The return of a 1950s detective strip, updated and spin-doctored by the *Ms Tree* creative team of Max Collins and Terry Beatty. This starts off as a straightforward hard-boiled sleuth tale, but takes a spin into the supernatural to great effect. Beatty's blocky, down-to-earth style makes the horrific events even more so by its matter-of-fact presentation. Involving Satanic deals and zombie gang-war, it can safely be said that you haven't read anything entirely like this before. Mitch O'Connell's hallucinogenic covers are the icing on the cake.~HS
Recommended: 1–4

JOHNNY NEMO
Eclipse: *3-issue miniseries 1985–1986*

Brutal hard-boiled detective in the future, as previously seen in *Strange Days*. Some nice lines, but otherwise slim fare. Nemo later resurfaced in *Deadline*.~WJ
Collection: *Johnny Nemo* (*Deadline* stories)

JOHNNY THUNDER
DC: *3 issues 1973*

This is one of the best of the reprint titles DC were issuing in the early 1970s. It featured the cream of the company's 1950s Western strips, with art by Alex Toth, Mort Drucker, Gil Kane and others at a fraction of the cost of the originals. With stories by Robert Kanigher as well you really can't lose with this comic.~DAR
Recommended: 1–3

THE JOKER
DC: *9 issues 1975–1976*

If character inconsistencies between the homicidal maniac seen in contemporary Batman comics and the merry prankster portrayed here aren't cause for concern this is a nice, if bizarre, series. Most issues guest-star other DC characters, with the best being the Creeper's appearance in 3.~FP

JONAH HEX
DC: *92 issues, 1 Spectacular 1977–1985*
Vertigo: *5-issue miniseries ('Two-Gun Mojo') 1993, 5-issue miniseries ('Riders Of The Worm And Such') 1995*

Although it's often credited to John Albano, it was Michael Fleisher who wrote the classic tagline: 'He was a hero to some, a villain to others, and wherever he rode people spoke his name in whispers. He had no friends, this Jonah Hex, but did have two companions. One was death itself, the other the acrid smell of gunsmoke...' It encapsulates 1870s bounty hunter Jonah Hex succinctly and accurately.

Fleisher starts the title by altering two constants from Hex's run in *Weird Western*, firstly introducing a thread of continuity while still producing largely single-issue stories. Hex is framed for murder by his old enemy Turnbull and becomes a fugitive, a plot that's very tired by its conclusion in 16 and is recycled to better effect in 44–45. He also introduces crooks who survive Hex's blazing pistols to return, El Papagayo (2) being the first. How Hex became hideously scarred is revealed in 7–8, and his start as a bounty hunter is told in 30. Fleisher continues to be gruesomely inventive throughout the early issues, never more so than in the one-shot *Jonah Hex Spectacular*. It details Hex's death and subsequent movements, and still brings a lump to the throat. The first forty-three issues are drawn by a variety of artists, with Luis Dominguez best at providing a gritty Western flavour, although the cleaner style of José Luis Garcia-Lopez and Vincente Alcazar is also appealing.

45 is a turning-point as Hex marries Mei Ling, introduced in 23, a condition of the nuptials being that he renounce his life of violence. By this time Dick Ayers is the regular penciller, inked by original Hex artist Tony DeZuniga, making an appealing combination who stay until 82, when DeZuniga manages another six issues solo. Of course, given the demands, Hex's marriage wasn't likely to last and he soon reverts to bounty hunting.

65–71 concern an army payroll robbery and its consequences, and reintroduce Emmy Lou Hartley (from 50), one of many attractive women inexplicably drawn to the gruesomely visaged Hex. Those issues see Fleisher recovering from an uninspired run. From 76 the emphasis switches to continuity-based plots as old characters return. Cliffhanger endings are the norm, and there are fine individual issues (80–81 resolve the Turnbull situation), but the soap-opera tricks are jarring in a title that survived so long with barely a nod to them. Gray Morrow draws the final four issues of the DC series, leaving dangling sub-plots featuring the supporting cast as Jonah is transported to an ignominious future postscript in the pages of Hex.

Joe Lansdale and Tim Truman's take on Hex's character for the 1990s miniseries is spot-on. Their plots stem from Jonah Hex once starring in a comic titled Weird Western, and if you can overlook the anomalous introduction of supernatural elements to the Wild West, the new stories are fine, but don't match the best of the previous run.~FP

Recommended: 1–3, 7, 8, 10, 11–13, 24, 27, 32, 42–45, 48, 51, 58, 65-70, 73–75, 81–84, 86, Spectacular

Collection: Two Gun Mojo (1–5)

JONNI THUNDER Aka Thunderbolt
DC: *4-issue miniseries 1985*

Based on 1940s character Johnny Thunder, who could summon a mystical being, this update is a tolerably scripted female-private-investigator story. Ironically, it's the extraneous supernatural elements that spoil the revamp, as writer Roy Thomas is unable to resist giving her superpowers. Dick Giordano illustrates in his usual ineffable fashion.~HS

JONNY DEMON
Dark Horse: *3-issue miniseries 1994*

Light-hearted romp through an era where magic and demons are as commonplace on earth as science today. Average stuff from Kurt Busiek.~FP

JONNY QUEST
Comico: *31 issues, 2 Specials 1986–1988*

Generally excellent and vastly underrated series based on the 1960s cartoon show, with the care and attention lavished on the series exceptional, from the double-sized cover illustrations on. The writing of William Messner-Loebs underpins everything, with meticulous plots encompassing a vast range of topics, always warm, humorous, and able to adapt to whichever artist is handling a particular issue. And there's a stellar selection of artists before Marc Hempel and Mark Wheatley draw most issues from 14. Doug Wildey and Steve Rude both draw strips in 1, and other highlights include Adam Kubert on 6's story of a great discovery at the North Pole and Murphy Anderson illustrating an undercover operation in 9. Jonny Quest is the pre-teen son of the widowed Professor Benton Quest, all-round boffin, accompanied by his Indian friend Hadji and his dog Bandit. Adventurer Race Bannon keeps a watchful eye on all parties during their travels, particularly when nemesis Dr Zin is in the vicinity. It's rare that a story runs two issues, so sample away. There shouldn't be a dry eye after reading 2's story of Jonny's mother, 11 has Jonny meeting the Princes in the Tower, 20's 'Time Storm' is a trans-temporal mystery and 25 is a Bandit solo. They're four very different stories, but each typical of the series. Loebs has no hand in the specials featuring alternate-reality *doppelgängers* of Jonny & Co and a re-animated Lenin. They're to be avoided, but check out the affiliated *Jezebel Jade* series.~WJ
Recommended: 2–12, 17–29, 31

JONNY QUEST Classics
Comico: *3-issue miniseries 1987*

Doug Wildey adapts three episodes from the original Jonny Quest cartoon series 'Shadow Of The Condor', 'Calcutta Adventure' and 'Werewolf Of The Timberland' ('The Invisible Monster' can be found in *Jonny Quest* 30). Wildey's art is, as always, top notch, but the material he's adapting doesn't have the depth or resonance of the stories written by William Messner-Loebs for the ongoing *Jonny Quest* title.~WJ

JONNY QUEST The Real Adventures
Dark Horse: *4 issues + 1996 to date*

The 1990s TV cartoon series has aged Jonny and Hadji to their early teens and added a female companion, Jessie, who appears to be related to Rand Race. Must cover the widest possible demographic spread, after all. Kate Worley writes the first story arc in 1–4, and throws in everything bar the kitchen sink, although Solano Lopez draws a very nice bathroom pail on issue 2's splash page. There are vampires, ancient castles, dancing bears, gypsies, pickpockets, computer crime and a miraculous hair-dye that washes in and out with no tell-tale traces. There are gaping great holes in the plot, and little logic throughout. One only hopes the second story, from 5, is an improvement.~WJ

She's... JOSIE
Archie: *44 issues 1963–1966.*

Archie artist Dan DeCarlo created Josie in a clear attempt to repeat the winning formula. Josie could have been Archie's long-lost twin sister: redheaded, attractive but wholesome, klutzy, well-meaning, bright and easily distracted by the opposite sex. The majority of her supporting cast were also introduced in 1: her long-suffering parents, wimpy boy-friend Albert, wisecracking best friend, Pepper, Pepper's boy-friend, the dimwitted Sock (short for Socrates), and... Melody. The traffic-stopping blonde bombshell Melody was the closest to a sex symbol one could have in a Comics Code-approved comic. The chaos caused by her inability to grasp facts was equalled only by the disasters that occurred when her startling figure was seen by drivers, traffic cops, or just about any male, who developed a sudden inability to focus on what he was doing. Hugely popular with readers of both sexes, she gave the book such a boost that a proposed *Melody* spin-off was rejected, for fear *Josie* would lose too many readers! The only significant later additions to the cast were resident villainous siblings Alexander and Alexandra Cabot, spoilt rich kids who, peculiarly, were the most inept practitioners of witchcraft ever seen in comics. For forty-four issues, Josie and her gang trundled along in teen-comedy misadventures, occasionally interacting with the Archie characters, but pretty much minding their own business. Come 45, the title was suddenly renamed *Josie & The Pussycats*.~HS

JOSIE & THE PUSSYCATS
Archie: *62 issues (45–106) 1966–1982, 2 issues 1993–1994*

Without explanation, Josie and Melody were two sides of a pop triangle. Albert, Pepper and Sock were gone, to be replaced by blond bimboy Alan M as Josie's new love, and a new character, Valerie, only about the fifth black person seen in Riverdale, as the third Pussycat. Though seen throughout the issue, Valerie's one line of dialogue was a less than groundbreaking 'Yeah!' Maybe Archie didn't want to traumatise the Mid-West by having her be too uppity. No longer students, the trio toured as an internationally famous award-winning rock band – except when the plot required that they be an obscure struggling garage band, in which case that's what they'd always been. Continuity has never been a hallmark of the Archie line! This was done to tie in with the 1970s *Josie and the Pussycats* TV show. Revamping the *Josie* cast to a pop milieu, the comic was obliged to hastily shoehorn the changes in to gain those TV-led readers. Some changes were for the better. Alan M couldn't be less fun than Albert, and Valerie, though no substitute for the acerbic Pepper – I've always imagined she and Albert eloped, after burying Sock under a patio! – did eventually develop a personality. The TV show was popular enough to come back as *Josie & The Pussycats In Outer Space*, whose premise was... oh, you guessed. Yep, accidentally launched into deep space, the Pussycats, Alan M. and the Cabots struggled to find their way back to Earth while entertaining bug-eyed monsters galaxy-wide with bubblegum rock. Clearly they did, eventually, make it back, as the title lasted until 106, and the group features in sporadic specials and one-shots to this day. Delightful fluff, usually drawn by either DeCarlo (early issues inked by his brother Vince, whose tragic death robbed DeCarlo of his most sympathetic finisher) or, later, Stan Goldberg, the Josie books are a fun read as long as you're not expecting deep thought... and let's face it, if you were would you pick up an Archie comic at all?~HS

JOURNEY
Aardvark-Vanaheim: *14 issues 1983–1984*
Fantagraphics: *13 issues (15–27) 1984–1986*

The life of early-19th-century frontiersman Wolverine MacAlistaire wasn't obvious subject-matter in 1983, but the deft writing and Eisneresque art of William Messner-Loebs make for a fine comic, with the entire series occurring over a year. From the extraordinary sixteen-page opening sequence of a bear chasing MacAlistaire, *Journey* stamps itself as unique. In the same issue he agrees to deliver a package to a community called New Hope, thus starting the journey of the title. MacAlistaire is fictional, but you wouldn't know it from the depth of research Loebs brings to *Journey*, conveying both historical accuracy and a real feeling for the knowledge of a trapper. Fanciful intrusions such as Sasquatch in 3 and a crossover with Normalman in 13 jar. A winter stopover with an old companion whose marriage is wilting through lack of communication in 8–11 is subtle and insightful while also harbouring some dangerous adventure: it's the highlight of the run. MacAlistaire's participation in 14–17 is minimal as the series concentrates on Fort Miami, an outpost precariously close to falling to Tecumseh, and the series is weaker without him. The predicament of folk at Fort Miami becomes dull, and Loebs seems to recognise this by an abrupt change of direction with 18, as MacAlistaire again takes centre stage. Refined Bostonian poet Elmer Alyn Craft plays an increasingly important role from 18, acting as narrator, foil to MacAlistaire's rough-hewn ways and partner as they reach New Hope in 20. The community seemingly belies its name, and conceals several deep secrets that begin to emerge once the package is handed over. The final seven issues are a dark and separate journey which considers just how much is acceptable in protecting a utopian vision, as Craft and MacAlistaire play a deadly game of truth and consequences. *Journey* is best read as a series from the start. There are few concessions to new readers and issues from 8 on are more or less one continuous story, although 12, 18 and 20 just about qualify as jumping-on points. A follow-up series titled *Wardrums* picks up on some of the supporting characters from the Fort Miami issues, and seemed very promising, but lasted only two issues of a proposed six, as more lucrative assignments came Loebs' way.~FP

Recommended: 1, 2, 4, 5, 7–12, 21–27
Collections: Tall Tales (1–3 plus *Cerebus* 48 & 49), *Bad Weather* (4–7)

JOURNEY INTO MYSTERY

Marvel: *Series one 127 issues, 1 Annual 1952–1966 (1–125), 1996 to date (503 on), series two 19 issues 1972–1975*

Despite a brief publication hiatus in 1958 and change of title to *Thor* from issues 126–502, *Journey into Mystery* is the longest-running Marvel comic. The standard horror/monster shorts in issues 1–82 are most notable for their presentation of the Hulk (no relation) in 62 and 66, a shaggy alien who menaced Earth. Cunningly disguising himself with a name change to Xemnu the Titan, he tried again during his reprints in *Monsters On The Prowl* 11 and 14 and made his formal introduction to the Marvel Universe in battle against the Defenders in *Marvel Feature* 3.

Weird shorts served as back-ups in 83–108 to the new lead feature: The Mighty Thor. Early issues in particular are ludicrously antiquated. Central plot themes involve Thor's love for mortal nurse Jane Foster, Odin's remonstrations with his son regarding non-revelation of his identity to her, and Loki's scheming machinations. The God of Mischief appears in over half of the Thor issues, and Odin's credibility as All-Father is stretched well beyond belief as Loki endlessly beguiles him into overlooking his treachery. Perhaps it is just as well; Stan Lee might have been hamstrung for plot ideas otherwise. He delivers dialogue with pomp and splendour and, with Kirby's power-packed pencils, ensures smooth improvement over the run. Many classic Marvel villains début in this strip.

Worthy issues introduce Grey Gargoyle (107) and Absorbing Man (114, 115), although the Carbon Copy Man is probably best left unmentioned. The finest two issues are 110 and 111, in which Loki enhances the powers of two of Thor's most formidable villains, Cobra and Mr Hyde. This story encapsulates all the vital elements of early Thor and, in a stirring climax, a desperate and noble Thunder God clings to Odin's mercy when powerless to save the dying Jane Foster, yet finally '… turns his back upon his defeated foes, and upon the house of darkness, as he walks into the shining light of morning!' They don't make them like that any more. 97–125 include five-page back-up strips of the 'Tales of Asgard'. Mostly set during Thor's boyhood, they feature many characters from the Norse pantheon, hordes of Frost Giants, Storm Giants and Trolls, and encompass the riotous, far-flung corners of Asgard.

The 1996 title change arose from Thor's revamp following Marvel's 'Onslaught 'saga. Tom DeFalco stews a potboiler of potentially amnesiac Norse Gods, a quest to resurrect them and some cheap opportunism to flash hot babes. The second series reprints 1950s weird shorts, although the first five issues are enlivened with new adaptations of stories by master writers of the macabre Robert E. Howard, Robert Bloch and H.P.Lovecraft.~APS

Recommended: 110, 111
Collections: Marvel Masterworks Vol 18 (83–100), *Marvel Masterworks* Vol 26 (101–110)

JUDGE DREDD

Eagle: *33 issues 1983–1986*
Quality: *Series one 2 issues (34–35) 1986, series two 77 issues 1986–1993*

For those who don't know, Judge Dredd lives in the future, where huge Mega-Cities exist, full to breaking point, with people living on top of one another. Outside the cities there are only radioactive wastelands, the 'Cursed Earth', full of mutants, outlaws and horrible, deadly wildlife, and the Black Atlantic, much the same with water. The Judges are this society's police force, with the right to pass sentence on the job, as it were, whether it be a death sentence or a long jail term. Mega-City One's main problems are the block riots caused by too many people living too close together and venting their frustrations against their neighbours, the Russian Mega-City (always prone to invade) and the normal, average working citizens who can get arrested for countless activities which we'd consider minor. The Law's the thing, here.

Dredd is the greatest of the Judges, totally incorruptible, never seen without his mask and as humourless a character as you could wish for. Fortunately, writers John Wagner, Alan

Grant and, sometimes at the start, Pat Mills inject humour (normally very black) into most of his adventures. They range from bizarre fads (like products to make you ugly in 25) that help keep the city's occupants sane (well…) to Dredd's robot helper Walter (who, through a speech impediment, calls him 'Dwedd').

The stories here are reprints from *2000AD*, the British weekly comic in which Judge Dredd first appeared (2). The Eagle run starts with the highly polished Brian Bolland-drawn stories, including Judge Death, who comes from a parallel dimension in which the Judges have decided that the only way to keep the law is to kill all humans. When they've finished with their own dimension they come looking for others to cleanse. By 4 we're onto Ron Smith as well as Bolland ('Father Earth', a messianic prophet who seems to be in communication with the Earth itself), and soon Mike McMahon is also represented with the 'Cursed Earth' saga (5–9), followed by the deranged Judge Caligula's takeover of Mega-City One. 'Block Mania' (18, 19) and its sequel 'The Apocalypse War' (20–24) deal with the almost total devastation of Mega-City One, and Dredd's visual creator Carlos Ezquerra draws most of these issues. 27 introduces Chopper, a character who'll later become very popular as a sky surfer, here a graffiti artist. Continuity isn't integral to Dredd, but there are elements, particularly stories sparking from previous tales. From 30 there's a policy of reprinting stories in roughly the same time-frame as originally published, balanced by the attempt to employ only a single artist for each issue. Eagle's final issue is a particularly good look at the ludicrous fads that sweep through the city, featuring 'The League Of Fatties', new food product Gunge and people having all facial features removed to become blobs. The Eagle issues have new Brian Bolland covers throughout. Quality take over the title, cancel it and later relaunch it (1986). From this point, *Judge Dredd* is printed on toilet paper and we're onto Steve Dillon's run on Dredd, apart from the first Dredd story, reprinted in number 2 (perhaps not a coincidence).

The poor colouring, appalling printing, and art stretched to fit the American comic page monopolise the Quality title, and the initial issues of its companion title *The Law Of Judge Dredd*. Anyone interested in seeing these stories, seemingly selected at random, is directed to the Titan Books black and white reprints. With 38 the logo changes from Quality Comics to Fleetway Quality but the publishers are listed as S.P.Q. Inc (as they have been for some time before). By 57, we're back to reprinting the first Dredd story again and the Steve Dillon werewolf story from 1, and the title becomes *Judge Dredd Classics* from 62.

Judge Dredd's politics are definitely suspect but the better writers have made the series a very black comedy, as much a satire on contemporary society as a science-fiction adventure.~NF

Recommended: Eagle 1–33

Collections: Apocalypse War Vol 1 (20–22), vol 2 (22–24), *Block Wars* (Eagle 18, 19), *The Cursed Earth* (5–9 – also available in two volumes), *Judge Caligula* Vol 1 (Eagle 10, 11), vol 2 (12–14)

JUDGE DREDD
DC: *18 issues 1994–1996*

As the Judge Dredd movie neared, DC signed up the character for their own series. They wisely opted to set the strip in the years before Dredd was fully established as the most respected Judge in an autocratic future, thus partially removing inevitable invidious comparisons with the British stories. Nevertheless, while the American version portrays the Judge as devoid of human emotion, being merely a law machine, there's a lack of the contrasting black humour that characterised the feature. Andrew Helfer's scripts are mediocre, whilst Mike Oeming's art is cartoon-like and colourful; later issues by other creators lose the plot completely. There's a change of direction from 11, which has Judge Dredd thrust fifty-four years into the future, and following issues show how he's forced to change to survive in a new time. By and large the Quality comics, reprinting the British version of Judge Dredd, are far superior. Read them instead.~SS

JUDGE DREDD Collections
Titan: *50 volumes 1982–1990*
Hamlyn/Mandarin: *12 volumes + 1991 to date*

Judge Dredd is particularly well served by the Titan reprint books. In addition to twenty-five volumes each concentrating on a single artist's interpretation of the character, and two combination tomes, there are a further fifteen volumes collecting longer stories. The best sample volume for those unfamiliar with the character is the first, just titled *Judge Dredd*. It's sixty-four pages of witty John Wagner scripts, illustrated by Brian Bolland, and features the first appearance of Dredd's arch-nemesis Judge Death (with the remainder of the Bolland Judge Death strips collected in *Judge Death*). Bolland-drawn stories are also part of *The Cursed Earth*, originally published as two separate editions, now collected in a single volume. The only early Dredd stories to strongly feature writers other than John Wagner and Alan Grant, *The Cursed Earth* sees Dredd having to travel across a mutant-infested wasteland to deliver a plague antidote. He encounters alien slave traders, robotic vampires and a tyrannosaurus rex among other oddities. It's consistently inventive, and the only shame is that the threat of legal action prevents episodes which used advertising trademarks and featured a burger war between McDonald's and Burger King ever being reprinted. With the exception of the *Judge Child Quest* (three volumes), which has a similar inventive quality to *The Cursed Earth*, successive extended Dredd stories reprinted by Titan are largely disappointing. *Judge Caligula* (two volumes) has a mad judge taking over Mega-City One and Dredd leading a desperate attempt to regain control. Despite several fine individual episodes and strong art from Bolland and McMahon, it lacks the thrust of *The Cursed Earth*. *Apocalypse War* (two volumes) and its precursor *Block Mania* see a full-scale invasion of *Mega-City One*, and while *Judge Dredd In Oz* (for a surf contest) works in places, there's too much padding. *City Of The Damned* picks up from the plot of *The Judge Child Quest*, as the predicted event from which the Judge Child would save Mega-City occurs.

The twenty-seven volumes spotlighting artists almost all contain strong and amusing John Wagner and Alan Grant strips, and that the massive disparity of artistic approaches all work with the character is a testament to the quality of the writing. Ron Smith (5, 6, 8, 10–12, 26) was the most prolific Judge Dredd artist of the late 1970s and early 1980s; the other featured artists are Mike McMahon (2), Carlos Ezquerra (4, 7, 23), Steve Dillon (9, 20), Cam Kennedy (13, 15, 17, Brendan McCarthy (16), Cliff Robinson (18) Ian Gibson (19, 25), John Higgins (21), Brett Ewins (22) and Barry Kitson (27). 3 pairs Mike McMahon and Ron Smith, while 14 is a combination of Smith, Robinson and Dillon. Stories by artists who haven't drawn enough Dredd to warrant their own album are collected in catch-all titles *Mega City Vice* (three volumes) and *Rough Justice*. Despite including Dave Gibbons, Kevin O'Neill, Bryan Talbot and Colin Wilson (largely unknown in the USA, but massively popular in Europe) alongside other material by artists whose work was already collected, they're hit-and- miss propositions, although each has some decent strips. The same applies to *Judge Dredd's Crime Files* (four volumes).

In the early 1990s Dredd's home, *2000AD*, went to full colour, Dredd was serialised in *Rock Power* magazine as 'Heavy Metal Dredd', and a companion magazine, *The Judge Dredd Megazine*, ensured there was more original Dredd material appearing than ever before. The downside was that John Wagner and Alan Grant cut back on their Dredd stories. The UK's Mandarin Books have been issuing colour collections of post-1990s Dredd material; their best volume by far is *America*, by John Wagner and Colin MacNeil. It's a

bittersweet story about love and revolution under tyranny. MacNeil also draws half of *Mechanismo* (completed by Peter Doherty), in which giant robot judges are introduced, and, inevitably, begin to malfunction. It's not the best Dredd, but certainly readable, which is more than can be said for *Heavy Metal Dredd*, which has Simon Bisley art, but very slight stories. *Three Amigos* is John Wagner back on form with some nice Mike McMahon-style art from Trevor Hairsine. It does prompt one to consider why McMahon wasn't asked to draw the story in the first place, though. The three amigos of the title are Dredd and his two most popular adversaries, Judge Death and Mean Angel, the unlikely teaming occurring in order to trap a redneck outlaw. The remaining volumes are lesser quality throughout, either because Wagner and Grant are retreading old ground, or because other writers lack inspiration. The previously high standard of art has also slipped, with too many artists hiding basic deficiencies behind layers of acrylic paint.~FP

Recommended: *America*, *The Cursed Earth*, *Judge Death*, *Judge Dredd* Vols 1–3, 5, 11, 13, 17, 19, 21, 25

JUDGE DREDD In 'The Judge Child Quest'
Eagle: *5-issue miniseries 1984*

Certainly a contender for the best Judge Dredd multi-parter, the *Judge Child Quest* was seemingly begun with an end in mind, yet is flexible enough to permit the eccentric detours that keep Dredd fresh. It also introduces the popular Judge Hershey and the Angel Gang, members of which have proved enduringly recurring foes for Dredd; artists Brian Bolland, Mike McMahon and Ron Smith are on top form. After a slow start, so is writer John Wagner, throwing out good ideas at such a clip there's a frenetic pace to the stories when collected from the originally published weekly versions. Precognitives see a time of great trauma when only Owen Krysler can save Mega City. Krysler is now a child able to see into the future, and has been kidnapped and flown off Earth by the Angel Gang. Dredd has to return him, encountering all sorts of strange beings and planets along the way.~WJ

Recommended: 2–5
Collection: The Judge Child Quest Bks 1–3 (1–5)

JUDGE DREDD The Early Cases
Eagle: *6 issues 1985–1986*

It took almost a year of continuous weekly publication before writer John Wagner fixed his concept of what Dredd was, how his world operated and how best to handle him. The system he settled on was Dredd as straight-faced foil to the lunatic goings-on around him. The early stories, while gradually developing

Dredd's world, are relatively primitive, as artists Mike McMahon, Carlos Ezquerra and Ian Gibson also develop their styles. Brian Bolland's first Judge Dredd story is reprinted in 3, and while there's a novelty in seeing a classic strip develop, there's plenty of better Dredd material available.~WJ

JUDOMASTER
Charlton: *10 issues (89–98) 1966–1967*
In the usual Charlton fashion, rather than renewing their magazine-rate postal permit they cancelled a title, in this case *Gun Master*, and merely started their new project by continuing the numbering of the old title. In the final months of World War II Sgt Rip Jagger becomes the freebooting Judomaster. From his island base he and his band of raiders foil Japanese sabotage attempts in the South Pacific in what was the first martial arts strip to appear in comics. Drawn by martial arts devotee Frank McLaughlin and débuting in Charlton Special War Series 4, Judomaster proved to be one of Charlton's best. The back-up feature, a revival of Sarge Steel, by Steve Skeates and Dick Giordano, was also very good, making for an eminently readable comic.~SW

JUNGLE ACTION
Marvel: *24 issues 1972–1976*
Jungle Action's original remit was to reprint stories of scantily clad male and female Tarzan rip-offs, and apart from some drawn nicely by Joe Maneely in 1–3 there's nothing of note. The Black Panther is the featured character from 6, and was immediately launched into the epic 'Panther's Rage' story until 18. The Panther was a blank slate for writer Don McGregor, who fleshed out the bare bones of his background from previous appearances. The Panther was the ruler of Wakanda, a technologically advanced hidden African society, from which McGregor extrapolated a complex culture, mythology and geography, devising a complete map of Wakanda and the surrounding area, and being consistent in sticking to it for the duration of his run. They may seem obvious pieces of preparation, but few comic creators at the time bothered with background to that degree. In the company of artists Billy Graham and Klaus Janson (from 10), McGregor wove a complex tale of an uprising led by the imposing Erik Killmonger. Mixing exotic characters, a Wakandan travelogue and political machinations, and still finding space for small human moments, it's a considerable achievement, albeit flawed by McGregor's florid writing style. McGregor cared about the feature, though, to the extent of preparing text and illustration pages more in keeping with the tone of the Panther's strip to replace the reprint back-ups, and including an extra level to some stories by, for instance, planting subtle clues as to the identity of a mystery assassin in 9. The complexity of McGregor's plotting and the ideas incorporated make 'Panther's Rage' a forerunner of the current crop of adult-oriented comics. 19 began another multi-parter with the Panther back in the USA confronted by the bigotry of the Ku Klux Klan. Unfortunately, McGregor's prolix tendencies run out of control, producing dull issues. The story was unfinished as *Jungle Action* was cancelled (to let Jack Kirby start his *Black Panther* title); Ed Hannigan completed it none too satisfactorily in *Marvel Premiere* 51–53.~FP
Recommended: 8–17

JUNGLE JIM
Dell: *20 issues 1953–1959*
King: *1 issue (5) 1967*
Charlton: *7 issues (22–28) 1969–1970*
The original comics featured adventures of Alex Raymond's syndicated hero Jungle Jim Bradley and his faithful companion Kolu in the greenery 'East of Suez'. Despite the newspaper strip being discontinued in 1954, the character's popularity was maintained due to movie B-features starring a post-*Tarzan* Johnny Weissmuller, and a TV series.
     The first two Dell comics are issues of *Four Color* (although Jim's name is large on the cover), and the series officially picks up with 3. They're largely drawn by Paul Norris and Frank Thorne in a conservative 1950s style, and the King issue reprints 5. Perhaps that's why it's numbered as such rather than 21. The only additional item of interest was the tantalising Wally Wood cover. When Charlton leased the feature they were given the unpublished art for stillborn future King issues, so 22, 23, and 27 have artwork by Wally Wood (and his assistant Wayne Howard) and Steve Ditko, inked by Wood (or Howard). The balance of the stories are by Joe Gill and Pat Boyette, who did an unconventional but highly reverential job on the strip. The Charlton series also features a one-page lesson on how to speak Swahili each issue.~SW
Recommended: 22, 23, 27

JUNGLE TALES OF TARZAN
Charlton: *4 issues 1964–1965*
This notorious unauthorised comic adaptation was forcibly discontinued by the Edgar Rice Burroughs estate after four issues. They seized practically the entire print run of issue 4 and destroyed them. The strips are adapted from Burroughs' original stories by writer Joe Gill and artist Sam Glanzman. The story is told entirely in captions, lettered by Charlton's dreadful 'A. Machine' device in the first issue, which really detracts from the comic's appeal. The drawings in 1–3 are nice, though hardly

Glanzman's best. Sadly, the ultra-rare issue 4 is drawn by Montes and Bache, guaranteeing more entertainment from the staples in the centrefold than from the rest of the comic.~SW

The Exploits of the JUNIOR CARROT PATROL
Dark Horse: *2 issues 1989–1990*
The whimsical surreality of Flaming Carrot is present and correct and Rick Geary's a better artist, yet somehow these junior crimefighters attempting to emulate their hero fall flat.~FP

JUNKWAFFEL
Print Mint: *4 issues 1971–1972*
Last Gasp: *1 issue (5) 1983*
One of the underground's most prolific artists, Vaughn Bodé produced a large body of work that was variously touching and bawdy, profound and cutesy depending on the strip. *Junkwaffel* was conceived as a receptacle for obscure, early or unpublished stories, and was inevitably a patchy affair, but certainly contained fine work. Highlights of the run include the powerful and violent anti-war strips 'The Machines' in 1, dating from his college days, and 'Cobalt 60' in 2, the chapters of which were later collected from disparate sources. By contrast the magazine-sized 5 reprinted Bodé's charming unpublished newspaper strip 'Zooks', the story of the first lizard in space. Some of the material now appears a tad sexist and inconsequential, but there's much of interest here overall. The issues have been kept in print by Last Gasp, and all are still available.~DAR
Recommended: 1, 2

Return to JURASSIC PARK
Topps: *8-issue limited series, 1 Annual 1995–1996*
Tom and Mary Bierbaum pick up where Englehart left off with the *Raptor* series, by introducing a story that parallels the events of the source film. Drs Grant and Sattler investigate the military occupation of Jurassic Park in 1–4. Two new scientists are introduced for 5–8, which features them abandoned on the island during a storm, and coming into conflict with the military. Armando Gil returns as penciller, but Michael Golden's covers are the artistic highpoint of the series. The annual (1995) and *Jurassic Jam* (1996) complete the Jurassic spin-offs, the latter a story by Keith Giffen illustrated with single-pagers from the likes of John Byrne, John Bolton, George Perez and Walt Simonson.~NF

JUSTICE
Marvel: *32 issues 1986–1989*
A memorable disaster area. How on earth did it last for so long? Archie Goodwin created a confused alien called Tensen who had been a law officer on his own world, Spring (the baddies are from Winterland), and continued to punish evildoers after arrival on Earth. He judged them by their black auras and battered and fried them with his electric shield and sword. Steve Englehart took over the scripting from 2, and it's not bad. The earth scenes are typical 1980s sub-Frank Miller mean-streets stuff, and the fantasy elements are by way of vintage Steve Ditko strips such as *Dr Strange* and *Shade The Changing Man*. The chief problem is the eccentric pencilling by Geof Isherwood, plainly inked by Vince Colletta. It looks a mess.

Keith Giffen, heavily under the influence of the South American master José Muñoz, drew some decent issues, written by old hand Gerry Conway (9–11). Then, after some rough fill-ins, halfway through the run someone decided to try some creators who weren't incompetent or clapped-out on the comic. It was revealed that Tensen had been under the hypnotic spell of a paranormal. The editors explained: 'Unfortunately, in the creative crunch to get the books done for Marvel's 25th anniversary, we accidentally let a few stray concepts – aliens and alternative dimensions – creep in, concepts we soon realised were "old universe".' Peter David wrote the strip to its end and packed in a lot of slapstick and digs at comic-book writing and cultural events such as *Live Aid*. Issues 16–32 are quite readable – even funny if you followed the title from the beginning. Lee Weeks and Mike Gustovich's art is clear and dynamic. Tensen learns to walk on his shields (i.e. fly) and the criminals still get incinerated.~GK

JUSTICE Four Balance
Marvel: *4-issue miniseries 1994*
No relation to the 1980s character, this Justice is a telekinetic teenage member of the New Warriors. Having suffered heavy beatings as a child, Justice is keen to investigate the death of a possibly abused teenager. The first issue is reasonably well handled, but precedes two issues padded with superfluous cameos and jarring 'fantasy' sequences to stretch the series to four issues. The concluding issue stands apart from the remainder, and is the best of the run, making every necessary point on its own.~WJ

JUSTICE INC
DC: *4 issues 1975, 2-issue microseries 1989*
A contemporary of The Shadow, and like his counterpart operating a pool of agents, The Avenger was created for 1930s pulp novels by writer Kenneth Robeson. An experimental operation by enemies of the state endowed Richard Benson with the ability to morph his features to resemble anyone he chose, a technique he used to the full in fighting crime.

The first series can't make up its mind if it's to be a home for adaptations of the novels or for original material, and the identity crisis resulted in an unsatisfactory series. Al McWilliams does a nice job illustrating the first issue and Jack Kirby draws 2–4, but they're strangely lacklustre, as Kirby often was when working on creations other than his own.

Andy Helfer wisely chose to have the microseries span twenty years from 1948, distancing it from the pulps to avoid invidious comparisons, but retaining the essential period feel. Helfer provides a dense plot, adding elements to the Avenger's origin and portraying him as a man manipulated by the security services from day one. In keeping with the tone of the feature, Kyle Baker's art is distinctly unsettling. He appears to have drawn in coloured chalks, adding black outlines on an overlay, for an overall ghostly and distancing effect. There's perhaps a little too much exposition and set-up beginning the second issue, but once Benson knows the truth about himself he embarks on an ingenious course of action that engrosses until the end. Baker and Helfer don't top their work on *The Shadow*, but they're even less reverential here and their take on *Justice Inc* is well worth reading.~WJ
Recommended: Microseries 1–2

JUSTICE LEAGUE AMERICA
DC: *113 issues, 9 Annuals, 1 Spectacular 1987–1996*

The previous version of the Justice League had been allowed to stagnate, and eventually died in mediocrity, so something radical was required to entice readers back. Writers Keith Giffen (plot and often art breakdowns) and J.M. DeMatteis (dialogue) came up with the goods. The new JLA's multinational mixture of characters were more likely to mess up before they came through, and had a difficult time taking the concept, or each other, seriously. Humour is paramount, in the way the characters mesh and the snappy dialogue, but it's backed up with strong plots and thoughtful characterisation, and it switches tone deftly to tragedy when required.

Of course, it helps that throughout most of their run Giffen and DeMatteis are blessed with gifted art teams. Pencillers Kevin Maguire (1–12, 16–19, 22–24, 60), Ty Templeton (20, 21, 24–29), Mike McKone (28, Annual 3, 4, 41, 42), and Adam Hughes (30–40, 43, 44, 51), and inkers Al Gordon, Joe Rubinstein and Art Nichols produce slick and dynamic superhero art that flows from page to page. It's likely that if you enjoy one of the issues written by Giffen and DeMatteis you'll enjoy most of them. Good samples are the Justice League moving into their new global embassies (8), the

ludicrous Injustice League (23), or 43–44, in which a novice wins the accoutrements of some of DC's daftest villains in a poker game and proceeds to cause havoc.

From 7 to 25 the title is called *Justice League International* (not to be confused with the later *Justice League International*), and the final Giffen and DeMatteis story arc, *Breakdowns* (53–60), switches back and forth between this title and *Justice League Europe* 29–37. By this time the previously successful formula is sagging a little at the seams, not least because Adam Hughes was never adequately replaced as pencil artist. The appointment of Dan Jurgens solves the art problem, and his writing is solid if unspectacular (which makes his début in the one-shot *Justice League Spectacular* an irony). Jurgens only sticks around for seventeen issues, but does turn in one excellent story, the first part of 'Destiny's Hand' (72–75), with the shocking return of the old Justice League of America.

After Jurgens it's downhill. Dan Vado (78–91), a good writer on more idiosyncratic projects, seems decidedly uncomfortable here, and Gerard Jones (92 on) only ever seems to rise above comics-by-numbers mode when writing miniseries. Their accompanying art teams, Kevin West inked by Rick Burchett, and Chuck Wojtkiewicz and Bob Dvorak, hold their ends up, but Jones' policy of constant guest stars and temporary members initially leaves little time for any individual focus. The title never reaches the depths plumbed by its predecessor, but the end was just as merciful.~FP
Recommended: 1–12, 16–28, 31–47, 51–54, 58, 72, Annuals 2–5
Collections: A New Beginning (1–7), The Secret Gospel of Maxwell Lord (Annual 1, 8–12)

JUSTICE LEAGUE EUROPE
DC: *50 issues, 3 Annuals 1989–1993*

The European branch of the Justice League was first introduced in the *Justice League International* (or *America*) 24, and follows the parent title's humorous bent. It works brilliantly… to begin with. Early issues concentrate on the problems the JLE had in settling down in France, and before the suitcases have been unpacked writer Keith Giffen begins to explain the history of Metamorpho. 11–13 show the real personality behind this wacky superhero in a fine story, with a cast well drawn by regular penciller Bart Sears. The Extremists are introduced in 15 and cause havoc for the JLE up until 20, returning later to more devastating effect in *Justice League America*. Their relationship with the French in perennial free-fall, the team move headquarters to London in 20, and 23 features the origin of the French heroine Crimson Fox, which has an interesting twist that explains her personality. The old Justice League villain Starro makes a welcome return in 25–28, attempting another scheme for world domination just prior to the 'Breakdowns' story-line, which alternates with issues of *JLA* between 29 and 35. This story features major upheavals for the group and changes the team forever. A new JLE team is formed in 37, but never really takes off under the new creators, and the title becomes tired and dull. In issue 50 the team is amalgamated back into Justice League International, and continues under that title. JLE started well but, following the departure of Bart Sears after 28 and Keith Giffen after 35, the title never got back on track, and with 51 became *Justice League International*.~SS

Recommended: 11–13, 15–19, 26–28

JUSTICE LEAGUE INTERNATIONAL

DC: *18 issues (51–68), 2 Annuals 1992–1994*

This shouldn't be confused with the earlier version of Justice League International, dealt with under *Justice League America*. This continued from companion title *Justice League Europe*. It's the same characters from that comic, produced by the same creative team. The stories don't change, with simple superhero action and some lighter-hearted humour paramount. Gerald Jones' scripting is passable but not spectacular, and the only real issue of note is 53, and then only if you're a Crimson Fox fan. 68 introduces Triumph, ties in with Zero Hour and draws the series to a close. It was for the best.~SS

JUSTICE LEAGUE OF AMERICA

DC: *261 issues, 3 Annuals 1960–1987*

Astounding as it may seem today with the proliferation of superteams, there was an era when the uniting of a company's top-of-the-line superheroes was distinctly novel. In the late 1950s DC's Justice Society of America in *All Star Comics* was still fondly recalled by long-time comic fans, despite the fact that the characters rarely did more than team in pairs or trios. Having successfully refurbished most of DC's more popular 1940s superheroes for the 1960s, editor Julie Schwartz took the next logical step in teaming them in *Justice League Of America*. Even then it was a tentative introduction, with the idea having to prove itself commercial through three try-outs in *The Brave And The Bold* 28–30.

Despite the revived characters and a concept exciting at the time, the early *Justice League* issues have aged badly. Schwartz co-plotted with writer Gardner Fox (author of many of the 1940s Justice Society tales) and they adhere rigidly to a four- or five-chapter formula. It has the unsophisticated, cleancut, radiantly

cheerful heroes teaming in pairs and trios to combat aspects of that issue's menace before uniting for the final chapter's dénouement. While the plots and means used to deal with villains are imaginative, and Mike Sekowsky's quirky art is oddly appealing, modern-day readers will find 1–20 formularised and naïve if read in bulk. This was, of course, never intended to be the case. Characterisation was never a priority, and, setting aside their respective limitations, Green Lantern, for instance, could have substituted for Martian Manhunter to little obvious difference. The origin of the League wasn't presented until 9. Aquaman, Batman, Flash, Green Lantern, Martian Manhunter (then more commonly known as J'onn J'onnz), Superman and Wonder Woman each dealt with a strange creature transforming the population and using Earth as a battleground to decide which would rule their native planet. It's a decently plotted tale that serves as the best sample of the first three years.

With the new versions of their characters now instituted, DC had begun to receive requests for further old heroes to be revived. The process began in *Flash* 123, where Flash met his 1940s counterpart. It established that the 1940s superheroes occupied a separate Earth, designated Earth 2, one dimension along from that on which the 1960s superheroes operated. From that moment it was inevitable that the Justice League would meet their predecessors, and the teaming with the Justice Society in 21 and 22 remains a landmark. It was the first continued *Justice League* story, and set a precedent. Until almost the end of the run the Justice League and Justice Society would team annually. These remain highlights of the Fox and Sekowsky run, with 29 and 30 introducing Earth 3, where the JLA counterparts are criminals; Earth A in 37–38 introduced an evil version of the JSA's Johnny Thunder.

By 23 Fox has begun integrating his heroes a little more, making for a more satisfying read, and by 40 there's more of a sense of a complete story. Although the stories are still split into chapters, they're no longer as formulaic. By this time the *Batman* TV show was at the height of its popularity, and Batman dominated the covers of issues in the 40s and early 50s. Inside as well there's reflections of the TV show, with wackier dialogue and more gimmicks, but Fox had the common sense not to let the issues become too entrenched in the times. 46 and 47's teaming with the Justice Society reflect this era, with an inventive menace, several jokes (both visual and verbal) and a decent plot, combined with some ludicrous dialogue.

65 was the last issue written by Fox, in which he upgraded another 1940s superhero in

Red Tornado, now a thinking robot with tornado-generating abilities. A good selection of Fox and Sekowsky reprints can be found in 39, 48, 58, 67, 76, 85, 93, the hundred-page JLA special, and the hundred-page issues 110–116, but the time had come for a change. It came with the appointment of Denny O'Neil as writer, who'd managed the miracle of making several Charlton comics fresh and interesting. Whereas Fox might have been a tad predictable, his well-plotted light superhero stories had characterised the JLA, and O'Neil's heavy-handed moralising and often overwriting just didn't suit the title. His lasting monument was the well-considered application of a character to Green Arrow, who'd spent forty years without one, in 75. Now no longer a millionaire playboy, he was a concerned and aware superhero. From this point he was the title's conscience, and often disagreed with his team-mates. O'Neil also rid the JLA of their enthusiastic teenage mascot Snapper Carr, now well past his sell-by date, in 77, in a plot that would have later ramifications. As ever, though, the best of O'Neil's run was the teaming with the Justice Society in 73–74. Despite a preposterous villain, there's a genuinely touching ending that sees the JSA's Black Canary transfer to the JLA, largely to replace the Martian Manhunter, who'd departed with 71 and wouldn't be seen again for over a decade. Sekowsky was also gone, replaced by Dick Dillin in 64. Dillin, very much an artist of the old school, turned out unpretentious pages characterised by consummate story-telling, finely inked by Joe Giella to 101, Dick Giordano to 116 and Frank McLaughlin thereafter. He was to draw every non-reprint issue until his death in 1980.

Mike Friedrich became writer with 86, but was no better. The idea of incorporating relevance into superhero stories was a largely ridiculous conceit that few pulled off successfully, and Friedrich wasn't among them. It should be noted that Gardner Fox had introduced issue-based stories to JLA with 57's unsubtle but well-meant tract on brotherhood. Although equally well-intentioned, Friedrich's heavy-handed and florid proselytising is almost unreadable today, and his best issues are those with no drum to beat. 87 introduces counterparts to Marvel's Avengers shortly after they'd encountered barely concealed JLA equivalents, and 98's desperate last battle against the invincible Starbreaker is okay. Ironically, the worst run of issues JLA was to have for many a year was largely graced by excellent Neal Adams covers, and Adams drew portions of 94.

Len Wein's appointment as writer with 100 immediately blew away the cobwebs, restoring the superhero aspects with stunning success in a three-part teaming with not only the JSA, but another 1940s group, The Seven Soldiers Of Victory. 107–108, introducing a group of heroes acquired from the defunct Quality line, in a world where the Nazis had won World War II, was another triumph, and from that point the annual team-up usually incorporated a third superteam. Wein's entire run to 114 was equally well conceived, and included a sentimental yet hard-edged Christmas story in 110, a tragic story of the original Sandman in 113, and a good old-fashioned superhero slugfest with the Shaggy Man in 104. On Wein's departure numerous writers took over, producing nothing above ordinary.

The arrival of Steve Englehart with 139 altered that. He defined the Justice League as no previous writer had done, establishing inter-dynamics for the team, noting which members were friends and which didn't get on. He additionally produced page-turning plots, including the real origin of the Justice League in 144, and mixed in unlikely characters such as the Phantom Stranger and Red Tornado to great effect. That the new villains he created were largely poor was of no concern when his use of existing ones was so deft, particularly the Key in 150. The new hero he introduced, The Privateer, formerly a Manhunter, and the plots stemming from his appearances, were excellent. Any of Englehart's issues are worth a look, but they're interrupted by an average JLA/JSA and Legion Of Super-Heroes team-up in 147–148. Gerry Conway wouldn't have been many people's choice to replace Englehart from 151, and he took a considerable while to settle in, but the unlikely plot of concluding loose ends from his cancelled Secret Society Of Super-Villains series in 166–169 seemed to spark something. He seemed to have tapped into the same conduit that had fed Wein, and from that point his plots were more inventive, and usually enjoyable. As was often strangely the case, among his best were the annual team-ups with the JSA. 171–172 was a locked-room murder mystery, and 183–185 was Conway's best ever use of Jack Kirby's New Gods characters, a cast he'd ritually abused in their own title.

Sadly, 183 was to prove Dillin's final issue. Never flashy but always solid, reliable, and versatile enough to be convincing no matter where a story was set, Dillin's art is woefully underrated. His replacement was George Perez, who had considerable experience with superteams and relished packing his panels with as many characters and as much detail as possible. Seemingly thrilled at drawing the title, his best sample is a strange tarot-related story in 194, but the art is stunning on every issue he illustrates (184–186, 192–197). Sadly, the same can't be said for Don Heck and Rich Buckler, and their regular contributions appear to dissipate Conway's inspiration. The Secret Society Of Super-Villains have a sprightly return in 195–197, but Conway's final decent issue is the celebratory 200. Many different artists contribute, a nostalgic joy being a return of pencillers to characters they once drew, such as Gil Kane on Green Lantern and Atom, Joe Kubert on Hawkman and Jim Aparo on the Phantom Stranger. The highlight, though, is Brian Bolland, in some of his first work for DC, illustrating a chapter starring Green Arrow, Black Canary and Batman.

With Conway off the boil and sales slipping down the tubes, radical surgery was required for the *Justice League*, and it came in the form of an idea successfully applied to Marvel's team title, *The Avengers*, early in its run. The top-of-the-line characters were displaced by a group of third-string heroes and new creations. Of the familiar cast only Aquaman, Elongated Man, Zatanna and the returned Martian Manhunter remained from 233. It was a disaster, creatively and financially. The audience hated the new characters, and with an uncharacteristic masochistic streak, DC gave the remaining readers what they wanted, with the decimation of the pretenders in the final four issues. Those were written by J.M. DeMatteis, and, all things considered, were a shabby end to what should have been a top-of- the-line title. The good news was the restoration of the idea as *Justice League America*.~WJ

Recommended: 21, 22, 100–102, 107, 108, 110, 113, 142–144, 146, 149, 150, 166–168, 171, 172, 183–185, 194–197, 200

Collections: *Justice League Of America Archives* Vol 1 (*The Brave And The Bold* 28–30, 1–6), Vol 2 (7–14), Vol 3 (15–22)

JUSTICE LEAGUE QUARTERLY
DC: *17 issues 1990–1994*

At the height of their popularity the Giffen and DeMatteis version of the Justice League spawned this oversize publication featuring solo and group tales of the superteam, their associates and their enemies. There's a fair amount of decent material, starting with 1's eighty-pager, with Booster Gold forming a new team, the Conglomerate, who appear to be a model of efficiency when compared with the League. 3–12 usually have Mark Waid writing the lead, although his best is the costumeless back-up 'When Titans Date' in 10, a generally excellent issue. When *JLQ* is bad, though, it's appalling: witness Paul Kupperberg and Don Heck's reduction of parody patriot General Glory to the level of the stories he was conceived to lampoon. Oddly enough, though, Kupperberg redeems himself in 16 with a touching story amid more half-assed homages. The Praxis series running in 11–15 chugs along nicely until a stupid

concluding episode, 3's mini-Justice League has excellent art from Mike McKone (also artist on 5), most of the assorted Fire and Ice shorts are worth a look, and Phil Jimenez and John Stokes provide stunning artwork for a Maxima solo in 17.~WJ

Recommended: 1, 3, 10

JUSTICE LEAGUE TASK FORCE
DC: *37 issues 1993–1996*

After the *Zero Hour* series, the Justice League was split into three titles, supposedly to represent different aspects of the 'Justice' in the title. *Justice League Task Force* began life as a UN police force, sent into trouble spots or assigned to investigate potentially dangerous organisations. J'onn J'onzz, the Martian Manhunter, provides the backbone. Little's been done with him for years and he links the team to the past. He's shown as a clever if manipulative leader, ideally suited to managing young heroes. The original premise creates a new group for each mission and the first story-line featured Nightwing, Flash and Aquaman. 5 and 6 tie into the Batman series 'KnightQuest: The Search', with Gypsy, Green Arrow and Bronze Tiger helping Bruce Wayne find a kidnapped doctor. 7 and 8, written by Peter David, have an all-female team investigating a race of lost women. Bizarrely, J'onn J'onzz, as leader, feels compelled to become a woman for the duration of the mission! Around 16 the permanent team of Gypsy, The Ray and L-Ron/Despero start to coalesce. This issue ties into the other *Justice League* titles and introduces Triumph, an original League member who's been missing (and apparently forgotten) since the League's first adventure. The next issue provides a recurring villain in Vandal Savage, and by 21, with Christopher Priest writing, they're all in matching costumes doing traditional superhero team stuff. Up to this point Sal Velluto had provided a real sense of continuity through his artwork. Though the overall quality is dependent on the skill of his inkers, Velluto's style (somewhere between Gene Colan and George Perez) gives the series a distinctive look. However, from issue 25 Ramon Bernado takes over the art chores, with a style far too close to Sal Buscema's to have much merit of its own (even if you like Buscema). Later issues rely on traditional DC team plots: fights for leadership, members being tried for criminal activity. They even end up crossing over with Travis Morgan, The Warlord and having a 'land that time forgot' adventure in 34–36, at which point another revamp of the *Justice League* books was announced, resulting in the title's cancellation.~NF

Recommended: 7, 8

JUSTICE MACHINE
Noble: *5 issues 1981–1983*
Texas: *1 Annual 1984*
Comico: *29 issues, 1 Annual, 1 Summer Spectacular 1987–1989*
Innovation: *3-issue miniseries 1990, 7 issues 1990–1991*
Millennium: *3-issue miniseries ('The Chimera Conspiracy') 1993*

The Justice Machine was and is artist Mike Gustovitch's baby. The original series in magazine size proved popular enough to spawn a role-playing game and accompanying sourcebook, but issues are so difficult to find that when the series was picked up by Comico in 1987 Gustovich decided to ignore past continuity and start again from scratch, with Tony Isabella handling the script.

The Justice Machine are the government enforcers of the unsubtly named planet Georwell. After meeting up with Earth's Elementals (who débuted in the Texas annual) in issue 4, *Justice Machine vs The Elementals* (1986), they begin to question their orders and when they push too far find themselves framed for treason. After that, it's time to team up with their former enemy, Maxinor, for Justice Machine vs the evil regime, via Earth, where the rebels have allies. The basic idea might not be the most original, but along the way the comic addresses issues of where you draw the line between heroic freedom fighters and evil terrorists. It also tackles drug addiction (Justice Machiner Demon's powers are derived from drugs to which he is addicted), albeit in a way which makes you feel you're being preached at rather than offering much advancement to the plot. Mostly, though, the Comico issues are a competent superhero romp, nothing special but a satisfying, easy read. The Innovation miniseries and subsequent seven issues, and Millennium's miniseries, are poorer quality and best avoided.~JC.

JUSTICE SOCIETY OF AMERICA
DC: *8-issue limited series 1991, 10 issues 1992–1993*

The 1991 series is set in 1950, towards the end of the JSA's original run in *All-Star Comics*, and is a real treat for ageing nostalgists everywhere. The team's immortal enemy Vandal Savage sets out to forcibly regress the world to the Bronze Age, eliminating the 'blights of modern life', which include electricity, atomic power and – gasp! – television. The artistic tag team of Parobeck, Burchett, Artis and Miehm evokes the style of the 1940s stories with a modern vitality, and Len Strazewski reveals a previously unsuspected skill and finesse in plotting and characterisation. Critical and commercial support for the series was such that an ongoing contemporary JSA series was launched. Strazewski returned as a writer and the late Mike Parobeck became sole artist. The series intelligently and unflinchingly addressed issues many readers had raised, such as whether the heroic ethos of the JSA was outdated or if a group of (on average) septuagenarian superheroes could be effective. It was also a big, splashy, witty adventure deftly put together, and the finest hour for both Strazewski and Parobeck. Although selling adequately, the title was cancelled when the powers that be decided that kids didn't want to read stories about old guys, and the JSA were more or less irrevocably destroyed in *Zero Hour* – a decision that reveals a contemptible attitude towards characters, and readers, over the age of 30.~HS

Last Days of the JUSTICE SOCIETY OF AMERICA
DC: *One-shot 1986*

Allegedly under instructions to eliminate the venerable Justice Society of America from continuity, writer Roy Thomas, rather than simply killing them, created this contrived affair. In order to stop a rip in time from eliminating All There Is (what, again?), the JSA-ers sacrifice themselves to an eternal limbo of fighting the battle of Ragnarok over and over again, forever (or at least until DC relents and wants them back). Lame, but at least his heart was in the right place.~HS

JUSTY
Viz: *9 issues 1988–1989*

Tsuguo Okazaki's sparse artwork, with its emphasis on facial expression and character, is what defines the quality of this Manga. Justy is an agent of the Galactic Patrol with super-psi powers. With his sister Jerna and companion Lieutenant Trever, Justy must fight pirates and renegade espers. Not first-class but well worth reading.~NF

KABUKI

Caliber: *One shot ('Fear The Reaper') 1994, 6 issue miniseries ('Circle Of Blood') 1994, one-shot ('Colour Gallery') 1994*
London Night Studios: *1 issue ('Dance Of Death') 1995*

A future Japan is bursting with criminal types following the Communist takeover of Hong Kong and the invasion of the Triads. The Noh is a secret government organisation dealing with gangster excesses and government corruption by turn, to keep the country's delicate economy in balance. It's run by an aged general who's officially dead, and staffed with shapely female operators, chief among these his own granddaughter, Kabuki, who kills mercilessly with a pair of scythes.

After introducing the character in 'Fear The Reaper', writer/artist David Mack settles down to the extremely serious business of recording her origin and epic fight with her father, the old general's Yakuza son, in 'Circle Of Blood'. The innumerable repetitions in the story, which begins with an origin tale better dealt with in eight pages rather than a whole issue, are no doubt intended to give it an epic feel, but are merely tedious. Mack has a lot of story-telling quirks that make the story's pacing jerky, and a number of drawing quirks which also stand in the way of your enjoyment. The strangest is his habit of putting lingerie-catalogue-style shots of the various agents posing with their weapons where you'd expect to see them slicing and dicing, while they describe what they've done to the various villains. Altogether there are far too many stiff splash pages and 'symbolic' full-page layouts with 1970s-style floating heads and images melting into each other. It's like looking at Paul Gulacy circa *Sabre* being advised by Steranko on particularly 'trippy' pages. Although well researched, the drama in *Kabuki* has too many moments of bathos to be affecting, and the violence is too controlled to be disturbing.~FJ

KAFKA

Renegade: *6-issue miniseries 1987*

A modern thriller, *Kafka* is an ambitious work with experimental elements to both story and art. Steven T. Seagle's script is full of silences and

gaps that need attention and Stefano Gaudiano's art-style owes much to Hugo Pratt, and though expressive is somewhat uncontrolled and inexperienced. The story concerns a criminal who undergoes experimental treatment at the hands of the CIA before being given a new identity after testifying against some terrorists. Overall, a well-written, thoughtful attempt to bring European sensibilities to American comics.~NF

KAKTUS VALLEY

Fantagraphics: *1 issue 1990*

Bizarre and quite frankly rather poor collection of material from people who could do much better. The intention appears to have been to produce a comic for children, but it's doubtful children came near this, and those who did surely wouldn't like the scratchy artwork from the two most notable contributors, Gary Panter and Mark Beyer.~WJ

KAMANDI

DC: *59 issues 1972–1978, 6-issue miniseries 1993*

This was Jack Kirby's most successful series for DC. He'd moved there amid great fanfare in the early 1970s, having made the largest contribution to the foundations for Marvel's lasting success. He immediately set to work on a grand saga encompassing four titles. Within two years every portion was cancelled or neutered, yet this, the simplest of his titles, outlasted everything else he created for DC by some considerable distance.

An unspecified great disaster (known as The Great Disaster) had rendered Earth a barren wasteland. In introducing this concept Kirby went one better than *The Planet Of The Apes* and bestowed sentience on a selection of the animals still populating the world. Others were mutated into huge and frightening versions of their previous forms. Most humans have been reduced to the state of animals, with Kamandi apparently the sole human to retain his intellect. This is due to his avoiding all tradition through having being raised in a bunker, Command D, from which he also derived his name. He wanders the globe, usually with a trio of mutated humans, including the dog-like Ben Boxer, encountering different mutated animals. There's the possibility of danger with every step, and Kirby's inventive mind creates an astounding array of life-threatening situations. While it goes without saying that Kirby supplies a fine portion of action (at an unusually frenetic pace) the old master is surprisingly adept at conveying the tender and wistful moments, making Kamandi more than just another fantasy comic. Kirby drags the reader along from adventure to adventure, with simple plots – like helping an intelligent dolphin across land to water (21) – taking an issue once Kirby has unleashed the assorted menaces. Mood is an important factor, as is mystery, with Kirby only dropping the first hints as to what The Great Disaster was in 16.

Kirby left the series with 40 and the tradition was adequately maintained by Gerry Conway and Chic Stone. Towards the end of his run Kirby seemed to be losing interest, providing skimpier and skimpier plots, and Conway beefed up the stories. Another of Kirby's creations, Omac, dropped by in 50, but Kamandi's unlikely saviour was writer Jack C. Harris. Harris took over the series with 52 and proceeded to raise it to its pinnacle. Many have tried, but few creators have managed to better a Kirby idea at DC, but Harris's plotting was excellent, and the art of Dick Ayers and Alfredo Alcala matched the plots. Harris even introduced a subtle humour to *Kamandi* in the form of dog versions of Sherlock Holmes and Dr Watson. The title was cancelled during a period of major cutbacks during 1978, and was certainly one of the sadder losses.

Kamandi was revived in 1993, bearing, in the new continuity-conscious atmosphere, an 'Elseworlds' label, thus indicating it wasn't to be considered part of the now rigid DC company-wide continuity. Writer Tom Veitch takes Kirby's disaster concept one step further and elaborates on his plots, giving Kamandi a possible origin (remember the 'Elseworlds' label). He's raised by a cybernetic mother, then sent on a quest to find the person responsible for the devastated Earth, Superman. On his journey he engages some unlikely allies and is pursued by Ben Boxer, no longer a friend, and his bio-mechs. It's a decent stab at the post-holocaust Earth, nicely illustrated by Frank Gomez and Mike Barriero, and the saga is continued in the *Superman At Earth's End* one-shot.~HY
Recommended: 1–6, 12–16, 21–23, 26–29, 52–59

The Legend Of KAMUI
Eclipse: *38 issues, 1987–1990*

A translation of Sanpei Shirato's ninja epic. Avenging sons, copyright wrangles over sword-techniques, and constantly shifting alliances. Many solemn quotes along the 'War is hell' line, yet it's a restful issue if the count of

severed limbs and heads is below twenty. It obviously has its fans, mostly martial arts enthusiasts to judge by the letter column, but the general reader is likely to find it unrewarding.~FC

KANE
Dancing Elephant: *14 issues + 1993 to date*

Paul Grist's self-published detective comic is a class act. The story opens with the eponymous detective Kane returning to duty after the investigation of his killing a corrupt partner. Amid a climate of ill-feeling the abrupt, confrontational detective makes no attempt to regain the confidence of his disgruntled colleagues, instead plunging into his work with near-maniacal fervour.

The comic ably combines ongoing plot-lines with satisfying individual cases as it slowly builds up a picture of life in the imaginary city of New Eden. The atmosphere is reminiscent of *Hill Street Blues*, as brutal murders are mixed with absurd criminal activities, including the superb silent-chase sequence in 5 as Kane's young partner Page hunts a man in a pink bunny suit. Grist develops character slowly within the main thrust of the story-line, rarely showing scenes outside the world of work. His sharp, minimal black and white artwork echoes Kane's brutal world-view. Keep your wits about you when reading: Grist uses some clever tricks to indicate flashbacks, fantasies and different narrators, which have befuddled people trying to skim through.~FJ
Recommended: 5, 6
Collection: Kane (1–4)

KAOS MOON
Caliber: *1 issue + 1996 to date*

David Boller's very appealing clean and detailed art is the highlight, but by no means the sole virtue of this story about a psychic investigator, Katja Zakov. She's inhabited by inner personalities who project an astral protector, Kaos Moon, and is investigating the disappearance of odd skulls. There's a wealth of background about the cast in text features, enabling plenty of interesting stories to come. *Kaos Moon* should appeal to the *X-Files* audience, and Boller is a name to watch out for.~FP

KAPTAIN KEEN And Kompany
Vortex: *6 issues 1986–1988*

Bill White's Kaptain Keen is an impossibly large-jawed, clean-cut, generic superhero accompanied by a silent moose sidekick in an alternate version of Bullwinkle and Dudley Doright. It's the 'and Kompany' bit of the title that's the better strip, though, with Gary Fields' cigar-smoking, heavy-drinking and copiously swearing porcine superhero Superswine raising more smiles. White and Fields are both talented cartoonists, but it's chuckles and grins to be found here rather than belly laughs. Superswine later had his own title.~FP

KARATE KID
DC: *12 issues 1976–1978*

Strange attempt to cash-in on the mid-1970s kung fu craze. Legion of Super-Heroes martial arts master Karate Kid becomes insecure with his role as a 'normal' human among superhumans (some of whom were the likes of Bouncing Boy and Matter-Eater Lad!) and exiles himself to the primitive 20th century to 'find' himself. Regular LSH scribe Paul Levitz set up the first issue, then fled, leaving the next nine to the presumably pseudonymous Barry Jameson, and Ric Estrada's scratchy artwork hindered the first eleven issues. With 12 a new team made a conscientious attempt at a new direction, but it was too late. Immediate plot threads were cleared up in *Kamandi* 58, and long-term story-lines were tied up in *The Brave And The Bold* 199.~HS

KATO
Now: *4-issue miniseries 1991–1992, 2-issue microseries 1992*

Green Hornet's companion steps out for some solo outings. In the Now continuity, this is the 1960s Kato, who made a series of Hong Kong action movies (in a nod to Bruce Lee, who portrayed the character on TV) after his American escapades. It's now the 1990s, and Mike Baron writes both series. The first takes Kato back to China where the monastery at which he was taught is under fire from government troops, and the second has him playing bodyguard to an obnoxious rock star under threat of assassination. Both are standard action adventure, with the more compact Val Mayerik-drawn second series, titled *Kato II*, better than the first tale, drawn by Brent Anderson.~WJ

KATY KEENE
Archie: *62 issues, 6 annuals 1949–1961*
Red Circle: *33 issues, 1 special 1983–1990*

Subtitled 'The pin-up Queen', brunette model and actress Katy was created by Bill Woggon as a back-up for the Archie title *Wilbur* in 1945. Identical to any number of other leggy-girl comedy strips, her gimmick of reader participation catapulted her to stardom and numerous spin-off titles. Readers submitted their suggestions for costumes in the hope of seeing their names in print, designs arrived by the sackful, and Katy Keene has been imitated by hundreds of girl-targeted strips since. Woggon's ornate and decorative art style apart, Katy's stories had little to offer, being very lightweight romantic comedies in which

she was squired by a succession of doll-like boy-friends. The occasional twist was Katy's chubby, bespectacled sister throwing a spanner in the works. Yup, Katy made *Millie The Model* read like Chekhov in comparison.

Unlike other girl strips, Katy never made even a token concession to the passing years. Her style remained resolutely 1946 right until the bitter end. Her fans knew what they liked, though, and they liked it a lot. Most of the time you could hardly follow the story for captions crediting 'contributing designers'. Under the Red Circle imprint Archie tried to update Katy for the 1980s, but despite some gorgeous artwork from Barb Rausch (a first-generation Katy fan) the series didn't gel. Reverting to reprints of the classic material with the occasional new strip, the title enjoyed a moderately successful run.~HS

KA-ZAR the Savage
Marvel: *Series one 3 issues 1970–1971, Series two 20 issues 1974–1977, Series three 34 issues 1981–1984*

Not only did Marvel have three goes at a title starring their blond, low-rent Tarzan and his pet sabre-tooth Zabu, he also starred in the first twenty issues of *Astonishing Tales*. First time around the series reprinted Ka-Zar stories (pronounced Kay-sar, true believers) from the original *X-Men* and early issues of *Daredevil*, including a run-in with Spider-Man. Yes, Ka-Zar was one of the many lame-brains J. Jonah Jameson persuaded to beat up the wall-crawler. There are also all new back-ups featuring Hercules (1) and the Angel (2–3).

The second series, set in Ka-Zar's Antarctic jungle home The Savage Land, suffered from an ever-shifting creative rollcall, after a less than distinguished start under Don Heck. John Buscema and a selection of inkers turned him into a peroxide Conan, and Russ Heath drew beautiful scenery but uninspired action in issue 8. At the end of the run Doug Moench made efforts to involve readers in a multi-issue plot more complex than the usual 'wizard sets monster on Ka-Zar, Ka-Zar kills monster' fare audiences had been suffering, aided by Val Mayerick's sensitive but warty artwork. Mayerick looked much more at home in the 'Tales of Zabu' backup in the third series, where he hardly drew any human beings. The title was cancelled mid-fight with issue 20, the story-line being finished off as a footnote when the X-Men visit the Savage Land in issue 114 of their own title.

When reviving Kazar yet again, third-series writer Bruce Jones swiftly introduced new characters and a new origin for the Savage Land, and lost the hyphen. Most significantly, however, he had Kazar act like a grown-up. You know something's good when 1 opens with the

muscular Lord Plunder questioning the point of his existence. Jones develops the plot swiftly but the many fights and revelations are merely dressing for the stormy and very adult relationship that springs up between Kazar and his sometime companion Shanna the She Devil. With Brent Anderson handling the pencils and co-plotting for the first fifteen issues, including an epic Dante's Inferno story-line, Kazar enjoyed a golden period. With issue 16 Ron Frenz took over and, while entertaining and often whimsical, the stories thereafter were never quite so involving, no matter how much Jones tried to wring the readers' hearts as Kazar and Shanna suffered trauma after trauma.~FJ
Recommended: Series three 2, 10–12

KELVIN MACE
Vortex: *2 issues 1985–1986*

Irresponsible and violent P.I. played deadpan by Ty Templeton and Klaus Schoenefeld, but loaded with gags. Schoenefeld was an excellent artist, but died before a third issue.~FP

KEYHOLE
Millennium: *2 issues + 1996 to date*

Interesting mix of travelogue, autobiography, observation and a daft superhero from Dean Haspiel and Josh Neufeld. Both are improving artists and their combined broad tastes ensure this selection is worth a look.~WJ

KICKERS, INC.
Marvel: *12 issues 1986–1987*

An intensifier process gives four members of a football team (plus one spouse) increased strength. They decide to use their powers for good by setting up a foundation (with tax-exempt status, natch) and thus Kickers, Inc. is born. Various assignments come through the foundation, mixed in with football games and politics, and it's all thoroughly boring and pointless. The creative team kept changing from issue to issue, but none of them managed to breathe life into the idea.~FC

KID BLASTOFF
Slave Labor: *One-shot 1996*

Very basic adventure about a dumb jock chosen to be a superhero and the smart girl who keeps getting him out of trouble when he realises there's more to it than looking good in tights. By Evan Dorkin and Sarah Dyer, this untaxing stuff originally appeared in *Disney Adventures* the year before.~FJ

Western Action Starring
KID CODY and The COMANCHE KID
Atlas: *1 issue 1975*

A cliché-ridden story starring Kid Cody, Gunfighter, was backed up by an equally fatuous tale of the Commanche Kid, a white boy brought up by Comanches. Both featured prominently on Atlas' house ads, but such was their lack of appeal they only ever appeared the once. 'Comics Are Entertainment,' proclaimed those ads. This wasn't, despite Doug Wildey art on the lead.~APS

KID COLT, Outlaw
Marvel: *229 issues, 3 Giant-Size 1948–1979*

Western genre strip. Kid Colt killed a man in self-defence in his youth and fled in panic, thus becoming an outlaw. The series is littered with every Western cliché imaginable, with particular emphasis on 'dead shot' bad guys who suddenly cannot hit the broadside of a barn whenever Kid Colt walks into the sights. From 140 onwards, almost all issues reprint earlier material.~APS

KID ETERNITY
DC: *3-issue miniseries 1991*
Vertigo: *16 issues, 1993–1994*

The original Kid Eternity was an adolescent boy who could conjure up historic figures by shouting the word 'Eternity' and was accompanied by a benign old spirit called Mr Keeper. His adventures were whimsical fun, light and innocent, making him, therefore, prime material for the late 1980s trend at DC to recreate any character they could as a grimmer, grittier, more horrible version of the old. Kid Eternity fared better than some. The miniseries, written by Grant Morrison and drawn by Duncan Fegredo, keeps the character's origin – taken to heaven by mistake, sent back to Earth with fantastic powers to compensate – more or less intact, except that it wasn't heaven he was taken to but hell, and the historical figures he summoned were actually demons (as was Mr Keeper) who just thought they were olden-days heroes. At the start of the miniseries, he's been trapped in hell for the last thirty years (as a result of which he's grown his hair, started wearing dark glasses and swears a lot) and enlists the help of a drunken and dying stand-up comedian to accompany him to hell, free Mr Keeper and set the world to Karmic rights by breeding the next generation of 'ascended children'. In other words, it's pretentious twaddle, though no worse that most Vertigo. It's better, though, than the continuing series by Ann Nocenti, largely drawn by Sean Phillips, which just tries to be pretentious, falls far short of the mark and doesn't even have the advantage of being nicely drawn. Do yourself a favour and stay well away.~JC

KID'N'PLAY
Marvel: *9 issues 1992*

Rappers Kid'n'Play star in a retelling of their rise to stardom written as if a TV sit-com. Sharply observed by Dwight Coye, with pleasing art from Chuck Frazier and Ron Boyd, it's very much a timepiece, though. Look back in 2002 to laugh at the hilariously outmoded street talk, styles and behaviour. Issue 2's morality play rather disturbingly equates dope and alcohol with the road to perdition.~FP

KILGORE
Renegade: 4 issues 1987

The idea of taking Sgt Bilko, planting him in World War II, restoring his hair and adding a Ronald Colman-style mustache is a pointless one, and Kilgore never develops enough character to progress from it. The concept is so obviously appropriated, and it falls way short of the material that inspired it, although there's a commendable variety of stories within the setting. Kilgore as army wheeler-dealer works best in 2's Hollywood sequences, although the best issue is 4, heavily Bogart-influenced and less dependent on Kilgore's character.~WJ

KILLER
Eclipse: One-shot 1985

Collecting some of Tim Truman's pre-Grimjack work, Killer contains two stories produced for gaming magazines and one collaboration with the legendary Gardner Fox. The latter is a red-blooded sword-and-sorcery adventure with monsters and beautiful women in distress. For Truman completists only.~NF

KILLER FLY
Slave Labor: 3-issue miniseries 1995

A dwarf clown in an unknown and, one suspects, unknowable circus falls in love with the violent knife-thrower's wife and tries to save her from her husband by spiriting her away, with the help of a mild-seeming boy who, when angered, turns into a giant fly. However, this unlikely trio soon discover that the freedom offered by escaping from a world in which they're reduced to ciphers is transient. It sounds preposterous, but this story has more in common with David Lynch at his strangest (and indeed Moebius' partner in crime Jodorowsky) than many comics one could name. Chris Butler writes with a fierce intensity and rare understanding of human nature. Artist Chris Hogg matches him frame for frame with bold, twisted graphics. An excellent combination: Angela Carter meets José Muñoz.~FJ
Recommended: 1–3

KILLING STROKE
Eternity: 4 issues 1991

A black and white anthology comic, presumptuously subtitled 'The Best In New British Horror'. Did anyone else call it that? 'A younger generation trying to break into the field' would be a fairer description. It started life

as a self-published fanzine by Shane Oakley and friends. Vampires, serial killers, suicide and gore abound. Mark Buckingham contributes a striking cover painting to 1, but the best content is in 3: Matt 'D'Israeli' Brooker's 'Floppity Bunny' story, which brings some much needed humour to the proceedings.~GL

KILLPOWER, The Early Years
Marvel UK: 4-issue miniseries 1993

The none-too-smart muscle-bound hitman and Genetix rumble back and forth through past and future, encountering Pharaoh Rama Tut, the Punisher and a mutant-populated wasteland. Pointless stuff.~WJ

THE KINDRED
Image: 4-issue miniseries 1994

Back in the days when Team 7 was a story still waiting to be told, this miniseries reunited three of the surviving members (Lynch, Grifter and Backlash) and was produced by Jim Lee, Brandon Choi, Brett Booth and Sean Ruffner – a WildStorm hall of fame roll-call. Jack Lynch and Alicia Turner are kidnapped by a mysterious group calling themselves The Kindred and Backlash is recruited to rescue them, with Grifter tagging along for the ride. The trail leads to Caballito, an island populated by evolved sentient animals, The Kindred, who were created as a result of test trials for the Gen-factor, the source of Team 7's powers. The creatures want revenge for the way they have been treated, and the team are left to fight their way free. Not as good as the real Team 7 stories which followed, but it was, at the time, a welcome taster and a competent action tale.~JC

KING LEONARDO and His Short Subjects
Dell: 3 one-shots 1961–1962
Gold Key: 4 issues 1962–1963

Based on a TV cartoon that ran between 1960 and 1962, invented by Mandrake artist Fred Fredericks, the Dell one-shots have no number and are issues of their ongoing Four Color series. Leonardo is a lion who is also the amiable monarch of the cartoon kingdom of Bongo Congo. He and his aide, a skunk named Odie Cologne, have their hands full with Biggie Rat's constant plots to dethrone Leo and replace him with his rather dim brother Itchy. Charming and witty, it's truly a cartoon strip among cartoon strips.~SW

THE KING OF PERSIA
Accordian Press: One-shot 1996

Bizarre fairy tale book by Walt Holcombe. The King Of Persia (the most un-regal being imaginable) falls in love, but his true love falls ill. To cure her he must obtain an emerald from a secret land and so on. Holcombe's cartooning is delightful and expressive and there's a joy in the incongruous whimsical elements he includes in his panels. Overall, though, the seemingly stream-of-consciousness nature of the story renders it too quirky.~WJ

KINGDOM COME
DC: *4-issue miniseries 1996*

Approximately twenty years into the future of the DC Universe, the world is a much bleaker place. Superman has turned his back on the human race to live in seclusion, and most of his generation of heroes followed his example and retired. But the new generation of 'heroes' is an ever-increasing threat to the survival of the world. Largely deprived of opposition, the surviving villains having retired or fled; they spend their days in violent conflict with each other, heedless of the harm done to civilians. When one such incident causes a nuclear accident that wipes out the state of Kansas, Wonder Woman forces Superman to emerge from retirement and lead the older heroes against their own rebellious offspring. This is not a simple battle of the generations, though; Wonder Woman has her own agenda, of which Superman is unaware, and Batman may get caught in the crossfire between them. Astonishingly, this fully painted series lived up to much of the hype. Mark Waid's story is complex and intriguing, although sharing many sparking points with the *Squadron Supreme* limited series. The reader is left guessing about characters' motives just long enough, the characterisation of the lead triumvirate is strong, and there are endless fascinating bits of side business and subplots – often expressed wordlessly in the background of panels – achieving a satisfyingly multi-layered feeling. More importantly, one feels genuine shock at some of the final conflict, and the ending doesn't seem anticlimactic, which is the major flaw of so many intended 'blockbusters'. The lavish and detailed artwork by Alex Ross withstands the inevitable comparisons to *Marvels* with credit. *Kingdom Come* knows its limitations: it doesn't aspire to be *Watchmen* or *The Dark Knight Returns*, but is mainstream superheroics, and proud of it. But it's probably one of the finest examples of mainstream superheroics ever.~HS
Recommended: 1–4
Collection: Kingdom Come (1–4 with new prologue and epilogue)

KINGS IN DISGUISE
Kitchen Sink: *6-issue miniseries 1988*

A young teenager runs away from home during the depression of the 1930s intending to find his father. What he finds instead is an education in the company of an eccentric hobo dying of

tuberculosis. Freddie Bloch witnesses the desperation and intolerance of humanity, and the lengths to which those with power will go to protect what they have, however little it might be. Writer James Vance and artist Dan Burr vividly evoke an unhappy period in American history, yet Vance is knowing enough to leaven the unrelenting hardship with comic moments as the naïve Freddie grows into an adult. The collection also includes material from *Dark Horse Presents* 42.~FP
Recommended: 1–6
Collection: Kings in Disguise (1–6)

Robert E. Howard's KINGS OF THE NIGHT
Dark Horse: *2-issue miniseries 1990*

Bran Mak Morn unites the warring British tribes against the Romans by promising they shall be led by an independent king. And guess what, the legendary King of Atlantis (presumably not named because Marvel still have the comics licence for Kull) is pulled through time. And he's just in time for the second issue's big battle. Dull, dull, dull.~WJ

KISS OF DEATH
Acme: *2 issues 1986*

Adaptations of horror stories and some original material, all drawn by John Watkiss in fine contrasting black and white. It's dark and moody stuff, though the writing is occasionally overwrought, and Gene Colan is an obvious artistic influence at times. Originally planned as three issues, a one-shot publication titled *The Last Kiss* concluded matters.~FP

KITCHEN SINK/TUNDRA Graphic Novels

It's not until they're considered as a list in their entirety that one realises that, volume for volume, Kitchen Sink's graphic novels, both originated and acquisitions, match the quality of those from any other publisher one cares to select from around the world. Furthermore, with few exceptions, most notably the inherited *Skin*, each of them is accessible to and suitable for anyone of adolescent age and up. The cornerstones of the line are the works of Will Eisner. A pioneer in popularising the graphic novel (a term he coined) in the USA with *A Contract With God*, over the past twenty years he's continued to produce thought-provoking stories. There are similar themes running throughout his works, most emphatically an optimism about life, the way in which people interact in cities, and a possibly over-sentimental view of the past, but in making a reader care about basically decent human beings he's the Frank Capra of comics. Anyone starting to read Eisner with even one of his lesser works would probably be charmed and captivated. His inordinately expressive artwork shimmers with movement and characterisation, and they're fine starting points for the non-comic-reading public.

Encouragingly, Eisner's best story is his most recent, *Dropsie Avenue*, reworking an idea used to lesser effect in *The Building*, that of taking a metropolitan area and charting its progression over a century. It's as if Eisner was unsatisfied with the previous exercise and decided to correct the faults. Incorporating themes of racism and integration, human greed and urban planning, along the way it also tells some fine stories. It's contrived to push all the right buttons, and the ending ought to bring a lump to the throat of all but the most cynical readers. *The Building* covers very similar territory in a far less satisfactory manner, although it's still immensely readable, due to Eisner's deft characterisation. *A Life Force*, originally serialised in *Will Eisner's Quarterly*, is an even earlier work covering much the same ground, even using Dropsie Avenue as its setting. The incorporation of newspaper clippings and correspondence, and some odd story-telling sequences, render it far less satisfactory. Try most of the others first and come back for *A Life Force. New York* expands the horizons of Eisner's observations beyond a neighbourhood to aspects of the city in the present day. Told largely in one- to three-page, often silent vignettes, with wry punchlines, Eisner's evocations of the minutiae of city life charm and captivate. They're not as satisfying, though, as his longer work. *City People Notebook* utilises previously unpublished research sketches, many of them produced for *New York*, and Eisner works them into short strips. There's the same bittiness, although the art is top-notch.

The Dreamer is a slim autobiographical recollection, detailing the early days of comics in the 1930s. It has an appeal beyond that to comics historians, as Eisner details his early days as a comic artist, from the struggling hopeful to the man ready to make a career jump. He's caustic in detailing the shoddy goings-on, and while the identity of many figures is transparent, there's a level of enjoyment to be had in guessing who others might be. *To The Heart Of The Storm* is similarly autobiographical, but a work of far greater depth. As a young man travels to join the troops in the early days of the USA's involvement in World War II the sights he passes on the train prompt recollections of family history. Very episodic and less sentimental than many of Eisner's other works, it also confronts racism far more overtly than his other material. *Life On Another Planet* was Eisner's second attempt at a graphic novel. Originally serialised in ill-advised

eccentric fashion in Eisner's *Spirit* magazine, it works far better collected. It takes as a theme the first signal from outer space, and the panic and other reactions it engenders. Lacking the subtlety of later work and decidedly trivial in places, it's a contradictory affair by also being far more knowing and darker than any of his other work, and markedly distrustful of authority and big finance.

A Contract With God was Eisner's first graphic novel, originally published in the mid-1978 by Baronet, but now part of Kitchen Sink's line. For a twenty-year-old step into the unknown it remains an affecting and powerful work, although the story-telling is occasionally clumsy and unrefined as Eisner stretches into a new format. It's a snapshot collection, remembered best for the title chapter, but the most affecting chapter is entirely uncharacteristic for Eisner, detailing the downfall of an unpopular and lonely building superintendent in a totally unsentimental fashion. *Invisible People* is a similar look at the lives of individuals, weaving very different but equally compelling stories about three undistinguished individuals faced with a crisis in their lives and the choice they make.

Artist Michael Ploog was heavily influenced by Eisner, so there's an apt coincidence (or possibly not) that he's also published by Kitchen Sink. Ploog's adaptation of Frank Baum's *Life And Adventures Of Santa Claus* is the undoubted artistic highlight of their list. Richly and stunningly rendered, elves, goblins and giants have never looked so appealing. Anyone not charmed by this has no further reason to live. And the same applies to anyone who can't laugh at Harvey Kurtzman's *Jungle Book*. This was originally published in the 1950s, post his editorship of *Mad*; Kurtzman turns an even more venomous pen towards TV detectives, magazine publishing, Westerns and the Southern states, where an ability to read is enough to prompt a lynching. Sadly, his 1980s collaborations with Sarah Downs, *Betsy's Buddies*, collected from *Playboy*, is far less satisfying. Carol Lay's collection *Now Endsville* is a skewed look at life with a strong fantasy element. She has a delightful cartooning style, and the mixture of caprice and observation in the 'Story Minute' is wonderful. In twelve panels, they're short modern fairy-tales, and largely unpredictable to boot. On the extended strips, though, she's not as deft, with the quirky ideas obstructing plots, but not strong enough to compensate. The title story in particular drags long before the end, but 'Invisible City', part ecological fantasy and part whimsy, is far stronger. Lay's second collection is better. There's a larger selection of 'Story Minute' strips, and the title strip, 'Joy Ride', is excellent, hanging on the idea of fat people being able to hire the personality of others to trim their bodies. James Robinson and Phil Elliott's *Illegal Alien* is a charming story concerning a dead American gangster being possessed by an alien, who then travels to Britain to stay with relations of the body he's inhabiting. They're pleased to find him a seemingly reformed character, and he transforms their lives, most particularly that of the adolescent Dino. It's a successful evocation of 1960s Britain that's exciting and suspenseful to boot.

A below-par graphic novel is *The Acid Bath Case*, a mannered and surreal story of people murdered in their bathtubs. The eccentric art of Kellie Strom is ill-matched with Stephen Walsh's writing, which in turn strives too hard to shock and to be different, but seemingly just for the sake of it. Altogether a disappointment, as is Erez Yakin's *Silent City*. It's a series of appallingly muddily printed black and white-toned illustrations telling a preposterously simple story of state brutality. One feels every sympathy for Yakin apparently having to live through such conditions, but this dull narrative doesn't disturb or stimulate in the manner intended. A far better European graphic novel is *Armed And Dangerous*, a sleazy and sweaty 1950s crime thriller from Mezzo and Pirus drawn in an odd hybrid style that combines elements of Charles Burns and Steranko among others. Also dwelling on crime is *Button Man*, an imaginative thriller, written by John Wagner, which concerns a hitman involved in a scheme beyond his previous experience. Wagner is masterful in dragging the reader in to his complexly constructed web, and the photorealist art of Arthur Ranson is astounding.

As Tundra was merged into Kitchen Sink, so were that company's graphic novels. Those bearing the *Heavy Metal* imprint are allocated a separate entry in this book, but more powerful than any of them was *Skin*. It's the story of a thalidomide skinhead. Brutal and offensive, writer Peter Milligan pulls no punches in a passionate script, without salving political correctness. Martin hates the world and decides to extract vengeance on the company responsible for his affliction in the only manner he knows. Artist Brendan McCarthy matches the brutality of the script, creating an escalating mood by forgoing panel borders, and Carol Swain's well-considered colouring is also vital to the atmosphere. Tundra also brought *Hugo Tate*, Nick Abadzis' comics road movie. It's an introspective look at America as Hugo accompanies a gun-toting hard man on a delivery across the USA. His growth as a person is signified by the strange method of an increasingly rendered face, but it's an engrossing and rewarding read. Bo Hampton's

adaptation of the Washington Irving story *The Legend Of Sleepy Hollow* is beautifully painted, but unlikely to thrill anyone today.~FP

Recommended: *A Contract With God, Button Man, The Dreamer, Dropsie Avenue, Hugo Tate, Illegal Alien, Invisible People, Joy Ride, Jungle Book, The Life And Adventures Of Santa Claus, Skin, To The Heart Of The Storm*

KITTY PRIDE & WOLVERINE
Marvel: *6-issue miniseries 1984–1985*

You read a series like this and think 'Who first had the bright idea to employ Al Milgrom as an artist?' Chris Claremont overwrites and Al Milgrom does what we might euphemistically call draw as Kitty Pride discovers her dad's involved with some evil Japanese gangsters. She presumes he's been strong-armed by the Yakuza and is horrified to discover he's actually been voluntarily in cahoots with them all along. Setting off to deal with the matter without the X-Men's help, she's promptly possessed by a demon Ronin called Ogun or, as Wolverine puts it when he's recovered from Ogun's attempt to kill him, 'by magic, or some form of psi-powers, he imprinted his psyche onto yours, created a sort of psychic clone of himself inside your skull'. So now you know. Having failed to drive Ogun out on her own she goes back to the US to enlist Professor X's help, much to Wolvie's disgust. When is it weakness to turn to your friends, and when is it wisdom? Chris knows the answer and he's sure as hell going to make sure we do by the end of this over-emotional nonsense.~FJ

KNIGHTHAWK
Windjammer: *6 issues 1995*

Originally planned as a Continuity title, this shares all the trademarks of that company's titles: superb artwork coupled with unreadable stories. For what it's worth, Knighthawk himself is a sort of cross between Batman and the Angel, but the stories never rise above perfunctory, and the dialogue is quite appalling. This is offset, however, by the breath-taking art of Ernesto Infante (aided by Continuity founder Neal Adams), who manages to combine exquisite figurework with incredible dynamism. Interestingly, Knighthawk's *alter ego* is named after famed romance artist J. Scott Pike. What can it all mean… ?~DAR

KNIGHTMARE
Image: *5 issues 1995*

He was Mafia muscle, but then married and started thinking it was time to get out, at which point his boss sent a hit squad after his family. So now he's made it his life's mission to destroy the Mafia. He knows that it is a mission as insane and deluded as that of Don Quixote, his childhood hero, and in recognition of this he's based his masked costume on medieval armour and named his motorbike after DQ's horse. The Don Quixote theme is well handled by writer Robert Loren Fleming, who manages to introduce some imagination and humanity in the spaces left in Rob Liefeld's plot-lines of Soviet warheads, Yakuza and demons. Still, it's a grisly, blood-spattered read, except for the scene in 3 where a hand is cut off with barely a drop spilled. Now that would have been a story: 'How I made it in the Mafia despite having negative blood pressure.' The artists (too numerous to name) are probably responsible for that particular stupidity, since they never display signs of intelligence elsewhere in the work.~FC

KNIGHTS OF PENDRAGON
Marvel UK: *18 issues 1990–1991*

Building on characters created by Alan Moore and Alan Davis in the ground-breaking Marvel UK comics of the early to mid-1980s, and by Roger Stern and John Byrne in *Captain America* 247–255, Dan Abnett and John Tomlinson attempted to create a very English corner of the Marvel Universe. While Captain Britain and his team-mates were no strangers to adventures culled from ancient British myths, combining the mystical threats with fairly heavy-handed environmental propaganda hindered what had the potential to be a cracker of a series. From the declaration on the inside front cover that the comic was printed on tree-friendly Scangloss paper onwards, the project was a bit too preachy to be fun and too unsophisticated to be taken as serious political comment. In short, it tried too hard to be relevant, ending up as the kind of story teenagers consider profound, but which leaves anyone else gagging.~JC

Operation: KNIGHTSTRIKE
Image: *9 issues 1995–1996*

US supersoldiers battle evil Soviets and sadistic scientists in this lively and jingoistic Rob Liefeld creation, replete with the usual giant guns, muscles and explosions.~GK

KNOCKABOUT
Knockabout: *14 issues 1980–1987*

Knockabout began in modest fashion with an un-numbered British-style equivalent of the American underground anthology. It's long on enthusiasm, but desperately low on structure and plot, a problem affecting all the first half-dozen comic-sized issues. The best of them is 4, published as a fund-raiser for one of Knockabout's sadly all-too-frequent appearances in court under the archaic provisions of Britain's Obscene Publications Act. That Knockabout have won every case doesn't appear to deter the authorities. By 4 Hunt Emerson has developed into an accomplished cartoonist, and his piece lampooning the ridiculous aspects of Britain's obscenity laws is the highlight, despite contributions from Gilbert Shelton, Robert Crumb and S. Clay Wilson. From this point Emerson's pieces throughout the run are delightful, whether dealing with the hapless Max Zillion, saxophone player *extraordinaire*, yet always ripped off, or Calculus Cat, he of the permafixed grin forever plagued by his television. Other notable contributors to early issues include Steve Bell, with the pointed political satire that he's known for, Cliff Harper, also contributing political strips, and Graham 'Pokketz' Higgins, whose excellent art was never quite matched with a decent script. Special mention must go to Mike Matthews, whose disturbing mix of sex and violence was obviously EC-influenced, but which contained material that would make even EC artists blanch. There's no *Knockabout 7 per se*. Another court appearance had necessitated the fundraising *Knockabout Trial Special* in its place. It must be the only publication in which you'll find the precise linework of Brian Bolland and the visceral stylings of Savage Pencil between the same covers. Other notable contributors include Phil Elliott and a text piece from Alan Moore, along with *Knockabout* regulars Steve Bell, Cliff Harper, Mike Matthews, Bob Moulder and the inevitable Hunt Emerson. Despite the good intentions it's very much a hotch-potch, although Pokketz' adaptation of a song, 'Drunken Uncle John', is a pleasant surprise.

With 8 Knockabout became a sixty-four-page large-sized paperback volume, each issue themed, which, one suspects, was conceived to add a needed structure to the comic without actually imposing any editorial interference on the creators. Emerson continued to astound, never more so than with his contribution to 8's theme of 'Hell On Earth'. It's a Max Zillion strip in which Max signs a contract with the devil, including an astonishing four-page sequence detailing the ills of the world today in ghastly, thought-provoking clarity, yet still unmistakably in Emerson's style. There are at least two of his strips every time from 7, almost all gems. 8 contained the last of Bob Moulder's well-researched tales of historical obscurities, always interesting, but out of place in the otherwise humorous content. By 10 *Knockabout* has settled into the formula for the final few volumes. Each volume contains some strips on the volume's theme, a section of classics reprinting old underground strips, part of Max's serialised *Peter Pank* strip (a punk version of *Peter Pan*, an odd idea that soon wears thin), and a section of non-themed comic strips. The latter category always included Emerson, along with a decent selection of Gilbert Shelton spread across all his characters, although the

Freak Brothers and Fat Freddy's Cat dominated. Mike Matthews continued to be an oddball contributor, Pete Rigg's strips hit the right humorous tone and Graham Higgins, whose art became ever better, managed some halfway decent scripts with Jack Alarum, 18th-century footpad, in 12 and 13.

Beyond Emerson and Shelton, the classics portion of every volume is almost always the most interesting. Kim Deitch's weirdness is in 10, there's Dave Sheridan in 11, an all-too- short Greg Irons spotlight in 12, Justin Green in 13, and Ted Richards' Dopin' Dan and 'The Forty Year Old Hippie' in 14. 14 also introduces the bizarre Edika, whose story of domestic strife is certainly unique. Beyond 14 Knockabout continued themed volumes, but issued them instead as collections. See below.~FP
Recommended: 8, 12–14

KNOCKABOUT Graphic Novels And Collections

Knockabout is a much loved British institution, having distributed underground comics in Britain since the early 1970s, and followed through with a publishing programme since 1980. Most of their book publications also have a Crack Editions logo on the front cover and spine. The majority of their original graphic novels are the work of Hunt Emerson, and rightly so. Due perhaps to an exaggerated bigfoot cartooning style he doesn't receive recognition commensurate with his talent, and should be revered as a national treasure. *The Big Book Of Everything* collects Emerson's work from his earliest days in arts-collective publications to the assured and confident early-1980s strips for *Knockabout* (the only work anyone really needs from those issues). As well as detailing his progress over ten years, it's also hilariously funny, and would be recommended were it not for a later collection, *Rapid Reflexes*, which is even better. By the early 1980s Emerson had reached the point where he would confidently lay down the most amazing and imaginative pages seen from a British comic artist since Ken Reid's 1960s heyday. His writing had developed to such an extent that almost every panel is a gag instead of leading up to one, although *Rapid Reflexes* also contains collaborations, and was more structured than previously. There's also a *Calculus Cat* volume and *Jazz Funnies*, collecting the downbeat strips starring Max Zillion, saxophonist. The former reworks the same theme (the pernicious influence of television – laudably produced by a man not possessing one) to good effect, but the strips are best sampled individually, as repetition dulls the effect. Max Zillion is a more individual and expressive strip, and also patchier. While some episodes are astounding, particularly that of Max

loosing the demons of hell onto Earth, there's also a fair amount of meandering space-fillers.

Emerson's ability to fill a page with inventive visual gags is even more apparent in his graphic novels. *Casanova's Last Stand* is his best. From the *double entendre* title to the final expiration it's excellent. It's based in part on Casanova's memoirs: the great lover is recounting past exploits as he plots one final grand seduction. There's both sympathy and relish to the fore in the graphic-novel equivalent of the British seaside-postcard tradition. The version of *The Rime Of The Ancient Mariner* reproduces the Coleridge poem exactly, accompanied by Emerson's visual interpretations and asides. It's his only colour work, and the influence of *Krazy Kat* is greater here than elsewhere, but one wonders at the appeal of the poem today, even as depicted by Emerson. One suspects the choice of *Lady Chatterley's Lover* as Emerson's first graphic novel was not without a nod to the travails of his publisher, often in court on obscenity charges (and always acquitted). It's excellent, populated with an extraordinarily characterised cast and plenty of jokes, and Emerson manages to make a largely tedious novel (despite its notoriety) immensely readable. He also illustrates *Hard To Swallow*, the stand-up comedy routines of John Dowie, but it's an awkward mix, with the patter devoid of the personality live delivery offers and unsteadily fused to the art.

Outrageous Tales From The Old Testament was a side-swipe at Knockabout's court cases, highlighting the number of astounding, intolerant, violent and possibly obscene stories to be found in the Bible. Knockabout regulars Emerson, Rigg, and a stellar cast including Dave Gibbons (on a decidedly unsalacious Sodom and Gomorrah), Dave McKean, Kim Deitch, and combinations of Alan Moore and Hunt Emerson, and Neil Gaiman and Mike Matthews (whose scenes of carnage and degradation have to be seen to be believed) participate. Graham Higgins turns in a nice Samson, and overall it's a good chuckle, but it's not as amusing as the title might suggest, and overall one is left disappointed. Sticking with a biblical theme, *Seven Deadly Sins* is just that, each one rendered as a tale, lovingly illustrated in comedic fashion. Emerson, Gaiman, Steve Gibson, Higgins, Matthews and Moore return, joined by Dave Gibbons, Lew Stringer and Bryan Talbot for the best of Knockabout's collections. The pairings of creators is imaginative – each makes an effort – and there are few duff pages. Attention should be drawn to Jeremy Banks and Davy Francis' 'Anger'. Both are top cartoonists, consistently producing very funny material, and neither receives the recognition they are due. Again, a tenuous thread connects to the following Knockabout collection, *Seven Ages Of Women*. It's a book issued to make the point that women cartoonists are marginalised, and there are plenty of talented female comic creators without a regular outlet for their work. There's no denying each of the contributors is a talented artist, but there's more to comics, and the cluttered layouts and story-telling of several are potentially off-putting when some editing might have made for a still better package. That said, on balance *Seven Ages Of Women* hits the mark, with 'The Lover' by Julie Hollings, and Jackie Smith's 'Old Age', being standouts.

Finally there's *Thrrp!* Oh dear. Leo Baxendale is a British comics legend, to British humour comics of the 1950s and 1960s what Jack Kirby was to American superhero comics of the same era, having revitalised them. Sadly, Baxendale suffered similarly from exploitation, and while it's assumed that the terms of a secret out-of-court agreement granted him some restitution for characters still appearing and now much merchandised, it can't have compensated for several decades of wait. He'd continued producing innovative children's strips throughout the 1960s and 1970s, his style metamorphosing all the time. By the late 1980s it had evolved to the point where Baxendale was drawing astonishing amorphous figures that almost wobbled on the page. Sadly, the writing was little more than a series of fart jokes extended over forty-eight pages. Whether he was making a point, or had lost the plot, *Thrrp!* was a decidedly unsatisfactory read. One Fat Freddy's Cat volume was also produced, and several Fabulous Furry Brothers collections, all dealt with under individual entries.~FP
Recommended: *Casanova's Last Stand, Lady Chatterley's Lover, Rapid Reflexes, Seven Deadly Sins*

KNUCKLES THE MALEVOLENT NUN
Fantagraphics: *2 issues 1991*

Knuckles graduated to her own short-lived title in 1991. Cornelius Stone and Roger Langridge's sacrilegious humour relies on surreal *non-sequiturs* and notes in the margins, peaking with outrageous outbursts of slapstick violence. The shorter pieces, haunting in their insanity, work best. The ongoing story-line, in which Knuckles' guardian angel (a penguin) and her pet fly attempt to rescue her from hell with the help of a hippy Jesus, strains the humour in places. If you like your fun cerebral but zany, get to know 'God's hand-grenade'.~FJ

KOBALT
Milestone: *16 issues 1994–1995*

For years, the non-powered vigilante Kobalt has terrorised the lowlife of Dakota City by maintaining a reputation as a 'secret defender'. Naïve young Richard Page daydreams of becoming a superhero. When Richard's dad, trying to scare him out of the idea, cashes in a favour and forces Kobalt to train Richard as an apprentice, hilarious consequences ensue. Or, at least they might have. But mostly not. Writer John Rozum never really develops Kobalt beyond the 'grim avenger' stereotype, and his current and former sidekicks, whether idealistic (Page), amorous (Clover), or twisted and homicidal (Harvest), are all more interesting than he is. Arvell Jones illustrates, competently but not in a manner to make one's pulse race with excitement. A stellar exception is issue 7, guest-illustrated by Jamal Igle, focusing on Page's adventures at high school – the same one Static attends – when a situation develops which demands the attention of both young heroes. Funny and astute, it makes you rather less appreciative of the rest of the run than you might have been. The series' end coincides with the end of both Kobalt and Page's heroic careers. They are operating out of their depth, and in an unexpectedly realistic conclusion to the book, that fact is brought brutally home to them.~HS
Recommended: 7

KOBRA
DC: *7 issues 1976–1977*

An interesting series about Siamese twins surgically separated at birth. One grew up to be a nice young man, but the other, Kobra, became leader of the evil cult that raised him back when evil cults in comics weren't a dime a dozen. Originated by Jack Kirby and carried through confidently by Martin Pasko, the plot-line naturally concentrated on the brothers opposing each other. An unexpected twist actually had the good brother dying! The saga continued in *5 Star Super-Hero Spectacular*, and Kobra has been a recurring DC villain since.~HY

KONA, Monarch Of Monster Isle
Dell: *21 issues 1962–1967*

Monster Isle is situated in a cavern beneath the sea bed, and contains a wide and varied form of indigenous wildlife, from giant insects to giant animals. Kona, cock of the yard, has his hands full protecting a group of adventurers from the isle's inhabitants. Giant insects and animals were the theme as further strange creatures turned up when the crew abandoned Monster Isle for the surface world. Sam Glanzman drew this bizarre series, and the oddly-written early issues are out-and-out tracts of survival philosophy for the most part. An acquired taste, with the early issues being the best.~SW

KONG

DC: *5 issues 1975–1976*

Along with DC's fantasy line came this attempt to upgrade the image of boring old caveman stories. This blond caveman's strip is only noteworthy for Alfredo Alcala's nice art, the stories never daring to rise above run of the mill.~FP

KONGA

Charlton: *23 issues 1960–1965*

Giant rampaging-ape comics. Steve Ditko adapts the 1961 movie for the first issue, in which nutty science transforms a chimp into a giant gorilla, and continues the good mindless fun until 16. Thereafter it's the appallingly lack-lustre efforts of Montes and Bache that see the title to cancellation.~WJ

Edgar Rice Burroughs KORAK, Son Of Tarzan

DC: *14 issues (46–59) 1972–1975*

Inherited from Gold Key, and continuing their numbering, there seemed to be a genuine pride at DC in ensuring that this licensed title showed up its ordinary predecessors (although the very early Russ Manning-created issues had been noteworthy). Editor Joe Kubert and writer Robert Kanigher deliberately differentiated *Korak* from their *Tarzan* work by adding a fantasy element to the stories, and it worked, as did Korak's 'origin' in 49. 46 has some nice Frank Thorne art, and Murphy Anderson drew a lovely Korak in 52–56, but later issues by Rudy Florese don't quite match them. The back-up strips were also well conceived and excellently executed, particularly the Carson Of Venus feature by Len Wein and Mike Kaluta in 46–56. The title changed to *Tarzan Family* with 60, and Korak continued there.~HY
Recommended: 46–56

KRAZY KAT

Eclipse/Turtle Island Foundation: *9 volumes 1988–1992*
Remco: *2 volumes 1990–1991*

Krazy is a cat of ambiguous gender in love with a mouse, Ignatz. Unfortunately Ignatz despises Krazy and expresses this by throwing bricks at his/her head. Krazy in turn interprets this as a sign of Ignatz' love and cannot understand why Officer Pup tries to protect him/her from being hit by locking Ignatz in prison whenever he catches him with a brick.

Beyond this bare-bones situation lies the finest comic strip in existence. Creator George Herriman's skill with pen and word is consistently amazing. His location, Kokonino County, evokes the great American landscapes of the Grand Canyon, Monument Valley and New Mexico, yet there's a surreal element to the whole that creates a constantly shifting 'reality'

where all sorts of odd things can happen. There's a large supporting cast that includes Kolin Kelly (millionaire brick merchant), Gooseberry Sprig (The Duck Duke), Mme Kwakk-Wakk, Joe Stork ('purveyor of progeny to prince and proletariat') and Gonzalo Gopher amongst others, but the basic triangle is always at the heart of each strip.

These volumes concentrate on reprinting the Sunday pages rather than the separate daily continuities, some of which can be found in *Comics Revue Magazine*. Each Eclipse volume includes a whole year's worth of strips, taking us from 1916 to 1924. The Remco volumes (subtitled 'The Komplete Kolor Krazy Kat') cover 1935 to part way through 1937. Remco decided to publish the colour Sundays in hardback editions (prompting a colour section in Eclipse's vol 7) but went out of business before finishing their projected seven volumes. Eclipse, too, had problems (and a rival publisher didn't help them, given that the colour Sundays, which they hadn't reached in continuity, had the greatest commercial potential) and didn't complete their projected series either.

Herriman's Krazy Kat is a constant reminder that comics as a medium can have literary value. His poetry and visionary graphics represent a peak of creativity which, while it has been rivalled, has never been surpassed.~NF
Recommended: Eclipse 1–9, Remco 1–2

KRUSTY Comics

Bongo: *3 issues 1995*

Uncharacteristic lapse into mediocrity from Bongo's *Simpsons*-related line. Krusty is Springfield's surly celebrity TV clown, always on the lookout for a fast buck. In this instance there's the opportunity to build a theme park as cheaply as possible on a nuclear waste dump, with predictable consequences. The plot is thin, the jokes are threadbare and the eccentric layouts dreadful. The title's good, though. Maybe The Levellers can use it.~FP

THE KRYPTON CHRONICLES

DC: *3 issues 1981*

This explored the history of Krypton, using Superman's ancestors as a focal point. Luckily they were all achievers in their chosen fields. Strangely though, the ancestors were dealt with in reverse chronological order, with the first of the El family appearing last in the series. Perhaps a bit confusing, but a must for Superman buffs.~HY

KULL and the Barbarians

Marvel: *3 issues 1975*

Short-lived black and white magazine, launched on the strength of *Savage Sword Of Conan*'s popularity, featuring various characters created by Robert E. Howard. There's Atlantean warrior King Kull, Conan's sometimes paramour Red Sonja, and obsessive Puritan Solomon Kane. Few of the stories, some written by Roy Thomas, others by Doug Moench, often working from Thomas' plots, shine. 1 is a disappointing black and white reprint of *Kull The Conqueror* 1 and is probably the most polished piece on offer. Otherwise the art, by the likes of Tony De Zuniga and Pablo Marcos, looks rushed. Howard Chaykin's work on Red Sonja is loose and spirited, but looks as though it was intended for colour. Better material featuring these characters appeared in *Savage Sword* itself.~FJ

KULL The Conqueror

Marvel: *29 issues 1971–1978, 2-issue miniseries 1982–1983, series two 10 issues 1983–1985*

Kull's the best Robert E. Howard hero after Conan, and God knows every Howard hero or heroine's had their own comic at some point. Set in a pre-Cataclysmic age, Kull's a proto-Conan, driven from his barbarian tribe for an act of weakness. The story starts when he seizes the throne of decadent Valusia in a bloody coup. Unlike Conan, Kull has to stay at home and worry about affairs of state. The main difference, though, is that Kull wears a vest. The first series, written chiefly by Gerry Conway, does little to differentiate between the characters. Kull's always going off to rid his people of some menace, and giant worms, octopodes, were-creatures and evil sorcerers loom large. If you've read all your *Conans* until they're falling to pieces, this is the next logical title, with some tasty, clean art from John and Marie Severin in issues 2–9 and 11. The miniseries is really two specials, one by Alan Zelenetz and John Buscema, the other by Doug Moench and John Bolton. Both writers are determined to make use of Kull's regal position. Zelenetz has him activate a curse while digging the foundations of a new civic centre (his choice of words, not mine), while Moench involves him in a politically expedient marriage and a gang of werewolves. John Bolton adds a delicacy to the art rarely seen since Barry Windsor-Smith's début on *Conan*.

Zelenetz obviously won the toss and gets to write the second series, which attracted richer artistic pickings, including Charles Vess, Bolton and Bill Sienkiewicz. He concentrates on political plots, develops stories around supporting characters, and has Kull spend as much time pondering the uneasy allegiance of his adopted subjects as he does hacking into eldrich monsters. Declining public interest in hefty men in fur boxer shorts killed the title after ten issues.~FJ

Richard Dragon, KUNG FU FIGHTER

DC: *18 issues 1975–1977*

Denny O'Neil's Richard Dragon creation was published far too late to make a good impression with early-1970s martial arts fans. While the series never attained black-belt status, it did get off to a reasonable start with fairly decent stories and art (Jim Starlin 2, Jack Kirby 3, Wally Wood 4–8), but rapidly declined into mediocrity with O'Neil and regular artist Ric Estrada possibly at their worst. Supporting characters included the stereotyped black fighter, Bronze Tiger, who was later redeemed in the excellent *Suicide Squad*, and a female sword-swinging expert Lady Shiva – and she certainly did. Richard Dragon later became a major player in O'Neil's *Question* series.~HY

KURTZMAN KOMIX

Kitchen Sink: *One-shot 1976*

Harvey Kurtzman is one of comics' great stylists, but his genius was expressed in dribs and drabs in late-1940s throwaway comics before it was recognised at EC. This title collects assorted shorts from that period, all drawn in the inimitable Kurtzman gag style. Pot-Shot Pete is an inept sheriff, Sheldon is a one-page feature about a plain nasty tyke. *Hey Look!* experiments with the comics format in often surreal fashion. *The Hey Look!* paperback collects all this material and plenty more besides and is heartily recommended.~FP

Recommended

Collection: Hey Look!

LA PACIFICA

Paradox: *3-issue miniseries 1995*

A pocket-sized-book format mystery novel in three parts. La Pacifica motel is the site of a seemingly mindless mass shooting by a Vietnam vet killed by police on arrival. The only survivor of the massacre is co-owner Don Cooper, and once recovered he finds himself inexplicably compelled to investigate the circumstances of the vet's breakdown. The only lead is a woman, Cameron, who moved to Las Vegas following the massacre. Shortly after Cameron arrives in Vegas events repeat themselves, and she's again involved before moving on. Joel Rose and Amos Poe write a good imitation Hitchcock movie concerning a gradual obsession, including enough well-placed asides to divert the attention. Turkish-born artist Tayyar Ozkan complements a fine script with an astoundingly convincing evocation of the USA, both rural and urban. A very satisfying read.~FP
Recommended: 1–3

LABMAN

Image: *2 issues + 1996 to date*

Based on Rudy Coby's TV series in which he plays the crimefighter/magician *Labman*. 1–2 tell the origin of Labman, including his discovery of four-legged chickens while he's held captive by shapely villainess The Hourglass. Drawn by Andy Suriano like a stylised cartoon, the strips are poorly paced and lack the wit they so desperately strive for.~NF

LABOR FORCE

Blackthorne: *4-issue miniseries 1986–1987*

Released at the height of the black and white comic glut, this execrable title was shoddily written by Greg Swan (who has the cheek to call himself 'a methodical, careful creative talent' in a first-issue text piece), and crudely drawn by future Malibu Ultraverse penciller David Ammerman. Labor Force are a superhero team who operate as a business venture. They have a marketing consultant, and an accountant who watches the team's budget. Rather than use this promising premise as the springboard for a timely satire on 1980s money culture, Swan and Ammerman rush straight into a series of

moronic superhero adventures that would be more at home in an amateur fanzine than in a supposedly professional comic book.~AL

LADY DEATH

Chaos: *3-issue miniseries 1994, 4-issue miniseries ('Between Heaven and Hell') 1995, 4-issue miniseries ('The Odyssey') 1996, 6-issue miniseries ('The Crucible') 1996–1997*

Débuting as Evil Ernie's object of veneration in his series, Lady Death is a pallid personification of the netherworld replete in ludicrous bra, stockings and panties. She resembles nothing as much as an underwear catalogue model, and certainly not the single-minded demoness wanting to eradicate all life on Earth. The first miniseries details how an innocent 15th-century teenager is transformed into Lady Death through the machinations of her father, a man not averse to consorting with demons. It sets the tone for the remainder, full of pitchfork-wielding villagers, burnings at the stake, and ludicrous dialogue bringing to mind nothing more than the typical early-1960s Hammer horror film. That's to rate this drivel too highly, though. In the first series and all sequels, creators Brian Pulido and Steven Hughes deem any but the most basic story superfluous, provided there's plenty of posing and tottering about in fetish gear. The plots for the second, third and fourth series run as follows: Lady Death, seemingly invincible at the start, is brought to near breaking point before summoning the last vestiges of her strength to grasp victory from despair. Hundreds of thousands of presumably contented purchasers who could buy a proper stroke mag for the same price seem happy enough with *Lady Death*, but it's not recommended to anyone with an IQ higher than their shoe size.~FP
Collection: *Between Heaven And Hell* (1–4), *The Reckoning* (first miniseries 1–3)

Neil Gaiman's LADY JUSTICE

Tekno: *11 issues 1995–1996*
Big Entertainment: *9 issues 1996*

The spirit of Justice empowers young women who've been wronged by men (usually with some sort of crime involved) and, while now blindfolded, they exact bloody revenge for these wrongs. In each story-line a new woman becomes Lady Justice. The best thing about this series is the covers, all by Daniel Brereton, who also supplies the final story-line 'Woman About Town' (6–8), the best of the series. What's gone before is rather simplistic and uninvolving and though Brereton really tries to make something of it, by now it's way too late.~NF

LADY RAWHIDE
Topps: *5-issue miniseries 1995–1996, 2 issues + 1996 to date*

An offshoot of *Zorro*, this scantily-clad woman rides around adventuring in a costume that, in real life in the 1800s, would have caused her to be arrested on sight. Mayhew and Palmiotti's artwork is pleasant, and Don McGregor's prose, despite the total lack of any artistic credibility in this project, is as purple as ever. Particularly amusing are his lengthy rationalisations in the text pages as to why he's working on this rubbish in the first place. The miniseries was sufficiently successful to provoke an ongoing series, with art, initially, by the Esteban Maroto studios. Sigh. Aren't most of the readers old enough to purchase real pornography if they need it?~HS

LADY SUPREME
Image: *2 issues 1996*

Having tempted Terry Moore (*Strangers In Paradise*) to write superheroes on the strength of his supposed understanding of female characters, Liefeld lets him loose on *Lady Supreme*. As far as these things go it's an average dopey superhero strip in which Lady Supreme learns that her mother is Glory. They have a good old mother/daughter chat and then do a bit of fighting. Next time Liefeld wants someone who particularly understands women he should remember that about 50% of the world's population are better qualified than Terry Moore.~NF

LAFF-A-LYMPICS
Marvel: *13 issues 1978–1979*

In the late 70s Marvel tried to build a children's line based on the cartoons of the Hanna-Barbera Studios. This was one of the longest running titles, but that's probably because it featured so many cartoon characters rather than because it was any good. The basic premise is to team up lots of familiar characters and have them compete against each other. Scooby Doo, Yogi Bear and Mumbley are the team captains and given that Mumbley's team includes Dread Baron and the Creepleys you know which team's going to cheat but never win. Mark Evanier does his best with the premise but it's tough going.~NF

LAFFIN' GAS
Blackthorne: *12 issues 1986–1987*

Taking a different theme or target each issue, a regular bunch of cartoonists turn in short stories. Beginning in decidedly lack-lustre fashion, the quality curve is upward throughout. Best of the bunch is 10, the anti-censorship issue.~FP

LANCE BARNES: POST NUKE DICK
Epic: *4-issue miniseries 1993*

A variation on the hard-boiled-detective theme sets Lance Barnes in a post-nuclear world, the twist being that he set off the missile that began World War III. Accompanied by his one-legged companion Peg (geddit?), Barnes wanders across the USA encountering the comic remains of humanity. Writer Stefan Petrucha turns in consistently witty dialogue, matched by artist Barry Crain's visual whimsy. The fourth issue, satirising state administration and confronting Barnes, is the best sample.~WJ

LASER ERASER AND PRESSBUTTON
Eclipse: *6 issues 1985–986*

Following on from Eclipse's reprints of the Laser Eraser adventures that appeared in British monthly *Warrior*, this series features new stories of pan-galactic assassination, all written by Steve Moore under the pseudonym Pedro Henry, featuring art from a wide range of British artists. Many of the stories revolve around space-opera clichés such as a mind-parasite invading the Laser Eraser's mind and forcing her to land on the planet, where it's trapped, or the telepathic assassination target who switches Pressbutton's circuits to keep him in a state of constant orgasm, finally defeated with the help of Zirk, a sexually obsessed telepathic blob that floats around on a flying platform. The scripts are quite sharp but rather dated. Towards the end of the series Moore started to work on the lead characters, inserting sexual jealousy into what had previously been portrayed as a light-hearted relationship.

Although Steve Dillon is associated with the strip he only drew the first issue of this series. David Lloyd looks uncomfortable on the second, while Jerry Paris and Garry Leach (who did the covers for 1, 2 and 6) run riot on the alien parasite story in 3. Jim Baikie's 'Twilight World', reprinted from *Warrior*, appears as back-up in the first four issues, and a Cam Kennedy-illustrated tale about Laser Eraser's mum fills up the last two.~FJ

The LAST AMERICAN
Epic: *4-issue miniseries 1990–1991*

The stunning, almost cubist art of Mike McMahon instantly characterises this story of Ulysses S. Pilgrim, put into suspended animation as nuclear war ravages the globe in

1999, and revived twenty years later. Accompanied by three robots, Able, Baker and Charlie, Pilgrim sets out on his quest to discover if anyone else has survived global warfare and if so, how he can contact them. That being the mission, there's little point in a first-issue resolution, resulting in a very bleak series as Pilgrim trundles through a countrywide wasteland in his army vehicle.

Wagner and Grant's writing is unlike anything they've attempted before, being resolutely downbeat, with few humorous touches, one being Charlie's speech-patterns, which stem from over-indulgence in television broadcasts. It contrasts well with Pilgrim's stiff formality and mood swings. Having made a leap into new territory, Wagner and Grant throw the doors open wide, particularly on the fantasy musical sequence in 2, in which a skeletal Uncle Sam leads his fellow skeletons on a song-and-dance tour through devastated New York. Musicals in comics is a trick Wagner and Grant have attempted before with less success, but here it's played to perfection, with McMahon's choreography outstanding. It's tragic, then, that somehow the pages have been printed in the wrong order. McMahon's art throughout almost looks as if he's carved his characters rather than painted them, and the resolutely dark and gloomy palette he uses to indicate the perpetual fall-out cloud covering the USA is masterful. It speaks volumes for the talent of all three that isolation has never looked so splendid.~FP
Recommended: 1–4

The LAST ONE
Vertigo: *6-issue miniseries 1993–1994*

An enigmatic person purporting to be an ancient sorcerer roams the streets of the city, selecting certain of the homeless and the hopeless, and trying to awaken them to the possibilities still open to them. A strangely compelling series, much less woolly than J.M. DeMatteis' usual fare. Yes, there are enigmas here, but you get the impression they're due to planning, rather than incompetent writing, and Dan Sweetman's illustrations have a pleasing luminous quality.~HS

LAUNDRYLAND
Fantagraphics: *4-issue miniseries 1990–1992*

Literally a soap opera, set in and around a laundromat run by the unbelievably cutesy Natalie, Forg and Jeans' mundane miniseries fails to deliver much in the way of humour or human insight. The predictable script isn't helped by Jeans' slapdash artwork and lettering.~AL

LAWDOG
Epic: *10 issues 1993–1994, One-shot 1993*

Lawdog is the comic equivalent of a road movie. It's the title character's journey down the inter-dimensional highway, where he discovers strange towns and alternative realities. Along for the ride is a blonde bimbo who acts as a contrast to the cold, lonely Lawdog. Chuck Dixon turns in a mediocre plot and the Lawdog's origin is so clichéd it reads like a bad soap opera. The saving grace is the talented artwork of Flint Henry, who provides some great layouts, although his grasp of the female anatomy is questionable. *The Law Dog vs Grimrod* (from *Alien Legion*) one-shot is low quality with a dire script. Avoid at all costs.~SS

LAZARUS CHURCHYARD
Tundra: *1 issue 1992*

Warren Ellis' grizzled cyberpunk hero got very few outings. Planned as the first issue of a miniseries, 1 collects together six short stories produced for British adult anthology *Blast!*, but offers no new material. The heavily painted art by D'Israeli is worth a look.~FJ

LEATHER AND LACE
Aircel: *25 issues, 1989–1991*

At a time when his Ripper comic was being lambasted for racism, the loathsome Barry Blair's other 'creative' input was full of unpleasant overtones of paedophilia. Most of the characters, although supposedly adults, resembled pre-pubescent children, usually clad – as the title suggests – in bondage gear and erotic underwear. Issues were sealed in plastic bags, and Blair also produced tamer versions of each issue for news-stand distribution. Guess which version sold best… ~JC

Tales from the LEATHER NUN
Last Gasp: *One-shot 1973*

A great title, that this underground anthology almost inevitably doesn't quite do justice to. Still, it does contain several morally reprehensible tales by the likes of Crumb, Spain and Jaxon, and a very nicely drawn lead story by the under-rated Dave Sheridan.~DAR

LEATHERBOY
Eros: *3-issue miniseries 1994*

Hard-core porn about a gay superhero who somehow manages to be less well drawn, less interesting and less erotic than artist/writer Craig Maynard's slice-of-life strips.~HS

LEAVE IT TO CHANCE
Homage: *4 issues + 1996 to date*

Chance Falconer is the daughter of the world's greatest magic user, and heir-apparent to his power and secrets. The trouble is, her dad doesn't want to know, because it's too

dangerous for a girl. Naturally unenthused by this Neanderthal attitude – although the loss of her mother, and his own human appearance in previous adventures goes some way to excusing Papa Falconer – young Chance goes adventuring on her own initiative. She's soon embroiled with dragons, shamans, goblins and spectres of the night, all standard urban furnishings of her city, as well as the more usual kidnappers and corrupt cops. Old World magic in a big city environment, with humour, charm and wit, *Leave It To Chance* is an engaging *tour de force* from James Robinson, lovingly illustrated by Paul Smith.~HS
Recommended: 1–4
Collection: Leave It To Chance (1–4)

LEFT-FIELD FUNNIES
Apex Novelties: *1 issue 1972*
Cartoonist Booby London's style is taken straight from Segar's *Popeye*, but he applies it to a distinctly hippy style stories of sexual politics, dope and revolution in his Merton strips, occupying half the issue. They're all very dated these days, but the art's great and if you've ever wondered about the sex lives of Popeye's cast this is the nearest you'll get. Fellow contributors Gary Hallgren, Gary King, Willy Murphy and Ted Richards (with a short Dopin' Dan strip) have a knockabout agenda for their material, and it stands up far better, particularly Hallgren's contribution, which is passably Cliff Sterrett in places. The highlight of the issue, though, is Shary Flenniken's delightful 'Trots And Bonnie'. Again influenced by older cartoonists, in this case largely Wilhelm Busch, it's a simple, disjointed, quirky piece. Never mind the stories: scan the art, and you should be delighted.~WJ

THE LEGEND OF MOTHER SARAH
Dark Horse: *8-issue limited series 1995, 7-issue limited series ('City Of The Children') 1996, 9-issue limited series ('City Of Angels') 1996–1997*
Written by Katsuhiro Otomo, and exquisitely drawn by Takumi Nagayasu, this is among the best Manga yet to be translated into English. Humanity has deserted a ruined planet for life in satellites, but some have returned to brave harsh conditions and military rule. Sarah has been separated from her three children, and wanders the desolate planet from isolated community to isolated community searching for them. Despite the Japanese origin, the first series is very much in the tradition of a Clint Eastwood Western, a simple story stylishly told, with the stranger in town setting events in motion that change everyone's lives. It surpasses Otomo's best-known work, *Akira*, by virtue of its meticulous planning and lack of any padding. This isn't a run that can be

dipped into halfway, it has to be started with 1 for full effect, as the mood and pace are excellently timed. That Otomo and Nagayasu have the confidence to begin the conclusion in 7 and continue it for a further twenty-five pages is astounding. Nagayasu effortlessly apes Otomo's style, possibly because as a former assistant he contributed heavily to that style. There's the same delicacy of line and effective layouts, and the occasional misproportioned figure is largely lost.

'City Of The Children' concerns, as the title suggests, a town ruled by teenagers. Borrowing points of Communist ideology, they also hold a belief that anyone over the age of forty is partially responsible for the barren state of the planet, and therefore should be made to work off a debt. This takes the form of unearthing an underground radioactive waste dump. As previously, Sarah's arrival sparks changes, and she's once again forced to fight for her life. The familiar structure, less original plot and greater reliance on a series of conflicts dilutes the effect if one has read the first series, and an insight into Sarah's current situation in 2 doesn't compensate.~WJ
Recommended: Series one 1–8

LEGENDS
DC: *6-issue miniseries 1986–1987*
Having discovered with *Crisis On Infinite Earths* that the idea of a series involving all their characters and tying into numerous titles was a sales success, DC were quick to concoct a follow-up, nominally to explore the idea of what their characters meant to the world around them. They launched *Suicide Squad*, and new *Justice League* and *Flash* titles, in which assorted DC heroes are manipulated and discredited. The need to focus on a large cast results in unsatisfactorily small sequences with each, and resulting events are depicted in shorthand fashion, thus ensuring that the underlying ideas never gel. The constant commentary from Darkseid and the Phantom Stranger is irritating and the method of bringing people to their senses is straight from cliché-land. On the positive side, John Byrne's art is never less than professional, but it's scant compensation.~FP
Collection: Legends (1–6)

Judge Dredd: LEGENDS OF THE LAW
DC: *13 issues 1994–1995*
DC's new Dredd material upped the page count from seven to twenty-two, but didn't add any more plot. Wagner and Grant repeat their all-singing all-dancing villain in 1–4, and not unexpectedly manage the best mixture of humour and action. The best actual story, though, is written by John Byrne with art from Tommy Lee Edwards and Gary Martin in 8–10.

You'll figure out where the plot is going long before the end, but at least there is a plot, and an interesting idea at that. With the failure of the Dredd movie this and its companion title were dropped with all due despatch.~FP

L.E.G.I.O.N.

DC: *70 issues, 5 Annuals 1989–1994*

The acronym stands for Licensed Extra Governmental Interstellar Operatives Network, an organisation which was launched by the son of Superman's enemy Brainiac, the green-skinned Vril Dox. As with the 30th-century Legion Of Super-Heroes, with which this is only superficially connected, he gathers 20th-century residents of assorted planets with superpowers. There's a shapeshifting Durlan, Larissa Mallor, able to project areas of darkness, and as this is a title written by Keith Giffen and Alan Grant it's not long until intergalactic wildman Lobo turns up. Their sense of humour comes through early with the leader of a drug ring named Kanis Biz.

Dox is a well-conceived character. His ambition is to set up an interplanetary police force, and he will stop at little to follow his aim through, feeling the end justifies the means. He's a brutal commander, often in conflict with his operatives and everyone else, a good example being 2. He manages to free his homeworld from the grip of the ruling computer tyrants, and in doing so nearly trashes the entire planet, an irrelevancy to him as the people are now free.

Dox is also strong-willed enough to control Lobo, by foul means if not fair, and they make a demonic duo. From the early days this is a good action-adventure series, possibly over-violent, but with a lot of black humour, and well illustrated by Barry Kiston. The abrasive relationships between the cast also make for interesting reading, with the writers still able to spring surprises even when characters seem familiar. The transformation of Stealth is an interesting case with an unpredictable outcome, resulting in Dox almost dying in 7. In 9 the mysterious Durlan disappears, to be replaced by a female with amnesia. She's actually the 30th-century's Phantom Girl, now named Phase.

From 13 Alan Grant is the sole writer, and in 16 he introduces the superstrong Lar Gand, later to step into his own series as Valor, and returns Captain Comet, one of DC's 1950s space heroes. With telepathic powers he was considered a man of the future, and left to explore space. The basic decency of this pair is thrown into the turbulent mix, with Lobo being a particular cause for concern. There's a death in 19, and 23 reveals the fate of the displaced Durlan, drawn by guest artist Richard Piers Rayner. In 28 Stealth gives birth to her son, who'll play an important part in the series for several reasons. Captain Marvel and

Lobo go head-to-head in 31, and in a smooth transition from 40 Kitson starts writing the title as well. Alan Grant returns for 51, in which Lobo is stuck on a remote asteroid along with fellow-L.E.G.I.O.Nnaire Telepath and a prisoner. To pass the time they recount their pasts, which makes for humorous and gruesome reading.

From 52 Mark Waid takes over the scripting (from Kitson's plots), working well with him, particularly in 59 and 60, where they spotlight Phase's homeworld. Waid flies solo on the black-humoured 56, featuring a villain very similar to Bouncing Boy of the Legion Of Super-Heroes. Arnie Jorgensen is the penciller from 49, and his dynamic artwork doesn't quite match Kitson's story-telling abilities. Tom Peyer (calling himself 'Tennessee') writes from 61, and his primary plot concerns Stealth's son Lyrl, who's developed advanced intelligence for a baby. Lyrl has an agenda of his own, involving taking over L.E.G.I.O.N., manipulating events to ensure his succession. The series thereafter continues as *R.E.B.E.L.S.* The annual that stands out is the fifth, with a number of alternative versions of the team. There's a 007 takeoff for Lobo, and a two-pager by Tom Peyer and old *Batman* artist Dick Sprang. Anyone who doesn't have a chuckle at it has lost their sense of humour. L.E.G.I.O.N. was well plotted, richly characterised and nicely illustrated throughout its run, but never gained the attention it deserved.~HY
Recommended: 4–6, 12, 13, 23, 26, 51, 56, 66, Annual 5

LEGION OF MONSTERS

Marvel: *One-shot 1975*

This black and white title was conceived to fill the gap after the mass cancellation of Marvel's horror-magazine line. Consequently it features the likes of Frankenstein and the Manphibion (from *Monsters Unleashed*), and a deliciously gruesome Gerry Conway short 'The Flies', drawn with relish by Paul Kirschner and Ralph Reese. The highlight, however, was another chapter of Roy Thomas and Dick Giordano's *Dracula* adaptation, continued from the pages of *Dracula Lives*, unsurprisingly. It remains sadly unfinished to this day. A nice little package.~DAR
Recommended: 1

The LEGION OF SUBSTITUTE HEROES

DC: *One-shot 1985*

In the convoluted Legion Of Super-Heroes history a number of folk who'd been rejected for membership in the first team banded together to form The Legion Of Substitute Heroes. They featured such luminaries as Stone Boy, who could turn into a statue, Infectious Lass, able to give people diseases, and Color Kid, able to change colours, and here to change gender as well. Unbelievably, there was a time when these characters were taken seriously, but not here. Then regular Legion creators Paul Levitz and Keith Giffen highlight the ridiculous aspects of this motley crew, producing a good few giggles along the way, the humour accentuated by Giffen drawing in the style used for the parent title.~WJ

LEGION OF SUPER-HEROES

DC: *Series one, 4 issues 1973, series two 55 issues (259–313), 3 annuals 1980–1984, series three 63 issues, 2 annuals 1984–1989, series four 87 issues +, 7 annuals 1989 to date*

Introduced as once-only foils for Superboy in *Adventure Comics* 247, something about the team of 30th-century teenage superheroes appealed to the readership. They began to recur in the Superman family of titles, eventually earning their own series in *Adventure Comics*. The first series of their own title reprinted four mid-1960s adventures to judge the viability for an ongoing series. Apparently there was a market, as they virtually took over *Superboy* that year, when the series became *Superboy and the Legion of Super-Heroes*. Seven years later they succeeded in booting the boy of steel out of his comic entirely, and the second run continues the numbering of that title, with 259's cover having Superboy flying off bidding a fond farewell to the Legion.

He was the lucky one being able to escape from this dreadful comic. Under Gerry Conway and Joe Staton the Legion had never known darker times, with inane sub-1960s-style plots involving evil space circuses and escaped genies. Successors artist Jimmy Janes (from 263) and writer Roy Thomas (from 277) were no better, with Thomas concentrating on developing a character only previously ever seen as a statue. The one bright spot in this run is one of the most beautifully illustrated *Legion* comics ever. Former artist James Sherman returned for 262 and inked his pencils for a gorgeous result that even made the Conway story bearable. Thankfully it was all change with 284, with the return of writer Paul Levitz and new penciller Pat Broderick. From the very ends of the cosmos you could hear champagne bottles popping. Levitz once again provided decent plots with excellent characterisation. He knew the personalities of all the Legionnaires and how they interacted. Broderick, while never a very fluid artist, was far more dramatic than his predecessors. However, it was the back-up stories, illustrated by Keith Giffen, that attracted more attention, and when he took over the art chores on the lead stories with 287 a new era for the Legion arrived. Giffen developed great designs and imagery that suited this futuristic series. He and Levitz created their first epic,

'The Great Darkness Saga', in 290–294. One of the Legion's deadliest foes returned, but pulling the strings is an infamous 20th-century villain. Throughout the action, Levitz and co-plotter Giffen add additional Legionnaires to the roll-call, and flesh out existing characters, a good example being Dream Girl. Always an underdog, her powers of premonition were never fully utilised, and half the time she just looked like a dumb blonde. But Levitz gave her a vibrant personality and intelligence and made her an effective leader of the Legion. Over succeeding issues she developed a vamp-like presence that made here even more unique.

The 300th issue was a special occasion, a giant-sized epic featuring art from past and present Legion artists including Curt Swan, Dave Cockrum and James Sherman. The future of the Legion, established way back in *Adventure Comics* 354, had obstructed what could be done with various characters, and in 300 it was finally laid to rest. 305 was another notable issue, concluding a long-running plot involving one of the Legionnaires being an impostor. The next epic was 307–310, featuring the 'Prophet and Omen' story-line, in which the mysterious Prophet arrives on a hostile world and warns them of impending doom in the form of a being called Omen. It didn't gel throughout, but is still an impressive adventure, and Giffen uses the opportunity to evolve his art still further with the aid of inker Larry Mahlstedt. 313 was the last issue in this series. From 314 it became *Tales Of The Legion of Super-Heroes*, running new stories to 325, and thereafter reprinting stories from the Legion's next series, printed on high-quality paperstock. The idea was to give readers two options, with those unable to afford the higher-priced version able to get the story a year later at the normal price. The series continued to 364. Before the title went reprint there were three good annuals. The first introduced new characters to the Legion, the second featured a Legion wedding illustrated by Dave Gibbons, while the third, in 1984, featured the birth of a character that would eventually have dire consequences for the Legion.

The new series began in great fashion with an all-action affair featuring the Legion's evil counterpart, The Legion of Super-Villains, and ending with the death of a Legionnaire in 5. Steve Lightle is the penciller from 3 and slips very well into Giffen's shoes. He's not as abstract as Giffen, but still draws excellent, colourful characters, and Levitz works equally well with Lightle. 7–8 feature a dimension-hopping story crossing over with *DC Presents* 80 starring Superman, while 11–12 have Legion founders, Cosmic Boy, Saturn Girl and Lightning Lad, deciding to leave the team. This makes way for new characters to join in 14, including two non-humanoid characters (the first ever in the Legion) and the mysteriously masked Sensor Girl, who is apparently an old character. There was much reader speculation as to her real identity. She naturally played a major role, as her identity was eventually revealed in a story-line featuring a new-look Fatal Five (one of the Legion's most deadliest adversaries) that ended with 26. Meanwhile the able Greg La Rocque pencils from 15, while 22 gives us the first hint of a possible lesbian relationship between two of the cast. 31 is a special issue featuring an untold tale starring some of the dead Legionnaires, and Levitz pulls off another epic in 32–35, where Universo once more uses his brainwashing abilities to gain power. He imprisons the four Legionnaires who are the most threat to him, i.e., the cleverest, and the story of how they escape and restore everyone's minds is a real treat. Perhaps Levitz's greatest inspiration was in resolving the continuity problems engendered by the necessary removal of Superboy because in 1986's relaunched Superman's continuity he'd never been Superboy. He dies in 37–38, wherein it's established that the Legion's Superboy existed in a parallel universe.

The Legion's thirtieth anniversary in 45 is a spotlight on the life and times of Legion founder Lightning Lad, and Levitz hits gold again when he begins the 'Conspiracy' story in 46. A number of Legionnaires conspire, against Legion code, to confront and destroy the Time Trapper, the villain who killed Superboy in 38. This saga comes to a head in 50, which has the return of Keith Giffen, who hadn't lost his touch, marking his return by giving all the Legionnaires a new look in 54. After the return of the Fatal Five villainess, the Emerald Empress, in a magnificent battle in 57–58, 59 offers another blast from the past, featuring an untold tale of some dead Legionnaires, and the 'Magic Wars' saga in 60–63 ends the series. Science is failing, with magic becoming a dominant force, and although they're reunited by the end of 63, the Legionnaires don't know what's in store for them. The best of the two annuals was the second, in which Curt Swan returns to pencil a story revealing the strange connection between married Legionnaires Saturn Girl and Lightning Lad, and Validus, brutal monster member of the Fatal Five.

The fourth series jumped five years for a dramatic new look instituted by Keith Giffen, who was joined by two new writers, Tom and Mary Bierbaum. A lot had happened during the five years. The Legion had disbanded, the Earth government is controlled by hostile aliens, the Dominators, some Legionnaires went missing, some presumably died, some fought each other, and some old-time fans were outraged. The

classic Legion of young colourful characters was gone, replaced by adults in a turbulent, unsettled world. It may not have been to everyone's liking, but it demanded attention as an extremely well paced, well plotted and exciting saga. The first few issues slowly introduce the old cast as the Legion begins to regroup, and in 4–5 the Legion's history is rewritten (the latter being an outstanding issue), with new characters now cast as major players in old Legion adventures. While this new series was grittier than ever before, there are great moments of humour, typified by the reintroduction of Matter Eater Lad in 11. His ability to eat anything was previously taken too seriously, but here the absurdity of the character is excellently explored in a witty but respectful fashion.

12 has the Legion back in full force, but there are still mysteries about the title, not least what's happened to some of the previous cast, presumed missing in action. More of them are gradually introduced, along with more information as to what occurred during the five years. 20 certainly offers new insights, and 25 introduces the Legion of the old *Adventure Comics* days from the 1960s! Called Legionnaires, they were first thought to be clones of the originals reared by the Dominators. The young Legionnaires become involved with a resistance force against Earthgov and even enlist the aid of their old adversary, Universo. Jason Pearson is now pencilling the series, but it's Colleen Doran and Curt Swan who illustrate the landmark issue, 31. The female lover of the Jan Arrah, Element Lad, reverts back to a man! Surely a first, and this question of sexuality is carefully handled. The war with the Dominators comes to a close with 35, and something unique happens to the Earth in 38. It's destroyed. This is Giffen's swansong, as he now leaves all the writing to the Bierbaums.

There's another new penciller in Stuart Immonen from 39, although it's guest-penciller Chris Sprouse who redesigns the youthful Legionnaires in 42 before they move into their own title. The Bierbaums meanwhile lead the adult Legion into epic battle with old foe Mordru in 43–48, featuring lots of dead DC characters. They end their run on the title in great form in the special fiftieth issue, and are replaced by the series colourist, Tom McCraw. He tries hard, but was outclassed by his predecessors, with his lack of writing experience showing. His best effort re-runs an old plot of the Legion being outlawed.

60 instigated another change, this time the end of an era, and crossed into both *Legionnaires* and *Valor*, while 61 tied in with the *Zero Hour* series. The next issue, numbered 0, was back to basics, with the Legion now only existing as

youngsters. The whole formation started again from scratch with the three founding members, Cosmic Boy, Saturn Girl and Livewive (now with a changed name). Experienced writer Mark Waid arrived to assist McCraw, and the combination worked, producing entertaining tales, helped from 62 by artist Lee Moder, who has a nice feel for the characters. Tom Peyer also joins the writing team with 70. While there's an element of history repeating itself, there are alterations to lessen the predictability. One Legionnaire even comes back as a snake!

The title can now be categorised as 'fun', but its bright appearance is deceiving, as it can at times be quite gruesome – witness a planet's entire population being murdered in 71. The new Superboy makes a welcome début as his title crosses over with 74, and stories are now regularly crossing over with *Legionnaires*. Old and extremely powerful adversaries the Fatal Five are reintroduced in a worthy battle (78), and a big change comes to the title with 85, as a number of Legionnaires are thrust back through time to the twentieth century. This is meant to be a temporary measure, but it does allow the Legion to integrate with the existing DC Universe. Overall, the change to the younger Legion has proved a positive step, as the Legion were conceived as a bunch of young, colourful characters. Of the seven annuals, the better ones are 1 and 3, revealing secrets about the old Legion.~HY

Recommended: Series two 262, 289–293, 298, 300–305, 307–310, Annual 1, 3, series three 1–5, 7–9, 11, 14, 18, 24–26, 30–35, 37, 38, 45, 50, 51, 53, 54, 57–63, series four 1–14, 19, 20, 25–32, 34–36, 38–41, 44–50, 59–61, 0, 62, 63, 66–68, 70, 71, 78–86, Annual 1, 3

Tales of The LEGION OF SUPER-HEROES

DC: 37 issues (314–350) 1984–1987

This continued the numbering of the second *Legion of Super-Heroes* title. The Legion moved into a new series printed on high-quality paper, and those stories were printed a year later in this cheaper title, starting with 326. Before that there were twelve new issues to complement the main series. Most stories were written by co-plotters Paul Levitz and Keith Giffen (with occasional assist from Mindy Newell), with some really nice art by Terry Shoemaker and Karl Kesel in 314–319. They emphasised the teenaged look of the characters, and Dan Jurgens carried on the pencilling admirably from 320. The opportunity was used to highlight a few characters in most issues, though not always successfully, as 321–323 show. Regular Legion adversaries the Dark Circle were featured in 314–315 and again to end the series in 324–325.~HY

THE LEGION OF THE NIGHT

Marvel: *2 issues 1991*

Fin Fang Foom. A depraved religious cult. Steve Gerber, Whilce Portacio and Scott Williams. Demons, sex and a modern-day witch. All sounds rather exciting, doesn't it? Sadly, it isn't. It's a formulaic old horror plot padded out to ninety-six pages with some mystical mumbo-jumbo.~FP

LEGIONNAIRES

DC: *40 issues +, 3 annuals 1993 to date*

1–19 chronicle the adventures of a bunch of superpowered futuristic teenagers who may be the clones of the 'thirty-something' members of the Legion of Super-Heroes, or may not. They protect New Earth, a collection of domed cities linked in space, which is all that remains of our planet in the thirtieth century after aeons of ecological abuse. The first several issues, written by Tom and Mary Bierbaum and exquisitely illustrated by Chris Sprouse, are a bouncy, fun read, entertaining adventures of neophyte superheroes. Sadly, after fill-in art by Adam Hughes (7) and Coleen Doran (8) the schedules continued to slip later and later, and Sprouse was forced to give up the title. From 20 reference must be made to *Zero Hour*, DC's time-warping 1994 crossover series. *Legionnaires*, together with its parent title *Legion Of Super-Heroes*, was deemed to have too much continuity baggage by the powers that be. Reading it, they thought, required too much prior knowledge, therefore putting off potential new readers. So, with 0 (Oct. 1994), everything was labelled 'never happened', and 20 on up crossed over and alternated with issues of *LSH*, both titles detailing the ongoing saga of empowered teenagers in spandex patrolling the galaxy. To those a tad older than sixteen, the current titles are 'Legion Lite', with a tacit agreement that no matter how long they run they'll never be the real thing. Nevertheless, they are generally well crafted, appealing and entertaining.~HS

Recommended: 1–7

LEGIONNAIRES 3

DC: *4-issue miniseries 1986*

The founding members of the Legion of Super-Heroes, retired from active service, face their greatest challenges from the Time Trapper and their own unresolved issues about their lives. Some logical flaws – if these folks are retired from heroics why are they still wearing their action costumes? – but a better than average LSH miniseries.~HS

LEMME OUTA HERE!

Print Mint: *One-shot 1978*

Anthology in which a top line-up of underground cartoonists post recollections of their childhood. Despite the presence of Justin

Green, Kim Deitch and Robert Crumb, it's Bill Griffith who steals the show, asking 'Is There Life After Levittown?' It's a resonant recollection of childhood mischief and adolescent alienation. Crumb's two-pager is charming, and Aline Kominsky's pages are, as always, a curious mixture of compulsive text and off-putting art. Her story of a holiday camp is curiously spliced with what seems to be an entirely different eight-pager about early dating experiences. Patchy, but certainly worth a look for the better material.~WJ

LES LIAISONS DELICIEUSES
Eros: *6-issue miniseries 1990–1991*

A pair of beautiful women in a strange great house welcome a series of lovers, often dressed in masks and costumes. At the end of each encounter the lovers are killed, either by their successors or by the women. Gender is obscured by satin and brocade, new amours take the guise of the men they have just killed. Richard Forg builds an indulgent, sensual world of black and white images without using words, paying particular attention to body language and facial expression, but clearly drawing at speed. The dashed-off quality of the drawings gives a feeling of tumultuous passion, even if the odd panel is clumsy. He's been looking at Manara, that's for sure, but brings an edge of roughness, and more than a hint of danger, to the scenarios.~FJ
Recommended: 1, 3

The LIBERATOR
Malibu: *6 issues 1987–1988*

An unnecessarily complicatedly told liberal tale of World War II supersoldiers growing old. One gets cancer and loses his wife to another, they criticise covert US involvement in Central America, blah, blah… It's crudely drawn and barely edited.~GK

THE LIBERTY PROJECT
Eclipse: *8 issues 1987–1988*

A project set up to rehabilitate superpowered criminals is an interesting idea. Beyond that, this is the usual group of bickering teens, although the ending to the final issue is unintentionally hilarious. For a similar idea well executed, see *Suicide Squad*.~FP

It's only a matter of LIFE AND DEATH
Fantagraphics: *1 issue 1990*

A collection of Peter Kuper material ranging from travel diaries through a wordless allegory of the banking system to a version of *La Ronde* starring a dollar bill. Kuper's strips are more thoughtful than most, and this is a fine selection.~WJ
Recommended

THE LIFE OF CHRIST
Marvel: *1 issue 1993*

Marvel present a radical origin of a new superhero by starting with his birth. The guy's name is Jesus, and my guess is that the angels who keep turning up give him superpowers, and the guy John, who's born a few months before, will be his arch-enemy. We'll never really know, though, because this was cancelled after one issue.~FP

LIFE OF POPE JOHN PAUL II
Marvel: *One-shot 1983*

Reputedly one of Marvel's best-selling comics ever, one wonders where the idea of doing a Popeography came from. Probably the same source that suggested *The Life Of Christ*, published the same year, perplexingly in February, rather than at Christmas. Short on action, unless you get all excited about Papal Bulls.~FJ

LIFE, the UNIVERSE and EVERYTHING
DC: *3-issue miniseries 1996*

Sequel to *Restaurant at the End of the Universe*, as Neil Vokes replaces Steve Leialoha on pencils. Adapts the pre-penultimate, third book of the Hitch Hiker's trilogy in an unevenly edited form that contains many passages which simply seemed like a good idea at the time.~APS

LIFE UNDER SANCTIONS
Fantagraphics: *One-shot 1994*

It's doubtful anybody really understands the reasons for the conflict that's torn Yugoslavia apart. In this one-shot Serbian cartoonist Aleksandar Zograf tries to make sense of what's occurring on a day-to-day basis, and the world's reactions to it, eventually evoking a memorable image of a land without Mickey or Donald as Disney uphold the international embargo.~WJ
Recommended: 1

THE LIGHT AND DARKNESS WAR
Epic: *6-issue miniseries 1988–1989*

A Vietnam veteran experiences flashbacks and hallucinations, causing him grave concern, especially when it transpires they may not be hallucinations, but trips into another dimension, where Leonardo Da Vinci and other dead geniuses rally forces for the ultimate battle. Imaginatively and lovingly put together, with stylised but meticulously crafted art by Cam Kennedy.~HS

LINDA CARTER, Student Nurse
Marvel: *9 issues 1961–1963*

An attempt at taking the 'fluffy girlie' comic style of *Millie The Model* and applying it to a more workaday environment. *Linda Carter,* drawn in a semi-realistic style by Al Hartley, didn't know whether to be soap or comedy, and failed to be either, though the stories now have a camp nostalgic charm. Hey, any comic featuring paper dolls emblazoned 'Let's Dress The Boys!' can't be all bad... ~HS

LISA COMICS
Bongo: *1 issue 1995*

An awkward attempt at presenting a teaching aid with *The Simpsons* cast, as Lisa Simpson is spirited away to an adventure in Wordland.~FP

LITTLE ITALY
Fantagraphics: *One-shot 1991*

This is one of Eddie Campbell's most charming collections, gathering together a number of scribbled strips produced during a series of visits to Australia to spend time with his prospective wife and her family. The two 'Pajama Girl' stories, reprinted from *Taboo*, sit a little uneasily against the observational pieces. At the heart of the book is 'Little Italy' itself, a cleverly constructed piece about Catholicism and mysticism where the author muses on tradition in families and how it really relates to religious belief, studded with gems of observational humour. Even better is 'This Happened Yesterday', in which the narrator's doctor tries to demonstrate, using his hands and mouth, how an infection got into the narrator's penis – a great piece of bigfoot cartooning.~FJ
Recommended: 1

The Complete LITTLE NEMO IN SLUMBERLAND
Fantagraphics/Titan: *6 volumes 1989–1991*

As the name suggests, this series of hard-backed collections reprints the complete run of Winsor McKay's masterful 'Little Nemo in Slumberland', which ran in the colour sections of Sunday newspapers from 1905 to 1911 (vols 1–4), and 'Little Nemo in the Land of Wonderful Dreams'. The latter is the same strip in all but name, continued for William Randolph Hearst from 1912–1915 (vols 5–6). The strip was revived again in 1924, these pages remaining unreprinted.

Little Nemo is widely considered one of the all-time classic newspaper strips. It deals with the surreal dreams of a small boy, the fantasy worlds to which those dreams take him, and the bizarre creatures he meets there. While the 'plot' advances little over the strip's entire run, the strength is in McKay's wonderful artwork. His fantastic cityscapes and innovative use of colour, impressive as they are today, were decades ahead of their time at in the first decade of the century, when sequential art was still in its infancy. These volumes, complete with historical notes on McKay's career, are unbelievably beautiful – even after April 1911,

when full colour is abandoned in favour of less sophisticated tints. Although it's difficult to single out any strips from the others when the overall quality remains so consistently high, the Christmas strips of December 1905 (vol 1), the storm-tossed houses of October 1908 (vol 3) and the airships battles of January 1909 (vol 3) stand out. It is a desperate shame that cinema animation and political cartooning eventually seduced McKay away from *Little Nemo*.

Although some of the depictions in the strip could be pulled up by today's standards of political correctness, the only real criticism which can be levelled against the run is that if you've read one *Little Nemo* you've really read them all, although you certainly haven't seen them all. At times the constant punchline becomes a familiar friend as the reader knows, as does Nemo himself, that whatever predicament he finds himself in he'll have escaped from by the coming morning when he wakes up. The popularity of the character over eighty years since his last appearance, and more than sixty since McKay's death, ise a fitting testament to the quality of the work. If you only ever buy one complete collection of newspaper strips, make it this one.~JC
Recommended: 1–6

LITTLE SHOP OF HORRORS
DC: *One-shot 1987*

An adaptation of the musical film about mild-mannered florist Seymour, and the way his life changes when he discovers a strange, alien plant with an insatiable appetite for... But that would be telling. The adaptation is competent enough, but without the songs and the musical razzmatazz, the weakness of the story becomes very apparent.~FC

LIVINGSTONE MOUNTAIN
Adventure: *4 issues 1991*

There's a living stone mountain where dragons and all kinds of unimaginatively designed humanoid creatures consort. *Fish Police* creator Steve Moncuse had a very good idea for a comic, but it wasn't this dull fantasy nonsense.~WJ

LLOYD LLEWELYN
Fantagraphics: *6 issues 1986–1987, one-shot 1988*

Before he created the rich and varied sources of amusement in *Eightball*, Dan Clowes was hung up creating the adventures of Lloyd Llewelyn, beatnik detective and coolest cat in town, whose stories came 'from the weird side of unusual'. Many of the Clowes trademarks are there, including strange characters, mad science and retro-1950s symbolism, but the stories never attain the absurd but genuinely thrilling intensity of his later mysteries. Style over content, and all that. Clowes' drawing at this stage lacks the clarity and assurance of his later work. Thin-line inking gives a mechanical look to the pages, which is further accentuated by the use of a single light grey tone for shadows, and although there's a lack of background detail many of the panels look too cluttered. The first six issues are magazine format, and the one-shot is traditional comic size.~FJ

Collections: The Lloyd Llewelyn Collection (1–6), *The Manly World Of Lloyd Llewelyn* (all *Lloyd Llewelyn* strips)

LOBO

DC: *32 issues +, 4 annuals 1993 to date*

Introduced in *Omega Men* 3, Lobo is the biggest, meanest bastich in the galaxy, a cigar-chomping, bounty-hunting, mercenary powerhouse able to go head-to-head with the DC Universe big guns. Wherever he goes, violence follows, with dismemberment and death portrayed in exaggerated cartoon fashion. Numerous *Lobo* miniseries sold enough to prompt an ongoing title, although Lobo's very much a one-note joke, albeit one that stands repetition. Luckily, writer Alan Grant can create a wealth of suitably ridiculous supporting characters and is possessed of a deft touch with comic dialogue, while artists Val Semeiks and John Dell (to 18) are adaptable enough to know when to play it straight and when to go for over-the-top slapstick violence. Most issues give a major bang for the buck, little plot, but quite a few good jokes strung together. Anyone enjoying one issue should go on looking. Start with 10's religious satire, featuring a good telling of the classic healing-the-sick joke, Lobo's birthday party in 25 or, for an atypical sample, start with the baby Lobo in issue 0 as the main man's full origin is told. From 19 it's different artists every issue, some of whom are more successful than others, with Carl Critchlow consistently good.~FP

LOBO Miniseries and one-shots

DC: *4-issue miniseries 1990–1991, One-shot ('Paramilitary Christmas Special')1991, 4-issue miniseries ('Lobo's Back') 1992, One-shot ('Blazing Chain Of Love')1992, 4-issue miniseries ('Infanticide') 1992–1993, One-shot ('Portrait Of A Victim') 1993, 4-issue miniseries ('UnAmerican Gladiators') 1993, One-shot ('Convention Special') 1993, One-shot ('Lobocop') 1994, 4-issue miniseries ('A Contract On Gawd') 1994, One-shot ('In The Chair') 1994, One-shot ('The Brave And The Bald') 1995, One-shot ('Bounty Hunting For Fun And Profit') 1995, One-shot ('Big Babe Spring Break Special') 1995, One-shot ('I Quit') 1995, One-shot ('Lobo Goes To Hollywood') 1996, 4-issue miniseries ('Death And Taxes') 1996*

In general the quality of the regular title is far higher than the one-shots and miniseries, which suffer from a paucity of plot and few supporting characters able to play off Lobo's one-string personality. The only essential *Lobo* is the first miniseries, in which Lobo is reacquainted with his school teacher. It says everything about the character while he's still fresh in four mindless-mayhem-filled issues drawn by Simon Bisley. *Lobo's Back* explains Lobo's immunity to death, but, a good joke with the covers of the first issue apart, the formula is becoming stale, and Bisley jumps ship with 3. The patchy 'Infanticide' is co-writer Keith Giffen's swansong, and he also draws the series as Lobo's many children come looking for him. The regular title's main art team of Val Semeiks and John Dell début on 'Portrait Of A Victim', and the 'Convention Special' has a high quota of very funny digs at the comics industry, and it's excellently drawn by Kevin O'Neill, taking labelled visual gags to new heights. 'UnAmerican Gladiators' is the best miniseries since the first – *Wacky Races* gone mad. Lobo participates in a televised celebration of violent excess, pitched against the survivors of the neglected *Outcasts*. John Wagner co-writes and Cam Kennedy's inventive visual gags, fused to a ridiculous cast, hilarious script and silly situations, make for a great read. 'A Contract On Gawd' has its moments, but is stretched thin over four issues. Martin Emond's art on the teaming with Deadman in 'The Brave And The Bald', and on 'Lobo In The Chair', is magnificently excessive, as is Carlos Ezquerra's for 'I Quit', but, as ever, story content is slim. *Caveat emptor.*~FP

Recommended: *Lobo* 1–4, *UnAmerican Gladiators* 1–4

Collections: *The Last Czarnian* (*Lobo* 1–4), *Lobo's Back's Back* (*Lobo's Back* 1–4)

LOGAN'S RUN

Marvel: *7 issues 1977*

An adaptation of the movie started by Gerry Conway, but completed by David Kraft (2–5) with art by George Perez. The plot remained faithful to the film, with a tight script and some of Perez's best art to that time, resulting in one of the best movie adaptations seen in comics. With 6 a new team took over and continued beyond the film, but the title was cancelled for licensing reasons. The Thanos solo strip pushing up the price of 6 is nothing special.~DWC

Recommended: 1–5

LOGAN'S RUN

Adventure: *6-issue limited series 1990–1991*

Adapting from the novel rather than the film means the story is told with scenes of rumpy-pumpy intact, but that's the only reason to search this out in preference to the Marvel film adaptation. On the downside, the story is adapted by the prolific Barry Blair, whose elfin figures detract from it. In its time, though, this was successful enough to prompt a follow-up series adapting the novel's sequel *Logan's World.*~FP

Superman's Girlfriend LOIS LANE

DC: *137 issues 1958–1974, 2-issue microseries 1990*

The cover to the first issue had Lois riding a broomstick, dressed in rags, for a story called 'The Witch Of Metropolis'. One could easily change the 'witch' to 'bitch', because she was the ultimate girl-friend from hell. Lois had débuted twenty years previously in the first Superman story in *Action Comics* 1, where she was introduced as a glamorous reporter who more or less took an instant dislike to Clark Kent, while fawning over Superman. A little while later, beginning with 'Man Or Superman' in *Superman* 17, she began to suspect that they might be the same person. Her snooping around the topic, and her character in general, proved popular enough for her to become the first of the Superman cast to have her own strip, 'Lois Lane, Girl Reporter', which ran in *Superman* 28–42. It took another fifteen years, though, before she had her own title, introduced after try-outs in *Showcase* 9 and 10.

1–79 present varying stories on a few regular themes. Throughout the 1940s and early 1950s Lois' character in *Superman* was as a gutsy reporter and a bit of a glamour girl. In the late 1950s and 1960s her adventures were more romantic in nature, with assorted plans to win Superman's hand in marriage, to which end she would go to almost any lengths. She's also portrayed as a snoop and spoiled brat, with her selfishness always at the forefront. She did, though, seem quite innocent and unaware of her bad traits. The terms 'implausible' and 'unrealistic' come to mind when considering Lois' adventures until the late 1960s, though they all made sense allied to the Superman mythos of the time. Lois' main aim in life was to marry Superman, but his affections sometimes swayed towards red-headed Lana Lang, Superman's childhood sweetheart, now a TV reporter. Many a story showed Lois and Lana confronting each other, rivals for Superman's attentions, and the cad just led them on. An example is 50, in which Lois goes back in time (something she managed as often as consuming hot dinners) to prevent Superboy kissing Lana and starting their romance. Lana was usually presented as a nicer person and a better dresser, with a flashier job, although the rivalry with Lois did get to her. She wasn't entirely innocent of schemes to deal with Lois, either, banishing her into the Phantom Zone in 33 so that only she would be around to benefit from Superman's attention. In 21, in one of many stories where the two gained superpowers, at least for an issue, there was a battle between Super Lois and Super Lana. Another time-travel story occurs in 37, in which Lois goes back to meet Leonardo Da Vinci. Guess who actually posed for the Mona Lisa? And here's Lucretia Borgia, looking incredibly familiar, with red hair. Lana lookalikes in the past was another common theme. In 59, though, she rather oversteps the mark by not only going back into Krypton's past before it explodes, but initiating a fling with Superman's father Jor-El.

This wasn't the first time she'd had her head turned, having courted Aquaman (as a mermaid) in 12, Astounding Man in 18, Titan Man in 79. The hussy. Some romances were hoaxes, one being 'The Irresistible Lois Lane' in 29, when she's caught snogging Aquaman (again), Batman and Green Arrow. Her intentions were good, though, as she was merely passing on some Red Kryptonite in her lipstick, enabling the heroes to neutralise a Green Kryptonite rock poisoning Superman at the time. Lois did actually marry Superman a few times, or so it seemed. For a really classic 1960s-style Lois Lane story you can do no better than 15, which features the 'Superman Family Of Steel'. For once it wasn't a hoax, imaginary story or dream as Superman and Lois tie the knot, except they're doubles! So what would happen if Superman and Lois did marry? This was tried and tested many times in 'imaginary stories', the first of which was in 19. She was also shown to have married Lex Luthor on occasions (34, 46). A classic Superman marriage story is 'The Three Wives Of Superman' in 51, in which he marries Lois, Lana and former mermaid sweetheart Lori Lemaris, and they all die!

As well as attempting to marry Superman and discover his identity, travelling in time and following her career as a reporter, she was also a volunteer nurse (43), she ran a fan club (50), and it's a little-known fact that she once ran for the Senate (in 63–64). Before leaving Lois' golden era there are two other issues of note. 70 features the début of the new-look Catwoman, and 73 offers us the infamous kinky cover with Superman bound to a bench by Kryptonite handcuffs while Lois is whipping a puppet of Superman. Anyone wanting to experience an average, absurd, yet charming tale should find 53, titled 'When Lois And Lana Were Brides'. Lois, Lana and Clark are in a secret valley in Britain, where they meet an ancient Celtic tribe. On meeting, Clark thinks to himself, 'Their language is similar to modern Welsh, which we've all learned.' Yeah, right, of course you have.

Almost every issue to 79 was drawn by Kurt Schaffenberger, who was matched to feature exactly. His semi-humorous yet realistic style suited the mood perfectly, and when other artists provided the odd fill-in they failed to match his panache. The writers remain uncredited, but it's known that editor Mort

Weisinger had a heavy hand in the plotting. The consistency of the issues is such that it's difficult to recommend any issue above the others, so prospective readers are directed to the giant-size issues that reprinted many a classic, 68, 77, 86, 95, 104, and 113. Before starting, put all disbelief to one side. A nice comfy armchair and a cup of cocoa also add to the ambience.

There came a time, though, when the comic had to progress: the first hint was 79's cover from Neal Adams, and in 1968 issue 80 presented a new-look Lois Lane. The cover said it all, with Lois ripping out the 'girlfriend' part of the logo and throwing it to the floor as the cover proclaimed, 'At last, the impossible come true! It's splitsville for Lois and Superman!' Lois is fed up with Superman and decides the time has come for a change. She gets a brand new wardrobe, including some sophisticated mini-skirt numbers, some sizzling bikinis, and a few 'Sun and fun sport outfits'. Things were never the same for the strip. Schaffenberger's art didn't suit the new, more plausible style of story, and from 82 Irv Novick took over the artwork, but seemed no more at home. There was the occasional glimpse of the new Lois DC were trying to project, such as when she joins a motorcycle gang in 83, but on the whole it was never entirely successful. The Lois and Lana rivalry came to a head in 99–100, with Lois on trial for the murder of Lana.

A change that was more than cosmetic came with 105, when we're introduced to regular supporting character and back-up strip, 'Rose And The Thorn'. It was a dramatic story, written by Robert Kanigher, about a young woman called Rose Forrest, who at night, unknown to her, takes on a different personality as the vigilante Thorn. As if to freeze her in the early 1970s, as illustrated by Ross Andru and Mike Esposito she wore a lime-green bikini outfit and green thigh-length boots. Despite discussion of sexist costumes being low on the agenda, this was the era of relevance in comics, and as a reporter Lois was better placed than some characters to participate. 106 has a story, now very dated, but well-intentioned at the time, in which Lois becomes black for a day, experiencing the problems faced by black people in the ghettos. The theme of racism and bigotry is taken up by Kanigher again in 110, when Lois becomes foster-mother to an orphaned Native American baby. By this time the arrogant snooper of the 1960s was gone, and Lois was thinking about things. Editor E. Nelson Bridwell ensured that *Lois Lane* reflected the changes in the other *Superman* titles of the early 1970s, with the *Daily Planet* taken over by a TV company run by someone operating for the

evil galactic conqueror Darkseid. Morgan Edge was also running Intergang, a powerful criminal organisation, and from 111 there's a succession of excellent stories by Kanigher and artist Werner Roth. The back-up strip is now being beautifully illustrated by Gray Morrow.

Lois also became involved in a fight against another criminal gang, the 100, also being fought by The Thorn, and they would occasionally meet, as they did in 114. 119–120 featured Lucy Lane, Lois' sister, who apparently dies in 120. 121 is one of the best-ever Lois Lane issues, as a grief-stricken Lois decides to change her life by becoming a freelance reporter writing about serious social problems. 112–123 are all fifty-two-page issues worth looking at not only for the decent Lois and The Rose And The Thorn strips, but for the reprints, including some 1940s stories in 115, 120 and 122, all minor classics. With the reversion to a standard-size comic there was also a reversion to the old themes, which just didn't work in the 1970s.

Over twenty years later, among DC's female characters only Wonder Woman has enjoyed a longer run. Lois continued as a solo feature in *Superman Family* and as a primary supporting character in the *Superman* titles.

A special two-part series from Mindy Newell and Gray Morrow used Lois to focus on the serious subject of missing and abused children. It was maturely written and gorgeously drawn, and involved Lois' relationship with her estranged sister Lucy (not dead after all), and with Lana, who is integral to the plot, and certainly not in trivial fashion. There are more plus points for the fact that Superman is nowhere in sight.~HY
Recommended: 15, 29, 33, 51, 110, 118–121, microseries 1–2

THE LONE RANGER AND TONTO
Topps: *4-issue miniseries 1994*

After re-inventing Jonah Hex for the 90s, Joe R. Lansdale and Tim Truman took on The Lone Ranger and Tonto – a pair that hadn't even made it past the 60s. It's not bad, with an origin of sorts worked into a good character piece about the relationship between the pair. But the plot, about an alien, mummified by the Aztecs and accidentally awakened by train robbers, is a weak reflection of Lansdale's roots as a horror writer. Having said that, Truman's artwork has a pleasing openness and there's a lot for Western fans to enjoy.~NF

LONE WOLF AND CUB
First: *45 issues 1987–1991*

Itto Ogami is the official executioner of the Shogunate, with a loving wife and child, until he falls foul of the political ambitions of the

Yagyu clan and is accused of plotting to overthrow the Shogun. His wife is killed and he's ordered to commit ritual suicide, but instead decides to seek revenge as an outlaw assassin. He offers his small son Daigoro the choice of sword or ball. When the sword is picked he embarks on the road to hell, taking his son with him. The pair travel together, Diagoro in a baby carriage, living off the land and by their wits, occasionally earning money as assassins. Kazuo Koike and Goseki Kojima's comic first appeared in Japan in 1970 and has enjoyed huge success, being made into films, plays and a television series. There are twenty-eight volumes (roughly 9,000 pages) of the strip in the original language, so First had plenty to go at, even with around sixty story pages an issue in this format.

Cited as an influence on the visual style of some of America's film-makers, *Lone Wolf And Cub* is notable in the comics world for inspiring Frank Miller (most obviously on *Ronin*), who provided introductions and covers for the first twelve issues. After Miller, Bill Sienkiewicz (13–24), Matt Wagner (25–36), Mike Ploog (37–44) and Ray Lago (45) drew the covers.

Ogami's 'origin' is presented in several tales (6, 13), and Diagoro's separation from his father on several occasions provides the impetus for the story (11, 33–39). Throughout, bushido, the warrior's code of honour, determines how the characters must react, even to the point where a messenger's job is more important than the life of a child (45). Stories are saved from repetitiveness by the presence of Diagoro, and by Koike's masterly story-telling, pitting Ogami against various members of the Yagyu clan (15, 16, 32, 43), the Kurokuwashu ninja (3, 26), yakuza and, of course, the elements themselves.

Visually the series is amazing, mostly pen-and-ink work with the occasional wash effect, constantly graceful and vital. Small actions can take pages and there's always time for creating atmosphere and setting. There's an expressionistic feel to the drawings which goes hand-in-hand with the story-telling. This is a violent and uncompromising work that nevertheless goes beneath the surface to the heart of the characters and the social mores of the age in which it's set. Not for the faint-hearted, but essential reading for anyone who loves the medium.~NF
Recommended: 1–45
Collection: Lone Wolf And Cub (1–7)

LONELY NIGHTS COMICS
Last Gasp: One-shot 1986

Dori Seda offers a mixture of autobiographical strips largely concerning her dog, with whom everyone assumes she has an unnatural relationship, and some further pieces on sex.

They're all perceptive, delightfully drawn and very funny, with the only mistake in the whole comic being the ill-advised *Weirdo* style photostrip.~WJ
Recommended: 1

LONER
Fleetway/Quality: 7-issue limited series 1990–1991

A big brute with a gun lands on a hostile planet and stumbles from one precarious situation to the next. Originally serialised in five-page instalments in a British weekly comic, the remit was obviously to end each segment on a cliffhanger, so *Loner* is plotted with no more than the following episode in mind, and as such doesn't make for a compelling read. 1–3 have some good David Pugh art, but standards decline thereafter.~FP

LONG HOT SUMMER
Milestone: 3-issue miniseries 1995

Try to work your way past the positively bizarre, off-putting and almost unreadable logo incorporating a city aflame. Once inside there's a worthwhile story about urban development and renewal, and the consequences of trampling wholesale over the wishes of the residents. Better still, despite the fact that it ties into all other Milestone titles for three months, it's easily read and understood on its own. The regular Milestone superpowered characters play their part largely outside the pages of this miniseries, and there's a decent attempt made to portray them as seen by the ordinary humans in Dakota.~FP

THE LONGBOW HUNTERS
DC: 3-issue miniseries 1987

Chiefly remembered today for writer/artist Mike Grell's somewhat prurient inclusion of a long sequence in which Black Canary gets strung up, whipped and abused, *The Longbow Hunters* was one of the jumpers on the 'grim'n'gritty' bandwagon in the wake of *The Dark Knight Returns*. Green Arrow becomes involved in some CIA jiggery-pokery, trading his usual collection of special-effect arrows for the more usual metal-tipped, deadly sort as Oliver Queen gets ready to face up to more 'realistic' dangers in the modern world. There's his usual 'I'm getting too old for this' worries followed by 'I want to be a dad'. Some critics have read into this an unpleasantly patriarchal agenda whereby the Black Canary, as soon as she's refused to have his child, spends the rest of the story getting abducted, beaten and generally abused. Although that's stretching it somewhat, there's a nasty, voyeuristic feel about this aspect of the book, which is otherwise eminently forgettable.~FJ
Collection: The Longbow Hunters (1–3)

LONGSHOT

Marvel: *6-issue miniseries 1985–1986*

One moment you're in Dimension A being chased by monsters and with no idea who you are, then some sparkly lights and you're in Dimension B being chased by monsters... etc. All that's apparent is that your luck is miraculously good (providing your motives are pure), and the name Longshot arises and you use it. After a while, you discover that Dimension B is called Earth. Writer Ann Nocenti says she created Longshot to be an innocent – a 'clean slate' – and a truly feel-good hero. It could easily have been feeble and saccharine, but instead, it's a delight: such imagination, such pace, and so strange. The writing peaks around Issues 2 and 3, then becomes fractionally more predictable (though still above approved safety limits), but Arthur Adams' artwork becomes steadily more assured and intricate with each issue. Wonderful.~FC

Recommended: 1–6

Collection: Longshot (1–6)

LOOSE CANNON

DC: *4-issue miniseries 1995*

Superman supporting character Loose Cannon is DC's version of the Hulk, big, brutish and ever more powerful the angrier he becomes. That he's a policeman in his civilian guise isn't enough to deflect the other similarities. There's disturbingly little in the way of a cogent plot, merely testosterone unlimited as Loose Cannon and Eradicator square off.~WJ

LOOSE TEETH

Fantagraphics: *3 issues 1991–1992*

Hilarious anthology that's the work of Scott Musgrove and Brian Sendelbach, either in collaboration or separately. Three strips occupy most of the comic. 'Fruitheads' has large-eyed fruit-headed characters committing or suffering acts of extraordinary violence. This juxtaposition of children's cartoons and uncharacteristic behaviour has a longer shelf life than you might expect, as do the scrawled cartoon stories and diary entries of Billy Mathers (age 7), who responds to the world with typical childish cruelty. The other regular feature is 'Fat Dog Mendoza'. Shaped like a curling stone and with a voracious appetite, Fat Dog is a surreal blend of matter-of-fact reportage and seemingly stream-of-consciousness ramblings. Visually he lends himself to hilarious images, such as when he becomes Pope, and he can also be found in a Dark Horse one-shot. At least one laugh a page is guaranteed, and how many comics can you say that about?~FP

Recommended: 1–3

LORD PUMPKIN/NECROMANTRA

Malibu: *4-issue miniseries 1995*

The first three issues of this comic tell two stories, Lord Pumpkin's return to his kingdom after striking a deal with Loki and Necromantra's acquisition of power and influence in the same kingdom whilst Pumpkin is away. The final issue brings the story-lines together for a rather unsatisfactory conclusion. Both characters are rather repulsive, which makes the story hard to enjoy and the outcome unexciting, but the fresh artwork by Gabriel Gecko (1–4), Kyle Hotz (1,2) and Jeff Lafferty partly compensates. The series is a spin-off from the Ultraverse's 'Godwheel Saga', Lord Pumpkin being a malevolent vegetable while Necromantra is Thanasi, the betrayer of Archimage, now, like Mantra, in a woman's body.~NF

LORDS OF THE ULTRA-REALM

DC: *6 issues 1986, 1 Special 1987*

Fantasy, owing much to Edgar Rice Burroughs, telling the story of Michael Savage, a tortured Vietnam veteran who is mystically transferred to the Ultra-Realm, a reality embodying all of the Earth's fears and hopes, ruled by Seven Princes of Light and Seven Princes of Darkness. Doug Moench's script doesn't really have anything to say, and Pat Broderick's florid but rather flat artwork, though distinctive, is only occasionally engaging.~NF

LOST CONTINENT

Eclipse: *6-issue miniseries 1990–1991*

Set in the mid-fifties, this is the story of the search for a lost Arctic nation. Hazekura, an archaeologist, and Hinata, a reporter, are opposed by a mysterious secret society that seeks the lost land for its own evil purposes. Thrills, spills, dinosaurs and sorcery add up to a fast-paced romp. This traditional adventure series in the manner of Burroughs or Haggard is written and drawn by Akihiro Yamada in a style that is an intriguing mix of Japanese and Western influences.~NF

LOST GIRLS

Kitchen Sink: *2 issues + 1995 to date*

Begun in the pages of *Taboo*, *Lost Girls* is Alan Moore and Melinda Gebbie's attempt to produce an intelligent, grown-up comic about sex which doesn't fudge the issue and appeals equally to both sexes. It's unrepentantly pornographic, with a segment of story followed by a balancing segment of sex, but ultimately comes over as cold and over-stylised, despite Gebbie's intensely coloured, Art Nouveau-influenced artwork. Her attention to detail over clothes, shoes and surfaces will engage some female readers, although others will find the artwork garish.

Almost too clever for its own good - as erotica, anyway - it re-examines three female archetypes from children's fiction: Pale, opium-addicted Alice from *Alice in Wonderland*, repressed Wendy from *Peter Pan*, and giggling good-time girl Dorothy from The *Wizard of Oz*. The three women meet in a luxurious hotel and, as they get to know each other, tell erotic versions of their famous stories.~FJ

LOST IN SPACE
Gold Key: *18 issues (37–54) 1973–1977, 5 issues (55–59) 1981–1982*
Formerly titled *Space Family Robinson, Lost In Space* appeared large on the cover from 15, and when the title switched when the idea was revived with 37. Buffeted through time and space, the Robinson family encounter a variety of aliens, almost invariably biped humanoids in predictable hokey old plots. This is largely dull, unimaginative material, although reasonably drawn by Dan Spiegle. The 1980s issues are reprints.~FP

LOST IN SPACE
Innovation: *18 issues 1991–1993, 3-issue miniseries ('Arrival') 1993, 1 issue ('Project Robinson') 1994*
The original Space Family Robinson returned with brand-new adventures, but fell victim to Innovation's constant belief that all painted artwork is good. It isn't, and substandard watercolours and airbrushes just don't wash. The scripts all have hooks and keep the 1960s kitsch factor, but it only emphasises that the TV series was supported by OTT performances and not decent writing. There are a few occasions when the stories shine, though, most notably those written by Bil Mumy, Will Robinson from the original show. 'Giving Thanks' in 9 tells a nice eco-friendly tale despite being marred by average line art and gaudy colours. Project Robinson, the early life of Maureen, may interest some, as it has very promising early art by cheesecake king Mike Deodato, but the story was never completed.~TP
Collection: Strangers Among Strangers (4–5)

LOST PLANET
Eclipse: *6-issue miniseries 1987–1989*
Earthman Tyler Flynn is transported to an exotic other-worldly locale where he encounters, among others, a woman and her chimpanzee, dinosaurs, a talking raven and Ambrose Bierce. This well-illustrated superior fantasy is obviously a labour of love from creator Bo Hampton, and the back-up stories give an added insight into the world and characters he's created. If fantasy comics usually make you barf take a look anyway. You might be pleasantly surprised.~WJ
Recommended: *1–6*

LOVE & ROCKETS
Fantagraphics: *50 issues, 1982–1996*
Love & Rockets (sometimes with ampersand, sometimes spelled out) was one of the earliest alternative comics written by and for young people. The Hernandez Brothers (Jaime, Gilbert and Mario, although he later faded away) began by writing a range of science-fiction and comic- inspired tales. Within a couple of issues they'd settled down to major story-lines, and although they would experiment with different stories from time to time, Jaime's Mechanics universe, and Gilbert's tales of a small Mexican town called Palomar (beginning in 5 with 'Heartbreak Soup'), would be the narratives that held the magazine together.

Jaime is perceived as the lighter-weight writer of the two, although perceptive readers will soon note he takes greater risks both in structuring his stories and in forcing the reader to make leaps of understanding between them. What begins in the first few issues as the funny story of punk mechanic Maggie, her crush on her new boss Rand Race and her possible lesbian relationship with her best friend, Hopey, complete with dinosaurs and robots (collected as the *Mechanics* miniseries), quickly turns into a harrowing examination of modern values. Nonetheless, the early tales, in which Maggie and her friend Penny Century imagine themselves superheroines, play with the conventions of comics in a revealing way.

The first real sign that Jaime is getting to grips with weightier matters comes in '100 Rooms', a brilliantly paced thriller set in a huge mansion that Maggie and Hopey are staying at, in which Maggie is 'kidnapped' and becomes enamoured of a man who may be no more than a simple vagrant but hints at being on the run. Jaime creates an electric atmosphere throughout the 'inside' scenes, where Maggie and her abductor hide from view, contrasting that with the open, sunny poolside frolics of her friends. For the first time her loyalty to Hopey comes into question, as do her motives for suddenly transferring her affections and her eroticism of violence – buy the comic, as the collection has some extra bits inserted which destroy the excellent, albeit obviously unconscious pacing. In all eventualities it turns out to be Hopey who abandons her to go on tour with her band. Slices of on-the-road life, like 'Crickets' in 20, bring humour back to the series before Jaime starts a number of tragic story-lines. Maggie, fat and working in a burger bar, faces up to the death of an old friend, the boy she never quite got off with, in the brilliant 'Vida Loca' (21–23). Audaciously, Jaime announces the event that will end the gang-war story, by subtitling it 'The Death Of Speedy Ortiz', allowing the mood of bittersweet regret to carry the tale.

Things are even less cheerful from then on. Jaime orchestrates a huge cast of characters over twenty-eight more issues, putting each into the spotlight in turn. The plot swoops around examining a younger generation via Hopey's pretty younger brother Joey and his friends, but always returns to Maggie. One of the best later stories, 'Chester Square', in issue 40, amazes the reader by digging still deeper into this character we've been reading about for forty issues as Maggie, abandoned in a neighbourhood she hasn't visited for years, is mistaken for a whore. Jaime draws in a wonderful, sexy *Archie* style, with hints of Kirby and Toth to sharpen it up. He has a great eye for spotting blacks and dramatic composition, not to mention slapstick effects, and even in the last issues, when Maggie has been through relationships and rejections, she can still have a screaming fit that involves steam coming out of her nostrils and goggling eyes. Jaime should be remembered for his ability to put ennui on paper. He studies the limitedness of life over and over, using his 'Chester Square' series of stories to go over significant events in the previous forty issues once again.

Gilbert (or Beto) is a comics version of Gabriel Garcia Marquez, a magic realist who mingles symbolic acts with everyday dramas in the small Mexican town of Palomar. After several science-fiction stories, including the ambitious 'BEM' (2), Gilbert settled into producing long story arcs, rather than series of short tales like his brother, which start with the arrival of the huge-breasted Luba in the small town, and end with her departure several decades later after an earthquake has destroyed it, serial killers have run amok, and many of her children, all by different fathers, have left home. He explores both the history of the town and Luba's past, again creating a large cast, all of whom will have important roles to play as the stories unfold. He is particularly good, given the number of years the story sweeps over, at confounding your expectations for his characters. He brings perspective to his stories with 'An American In Palomar' (13–14), in which a photographer is delighted to discover such a run-down, backward place and intends to take portraits for a coffee-table 'exposé' of the poor peasants. He surfaces again at the end of the symbolic serial-killer story 'Human Diastrophism' (21–26), which begins with the residents of Palomar joining together to bludgeon a plague of monkeys and ends up with the illiterate Tonantzin, always portrayed as a sexy airhead, immolating herself on television, watched by the photographer. The liberal nonsense he spouts as he ignores his girl-friend being genuinely moved by the scene is one of Gilbert's finest moments.

Although of significance in understanding Luba's character, the long story arc 'Poison River' (29–40), which deals with her life before she sought refuge in Palomar, is probably Beto's least successful work. It has a deliberately chaotic structure, in which Luba's reactions to a hasty marriage to a gangster, and being taken from a quiet life into the glitz and danger of a big-city underworld, are echoed in the story-telling. The reader meets dozens of characters, eavesdrops on incomprehensible conversations between her husband and his operatives, and watches her get hooked on drink and drugs, with all the distortions they cause. It's just too much, panels packed onto the page to get through a huge amount of narrative. The graphic novel, with fifty extra pages, may be even longer but it allows the story some room to breathe.

Generally, though, there is a much greater sense of control and intention in Gilbert's plotting, which is why you can't really avoid reading 'Poison River'. Few stories are insignificant, even delightful shorts like 'The Whispering Tree', in which one of Luba's daughters convinces her sister that a tree's branches rubbing together are the voice of a bruja, or witch. Some of his most touching stories centre around the children of Palomar and their untimely, not to say peculiar ends, and he has a particular gift for drawing gangly-limbed, huge-headed kids. Gilbert is a much more workmanlike artist than his brother, less crowd-pleasing, except in his fondness for women with big hooters. He pushes the story along with the art, using expression and pose to tell half of it, inking freely with a brush and drawing barren landscapes and children with great freedom and beauty.

Love and Rockets contains two of the best dramas you'll find in comics to date. The main stories complement each other perfectly. Both are semi-fantasies which, understandably, have drawn a lot of female readers, attracted by the high number of strong female leads. The Hernandez Brothers share the ability to make you care about their characters deeply and to handle big issues with a personalized touch that gives them impact.

The British collected editions of *Love and Rockets* (from Titan and Penguin) differ in content from their American counterparts, often confusingly using the same titles. They split the work of Gilbert and Jaime into separate editions more than the Fantagraphics editions, so each is listed with the corresponding creator. Many also include additional material, some of which is published in magazine form as the *Love & Rockets Bonanza*, alongside stories prepared for other publications.~FJ

Recommended: 2–26, 37, 40, 48, 50

Collections: Ape Sex (J 18–25+ short from *Mechanics* 1), *Blood Of Palomar* (G 21–26), *Chelo's Burden* (G+J 3–4), *Chester Square* (J 40–50), *The Death Of Speedy* (J 21–27), *Duck Feet* UK (G 11–18), US (G+J 16–19), *Flies On The Ceiling* (G 27–28, J 29–32), *Heartbreak Soup And Other Stories* (G 1–8), *House Of Raging Women* UK (J 26–32), US (G+J 12–15), *Human Diastrophism* (G21–26), *Las Mujeres Perdidas* (G+J 5–10), *The Lost Women* (J 9–16), *Love & Rockets* (J 1–8), *Love And Rockets X* (G 31–39), *Luba Conquers The World* (G 43–50), *Music For Mechanics* (G + J 1–2), *Poison River* (G 29–40), *The Reticent Heart* (G 9–16), *Tears From Heaven* (G+J 11–15), *Wigwam Bam* (J 33–39)

LOVE LETTERS In The Hand
Eros: *3-issue miniseries 1991–1992*

A positive rarity this, a series for a sex comics imprint in which the sex is essential to the story, and furthermore there's a story to be told. David Hodson contrived a simple but beguiling plot involving the maximum amount of sex, with the assorted couplings occurring in a small 1960s Australian town. A drifter named Stan arrives to bury himself away from trouble, but becomes embroiled in a relationship, the outcome of which is inevitable. There's a wry sense of humour involved, as evinced by 1's postcard pastiche depicting who's fucking whom, and by the daft 'Surferman' strip in 2, but it's the finely paced, almost film noir aspects that see the story through.~WJ

LOVE STORIES
DC: *7 issues (147–153) 1972 –1973*

A retitling of the long running *Heart Throbs* for its final few issues. The 'mod' new name didn't help much.~HS

LOWLIFE
Caliber: *2 issues 1991*
Aeon: *3 issues (3–5) 1993–1996*

Lowlife's lead character Tommy is a whining and self-pitying introspective who prefers to pontificate about life than to participate in one. Unfortunately, after a first issue of autobiographical material, one suspects that creator Ed Brubaker is merely applying a thin veneer of fiction over further auto-biographical sequences. Anyone who can read *Lowlife* without wanting to reach into the comic and throttle Tommy screaming 'Wake up and smell the coffee' ought to question their reading habits. Brubaker's art, though, is

very simple, open and appealing, and at his best (3's story of ripping off the shop he works in) he can be engaging. If you're a selfish wastepail borrow this comic and see your lifestyle justified and vindicated.~FP

LUCIFER
Trident: *3-issue miniseries 1990*

This miniseries from writer Eddie Campbell and artists Phill Elliott (1) and Paul Grist (2–3) just about sustains its whimsical tone over three thinly plotted issues. Lucifer is a wicked young man who enters hell through a monstrous wart extracted from a man's nose. After bumping off the devil Lucifer becomes the new ruler of the underworld, and sets about creating hell on Earth. Grist's smooth artwork particularly complements Campbell's soup of bad puns (like that one), absurdist humour and mild-mannered satire.~AL

LUCKY LUKE
Hodder and Stoughton: *8 volumes 1972–1982*
Ravette: *1 volume 1991*

This highly popular comedy Western strip first appeared as a one-off in the 1946 French anthology *Almanach De Spirou*, written and drawn by Belgian cartoonist Maurice de Bevère, aka Morris. Born in 1923, Morris had previously shared an animation studio with two other giants of the Franco-Belgian comics scene – André Franquin, creator of accident-prone office boy Gaston Lagaffe and the exotic animal strip The Marsupilami, and Joseph Gillain (aka Jijé), influential artist on the Jerry Spring Western adventure and a mentor to modern-day master Jean 'Moebius' Giraud. When Lucky Luke proved to be an immediate hit he graduated to his own weekly strip in *Spirou*, and from there to a series of best-selling collections, animated feature films, TV programmes, and numerous spin-offs and tie-ins. Lucky Luke is a laconic, do-gooding drifter, 'a poor lonesome cowboy a long way from home' who can 'shoot faster than his own shadow'. He was always accompanied by his faithful but cynical horse Jolly Jumper. Luke's adventures were meticulously researched historical farces that showcased Morris's clear linework and gift for character comedy. Like other European creators Morris was captivated by the sense of freedom, optimism and newness that America, and the American Wild West, represented. In 1948 Morris joined Franquin and Gillain for a six-year sojourn in North America, incorporating his experiences and insights into the new Luke stories that continued to appear in France. Morris also met the French writer René Goscinny in New York, where Goscinny had been exchanging ideas with Harvey Kurtzman. Morris returned to

Belgium in 1954, and began collaborating with Goscinny on a run of exquisite Luke stories – 'The Stage Coach', 'Western Circus', 'Curing The Daltons', 'Dalton City', 'The Tenderfoot' and 'Apache Canyon' amongst the best of them. Like Goscinny's other famous creation Asterix, Lucky Luke became a vehicle for the writer's satiric imagination, with Goscinny poking gentle fun at the conventions and clichés of numerous Western movies, while thankfully avoiding Asterix's torturous punning. The strip's supporting characters grew, with the introduction of psychotic bandits The Daltons and dumb dog Ran-Tan-Plan, appearing alongside such historical figures as Judge Roy Bean, Calamity Jane and Jesse James.

Since Goscinny's death, Morris has continued to produce occasional Lucky Luke adventures with the assistance of writers like Fauche and Leturgie. In 1983 Luke's ubiquitous cigarette was abandoned in favour of a more health-conscious blade of grass, although some covers on the 1970s English editions of *Lucky Luke* already have the offending snout clumsily removed. These translations, by Frederick W. Nolan, are witty and concise, but have been out of print for years and are now tough to find. In England Ravette also published a single, post-Goscinny story in 1991, 'The Dalton Brothers Memory Game', which showed that Morris' style had barely altered since the 1940s. Translated into twenty-three different languages and still one of the most instantly recognisable characters in European comics, Lucky Luke remains perennially underappreciated by English-speaking comic fans.~AL

Recommended: *Apache Canyon, Curing The Daltons, The Dalton Brothers Memory Game, Dalton City, The Dashing White Cowboy, Jesse James, The Stage Coach, The Tenderfoot, Western Circus*

LUGER
Eclipse: *3-issue miniseries 1986–1987*

One of Bruce Jones' ongoing attempts to bring old-fashioned pulp adventures to an unwitting (and, one suspects, often unwilling) public. Luger is a big-game hunter with an insane sister who gets involved in a search for a missing heiress. Good, risqué fun on the whole, with atmospheric art by Bo Hampton and Tom Yeates.~NF

LUM
Viz: *8 issues 1989–1990*

Young Ataru Moroboshi has a face shadowed by misfortune, or so says an ancient (and greedy) Buddhist monk called Cherry, who accidentally pushes him into a river while trying to stop him committing suicide. Ataru

has had a bust-up with his girlfriend Shinobu, but he's hardly suicidal. However from that moment forward Ataru's life is dogged by misfortune. Returning home he finds he's been chosen by space demons to fight their champion Lum for mastery of the earth – by playing tag. In the course of winning the contest, which occupies the early issues, Ataru accidentally asks her to marry him. The rest of the series recounts his attempts to convince Lum he doesn't love her and Shinobu that he does, a classic Rumiko Takahashi love triangle which is soon complicated by the arrival of various other suitors for the hands of all three of them.

Takahashi's plotting is playful, as Ataru's home is overrun by demons (part 3), his mother falls in love with Lum's sexy fiancé, Rei, who has a habit of turning into a huge monster when riled (part 6), Lum kidnaps him to attend a cosmic war with the good gods, which he loses for her side (part 8), and Lum accidentally sends him twelve years into the future, to his own school reunion, when trying to create a short-cut to the school building (part 11). But best of all is part 16, Disco Inferno. Cherry's beautiful niece Sakura asks Ataru to go dancing with her, where they're confronted by Tsubame Ozuno, her magician lover, who's been studying black magic in the west. Ozuno's first attempt to conjure Satan results in Ataru turning into Santa, but soon it's a stand-off between Rei in monster form and the lord of darkness, much to the puzzlement of the assembled groovers. Takahashi's art is simple and straightforward. Her story-telling's very direct, but she has the talent of portraying emotion in small details, as well as creating broad, slapstick sequences. Lum's not quite as manic as *Ranma 1/2*, but it's very much in the same, pleasantly confusing vein.~FJ

Recommended: 1–8

Collections: Lum vol 1 (1–4), vol 2 (5–8), The Lum Perfect Collection (1–8)

LUNATIK
Marvel: *3-issue miniseries 1995–1996*

There was previously no Marvel Universe equivalent to DC's Lobo. Now there is. Originality not at a premium, then.~WJ

LUST OF THE NAZI WEASEL WOMEN
Fantagraphics: *5 issues 1990–1991*

Entertaining adventure series that pits a burned-out alcoholic pilot who tells tall tales of fighting The Dragon Queen and Leonard, The Easter Bunny (no, really, but it's a good story), against Hitler, who's currently got the body of a parrot, and his Weasel women. Mitch Manzer doesn't always manage to pace his jokes but the bigfoot art style is pleasing on the eye.~NF

The Adventures of LUTHER ARKWRIGHT

Valkyrie: *10-issue limited series 1987–1989*
Dark Horse: *9-issue limited series 1990–1991*

In one version of reality, the (English) Civil War is still being fought in the 1980s. The agency that keeps track of a myriad different probable realities has dispatched a psychically gifted agent to assassinate the parliamentary leader, a hypocrite descending into madness, and thus bring time back into line with the future, putting a stop to cataclysmic events in other realities. That agent is Luther Arkwright, dashing adventurer, sensual lover, deadly assassin.

Based around the universes suggested in Michael Moorcock's *Jerry Cornelius* tetralogy, Bryan Talbot has woven a complex religious and political story that takes us from the painful awakening of Arkwright's mental powers in another dimension through to his god-like transcendence at the end of the tale. The art is packed with imagery, shot through with British mythology and informed by a comprehensive knowledge of world religion. That it is also drawn in Talbot's detailed, elaborately structured style is a bonus. Early issues show too much dependence on design tricks, leading to a stiffness in the action, but later ones put Talbot's theatrical sense of page layout to good effect, using chequerboards of panels to flicker between two simultaneous scenes, or slowing down the moment of assassination to half a dozen pages, each panel only fractionally different to the rest. Some readers may find it all a bit too much to assimilate, with information packed into every drawing and innumerable 'reports' on other realities threading like ticker-tape between the panels. It's a work that repays repeated reading, a love story, an allegory, a philosophical treatise: make of it what you will.

The story runs in 1–9, with Valkyrie's issue 10 (ARKeology) being a series of essays, sketches and notes. Dark Horse republished the comic on much better quality paper than the Valkyrie, but the quality of printing is poor. Go for either the limited-premium hardback or graphic novel reprints.~FJ
Recommended: 1–9
Collections: The Adventures Of Luther Arkwright Vol 1 (1–3), vol 2 (4–6), vol 3 (7–9), *The Complete Luther Arkwright* (1–9)

LUX & ALBY Sign On & Save the Universe.

Acme: *9 issues 1992–1993*

Lux the Poet & Alby Starvation, protagonists of novels by Martin Millar, are brought to comics by him and illustrator Simon Fraser. Living in a Brixton squat, airhead Lux and paranoid Alby are fair game for any strange character who comes along. Their house alone has a belligerent student of the I-Ching who wants to force his way into Nirvana, a cult who worship the goddess Ishtar (who handily becomes a major player in the series), a philosophical plant, a contented hamster, and visiting drug addicts. Throw in a drunken handmaiden sent on a holy quest to become the best kisser in the universe, a paraplegic bicycle thief and sundry fairies, and you have a fascinating and rewarding read. It's shot through with eccentric humour and unusual parallels, as the battle for Nirvana is compared with the struggle for chairmanship of a housing co-operative. Fraser's art is charming, though he seems rushed towards the end of the series.~HS
Recommended: 1–9

M
Eclipse: *4-issue miniseries 1990–1991*

John J. Muth's atmospheric painted adaptation of the Fritz Lang film, based on the screenplay by Lang and Thea Von Harbou, co-writer (also with Lang) of *Metropolis*. Put under pressure by the police, Berlin's underworld criminals begin their own search for a child-murderer. When he's captured they decide to put him on trial themselves. The painted artwork attempts to bring a photo realism to the title, but sadly detracts from the story.~NF

M.A.C.H. 1 Secret Weapon
Fleetway/Quality: *9 issues 1991*

When British weekly *2000AD* launched in 1977 with four new series, Judge Dredd took off, and this third-rate *Six Million Dollar Man* was gone within the year. Over a dozen creators worked on the series, none of them with an ounce of inspiration, and why anyone thought an American audience would buy this fifteen years on is a mystery.~WJ

THE MACHINE
Dark Horse: *4 issues 1994–1995*

Having débuted in *Comics Greatest World* and hogged a fair part of early *Barb Wire* issues, The Machine stepped into his own title still hunted by the CIA. A fusion of flesh and machinery, Avram Roman can tap into any computer, has an outstanding regenerative capacity and is stronger than your average bear. It's a concept with great scope and worked well for the title's short life.~WJ

MACHINE MAN
Marvel: *9 issues 1978, 10 issues (10–19) 1979–1981, 4-issue miniseries 1984–1985*

Machine Man was one of Jack Kirby's more successful 1970s creations: a thinking robot able to elongate his limbs, he searches for a place among humanity that rejects him. It's not an original theme, and Kirby appears to be going through the motions. The art's still powerful, particularly the covers, but there's no heart. There couldn't be a bigger contrast in style between Kirby and Steve Ditko, who draws the title when it's revived a year later, but it works. Sadly, the stories, integrating Machine Man fully into the Marvel continuity,

are functional at best. Where Machine Man came into his own is the miniseries. Tom De Falco, who'd written the final few issues of the previous series, achieves a quantum leap in plotting, but it's the stunning art by Barry Windsor-Smith over Herb Trimpe's breakdowns that ensures this incarnation is memorable. The final masterful touch is having Smith also colour the issues, as his sympathetic and muted tones are essential to the evocation of a depressing future. By 2020 Machine Man has been dismantled, while his most persistent enemy owns an influential robotics corporation whose tentacles extend everywhere. Discarded by computer error, the restored Machine Man leads an uprising against the company which was founded on technology stolen from him. Ten years on, these issue were reprinted as two issues of *Machine Man 2020*.~FP
Recommended: Miniseries 1–4
Collection: Machine Man (miniseries 1–4)

MACKENZIE QUEEN
Matrix: *5 issues 1983–1984*

Mackenzie Queen lives happily in a castle. Day-to-day subsistence is not too bad, thanks mainly to his isolated location, but also because of those powers of total wish fulfilment at his command. Then those bothersome agents of the Brotherhood show up and volunteer him to help repel the Ice Men, who are giving a spot of trouble. Oh, they're also about to invade Earth. Luckily, he's assisted by his interplanetary Volkswagen Beetle and Ududu, a sort of personification of the devil: 'Have any meat? I like it drippy… What's this? – Cornflakes – This isn't meat! No… but they drip.' It's by Bernie Mireault. It's in black and white. It's underground. It's sparse. It's crude. It's vulgar. It's very, very funny.~APS
Recommended: 1–5
Collection: Mackenzie Queen (1–5)

MACROSS
Comico: *36 issues, 1984–1989*

The original *Macross* was a Japanese animated series featuring 'mecha' – planes and other equipment that transformed into robots. The comic started as an adaptation of that Japanese series (1), but then the *Robotech* TV series was created as an English-language adaptation of

Macross and two other Japanese mecha series and the comic had a change of title to *Robotech: the Macross Saga*, and also of style. The story centres around the Macross battle fortress. This was built by unknown aliens and crashed on Earth in 1998. Humans put a lot of effort into mending it, and it repays them by powering up its automatic defence systems when it senses that its old enemy (the Zentraedi) are in range, and then blasting half of the Zentraedi fleet out of the sky. This means that the Zentraedi immediately wage war on Earth, and the humans make no attempt to explain but simply launch the Macross and pursue the battle out in space. This launch drags most of the surrounding city along with the ship, so the stories can feature a lot of domestic urban detail (beauty contests and teenage recording stars, mostly) mixed in with the heroic teenage fighter-pilots. This plot doubtless seems really clever and cool when you're about ten, and as entertainment for children goes, it's well crafted (apart from 1, which had ghastly artwork), though one hopes that any girl-child who picks it up already has enough self-confidence to shrug off the relentless undermining that's inflicted on the female characters. However, if your tenth birthday is but a dim memory and you're not in the advanced stages of Manga addiction, you can safely give this one a miss.~FC

MACROSS II
Viz: *10 issues 1992–1993*

Tsuguo Okazaki and Sukehiro Tomita produced a Japanese comics adaptation of the video series *Macross II*, and this title is an English translation of that comic. The story takes place eighty years after the first Macross story, and Earth has been successfully keeping the enemy Zentraedi at bay with recordings of pop songs. However, the enemy's own singers have now arrived and in this story one of them is captured by a shallow young journalist and brought to Earth, causing changes in the singer, the journalist and the war. This isn't a humour series, though it's hard to describe without making it sound like a joke. The pop-song defence was inherited from the first series, where it went almost unnoticed among all the other idiocies designed for the ten-year-old brain. Transplanted to a comic for adults, though, it looks very strange, and that does seem to be much of the point of the story: redesigning the enemy's culture so that their reaction to the pop songs makes sense. The redesign works well, and the comic has a much more alien feel than the first series. Other changes: there's far less emphasis on the transforming machines, and far more on character development (though the characters still struggle to get to two dimensions), and the artwork is much more varied and dramatic. No

change, though, in the action sequences, which are almost impossible to follow. Read an issue or two for the atmosphere, but don't expect much of the narrative.~FC

MAD-DOG
Marvel: *6 issues 1993*

The 1990s *Bob* TV show cast Bob Newhart as a comic artist given the opportunity to revive his homely 1960s character Mad-Dog provided it was given a grim and gritty reworking more in keeping with the name. *Mad-Dog* is a flip comic offering both versions. Ty Templeton's humorous take on the naïvety of 1960s comics, with the original Mad-Dog, is more successful than the updated version, which isn't far enough removed from the ultra-violent 1990s superheroes it parodies.~FP

MAD DOGS
Eclipse: *3-issue miniseries 1992*

Violent thriller in which the cops are as reckless as the gangsters, hence the title. Excellent Victor Toppi artwork promotes this above average.~FP

MAD HOUSE
Archie/Red Circle: *130 issues, 11 Annuals 1959–1982*

Probably best known for its short-lived incarnation as a serious horror anthology (95–97), *Mad House* started life as *Archie's Mad House* from 1–66. 1–17 featured the regular Archie crew (with Betty and Veronica, Jughead *et al.*), but largely in stories of vampires, werewolves and so on, since the Universal horror films were being revived on TV at the time. After 18 it became modelled on the original satire comic/magazine, *Mad*, but mostly did parodies of superheroes and other comic-book genres, again cashing in on the current trends. Sabrina the Teenage Witch first appeared in 22, and became a lasting Archie star. Captain Sprocket followed in 25, and remained the lead superhero parody until the next remodelling. Hippies, mods and pop groups started making more and more appearances as the 1960s went on. A name change to *Madhouse Ma-ad Jokes* took place from 66–70. By now the year was 1969, so up-to-date Archie Comics made with the 1960s slang, daddy-o, changing the name to *Madhouse Ma-ad Freakout* from 71. 72 features the Archies, cartoon pop stars who topped the real-life charts, but from 73–94 the name was *The Mad House Glads*, and the comic featured its own pop group of the same name. Their groupie, Fran the Fan, and her pal Rod The Mod (not looking a bit like Rod 'the mod' Stewart), both starred in strips of their own.

95–97 must have come as something of a shock to regular readers, as the name reverted to *Mad House* and humour went out of the window, replaced by the trend *du jour* once again. In 1974 horror comics were big. Art and stories by old pros like Gray Morrow sat well next to the work of up-and-comers like Bruce Jones and Sal Amendola. 97 saw the first appearance of Sherlock Holmes lookalike Henry Hobson, drawn by Frank Thorne and perhaps intended as a series. It was not to be, however, as 98–130 saw the return of the humour format, without the Glads this time, but concentrating again on media and TV parodies. Some reprint material, including Captain Sprocket, was now included. All the Annuals are humour, and 11 is noteworthy for a Wally Wood reprint, mixing the perennial *Mad House* subject-matter of monsters, hippies/mods and pop music, as Frankenstein's Monster goes Flower Power and his creator opens a disco. Curiously, the punchline of this strip was used as the cover gag of 114, which doesn't contain the story.

The particular challenge of attempting a *Mad Magazine* format, while retaining an Archie house-style, was always going to cause problems. One major stumbling-block is that Archie humour simply isn't very funny. The comics' strengths, such as they are, lie with their continuing characters. Without the core Archie gang it's amazing that *Mad House*, in its various guises, lasted as long as it did.~GL

MAD RACCOONS

Mu Press: *6 issues + 1991 to date*

Cathy Hill's Mad Raccoons is an annually published anthropomorphic series that manages the difficult task of staying this side of cute, but retaining good, old-fashioned charm. Virgil is constantly frustrated, ever ready to fall into a tantrum, Uncle Erf has a personality disorder that makes him act at times like his own son, his own wife or his own dog, Orly and Poppyseed are the youngsters, while Cousin Lemur is a wandering minstrel. The strips are generally light-hearted explorations of the raccoons' world, but alongside these are features on Raccoons in Literature or The Philosophy of Raccoons. The black and white cartooning is simple but visually inventive, with an acknowledged debt to such greats as Walt Kelly, Carl Barks and George Herriman.~NF

Recommended: Collection

Collection: Mad Raccoons (1–4 plus additional material)

MADAME XANADU

DC: *One-shot 1981*

Much was expected from the *Detective* dream-team supreme of Steve Englehart and Marshall Rogers in the first comic to be sold only through direct-market outlets and thus free from Comics Code restrictions. Englehart offers up those subjects he likes best: the Tarot, drugs and demonology in a lead feature that might have held water had it been published in flower-power days. Ironically, it takes backstage to DeMatteis and Bolland's poignant seven-page science-fiction back-up.~APS

MADMAN

Tundra: *3-issue miniseries 1992, 3-issue miniseries (Madman Adventures) 1992–1993*

Dark Horse: *11 issues + (Madman Comics) 1994 to date*

Infused with the spirit of 1950s science-fiction films, *Madman* is also partially a return to the innocent superheroes of yesteryear. Writer and artist Mike Allred convincingly presents a world of benign and eccentric inventors creating strange robots, touching and friendly relationships, and although starring a costumed lead, there are no supervillains and this is no traditional superhero series.

The first squarebound Tundra series is grey, black and white, and Allred has yet to refine the elements of his strip. There's a darker than usual tone throughout with some resolutely unpleasant (and now uncharacteristic) scenes, but Allred's art is already polished, and it's a fine B-movie style plot. The socially dysfunctional Frank (Madman – although he's never referred to as such, it's just a catchy title) is full and present in costume, and must locate a scientist to revive his scientist pal, knocked down by a car. The story establishes the main cast, some of whom were introduced in Allred's previous series, *Grafik Musik*, is enjoyable, and from many others would stand alone as excellent, but for Madman it's more a prelude. The second Tundra series is pretty much the finished article, featuring a more mature Frank, and a much lighter tone; Laura Allred's vibrant colours provide the final step to an entirely charismatic package.

The continuing series is titled *Madman Comics*, and is a success from the off. In the first few issues there's a plethora of bug-eyed monsters, inventive robots and aliens. Hellboy is in 5, and The Big Guy assists Frank (or vice versa) in 6 and 7. The entire series is a triumph, and anyone who's going to like *Madman* will be instantly drawn to it. 9 is a tale, pretty much complete in one issue, of Madman shrunk to minute stature having to make his way home; this is a good representative sample. Such is the Madman's popularity and visual appeal that there are also two series of bubblegum cards (without the bubblegum), offering interpretations of the character from some of the greatest artists around. Allred's been using the illustrations as back-cover pin-ups, but they're entirely worth a separate purchase.~WJ

Recommended: *Madman Adventures* 1–3, *Madman Comics* 1–11

Collections: Madman Adventures (1–3), *The Oddity Odyssey* (Madman 1–3)

MAEL'S RAGE
Ominous: *1 issue 1994*

Artist Bart Sears strikes out on his own and rapidly proves he can turn out plotless big-bicep nonsense with the best of them. A career move to Extreme Studios surely beckons.~FP

MAGE
Comico: *15 issues 1984–1986*

Reading *Mage* can be very refreshing if you like fantasies but are fed up with soft-centred fairies and hobbits. If you don't, you'll probably find it twee. Matt Wagner has a direct approach to story-telling. His hints are very heavy, and most of the time he has one of his characters explain anything that might be confusing to another. His art's bold too, with lots of black backgrounds and bold brush-strokes; Sam Kieth played to this when he took over inks with 4, but added his own finesse. *Mage* is a quirky updating of Arthurian myth, fast-paced and engaging (if you can stomach whimsical touches like calling the hero Kevin Matchstick). It's unsophisticated but well-structured and full of likeable characters, from Mirth, the teasing wizard, to Sean, the morose ghost. It has all the appeal of films like *Highlander*, but takes itself less seriously, with the characters periodically aware of how silly they sometimes appear. Wagner's art improves throughout. In 1 his action scenes are jerky, but by 5 the comic's become a breathless read. Kieth's inks are dazzling, but the effect is undermined by the garish application of colour. From 6 there's a regular Grendel back-up (and indeed Mage features as back-up in some issues of *Grendel*). The advertised second series never appeared.~FJ
Recommended: 5–8
Collections: Mage Vol 1 (1–5), Vol 2 (6–10), Vol 3 (11–15)

MAGGIE THE CAT
Image: *2 issues 1996*

Arguably Mike Grell's best character, cat-burglar Maggie gets a chance at her own title on the strength of the general interest in 'bad girls' as female leads. Grell's scripting has never been particularly focused and his artwork on this title is looser than ever. Originally a light-hearted sparring partner for Grell's pseudo-Willie Garvin, Jon Sable, for this series Maggie is thrust into a world of spies and international intrigue which doesn't particularly suit her character or her abilities.~NF

Calling John Force MAGIC AGENT
ACG: *3 issues 1962*

Force was a sort of one-man *X-Files*, investigating supernatural threats with a few tricks up his sleeve to stop them. There are three short stories each issue, but the occasionally inventive plots of Richard E.Hughes are dulled by the art of Pete Contaza and, particularly, Paul Reinman. Force later settled into occasional appearances in ACG mystery title *Unknown Worlds*.~WJ

THE MAGIC FLUTE
Eclipse: *3-issue miniseries 1990*

Mozart's *Magic Flute* is a perennially popular opera, conveying tragedy, farce and romance; here the spectacle is rendered in exquisite fashion with an extraordinary delicacy by P. Craig Russell. He is, however, ploughing a lonely and eccentric furrow in adapting operas to comics. While they have the capacity for pomp and pageantry bestowed by an unlimited budget, the missing sound and fury renders them an unsuitable receptacle for opera, and with little to clothe bare-bones plots one is left with a hollow item of great beauty.~FP

MAGIC: THE GATHERING
Armada: *4-issue miniseries ('Shadow Mage')1995, 2-issue microseries ('Arabian Nights') 1995, One-shot ('Homelands') 1996, 2-issue microseries ('Legend of Jedit Ojanen') 1996, 2-issue microseries ('Shandalar') 1996*

These are comics based on the collectable card game that took the world by storm. Although better produced than the similar role-playing-game comics that preceded them by half a decade, they remain pedestrian sword-and-sorcery material.~HS
Collection: Shadow Mage (1–4)

MAGIK
Marvel: *4-issue miniseries 1983–1984*

In *Uncanny X-Men* 160, seven-year-old Illyana Rasputin is transported to the magical realm of Limbo, ruled by the demon Belasco. She returns to Earth in a second, twice the age she should be, with fantastic powers. This series by Chris Claremont, John Buscema and Tom Palmer fills in the story of what happened in the seven years she spent in Limbo, with liberal sprinklings of alternate-world versions of familiar characters and all the trademark Claremont *angst*.~JC

MAGNETO
Marvel: *One-shot, 1994, 4-issue miniseries 1996–1997*

The début one-shot was a embossed cover reprint of two Claremont/Bolton back-ups from *Classic X-Men* with a framing sequence and a pin-up gallery. The second attempt to give one of Marvel's potentially most interesting characters his own title was not as prettily drawn and nowhere near as well written. An amnesiac Magneto, now reformed and calling himself Joseph, meets his former followers the Acolytes once again, and Peter Milligan proves once again that while he can be a talented writer, he and the Marvel mainstream just don't mix.~JC

The Mighty MAGNOR
Malibu: *6-issue miniseries 1993–1994*

Sergio Aragonés attempts to recreate the success of his *Groo The Wanderer* with this tale of an amnesiac spaceman who ends up in the hands of two struggling comic artists. Seizing the opportunity, they set him up as a real-life superhero, claiming ownership and responsibility, at least until the lawsuits for property damage start coming in! Hilarious stuff.~HS
Recommended: 1–6

MAGNUS/NEXUS
Valiant/Dark Horse: *2-issue microseries 1993*

Prettily drawn by Steve Rude, former assistant to Magnus creator Russ Manning, but otherwise fairly inconsequential team-up between the two characters. Written by regular Nexus scribe Mike Baron, the story deals with Arkon, an alien who arrives on Magnus's planet and goes about curing the population of all ills. Predictably, all is not what it seems and Nexus soon turns up to save the day.~JC

MAGNUS, ROBOT FIGHTER
Gold Key: *46 issues 1963–1977*

Given the brief of creating a science-fiction strip of the type that would be too costly for television, Russ Manning came up with Magnus. Raised from the cradle by all-wise robot 1A, Magnus combats renegade robots in an otherwise idyllic 40th century. Manning plotted and drew the first twenty-one issues (with Mike Royer assisting towards the end of his tenure), and never put a foot wrong. His fluid, controlled artwork enabled him to switch from action scenes to everyday moments with naturalistic ease. His characters were clean and heroic, his villains had a distinctive silent-film quality, and his robots, though seemingly fragile, were well designed, but Manning's plots were really only showcases for the action and the art. 22 reprints the first issue, and with the exception of the substandard 42 and 44 the remaining issues are all reprint. Valiant issued a further series of reprints with four issues of *Vintage Magnus, Robot Fighter* to accompany their revival of the character. The back-up strip 'Aliens', also by Manning, also ran in 1–22, and early strips were reprinted as a one-shot.~SW

MAGNUS Robot Fighter
Valiant: *65 issues (0–64), 1 Yearbook 1991–1996*

This revival of the old Gold Key character is surprising in many ways. Apart from true diehard comics fans, very few of the 1990s generation had heard of, let alone seen, the original, and a bloke beating up robots seemed an odd choice of character with which to launch a new line of comics. But Valiant were right to do it. With a deliberate retro-1950s science-fiction look and crisp, clean, art the series was very distinct in the 1990s.

The plots, initiated by Jim Shooter, elaborate on the simpler original series. Magnus is a nigh-invincible human living in a huge 41st-century conurbation called North-Am. There are millions of robots to perform every conceivable menial task, and they act as police and ambulances and do all the manual labour. The only problem is when they go haywire and start killing people. That's where Magnus comes in. He's been specially trained from birth, and has the speed and power to punch right through rogue robots, thus being appointed the people's hero by the high council. The society is far from perfect, though, with two classes separated by a huge gap: the wealthy élite and the downtrodden proles, known as Gophs. Many of the early issues are overwritten, but give glimpses of the council's political machinations, internal feuding and attempted coups that form the basis of the series. Along with robot bashing, of course.

Rai débuted in 5, and occupied a back-up strip before moving into his own title. He'd turn up several times to help out Magnus, in more ways than one in a later episode. Magnus' love interest, as in the original series, is councillor Leeja Cane, and their affair runs hot and cold throughout the series. The writers changed with great frequency, but without affecting the title as a whole, and 13–14 reintroduced old enemy Merkman from the original series just before Magnus was whisked off to save the world as part of the *Unity* crossover, with his hitherto unrevealed parentage featuring in 16. Throughout the run the interesting concept of robot rights is raised, as several robots develop emotions and feelings and demand equality with humans. These 'freewills', one of whom raised Magnus, escape oppression and form an autonomous state, with their leader Tekla, a female robot. Steve Ditko is given the topic of robot rights in 19, and supplies a nice discussion and pencils.

There's a big change of direction from 21, when the Malevs (an equivalent to *Star Trek's* Borgs) descend to wipe out massive portions of North-Am. 25 crosses over with Rai and The Future Force, a team devoted to wiping out Malevs, and Magnus leads the survivors to South-Am, only to confront the Neo-Nazi homeland of Aryantania in a very silly story occupying 29–31. Shock surprises include Leeja shagging Rai on the sly, and Tekla confessing her undying love for Magnus. By 33 he's back in North-Am leading the resistance movement, a revolution that only works with the assistance of the freewills. A pregnant Leeja returns, and in the mopping up Magnus is made president, and the humans, in a knee-jerk reaction, decide to wipe out all robots.

A bizarre, but required, change of direction with 49 has the title leaping sixteen years further into the future. Magnus now has distinguished grey tufts of hair and a brooding teenage son. Most of the freewills have been wiped out, the exceptions being an élite band who've transferred their minds into human bodies, which prompts the question 'Why are they still fighting?' At this point Keith Giffen became writer, but his usually inventive plotting abilities deserted him here, and the best he can do is ship Magnus over to Japan with Rai in order to have him beaten to a pulp by some old enemies in 56. Finally everything went cosmic with the introduction of the Psi-Lords, and Leeja being captured by the Malevs and converted to the cause. The climax occurs on the Malev homeworld, but it's an ignominious end to a series which began as an intriguing political thriller about smashing up robots! Even the look had changed, from the appealing retro designs to high-tech 1990s, so it ends up looking like every other comic on the shelves.~TP

Recommended: 1–5, 19, 33
Collections: *Invasion* (5–8), *Steel Nation* (1–4)

MAI THE PSYCHIC GIRL
Eclipse: *28 issues 1987–1988*

Mai is a Japanese schoolgirl who has inherited powerful psychic abilities from her dead mother, abilities the Wisdom Alliance, bent on world domination, want to train and harness. In order to escape them Mai must leave behind her ordinary life, her school-friends and her father, and take a journey, both physical and spiritual, to learn how to best use her inheritance. Kazuya Kudo's script blends the everyday, the mystical and the futuristic effortlessly. Mai is perfectly portrayed on the cusp of adolescence, feisty but needing guidance, alternately exulting and horrified by her powers, laughing with her school-friends over a crush but knowing, simultaneously, that her mind has huge destructive potential. Kudo keeps the comic full of surprises, bursts of humour interspersing epic mental battles and people being injured and killed when you're not sure they're too intrinsic to the plot, and too likeable, to deserve such a fate. Ryoichi Ikegami matches these abrupt changes in his artwork. Full of splash pages for confrontations, he also has plenty of time for slapstick sequences and tender scenes. His art is a little more cartoony than usual, particularly in the humour scenes, but it's a lot more realistic than the traditional wide-eyed look he's chasing in his depictions

of Mai. Titan reprinted the series in four very handsome Japanese-format graphic novels.~FJ
Recommended: 1–8
Collections: *Mai The Psychic Girl* Vol 1 (1–7), vol 2 (8–14), vol 3 (15–21), vol 4 (22–28)

MAISON IKKOKU
Viz: *Part One 7 issues 1993–1994, Part Two 6 issues 1994, Part Three 6 issues 1994, Part Four 10 issues 1995, Part Five 9 issues 1995–1996, Part Six 11 issues 1996–1997*

The new manager of a small boarding house called Maison Ikkoku, Kyoko Otonashi is a young widow with a dog, Mr Soichiro. Her tenants are an odd bunch and include Yusaku, a student drop-out, Yotsuya, a mysterious young man who spends most of his time scrounging off the rest of the tenants, Akemi, a young woman who works at a local bar, and Mrs Ichinose and her son, who has shown no sign yet of the madness that seems to afflict the rest of the household. From this, Rumiko Takahashi has created a romantic soap opera in which the tenants are comic foils for the nearly-on-mostly-off relationship between Yusaku and Kyoko. Constant misunderstandings dog their lives and each is pursued by other suitors to prolong the suspense.

Part One sets the scene and introduces Mitaka, tennis coach and all-round good guy who becomes Yusaku's rival for Kyoko, and Kozue, a young girl student who starts to go out with Yusaku (when he decides that he does need an education after all) and can't understand why he won't take advantage of her. Part Two continues the will-they-or-won't-they nature of Yusaku and Kyoko's relationship, as Kyoko's parents try to persuade her to give up her job and move back with them. Yusaku meets Kozue's very friendly parents, which makes it all the more difficult for him to tell her he doesn't want to go out with her any more. Part Three begins with the loss of Mr Soichiro (named after Kyoko's late husband), but is mainly about Yusaku's misfortunes when he leaves Maison Ikkoku and ends up sharing an apartment with a masseuse and her Yakusa boy-friend. Fortunately, his friends decide to help him out of a bad situation.

The rest of the series settles into a pattern of sorts. A drunken kiss from Akemi for both Yusaku and Kyoko causes complications. Mitaka and Kozue unknowingly create the wrong impression when Kozue asks for his advice about Yusaku. Then there's an impromptu costume party when Kyoko tries on her old school uniform and Yusaku's grandmother arrives to create some inspired interference. After Grandma's return to her home in Part Five, Yusaku breaks a leg trying to rescue Kyoko from the roof and there follows a series of misadventures in the hospital that eventually includes even Mitaka. There's a change of pace with Part Six, when Maison Ikkoku gets a new resident. Nozomu is a rich trouble-maker who's there by accident but decides to stay to be close to Kyoko. Meanwhile, Yusaku lands a job as a trainee teacher at Kyoko's old school and finds himself the object of Yagami's affections, much to his consternation.

Takahashi's artwork is simple but effective, especially in the expression of emotion. The story-telling is fast-paced and full of slapstick but capable of drawing back for quieter, more intense scenes that mostly avoid seeming too manipulative. Whether you'll enjoy the series depends on your tolerance for being teased and for the unsympathetic nature of Yusaku. Everyone treats him like a doormat and his actions generally mean he deserves such treatment. There are signs, however, that as the series progresses Yusaku is growing up and as he does so, his chances with Kyoko can only get better. If you enjoy one part of the series, you'll enjoy all of it.~NF
Recommended: Part Three 1–6, Part Four 1–10, Part Five 1–9
Collections: Empty Nest (Part Four 6–10), *Family Affairs* (Part Two), *Good Housekeeping* (Part Four 1–6), *Home Sweet Home* (Part Three), *Maison Ikkoku* (Part One)

MAJOR POWER AND SPUNKY
Eros: *One-shot 1994*

Cheerfully smutty *Carry On* style romp, with no nudity or bonking, but bags of innuendo with a gay twist. Scripter Malachy Coney brings up all the old Batman and Robin camp jokes and artist Sean Doran has a real comic gift. A very funny comic if you're not narrow-minded.~HS
Recommended: 1

MALCOLM X The Angriest Man In America
London Publishing: *One-shot 1992*

Worthy but dull effort to bring the teachings of Malcolm X to a comic-reading audience. The problem lies with the illustrations, which add nothing to the text, and an unimaginative talking-heads format studiously applied throughout. You're better off buying a book.~FP

MAN
Nicotat: *1 issue 1989*

Pastiche of the ultra-violent comic characters populating comics in the 1980s, positing that the deadliest creature on Earth is Man. Inside an ultra-brute (™ & © but I'll sell at the right price) proceeds to demolish an entire town. It's a joke stretched too far, unlike the two-page back-up, in which Gerard Jones redialogues an old war story to far funnier effect.~WJ

THE MAN
Print Mint: *One-shot 1972*

Completed in 1966 while in college, this collects one of Vaughn Bodé's earliest works. It details several days in the life of a caveman, in which he simply hunts, eats and eventually finds a companion, a lizard. Taking this simple premise Bodé uses it as a means to ask some very profound questions about our relationship with the planet and life itself. Both touching and insightful, this is quite possibly the first existential comic.~DAR
Recommended: 1

MAN AGAINST TIME
Image: *6-issue limited series 1996*

An intriguing, dream-like story starring Law, a mysterious hooded figure who creates and destroys timelines at whim so he can have 1940s pilots in space and 19th-century Arizona lawmen fighting ancient Romans. Perhaps he will stop world war erupting in the Balkans a fourth time. The art by Gino DeCicco is the only clear thing in it.~GK

MAN-BAT
DC: *2 issues 1976, 3-issue miniseries 1995, 3-issue miniseries 1995–1996*

Drinking a serum that transforms him into a mixture of man and bat, Kirk Langstrom débuted in *Detective* 400. He proved popular enough to merit regular guest appearances in Batman titles thereafter, but not to sustain his own series beyond two wildly different stories, almost unconnected beyond the title character, in 1976. Back-ups in *Batman Family, Detective*, further guest shots and a one-shot reprint of his Neal Adams-illustrated appearances in *Detective* 400 and 402 were the order of the day until 1995. Featuring sumptuously painted art from John Bolton and a slim plot well paced and dialogued by Jamie Delano, the 1995 miniseries is a good read with a conservation subtext. Delano enjoys gently ridiculing Batman by giving him an investigative visit to a whorehouse and a speeding ticket, and the Man-Bat has a previously unseen agenda. The 1995–6 miniseries has Man-Bat back in Gotham and is very ordinary.~WJ
Collection: Man-Bat (1995 miniseries 1–3)

MAN-EATING COW
NEC: *10 issues 1992–1993*

Wisely realising the one-note joke of the silent title character, the series concentrates as much on the stupid superheroes populating the city, most prominently the wonderfully conceived Crime Cannibal, who eats malefactors. Presented with the po-faced sincerity of the *Airplane* movies – the police department includes an undercover clown squad – this is a different type of humour from its progenitor,

The Tick. The best sampler is 6, where cattle mutilations and UFOs plague the middle-American town of Dullsville, 'where scientists find more creative household uses for isotopes'. The final two issues form part of a longer story with the concluding issues of *Paul The Samurai*.~WJ

The Saga of the MAN ELF
Trident: *5 issues 1989–1990*

The title may sound cutesy but Guy Lawley's Michael Moorcock-inspired near-future fantasy has a very hard edge indeed, as well as enough in-jokes and references to satisfy the biggest Moorcock fan. Using the cast of the Jerry Cornelius tetralogy (and handling them better than most writers who've had a go at adding to the Cornelius canon over the years), Lawley crafts a semi-absurdist political adventure somewhere between *Luther Arkwright* and *V For Vendetta* (very English in its frame of reference, including the humour). The first two issues are beautifully illustrated by Steve Whitaker, the comic world's answer to Harold Brodsky: those in the know revere his abilities although he's hardly published a thing. *Man Elf* is drawn in an open and European style, which late-substitute artist Richard Weston tried his best to assimilate for the final three issues; unfortunately his take on it looks blocky and clumsy.~FJ
Recommended: 1–2

The Uncanny MAN-FROG
Mad Dog: *2 issues 1987*

The idea of setting a comic in a circus freak show is just so apt you wonder why no one's done it before. Perhaps considering a comic named after a single character would be more attention-grabbing, the team of John Wooley and Terry Tidwell title their series after just one member of their eccentric cast. Sadly short-lived at just two issues, this is an engaging mixture of drama and humour.~WJ

MAN FROM ATLANTIS
Marvel: *7 issues 1978*

A survivor of Atlantis aids an undersea research organisation, encountering assorted villains and anomalies. Creators Bill Mantlo and Frank Robbins seem uninspired by the mundane TV show on which this is based, and cancellation of both show and comic was swift.~FP

The MAN from U.N.C.L.E.
Millennium: *2 issues 1993*

Prosaic and unmemorable affair of Kuryakin and Solo turning out for U.N.C.L.E. to combat a latent T.H.R.U.S.H. menace, years after their active service retirement. The opening line sets the standard for the story: 'April 31st'.~APS

THE MAN IN BLACK
Harvey: *4 issues 1957–1958*
Lorne-Harvey: *1 issue 1990*

Mr Twilight, The Man In Black, variously Fate, Luck or Death,   presents short tales, some 'true', that illustrate how fate can move in mysterious ways. An eagle mascot saves a life in the American Civil War; an outlaw kills a messenger who carried a peace offering on the eve of the battle of Little Big Horn and thus ends up on the battlefield himself. The Weaver ('she who weaves the patterns of life') or Time are his opponents in these tales, urging on the worst possible conclusion, always above the action but trying to influence it. An odd idea, but always strikingly illustrated by the great Bob Powell. The 1990 issue reprints various stories from the first three issues.~NF

MAN OF WAR
Eclipse: *3-issue miniseries 1987–1988*

A centuries-old fight between aliens is finally resolved in the 1980s. Wafer-thin, muddled story that's nothing more than an exercise in page-filling from creator Bruce Jones.~WJ

MAN OF WAR
Malibu: *8 issues 1993–1994*

Malibu's flag-clad patriot steps out from *The Protectors* to progress from one punch-'em-up to the next with very little plot over eight issues. Bryan Lee and Mike Miller's art in early issues is so appalling it needs to be seen to be believed.~FP

MAN-THING
Marvel: *Series one 22 issues, 5 Giant-Size 1974–1975, series two 11 issues 1979–1981*

Continuing from *Fear*, Steve Gerber expanded his horizons to experiment with weirder and more outrageous ideas. As it's impossible to characterise Man-Thing himself, Gerber's successful line of attack was to infuse personality and depth into the supporting characters and then examine how Man-Thing reacted to their actions and, specifically, emotions. The virtual absence of superheroes and villains enhanced the whole run, and its suitability for stories of all genres was a great asset. Many issues failed but this was an acceptable by-product of the book's empirical nature. The series declined slightly after half-time, particularly as artistic instability set in and the talents of Val Mayerick and Mike Ploog were lost. Giant-Size 4 and 5 are usually remembered for the first two Howard the Duck solo stories. This does no justice to Giant-Size 4. Words are inadequate to describe the magnificent Man-Thing lead story, Steve Gerber's personal favourite issue. The Man-Thing is drawn towards a funeral, feeding off the strong emotions and recriminations, and the story goes on to relate the circumstances of death.

The revival was mostly crafted by Chris Claremont, who never came to terms with the concept. His approach was much as Gerber's in the first series, but failed to match the bizarre mood. Whereas Man-Thing was an integral part of Gerber's scripts, Claremont's gave the impression that the swamp-dweller was dispensable. Issue 10 is the most impressive, thanks to a guest-starring role by John Kowalski from *War is Hell*.~APS

Recommended: Series one 2–6, 11, 16–18, Giant-Size 2–4

Daredevil: THE MAN WITHOUT FEAR

Marvel: *5-issue miniseries 1993–1994*

As part of the revamping of Daredevil's character, this miniseries presents his definitive origin. The story is fast-paced and detailed, with his initial meeting with Elektra (4) particularly well handled, mixing mystery, love and an overwhelming sense of anticipation. The end-product is a brilliant portrayal of the man behind the costume. Frank Miller's words give real emotional depth to the cast, while John Romita Jnr's pencils have never been as truly brilliant as they are here, displaying striking characters and wonderful backdrops. One of the finest comics of recent times.~SS

Recommended: 1–5

Collection: Man Without Fear (1–5)

MANDRAKE

King: *10 issues 1966–1967*

A classic old comics character is ill-served in this 1960s revival, notable only for four pages of early Jeff Jones art in 8 and a reprinted Alex Raymond strip in 10.~FP

MANHUNT

Print Mint: *1 issue 1973*
Cartoonists Co-Op: *1 issue (2) 1974*

An interesting but only partially successful comic about relationships, produced by a mixture of male and female cartoonists. The most talented cartoonists were certainly Gary Hallgren, Ted Richards and Bobby London, but their material here is disappointingly trite. More interesting by far was Aline Kominsky's crudely drawn 'Fat Came Between Us' in 1 and 'I Was A Teenage Intellekshul!', a presumably autobiographical piece by the great Lee Marrs in 2. Quite a lot of the material was clearly designed to be shocking – Leslie Cabarga's 'Child Molester' in 2, for instance – but what once seemed far gone can leave a contemporary audience rather unsettled.~DAR

MANHUNTER

DC: *24 issues 1988–1990*

No relation to the previous Manhunters (for which see *Detective*), Mark Shaw was introduced in *First Issue Special* 5 as a wannabe superhero manipulated by alien masters. Everything came to a head in the *Millennium* series, leaving Shaw independent, with a mask full of gimmicks but with his identity public knowledge. 2 is a rare occurrence, mostly occupied by a genuinely suspenseful and inventive fight sequence, but the diluted reprise that concludes the series is disappointing. There's minimal continuity between 4 and 18 (although 14 is a chapter of the 'Janus Directive' crossover) and all are decent superhero comics. Those who prefer final resolutions to the happy ending closing the series should check *Eclipso* 13.~WJ

Recommended: 2, 4

MANHUNTER

DC: *13 issues (0–12) 1994–1995*

With the name once again up for grabs, DC unleashed this musician bonded with an eldritch entity called The Huntsman. A difficult-to-follow origin story occupies 0–3, and it turns out to be a mixture of selling one's soul to the devil and your basic revenge plot. In 4 the villain says 'You're supposed be something new. Show me something different', and that really sums up the series. The stylised art and non-linear story-telling are mere trickery disguising the banal, clichéd and obvious. Steven Grant and Vince Giarrano managed far better with *Badlands*.~FP

MANTRA

Malibu: *Series one 24 issues, 1 Giant-Size 1993–1995, 2-issue microseries ('Spear Of Destiny')1995, series two 7 issues 1995–1996*

The tragic (in every sense of the word) story of a man trapped inside a woman's body, a plot device also used by writer Mike Barr in *Camelot 3000* a few years previously. Is he trying to tell us something? Mantra is an age-old mystic named Lukasz who finds himself trapped in 20th-century Eden Blake's body. There's lots of sub-Adam Hughes cheesecake artwork, giving the series the feel of a mystic *Ghost*. The majority of issues take place firmly in Malibu's Ultraverse version of Earth, but 9–14 are a tedious fantasy epic, 'The Archmage Quest', set on a planet where mystics rule and men and women only shag once a year. Particularly naff plot-lines involve Mantra getting married (4), and pregnant (18)! The starter for the second series is numbered with an infinity symbol and introduces a new Mantra and new writer. It doesn't help, and that series has even less to recommend it.~TP

MARA OF THE CELTS

Aircel: *First series, 4 issues 1990–1992*
Rip Off: *1 issue 1993*

Most people don't care if porn makes sense or has a good story, but this really is one of the most stupid erotic tales ever produced. Mara lives on another planet but hops from one dimension to another whenever it looks like anything remotely interesting might happen to her on her quest for revenge against the slaver who's kidnapped her sister. Dennis Cramer's scripting is very poor: most captions tell you exactly what's happening in the pictures, and the story relies far too heavily on *deus ex machina* rescues. Nil for story-telling effort. Cramer draws in a stilted style mixed from equal parts Aubrey Beardsley and Vaughn Bodé. His ability to draw facial expressions is particularly poor. Mara's always vogueing with her tits stuck out, and despite being set up as a positive figure of a woman she's rather offensively passive in the final analysis. Not the best choice for a quiet evening in, I'm afraid.~FJ

Collection: Mara of the Celts (1–4, one-shot)

THE MARK

Dark Horse: *6 issues 1987–1988, 4-issue miniseries 1994*

The potentially interesting idea of a man branded 'genetically impure' waging a war against a fascist state, Lutzania, is strangled at birth by a change of either writer or artist every issue. The succeeding stories in *Mayhem* were better, and the story continues in *Dark Horse Comics* 14–15 before the miniseries, which is much improved. In what was designed as a four-issue story, the Mark travels to the USA to kill the deposed Lutzanian dictator.~FP

MARS

First: *12 issues 1984–1985*

Mark Wheatley and Marc Hempel's metaphysical science-fantasy series ponders such abstract ideas as the nature of reality, the power of memory and the lure of dreaming. It's told in a mysterious and often metaphorical manner; some readers may well find the series simply pretentious or bafflingly obscure. However, those unfazed by the unconventional should appreciate *Mars'* pleasingly thought-provoking, mysteriously seductive qualities.

The first issue briskly introduces heroine Morgana Trace, a paraplegic able to walk in zero gravity, courtesy of a computer mindlink process invented by her late scientist father. Selected for a mission to Mars, Morgana and a crew of six are forced to hibernate for 10,000 years after all contact is lost with Earth. Finally awakening on the red planet, Morgana is immediately lured into a series of surreal and often disturbing adventures. Mars is not the bleak landscape of fact, but a lush Garden of Eden populated by fawns, alien predators, strange gods and, in issue four, the artists Van Gogh, Gauguin and Norman Rockwell!

As the series progresses Wheatley and Hempel dispense with even the pretence of linear narrative and the comic acquires a dreamlike quality, so that Mars becomes a state of mind, or perhaps even a nightmare dreamt by the dying Morgana. Underneath the simple, cartoonish artwork lurks something dark and disturbing. Wheatley and Hempel seem obsessed with decay, destruction and betrayal, themes also explored in their subsequent DC miniseries, the equally fine *Breathtaker*.~AL

Recommended: 1–12

MARS ATTACKS

Topps: *Series one 5 issues 1994, Series two 6 issues +, 1 Special 1995 to date*

Robust, often perversely hilarious gross-out spin-off from the popular 1950s bubblegum cards, released in anticipation of a movie deal. Charlie Adlard's art on the miniseries is much more fun than the needlessly sedate *X-Files* gig he moved on to, and the dark, twisted humour makes this very entertaining reading.~HS

M.A.R.S. PATROL

Gold Key: *10 issues 1965–1969*

The first two issues were titled Total War 'featuring the fighting four of M.A.R.S. Patrol'. Lt Cy Adams, Sgt Joe Striker, Cpl Russ Stacy and Sgt Ken Hiro are military specialists for the Marine Attack and Rescue Service, and the strip is 60s military paranoia with a twist. The Earth is invaded by alien troops, and it's the job of Adams and his men to thwart the attempt of the aliens to take over. The twist? The men from M.A.R.S. vs the men from Mars. 1–3 are written and superbly drawn by Wally Wood, with a further seven issues by Dan Spiegle following. The series would have been validated by some kind of conclusion, but, as it is, the first issues have better continuity than the later ones.~SW

Recommended: 1–3

MARSHAL LAW

Epic: *6-issue miniseries 1987–1989, One-shot ('Takes Manhattan') 1990*
Apocalypse: *One-shot ('Kingdom Of The Blind') 1990*
Dark Horse: *One-shot ('Super Babylon') 1992, 2-issue microseries ('Cape Fear') 1993*

The vigilante, Marshal Law, sees himself as standing alone against the decay caused in the city of San Futuro by the corrupt élitist superheroes. Some, the most powerful and popular, he tolerates publicly, derailing their schemes covertly. Others, he kills. The first series, a story of politics, power-games and serial murder, is a compelling read, dark, twisted and shot through with bleak humour. Pat Mills' mordant scripting and Kev O'Neill's disturbing art are on top form. The 'Takes Manhattan' one-shot is a parody crossbreed of the Marvel Universe with *One Flew Over The Cuckoo's Nest*, and while readable, lacks bite. 'Kingdom Of The Blind', on the other hand, has all the bite you can hope for, a savage yet perversely amusing tale of vivisection and vengeance. From there, the strip went into a run in the British comic *Toxic*, and emerged into 'Super Babylon', a superbly vicious attack on 1940s superheroic ideals and their relationship to the realities of war. After that, the Marshal started to look a bit tired. 'Cape Fear', though containing amusing sideswipes at both the 1960s incarnation of the Legion of Super-Heroes and the plethora of current X-Men titles, was just a succession of nasty gags, with everybody seemingly going through the motions.~HS

Recommended: Epic 1–6, 'Kingdom of the Blind', 'Super Babylon'

Collection: Blood, Sweat And Fears (Kingdom Of The Blind, Super Babylon + Toxic material), Crime And Punishment (Epic 1–6), Fear And Loathing (Epic 1–6, Takes Manhattan)

MARTHA WASHINGTON

Dark Horse: *5-issue miniseries ('Goes To War') 1994–1995, One-shot ('Happy Birthday') 1995, One-shot ('Stranded In Space') 1996*

Frank Miller and Dave Gibbons' war story from *Give Me Liberty* returns with more instalments from the career of Martha Washington, a poor black girl whose courage, ingenuity and fighting spirit take her from strength to strength in an army whose integrity isn't a patch on her own. It's 2014 and the USA is split into several states. Martha's lover, family and psychic friend have been killed in the nuking of Chicago, although she'll later discover some surprises on that score.

Frank Miller tells his stories using magazine covers, newspaper snippets and other print media, as well as cartoon strip, guiding his Everywoman heroine through a maze of global threats and personal attacks to emerge, mentally and physically scarred, but always alive, at the end. Dave Gibbons' lushly detailed art is admirably suited to the chases and battles that make up a large part of the story. 'Stranded In Space' is a weak one-shot with a lead story in which Martha, investigating a strange hole in space that leads to other probabilities, sees a vision of what her polluted future earth could look like. In the back-up tale, the spoofy 'Attack Of The Flesh Eating Monsters', Martha and her co-pilot are picked up by a group of flesh-eating aliens, only to find they aren't what they seem.~FJ

Collection: Martha Washington Goes To War (1–5)

MARTIAN MANHUNTER

DC: *3-issue miniseries ('American Secrets') 1992, 4-issue miniseries 1994, Special 1996*

Débuting in *Detective Comics* 225, there's a case for the Martian Manhunter being the start of the 1950s superhero revival. Despite this and being a founder-member of the Justice League in both incarnations, he's always been a second-stringer. The problem is that he's a near-omnipotent alien with a fatal weakness (when encountering fire), and DC already have a far more popular near-omnipotent alien with a fatal weakness. Gerard Jones circumvents this for the first series by concentrating on Martian Manhunter's assumed identity: John Jones, Denver police officer. It's set soon after his arrival on Earth and the plot is a checklist of the 1950s in hindsight. Payola, quiz fixing, UFO scares, a pink Cadillac, *Mad* magazine, the fear of Communism, the new suburbs, Elvis Presley (or as near as his estate's lawyers will permit) and *Leave It To Beaver* are all thrown into the mix for a dark and atmospheric story, lifted further by Eduardo Barreto's art. The succeeding series is dull stuff, as suppressed memories rise to the surface and, yawn, the Manhunter must confront his true identity. A spiritual quest also starts the 1996 Special, but it soon degenerates into fights.~FP

Recommended: Miniseries one 1–3

MARVEL ADVENTURE

Marvel: *6 issues 1975–1976*

If you want *Daredevil* 22–27 edited by a few pages per issue to fit the lower 1970s page-count this is the title for you.~FP

MARVEL CHILLERS

Marvel: 7 issues 1975–1976

The first two issues starred Modred the Mystic, an apprentice of Merlin revived from suspended animation. He would have been better left there. Previously Cat by name, Tigra prowled 3–7 after her feline transformation in *Giant-Size Creatures* 1. Tigra, Red Wolf and the sleepy outback setting collided inelegantly with robots and the Super Skrull. The only positive spark arose from her attempts to reconcile her human and feline personae. Three writers and four pencillers in five issues rarely bodes well. This series proved the point.~APS

MARVEL CLASSICS COMICS

Marvel: *36 issues 1976–1978*

The majority of these forty-eight-page literary adaptations are reprinted from the sixty black and white *Pendulum Illustrated Classics* produced by Filipino artists between 1973 and 1978. Artwork from the likes of Nestor Redondo on *Dr Jekyll And Mr Hyde* (1) and

Dracula (9), Alex Niño on *The Time Machine, Moby Dick, The Three Musketeers, War Of The Worlds* and *The Invisible Man* in 2, 8, 12, 14 and 25, and Rudy Nebres' *Treasure Island* in 15 accompanied undistinguished scripts. Only nine titles were originated by Marvel, all with equally lifeless writing. Most noteworthy for their artwork are John Buscema's *Count Of Monte Cristo* (17), Gil Kane's *Master Of The World* and *She* (21 and 24), Alfredo Alcala's *Robin Hood* (34), Frank Bolle's surprisingly faithful *Alice In Wonderland* (35) and some of Mike Golden's earliest professional work in *The Pit And The Pendulum* (28). It's hard to recommend any of these condensed classics and one has the feeling that the addition of colour may not have done the highly detailed Filipino artwork any favours.~SW

MARVEL COLLECTORS' ITEM CLASSICS
Marvel: *22 issues 1965–1969*

This double-size title reprints runs of Doctor Strange, Fantastic Four, Hulk and Iron Man, almost from the beginnings of their own strips. The title changed to *Marvel's Greatest Comics* with 23.~APS

MARVEL COMICS PRESENTS
Marvel: *175 issues 1988–1995*

This anthology covered just about every single Marvel hero from their top sellers, Wolverine and Ghost Rider, to their more obscure, Shooting Star and Le Peregrine. Covers were supplied by just about every big name in the biz, from Kevin Nowlan and John Romita Jr to George Pratt and Simon Bisley. With a combination of one-off strips and ongoing story-lines of varying lengths, it is a very mixed bag. Much is pretty basic but a few issues shine out. 1–12 have Steve Gerber back on the character he created, Man-Thing, with grisly art by Tom Sutton, exploring genetics and politics in the Deep South. Peter David and Sam Kieth tell an amusing and exciting Wolverine tale in 85–92, and 164–167 has Simon Jowett and Paul Johnson retelling the origin of Man-Thing with a fresh perspective not seen since Gerber was writing. The true diamond in the rough, though, is Barry Windsor-Smith's opus, 'Weapon X'. This definitive origin of Wolverine ran from 72 (double-size issue) to 84 and marked a change in the schedule to bi-weekly, a rarity in American comics. Told in a series of back-and-forward flashes, the narrative is confusing at first, especially in fractured instalments, but Windsor-Smith pulls it off with aplomb. His script, art and colours give it a unique look: this is some of his finest work since the seventies. Truly the man deserves the title *auteur*. Also of note is Sandy Plunkett's solo

Ant-Man strip in 131, which is as good as an Ant-Man story can get.~TP
Recommended: *1–12, 72–92, 164–167*
Collections: Acts of Vengeance (Ghost Rider and Wolverine from 64–71), God's Country (Colossus story from 10–17), Save The Tiger (Wolverine story from 1–10), Triumphs and Tragedies: Wolverine Vs Spider-Man (Wolverine story from 48–50), Typhoid's Kiss (Wolverine story from 108–116) Weapon X (Wolverine from 72–84), Wild Wild Life (Excalibur story from 31–38)

MARVEL DOUBLE FEATURE
Marvel: *21 issues 1973–1977*

Reprints the Captain America and Iron Man stories from the latter twenty-odd issues of *Tales of Suspense*.~APS

MARVEL FANFARE
Marvel: *Series one 60 issues 1982–1991, series two 6 issues + 1996 to date*

In 1982 Marvel were taking their first steps to producing titles for exclusive distribution to comic fans through comics shops, sidestepping the traditional news-stand market altogether. They reasoned that fans would pay more for stories on better-quality paper written and drawn by their favourite creators, and hence issued *Marvel Fanfare*. The opening story in 1–4 exemplifies the ideal, featuring a teaming of Spider-Man, perennially Marvel's most popular character, and the X-Men (then selling very strongly in comic shops, but not so well outside) with Ka-Zar, written by Chris Claremont, started by the highly regarded Michael Golden (1, 2), and completed by recently departed *X-Men* artist Dave Cockrum (3) and the then little-known, but very talented Paul Smith (4). However, beyond a certain point (around halfway), and with the comic-shop market established as an outlet for high-volume sales, *Marvel Fanfare* rather slipped into becoming a try-out title or a home for previously commissioned but unpublished stories, although the editorials kept denying that it was an 'inventory' title.

Apart from the opening story, there really was very little strong material, and only a handful of issues that are worth tracking down. 7 has an unusually downbeat Daredevil story about a missing guide dog, from generally unsung writer Bill Mantlo and artist George Freeman, and 15's 'That Night...' is a clever and amusing Fantastic Four story from Barry Windsor-Smith, with the Thing prominent. 27 has Marc Hempel's take on Spider-Man coping with boredom, and 40 features the haunting 'Chiaroscuro' by Ann Nocenti and Dave Mazzuchelli, tying into the Mephisto limited series. Of lesser interest are Gil Kane's adaptation of *The Jungle Book* in

8–10, Charles Vess' story about a lost poet inadvertently gathering material (13), and a Captain Universe story (25) in which a bullied schoolkid acquires the powers just long enough to see him through a bad day. There's also a John Byrne Hulk story in 29 in which every page is a splash page, a Dr Strange story by Walt Simonson and Dave Gibbons in 41 and the all-pin-up issue 45. Elsewhere there is a small amount of material that might be of interest to completists: more Charles Vess in 6 and his Warriors Three story in 34–37, with some nice rose bushes but little plot, Coleen Doran's music-based story and portfolio in 38, and a Power Pack tale in 55. In general, don't get your hopes up.

The draw of the second series is presumably meant to be the price, which is very low at 99 cents. It's still not worth it, though. There's a Hulk/Wolverine story (2–3) that is just about readable, but Pop Mhan's cutesy style of artwork is distractingly inappropriate. Fans of Longshot's innocent charm might be tempted by 4 and 5, but should resist the temptation with all their might.~FC

Recommended: Series one 7, 15, 27, 40
Collection: X-Men: Savage Land (1–4)

MARVEL FEATURE

Marvel: *Series one 12 issues 1971–1973, Series two 7 issues 1975–1976*

The first series is a showcase comic. 1–3 feature the first appearances of the Defenders (Doctor Strange, Hulk, Sub-Mariner), by Roy Thomas and Ross Andru, before the team moved to its own title. 1 includes a significant back-up strip in which Doctor Strange returns to his role as a sorcerer after having renounced the mystic arts in *Incredible Hulk* 126. 4–10 spotlight Ant Man in a strange solo run by Mike Friedrich. Hank Pym retrospectively narrates the whole series, in contrast to conventional story-telling, but the ludicrous concepts, plot and dialogue insult the intelligence of a seven-year-old. 11–12 are the first Thing team-up stories, an immediate prequel to *Marvel Two-In-One*. Both drawn by Jim Starlin, 12 spins off from the Thanos war story line in *Captain Marvel* 25–33.

The second series was won by Red Sonja after a popular introduction as a supporting character in *Conan the Barbarian*. As a young girl, she was transformed into a warrior by a goddess after her home and family had been pillaged and slain and she herself raped. The goddess imposed a condition: that she could love no man unless he had first defeated her in fair combat. Written by Bruce Jones and drawn by Thorne, the series suffers from uninspired plotting and cartoonish artwork, although the odd nice human touch surfaces sporadically. Red Sonja continues in her own title.~APS

Recommended: Series one 2

MARVEL Graphic Novels

Any graphic novel featuring characters with their own series is dealt with in that series' entry. Considering the other superhero volumes first, the best of them is the Black Widow story *The Coldest War*, written by Gerry Conway and pencilled by George Freeman. The Widow is manipulated by the KGB into performing a job for them. Conway's on better-than-average form, but Freeman's art varies according to the inker on any particular page, and there are five credited in all. The production's shabby as well, with the art printed at differing sizes. *The Aladdin Effect* starts well enough, with a Wyoming town enveloped by an impenetrable force field and the consequent reactions of the inhabitants. She-Hulk may not be able to batter a hole in the force field, but she could throw a bus through the holes in the plot, and there are even bigger contrivances as four superheroines are plucked from their outside lives to help. *Revenge Of The Living Monolith* and *Emperor Doom* both concentrate on familiar villains. Dr Doom actually succeeds in taking over the world in the latter. It's a clever plot poorly executed, which ranks it higher than the former, but it relies on a particularly daft ending.

Taking *Thor* supporting characters Fandral, Hogun and Volstagg on a quest, *The Raven Banner* has the benefit of Charles Vess art, but a merely functional plot. The Mike Mignola-illustrated teaming of *Dr Doom and Dr Strange* is also excellently drawn, but every time the plot becomes interesting another bunch of demons are thrown in as Doom investigates the mystical side of his nature. Even less commendable is *Blood Truce*, a comic-sized teaming of Captain America and Nick Fury, which might have made for a worthwhile annual, but not a $6 one-shot.

Rick Mason, The Agent isn't superpowered, but his adversaries are. Supervillains occupy a small South American country, transforming it into a drug-supplying haven, and Mason is sent in to sort them out. James Hudnall and John Ridgway supply a decent suspenseful spy thriller concentrating on character, with Mason a heroic-fiction tough guy archetype. So is *Absalom Daak, Dalek Killer*, a gung-ho testosterone-propelled brute. Emanating from the British *Doctor Who Magazine*, he takes a violent pride in his work. More in the mode of a traditional British annual with other features and text pages in addition to the lead, *Daak* is probably most notable these days for the Steve Dillon art. Also published by Marvel's British office was the *The Chronicles of Genghis Grimtoad*. Optimistically labelled 'volume one', John Wagner and Alan Grant stitch a plot by stringing together every fantasy cliché in the book and appending a few moments of slapstick. The shipshod affair is almost redeemed by the gorgeous Ian Gibson artwork, but not to the point of ensuring a second volume.

Actors Billy Mumy and Miguel Ferrer write *The Dreamwalker*, modelled on the 1930s pulp heroes, and woven into a world of gangsters and government agency revenge. It's a readable page-turner that rather falls to pieces at the end, although Gray Morrow's art throughout is excellent. More effectively redolent with the seamy pulp atmosphere of the 1930s is *Nightraven: House Of Cards*. It's available in both book and traditional comic size, and the titular hero is a lurking background figure as the focus is on gangster Soldier Jack, gradually being drawn into a situation beyond his control. Jamie Delano populates the story with a fine sleazy supporting cast and David Lloyd's moody art evocatively portrays the bygone era.

A frequent problem is that Marvel's graphic novels are technically proficient, yet fail to engage emotionally, with Sam Glanzman's *A Sailor's Story* foremost among them. It's two beautifully drawn volumes of Glanzman's navy experiences during World War II, with some fine moments, but overall too bitty and prolonged to captivate. *Hearts And Minds* is similarly reality-based, this time a tragic Vietnam war story drawn by the worthy Russ Heath, yet strangely uninvolving. There's nothing wrong, either, with *Greenberg The Vampire*, previously seen in *Bizarre Adventures*. The idea of a Jewish vampire has a novelty, but beyond that there's nothing to make it an essential purchase, with J.M. DeMatteis treading familiar territory regarding families and writing, and functional art from Mark Badger.

Super Boxers is a step down. Among the first Marvel graphic novels to stray from established characters, it's difficult to imagine the intended audience for this almost plotless boxing tale in a corporate-controlled future. Stale from the off, it wheezes towards a predictable conclusion in the manner of a consumptive asthmatic. Far better is *Arena*, written and drawn by Bruce Jones. It's a simple combination of time-gates in the Ozarks with hillbillies looking for a wife, and a mother/daughter relationship in need of some repair. *Heartburst* blends science fiction and Aboriginal myth with some New-Age sentiments, to concoct a story of one man against the world, persecution and spiritual enlightenment. Rick Veitch writes and draws, and sometimes loses his way, but it's largely very readable. *Ax* is bizarre fantasy, entirely the work of Ernie Colon, down to the lettering. Science-fiction elements are merged into a muddy, vaguely moralising, script through which the title character wanders, seemingly impervious to harm. The art's great, though, vibrantly coloured and illustrative. *Marada The She-Wolf* collects the warrior woman's first appearance in *Epic Illustrated* 10–12, now with a fine palette enriching John Bolton's excellent art. Chris Claremont's plot of Marada bewitched and stripped of her character makes for a fine fantasy story, and it's followed by a tale detailing a glitch on the journey home.~FP
Recommended: *Marada The She-Wolf, Night Raven*

MARVEL HOLIDAY SPECIALS
Marvel: *3 issues 1991–1993*

Anthology comics featuring various Marvel characters in stories set around the winter solstice. The stories in the 1991 issue are mostly indistinguishable in their mixture of sentimentality and violence, but the 1992 issue has some gems. There's a wordless Wolverine story that says a lot about the vividness of childhood imagination, then a hilarious Doc Samson story in which he's supposed to be telling the story of Chanukah to a class at a Hebrew school, but is forced to make some drastic revisions, and finally a Daredevil story written by Ann Nocenti. It follows the thoughts of a toy lamb that Daredevil has just bought as a present, but Nocenti keeps the story on the correct side of cute throughout, and that's a real achievement. The 1993/1994 issue isn't up to this standard, though it's worth a look for two strips: a Nick Fury story, by Howard Chaykin, which is ultimately sentimental but has a compulsive rhythm to it, and a Ghost Rider story, written by Ann Nocenti, which has a nice idea about a timid office worker getting a chance at revenge, but is let down by the ending.~FC
Recommended: 1992

MARVEL MYSTERY Comics
Timely/Marvel: *92 issues 1939–1949*

The title that launched the careers of the Human Torch and the Sub-Mariner, and thus the entire Marvel Universe, this series is unquestionably significant. Historic. Nay, even iconic. It's not actually very good, though. You see, in the early 1940s, Timely, the antediluvian ancestor of Marvel, was the Poverty Row production company, employing mostly folks who jumped ship as soon as they got a more lucrative gig, or those who couldn't get work anywhere else. This did improve by 1944 or so, but apart from the ornate and insanely convoluted Alex Schomburg covers, most of these early *Marvel Mysterys* are rough, thrown-together ragbag comics, with a crude vitality but very little artistic merit. In addition to the Human Torch (1–92) and the Sub-Mariner (1–91), *Marvel Mystery* featured Captain America (80–92) and a host of lesser strips. Among the most popular was Ka-Zar (1–27), a blond Tarzan later recreated for 1960's Marvel, and The Angel (1–23). Inspired by Leslie Charteris' Saint, this costumed but non-

powered detective's sedate adventures were unaccountably popular with the Marvel staff, to the extent that he was given several early covers. The Vision (13–48) was a supernatural being who entered and exited the Earthly plane in bursts of smoke; this low-rent Spectre was best known for being created by Joe Simon and Jack Kirby, who drew his early adventures. The Patriot (21–74), crusading reporter Jeff Mace, filled the Captain America-type slot until it dawned on *Marvel Mystery*'s editors that they could just as easily import the real thing. Miss America (49–85) was teenager Madeleine Joyce, caught in an electrical experiment and emerging with superstrength, flight, X-ray vision and the wisdom of the ages. As you do. None of these powers helped her failing eyesight (must be the strain of the X-ray vision), and by 1946 she was proudly the first four-eyed superheroine. The Blonde Phantom (84–91), alias Louise Grant, mousy secretary, let down her hair, doffed her glasses, and slipped into a thigh-slit, bare-bellied, low-cut red silk evening dress to fight crime. Surely, by the time she got all dolled up, most emergencies would be either over or beyond control? So, historically significant, funky, nostalgic – and most issues beyond number 50 were even consistently competent, but, unless you've a real taste for the cruder or stranger side of superheroics, not worth the hugely inflated prices generally demanded.~HS
Collection: Marvel Comics 1 (reprints 1 only)

MARVEL PREMIERE
Marvel: *61 issues 1972–1981*

Although designed as a try-out series featuring new lead characters every few issues, Doctor Strange (3–14) and Iron Fist (15–25) shanghaied the title until both were promoted to their own books. 1–2 witness the transformation of supporting character 'Him' into Adam Warlock. 3 contains a lovely, surreal Stan Lee story with exquisite Barry Smith art, but Gardner Fox follows with a horribly convoluted plot-line that was mercifully laid to rest by Steve Englehart. He and Frank Brunner then produced a highly original time-travel story in 12–14. 15 introduced Iron Fist as Daniel Rand, a youth who entered the mystic city of K'un Lun and was taught oriental fighting skills by the race of immortals who dwelt there. The continuing story-line narrating his origin suffers from a suicidal maximum-three-issues-per-writer syndrome. 25 sports early John Byrne artwork.

From 26, the try-out concept genuinely took over, with no character holding centre stage for more than four issues. *Marvel Premiere* was designed to feature brand-new concepts whilst its sister title, *Marvel Spotlight*, showcased established characters. In practice, the

difference was hard to distinguish. 31 features Bill Mantlo and Keith Giffen's Woodgod, a marvellously original treatment of the Frankenstein theme told in an ingenious, unorthodox first-person narrative by the hybrid creature. Howard Chaykin's space mercenary, Monark Starstalker, delivers competent action adventure in 32, whilst Roy Thomas' 3-D Man in 35–37 has one of the most ludicrous origins and costumes in any comic book. Doug Moench and Mike Ploog deliver the second *Weirdworld* appearance (following *Marvel Super Action* 1) in 38; a warm elven fantasy tale told with charm and a certain degree of tongue in cheek. However, Moench's Seeker 3000! science-fiction strip in 41 is immature and scientifically inaccurate.

Don McGregor's portrayal of Paladin, the Daredevil supporting character, in 43 is muddled and self-indulgent. Whilst Bill Mantlo and Keith Giffen's Jack of Hearts in 44 makes the grade, it is seriously at odds with the character's treatment in the later miniseries. Alarmingly, Dave Kraft chooses a sword-and-sorcery setting to tie up the loose ends of the Man-Wolf story so rudely interrupted by the cancellation of *Creatures On The Loose* three years earlier. Amazingly, he pulls off a blinder, laced with restrained humour, John Jameson's reluctant acceptance of promotion to godhood and George Perez's usual gorgeous pencils. Scott Lang's début as the new Ant-Man in 47–48 is acceptable superheroics and a wild contrast to Alice Cooper's début in 50, which Alice co-plotted. 51–53 tie up the Black Panther loose ends from the cancellation of *Jungle Action*. 54 sports a new Western hero, Caleb Hammer, as Peter Gillis presents a fine, melancholy tale and Gene Day's five-star pencils serve up a dead ringer for Clint Eastwood. 57–61 reprint British Marvel Dr Who strips by Dave Gibbons, and the title bows out with Doug Moench and Tom Sutton's outstanding Starlord science-fiction story. Much food for thought is provided by the vastly different interpretations of the same events experienced by Starlord and the sentient planet he visits.~APS
Recommended: 1, 3, 12–14, 31, 45–46, 54, 61

MARVEL PRESENTS
Marvel: *12 issues 1975–1977*

Best to ignore the *Bloodstone* strip occupying the first two issues. Suffice it to say he went on to better things in the rear of *Rampaging Hulk*. The Guardians of the Galaxy took up residency with issue 3, continuing their story from *Defenders* 26–29. Steve Gerber wrote fun space opera with engaging characters, illustrated by Al Milgrom seeming like he cared for once, with their best issue being Gerber's satire on 1970s New York in 5. Roger Stern becomes

writer with 10, but lacks Gerber's light touch, and although not bad, his issues suffer in comparison. Beware the reprint in 8.~FP
Recommended: 3–7

MARVEL PREVIEW
Marvel: *24 issues 1975–1980*

Another Marvel try-out comic, in this case a black and white magazine whose contents were sometimes inspired and occasionally bizarre. The first feature was the Erich Von Daniken-inspired 'Man Gods From Beyond The Stars', a spacemen and cavemen epic by Doug Moench and the brilliant Alex Nino. Contrary to expectations it effortlessly transcended its rather ludicrous premise, as did its EC tribute back-up, 'Good Lord', wherein a group of spacefarers meet God... and kill him! 2's headliner, The Punisher, was overshadowed by a lovely Howard Chaykin 'Dominic Fortune' short, while 3's 'Blade' strip (a refugee from *Vampire Tales*) was well drawn by Tony DeZuniga among others. With 4 the title discovered its only real success in Steve Englehart and Steve Gan's *Starlord*, a (for its time) downbeat space-opera strip. The next instalment, in 11, featured the crowd-pleasing line-up of Chris Claremont, John Byrne and Terry Austin and a far more conventional superhero slant. Subsequent appearances were less bombastic and boasted nice art from Carmine Infantino (14–15) and a young Bill Sienkiewicz (18).

Sienkiewicz reappeared for the superhero strip Moon Knight (in 21), which followed another colour comics transplant, Thor (10), though neither gained much from the format change. More successful were the natural inhabitants of the magazine format, the horror issues, with none more so than 7's Claremont-scripted Satana with the superbly atmospheric art of Vincente Alcazar. 'The Legion Of Monsters' in 8 boasted Gene Colan and Mike Ploog artwork and an epic tale of Morbius, the living vampire, while 12 – 'The Haunt Of Horror' – starred Dracula, Lilith (with a typically strong Steve Gerber script) and a terrific Mike Kaluta short. The most impressive collection, however, was 16's 'Masters Of Terror', with three Colan strips, the best of which was another Gerber Lilith story, the cutting dissection of 1970s mores 'Death By Disco'.

Many of the remaining issues were decent, but uninspired reads. Sherlock Holmes headlined 5 and 6, 9's Man-God was an adaptation of Philip Wylie's 1930s novel *Gladiator*, *Blackmark* in 17 was a below-par Gil Kane, and Kull in 19 and Merlin in 22 were equally undistinguished. 20 and 23 were both titled 'Bizarre Adventures', with the first all reprint and the second a collection of stories by

an all-star cast (including Frank Miller, Gene Colan and John Buscema) that proved surprisingly unsatisfactory. Preview's final story, the science-fiction Paradox strip, mixed sex and drugs and was considered quite daring for the day, though contemporary audiences may well wonder what the fuss was about. Undoubtedly the comic's strangest hour, though, was 13's 'UFO Connection', a heady brew of alien abductions, time- shifting and pyramid power from David Anthony Kraft and Herb Trimpe (great aliens, Herb!). From 25 the comic was retitled *Bizarre Adventures*.~DAR
Recommended: 1, 2, 7, 16

MARVEL SAGA
Marvel: *25 issues 1985–1987*

Retells the significant events of the Marvel Universe to early 1966, concluding with the origins of Galactus and the Silver Surfer. Researcher Peter Sanderson writes new framing text around cut and pasted panels from comics of yesteryear. All events are presented in order of internal chronology, including those not revealed until many years later, thus creating heaven for continuity freaks. Full source and creator credits contribute to a professional product. A fine, shortcut revision guide for boning up on early Marvel history.~APS

MARVEL SPECTACULAR
Marvel: *19 issues 1973–1975*

Reprints Thor stories sequentially commencing with *Thor* 128.~APS

MARVEL SPOTLIGHT
Marvel: *Series one 31 issues 1971–1977, Series two 11 issues 1979–1981*

The companion title to *Marvel Premiere* was also a showcase for new strips, albeit initially with a pronounced horror bent. The exception was 1's Red Wolf feature, an unremarkable Western by Gardner Fox, Syd Shores and Wally Wood, but popular enough to spawn its own series. More successful was 'Werewolf By Night' in 2–4, blessed with gorgeous art from Mike Ploog; typically for Marvel monster features it took a rather superheroic approach to the age-old concept. The giant-sized 2 also featured a lovely Bill Everett Venus reprint from the 1950s. The talented Ploog was on hand again for Ghost Rider, which ran in 5–11 before inexplicably going on to become Marvel's longest-running horror title. Clearly any series about a stunt cyclist selling his soul to the Devil was never going to have much intellectual depth, but Gary Friedrich's scripts were vigorously fun, and Ploog's visualisation of the fiery-skulled motorcyclist had an undeniable, if kitsch, resonance. Friedrich's next creation was even more bizarre, none other than the Son Of Satan. How on Earth did Marvel ever get away with it? And again, its lengthy run (12–24) spawned its own series. With *Hulk* artist Herb Trimpe on pencils, as inappropriate a choice as its possible to imagine, the strip revelled in scenes of the suffering denizens of Hell and innumerable very muscular demons. Oh, and Satan looked peculiarly like the Human Torch! Creative successors Steve Gerber and Jim Mooney calmed things down a bit before Gerber and Gene Colan gave the strip its only brief sense of direction with a very powerful exorcism two-parter in 18 and 19. The strip's final creative team, Chris Claremont and Sal Buscema, did little, and the next few issues, with Sinbad (25), The Scarecrow (26), Sub-Mariner (27) and Moon-Knight (28–29), proved equally unexciting. The last few issues of *Spotlight*'s first run were a mixed bag. The Warriors Three from the pages of *Thor* in 30 had nice John Buscema artwork, 31's Nick Fury story by Jim Starlin and Howard Chaykin saw neither at their best, and 33 continued *Deathlok* from *Astonishing Tales*. All failed to catch the public imagination. Only 32's Spider-Woman went on to bigger things, though this first appearance was perfunctory.

The second series was like much of Marvel's early 1980s material, humdrum in the extreme – with two notable exceptions. 1–4 printed left-overs from the recently cancelled *Captain Marvel* to no great effect, though 8's Captain Marvel tale at least boasted some nice early Frank Miller art. Steve Ditko's efforts on Dragonlord in 5 and Captain Universe (9–11) remain unforgivable exercises in abject hackery that he should be suitably embarrassed about. On the other hand, Doug Moench and Tom Sutton's Starlord in 6 and 7 was well crafted and quite touching space operatics of the highest order.~DAR
Recommended: Series one 2–4, 18, 19

MARVEL SUPER ACTION
Marvel: *One shot 1976, 38 issues 1977–1981*

The black and white magazine one-shot leads off with a decent Archie Goodwin Punisher story, the follow-up to his origin in *Marvel Preview* 2. Back-up tales are the Huntress (who later became Mockingbird), Dominic Fortune by Howard Chaykin and the incongruously placed first appearance of *Weirdworld* by Doug Moench and Mike Ploog.

The second incarnation reprints Captain America stories starting with 100. 12 and 13 reprint the first two Steranko issues (110, 111) with pages cut. Issues 14 on reprint Avengers 55–77, continuing from where the deceased *Marvel Triple Action* left off. From 27 most issues also carry back-up Hulk stories previously seen only in British comics.~APS

MARVEL SUPER-HEROES
Marvel: *One-shot 1966, Series one 95 issues (12–106) 1967–1982, series two 15 issues, 1 Special 1990–1993*

The 1966 one-shot reprints 1940s Sub-Mariner and Human Torch stories alongside *Daredevil* 1, and the title was resurrected to replace *Fantasy Masterpieces* a year later. The policy of reprinting 1940s material was continued, backing up one new feature per issue until 20. There's the Black Knight in 17, Medusa in 15 and Dr Doom in 20, but the introduction of the Guardians of the Galaxy in 18 is as good as it gets, although 12–13 are notable for Captain Marvel's first appearances. Thereafter it's reprints all the way, with *Uncanny X-Men* 1–8 and *Daredevil* 2–7 featuring in 21–27, then Hulk reprints running sequentially until *Hulk* 157. The third series revived the giant-sized format to feature at least three stories each issue, encompassing a variety of Marvel characters right down to third-stringers like Sabra and Spitfire (well treated in 4, which also has an Alan Davis Black Knight strip) along with the top-of-the-line mainstays. There's a fair selection of irredeemable rubbish, but while never remarkable, it's not the total disaster one might assume given the prevailing standards at early 1990s Marvel. Freed from the constraints of continuity, crossovers, guest appearances and tie-ins, many of the stories display a spirit absent elsewhere in the line. The inventory material also featured isn't quite as good, although Ms Marvel fans will want to pick up 10 and 11, featuring what would have been the 24th and 25th issues of her title. 3 contains a story prepared for *Captain Marvel's* late 1970s run.~WJ

MARVEL SUPER SPECIAL
Marvel: *41 issues 1977–1986*

Don't look for the title *Marvel Super Special* on the cover, as it was an umbrella title under which numerous features appeared. Much trumpeted higher production values on the launch led to high expectations, but the reality is that most issues are little more than magazine-size comics. It launched with a coup, the first comics story featuring inordinately successful glam rock band Kiss. With their greasepaint personae Kiss were heavily comics-influenced, and the creative team of Steve Gerber, pencillers Al Weiss, John and Sal Buscema and Rich Buckler (one for each member of the band) and inker Al Milgrom produced a largely enjoyable slice of nonsense about Kiss fighting Marvel villain Dr Doom. The series incorporated song titles throughout and Kiss as superheroes; in keeping with the band's over-the-top persona, each member donated a vial of blood to be added to the red printing ink. The comic's success was such that a quick reprise was prompted in 5, but by lesser talents.

Warriors Of The Shadow Realm is a fantasy series occupying 11–13, where, again, much was made of the comic's production in the editorial pages, presumably to deflect attention from the dull content. The space opera of *Battlestar Galactica* (8) and *The Empire Strikes Back* (16) works well, and *Conan* fans might want to find 2 and 9, the latter with a decently drawn Red Sonja strip by Howard Chaykin. George Perez draws the story of the Beatles well enough in 4, and 7 allegedly features an adaptation of *Sgt Pepper's Lonely Hearts Club Band*, but was withdrawn from US and British publication when the film proved an all-time turkey. It was allegedly published in Japan, and listed as such in several price guides: do you actually know anyone who's seen a copy?

From 14 it's film adaptations all the way, with highlights difficult to locate. Few of those working on these adaptations made much effort, although Gray Morrow's *Sheena* in 34 is, at least, a visual treat. Walt Simonson and John Buscema turn in an acceptable *Raiders Of The Lost Ark* for 18, and Bill Sienkiewicz draws *Dune* for 36. Perhaps fittingly, the series closed with an adaptation of *Howard The Duck*, another all-time turkey, but the only other comic in which Kiss appeared.~FP

MARVEL TALES
Marvel: *291 issues 1964–1994*

Marvel's longest-running reprint title deals almost exclusively with Spider-Man. The first two double-size issues are titled *Marvel Tales Annual* and reprint the origins of most of the early Marvel superheroes. 3–33 are also oversize, as *Amazing Spider-Man* reprints are backed up by Thor and Human Torch in 3–27 (from the beginnings of their runs) and miscellaneous features, most notably 1950s Marvel Boy stories in 13–16. From 34, Spider-Man assumed the solo feature until 136, which reprints *Amazing Spider-Man* 159. 131–133 reprint the British *Captain Britain* 1–2, not previously published in the US, and 134–137 feature Doctor Strange's first four appearances from *Strange Tales*.

With 137, *Marvel Tales* rewound its reprints to *Amazing Fantasy* 15 and re-presented all the early issues of *Amazing Spider-Man* until 190 (reprinting *Amazing Spider-Man* 50). These are laudably free of edited pages, but suffer from the smudged production typical of Marvel's early 1980s output. *Spider-Man Digest* continues reprints of *Amazing Spider-Man* from 51 onwards. *Marvel Tales* then went hot, reprinting random issues featuring Spider-Man stories guest-starring popular characters, namely the John Byrne *Marvel Team-Up* issues to 208, Punisher to 222, X-Men to 244 and then

scattered Morbius, Ghost Rider, Hobgoblin and Black Costume appearances until its finale.

A handful of new back-up stories, paradoxically rarely featuring Spider-Man, have filled out occasional issues: Angel in 30, concluding his story-line from *Ka-zar* 3, Hawkeye and Two Gun Kid in 100, Spider-Man and Thing in 198, X-Men and Sunstroke in 262 and Woodgod in 263. Owing to their minute page-count (5–10 pages), all are inconsequential aside from the Woodgod tale, which serves as an eloquent epilogue to his origin in *Marvel Premiere* 31.~APS

MARVEL TEAM-UP
Marvel: *150 issues, 7 Annuals 1972–1985*

Taking a leaf from DC's success in teaming Batman with other superheroes on a regular basis in *The Brave And The Bold*, Spider-Man was given his own team-up title in 1972. Early issues are only noteworthy for some fine Gil Kane art, particularly in 4's X-Men guest-shot. Writers Len Wein and Gerry Conway show little interest, bottoming out with Conway's all-time stinker in 28 as Manhattan Island is towed back into place by Hercules, having been held for ransom in the Atlantic. Between 21 and 32 Spider-Man got every third issue off, with the Human Torch filling in. It was probably a similar contractual deal to that of talk-show hosts. Bill Mantlo and Sal Buscema couldn't be worse than what went before, and in 41–44 turn out an interesting tale involving the Scarlet Witch, Dr Doom and the Salem Witch Trials, but it was merely a blip among the mediocrity, as was Daredevil's appearance in 56.

With 57 Chris Claremont became writer, joined by regular penciller John Byrne, who'd already drawn 53–55, and *Marvel Team-Up* became an interesting title. More off-beat guest stars like Yellowjacket and the Wasp (59, 60), Captain Britain (65, 66), and even the cast of *Saturday Night Live* (74) became the order of the day, and it seemed as if the creators actually cared about more than meeting a deadline. Highpoints are the conclusion to the *Iron Fist* series in 63–64, the unusual appearance of Red Sonja in 79 and, artistically, Thor and Havok in 69–70. Sal Buscema and Steve Leialoha draw up a storm for a story involving the Black Widow, Nick Fury and Shang-Chi (82–85), and 86's Guardians of the Galaxy appearance is also worth a look. Byrne was already gone when Claremont left with 89's Nightcrawler story. From 90 an assortment of creators sent the title spiralling back into a panache-free zone, brightened only by Claremont returning in the company of Frank Miller to team Spider-Man with the Fantastic Four and introduce New Mutant, Karma, in 100.

The appointment of regular pencillers Herb Trimpe (106–118) and Kerry Gamill (119–133)

along with writer J.M. DeMatteis (111–133) doesn't lift the title – with one glorious exception. In 119 there's no supervillain and Gargoyle and Spider-Man spend little time in each other's company, but each is involved in a situation pertaining to old age, resulting in a very touching story. DeMatteis appears to have been resolving some questions regarding his relationship with his parents during his time writing *MTU*, as the gulf between parent and offspring is a recurring theme, even in 131's deliberately ridiculous Frog Man story. From that point the only other issue worth mentioning is the silliness of 137, in which Spider-Man's aged Aunt May and Franklin Richards team up to save Earth from the planet-devouring Galactus. By 1985 a team-up title was no longer required as guest appearances were commonplace at Marvel, while crossovers were about to become the norm rather than the exception, and *Marvel Team-Up* departed with a whimper, only to be revived in all but name as *Spider-Man Team-Up* in 1996.~FP

Recommended: 56, 63, 64, 69, 70, 79, 82–86, 100, 119

Collected: Spider-Man and the X-Men (Annual 1 & 150 plus other material)

MARVEL TRIPLE ACTION
Marvel: *47 issues 1972–1979*

Where the triple action came from no one knows. 1–4 reprint Kirby *Fantastic Four* issues, and from 5 it's *Avengers* reprints all the way, encompassing the final Lee and Kirby period, through Thomas and Heck to John Buscema's earliest days on the comic. Fewer pages in the 1970s comics meant that all stories are edited by at least a page, some none too sympathetically.~FP

MARVEL TWO-IN-ONE
Marvel: *100 issues, 7 Annuals 1974–1983*

This team-up title stars the Thing and a different superhero guest every issue. Such titles are difficult to write well. The traditional formula has the co-stars battling each other before collaborating against the villain, and *Marvel Two-In-One* has more than its fair share of these potboilers. Steve Gerber started on a sound footing for its first nine issues, although most stories are heavily tied to other titles he was writing contemporaneously. His depiction of the Thing's artful sense of humour provided a refreshing change from the continuous wisecracking machine often portrayed. The title's nadir swiftly followed, with most issues in the teens hitting absolute rock bottom.

Sporadic signs of promise surfaced in issues 42–43 and 50–51 before Mark Gruenwald and Ralph Macchio taught all other scripters a lesson on how to write team-up titles. Their run in 53–58 and 60–74 seamlessly melds rotating guest stars into multi-issue story-lines, punctuated with such delightful one-off stories as the touchingly humorous Impossible Man tale in 60. The Project Pegasus saga serves as the crux of their run, fostering several meaty sub-plots, all of which are resolved by the end of their tenure, a rare event in more modern times. Regrettably, the output fades towards average over their final few issues. The visual side is spoilt by the presence of too many artists in the twenty-one issues, although work by Byrne, Perez, Day and Bingham is of high quality. Tom DeFalco failed to heed their lesson. 75 onwards churn out mediocrity at best. His only issue worthy of mention is 86, in which Sandman goes straight. Annual 2 by Jim Starlin chronicles the final chapter in the Warlock/Thanos feud that began in Warlock's first series. Although not the best issue of that run, this fine story depicts one of Thanos and Warlock's many deaths. All the other annuals are forgettable.~APS

Recommended: 6–7, 10, 51, 53–58, 60–67, Annual 2

MARVEL'S GREATEST COMICS
Marvel: *74 issues (23–96) 1969–1981*

Carrying on directly from *Marvel Collectors' Item Classics*, issues 23–34 are double-size and continue reprints of Doctor Strange, Fantastic Four and Iron Man. Also included are Captain America's early stories from *Tales of Suspense*. From 35 on, the book shrank to a thirty-two-page *Fantastic Four* reprint title. 116 is the last issue reprinted before cancellation.~APS

MARVELS
Marvel: *5-issue limited series (0–4) 1994*

This groundbreaking series by Kurt Busiek and Alex Ross retells early events in the Marvel Universe through the eyes of news photo-journalist Phil Sheldon. Like his ordinary fellow-men, he has to come to terms with the appearance of superbeings and the effects they have on day-to-day life. Through him, his family, colleagues and strangers he meets, we see mankind's fear, insecurity, helplessness and prejudice laid bare by these awesome Marvels whose conflicts wreak millions of dollars of property damage with apparent disdain for the misery heaped upon affected innocents. Every piece of superheroic action is sourced from an existing Marvel comic. Each issue focuses on a major event from a different period in Sheldon's life. These events and real-time publication dates are: 1 – the first appearance of the original Human Torch (1939), 2 – anti-mutant hysteria (1965), 3 – the coming of Galactus and the Silver Surfer (1966) and 4 – the death of Gwen Stacy (1973).

Ross's painted artwork is magnificent. Realism and lavish attention to detail underlie every panel, particularly exemplified by 1's late 1930s period setting – the cars, the dress styles, everybody smokes. Backgrounds are meticulous. Spot the Beatles at Reed and Sue's wedding in 2 and Pete Townshend in 4. Busiek's script is low-key and understated. A young J. Jonah Jameson makes a guest appearance in 1, yet his name is never mentioned. Issue 2 is the strongest. Sheldon is involuntarily swept up in a frenzied wave of anti-mutant hysteria and subsequently has to reassess his stance when he meets a defenceless, innocent mutant child face to face. Later, Sheldon writes a book titled 'Marvels' which contains many of his news photos.

Issue 0 was published some four months after the regular series and is not essential. It contains short text pieces describing how the project came to be, an eleven-page prototype story with a more detailed origin of the Golden Age Human Torch, and pin-ups and character sketches by Ross during development.

Marvels' success can be gauged by the spin-offs and reprints it has generated. 1–4 were reprinted individually during 1996. All five issues have been collected in softcover, hardcover and limited-edition variants. The softcover boasts the same cover as Sheldon's fictional book, provides further details of the project's design stages and, for complete fanatics, lists the source of every recaptured event right down to issue and page number. Spin-offs *Ruins* and *Tales of the Marvels* were published during succeeding years and maintain the same theme. Busiek has since adopted a similar approach with unfamiliar superheroes in *Astro City. Marvels* cannot be recommended too highly, although unfamiliarity with the early, retold stories does slightly lessen its appreciation. It is an adult comic in the true meaning of the word, with neither an ounce of exposed flesh nor exposed innards in sight.~APS

Recommended: 1–4
Collection: Marvels (0–4)

MASK

DC: *4-issue miniseries 1985–1986, 9 issues 1987*

One third of the cartoon series and toy triumvirate, *Mask* is pretty simple car-and-vehicle-related adventures scripted, seemingly in his sleep, by Michael Fleisher. What makes this of passing interest is the team of classic Superman artists Curt Swan and Kurt Schaffenberger still on good form.~FP

THE MASK

Dark Horse: *5-issue miniseries (0–4) 1991, 4-issue miniseries (The Mask Returns) 1992–1993, 2-issue microseries ('The Movie') 1994, 12 issues + 1995 to date*

Long before Jim Carrey inherited the ancient face-gear the original comic series existed, and

was a very different beast, running as The Masque in *Dark Horse Presents* 10–15 and 18–21. A makeover resulted in a more familiar version, where ultra-violence with high body counts and rivers of blood is tempered with slapstick humour and bad jokes. The first miniseries has Stanley Ipkiss, a loser bank-teller from Edge City, discovering an old mask. When he puts it on he's transformed into a maniacal, bloodthirsty, wisecracking vigilante. To prevent some gangsters robbing his bank Stanley destroys half the city, and consequently makes an enemy for life in the mute, unstoppable thug known only as Walter. The strengths of the series lie in the ludicrous props the Mask seems to pull from thin air, and the imaginative way he dispatches his enemies in the fashion of an acid-crazed merging of *Tom And Jerry* and Charles Manson. The second series is much the same and still has some laughs, but by the ongoing series the formula has become repetitive. All written by John Arcudi, the plot of Mask up against a bunch of nasty villains whom he kills in the name of justice and comedy has become only mildly amusing and a tad too predictable. By now Dark Horse had begun heavily cover-numbering each new story arc with a 1, while continuing the regular series, and from 6 Evan Dorkin writes 'The Hunt For Green October', injecting some of the anarchic humour that makes his *Milk And Cheese* so good. The ownership of the mask is transferred to film buff Ray Tuttle and his daughter, but the new story-line falls into the same trap as the others; but by this time any reader will know what they're getting. 'Southern Discomfort', the most recent story arc, has Eric Martin, the latest Mask owner, searching for his missing sister in a voodoo-infested New Orleans. The two-issue movie adaptation is toned down for the kiddies, and has some very nice Killian Plunkett art, and there's also *Adventures Of The Mask*, based on the Saturday morning cartoon series, taking the mask back to its original owner with the original cast. Lighter in mood, there's no gore.~TP

Recommended: Miniseries one 1–4
Collections: Hunt For Green October (6–9), *The Mask* (miniseries one 1–4), *The Mask Returns* (miniseries two 1–4), *The Mask Strikes Back* (1–4)

THE MASK Graphic Novels

Appealing to the younger audience for the film, there are three seasonal hardcovers: *The Night Before Christmask, Summer Vacation* and *School Spirits*, all written and drawn by Rick Geary. All three have a very different tone from the comics, more akin to children's picture books, and are light-hearted romps, with L'il Mask playing an alternative Santa Claus,

fighting spooks etc. Beautifully drawn, they are compelling despite the short content.~TP
Recommended: *The Night Before Christmask, School Spirits, Summer Vacation*

THE MASKED MAN
Eclipse: *9 issues 1984–1985*

As a child, Dick Carstairs saw his mother shot dead, so now he runs a detective agency and sometimes he rolls his sleeves up to his armpits, puts a mask on, and hits people. B.C. Boyer's hero débuted in *Eclipse Monthly* as an obvious homage to Will Eisner's *Spirit*; there are refreshing aspects, in that Carstairs is desperately puppy-like and gormless, and the mask never stops anyone recognising him. But the stories are feeble and ponderous, and the artwork stiff, at best. The final issue, though, is unintentionally hilarious. You would have to be lost to all finer feelings not to laugh out loud at the death scene.~FC

MASTER OF KUNG-FU
Marvel: *109 issues (17–125), 1 Annual, 4 Giant-Size 1974–1983, One-shot 1991*

The potential for disaster was immense. Not only was the comic to tie-in with a 1970s fad, the lead was the son of oriental pulp-novel villain Fu Manchu. Given the inauspicious conception, it's astounding that this survives as a highspot of 1970s Marvel output. The title continues the numbering from *Special Marvel Edition*, which saw the début of Shang-Chi, Master of Kung-Fu. The original creators departed rapidly, and replacement writer Doug Moench overcomes a faltering start to infuse the comic with a lyrical blend of philosophy, a well conceived and fleshed-out supporting cast, and action that's questioned and justified *in situ*. For large portions of the run Moench is accompanied by excellent artists. Paul Gulacy (most issues between 25 and 50), Mike Zeck inked by Bruce Patterson then Gene Day (67–101) and particularly Gene Day (102–120) are the pick of the bunch.

The comic takes off once Moench and Gulacy dispense with all-out butt-kicking kung-fu action and opt for spy thriller as the apt genre for the title. Shang-Chi is a man raised to be a living weapon in his father's service, but discovers Fu Manchu's true intentions in early issues. He adopts Denis Nayland-Smith, also inherited from the Sax Rohmer Fu Manchu novels and head of the British government anti-terrorist branch, as a surrogate mentor. Smith's right-hand man, Black Jack Tarr, and agents Leiko Wu and Clive Reston (dropping claims of Sherlock Holmes and James Bond among his ancestry), round out the main cast for the entire run. Shang-Chi is a consistently reluctant combatant but constantly finds circumstances lead him down that path.

Probably the best issues of the title came relatively early into the run, with a tragic love affair in Hong Kong providing the background for 38–39, and an epic battle against Fu Manchu narrated in turn by involved cast members in 44–50. That's not to say, however, that later issues are substandard. Almost the entire run attains a level of quality rarely seen today, and if some of the philosophising seems dated, and the martial arts villains contrived, there's always something to compensate. Moench and Day left the title with 120, and that it was cancelled a mere five issues later speaks volumes. An ill-advised return by Moench, initially serialised in *Marvel Comics Presents*, was issued as a one-shot in 1991, and he followed that with the *Moon Knight Special* in 1992, with Shang-Chi taking an equal part.~FP
Recommended: 29–31, 33, 34, 38–40, 42–51, 71, 76–80, 83–89, 96-98, 100, 109–111, 114–118, 120

MASTERS OF TERROR
Marvel: *2 issues 1975*

A black and white reprint magazine that drew its material from the likes of *Supernatural Thrillers* and *Journey Into Mystery*. Of the two, the first issue is the best, with strips by Gil Kane, Frank Brunner and Esteban Maroto, although either is a nice introduction to Marvel's horror titles.~DAR

MATT CHAMPION
Metro: *2 issues 1987*

The world of wrestling in the 1930s is the theme of Ernie Colon's series, but don't let that put you off. The central character has evolved into a powerful wrestler by means of illegal injections administered by his chemist father, and the story deals with the corrupt nature of wrestling in general, though not without a sense of humour. Matt is a kindly soul who rebels against the crooked promoters, and when dealing with gangsters it's as well the injections have also made him bulletproof. If you're looking for something different, this may be for you. Sadly it was never completed.~HY

MAUS
Pantheon/Penguin: *2 volumes 1986, 1991*

art spiegelman (who prefers lower-case) covered quite a few bases in shunting comics forward another level. On the face of it he was an unlikely candidate. Certainly a man who cared about his artwork, this was often to the detriment of any narrative or popular appeal. *Raw* magazine, which he co-produced and edited, presented strips almost wilfully teetering on the fine line that separates the King's new clothes from works of genius, yet – at odds with much of the other content – it was here that he began *Maus*. It's a work that replays the horrors and fear accompanying

Nazi occupation during World War II, and eventually the death camps which resulted from their ethnic cleansing programmes. Instead of selecting a straightforward portrayal, spiegelman elects to depict the Jews as mice, and the Nazis as cats, following the metaphor through with other, often inexplicable, depictions (Poles as pigs?). Given the sensitivity of the topic, it demands a serious approach, and spiegelman never flinches from portraying events as they're told to him, political correctness be damned. These sequences alone, the topic they cover and the story they tell would mark *Maus* as a landmark.

But there's another level. spiegelman is conveying the experiences of his father Vladek, a death-camp survivor, who's relating the story in segments at his son's prompting. Father and son have had a fractious relationship over the years. While *Maus* is the story of Vladek's experiences in the 1940s, it's also the story of a then twenty-something and now thirty-something art attempting to reconcile and make sense of the contradictory emotions he has regarding his father, and come to an understanding of what shaped the man he knows. It's this extra level that elevates the entire project, with each chapter of horror sandwiched by sequences with art and Vladek. *Maus* is an extraordinarily honest work: implicit in its presentation is art's admission of badgering his father for his own ends, although there's no way he could have foreseen the critical and financial success his father's story would bring. For all the introspection and worthiness, spiegelman always sticks with a simple, accessible narrative. There have been few comics as intensely involving as *Maus*, and none as harrowing. It's widely acknowledged as a masterpiece; the only shame is that in ten years since the publication of the first volume few works have come anywhere close to equalling it.~FP
Recommended: 1, 2

MAXIMAGE
Image: *7 issues 1995–1996*
There has, apparently, always been a mystical entity known as the Maximage. This time the Ancient, recently released from incarceration by aliens, selects Lori Sanders, a street urchin, to do the job. Knowing nothing about her new powers, Lori has to confront the aliens in the 'Extreme Destroyer' multi-title crossover (issue 2) and then gets involved in the battle between Glory, Angela and Celestine (4). Pretty much what you'd expect of a Rob Liefeld character, but with scripts by Bill Messner-Loebs (from 2) the title's at least better written than most Extreme offerings.~NF

MAXIMORTAL.
Tundra/Kitchen Sink: *7-issue limited series 1992–1993*
Continuing Rick Veitch's deconstruction of the superheroic genre, *Maximortal* tells of an alien creature who is used as the ultimate weapon, but turns the tables on his abusers. It's also the story of two naïve young cartoonists who lose the rights to their character 'True-Man' when they sign a contract without looking at the small print. It's also seemingly about several other things, but frankly, it just doesn't tell any of the stories very well at all. The segments involving Spiegal and Schumacher, the cartoonists ripped off by Sidney Wallace, are the strongest, but whenever the action moves away from them it becomes incoherent and metaphysical. And it's got another of those irritating The-End-Is-The-Beginning cop-out conclusions. After the power and drive of *Brat Pack*, this woolly meandering is simply annoying, not meaningful.~HS
Collection: Maximortal (1–7)

Joe Sinardi's MAXWELL MOUSE FOLLIES
Renegade: *6 issues 1986*
If there's an artform entirely inappropriate for treatment in comics it's song and dance, yet Renegade belly flopped *two* such titles into the shops (the other being *Neil The Horse*). This has a mouse society in 1930s New York flourishing as a scaled-down version of the real thing, but every time the plot starts to spark, a musical number grinds it to a halt.~FP

The MAXX
Image: *27 issues + 1993 to date*
This sticks out of the Image range like a mountain in Holland. William Messner-Loebs and Sam Kieth have crafted a fine example of what a comic is capable of. Initially the story appears to concern a massive purple character with big teeth and a giant claw extending from each hand who is referred to as the Maxx. It's not long before this idea is thrown on its head and we are forced to readjust our view of the characters. The creators don't rest there: they constantly try to keep the readers on their toes. The story takes place in two different locations, the first an American city, while the rest occurs in 'The Outback'. The script implies that the city is reality, but we are forced to question this at every turn. 1–20 features the purple Maxx and a social worker named Julie, examining their relationship and explaining the main ideas of the two locations. Thereafter the story jumps ten years and the focus shifts to a young girl named Sarah and her links with the Outback. The Maxx appears under a different guise but the stories continue to look at the central characters and their interaction. *The*

Maxx is fast-paced and always intriguing, although the complexity of the plot means some elements are difficult to understand without reading the entire series.~SS.
Recommended: 1–3, 7–8, 20

MAYHEM
Dark Horse: *4 issues 1989*
Anthology title featuring strips from two cancelled titles and the first version of the Mask in his current madcap form. An attempt to blackmail the Archon in The Mark goes wrong, and the Mecha crew locate more giant robots in the only dull strip.~WJ
Collection: The Mask (Mask strips from 1–4)

MAZE AGENCY
Comico: *7 issues 1988–1989*
Innovation: *16 issues (8–23), 1 Annual, 1 Special 1989–1991*
Each issue of *Maze Agency* features a mystery to be solved in the classic whodunnit manner. Private detective Jennifer Mays and her partner Gabriel Webb, true-crime writer and amateur sleuth, sort through the clues and red herrings in this cleverly-crafted series, written by Mike W. Barr. As the series progresses we learn more about the lead characters and their developing relationship, leavening the Ellery Queen-style pat detection with romance. The whole is as light-hearted as a series dealing with murder could be.
  Maze Agency introduced artist Adam Hughes to an appreciative public. He drew the first dozen issues, and after he left there seemed to be a new artist on every issue. Though Barr's scripts remained consistently good the book lacked visual appeal and suffered from being published by the relatively obscure Innovation. The 1990 annual has a terrific cover and homage to *The Spirit* by Mike Ploog; a special includes stories drawn by Joe Staton, the Pander brothers and Alan Davis.~NF
Recommended: 1–5, 8, 9, 12

'MAZING MAN
DC: *12 issues 1986, 3 Specials 1987, 1988, 1990*
'Mazing Man is an impossibly genial little guy who believes he's a superhero and wanders his Queens neighbourhood in home-made regalia performing good deeds like unclogging drains and keeping a watchful eye on the local infants. The other residents of 'Mazing Man's block make for a fine supporting cast. The series resembles nothing so much as a superior sitcom, rich in whimsy, sensitivity and observation, and able to elicit laughter and sympathy while bringing a glow to the heart. Stephen DeStefano's cartooning is excellent, and Bob Rozakis more than atones for all the drek he wrote in the 1970s. Every issue is a gem. A delightful series.~FP
Recommended: 1–12, Specials 1–3

M.D.
EC: *5 issues 1955*
Another peculiar choice of title from EC, but the intentions are plain from the first page of issue 1, which has a ghastly Graham Ingels-drawn screaming caveman heralding a story about the practice of medicine through the ages. It's well researched and beautifully illustrated by the likes of Reed Crandall, George Evans, Ingels and Joe Orlando; the contents veer between domestic dramas and medical emergencies in the fashion of TV medical shows since day one. They are, though, far too reliant on authenticity at the cost of tension. Three pages of meticulously detailed operations don't carry the same tension they would on television. 3 is the most diverting issue, with an Ingles story of a hillbilly community coming as an antidote to the antiseptic tone, and an unusually moralistic examination of now discredited electroshock therapy.~FP
Collection: M.D. (1–5)

MECHA
Dark Horse: *6 issues 1987–1989*
In as much as it offered insights into the occupants, this is a better-than-average giant-robot comic, although that's not saying much, and Harrison Fong's artwork is excellent. *Mecha* continues in *Mayhem*, and bears no relation to the character of the same name introduced during *Comics Greatest World*.~WJ

MECHANICS
Fantagraphics: *3-issue miniseries 1985*
Fantagraphics' first attempt to bring the Hernandez Brothers to the attention of a wider audience. This reprint of Jaime's first sustained story, about Maggie the pro-solar mechanic on assignment with Rand Race, the boss she's infatuated with, in a far country where dinosaurs and robots share the same landscape, loses a great deal of impact by being coloured. Paul Rivoche did the crisp, sensual artwork few favours by smearing dark watercolours over it, detracting from the postcard-home format of the strip. Jaime's writing is feeling its way, but manages to both make you laugh and worry about his characters' fates.~FJ

MEDAL OF HONOR
Dark Horse: *1 Special 1994, 4 issues 1994–1995*
The series recounts the individual exploits of the people who've won the USA's highest military award, the Congressional Medal of Honor. Reducing the actions of extraordinarily brave people to a succession of dialogued panels has to be deftly handled to avoid cliché, and sometimes Doug Murray's scripts don't cope. That said, every issue contains at least

one excellent tale, with the most poignant being those of Richard Bong (1) and the lost battalion (4). It was advertised as a 5-issue miniseries, but the fifth issue was never published.~FP
Recommended: 1, 3, 4

MEGALITH
Continuity: *Series one 9 issues 1989–1992, series two 8 issues (0–7) 1993–1994*

The first run of *Megalith* differed from other Continuity titles by dint of its resolutely urban setting, concentrating on smaller issues like gang warfare, gun control and kidnap. Unfortunately, Peter Stone and Neal Adams' bombastic writing style totally scuppers every chance at credibility. Artistically Mark Texeira (1–3), Trevor Von Eeden (4, 5), Mike Netzer (6, 7), Dave Hoover (8) and Sal Velluto (9) acquit themselves well enough, with Texeira's fully painted job on 3 particularly noteworthy. 0–3 of the second series are portions of the 'Deathwatch 2000' story-line, of which we're still awaiting the concluding part, and 4–7 part of 'The Rise Of Magic'. Far more significant is the work of Ernesto Infante, an artist as talented as he is shamefully unknown. Incoherent as the story is, issues 0, 1 and 3–6 are worth buying for his art alone.~DAR

MEGATON MAN
Kitchen Sink: *10 issues 1984–1986, 3-issue miniseries 1988, one-shot 1989*
Fiasco: *One-shot, 1 issue + (0) 1996 to date*

Don Simpson's satirical and parodic *Megaton Man* is well sustained over ten issues, though the contents start to become what they're commenting on before too long, however funny they might be. Trent Phloog is secretly Megaton Man and meets the Megatropolis Quartet, who're soon down a member when the See-Thru Girl gets liberated along with Trent's reporter partner Pamela Jointly (who used to fall off skyscrapers). The search for the Cosmic Cue Ball takes up most of what passes for plot, but the stories are none the less fun for all that. 6–10 contain the first episodes of Simpson's 'Border Worlds'. A less heavily rendered and more naturalistic style helps make 'Border Worlds' a turning point in Simpson's artistic growth. It continues in *The Return Of Megaton Man*, a three-issue miniseries. Trying to retire, Megaton Man is reactivated by the government only to find himself thoroughly merchandised by Bad Guy. In the meantime the See-Thru Girl is pregnant and her ex-boy-friend, Rex Rigid, has revived the Golden Age Megaton Man with a view to getting revenge on the current version. Tighter scripting and a plot help make this more consistent and entertaining than the previous series.

Megaton Man Meets the Uncategorizable X+ Thems sees the introduction of Ms Megaton Man (supposedly the result of a sexually transmittable mega-serum) during a battle against god of war Mars in the Collision of All Conceivable Comic Book Universes at Once Wars. *Megaton Man vs Forbidden Frankenstein* is a meeting between Simpson's *Bizarre Heroes* characters and those from his Eros series, though they're played as 'straight' super characters. *Megaton Man 0* is a sort of synopsis of everything that's gone before, and part of the continuing *Bizarre Heroes* story-line, which gets more and more complex and less like a parody the longer it continues. On the other hand, the ridiculous nature of the strip doesn't preclude a desire to see where on earth Simpson will take the series next.~NF
Recommended: 6–10, 0
Collection: Megaton Man (1–4)

Marvel Super-Heroes MEGAZINE
Marvel: *6 issues 1995*

The best of Marvel's 1980s output collected in a value-for-money package. In each issue there's Frank Miller Daredevil (159–164), John Byrne's Fantastic Four (232–237) and Hulk (314–319), and Iron Man by Michelinie and Layton (115–120). If you've not read the originals, this is worth a shot.~WJ

MELODY
Kitchen Sink: *10 issues + 1988 to date*

The autobiographical stories of Sylvie Rancourt, and how she became a nude dancer under the name Melody. Initially from a small French Canadian rural community and living with her wastepail boy-friend Nick, Melody encounters hostility from all around for pursuing a sexually hedonistic lifestyle. Moving to Montreal, she finds it's harder to make ends meet, and Nick makes little effort other than to suggest Melody takes a job in a strip bar. Sexual content is high, but as drawn by Jacques Boivin astonishingly unarousing and antiseptic for a comic salaciously cover-blurbed 'The true story of a nude dancer'. That being the apparent reason for publication, and characters other than Melody and Nick being largely ciphers, it makes for dull comics.~FP
Collection: The Orgies Of Abitibi (1–4)

Havok and Wolverine MELTDOWN
Marvel: *4-issue miniseries 1988–1989*

Wolverine and Havok are on holiday in Mexico when they become involved in a convoluted and diabolical ploy to destroy the world. Pretty usual stuff, you might think, but with a major difference. This prestige-format miniseries had sublime art by some of the best painters in the industry, Jon J.Muth and Kent Williams. The duo work well together, using the unusual technique of each painting one character (Muth/Havok, Williams/Wolverine)

even on the same page. They complement each other, and the whole project is a joy to behold, despite Walt and Louise Simonson's predictable script.~TP
Recommended: 1–4
Collection: Meltdown (1–4)

MELTING POT
Kitchen Sink: *4 issues 1993–1994*

A harsh and brutal planet is populated with the worst specimens of assorted alien races. Daily survival is the best most can hope for, and the biggest and baddest rules the roost. Eric Talbot and Simon Bisley provide Corbenesque art over Kevin Eastman's script, but story content is slim.~WJ
Collection: *Melting Pot* (1–4 + *Heavy Metal* preview story)

MEMORIES
Epic: *One-shot 1992*

One-shot publishing Otomo's first major story, a lyrical science-fiction thriller in which a crew investigating a derelict ship in the shape of a rose discover that it's filled with physical recreations of its dead mistress' memories, kept alive by the ship's computer. Simply drawn, but well plotted.~FJ

MEN OF WAR
DC: *26 issues 1977–1980*

DC tried to prolong war-genre comics with this title featuring Code Name: Gravedigger, a black soldier used as a special agent. The earlier issues, written by David Michelinie, are worth looking at, but overall nothing too special. Back-up features included Enemy Ace, Dateline: Frontline and Rosa, Master Spy.~HY

MEPHISTO
Marvel: *4-issue miniseries 1987*

The Marvel Universe's Satan-lite works his way through four superteams, the Fantastic Four, X-Factor, the Avengers and the X-Men, trading up souls. It's a pitifully laboured analogy to comic collecting, including 'Mystic Mylar' bags in which to store his acquisitions.~HS

Mark Hazzard: MERC
Marvel: *12 issues, 1 annual 1986–1987*

No, Mark Hazzard is not an expensive German car, he's a mercenary. The comic is eager to convince you he's also a modern-day saint: all those emerging alive from an encounter with Mr Hazzard thereafter give high priority to sitting around and telling each other how Mark changed their lives and saved their souls. It's all completely objectionable, and yet...there's always enough happening in each issue to make you pick up the next one. It's at its best with Peter David's writing (1–4), when

there are fleeting moments of ambivalence, but once Doug Murray takes over from 5, it's full speed ahead for canonisation.~FC

MERCHANTS OF DEATH
Eclipse: *4 issues 1988*

Magazine dedicated to adventure strips from Europe and America. Each issue features a colour episode of 'Soldier Of Fortune' by Grassi and Breccia. The stories are hard-hitting but not particularly outstanding, featuring a taciturn mercenary hero, and the awful colouring does not improve matters, but the pared-down artwork survives it. Less exciting is 'Ransom', an adventure story set in Europe, written by Kurt Busiek with art by Rick Howell and the young and rather rough Dan Brereton. You can see the bones of Brereton's style, but overall the art is rather chunky and clumsy. Ransom's a secret-agent type hired by a mysterious Rumanian to steal back a family heirloom. At least, that's what he's told. Rounding out the issues are shorter pieces written by Trillo and illustrated, in a fine line style, by José Luis Salinas, set during the American Civil War; and there's a French Foreign Legion strip, also by them.~FJ

MERMAID
Viz: *Mermaid's Forest 4 issues 1994, Mermaid's Scar 4 issues 1994, Mermaid's Promise 4 issues 1994, Mermaid's Dream 3 issues 1994–1995, Mermaid's Gaze 4 issues 1995, Mermaid's Mask 3 issues 1995*

Very dark and disturbing stories from Rumiko Takahashi, better known for her lighter material. Partaking of the flesh of a mermaid renders one both immortal and immune to harm. This is discovered the difficult way by Yuta, who's been around for centuries. Unfortunately this only works for a few, and a horrible demise awaits the failures, although there's no shortage of those willing to try. The mermaids aren't necessarily the glamorous and friendly sirens of myth either: they're altogether more unfriendly and vicious, particularly when it's apparent that their flesh is at stake.

Mermaid's Forest continues from material published in the Manga magazine *Animerica*, with Yuta having rescued Mana, a fellow-immortal raised in isolation by mermaids to become one of them. Separated from Mana, Yuta finds her again captured by two sisters, one of whom is also immortal, but at a price. The story delves deep into some rather murky motivations, and ought to surprise with its conclusions. Unfortunately, with minimal changes, that's also the plot of *Mermaid's Promise*, and the impact is very much lessened by repetition. The intervening series, though, is another shocker, playing off the innocence of youth against the horrific consequences of consuming mermaid's flesh. It's padded towards the end, with 3's *Home Alone* sequence jarring, but there's just enough momentum to see the story through.

Mermaid's Dream is two individual stories, with the better of them being 'The Ash Princess' in 2 and 3. It's a powerful and spooky tale of life, legend and trickery, and the best of the *Mermaid* canon. By the time of *Mermaid's Gaze* one begins to wonder just how many people aren't familiar with mermaids and their legend, as Yuta and Mana unerringly home in on those that are everywhere they visit. Containing the requisite mixture of threat and horror, it's functional, but familiarity dilutes the idea, and one gets the feeling Takahashi had her mind on other projects. *Mermaid's Mask*, though, is a partial return to form. Lacking the complexity of previous tales, and relying once again on childhood innocence as a counterpoint to grim events, it incorporates a resonant and gruesome streak of horror.

If there's a theme to *Mermaid* it's that immortality comes at a price, and those who lust after it rarely attain it in the form they desire. It also strays far from the whimsy and adventure so associated with Japanese comics, yet for all her individuality in approach, Takahashi is distressingly traditional when it comes to presenting role-models. The female Mana is always the abducted victim and the male Yuta her rescuer. Takahashi's delicate artwork is far removed from the cartoon exaggeration of *Ranma½* and if on occasion there's a little too much wide-eyed innocence it all serves to contrast the horror of the stories. Largely underrated, *Mermaid* is well worth anyone's time, and is particularly recommended to people not usually very keen on Japanese material.~WJ

Recommended: *Mermaid's Forest* 1–4, *Mermaid's Scar* 1, 2, *Mermaid's Dream* 2, 3

Collections: Mermaid's Forest (*Mermaid's Forest* 1–4 + material from *Animerica* magazine), *Mermaid's Scar* (*Mermaid's Dream* 1–3, *Mermaid's Scar* 1–4, *Mermaid's Promise* 1–4), *Mermaid's Gaze* (*Mermaid's Gaze* 1–4, *Mermaid's Mask* 1–3)

META 4
First: *3 issues 1991*

Altogether lack-lustre early attempt at incorporating Fortean topics into comics. Stefan Petrucha would go on to write far better material along the same lines for *X-Files*, while artist Ian Gibson obviously couldn't give a toss.~WJ

METACOPS
Monster: *3-issue miniseries 1991*

Historical characters like The Queen of Sheba, Jimi Hendrix and Albert Einstein didn't die, they were recruited into a time-travelling police force. Humorously re-creating and distorting the past, *Metacops* is just a bit of fun with history.

Unfortunately it's rather wordy (courtesy of Link Yaco) and the artwork (by John Heebink) is both fussy and unappealing.~NF

METAL MEN
DC: *56 issues 1963–1970 (1–41), 1973 (42–44), 1976–1978 (45–56), 4-issue miniseries 1993–1994*

One of DC's most endearing creations, the Metal Men were introduced via four try-out strips in *Showcase* 37–40, before being granted their own series. Pipe-smoking and orange-checked-jacket-wearing government scientist Dr Will Magnus manufactures a bunch of robots each with the ability to mimic the chemical properties of the metal they were constructed from. All were also implanted with a 'responsometer', enabling them to have human characteristics to complement their respective metals. Gold, the dependable leader of the gang, can stretch himself for miles, the hot-tempered Mercury can melt himself at room temperature and the female Platinum, nick-named Tina, proves tough and resilient. The stocky and dense Lead always acts as a good barrier, especially against radiation, while Iron is the strong-man of the team, and the flexible and stuttering Tin the weak spot.

Creator Robert Kanigher worked in perfect harmony with artists Ross Andru and Mike Esposito to produce some wonderful light-hearted tales. Most Metal Men adventures dealt with other robotic adversaries: there were robot amazons, spider-robots, robot dinosaurs, etc., and then there were foes made from plastic: Plastic Perils, The Gas Gang (belch), not forgetting the giant chemical creature, Chemo. And we mustn't forget the other elemental robotic creations – Barium, Zirconium, Sodium, Osmium, Gallium, Iridium and the like. Who says comics aren't educational? Chemistry lessons in school would've been a lot more fun if *Metal Men* had been part of the curriculum!

The adversaries played their part, but the core of the series was the interaction between the group, all of whom were disturbingly human. Platinum was in love with Doc Magnus, while poor Tin often felt out of things, so even invented his own stuttering girl-friend, Nameless, who shared some of his abilities. On the downside, the formula plots, charming as they were, ensured a predictability. This slowly began to change with 30, when the creative team of Otto Binder and Gil Kane arrived. Things took a further step up when Mike Sekowsky took over the art with 32, and Kanigher returned to write. In an obvious attempt at stopping declining sales *Metal Men* was given a new direction. Sekowsky continued the plot when he also became writer with 37, his first act being to put the Metal Men on trial and have them destroyed. During this time Doc Magnus was in a coma, and the team are rescued by the mysterious Mister Conan in 37, a billionaire who wants to use his wealth to combat chaos around the world. In order for the Metal Men to act successfully and covertly they're given human disguises. Gold becomes Guy Giden, a philanthropist and Wall Street genius; Platinum becomes Tina Platt, a beautiful model; Lead and Tin become Ledby Hand and Tinker, a singing sensation; Mercury becomes the red-haired, red-bearded, temperamental artist and sculptor, Mercurio; and Iron becomes successful construction engineer Jon 'Iron' Mann. Don't you just love Sekowsky's sense of humour? Oddly, though, there was nothing humorous about this group. *Metal Men* was now played straight, and it worked. The issues concluding the first run came to a head with Doc Magnus coming out of his coma, but with a decidedly different personality. He's now a would-be despot, constructing robots to take over the world, which forces his original creations into conflict with him. Sadly, this interesting plot was never concluded, as the axe fell.

The title returned in 1973 featuring reprints to see if the group had any pulling power. Apparently not, but they were revived in *The Brave And The Bold* 103 in their original robot bodies, and would return a number of times to team with Batman before their title picked up again with new stories from 45. Writers Steve Gerber and Gerry Conway kicked off proceedings with the excellent stylised art of Walt Simonson, and Doc Magnus regains his sanity. Slightly wackier stories emerge from the mind of Martin Pasko (52's 'Dr Strangelove and the Brain Children' is a good example), but artist Joe Staton fails to impress as much as Simonson, despite his cartoony style. Conway returns for the last three issues and once more tries to humanise the team, but it proves a failure.

Besides the occasional guest appearance not a lot was heard from the Metal Men until the 1993 miniseries. Without giving the plot away, let's just say the Metal Men were far more than they seemed to be, as were their alleged 'responsometer'-granted personalities. Mike Carlin's plot added considerable depth to the Metal Men's origins and characters. Artists Dan Jurgens and Brett Breeding held their end up, and the miniseries was the most enjoyable run since the Mike Sekowsky stories.~HY

Recommended: 6, 10, 13, 21, 31–33, 37–41, 45–47, miniseries 1–4

METAMORPHO, The Element Man

DC: *17 issues 1965–1968, 4-issue miniseries 1993*

After trying out in *The Brave And The Bold* 57–58, Metamorpho moved into his own title, a fine, light-hearted, inventive and somewhat tongue-in-cheek series written by Bob Haney and originally drawn by Ramona Fradon. An

ancient artefact changed Rex Mason into Metamorpho, a striking but freakish-looking character able to transform his body into any element or structure. Along with some adversaries of decidedly bizarre appearance, the series featured a great supporting cast. Sapphire Stagg was Metamorpho's naïve, poor-little-rich girl-friend; Simon Stagg her wealthy, scheming father who tried to use Metamorpho for his own purposes; Java a stone-age man restored to life by Stagg and also in love with Sapphire; and there was Metamorpho's female counterpart and other 'romantic' interest, the beautiful green-haired Urania, the Element Girl. This entertaining series was unfortunately cancelled halfway through a story. Metamorpho popped up some years later as a back-up in *Action Comics* (413–418) and *World's Finest* (218–220) and was a regular in *Batman And The Outsiders* and later *Justice League Europe*, but it wasn't until 1993 that he was given another title. Scripter Mark Waid continued the saga well, though he concentrated on the darker elements (no pun intended) of the turbulent relationships between the major characters, with plenty of surprises. Alas, no Element Girl. Her final fate was revealed in *Sandman* 20.~HY

Norm Breyfogle's METAPHYSIQUE
Eclipse: *2 issues 1992*
Bravura: *6 issues 1995*

The Eclipse issues prove that Norm Breyfogle can turn out nicely drawn *House of Mystery*-style stories with the best of them. The Bravura series is an entirely different kettle of fish. A group of people continually plagued by deeply disturbing nightmares are to participate in a project exploring their dreams, only all is not what it seems. The story plays with the reality of dreaming, uniting the experience with virtual reality, setting up an interesting scenario amid a plethora of contrived buzzwords, with the mysterious vanished superhero Metaphysique apparently at the centre. Sadly, though, Breyfogle cops out and we're left with an interesting, but fatally flawed, superhero title.~WJ

METEOR MAN
Marvel: *6 issues 1993–1994*

Feeble follow-up to Robert Townsend's movie, transforming Meteor Man into a typical *angst*-ridden, self-doubting, Marvel-style superhero. Marvel also released a dashed-off movie adaptation.~FP

METROPOL
Epic: *Series one 12 issues 1991–1992, Series two 3 issues 1992*

Although some readers may find Ted McKeever's religious allegory *Metropol* perplexing, take heart from the fact that it is considerably less obtuse than his previous series *Transit* and *Eddy Current*. Characters from *Eddy Current* turn up throughout *Metropol*, and *Transit*'s story-line is concluded there. McKeever depicts the transformation of a grim, ugly city whose inhabitants have lost faith in themselves into a primeval battleground for angels and devils. As a plague rips through the populace some individuals find themselves reborn as angels, and others as devils. Unfortunately there are 80,000 demons, and only five angels to protect the remaining humans. McKeever writes, pencils, inks and colours all issues (except for the *Eddy Current* back-up strip in 9–11, drawn by Mike Mignola), allowing him very close control of the look of the book. His style here is more blocky and powerful than earlier, very confidently inked with flowing, heavy lines. His colouring is excellent; flat colours slightly dulled with black are used to suggest an environment that is dirty at the edges.

In the second series, titled *Metropol AD*, a year and a half has passed since the demons overran the city, one of the angels has given birth (!) and the few surviving humans are planning to try to break through the wall which was erected around the city in the first days of the plague to contain the contagion. Also, the angels are beginning to show dangerous signs of human weakness. *Metropol* is an extraordinary piece of symbolic writing in which Milton meets Kafka, built up from short, seemingly unrelated incidents, dream fragments and visions.~FJ
Recommended: 1–3, 8, 12

METROPOLIS S.C.U.
DC: *4-issue miniseries 1994–1995*
An intelligent and entertaining use of supporting characters from Superman. Lois Lane joins the Special Crimes Unit, the team that deals with Metropolis' supercriminals, to investigate the death of an officer. Maggie Sawyer, commander of the S.C.U., is having increasing trouble separating her personal and professional lives, a situation exacerbated by the fact that her girl-friend Tobie, also a journalist, is jealous of Lane's access to the S.C.U. Throw in Maggie's ex-husband and a crazed eco-hermit and you've got a thoroughly readable miniseries, courtesy of Cindy Goff and artist Pete Krause.~HS
Recommended: 1–4

MIAMI MICE
Rip-Off: *4 issues 1986–1987*
If you're busting a gut laughing at the idea of a rodent-infested TV parody this is the comic for you. And if you're a *Cerebus* completist you'll have to pick up the fourth issue.~WJ

The New Crime Files of MICHAEL MAUSER, Private Eye
Apple: *1 issue 1992*
From the pages of *E-Man* comes Michael Mauser, a rat-faced private detective with a mauser gun. This was the first full-length story after he'd appeared as back-up in Charlton's *Vengeance Squad* and made guest appearances in *E-Man*. Scripted and drawn by co-creators Nicola Cuti and Joe Staton, this one-shot, in the tradition of Mike Hammer, concerns Mauser's attempt to find a serial killer who may or may not be himself. Staton's art looks great in black and white.~NF

MICKEY AND DONALD
Gladstone: 18 issues 1988–1990
As you would expect from a Gladstone title, Carl Barks is represented in each issue, mostly by stories reprinted from *Walt Disney's Comics And Stories*, though he also illustrates Mickey Mouse in 17. With the Mickey Mouse title reprinting Floyd Gottfredson's Mickey Mouse newspaper strip, this title offered an outlet for later Mouse artists, Bill Wright (1, 5, 9–11, 15), Jack Bradbury (2, 3, 11, 13, 14), Romano Scarpa (6–8) and Paul Murry (1, 12, 17). Of these, Scarpa's 'The Blot's Double Mystery' is an excellent Phantom Blot story. Gottfredson is also represented with 'The Man of Tomorrow' (3, 4), 'The Santa Claus Bandit' (13) and 'The House of Mystery' (18), as well as by various one- and two-page gag strips. William Van Horn (2, 9, 17), Daan Jippes (2, 5) and Don Rosa (1, 17) contribute good examples of their work but they are really quite slight strips.~NF
Recommended: 3, 4, 6–8, 13, 17, 18

MICKEY RAT
LA Comics: *1 issue 1971*
Kitchen Sink: *1 issue (2) 1972*
Last Gasp: *2 issues (3–4) 1980–1982*
Mickey Rat was Robert Armstrong's amoral, beer-swilling antihero whose adventures comprised the bulk of the issues. The first two are entertaining enough, though lacking in focus, but by 3 Armstrong had matured into a fine satirist and the writing is much sharper. Mickey Rat's exploits are utterly reprehensible, but thoroughly compelling at the same time, never more so than when shared with the Couch Potatoes. This TV-addicted group of losers proved popular enough for their own feature in 4, and *The Official Couch Potato Handbook* was published in 1983. Another back-up strip, the jazz-based Dizzy Ratstein, never quite comes to life, but overall the last two issues make fine reading.~DAR
Recommended: 3, 4

M.I.C.R.A.
Comics Interview: *6 issues 1986–1987*

The acronymically titled Mind Controlled Remote Automaton is experimental technology used by a woman paralysed in a terrorist attack. It's initially designed merely as a form of mobility for her, but she's gradually applied as a weapon, and manipulated by army officers keen to learn the technology. Manga-influenced long before it was common in the USA, M.I.C.R.A. was a decent blend of mystery, action and soap opera, that started well and improved. The premature cancellation was a shame.~FP

MICROBOTS
Gold Key: *1 issue 1971*

Jeff Micron emerges from cryogenic freezing to a new world, accompanied by miniature indestructible working robots allegedly designed by his father. This being the days before video and toy tie-ins, they actually look like they were designed by a three-year-old with building bricks. Dull.~FP

MICRONAUTS
Marvel: *59 issues, 2 annuals 1979–1984, series two ('The New Voyages') 20 issues 1984–1986*

The Micronauts were a curious set of toys to give to small children, including as they did human/animal hybrids, a race of insectivoid hominids and all sorts of other strange figures. And those were just the good guys. In a superpowered take on *Land Of The Giants* a group of royal rebels from various planets in the Microverse escape into our huge universe and then discover they're trapped, while back on their own plane the evil Baron Kaza takes over planet after planet, filling them with his evil bodybanks, where he grows hideous, mutated dog soldiers.

For a comic based around a set of toys, The Micronauts wasn't bad. Possibly inspired by the art of the young and then unknown Michael Golden, his drawing heavily influenced by Berni Wrightson, on the first dozen issues of the book, Bill Mantlo turned in the finest scripts of his career, quickly establishing the scenario and putting in plenty of excitement. The characters are visually striking but their characterisation remained vague and shifted to suit the plot. Bug, the insectivoid member of the team, has a speech impediment in place of a character, and most of the others aren't much better. Later inclusions to the line included Devil, a big red hairy alien, and in the second series Hunter, a big knobbly alien. Things would no doubt have been better if most of the villains weren't lumpen plastic things created by toy designers rather than writers. Since the bodybanks could turn out all sorts of mutations, ludicrous villains that

matched each hero were constantly being wheeled out. And for some reason, instead of all swapping and fighting menaces not specifically grown to neutralise their power, the Micronauts duly took them on in order.

The origin of the Microverse is revealed in 35 as being the creation of a race of various aliens who'd banded together to seek sanctuary, and in the process of creating the microscopic universe had also imprisoned the demons then ruling Earth. Once the team are back there the series builds to an epic climax as the Micronauts' leader, Commander Rann, attains god-like powers along with his arch-enemy, but rejects them. Rann is a rather pompous philosopher, who tends to spend a lot of the series deep in thought, in trances, or floating around in space capsules doing cosmic things. At one point he even joins spirits with Dr Strange to become Captain Universe! Mantlo has great fun with the fact that he never seems to notice his mate, Princess Marionette (those names, huh?), being seduced left right and centre by his friends.

'The New Voyages' carried on where the first series left off. One suspects Marvel were hoping to refresh the book's audience by offering a new first issue, but the plots are very similar, with the war still raging, and the Micronauts continually having problems staying in their universe. Peter Gillis' scripts are not particularly inspired. He has the Micronauts irradiated inside a giant insect, visiting their various home planets – to find their friends too busy fighting local wars to help in the coming struggle – and trying to come to terms with the mysterious Scion. He pops up out of nowhere, claims their leadership and appears to be willing to die to get them back through the space-wall into the Microverse. Kelley Jones' art was undeveloped, although by comparison to some of the later 'creators' let loose on the first run he's a definite improvement. There were artists of note in the first series – Howard Chaykin from 13–18 and a hurried Gil Kane – but there was also the likes of Danny Bulanadi to come to terms with.

The Micronauts Special Edition series was simply a reprint of issues 1–5 of the original series.~FJ

MIDNIGHT EYE
Viz: *6 issues 1991–1992*

Set in the technologically advanced future so ubiquitous in Japanese comics, the Midnight Eye is Gokü, whose right eye has been replaced with a device permitting him to interface with any computer in the world. A Japanese take on the hard-boiled detective, with stories named after the featured female lead, it's a well drawn title, but ultimately unmemorable.~FP
Collection: Midnight Eye (1–6)

MIDNIGHT MEN
Epic: *4-issue miniseries*

Very familiar territory indeed for creator Howard Chaykin as his square-jawed, fallible hero Barnett Pasternack discovers he's inherited a role as the latest of a long line of protectors of Hollywood throughout the century. There's also a nutter on the loose slicing out thyroid glands, and tied in with a rich businessman. It's sharply observed, well plotted, tautly dialogued with added quirky bits and somewhat sketchily illustrated, but one gets the impression Chaykin can knock this stuff out in his sleep by now. It's about time he changed his tune, and it's about time the rest of the comics industry caught up.~WJ

MIDNIGHT MYSTERY
ACG: *7 issues 1961*

This is a science-fiction and supernatural themed anthology. None of the stories are exactly strong, but they have more humour than most of their kind. The best is 'Spacemen Against The Supernatural' (2), featuring a man with no grasp of science who makes inventions by bolting things together any old how, and doesn't realise that they only work because of the magic charm he inherited from his uncle. His shining self-confidence is nicely handled. And there's 'Clem Never Does Anything Big' (6), which pits a Kentucky hillbilly against an alien invasion. Don't devote any time to finding them, but skim through them if they come your way.~FC

MIDNIGHT SONS Unlimited
Marvel: *9 issues 1993–1994*

Midnight Sons was the collective name applied to Marvel's supernatural and horror characters in the early 1990s, and this oversized title featured all of them either teamed or in individual stories with framing sequences. Despite the use of some popular creators, the content hardly rises above bland, and only 7 possesses any spark, featuring the return of Brother Voodoo in a touching tale. 9's story of the Blazing Skull provides welcome relief from the unrelenting grim earnestness to most of the material, which is rarely leavened by any humour. Should you care, the crossover 'Siege of Darkness' story concludes in 4.~WJ

MIDNIGHT SURFER
Quality: *One-shot 1986*

Very sympathetic re-jigging permitted a Cam Kennedy story drawn for a different page-size and spread over several short episodes to be presented in a single American-sized comic in seamless fashion. Although nominally a Judge Dredd story, writer John Wagner, as

ever, is more interested in the supporting characters and their escapades, and Chopper is the star of the show. He's a participant in the illegal sky-surfing world championship which is occurring in Dredd's Mega-City One, and as well as completing a difficult course he must evade the Judges attempting to bring him down. There's very little plot, but this is strangely poetic for a Judge Dredd story, and Wagner was to return to the theme several times afterwards.~FP

Milton Knight's MIDNITE The Rebel Skunk
Blackthorne: *2 issues 1986–1987*

Milton Knight brings the madcap world of 1920s animation to comics with his stories of a female skunk protector of the good. Knight's art leaps off the page, and in 2 he draws a testosterone factory of a superhero, but once you've got past how stunning the art is, there's very little else to his tales of the glamorous sex-bomb skunk.~WJ

MIDNITE TALES
Charlton: *18 issues 1972–1976*

One of Charlton's innumerable horror titles, this was as anaemic as its companions, although occasionally enlivened by some nice art. Each cover and much of the contents were provided by notorious Wally Wood imitator Wayne Howard, though Tom Sutton and Joe Staton were usually also present. The most notable artist to contribute was Don Newton, whose art in 11–14 is quite gorgeous.~DAR

MIGHTY COMICS PRESENTS
Mighty: *11 issues (40–50) 1966 –1967*

Archie's attempts to emulate Marvel moved into high gear as they cancelled *Fly-Man*, but continued the numbering with a changed title to feature revivals of a whole host of obscure 1940s superheroes. Back came the Black Hood, The Fox, The Shield, Steel Sterling, The Web and several more, each of them with a personality interchangeable with the others, being fast-mouthed crime-fighting athletes. The appalling art (take a bow, Paul Reinman), ludicrously contrived plots and camp dialogue make for a chucklesome read at the comics rather than with them, and the only strip displaying a modicum of genuine humour is the Web (in 40, 43, 45, 46 and 50). The camp superheroics are present in full quantity, but the scenes of the superhero returning home to be henpecked by his wife and having to dodge the mailman on his way out to fight crime have an acceptable slapstick quality. Overall the run isn't quite as preposterous as the Mighty Comics' stab at the *Mighty Crusaders*, but there's plenty of cheap laughs to be had.~WJ

THE MIGHTY CRUSADERS
Mighty: *7 issues 1965–1966*

The Mighty Crusaders was an unashamed attempt to cash in on the twin successes of Marvel's superheroes and the Adam West *Batman*. Superman creator Jerry Siegel gathered together Archie Comics' superheroes Fly Man, Fly Girl, The Shield, The Black Hood and The Comet for this bizarre version of Marvel's popular team book *The Avengers*. Siegel and 'artist' Paul Reinman may well have been sending up Stan Lee's bickering, neurotic loser heroes, but their attempts to be swinging and camp are pitifully middle-aged and ungroovy. Not that this stops *The Mighty Crusaders* from being a wonderfully dopey piece of 1960s kitsch. Who could resist lines of dialogue like these deep musings from troubled superspook Mr Justice in 5: 'Ah, yes… There is so very much I know… an overvoid awareness of the infinitum intermingling of timelessness, everlastingness and grandeur parellsected by diabalkarm trogs culminating in a terrible awareness'! Outta sight, Daddy-o! Although 3's villain has a great silly name – The Deathless Smiler – 5 is probably the 'best' of the series. It features a ludicrous parade of 'guest appearances' from such heroes and villains as D.E.M.O.N. ('the code-name of the international terror organization which furthers Destruction, Extortion, Murder, Oppression and Nefariousness'), The Fox, The Web and Captain Flag, aka The Ultra-Men, The Agents of A.U.N.T.I.E. ('Amalgamated Universal Network To Inhibit Evil'), The Spider, The Terrific Three (Steel Sterling, The Jaguar, the aforementioned Mr Justice) and chief baddie The Nameless One, all in nineteen dense pages. Forget about the final issue, in which the Crusaders are displaced from their title by the witless Steel Sterling, but otherwise *The Mighty Crusaders* is about as 'authentic' as *The Monkees*, and nearly as much fun.~AL
Recommended: 5

The MIGHTY CRUSADERS
Red Circle: *5 issues 1983–1984*
Archie: *8 issues (6–13) 1984–1985*

After the camp triumph of the 1960s incarnation there's an immense disappointment when beginning to read this series. Oh yes, there are daft plots and daft characters, particularly The Brain Emperor (a guy with a transparent dome covering an otherwise exposed brain), but this is an attempt to play the characters straight from creators not able to transcend mediocrity. Bizarrely, though, instead of forgetting the previous series entirely, there are attempts made to reconcile the continuity of a twenty-year-old, universally ridiculed comic. Fans of the 1960s material shouldn't despair, though, because in the final issues Rich Margopoulos tries his level best to write a 1980s equivalent. You are referred to 12's splash page featuring the Crusaders' building-block flying train, and 13's lump of red-rock villain. The dialogue is gloriously pompous and expository, and only the competent, although far from exciting, art of Dick Ayers and Chic Stone prevents a total lapse.~WJ

The MIGHTY HERCULES
Gold Key: *2 issues 1963*

This curious, angular Hercules starred in a kids' TV cartoon, and the stories reflect the juvenile origins.~FP

MIGHTY MARVEL WESTERN
Marvel: *46 issues 1968–1976*

Poorly Marvel Western more like, as there's little in this collection of reprints, culled from 1950s and 1960s titles, to set the heart racing. There's a longish Rawhide Kid story in every issue, and shorter Two Gun Kid (every issue), Kid Colt (1–24) and Matt Slade (25 on) back-ups.~FP

MIGHTY MOUSE
Marvel: *10 issues 1990–1991*

Surprisingly very funny update on the old 40s cartoon series. Instead of re-telling of old stories it found its niche in parodies of current titles. Everything from *Crisis on Infinite Earths* to Spider-Man are lampooned to good effect.~TP
Recommended: 1, 2, 6

MIGHTY SAMSON
Gold Key: *31 issues 1964–1970 (1–21), 10 issues 1973–1976 (22–31)*
Whitman: *1 issue (32) 1982*

Post-holocaust adventure with Samson and his companions Mindor and Sharmaine. The resemblance to the later *Hercules Unbound* from DC is too strong not to be mentioned, although the quality of this title is considerably lower. Early issues are drawn by Frank Thorne, but thereafter Jack Sparling hacks out one issue after another. The 1970s issues are reprints, as is the 1982 Whitman comic.~SW

Mickey Spillane's MIKE DANGER
Tekno: *11 issues 1995–1996*
Big Entertainment: *9 issues 1996*

Before he came up with Mike Hammer, Spillane outlined a cartoon series, which Tekno saw fit to dig up, with Max Allan Collins in charge of the scripts. Tough guy P.I. Mike Danger wakes up in the future, where he's told he's been in suspended animation. And people start trying to kill him. Obviously all is not what it seems, you say to yourself, and by the end of the series you discover you were right. In this synthetic, carefully controlled world Danger's the only 'real' man around and women start falling all over him. Eduardo Barreto, who provides most of the early artwork, plasters the strip with Betty Page lookalikes and deals with the action in a workmanlike fashion. Unfortunately there's not a lot of it – several pages of explanation followed by an attempt to kill Danger is the usual form. When Peter Gran takes over with 7 the art turns slippery but simultaneously wooden. Disappointing overall.~FJ

MIKE MIST MINUTE MYSTERIES
Eclipse: *1 issue 1986*

A collection of single-page puzzlers by Max Allen Collins and Terry Beatty, where the idea is to guess who did it before reading the final panel, upside down. Fine as a back-up in Collins and Beatty's *Ms Tree*, slight and sometimes unconvincing here.~NF

MILK AND CHEESE
Slave Labor: *6 issues + 1991 to date*

Evan Dorkin presents tales of dairy products gone bad. A cartoon lump of cheese and a cartoon carton of milk come to life and cause all kinds of havoc as they rail about the plastic aspects of society. It's a thinly veiled opportunity for Dorkin to make his own comments on anything and everything. The one- and two-page strips are generally funny but after half a dozen monotony begins to set in. It's well worth reading one issue, but more than one could leave you with a fear of dairy products for life. As an added comment on the ridiculous practice of restarting comics from the first issue, *Milk And Cheese* has four different number one issues, 'our first number two' and issue 666.~SS
Collection: Milk And Cheese (1–3)

MILLENNIUM
DC: *8 issues 1987*

Yes, it certainly read like it. This was a long haul. The premise for DC's 1987 company-wide crossover was the emergence of a three-billion-year-old android cult, the Manhunters. Originally created as a force for good by the Guardians of the Galaxy, they turned bad and had now returned etc., etc. An interesting facet was that a few long-standing DC characters turned out to be androids, or human acolytes serving the Manhunters. In order to defeat them ten humans had to be advanced and… oh, it's too tedious to bear repetition. If you like to see dozens of DC heroes drawn by Joe Staton in every panel this is the series for you, but both Staton and writer Steve Engelhart had seen better days.~HY

MILLENNIUM FEVER
Vertigo: *4-issue miniseries 1995–1996*

Millennium Fever starts off as a comic about the everyday worries and joys of a young student's life. Of mixed parentage, his mother's going off the deep end after the death of her baby and his father's turned into a brick wall. He wishes either of his grandmothers were alive to advise him, and worries that he'll never lose his virginity. Eventually he answers a personal ad and meets the perfect partner. Until, that is, she turns out to be an embodiment of the soul of the universe, or something like that.

Nick Abadzis' script scores highly for authentic street language and emotional honesty, but loses points for getting wrapped up in ecological mysticism towards the end. His propositions are no odder than a common-or-garden *Sandman* story, but by being so convincing in the early pages he leaves the reader unprepared for the weird shit. The story uses long chunks of narrative to progress and comment on the behaviour of the characters, rather than dialogue, which makes it text-heavy in parts. Duncan Fegredo draws modern people in a modern style and by this stage has learnt to control some of the scribbly excesses of his early work. He suits the tone of the story well, able to draw cosmic encounters as well as London street scenes with conviction. Pity he wasn't left to do a bit more of the work.~FJ

MILLIE THE MODEL
Marvel: *207 issues, 10 Annuals 1945–1973*

The misadventures of daffy blonde model Millie Collins, her photographer boy-friend Flicker Holbrook, her red-haired rival Chili Seven, and their friends delighted generations of comic-reading girls (and more than a few furtive boys) for generations. Switching styles between cartoon comedy and semi-realistic soap as tastes changed, Mil lasted through the desert years of the 1950s with minimal alteration. Her boy-friend's name was changed to Clicker when it was pointed out that the second two letters of 'FLICKER' might run together on the printing press to unfortunate effect, and her rival Chili's surname was changed to Storm for no reason at all. Our heroine remained serenely untroubled, dispensing wisecracks and fashion tips in her own comic and the companion titles *A Date With Millie* (7 issues 1956–1957 and another 7 issues 1959–1960), *Life With Millie* (13 issues, 1960–1962), *Mad About Millie* (17 issues, 1969–1970, 1 Annual, 1971), and *Modelling With Millie* (33 issues 1963–1967). Unlike Patsy Walker, Millie was never mixed into the Marvel Universe proper, only sticking her head into guest-shots in *Defenders* and *She-Hulk*. It's become fashionable to belittle frivolous 'girls' comics' like *Millie* and *Patsy*, but without the dollars they brought in, Marvel wouldn't have survived until the 1960s to usher in the 'Marvel Age of Comics', so all you little mutant zombies better show some respect, you hear?~HS

MINIMUM WAGE

Fantagraphics: *One-shot 1995, 5 issues + 1996 to date*

Bob Fingerman works a fair amount of autobiographical experience into his stories of Rob Hoffman, struggling New York cartoonist specialising in obsessing over trivia, and being a damning silent critic of humanity's foibles (as all good cartoonists should be). Many of the tribulations depicted are seemingly common to half of New York, but the level of charm and wit, and occasional sequences of gut-busting hilarity, ensure that otherwise mundane events are promoted beyond their status. Despite the attractive, clean cartooning style, the grime and sleaziness of some characters still oozes off the page, which is a remarkable achievement. Densely written to the standard of a quality sit-com, this differs from similar material in that it's largely an upbeat title. Rob is relatively content with his lot and has an attractive partner, and much of the humour stems from the misfortunes of others. The introductory one-shot is excellent, but expensive, so sampling is best begun with the stand-alone issues of the regular series. Come back for the one-shot, though.~FP

Recommended: One-shot, 1–5

The MIRACLE SQUAD

Upshot: *4 issues 1986–1987*
Apple: *4-issue miniseries ('Blood And Dust') 1989*

Set in late 1930s Hollywood, this is a fast-paced adventure strip based around Miracle Studios. The first series introduces Sandra Castle searching for her twin sister and involving the studio and its boss, Mark Barron, in a takeover battle with gangster Sweets O'Hanlon. 'Blood And Dust' sees the studio trying to make a film about the poverty of dustbowl America and encountering Ku Klux Klan-type prejudice. Briskly written by John Wooley, who knows his period, and cleanly drawn by Terry Tidwell, there's humanity in the stories but it lacks a little sophistication.~NF

MIRACLEMAN

Eclipse (with Quality, 1–6): *24 issues + 1985 to date*

Starting out life in the 50s as a blatant Captain Marvel rip-off, Mick Anglo's Marvelman was the recipient of an Alan Moore overhaul in the enormously influential British anthology comic *Warrior*. The story was reprinted by Eclipse under the title *Miracleman* to stave off threats of legal action from Marvel Comics.

In Moore's hands, the innocent 50s hero grew up into an unsuccessful and insecure freelance reporter whose memory of his powers existed only in dreams. When reawakened, Mike Moran's *alter ego* makes the mistake of contacting his former sidekick, who has used his own abilities to build up an incredibly powerful multinational corporation. Things go from bad to worse. Kid Miracleman is an unbalanced sadist with the powers of a god, and the steps taken to stop him send Moran down an irreversible path that leads to him assuming absolute control of Earth. Along the way, startling revelations about his origin further destroy the cosy world he thought he knew, and the more he embraces the god-like side of his nature the further removed from reality (and his own humanity) he becomes. Miracleman may be a benign dictator, but neither the reader nor the character are allowed to forget that he has chosen to place himself above the mortals. When Moore brings his story to a conclusion in 16, the Miracleman he leaves not only knows what he has gained, but is all too painfully aware of what he has lost. Sadly, the artwork doesn't always live up to the consistency of Moore's writing. Early episodes, drawn by Garry Leach and later Alan Davis for reproduction in black and white, do not always take colour well. There are some ugly issues by Chuck Beckum when the reprint material runs out, and it is not until John Totleben comes on board with 11 that the title re-acquires a consistent look.

Despite a rocky publishing history (the first sixteen issues are spread over more than four years), the critical acclaim and high standards ensured the title's survival and cemented Moore's reputation in the American market. It is perhaps regrettable that Eclipse chose to continue the series after Moore's departure. Neil Gaiman and Mark Buckingham did an admirable job, presenting a series of vignettes (17–22) exploring what the world Miracleman has remade in his own image is like for those who have to live in it, not all of whom necessarily want him as their god. But the central character is noticeably absent, and there is a feeling that even they have admitted that Moore's act is impossible to follow, although their obvious love for the character carries them through.

From 23, Gaiman and Buckingham begin continued stories, once again focusing on the title character, now more god-like, omnipotent and self-absorbed than ever. Production problems continue to be the book's main fault and, by 1993, the numbering had progressed only as far as 24. It says something about Miracleman's history that his readership is prepared to wait for 25 onwards, and still believes they will come. ~JC

Recommended: 1–16

Collections: A Dream Of Flying (1–4), *The Red King Syndrome* (5–10), *Olympus* (11–16), *The Golden Age* (17–22)

MIRACLEMAN APOCRYPHA
Eclipse: *3 issues, 1991–1992*
This series of short 6–8 page vignettes from the past and present of the Miracleman family, by various creators, suffers as all such projects do from fluctuating quality. Okay for die-hard collectors, but the whole idea was largely superfluous.~JC

MIRACLEMAN FAMILY
Eclipse: *2 issues 1988*
Reprints of Mick Anglo stories from the 1950s, heavily influenced by the golden age Captain Marvel comics that inspired the characters.~JC

MR A
Comic Art Publishers: *1 issue 1973*
Bruce Henderson: *1 issue (2) 1974*
Mr A was the venue through which Steve Ditko expounded his views on life, society and politics. Mr A himself most closely resembled Ditko's Charlton character The Question, but that strip was at least hemmed in by thoughts of commerciality. These strips, many of them reprinted from fanzines, make no such concession. Ditko's philosophy was a form of right-wing absolutism, or, as Mr A says in 1, 'A is A. A thing is what it is. No man can have it both ways. Only through black and white principles can man distinguish between good and evil.' And so on. And on. And on. To anyone not sharing Ditko's views, which, let's face it, is most of us, this is all completely mad. At the same time, though, it makes compulsive reading and Ditko's art is absolutely top-notch throughout. The second issue is actually number 4 in 'The Ditko Series', 2 and 3 being *The Avenging World* and *Wha...?*~DAR

MR DAY AND MR NIGHT
Slave Labor: *1 issue 1993*
Previously seen as the back-up in *Paris, Man Of Plaster*, this is a superhero spoof (sort of) written by Glenn Dakin and drawn by Phil Elliott. Ponderous in places, but builds up to some good points about the value of scepticism.~FC

MISTER E
DC: *4-issue miniseries 1991*
There's a mystery here all right. It's how a comic about a psychotic blind psychic, whose father scooped his eyes out with a spoon when he caught him reading a nudie mag, confronting his guilt and repression could be so stultifyingly dull.~FP

MR. FIXIT
Apple: *2 issues 1990*
As different areas of the USA slip into different time-zones it's up to the best mechanic in the country to put things right. Strangely old-fashioned and light-hearted, competently written and drawn, there's nothing outstanding here, and as such it's only worth investigating as a bargain-box cheapie.~WJ

Neil Gaiman's MR HERO, The Newmatic Man
Tekno: *Series one 17 issues 1995–1996, Series two 5 issues + 1996 to date*
Museum curator Jenny Hale discovers a Victorian steam-powered robot, Mr Hero. It has two personalities according to which of its two heads is fitted. There's the simple blue-collar protective type, and the logical and superior detective. The downside is that Mr Hero is the property of the terrible Mr Henry Phage, other-dimensional dictatorial dinosaur with influence everywhere, and, retaining only his left hand, he wants Mr Hero back. Generally a fun title with appealing pencils from Ted Slampyak.~FP

MISTER MIRACLE
DC: *Series one 25 issues 1971–1974 (1–18), 1977–1978 (19–25), One-shot 1987, series two 28 issues 1989–1991, series three 7 issues 1996*
'Mister Miracle. He cheats death! He defies man! No trap can hold him! The making of a Legend!' exclaimed the first issue's cover, while tucked away in the top corner was one of the great understatements of the comics century: 'Kirby's Here'. Inside we're introduced to Thaddeus Brown, an escape artist who's trying to make a comeback, and the mysterious young man Scott Free – Kirby always had a way with names – and his mysterious technology. When Brown is executed by gangsters Scott assumes the mantle of Mister Miracle, super escape artist, assisted thereafter by Oberon, short, feisty and middle-aged. It's your basic superhero story with Kirby's art magnificent, even inked by Vince Colletta, although the infinitely more sympathetic Mike Royer inks from 5, completing the dynamic flair of the series.

The first issue makes little reference to the connected story Kirby was also telling about the world of Apokalips and New Genesis in the pages of *New Gods* and *Forever People*, but Scott Free was an integral part of that story. 2 steps right in with the boots on as gruesome old-age-pensioner Granny Goodness turns up. Granny heads up the Apokalips orphanage from which Scott Free has recently escaped, and since he's the first ever to do so Granny is out to punish him. 2–10 introduce an amazing gallery of Apokalips villains still used to this day. Besides Granny we have Dr Bedlam, a mind-manipulating scientist with a host of bodies, Kanto the assassin and Virman Vundarbar, a mock-Prussian military genius. Then there are Granny's élite soldiers, those

Female Furies, Lashina, Stompa, Bernadeth and Mad Harriet. Into this mixture Kirby throws a thinly disguised parody of his former Marvel partner Stan Lee, here named Funky Flashman. 7 and 8 have Mister Miracle back on Apokalips and really show Kirby at his story-telling best, with great action and marvellous dialogue. 9 temporarily pauses the action for one of the best-ever superhero comics, 'Himon', relating the story of Scott Free's parentage, his Apokalips upbringing, and how he escaped with the aid of Big Barda. Once head of the Female Furies, she was introduced in 4 as Scott's love interest, the cover proclaiming 'Big bonus! Big Surprise! Big Barda!', and she certainly is, especially with her megarod.

After 10, with the backstory told, *Mister Miracle* becomes a straight superhero adventure title, but that doesn't stop the Kirby creativity, and, with the Female Furies on Earth, he just can't stop the fun. Adversaries for the next few issues included The Floating Head and, as proclaimed on 14's cover, 'The weirdest villain ever seen in comics: Madame Evil Eyes', alas never seen again. Unfortunately, the marvellous Female Furies were ousted as supporting characters by the son of the original Mister Miracle, and a young kid, Shilo Norman, an irritating little runt, but the catalyst for a few good adventures. 18 returns the Apokalips crew for Scott and Barda's wedding in Kirby's (and the series) finale.

Mister Miracle returned in magnificent form in 1977. It's not easy to outdo Kirby, but writer Steve Englehart and artist Marshall Rogers had a good stab. The action centred on the Apokalips villains, with Granny Goodness still holding a grudge. The stories had a grittier feel, but the team didn't last long, Englehart even being so dissatisfied with 22 he was credited under an alias. Steve Gerber and Michael Golden are in place for 24, and produce two very good issues, but were unable to prevent cancellation halfway through a story. All the creators on this run had very different approaches to Kirby, but do justice to his character. A decade later a *Mister Miracle Special*, appeared written by Mark Evanier, at one time an assistant of Kirby's, and beautifully illustrated by Steve Rude and Mike Royer. Very much in Kirby style, it was an amusing story featuring Darkseid, and Funky Flashman.

The next series outlasted the previous two runs put together. Written by J.M. DeMatteis, it was intricately connected with the Justice League, of which Mister Miracle was a core member, also written by DeMatteis. The stance here was domestic comedy of sorts, as Scott and Barda set up home in a quiet town, but there's never anyplace quiet when the inhabitants of Apokalips and New Genesis are involved. Ian Gibson illustrated 1–7, but obviously didn't enjoy it, and DeMatteis forced the humour too far for what had until now been an adventure title, taking liberties with previously noble characters, particularly the Highfather. Keith Giffen and Len Wein take the comedy even further, but in better-conceived stories, and Joe Phillips' art from 8 is an improvement. Wein begins a plot-line with lots of ramifications in *Justice League* as Mister Miracle signs a binding agreement for an interplanetary tour that runs in 13–18.

Back on Earth in 19 Shilo Norman returns, less annoying than before, to become a new Mister Miracle in training in 20–22. Scott and Barda want to live as a normal couple, but Barda needs to work and becomes a wrestler, turning up the amusement factor another notch. Inevitably successful given her background, Barda wins a championship and creates a new group of Female Furies, wonderful busty, colourful-looking wrestlers. Everything comes to a head in the final issue, with Scott and Barda realising that they're unable to have a comfortable suburban existence: Scott has to fulfil his New Genesis heritage. Overall there weren't too many bad issues, but neither was this Mister Miracle as originally intended.

The 1996 series from Kevin Dooley and Steve Crespo continues where the previous run left off, more or less. There's trouble in New Genesis when Scott decides perhaps he doesn't want to become a god after all, preferring to live up to his name rather than have his destiny plotted out for him. Along the way there's a trip to the land of the dead and marital problems for Scott and Big Barda. She leaves for Wonder Woman's Paradise Island, while Scott joins Oberon's Miracle Workers, a charitable organisation assisting people in need. The series was prematurely cancelled, but the plot-lines continue in the most recent *New Gods* title.~HY

Recommended: Series one 1–10, 18–21, *Mister Miracle Special*, series two 13–18

MR MONSTER

Eclipse: *10 issues 1985–1987*
Dark Horse: *8 issue limited series 1988–1991*
Tundra: *3 issues 1992*

Michael T. Gilbert's Mr Monster is in large part a revival of a 1940s Doc Stearne, Mr Monster who appeared in *Super Duper Comics*. Mr Monster is played for laughs as a gung-ho superhero who shoots first, and kills all known monsters. His beautiful assistant, Kelly, sometimes has to stop him killing his own patients in this quest to rid the world of evil creatures. Artistically you might be forgiven for thinking Gilbert the president of the Will Eisner Appreciation Society. Gilbert's own work is a little more ornate than Eisner's but he gets a lot of help from his friends. Bill Messner-Loebs draws the first issue, and several others chip in as the series progresses (Keith Giffen in 6, Don Simpson in 6 and 10, Mark Pacella in 7, 8 and 10, Bill Wray for 8, Gerald Forton for 9 and Batton Lash in 9 also – a delightful *Wolff and Byrd* crossover). Gilbert writes most of the scripts but he's not afraid to hand over the typewriter to the likes of Alan Moore (3), and often co-scripts stories. It's all good, outrageous fun. 10 is in 6-D (because it's twice as good as ordinary 3-D), 3 has a Basil Wolverton reprint, 4 reprints a Jerry Grandinetti Dr Drew story and 6 contains a reprint of Steve Ditko's first comic work from 1954.

Anyone who'd read the Eclipse series was not well prepared for Mr Monster's return under the Dark Horse banner. In place of the humour, 'Origins' is two hundred highly serious pages delving into the legacy of Mr Monster. There's always been a monster fighter in the family, but Mr Monster's dad was seduced into renouncing his monster-slaughtering crusade by a vampiress who couldn't have children. Or that was the theory, anyway. Entirely Gilbert's own work, 'Origins' sees his artwork move away from pure Eisner into P. Craig Russell territory, more ornate, but still dark. It's an ambitious saga, not entirely without humour, but a far cry from the gruesome hilarity of the first series. The two known Mr Monster tales from the 1940s are reprinted in issues 1 and 2, with another Dr Drew tale by Grandinetti filling out 6.

The Tundra issues, titled *Mr Monster Attacks*, are a return to the boisterous antics of the Eclipse series, with the emphasis on space monsters. Collaborations are back too. Dave Gibbons contributes to 1, Sam Kieth does 2, and Simon Bisley and Dave Dorman both work on 3, among many others. A Kelly solo story, drawn by Tom Buss, was a prelude to her own series, which never appeared. Artistically Gilbert himself shows signs of continued development, although his scripting is disappointing after the darker 'Origins' story-line.~NF

Recommended: Eclipse 3, 4, 6, Dark Horse 1–8
Collection: Origins (1–8)

MR MONSTER Specials and One-Shots

Although not numbered as such on their covers, everything in this entry is identified as an issue of *Mr Monster Super Duper Special* in its indicia. All were published by Eclipse in 1986 and 1987. The name of Mr Monster is procured from an obscure 1940s hero, and many of these specials hark back to the past, with Mr Monster introducing reprints of horror, crime and science-fiction stories. The 3-D 'Hi-Octane' special reprints the first 3-D horror story, by Joe Kubert, dating from 1953, plus Bob Powell's 'The Blind, The Doomed... And The Dead!' from 1952. The other is full of classic tales by George Evans, Jerry Grandenetti and Basil Wolverton. *Mr Monster's True Crime* 1 and 2 concentrate on the work of Jack Cole. His true-crime tales are thrilling and entertaining but most certainly prove that 'crime does not pay'. *Hi-Voltage Super Science* features Bob Powell's Vic Torry and his Flying Saucer (originally a Fawcett one-shot from 1950 and less dumb than it sounds), while *Hi-Shock Schlock* 1 and 2 contain stories 'too weird or silly to fit anywhere else', including Flatman (1), Dick Briefer's 'Frankenstein And The Mummies' (1), Norman Nodel's Toni Gay (and her friend Butch Dykeman. No, this is for real) and Frank Thomas' 'The Eye Sees', a 1940s tale about a floating eye. The final special is *Weird Tales Of The Future*, all Basil Wolverton reprints from the series of the same name from 1952–1953, including such classics as 'The Brain Bats of Venus' and 'Nightmare World'. Quite apart from the appeal to Mr Monster completists, these comics reprint classic stories and are well worth looking for.~NF

Recommended: 1–8

MR NATURAL

San Francisco: *2 issues 1970–1971*
Kitchen Sink: *1 issue (3) 1977*

By the time Robert Crumb's legendary Mr Natural graduated to his own title he was already an underground veteran. Whilst the first issue is credible enough, full of Natural's obdurate homilies, by the second Crumb was beginning to grow disenchanted with the hippie movement. Much of the comic pokes fun at cults and movements in a rather jaded way, although 'Mr Natural Does The Dishes' is almost worth the price of admission on its own. After a gap of six years 3 collected the complete run of the character's weekly strip in *The Village Voice*. Coming so many years after his heyday, the character had inevitably become an anachronism, but for all that Crumb invested it with a vigour and intelligence lacking in the earlier comics. To top it all off the art is absolutely terrific. Mr Natural was revived in the early 1990s in the pages of *Hup*.~DAR

Recommended: 3

MR T AND THE T FORCE

Now: *14 issues 1993–1994*

You may have thought (hoped, even) that the ex-wrestler festooned with gold chains who delighted many very small children in *The A-Team* years ago would not warrant his own comic book in the 1990s, especially one co-written and drawn by Neal Adams and his studio. You reckoned without the power of Saturday-morning cartoons, which extended Mr T's shelf life. Yo, Suckas! as the man with the bog-brush hairstyle would put it.~FJ

MISTER X
Vortex: *Series one 14 issues 1984–1988, series two 12 issues 1989–1990, One-shot 1990*
Caliber: *3 issues + 1996 to date*

Dean Motter's brainchild, Mister X, is a confounding, slowly-paced series, where style is often as important as content. The mysterious central character, a bald, mirror-shaded junkie who never goes to sleep, returns to Radiant City because he believes he has created an environment which twists its inhabitants. The city's underworld is controlled by Mr Zamora, a crooked businessman who seems unreasonably interested in the anarchic architect. 1–4 are by the Hernandez Brothers, with stunning covers by Paul Rivoche on the first three. Gilbert and Jaime give us a 1950s vision of the future, with finned flying cars, benevolent servant robots and slick suits. After this the title was beset by difficulties throughout the first series, as artist after artist joined and then left suddenly, although Motter's scripting provided continuity. Of course the story is as twisted as the architecture and as we meet more and more characters claiming to know who Mister X is and who he once was, the 'save the city' plot is soon subsumed by the mystery of his identity. Although this never becomes clear, some light is shed on his motivations by Pete Milligan and Brett Ewins' bizarre one-shot, 'Mister Insect X'. Mister X substitutes the sound of insects for the noises he associates with his most traumatic experience in the dreams he creates with a dream machine he's building, and while this isn't much plot for a special, Milligan works it very well.

The third series is written by Deborah Marks in a manner guaranteed to confuse even those familiar with the series, as Mister X investigates the strange phenomenon of people becoming transparent and then disappearing completely. The artwork by Gene Gonzales is clean and simple but isn't as stylish as it wants to be. Basically, it lacks atmosphere but tries to make up for it in mystery.~FJ
Recommended: Series one 1–4
Collection: The Return Of Mister X (Series one 1–4)

MISTY
Star: *6 issues 1986*

Young Misty Collins struggles through the trials of a high-school student and teen model's life, although in the last department she has an advantage: her aunt is the world

famous Millie The Model! Produced by writer/artist Trina Robbins for Marvel's short-lived line of children's comics, Misty's adventures are lightweight, but affable.~HS

MOBFIRE
Vertigo: *6-issue limited series 1994–1995*

A Mafia-style London Godfather dies leaving his empire in son Jack Keller's hands. Jack's guilt feelings and desire to dissolve the Mob are complicated by his inheritance of right-hand magician Bocor, whose loyalty to the son is somewhat cooler than it was to the father. The gritty, sardonic, jet-black story by British creators Gary Ushaw and Warren Pleece makes no concessions to its native audience. How many American readers appreciated the crossed hammers and WHUFC graffiti on issue 2's cover? This British version of *Reservoir Dogs* takes a turn for the perpendicular half way through when the mystical elements kick into gear; these sit ill with the gangland setting. Pleece's artwork is ugly, yet still fails to match the script's mood. Has its moments. 18 certificate.~APS

Tales Mutated For The MOD
Kitchen Sink: *1 issue 1981*

Terry Beatty edits an old-fashioned under-ground anthology, either writing or drawing most strips himself, and proving adept at aping other styles. There are also early Bob Burden strips, and the comic is rounded out by Bill Griffith and Zippy the Pinhead. Chuckles rather than belly laughs are on offer, but there's plenty worse out there.~FP

MODESTY BLAISE
DC: *One-shot 1994*

Surely a must for all Modesty Blaise fans, written by creator Peter O'Donnell and illustrated by Dick Giordano. It's the usual espionage adventure associated with the 'sexy... seductive... deadly...' (so the back cover blurb tells us) crime boss. Modesty is lured out of retirement to rescue her old chum Willie Garvin. Naturally she does so with ease, and in return for their help, she in turn must help the British secret service on one of their missions. And that's when all the fun and action start. Fans of Dick Giordano's art won't want to miss this. His style is spot-on for the genre and very reminiscent of the wonderful Diana Prince, Wonder Woman stories he illustrated in the early 1970s.~HY
Recommended

MOEBIUS COMICS
Caliber: *3 issues + 1996 to date*

If you think Moebius is one of the greatest artists comics have yet produced you'll be interested in this collection of intriguing odds and sods. If you're not so sure, go and read some of his masterpieces. Highlights include the follow-up to 'The Man From Ciguri' (itself the follow-up to the seminal 'Airtight Garage Of Jerry Cornelius'), a labyrinthine, confounding tale that you have to let wash over you rather than try to understand, and old Arzach roughs, pencilled and inked by an interesting variety of artists, including Bill Stout in issue 1.

Less promising is the serialisation of the storyboards for 'Internal Transfer', a proposed full-length animated science-fiction film expounding the philosophy of French parapsychologist and New Age guru Jean-Paul Appel-Guéry, whose ideas have influenced Moebius' work since the 1980s. In general, credos that are best put over as science-fiction epics are probably laughable, but you should make your own minds up.~FJ

MOEBIUS Graphic Novels
Epic: *12 volumes 1987–1995*
Dark Horse*: 1 volume (0) 1992*
Graphitti: *1 volume 1991*

The career of French artist Jean Giraud neatly divides into two halves. As Gir he is the artist of the phenomenally successful Western series *Lieutenant Blueberry*, and as Moebius he is a more experimental science-fiction artist. Books 1, 5, 7 and 9 of the Epic series comprise the lengthy 'Gardens Of Aedena' serial and all too potently illustrate Moebius' principal failing: he may well be a superb artist, but his stories all too frequently succumb to unfocused meanderings and unreconstructed neo-hippy waffling.

Luckily Epic's other albums are far better. *Arzach* (volume 2) contains some of his most breath-taking artwork and rather more incisive writing. Its eponymous pterodactyl-riding hero is also one of comics' most potent icons. *The Airtight Garage* (3) might well meander, but it's exquisitely drawn, while *The Long Tomorrow*'s (4) lead strip benefits from a terrific Dan O'Bannon script and an unusually dystopian feel. *Pharagonesia* (6) mops up the remaining science-fiction strips drawn by Moebius in the 1970s, and is generally a less essential purchase than its predecessors, though the short 'Rock City' tale is particularly good. By contrast, 8's *Mississippi River* is a Western written by *Blueberry* scribe Jean Michel Charlier, and although the art is rather rushed, the story is top-notch.

Elsewhere Dark Horse's *Horny Goof* (0) collects Moebius' more *risqué* material, while Graphitti's *Early Moebius*, numbered ½, effectively mops up the leftovers. Both are for completists only, although that's not to say there's nothing of interest. Of wider appeal are the three Epic volumes not comprising part of the numbered series, *Chaos, Metallic Memories*

and *Fusion*. These are lavish collections of his art that are never less than amazing. Whatever his shortcomings as a writer, Moebius has always possessed an extraordinary technical ability, and one of the most unfettered imaginations in the business. For those uninterested in his writing these collections are the best place to appreciate his art.~DAR
Recommended: *2–4, 8, Chaos, Metallic Memories, Fusion*

MOM'S HOMEMADE COMICS
Kitchen Sink: *3 issues 1969–1971*

Of historical interest as the first Kitchen Sink comic, 1 was a solo outing by Denis Kitchen, but a very tepid affair indeed. 2 featured a couple of nondescript non-Kitchen strips, so 3 remains the most interesting of the run. By then Kitchen had developed into a fine cartoonist and his fellow-contributors had grown to include Skip Williamson, Pete Poplaski and the underrated Jim Mitchell. Sadly, the writing was uniformly poor, making this one for completists only.~DAR

MONKEYMAN AND O'BRIEN
Dark Horse: *One-shot 1996, 3-issue miniseries 1996*

A laboratory accident creates a dimensional rift that pulls through a giant intelligent ape, and has the side-effect of transforming Ann O'Brien into an Amazonian woman. The ape is called Tiberius, and, once he's learned to speak English, he and Ann concentrate on finding the means to send him home. Unfortunately, other matters keep cropping up, including an invasion of Earth by frog-like creatures and a humanoid shrew and his army of animals. It's all light fun stuff very nicely drawn by Art Adams, with heavy references to old Marvel monster comics. The one-shot collects the original stories from *Hellboy*, and the odd couple also appeared in *Dark Horse Presents* 80. All things considered it's the best talking-monkey-and-female-partner comic since *Angel And The Ape*.~FP

MONOLITH
Comico: *4 issues 1991–1992*

Daft plot, bad art and gratuitous gore make for a poor solo outing for the Elementals' Monolith, the 14-year-old able to transform into a three-ton stone giant.~WJ

MONSTER HUNTERS
Charlton: *18 issues 1975–1979*

Anthology loosely tied together by the title theme. Even the surprise of coming across early work by later respected artists such as Paul Kirchner (in 1) and Mike Zeck (several early issues) doesn't compensate for the feeble 'horror' stories on offer throughout. 12–18 throw up earlier material again.~FP

MONSTER MASSACRE
Blackball: *One-shot 1993*

An anthology of gore. Intended to be tongue-in-cheek and with some good ideas here and there. 'Well, well. I never knew you could do that with the lower intestine,' you'll say to yourself as you rush off to be sick. If it does come your way and you want to retain your last meal, skip to the last story, 'Snakedance', which is the most restrained, and easily the best bit of story-telling.~FC

MONSTER MENACE
Marvel: *4-issue miniseries 1993–1994*

The brainchild of reprint editor Mort Todd, this anthology reprinted Stan Lee 'stinger' mystery stories from the early 1960s. Fans of Kirby, Ditko, Heck and Ayers could enjoy new drawings done by some of the surviving artists. Todd's imaginative packaging emphasised the kitsch appeal of pre-Marvel monster stories in the 1990s, including tongue-in-cheek covers by the likes of Kyle Baker to go with the title's over-the-top name.~SW

MONSTERS ON THE PROWL
Marvel: *22 issues (9–30) 1971–1974*

The numbering continued from *Chamber Of Darkness*, as the title slowly phased out new contributions to become another of Marvel's myriad 1970s titles reprinting their 1950s and early 1960s mystery shorts. What differentiated *Monsters*, though, was that the stories were slightly longer than the usual five-page shorts. And, of course, they had such magnificent titles as 'I Defied Gomdullah, The Living Mummy' (in 12 if you really want to know). The last vestiges of the new material were unremarkable shorts in 9–15, the latter being Steve Englehart's first published comics, and 11 being drawn by Ralph Reese. 16 has a Kull The Conqueror story, and thereafter it's reprints all the way, with Ditko and Kirby in most issues.~FP

MONSTERS UNLEASHED
Marvel: *11 issues, 1 annual 1973–1975*

These are large-format, seventy-four-page horror comics, heavily dominated by werewolf stories. Only a few stories really stand out. The very best have artwork by Ralph Reese: 'Skulls In The Stars' in 1 (written by Roy Thomas) and 'The Roaches' in 2 (written by Gerry Conway). 'The Strange Children' in 6 (uncredited) puts an unsettling twist on the Pied Piper story, and 'Beauty's Vengeance' is a well-told tale about inner value versus outer glamour – it's a shame that the artwork has the two women looking almost identical (or is that the point?), but the story still works.~FC
Recommended: 1, 2

MOON KNIGHT
Marvel: *Series one 38 issues 1980–1984, 6-issue miniseries ('The Fist of Khonshu') 1985, series two ('Marc Spector...') 60 issues, 1 Special 1989–1994*

Introduced in *Werewolf By Night* 32, to all intents and purposes Moon Knight was Batman in white. More *Werewolf* appearances led to numerous guest spots and a solo tryout in *Marvel Spotlight* 28–29 before a back-up slot was allocated in *Hulk Magazine*. Writer Doug Moench, who'd created Moon Knight, was teamed with artist Bill Sienkiewicz, then still very much the Neal Adams imitator, for stories reprinted as *Moon Knight Special Edition* 1–3. Another solo in *Marvel Preview* 21 prefaced series one, the best run, keeping Moon Knight detached from the Marvel Universe, and usually from costumed foes. 1–12 are okay and 14 and 15 a false glorious dawn, but stay well away from the extremely pedestrian 16–21. The series begins to peak with 22, by which time Sienkiewicz is inking his own pencils and developing into an artist of singular stature with a recognisable individual style complementing his always bold layouts. By this point there's an undercurrent of emotional tension, combined with startling plays on tired themes. Try 'Stained Glass Scarlet' in 14, 15's 'Ruling The World From His Basement' or 'Hit It' in 26 for very different stories, each imparting the feel of the series. Even after Sienkiewicz the artwork is class, with Bo Hampton on 34 and 36–38 and Kevin Nowlan making an excellent début in 31–32, but Moench's departure with 33 hurts. He returns for the 1992 special, but it's of greater interest to *Master of Kung-Fu* readers.

In the miniseries Alan Zelenetz reinforces Moon Knight's ties to the Egyptian Moon God Khonshu, a theme introduced towards the end of the first run, and reduces what was once a vibrant title to the mundane. The second ongoing series has Chuck Dixon, Sal Velluto and Mark Farmer (later Tom Palmer) conveniently forgetting the Egyptian mythology and returning Moon Knight to the streets. There's an emphasis on the costume and guest stars, and the introduction of a Robin figure is a definite mistake, but rectified in gruesome fashion. In 15–18 Moon Knight is tried for a crime committed when he was a mercenary, and those enjoying it will probably like any issue before 25. While Dixon turns out a good adventure yarn, characterisation's not his forte, so J.M. DeMatteis is a welcome change. 'Scarlet Redemption' in 26–30 closes the entwined destinies of Scarlet and Moon Knight in poetic fashion for the best story of the run, helped along by sympathetic art from Ron Garney and Tom Palmer. A sprightly one-shot return from Dixon in 34 paves the way for new writer Terry Kavanagh, under whom

Moon Knight receives a new supporting cast and is transforrned into a gimmick-laden, heavily armoured fighter. Maybe Kavanagh wanted to write *Robocop*, but missed out. That apart, his tenure features novel concepts, some of which work while others stink up the house (Frenchie's unknown past in 50, for instance: if his was an important, guarded bloodline would he really have been a mercenary?) Of the more workable concepts, 42 showcases alternate Moon Knights and 46 features a quest for a possible successor. Unfortunately, it's Knights Templar and demons galore that come to dominate, although Stephen Platt's distinctive art in 55–57 and 60 goes some way to compensating.~WJ

Recommended: Series one 14, 15, 24–26, 31–33

MOONSHADOW

Epic: *12 issues 1985–1987*
Vertigo: *12 issues 1994–1995, one-shot ('Farewell Moonshadow') 1997*

Dire piece of whimsy, mistakenly hailed as a work of genius by out-of-date Goths and mawkish fops everywhere. John J. Muth illustrates, rather than draws a comic, but this is unsurprising given the meandering nature of J.M. DeMatteis's script, which lends itself to paneless pictures and floating word balloons. The series' coda, 'Farewell Moonshadow', is more a story book, with full-page illustrations against pages of text. The tale's all about the wonder of childhood and escaping harmful reality through your own fantasy world until you reach your personal nirvana, and is shot through with references and endless quotes. Like so many others, DeMatteis had been impressed by Alan Moore's technique of enriching a regular comic story with the cultural baggage of western civilization via a medley of quotations. Unfortunately he can't tell the difference between an apposite phrase that replaces dialogue and a meaningless repetition of the narrative in someone else's words. Not that his own are up to much. Is '"Sometimes," Moonshadow replied, "I love you so deeply, I don't know where you end and I begin"' ironic, do you think? Or is it simply that in the 1990s rehashed 'Obsession for Men' commercials can aspire to high art? Probably the most pretentious twaddle ever produced in comics.~FJ

Collection: Moonshadow (Vertigo 1–12)

MORBIUS

Marvel: *32 issues 1992–1995*

Briefly the star of *Fear* in the 1970s, Morbius returns for a creatively more successful run. The series starts out as a standard slasher title, but around 5 penciller Ron Wagner seems to have read a stack of Russ Heath-drawn comics and the visuals get a great deal better. The attempts of Morbius to rid himself of 'Living Vampire' status and regain his humanity are genuinely poignant and some of the twisted individuals he encounters on the way disturbing in the extreme. Sadly the book peters out in a slew of inferior artists and pointless crossovers towards the end.~HS

MORLOCK 2001

Atlas: *3 issues 1975*

Those looking for that elusive *Fahrenheit 451*/hideous-plant-creature crossover comic need look no further, though for less committed readers this remains a fun, if undemanding, title. 2 features mainstream comics' only *Clockwork Orange* tribute and 3 boasts the unique artistic pairing of Steve Ditko and Berni Wrightson!~DAR

MORT The Dead Teenager

Marvel: *4 issues 1993–1994*

Teenage life as seen by wrinkly Larry Hama and almost as wrinkly Gary Hallgren. Mort cops it in true teenage fashion playing chicken in his dad's car, but is returned to haunt family and friends. No classic, but some amusing moments. The best issues are the first, featuring Teen Death, and the last, in which Mort sees how his life would have turned out had he not died.~WJ

MORTAL KOMBAT

Malibu: *7-issue limited series (0–6) ('Blood And Thunder') 1994, 3-issue miniseries ('Goro, Prince Of Pain') 1994, 2-issue microseries ('Tournament Edition') 1994–1995, 2-issue microseries ('U.S. Special Forces') 1995, 3-issue miniseries ('Rayden/Kano')1995, 6-issue miniseries ('Battlewave') 1995, One-shot ('Kung Lao') 1995, One-shot ('Baraka')1995, One-shot ('Kitana And Mileena') 1995*

Taking the characters from the favourite videogame punch-'em-up and attempting to give them life and motivation was never a promising idea likely to produce top literature or art, but it didn't have to be quite this dreadful. 'Blood and Thunder' 1 sets up a good vs evil scenario from a martial arts tournament, and from that point more characters are introduced in more series, and they fight. Appalling throughout, with no single redeeming feature.~FP

Green Lantern MOSAIC

DC: *18 issues 1992–1993*

This spin-off from *Green Lantern* had John Stewart, the first black Green Lantern from Earth, sent by the Guardians to look after a planet inhabited by various creatures from around the universe. Set up as a keeper/peacemaker in this social-experiment-cum-cosmic-zoo, Stewart has a hard time preventing the individual races from destroying each other. A nice touch is the human colony, an entire town stolen from Earth, who, understandably, resent their kidnapping and demand to be returned. Unfortunately, overall the series isn't particularly well handled and not even guest appearances by Flash, Martian Manhunter, Hal Jordan and Guy Gardner could prevent it from cancellation.~TP

MOTORHEAD
Dark Horse: *1 issue 1993, 1 Special 1994, 6 issues 1995–1996*

Introduced as part of the *Comics Greatest World* series, Motorhead saves the day in the Steel Harbour section, and his 1994 special is more a Steel Harbour special, featuring Wolf Pack and serving as an introduction to the *Barb Wire* series. Frank Fletcher is empowered by an alien presence in his head calling itself The Motor, and although Motorhead appears virtually all-powerful it comes with a price of constant cerebral chatter. For the series The Motor is personified as a sort of mental Joker, Fletcher is given an old-fashioned carnival as a supporting cast and there are regular glimpses into his past. Kudos to Dan Chichester, Karl Waller and Timothy Bradstreet for attempting something different, but the series is as irritating as it is innovative.~WJ

MOTORMOUTH
Marvel UK: *12 issues 1992–1993*

Foul-mouthed street urchin Harley Davis finds a new pair of sneakers with dimension-hopping capability. Yep, it's those wacky Mys-Tech evil scientists looking for test subjects again, with their loopiest scheme yet! Nicknamed 'Motormouth' for no particular reason, Harley rapidly acquires sonic powers as a result of Mys-Tech interference, and a sidekick looms in the form of lovable homicidal maniac Killpower, who shares cover billing from 5. Art by Gary Frank, in 1–4, doesn't save this ill-advised attempt at a superheroic Tank Girl from meandering to an early end.~HS

MS. MARVEL
Marvel: *23 issues 1977–1979*

Another of Marvel's attempts at a liberated superhero. Carol Danvers was a love interest in the late 1960s *Captain Marvel* series. In 1977 a near-fatal attack led to Carol's dying wishes being fed into a nearby 'Psyche-Magnitron'. She became a female copy of Captain Marvel… but with bare legs and midriff. Hence the sobriquet 'Ms.', presumably. Now with the powers of superstrength and flight, she was also possessed of a precognitive '7th Sense', possibly intended as a magnified women's

intuition. The numerous similarities between this and DC's Supergirl – same surname, male counterpart, cheesecake costume, and penciller Jim Mooney – are hard to ignore. Scripter Gerry Conway should take most of the blame for the utterly unreadable early issues. Fortunately, he was relieved by Chris Claremont with 8, who gave Carol a family, a past and a supporting cast, and allowed her to come to terms with her Kree superpowers in 13. The subsequent build-up to 19's climactic meeting with Captain Marvel and the Kree Supremor displayed all of Claremont's skill as a weaver of sub-plots and characterisation. He also introduced many characters of later significance to his *X-Men* milieu, which indeed also featured Carol herself, who eventually became The Starjammers' Binary. Villainesses Deathbird and Mystique (then known as Raven Darkholme) débuted in 8 and 16 respectively. Numerous guest appearances include The Avengers in 18 and Vance Astro in 23. Dave Cockrum stepped in with a spectacular redesign of the character in 20, but the series only survived three more issues. The next two stories, originally drawn in 1979, featured appearances by Sabretooth and Rogue and surfaced in *Marvel Superheroes* 10 and 11 in 1993.~SW
Recommended: *13, 19–21*

MS MYSTIC
Pacific Comics: *2 issues, 1982–1984*
Continuity: *Series one 9 issues 1987–1992, series two 3 issues 1993*

It's hard to believe that at one point comics fans 'in the know' thought that Neal Adams' *Ms Mystic* (announced years before it actually surfaced) would be the future of ground-breaking comics. Instead it was a load of New Age nonsense vaguely articulated by a superheroine who, despite coming to save the world, seemed to do nothing, exciting or otherwise. Neal Adams' Continuity Comics reprinted the Pacific issues before offering seven more tiresome instalments of her adventures. The second series was a 'Deathwatch 2000' crossover which looks like it was knocked out in a hurry, with more 'Continuity Studios' than Neal Adams input.~FJ

MS TREE
Eclipse: *9 issues 1983–1984*
Aardvark-Vanaheim: *9 issues (10–18) 1984–1985*
Renegade: *32 issues, 1 Special (19–50) 1985–1989*
DC: *10 issues 1990–1993*

Crime novelist Max Allen Collins is responsible for this hard-boiled detective strip, very much patterned after Mike Hammer but with a much greater emphasis on detection and mystery (as you might expect given the detective's name). Michael Tree's husband is a detective who's killed by the mob, specifically the Muerta family, and throughout the series her vendetta against them is a constant factor that provokes trouble with the law on several occasions. It culminates in an arrangement of sorts when Ms Tree's adopted son falls in love with Dominique Muerta's daughter and the two team up to rescue their kidnapped children. This running theme of vengeance helps maintain momentum in the strip, but doesn't distract from other, non-Mob-related cases that are often picked out as having a particular resonance at the time (crimes against children are a special bug-bear), and Collins regularly has to question Ms Tree's readiness to exact her own, lethal justice, even having her committed at one stage. Overall, an impressive series that's willing to tackle many different aspects of crime and punishment, always in an unsentimental but not detached manner. Terry Beatty's artwork is rather stiff and unexpressive but works well in context.

Mike Mist is also a detective, again by Collins and Beatty, whose back-up strip involves short mysteries which you're invited to solve before the final (upside down) panel reveals all. From 36, Johnny Dynamite was added for financial reasons. Unfortunately, Pete Morisi's tough detective, reprinted from the Charlton series, has dated rather badly. There are also three specials, *1950's 3-D Crime* (1987), primarily Johnny Dynamite in 3-D, *Rock & Roll Summer Special* (1986) and *Ms Tree 3-D* (1985), both of which feature Mist and Tree together. They're all worth reading, though none stand out as being exceptional.

At DC the title changed to *Ms Tree Quarterly*, giving Collins and Beatty the time and space to produce single (but not completely unconnected) stories for each issue. Leaving aside most of the Mob connections, Ms Tree is still involved in murder mysteries but there's also a haunted house, Ms Tree's pregnancy and her subsequent fight to keep the child from its grandfather (4–10). 'Midnight' was revived as a back-up, written by Ed Gorman, but it's hardly compulsive reading. 1–3 include illustrated text stories: Batman by Denny O'Neil and Mike Grell in 1 and The Butcher by Mike Baron and Shea Anton Pensa (2–3). 6 is probably a good place to start and is less reliant on knowledge of Ms Tree's past.~NF

MUNDEN'S BAR
First: *2 issues 1988 & 1991*

Annuals spun off from the popular back-up in First's *Grimjack*. No 1 features a Fish Police crossover by Steve Moncuse, plus some nice art by Steve Rude and Brian Bolland, while the second has both Omaha and Teenage Mutant Ninja Turtle stories.~FJ

MURDER
Renegade: *3 issues 1986*

Actually a continuation of Robin Snyder's *Revolver*, *Murder* is a showcase for some of Steve Ditko's early to mid-1980s short, EC-style stories and Rich Margopoulos' adaptations of Poe's 'Eleanora', 'Ligeia' and 'Morella' (mainly text with illustrations by Dan Day). Single-page strips by Henry Boltinoff seem out of place but are good for a bit of nostalgia, while Alex Toth's two-pagers on the nature of drawing in 1 and 2 are slight but gorgeous. Issue 3's 'I Wonder Who's Squeezing Her Now' by Wally Wood, Nick Cuti and Ernie Colon turns the predictable shock ending on its head and is the highlight of the series.~NF

The MUTANT BOOK OF THE DEAD
Starhead: *1 issue*

Absolutely demented stuff from Mack White about the community of Chester County, Texas. It's populated by the mutant results of generations of inbreeding, resulting in horned women, pencil-neck geeks, and a brute with a smaller speaking head on each shoulder. White's stories rip right into the hypocrisy of rural communities, and stand a good chance of offending most people somewhere along the way. Excellent.~FP
Recommended: 1

MUTATIS
Epic: *3 issues 1992*

On promise of a cure, an infected former police officer has to track down and kill three carriers of a deadly virus before they infect an entire city. Writers Dan Abnett and Andy Lanning write a script that sustains tension and create a well-conceived future world, and John Higgins' claustrophobically designed city completes a top-notch package.~FP
Recommended: 1–3

MY GREATEST ADVENTURE
DC: *85 issues 1955–1964*

Not perhaps the greatest adventure series ever produced. On first inspection most stories could be filed under 'dull', but there was always the occasional interesting mystery or science-fiction tale of the type at which DC excelled. By the mid-sixties, the comic's appeal began to wane, but it was saved by the appearance of the Doom Patrol. DC's attempt by scripter Arnold Drake and artist Bruno Premiani to create a more Marvel-style super-team, where personalities took centre-stage, proved very successful. So much so in fact that from 86 the title changed to *Doom Patrol*.~HY
Recommended: 80–85

MY LOVE

Marvel: *Series one 4 issues 1949–1950, series two 39 issues, 1 Special 1969–1976*

The first series, launched in the wake of Simon and Kirby's *Young Romance*, was routine moonlight-and-flowers fluff. The only noteworthy feature is that the model for 4's photo cover is the notorious Betty Page. The second series featured an initially strong and imaginative run of lovelorn tales from Marvel mainstays. Buscema, Colan and Heck all chipped in, and did creditable work on stories largely written by Stan Lee. Although intuitively in touch with the times in most respects, Lee's take on feminism in 10 is a total hoot. Soon, however, it became clear that the dwindling pool of romance readers didn't care whether all this effort was made or not, and the series became all-reprint from 11. The 1971 Special reprints the much-sought- after Jim Steranko romance story from *Our Love Story 5*.~HS

MY NAME IS CHAOS

DC: *4 issues 1992*

A reclusive scientist discovers a secret colony of genetically created superbeings, and is forced to take a moral stand. Creative reworking of *Dr Moreau* with sumptuous John Ridgway art.~HS

MYS-TECH WARS

Marvel UK: *4-issue miniseries 1993*

This combines X-Men, the Avengers and various Marvel UK characters against the evil Mys-Tech organisation and its plot to control the world. The story-line is mindless (stuck for an idea? Send another character in to the attack) and the resolution pure technobabble, but there is some (small) entertainment value in seeing the various teams coming together, and then in monitoring the body-count. Still, you must have better things to do with your time.~FC

MYSTERIOUS SUSPENSE

Charlton: *1 issue 1968*

Originally intended as a series of back-ups for *Blue Beetle*, the four chapters merge seamlessly, and creator Steve Ditko makes his points about what constitutes a hero without resorting to the didacticism that sometimes characterised his later work. The compelling nature of the comic is all the more remarkable considering the amount of text-heavy talking-heads panels used. Crusading TV journalist Vic Sage is the focus rather than his costumed *alter ego* the Question, as he comes under fire for refusing to accept a new sponsor. Sage knows the man to be associated with a gangster, and is prepared to sacrifice his job to prove a point as all around him bay for his head. A magnificent one-shot that sees Ditko at the peak of his creative ability.~WJ

Recommended: 1

Tales Of The MYSTERIOUS TRAVELER

Charlton: 15 issues, 1956–1959 (1–13), 1985 (14–15)

There are many story-telling hosts in comics but none was ever more elegantly woven into the tales he told than, or had the sheer presence of, Steve Ditko's Mysterious Traveler. Usually, the only pleasure to be derived from Charlton's 1950s mystery and science-fiction anthologies comes from the stories drawn by Ditko. This is no exception, but here we have the added attraction of watching Ditko's development of the title's host between 2 and 11. After simply introducing early stories with an opening panel, the Traveler is gradually insinuated into skies, mists and shady backgrounds throughout the story. He walks the gutters between panels, sometimes splitting the whole page vertically. Some pages have a scatter of images held together by a huge shadowy portrait. 'Above The Top Most Peak' in 5 features the Traveler in every panel! There are too many notable Ditko stories to list here but 'Inside The Crystal Globe' in 11 is noteworthy for its experimental inking style (signed J. Kodti).

Charlton revived the title in 1985 for two issues: reprints, with one new Ditko story apiece. These new stories aren't in the 1950s format and are a little disappointing by comparison. Interestingly, some of the reprint stories are told by Dr Haunt, Ditko's other horror host from *This Magazine Is Haunted*, who has been recoloured to resemble the Traveler.~SW

Recommended: 4, 5, 6, 10, 11

Collection: Tales Of The Mysterious Traveler (2, 4, 6–9, 11)

MYSTERY IN SPACE

DC: *117 issues 1951–1966 (1–110), 1980–1981 (111–117)*

Characterised by superior artwork, DC's 1950s science-fiction stories generally displayed a little more imagination than those of their competitors. Surrendering its crown to the EC science-fiction comics for a short while, *Mystery In Space* was otherwise the top science-fiction comic of its era. Unfortunately, the stories now have a dated optimism, typified by the long-running 'Space Cabby' feature (21, 24, 26–47), although the art from the likes of Murphy Anderson, Carmine Infantino, Gil Kane, Mike Sekowsky and Sid Greene (all in most issues to 91), and one-offs from Virgil Finlay (19), Frank Frazetta (1) and Alex Toth (13), can still delight.

Beginning with 53 and running for most of the 1960s, Adam Strange was the cover feature. He'd been introduced in *Showcase* 17–19 as an Earthman transported by zeta beam to Rann, where he met his beloved Alanna. Alongside her he battled any planet-shaking menace that reared its ugly head. Gardner Fox and Carmine Infantino gave five years of consistent good taste and quality to what's acknowledged as DC's most elegant science-fiction strip. The earlier Adam Strange stories run between eight and fifteen pages; 75 is notable for a teaming with the Justice League, while the back-up strips include many of DC's best, notably Sid Greene's 'Star Rovers' (66, 69, 74, 77, 80, 83, 86). Sadly the Jack Schiff-edited 92–102 don't match the departed Fox/Infantino magic on Adam Strange, and later features such as Ultra The Multi-Alien (a being combined from four alien species!) should be avoided. Rather strangely, the Fox and Anderson Hawkman appeared in 87–90 before graduating to his own title in 1964. *Mystery In Space* was revived as a showcase for science-fiction short stories, and despite several distinguished strips from the likes of Marshall Rogers and Joe Kubert, the time for science-fiction anthologies seemed to have passed.~SW

Recommended: 53–58, 65, 66, 68, 72–86, 90, 91
Collection: Mysteries In Space (Frazetta story from 1, shorts from 8, 11, 19, 22, 35, 49, 61, Space Cabby from 42, Star Rovers from 74, Adam Strange from 75)

THE MYSTERY MAN
Slave Labor: *2 issues 1988*

These two issues intrigue and mystify, not least as to the identity of the Mystery Man of the title, who seems nowhere in sight. Stylishly drawn and inventively plotted by Scott Saavedra, sadly the story remained incomplete. This is a shame, not the least because few other comics have scenes with a cave leading to the bowels of the earth opening up behind the shower curtain.~WJ

MYTH ADVENTURES
Warp: *10 issues 1984–1986*
Apple: *2 issues (11–12) 1986*

Based on the popular series of fantasy novels by Robert Asprin, this undemanding humour title might well appeal to fans of Terry Pratchett, *Red Dwarf* and other allegedly sidesplitting genre comedies. 1–8 of *Myth Adventures* adapt Asprin's novel of the same name, 1–4 being magazine-sized. The story introduces sorcerer's apprentice Skeeve and his wily demon pal Aahz. Setting out to defeat evil wizard Isstvan, Aahz and Skeeve become caught in a series of tangles with dragons, unicorns, imp assassins and rapacious merchants. Writer/penciller Phil Foglio has a pleasantly cartoony style, occasionally undermined by slapdash inking and lettering from Tim Sale, but his reverence for the source

material makes the strip unnecessarily drawn-out. 9–12 feature new artist Valentino, in a four-part story written by Asprin especially for the comic. The level of humour never rises much above feeble puns, vulgar slapstick and mystifying in-jokes. 11 includes a particularly obvious satire on comic-book conventions.~AL

MYTH CONCEPTIONS
Apple: *8 issues 1987–1989*

The further comic adventures of Aahz and Skeeve, a crusty demon and his bungling apprentice first seen in *Myth Adventures*. It's adapted from a novel by Robert Asprin; new writer and artist team Ken and Beth Mitchroney ensure that previous standards are maintained, if never exceeded.~AL

MYTHOS: The Final Tour
Vertigo: *3-issue miniseries 1996–1997*

John Ney Rieber scripts the tale of Adam Clay (geddit?), a Kurt Cobain-like figure who's being manipulated by various Old Gods, some of whom are trying to bring about the End Of The World. Adam may or may not be the reincarnation of Osiris and Tammuz himself… sorry to be vague, but it's that kind of comic. It's got its moments, the best being in 2, when *Hellblazer's* John Constantine guests. 3 has the baby Black Orchid from *Black Orchid*, and Sandman's sister/brother Desire is lurking in the background. It's an honest attempt to look at the way rock stars have become myth figures of the late 20th century, but it's too mired in the myths of the past, and much too male-centred. It has some of that essence of male adolescent *angst* that fired *The Crow*, but lacks that title's simple plot and concentrated emotional punch. Another point against: the hero is messed up because of his evil father, but also because he killed his pet puppy when he was little. At the end, he not only gets the girl, but a new dog too. Typical over-sentimental silliness: the hated father-figure was plenty of motivation. Is Rieber working out some puppy-loss trauma of his own here? If you're prepared to entertain the notion that Kurt Cobain died for your sins, and you really, really love dogs, this book is for you.~GL

The 'NAM

Marvel: *84 issues 1986–1993*

The 'Nam was conceived as an attempt to portray the Vietnam war as it was for the American soldiers fighting there, progressing in real time with characters moving in and out, and little sentimentality when it came to killing the cast. In 1–11 Doug Murray and Michael Golden set the scene admirably, combining anecdote and experience, and by concentrating on a relatively small cast they're able to focus on emotion and fear as part of the larger picture. The first half-dozen issues are more action-oriented, convincingly conveying the suspense and tension of warfare, and thereafter the action is mixed with quieter moments as the characters come more to the fore. Wayne Vansant is the artist from 13 (after a fine John Severin fill-in on 12). His art's more static and less expressive, but he's nonetheless suited to the tone of the comic.

Once the parameters have been established the scope is broadened, and Murray's choice of occasionally referring back to Ed Marks, through whose eyes the scenario was introduced in 1, allows for different perspectives from outside Vietnam. More unusual events come to the fore, and it becomes apparent that there wasn't always an all-for-one attitude between the ground troops, with 18 depicting one way of dealing with unpopular officers. 1–20 are reprinted in black and white at two stories per issue in *The 'Nam Magazine*.

The major downside to *The 'Nam* is that it's one-sided, written very much from the viewpoint that the American presence in Vietnam was essential in seeing off the godless Commies, whereas hindsight tends to indicate otherwise. After 7's history lesson (an audition for Vansant) explaining why the Vietcong are fighting, there's no attempt made to suggest that, setting aside Communist ideology, the aim of freeing Vietnam from the remnants of colonialism was justifiable in its own right. Although never glorifying war, the sub-text disturbs. To Murray's credit, though, he doesn't shy away from the unsavoury US tactics as in 35, and he's patently sincere in wanting to ensure his stories are as authentic as possible.

Unfortunately there was a shabby decline for this well-intentioned project during issues in the 40s. Out went the idea of following a single troop and its changing personnel throughout the war, as the spotlight shifted to other branches of the US forces in Vietnam, and the chronological timescale was also shelved. The first nail in the coffin was 41's cover, prominently featuring Marvel superheroes, and an accompanying story about how they might affect the war – sympathetically handled, but nonetheless an obvious attempt to attract new readers at the risk of alienating the old. Chuck Dixon's fill-in in 43 signalled the beginning of a more jingoistic stance, and from 46 Murray's more sensitive scripts are few and far between, with Dixon the most regular writer. The final nail was the Punisher in 52–53, albeit in pre-vigilante days and civilian identity, in a story based on the novel *Sniper*. It could have been fitted around any character, but declining sales demanded a high-profile guest star. The Punisher was to return in the inferior 67–69, although the title already had Joe Hallen, a character who typified the new gung-ho attitude permeating the series, and who could have been the Punisher. 'The Death Of Joe Hallen' in 54–58 is the only story extending beyond three issues, yet after a promising start with Hallen's return home in 54 it becomes a standard mid-period 'Nam effort, although with an unpredictable conclusion. It's followed in 59 and 60, though, by Dixon's best contribution, detailing what could be expected when a US serviceman was captured by the Vietcong, and returning a soldier from the early issues. 'Creep' in 66 is also a decent story, about a deadshot sniper.

70 is a revelation. Vansant began heavy use of photo reference for his art, which may have silenced the odd letter-column carper, but didn't really improve on his more natural style, and Vietnam vet Don Lomax was appointed the regular writer. Although not reverting entirely to the original premise, they return the integrity of the title, stamping their intention by reintroducing Ed Marks, now a reporter. Lomax uses him as an observer in similar fashion to the writer in *Vietnam Journal*, and his coping with the concept of reporter's objectivity at the cost of lives is powerfully portrayed in 72. From 71 Lomax also introduces a back-up

feature looking in on the lives of former cast members. 75's examination of the My Lai massacre has an astonishingly callous conclusion encompassing the monk who set fire to himself as a protest against the war. Neither Lomax nor Vansant are responsible, and their back-up strip is far more effective. They also provide a decent account of the 1968 Tet offensive in 79–81, but never quite match the warmth of the earlier issues. Ironically, Lomax's best story in 84 isn't illustrated by Vansant; it takes as its topic the experiences of the North Vietnamese guerrillas. It's a sympathetic and rounded conclusion to a largely decent series, and probably for the best, as the already completed stories which were originally intended to occupy 84–86 can be found in *The Punisher Invades The 'Nam*. It's a typical Punisher story, offering little concession to the title in which it was appearing.

Finally, mention must be made of *The 'Nam's* covers, which were regularly attention-grabbing and memorable. Michael Golden's initial efforts set the standard, with a unique use of colour, and he continued providing occasional covers after ceasing to draw the title. Kevin Kobasic, Ron Wagner, Andy Kubert and Joe Quesada all deliver stunning illustrations, and Vansant, as he was inside, is a model of consistency and excellence.~WJ
Recommended: 1, 3, 5, 7, 10, 12, 15–18, 23, 35, 38, 39, 59, 60, 66, 72, 80, 84
Collections: The 'Nam vol 1 (1–4), vol 2 (5–8), vol 3 (9–12)

NAMOR
Marvel: *62 issues, 4 Annuals 1990–1995*

The undersea prince is one of Marvel's oldest characters, and was given a total revamp from the master of makeover, John Byrne, who both writes and draws. There's a fun start with Byrne pushing all the right buttons, including the bizarre resurrection of Marvel's 1970s kung-fu characters, including Iron Fist, Thunderer and Master Khan. Namor's cousin Namorita was also a major character, as the Sub-Mariner decides to deal with humanity on its own terms, founding a successful corporation called Oracle Inc.

From 25 there's a radical change, as Byrne relinquished the art to newcomer Jae Lee, whose darker and more sinister style alters the look of the series. He also transforms Namor, giving him a ponytail and goatee, and the stories become rougher, with Namor becoming ever more embittered. Byrne left after 34, and Lee continued with an assortment of writers, including some dismal scripts from Roy Thomas, before heading off to pastures new ten issues later. From 44 Glenn Herdling, Geof Isherwood and Jeff Albrecht are the creative

team, starting with the bizarre 'The Rime Of The Ancient Sub-Mariner', but they couldn't halt flagging sales. Their highpoint was 50's long, unfulfilled love affair between Namor and Sue Richards, the Invisible Woman. Fickle monarch that he is, though, in 54 another of Namor's longtime love-interests, Llyra, gave birth to his son.~TP
Recommended: 1–25, 50

NATHANIEL DUSK, Private Investigator
DC: *4-issue miniseries 1983, 4-issue miniseries 1985*

Don McGregor and Gene Colan's *Nathanial Dusk* was a classic Chandleresque piece of noir for which McGregor put away his purple prose and bleeding heart, while DC obligingly printed the strip from Colan's extra tight (but still wonderfully fluid) pencils. The lack of black contrasts and the washed-out colour palette gives the art an emotional sensitivity that reflects McGregor's humanist approach to the genre. Colan draws great characters, while McGregor's stories, set on the cusp between the Great Depression and World War II, hammer home a 'do the right thing' message. The first series, which concerns Dusk's search for revenge when his lover is murdered, is fuelled by the character's rage, giving it a sense of inevitability. It's straightforward but well told, supported by excellent artwork, although the second series was, if anything, better drawn. Although the second story is more complex, Dusk's motivation is forced, and the eventual dénouement is rather obvious. It's unfortunate that one miniseries has the best art while the previous one had the sharper story. They're still a cracking read, however.~FJ
Recommended: Series one 1–4

Roberta Gregory's NAUGHTY BITS
Fantagraphics: *21 issues + 1991 to date*

Despite the salacious title, anyone looking for titillating material will be sorely disappointed. Come for a scathing and hilarious dissection of the seething underbelly comprising office life, or relationships for the late-thirtysomething woman in the 1990s, and you'll be more than satisfied.

Gregory's central character is Bitchy Bitch, who begins as a barely repressed manic mass of outrage and resentment prone to fearsome vocal outbursts and tantrums. Over the course of the series, though, she becomes a more fully-rounded character, particularly through glimpses back into her past. As the enquiring and uncertain teenage Midge she has a plastic mother impregnated with the values of the 1950s, and a brutal father (6–8, 15–17). Breaking free of their values is an important growth stage. The *Naughty Bits* supporting cast is small, but defined in wonderfully irritating fashion, with the beatific God-absorbed Marcie and the contented New Age Sylvia (who gets a solo in 20) predominant, although an early quick shag, the exquisitely named Toadman, is also a memorable creation (1, 5). There is explicitly depicted sex, including 1's infamous Bobbitting, but Gregory's renditions, in one sense simple, in another more realistic than the perfect bodies found in sex comics, are far from erotic. It seems to be a case of acknowledging that sex is an important part of people's lives. She also takes far more trouble with her editorial pages than most, to the point of usually including introductory or postscript strips talking directly to the reader. They're an endearing addition. 4's 'Unhappy Holidays' is a good representative issue, contrasting a childhood Christmas visit to the molesting Uncle Stanley with an adult family Christmas twenty years on.

Through Bitchy Bitch's aggressive character *Naughty Bits* often engenders accusations of being man-hating, which is a frankly ludicrous assertion. Although versions of many of the planet's prime male slimeballs are depicted, Gregory's is an equal-opportunity caustic wit, and her portrayals of female characters are no more flattering. Furthermore, she manages to insert vast doses of common sense into all the subjects she tackles. Anyone with a strong anti-abortion stance should read 8, and her issue dealing with people's reactions to a lesbian in the workplace (14) is a treat.~FP

Recommended: 1, 4, 5, 8, 10–12, 14, 17, 20
Collections: As Naughty As She Wants To Be (1, 2, 5, 9 plus back-ups), *At Work And Play With Bitchy Bitch* (10–14), *A Bitch Is Born* (3, 4, 6–8)

NAUSICAA of the Valley of Wind

Viz: *Part One 7 issues 1988–1989, Part Two 4 issues 1989, Part Three 3 issues 1992–1993, Part Four 5 issues 1994, Part Five 8 issues 1995–1996*

In the far future, humanity struggles to survive in a harsh, unforgiving environment. Some still try to use ancient technologies but those close to the Sea of Corruption, a forest of fungi and mould inhabited by enormous insects, the Ohmu, and poisonous to people, have grown used to the dangers of nature and show in their lives their respect for its power. *Nausicaa* tells the story of a war between the Torumekian and Dorok empires, of one side's unleashing of a biotechnical weapon that threatens to overwhelm everything, of a crypt wherein lie the secrets of the past, and of a plan to repopulate the Earth after its cleansing by the Sea of Corruption. Most of all, however, it's about Nausicaa herself, chief of the tribe of the Valley of Wind, conscripted into the war but increasingly associated with The Blue Clad One, the messiah who will save the world. Nausicaa is a warrior but more than

anything else she is at peace with nature and she alone can communicate with the insects of the forest.

The first part introduces Nausicaa to the war between the Doroks and the Torumekians. She meets the Torumekian Princess Kushana, commanding forces that have been sent to confront the Doroks but which are no match for the miasma that has been spreading from the forest. Kushana's other worry is the plotting against her of her brothers and her father, the Emperor. As Nausicaa defies Kushana's orders in order to help those ruined by the warfare or the miasma, she finds herself falling into the role of The Blue Clad One.

In Part Two, after being an unwilling participant in pitched battle, Nausicaa leaves Kushana's army and heads off on her own. One of the ancient God-Warriors has been unearthed but is in stasis, and the Dorok scientists have been experimenting dangerously with the spores from the forest, creating a mutant mould they can't control. Kushana is forced into a marriage pact with Namulith, true Dorok Emperor, in Part Three, in which Nausicaa discovers that the Ohmu are sacrificing themselves in order to destroy the mould. In Part Four, Nausicaa takes a spiritual journey on which she learns the secret of the Sea of Corruption. Returning to the outside world, she accidentally awakens the God-Warrior, which promptly mistakes her for its mother. Part Five concludes the series after confronting the plans of those who created the Sea of Corruption. Nausicaa refuses to accept that the only way forward is to recreate the past, and ultimately she denies it.

Hayao Miyazaki is modest about his comic skills, being better known in Japan for his animation, but this is quite frankly a masterpiece that deserves to be read by anyone with an interest in the medium. His humane scripting, sense of action, deftness of characterisation and story-telling and his control of the emotional highs and lows are all first-rate. This is an epic story, told in epic style; to compare Miyazaki with Moebius does neither a disservice. You thought *Akira* was as good as Japanese comics got? How wrong you were.~NF

Recommended: Part One 1–7, Part Two 1–4, Part Three 1–3, Part Four 1–5, Part Five 1–8
Collections: Nausicaa Vol 1 (Part One 1–3), Vol 2 (Part One 4–6), Vol 3 (Part One 7, Part Two 1, 2), Vol 4 (Part Two 3, 4), Vol 5 (Part Three 1–3), Vol 6 (Part Four 1–5)

NAZA

Dell: *9 issues 1964–1966*

The adventures of a Stone-Age warrior didn't sell back in the 1960s either. Bad stuff.~SW

THE NAZZ

DC: *4 issues 1990–1991*

Faintly disappointing miniseries about a sexy guru who turns out to be a power-hungry monster. Tom Veitch over-complicates his strip by hiding his central character's real agenda behind a series of smoke-screens and using a different character's viewpoint in each issue, which makes the story feel more profound than it is: power corrupts, and all that. Nonetheless, it's a very interesting read, and it makes a change to have someone musing about godliness from an Eastern rather than a Western point of view. Bryan Talbot is a sympathetic artist for this material, able to draw in a super-realistic, detailed style that avoids reminding you of superheroics (although The Nazz would probably qualify as a superhero by most people's definitions). Apparently readers deserted the book in droves when the 'hero' stopped looking cute and acting nice, which is a sad reflection on the state of comics today.~FJ

NBM Graphic Novels

NBM's extensive graphic-novel line, increased by a large number of titles they inherited from Catalan when that company closed, is now formally divided into two main areas: erotic and literature, as previewed in their *Comics Lit* magazine. The erotica is separated into two imprints, the extensive Eurotica and the poorer Amerotica, each encompassing work from the continent that the names imply, with the former featuring artists first published by Catalan. The Lit line again features both European and American creators, and by contrast with the obviously popularist soft-porn choices features some difficult creators.

Regarding the Eurotica line: however complex his page structure, and however freaky his sexual interests, NBM discovered that American readers liked Guido Crepax's peculiar, elongated women as much as Europe had, and rapidly published his erotic work. The best of these is *The Story Of O* (3 vols), an adaptation of Pauline Réage's classic of domination about a young woman who allows herself to be taken to a strange house, where she is beaten and abused by a group of masked men. Crepax adds a great deal of detail to the original while not losing the curious, detached quality of the heroine's narration. He also brings something new to his version of the notorious skinflick *Emmanuelle*, giving it an elegance and fetishistic grandeur which the film lacked (2 vols). Volume 1 has a particularly useful introduction for new readers, including samples of Crepax's art from his different periods.

Less satisfying are the *Anita* collections, erotic encounters based around TV and video technology. For some reason the first two-thirds of *Anita Live* are in one volume, with the conclusion and another, shorter story in volume 2. As *Anita* is somewhat fluffier and less plot-driven this is not an insurmountable problem, and the reprints retain the partial use of colour that's about the only innovative aspect of the strip. NBM took longest in reprinting Crepax's early masterwork, *Valentina*, the erotic adventures of a pretty female photographer. Surreal and full of 1960s iconography, as well as fabulous sado-masochistic imagery, they're drawn in a less linear style than the later works. At this stage Crepax is just finding his artistic feet and pushing at the boundaries of the strip format, making for some incredibly exciting art.

The last Crepax volume to appear is not particularly fine. Although many of his literary adaptations bring a great deal to the existing story, others, like this strange, oversexed version of Henry James' chiller *The Turn Of The Screw*, do not work. Updated to the 1920s, completely missing the fact that the stiff reserve of hooped skirts and buttoned-up suits adds immeasurably to the sense of seething, hidden desires in the original, Crepax's version shows too many of the acts that are much more disturbing when left to the reader's imagination. Why no one has translated his magnificent *Dracula* instead is a mystery.

Some people will find Crepax's interest in sado-masochism a little disturbing. If so, they will not want to come within a hundred miles of George Pichard's more extreme efforts such as *Marie Gabrielle, Madaleine* and *The Red Countess*. The first is a fake picaresque morality tale centring around a nunnery where women are tortured to punish them for their sins. There's a strong anti-religious undercurrent and a number of digs at hypocrisy to the tale, which excellently captures the voice of the genre it pastiches. However, one suspects that most readers will be buying it for the rampant sadism. *Madaleine* is a less convincing retake on the theme, set on an alternate earth where women who commit sexual crimes are incarcerated and punished. *The Red Countess* is a particularly detailed account of the outrages committed by Elisabeth Bathory, whose story gave rise to a number of vampire legends. She was outstandingly cruel even by the standards of her day (16th century); Pichard delights in recreating her excesses in pointillist detail.

Ulysses (2 vols) is an early work, adapted by Lob from *The Odyssey*, from the period when the artist was less obsessive about the female form, the art giving a nod towards Greek painting. Although Pichard again adapts his drawing style for *The Illustrated Kama Sutra* (2 vols, text and illos rather than strip), it's still very clearly his work. The Indian liking for fleshy women fits in well with his own particular interest in well-curved victims. Bridging the gap between these and Pichard's later style is his 1981 rendition of

Carmen, an earthy tragedy much closer to Prosper Merimée's original than the operatic story we're more familiar with.

To a large existing body of work which they keep in print, NBM added Manara's *Click* 2 and 3, not quite so ground-breaking as the original, but satisfyingly horny. No doubt Manara's sexy version of *Gulliver's Travels*, *Gulliverana*, will be heading our way shortly. In a similar vein, and equally lightweight, we have Leroi and Gibrat's *Pinocchia*, a dirty version of the wooden-boy story, in which a lusty Gepetto carves himself a wooden mate who is brought to life by magic. Finally there's *Angel Claw*, a collaboration between Moebius and Jodorowsky, consisting of full-page black and white illos and short accompanying text. What's peculiar, apart from the overtly sexual nature of the pictures, is that Jodorowsky constructed the order and story after Moebius had done the drawings, creating an artificial excuse for us to have a look at Moebius's fantasies. Needless to say the drawing's very fine indeed, and the symbolism is revealing.

The Amerotica line hasn't been productive in terms of quality or quantity. Elaine Lee's long-planned series of erotic science-fiction stories, which promised to be real tales rather than just excuses to bonk, turn out to be a load of clichés, indifferently and often poorly illustrated in 2 vols of *The Skintight Orbit* , while Amerotica's only 'discovery', Michael Manning, creates a world of weird sado-masochistic creatures, aliens, horse people and dominatrixes. Pity he can't draw. *The Spider Garden* has some sort of plot, *Hydrophibian* creates a world of bondage mermaids, while the *Lumenagerie* is a collection of sketches. As S&M goes, his imagery is rather stale. Before the division, about the only saucy US creator they'd published was Will Desberg, whose *The Garden Of Desire* is a sexy world tour about a man searching for his ideal woman, drawn in a simple, cartoony style.

NBM have always supported a handful of rather serious authors, now allocated to the Comics Lit imprint. The most notable among them is Hugo Pratt, whose *Corto Maltese* series is dealt with in a separate entry. As well as keeping *Indian Summer*, Pratt's first collaboration with Manara, in print, NBM also published his last work, *El Gaucho*. While it's perhaps not the best thing he's ever written, Pratt's script for this tale of rebellion and political manoeuvring in South America in the early 19th century, seen through the eyes of a young seaman, is a sweeping history lesson, beautifully illustrated by Milo Manara. Manara puts in even more detail than usual, creating wonderful character studies and drawing every fibre of the rigging as mighty ships set sail. Miguelanxo Prado's stories are closely comparable to the shorter stories of the Italian master of bitterness and wasted opportunities, Alberto Moravia, and like Moravia, Prado goes over the same ground again and again, adding tiny touches of characterisation, giving each story a new twist. *Streak Of Chalk* and *Tangents* are both relationship-based books about mature people reflecting on their unfulfilled lives, and learning how best to hurt each other. Prado succeeds in keeping your interest in characters to whom you are not supposed to warm, using a soft pastel technique on dark backgrounds, and drawing accurately observed human mannerisms to match his subtle stories.

A number of NBM's books were reprinted following the appearance in *Cheval Noir* either of the work itself or of the creator. Andreas's *Rork* series (3 vols: 'Fragments', 'Passages and 'The Graveyard of Cathedrals/Starlight') is about a mysterious, white-haired psychic who, the pawn of fate, features in subtle, almost Lovecraftian tales of lurking evil. The first two volumes are slight but the third, featuring two of a series of linked stories, part of a major plot-line, is a huge creative step forward for Andreas. The premise of 'The Graveyard of Cathedrals' – that the heretic Roman Catholic cult the Cathars, banished to the New World for their radical thoughts on architecture, founded a settlement in an ancient place of power in Mexico, which Rork stumbles upon along with a band of adventurers – allows Andreas scope to draw the most amazing landscapes. *In Search Of Shirley*, by Cosey (2 vols), is a direct reprint from *Cheval Noir*, where the series was called *Voyage To Italy*, as is *The Six Voyages Of Loan Sloane*, spaced-out acid adventures from Phillipe Druillet. NBM recently published another book by Cosey, *Lost In The Alps*, the tale of a young English writer's search for his elder brother, who last contacted him from an Alpine resort. Although not typical of his output, Jacques Tardi's work on *Roach Killer* is outstanding, especially his use of spot red. Written by Legrand, it brings all the brooding atmosphere of a film noir to the story of a New York exterminator. Very different are the two volumes from the *Adele Blanc-Sec* series which he both wrote and drew, also taken from *Cheval Noir*. *Adele And The Beast* and *The Demon Of The Eiffel Tower* are inventive, almost playful detective stories which subvert the forms of the genre. The series of architectural fantasies by Schuiten and Peeters, in which the phantasmagorical landscapes carry as much meaning as the 'plot', look complex but repel reading. *Fever In Urbicand, The Great Walls Of Samaris* and *The Tower* are all dense, multi-layered books crammed with detail.

Then there are a small group of adventure stories. Marvano turns Joe Haldeman's anti-war space novel *The Forever War* into a three-volume series. He doesn't add much, but it's competent science fiction. NBM also collected Richard Corben's globular adaptation of Harlan Ellison's classic holocaust-survivor story 'One Man And His Dog' as *Vic And Blood*, following the film of the same name. Segrelles' detailed painted style and rather classical knights-and-maidens fantasy stories would please boys raised on *The Eagle*, although the language is modern, despite the setting. The three volumes of *The Mercenary* (Vol 1: *The Cult Of The Sacred Fire* and *The Formula*, Vol 2: *The Trials* and *The Sacrifice*, Vol 3: *The Fortress*) are largely unexciting but workmanlike.

Recently the line has lost some of its direction and distinction, and there are signs that the editors are trying to find new avenues to explore. The 1996 output has been scattershot in its appeal and quality, with some of the best work coming from American creators. Michael Cherkas and John Sabljic's *The New Frontier* is in the same vein as their earlier *The Silent Invasion*, a complicated but engrossing conspiracy story pre-dating *The X-Files* and its copyists by several years. Unusually for such stories it's drawn in a broad, 1950s style reminiscent of Yves Chaland, with no attempt at realism whatsoever. Rick Geary's *Jack The Ripper*, a handsome volume which contrasts cosy and often comic Victoriana with the brutal slayings, to great effect, is expensive but rewarding, if you like Geary's lumpy illustrative style. Similarly slight but worthwhile is *Give It Up*, in which Peter Kuper takes on Kafka. And wins.

The Worst Thing I've Ever Done is an amusing 'true life' collection from Ted Rall, very much in the vein of Daniel Clowes' *Duplex Planet* pages from *Eightball*. People tell Rall exactly what the title suggests, ranging from minor nastiness to murder. It works, but you're beginning to get a bit tired of the format by the end. In a similar format there's the less successful *Classics Desecrated* by Doug Wheeler and a host of artists, which is well-executed but kind of a tired idea. *Verdilak*, by Bo Hampton and Mark Kneece, is an awful vampire tale, based on Tolstoy's *La Famille de la Vourdalak*, painted in drab and often clumsy watercolours, and featuring pompous nonsense like 'The systolic rush, embarrassingly conspicuous, pounds in her ears and carries on the raging winds of the storm.' It recalls the earlier *Dracula* by Jon J. Muth, more arty-farty daubings, but this time illos for a play script. Both Bo and Scott Hampton make a much more respectable contribution to *Confessions Of A Cereal Eater*, a collection of reminiscences by Rob Maisch. The other illustrators are Rand Holmes and Sandy Plunkett, and all are fine in their own way. What shines through, however, is the seemingly artless story-telling. Maisch tells us of his malignant behaviour towards a neighbour as a child, his problems as a mall manager when a childhood cowboy hero turns up for a personal appearance, now aged, foul-mouthed and drunk; and he lays out for us the bizarre mating rituals involved in school dances in the first story, 'Slow Dance', excellently illustrated in loose black and white by Scott Hampton. Both brothers have a hand in 'adapting' Maisch's stories, whatever that means, but the collaborations are extremely fruitful.

What's worrying is that NBM haven't 'broken' any new European talents for quite a while. Hopefully their investment in Prado will reap rewards and encourage them to pursue truly adult works, rather than adventure stories.~FJ

Recommended: *Adele And The Beast, The Demon Of The Eiffel Tower, The Graveyard Of Cathedrals, In Search Of Shirley, Roach Killer, The Silent Invasion, The Story Of O, Streak of Chalk, Tangents, Valentina*

NEAR MYTHS
Rip Off: *1 issue 1990*

As its title suggests, this is a collection of mythological tales, here interpreted (or reinterpreted) by Trina Robbins. Though not a major work, it retains her usual charm and economic line.~DAR

NEAT STUFF
Fantagraphics: *15 issues 1985–1989*

Within the first four issues of his black and white magazine *Neat Stuff*, Peter Bagge went from an underground (particularly Crumb)-influenced doodler to a master story-teller. It's a delight to watch him feeling his way and developing his characters. Early issues are more manic, centring around Girly Girl (the most fearsome small child ever created) and Chuckie Boy (an incompetent wimp), followed by The Bradleys, his enduring creation. The Bradleys are the ultimate imperfect American family, in which the members spend most of the time hating each other. The stories revolve around teenage Buddy and his viewpoint, without being blind to his many failings. By 6 Bagge was producing extraordinary comic *tours de force* like 'Mom Power', in which Buddy's long-suffering mother goes bananas, downs tools and gets pissed on the front lawn, and 'Brotherly Love', an extended chase sequence in which Buddy and his annoying little brother Butch act out *Tom And Jerry* cartoons. Each character is fully rounded; each is awful in their own special way.

Neat Stuff also introduced us to the delights of Junior, a hopeless loser whose dry and rather dumb commentary on the world passing by is both touching and funny, Studs Kirby, a parsimonious braggart who runs a talk radio show, and Chet and Bunny Leeway, young professionals whose guiding force is a mixture of social climbing and ennui.

Bagge's sympathy for his characters is displayed in the gut-wrenchingly embarrassing 'Studs Kirby's Big Break' in 7, where Studs, mostly out of fear, screws up his chance to impress a big city radio star by getting drunk and insulting him. All the character's insecurities and the way he compensates for them are laid out for us to realise that what we've been laughing at is weakness. Other excellent stories include the thirty-two-page Buddy story, 'Hippy House', in 9, 'You're Not The Boss Of Me' (Buddy's self-obsessed sister Babs throws the mother of all strops), and Girly Girl and Chuckie Boy putting the boot into political correctness in 'Summer Camp' in 13.

Neat Stuff blends the screamingly funny with warm, understanding humour that succeeds so well because it's character-driven. Bagge's manic drawing style perfectly matches the sudden outbursts, screaming fits and fights with which the stories are punctuated.~FJ

Recommended: 6, 7, 9, 11–13, 15

Collections: The Bradleys, Junior And Other Losers, Studs Kirby, Stupid Comics

NECROSCOPE

Malibu: *5-issue miniseries 1992–1993, 5-issue miniseries ('Wamphryi') 1993–1994*

Two miniseries adapting Brian Lumley's novels. The Necroscope of the title is Harry Keogh, able to speak with the dead and instantly learn anything from them, which is just as well because a Russian ESP operative is attempting to raise a vampire. Dying in the first series is a minimal hindrance to Keogh, who faces an older and infinitely more terrifying vampire in the second series. Martin Powell's adaptations make for good comics, with the first being superior by virtue of Daerick Gross' more appealing artwork. In the second Dave Kendall disguises a lack of basic anatomical knowledge under his painting.~WJ

Collection: Necroscope (miniseries one)

NEGATIVE BURN

Caliber: *40 issues + 1993 to date*

Despite attracting work by some of the great and good, *Negative Burn* remains rather indulgent. The diversity of the stories is laudable but too often they rely on supposedly humorous punchlines or else are let down by amateurish artwork.

There are several main strands to the likely content of any issue; from 28, the page-count was increased to sixty-four pages, so there's plenty of room. There are the regular series: 'Mr Mamoulian' by Brian Bolland (all issues), dealing with park-bench philosophy; 'Classics Desecrated' by Doug Wheeler and various artists (4–18, 20, 21, 23, 24), in which literary

classics are trashed (sorry, adapted) in one or two pages, and 'Alan Moore's Songbook' (9–14,16–19, 25, 26, 28, 35, 37), where his lyrics are illustrated by different artists, more or less successfully. There are also early or unpublished works by a number of better known creators, P. Craig Russell (4, 8, 30,37), David Lloyd (6), Michael T. Gilbert (14) and John McCrea (37, 39).

A major proportion of the remaining material consists of strips from existing or upcoming Caliber titles or else examples of small-press titles that Joe Pruett, as editor, feels deserve wider exposure. Most of the following strips are well worth investigating, either here or in their own titles. In the former category we have Kilroy Is Here (1, 4, 6, 13, 18, 24), Boneshaker (1, 8), The Wretch (38), The Trigger Man (4), Dominique (9, 13, 25, 34), Twilight People (9–13), Exit (12, 22), Baker Street (25), The Jam (25), Nowheresville (33) and The Kingdom of the Wicked (38). In the latter, Flaming Carrot (1, 14, 19), Jazz Age Chronicles (7, 12), Strangers In Paradise (13), Suburban Nightmares (25–27), Trollords (21), Replacement God (29, 35), Strangehaven (24), Very Vicki (26), Rob Hanes (30, 39), Shades of Gray (32) and The Trespassers (38). There's nothing particularly wrong with this but the short-story format doesn't always do the strips favours and it's not always obvious whether the story's been produced specifically for *Negative Burn*. Other strips that fall into the above categories but which are less successful are The Black Mist (3), The Apparition (1, 25), Sojourn (5), Kabuki (16, 25) and Milk & Cheese (13).

Outside the categories above, one or two creators deserve mention. Phillip Hester's artwork is constantly surprising, changing shape to suit story or genre, whether it be odd short stories, like Boneshaker, the Creep (29, 37) or longer ones like 'The Wretch', and he can be found in many other issues. Jeff Nicholson's disquieting studies of human behaviour are very effective (15–18, 30–36). Joe Pruett and Philip Xavier's 'Lost Paradise' (22) and Ian Carney and Dave Taylor's 'Mr Murray' are both heavily, but interestingly, Moebius-influenced. Joe Pruett and Andrew Robinson's 'Dusty Star' (28, 37) is a Western with robotic trappings, but regrettably reduces itself to a gag strip for the second episode (though it's now been scheduled for its own title). Kevin O'Neill turns in some interesting experimental artwork in 31 and James Owen's 'Little Neil In Slumberland' neatly parodies *Cerebus* and Neil Gaiman. Star of the show, however, is Paul Pope, whose 'Eulogy To Marx' (12) and 'Triumph Of Hunger' (13) are terrific political strips, and whose non-related short stories in 18, 20, 21 and 23–25 are worth looking out for.

Finally, many issues have sketchbook pages, some of which may be of particular interest – Mike Kaluta (4), Jeff Smith (3), Arthur Suydam (5), P. Craig Russell (10), Tony Harris (13), David Mazzuccheli (17), Jaime Hernandez (31) and Neil Gaiman (25). There are two collections of the *Best of Negative Burn Year One* and *Year Two*, which are a good place to start for those who want to see why the title is generally well regarded; but on the whole there are no single issues that can be wholly recommended.~NF

NEIL THE HORSE Comics And Stories
Aardvark-Vanaheim: *10 issues 1983–1984*
Renegade: *5 issues (11–15) 1984–1988*

Beginning life as a syndicated newspaper strip (1975–1979), Arn Saba's eclectic creations made a brief appearance in *Charlton Bullseye* 2 (1981). The title is dedicated to Carl Barks and inspired by the musicals of Fred Astaire, indicating that this is a very unusual comic. Based in format on *Walt Disney's Comics And Stories*, it mixes comic strips, annotated music scores, illustrated text and paper-doll pages. Neil himself is a big-hearted omnivore with a real love of bananas; his companions are Madame Poupee, a puppet, and Soapy, a cigar-smoking, cynical cat. Saba is assisted by a number of friends who contribute stories or lyrics or paper dolls (Barb Rausch). Her *Great Women Of Comics* dolls include the Dragon Lady, Modesty Blaise and Phantom Lady. The stories are full of *Little Nemo*-like surrealism, totally out of this world, with touches of parody and plenty of romance. This is a unique series that's a joy to read, pushing what you expect of a comic book to the limits.~NF
Recommended: 3, 11, 14

NEMESIS the Warlock
Eagle: *7-issue limited series 1984–1985*
Fleetway/Quality: *19 issues 1989–1991*

On a far-future, radiation-scarred Earth, mankind dwells underground, courtesy of the alien invasions that have devastated the surface. Transportation is provided by a fantastic system of Travel Tubes monitored by Chief of Tube Police, Torquemada. Named after, and later revealed as a reincarnation of, the 15th-century Spanish monk who tortured thousands of heretics, this righteous, evil bigot graduates to Earth ruler and later godhood as he fans xenophobia against all non-humans and drives his crusade to the stars. His nemesis is Nemesis, a bipedal equine alien who assists any alien or Earth resistance movement subjected to Torquemada's attentions. Outrageous, wacky, undisciplined and juvenile, the strip is littered with throwaway gags, both verbal and visual, such as the flying machine based on a Penny Farthing design in the Gothic Empire sequence. Fine character development unfolds leisurely; it is not until 'Purity's Story' (16–17) that Nemesis'

full motives are revealed to be not quite as pure as initial appearances suggest.

The publishing history of *Nemesis* is convoluted. It débuted during 1980 as a few isolated shorts in the British weekly comic *2000AD*. The regular strip began as a series of serials in *2000AD*, each serial labelled a 'Book' and comprising around twelve to fifteen consecutive issues of five-page episodes. The Eagle series reprints Books 1–3 in colour for the first time, and Fleetway/Quality reprint Books 1, 3–9. In both cases, the originals have been resized and partly redrawn to fit standard comics, much to the detriment of the artwork. The best and most accessible format is presented in Titan's *Nemesis* compilations, also designated as 'Books'. These fail to collect Book 2, which means that their numbering is out of sync with the original Nemesis numbering. More sporadic episodes have appeared in *2000AD* subsequent to Book 9. Pat Mills is Script Robot on all and Kevin O'Neill co-creates and draws Books 1, 3 and 4. Indeed, some of their previous creations (most prominently ABC Warriors) find their way into later stories. Bryan Talbot is the other major artistic contributor (Books 4–6). Jesus Redondo (2), John Hicklenton (7, 9) and David Roach (8) complete the roll call.

Books 1, 3, 4 head the class, as later tales are burdened by the increasing political conscience that the series develops. And the kindest comment that can be attributed to Hicklenton's artwork is to describe it as an acquired taste.~APS
Collections: Nemesis vol 1–9 (Fleetway/Quality 1–19)

NERVOUS REX
Blackthorne: 10 issues, 1985–87

Rexford is a mild-mannered Tyrannosaurus Rex who would rather eat oatmeal than hunt and rend and tear. This wouldn't be a problem, except that his huge wife, Dearie, has ambitions for him. It's the old hen-pecked husband gag – with the jokes rationed to about one every two issues, so it's just a portrait of an ugly marriage in urgent need of a divorce lawyer. Once in a while, however, William Van Horn manages to keep an idea pinned down for long enough to build a story, and he has a nice way with moons and planets.~FC
Recommended: 5

NEUTRO
Dell: *1 issue 1967*

Had notoriously inept film maker Ed Wood ever turned his hand to comics he'd have created *Neutro*. It's gloriously incompetent in every fashion, from Jack Sparling's appalling art (if the hand he's drawn on page 16 is based on his it explains a lot) to the anonymous

script. That reads like it's been dashed off on dictaphone by someone who's just consumed more speed than is good for them. Neutro is a giant robot, buried on Earth in component parts centuries ago by aliens for an obscure purpose. Uncovered by archaeologist John Dodge, Neutro is reconstructed, and there follows twenty-two pages of dementia, starting with speculation on Neutro's possible destructive capacities and continuing with a spectacularly badly illustrated sequence of assorted powers attempting to bring Neutro under their control. Truly an all-time turkey, and only recommended for kitsch value.~FP
Recommended: 1

NEW AMERICA
Eclipse: *4-issue miniseries 1987–1988*

A story spun-off from Eclipse's *Scout*, set in the early 21st century, when America is ravaged by a twelve-year civil war and partitioned into independent kingdoms as political factions fight for control. *New America* focuses on anti-heroine Rosanna Winters, general in the Southwestern Free States, as they conduct assassinations and sabotage raids to play off the political cabals. Creators Ostrander, Yale and Kwapisz depict a grippingly realistic scenario, bereft of superpowers, spandex, magic or unforeseeable technology. Character motivations are powerfully defined. It is bleak, sober, political, adult, uncompromising and devoid of humour. You cannot dance to it and it will never spawn a hit single. A classic in its field.~APS
Recommended: 1–4

NEW FORCE
Image: *4-issue miniseries 1996*

Filling the gap during a hiatus in the publication of *Newmen*, this was intended to stimulate interest in one of Image's longer running titles. The Newmen spend much of the series captured by one organisation or another, but by the end of the series the team has been refreshed and retooled for continuation in *Newmen* 21. Penciller Todd Nauck shows promise, although he'll have to learn to stop swiping.~WJ

THE NEW FRONTIER
Dark Horse: *3-issue miniseries 1992*

A dense and complex political thriller starting with the 1963 death of a beloved Marilyn Monroe figure and extrapolating from there to a 1980s in which there's an annual pageant in her honour. Such is the winner's popularity that her affiliation with a dark-horse presidential candidate boosts his ratings considerably, at which point past secrets begin to emerge. With *Suburban Nightmares*, *Silent Invasion* and this title, artist Michael Cherkas has a solo franchise on the conspiracy-theory section of the comic market, but his stylised art won't be to

everyone's taste. There's no really sympathetic characters and the third issue lacks breathing space, but otherwise top-notch.~FP
Recommended: 1–3

NEW GODS
DC: *Series one 19 issues 1971–1972 (1–11), 1977–1978 (12–19), 6-issue miniseries 1984, graphic novel 1985, series two 28 issues 1989–1991, series three 15 issues 1995–1996*

'An epic of our times', proclaims the cover of *New Gods* 1, and how true it was. The series inside audaciously begins with an epilogue explaining how when the old Gods died their planet split in half, one portion becoming New Genesis, the other Apokalips. This was the setting for what would be known as Jack Kirby's 'Fourth World Trilogy', the most magnificent space saga ever to appear in comics. When reduced to basics, the series concerns good vs evil, and whether upbringing or genetics determines character. The population of New Genesis live in harmony with themselves, each other and their world, and largely occupy a beautiful city, floating above a lush, green, unspoiled world. The inhabitants of Apokalips, by contrast, are ruled by the dreaded Darkseid, and the constantly churning energy pits cloud the planet with noxious fumes, blotting out most light.

The plot propelling Kirby's *New Gods* was Darkseid's quest for the Anti-Life Equation, which would give him power over the entire universe. The Gods from New Genesis want to prevent this, led by Highfather, visually a very biblical-style character. The main character, though, was Orion, who was Darkseid's son, but who, as the result of a pact, was raised on New Genesis. The full story is told in 7, perhaps the most powerful and moving superhero story ever, detailing the origin of the conflict between New Genesis and Apokalips. Orion's upbringing imbues him with decent values, but his endemic ferocity had to be curbed by machine. The Anti-Life Equation is to be found on Earth, and while it serves as a setting for Orion and other New Gods we also learn more about New Genesis and Apokalips. Kirby populated the series with further memorable characters such as Orion's right-hand man Lightray, a name describing his powers and personality, Darkseid's scientific minion the sadistic Desaad, and a personification of death on skis named The Black Racer. It's Darkseid, though, who's remained his most memorable creation. Although almost a personification of evil he retains the grandeur of a ruler, and a perverse sense of justice

New Gods was Kirby at his best. The grandeur of his designs completely convinces, and the comics are packed with magnificent imagery. The only downside is the subdued inking of Vince Colletta in 1–4. Mike Royer's arrival with 5 cemented a perfect look. Kirby's plots and characterisation were equally excellent, and although he was often criticised for unrealistic dialogue in other titles, such comments have no place regarding *New Gods*. 6's 'Glory Boat' is a great delve into the depths of the human psyche, and there's more human interest in 8's 'The Deathwish Of Terrible Turpin', a study of how much a human will endure. Kirby also surprises throughout, particularly with 9's revelation that New Genesis is not the paragon of integrity thus far presented. Sadly, Kirby was unable to finish his story, and Orion's claim in 11 that when he and Darkseid clash the war will finally end is a tantalising teaser. In 1984 DC reprinted Kirby's issues as a 6-issue miniseries, featuring an all-new conclusion in the final issue. With a twelve-year gap Kirby's art wasn't as strong as previously, but his plotting was as good, with an ending that defied all predictions. The saga didn't finish there, though, as Kirby then wrote and drew the graphic novel *The Hunger Dogs*. It's frankly disappointing, with Kirby's intention of killing some major characters vetoed in the face of toy-company interest, requiring extensive alteration to plot and art.

Little was seen of the New Gods until *First Issue Special* 13 announced their return, leading to the restoration of the regular series, now titled *The Return Of The New Gods*. Those hoping for a return of the glory days were sorely disappointed. Gerry Conway was seemingly under instructions to go mainstream superhero and redesigned characters and concepts accordingly, introducing new cast members along the way. If one can forget Kirby it's a solid, if unspectacular superhero series, very nicely drawn by Don Newton. Ultimately, though, the characterisation is very much at odds with what had been established, the uniform dialogue patterns being particularly out of place. Again cancelled midway through a story, this time it was concluded a little sooner in *Adventure* 459 and 460.

By the time of the second ongoing series the *New Gods* cast were intimately connected with the DC Universe as recurring characters. The appointment of respected TV scriptwriter Mark Evanier boded well as his credentials included a period as Kirby's assistant when the original series was conceived. Strangely, though, his work fails to impress. Part of the original appeal of *New Gods* lay in the gradual unfolding of a mystery, but Evanier lays everything out on a plate, sometimes complicating stories with superfluous explanation. He gave the characters a greater depth, though, and his best story is 7–12, in which Orion infiltrates Apokalips to search for his imprisoned mother. Evanier's scheming Desaad was also well characterised, plotting to usurp his master Darkseid throughout the

series. 17 introduces Darkseid's father, an equally unsavoury character, completing three dysfunctional generations. Paris Cullins drew 1–18, and, while able to tell a story and draw a good action scene, he was incapable of imparting the grandeur of New Genesis or the squalor of Apokalips. The same applied to his successor, Rick Hoberg. The problem throughout *New Gods* is that Kirby defined his worlds and characters so well that no following creators have been able to match him, few having his imagination and scope. Jim Starlin also paints a grand picture, though, and was originally intended to produce the entire series. What remained of his plots filled 2–4. When cancellation arrives with 28, the primary thought is 'oh well, never mind'.

The bulk of the 1995 series is written by Rachel Pollack, and the usual plot of Orion and Darkseid in opposition isn't dragged out. The astonishing conclusion in 2 results in some of the Gods going mad, particularly Lightray. This is where the series becomes disjointed, with the redeeming plot-line being Desaad masquerading as Darkseid, and despite dramatic artwork from Luke Ross the series failed to gather pace. 9 is a noteworthy Keith Giffen-illustrated fill-in, Giffen having begun his career with nice Kirby impressions. Pollack ends her run in 12 with a big bang, leaving John Byrne a bit of a problem to tie up in the final three issues. He does so with aplomb, his interpretations of the characters being closer to Kirby's than anyone else's. He provides a well-paced plot involving the destruction of Apokalips and New Genesis, guest-starring other related Kirby characters Mister Miracle, Big Barda and the Forever People. Byrne's pencils, inked by Bob Wiacek, are clear, crisp and expansive. It seems as if Byrne is the first worthy successor to Kirby. He concludes the series with a cliffhanger to be resolved in a forthcoming comic showcasing all of Jack Kirby's early 1970s creations for DC. If you want to experience the New Gods saga at its best read the recommended issues and don't bother with any of the rest.~HY

Recommended: Series one 1–11, miniseries 6, series three 12–15

Collection: Jack Kirby's New Gods (First series 1–11)

NEW GUARDIANS
DC: *12 issues 1988–1989*

Assembled during *Millennium*, this bunch of oddballs and misfits was supposed to 'bring about the next evolutionary step for mankind'. This rapidly became a moot point, as they featured the most embarrassing collection of stereotypes ever to be assembled in one team. The Chinese woman is in touch with the 'Dragonforce' of ley lines, there's a tech-obsessed Japanese man and the streetwise black chick from 'Fascist Britain', the Aboriginal mystic who became 'one with everything', and the embarrassingly nellie South American mystic who became comics' first visible homosexual, thereby reinforcing everybody's favourite stereotype about gay men. Realising they were on a highway to doom, the creators flailed about, trying a succession of 'quick fixes'. Jet sacrificed her life heroically during an *Invasion* crossover and Extrano butched up his act, becoming more Dr Strange and less Carmen Miranda, but it was still all going horribly wrong. Eventually, the DC cut their losses and decided that they were instead supposed to be the protectors of the next generation of humanity, dumping the team on an island with a bunch of mutants and forgetting all about them. No bad thing, either.~HS

NEW MAN
Image: *4-issue miniseries 1996*

A spin-off from the 'Extreme Destroyer' crossover, New Man is trapped in the present, having been a servant of the alien Keep who chose to help the Earth's defenders against them. 2 sees him trying to recruit the Wildcats against another alien who's controlling all human minds, but by the time he's convinced Majestic to join him the crisis has been averted. Told straight by Eldon Asp but actually quite funny. The rest of the series is about starting over on a new world. The last issue is a 'Shadowhunt' crossover. Daft name, but not without promise.~NF

NEW MUTANTS
Marvel: *100 issues, 7 Annuals, 1, Special, 1 Graphic Novel 1983–1991*

Débuting in 1983 in the graphic novel, *New Mutants* was one of the earliest *X-Men* spin-off comics. Originally by Chris Claremont and Bob McLeod, it returned to the very roots of the X-Men, bringing together the second generation of students at Xavier's School for Gifted Youngsters. A group of young mutants were learning both to use their powers and to function in a world which hated and despised them. The title also built on the New X-Men concept of a multi-racial, multi-national team boasting members from as far afield as Brazil, Scotland, Asia and Nova Roma, a throw-back colony to ancient Rome. Early issues are a light, solid read, not as angst-ridden as the adult team's book and generally entertaining. An evil teen nemesis team, the Hellions, add to the fun and games. The straightforward superhero fun goes out the window with the arrival of Bill Sienkiewicz on 18, when the stories take on a darker, weirder edge. Sadly, the low-grade paper and basic printing aren't enough to do Sienkiewicz's art credit – the gorgeous covers serve to show us what we're missing – but the stories make up for it, particularly the 'Demon Bear' issues starting with 19.

After Sienkiewicz leaves with 28, issues are mediocre and best avoided, although, if you haven't already had your fill of X-Men-related time paradoxes, the look at alternate futures around issue 50 is worth the time. The next notable period comes with the arrival of Rob Liefeld, who, like him or loathe him, certainly stamped his mark on both the *New Mutants* and the entire comics industry. Liefeld gave the book a much harder, more violent edge, action-packed, fast and furious, with little time for boring stuff like characterisation. Introducing Cable, the warrior from the future with the gun twice his size, the New Mutants moved further and further away from Professor X's ideals under the guidance of their new mentor. Appealing to a younger audience, and filling long-term fans with horror, Cable quickly became one of the most popular characters in the Marvel Universe. Before long, Cable had his own comic, the *New Mutants* had become *X-Force*, and Liefeld had left to become one of the founders of Image Comics, ushering in a new era for the comic book industry. Arguably, comics would never be the same again.

In addition to the annuals, there's also a 1990 one-shot titled *Mutant Summer Fun*, which is, to all intents and purposes, a *New Mutants* Special.~JC
Recommended: 18–28
Collections: Cable and the New Mutants (87–94) *Demon Bear Saga* (18–21); see also Uncanny X-Men

NEW TALENT SHOWCASE
DC: *19 issues 1984–1985*

New Talent Showcase stemmed from DC's commendable encouragement of new creators under talent co-ordinator Sal Amendola. The best overall strip is 'Class Of 2064' in 1–3, in which a school trip runs contrary to expectation. It's written with a pleasing lightness by Todd Klein, already well employed as a letterer, and illustrated by Scott Hampton, already top of the form. It's reprised in 7–8, drawn by Terry Shoemaker. A high percentage of contributors go on to better things, with Dan Day, Stephen DeStefano, Geof Isherwood, Karl Kesel, Rick Magyar, Tom Mandrake, Mindy Newell, Graham Nolan, Javier Saltares and Eric Shanower among the successful graduates, but plenty of perspiration with little inspiration is the order of the day. The title changed to *Talent Showcase* with 16.~WJ

NEW WARRIORS
Marvel: *75 issues, 4 Annuals, 1990–1996*

Writer Fabian Niciezia and artist Mark Bagley co-brainstormed this premise, a team of unemployed young Marvel heroes, and got away with it for far longer than you'd imagine possible. The origin parallels, entirely coincidentally, we're sure, that of the most popular incarnation of the Teen Titans. Firestar (former *New Mutants* opponent), Namorita (shapely younger cousin of Sub-Mariner), Marvel Boy (former supporting character of *The Thing*) and Nova and Speedball (stars of their own short-lived series) are summoned from comic limbo by a new, mysterious character with an agenda of his own. The first laugh occurs when the mysterious individual turns out to be a skate-boarding martial artist with the jolly name of Night Thrasher! Maybe it means something different in the USA. Night Thrasher's sister Silhouette also joins the cast, a plucky young thing who melts into the shadows and reappears to beat up bad guys with her crutches. Yep, a paraplegic streetfighter. Oh well. The stunning idiocy of these two characters aside, the book's kind of fun, in a bogus way, lots of light-hearted superheroic hi-jinks, and when you think you've got its tone sussed it turns around and bites you.

An example is the sequence in 20, when Marvel Boy, Vance Astrovik, has to deal one time too many with his abusive father, and retaliates with his telekinetic powers. Rather than the usual cliché of 'Oh no! What was I thinking? I stopped myself just in time!', Vance lets dad have it full force... and Astrovik senior dies next issue. 21 also sees the additions to the team of Rage (briefly of *The Avengers*, until his true age was revealed) and Darkhawk, from another failed title. In 'Nothing But The Truth' (22–25) Marvel Boy is arrested, tried and convicted for negligent homicide, and interestingly is shown as having the maturity to accept and face the consequences of his actions, preventing the other New Warriors from breaking him out. The sub-plot concerning Night Spanker's agenda is resolved concurrently with Marvel Boy's trial. It's a tedious business involving an ancient cult whose female members are assigned to have children by Americans to fulfil a higher destiny, blah, blah. It's Vance's trials, literal and otherwise, that stick in the mind.

Bagley quits the series after 25, but Darick Robertson proves a capable replacement. 28 gives us yet another team member, or possibly two, as the young man and woman who share the Turbo costume and persona climb aboard. In 36 the incarcerated Vance Astro decides to change his *nom de guerre* to Justice, and starts seeking that same commodity for his fellow-prisoners, trying to change the reform system from within. The next significant story is 'Time and Time Again' (43–50), wherein the main Warriors are scattered in time and space,

courtesy of old Nova foe the Sphinx. A team of emergency reserve Warriors, including Dagger (*sans* her partner Cloak), Powerpax (oldest of the Power Pack, having stolen his sibling's powers), Timeslip, Powerhouse, Helix, Bandit and Hindsight Lad – that last an unkind parody of the fanboy stereotype – are called in to assist. During the action, Justice is thrown into the recent past of his own family, and discovers the reasons why his father became an abuser. Does he try and alter the course of events, saving his mother years of misery but perhaps preventing his own birth, or does he let history take its course?

Shortly after, both Nicieza and Robertson left the title. Evan Skolnick and Patrick Zircher did their best, but the decline was already in place. Desperate measures such as inducting the Scarlet Spider, in an attempt to tie into the 'Maximum Clonage' hoo-hah, were not well received by readers already sick of the Spider-Clone business. The one entertaining issue, however, was 66, 'The Speedball Revenge Squad', a light-hearted issue dealing with our bouncing buddy's inadvertent reunion with all the foes from his solo title – and Niels, the Bouncing Cat – during a visit to his home town. That was about the last hurrah for *New Warriors*, but the team still pops up in other Marvel titles, angling for a comeback.~HS

Collection: New Warriors (reprints issues 1–4)

THE NEW WAVE
Eclipse: *14 issues, 1986–1987*

Fairly uninspired superhero fare from the period when Eclipse came close to being a major player in the market. The Mindy Newell plots were mostly clichéd and never anything special, but some issues have early art from creators who were to go on to greater things, including Ty Templeton, Erik Larsen and Rob Liefeld.~JC

NEW YORK: YEAR ZERO
Eclipse: *4-issue miniseries 1988*

There are initial allegories to the Vietnam war as soldier Chester Brian, used to surviving on his ingenuity, returns from war on Venus to a hostile New York. It's a place where snipers are common, and the haves spend vast amounts of money on protection from the have-nots. Brian lucks into a job, but it comes with a high danger level. Uniformly poor covers by American artists probably prevented many from seeing the gorgeous and detailed interior art of Juan Zannotto. He enjoys illustrating his military hardware, and brings a real filthy quality to his street scenes. Ricardo Barriero's script throws in dozens of decent ideas, yet they're more diversions from a very thin, but action-packed plot. Anyone who enjoys gun-toting action heroes should sample *New York:*

Year Zero. There are guns and explosions aplenty, and they're better drawn than most.~FP
Recommended: 1–4

NEWMEN
Image: *24 issues + 1994 to date*

An alien race called The Keep have created the nu-gene, which gives some people abilities beyond those of normal humans. Having released the gene on Earth, they return from time to time to harvest the latest crop of superpowered beings as slaves. The Newmen are all young people affected by the gene, gathered together by the Proctor to repel The Keep when they next visit.

Most of the series depends for its dynamism on the conflict within the group as they come to terms with what they are. First appearing in 'Extreme Prejudice', *Newmen* 9–11 are part of the 'Extreme Sacrifice' crossover story-line; 20's conclusion was part of the 'Babewatch' crossover that was also the prelude to the 'Extreme Destroyer' crossover (see the pattern?) At this point the series went into hiatus while the *New Force* miniseries attempted to generate new interest in the constantly bickering team. Written throughout by Eric Stephenson (though created by Rob Liefeld), the premise is far too close to that of The X-Men to be comfortable – a teen group hated and feared by mere humans whom they seek to protect etc, etc. With 21 Chris Sprouse and Al Gordon brought a fresh, clean look to the series, with several nods to Alex Toth, which might augur well if Stephenson can continue the improvement also evident in the scripts.~NF
Collection: Newmen (1–4)

NEXT MAN
Comico: *4 issues 1985*
Comic Company A: *1 issue 1993*

A Vietnam soldier preserved after a near-fatal explosion is revived twenty years later, having been genetically altered. Minimalist plotting and artwork. The Comic Company A issue was to have been Comico's fifth issue.~FP

John Byrne's NEXT MEN
Dark Horse: *31 issues (0–30) 1992–1994*

The scene for *Next Men* is set in the one-shot *2112* graphic novel, highlighting the career of one cadet, Thomas Kirkland. His apprenticeship pits him against Sathanas, who leads a large band of mutated human beings, the results of genetic experiments a century previously known as the Next Men Project. It's thought that Sathanas is destroyed at the end, but the reality is that he's journeyed back in time to the present day. That's where *Next Men* takes off, but not before some

appearances in *Dark Horse Presents* 54–57, reprinted in the zero issue.

The plot concerns five youngsters with special abilities who were part of an unauthorised superproject funded by Senator Hilltop, with a mysterious ally. The youngsters escape, are separated, then reunited in an organisation run by 'Control', who gives them costumes and codenames – Sprint, Brawn, Bounce, Scanner and Hardbody. 7 has them investigating a group of Russian mutants at the behest of the Russian government. These characters are their counterparts indoctrinated with Communist ideals, and unhappy at the way the country has been developing recently. 13 starts a more character-based story inspecting relationships between the Next Men, specifically sexual tension disrupting the team, while the youngest member, Sprint, wants to learn more about his biological mother, and travels to New York to do so. There he's exploited by the head of a comic company, who sees extensive profits to be had by publishing a comic about a real superhero. The others follow, but their new-found fame leads to complications, most particularly a case of murder relating to their original escape.

From 19 Byrne begins writing four-issue story arcs, numbered as such on the covers, which also continue the regular numbering of the series. The first, 'Faith', sees the team joining an underground community of homeless people, and Mike Mignola contributes pages of Hellboy to 21. More comic characters come to life during 'Power', most pertinently the evil Dr Trogg, but also a guest shot from Concrete, manifestations created by a young woman whose latent powers have recently surfaced. 'Lies' (27–30) reveals that all is not what most believed to be the case. Overall, *Next Men* is a masterful exercise in sub-plots and subterfuge, full of twists and turns. Initial confusion will give way to understanding, as John Byrne is at his best, with excellent writing and great illustration.~HY
Recommended: 0–30
Collections: Collection 1 (1–6), Collection 2 (7–12), *Faith* (1–4), *Fame* (13–18), *Power* (1–4)

NEXUS
Capital: *Series one 3 issues 1981–1982, series two 6 issues 1983–1984*
First: *74 issues (7–80) 1985–1991, 4-issue miniseries ('The Next Nexus') 1989*
Dark Horse: *One-shot 1992 ('The Origin'), 4-issue miniseries ('The Liberator') 1992–1993, 3-issue miniseries ('Alien Justice') 1992–1993, 4-issue miniseries ('The Wages Of Sin') 1995, One-shot ('Nexus Meets Madman') 1996, 4-issue miniseries ('Exterminator's Song') 1996*

The first *Nexus* series was a black and white magazine that introduced a mysterious, immensely powerful hero and the planet where he lived, Ylum. Nexus is driven by terrible dreams to kill mass murderers. In telling his new lover, Sundra Peale, the story of his life, Nexus explains that his first execution was that of his father, Theodore Hellpop, who had destroyed a whole planet before escaping with his wife to Ylum, where Horatio was born. Writer Mike Baron swiftly introduces Dave, a Thune alien, the groups of political refugees led by Tyrone, and the bodiless heads which have been used to generate fusion energy by evil slavers. Beautifully drawn by Steve Rude, from the very beginning this was an excellent foray into science-fiction territory, albeit with a costumed central character.

The second Capital series was comic-sized and in colour, and introduced Judah Maccabee, The Hammer, who has modelled his life on Nexus and happens to be Dave's son. Briefly relieved of his head by the slaver Clausius, Judah joins the regular cast as Sundra is revealed as an ex-spy for the Cohesive Web, the Earth-based government. A drugged Nexus is seduced by Web ambassador Ursula Imada, and, as Nexus continues his murderous crusade far afield, trouble is brewing on Ylum as Tyrone seeks political power. Nexus always had a humorous side (though whenever Clonezone the Hilariator started cracking jokes this mysteriously evaporated) and the guest appearance of Badger (6–8) set the tone for the comic adventures of Judah that punctuate the more serious story-lines.

Tortured by the executions he must undertake, Nexus tries surgery to keep himself awake, but the resultant insomnia nearly destroys him, until he answers the dream calling him to kill the President of the Web (16). He's further shaken when Ursula turns up with their twin daughters. Locking himself away with his new family, protected by the Quatro Assassin, Kreed, Nexus is unprepared for Judah and Sundra's intrusion and the subsequent discovery of the secret behind his powers that causes the dreams in 18 and 19.

Steve Rude needed the occasional guest penciller (including Eric Shanower and Keith Giffen) to keep up a monthly title, but with 27 he took a longer leave of absence, returning to 33. Mike Mignola, José Luis Garcia-Lopez and Rick Veitch all filled in as Baron's plots became more and more convoluted. Judah becomes bodyguard to Ursula, and the twins, Nexus and Sundra, get back together, but Nexus' hit-list still seems never-ending, provoking all sorts of repercussions, and everyone fears him wherever he turns up because they assume he's out to assassinate someone.

Paul Smith draws 37, 38, 43 and 44 to give

Rude more time and Badger makes another appearance in 45–50, culminating in the death of a major character. With 51 Smith becomes the regular penciller, Nexus decides to shove his job as avenging angel, and the race for the presidency of Ylum is in full swing. Tyrone emerges as the victor, and the Merk recruits another Nexus, Stanislaus Korivitsky, as Horatio leaves for Flatlandia. This ties into the Next Nexus miniseries, in which an old enemy's daughters, with Nexus' powers, try to kill Horatio.

Rude returns (58–60) for the first part of the new Nexus' mission, but after his departure the book starts a high turnover of artists which seriously disrupts the quality. In an effort to kick-start things Baron has the new Nexus killing innocents as well as murderers, with the Web blaming Ylum for his murderous sprees. Horatio's old powers are restored in 75. Hugh Haynes draws the last issues of the regular series (72–80), but you miss Rude's smooth, dynamic artwork. Rude's departure seemed to demotivate Baron too, with the humour element all but disappearing from plots that seemed to drag on from issue to issue.

Nexus: The Origin is an all-new retelling of the hero's life by Baron and Rude, in preparation for the title transferring to Dark Horse. When Nexus returned it was in the hands of Stefan Petrucha and John Calimee, and, in 'Nexus The Liberator', considers what happens to the masses when someone kills their leader. Baron and Rude return for 'Alien Justice', in which Nexus must travel to the Thune home world in search of Dave's wife. Baron and Mike Allred co-write 'Nexus Meets Madman', with art by Rude, and it's a delightful if inconsequential episode that doesn't impinge on either of their ongoing plot-lines. 'Executioner's Song' is presented as a miniseries but numbers itself as Nexus 89 in the indicia. It begins with the desecration of Horatio's parents' graves as Michana Loomis goes on a rampage, still upset by her father's execution at his hands.

Throughout Nexus, Baron tried to create a complex universe where Nexus' actions are not only important but where Nexus is part of a society in which freedoms have been hard-won and must be constantly defended. Nexus chooses Ylum as a home precisely because it is in a state of flux, a place where refugees with all sorts of different beliefs gather for refuge. The interplanetary intrigues and personal vendettas that make up most plot-lines keep the level of adventure and excitement high, but the heart of the book is in its rich depiction of misfits and tortured souls, from Horatio himself to Judah and even Ursula. Without Steve Rude, however, Nexus is hard to read. His inspirational artwork lifted the series way above its competitors, and no one else can make the series as resonant as he can.~NF

Recommended: 1–20, 45–50, 'The Next Nexus', 'Nexus Meets Madman', 'Alien Justice', 'Executioner's Song'

Collections: Nexus vol 1 (1–5), vol 2 (6–10)

NFL SUPERPRO
Marvel: One-shot 1991, 12 issues 1991–1992

Let's quote from Marvel's blurb: 'Phil Grayfield's career as a pro football player ended soon after it began due to injuries. Now, as a result of a fantastic accident, he has a new career, as a super-powered hero who uses his amazing abilities to fight crime and defend the sport he loves from those forces that would seek to corrupt it.' Not a joke, not a parody, not a hint of tongue wedged in cheek. Redefines the term 'low concept'.~WJ

NICK FURY, AGENT of S.H.I.E.L.D.
Marvel: Series one 18 issues 1968–1971, Series two 47 issues 1989–1993

Splitting Strange Tales into two books gave Jim Steranko the chance to write and draw full-length S.H.I.E.L.D. stories at his psychedelic best. Frankly, his plots rarely made much sense but are vindicated by the sheer style that made 1–3 and 5 seminal comic-book works. They're reprinted as two issues of Nick Fury Agent of S.H.I.E.L.D. Special Edition. Sadly the creators who followed attempted to mimic his work, but Steranko is inimitable.

Gary Friedrich wrote most of the succeeding first series issues, yet the run suffers from a lack of continuity: for instance, Countess Valentina and Laura Brown are unaware or unconcerned that Nick Fury dates them in alternate issues. 12–14 are the best efforts but were not enough to stave off cancellation with 15. 16–18 were published a year later as all-reprint issues of the S.H.I.E.L.D. stories in Strange Tales 136–144.

Not once in forty-seven issues does the second series strike the right chord. S.H.I.E.L.D. distinguishes itself from the staple diet of comic-book superheroes when focused on the espionage/James Bond approach. This run gorges on aliens, resurrected characters, excessively recurring villains and superpowered S.H.I.E.L.D. agents. Bob Harras' first six issues continue in the same questionable vein he initiated in Nick Fury vs S.H.I.E.L.D. Relief arrives in the form of D.G.Chichester, who scripts most tales to 31. It is no coincidence that the series' best run, in 20–23, 25 and 26, is accompanied by Jackson Guice on pencils. The story is another Red Skull, Baron Strucker and HYDRA conspiracy, but nevertheless just manages to scale the dizzy heights of

mediocrity. The epilogue in 27–29, guest-starring Wolverine, disappoints as Chichester's fight dialogue exerts unreasonable demands on readers' credulity and Ernie Stiner takes over on artwork. A strip less suited to his cartoonish style is hard to imagine. Scott Lobdell's run from 32–37, 40–41 is disastrous, as all pretence of sub-plot, supporting cast and characterisation goes out the window. Gregory Wright handles the swan song (42–47) and achieves something of a resurgence, but he wields his powers of resurrection far too freely.~APS

Recommended: Series one 1–3, 5

NICK FURY vs S.H.I.E.L.D.
Marvel: 6-issue miniseries 1988

Bookshelf-format series in which Bob Harras pens the second most controversial story in the annals of S.H.I.E.L.D. (see Marvel Spotlight 31 for the first). Half the S.H.I.E.L.D. regulars die before 1 starts, as Nick Fury discovers corruption and subterfuge within the organisation in a highly promising first two issues. But Harras loses everyone with a rationale so questionable that even Marvel decided it was necessary to 'correct' portions of the story in the second regular series and the 1994 Fury one-shot. Internally shattered, S.H.I.E.L.D. is disbanded at series' end and not revived until Nick Fury, Agent of S.H.I.E.L.D. (second series) a year later. Paul Neary's polished pencils take no part of the blame.~APS

Collection: Nick Fury Vs S.H.I.E.L.D. (1–6)

THE NIGHT
Amaze Ink: One-shot (0) 1995

Dan Vado and Norman Felchle consistently turn out intelligent superhero action stories when allowed to plot them without the constrictions of company continuity. They're long overdue for a massive hit, and have contrived a title combining two currently popular elements. There's the starkly contrasting shadowy black-and-white-style artwork as used by Frank Miller in Sin City, and the impossibly proportioned hero with even more impossibly proportioned guns. Even better, there's a good story with a nod to the Ditko heroes of yesteryear.~FP

NIGHT FORCE
DC: Series one 14 issues 1982–1983, series two 1 issue + 1996 to date

The mysterious Baron Winters, who never seems to leave his spooky old Washington townhouse with its back garden leading into history, draws to himself people who will be able to help him deal with occult problems whether they like it or not.

Marv Wolfman kicked off the series with a

long story about Vanessa Van Helsing, grand-daughter of the vampire-slayer, who acts as a psychic conduit and is therefore in great demand with various nefarious organisations. Unfortunately the normal world thinks she's mad. To rescue and cure her The Baron recruits Jack Gold, a washed-up journalist whose promising career was cut short by alcohol addiction, and Donovan Caine, a professor of parapsychology. In later stories he uses a serial killer to destroy a strange monster that's imprisoned the inhabitants of an apartment building by taking away their will to resist, and has to call upon an old lover to rescue Vanessa when he sends her on a mission to exorcise the ghosts of Nazi plotters from an old house without seeing it's a trap. In the new series a Persian demon has possessed several young children, who start killing their parents.

Wolfman's scripts are very strong. His characters are by no means perfect – especially the Baron, a fascinating occultist always two steps ahead of the police, who think he's a charlatan. The Baron lies and manipulates freely, and is willing to send his 'force' to their deaths if necessary. The first series was atmospherically illustrated by Gene Colan, using a very light inking technique and relying on colour to bring to life the monstrous acts depicted and suggesting rather than showing most of the violence. The second is by Brent Anderson, and is a little more visceral but generally restrained enough to remain scary.~FJ
Recommended: 11–14

THE NIGHT MAN
Malibu: *23 issues, 1 Annual 1993–1995, 4-issue miniseries 1995–1996*

Created in the same accident that created the Strangers, the Night Man's took a little longer to develop his abilities, largely because he spent months in a coma. When he recovers, Johnny Domino finds that his eyes are extremely light-sensitive, and that he can tune in to the evil thoughts of those nearby. Given that he's not got much else in the way of abilities to start with, his one-man war against criminals has interesting and not always favourable repercussions. The ever-changing artists are distracting, although no-one terrible works on the title, but overall *The Night Man* is a decent if inessential superhero title. The miniseries, involving parallel dimensions and assorted mystical mumbo-jumbo, is plain dreadful.~WJ

NIGHT MUSIC
Eclipse: *3 issues 1984*

A collection of rare and early works by P. Craig Russell, whose detailed, highly illustrative style is at once realistic and fantastic. The first issue includes a science-fiction tale from 1979 and adaptations of songs by Mahler, the

second has two stories about dreaming and 'Dance On A Razor's Edge', about the dreams and death of Yukio Mishima. 3 is an adaptation of Rudyard Kipling's *Jungle Book* story, 'The King's Ankus'. Though these are immature works they are not without interest and are still beautifully illustrated.~NF
Recommended: 3

NIGHT NURSE
Marvel: *4 issues 1972–1973*

This series, by Jean Thomas and artist Win Mortimer, tells the story of three young nurses. There's a plucky black girl working her way out of the ghetto (oy vey!), a spoiled débutante slumming in the working world, and a nice middle-class blonde girlie. They face the hazards of everyday life on the wards: stopping terrorists from taking over the operating theatres, being summoned to care of elderly recluses in spooky Gothic mansions, being propositioned by hunky visiting millionaire playboys… yeah, right, that happens all the time! In the category of 'So bad it's a must-have item' this series, thanks to initially limited print runs and the fact that most readers destroyed it in disgust, is now achieving some desirability as a kitsch collector's item.~HS

NIGHT STREETS
Arrow: *5 issues 1986–1987*

A well conceived and produced story about criminal life in an un-named city. It's a place protected by the Black Dahlia, a vigilante in fishnets, and has a protection racket run by a six-foot tall talking cat with a feral nature. Trouble starts when another organisation attempts to assume the role of Katt and Associates. The high story content prevents excess talking heads becoming boring and more than compensates for the shortcomings of the art, although Mark Bloodworth improves throughout. Unjustly neglected, this puts many more professional titles to shame. Caliber published two collections, and you'll need to buy the second for the conclusion.~FP
Recommended: 1–5
Collections: Night Streets Bk 1 (1–4), *Night Streets* Bk 2 (5 + new material)

NIGHT THRASHER
Marvel: *4-issue miniseries ('Four Control') 1992–1993, 21 issues 1993–1995*

The queue for the most ridiculous name ever bestowed on a comics character starts with Dwayne Taylor, intense poor-little-rich-boy armoured teenager who founded the *New Warriors*. The miniseries is a successful mix of corporate mystery and superhero action as Taylor searches for the person behind a takeover attempt on his family foundation.

1–14 of the ongoing title are bereft of any spark, with the well-intentioned but miserably executed polemic about racial division in 6 typical. Kurt Busiek becomes writer with 15, and improves the title, applying practical solutions to villainy using Taylor's wealth. The final two issues are the best of the series, with Night Thrasher at odds with his charge Rage, a 14-year-old built like the Hulk, unhappy with his lot and reacting the only way he can.~FP

NIGHT ZERO
Fleetway/Quality: *4-issue miniseries 1989*

By the time they reached this old tosh Fleetway/Quality had dredged right through the bottom of the barrel and into the compost beneath as far as *2000AD* material was concerned. With a he-man hero and dealing with the problems of succession in the dystopian Zero City, there's a total lack of inspiration, and, violence apart, it both reads and looks as if it had been produced in the 1950s. It's distressing to consider how many trees died so that this pap could see print on two separate occasions.~WJ

Clive Barker's NIGHTBREED
Epic: *25 issues 1990–1992*

Charged by an otherworldly entity with locating a homeland for monsters on Earth, the Nightbreed travel the remote back streets of North America searching for sanctuary, often encountering other Nightbreed who aren't prepared to follow the leader. 1–4 adapt the *Nightbreed* film, which was Barker on autopilot, and those are the best issues. A contender for Most Ridiculous Character Seen In Comics is the guy who rips out his spine to use it as a lasso in 7. Wouldn't a rope be easier? Gratuitously gory, with an almost child-like desire to shock, there's little to be recommended beyond the violence. A two-part series *Jihad* pits the *Nightbreed* cast against the Cenobites from *Hellraiser*, and is better than any regular issue, with excellent art from Paul Johnson.~WJ

NIGHTCAT
Marvel: *One-shot 1991*

This one-shot was the result of a deal struck by Marvel with one Jacqueline Tavares, a singer who thought that dressing up as a superhero would enhance her career. Oops. Using her likeness, but presumably not her actual biography, the Mighty Marvel Monolith created a comic only Helen Keller could love, exhuming every cliché in the comic to generate another feline *femme fatale* in a Marvel Universe already overstocked with same. The real life Ms. Tavares allegedly sued Marvel for failure to deliver the further adventures of *Nightcat*, as stipulated in her contract. She should have sued them for ending her career by putting her in this piece of tat in the first place.~HS

NIGHTCRAWLER
Marvel: *4-issue miniseries 1985–1986*

This inoffensive little tale has Kurt, then of the X-Men, now of Excalibur, subject to a freak accident in the X-Men's Danger Room. He's transported to a bizarre dimension where there are miniature versions of the X-Men called Bamfs. With hindsight Dave Cockrum and Joe Rubenstein's script and art seem a little dated, but the light-hearted tone makes this worth a read if you've nothing else in the house.~TP

NIGHTMARE
Marvel: *4-issue miniseries 1994–1995*

Edvard is the monarch of the Realm of Nightmare, and, as a long-time foe of Doctor Strange, feeds off human terrors. However, when he falls in love with Roxanne, star of countless horror films, he leaves his realm in order to be with her, and this causes disturbance in many quarters. The parts involving Roxanne work very well, as she emerges from her initial romantic daze and realises Edvard is less than pleasant, probably not human, and not at all good for her. The greater part of the story, though, concerns an attempted coup in the Realm and Edvard's plans to establish a base of operations on Earth. The action really doesn't make much sense, as the rules are never clarified – you're told that X (or Y) won the last fight, and you can't really see why, but just have to accept it. It's not Ann Nocenti's best writing. The artwork by Joe Bennett and Mike Witherby meets the needs of the story well: plenty of Gothic extravagance and a truly frightening Edvard. All in all, it's above average, but the plotting weaknesses make for a frustrating read when it's clear that Ann Nocenti can do so much better.~FC

NIGHTMARES ON ELM STREET
Innovation: *6 issues 1991–1992*

New stories for those who can't get enough of Freddy Krueger and his bloody habits. Successfully conveys the remorselessly nasty spirit of the films, but much better is the three-part *A Nightmare on Elm Street: the Beginning*, in which Freddy's early days are recounted.~WJ

NIGHTMASK
Marvel: *12 issues 1986–1987*

Using a character who lives and operates in dreams there's always the option of ethereal left-field encounters and shaded revelations, and so it is here. Directionless from the off, when the Haitian in the supporting cast suddenly becomes involved in voodoo you know the barrel is being scraped. The only surprise is why the editors let this pelt headlong into mediocrity so swiftly.~FP

NIGHTSTALKERS
Marvel: *18 issues 1992–1994*

On the face of it, teaming three of *Tomb Of Dracula*'s supporting cast as hunters of the supernatural wasn't the brightest idea for a series, but it works. Frank Drake is Dracula's descendant, Hannibal King is a vampire who resists his craving for human blood and Blade is a single-minded vampire hunter. Given to fighting among themselves as much as with supernatural menaces, this is the best of the *Midnight Sons* titles, largely due to writer D.G. Chichester's gruesome imagination and facility for dialogue over the first eleven issues. 14 and 15 are *Siege of Darkness* chapters and 16–18 returns more characters familiar *to Tomb of Dracula* readers, and ends the series in style.~FP

NIGHTVEIL
AC: *7 issues 1984–1985, 1 Special 1988*

The sorceress member of Femforce stars in solo adventures, meant to be trippy and supernatural, but mostly lame and clichéd. The special had a rather nice Mike Kaluta cover. Two spin-off issues of *Nightveil's Cauldron Of Horror* appeared in 1989 and 1990, black and white 1950's horror reprints with our heroine appearing in a framing sequence.~HS

NIGHTVISION
Rebel: *3-issue miniseries 1993*
London Night: *One-shot 1996*

The night vision is Blythe's ability to instantly recognise other vampires. Alluring and deadly, she's on a quest to deal with them all. David Quinn's distinctive narrative is at times poetic, but more often tiresome, and occasionally wanders up his own arse in a succession of hollow soundbites like 'Fetish freaks in the Hollywood babe machine'. The art is standard seductive babes for boys too young to buy a proper sex mag.~WJ

NIGHTWATCH
Marvel: *12 issues 1994–1995*

Pity poor Kevin Trench, Nightwatch. Designed as a blatant copy of Spawn, he encounters a succession of ridiculously named villains, while his supporting cast becomes ever more ill-proportioned. The short run indicates that *Spawn* readers obviously didn't fall for the con. After his title was cancelled it's likely that Nightwatch went into demolition, as he averaged the destruction of one building per issue.~WJ

NIGHTWING
DC: *4-issue miniseries 1995, 3 issues + 1996 to date*

The miniseries begins with Dick Grayson's resignation from the superhero business, but he receives a mysterious letter that suggests that his parents may have been killed by someone other than the man he's always thought responsible. He puts on a new costume and heads off to the despotic country of Kravia, where his family, the Flying Graysons, had apparently seen something they shouldn't have during a circus tour. Written by Denny O'Neil, it's about tidying up the past and clearing the way for a new life. So Dick has to come to terms with his parents' deaths, his upbringing, his relationship with the Batman and what he wants to do next. Initially, it reads poorly. However, it does its job without fanfare, though the artwork, by Greg Land, is clunky and unattractive.

In his own series after many years, during which a very devoted fan base has built up, Dick Grayson moves into Bludhaven, a place in need of a superhero: it's had a corrupt government for a long time and has now become home to Black Mask and his (large) criminal organisation. Written by Chuck Dixon, who's made a career of action-adventure strips, and drawn by Scott McDaniel, it's got the makings of a rather dull, common-or-garden superhero title. It's going to take much more than this to prove that Nightwing can have life beyond the Teen Titans or outside the shadow of The Batman.~NF
Collection: Ties That Bind (miniseries 1–4)

NINA'S ALL-TIME GREATEST...
Dark Horse: *One-shot 1992, one-shot 1994*

Nina Paley's underground style strips have 'self-publishing' written all over them. This isn't a personal mini-comic, however, and no matter how much these strips resemble the comix of the mid-1970s, there's no bite whatsoever. In fact, despite their charm and high degree of craft, their observations on cartooning and sexual politics are crass and somewhat asinine.~SW

NINE PANEL GRID
James Pyman: *6 issues + 1994 to date*

The title is the format for every page in this self-published comic. Each issue contains a chapter of the meandering ongoing 'Greetings From Asbury Park', the story of a couple taking a trip to Asbury Park and hanging out there. He's English, she's American and it's all very dull. It's combined with individual short observation and mood pieces in which Pyman wanders the streets of London, or details a night in the pub as seen through the eyes of a drinker. As much as anything *Nine Panel Grid* appears to be a form of story-telling discipline for Pyman, whose art progresses from issue to issue, although perhaps not as much as he might like. For someone basing his stories in the everyday world, his stiff and often incorrect figurework doesn't yet match his ambition and requires more attention.~FP

1963

Image: *6-issue miniseries 1993*

It's a matter of record that having written the ground-breaking *Watchmen*, Alan Moore came to despair of the grim and downbeat superhero comics it spawned. Here he takes the opposite tack, by pretending it's 1963 (right down to fake ads and editorial pages), to produce a pastiche of early Marvel comics in all their enjoyable simplicity. What elevates this beyond affectionate parody is that while aping the early Marvel style – artists Steve Bissette, Dave Gibbons, John Totleben and Rick Veitch obviously have a fine old time imitating Jack Kirby and Steve Ditko – Moore brings his own plots and characters to the party. Each issue spotlights different characters, maintaining that they're issues of an ongoing run, complete with footnotes referring back to hilariously titled non-existent comics and Marvel-style letters pages. The issues can easily be read individually, but chronologically they're titled *Mystery Incorporated, No One Escapes The Fury, Tales Of The Uncanny, Tales From Beyond, Horus Lord Of Light* and *The Tomorrow Syndicate*. The best stories are those with but a superficial similarity to Marvel characters, such as the gloriously beat Tibetan-trained mystic Johnny Beyond in *Tales From Beyond*. The clash of 1960s beatspeak with New Age waffle from the 1990s provides both the funniest moments and the best story. The ongoing plot running through all issues was leading towards a giant-sized issue contrasting the 1963 heroes with the 1993 Image counterparts, to be drawn by Jim Lee. Sadly, the lazy bugger never got around to it.~WJ

Recommended: 1–6

1984

Warren: *29 issues 1978–1983*

This magazine-format title bills itself as 'illustrated adult fantasy', which here translates as 'porn with a science-fiction theme' or 'Hey! If I set this in the future or another planet, I can cram in any amount of rape, torture, bestiality, cannibalism and compliant robot women, and claim it's daring and progressive fantasy.' This really is a foul series, reeking with hatred and resentment for women and sex – and apparently convinced that these attitudes are normal and universal. Let's take 'Little Beaver' in 26 as an example. A group of men take a pubescent girl, place a bomb inside her vagina, and send her to the enemy in the expectation that she will be raped by the commanding officer, thus triggering the bomb. And the style of the artwork (and previous 'Little Beaver' stories) leave you in no doubt that this is intended to titillate, which is deeply frightening. Presumably there are men who can read this comic without feeling ashamed to be male, but one wouldn't care to meet them. Admittedly, not all of the comic is that extreme, and many stories aren't porn at all, though they're all weak and poorly told. In the whole series, there's only one story genuinely worth reading, 'The Missionary' by Carlos Gimenez in 15, which makes a good point about the fixation on pain and suffering in certain aspects of Christianity. Are there other reasons for opening any of these issues? Well, if you must, there's artwork by Alex Nino (every issue), Richard Corben (1–8) and Frank Thorne (7–29). And let's not forget Peter Hsu, whose 'Ariel Hart' stories (22, 26) are easily the most explicit in the series, and whose frankness deserves some kind of recognition – it's not every artist who would want the world to know that he's a graduate of the Barbie Doll School of Anatomy, and has only the vaguest idea of how the female pelvic area is put together. The title is updated to 1994 with 11, but avoid.~FC

NINJA HIGH SCHOOL

Antarctic: *2 issues 1986*
Eternity: *40 issues (1–3, 3½, 4–39) 1988–1993*
Antarctic: *14 issues + (40–54), 2 Yearbooks, 1994 to date*

This is a spoof and celebration of Manga created by Ben Dunn, who writes and draws almost every issue. At the centre of the story is Jeremy Feeple, a student at Quagmire High School. In the space of one day, two young women arrive in town, each determined to marry him: there's Ichi Kun, heir to a ninja empire, who has been ordered to marry him as a condition of her inheritance; and there's Asrial, princess of a furry alien race, whose advisors tell her she must marry Jeremy in the name of intergalactic peace. Does Jeremy have a say? Of course not. His job is to be shiningly innocent, and to be fought over and taken hostage. It's a delightful spoof, handled with a light touch and lots of imagination. The freshness does fade after a while – from about 14 on – as the plots become more earnest and the surprises less frequent, though the comic is still above average, with entertainment in every issue.~FC

Recommended: 1–13

Collections: Beans, Steam And Automobiles (8–11), Blood And Irony (20–23), The Ides Of May (24–27), Long Distance Battle (32–35), Ninja High School (1–3½), Of Rats And Men (12–15), Shades Of Grey (Antarctic 1–4), That Old Black Magic (4–7), Sheesh, Boom, Bah (28–31), The Toughest Contest In The World (16–19)

NINJAK

Valiant: *28 issues (2 x 0, 1–26), 1 Yearbook 1993–1995*

Independently wealthy Colin King maintains a dual career as the crimefighting Ninjak, concentrating his efforts on infiltrating seemingly impregnable secret organisations.

As his name suggests, he's an accomplished swordsman and martial artist, and is also adept at espionage. He often works, reluctantly, under the sponsorship of Neville Allcott and the British secret service. This is all established in 1–4, written by Mark Moretti and drawn by the team of Joe Quesada and Jimmy Palmiotti, and together with the Moretti-written and drawn 0 and 00 issues, running through his background and origins, they're the best of *Ninjak*. Beyond that point it's not until 11 that a regular new writing team of Dan Abnett and Andy Lanning take over, with artist Andrew Currie joining them in 13. The trio's dry run in 7 is the best of their work here, and no sooner have they settled in than they're displaced by José Gonzales, who lasts until the final issue. Lack of any cohesive direction is a constant problem, with almost every issue changing one member of the creative team. While *Ninjak* never plummets into mediocrity, there's little inspiration beyond the early issues either. The series is abruptly cancelled mid-plot.~FP
Recommended: 0, 00, 1–4

NO DUCKS!
Last Gasp: *2 issues 1978–1980*

Anthropomorphic underground that Walt certainly wouldn't approve of! Packaged, like *Commies From Mars*, by Tim Boxell, a lack of big names makes this even patchier than a normal underground, but Hunt Emerson and J. Michael Leonard offer good fun, and issue 2's Moebius parody by Steve Leialoha is well worth searching out.~NF

NO GUTS OR GLORY
Fantaco/Tundra: *One-shot 1991*

Set a challenge to produce a twenty-four-page in twenty-four hours with no prior thought, Kevin Eastman did just that. Good for him. To then package the resulting old tosh and try to sell it at $3 a pop shows a more than a little cheek.~WJ

NO HOPE
Slave Labor: *9 issues 1993–1995*

Jeff Levine's cartooning is basic, and his stories are often unrounded, dealing as they do with everyday incidents, but there is something curiously gripping about *No Hope*. It's well-dug ground – going to punk gigs, having a dead-end job, drinking too much, watching TV – but Levine injects moments of self-revelation into his ongoing diary of pointless youth. With 7 his style changes dramatically from increasingly smooth cartoony figures to rough, brush-rendered portraits and street scenes, relying more on observation. From this point the stories cease to centre around the same characters and the book loses cohesion, but there's some good drawing, particularly in the dialogueless strips.~FJ
Recommended: 3, 8

NOCTURNAL EMISSIONS
Vortex: *4 issues 1991–1993*

Cross-pollinate prime, late 1960s S. Clay Wilson and Mary Fleener at her most oblique and you still don't have an adequate handle on Fiona Smyth's work. *Nocturnal Emissions* is a forum for her curious mix of graffiti and underground-style stories. Two continuing series begin in 1. 'Toad in the Hole' is a sort of 'acid in wonderland' trip strip, while 'The Mannequin' chronicles the amorous misadventures of city girl Gert in Nevada. As well as some other aggressively idiosyncratic strips, a third series, 'Skin Of Fate', begins in 3, which involves protagonists Pussy & Roach and a much-sought-after human tattoo-hide.~SW

THE NOCTURNALS
Bravura: *6 issues 1995*

Written and drawn by Daniel Brereton as part of Malibu's creator-owned Bravura line, this is a pulp-influenced tale of 'monsters' who have escaped from The Narn K Corporation's laboratory where they were created. Doc Horror leads a group comprising Komodo, Halloween Girl, Polychrome, Firelion, Starfish and The Gunwitch who are caught between factions fighting for control of the Mob and hunted by Mister Fane and the Corporation. Perhaps not completely at ease with scripting, Brereton nevertheless has a good ear for dialogue and has created a strong story that benefits enormously from his atmospheric painted artwork.~NF
Recommended: 1–6

NOCTURNE
Marvel UK: *4-issue miniseries 1995*

A film-maker discovers an old costume that grants him extraordinary powers, but that seems to be taking over his mind. Very stylishly drawn by José Fonteriz, fresh from his sojourn on *XXX Women*, and written by Dan Abnett. This enjoyable sequel to the old Night Raven character was sadly a victim of one of Marvel UK's periodic cutbacks and never really received a fair chance at distribution.~HS

NOMAD
Marvel: *4-issues miniseries 1990–1991, 25 issues 1992–1994*

Possessed of a complicated background (explained in the first issue of the ongoing series), Nomad appeared periodically from *Captain America* 282 as Cap's costumed assistant. The costume has gone by the time of this well-conceived miniseries from Fabian Nicieza, James Fry and Mark McKenna, as Jack Monroe is developed into an armed vigilante with a conscience following a drug trail. Unfortunately it also lands him with an infant, leading to ludicrous scenes as Nomad dukes it out with assorted groups of ne'er-do-wells with a baby strapped to his back. The ongoing series begins well, with Nomad following the peripatetic inclinations of his namesake, but quickly becomes bogged down in crossovers and mundane plots. It takes notice of the title's cancellation for matters to improve with the 'American Dreamers' story in 22–25. Nomad is reunited with his sister to confront his past, but there's plenty who don't want him to have a future. A captivating plot and unpredictable conclusion make it a shame the title was permitted to slip.~FP

NOMAN
Tower: 2 *issues 1966–1967*

The second T.H.U.N.D.E.R. Agent to go solo, Noman can switch his mind from one artificial host body to the next, with one of the androids also having a cloak of invisibility. As with all Tower titles, the art, largely from Ogden Whitney, is excellent but the stories let the comic down.~DWC

NORMALMAN
Aardvark-Vanaheim: 8 *issues 1984–1985*
Renegade: 4 *issues, 1 Annual (9–12) 1985–1987*

Jim Valentino's first major comic series is a protracted satire on the superhero comic. Normalman has been rocketed from Arnold by his parents (only Arnold didn't blow up) to Levram, where he's the only non-superpowered person. The Ultra-Conservative takes exception to this, and Normalman finds himself relying on Sgt Fluffy, Captain Everything, Sophisticated Lady and the Countess of Monte Crisco to get him safely back to Arnold. Each issue concentrates on a particular company or genre (EC in 3, Disney in 4, team comics in 7, Cerebus in 10, American Flagg in 11, Archie in 12), and as parodies go it benefits from having a real story and not relying too much on the same sort of material every issue. It's not hilarious but it is good for a laugh. The series concluded in *Normalman 3-D Annual*, which is a rare comic making good use of 3-D.~NF

Collection: Normalman: The Novel (1–12, Annual)

NORMALMAN – MEGATON MAN
Special
Image: *One-shot 1994*

Jim Valentino and Don Simpson get together to parody the then current state of comics as Megaton Man and Captain Everything (two of the stupidest characters around) decide to join a successful comics universe and make some real money. With assistance from Larry Marder and Bob Burden, who draw their own creations (from *Tales Of The Beanworld* and *Flaming Carrot*) throughout, Valentino and Simpson manage to throw pretty much

everything but the kitchen sink at the issue. Unfortunately, it's only okay, because, fun as it is to see lots of cameos of characters, the targets have been hit so many times before that the script's practically one big cliché (though the Neil Gaiman section's vicious enough).~NF

NORTHSTAR
Marvel: 4-*issue miniseries 1994*

Having gone to such great pains to out Northstar as the first openly gay superhero in *Alpha Flight* 106, Marvel then seemed to change their mind about the whole issue. Their second-string mutant speedster engages in perfectly pedestrian anti-terrorist activities. Leaden.~HS

NOSFERATU
Dark Horse: *One-shot 1991*

Reprint of Phillipe Druillet's extraordinary Gothic adaptation of the Nosferatu legend, drawn in his customary, highly decorative style featuring flowing forms and pattern making. A quintessentially 1970s artist whose work is free-form and original, if sometimes frustratingly visually led, Druillet was introduced to a new audience by *Cheval Noir*.~FJ

NOSFERATU: Plague of Terror
Millennium: 4-*issue miniseries 1991*

Why were people so mad-keen for *Nosferatu* comics in 1991? Millennium pitched in with this series by Mark Ellis and Rik Levins, in which the bald old ghoul is on the rampage once more, in search of attractive victims to bite. Brings nothing new to the vampire genre.~FJ

NOT BRAND ECCH
Marvel: 13 *issues 1967–1969*

'Brand Ecch' was the tongue-in-cheek editorial manner in which Marvel referred to the product of their competitors in the mid-1960s. 1–8 caricature Marvel and occasionally DC superheroes with varying degrees of success. From 9 the page-count increases and the emphasis broadens to encompass general parody. There's pleasure to be derived from seeing the regular Marvel artists lampooning their characters, with Jack Kirby proving surprisingly adept at parodying his own Thor (3) and Fantastic Four (7) origins. Marie Severin's demonstration on how to draw the Marvel way in 13 is hilarious, but the best issue to sample is 7, also including Roy Thomas and Severin's Superman parody.~WJ

NOT QUITE DEAD
Rip Off/Knockabout: 3 *issues + 1993 to date*

Gilbert Shelton has a rightful place among the all-time-great comic creators. His Fabulous Furry Freak Brothers and Fat Freddy's Cat strips, although evolving from the underground comics of the 1960s, have transcended generation gaps to become universal crowd-pleasers, and Shelton's cartooning has developed into an appealing and expressive shorthand. Until *Not Quite Dead*, he'd been recycling his 1960s characters, and the first issue reads like the work of a man trying to create something new, but with little new to say.

Not Quite Dead are the longest dues-serving band in existence, hauling their equipment to whichever dive will provide beer, pizza and a little money. Shelton, with French cartoonist Pic contributing to the art, doesn't really hit the spot in 1, where the one-pagers are okay, but the longer strips string together a succession of punchline gags, and don't work. There's a slight improvement with the second issue, but things really begin to come together in the third, where Shelton plays a variation on the myth of Robert Johnson meeting the Devil at the crossroads. It's sustained, funny, makes a point and bodes well for the future. The cover paintings to all three issues are magnificent.~FP

Recommended: 3

NOVA
Marvel: *Series one 25 issues 1976–1979, series two 18 issues 1994–1995*

Nova was originally conceived as a way to get back to basics, to the freshness and youthful fun of the early Spider-Man. Enter Richard Ryder, who stumbles upon an alien helmet that confers on its wearer superstrength, the gift of flight and sundry other superpowers. Rich is just a student, unsure about his role, lacking in confidence, and finding it hard to explain his late homeworks and mysterious absences while out fighting second-string villains like Diamondhead and The Living Pharaoh, not to mention various heroes who initially mistake his intentions, in the time-honoured Marvel tradition. Marv Wolfman gave Nova an (unintentionally) funny supporting cast full of comedy racial stereotyping. While establishing his own set of villains, Wolfman also had him meeting Thor in 4 and Spider-Man in 12 (continued in *Spectacular Spider-Man* 171). At one point Nova even pops up in the Marvel offices, suggesting they should do a comic about him in one of those uncomfortable 'superheroes are real, kids' scenes. However, there was too much reworking of an old formula and not enough fresh ideas to make the character popular. Sal Buscema's by-numbers artwork didn't help, although latter issues pencilled by Carmine Infantino are an improvement.

Marvel decided to have another go at the character following the success of the New Warriors, in which he appeared with new powers and a new costume. It was unlikely there was a great deal of fan recognition out there so they might as well have created another character altogether.~FJ

Nth MAN
Marvel: *16 issues 1989–1990*

As strange a comic as Marvel has ever produced, being partly a war title, partly a superhero title, and partly a treatise on the abuse of power. John Doe and Alfie O'Meagan spent their 1960s pre-teens in an Iowa orphanage, and events shaping them are interspersed with their current situation. Doe has become the Nth Man, a CIA-sponsored ninja, and O'Meagan is a near-omnipotent being able to erase the world's nuclear arsenal with a thought (unwittingly precipitating World War III), and to manipulate time and reality. The bizarre ending is completely in keeping for Larry Hama's continuous story, often confusing, but never dull. You're best advised to start with the first issue.~FP

NUKLA
Dell: *4 issues 1965–1966*

A US spy pilot is blown to smithereens by an enemy's nuclear defences, but manages to re-assemble himself and his plane by sheer force of will. Thus is born Nukla, the atomic spy, in a complete copy of Captain Atom's origin. The stories are predictably poor, but there was some above-average artwork by Dick Giordano, Steve Ditko and Sal Trapani.~SW

NUT RUNNERS
Rip Off: *2 issues 1991*

Bizarre, meandering fantasy about escalated competition between burger and pizza franchises. From the unreadable logo through the confused story to Stuart Immonen being unable to differentiate the look of his cast adequately, this is missable.~FP

OBLIVION
Comico: *2 issues 1995–1996*

When the first issue's editorial is arrogant and foolish enough to claim that 'two talented individuals' have created 'a stunning amalgamation of superheroics, science fiction, espionage and cold war intrigue' it's inviting contradiction. What writer Jack Herman has done is read Jim Starlin's *Dreadstar* and some Clive Barker books, and what artist Andrew Dimitt has done is to watch Clive Barker films when he should have been paying attention in his anatomy classes. Utter bollocks, and derivative bollocks at that.~FP

OBNOXIO THE CLOWN
Marvel: *1 issue 1983*

First seen in *Crazy* magazine, Obnoxio's refreshingly disreputable and cynical, and here we see how he fares in the X-Men's Danger Room, and then against the horrors of jury duty. Alan Kupperberg has fun in both writing and art.~FC

OFFCASTES
Epic: *3-issue miniseries 1993*

Good-looking but derivative coming-of-age science-fiction adventure with thefts – 'scuse me, homages – from Moebius' *Airtight Garage*, *Blade Runner* and *American Flagg* among others.~HS

OH MY GODDESS!
Dark Horse: *Series one, 6 issues 1994–1995, series two 8 issues 1995, Series three 5 issues 1995–1996*

Whimsical humour from writer/artist Kosuke Fujishima about a student who accidentally rings the 'Goddess Help Line' and wishes that the rather personable Belldandy who visits him to grant a boon would stay with him forever. In doing so he neglects to consider the practical ramifications – like the fact that he lives in an all-boys dorm.

Dark Horse screwed up the first series by reprinting stories out of order but rectified this in their collected version. It doesn't actually make that much difference as the stories jump about a lot anyway. Fujishima's artwork is very pretty, more detailed and decorative than many Manga artists, but his humour is weak. The stories revolve around romantic tension and this soon becomes annoying: they're slight and fluffy, and you can usually see the joke coming as fellow-students and Belldandy's sister all jealously work to stop anything more chaste than a kiss.~FJ
Collections: *Oh My Goddess*

OINK
Kitchen Sink: *3-issue miniseries 1995–1996*

Not to be confused with the British humour comic of the same name, this *Oink* is a painted miniseries about a mutant pig seeking revenge on his totalitarian masters. Writer/Artist John Mueller is clearly influenced by the work of Bill Sienkiewicz and particularly Simon Bisley, but his dour début cries out for stronger scripting. Mueller wants to say big things about religion, politics and science, but the emphasis on nihilistic gore simply makes *Oink* an exercise in pretentious Gothic melodrama.~AL
Collection: Heaven's Butcher (1–3)

OKTANE
Dark Horse: *4-issue miniseries 1995*

Broad-based satire extrapolating on the current condition of federal and local government administration and finance, and taking sideswipes at political correctness, rednecks and plenty of other targets along the way. In the middle of all this it's also an action comic, with the dispossessed and downtrodden mad as hell and not going to take it no more, led by a giant black man-machine Oktane. Gerard Jones casts his net far too wide actually to catch anything, and the convoluted pastiche elements prevent this from being a satisfactory action story either – though that isn't the aim. There are plenty of decent ideas lost in the muddle, and some very funny lines and scenes. Oktane constantly revising his background to engage the sympathies of those he's with is amusing, and Gene Ha and Andrew Pepoy's art is excellent throughout. Better *Oktane* than yet another assembly-line superhero, but overall unsatisfying, although Jones' editorial in the final issue should be required reading for all aspiring comic writers and plenty of those already employed as well.~WJ
Collection: Oktane (1–4)

THE OLYMPIANS
Epic: *2-issue microseries 1991–1992*
Oh dear. Superhero parody that's neither big nor clever. The only item of note is that Todd McFarlane inked 2 just before hitting the big time with *Spider-Man*, but I wouldn't bother if I were you.~TP

OMAC
DC: *8 issues 1974–1975, 4-issue miniseries 1991*
Yet another great concept from Jack Kirby. Menial Buddy Blank is transformed into a One Man Army Corps powered through a psychic link with a satellite, Brother Eye. Poor pacing and weak scripting dilute strong plots and artwork in the first series, after which Omac is given a couple of back-up slots in *Warlord* 37–39 and 42–47. John Byrne remains true to Kirby's ideas in the second series, now in black and white, and produces an excellent tale concerning the consequences of dabbling with time. Byrne switches the emphasis with each issue, the most effective being Omac trapped without memory on Earth in the 1930s, and leading a completely different existence. The story is finished in style, and the entirety ties in well with everything established by Kirby with altering anything, but can be understood without reference to any previous issues. A gem.~FP
Recommended: Miniseries 1–4

OMAHA The Cat Dancer
Steeldragon Press: *2 issues 1984–1986*
Kitchen Sink: *18 issues (3–20) 1986–1993*
Fantagraphics: *4 issues + 1994 to date*
You would think that any comic that dealt intelligently and in a thought-provoking manner with gay, bi- and disabled issues, political scandal and attitudes to pornography, mental health and prostitution would be far too 'politically correct' to be fun. You'd also think that with more plot and characters than your average episode of *Coronation Street* it wouldn't have time to fit in frequent sexual encounters between characters. And you'd think an issue packed soap-full of bonking cats, birds and dogs wouldn't be very hot. You'd be wrong on all counts. *Omaha*, which débuted in *Bizarre Sex* 9 (reprinted as *Omaha* 0), is produced by a well-informed, liberal couple who obviously know their way around the bedroom. Its strength lies in the emotional resonance of the characters, which carries you through various dramatic plot twists. For an exotic dancer Omaha sure does get involved in her fair share of kidnappings, murders, secret inheritances, 'dead' parents who suddenly reappear, etc.

Kate Worley writes decidedly superior melodrama and Reed Waller draws the sexiest cat/human hybrids you'll ever see. Whatever *Omaha* lacks in depth it makes up for in honesty as one of the few truly 'adult' sex comics

around. Kitchen Sink reprints of the first two issues are also available, and they also publish two issues of *Images Of Omaha*, collections of illos and short strips by other creators, published to benefit Waller while he was being treated for cancer. See also *Dope Comix* 5.~FJ
Recommended: Series one 3–7, Series two 2, 3
Collections: Vol 1 (1–2 plus material from anthologies), Vol 2 (3–6), Vol 3 (7–10), Vol 4 (11–14), Vol 5 (15–18)

OMEGA the Unknown
Marvel: *10 issues 1976–1977*
A large mute humanoid alien wearing a blue and red costume and endowed with superstrength lands in New York, and is somehow connected with a young boy whose parents are revealed as robots. This was off-the-wall stuff even for the experimental mid-1970s Marvel, but unfortunately only writers Steve Gerber and Mary Skrenes knew what was going on, and they never had a chance to finish the story. Avoid the hack fill-ins (7–8); loose ends are poorly tied up in *Defenders* 76 & 77.~FP

OMEGA MEN
DC: *38 issues, 2 Annuals 1983–1986*
Now only remembered for Lobo's début in 3, there are many worthwhile issues of *Omega Men* later in the run. Introduced in *Green Lantern* 141, they began as spacefaring superheroes united by a desire to free their occupied homeworlds. Led by the utterly charisma-less Primus, the remainder of the crew were from Grim'n'Gritty Central Casting, with the only element of suspense coming from whether or not the serpentoid Demonia would betray the team to their enemies. Long directionless and meandering, the comic finally took off when the creative team of Todd Klein and Shawn McManus arrived with 26. Their decision to sideline the previous heroic archetypes in favour of more interesting secondary characters and well-conceived new ones was wise, as was emphasising science-fiction elements instead of superheroics. When the familiar cast return Klein's given them a personality boost. There's also a varied selection of back-ups focusing on the planets in the Omega Men's solar system, with Steve Parkhouse's contribution in 28 a gem, and Dave Gibbons' dry run for *Watchmen* in 33 also worth a look. Unfortunately McManus' deadline problems mean there are art fill-ins aplenty after 30, with the best being the Dan Spiegle-illustrated mystery story in 32 with not one, but two good revelations. The series' conclusion is excellent, and should bring a glow to the heart of anyone who's been following the plot, but loses some effect when read cold. There's a disappointing coda in *Teen Titans Spotlight* 15.~WJ
Recommended: 26–30, 32–34, 38

THE ONE
Epic: *6-issue limited series 1985–1986*

The first series to seriously deconstruct the superhero and, by Alan Moore's own admission, a major influence on *Watchmen*, although largely ignored by the public when released. Rick Veitch's brutal black and white art and savage scripting weave an epic tale of Nazi genetics, New Age mysticism and superhero psychosis. The USA goes to war with the Soviet Union using superheroes instead of atomic bombs, but with equally devastating results. As the protagonists learn that they are genetically enhanced beings they start to question everything from their emotions to their country's motives, with gruesome results. The story's strengths lie in the interweaving of ordinary people caught in circumstances beyond their control with that of the *übermenschen* flying around oblivious to the destruction they cause. Throw in a giant killer rat and you've got a classic! Veitch's covers are masterpieces of design, using familiar icons – coke cans, washing powder boxes – to create a unique look, and his interior art portrays leaders and politicians as horrific caricatures reminiscent of Gilray. Grotesquely funny and chillingly realistic, *The One* is essential reading, but not for the delicate.~TP
Recommended: 1–6
Collection: The One (1–6)

ONE-FISTED TALES
Slave Labor: *10 issues 1990–1994*

Sadly, the funniest thing about *One-Fisted Tales*, the humorous, sexy anthology, is its title. That, and the joke brown paper cover on issue 1. The quality of the art lets it down most of all: badly-drawn, anatomically incorrect people getting it on don't get most of us hot under the collar. There's a Cherry story in 3, and 8 has a particularly pointed, if unerotic and poorly drawn, piss-take of Madonna's *Sex*.~FJ

ONE MILE UP
Eclipse: *2 issues 1991–1992*

There's a Manga and Robert Heinlein feel to this prematurely cancelled tale of armoured federation troopers protecting the galaxy. From the promising artwork one might have expected to see more of Shepherd Hendrix.~WJ

ONYX OVERLORD
Epic: *4-issue miniseries 1992–1993*

A tale of Moebius' Airtight Garage, with story by Moebius but script and art by others. Two characters are trying to save the Airtight Garage from the Onyx Overlord, but their efforts are hampered by the fact that they've stumbled into an area of alternate realities, which basically means a lot of rushing around,

leaping from steam trains while pterodactyls fly overhead. The artwork's attractive, particularly the colouring, but the story is weak and muddled.~FC

OPEN SEASON
Renegade: *6 issues 1986–1988*
Strawberry Jam: *1 issue (7) 1989*

Domestic comedy that begins with the unprepossessing Jim moving into a new flat at the invitation of Cliff. Jock of the Year Cliff neglected to mention this to already-in-place flatmate Robin, a woman with the ability 'to piss people off with little effort at almost any time'. *Open Season* is an impressively mature title, as creator Jim Bricker brings a hint of Jules Feiffer and more than a little Berke Breathed (implicitly acknowledged) to both his art and his writing. He takes on board more influences as the title progresses, and having sketched his cast exceedingly well from the off, he manoeuvres them effortlessly and mercilessly through plots that reveal different and surprising facets of each. The series was briefly adapted for the stage (although a one-shot adapting the play was solicited but never published). Also of note are back-up strips by the equally talented and largely unknown Basilio Amaro (2) and Doug Gray (7).~FP
Recommended: 2, 3, 5–7

OPEN SPACE
Marvel: *4 issues 1989–1990*

Coming in a period when many companies were toying with the idea of science-fiction anthologies, this one had little to rave about. There is a nice Steve Yeowell-drawn strip in 1 but nothing else of note.~TP

OPTIC NERVE
Drawn and Quarterly: *3 issues + 1995 to date*

Springing from the self-publishing scene, Adrian Tomine's *Optic Nerve* is a refreshing and stimulating title. The comic consists mostly of vignettes of relationships and tantalising glimpses into lives, told with a unique detachment. Imagine Edward Hopper as a cartoonist. Tomine is a also a skillful artist, drawing in a number of styles, and each issue is enjoyably varied. A collection of all seven previously published minicomics titled *32 Stories* is also available. Tomine is a talent to watch.~DAR
Recommended: 1–3

ORBIT
Eclipse: *3 issues 1990*

Adaptations of prose fiction to comics generally result in dashed expectations. To those who know the stories the thrill of seeing them visualised is usually offset by the disappointment incurred by the necessary contractions. Those unfamiliar with the original work have very little reason for sampling, leaving only staunch fans of the artists concerned likely to be happy. So it is with *Orbit*, in which stories originally published in *Isaac Asimov's Science Fiction Magazine* are realised by artists of the quality of John Bolton and Tom Yeates. Both artists feature in 3, along with John Estes illustrating one of Asimov's better-known stories 'The Last Question', making the best sample.~WJ

Masamune Shirow's ORION
Dark Horse: *6-issue limited series 1992–1993*

Over-exaggerated, vomit-inducing, saccharine whimsy is blended with the Manga standbys of scientific technobabble and mystically summoned demons for a story set in the Orion galaxy. Shirow's artwork is adept in both cartoon and pseudo-realistic modes, but the slapstick Japanese humour doesn't translate well, and his cutesy heroine Seska is irritating beyond belief. *Orion* is very highly regarded, and the background detail is immense, so those predisposed to Manga might consider investigating, but it won't make any new converts.~WJ
Collection: Orion (1–6)

THE OTHERS
Image: *5-issue miniseries (0–4) 1995*

There's this race of humanoids under the Earth, all descended from different kinds of animals. There's a bull, a few dinosaur types, goats, birds etc, so it's rilly cool, and the guys all look like the animals and the chicks are all, like, total babes. Who cares about funny ears when you see their gazongas! And you almost do a couple of times, 'cos there's not much covering their lady bumps. First the animals beat up on the humans, and then on each other, with this big fight between the wolfman and the cockroach in 3. I reckon all the creators must be fourteen 'cos it's mega.~FP

OUR ARMY AT WAR
DC: *301 issues 1952–1977*

As DC's flagship war title, *Our Army At War* not only outlasted its companions (in one form or another), but in Sgt Rock it also presented the genre's most important character. In keeping with their fellow DC war titles 1–80 comprised short one-off strips initially drawn by company stalwarts such as Carmine Infantino, Gil Kane, Bob Oksner and Gene Colan. EC regular Bernie Krigstein was an early contributor, with beautiful work in 8–11, 13 and 14. Gradually the company's regular war-story artists arrived, and issues from 32 on are predominantly drawn by Joe Kubert, Irv Novick, Mort Drucker, Jerry Grandenetti, Russ Heath and the team of Ross Andru and Mike Esposito. As ever, the standout

artist was Drucker, who produced a substantial body of work here in 2, 7, 25, 29, 37, 41, 67, 68, 70–72, 76, 79, 82. 83, 87, 96 and 100. The principal writers were Robert Kanigher, Ed Herron, Bob Haney and Hank Chapman, assuring that pretty much every issue contained entertaining, if rarely exceptional, stories, and artistically there's barely a bad issue among them.

From 61 the title occasionally featured the adventures of Easy Company, and 81's 'Rock Of Easy Company' by Haney, Andru and Esposito starred a Sgt Rocky, and gave a glimpse of what was to come. The real Sgt Rock first appeared two issues later in 'The Rock And The Wall', by the definitive team of Kanigher and Kubert. Over the next few years Rock's colourful battalion was introduced, until Easy Company consisted of Bull Dozer, Zack, Wild Man, Ice Cream Soldier, Jackie Johnson and Little Sure Shot. Rock himself was the perfect Sergeant, gruff but compassionate, possessing a keen battle sense, but ultimately vulnerable, and above all tough!

For the most part Kanigher's early stories were quite realistic, and Easy's new recruits, though never the regulars, suffered from a frighteningly high mortality rate. Occasionally, however, his quirkiness got the better of him, notably in 124, in which Rock is brainwashed into thinking he's a Nazi, and 146, which had a story narrated solely by Easy Company's guns. Kanigher's nadir (or peak, depending on one's taste for the bizarre) was in 162–163, teaming Rock with medieval Viking Prince. 158 had the creation of Rock's nemesis, the Iron Major, named for his metal hand, who would periodically reappear to great effect. Another notable tale starred Easy's only black soldier, Jackie Johnson, an ex-boxer, involved in a fight with the star Nazi sparrer. The anti-racist message was thunderously obvious, right down to the inevitable climax of Jackie having to give his injured opponent a blood transfusion, but the story was no less powerful for it.

As issues prior to 100 had revelled in a succession of fine short stories, back-ups after then were surprisingly mediocre. Notable exceptions were art jobs by Heath (104, 120), Colan (169, 173) and some glorious work by a young Neal Adams in 182, 183 and 186. More significantly, 151 introduced the world to another great Kanigher/Kubert creation, the Enemy Ace, also in 153 and 155, who went on to greater things in *Showcase* and *Star-Spangled War*. Creatively the Sgt Rock strip was largely stable throughout the 1960s. In fact from 83 to 193 Kanigher only missed one issue (86, by Haney). Artistically, Kubert produced a vast body of work, although he, at least, needed the occasional break and Novick (84, 106), Grandenetti (88, 89, 123) and Heath (108, 118) all pitched in. At one point, however, Kubert began work on the 'Green Berets' newspaper strip, which owed a lot to Sgt Rock, and Heath admirably took over for 172, 175, 178, 180–183, 185 and 187, giving a taste of what was to come.

A major turning-point came with Kubert replacing the long-serving Kanigher as editor. While essentially a realistic strip, Sgt Rock had long had its faults, typified by Easy Company's tendency to punch out the enemy on a regular basis in ever more fevered tableaux of fisticuffs. While never less than professional, Kubert's mid-1960s strips had lacked the conviction of his earlier work, and the Heath issues had rather overshadowed him. With 196's 'Stop The War, I Want To Get Off', Kubert, acting as both artist and writer, delivered the series' first significant story. Decidedly unconventional, it was a look at the horror of war through the ages, and was immeasurably enhanced by its emotionally charged art, Kubert's best on the strip so far. From that point on Sgt Rock gradually became more realistic and Kubert's art returned to its typical high quality. It didn't last, though, with editorial duties meaning that Kubert gave way to Russ Heath with 208, although occasionally filling in to great effect (217, 220, 222, 224, 228, 233, 238). Heath is undoubtedly DC's most underrated artist, and seems quite incapable of drawing badly. Consequently each issue containing his work is worthy of a place in any serious collection. His draughtsmanship, story-telling and detailed inking style made for excellent artwork on every strip, and from time to time he was capable of almost superhumanly good art jobs that surpassed even his high standards; it is these that are recommended. 208 also saw Kanigher's position as principal writer usurped by Kubert, who, along with occasional scripts by Heath, wrote most issues until 230. After returning, Kanigher delivered one of his best-ever stories, 'Head Count', in 233, clearly inspired by the My Lai massacre. To further emphasise the title's anti-war tone, from that issue each strip would end with the legend 'Make war no more'.

Other notable stories of this period included Heath's magnificent solo job on 'Easy's First Tiger' in 244 and a continued Iron Major story in 251–253. Kanigher and Heath also excelled themselves in an extended continuity (256–260) that had Rock stranded in the South Pacific, though 247's Joan Of Arc story was a return to the gimmicky days of old. Editor Kubert ensured that the back-up strips were of a similarly high standard, with contributions from Frank Thorne (199, 227, 236, 260), Wally Wood (249), Neal Adams (240) and Alfredo Alcala (251). As always, the great Alex Toth provided some of the title's finest back-ups in 235 and 254, particularly with Bob Haney's 'Dirty Job' in 241, which powerfully described the Crucifixion through the eyes of three Roman centurions. Generally, however, the back-ups were one of several alternating series, all of which were well crafted.

Ric Estrada's 'Great Battles' series ran occasionally between 213 and 224, and Estrada later went on to become principal artist on 'Robert Kanigher's Gallery Of War', which ran from 251. It alternated with Norm Maurer's rather more factual 'Medal Of Honor' series, which began in 233, and Sam Glanzman's 'U.S.S. Stevens'. Glanzman was a veteran sailor who was actually stationed on the real U.S.S. Stevens throughout World War II, and his stories were palpably autobiographical, mixing his punchy writing with a Kubertesque art style. It's every bit as good as the lead strip; any episode is worth looking at, with the series running in many issues between 218 and 298. The short-lived 'Sam Glanzman's War Diary' (242, 244, 266, 269) was, if anything, even more powerful, since it consisted of actual letters, translated into short strips, written by the artist during the war.

264 was the last regular issue by Heath, and, though always readable, later issues were never again quite as essential. Heath continued to draw the occasional story (268, 271, 273, 275, 277, 279, 281), for a while alternating with George Evans and John Severin (265, 272), but after his finale the strip was passed from hand to hand. Ric Estrada in 282 was inked by Kubert, Doug Wildey in 283–285 and 287 was hampered by spectacularly bad Mike Grell inking, and eventually Kubert settled on Frank Redondo, an artist very much in his own tradition. Redondo went on to draw the strip for almost ten years (although Kubert himself drew 300). From 302 the title became *Sgt Rock*, though in all other matters it was identical.

164, 177, 190, 203–205, 216 and 242 are all 100% golden reprints, and oversize issues 229, 235–241, 243–245, 269, 275 and 280 all mix new material with classic reprints.~DAR

Recommended: 8–11, 13, 14, 83, 151, 153, 155, 160, 182, 183, 186, 196, 233–235, 240, 241, 244, 248–260, 262, 279

OUR FIGHTING FORCES
DC: *181 issues 1954–1981*

The last and least of DC's major war titles, this nonetheless featured some fine material, but a higher percentage of dross than its companions. In common with them, though, it started by running short one-off stories, often composed around a particular theme each issue, and written and drawn by the same highly talented pool of contributors as worked on the other titles. As ever, the most outstanding art of this early period was that of Mort Drucker (10, 27, 28, 32, 36, 39, 42–44, 49, 53, 55), though a special mention should be made of former EC artists Wally Wood (10) and John Severin (32, 35, 37).

Our Fighting Forces' most prolific artist in the

early days was Jerry Grandenetti, so not surprisingly he was assigned to draw its first regular series, Gunner And Sarge. They'd débuted in *All American Men Of War* 67 before transferring here to run between 45 and 94. Written by Robert Kanigher, it was a fast-moving, humorous affair that had a tendency to go way over the top. From 47 the two stars were joined by Pooch, their canine sidekick, which only heightened the strip's sense of unreality. Still, if you can overcome scenes like our heroes single-handedly blowing up a submarine (underwater, of course), the feature was undemanding fun. Grandenetti at his best could create wonderfully kinetic, expressionistic and powerful art, but he had a tendency towards over-cartooning, and visually the early episodes are by far the best. Other artists included Joe Kubert (51, 52, 74), Irv Novick (67, 68) and Jack Abel (85–94), the latter's contributions being woefully poor and heralding the comic's decline.

Gunner And Sarge was finally followed by Sgt Rock's brother Larry Rock, 'The Fighting Devil Dog' (95–98), and the ill-judged Vietnam strip 'Hunter' (99–107), both by Kanigher and Novick. Novick was soon replaced by Jack Abel, who teamed with Howard Liss to create 'Hunter's Hellcats', World War II strips of the same Lieutenant Hunter. The Hellcats were a bunch of former convicts, and the strip was every bit as unappealing as the premise suggests. Its only notable episodes were courtesy of fill-in artists Russ Heath (114) and Frank Thorne (115–117). Sadly none of the strips had much merit and probably the most outstanding element of this era was the occasional appearance of a Gene Colan back-up (86, 87, 95, 100).

Matters improved with 123 and the first instalment of yet another Kanigher series, The Losers. This brought together the team of Gunner and Sarge, Johnny Cloud (from *All American Men Of War*) and Captain Storm from his own 1960s title, all losers of one sort or another, hence the name, although cynics might suggest that their main losses were their own strips. After a first instalment drawn by Ken Barr, Ross Andru and Mike Esposito became the art team. It wasn't until John Severin took over in 132 that the series really took off. Kanigher's early stories were jokey, insubstantial affairs, with the lead characters whining on about being losers; the turning-point was 135, where the female freedom fighter Ona was introduced and Capt Storm was (temporarily) killed off. Subsequent episodes had significantly more continuity and 135–150 make entertaining reading, not least because of Severin's beautiful art. The improved lead feature was matched by a nice variety of back-up strips, including work by veterans Russ Heath (123, 130), Frank Thorne (136) and Severin himself in 124. Younger artists

also cropped up, including Bruce Jones (139), Tom Sutton (144) and the underrated Ed Davis (150), but, as ever, the best strips were drawn by the wonderful Alex Toth (136, 144). In fact 'Burma Sky' in 146, a poignant tale written by Archie Goodwin about the Flying Tigers fighter squadron, is the finest war strip DC produced. Toth's art was quite breathtaking.

From 151 to 162 the comic was written and drawn by Jack Kirby, who promptly disregarded everything that had previously occurred in taking the Losers in another direction entirely. Kirby had little interest in continuity or characterisation here, and his writing was at times simplistic, although he did bring an astonishing vitality to the strip. On Kirby's departure Kanigher once again assumed control, this time with George Evans on art, but these were strictly by-the-numbers issues, and none were exceptional in any way.~DAR

Recommended: 10, 27, 28, 32, 36, 39, 42–44, 49, 53, 55, 123, 130, 134–150.

OUR LOVE STORY
Marvel: *38 issues, 1969–1976*

As with its sister title *My Love*, this series started out strongly, with brand-new stories by Marvel's top-line artists. Buscema, Colan and Heck all appear, but it quickly became a mixture of reprints and a showplace for newcomers (Al Weiss) or old-timers making a comeback (Tarpe Mills, in a peculiarly dated story in 14). It turned all reprint from 18, relying on Marvel's vast inventory of material to fill the pages and satisfy the dwindling romance market until it closed down. A sought-after issue is 5, featuring Jim Steranko's only known work on a romance story.~HS

OUT OF THE VORTEX
Dark Horse: *12-issue limited series 1993–1994*

Disappointingly ponderous conclusion to *Comics Greatest World*'s introduction of a new world of superheroes. A shaggy dog story is padded over a dozen issues, and after the final issue you'll probably wonder why you bothered with any of it. If you *really* like the characters introduced in *Comics Greatest World* , then plenty feature here, but avoid otherwise.~WJ

The OUTCAST
Valiant: *One-shot 1995*

The introduction of a new character to Valiant's continuity. Former A-grade student Lenny is retarded after an accident, but, as compensation for his reduction in mental acuity, he can transform into a nine-foot superstrong creature. In addition to a nod in John Steinbeck's direction, Lenny's home town is called Valiant. It's all competently produced, and might have had a greater resonance had Valiant's entire line not been cancelled soon afterwards.~WJ

OUTCASTS
DC: *12-issue limited series 1987–1988*

When all around them were turning out grim, gritty and 'realistic' titles, the writing team of John Wagner and Alan Grant put the comedy back into comics. *Outcasts* is hilarious, packed with black humour, funny dialogue and enough good ideas to keep lesser writers in plots for years. It starts slowly as the team is formed to combat administrative corruption after the assassination of a leading political figure. Once the plot is set in motion, though, the characters take over, and it's fun, fun, fun all the way. Top moments include Al the Human Anaconda (2), trench-coated robot assassins The Satan Brothers (6, 10–12), punch-drunk former Slaughterbowl player B.D. Rickenbacker having to re-form the team with old colleagues (7), Suicide Park (9), and surely the only hero in a bucket ever. And there's plenty more where that lot came from. Artists Cam Kennedy and Steve Montano depict the ongoing lunacy in magnificent fashion, as the surviving Outcasts cross paths with the Satan Brothers again in the Lobo miniseries *UnAmerican Gladiators*.~FP
Recommended: 6–12

OUTLANDER
Malibu: *5 issues 1987–1988*

Surprisingly well conceived and interestingly executed thriller concentrating on Adam Gallow, the Outlander of the title. He's been trained by The Institute to become their foremost weapon, but rejects the idea and breaks loose. As he searches for Cassandra, a powerful empath, so he's stalked by The Institute, which isn't about to give up on their prized asset so easily. If not entirely successful, writer Scott Finley is attempting a little more than the recycling of old ideas, and the same can be said for artist Brooks Hagen, whose style is seemingly European-influenced. Try 3, in which Gallow's participation is minimal, as Cassandra encounters a mad motorcyclist.~FP

OUTLANDERS
Dark Horse: *34 issues (0–33),1 Special 1988–1991*

When the Earth is invaded by its original inhabitants, the Santovasku Empire, who believe that humans are little more than vermin polluting their Sacred Mother Planet, there's a faction within the military establishment who seem to have been expecting their return. Tetsuya, a photographer, finds himself in the company of the invading emperor's runaway daughter Kahm, and *Outlanders* is principally the story of their romance, set against the backdrop of the Earth's desperate defence as loyalties shift on both sides.

Truly epic in scope and vision, Johji Manabe's story-telling is pacey where it needs to be but full of humour and character that

counterpoints what might otherwise be a grim tale. More space opera than hard science, it's still innovative and colourful. Issue 0 (1992) is a one-off Kahm (mis)adventure set before she arrives on Earth; the 1993 special stars Battia, Kahm's best friend. *Outlanders Epilogue* (1994) is the strip's final appearance, a moving reunion between the survivors of the war and the spirits of those who died.~NF

The OUTLAW KID
Marvel: *30 issues 1970–1975*

A popular title in the 1950s, this 1970s series began by reprinting some classy Doug Wildey (1–9) and Al Williamson (in 3 and 9) drawn four- and five-page strips. They proved so popular that Marvel commissioned new material, starting with an origin story in 10, but it wasn't up to the high standards of the reprints, to which the title reverted with 17. It's comforting to note that for once the continuing plot-line was actually concluded first. Any of the early reprint issues is worth sampling for the moody art, but the stories are standard stuff, so you don't need to look at more than one.~SW

OUTLAWS
DC: *8 issues 1991–1992*

Michael Jan Friedman's intelligent script, set in a dystopian feudal society following a plague, uses elements from versions of the Robin Hood story but gives it a twist by making protagonists aware of the fact that they are aping the actions of a legendary hero. Unfortunately, Luke McDonnell's artwork is scratchy and unappealing. If the script aspires to Richard Carpenter's *Robin of Sherwood* the artwork's sub-Kevin Costner.~NF

THE OUTSIDERS
DC: *Series one 28 issues, 1 annual 1985–1988, series two 26 issues (0–24, 2 x issue 1) 1993–1995*

The luxury-format glossy paper and lack of Batman was a sure sign that the Outsiders were on a roll after the success of *Batman and the Outsiders*. Batman has departed after a bust-up, and Mike Barr and Jim Aparo continue the story of the team as they relocate to Los Angeles. Black Lightning, Geo-Force, Halo, Katana and Looker (possibly the sexiest/most sexist mainstream superheroine ever) have their further adventures sponsored by the Markovian government, who buy them a nice oil rig just off the Californian coast. No sooner are they settled in when a nutty professor and his robot family try to nuke L.A. He and the likes of the robotic Duke Of Oil in 6 and 7 obviously did nothing for sales, as Batman is shovelled back in from 18. He's also there in the beautifully drawn annual, in which Kevin Nowlan adds to the effect of his already superlative artwork with suitably moody colouring.

The sad finale for the first series is a *Millennium* crossover drawn by Erik Larsen. Although the series is competent throughout, and has some very nice Brian Bolland covers, it lacks the fun and punch of *Batman and the Outsiders*, and is missing the Alan Davis artwork. From 39 that title began reprinting this from 1 for the further eight issues it lasted.

The relaunch is very poor. It seems Mike Barr underwent a lobotomy before beginning work, not least in the idea of two first issues, with four pages in common, each uniting half the team. The old cast are all present, although one of them not for long, and there are new bods in Faust, Technocrat and Wylde. Who comes up with these names? Things don't go well at first, with Geo-Force accused of murder in 1–2, and after another falling-out with Batman in 9 half the team are behind bars. After a breakout, the Outsiders live up to their name and go underground to locate the person who fitted them up. Factions split the team in 10 as Katana, Geo-Force and Technocrat go it alone and the Eradicator, from Superman titles, takes up the leadership of the remainder. Barr fails to come up with an original idea for this series, so we're reduced to endless fights with giant fish, evil sorcerers and the perennial bad guys in the employ of old enemy Kobra. Metamorpho is reunited with his old teammates in 20, but, throughout, lack-lustre artwork hampers the little spark possessed by the writing, and the series ended with a whimper.~TP

THE OWL
Gold Key: *2 issues 1967–1968*

1940s hero in a grey costume is revived, given a camp workover and relaunched to cash in on the *Batman* craze that's sweeping the USA. Feeble stuff that falls shy of being so bad it's good.~FP

OWLHOOTS
Kitchen Sink: *2 issues 1991*

Short-lived, unfinished attempt at something different by James Vance and John Garcia. Illustrated as though a series of sepia photographs, the story explores the relationship between early cinema and the Western heroes who were starting to feel out of place in an increasingly 'civilised' world and found a ready audience for their stories in Hollywood.~NF

OZ
Caliber: *18 issues +, 4 Specials 1994 to date*

A magical tome transports three adolescents and the obligatory dog to the land of Oz, several years after Dorothy's jaunt. The land is now dark and foreboding. Evil rules in the form of the Nome King. The original heroes are under his thrall. Writers Stuart Kerr and Ralph Griffith extrapolate from Frank L. Baum's concepts, introducing new, fantastic creatures and endowing them with much of the charm of the original stories. 1–15 form a tightly plotted continued story in which the new heroes trigger the revolution to restore to Oz all that is good and right. Although rather stiff at first the story does grow on you, albeit hampered by some questionable plot developments and Bill Bryan's art, which is too cluttered for a black and white production. Much care and thought has gone into this classically styled fairy tale, which is suitable for young and old kids alike. 16 starts a new story arc in which the Earthlings go home and a liberated but weakened Oz must fend for herself against the gathering menaces of the Goblin King and the Wicked Witch. The double-sized, normal-priced 17 has a full-length 'Boston Bombers' back-up strip.

The cover month policy (there aren't any) and numeration (all the Specials are numbered 1) create a nightmare for back-issue readers. The internal chronology is: issue 0, *Scarecrow Special, Lion Special, Tinman Special, Freedom Fighters Special, Romance in Rags* limited series 1–3, regular issues 1–17. All bar the regular issues are second-string, unessential background reading.~APS
Collections: *Mayhem in Munchkinland* (1–5), *A Gathering of Heroes* (6–10)

OZ: ROMANCE IN RAGS
Caliber: *3-issue miniseries 1996*

A tale of courage and sacrifice featuring Scarecrow and his fair lady, Scraps the patchwork girl, set during the time when Scarecrow was under the Nome King's thrall. Issue 1's cover shows just how good Bill Bryan's art looks in colour.~APS

THE OZ-WONDERLAND WAR
DC: *3-issue miniseries 1986*

Funny-animal superheroes Captain Carrot and his Amazing Zoo Crew find themselves caught up in a long-winded adventure featuring the characters of Frank L. Baum and Lewis Carroll. Although presumably intended for a young audience, the complicated script by E. Nelson Bridwell and Joey Cavalieri – about an evil wizard named Roquat and his attempts to enslave the entire land of Oz – seems like pretty musty stuff compared to a good computer game. Crammed full of pointless in-jokes and obsessive continuity, the series is further hampered by Carol Lay's crowded artwork, which needlessly tries to re-create the work of original book illustrators John Tenniel and W.W. Denslow.~AL

PACIFIC PRESENTS
Pacific: *4 issues 1982–1984*

The first three issues of *Pacific Presents* feature one of Steve Ditko's oddest creations, the Missing Man, a superhero whose head, arms and legs are the only parts of him visible. The stories are the usual moral, overwrought dramas, beautifully drawn. The other star of this title was only in the first two issues: Dave Stevens' Rocketeer story, continued from the back-up in *Starslayer*, was intended to be in three issues but was eventually completed in a Special. A return to the action-adventure atmosphere of the 1930s, The Rocketeer looked ravishing (as did Stevens' wife, drawn to resemble Betty Page), and though hardly demanding it's full of good story-telling. The first appearance of Will Meugniot's Vanity (3) can't disguise the weakness of the material in the two final issues.~NF
Recommended: 1–2

The PACT
Image: *3-issue miniseries 1994*

Mindless violence between preposterously proportioned individuals.~FP

PALESTINE
Fantagraphics: *9 issues 1993–1995*

Palestine is almost unique, being a form of emotional comics journalism. In 1991 Joe Sacco spent two months in the Israeli-occupied areas of the West Bank (1–5) and Gaza Strip (6–9), learning about the repressive conditions the Palestinians had to live under, events rarely reported or known to the outside world. He was told of detention and deprivation without due reason, the appalling conditions in the prison camps and government-sanctioned torture, and relates it all with a passionate sense of horror. There's no lack of harrowing experiences. In 4 a Palestinian is forcibly removed from his home at night by security troops, chained to a pipe with a dried-urine-smelling sack over his head, and held without good reason for nineteen days. In 8 an old lady recalls the loss of two family members and the appalling attitude of the occupying troops: the policy of depriving already poor families of what little livelihood they have by chopping down their olive groves is a resonant image of persecution. The final issue takes some space to examine the situation from the Israeli viewpoint, but the sequence is clumsy in comparison with the remainder of the run.

Sacco's is a powerful voice in relating these stories. Fully cognisant of his own shortcomings, and of the voyeuristic-ghoul aspects of what he's doing, he has a sympathetic outsider's perspective on events, but maintains an awareness of the conflicts within Palestinian society. The short sequence in 5 concerning women wearing traditional Koran-approved dress is both informative and puzzling from the Western viewpoint, as is 6's discussion of Koran-approved methods of retribution that seem barbaric to Westerners.

The art can initially be off-putting, with Sacco's self-caricature sitting ill alongside the more naturalistic portrayal of others, but it sucks the reader in very quickly, and by later issues there's some excellent work. The depiction of the squalid Gaza refugee camp opening 6 is an exceptionally well noted (and depressing) panorama. It's harder to adjust to the blocks of handwritten lettering pasted over the art. This has the deliberate effect of adding an urgency to the text not available by more conventional placing, but it's also often a distraction, inhibiting the story it's supposed to enhance. This is, though, a minor caveat concerning an otherwise excellent title. One hopes somehow it's had an effect beyond being fifteen minutes reading per issue.~FP
Recommended: 1–9
Collections: A Nation Occupied (1–5), *In The Gaza Strip* (6–9)

PALOOKAVILLE
Drawn & Quarterly: *10 issues + 1991 to date*

There are so many cartoonists telling tales of their everyday lives in downtown Toronto, it's a wonder you can tell them apart. Seth stakes a very different ground to Joe Matt or Chester Brown in his quiet, driven stories of searching for obscure editorial cartoonists and failing to bother about the demise of his latest relationship. Both tone and drawing are extremely cool, yet somehow charming. Seth's 1950s-influenced style, which draws upon advertising art as well as the work of gentle humorists like Raymond Peynet, adds even more balance and distance. The strip occasionally teeters on the brink of becoming self-aware and is the epitome of what people who hate autobiographical works complain about. However, it remains clever, sharply observed, and dryly humorous.~FJ

Collection: It's A Good Life If You Don't Weaken (4–9)

PARAGON
AC: *4-issue miniseries 1993*

Paragon (originally *Captain Paragon*) is to AC what Superman is to DC, and in the year of AC's tenth anniversary this miniseries was intended to reintroduce and redefine his character for the 1990s. These issues can be read on their own, but the story does cross over into issues of *FemForce* (58–60) as Paragon is manipulated into frustrating the Black Commando's vengeance on those he believes ruined his life. Bill Black's love of Golden Age superheroes is evident in all that he (and AC Comics) do, but the convoluted plot and dull artwork combine to make this one for *FemForce* completists only.~NF

PARIS The Man Of Plaster
Harrier: *6 issues 1987–1988*

Glenn Dakin and Steve Way's daft Parisian crimefighter is the lead strip, backed up with assorted superhero spoofs. It's all reasonably enjoyable, but pales in comparison to the consistently excellent 'Temptation' one-pagers in which the Devil attempts to obtain a soul by deceit, bribery or any other means.~FP

PARSIFAL
Star*Reach: *1 issue 1978*

Collection of the first two episodes from the *Star*Reach* series with the third and final part of Patrick Mason and P. Craig Russell's adaptation of Richard Wagner's opera. Parts one and two are recoloured here for consistency and though the paper on which the title is printed isn't very good, the muted colours provide some lovely images. On the whole, this is perhaps too much of an early work for Russell, his rendering sometimes tentative and his characters' expressions too wide-eyed or inelegant.~NF

PARTICLE DREAMS
Fantagraphics: *6 issues 1986–1987*

Vehicle for some of Matt Howarth's science-fiction strips. 'This Fear Of Gods' (2–3), telling of the Galation Empress War, is part of Keif Llama's ancient history. Howarth continues with stories about Keif, a resourceful woman whose job it is to resolve conflicts with aliens, which requires her to keep all her wits about her. Howarth's straightforward, heavily crosshatched artwork perfectly suits the alien

landscapes Keif frequently finds herself dumped in. Diverting if you like traditional science-fiction stories rather than fights in space.~NF

Recommended: 4, 5

PARTS UNKNOWN
Eclipse: *4-issue miniseries 1992, 1 issue 1993*

Remember the tongue-in-cheek camp humour film *Mars Needs Women*? Well, someone thought it would be a good idea to re-work the plot with plenty of underwear shots and extra violence. It wasn't. The second series, titled 'The Next Invasion', was left uncompleted.~WJ

Siegel + Simon's PARTY Comics
Siegel & Simon: *One-shot 1980*

Very feeble self-published humour comic. It's as if two ageing hippies half-remember Robert Crumb strips, have thought 'We can do that', and have gone on to prove they can't. There's the oldster making a fool of himself at a punk gig (Oh, my aching sides), the sad cartoon freak (I think they're splitting now), the 1950s sit-com parody (Nurse, nurse), and the drug tragedy as cartoon inspiration (sutures, please). The strips are all well illustrated, and in most there's a different pair of smug fuckers pulling the strings. Not worth a wank.~FP

PATHWAYS TO FANTASY
Pacific: *1 issue 1984*

Editor Bruce Jones rounds up an entirely predictable selection of the more sensitive members of the comics community to deliver an arty-farty first issue which, to no one's surprise, turned out to be a one-off. However, it's a lesson for all publishers, containing as it does a lot of well-respected names (Windsor-Smith, Jeff Jones, Scott Hampton, John Bolton and portfolio queen Lela Dowling – too bad she can't actually draw). On the whole, pretty, lacking stories and awfully wet.~FJ

PATSY WALKER
Marvel: *125 issues 1945–1965, Fashion Parade 1 issue 1966*

'The Girl Who Could Be You!' reads the blurb above early issues of this title. Not without some major liposuction, babe. Anyway. Attractive, red-haired teenager lives in Centreville, USA with her long-suffering parents. Her best friend, and deadliest rival, is scheming brunette Hedy Wolfe. Her high-school sweetheart is Buzz Baxter. And... that's it, really. Amazingly, these innocuous tales of comedic romance, without either the diverse cast (!) or the overtly cartoony style of *Archie*, became his closest rivals for longevity, sustaining not only 125 issues of Patsy's own comic, but also starring roles for Patsy and her pals in *Patsy And Hedy* (110 issues, 1 annual

1952–1967), *A Date With Patsy* (1 issue 1957), *Girl's Life* (6 issues 1954), *Miss America Magazine* (93 issues 1944–1958), *Patsy And Her Pals* (29 issues, 1953–1957) and *Hedy Wolfe* (1 issue 1957). Patsy Walker was one of only two Marvel characters to be published uninterrupted from the 1940s to the 1960s (the other being Millie the Model), and, at the time of her cancellation, had appeared in more stories than any other Marvel character. One of her spin-offs, *Patsy And Hedy*, survived slightly longer than the parent title, but only thanks to the novelty of the girls finally graduating (after twenty years!) and setting out as 'Patsy & Hedy, Career Girls'. An oddity was the one-shot *Patsy Walker's Fashion Parade* of 1966, published a full year after Patsy's own comic folded. It featured not a single story, but instead page after page of pin-ups, hairdos and 'Fashions From Fans'... a sad, final collection of sweepings from the hairdresser's floor. In the early 1970s, Patsy and her husband, Buzz, were brought back from limbo as supporting-cast members in the Beast's solo strip in *Amazing Adventures*, after which she went on to become, bizarrely, the superheroine Hellcat in *Avengers* and *Defenders*.~HS

PAUL The Samurai

NEC: *3-issue miniseries 1990–1991, 10 issues 1992–1994*

What makes this series funny is contrasting the ludicrously pompous Paul, attempting to follow his warrior's code of honour, with his mundane existence in American society, where Japanese culture is typified by a ninja-themed sushi takeaway. Spinning off from *The Tick*, this is very much in the same mould, with preposterous characters played as relatively straight superheroes with portentous dialogue. There's plenty of neat touches from writer Clay Griffiths initially (Paul conceals his sword in a baguette to avoid arrest), but midway through the ongoing series it runs out of steam. The final two issues form one long story with the final two issues of *Man-Eating Cow*, and guest-star the Tick. Sample the first two issues of the regular series featuring a trip of silly superheroes based on other Japanese stereotypes, and if you like them dive in further.~WJ
Collection: The Collected Paul The Samurai (miniseries 1–3)

PEACEMAKER

Charlton: *5 issues 1967*

The bizarre concept of the man who loves peace so much he's willing to fight for it falls on US UN envoy Christopher Smith. Joe Gill and Pat Boyette turn out frankly dull stories, but masterpieces in comparison with the *Fightin'* 5 back-ups. Peacemaker began as a back-up in *Fightin'* 5 40 and 41, so presumably had a debt to repay.~FP

PEACEMAKER

DC: *4-issue miniseries 1988*

At DC there was no compunction about exploiting the inherent illogic of Peacemaker's stance as the man who loves peace so much he's willing to fight for it. Smith is portrayed as a man diving over the edge on a regular basis, tormented by the ghost of his Nazi father, yet still somehow able to function effectively as a vigilante. It's not outstanding, but there's enough action and ideas to see out four issues. He later becomes part of *Checkmate*.~FP

Joe Matt's PEEP SHOW

Drawn And Quarterly: *9 issues + 1992 to date*

The one page 'Peep Show' strips were a highlight of anthology titles such as *Snarf* and *Drawn And Quarterly* in the late 1980s and early 1990s. Frankly confessional in nature, the diary-style pages of anything up to forty panels revealed Joe Matt as a parsimonious, compulsive obsessive with plenty of personal habits to make the average reader squirm, yet were all the more compelling for doing so. All the strips originally published in anthology comics are compiled in the essential *Peep Show* collection. For the regular title, Matt dropped the minute panels in favour of a more traditional format, but initially the content still examined his day-to-day life and relationships. Expanding stories over an entire issue permits more in-depth exploration of Matt's motivations for his often unsavoury behaviour, while reservations concerning the fly-on-the-wall position of the readership are dispelled by Matt's continuing compulsion to portray himself in the worst possible light. Although surely not his intention, Matt has tapped into elements of the 'new lad' persona, wanting his cake and a fair proportion of other people's as long as he doesn't have to pay for it. Of course, if not in financial terms, payment is always due, and the first three issues chronicle the disintegration of his long-term relationship. The consequent thrashing around is detailed in 4–6. There's an abrupt change of tack from 7, as Matt begins relating events that occurred when he was ten years old. So far it retains the car-crash-style compulsion as developing facets of Matt's character come to the fore, but an increasingly erratic publication schedule (only three issues since 1994) leaves it thus far incomplete. Though he's accomplished as a cartoonist, the appeal of Matt's work lies strongly in his acknowledging that plenty of his habits and facets of his personality are off-putting and distressing to others, yet presenting them without shame, leaving one to wonder about further horrors he's not revealing. This is coupled with constant agonising over why people don't get on with

him. Lacking the expressive art and constant seam of humour there might be nothing endearing about Matt's work, yet as it is he's compulsive reading.~WJ
Recommended: 1–6

PELLESTAR
Eternity: *2 issues 1987*

There's a decent enough story going here about Brian, on the cusp of adulthood and unsure where life's going to take him. The problem is, he's been having these dreams involving a vicious beast. When his grandfather dies Brian begins to learn the truth about what he is, and what the old stuff in the attic is, and it's quite a shock. The fantasy elements are minimal beyond the dreams, and the potential of this series was never realised, as it remained incomplete. That being the case, it's chiefly memorable for the early pencilling of Richard Case and the early inking of Doug Hazlewood and Jimmy Palmiotti. One wonders what happened to writer Peter Palmer, who definitely showed promise.~WJ

Knights Of PENDRAGON
Marvel UK: *15 issues 1992–1993*

Few traces of the ecological subtext of the previous series (for which see under 'Knights') remain by the new first issue. The Arthurian legend aspects are played up, though, with all sorts of tiresome exposition on what it means to be a Pendragon, with new abilities and members popping up all the time. On the positive side, at least Grace gets to wear something other than her sci-fi slut gear. Writers Dan Abnett and John Tomlinson have put a lot of thought into the background, but given the grand idea that the Knights are the 20th-century equivalent of the Round Table, protecting Britain in her hour of need, there's an awful lot of basic superhero punch-'em-ups. John Royle is the main penciller, starting with 3, and begins in a nice sub-Alan Davis style devolving into a ghastly lines-all-over-the place format by the end. Altogether unmemorable.~FP

PENTHOUSE COMIX
Penthouse: *17 issues + 1994 to date*

If anyone could set up a successful soft-porn news-stand comic you'd have thought it would be *Penthouse*. And when *Penthouse Comics* débuted in 1994 it looked great – very slick and shiny, and benefiting from artwork by the likes of Gary Leach, Arthur Suydam, Kevin Nowlan, Gray Morrow and Adam Hughes. Apart from Mark Beachum, whose painted artwork appears in 4–8, 11 and 12, and Arthur Suydam, whose fantasies grace 1–8 and 13, the art tended to be tight, highly finished and realistic. The early stories were a different matter. Largely written by editor George

Caragonne, they were repetitive and poorly paced takes on superheroes and space opera, featuring aged jokes and heavy-duty bondage. Caragonne persuaded some interesting artists to work with him, however, including Russ Heath and Curt Swan in 5. The high point of the early issues was 'Scion', a series about psychics in Russia drawn, with great elegance and grace, by Kevin Nowlan in a pared-down, controlled version of his earlier fine-lined style. The sex was restrained but erotic, and there was an interesting thriller plot. Unfortunately it disappeared after issue 5, unfinished.

When experienced letch Dave Elliott replaced Caragonne the title became softer and more humour-driven, but it attracted a still more glittering array of names, including Moebius and Steranko (11), Richard Corben (15–17) and John M. Burns (17). Apart from a preview of Milo Manara's *Click* 3 which landed it in trouble with British distributors, *Penthouse Comix* had steered clear of reprints, but Elliott began a series of quality European reprints. These included Leroi and Gibrat's Pinocchia (14–16) and Manara's 'Hidden Camera' (17 on).

Essentially *Penthouse Comix* is *Heavy Metal* with a higher tits-and-ass quotient, concentrating on parodies, sexy superheroes and space-bondage fantasies. It's fine for whiling away a quiet afternoon, but don't look to it for insights.~FJ
Recommended: 1–5 for the Kevin Nowlan artwork

PENTHOUSE MAX
Penthouse: *1 issue +, 1 special 1996 to date*

After the failure of *Penthouse Comix* spin-off *Men's Adventure*, Penthouse International made another go at developing a second title by concentrating on popular, established characters. The first issue featured Hericane, a ballsy superwoman with nymphomaniac tendencies. The Election Special was very different, a series of short skits in flip-book format, one half and cover lampooning Clinton and the other half sending up Dole. Numerous comics names contributed, including many of the *Penthouse* regulars, plus Dan Jurgens, Dick Giordano, Scott Hampton, Bill Sienkiewicz, Keith Giffen, Lovern Kindzierski, Rick Geary, Kev O'Neill and Hilary Barta.~FJ

THE PEOPLE'S COMICS
Golden Gate/Kitchen Sink: *One-shot 1972*

A one-shot by a Robert Crumb in transition. By 1972 he'd been the most fêted underground cartoonist for over five years, and was obviously feeling pigeonholed by his standing and his characters. The boorish Fritz The Cat was being adapted, none too successfully, for a movie, and Crumb's images and catchphrases had propelled him to a public-awareness factor way beyond most counterculture creators. It's with *The People's Comics* that he begins to turn away from the underground, leaving Fritz's tombstone at the conclusion of a vitriolic strip concerning his perception of Hollywood types. It contains the usual dose of wish-fulfilment sex, as does the remainder of the comic, but what marks this is as turning-point is Crumb producing personal material moving beyond sexual fantasy and distancing himself from his presumed associations. It's the half-hearted manner in which he does so that makes this inessential Crumb. Always portraying himself as insecure, he seems uncertain about straying too far away from the market he no longer felt in tune with. Originally published by Golden Gate Press, there have been numerous reprints over the years, the most recent being Kitchen Sink's 1995 edition.~WJ

PEDESTRIAN VULGARITY
Fantagraphics: One-shot 1990

Certainly living up to the title, this reprints short strips created by Dennis Worden between 1981 and 1989. Quality varies wildly, but there are plenty of laughs and it isn't always the later material that's superior.~WJ

PELLEAS AND MELISANDE
Eclipse: 2 issues 1985

Pelleas and Melisande (also known as *Night Music* 4 and 5) is adapted from the stage play by Maurice Maeterlinck, which was written in 1892. It's the story of Melisande, married to Golaud but, seemingly inevitably, drawn to Pelleas, Golaud's half-brother. As Pelleas declares his love, however, he is killed by Golaud, who has been watching the couple's growing intimacy with anger. Maeterlinck asks questions rather than offering solutions. His strongest influences are the French Symbolist poets; it is the expression of their ideas that concern him and which P. Craig Russell so carefully captures with his artwork. If the text is oblique, the story is carried by image and gesture. Russell's rich, sensitive artwork provides the emotional intensity to carry a play that is best known for Debussy's opera based on it.~NF
Recommended: 1, 2

PERRAMUS
Fantagraphics: 4-issue miniseries 1991–1992

The late Argentinian artist Alberto Breccia began this complex political fable in 1984, towards the end of a long and distinguished comics career. Born in Uruguay in 1919, Breccia drew his first professional cartoons in 1936. By 1945 he'd joined the staff of *Patoruzito*, Argentina's first comic book, where he began his début feature, Jean de la Martinica. Breccia made his name with the 1956 strip *Sherlock*

Time, written by the prolific Hector Oesterheld, who also scripted Breccia's most popular work, *Mort Cinder*, first published in 1964. The artist's continuing mastery of the black and white medium was now complemented by restless technical experimentation, a highly influential blend of collage, photography, painting and breath-takingly assured line-work, techniques which also help to make *Perramus* such a visual treat.

Written by Juan Sasturain, *Perramus* concerns a man without a memory searching for his real identity, in a post-Peron Argentina, haunted by the memory of those 'disappeared' (murdered) radicals who dared to oppose the 1977 military dictatorship. Oesterheld, who once produced a biography of Che Guevara with Breccia, was himself 'disappeared' in 1977, along with his four daughters. Conceived in the aftermath of the Falklands War, *Perramus* is a complex, teasing, often obscurely allusive fantasy which features a guest appearance from Argentinian writer Jorge Luis Borges in 2. Borges was obsessed with games, riddles, enigmas; *Perramus* shares some of the same concerns. This also serves as a fine introduction to the peerless artwork of Breccia, one of the greatest of all comic artists.~AL
Recommended: 1–4

PETER PORKER, SPIDER-HAM
Marvel: *One-shot 1981*

Anthropomorphic humour. Allegedly. The title says it all, really.~FJ

THE PHANTOM
Gold Key: *17 issues 1962–1966*
King: *11 issues (18–28) 1966–1967*
Charlton: *45 issues (30–74) 1969–1977*

Lee Falk's famous jungle detective has had a chequered career in comics. Gold Key's handling of the character was characteristically lack-lustre, despite starting promisingly by having Russ Manning illustrate the first issue. Things remained poor under King Features, where all but a couple of issues were drawn by erstwhile Phantom strip artist Bill Lignante. What makes the King issues an improvement is the superior quality of the back-up features: Flash Gordon by Wally Wood, then Gil Kane (18–20), Brick Bradford by Paul Norris in 26, and a couple of Civil-War strips by a very young Jeff Jones.

Charlton began their tenure by forgetting all about issue 29, starting with 30. Early issues were written by Steve Skeates as 'Norm DiPlume' and were imaginatively drawn by Jim Aparo. Sadly, 39 onwards, by writer Joe Gill, were no better than those of Gold Key or King. Lee Falk disliked what Charlton was doing with his character so much that he insisted they farm the work out to Spanish artists. Unfortunately, this produced little change. With 67 the title was resuscitated by Don Newton, who managed to breathe new life into the character with dynamic and moody artwork and by setting the stories in unusual locations. He also played up the dynasty aspect of the character by utilising various historical settings. Particularly recommended are 70, a delightful gangster-movie pastiche co-starring a Humphrey Bogart lookalike, and 74, which was arguably the best bicentennial story published in 1976.~SW

Recommended: 70, 71, 74

THE PHANTOM

DC: *4-issue miniseries 1988, 13 issues 1989–1990*

One of the many comics adaptations of Lee Falk's newspaper strip superhero, started in 1934 and still going. Being the Phantom is a family business: 400 years ago, the original Phantom saw his father murdered by pirates and vowed to dedicate his life and those of his son, grandson, etc., to revenge and justice (with priority given to pirates). Here in 1988, Kit Walker is the twenty-first of this unbroken line. The miniseries acts as an introduction to the dynasty, recounting exploits in the careers of Phantoms 1, 13 and 21. Peter David's writing is leaden and Joe Orlando's story-telling confused, with at least one serious mistake at a critical moment. A thoroughly tedious read, unleavened by humour or any genuine human contact, and full of smug, self-important lectures. The Phantom may have the worst case of a God Complex in all of superherodom: he has his Chosen People tattooed with a sign that shows they are under his protection, and he can be found saying 'There are man's laws, there are God's laws, and there are the Phantom's laws.' Really, there's no reason to read this comic, except as a study of twenty-one generations of mental illness – that's one hell of a persistent gene on that Y chromosome. The ongoing series by other creators is mostly one- or two- issue stories, but each is so boring, it feels about four times the length. It earns some points for continuity in preserving all of the faults of the 1988 series and resisting any urge to make improvements.~FC

PHANTOM FORCE

Image: *2 issues 1993–1994*
Genesis West: *9 issues (0, 3–10) 1994–1995*

Poor old Jack Kirby must be doing somersaults in his grave over this. He developed some characters for Richard French and Mike Thibodeaux instead of paying them for some inking work. The gruesome twosome then took Kirby's concepts and made a real cack-handed job of adapting them. The Image-published issues are, without a doubt, superior, with Kirby having some control (being alive at the time),

and having been inked by Image mainstays Erik Larsen, Jim Lee, Rob Liefeld and Todd McFarlane. The story is typically Kirby, a great cosmic epic almost reminiscent of his early 1970s DC titles, but something doesn't gel, rendering the misfit superhero team two-dimensional and bland. The main plot, concerning an evil alien attempting to take over the galaxy, is also rather ho-hum. Once the title returns to French and Thibodeaux it's mindless all the way. Seek out the 1960s and 1970s work by Jack Kirby and ignore this sad footnote to one of comics' legends.~TP

PHANTOM LADY

Fox Features: *11 issues (13–23) 1947–1949*
Verotik: *1 issue 1994*

The 'good-girl' art of Matt Baker is what most distinguishes *The Phantom Lady*, though her adventures (against everything from thieves and murderers to werewolves) are a cut above most others of the period with their emphasis on detection and mysteries. Phantom Lady herself is Sandra Knight, senator's daughter, who puts on a skimpy costume (but manages to avoid recognition without a mask) and wields a ray of black light against her adversaries.

The Verotik issue contains reprints from 14–17 and two from *All-Top Comics*, with pin-ups by Adam Hughes.~NF

PHANTOM OF FEAR CITY

Claypool: *12 issues 1993–1994*

A supernatural romance, this twist on the Flying Dutchman legend starred Juup Van Derdecken as the eponymous spirit, cursed to wander the earth, but every seven years made flesh, briefly, to seek the love of a woman who might free him. Along the way he encounters business sharks, serial killers, opera divas and more in a blend of *Dallas* and *Dark Shadows*. Steve Englehart's script is painstaking and evocative and the artwork, initially by Matt Haley, later by Nick Choles, quite lovely.~HS

Recommended: 1–12

THE PHANTOM STRANGER

DC: *Series one 6 issues 1952–1953, series two 41 issues 1969–1976, 4-issue miniseries 1987–1988*
Vertigo: One-shot 1993

Débuting earlier than most people realise, the first series by John Broome, Carmine Infantino and Sy Barry had the Stranger solving mystical mysteries and supernatural happenings, and exposing fakes. Although visually similar to later versions in slouch hat, black suit and cloak, he had no particular abilities other than being able to manifest like a phantom. One of these stories is reprinted in *Showcase* 80 with a new framing sequence

1–3 of the second series are also reprints with framing sequences, as our man, in the company of Ghostbreaker Terry Thirteen, argues the merits of the super-natural cases represented. Robert Kanigher and Neal Adams provide all new material in 4, introducing a regular adversary in sorceress Tala. The strange combination of Mike Sekowsky and Murphy Anderson draws 5, which is monopolised by a group of youngsters resembling nothing so much as the human cast of *Scooby Doo*. Regular artist Jim Aparo arrives on 6, and writer Gerry Conway's début in 10 rids us of Tala and the annoying teenagers while retaining the skeptical Terry Thirteen back-ups, now drawn by Tony DeZuniga, and introducing a new mystical menace, Tannarak. Except for Kanigher's brief return on 12 and 13, The Stranger was now an active participant in the stories.

Len Wein becomes writer with 14, and 17 is the first appearance of Cassandra Craft, a blind girl with telepathic abilities who cares for the Stranger after he's been mugged in the subway! Tannarak is also on hand, obsessed with attaining immortality. Wein was at a peak here between 18, nicely drawn by DeZuniga, and 25. 20 introduces the evil mystical organisation The Dark Circle, who would recur throughout, and 22 begins the best story of the run, with Cassandra kidnapped and controlled by the Dark Circle. In order to locate them, the Stranger must seek the aid of Tannarak, by now a marvellously sarcastic character. The conclusion in 24 reveals another familiar face. If this isn't enough to excite, 23 starts a back-up strip called 'The Spawn Of Frankenstein', written by Marv Wolfman and drawn by Mike Kaluta. Both were in their prime for a marvellously produced series, which progressed to a full-length teaming with the Phantom Stranger in 26. It continued in 27–30, drawn by Bernard Bailey.

Wein left with 27, and the comic began a slow decline as the Stranger once again reverted to small cameo appearances in mystery stories mainly illustrated by Gerry Talaoc under a huge procession of writers. Subsequent issues are notable for the Black Orchid back-up, which has an irregular run in 31–41. Continued from *Adventure*, by Sheldon Mayer and Tony DeZuniga, it maintained the mystery of this crimefighter in moody stories. In 38 the strip was drawn by Fred Carillo, now also drawing the lead feature. In an effort to increase sales, Deadman, drawn by Mike Grell, appeared in 33 and was popular enough to return for 39–41, along with Cassandra Craft.

After cancellation the Phantom Stranger popped up in guest roles in other series, including the seemingly incompatible *Justice League*. For the 1987 miniseries Mike Mignola and P. Craig Russell ensure that he looks excellent, but much detail is lost in the printing.

Despite a lack-lustre start from writer Paul Kupperberg, the series ends in spectacular fashion. The villain was Eclipso, a largely tedious DC evildoer inflicted on everyone at one time or another. The Stranger's super-natural powers are rescinded by the Lords of Order, who've decided that the time of Chaos should inflict Earth. The series works on two levels, as a supernatural battle and as a crime thriller, but is severely hampered by the strange dialogue inflicted on the Stranger, who sounds more like Marvel's Thor than any previous incarnation. The Stranger later had another short solo run in the back of *Action Comics*, but it never matched this series.

The Vertigo title has the Stranger as never seen before from Alisa Kwitney, and illustrated by Guy Davis. It's an atmospheric and creepy story, with the Phantom Stranger trapped in a strange house and separated from his body. It involves all manner of strange demons and creatures in a to-hell-and-back saga.~HY

Recommended: 4, 17, 18, 20–26, one-shot

THE PHANTOM ZONE
DC: *4-issue miniseries 1982*

Before Superman's home planet Krypton exploded, The Phantom Zone was a special dimension where Kryptonian villains were imprisoned in phantom form as a humane alternative to execution. This epic miniseries, masterfully written by Steve Gerber and beautifully drawn by Gene Colan, deals with the many mysteries surrounding the Phantom Zone and its prisoners. While Superman is trapped in the zone, the escaped Kryptonian villains, all superbly characterised, cause havoc on Earth, and both the Justice League of America and Supergirl are required to stop them. Nuff said?~HY

Recommended: 1–4

PHAZE
Eclipse: *2 issues 1988*

A candidate for All-Time Stinker. The germ of a decent time-travel plot is successfully buried as writer Fred Burke attempts a complex story before he can manage a simple one. *Phaze* exhibits appalling story-telling amid a plethora of talking heads. It's a rare character that can be recognised from panel to panel, never mind from page to page, a confusion compounded by the decision to colour directly over Rafael Kayanan's pencils, then to use at least three colourists an issue so there's no consistency. Just in case someone does start to figure out what's going on, there's a succession of confusing montage pages. Eclipse wisely gave this a premature burial two issues into a planned six-issue run.~FP

PHOENIX
Atlas: *4 issues 1975*

Much like Marvel's Warlock series, Phoenix was a futuristic superhero with strong messianic overtones. 1–3 were decently written by Jeff Rovin and well drawn by the under-rated Sal Amendola, though perhaps the comic's greatest claim to fame is featuring Carmine Infantino as one of its characters. With 4 the title changed to *Phoenix The Protector* and gained a far less impressive costume and creative team. It's worth noting 3's back-up, The Dark Avenger, wryly written by John Albano and well drawn by Pat Broderick and Terry Austin.~DAR
Recommended: 3

PHOENIX The Untold Story
Marvel: *One-shot 1984*

In the planned ending to the *Dark Phoenix Saga* (*Uncanny X-Men* 129–137), Jean Grey was stripped of her powers and returned to her team-mates to live happily ever after. Editor-in-chief Jim Shooter objected: she had committed genocide and this amounted to little more than having her wrists slapped, so he forced Chris Claremont and John Byrne to rethink. This presents the story that would have appeared in *X-Men* 137 without Shooter's interference, and is surprisingly bland and anticlimactic next to the 'real' version. There is also an interview with Byrne, Claremont and Shooter, and scenes from the issues that would have followed. An interesting collectors' piece.~JC

THE PHOENIX RESURRECTION
Malibu: *3-issue miniseries 1996*

Previously purged in the memorable *X-Men* 137, Phoenix is an all-powerful symbiotic alien entity that bonds itself to an appropriate host. A big event was required to promote the merging of the Malibu Ultraverse into Marvel's titles following a corporate buyout, so Phoenix was revived. Trailed in the second issues of all the relaunched Ultraverse titles, this series sees Phoenix once again manifesting to fight the X-Men, Exiles and Ultraforce in the first two un-numbered issues, titled *Genesis* and *Revelation*. No obvious biblical title was available for *Aftermath*, and it's also very little to do with the remainder of the series, a pointless coda set in the future introducing Foxfire. Overall this is no better than average, and although the art is decent, the continuous switching of pencillers jars.~FP

THE PHONY PAGES
Renegade: *2 issues 1986*

This spoofs famous strips and characters from throughout the history of comics. Starting with 'The Blue Kid' (mixing Gainsborough's 'Blue Boy' and Outcault's 'Yellow Kid'), there's 'Little Nimoy in Slumberland' (cue *Star Trek* gags in the style of Winsor McKay), through 'Prince Valium' to 'Brooke Shields, agent of F.U.R.Y.' As artwork, Terry Beatty's pastiches are accomplished, but the jokes just aren't funny enough.~FC

PICTOPIA
Fantagraphics: *4 issues 1991–1992*

On the basis of the first issue one might almost think publisher and co-editor Gary Groth was running an experiment to see how far he could push his audience before a cry of 'King's new clothes' issued forth. Almost wilfully empty and insubstantial strips jostle for place with material that its creators seem to consider avant-garde, and the only notable content in seventy-two squarebound magazine-sized pages is Solano Lopez and Panosetti's harrowing strip about the Argentinian police junta. As Ambrose Bierce had it, the covers are too far apart. 2 starts off with much more of the same before being redeemed by a glorious Jim Woodring 'Frank' strip, and the hefty opening chunk of Jacques Tardi's 'Griffu', which concerns a 'legal adviser' for whom a simple case becomes a complex web of property fraud and murder. Tardi's on top form interpreting Manchette's well-paced plot, and it's the highlight of the following two issues. They're also blighted by substandard filler material from known and obscure alike, although, covers apart, there's a rare chance to see Chris Ware's work in colour. It's oddly distracting and sadly disappointing. There's so much poor content, no issue can be wholeheartedly recommended, but the Tardi strip is worth anyone's time.~FP

PINEAPPLE ARMY
Viz: *10 issues 1988–1989*

This is a translation of the Japanese comic written by Kazuya Kudo and drawn by Naoki Urasawa. Jed Goshi has bushels of combat experience, and now he lives in New York offering combat instruction to civilians. At the beginning of each assignment he sternly tells the client that he'll teach them to fight but won't do their fighting for them – but guess what's happened by the end of the issue. The first few stories (1–3) are fairly down-to-earth, dealing with ordinary New Yorkers faced with trouble they can't face alone. These are quite fresh and imaginative, especially 1, although the logic and psychology in each is... eccentric. However, from 4 on, it's all foreign governments and guerrillas, spies and gangsters and heroic mercenaries, and we go from eccentric to boring and witless. The art is consistent and effective throughout, and particularly good at differentiating characters with just a few lines.~FC
Recommended: 1
Collection: Pineapple Army (1–10)

PINHEAD
Epic: *7 issues 1993–1994*

Spin-off from Clive Barker's *Hellraiser* series starring eponymous demon and sundry Cenobite pals'n'gals. Leaden writing and sub-professional artwork make what should be stomach-turning violence seem very dull indeed.~HS

PINHEAD/MARSHAL LAW:
Law In Hell
Epic: *2-issue microseries 1993*

Pat Mills and Kev O'Neill's vigilante takes on the villain from the *Hellraiser* movies, in a pointless crossover that just proves both characters are way past their sell-by date.~HS

PINKY AND THE BRAIN
DC: *1 Special 1995, 2 issues + 1996*

Taken from the successful cartoon show *Animaniacs*, Pinky and the Brain are two lab mice. One was given a vast intellect and the other is insane, and the comic continues the plot of the cartoon, with Brain trying to take over the world. This has a much more subtle humour than its sister title *Animaniacs*, which makes it better suited to a comic medium. The long-term appeal is dubious as originality is at a premium and the comic may find itself becoming repetitive very quickly.~SS

PIRACY
EC: *7 issues 1954–1955*

Commonly perceived as a title introduced by EC when forced to discontinue their horror and crime lines, this was actually published as a complementary title, not a replacement. Historical seagoing stories obviously appealed to artist Reed Crandall, who is excellent throughout the run, with his finest tales being the mystery of pirate Jean Lafitte in 5, and Blackbeard's encounters with the scheming Stede Bonnett in 3. Wally Wood's tale of mutiny in 1, and the work of George Evans throughout, are also excellent, while mention must be made of Bernie Krigstein's simple yet stunning cover to 6. A blazing orange sun shines down on a floating castaway, and Krigstein's bold use of colour and space are outstanding. His interior work also continues his tinkering with the approved format for comic pages, and he's given strong material, the best being 'Salvage', a superior EC-style story of revenge and retribution. Sadly, over the entire run there are a few too many of these stories along with dumb twist-in-the-tail features, and Graham Ingels is wasted on a fair proportion of them. His best is 3's 'Slave Ship', concerning a kidnapped farmer. For some reason the odd numbered issues are consistently superior to the even, but all are

collected hardbound in a slipcase alongside collections of *Aces High, Extra!* and *Psychoanalysis.*~WJ
Recommended: 1, 3, 5, 7
Collection: Piracy (1–7)

PIRANHA PRESS Graphic Novels

DC's early 1990s Piranha Press imprint thrashed around with little identity beyond the cover designs, stringing together such disparate items as children's fairy tales and drug-fuelled private detectives. By and large wilfully uncommercial and seemingly unedited, the list appears to have taken the 'throw it at the wall and see what sticks' approach. The pick of the bunch is Kyle Baker's *Why I Love Saturn*, a wryly observed dissection of twenty-something values and relationships with astonishingly sharp dialogue and stunningly expressive, yet simple art. It's also screamingly funny, commendably unsentimental and just waiting to become a movie (without a word changed, please). *The Hiding Place* is also noteworthy. Sumptuously illustrated by Steve Parkhouse, Charlie Boatner's modern fairy-tale mixes a human child with mythical and extinct creatures, the last of whom gravitate towards this hidden land. Having to save the hidden world from troglodytes causing industrial pollution, Jonathan proves resourceful. If the allegories to reality are occasionally a little too marked, Parkhouse's excellent cartooning always compensates, and there's a refreshing lack of the twee factor which often scuppers similar ventures.

As for the remainder, well, it's difficult to love or cherish any of them. The work of Alec Stevens is very much an acquired taste. *Sinners* has a knowing narrative as the errors of youth are contemplated with hindsight, drawn in a delicate, heavily contrasted style, and *Hardcore* concerns a gang of skinheads and what occurs when a member wants a change of life-style. Stevens' art is stylised gloom, and largely inappropriate for both of his stories. *The Wasteland* is a collection of one-page cartoons from the people responsible for the illustrated fiction of *Beautiful Stories For Ugly Children*. Dave Louapre writes, and Dan Sweetman illustrates largely pithy downbeat comments on the human condition. Infuriatingly recondite references mixed with shallow observation makes for an unsatisfying and rarely funny combination. If you want to read about a delusionary psychotic who believes he's a private eye, don't bother with *The Drowned Girl*, get *The Bogie Man* instead. The former's combination of ugly art and nonsensical story is intended as a commentary on the hollow values of society, but the total lack of any wit in making the point renders it impotent. If you ignore the advice, and enjoy *The Drowned Girl*, there's plenty more thrashing at society with a balloon on a stick in Jon Hammer's following graphic novel, *Nation Of Snitches*. *Mars On Earth* is mundane prose with illustrations. Straining to be hip and knowing, it's derivative and obvious, with not an original observation in sight.~WJ

Recommended: *The Hiding Place, Why I Love Saturn*

PIRATE CORP$!

Eternity: *Series one 4 issues 1987–1988*
Slave Labor: *Series two 6 issues + , 1 Special 1989 to date*

Pirate Corp$!* began as an interstellar adventure strip with a dash of humour, and the Eternity issues follow that through. In his introduction to Slave Labor's reprinting of these issues as *Pirate Corp$!: The Blunder Years, creator Even Dorkin calls them 'awkward and amateurish'. He's lying. They're solidly crafted stories displaying a precocious talent and a very confident début, their only failing being that they don't match the later material. The science-fiction adventure aspects are minimised in the special which bridges the first and second series, and the Slave Labor issues concentrate more on the cast, with Dorkin's *alter ego* Halby more often than not centre stage. 3's trip to the supermarket or 6's trying time in police custody give a good feel of the series as a whole. The one-shot *Vroom Socko Special* reprints a story originally run in the UK's *Deadline*, featuring the most unpleasant of the other pirate-ship captains. From 6 *Pirate Corp$!* is retitled *Hectic Planet*, as belated affirmation of the change of emphasis, and 7 is promised in 1997, as are *Hectic Planet* stories in *Dark Horse Presents*.~FP

Recommended: Series one 4, Series two 1–6

The P.I.'s

First: *3-issue miniseries 1983–1984*

Detective title shared by Michael Mauser, seedy detective from *E-Man*, and Ms Tree. The mixture of humour and pathos essential to Mauser strips doesn't mix well with the more traditional detective fiction of Ms Tree.~WJ

PITT

Image: *9 issues 1993–1995*
Full Bleed: 3 issues + (½ 10–11) 1995 to date

This is a blend of science fiction and all-out action adventure. After picking a fight with a group of aliens, Pitt is chased from his home planet and the series follows his adventures upon landing on Earth. Dale Keown's art is strong and vivid, but the main figure is visually very similar to Marvel's *Hulk*, which Keown also drew, bringing a lot of unfair criticism to the title. The character is a lot more complex than his Marvel counterpart, and

displays a psychic link with an Earth child. The later issues are more interesting as the characters are developed further, and under the Full Bleed banner the emphasis has shifted more to the plot, much to the improvement of the comic.~SS

The PITT

Marvel: *One-shot 1988*

This one-shot ties into the *Starbrand* and *DP7* continuities, although it's characters from *Spitfire* that play the largest part. It details an explosion that turns Pittsburgh, and several miles surrounding the city, into radioactive mutagenic goop, and the aftermath thereof. It sets up tragic repercussions for several characters, and the story continues in another one-shot *The Draft*. It's formula material throughout.~HS

PIXY JUNKET

Viz: *6-issue miniseries 1993*

A mythical women buried for centuries emerges alive and well, causing a six-issue chase between assorted parties interested in controlling her. The pay-off in 6 is interesting, but the remainder is one long chase.~WJ

P.J. WARLOCK

Eclipse: *3 issues 1986–1987*

What few royalties this outrageously wholesale *Cheech Wizard* rip-off may have earned should have been passed to Vaughn Bodé's estate. Lame humour abounds from newspaper cartoonist Bill Schorr.~FP

PLANET OF THE APES

Marvel: *29 issues 1974–1977*

Movie adaptations are always very tricky to handle, and with a licensed title like *Planet Of The Apes* the results could have been disastrous. Luckily, writer Doug Moench was just the man for the job. In addition to adapting all five films, he successfully expanded the Apes concept with his own highly inventive spin-offs that at time even transcended the source material.

Of the adaptations, *Planet Of The Apes* (1–6) was hampered by George Tuska's totally inappropriate artwork, while *Battle For The Planet Of The Apes* (23–28) was scuppered by a very unsettled creative team. On the other hand *Escape From The Planet Of The Apes* (12–16), drawn by Rico Rival, was suitably poignant, while *Beneath The Planet Of The Apes* (7–11) and *Conquest Of The Planet Of The Apes* (17–21) were both extremely successful, thanks in no small part to Alfredo Alcala's beautiful visuals. The first two adaptations were reprinted in colour as eleven issues of *Adventures On The Planet Of The Apes*.

The magazine's highspot, however, was Moench's original creation 'The Chronicles Of

The Planet Of The Apes', which was effectively a highly imaginative fantasy strip only tangentially ape-based. In Tom Sutton he had an artist of seemingly limitless imagination, and all its instalments (12, 15, 17, 24, 29) are well worth a look. Moench's other original strip, 'Terror On The Planet Of The Apes' (1–4, 6, 8, 11, 13, 14, 19), also had an excellent start due to Mike Ploog's superb artwork. While these early instalments kept closely to the milieu of the first two films (and, indeed, to the TV show), the strip went horribly askew with the introduction of some very inappropriate science-fiction elements, and the post-Ploog issues (20, 23, 26–28) are simply a mess.~DAR
Recommended: 1–4, 6, 8, 11–15, 17, 24, 29

PLANET OF THE APES
Adventure: *24 issues, 1 Annual 1990–1992*

Given the concept of *Planet Of The Apes*, it's a curious editorial decision to present it as episodes of *Dallas* (and occasionally *The Waltons*) with apes and the occasional bout of violence. Even stranger then that the cast are consistently bland, with only the morally questionable scientist Dr Moto evincing any strong characteristics. Starting the run with a battle for control of Ape City, 6 follows, serving as a primer to the city and its inhabitants. Thereafter it's largely soap opera all the way. The initial Kirbyesque art of Kent Burles and Barb Kaalberg succeeds in creating an individual world, but their successors, M.C.Wyman and Terry Pallot (from 12), stick closer to the look familiar from films and TV. Charles Marshall writes the entire series, and his most successful effort is the concluding story-line in 21–24. It returns the vindictive Governor Breck from the film *Conquest Of The Planet Of The Apes* (which was reprised from a different viewpoint in 19). It also evokes the atmosphere of the films for the first time, and sheds the complacency affecting the title by dispensing with some regular characters. Unfortunately, by this point Wyman is being inked by Peter Murphy, resulting in substandard art. Those wanting more of this version should also look for the *Ape City* and *Urshak's Folly* miniseries, and a teaming with the characters from *Alien Nation* in *Ape Nation*.~FP
Collection: *Monkey Planet* (1–4)

PLANET OF VAMPIRES
Atlas: *3 issues 1975*

A team of astronauts return from a ten-year mission to discover there have been some changes back home. Humanity now consists of a small group of technologically advanced vampires, and the scavenging majority living in ruins. As a variation on *Planet of the Apes* it's dull stuff, not at all redeemed by lack-lustre Russ Heath art in the third issue.~FP

PLANET TERRY
Star: *9 issues 1985–1986*

Marvel's Star line was a blatant attempt to develop characters for young children that could be licensed for the lucrative TV and toy market. They were almost all awful, the contrived nature of the project resulting in the vomit-inducing likes of *Strawberry Shortcake*. The one concept to transcend the creation-by-committee origin was *Planet Terry*. Make no mistake, it's a still a strip intended for the very young, but, as written by Dave Manak, from the title pun on down there's a charm and innocence that works. The basis of the series is that Terry is searching the universe for his parents, accompanied by surrogates in the form of the alien Omnus and a decidedly female robot. The simple art is ideal, and the stories fun. If you have to investigate the Star line this is the title to find, and any issue will do as a sample.~FP

PLASMER
Marvel UK: *4 issues 1993–1994*

Evil scientist attempts to give herself superpowers, but the experiment goes awry, generating a separate, powerful being embodying her darkest secret... her conscience! Probably the worst art ever in an allegedly professional comic from Pascual Ferry, but wacky, irreverent scripting by Glenn Dakin makes this a fun read.~HS

PLASTIC FORKS
Epic: *5-issue miniseries 1990*

In this short and simple story Ted McKeever asks some very big questions. Like: 'What is humanity?' The plastic fork of the title is a metaphor for a society so throwaway that it's losing a grip on what makes us human. All this within an adventure story about the not very heroic or sympathetic Henry Apt, who, like Dr Frankenstein, realises his mistake in dabbling with nature too late. He tries to make a device that allows a single person to create and fertilise their own eggs. His mad partner grafts it onto Henry's groin when he's attacked by the lab animals he's been experimenting on and he's suddenly transformed from God-like doctor to victim of science. Issue 1 kicks off with a load of nonsensical technobabble, which doesn't matter because it's all symbolic anyway. Bear with it. After this slow start the pace of the series builds inexorably to a crushing climax. McKeever's painted art for the series is bright, lush and expressionistic, making bold use of splash pages and half-page frames to tell his fable. An excellent – and deceptively simple – series.~FJ
Recommended: 1–5

PLASTIC MAN

DC: *20 issues 1966–1968 (1–10), 1976–1977 (11–20), 4-issue miniseries 1989*

Jack Cole's Plastic Man is one of the standout comic strips of the 1940s. Small-time crook Eel O'Brian escapes in the wrong direction after a robbery, standing under a tipped acid vat, stumbling through a swamp and awakening in a monastery able to stretch or mould his body into any shape or form. Instantly repenting, he decides to use the ability for good. That was the origin from *Police Comics* 1. Cole wasn't interested in straight superheroics. His Plastic Man was a gag vehicle from the off, and his penchant for slapstick was astounding, matching the best cartoon shorts. Accompanied by rotund, inept helper Woozy Winks, a man who couldn't be harmed in any fashion, Plastic Man's career was further complicated by maintaining his O'Brian persona to ingratiate himself with the underworld for information. A decent selection of Cole's Plastic Man is reprinted in *DC Special* 15, and there are also three bootleg comics reprinting Cole's Plastic Man issued by a company called Super, who'd acquired the printing plates of the originals.

Cole's Plastic Man set the standard for all humorous superheroes to follow, and DC's 1960s revival just wasn't up to scratch. A try-out of sorts had been planted in *House Of Mystery* 160, as the 'Dial H For Hero' feature saw the lead transformed into Plastic Man. Reader reaction was very positive, and the series followed. Win Mortimer's stiff art wasn't suited to the wacky cartooning expected, and the scripts concentrated far too much on TV, film and comics parody, shoehorning Plastic Man into uncharted territory. DC might as well have created a new character for all the relation this had to the original. There were some surprisingly successful team-ups with Batman in *The Brave And The Bold*, all the more astonishing for Plastic Man being played straight in 95, and the idea working. The 1970s continuation was far better. While the scripts were generally weak, Ramona Fradon was surprisingly successful at recreating the visual gags and cartoon style. Sample any one for the art. Also of an acceptable standard was an early 1980s run in *Adventure Comics*.

The 1980s miniseries was excellent and controversial. While sticking largely to Cole's vision, with some brilliant cartooning from Hilary Barta, it attempted to rationalise Plastic Man as part of DC's ongoing continuity. That being the case, though, it was clear Plastic Man's wacky, distorted world couldn't be the same one that Superman and Batman occupied. Or could it? Sadly, it could, and while one should be thankful that the contrived explanation leaves Plastic Man and his world intact, it seemed pointless. It did

allow for some nice 'reality check' pages from Kevin Nowlan, and, the continuity apart, Phil Foglio writes a great Plastic Man. Starting with a revised origin, it's manic gag-filled heaven from beginning to end, and one suspects Cole would have been pleased with the results.~FP
Recommended: Miniseries 1–4

PLASTRON CAFÉ

Mirage: *5 issues 1993*

Sooner or later every publisher seems compelled to issue an anthology. Mirage's seems a little more eclectic than many. Primarily science-fiction-based, it resurrects some good, defunct series as well as previewing new titles. In the former category are Anthony Smith and Eric Vincent's 'Alien Fire' (reprinted in *Alien Fire: Pass In Thunder*) and Tom Stazer's 'Spaced', both short-lived series from the mid-1980s, which appear in 3 and 4. Best of the new material, 'North By Downeast' is a spin-off from *Teenage Mutant Ninja Turtles* featuring space lobsters, written by Kevin Eastman and drawn by Rick Veitch (1–5). Previews include A.C. Farley's 'Bioneers' (4,5) and 'Xenotech' by Michael Dooney, both of which are promising.~NF

PLEASANTLY DISTURBED

La Comédie Illustrée: *1 issue + 1996 to date*

A French production translated into English, it details that awkward dinner at which a young man introduces his fiancée to his family. Sharply observational writing from Christopher and almost cubist freehand cartooning from Jean-Philippe Peyraud make for an appealing dish. Adding that final touch of elegance, recipes for each course consumed are included as text pages. Fine stuff.~WJ
Recommended: 1

PLOP!

DC: *24 issues 1973–1976*

A wonderful humour title strongly influenced by *Mad* artist Sergio Aragonés, who contributed to every issue and usually drew the amusing framing sequences staring Cain, Abel and Eve, hosts of DC's more realistic mystery titles. *Plop!* was subtitled 'The magazine of weird humour', and on the whole lived up to it. Besides many one-panel gags, there were lots of amusing, macabre tales by some top talents. 1–19 featured unique covers either by Basil Wolverton or Wally Wood. Inside you could find the art of Berni Wrightson in 1 and 5, Nick Cardy in 4, Mike Sekowsky in 6, George Evans in 1, Murphy Anderson in 5, Frank Robbins in 4 and 17, Ramona Fradon in 8, Alex Toth in 11, Steve Ditko in 16 and Wally Wood in 4. Mainstays were Lee Marrs and David Manak, while the most prolific regular scripter was

Steve Skeates, who worked wonderfully with Aragonés, the comic's real star. The earlier issues are the more amusing, as when the title became a giant-size from 21, with new strip-gag covers, it began to lose its appeal. Nevertheless *Plop!* remains a milestone in DC humour publishing.~HY
Recommended: 1–6, 8, 11, 14, 16

POISON ELVES
Mulehide: *13 issues (8–20) 1993–1994*
Sirius: *17 issues + 1995 to date*

The Mulehide issues continue numbering from *I, Lusiphur*, and also continue the magazine format to 15. There's a gradual progression in both the writing and drawing abilities of creator Drew Hayes, who very much seems to be basing his title on *Cerebus*. Similar page layouts and graphic elements recur, the pacing is of a similar nature, the deliberately ridiculous recurring character Purple Marauder behaves in similar fashion to the *Cerebus* loony and Hayes also has a story of several hundred issues to tell. Sadly, he's not the story-teller, artist or satirist that Dave Sim is. The change from self-publishing to Sirius enables him to take stock, and the title is stronger for it. Lusiphur joins a rogues-and-assassins clearing house in 2, broadening the supporting cast and providing him with a partner. Lusiphur is largely one-dimensional, but the issues offering insight into his often unsociable behaviour are among the best in the series, particularly the harrowing recollections as he's confronted by his inner self while unconscious in 8. Otherwise *Poison Elves* is a curious blend. Some issues are little but fights (3, 15), while others are more interesting pub conversations (11), and every now and then Hayes will throw in a completely contradictory element to shock (1). Best noted as an acquired taste, *Poison Elves* is a vastly overrated title.~FP

POLICE ACTION
Atlas: *3 issues 1975*

A feeble attempt to produce a detective comic emulating the TV police series prevalent at the time. Lead feature *Lomax* is a non-starter, and even worse is back-up *Luke Malone – Manhunter*, drawn by Mike Ploog who seemed to have required something to keep his feet occupied while using his hands to draw *Man-Thing*.~FP

POLLY AND HER PALS
Kitchen Sink: *2 volumes 1990–1991*

Cliff Sterrett's *Polly and Her Pals* newspaper strip ran for forty years, was consistently inventive and innovative, and remains a highspot in comics. The colour Sunday pages show Sterrett's graphic innovation and whimsy to best effect, and these volumes collect those from 1926 to 1929. By this stage Sterrett had been drawing the strip for over fourteen years, and was combining elements of surrealism and cubism with straightforward narrative. The title is a misnomer, as the strip concentrates on Polly's father Pa Perkins, and his constant search for a quiet life in a house populated by an endless stream of Polly's suitors, dopey relatives, misbehaving pets and his dominant wife. Pa's a natural enemy of any mechanical contrivance and can be relied upon to fall asleep at the most inopportune moments, but has his wits about him and is generally more than a match for any situation. The combination of first-class slapstick humour and strikingly designed artwork, the like of which wasn't seen again until the underground comics of the 1960s, makes for a neglected masterpiece, and it's tragic that sales apparently only warranted two collections.~WJ
Recommended: vols 1 and 2

POPCORN
Discovery: *One-shot 1993*

The term 'wholesome children's comic' is likely to cause grimaces in these days of political correctness, indicating an item devoid of any intellectual content or amusement value. Thankfully, *Popcorn* is precisely the opposite. In the manner of the best Disney material it's an absolutely delightful tale, to be enjoyed by everyone. Scott Deschaine's simple layouts and Bob Donovan's expressive cartooning ensures the younger readers won't be alienated, while Deschaine's plot about a department-store salesman working for a tyrannical, child-hating owner is sentimental in the best sense of the term. If only everything that can be categorised under old-fashioned values was as much fun.~FP
Recommended: 1

The Complete E.C. Segar POPEYE
Fantagraphics: *11 volumes 1986–1990*

In 1919 Elzie Crisler Segar started a newspaper strip for William Randolph Hearst called *Thimble Theatre*. Initially a gag strip about members of the theatre, it soon developed a strong cast, including Olive Oyl, Castor Oyl and Ham Gravy, and began to include longer adventures, without, however, neglecting the need for humour and a daily joke. Rumoured to be published by Hearst because he liked it (like *Krazy Kat*) rather than because it had a large initial following, all that changed with the introduction of an ugly sailor in January 1929.

In this story Popeye is employed as a one-man crew to take Ham and Castor (and a stowaway Olive) to a Pacific island that has a gambling den, where Castor intends to break the bank with the help of a magic whiffle hen. After he's done so, the boat is bordered by the villain, Jack Snork, who shoots Popeye fifteen times and takes the others captive. Rather than his famous spinach, it is rubbing the head of the whiffle hen that restores Popeye and gives him his wondrous strength. Popeye then quickly beats Snork and, after getting everyone home, leaves the strip. Just over a month later, however, he's back to rebuff one of Olive's suitors – and the strip would never be the same again.

The first four volumes of Fantagraphics' reprint series are large-size books which contain all Segar's Sunday pages featuring Popeye. The Sundays were kept as a separate continuity from the daily pages and normally contained single gag strips, but occasionally longer stories were included, such as those involving the Sea Hag (the marvellous 'Plunder Island', December 1933 to July 1934, which introduces Alice The Goon and Popeye's old friend, Bill Barnacle) and a sequence with the cast out West, both in volumes 2–3. Volume 5 starts a series of more traditional-sized paperbacks, and begins with the sequence that introduces Popeye in the dailies, and successive volumes, each containing about sixteen months of strips, run through to Segar's final episode on 17 February 1938.

Segar takes Popeye through his paces as a prize-fighter, and feats of strength become an important element of the strip, but not to the detriment of story-telling or humour. Along the way we're introduced to J. Wellington Wimpy, a scoundrel forever looking for a free meal or handout, Swee'Pea, a child delivered in a wooden crate whom Popeye adopts, Eugene the Jeep (Popeye not only named the first major hamburger franchise, it also added the words 'jeep' and 'goon' to the English language), an orchid-eating creature that is able to move through dimensions and has magical abilities. Later, Popeye's father Poopdeck Pappy arrived to dominate much of the action in Segar's final year, and was even more anti-social than Popeye himself. Snork returns for the 'Mystery House' (vol 6), while King Blozo and the nation of Nazalia are featured in several episodes in 6, 7 and 9. Vols 9 and 10 contain an eleven-month story ark which sees Popeye the dictator of Spinachola, while 'The Search for Popeye's Poppa' rounds off volume 10.

Segar's *Thimble Theatre* is a great work by a true master of the medium. His stories are elaborate adventures full of drama, romance and humour, and if the plot drifts for the sake of some joke then it's well worth the detour. His drawings might seem simplistic to those who expect more 'realism' in their artwork but Segar understood his craft completely – no lines are wasted. Few comics have bettered this.~NF

Recommended: 2, 3, 5–10

PORTIA PRINZ
Eclipse: *6 issues 1986–1987*

'The World's Foremost Pseudo-Intellectual Super-Heroine' is the somewhat misleading tagline for Richard Howell's witty and loquacious series. Certainly, the pseudo-intellectual appellation is appropriate, though Portia herself would dispute the 'pseudo'. The 'super-heroine' line is inapt, as the Princess of the Glamazons doesn't don a distinctive outfit and fight crime, but devotes herself to the pursuit of social engagements and philosophical debates, in which she can show off her education and accomplishments. Those who don't like *Portia* hate it a lot. They find the oratorical and declamatory style pretentious and off-putting. Others warm to the charm and engagingly flawed characters. Don't expect any brain-busting battle scenes in what is probably the single most word-crammed comic to date.~HS

POSSIBLEMAN
Blackthorne: *2 issues 1987*

William Van Horn's humorous super-hero. Comic fan Dexter Smeal becomes the 'puffacious' Possibleman, defender of Squatsburg, USA. Charming, lightweight stuff from the future star of Disney's Duck strips in the 1990s.~SW

Those Annoying POST BROTHERS
Vortex: *18 issues 1985–1990*
Rip Off: *20 issues (19–38) 1991–1994*
Aeon: *16 issues + (38–53), 2 annuals 1994 to date*

Ron and Russell Post are the two people most of us would least like to meet, any time, anywhere. Inhabitants of Bugtown (where, if you die, you just regenerate), with the ability to shift effortlessly between all possible realities, they're mad, bad, dangerous to know and extremely trigger-happy sadists. On the plus side they are fond of the Bulldaggers, a musical combo that includes their friend Savage Henry (as well as the great god C'thulu, which makes touring interesting, to say the least). Initially co-scripted by Lou Stathis, from 5 Matt Howarth took over complete control of the strip. Shorter stories are mixed with long epics such as 'The Shell Game' (10–14), which involves among other things Ron being sealed in his girl-friend Jeri's house by the landlord, Big Al, who's about the only person the brothers respect. 'Video Party' (17–20) leads up to Ron and Jeri's marriage and 21–26 has a rematch with the very nasty Hiroshima, who used to be in the Bulldaggers but was ejected for being power-mad.

The stories develop in much the same vein, as the Post Brothers reputation makes them hated and feared wherever they go. Russell is always looking for the angle to gain any sort of advantage, and Howarth continues to create imaginative ways for them to kill, be killed or be transformed as they (mis)use their reality-shifting powers. It's all good fun, but becomes repetitive once you know the characters, although Howarth's humour and musical references (a very important part of the work) help keep it fresh. His artwork is unique – tight, spiky lines heavily and roughly cross-hatched with few blacks, which gives the book an other-worldly feel. It's not for the squeamish, and not to all tastes, but it's worth sampling. Try the 1995 annual, co-written by Nancy A. Collins (there's also one in 1996) or 27, set at a comic convention.~NF

Collections: Das Loot (1–5), *Disturb The Neighbours* (6–10)

POWDERED TOAST MAN!
Marvel: *One-shot 1994, One-shot 1995*

Displaying no shame following the success of their *Ren and Stimpy* comics, Marvel issue comics starring the preposterous super-hero from the cartoon, created to satirise mundane superheroes. The wackiness doesn't work on the printed page, and the idea of encompassing film pastiches is daft. The best sections are the 'ad' pages featuring Ren and Stimpy.~WJ

POWER Comics
Eclipse/Acme: *4 issues 1988*

Both Brian Bolland and Dave Gibbons cut their professional teeth on the Nigerian superhero strip collected herein. Each issue features a story from both artists, and it's surprisingly confident and competent work. The tales of Powerman (or Powerbolt as he was called for the US market), however, are aimed at a very young audience, so don't expect much in the way of intellectual stimulation.~FP

POWER AND GLORY
Bravura: *4-issue miniseries 1994*

Howard Chaykin returns with guys in funny lycra outfits, chicks with big tits, and lots of gratuitous sex and violence. Par for the course for Chaykin, as one-dimensional characters get involved in a complex story involving government agencies and corporate politics in a world where everyone wants a piece of a Captain America clone.~TP

Collection: *Power And Glory* (1–4)

POWER FACTOR
Innovation: *3-issue miniseries 1990–1991*

A rather disjointed series, but with several good ideas among the chaos. It introduces a new world with plenty of superheroes, a place where the term 'organised crime' has a more literal meaning than usual, as the superheroes are murdered one by one in the first issue. The few survivors gather some time later, and begin swapping costumes to instil the idea that there are more of them around than anticipated. Carmine Infantino's art in 2 and 3 is a treat.~WJ

POWER GIRL
DC: *4-issue miniseries 1988*

Following *Crisis On Infinite Earths*, the former alternate Earth Supergirl needed a new identity, background and history. No longer Superman's cousin, she becomes instead Karen Starr, business woman and granddaughter of Arion, Lord of Atlantis, in one of DC's more ludicrous continuity rewrites. Four issues of battling fourth-rate villains are little more than pointless fight scenes to remind readers that she exists. It might have been kinder to let us forget.~JC

POWER MAN
Marvel: *33 issues (17–49), 1 annual, 1 Giant-size 1974–1978*

Changing the title from the presumably less commercial *Hero For Hire* didn't do much for the quality, with cliché and conflict the order of the day. To his credit, writer Don McGregor attempted to bring a more poetic and introspective quality to the title, but it only stands out because the remainder is so dire. His peak was in 28, 30 and 31, the best issues until the arrival of Chris Claremont and John Byrne with 48. In a story reprising and repeating the experiment that created Luke Cage, Power Man, and introducing Iron Fist to the title, they provide more tension and excitement than in the entirety of the run to that point. The editors recognising a good thing, Iron Fist stayed and the title was changed to *Power Man and Iron Fist* with 50.~FP

Recommended: 48, 49

POWER MAN AND IRON FIST
Marvel: *76 issues (50–125) 1978–1986*

With the cancellation of his own title Iron Fist and supporting cast moved in with Power Man as the two ran their own investigations agency. Having revitalised the title, Claremont and Byrne turn in a good story in 50 before a rapid exit, and after some floundering Jo Duffy and Kerry Gammill combined for serviceable material. Any issue between 59 and 85 is likely to be of a reasonable standard. Duffy's characterisation played off the awkward mixture of white, rich-kid martial artist Iron

Fist and the black, ghetto-born Power Man, used to surviving on his wits, and Gammill's art is solid and consistent. After their departure, the title sank back into mediocrity, and although there's a spark of improvement over the final year of the run it's too little too late. 66 has an early appearance of Sabretooth, but a better sampler by far is 72's story of Oriental gang wars.~FP

Recommended: 60, 67, 72, 74, 75

POWER OF PRIME

Malibu: *4-issue miniseries 1995*

A tedious six-part origin of Prime (parts 2 and 3 are issues 25 and 26 of the regular Prime series), which sees lots of characters with Prime-like powers (i.e., god-like bodies of slime around a mortal frame) fighting on the planet that first created the Prime process. Gerard Jones and Len Strazewski must have written this in their sleep.~NF

THE POWER OF SHAZAM

DC: *Graphic Novel 1994, 24 issues + 1995 to date*

Contrary to the usual practice of riding rough-shod over past history when starting a new series with a well-established character, Jerry Ordway's Captain Marvel revamp seems determined to do everything exactly by the book. The hardback graphic novel, drawn as well as written by Ordway, is beautiful to look at and a joy to read, taking the character back to his 1940s roots and keeping almost all the long-standing continuity intact. This trend continues into the ongoing series, written by Ordway and drawn by artists very much like him, but after a while the novelty starts to wear off. It's nice to see all the old characters re-introduced and all the old situations re-established, but not at the expense of anything new at all. If you've loved Captain Marvel for years, everything's here: Mary, Junior (whose solo issues are drawn by Gil Kane), Uncle Dudley, Mr Tawky Tawny, Dr Sivana... but we've seen it all before and there's nothing but nostalgia holding it all together. It's nice but, at the end of the day, just a little bit dull and a little bit too reverential.~JC

POWER PACHYDERMS

Marvel: *One-shot 1989*

At the height of the fad for multi-adjectival anthropomorphic features, Marvel published their cash-in, attempting to make doubly sure of success by parodying their own superheroes. And, surprise, there are quite a few giggles to be had. If the thought of an elephant version of Cyclops who has to plug his trunk doesn't raise a smile, stay well away.~WJ

POWER PACK

Marvel: *62 issues 1984–1991, 1 Special 1992*

Behind *Power Pack* lies a very stupid idea, and possibly a rather dangerous one. The four Power children – yes, their father has a convenient surname – are each given a superpower by a dying alien resembling a horse, in order to destroy the anti-matter device their father has created, which the government want to use as the ultimate weapon. The cute-looking aliens, Kymellians, are up against a nasty, lizardy race, and throughout the series they periodically attack the team. The morality of *Power Pack* is very simple. The kids bicker and have problems getting their homework done; many of the stories come out of childish things like trying to rescue a kitten. It requires a certain suspension of disbelief to get into a series where the youngest (and most powerful) character has just started kindergarten. However, if you can get your sense of wonder going, the early issues of *Power Pack* are rewarding.

Louise Simonson's scripting is fresh, with particularly strong interaction between the characters, although she does have a tendency to get sentimental – witness 19, where Katie causes havoc by inviting their superhero friends over for Thanksgiving while their mother's in hospital. Yes, lots of superheroes know about them, but none of them seem concerned about five-year-olds fighting crime. Frequent co-stars include Cloak and Dagger, various X-Men – especially Kitty Pryde and Wolverine – Spider-man and The Morlocks, and they often go adventuring with Franklyn Richards, Fantastic Four Jnr.

1–21, largely illustrated by June Brigman with occasional issues and art assists from Brent Anderson, are probably the only comics in which young children are drawn with the bodies of children, rather than as shrunken adults. Brigman is a delicate penciller, as adept at action sequences as she is at conversations. For crossover-addicts, 12 is a Morlock two-parter that concludes in *X-Men* 195, 18 is a *Secret Wars* crossover, 27 is a 'Mutant Massacre' crossover, 35 is a 'Fall Of The Mutants' crossover, issues 42–44 tie in with 'Inferno', and 53 ties in with 'Acts Of Vengeance'.~FJ

Recommended: 6, 12

POWERLINE

Epic: *8 issues 1988–1989*

Part of the 'Shadowline' series that also introduced Dr Zero and St George. A brother and sister discover they have latent abilities and go on the run... Wait a second, that sounds familiar. Decent artwork, largely from Gray Morrow, but otherwise unmemorable. The dangling plot-lines concluded in *Critical Mass*.~TP

POWERLORDS

DC: *3-issue miniseries 1983–1984*

Another toy-based series, this time from Revell. Drawn by a young Mark Texeira, it's of no interest to comics buffs whatsoever, even if you do like his artwork.~NF

POWERS THAT BE

Broadway: *6 issues 1995–1996*

The cover star of the first issue is the big-bosomed, all-powerful Fatale, who has the interesting ability to drain the energy from anyone she touches to enhance her own capacities. Hmm… Certainly an interesting date. Fatale's introduction is a witty, fast-paced, action-packed adventure, reading like a James Bond script, with operatives appearing right, left and centre to apprehend her. Her story continued in *Shadow State*, then her own title. This title's lead feature, 'Star Seed', also had a great start. It's an excellently paced story of a young man who's trying to locate his alien father. He has impressive superpowers, but he's apparently not the only one. All the intrigue and an interesting supporting cast combine for a well-plotted and executed series, but you'd expect nothing less from guiding force Jim Shooter. The title changed to *Star Seed* with issue 7.~HY
Recommended: 1–6

PRAIRIE MOON and other stories

Dark Horse: *One-shot 1992*

Rick Geary is one of the great eccentrics of the comics world. He uses simple but elaborately decorated images, which often make his strips feel more like illustrated stories than sequential comics. When he wants to, however, he can do marvellous things with simple images. This collection of three longer strips and a number of single-pagers is a good showcase for his odd sense of humour. *Prairie Moon*, for example, is about a travelling sheet-music salesman whose demonstrations of popular songs bring about various natural disasters, but who is welcomed wherever he goes. Another highlight is *A Survey Of The Twentieth Century*, a single page of twelve panels, each one labelled with a year, each image suggesting that the years are entirely interchangeable.~NF

PREACHER

Vertigo: *20 issues +, 1 Special 1995 to date*

The Reverend Jesse Custer is searching for God, in a literal rather than symbolic sense, since God has abrogated his responsibilities and gone walkabout. Complicating matters is that Custer has been united with the celestial offspring of angel and demon and is possessed of the ability to compel people to do what he says. Also along for the ride are Custer's former girl-friend Tulip, and Cassidy, an Irish vampire with a conscience.

Stunning Glenn Fabry covers welcome readers to each issue, while inside Garth Ennis and Steve Dillon combine to produce a mélange of sex, violence and horror, which attracts frequent criticism, with most critics failing to notice the violence is generally used to very comic effect. What astonishes is the continuing capability of Ennis and Dillon to shock and surprise on a monthly basis. Almost every issue contains at least one scene that should have eyes popping out on stalks in almost cartoon fashion. Don't come to *Preacher* expecting a dense plot, though, as it's very much in road-movie style with detours. The wonder of the title is in the dialogue, the comedy, the bonding and the shocks. There are few dud issues so far, although, having backed himself into a corner in 10, Ennis cops out in 11 in the certain knowledge he's presented his characters so well the readership wouldn't have it any other way. Most stories are multi-part, with only 18, an atypical Vietnam story, being relatively complete in itself. If you don't want to start with the now expensive early issues, try 'Naked City' in 5–7. Jesse, Tulip and Cassidy arrive in New York as a pair of insecure and gung-ho New York police detectives are investigating a serial killer. The *Preacher Special* features Arseface, a teenager who blew half his face off in an abortive suicide attempt, and is more downbeat, but every bit as twisted as the regular title.~FP
Recommended: 1–7, 13–17, 20
Collection: *Gone To Texas* (1–7) *Until The End Of The World* (8–17) *Proud Americans* (18–26)

PREDATOR

Dark Horse: *4-issue miniseries 1989–1990, 2-issue microseries (Predator 2) 1991, 4-issue miniseries ('Big Game') 1991, 4-issue miniseries ('Cold War') 1991–1992, 2-issue microseries ('The Bloody Sands Of Time') 1992, 2-issue microseries ('Predator Vs Magnus') 1992–1993, 5-issue miniseries (0–4) ('Race War') 1993, 4-issue miniseries ('Bad Blood') 1993–1994, One-shot ('Invaders From The Fourth Dimension') 1994, One-shot ('Jungle Tales') 1995, 4-issue miniseries ('Kindred') 1996–1997*

If you've not seen the *Predator* film or its sequel it's pertinent that the Predators of the title are deadly alien hunters who stalk humans for the challenge. In the first film Arnold Schwarzenegger was on the menu. *Predator* is set after that movie, and plays safe by introducing Big Arnie's brother. Mark Verheiden's script is an engaging blend of hokey dialogue and over-the-top violence; very cinema action film in fact, and far superior as such to the eventual sequel adapted in two ordinary issues. He returns his cast and formula for *Cold War*, largely set in Siberia, for another action-packed romp. Ron Randall's not the penciller Chris Warner is, but he's adequate. Warner inking Dan Barry on *The Bloody Sands Of Time* provides better art, but the story of a Predator interfering in World War I's trench warfare is ordinary, as is the battle between Predator and Magnus, Robot Fighter. *Big Game* is neither John Arcudi nor Evan Dorkin at their best as a Predator targets a desert military base, and *Race War* switches the action inside to a tinder-keg prison. Considering the scenario and that it's plotted by crime writer Andrew Vachss, tension is minimal. *Bad Blood* is little other than a 4-issue massacre, and would have been better restricted to its preface in *Dark Horse Comics* 12–14. By *Invaders From The Fourth Dimension* the basic hunters-and-killers plot has worn threadbare, and *Jungle Tales* reprints stories from *Dark Horse Comics*. Try the Verheiden-written stories, but only go further if you're a major *Predator* fan.~WJ

Collections: Big Game (1–4), *Cold War* (1–4), *Predator* (1–4), *Race War* (0–4)

PREZ
DC: *4 issues 1974*
Vertigo: *One-shot 1994*

After the failure of *Brother Power, The Geek*, Joe Simon, a true visionary if there ever was one, returned to DC with artist Jerry Grandenetti, and created one of the most original series ever seen in comics, as the eighteen-year-old Prez Rickard becomes President of the USA. To an audience used primarily to superhero, war and mystery comics Prez was a bizarre departure. Naturally his term in office was fraught with danger, and those wanting him out off office included Boss Smiley (a man with a smiley badge head) and a crippled vampire. How weird and wonderful! The 1970s Prez made one other appearance in *Supergirl* 10.

His revival was in the more mystery-oriented *Sandman* 54. This led to a Vertigo special in 1994. This was a coming-of-age road movie in which three young men travel across the USA to locate the long-disappeared Prez, whom one of them firmly believes to be his father. This is a far cry from the Simon issues, with the whimsy replaced by a haunting and powerful plot from Ed Brubaker and excellent art from Eric Shanower. Don't come expecting anything like the wackiness of the original series, but as a homage to that and an exploration of 1960s and 1990s values it's very good.~HY

Recommended: 1–4, one-shot

PRIEST
Maximum: *3-issue miniseries 1996*

Whether he's read it or not, Rob Liefeld cannot be unaware of *Preacher*'s success. It therefore speaks volumes for his level of incompetence that he issues a comic with the ludicrous concept of a priest by day becoming a bloodthirsty armed vigilante by night. Liefeld's obviously working through some confused feelings about organised religion, with Mafia-style bishops and dying nuns. There is one redeeming factor in the pencils of Mark Pajarillo, who has the makings of a dynamic action style and could be worth looking out for in the future.~FP

PRIMAL
Dark Horse: *Graphic novel, 2 issues 1992*

In the early 1990s it seemed as if comic companies were bidding to adapt anything written by Clive Barker. These half-baked stories about creatures embodying fear are a notch above his shopping list. It's meagre fare indeed, with cut-and-paste artist John Van Fleet trying his utmost to obfuscate the slim element of plot present.~FP

PRIMAL FORCE
DC: *15 issues (0–14) 1994–1995*

An uneasy blend of mysticism and superheroics uniting a deliberately tenth-rate collection of characters. Until the arrival of Black Condor, Red Tornado is the best known, in this incarnation oddly mute and battered. They're allied with a new Claw, a novice Jack O'Lantern, the Golem and a previously unseen character called Meridian. Tying in the team with old Earth beliefs and superstitions is an interesting idea that never quite gels in practice. Writer Steven Seagle seems as uncomfortable with the required superhero action as he is well-versed in supplying small characterisation slots.~WJ

PRIME
Malibu: *Series one 26 issues, 1 Annual 1993–1995, series two 15 issues 1995–1995*

Prime is a superhero whose adult, heavily over-muscled body is actually a mass of green slime encasing the thirteen-year-old Kevin Green. The body is very strong but is susceptible to breaking down after too much strain is placed on it, forcing Kevin to rest before he can become Prime again. Supposedly the result of genetic experiments by Doctor Gross, Prime retains the mind of Kevin and his attempts at superheroics are subject to temper tantrums and inexperience. His father tries to protect him from the military, and prevent his mother from finding out just what's causing their son to wander off and then turn up naked on the doorstep. Meanwhile Kevin tries to romance Kelly, a school-friend, as Prime, whom he sees as the answer to all his childhood problems.

The major villains are the military (both conventional and governmental, in the form of the Aladdin organisation) and Doctor Gross, who wants to discover why Prime's body is 'perfect' when all his previous attempts have resulted in hideous monsters. A crossover with Mantra (8) established a rapport between them and attempted to give Kevin someone that he could call on for advice – something he desperately needs when he decides he's had enough of trying to be good but always being misunderstood (he tends to destroy things and is seen by school authorities as a potential child-molester because of his attentions towards Kelly). This bad-boy attitude lasts until he and Hardcase defeat Doctor Gross together in the annual and Kevin begins to understand what it means to be a hero, rather than just someone with a lot of power who does whatever he pleases.

One of his old skins gains a life of its own: as Primevil, in 22, he discovers a couple of friends, Turbo Charge and Phade, who vie for his attentions; the final two issues see them all involved in the crossover with *Power Of Prime*, which answers all of the questions about his true origin. Written by Len Strazewski and Gerard Jones, 1–12 are drawn by Norm Breyfogle, but after that it's practically a different artist on every issue. The premise is a variation on the original Captain Marvel with a modern twist but it's not handled well. Prime and Kevin are both very unsympathetic as written, and neither the supporting characters nor the artwork are good enough to overcome the scripts' faults. 'Prime Infinity' (1995) sets up the second series by having Prime so impressed by Spider-Man that he adopts a similar form and then takes on the Lizard. By 13 his secret identity as Kevin has been broadcast to the world after a long struggle with Aladdin. Frankly, not worth the paper it's printed on.~NF

PRIME CUTS
Fantagraphics: *10 issues 1987–1988*

A lack-lustre anthology for intellectuals, which has its moments but lacks consistency. Editor Gary Groth used it to showcase various other Fantagraphic projects to great effect; thus in various issues you'd get some *Polly & Her Pals* reprints, or a story from the *Complete Crumb* series. Generally this material was among the most desirable in the collections. Gabriel and F. Solano Lopez's harrowing *Ana* is serialised in 6–9, and there are occasional appearances by then newcomers such as Susan Catherine and Chester Brown, but on the whole the anthology concentrates on a central rota of contributors like Drew Friedman, Richard Sala, Michael Dougan and Dori Seda (whose contributions are uncharacteristically poor). Groth takes a multi-media approach to magazine editing,

reprinting Flaubert's chucklesome *Dictionary of Received Ideas*, illustrated by Rick Geary and including short stories. While contributions by the likes of Herman Hesse and Djuna Barnes shore up the mag's literary pretensions they can't help but show up the quality of most of the strips' scripts.~FJ

PRIME SLIME TALES
Mirage: *4 issues 1986*

In which a new genre is conceived: Mirage give you the unfunny animal comic.~FP

Comico PRIMER
Comico: *6 issues 1982–1984*

The first Comico title was essentially a fan publication. A very basic black and white anthology, it introduced Az, Skrog and Slaughterman, all of whom graduated to their own titles and disappeared quickly, and Mr Justice, who never got even that far. If the title is to be remembered it's for the first Grendel story in 2 and the first appearance of The Maxx in 5. Unless you've got more money than sense only Matt Wagner and Sam Kieth completists are advised to search out the issues in question. Both display early talent, but *Neutro* would sparkle amid some the other material present.~FP

Leonard Nimoy's PRIMORTALS
Tekno: *16 issues 1995–1996*
Big Entertainment: *6 issues + 1996 to date*

It transpires we are not alone, and our forebears were a group of mammals genetically mutated to increase intelligence and then removed from Earth. Now they've returned, bringing their conflicts with them. Despite his name being part of the title, Mr Spock has little to do with anything beyond the concept (although he did plot the two-issue *Primortals Origins* spin-off). It's left to an ever-changing cast of artists and writer Christopher Manley (from 3) to tell this story of Earth's first contact. It's all competent enough so far, but only really comes to life with the final issues of the Tekno series. A company change of name serves as an excuse to re-start the series, and Doug Wheeler writes the first six issues. 1 and 2 tie-up loose ends from the previous story and 3–6 have an alien plague loose on Earth, with little involvement from the aliens.~WJ

PRIMUS
Charlton: *7 issues 1972*

The undersea adventures of Ivan Tors's TV hero Carter Primus, 'the first man of the sea'. Accompanied by his lovely assistant Toni, Primus deals with foreign intrigue and marine mysteries in his mini-submarine, The Orca. The paper-thin stories by Joe Gill boast some of

Joe Staton's earliest comic art, and that's about as interesting as it gets. The appearance of a presidential stand-in named Richard N. Mixon in 7 has some curiosity value.~SW

PRINCE

Piranha/Titan: *One-shot ('Alter Ego') 1991, One-shot ('Three Chains Of Gold') 1994*

The first title should have been 'Super Ego', as it was surely only produced to pamper the purple one's ego. The nonsense has our 'hero' driving around Minneapolis playing concerts and righting wrongs on his motorcycle. There's no story to speak of, just promotional stuff for his *Diamonds And Pearls* album, and only bread-and-butter work in the art department from Denys Cowan and Kent Williams. The best thing about the whole sorry fiasco is a lovely Brian Bolland cover. The follow-up at least has the decency to amuse. Prince helps a Middle Eastern princess claim her throne from the wicked Vizier. Lots of sword fights and snogs ensue, all in a post-Adam Hughes style. Truly one for diehard Prince fans only.~TP

PRINCE VALIANT

Fantagraphics: *31 + volumes 1984 to date*

These volumes reprint the weekly newspaper strips begun by Hal Foster in 1937, with the intention of collecting every strip he contributed until his 1982 retirement (although he surrendered the art to John Cullen Murphy in 1971). In the strictest sense, *Prince Valiant* isn't a comic, being illustrations accompanied by blocks of text, but it's nevertheless stylish, influential, and an exceptional body of work. A skilful blend of imagination, legend and reality, Prince Valiant is a 5th-century adventurer, travelling the known world, usually as part of a mission for either King Arthur or for his father, the ruler of the Northern kingdom of Thule. A rare instance of the passage of time being incorporated into the strip, over the years Val develops from a hotheaded youth into a respected knight and leader and then a doting father. In later years his eldest son Arn is the focus.

The earliest work on the strip, although good, doesn't compare with what was to come, with Foster still developing his feature, although there's a greater fluidity to his art, which becomes more and more static as the series continues. The progress over the first six months is noticeable, as Foster eschews cluttered small panels for a more expansive layout, and his illustrative background is apparent from the start. Meticulous depictions of castles, battles, pageantry, scenery and sweeping panoramic views, the strong repertoire of postures and expressions, and the extraordinary detail characterising the feature

are all in place by the end of his first year. During the second year he's permitting more reflective moments to counterpoint the action, and by volume 5, 'The Sea King', reprinting stories from 1940, the art has begun to hit a peak from which it doesn't descend in the volumes so far collected. 9 and 10, otherwise good starting samplers as Valiant first meets his wife Aleta, see the lead strip reduced to two-thirds of a page by the introduction of a second feature, 'The Medieval Castle', depicting life as it was at the time.

Foster's artistic mastery tends to reduce the attention given his writing. The collections over-emphasise the skeleton upon which Foster hung them, with Valiant forever embarking on a new quest or mission, a weakness that wouldn't have been apparent reading the strips weekly over a period of years. The plots are well-conceived, exotic travelogues, with Foster never condescending towards other nations in the manner typical of the time at which they were created. He sets up tough problems and provides ingenious solutions, whether researched or imagined, and while his depiction of 5th-century life may diverge from reality, particularly in the area of cleanliness, it falls well within the bounds of artistic licence. He convinces by the well-researched artefacts and weaponry and the engagingly portrayed day-to-day life: small details such as mosquitoes being attracted by the damp animal skins being used for canoe-building characterise the extraordinary thought behind *Prince Valiant*. Foster's not above a chuckle at the superstitions of the past, and most mystical menaces introduced are revealed to have prosaic origins, unless Merlin is involved. The application of hindsight in those instances serves to authenticate the remainder of the strip.

There's week-to-week continuation of stories, although campaigns and missions are generally punctuated by less monumental activities. These ideal jumping-on points rarely coincide with the start and finish of individual collections, but events are easily picked up, meaning that one volume is as good a sample as another. Volumes relatively complete in themselves are 12, 'The New World', in which Valiant arrives in North America, or 15's story of a youngster introduced to Camelot and a war with the Picts. Both reprint pages from the late 1940s.

Despite the astounding amount of work involved in each weekly page, it's fifteen years before Foster resorts to reprinting (for four pages in 18), and even then it's framed with some new material. Unfortunately, limited access to the original art or good-quality copies means there's the occasional lapse in reproduction standards, but Fantagraphics are

to be commended for a high-quality reprint package befitting the material. Prince Valiant is rightly regarded among the top tier of American comic strips, and should be sampled by anyone interested in great art.~FP
Recommended: 5–31

Hal Foster's PRINCE VALIANT
Marvel: *4-issue miniseries 1994–1995*
As he dies, King Arthur asks that Excalibur be returned to the lake. Before he can do so, however, Gawain is set upon and the sword is taken by Morgause, who has also abducted Ingrid, Valiant's granddaughter and heir to the throne of Camelot. It's extremely faithful to the newspaper strip, to the extent of working with captioned illustrations: surely Foster couldn't have asked for better successors than Charles Vess, Elaine Lee and John Ridgway. There's a darker tone prevalent in this story, though, and the glory of battle is subsumed by its effects. Vess plots well enough to allow for plenty of diversions to interrupt the main quest, acknowledging the passage of time, and Ridgway's art is sumptuous.~FP
Recommended: 1–4

PRIORITY: WHITE HEAT
AC: *2 issues 1986–1987*
White Heat's a female James Bond type, who gets mixed up with Nazis trying to revive the Third Reich. Competent but uninspired.~NF

THE PRISONER
DC: *4-issue miniseries 1989*
A familiarity with cult TV series *The Prisoner* is essential here, but you'll be disappointed if you're looking for adaptations of episodes, because, although the title is based on the series, there's a new prisoner. The action takes place twenty years after the conclusion of the TV story. The mysterious village is now abandoned except for the sole occupant, the former number six. It doesn't stay that way for long, though, as back in the hush-hush world of the secret service, a female agent resigns and arrives at the Village. She's joined by the midget butler and the former number two, just released from prison. Meanwhile, back in London, the new prisoner's husband, also a secret agent, has been researching the secrets of the Village, and plans to rescue her. Fans of *The Prisoner* may not appreciate new characters being added to the scenario, but the known cast are excellently portrayed by writers Dean Motter and Mark Askwith, and Motter's imagery captures the mood of the series perfectly. The final issue reveals the real secret of the Village, but then is anything what it appears to be?~HY
Collection: Shattered Visage (1–4)

PRIVATE BEACH
Antarctic Press: *3 issues 1995*
Would-be Jaime Hernandez, writer/artist David Hahn, makes a good stab at reproducing the attitude and atmosphere of Hernandez's 'Mechanics', but there's something a little deliberate about it all. The plot concerns a freewheeling young woman's search for an extra-dimensional being who's forgotten who and what he is. Prodded by voices in her head, she's always been regarded as a bit of a freak by her friends. Too cute for many people's tastes, perhaps, but there is promise here in the lightness of touch and story-telling.~NF

The Double Life Of PRIVATE STRONG
Archie: *2 issues 1959*
Jack Kirby and Joe Simon rework their Captain America concept of an army joe with a secret costumed identity to revamp 1940s hero The Shield. Kirby's gone by the second issue, and oy, Archie, nooooo George Tuska is not an adequate replacement. It's pretty ordinary stuff from all concerned.~WJ

THE PROFESSIONAL Gogol 13
Viz: *4-issue miniseries 1991*
James Hudnall adapts a story from one of the earliest Manga successes by Takao Saito, drawn in what now looks quite a primitive style which, nonetheless, allows the story to flow smoothly. The Professional is a master assassin, here called upon to execute a man who, we are told, is a Nazi war criminal, now in a sanatorium. Like all good thrillers, nothing is what it seems. Initially Saito concentrates on the procedure of assassination as his hero grows on you, so that when the dénouement comes it will mean something.~FJ

PROFESSOR OM
Innovation: *1 issue 1990*
The Professor and a boxing champion are teleported by a strange force to an alien planet. Once on the planet the two characters fight jungle animals and barbarians before being captured by intergalactic gamblers and forced to fight for their lives. The artwork and the layouts are truly terrible, but the entire package makes excellent carpet underlay.~SS

PROFESSOR X & The X-MEN
Marvel: *17 issues, 1996–1997*
Marvel cancelled the successful reprint series *X-Men: The Early Years* series to make way for this soulless MTVisation of the early X-Men stories, complete with broken-backed Image-style art and mindless posturing. Most annoying is the participation of Jan Duursema on the early issues. Judging from her work

elsewhere, she's someone who can draw, but, judging by this, was ordered not to. Fortunately, the comics world failed to take this drivel to its collective bosom.~HS

THE PROJECT
Paradox: *2-issue microseries 1996*

The two paperback-sized issues comprising *The Project* are an ambitious work telling connected stories from a twenty-year period of an inner-city housing project. Characters are shown in one aspect, then, pages later, seen earlier or later in their lives. One presumes writer John Figueroa kept charts when plotting, such is the complexity of the intertwining. The largely depressing stories are illustrated in appropriately gritty style by Kirk Albert, and they're certainly heartfelt, but the first book doesn't present anything that most readers won't already have seen in countless TV shows. Beyond the narrative leaping back and forth through time Figueroa doesn't seem up to giving his stories an individual flavour. The best of the first volume concerns a woman deciding that the atrocities in her apartment block have gone on too long, and the time has come to take a stand, although the outcome is predictable. The second book, though, is a vast improvement. There's a greater originality to the stories, as Figueroa moves beyond examining crack dealers, junkies and gangsters and on to the system which lets them proliferate. There's less predictability, a greater emphasis on caring and a far greater warmth and understanding from both characters and author.~FP

PROPELLER MAN
Dark Horse: *8-issue limited series 1993–1994*

Propeller Man has huge gaps in his memory, armour in place of skin, and he flies with the aid of the propeller on his back and his wing-shaped jet-board. When a heavily armed monster escapes from an Antarctic lab and rampages through the city, Propeller Man feels that he knows it, and the monster seems to know him too, and, as events develop, Propellor Man starts to reconstruct his past. This makes the series sound far too interesting. When Matthias Schultheiss tells the story, it's a lot of gratuitous violence, corporate conspiracies, endless scenes with Propellor Man's friends (smug gits, to a man), and preposterous dialogue along the lines of 'Since she found that paper swallow with the poem on it, she's changed' and 'Eat my rotating blade'. Damn, it sounds too interesting again. Avoid.~FC

PROPHET
Image: *Series one 11 issues (0–10) 1993–1995, Series two 9 issues +, 1 Annual, 1 Special 1995 to date*

Prophet is a supersoldier empowered by a satellite, created in 1940s Germany and then left in suspended animation until revived in

Youngblood 4. Rob Liefeld might acknowledge this cobbling together of *Captain America* and *Omac* by having a supporting character named Kirby, but that doesn't excuse it. The forced biblical allegories of the first series wear thin, and Stephen Platt's trumpeted art in 5–10 is distorted and gruesome. Series two, written by Chuck Dixon, recasts Prophet and reveals he's far more than originally conceived, and Platt's reined in to good effect. It's still no masterpiece, but much improved. Pompous and overbearing villain Drakmordrid is a hoot and a half, offering self-obsessed soliloquies that one assumes Dixon considers poetic, dramatic and soul-searching. Try 8 for a particularly spectacular session.~FP
Collection: Prophet (series one 1–7)

PROTECTORS
Malibu: *20 issues 1992–1994*

A group of extremely obscure 1940s super-heroes revived and banded as a team. 1–9 are moderately intriguing, with enough mystery to ensure readers return for more, and 5 has a tacky novelty bullet-hole drilled through the entire comic to commemorate the death of a team member. Beyond that, the plethora of characters and an intrusive crossover ensure that little time is devoted to anything other than fighting. Full credit, though, for a final issue that runs contrary to all expectations.~WJ

PROTOTYPE
Malibu: *19 issues (0–18), 1 Giant Size 1994–1995*

It's hard to believe it took two writers, Len Kaminski and Tom Mason, to conceive this lame knock-off of Marvel's Iron Man. Naïve teenager Jimmy Ruiz is Prototype, the 'corporate spokesman' for devious organisation Ultratech. Ruiz, a superpowered 'Ultra' with a fondness for steroids, replaced original Prototype Bob Campbell, a crippled ex-stunt man now bearing a healthy grudge against his former employers. The first four issues were drawn by the team of David Ammerman and James Pascoe, before Ammerman left to plot and draw the crappy *Wrath* (another Ultraverse hero who first appeared in *Prototype* 4). After that, slightly more pleasing penciller Roger Robinson hung on until almost the bitter end. The idea of superhero as media darling dates back at least as far as Grant Morrison's *Zenith* circa 1987, and Kaminski/Mason don't have anything very new to say on the subject. In other words, a modish gimmick is used to prop up more witless superhero fisticuffs.~AL

PROWLER
Eclipse: *Miniseries one 4 issues 1987, Miniseries two 4 issues 1988*

Prowler is an ambitious attempt to create a new character that retains the mystery and adventure of the early pulps but that is capable of bearing some of the weight of 'modern' questioning of motives. Leo Kragg, the original Prowler, takes on a young apprentice, Scott, who's not at all ready for the violence and ruthlessness that being around the Prowler entails. Faced with an old adversary who commands an army of zombies and children, Scott does his best to avoid killing his enemies, nearly getting Leo killed in the process. Tim Truman's script is taut but occasionally obvious, while John K.Snyder III's artwork is mechanical and rather soulless. He obviously knows all the tricks of the trade and he captures expression well, but his figures never seem quite right. Tim Truman continues the adventures of his modern pulp hero in *Revenge Of The Prowler*. Unfortunately, though working hard on characterisation, he includes too much daft technology to make the plot work. Snyder's artwork looks rushed. As an added bonus, issue 2 has a flexidisk soundtrack to accompany the story.~NF

The PROWLER

Marvel: *4-issue miniseries 1994–1995*

Long-time occasional Spider-Man ally is forced to ask some soul-searching questions as to his priorities in life. Complicated by a murderous *doppelgänger* using his technology and a familiar villain, the miniseries, produced by the creative team of Carl Potts and Bill Reinhold, is better than its company contemporaries, although that's not difficult.~FP

PRUDENCE AND CAUTION

Defiant: *6 issues 1994*

Written by Chris Claremont and drawn by Jim Fern, this ties in with *Warriors Of Plasm*, starring Rick Tietz from that series. Prudence is a strange creature, perhaps the deadliest in the Universe, and is accidentally freed by Tietz in *Warriors* 6. Starting on Earth she has an interest in Rick, but she's not the only one. It's professional, but not outstanding.~HY

PSI-FORCE

Marvel: *32 issues, 1 Annual 1986–1989*

Marvel's 'back to basics' thrust in 1986 created the New Universe, the concept of which strove for even more realism than the mainstream Marvel Universe did in 1961. The New Universe is based on the real world until the White Event (see *Starbrand* 12) induced paranormal powers in two out of every million people. In *Psi-Force*, Emmett Proudhawk assembles five altered and unwilling teenagers. He dies at the end of issue 1, but collectively they are able to summon his spirit as a giant psionic hawk. Refreshing as it is to encounter characters without secret identities and code names, and who wear their underpants on the inside, crafting quality stories about superheroes without the trappings of a superhero universe is highly demanding, and the creators fail to rise to the challenge. There is plenty of characterisation, background and emotional *angst* in the first fifteen issues, mainly written by Danny Fingeroth, but dreary plots reiterate attempts by political and corporate entities to subvert the kids' abilities for their own goals. Furthermore, Wayne Tucker's mind-wiping powers mirror those of the *X-Men's* Professor X, are used with far less restraint and are far too convenient.

Fabian Nicieza writes all issues from 16, initiating a new and downhill direction from 18 as the team is involuntarily disbanded for six issues and reformed with changed personnel. The kids' streetwise maturity with their powers dissolves any charm of the earlier issues, where tentative fumblings often produced unpredictable results. The title rolls on like a telephone book but without the plot, until cancellation strikes mercifully in 32.~APS

PSI JUDGE ANDERSON

Fleetway/Quality: *15 issues 1989–1990*
2000AD Books: *1 Graphic Novel ('Shamballa') 1991*
Mandarin: *2 Graphic Novels + ('Childhood's End', 'Satan') 1993 to date*

With Judge Dredd by far and away the most popular strip in Britain's *2000AD* comic, it became inevitable that further strips would be spun off from the concept. The first of these was Judge Anderson. She was introduced as a freethinking woman whose individuality was indulged by the repressive Judge system due to her prodigious mental abilities. Alan Grant has written (or co-written with John Wagner) all her solo stories way beyond what's reprinted here, and from the start advisedly adopts a completely different tone to Judge Dredd. Anderson's stories are action adventure, and although there are moments of humour, they're more to contrast the darker mood than on the level of the farce prevalent in *Judge Dredd*. There's also no doubt that she's the focus of the stories.

Brett Ewins illustrates the earlier issues, but is uninspired by weak material, including demonic possession from a dimension beyond Earth. One of Mega-City One's greatest foes returns in 6 and 7, illustrated by Barry Kitson, with Anderson having premonitions of a wolf. The quality line is curving upward, but this is still perfunctory material. 'Helios' in 8 and 9 is the first really good Anderson story. Exquisitely drawn in neo-realist fashion by David Roach, it offers more of Anderson's character beyond the uniform amid a disturbing tale of revenge. 10 and 11's 'Triad', illustrated by Arthur Ranson, continues a fine run, touching on child abuse as childhood nightmares prove a very real threat to Anderson and the city as whole. Ranson's illustrative, almost photographic, art style is astoundingly detailed, yet fluid and emotional, and elevates the story, shaking loose any remaining tenuous associations with Dredd. 13–15 continue a tale begun in 12, which is actually a Judge Dredd story in which Anderson plays a large part. 'City Of The Damned' had already been reprinted as *Judge Dredd* 15–18, and is a lack-lustre effort about a mutant destined to rule Mega-City One.

Unfortunately the entire series suffers from shoddy reproduction, blurring the artwork. Interested readers are directed instead to the better-quality Titan reprint volumes.

Anderson has continued appearing in British strips since the conclusion of this story, and three collections of these later stories are available. They represent a period of progression for Anderson as the spiritual side of her nature comes increasingly to the fore, and she gradually becomes more disenchanted with the system which the Judges uphold. The Arthur Ranson-drawn 'Shamballa' proves him to be as masterful in colour as he is in pen and ink. Manifestations of strange phenomena allied with brutal deaths lead to a teaming of Anderson and a Soviet counterpart on a mission to a long-hidden subterranean city. In 'Childhood's End' Anderson investigates a pyramid on Mars in a story offering a solution to life on Earth. It's weak, and the substitution of Ranson's Anderson by Kev Walker's more muscly figure is initially jarring, although it's equally well drawn. 'Satan' has Anderson back on Earth, and Ranson back on the art, for a story involving an alien claiming to be Satan, an improvement on its predecessor, but not up to the best Anderson material.~FP
Recommended: 8–11, 'Shamballa'
Collections: Judge Anderson Vol 1 (1–3), vol 2 (4, 5), vol 3 (6, 7), vol 4 (8, 9), vol 5 (10, 11), *Judge Dredd: City Of The Damned* (13–15)

PSI-LORDS
Valiant: *10 issues 1994–1995*

The Psi-Lords are a team of ageless beings who've set themselves up as protectors of the universe. They're aloof, detached and feared. The first issue's introduction to the team (also known as Starwatchers) is very well handled. Despite 2–3 tying into 'The Chaos Effect' crossover, more information about the team is imparted, filling in most essential background detail. A fallen Starwatcher returns in 4, and 6 and 7 have an invasion by the frog-like Sirians, revealing an alternative agenda on the part of the Psi-Lords. This intriguing plot is dropped for the final three issues, which are a great disappointment, as they're nothing more than standard action material. The success of the

early issues is very much to do with writer Anthony Bedard choosing to have the reader see the Psi-Lords through the eyes of Earth ambassador Danae Del Sol. Her narrative, experiences and interpretations give a unique viewpoint for the title, and artist Mike Leeke is excellent throughout the first seven issues. All of those are worth picking up, but start at the beginning.~WJ
Recommended: 1–3, 6, 7

THE PSYBA-RATS
DC: *3-issue miniseries 1995*

The Psyba-Rats are criminal computer hackers led by Razor, who was given superpowers when bitten by an alien during DC's *Bloodlines* saga. With Hackrat and Channelman (who is trapped in Cyberspace) Razor sets out to find the formula for Zesti-Cola. A guest appearance from Robin helps set the series firmly amongst DC's youth titles. The story's not without its pleasures and the artwork, by Michael Dutkiewicz and Andrew Kent, is a delightful mix of old and new influences.~NF

THE PSYCHO
DC: *3-issue miniseries 1991*

James Hudnall spins a tale of what might have happened if a superpowered being had killed Hitler, shortening World War II and changing the political future of the West. Jack Riley is a non-powered spy sent to keep tabs on one country's stockpile of superbeings. When his cover is blown and his girl-friend, Sonya, captured he takes a drug that might or might not kill him and emerges as The Psycho, determined to rescue Sonya and clear his name. The story is uncompromising in its depiction of the lack of respect for life exhibited by both government and superbeings as they jostle for power in a world heading for a bloody war, where the country with the most superhero soldiers will win. Dan Brereton's painted artwork is stunning and his character designs are clearly precursors of his own *Nocturnals* series – he seems particularly taken by amphibian characters. These 'heroes' are the stuff of nightmare.~NF

PSYCHOANALYSIS
EC: *4 issues 1955*

Public pressure closed down EC's mainstay horror and crime titles, and this was the oddest of their replacements. On the face of it not the ideal choice of material for a comic, so it proved, although the stories do become more involving as they continue. Three patients are psychoanalysed, each having one session per issue. Freddy Carter resents his parents' attitudes towards him, Ellen Lyman is plagued by nightmares, and Mark Stone, ostensibly a successful writer, fears he's a hack

and is overly concerned with death. Jack Kamen makes a sterling attempt at injecting excitement and variety into a dry topic requiring plenty of talking-heads shots, but can only cope with so many of them no matter how good he is.~WJ
Collection: *Psychoanalysis* (1–4)

PSYCHOBLAST
First: *9 issues 1987–1988*
Psychoblast can do almost anything with the power of his mind, making him a desirable item for plenty of folk. Unfortunately he only exists when his host body, Brian Burke, sleeps. There's blood and thunder galore, but it all amounts to little in the end.~WJ

PSYCHONAUTS
Epic: *4-issue miniseries 1993*
Produced as a joint effort between America and Japanese creators, the story features a group of six telepaths landing on a diseased earth in search of a new home. Essentially boring, and Motofumi Kobayashi's artwork is more suited to Manga than the washed-out form he displays here.~SS.

PTERANO-MAN
Kitchen Sink: *One-shot 1990*
A superhero parody on a grand scale, Don Simpson's *Bizarre Heroes* include Pterano-Man, The Phantom Jungle Girl, Megaton Man and the See-Thru Girl. The one-shot prelude to the regular *Bizarre Heroes* series features three stories introducing the first two characters above. Pterano-Man battles ecological disaster and a man-dinosaur while Phantom Jungle Girl gets her mind switched with the Cowboy Gorilla's. Good, mostly clean fun.~NF

PUMA BLUES
Aardvark One International: *17 issues 1986–1988*
Stephen Murphy & Michael Zulli: *3 issues (18–20) 1988*
Mirage: *3 issues (21–23) 1989*
In the year 2000, Gavia Immer is a soldier sent out into the wild to observe and sample nature. It's a world where racist fantasies have nuked the Bronx and the rivers need regular doses of alkalines in order to offset the effects of acid rain. A flying mantra ray has stirred political interest and Gavia is beset by memories of his father (whom he re-encounters through videos) and conversations with a trespassing cowboy, which are recorded by a wandering robotic chauffeur.

Puma Blues is a complex, increasingly abstract work, undoubtedly heartfelt. At times it seems there's no plot, just a series of observations on nature, human or otherwise. It's also an intense plea for the protection of the environment from future depredation. Zulli's artwork is detailed, like Barry Windsor-Smith's, but he has also picked up the scratchiness of an Eddie Campbell. It's certainly very illustrative, particularly in 5, a wordless trip through the forest at night, with short vignettes about the creatures still abroad. 20 is a benefit book (with contributions from Dave Sim, Steve Bissette, Chester Brown, Peter Laird, Tim Truman, Tom Sutton, Alan Moore, Kev Eastman and Rick Veitch) to show solidarity in a dispute between publishers and distributors.~NF
Recommended: 5

PUMPKINHEAD
Dark Horse: *4-issue miniseries 1993*
An ages-old entity is summoned by magic in the backwoods to take revenge for murder. Throw in a superstitious local community, some teenage hoods, a woman with arcane abilities, and a mysterious stranger with a secret and you have all the ingredients of a horror plot. The trouble is that it's a plot used to excess through the ages, and there's nothing new added here, although Shawn McManus, as ever, produces functional and decorative artwork. Despite the name, though, the head of the title creature only resembles a pumpkin in colour. Very disappointing.~FP

THE PUNISHER
Marvel: *5-issue miniseries 1985–1986, Series one 104 issues, 7 Annuals, 10 Specials 1987–1995, Series two 14 issues + 1995 to date*
The Punisher spent over a decade as a supporting character, primarily in *Spider-Man* titles, before Steven Grant and Mike Zeck's miniseries made him a headliner. Introduced in *Amazing Spider-Man* 129, the Punisher is a composite lifted from popular 1970s paperback fiction: Vietnam vet turns heavily armed hitman driven to kill criminals, having seen his family wiped out by gangsters. If you can accept the debatable ethics of the series, *The Punisher* provides generally reasonable stories issue after issue without ever being outstanding.

The exception is the first issues of the miniseries. Steve Grant and Mike Zeck explain previous inconsistencies in the Punisher's behaviour, have him settle a few scores in jail, and escape with the complicity of the warden. Thereafter the story slipped a little, but reflected the trend towards more violent comic heroes, and its success seemed to catch Marvel on the hop. It was over a year before the start of an ongoing title (although they made up for lost time, as the plethora of other *Punisher* titles testifies). Retaining the first-person narrative as exposition, Mike Baron writes most issues to 62 of the first series. He provides action thrillers with the requisite high body count, initially liberally adapting contemporary news. The likes of the Reverend Jim Jones, blackmailers tampering with pharmaceutical products and insider traders all get theirs in suitably brutal fashion. Stories rarely stretch beyond two parts, and there's little continuity, making sampling relatively simple. Best of the earlier issues is the Whilce Portacio and Scott Williams-illustrated cat-and-mouse with the Kingpin in 15–18, but none match the power of the miniseries.

That Baron was running out of ideas after nearly five years can be seen by the conclusion to a multi-parter in 59, in which The Punisher is transformed into a black guy, albeit only for three issues. New writers Dan Abnett and Andy Lanning (and penciller Dougie Braithwaite to 75) offer more multi-part stories, starting with the Punisher in Europe in 64–70, and while maintaining the body count their stories aren't so relentlessly grim. 'Fire Fight' in 82–84, well pencilled by Hugh Haynes, is their best effort, and it also features Vigil, the New York anti-vigilante squad who've been after Castle since 72. 86–88 are this title's chapters of 'Suicide Run', which crosses over with both other Punisher monthlies, and leaves an assortment of Punishers running around in the wake of Frank Castle's apparent death. He's not dead, of course, and after 'Suicide Run' there are different creative teams almost every issue to the end of the run, with Frank Teran's astoundingly distorted art in the brutal 94–95 worthy of note. Bullseye turns up in 102 to set in motion events that have far-reaching consequences for both the Punisher and S.H.I.E.L.D., and end the first ongoing series.

For the second series John Ostrander and Tom Lyle realise that the Punisher of old has fallen into disarray and modify his method of operation. Concluding that he'll never eradicate crime, he takes control of a crime family to fight the war from within. Unfortunately, there's still some business outstanding with S.H.I.E.L.D. that comes to occupy the title. This version is consistently more interesting than at any time since the miniseries.

At the height of the character's popularity Marvel issued The Punisher Magazine, a black and white title reprinting the miniseries and early issues of this and Punisher War Zone.~WJ
Recommended: Miniseries 1
Collection: The Punisher - Circle of Blood (Miniseries 1–5)

PUNISHER Graphic Novels, One-Shots and Microseries

Whether Marvel believed that banging out Punisher stories in a more expensive format would introduce the character to a new audience or whether they just wanted more money from the already captured punters is debatable. They certainly instituted a hectic

schedule from 1987. The best of the bunch is the oversized Assassins Guild. It's a well-plotted story from Jo Duffy in which our man teams with the titular guild to eradicate a company protecting rich criminals. It's lifted to great heights by the excellent Jorge Zaffino artwork, and if ever another Punisher movie script is required the studios could do far worse than this. Zaffino returns in fine form in the company of Chuck Dixon for the less successful Kingdom Gone. Blood On The Moors shows none of the creators at their best, and the idea of transporting the Punisher to the Scottish highlands is daft. That said, it's a rare story by John Wagner and Alan Grant that lacks any leavening humour, and Cam Kennedy is never less than professional, which ranks this near the top of the list. It's a shame, then, that Marvel only ever published the story in expensive hardback format. Dan Chichester, John Romita Jnr and Klaus Janson turn in an acceptable exercise in compare-and-contrast in Punisher/Batman.

Jim Starlin's decent plot combats Tom Grindberg's shockingly distorted figurework in the two-part Ghosts Of The Innocent with an interesting twist on the school-bus-caught-in-gangster-shootout scenario, and The Punisher's creator, Gerry Conway, returns with Dave Cockrum and Jeff Albrecht for a somewhat predictable but nonetheless spirited Bloodlines. The Grant/Zeck team that elevated the Punisher to star status are back for Return To Big Nothing. It's taut and well constructed from a string of clichés including (but not limited to) the guy who was always tougher than Frank Castle in Vietnam, the matchbook clue, the whore with the heart of gold, the Saigon withdrawal and the fixed casino. Divorced from the idea that it was originally intended to occupy three issues of Marvel's restrained and sober The 'Nam, Castle romping around the jungle in The Punisher Invades The 'Nam has its moments, although it's little more than a shoot-'em-up. Absolutely nothing more than a shoot-'em-up is The Punisher Kills The Marvel Universe. Not literally, you understand, but he does off almost every superhero and supervillain. Switch off your brain before entering.

Of the less memorable series and one-shots, Blood And Glory might have worked in one issue, but drags over three, contrasting the Punisher with Captain America as they forge a mutual respect, and also featuring Terror. It's better, though, than the meeting with Cap's more gung-ho counterpart, the USAgent, in No Escape, in which Paladin has to assassinate our man. Strangely, he fails. The Origin of Microchip tells in rather prosaic fashion how the Punisher's techy pal hooked up with him, in what would at any other time have been two issues of a regular title, as would G Force. Slim

plot sees off *Die Hard In The Big Easy* and the team-up with Black Widow in *Spinning Doomsday's Web*, while there's a fine twist to *The Prize*, but getting to it through dull story and pedestrian art is hard work. The same applies to *Intruder*, with its strained religious symbolism and stupid plot, from Baron and Reinhold on autopilot. Their efforts on *Empty Quarter*, the Punisher in the desert, are only marginally better. Teaming the *Punisher and Archie* was an idea best left in the bar, while *A Man Called Frank* is a pointless reworking of the Punisher's origin in 1910 to create a late Western version of the character.~FP
Recommended: *The Assassins Guild*

PUNISHER P.O.V.
Marvel: *4-issue miniseries 1991*

Jim Starlin and Berni Wrightson concoct a better-than-average Punisher story in which pragmatism allies him with the Kingpin's men. This is to deal with the son of an industrialist, hideously mutated by toxic waste, with a penchant for draining women's blood. Plot complications ensue with the involvement of a deranged vampire-hunter, prompting the interest of Nick Fury.~FP

PUNISHER 2099
Marvel: *34 issues 1993–1995*

You've got to have some sympathy with the guy who wipes out Jake Gallows' family. As caricatured by writers Pat Mills and Tony Skinner they're the most saccharine bunch this side of the Care Bears. Sadly, this shorthand characterisation extends to the entire cast. Despite some inventive wrinkles on the Punisher legend, like Gallows keeping a prison complete with molecular disintegrator chair in his basement, it's basically little more than line-them-up-and- blow-them-away for the first twenty-seven issues. With 28 Doom's takeover of the USA in *Doom 2099* has repercussions here, as the Punisher is appointed to head an anti-criminal squad called S.H.I.E.L.D. The final few issues, by Chuck Dixon and Rod Whigham, are a marginal improvement as Gallows has to fight his robotic *alter ego* and escape Doom.~WJ

PUNISHER WAR JOURNAL
Marvel: *80 issues, 1988–1995*

Since his earliest appearances, a narrative format used for The Punisher is captions detailing his 'War Journal' entries, or 'Punisher's Diary', with the pretence stripped away. 'Dear Diary, today I protected the innocent (apart from the ones killed in the crossfire), thwarted the guilty (apart from the ones who are smarter than me, which is most of them), and made the country safe (after everybody pulled themselves out of the

smouldering wreckage).' Exaggeration perhaps, but certainly not by much. In what was touted before its début as the 'quality' *Punisher* title, Frank Castle goes around the world having adventures in picturesque foreign parts, reducing them to rubble in partly-successful attempts to right wrongs. Jim Lee drew most of 1–19, presumably the reason for the title's misapplied 'quality' tag. His presence, though, doesn't disguise the rushed, slipshod, second-rate nature of most of the stories. Once he leaves, the most notable issues artistically are the teaming of Andy Kubert with father Joe in 31–33. Most superheroes look out of place in Punisher's gritty urban milieu, but that doesn't stop the writers trying to sneak them in. There's the inevitable Wolverine (6,7), Daredevil (2, 3, with Nomad in 45–47), Ghost Rider (29–30, 57–58), and Daredevil and Ghost Rider (57,58). 61 begins the 'Suicide Run' story, which crosses through numerous issues of both other ongoing Punisher titles before concluding here with 64. It begins with Castle's apparent death, and, adopting the similar idea from the *Superman* titles, four surrogate Punishers appear to take his place, a frightening equation. Thankfully the market for obsessive gun-toting murderers appeared to have declined by 1995, sweeping most of the Punisher's titles away.~HS
Collections: The African Saga (6–7), *An Eye For An Eye* (1–3)

PUNISHER WAR ZONE
Marvel: *41 issues, 2 Annuals 1992–1995*

Punisher exploitation hit a peak with the launch of this third ongoing title. Its distinguishing aspects are a monopoly of multi-issue story-lines and avoidance of superhero guest stars. Only Wolverine, in 19, breaks the rule, and even then stays out of longjohns. All the stories reflect Punisher's violent, obsessive vendetta against the criminal fraternity and many have some degree of merit, but the run suffers from repetition.

Chuck Dixon writes the majority (1–11, 26–37, 41, both annuals) and leads the field, mainly by endowing Frank Castle with curt, black humour. 1–6 set a standard that the book never subsequently regains. Punisher goes undercover, has a domestic with Microchip and confronts a chilling new nemesis, Thorn, whose major reappearance in Annual 2 sadly disappoints. Dixon's sequel in 7–11 is still reasonable, although lessened by John Romita Jr's departure from pencils. Dan Abnett and Andy Lanning break the formula in 12–16, but their narrative of Punisher's brain-washing does not quite hang. Writing Punisher requires a fine art in displaying his escapes from certain death cliffhangers – after all, the man has no superpowers – and Larry Hama's run (20–25) overstretches suspension of disbelief. His

'Suicide Run' (23–25) and 41's 'Countdown'
are the only stories to directly crossover with
Punisher's other ongoing titles.~APS
Recommended: 1–6

THE PUNISHER YEAR ONE
Marvel: *4-issue miniseries 1994–1995*

Picking up with the murder of Frank Castle's
family, this is really the first couple of weeks
for the Punisher, and it's not until the final
issue that he dons the skull shirt. Feeling
betrayed by the law he resolves that those
seemingly beyond judgement will be
punished. Adequate, but Dale Eaglesham's
covers apart, not spectacular, which it really
should be.~WJ

PUNX
Valiant: *4 issues, 1 Special 1995*

Keith Giffen masterminded this parody
comic, centred nonetheless firmly in the
Valiant Universe. A bunch of the most futile
and occasionally disgusting paranormals
imaginable, (Ma'am Marie? The Crimson
Pigeon? P.M.S. The Para-Military Shrew?)
offshoots of the Harbinger programmes,
thwart (mostly inadvertently) the plans of an
evil collective creature, the Veil. Some cute
touches, including sarcastic digs at Valiant's
increasingly desperate 'relaunch' attempts,
but largely muddy and incoherent. The
Manga Punx one-shot, printed back to front,
followed, and subsequent one-shots were
solicited, but never issued.~HS

PURGATORI: The Vampires Myth
Chaos: *3 issues 1996*

An excuse for big-titted vampiresses to lose
what few clothes they have as they fight
amongst themselves. Brian Pulido includes
Purgatori's origin, working in a bit of ancient
Egyptian lesbianism for the lads, and Jim
Balent's artwork isn't actually that bad if you
like that sort of thing, but, really, who's got
time?~NF

PURGATORY USA
Slave Labor: *1 issue 1989*

Début for Ed Brubaker, with vignettes about
the fictional Maynardville, middle USA.
Although it's well drawn, the enduring feeling
is 'so what?' The one story with the potential to
avoid this, 'The Rain', begins with six pages of
unnecessary exposition, and the chapter
ending occurs as the story had taken off, never
to be completed. Brubaker left this behind for
the more successful *Lowlife*.~WJ

QUACK
Star*Reach: *6 issues 1976–1977*

Mike Friedrich's Star*Reach Productions did much to pave the way for the independent boom of the early 1980s. Giving creators copyright and creative freedom, the aim was to try to reach a more mature audience but retain some of the sense of fun that brought them into the comics business in the first place. *Quack*, nominally a funny-animal anthology that features ducks, never bothered too much about keeping to the rules. Three strips stand out from the series. Michael T. Gilbert's 'The Wraith' began life as a Spirit parody/homage and quickly improved as Gilbert's art skills developed. 'Newton The Wonder Rabbit' from 2 is a madcap space adventure written by Sergio Aragonés and drawn by Steve Leialoha, and 'The Beavers' is an early, very rough Dave Sim strip commenting on Canadian stereotypes and taking potshots at family life. No single issue has enough meat to make you feel it's a great title, but there are many interesting contributions from the likes of Frank Brunner, Mark Evanier, Scott Shaw and Dave Stevens.~NF

QUADRANT
Quadrant: *8 issues 1983–1986*

If you like sword-and-sorcery and naked women there's a chance you'll enjoy this half-arsed, sub-John Norman tale of warrior women, elven thieves, dire gods and dim (or undead) swordsmen. What separates *Quadrant* from most other strips in the genre is the scattershot attempt to make it sexy, with everything from open-crotch shots to bondage and lesbian encounters. Its utter triviality is demonstrated by the concept of hordes of women going into battle wearing nothing but high heels.~NF
Collection: The Hellrazor Saga (1–8)

QUANTUM LEAP
Innovation: *12 issues 1 Special 1991–1993*

This is the comics version of the TV series, telling additional stories of Sam Beckett as he leaps from life to life, inhabiting each person's body for long enough to 'put right what once went wrong'. The comic captures the characters and the feel of the series very well,

and with each story limited to a single issue (or half-issue), even the weaker ideas don't make unreasonable demands on your patience, which is more than can be said for the series. Of the stronger ideas, some explore the rules of the format (6, where Sam becomes one of a pair of twins), whereas others tackle particular issues (9, on the gay rights movement, written by Andy Mangels). During the first flush of popularity the first issue was reprinted with some extra pages of text material.~FC

QUASAR
Marvel: *58 issues 1988–1994*

One of the many series which manages to be entertainingly average without rising far enough above that to receive any recognition, *Quasar* was written for most of its run by the reliable Mark Gruenwald, and is a bargain-box gem. The soap-opera plot, centring around the title character and his friends – including his girl-friend Kayla and the (never actually stated but obviously gay) Eternal, Makkari – always trotted along with an air of light-hearted fun. The plots were never as cosmic as they aspired to be but were nonetheless never dull, augmented by a plethora of jokes milked out of the fact that in his civilian identity of Wendell Vaughn, Quasar rented office space in the Fantastic Four's Baxter Building headquarters. It was the perfect cover: if a villain attacked at an inopportune moment, Vaughn would protect his identity by claiming they were after the FF instead. 17, featuring a race to determine the fastest character in the Universe, is full of great in-jokes for sad old fanboys.~JC
Recommended: 17

QUEST FOR DREAMS LOST
Literary Volunteers Of Chicago: *One-shot 1987*

As the publisher suggests, this was intended to raise money to promote the importance of literacy, with many creator-owned properties occupying short chapters in which they must locate a well-known fictional object. The most prominent among them are the Teenage Mutant Ninja Turtles, by Eastman and Laird, retrieving Arthur's legendary sword Excalibur, but of most interest is the early artwork from Mike Parobeck and Guy Davis.~WJ

THE QUESTION

DC: *Series one 36 issues, 2 Annuals 1987–1990, Series two 5 issues 1990–1992, One-shot 1997*

An excellent and vastly underrated series. Continuing from the premise of the Question's previous solo outing almost twenty years previously in *Mysterious Suspense*, the stated editorial aim was to present a world as real as possible. The only anomalies are the minor scientific gimmicks used to transform crusading TV journalist Vic Sage into the crimefighting Question. Astonishingly, *The Question* lived up to the promise, over thirty-six issues becoming a compulsive drama that can stand with the best TV output. Even bit-players are multi-faceted, with motivations consistent with their actions. Sage himself is exceptionally well drawn, a far from likeable individual who nonetheless cares deeply about the disintegrating industrial wasteland his city is becoming.

The first series can be broken down into four distinct phases, with 1–5 filling in Sage's background and giving him a philosophy about life, while remaining consistent with the 1960s Steve Ditko stories about the character. Issues up to 14 have the Question confronting a variety of unsavoury individuals as plots address social concerns such as pollution, military patriotism, TV evangelists and ubiquitous drugs, while Sage rekindles his relationship with old flame Myra Fermin, now married to Hub City's drunken and ineffective mayor.

The third phase of the series starts with 14, as Myra announces her candidacy for mayor of the city she runs in all but name anyway. The election is decided in issue 24, and from that point the ongoing and seemingly irrevocable decay and corruption in the pseudonymous Hub City (Detroit?) underscore the remainder of the title's first run to an unpredictable conclusion (although most stories occupy only one or two issues). That writer Denny O'Neil (all issues) and penciller Denys Cowan (most issues) stuck with the title throughout its run goes a large way to explaining why, after a no-better- than-average introductory phase, almost every issue is worth a look. Worthwhile sample issues are the story of a racist investigator in 15, or 32's story about someone trying to redeem a mistake made during the Vietnam war.

The gap between first and second series (titled *The Question Quarterly*) is bridged by an appearance in *Green Arrow Annual* 3. The first new issues see Sage in South America, and facing a new challenge. He does return to Hub City, but the undercurrent of political intrigue is underplayed, and the stories suffer as a result. The best of them is 3, in which a movie crew hits Hub City. The Question is next seen in *Showcase '95* 3. The 1997 one-shot, titled *The Question Returns*, almost reaches the standard of the initial series, although purists may carp that the Question's distinctive featureless face-mask now has eye slits. Several years have passed since the conclusion of the previous series, and O'Neil pens a tale requiring Sage to return to Hub City, illustrated in fine, restrained fashion by Eduardo Barreto.~FP
Recommended: 7, 8, 12–16, 20–24, 26, 28–36
Collection: Thunder Over The Abyss (1–5)

QUESTPROBE

Marvel: *One-shot 1993, 3 issues 1994–1995*

Bizarre attempt to promote computer games featuring Marvel characters. In each issue a superhero passes through a portal that probes, assesses and drains their power, at which point you're supposed to rush off and buy the computer game to discover what happens next. Infrequent publication tied into the release of the games and bog-standard comics ensured an early cancellation, although the planned fourth issue eventually turned up as *Marvel Fanfare* 33.~FP

Q-UNIT

Harris: *1 issue 1993*

The Braxis have developed a new weapon: a chip that can store psi energy. A blast of psi energy will destroy the electronic brains of the terrorist enemy, the Renegade Synthetics. However, the Synthetics know of this chip and they've stolen a prototype. For the dangerous mission of getting it back, the Braxis form Q-Unit, a team of prisoners with psi powers offered the choice between Q-Unit and execution. The story-telling is cluttered, needlessly convoluted, and very hard to follow, and for 'characterisation' we have the male members of Q-Unit staring each other down, and the female members reminiscing about their lives as slaves. Had it run for a few more issues all would have become crystal-clear and endearing. Maybe.~FC

RACE OF SCORPIONS

Dark Horse: *4-issue miniseries 1991*

Continuing from its appearances in *Dark Horse Presents* 30–34, *Race Of Scorpions* is a series of stories about characters in a far future where most animals no longer exist and water is the most precious commodity. Pirates, tales from the past and a mine manned by children are the major features of Leo Duranona's unsettling adventure here. The artwork's like a loose Moebius in style, but not so compelling.~NF

RACER X

Now: *Series one 11 issues, 1 Special 1988–1989, Series two 10 issues 1989–1990*

Launched with an oversize special before beginning a regular series, Racer X is the ridiculous combination of top racing-car driver and global peace agent. Complicating matters further, he's also Speed Racer's older brother, long believed dead, and can't reveal his real identity for fear of compromising his security. Whereas the *Speed Racer* companion title just about passes muster, *Racer X's* first run insults the intelligence, even of the pre-pubescent readers it's aimed at. The second series is slightly more successful, with Chuck Dixon's scripts dispensing with the neither-fish-nor-fowl aspect of the title and concentrating on the action adventure aspects.~WJ

RACK AND PAIN

Dark Horse: *4-issue miniseries 1994*
Chaos: *2 issues + 1996 to date*

Lobo teams with the Terminator as their exploits are beamed back for the viewing pleasure of millions. Except ratings are slipping, so Rack and Pain are set up against foes they can't beat. Maybe. Cartoon violence, so don't expect a lot of plot, but Leopoldo Jimenez's art is extraordinarily detailed in places. The Chaos series is more mayhem and brutality.~WJ

RADICAL AMERICA KOMIKS

Print Mint: *1 issue 1969*

Despite being a spin-off from *The Journal of U.S. Radicalism*, this is for the most part not particularly political. Apart from several minor strips from underground stalwarts like Rory Hayes and Jack Jackson, the bulk of the comics is given over to Gilbert Shelton, who thoroughly entertains with an early Freak Brothers strip and the unique 'Smiling Sergeant Death And His Merciless Mayhem Patrol'!~DAR

RADICAL DREAMER

Blackball Comics: *2 issues (0–1) 1995*
Mark's Giant Economy Size Comics: *7 issues + 1995 to date*

Very good, rough artwork from Mark Wheatley combines with a dunderheaded plot, unfortunately also by Mark Wheatley, to produce a comic only worth looking at. In the 30th century the ultra-rich control everything and the underclass are very repressed indeed. They even have their dreams piped in, via DreamNet. Our hero (its inventor), full of ideas about uprisings and educating the masses, enters his own virtual-reality world in order to try to reach them through their dreams, but once there comes under attack from all sides. The script is by turns histrionic and didactic. Turn the sound down for this one.~FJ

RADIOACTIVE MAN

Bongo: *6 issues, 1 special 1993 – 1995*

Bart Simpson's favourite comic character is Radioactive Man, and his comic frequently cameos on the cartoon, which made it a sure bet for publication once Simpsons comics began appearing. In a very funny six-issue series, co-plotters Cindy Vance, Steve Vance (script and layouts) and artist Bill Morrison go Alan Moore's *1963* one better: instead of parodying Marvel Comics from 1963 alone, they spoof five decades and three comics companies. The numbering of the comic is likely to confuse, as the covers only show the issue number they are pretending to be. 1 is an atom-age origin issue, supposedly from 1952, in which Radioactive Man helps the US Senate destroy an EC-type horror comics line. 2 (pretending to be 88, from 1962) is a Marvel parody, with some witty Lee/Kirby and Lee/Ditko references. 3 is '216, August 1972', a 'relevant' story in which our hero's teen sidekick becomes a hippy (closely paralleling some of DC's *Green Lantern/Green Arrow* issues, complete with Neal Adams art gimmicks). 4

(or '412') and 5 ('679') are respectively *X-Men* (1980) and *Watchmen/Dark Knight Returns* (1986) spoofs. 6, or '1008', is an Image Comics 1995 issue in which our hero trips over his billowing, Spawn-style cape. Each issue's art style imitates its respective era and artist pretty closely, while still sticking to the look of *The Simpsons* TV show, which is no mean achievement. A villainous Richard Nixon appears throughout the series, as Senator, President and finally a disembodied head in a jar. The real Nixon died during the run of the book; maybe someone showed him a copy. The '80pg. Colossal' parodies DC's *80pg. Giants*, and is labelled 'No.1, Summer 1968'. The Vances had left Bongo by this point, and as with *1963*, the cod small ads and house ads in this one-off Special are often funnier than the strips.~GL
Recommended: 1–6

RAGAMUFFINS
Eclipse: *One-shot 1985*

Don McGregor and Gene Colan look back on incidents from a 1950s childhood in stories originally published in *Eclipse Magazine*. What makes these more than nostalgia-fests is the ending to each, contrasting the childhood experience with an event in the lead character's adult life. The first two stories lack bite, but the third is excellent. In 1951 Bobby McIlroy weighs being forbidden to cross the road against the toy shop on the other side, while fifteen years later he has to visit his dying aunt. It's a story raising familial ethical dilemmas, with no real correct answer, and all the more satisfying for doing so. Further Ragamuffins tales appeared in *Eclipse Monthly*, but none were as powerful as this.~FP
Recommended: 1

RAGMAN
DC: *Series one 5 issues 1976–1977, series two 8 issues 1991–1992, 6-issue miniseries ('Cry Of The Dead') 1993–1994*

The Ragman was created as a hero for the common man, set in a ghetto where he protected the poor, hungry and homeless. His civilian life was spent as Rory Reagan, pawn-shop owner, endowed with extra strength, agility and fighting ability through an origin explained in the first issue. Robert Kanigher writes human-interest stories about the harsh realities of living in the ghetto, with a sparse cast, and he weaves a fine mystery throughout the series concerning an abandoned mattress stuffed with $1,000,000. As assorted crooks attempt to retrieve it they're confronted by Ragman, who is unaware of the secret hoard. The final fate of the money is well considered and in keeping with the unusual tone of the series. The art is largely by the Redondo Studios, with co-creator Joe Kubert chipping in

for the final two issues, and is excellent throughout.

The themes and cast of the original series are reworked entirely for the second series, which bears little relation. This Ragman was rooted in Jewish folklore, with his abilities now in the suit, not the person, and the rags comprising the suit entities in themselves. Writers Keith Giffen and Robert Loren Fleming reveal Reagan wasn't the first Ragman, merely the latest in a succession. Besides the local Mob wanting to turn the pawn shop into a front for drugs, Ragman must also confront an old Jewish legend, the Golem. This was a well-constructed story, and decently drawn, although Pat Broderick's art over Giffen's breakdowns was a little stiff when it came to a fluid character like Ragman.

The third series has Rory Reagan established in New Orleans, a town with a mystique suited to Ragman. Of course, it's an unwritten rule that every comic set there has to introduce voodoo at some point, and writer Elaine Lee isn't slow off the mark. Despite the clichés, Gabriel Morrisette's art captures the eerie mysticism of New Orleans. The Golem returns, and numerous people and objects are possessed in an interesting, but convoluted, plot. All three series have their points of interest, but the original remains the best.~HY
Recommended: Series one 1–5

RAI
Valiant: *34 issues (0–33) 1992–1995*

Introduced in the flip-book format in *Magnus* 5–8, Rai was the hereditary protector of Japan in Valiant's 41st century, a samurai infused with nanite-rich blood empowering him. The first (or, to be precise, 42nd) Rai in 1–8 is extremely dull, and in recognition of this Valiant give him an early demise in suitably heroic fashion.

The next Rai, Takao Konishi, is able to influence people through force of belief, and from 9 the title changes to *Rai and the Future Force* as Rai is joined by assorted other super-types battling to rid the planet of robot invaders. They face off against one lot of robots here and another bunch there and when variety is required cyborgs are served up. It took Valiant a little longer to realise this Rai was also terminally dull, and he lasted until 22 before shuffling off the old mortal coil. The novice Rai in 23–33 encounters sibling rivalry, a harsh teacher and the X-O armour in the best of the run, but by that point the damage had been done.~FP
Collection: Rai (0–4)

RAIN
Tundra: *5 issues 1991*

Rolf Stark's largely autobiographical *Rain* is a bleak and uncompromising look at unpalatable topics. If you can work through the apparently deliberately confused story-telling and cluttered, ugly art, there's some harrowing autobiographical glimpses of a German childhood towards the end of World War II and a mercenary career in Africa thereafter. Although six issues were planned, only 1–5 saw publication.~WJ

RALPH SNART ADVENTURES

Now: *3-issue miniseries 1986, Series one 9 issues 1986–1987, Series two 31 issues, 1 3-D Special 1988–1992, 3-issue miniseries 1992, 3-issue miniseries ('The Lost Issues') 1993, Series three 12 issues, 1 Special 1993–1994, One-shot 1994*

Ralph Snart is short, stupid, ugly, socially inept and… no, that's about it. Somehow this slender premise has been stretched into sixty-four issues. Creator Marc Hansen's work certainly looks as if it ought to be funny; his bigfoot cartoony style is very appealing, but sitting stony-faced and bored witless throughout the run is easily achieved. If there is any appeal, and there must be given the number of issues, it's on a Three Stooges level. Imagine sitting through an entire series of the worst sitcom you've ever seen – *Bottle Boys* or *Comfort And Joy*, for example: that numbness, ennui and lack of desire to go on living. That's what reading Ralph Snart does.~HS
Collections: Ralph Snart Vol 1 (Series two 1–3), Vol 2 (Series two 4–7)

RAMBA

Eros: *14 issues 1992–1994*

These sexually explicit adventures of a female assassin offer far more than the usual Eros fare. Although the nature of the product demands several pages of detailed sex each issue, there are action-oriented plots, and Ramba herself has a nice sense of eye-for-an-eye justice. Most issues are exceptionally well drawn by the presumably pseudonymous Marco Delizia, and even those he doesn't illustrate maintain a reasonable standard. If you like sexually oriented comics, they don't come better drawn than *Ramba*. Tying in with the questionable association of sex and violence, 14 features possibly the most bizarre and offensive execution seen in comics.~FP
Recommended: 9, 13, 14
Collection: Ramba Vol 1 (1–3, 5, 6), Vol 2 (4, 6–10)

RANMA½

Viz: *Part one 7 issues 1992–1993, Part two 11 issues 1993–1994, Part three 13 issues 1994–1995, Part four 11 issues 1995, Part five 7 issues + 1996 to date*

Ranma½ is your basic martial arts transsexual romantic comedy. What? You want more? Oh, okay… Teenage studmuffin Ranma Saotome is a martial arts expert from China, affianced at birth by agreement between the fathers to one of the three Tendo girls, heiresses to a martial

arts dojo in Japan. When Ranma shows up to meet his putative brides the girls get a shock. He appears to be a girl. Furthermore, his father appears to be a panda. This is due to an accident in training at a group of legendary cursed springs. Ranma and Saotome senior can revert back to their normal forms, but, needless to say, circumstances conspire to make Ranma girl-out at the least appropriate moment. Before long the strip is awash with similarly afflicted characters, transforming willy-nilly, as well as sundry non-transforming, but equally bizarre friends, foes, rivals for Ranma's affections and so on.

This is whimsical slapstick, elegantly executed by Rumiko Takahashi, which never loses sight of the core of attraction and exasperation between Ranma and Akane Tendo that makes them, in the middle of all this chaos, solid and appealing characters.~HS
Recommended: Part one 1–7, Part two 1–11, Part three 1–13, Part four 1–11, Part five 1–7
Collections: Vol one (Part one 1–7), Vol two (part two 1–6), Vol three (part two 6–11), Vol four (part three 1–7), Vol five (part three 8–13), Vol six (part four 1–6), Vol seven (part four 7–11)

Jurassic Park: RAPTOR

Topps: *4-issue miniseries 1993, 4-issue miniseries ('Raptors Attack')1994, 4-issue miniseries ('Raptor's Hijack') 1994*

Steve Englehart continues the story where the film left off in the *Jurassic Park* miniseries, with Doctors Grant and Sattler trying to round up the missing raptors. In keeping with the 'horror' elements of the film, the good doctors end up stuck on a cargo plane with the beasties, having been captured themselves by a mercenary hired to smuggle out the dinosaurs. Michael Golden covers promise more than the Armando Gil and Dell Barras artwork delivers. Gil's usually tight pencils are woefully mismatched with Barras's fitful inking, which varies in quality from page to page. In 'Raptors Attack' Englehart continues the story, naming the three remaining Raptors (Alf, Betty and Celia) and having them chased through the jungle by Alan Grant, Ellie Salter, Ian Malcolm and Robert Muldoon. Englehart's anthropomorphism is irritating, while Chas Truog's artwork (replacing the acceptable Armando Gil from 2 onwards) is unimaginative. The third series is again written by Englehart, who introduces a talking raptor, stretching credibility even further. Now down to two, the raptors are protected by business rivals of the original backers of Jurassic Park, while the heroes get progressively more lost in the jungle. Neil Vokes provides more interesting visuals than previous artists, but the whole thing is sketchy and unfocused.~NF

RARE BIT FIENDS
King Hell: *19 issues + 1994 to date*

The comic is like a group workshop on dreams: Rick Veitch starts by recounting one of his, then in the letters page people write in with one or two of their own, and finally there are stories about dreams from other creators (e.g. Al Davison in 11, Lee Kennedy in 19). It's interesting, and done with a spirit of lively curiosity untainted by analysis or navel-gazing. Have a look at any that come your way, but you probably won't feel the need to hunt them all down.~FC

Collections: Pocket Universe (9–14), *Rabid Eye* (1–8)

RASCALS IN PARADISE
Dark Horse: *3-issue miniseries 1994*

On the frontier of the universe a duplicate Earth, circa 1932, has been created as a giant resort by the civilised planets of the 24th century. Unfortunately, due to a computer error the world has been covered with tropical jungles, sparsely populated by ancient civilisations. In the tradition of Edgar Rice Burroughs, Jim Silkie crafts a tale of lost treasure, tribes of apes and damsels in distress. Magazine-sized, it's a beautiful production with engaging characters – including one based on the director, Sam Peckinpah.~NF

Collection: Rascals In Paradise (1–3)

RAVAGE 2099
Marvel: *33 issues 1992–1995*

Stan the Man came back! In his first 'writing' job for some while Stan Lee ran up this sad little number between television appearances. It's set in Marvel's 2099 era; Paul Ravage is a man who takes it personally when he discovers the evil that the Alechemax Corporation are up to. Lots of street fighting and corporate backstabbing occur, but nothing of note until 3, when Ravage is forced to rescue his compatriot Tiana from his nemesis Deathstryk, who never learned to spell at school. At Hellrock, an area occupied by humans mutated by radiation and toxic fumes, in a selfless and noble act he (choke) sacrifices himself for Tiana and exposes himself to deadly chemicals. Amazingly, though, he departs from Hellrock seemingly intact and with a new range of powers, including glowing hands. Cool! By now Stan only provides the plot, which he seems to have lost years ago, and Pat Mills and Tony Skinner take over the scripting. Not that there's much improvement. By 10 Ravage's transformation is complete and he's able to transform himself into an huge 'Beast Man', a Hulk-like monster with horns. Luckily, it's not permanent, and he returns to corporate politics with 12, forming his own company with members of his devious family. As the series progresses Mills and Skinner become more interested in the primal side of Ravage, and he eventually becomes an immense creature. A showdown with Deathstryk is inevitable, and Ravage raises an army of disaffected mutoids to rise up against his enemy in 28. It's all over by 30 – guess who wins – leaving the final three issues as a mopping-up exercise. What started as a one-man-against-the-world story became a techno fantasy complete with demons and castles. Why Mills and Skinner chose this path is unknown, but it certainly killed the title. A point to note is that as the series became sillier the art improved: is some kind of bizarre equation at work here?~TP

RAVEN CHRONICLES
Caliber: *10 issues + 1995 to date*

Aimed squarely and obviously at the *X-Files* fans, Raven Inc is a group of paranormal investigators looking into assorted Fortean topics. Spontaneous human combustion, vampires and pyrotechnics feature in the earlier issues, all of which are marred by clumsily inserted infodumps. 5 gives background information about the team, and ironically the best issue is 4, the most obviously similar to an *X-Files* episode. Only two of the team participate in the investigation of a ghostly hitch-hiker, elegantly drawn by Rick Taylor. Further commendable artwork is to be found from David Hill, David Boller and Galen Showman in 7, 8 and 10 respectively, but the writing doesn't reach a similar standard.~FP

Recommended: 4

RAVENS AND RAINBOWS
Pacific: *1 issue 1983*

Showcase for the early work of Jeff Jones, containing a collection of short strips and some portfolio pages. A number of different styles are on show, but his predilection for single-page strips is already in evidence; his fantasy is more successful than his science fiction. The most fully realised piece is the washed-out, sombre 'Spirit of 76'.~NF

RAVER
Malibu: *3-issue miniseries 1993*

It's difficult to conceive that Malibu were so desperate for the minor celebrity cachet a comic written by *Star Trek* and *Babylon 5*'s Walter Koenig might bring that they unleashed this pitiful hotchpotch of seemingly stream-of-consciousness trash.~FP

RAW
Raw: *8 issues 1980–1986*
Penguin: *3 books 1989–1991*

Emerging from the ashes of *Arcade*, *Raw*, under editor Art Spiegelman, was a ground-breaking anthology magazine that brought to prominence a whole generation of cutting-edge cartoonists. Its lavish tabloid size and high production values engendered experimentation rather than narrative, and the first issue suffered from a certain preciousness that occasionally resurfaced throughout the run. By 3, however, Spiegelman had assembled a roster of exceptional talents that brought an intelligence and breadth of vision rarely previously seen in the field. The most prolific contributors included the neo-primitive Gary Panter (3–6, 8), savagely pointillist Drew Friedman (1, 2, 6), the wistful chronicler of urban decay Ben Katchor (2, 3, 6) and the 1950s-influenced Charles Burns (3–8). Spiegelman, with co-editor Françoise Mouly, was also concerned to bring European artists to a larger English-speaking audience, most notably Jacques Tardi (1, 5), Joost Swarte (1–3, 5–7) and Muñoz and Sampayo (3, 6).

Almost inevitably in a magazine of predominantly short stories, the few lengthier pieces stand out, and it was Muñoz and Sampayo's epic 'Mister Wilcox, Mister Conrad' in 3 that was one of the comic's highpoints. Other notable extended works included Pascal Doury's frenzied and frankly indescribable 'Theodore Death Head' in 5, and Robert Crumb's biographical 'Jelly Roll Morton's Voodoo Curse' in 7. Above all else, though, *Raw* was home to Spiegelman's masterpiece, the harrowing Holocaust-based 'Maus', which ran in instalments from 2. The first chapters were collected by Pantheon/Penguin in 1987, causing an immediate sensation and eventually winning the Pulitzer Prize. Buoyed by its success, Penguin initiated the Raw Books line, the flagship title of which was a revived and expanded *Raw*. Under Penguin *Raw* was paperback-sized and 200 pages long, causing an immediate re-positioning towards extended narratives, which made the title more substantial than ever. All the previous incarnation's principal cartoonists returned, and were joined by new contributors Loustal (1), Baru (1) and Chris Ware (2, 3). Rounding out the package were judicious reprints (with Basil Wolverton in 1 and a lengthy Krazy Kat section in 3) and showcases for the bizarre, notably the obsessive and troubling art of Henry Darger. The comic is absolutely essential, and repays repeated viewings.~DAR
Recommended: Raw 3–8, Penguin 1–3
Collections: Maus Vol 1 (Maus from 1–6), Vol 2 (7, 8 and Penguin 1–3 plus concluding material), *Read Yourself Raw* (Raw 1–3)

RAWHIDE KID
Marvel: *151 issues, 1 annual 1955–1957, 1960–1979 (17–151), 4-issue miniseries 1985*

Oddly for the comic that went on to become the longest running of all Marvel's Western titles, the first run for *Rawhide Kid* was a decided flop. And no wonder, with template stories and dull art. The revival in 1960 was a different story, as the combination of Stan Lee and Jack Kirby honed the style later so successfully applied to the early Marvel superheroes. By and large Rawhide Kid was indistinguishable from other Marvel sureshots roaming the Wild West, but some sprightly dialogue and the occasional inventive plot from Lee and Kirby between 17 and 32 provided the best of the run. Thereafter it's mediocrity all the way, and don't be suckered in by inferior art from the likes of Jack Davis and Al Williamson. From 115 the first series is all reprint, and few are likely to have noticed. The 1985 miniseries jumps forward a few decades, when the appellation 'Kid' is a more than a tad in error. It's plotting by numbers as our man acquires a sidekick towards the end of his life.~WJ

THE RAY
DC: *6-issue miniseries 1992, 28 issues 1 Annual 1994–1996*

The series that launched polished artist Joe Quesada to an adoring public. Written by comics veteran Jack C. Harris, the series takes up the story of the original Ray, seen in the 1940s Quality comics and DC's *Freedom Fighters*. His son, Raymond Terrill, has been told all his life that he was allergic to the sun, but when his father dies he discovers this was to prevent him discovering his natural ability to control light. Confused and angry, Ray comes to terms with his new role in society as a potential hero. The script twists, turns, and keeps you guessing throughout, especially when the ghost of the 1940s Ray turns up as Terrill's mentor. Quesada's Mignolaesque art is slick and perfectly matched with the story.

Sadly he didn't stick around for the regular series. Christopher Priest, apparently Jack C. Harris by any other name (see the confusing editorial in the first issue), continued the writing, but seemed to have been drained of any further inspiration. The best issues have Ray travelling through time to confront his father in 9 and 10, but overall there's sloppy art until the final issues and far too many team-ups with other DC superheroes clogging up the pages.~TP
Recommended: Miniseries 1–6
Collection: In A Blaze Of Glory (Miniseries 1–6)

RAY BRADBURY COMICS
Topps: *5 issues 1993*

As the title suggests these are adaptations of Ray Bradbury's short stories, including in 1 and 2 reprints of EC stories by Al Williamson and Jack Davis ('A Sound Of Thunder' and 'The Black Ferris' respectively). The first and third issues have dinosaurs as a theme. Highlights here include another version of 'A

Sound Of Thunder' by Richard Corben in 1 and an adaptation of the classic 'The Fog Horn' by Wayne Barlowe in 3. The second issue concentrates on horror and provides the highlight of the series, Harvey Kurtzman and Matt Wagner collaborating on 'It Burns Me Up'. 4 includes excellent work by Mike Mignola and Ron Wilber but 5 is a letdown, despite a frontispiece by Moebius and Ross MacDonald's imaginative attempt at adapting 'The Trapdoor'. There's also a one-shot titled *The Illustrated Man*.~NF

Recommended: 2

Everette Hartsoe's RAZOR
London Night: *19 issues 1992 to date, 3-issue miniseries ('The Suffering') 1993–1994, 5-issue miniseries ('Burn') 1994–1995, 4-issue miniseries ('Torture') 1996*

Beginning as a black and white violent-babe title, the fact that it was marginally better drawn than many self-published efforts and came out at regular intervals ensured this title a following. Razor, named after the distinctive blades she wears on her arms, is Queen City's defender of the weak, preying on criminals in a particularly unpleasant fashion. Any inventiveness is in the way she tortures, maims or kills them. The colour miniseries expands the horizons a little by restoring Razor from the dead and introducing ongoing supernatural elements. Exploitative and titillating art throughout ensures continued purchase by adolescents.~WJ
Collection: Burn (1–5)

READ THIS BOOK AND DIE (LAUGHING)
Art & Soul: *One-shot 1995*

A sampler for Marc Hempel's *Tug and Buster* and for Mark Wheatley's *Radical Dreamer*. In *T&B*, Big Tug is the silent manly type, and little Buster idolises him and lives for their joint babe-quests. Nice comments on 'male bondage' (as Buster calls it). *Radical Dreamer* is probably about some conspiracy to exploit dreams, but it's unreadable, so who can be sure?~FC

REAGAN'S RAIDERS
Solson: *3 issues 1986*

An extraordinarily unfunny 'parody', this has President Ron and his cabinet getting costumes and superpowers à la Captain America and fighting terrorists and Commies. Writer Monroe Arnold clearly thinks Reagan really is some kind of hero, or else wants to reach readers who think that way. Artists Dick Ayers and Rich Buckler, on issue 1, only have about three photos of the Prez to work from, but try to make up for it by drawing his face in ten times more detail than everything else. The 'humour' is indistinguishable from the patriotic gushing, and it's all rubbish. So bad it's... bad.~GL

THE REAL GHOSTBUSTERS
Now: *3-issue miniseries 1989, series one 28 issues 1988–1990, series two 8 issues, two specials 1990–1991*

The main series is an adaptation of the TV cartoon, written by James van Hise with art mostly by John Tobias and Brian Thomas. At the start the pacing was poor and the dialogue very disjointed, but things soon improved and from 3 most stories are quite readable if not remarkable, with 4 having some art Evan Dorkin would surely sooner forget. 6 stands out with some amusing spoofs when TV programmes are invaded by ghosts, though the fun's over about halfway through. Also of interest is 21, a special containing three stories by different writers and artists, including Phil Elliott. The variety is refreshing, and the stories seem much stronger when corseted into eight pages. The miniseries is an adaptation of *Ghostbusters II* by Van Hise, Tobias and inker Rich Rankin. It's quite lively and amusing, with a much tighter story than most in the main series. Save it for a rainy day, though. The art on the second series is better, and there's the extra care taken in presenting puzzles and activities for the core pre-teen readers, but that being the case perhaps they shouldn't have stretched the first story over four issues.~FC
Recommended: 6, 21

REAL LIFE
Fantagraphics: *1 issue 1990*

The work of Mark Zingarelli was a pleasing sight in late-1980s anthology titles, and this one-shot collects several of his strips, most dwelling on the morbid side of life. Good as his strips about killers are (with an excellent, and possibly apocryphal, tale about the King of Ethiopia and the electric chair), the highlight is the remorseful tale of Augie's Miracle Meats. It combines happy childhood memories with sad decline, and is told in memorable fashion. The writing and art are engaging throughout, and those looking for more intelligent comics could do far worse than sample *Real Life*.~WJ

REAL STUFF
Fantagraphics: *20 issues 1990–1994*

Dennis Eichorn's work stands out from the introspective autobiographical crowd because he appears to have experienced more of life: the majority of his stories are anecdotal with no particular message, and he's far more in-your-face than many of his proselytising colleagues. At times he's an asshole, in fact. Notwithstanding, an excellent choice of artists contribute to *Real Stuff*, and interestingly enough, considering there's a minimum of five stories each issue, the material becomes stronger towards the end of the run, exemplified by the reminiscences about nutty 'musician' Wild Man Fischer. Expressively drawn by J. R. Williams, they're in 14 and 16–20. At his best Eichorn's anecdotes are good comic material, at his worst vainglorious boasting, but there's something worthwhile in every issue. When Fantagraphics began their Eros line, Eichorn's sexually based stories were cleaved off into six issues of a companion title, *Real Smut*. Isolated from the diversity of his other vignettes, the theme is strained, with 4's disturbing story of childhood vaccination an exception. There's also a single issue of *Real Schmuck*, published by Starhead, featuring a tale relating to a story about a McDonalds heiress printed in *Real Stuff* 9, and allegedly turned down as an issue of *Real Stuff*. It's a good selection, worth looking out.~FP

Recommended: 1, 4–8, 12, 16, 18–20, *Real Schmuck* 1

REAL WAR STORIES
Eclipse: *2 issues 1987 & 1991*

The Department of Defense tried to stop the distribution of *Real War Stories* 1, published on behalf of the Central Committee for Conscientious Objectors. The second issue highlighted the work of Citizen Soldier, an organisation dedicated to protecting the civil and human rights of its GI/veteran members. Neither volume is successful as a comic. Both have good writers and artists (Joyce Brabner, Brian Bolland, Steve Leialoha, Bill Sienkiewicz, Paul Mavrides) but only rarely do they attempt anything interesting as far as the form goes. In 1 Alan Moore effectively contrasts an ex-soldier's past and present life, while 2's highlight is Greg Baisden and Stephen DeStefano using *Alice In Wonderland* to satirise arguments about the use of military force. This is not to say that the title fails in its objective of expressing the tragedy of war, it's simply that the impulse to teach us this often outweighs artistic considerations.~NF

THE REALM
Arrow: *12 issues 1986–1988*
Weegee: *1 issue (13) 1989*
Caliber *8 issues (14–21) 1989–1992, Series two 13 issues 1993–1995*

Four earth teenagers are transported to The Realm, populated by magic, demons, elves, dwarfs and orcs. There they discover they also have dormant mystical talents, which one parlays into a position of great power. Guy Davis draws the first twelve issues (not very well) of this complex saga featuring so many characters and locations it becomes difficult to keep track of them. It's likely only fantasy fans will enjoy the initial material, but anyone starting the second series from 5 can pick up what's going without having to concern themselves about the meandering earlier

stories (although there is *The Realm Handbook* for the curious). By that time new writer Brent Truax has whittled down the cast and set up intriguing political scenarios. 9 is a flip-book sharing space with *Deadworld* 12; it's in issue 4 of the first series that *Deadworld* premiered. 10 does the same with *Zone Continuum* 2.~FP

Collections: Vol 1 (Series one 1–4), Vol 2 (5–8), Vol 3 (9–12), Vol 4 (13–15)

REALM OF THE DEAD
Caliber: *3-issue miniseries 1993*

The *Deadworld* characters invade *The Realm*. Only of interest to diehard fans of either series. Issue 1 comes with two alternative covers, each featuring characters from one series.~FP

Collection: *Realm Of The Dead* (1–3)

REBEL SWORD
Dark Horse: *6-issue miniseries 1994–1995*

A loose drawing style, reminiscent of Gene Colan's later pencil-only artwork, enhances the odd story of a young Japanese teenager getting involved with Kurdish rebels in Turkey. Yoshikazu Yasuhiko's artwork is well worth a look but his script is rather overwrought and meandering. A curiosity.~NF

R.E.B.E.L.S.
DC: *17 issues 1994–1996*

Virtually impenetrable sequel to *L.E.G.I.O.N.*, featuring lots of pointless fight scenes, often involving the equally pointless Lobo. It's about a group of rebel superheroes taking on the sinister interplanetary security agency L.E.G.I.O.N. Seventeen issues of bickering nonentities and ugly artwork by artists named Arnie Jorgensen and Derec Aucoin – truly for hard-core *Legion of Super-Heroes* fans only.~AL

Rudyard Kipling's RED DOG
Eclipse: *One-shot 1988*

Mowgli and the *Jungle Book* animals prepare for the arrival of a fearsome pack of Indian wild dogs. In attempting to remain faithful to the source material P. Craig Russell has produced a densely verbose comic. His art is beautiful, though, unmarred by the vivid colouring that often characterises Russell's work.~WJ

RED MASK of the Rio Grande
AC: *3 issues 1990–1992*

Fifties Western reprints from *Tim Holt*, a Magazine Enterprises comic based on the RKO Western star, which from 42 was retitled *Red Mask*, by Gardner Fox and Frank Bolle. 1 is in colour but 2 and 3 revert to black and white, including a peculiar simulated 3-D effect. Fox's clever mysteries and Bolle's rugged artwork make *Red Mask* one of the better Western series of the period.~NF

RED RAZORS

Fleetway/Quality: *2-issue microseries 1991*

Extrapolating on the world of Judge Dredd, Razors is a Sov Block Judge, transformed from criminal to the judiciary courtesy of some selective neurosurgery. Accompanied by his talking horse, inevitably named Ed, he's something of a maverick, and must retrieve the stolen remains of Elvis Presley and stop a Stalinist coup. All too self-consciously wacky writing from Mark Millar includes too many throwaway elements that just don't gel (simulacrums of the *Scooby Doo* cast for one), but artist Steve Yeowell more than holds his end up.~FP

RED SONJA

Marvel: *Series one 7 issues 1975–1976, series two 15 issues, 1976–1979, 2-issue microseries 1983, series three 13 issues 1983–1986, One-shot 1995*

Sonja is a redheaded swordswoman created by Robert E. Howard, who also created Conan the Barbarian. Howard may or may not have dressed her in a chainmail bikini, but that's what she wears throughout this series, which suggests that European winters were a lot warmer in those days. Some issues of the first series were written by Roy Thomas and others by Bruce Jones, both producing lively, straightforward stories of clashing steel and hell-spawned horrors which catch the spirit of Howard's yarns very well. Dick Giordano draws the first issue, and Frank Thorne the remainder. Giordano's work is fine, but Thorne's is exceptional: he draws backgrounds full of period texture and stink, and gives Sonja a wild, unapproachable look that's at least half gorgon, with personality that simmers off the page. Of its type, a classic.

Sonja's still in her chainmail bikini for the second series, which can be divided roughly into two parts: issues 1–11, written by Roy Thomas and Clara Noto, with artwork by Frank Thorne, and 12–15, mostly written by Thomas, with artwork usually by John Buscema. In both parts the stories have lost the fun of the earlier series and are sprawling and pointless, though the occasional scene shows genuine imagination, such as the giant imprisoned queen of the bee-creatures (6), the dream-like details of the enchanter's house (10), and Sonja's trip across the 'River Of Death' (14). Thorne's artwork is the main reason for reading, and it's not enough reason to persist issue after issue. Don't bother with the 1983 microseries as the only point of interest is that Sonja has abandoned the bikini in favour of a gymslip. Don't bother with the third series either, for that matter. It's tedious, rambling stories by various writers, and a succession of artists who seem to have been given no directions to her appearance other

than: 'She's got long red hair. And she looks like a porn starlet.' By the end you're wondering if Thorne's artwork was just a figment of your imagination. Could there really have been an artist who respected her enough to make her frightening? The 1995 one-shot, 'Scavenger Hunt', is no better.~FC
Recommended: Series one 1–7

RED TORNADO

DC: *4-issue miniseries 1985*

An ill-advised series, featuring early Kurt Busiek scripting and lacklustre Carmine Infantino art, in which the android member of the Justice League of America thwarts a takeover of the world by an intelligence that unifies every machine on Earth. The Tornado's always been a stultifyingly boring character, and, sadly, this series does nothing to help.~HS

RED WOLF

Marvel: *9 issues 1972–1973*

Although he's the ancestor of the character in *Avengers* 80–81, to all intents and purposes it's the same guy: a Native American and his faithful wolf. The final three issues return to the modern-day character. Certainly not a bad comic, but certainly not a good one either.~FP

REDBLADE

Dark Horse: *3-issues miniseries 1993*

The demon Engetsu crosses over to the material world, and the undead samurai Redblade is sent back to life to thwart him. Fast-paced, action-packed and not without moments of interest, but let down by writer Vince Giarrano's mediocre art. The story-telling is so bad you have to check you're reading the series in the correct order and not missing an issue.~HS

REDFOX

Harrier: *10 issues 1986–1987*
Valkyrie: *10 issues (11–20) 1987–1989*

Redfox began life as a strip in a role-playing magazine and to the end remained a comic in the *Elfquest* mode, squarely aimed at fantasy fans. There are wizards and wicked sorceresses, quests, a cute anthropomorphic companion and a basque-clad heroine with a big sword. However, it was a million miles away from 'babe' titles like *Shi*, and later issues were written with a lightness of touch that sometimes makes up for the pedestrian story-lines and wooden artwork.~FJ

REESE'S PIECES

Eclipse: *2 issues 1985*

A collection of short horror stories with art by Ralph Reese, and with various writers. It's standard stuff: carnivorous plants, cannibals in the sewers, yetis and curses – and with consistently weak endings. The artwork's quite versatile, but it doesn't make enough of a difference.~FC

REGULATORS
Image: *3 issues 1995*

The first series about the day-to-day life of a group of supervillains, spotlighting one member of the team each issue. Well written and drawn by Kurt Busiek, Ron Randall and Dan Davis, the best issue is 3, looking into Arson's head and extrapolating the difficulties of life while constantly on fire. Advertised as six issues, for some reason only three were published.~WJ

REID FLEMING, World's Toughest Milkman
Last Gasp: *One-shot 1980*
Eclipse: *5 issues 1986–1990*
Deep Sea: *7 issues + 1996 to date*

Reid Fleming is a great comic creation, bridging the gap between the underground and Slacker generations. David Boswell's pugnacious anti-hero, a confrontational, hard-drinking every(milk)man, treats his employers and customers with equal contempt, and has a long history, first appearing as a weekly page in an underground newspaper in 1977. The Last Gasp magazine includes a number of these early adventures, as well as extended stories. The lead, 'A Day Like Any Other', contains all the key elements of a good Reid yarn: he terrorises passers-by who make fun of him, threatens customers – '78 cents or I piss on your flowers' – tangles with his obsessive, square-headed supervisor and goofs off with his narcoleptic best mate, whose manhood he constantly demeans. Boswell manages to keep up a high standard of humour throughout the extended five- issue story-line in the Eclipse issues, simultaneously developing his considerable drawing abilities. Two-fisted humour at its best. Reid also appears in the one-shot *Heartbreak Comics*, and the Deep Sea series reprints all the previous issues before beginning new material with 7.~FJ
Recommended: One-shot, 1–5

RELENTLESS PURSUIT
Slave Labor: *4-issue miniseries 1989–1990*

One of many injustices against the Native American population in the nineteenth century was the forced removal of the Nez Percé tribe from their Oregon homelands. The resulting conflict spread through four states as the tribe attempted to flee. In telling this tragic story Jeff Kear's enthusiasm and research more than compensate for art that could be improved.~FP

REN & STIMPY
Marvel: *43 issues, 8 Specials 1992–1996*

Developed in association with Nickelodeon, the cable station that produced the madcap serial, the comic-book version lacks the violent edge that the cartoon has. The relationship between the two characters (a snarling chihuahua and his big, dumb, rather disgusting cat friend) is nowhere near as acidic as in the show and a lot of the jokes are rather hoary. One gets the impression that it's being written for a slightly younger audience. Certainly it's a corporate product, with numerous hands writing, pencilling and inking in each issue, although the success of *The Simpsons* suggests that this doesn't have to be a drawback. The art is heavily stylised, but again not as eccentric as the cartoon, and lacks the energy of the original, possibly because that is so fast-moving any paper representation would be a little 'flat'. Pretty good if you really like *Ren & Stimpy*, but unable to stand up on its own without a knowledge (and enjoyment) of the show.~FJ
Collections: Don't Try This At Home (9–12), *Pick Of The Litter* (1–4), *Seeck Little Monkey* (17–20), *Tastes Like Chicken* (5–8), *Your Pals Ren & Stimpy* (13–16)

RENEGADE ROMANCE
Renegade: *2 issues 1987–1988*

Charming covers from Gilbert (1) and Jaime Hernandez lead into a delightful short series. Realising the old romance comics formula was redundant in the 1980s, the contributors to this anthology were people with individual visions. The quality of the art throughout is excellent, but there are far more decent plots to match the art in the second issue. The exceptions in 1 are Trina Robbins' adaptation of a novel concerning love during the Russian revolution, continued in 2, and the charming Bob Rozakis and Stephen DeStefano strip in which a woman waiting on a park bench sees her life parade before her. That team also contribute to the second issue, with DeStefano completely changing style for a humorous recitation of marriage vows. Other highlights of the second issue include David Hine's story of an old romance comic being passed around current-day Brixton, Deni Loubert and Steve Leialoha's spotlighting a man torn between two loves and the woman he leaves, Colleen Doran's Beardsleyesque stylings, and the tearful 'Dreams' from Jackie Estrada and Barb Rausch.~WJ
Recommended: 2

REPTISAURUS
Charlton: *6 issues (3–8), 1 Special 1961–1963*

Continuing from two issues of *Reptilicus*, the first of which adapted a B-movie in which a giant dinosaur is grown from a frozen preserved limb. Most of Charlton's giant monster comics at least had the saving grace of some Steve Ditko art somewhere along the way, but Reptisaurus goes for all out mediocrity.~WJ

Artemis REQUIEM
DC: *6-issue limited series 1996*

Artemis is a more headstrong and callous version of Wonder Woman; she appeared in issues leading up to 100 of Wonder Woman's second series. Clawing herself from the grave in 1, she adopts the new identity of Requiem and joins a group called the Hellbinders, who combat assorted mystical creatures. It's uninspired stuff from writer Bill Messner-Loebs, and the distorted figurework of pencil artist Ed Benes moves beyond styling into hilarity. Still, at least *Requiem* provides the answer as to why superheroines wear such preposterous costumes. They obviously can't find real clothes to fit those peculiar bodies.~FP

RESTAURANT at the END of the UNIVERSE
DC: *3-issue miniseries 1994–1995*

Continues from *Hitch Hiker's Guide to the Galaxy*. Adapts the book of the same name (inaccurately) or the last eight radio episodes (extremely inaccurately). Reassuringly, however, where the comic book version is inaccurate, it is at least definitively inaccurate. Sequel: *Life, the Universe and Everything.*~APS

Warlock Silver Surfer RESURRECTION
Marvel: *4-issue miniseries 1993*

Continuing from the Silver Surfer graphic novel *The Homecoming*, the Surfer is offered the chance to resurrect his recently deceased love Shalla Bal. The price? A favour to be called in at a later date by Warlock. The Infinity Watch, Death and Mephisto all appear in a rather padded script by Jim Starlin, who also pencils. If you're already a fan you'll probably have bought this, otherwise it's not the place to start.~WJ

THE RETALIATOR
Eclipse: *4-issue miniseries 1992*

Morality play about the validity of vigilante justice and the evils of child abuse. Not a bad comic, but the worthiness and research are hammered home and the often amateurish artwork is a distraction.~FP

Keith Laumer's RETIEF
Mad Dog: *6 issues 1987–1988, One-shot ('Retief Of The C.D.T.')1988*
Adventure: *6-issue limited series 1989–1990, 4-issue miniseries ('Retief and the Warlords') 1991, One-shot ('Grime And Punishment') 1991*

Earth diplomat Retief is oddly fair-minded for his chosen calling, and adept at outflanking both his superiors and alien races in interplanetary dealings. A fine satire on administrative prevarication and procrastination, there's little to fault the Mad Dog adaptations of Laumer's short stories. They're working with very witty material, but Jan Strnad's writing is faithful and Dennis Fujitake's Moebius-influenced art is ideally suited to the mix of human and alien in the stories. Well-considered and never dull, it's a testament to Fujitake's style, considering the number of talking-heads shots required each issue. The switch of artists to Steve Vance with the Mad Dog one-shot is jarring, and the spiral downwards continues from there as less and less talented individuals come to work on the adaptations.~WJ
Recommended: Mad Dog 1–6

REVENGERS
Continuity: *6 issues 1985–1989*

The confused consumer should be warned that the first four issues of this title have Revengers in very small lettering above a large Megalith logo, and, indeed, the first issue is a Megalith solo comic. Not that this matters overly, though, as the writing rarely rises to the level of competency and the sole appeal is the art. For 1–5 that was provided by Neal Adams and is probably his best of the 1980s, and even Larry Stroman's work on 6 is quite presentable. The first two issues also contain back-ups, Crazyman in 1, his first appearance, and Shadow Hunter in 2, strangely reprinted from Marvel's *Bizarre Adventures*.~DAR

The REVIVAL
Bare Bones: *One-shot 1996*

An account of the early days of Christianity in the USA. A large crowd gathering to hear a preacher in East Kentucky witnesses a number of extraordinary events, and the clever pun and full horror of the title aren't apparent until the end. Either ingenuously faked or taken from contemporary accounts, *Revival* falls short of being compelling, largely due to the limitations of James Sturm's art. Neither does it have anything original to say about religion, but it's nonetheless a unique story worth a glance.~FP

Robin Snyder's REVOLVER
Renegade: *6 issues, 1 Annual 1985–1986*

Starting out as a science-fiction anthology (1–3) and then switching to 'Fantastic Fables', *Revolver* perhaps failed by trying to reach too many readers. Certainly, the main attraction of the title has to be Steve Ditko's sharp, detailed strips, whether the Jack C. Harris-written space adventure of Star Guider that harks back to the 1950s (1, 2) or Ditko's own, EC-style 'The Hand of Ages' (4). Nothing else really stands out, though early work by graduates of the Kubert School (Mandrake, Bissette) can be found alongside the work of old pros like Henry Boltinoff (1, 2, 4, 5), Vicatan (1), Adolpho Buylla (4, 6) and Irwin Hasen (2). The annual, with a wonderful Alex Toth cover, contains a mixture of old and new material under the banner 'Frisky Frolics'. Ditko's very literal Killjoy rubs shoulders with Moench and Colon, Kanigher and Hasen, and several one-pagers from the regular series. *Ditko's World*, featuring *Static* numbers 1–3 and *Murder* 1–3, is also known as *Revolver* 7–9 and 10–12 respectively, while the annual is 13.~NF

The Adventures of REX the Wonder Dog
DC: *46 issues 1956–1959*

Originally a fighting (K-9) dog, Rex soon progressed to wholly civilian adventures with his owner, Danny Dennis. Ever ready to fight crime or rescue someone from distress, Rex found himself travelling all over the world (and sometimes off it in later, sci-fi-driven episodes), usually fêted as his reputation preceded him and generally behaving like a comic-book version of Lassie. Each issue contained two Rex stories, usually drawn by Gil Kane, often heavily but not unattractively inked. The third story, however, was Detective Chimp. Bobo, deputy to a Florida sheriff, always seemed more capable of solving local crimes and capturing crooks than his owner. Over the series, the developing artwork of Carmine Infantino is a delight until his command of movement (for example in 41's skiing adventure) clearly foreshadows his upcoming work on *Flash*.~NF
Recommended: 40–46

RIBIT
Comico: *4-issue miniseries 1989*

Magic is being driven out by science, and Sahtee, the last remaining sorceress, decides to fight back by creating a warrior woman. The recipe is nearly finished when Ribit, a lizard-like familiar of Sahtee's, jumps into the cauldron. Ribit does indeed turn into a warrior woman, but she's only three feet tall, and she's bright green. Not that this stops her fighting – it just stops people taking her seriously. Frank Thorne's story has its self-indulgent moments, but is generally quirky fun, and the ending is a true surprise.~FC
Recommended: 1, 4

RIMA The Jungle Girl
DC: *7 issues 1974–1975*

Nestor Redondo's finest work appears in this Amazonian jungle-girl story, based on W.H. Hudson's turn of the century novel *Green Mansions*. Considered rather fast in its time, the story of a young freedom fighter who escapes into the jungle after a rebel defeat and is rescued by a mysterious white-haired woman has great charm and poignancy. Robert Kanigher recounts Rima's origin faithfully and only throws in one or two sub-Tarzan story-lines to extend the plot, which is mostly concerned with the blossoming but guarded relationship between Rima and the narrator. Redondo is the star, however. His version of the South American jungles is a *terra incognita* full of sinuous big cats and snakes, his Rima a ghostly figure who is both majestic and innocent. Top all this off with covers by Joe Kubert and you have one of DC's great, overlooked masterpieces. Various Kanigher-scripted science-fiction tales, usually illustrated by Alex Nino, fill the back-up slot in the book.~FJ
Recommended: 1–7

THE RING of the Nibelungen
DC: *4-issue miniseries 1989–1990*

Roy Thomas has always been fond of adapting the works of others, whether they be by R.E. Howard, E.R. Burroughs or Michael Moorcock. This is probably his most daring and, in some respects, his most successful. Few would have attempted Richard Wagner's Ring cycle – it's four operas, sixteen hours of theatre and music. Yet Thomas manages to retain a sense of the poetry behind the plot, and Gil Kane's dynamic artwork brings the fantastic elements to life in ways that the stage couldn't emulate. Welcomed by opera critics as a faithful vision, Kane's artwork is perhaps too overwrought in places, but Jim Woodring's subtle colouring helps to create an appropriately heroic but tragic atmosphere. It can't really compare to hearing or watching Wagner's original operas but it's a worthy attempt to create a comic for a different audience.~NF

RING OF ROSES
Dark Horse: *4-issue miniseries 1992–1993*

In an alternative Britain where monarchy was not restored with Charles II, by 1991 the country is still in dispute with the Vatican. Lawyer Samuel Waterhouse is asked by the Catholic church to investigate the disappearance of ten priests from a boat on the Thames. Das Petrou's complex setting includes a plague of rats, radio technology which is brand new, and the secret Brotherhood of the Rosie Cross. John Watkiss' artwork is full of shadows and heavy blacks, but it's completely appropriate to this moral thriller. Unusual and well worth a look.~NF
Recommended: 1–4

The RINGO KID
Marvel: *23 issues 1970–1973, 7 issues (24–30) 1975–1976*

What distinguished The Ringo Kid from other Marvel Western characters was that he was half Native American and half white. Unfortunately,

this intriguing springboard for stories was used
for little more than the occasional epithet
prefacing a fight, and, while they're never bad,
there's nothing to make these an essential
purchase. Reprinted from the 1950s *Ringo Kid
Western*, there's plenty of John Severin art
throughout, but he seems to have knocked it out
over breakfast before starting work on his EC
assignments. Joe Maneely's art is far more
impressive.~FP

RIO
Comico: *Graphic Novel 1987*
Marvel: *Graphic Novel (Rio Rides Again) 1990*
Dark Horse: *2-issue miniseries (Rio At Bay) 1992*
Former outlaw Rio now wanders around late-
19th-century USA seemingly unable to avoid
adventure wherever he arrives. Doug Wildey's
'realistic' art is glorious, whether pencilled and
inked for the first novel, or richly painted for
the others. A master at work, he's able to
convey emotion through expression like few
others. All the stories are good, but the first is
best, a story of abusing the power granted to
the railroad pioneers, encompassing war with
Native Americans and Mexican bandits. Rio
becomes sheriff of a town hiding a celebrity in
Rio Rides Again, and *Rio At Bay* finds him in San
Francisco.~FP
Recommended: *Rio, Rio Rides Again, Rio At Bay*
Collection: *Rio At Bay* (1–2)

RIOT
Viz: *6-issue miniseries 1995–1996, 7-issue
miniseries ('Act Two') 1996*
Riot is an ancient book that possesses many
secrets and the magical key to a vast treasure.
Billy The Kid, trying to steal the book, is
mortally wounded by the book's guardian,
Axel, but the book offers him knowledge and a
second chance if he will protect Axel for the
rest of his life. The first series introduces a
rivalry between the Eastern and Western
churches and explains that Axel has a brother,
Abel, whom Cain (a high priest of the Eastern
Church) is hoping to revive by combining the
power of Riot with another magical tome,
Phantom. The second story sees Billy The Kid
facing off against the Lion King while Cain
tries to use the witch Cyphone to bring the
Moon crashing down on the Western Church.

An updated spaghetti Western set in a ruined
world, Satoshi Shiki's *Riot* is a classic love story
as well as a violent adventure, pitting against
each other a group of characters whose
relationships seem sometimes overly complex.
It's not an easy read but rewards patience.

Shiki's detailed artwork is firmly within
Manga traditions, yet its decorative nature and
design set it apart. On hiatus in Japan, Viz
promise to continue the series as soon as it's
available.~NF

RIP HUNTER TIME MASTER
DC: *29 issues 1961–1965*
Débuting in traditional DC fashion in their
anthology title *Showcase* (20, 21, 25, 26), Rip
Hunter and his time-travelling exploits sold
well enough to ensure promotion into his own
title. Rip and associates drop back (rarely
forward) through time to moments of
historical importance, and encounter any
number of renowned figures from the past,
only to reduce them all to trivialities. We're
firmly in the hangover period from 1950s DC
titles, where there was an internal logic and
consistency that bore little reality to the outside
world, writers assuming that if there was an
anomalous element, in this case time travel,
then any further need to conform to logic
could be thrown out. A typical example is 21,
which has Helen of Troy, Scheherezade and
Cleopatra among those gathered for a beauty
contest to promote a movie. That said, there's
an enjoyable daft consistency to the stories,
most drawn by Bill Ely, and any issue at
random will provide a chucklesome five
minutes.~WJ

RIP IN TIME
Fantagor: *4 issues 1986–1987*
This is written by Bruce Jones and drawn by
Richard Corben. A killer and his girl-friend are
pursued through the past by a hard-headed
detective and his own, upper-class girl-friend.
Due to a temporal mix-up each girl ends up
with the wrong man in a world of dinosaurs
and prehistoric dangers. Then a government
killer from the present is sent back to hunt the
detective, who thinks he's still the hunter, in
order to protect the secret of time travel and
make sure that no one survives. Unusually for
Corben the art's in black and white.~NF
Recommended: 1–4

RIP OFF COMIX
Rip Off: *29 issues (1–12, 14–30) 1977–1983
(1–12), 1987–1991 (14–30)*
In its long and convoluted history *Rip Off Comix*
went from being a collection of underground
syndicated strips to an international showcase to
a scattershot presentation of new talent. For 1–7
its material consisted of consistently amazing
Freak Brothers, Fat Freddy's Cat and Wonder
Warthog strips by Gilbert Shelton, the self-
explanatory Dealer McDope by Dave Sheridan,
and 'The 40 Year Old Hippie' by Ted Richards.
Most importantly, it also featured Bill Griffith's'
superbly acerbic 'Griffiths Observatory', a career
highlight from one of comics' premier talents
and later collected as a one-shot.

Between 8 and 12 the title was split 50/50
between Shelton's work and the best of
European humour strips, such as *El Vibora* and
Fluide Glacial, with each issue spotlighting a

separate country's work. 11 and 12 are large-format, lavish magazines with a colour section and the initial instalments of Shelton's 'Idiots Abroad', later featured in the *Freak Brothers* comic.

Following a gap of four years *Rip Off* returned minus the colour and the foreign artists, reinventing itself as a more contemporary anthology, combining new and established cartoonists with the inevitable Shelton. Early issues rejoiced in the fine, predominantly autobiographical work of Dori Seda (14, 16, 17), The Fizz (17, 26) and Dennis Worden (17, 19), as well as better-known artists like Spain Rodriguez, who had a particularly fine war strip in 14. Spain also appeared in the anniversary issue 20, which also has strips by Shelton, Jaxon and Trina Robbins and a text feature on the chaotic history of Rip Off Press. Sadly, the magazine lost edge after this, and later issues are very patchy indeed, despite the occasional new discovery like Mack White in 26.~DAR
Recommended: 1–7, 20

RIPCLAW
Image: *4-issue miniseries 1995, One-shot 1995, 6-issue limited series 1995–1996*

Spin-off from Marc Silvestri's *Cyberforce*. Ripclaw is a Native American, Robert Bearclaw, whose cybernetic claws coupled with the mystical overtones of his origin mean that the character works equally well in supernatural thrillers and more straightforward superhero tales. The special was meant as a prelude to the regular series, and introduced Ripclaw's brother Michael who, though he could summon trans-dimensional creatures, was invariably possessed by them. Ripclaw repulses one creature but loses Michael in the process. The regular series established some sort of civilian life for Ripclaw and introduced Kildare (a sort of Madame Xanadu figure). Kildare aids Ripclaw in a battle between sinister cults for the Ptiorrsh Mirror (1–3), and then Ripclaw becomes the target for a number of assassins (4–6), leading to the return of Misery and continued in the Cyberforce series. David Wohl and Christina Z make a promising start at defining Ripclaw as more than just a Wolverine clone, and Anthony Winn's artwork, with occasional hints at a Manga influence, avoids most of the confusing story-telling mannerisms that sometimes seem to define Image titles.~NF

RIPFIRE
Malibu: *One-shot (0) 1995*

Created, written and drawn by Darick Robertson, *Ripfire* is the story of a youth possessed by an alien and granted superhuman powers who, after fighting another alien in the desert, sets out on a road trip, roughing up some rednecks along the way. Robertson's artwork is greatly enhanced by Dennis Jensen's inks on the final chapter of the issue, but overall there's really nothing to inspire the desire to see more of the character. Reprinted from the Ultraverse Premiere series, published as a flip-book with the various Ultraverse titles.~NF

RIPLEY'S BELIEVE IT OR NOT
Gold Key: *3 issues 1965, 91 issues (4–94) 1967–1980*

Believe it or not, the first two issues were subtitled 'True Ghost Stories' and the third 'True War Stories'. The first half of the run is quite readable, but uninspiring as anthology titles go, with some durable uncredited scripting, and art by the likes of Crandall, Evans, McWilliams, Orlando, Williamson and Wood. Once into the 1970s, though, the title becomes pure dreck.~SW

RIPPER
Aircel: *6-issue miniseries 1989–1990*

Extremely offensive, ultra-violent racist nonsense from Barry Blair, who left a trail of controversy behind practically every comic he ever worked on. Blair's twisted worldview leaves no room for enjoyment for anyone who doesn't share his opinion that all black men are rapists, muggers and/or thugs.~JC

RIPTIDE
Image: *2 issues 1995*

Youngblood's resident aqua-bint faces the consequences of having posed for a nude centrefold. Jeez. GET a LIFE, already! This would qualify as soft porn, if it weren't so execrably drawn.~HS

ROACHMILL
Blackthorne: *6 issues 1986–1987*
Dark Horse: *10 issues 1988–1990*

Rich Hedden and Tom McWeeney create a believable seedy, grimy world where gang bosses are bloated monsters, robots and mutates go about their business, and humans and a veritable platoon of assorted aliens mix freely. At the centre of this lunacy is Roachmill, an investigator possessed of an extra pair of insectoid arms, part of the joke being that while all around him is madcap Roachmill himself is forever grim-visaged. The plots are sometimes thin, but masked by Hedden and McWeeney's rich repertoire of visual gags and general inventiveness. If you like one issue you'll enjoy them all.~FP
Collections: *Roachmill* (Blackthorne 1–4), *The Greatest Roachmill Stories Ever Told* (Blackthorne 5–6 + *Dark Horse Presents* 17, 28)

ROBIN

DC: *4-issue miniseries 1991, 4-issue miniseries ('Joker's Wild') 1991–1992, 4-issue miniseries ('Cry Of The Huntress') 1992–1993, 32 issues +, 2 Annuals 1993 to date*

Batman's third Robin was the first to acquire his own title. He was relatively new to the position: the first miniseries features his training. Tim Drake is sent by Batman to Paris to be taught to be a crimefighter, and becomes involved in a confrontation with King Snake and Lady Shiva. It's drawn by Tom Lyle in a similar style to his Batman work; Chuck Dixon's script is focused and provides a decent insight into the character. The second miniseries has Batman out of town while Robin must tackle the Joker, fully aware that his predecessor had died at the hands of the twisted madman. As the title suggests, the third solo run co-stars the Huntress and sees the two working together.

The regular series spends time on characterisation, but not wanting to stray too far from a successful formula they're similar to Batman comics, using many of the same villains. Stories are aimed at a younger audience, and focus on the problems of simultaneously dealing with puberty, school and a secret double life. 8–9 show Robin's relationship with Batman, and are decent representative issues. Artist Tom Grummett captures the feel of the character and makes him look his age rather than like a small adult, which had previously been a problem. 28–29 are chapters of the 'Contagion' crossover from the Batman titles. Always a decent adventure title, *Robin* is well worth reading if you are a Batman fan or liked the Teen Titans.~SS

ROBIN HOOD

Eclipse: *3-issue miniseries 1991*

Gloppy, pale and insipid retelling of the Robin Hood legend, which only serves to illustrate the dangers of the craze for fully painted comics.~HS

ROBIN 3000

DC: *2-issue microseries 1993*

The Robin of the future has a chance to shine in as the latest incarnation of Batman is killed by alien oppressors. Thomas Wayne, Bruce's umpteenth nephew, continues the struggle. Byron Price's script is overwritten and a tad clichéd, but P. Craig Russell's vaguely homo-erotic renditions of the boy wonder and his retro-futuristic settings are pleasant.~TP

ROBO-HUNTER

Eagle: *5-issue miniseries 1984–1985*

Escaping from the black and white pages of *2000AD*, Sam Slade, Robo-Hunter, receives the full colour treatment in this collection of his first adventure. Armed with Cutie, a robotic robot detector, and Stogie, his artificial talking cigar, Sam travels to an all-robot planet to discover the fate of lost colonists. Pure hokum and lots of fun; the jokes come thick and fast with just about everything on the planet from handcuffs to boots having a wacky personality. Ian Gibson's slightly confused artwork is clarified by the colour, and the series is definitely worth perusing. Sam later returned in Quality's *Sam Slade* series.~TP

Recommended: 1–5

Collection: Robo-Hunter Book 1 (1–5)

ROBOCOP

Marvel: *23 issues, 1990–1992*

Considering that Robocop was only ever, at best, a watered-down version of Judge Dredd, Alan Grant seems a particularly apt choice to write Marvel's attempt at stories beyond the movies. Pedestrian (though competent) art from Lee Sullivan gives the series a consistency, but the stories are well below Grant at his best – hacking it out with the minimum of effort. Despite himself, the fact that Grant is much better than this can't help but come through, mostly in the TV news interludes and the dark, sarcastic humour of the in-jokes which pepper the main plots. For all Grant's apparent lack of interest in the character, he does a better job than his successors. After an unremarkable fill-in by writers Evan Skolnick and Stephen Ripinski, illustrated by Herb Trimpe (over Alex Trimpe layouts), Simon Furman takes over the series from 12 until the end. This makes it all too obvious that Grant's humour was the only thing the series had going for it, and Furman's attempts to continue the inter-panel banter fall way short of the mark. If the film left you thinking that there were likely to be any good stories to be had in giving Murphy some characterisation, you were wrong. He's a lump of metal with a heart because he's a Hollywood lump of metal and not even the most vicious Hollywood killing-machine is allowed to be totally schmaltz-free. Do yourself a favour and go read some *Judge Dredd* comics instead.~JC

ROBOCOP

Dark Horse: *4-issue miniseries ('Robocop vs Terminator') 1992, 4-issue miniseries ('Prime Suspect') 1992–1993, 3-issue miniseries (Robocop 3) 1993, 4-issue miniseries ('Mortal Coils') 1993, 4-issue miniseries ('Roulette') 1994*

Dark Horse carried on the adventures of Alex Murphy, the cyborg future cop, long after the movies left off. The adventures are presented in self-contained miniseries, with the first, *Robocop vs Terminator*, the best of the bunch, written by Frank Miller, who also wrote *Robocop* movies, and drawn by Walt Simonson. Miller plays on the time paradoxes of the *Terminator* films and the themes of humanity from *Robocop* to craft a clever tale of time travel and big explosions which will no doubt please those who like more of the same on the big screen. 'Prime Suspect', in which a framed Murphy tries to clear his name, is also of a decent standard. In general, give the miniseries a try and avoid the film adaptation. Somewhere buried in at least the first *Robocop* films was a half-decent story, and Dark Horse do a good job of tapping into it to produce some half-decent comics.~JC

ROBOT COMICS
Renegade: One-shot 1987

Described by creator Bob Burden as 'experimental literature guised as a leaking barrelful of rip-snorting, foot-stomping belly laffs' *Robot Comics* is as surreal as he gets. Barely the story of one night at a bar populated by the weirdest of the weird (robots, a man carrying his own tombstone, the Banjo Mummy, Uncle Billy with a pie crust on his head), it's really a series of one- or two-page vignettes, exercises in character. Bizarre but recommended.~NF
Recommended: 1

ROCKET RACCOON
Marvel: *4-issue miniseries 1985*

It's a funny-animal comic in a science-fiction setting, with space battles and killer robot clowns and deadly struggles for control of two rival toy producers for the hand of the beautiful otter princess. The setting shows above-average imagination, and this makes the series readable despite a weak story-line. Readable, but no classic.~FC

THE ROCKETEER
Pacific: *2 issues (Pacific Presents) 1983–1984*
Eclipse: *One-shot 1984*
Comico: *2 issues 1988*
Disney: *2 issues 1991*
Dark Horse: *1 issue (3) 1995*

Dave Stevens' *Rocketeer* is a labour of love, indulged by fans because it's the best chance we're ever likely to have of seeing more than covers and posters from this meticulous and beautiful artist. The character first appeared in the back of the otherwise forgettable *Starslayer* (2 and 3), and The Rocketeer of the title is Cliff Secord, a young pilot who lives in a world Stevens has crafted from 1930s pulp fiction and 1940s whimsy. It's a world of rocket jetpacks, gangsters, high adventure and model girlfriends who look exactly like 1950s pin-up Betty Page. The period feel of the book is pure nostalgia, the plots light but perfectly weighted, and the art is a dream. Sadly, the production schedule is less so. Even though there's almost always a back-up (by Steve Ditko in the Pacific issues, Mike Kaluta in the Comico ones), Stevens still has trouble turning out an issue more than once every

couple of years. One interesting feature of this is that you can almost follow the history of colouring technology improvements from one issue to the next, and by the Dark Horse issue (the most recent to surface, though more are promised), you wish all the issues had had such slick production. For completists, there's also the Disney-published *Rocketeer 3-D Comic* by Neal Adams and a graphic novel adaptation of the (surprisingly faithful) movie by Russ Heath. Plus more posters and merchandising than has ever before been lavished on a comic yet to reach double figures. But then, the Rocketeer's worth it. ~JC
Recommended: Pacific 1–2, Eclipse one-shot, Comico 1–2, Dark Horse 3
Collections: The Rocketeer (Pacific 1–2, *Starslayer* 2–3), Eclipse one-shot, *Cliff's New York Adventure* (Comico 1–2, Dark Horse 3)

ROCKETMAN King Of The Rocket Men
Innovation: *4 issues 1991*

Adapting the serial *King Of The Rocket Men*, this romps along encompassing action, suspense, red herrings and a fine selection of serial nasties. The Rocketman of the title is security officer Jeff King, who wears a flying suit developed in secret by one member of a group of scientists he's investigating. Another of them is the mysterious Vulcan, supplying information to the Nazis. Chrisopher Moeller's shades-of-brown painted art, intended to evoke the period, occasionally turns to mud, but it's largely effective. Tune in, turn off, and enjoy.~WJ
Collection: Rocketman (1–4)

ROCK'N'ROLL Comics
Revolutionary: *71 issues 1989–1994*

It's hard to conceive that even the most devoted of fans will want these rock-star and band biographies. Art is largely hackwork and sometimes appalling (although Chas Gillen makes a brave effort), and while issues written by Jay Allen Sanford from 22 are an improvement on Todd Loren's scripts they're still pedestrian. For British readers the Rolling Stones issue 6 is a hilarious must, with its shorthand presentation, wonderfully bad imagined dialogue and misuse of English terms. The back-up one-pagers in early issues, featuring gags about rock star Stan Back, are actually better than the feeble title pun would suggest.~FP

ROGUE
Marvel: *4 issues 1995*

Summoned away from her fellow X-Men by the kidnapping of her childhood sweetheart, our power-draining heroine is forced to confront some remarkably tangible ghosts from her past. Although the Howard Mackie/Mike Weiringo team create an affable romantic adventure, the hackles are prompted to rise by the fact that Rogue's lover Gambit occupies nearly half of the series, despite an earlier miniseries of his own in which Rogue didn't get a look in. It appears that the Merry Marvel Misogynists didn't have faith in Rogue's pulling power without the ol' clichéd Cajun lurking about to shore her up.~HS

Collection: Rogue (1–4)

ROGUE TROOPER

Quality: 49 issues 1985–1990
Heavy Metal: Graphic Novel 1993

Created when readers of 2000AD selected 'future war' as their preferred topic for a new series, there's a decent concept to Rogue Trooper. He's a Genetic Infantryman impervious to many of the dangers threatening regular human soldiers. Even if they're killed, the accrued experience and personalities of the GIs can be saved on datachips for eventual restoration, and Rogue is accompanied by three deceased comrades in this fashion. Sadly, despite the potential, Rogue has always been the runt of the 2000AD litter. Perpetually dull scripts only ever inspired functional artwork, even from the likes of Dave Gibbons, Cam Kennedy and Steve Dillon, as Rogue staggers from one conflict to the next, although Colin Wilson makes a brave stab at rendering the stories in entertaining fashion in early issues, particularly 4. The enticing combination of Dave Gibbons (script) and Will Simpson (art) for the graphic novel also fails to deliver, and one must wonder if all creators are rendered brain-dead upon starting work on the character.~WJ

Collections: Rogue Trooper vols 1–6 (1–24)

ROLLERCOASTER

Fantagraphics: 1 issue + 1996 to date

Rich Tommaso is one of the more interesting comic creators to emerge over the past few years, combining the detached narratives of Daniel Clowes with a more optimistic worldview. That isn't immediately apparent, however, from this extended narrative about the final night of a four-day pizza delivery shift. There are plenty of wordless illustrations of scenery and expressions in the nine-panel grid used to tell the story, which might not make for a long read, but works in conveying the sheer exhaustion of the nameless deliverywoman. The odd back-up is a muddied musing on the old ways, and altogether less satisfactory. One hopes this is a regular showcase for Tommaso's work.~FP

Recommended: 1

ROM

Marvel: 75 issues, 4 Annuals 1979–1986

Rom was conceived to promote a toy launch but proved far more successful than its parent product, outliving it by years. Full credit to Bill Mantlo for reworking an old science-fiction concept with new wrinkles. Armoured space-knight Rom arrives on Earth already infiltrated at all levels by evil beings known as Dire Wraiths, who seem human in every respect except to Rom's analyser. When he starts blowing away bastions of the community in a small West Virginia town it understandably raises eyebrows. His neutraliser actually banishes Dire Wraiths to limbo rather than killing them (wouldn't want to upset the younger readers, after all), but the effect is the same and Rom finds himself trying to save people who're after his head.

Mantlo writes the series from start to finish. Beyond the surface his plots often fail the logic test. Why would a Dire Wraith want to marry Rom's friend Brandy Clark disguised as her boy-friend (14)? Why would a prisoner containment van able to fly be driving along snowbound roads (31)? The strength, though, is that there's enough going on, if not to disguise the flaws, certainly to negate them. The always reliable Sal Buscema pencils 1–58 (best inked by Akin and Garvey in 36–50), and Steve Ditko, most often inked by P. Craig Russell in an interesting combination, handles the remainder. There's no single classic issue of Rom, but they're almost all okay, if undemanding, with plenty of Marvel guest stars along the way. Stories rarely continue beyond two issues, so sampling is simple.~FP

RONIN

DC: 6-issue miniseries 1983–1984

Many people were disappointed by Ronin, Frank Miller's first major work after a revolutionising stint on Daredevil. Others dismissed its artistic mixing of rounded, Moebius-esque forms and Manga influences as a necessary evil in the development of Miller's more acceptable, angular style for Dark Knight Returns. They are all wrong. Ronin has a straightforward plot. A young samurai whose master is murdered by a demon has to kill himself in order to also kill the demon, as his magic sword can only be activated by spilling innocent blood, and he is unwilling to kill a bystander. With its dying breath the demon curses them to meet and fight again down the centuries. Fast forward to a near-future New York in the grip of riots and public unrest. The Ronin – masterless warrior – possesses the deformed body of an adolescent to continue the fight.

Ronin's story is often overshadowed by the richness of its artwork, and Miller undoubtedly wears his influences on his sleeve, particularly in the Koike-inspired Japanese sequences. He uses a very rough line but rounded forms for the 'present', suggesting a perfect plastic future gone bad, and concentrates on building his main characters as the book ploughs towards the inevitable showdown and a tremendously touching climax. He also employs numerous experimental drawing and inking techniques that would provide him with an armoury of expressiveness for the next ten years.~FJ

Recommended: 1–6
Collection: Ronin (1–6)

ROOK
Warren: *14 issues 1979–1982*

Bill Dubay's time-travelling hero proved popular enough in *Eerie* to warrant his own title, where the emphasis was very much on rollicking adventure rather than Warren's staple horror fare. The Rook strip itself was generally entertaining, with nice art from Lee Elias for 1–6, but it was the back-up strips that provided the comic's real highpoints. Chief among these was Alfredo Alcala's barbarian epic 'Vector' (2–7), *Sherlock Holmes*, beautifully drawn by Anton Caravana in 10, Noly Panaligan in 13–14 and 'Bolt' by Alex Nino in 1. Other features of note include Nestor Redondo's gorgeous *Bat*, and a couple of features from Joe Kubert's obscure *Sojourn* comic, Lee Elias' detective strip 'Kronos' (8–11) and John Severin's Western *Eagle* (12–14). For the less committed reader, however, the magazine's best strip is Alex Toth's 'Bravo For Adventure' in 3–4, a superb 1930s adventure strip by one of comics' finest creators that should have a place in everyone's collection.~DAR

Recommended: 3, 4

The ROOK
Harris: *5 issues (0–4) 1995*

An altogether different proposition from his Warren predecessor, but no improvement. The Rook is now master of the reality flow, involving himself in alternate realities instead of contenting himself with hopping back through time. The first two issues have him fighting the undead in the old West, though, while the latter two see him fighting hoods possessed by a piece of chaos manifesting as a spider embedded in one of them. Oh yes, indeed. The zero issue prints two versions of a try-out strip, one by Kirk Van Wormer, who got the job, and the other by Caesar, who didn't. Shockingly overwritten throughout by Tom Sniegoski in the manner of a schoolboy's creative-writing assignment, the plots are much ado about nothing. Good name, good idea, but mucked up once again.~WJ

ROSCOE! The Dawg, Ace Detective
Renegade: *4-issue miniseries 1987–1988*

Australian not-funny-animal Raymond Chandler pastiche by Martin Trengove. The simple drawings, especially in the first issue, show some life but there are no good ideas here.~GK

THE ROVERS
Malibu: *6 issues 1987–1988*
Eternity: *1 issue (7) 1988*

The future is always a grim and desolate place in comics, and there's no trend-bucking for this gang of bounty-hunting teens. Starting from the clichéd scenario, matters improve with an endearing cast and decent art from the team of Scott Bieser and Mike Roberts. *Rovers* never really moves beyond Troma teens at play, but there's plenty worse. 6 is an origin story of sorts, and a good place to start if you can't locate the first issue.~FP

ROWLF
Rip Off: *1 issue 1971*

A rollicking good read from an on-form Richard Corben, and to date the only comic to feature Esperanto-speaking Nazi goblins! The story of a dog transformed into a man (sort of) veers from finely etched romanticism to literally bone-crushing action, and remains one of Corben's finest strips. It was later serialised in *Heavy Metal*.~DAR

Recommended: 1

RUBBER BLANKET
Rubber Blanket: *3 issues 1991–1993*

When David Mazzucchelli left the mainstream he didn't do it by halves. These oversized annuals represent a complete change of style, whether it be the minimalist 'Hope and Grope' (a newspaper strip pastiche) or the blocky expressionism of longer stories like 'Dead Dog' (1), 'Near Miss' (1), 'Discovering America' (2) and 'Big Man' (3). His stories are not simple but concern everyday things twisted by obsession. The superb 'Big Man' is about a giant washed up on a shore and taken in by farmers. He preys on their minds, simply by existing, until they betray him to the authorities. Though the title is primarily a vehicle for Mazzucchelli's own work there is also material by Richmond Lewis (1, 2), Ted Stearn (2, 3) and David Hornung (2, 3).~NF

Recommended: 1–3

RUINS
Marvel: *2-issue microseries 1995*

Journalist Phil Sheldon stumbles through a counterpart to *Marvels* set in a parallel universe where all the events that created superbeings happened with a difference and superhuman abilities work disadvantageously. The world is populated with diseased, mutated heroes, a

Kree concentration camp, a prostitute Jean Grey, mutants in 'correctional facilities' and the last Avengers quinjet is shot down by the military. An intriguing concept is poorly executed, as Warren Ellis goes for maximum shock value at all costs. Improbably, every character bar Sheldon is thoroughly disagreeable. Cliff and Terese Nielson only manage one and a half issues of gritty, abstract, painted artwork, and the awful contrast of Moeller's completion strikes like a bucket of iced water.~APS

Batman: RUN RIDDLER RUN

DC: *3-issue miniseries 1992*

Batman is briefly allied to his old foe the Riddler as he tries to clear his name after being framed for murder by an armoured private-security force. The three issues are drawn very stylishly by Mark Badger and the story, by Gerard Jones, is okay, but they don't really suit each other.~NF

RUNE

Malibu: *Series one 10 issues (0–9), 1 Giant-Size 1994–1995, 4-issue miniseries (The Curse Of Rune) 1995, series two 7 issues 1995–1996*

This intriguing character was created by Barry Windsor-Smith, and introduced in three-page segments of all Malibu's Ultraverse titles in 1994. It started out well. Rune is a savage, eternal vampire, more than a little influenced by Marvel's old vampire series *Morbius*. Including lots of blood'n'gore and drawn beautifully by one of the true masters, it fell the way of so many promising titles when Windsor-Smith left after the first series. New writer Len Kaminski neutered Rune by merging him with a superhero and concocting a ridiculous story about computers, cybernetic vampires and yet more superheroes. It's not at all helped by a change of artist almost every issue.~TP

Recommended: Series one 1–4
Collection: The Awakening (1–5)

RUNE Miniseries and One-Shots

Doug Moench provides a partial origin and a turning-point in Rune's existence in the three-issue *Hearts Of Darkness* miniseries drawn by Kyle Hotz in a style similar to that of Kelley Jones. This is an intelligent attempt to move the Rune series on while retaining the vampiric nature of the lead character. The back-up, 'In Dread Memory' by James Felder, is a rather uninspired battle between Rune and A'Charr, though the artwork (by the Pander brothers) has its moments. In the four-issue *Curse Of Rune* (by Chris Ulm and Kyle Hotz) Gemini and Rune are possessed in turn by Warlock's soul gem. The Aladdin Agent Shuriken and Janus are spectators only to a battle which sees Rune cast out of the Ultraverse in a story

bridging the first and second *Rune* series. *Rune vs Venom* typifies the dull crossovers between Malibu and Marvel characters. Rune is accidentally brought into the Marvel Universe and is possessed by one of the alien symbiotes that created Venom. In an attempt to discredit Venom, the symbiote takes Rune on a murder spree, culminating in the kidnapping of Venom's girl-friend. Written by Chris Ulm but with a depressing rota of three artists and two inkers, there's actually very little of Rune in this. *Rune/Silver Surfer* features two stories with the same conclusion as Rune takes the six Infinity gems from Warlock and the Infinity Watch, and The Living Tribunal taxes the Silver Surfer with preventing Rune from using all the gems together. At the end of each tale, in a brief fight, the Silver Surfer blasts the gems from Rune's hand but they fall into the Ultraverse, thus paving the way for Loki to find them, leading to the 'Black September' story that ran through all Malibu's Ultraverse titles. The Surfer story is drawn by John Buscema but that's the only hint of quality about this overpriced nonsense.~NF

RUST

Now: *Series one 13 issues 1987–1988, Series two 7 issues 1989*
Adventure: *4 issues 1992*

Prolonged contact with toxic waste didn't kill Scott Baker, but left him deformed, with acid running through his blood vessels, while anything he touches either dies or rusts. As no one in comics comes away from an encounter with toxic waste without some ability, he's also impervious and strong. Pathos comes naturally considering the traumatic existence of the title character, but Fred Schiller's consistently unconventional scripts reach beyond, making it a shame there's no artistic continuity. Inventive story-telling for its own sake does intrude, particularly when a climactic confrontation is related by talking heads in 9. Series one focuses as much on Baker's pre-teen niece Cheryl as on him, and 6–8 deal with her fears, with a surprising conclusion. Civilisation disintegrates in 13, leading into the appalling series two. Baker becomes a figure of redemption for the downtrodden in a series characterised by poor artwork and deliberately abstruse writing. Series three returns to the beginning once again, and while not bad is only noteworthy for the early pencilling of Philip Hester.~WJ

SABLE
First: *27 issues 1988–1990*

Restarted and retitled to coincide with a brief TV series and the desertion of creator Mike Grell, this is a new Jon Sable. The harrowing consequences of an AIDS victim returning to Iran in 1–2 has the subtlety of a kick in the teeth, but with more issues under his belt writer Marv Wolfman improves. He never manages to be convincing about Sable's mercenary missions and relies too heavily on loose ends from the previous series, but does keep the pages turning. In 6 Sable meets Myke's family, in 9–10 he must rescue his former father-in-law in Kenya, and 19 has the return of Maggie the Cat. Most issues to 19 are pencilled by Bill Jaaska, attempting to be Paul Gulacy but not quite pulling it off (and greatly benefiting when inked by E.R. Cruz). The final three issues provide a definite conclusion to the series, with new writer Steven Kaye adeptly tying up most loose ends, but the impact of an otherwise excellent story-line is severely restricted by substandard art. Sable and Myke reappear in *Shaman's Tears* 5–8.~FP
Recommended: 6, 9, 10

Jon SABLE Freelance
First: *56 issues 1983–1988*

Sable is a mercenary with a conscience who, as a cover for his day job, writes children's books. Despite this piece of whimsy writer/artist Mike Grell ensures that this incarnation of Sable is a thriller that lives up to the genre title. Never bogged down by continuity, the consistently well-plotted stories ensure that Grell's questionable grasp of bodily proportions isn't noticed after a while. The series is populated with engaging characters, particularly police captain Josh Winters, envious of Sable's ability to work outside the law. Septuagenarian stunt-man Sonny Pratt provides a toned-down comic relief, while the relationship between Sable and his illustrator Myke Blackman forms slowly but eventually surely. Sable himself is a man torn between the thrill provided by putting his life on the line and the comfort available.

3–6 are an origin tale establishing Sable's background as an Olympic pentathlete who later ran African safari tours. When his family are murdered by poachers he has his revenge and becomes a soldier of fortune. The story provides a plausible (in context) reason for Sable's dual career, and has a sequel of sorts in 19. Any issue before 34 is worth a look and 2, 7 or 20 are good single-issue samplers, with the best being 11, with the introduction of enticing burglar Maggie the Cat (also in 16, 50 and later her own series). 33 is a Sergio Aragonés guest-shot starring the leprechauns from Sable's children's books, but from that point Grell obviously has other projects on hand. His artwork becomes sketchier and more distorted, and it loses backgrounds, while plots are spread very thin. The problem's rectified by engaging a succession of fill-in artists from 44, but none are able to emulate Grell's mood, Mike Manley coming closest in 46–49. 1–10 are reprinted as *Mike Grell's Sable* in 1989–1990, and a glimpse of an alternate Sable is seen in Grell's *Green Arrow* 15 and 16.~FP
Recommended: 1–14, 17–33, 46, 47

SABRE
Eclipse: *Graphic Novel, 14 issues 1982–1985*

Tired of the constraints of mainstream companies, Don McGregor created a black freedom fighter (who looked suspiciously like Jimi Hendrix as drawn by Paul Gulacy) in a post-holocaust world of animal/human hybrids, nuclear spills and villains with extremely silly names. Sabre is peppered with scenes designed to upset the apple cart: gay sex, (lots of) straight sex, and childbirth. Sabre's one of the few serious comic characters shown changing nappies.

McGregor deals with important issues, albeit in a rather grandiose way, and makes you care about his somewhat sentimental characters despite saddling them with monikers like Deuces Wild and Midnight Storm. Paul Gulacy's art is stiff and detailed in its search for realism. Billy Graham's art on 3 is pretty awful, although it's getting slightly less so by 10, when José Ortiz takes over. Ortiz' art is much more confident but rather slapdash. He's clearly not inspired by the rather nauseating 'Sabre enjoys being a dad' story-line. When, instead of evil oppressors, Sabre's called upon to fight giant sand-bugs you know there's something wrong. Thankfully it was cancelled before McGregor could get any more mawkish.~FJ
Recommended: 1–2

SABRETOOTH
Marvel: *4-issue miniseries 1993*

Sabretooth grunts his way through scratchy Mark Texeira artwork and a Larry Hama script so geared towards exorbitant violence and shock value that a thoroughly illogical story emerges. Some facets of Sabretooth, Mystique and Wolverine's pasts are revealed.~APS

Collection: Death Hunt (1–4)

SABRETOOTH Classics
Marvel: *15 issues 1994–1995*

Reprints Sabretooth's early guest appearances in chronological story order starting with his second appearance in *Power Man And Iron Fist* 66. His first appearance (*Iron Fist* 14) is reprinted in a Marvel Milestone edition.~APS

SABRETOOTH Special
Marvel: *One-shot 1996*

An *X-Men* issue guest-starring Sabretooth that escaped under the latter's title. This acceptable if overlong story imparts some empathy to his character and, under Gary Frank's admirable (if somewhat Byrnesque) pencils, Sabretooth has never looked more feral.~APS

SABRETOOTH and MYSTIQUE
Marvel: *4-issue miniseries 1996–1997*

Jorge Gonzalez and Ariel Olivetti churn out a fairly routine S.H.I.E.L.D.-A.I.M.-HYDRA-world-domination scenario as the two uneasy allies follow up a mission from their distant pasts. Gonzalez constructs a few too many unlikely coincidences merely to further the plot, and Psycho spends four issues doing what he does best.~APS

SABRINA THE TEEN-AGE WITCH
Archie: *77 issues, 1977–1983, 1 Halloween Spooktacular 1993, 1 TV Special 1996, 2 issues + 1997 to date*

Conceived as a short-run gag feature in *Archie's Madhouse* in 1962, Sabrina's popularity was such that this muddling-through, apprentice magic-user made many appearances there and in *Archie's TV Laugh-Out* before her own title was launched on the strength of her segments in the animated *Archie* show of the late 1960s. Her supporting cast was limited to her Aunts Zelda and Hilda, her Cousin Ambrose, and her talking cat Salem, all, including the cat, better at magic than she, and her puny mortal boyfriend Harvey, but the Archie gang frequently dropped over. After a healthy seventy-seven issues, her title quietly ended; but sporadic attempts were made to revive the character. Her strip in the 1990s *Laugh* revival made the mistake of taking her out of Riverdale, giving her two new best friends – Cleara, an invisible girl, and Eyeda, a lady Cyclops – and sending her to Monster High. Quickly realising that the

fun in Sabrina was in seeing her interact with mortals, not other supernatural beings, Archie recanted and put her back amongst humans. The 1996 live-action TV pilot, resulting in an ongoing series, led to a further one-shot comic, with an ongoing series just announced.~HS

SACHS AND VIOLENS
Epic: *4-issue miniseries 1993–1994*

Peter David conducts a guided tour of the world of sleaze, starring soft-core porn model J.J. Sachs and Vietnam veteran Ernie 'Violens' Schultz. The lashings of sex and violence are thoroughly warranted and David's wit is not the only razor-sharp ingredient. George Perez's gorgeously detailed artwork demands lingering attention. Regrettably, the momentum of the first two issues does not quite sustain to the climax, but the series is still a cut above the average. Not for the faint of heart.~APS

Recommended: 1, 2

THE SAFEST PLACE
Dark Horse: *One-shot 1993*

Steve Ditko, outside the mainstream of Marvel or DC, has never been afraid to be political. *The Safest Place* is a Cold War thriller set in a totalitarian (probably Communist) country where secrets are being smuggled to the West, an activity in which an innocent woman is implicated. Ditko expertly captures the climate of fear among those searching for the traitors and those whose eagerness to support the *status quo* causes them to hate others who are still trying to think for themselves.~NF

Recommended: 1

ST GEORGE
Epic: *8 issues 1988–1989*

This brainchild of Archie Goodwin is the best of the 'Shadowline' titles. Beautifully moody and dark art from Klaus Janson tells the story of a down-and-out chosen by an ancient secret society to be their champion. The Brotherhood Of St George is based in Greece, and the reluctant hero dons special armour and wields a staff against enemies who threaten to reveal, and thereby destroy, the society. The cantankerous mentor Barnabas is a particular treat. Sadly, poor sales saw the series cancelled, but not before a young Jim Lee had a chance to work on 8. Plotlines were concluded in *Critical Mass*.~TP

Recommended: 1–8

SAINT OF KILLERS
Vertigo: *4-issue miniseries 1996*

The Saint of Killers is a memorable member of *Preacher*'s early cast, obviously based on Clint Eastwood's Western loners, a merciless and remorseless agent of celestial vengeance. As such he hardly required an origin, but we get it here anyway, and it's Garth Ennis on autopilot, stringing together familiar movie scenarios. The exception is the third issue's detour into Hell, which is sadly no improvement. Interior art from Steve Pugh and Carlos Ezquerra, and excellent Glenn Fabry covers, don't compensate for the ordinary scripts.~FP

SAINT SINNER
Marvel: *7 issues 1993–1994*

This was introduced as part of the Clive Barker-created Razorline range of titles. It's a psychological thriller about a boy trapped between entities from opposite dimensions and forced to fight for his life. The two entities are opposites, one representing good, while the other is evil, and their conflict turns the boy's mind into a battleground, with often terrible consequences. Larry Brown's art is dark and moody and the script by Elaine Lee is intelligent. This is the best of Clive Barker comics and is well worth a read.~SS
Recommended: 1–3

ST SWITHIN'S DAY
Trident: *One-shot 1990*

Although comparatively early published work from Grant Morrison, this remains one of his most effective pieces. Adapting extracts from his own teenage diaries, Morrison makes his protagonist an alienated, introspective teenager who travels to London in order to assassinate British PM Margaret Thatcher. Excellently drawn by Paul Grist, it's a fine study of teen angst, impotence and idealism and was previously serialised in *Trident*.~FP
Recommended: 1

SALLY FORTH
Eros: *8 issues 1993*

Engagingly dumb teasing stories originally produced in newspaper strip format by Wally Wood, whose heart was certainly in it. Sally's a member of the Co-Ed Commandos and, like all good cheesecake heroines, she gets her kit off at every opportunity, running into characters like Rock Buggers as Wood works his way through parodies of *Flash Gordon* and *Buck Rogers, Tarzan, Barbarella* and *King Kong*, to name but a few. Wood luxuriates in drawing his buxom character in classic EC style, beautifully inked and toned; such is his skill at pacing that the re-pasted panels read smoothly as a comic book.~FJ

SAM & MAX, Freelance Police
Fishwrap: *1 issue 1987*
Comico: *1 issue 1989*
Epic: *2 issues 1992*

Now better known for the excellent computer game, Sam & Max are a big cuddly dog and a cute psychotic rabbit. Inspired lunacy and ultra-violence abounds, courtesy of creator Steve Purcell. May he earn riches beyond his wildest dreams. One Epic issue reprints the Fishwrap comic in colour with extra material, and the Marlowe book collection reprints everything, but in black and white, while containing nine new colour one-pagers.~WJ
Recommended: Comico, Epic 1–2
Collection: Sam & Max: Surfin' The Highway (all issues)

SAM SLADE Robohunter
Quality: *31 issues 1986–1989*

Sam Slade returned in 1986, quickly following on from his Eagle series as *Robo-Hunter*. For some reason, though, Quality chose to run the stories out of sequence, opening with Sam Slade arriving in Britain, his robohunting trade having been outlawed in the USA. In the company of his assistant, the gormless Hoagy, and his talking Cuban robo-cigar he sets up as a private eye. The same creative team produce the lead strip throughout, writers John Wagner (under the alias of T.B. Grover) and Alan Grant, and artist Ian Gibson. Gibson's fluid and expressive cartooning perfectly matches the quirky nature of the writing, and he brings more life and character to robots than anyone might believe possible.

'The Day Of The Droids' starts in 5. Sequentially this predates 1–4, and is the peak of Slade's long career. Citizens all over the USA are being replaced by robots, and Wagner and Grant have created a lunatic population of droids including gangster robots complete with a godfather, a robot football team complete with maniac coach, and a Unionist cocktail-shaker robot. It's a hilarious story that tops all but the best Judge Dredd work by the same creators. Sadly it's downhill from there, due more than anything to a change of publisher (although the name and numbering remain intact). Whereas the artwork produced for British comic pages had been sympathetically resized and coloured for US publication, from 12 it's downright shoddy reproduction all the way, and readers are advised to seek out the stories in their original British editions or the British reprints in *The Best Of 2000AD*.

12–13 have the return of Joe Kidd from the *Robo Hunter* 1–5, now a successful TV star as a baby, but there's someone out to kill him, and no shortage of candidates. 14 and 15 feature 'Football Crazy', many elements of which will make little sense to those unfamiliar with British football, particularly the TV pundits satirised throughout. It's a good story though, and certainly an improvement on the all-singing, all-dancing 16–19, in which alternative lyrics are applied to familiar tunes. The musical aspects just don't work unless you sing along, and who's going to do that? 20–25 contain 'The Slaying Of Slade', which is the weakest of the long Robo-Hunter serials. Slade dies, returns as a ghost, occupies his clone and solves the mysterious Crown Jewels robbery. There are too many disparate elements strung together, and the humour, previously natural, is often forced. 'Slade's Last Case' in 26 and 27 is only a little better, with Sam, having retired on the proceeds of the previous case, now obese. Hoagy and Carlos Sanchez Robo-Stogie decide his life needs pepping up. When he emerges from a health farm in 28 Slade's back to his old self, but it appears his assistants have run off with his fortune. Discovering why involves Slade in a story that's a return to form.

There are decent back-up strips included in every issue. 'Ro-Busters' is a thinly disguised version of *Thunderbirds*, with excellent Dave Gibbons art in 1–6. ABC Warriors also feature before moving into their own title, and Ace Trucking Company take up occupancy in 20–25. Also humorously written by Wagner and Grant, they're a bunch of space truckers with a vast capacity for involving themselves in perilous situations.~FP

Recommended: 1, 2, 5–15, 28–31
Collections: Robo-Hunter Bk 3 (5–7), Bk 4 (8–10)

SAMURAI
Aircel: *20 issues 1985–1987*

A black and white series amateurishly drawn and pretentiously written by Barry Blair. Features punks, motorbikes, women in uniform, young boys, ludicrous cockney dialogue, and, yes, giant UN robots. There may not be a plot in it.~GK

SAMURAI CAT
Epic: *3-issue miniseries 1991*

Based on a novel of the same name, the action is very similar in style and humour to *Groo* but without the quality. In the third issue there's a *Star Wars* parody which does raise a few laughs, but nothing major.~SS

SAMURAI JAM
Slave Labor: *4 issues 1994*

In-line skating and all things Japanese obsess the characters in Andi Watson's quirky but likeable one-man title. Not a lot happens, and his insights aren't startling, but it's a pleasant read, drawn in a blocky, angular style that's very striking, although it can make for inexpressive faces.~FJ

SAMUREE
Continuity: *Series one 9 issues 1987–1992, series two 4 issues 1993–1994*
Windjammer: *2 issues 1995*

As one would surmise from the title, this is a superhero comic with martial-arts overtones, and, as one would expect from the publishers, it

marries beautiful artwork with nonsensical stories. 1–4 are particularly notable for the bottom-obsessed pencils of Mark Beachum that are as near pornographic as they are accomplished. As ever with a Continuity title, the hand of Neal Adams is rarely far away, and the other artists, S. Clarke Hawbaker (5, 6), Rodney Ramos (7) and Dave Hoover (8 and 9) all benefit from his touch.

The second series is four chapters of 'The Rise Of Magic' crossover; it's less superhero-oriented, aiming instead for a supernatural theme and ending up even more impenetrable than before. Rudy Nebres inks some very poor pencils in 1, 2 and 4, and future star Mike Deodato enlivens things in 3. Another great Adams discovery, Rodolfo Damaggio, drew both Windjammer issues with some aplomb, rounding off a series that offers the occasional treat for the eyes, if not the brain.~DAR

SAN FRANCISCO COMIC BOOK
Print Mint: *4 issues 1969–1973*
Last Gasp: *3 issues (5–7) 1975–1983*

A rather aimless underground title specialising in minor pieces by well-known artists (possibly rejected elsewhere), and consequently of great interest to dedicated collectors but of little to more casual readers. Later issues were also something of a showcase for new artists, with Melinda Gebbie (6, 7) and the talented but obscure John Burnham (5–7) particularly shining. By far the series' best strip was from the established Bill Griffith with 5's brief but poignant tribute to the legendary (if unbalanced) artist Rory Hayes.~DAR

SANCTUARY
Viz: *Part one 9 issues 1992–1993, Part two 9 issues 1993–1994, Part three 8 issues 1994–1995, Part four 7 issues 1995–1996, Part five 13 issues 1996–1997*

Question 1: Can you identify with adolescent fantasies about being a flawlessly pretty gangster who can get away with anything? Question 2: Does it seem reasonable to you that a police inspector should be unable to tell the difference between blood and tomato juice? If you can answer 'Yes' to both questions, then you have a good chance of being able to read *Sanctuary* on its own terms, and of enjoying the meticulous artwork, and the dense, far-seeing and comprehensive plot-work, which includes power-bids inside gangs, extravagant political ambitions, international expansion, youth against age… However, if your answers are 'No', then you may find yourself throwing the book across the room midway through Chapter 2, shouting, 'This is an insult to my intelligence!' Of course, we all have comics that are utterly stupid and that we still love, but it's difficult to feel affection for something as humourless and self-important as *Sanctuary*.~FC

Collections: *Sanctuary* Vol 1 (Part one 1–9), vol 2 (Part two 1–9), vol 3 (Part three 1–8), vol 4 (Part four 1–7)

THE SANDMAN
DC: *6 issues 1974–1975*

In 1947 Joe Simon and Jack Kirby recreated Adventure Comics' Sandman as a streamlined superhero with kid sidekick. Given another chance with the name in the 1970s, their new Sandman, in his baroque red and yellow costume and cape, is the friendly guardian of our sleep. It's his job to stop baddies using people's dreams (often those of his young pal Jed) to do evil things like invade Earth etc. Jed provided the identification figure for the children who were the comic's intended readers. Michael Fleisher wrote the poor 2–3, with Ernie Chua and Mike Royer providing substandard, if Kirbyesque, artwork. Only with the return of Kirby in 4, as plotter and penciller, did the series start to sparkle; this is the alien-invasion issue, and it reads like a 1950s science-fiction short expanded, quite delightfully, into a little classic of the form. Unfortunately, it's downhill from there; Jed's kindly Grandpa is killed by a totally gratuitous sea-monster in 5, and even Wally Wood's inks can't save 6 from damp-squib-hood. With his HQ in the Dream-Stream, and his ability to move from dream-realm to reality, this Sandman is a direct precursor of the far more adult Neil Gaiman character, and reappears in 11 and 12 of that Sandman's title.~GL
Recommended: 4

SANDMAN
DC/Vertigo: *75 issues, 1 Special 1989–1996*

Sandman is Morpheus, the Lord of Dreams. He is a member of the family of the Endless, along with Desire, Despair, Destiny and others. This provides a very broad setting for the telling of fantasy stories, and the comic makes good use of it. The seventy-five-issue run mixes single-issue short stories and longer story-lines of six issues and more, covering horror, humour, family drama, metaphysics... you name it – as long as you name horror twice, since it was particularly dominant in the beginning, frequently to scorching effect. It's a comic crammed with ideas and a large cast of memorable characters, who are given some great dialogue (particularly Delirium), and Neil Gaiman writes with an impressive command of styles and techniques. Add to this the artwork to match and amplify, and at its best it is a startling, invigorating read.

1–9 begin with Morpheus imprisoned on Earth for nearly a century, causing disturbances in human dreams and in his realm, and there's considerable work required to restore order. 1–4 are mediocre, with the writing barely compensating for Sam Kieth's shambolic artwork, but with 6 original inker Mike Dringenberg begins pencilling and the writing and art start working together. The result is some genuinely dreamlike sequences (5, 7), a horrific hostage story (6), and a poignant introduction to the first of Morpheus' siblings in 8. Although they're connected, no story lasts longer than two issues.

'The Doll's House' is the first really lengthy continued sequence, concentrating on Rose Walker, a young woman whose family was affected by the disturbances during Morpheus' imprisonment. In 10–16 this involves her, unwittingly, in some dangerous Dreamworld politics. It's a weak story, but introduces more of Morpheus' siblings and human characters, who later become important: Lyta Hall and her son Daniel; and Hob Gadling, who meets Morpheus in a tavern also frequented by Marlowe and Shakespeare in 13, independent of the main story-line. 14 is possibly the best of the entire series – the sickest, funniest parody of a fan convention you'll ever read.

One-issue stories under the collective title of 'Dream Country' occupy 17–20, generally with little involvement from Morpheus. The strongest is 17's 'Calliope', with art by Kelley Jones, which has much to say about creativity and maturity, and some dazzling verbal fireworks. 'A Midsummer Night's Dream' (19), illustrated by Charles Vess, depicts a unique performance of Shakespeare's play and won a World Fantasy Award. 'A Dream Of A Thousand Cats' (18) makes good points about fantasies of a Golden Age, though some find it too cutesy, and 'Façade' in 20 returns the obscure DC character Element Girl under tragic circumstances. Another collective title, 'Distant Mirrors' (29–31), encompasses another sequence of short stories. 29's 'Thermidor' is set during the French Revolution and introduces Orpheus, of Greek myth (told in the 1991 Special), and his relationship to Morpheus, which will become very important later. 'August' (30) features the Roman Emperor Augustus and events leading him to make an unusual decision in a strong and thought-provoking story. 'Three Septembers And A January' (31) is a nice piece about the protective properties of fantasy, but worrying for its signs that the Endless are never going to rise above their soap-opera behaviour. 'Convergences' (38–40) is another sequence of short stories. None are particularly strong, though 40 is significant in the Grand Scheme, with its focus on Lyta's son, Daniel.

Morpheus is forced to accept an unwanted responsibility in 'Season Of Mists' (21–28), and deputations arrive from several supernatural realms with the purpose of persuading him, by threats or bribes, to hand it over. There are many lively and inventive scenes with the various ambassadors (Norse gods, Egyptian gods, representatives of Order, of Chaos, etc), and hints are dropped about a missing member of the Endless. However, the story sprawls, and it's difficult to pick any outstanding issues, other than 25. Drawn by Matt Wagner, it's a detour from the main story-line: a ghost story, set in an English public school, introducing characters who later return in The Children's Crusade. 'A Dream of You' (32–37) focuses on Barbara (a character introduced in 'The Doll's House') and the rich Narnia-style fantasies she had as a child, with artwork mostly by Shawn McManus. The scenes set in the fantasy world (32 and 35, particularly) are excellent, aching with betrayal and failure and a loss of childhood faith, but the scenes involving humans are a test of patience. The story touches on issues of gender and identity, but only in passing and from a safe distance.

The earlier hint about a missing member of the Endless is picked up for 'Brief Lives', and in 41–49 Morpheus and Delirium indulge in an eccentric search. There's some terrific dialogue from Delirium, especially in 47, and appropriate artwork from Jill Thompson, but the story is twice the necessary length. The essence is imparted in 47–49, which are also the most critical to the Grand Scheme. Another of the 'Distant Mirrors' sequence is in the oversize 50. 'Ramadan' is a short story with an Arabian Nights feel. It's pretty, with artwork by P. Craig Russell, but not outstanding.

'World's End' (51–56) involves travellers from various realms who have taken refuge in an inn during a strange storm, and pass the time by telling stories. Bryan Talbot and Mark Buckingham draw the framing sequences set in the inn each issue, and every story told has a different artist. The most striking are 51, an atmospheric story about a strange city, with very effective art by Alec Stevens, and 53, an interesting Hob Gadling story with art by Michael Zulli.

The culmination of the Grand Scheme occurs in 'The Kindly Ones', with nifty artwork, principally by Mark Hempel. The boy Daniel is missing in ominous circumstances, and his mother, Lyta, embarks on a delirious mission to find him or seek vengeance. Tons of ideas and clever sequences, but it seems to go on forever. Still, you probably have to read it just to say you have, and to put your mind at rest. After this point nothing further needs to be said, but unfortunately we have an almost entirely self-indulgent and pointless coda in 'The Wake'

(71–74). Michael Zulli's artwork in 71–73 looks pretty at first, but the characters become more and more wooden. Jon J. Muth's Chinese style artwork in 74 is worth a look, and there's a moment that has a genuine feeling of dream logic, but the story has little reason to exist.

'The Tempest' (75) revisits 19's Shakespearean theme, including the return of Charles Vess as artist, and has Shakespeare back in Stratford at the end of his career, working on his last play. There is no sign here of the imagination that fired the early issues – if there's an obvious way of tackling a character or a conversation, that's what Gaiman chooses, every time. One to keep by your bed in case of insomnia.

As you will have gathered from the list above, the comic has its weaknesses, and they become more apparent and frustrating on each re-reading. Most obvious is the tendency towards self-indulgence, which by the end is a full-blown lifestyle rather than a tendency. Anyone able to read the last few issues without muttering, 'Oh, get on with it!' every two pages is definitely a hardened fan. Then there's the persistent weakness of plot in longer story-lines, which may either kick off with a threat that is sheer fantasy-babble ('There's a new Dream Vortex!' – you have to take Morpheus' word that this is A Bad Thing), or end on any tension-destroying pretext up to and including the direct intervention of God. Sandman contains treasures along the way, but you'd best be warned not to read for plot. Finally, there's Gaiman's reluctance to clarify the relationship the Endless have with the mortal world, or to make a distinction between the different ideas for which the English language uses the word 'dream'. Are the Endless simply ambulatory ideas or are they personalities in their own right? Sometimes they talk as if it's the former (in 8, one calls another an 'anthropomorphic personification'), but they always behave as if it's the latter, and the interactions between them have everything of soap opera, and almost nothing of commentary on the nature of human desire or despair or madness. As for the different meanings of the word 'dream', surely there's no real connection between the images our brains generate during sleep and our waking wishes and ambitions (the 'Dream House' or the 'Dream Vacation'). Both, though, come under Morpheus' jurisdiction, and the distinction is never made. These last objections may seem like nitpicking, but they must count against any claim that Sandman is a classic piece of fantasy literature. Unusually clever and entertaining by the standards of comics, yes, but the standards in prose have been set by writers who will make the effort to clarify and to make those important distinctions; let's not rush to forget how high those standards can be.~FC

Recommended: 5–8, 13–14, 17–19, 25, 30, 32, 35, 47

Collections: Brief Lives (41–49), *The Doll's House* (8–16), *Dream Country* (17–20), *Fables And Reflections* (29–31, 38–40, 50, Special 1), *A Game Of You* (32–37), *The Kindly Ones* (57–69), *Preludes And Nocturnes* (1–8), *Season Of Mists* (21–28), *The Wake* (70–75), *World's End* (51–56)

SANDMAN MYSTERY THEATRE

Vertigo: *45 issues, 1 Annual + 1993 to date*

Despite the title, the series has almost nothing to do with Neil Gaiman's popular Sandman character. This is the 1940s Sandman, Wesley Dodds, in new, *noir*ish tales by Matt Wagner (1–12) and then Wagner and Steven T.Seagle. There's a strong pulp feel to these dark stories, with hate (racial, sexual or otherwise) playing a large part in the motivation of some extremely nasty villains. Each story-line is told over four issues, but running throughout, to give a strong sense of continuity, is Dodds' increasingly intimate relationship with Dian Belmont, his development as a crimefighter, and his battles of will with the police department.

Episodes are named after characters: 'The Tarantula' (1–4), 'The Face' (5–8), 'The Brute' (9–12), 'The Vamp' (13–16), 'The Scorpion' (17–20), 'Dr Death' (21–24), 'Night Of The Butcher' (25–28), 'The Hourman' (29–32, introducing the two characters to each other), 'The Python' (33–36), 'The Mist' (37–40, the Starman villain), 'Phantom of the Fair' (41–44) and 'The Blackhawk' (45–48), which is a pre-war version of the famous character). There's a good balance in the stories of traditional 'super' characters and 'ordinary' criminals, since the Sandman's a better detective than he is a fighter.

It's mostly drawn by Guy Davis in his scratchy, many-lined but effective style, but there have been guest artists, including John Watkiss (5–8), R. G. Taylor (9–12), Warren Pleece (33–36) and Matthew Smith (45–48). One annual (1994) contains a story about a search for a Central Park mugger. Written by Seagle and Wagner, it's illustrated over nine chapters by Guy Davis, David Lloyd, John Bolton, Stefano Gaudiano, George Pratt, Alex Ross, Peter Snejbjerg and Dean Ormston. *Sandman Mystery Theatre* is a brave series for Vertigo, but it seems to be paying off. Wagner and Seagle have crafted some fine mysteries, raised some difficult issues through the situations, and in Wesley and Dian created an adult, compelling couple.~NF

Recommended: 13–16, 21–24, 29–32, 37–44, annual 1

Collection: The Tarantula (1–4)

SARGE STEEL

Charlton: *10 issues 1964–1967*

James Bond-style milieu starring a private investigator whose severed hand was replaced with a steel substitute up to the wrist. Last minute, death-defying escapes abound in this competent but unoriginal series. The title changed to *Secret Agent* with issue 9.~APS

SATAN'S SIX

Topps: *4-issue miniseries 1993*

Based on characters and concepts created by Jack Kirby, the first issue also featured a number of pages drawn by 'The King' and inked by such luminaries as Frank Miller, Todd McFarlane, Steve Ditko, Mike Royer and Joe Sinnott. Neither Jack nor his inkers are working at the height of their powers, and the thinly conceived characters are frankly laughable. Writer Tony Isabella obviously thought so, deciding to fashion a hopelessly jokey story-line around the completed, basically incomprehensible Kirby pages. Every issue is introduced and interrupted by Pristine, Angel of the comic book, who exists solely to make editorial comments like 'Don't let the occasional style change confuse you. This place was never big on consistency.'

So, we have Satan's Six – Brian Bluedragon, Hard Luck Harrigan, Doctor Mordius, Kuga The Lion-Killer, Dezira of Babylon and Frightful – escaping from the tedium of Limbo and causing havoc on Earth, after striking a deal with the Devil to recruit human souls for Hell. Penciller Jon Cleary is clearly a worshipper at the altar of McFarlane, his grotesquely distorted figures unable to hide a lack of drawing skills. To make this title even more of a ghastly cash-in, 4 features a horrendously inappropriate appearance from *Friday The 13th* psycho Jason, also being published by Topps. All in all, a tacky rip-off.~AL

The SATURDAY MORNING Comic

Marvel: *One-shot 1996*

Utterly mad promotional effort to tie in with an album on which a bunch of slightly left-of-mainstream artists record versions of old Saturday-morning-cartoon theme tunes. For the comic's purposes it seems the future needs saving, and this can only be done by providing the kids with some decent music, inspiring them to rise up against The Suits. Slipshod likenesses of rock musicians from otherwise decent artists vie with an inane script and the bizarre concept for the silliest aspect of the comic. Just say 'no'.~WJ

His Name Is SAVAGE

Adventure House: *1 issue 1968*
Fantagraphics: *One-shot 1984*

Boiled so hard he's stuck to the bottom of the pan, Savage is Gil Kane's brutal government covert agent. This was issued as a black and white magazine during a period of popularity for spy fiction and TV; Kane's contribution is certainly a little more sophisticated than contemporary mainstream comics, but has dated badly. The saving grace is the excellent artwork. Freed from the constraints of monthly superhero comics, the fluidity and expression is amazing, and certainly beyond anything he'd produced to that point. The Fantagraphics edition is a reprint on better-quality paper.~WJ

THE SAVAGE DRAGON

Image: *5-issue limited series (0–4) 1992–1993, 33 issues + 1993 to date*

The Savage Dragon begins with police lieutenant Frank Darling questioning a green-skinned, fin-headed amnesiac recently found in a burning parking lot. While Dragon, as he is soon nicknamed by hospital staff, is recovering, reports start to come in of superheroes being maimed and murdered. Darling asks Dragon to help the police, but he initially refuses until the warehouse where he is working is blown up by 'freaks', the superpowered villains who, unchecked, are terrorising the city. Provoked into action, Dragon joins the police force as a regular cop, albeit an unusual-looking one, waging war on the city's seemingly endless supply of bizarre and freakish ne'er-do-wells. From here on in, to the end of the mini-series and on through the regular series, you never lose the feeling that, first and foremost, writer/artist Erik Larsen is having a great deal of fun. The fights are spectacular, the action unrelenting and yet in the middle of it all there's still plenty of time for characterisation, both with Dragon and his police colleagues, who become valuable members of the strong supporting cast, and with the members of Freak Force, the other superpowered operatives the cops get onto the payroll, but who eventually quit for their own short-lived title. Some of the best story-lines revolve around the relationship between Dragon and his possessive, jealous, ex-hooker girl-friend Rapture – always full of surprises and never afraid to challenge comic conventions. The humour is strong, the stories entertaining and the characterisation top-notch, making *The Savage Dragon* a hugely entertaining title, marred only by the fact that guest-stars turn up a little too regularly. 13, by Jim Lee, was part of Image's crossover week which saw creators swapping books, and guest-stars Grifter in the first appearance of Condition Red (later of WildCATs). Larsen later printed what he originally planned for issue 13, explaining the two versions of that issue. Other than this, the only time the character has been handled by anyone other than Larsen is in the three-issue miniseries *The*

Dragon: Blood and Guts (1995) by Jason Pearson, which sees Dragon playing bodyguard to an old friend of his police partner who married into the Mob.

The original miniseries is available as both reprints, called simply *The Dragon*, on lower-grade paper or in a collected graphic-novel edition. ~JC.
Recommended: 4–6, 10, 27, 28
Collection: Blood And Guts (miniseries 0–4), *A Force To Be Reckoned With* (1–6)

SAVAGE HENRY

Vortex: *13 issues 1987–1990*
Rip-Off: *17 issues (14–30) 1991–1993*
Iconografix: *3 issues 1994, 3-issue miniseries ('Headstrong') 1994*

A spin-off from *Those Annoying Post Bros*, this is really a series about The Bulldaggers, a group of musicians that includes Savage Henry as well as Monsieur Boche (Samoan synthesist), Caroline (a clone), the Lord C'thulu (Elder God) and Conrad Schnitzler (German synthesist). The latter is in fact a 'real' musician, much beloved of creator Matt Howarth, who uses this title both to plug all sorts of brilliant music (in comic strip reviews after the main story) and also to pay homage to any musicians he happens to like. The Residents turn up a couple of times, Nash the Slash, Wire, Dieter Meier, Clint Ruin and others all share adventures in Bugtown with the Bulldaggers.

Hiroshima kills everyone in the first major story (2–7) but our heroes persevere, except that there's only one Caroline left at the end. 14–16 is a history of the band while 17–22 is a dreamtime adventure inside Ayers Rock, where the city of Harmony has been invaded by Headbangers. Harmony, by the way, is a Xanadu for experimental musicians. Caroline is kidnapped (24–25) and Hawkwind guest-star in 26. 'The Blue Bunker Ruse' (28–30) features the Post Bros themselves and concludes with Hiroshima ruling a world devoted to the music of the Bulldaggers, which she hates despite once being a member herself.

After moving to Iconografix, the series comes in shorter bursts but is otherwise unchanged and unchanging. Musicians continue to guest (Moby, Richard Pinhas) and the stories continue to revolve around music and the activities of the band. For those who find the violent anti-social antics of the Post Bros unamusing, this title is easier on the conscience but it's still seriously weird (in the nicest possible way).~NF
Recommended: 2–7, 17–22

SAVAGE LOVE

Bear Bones: *2 issues 1994*

Dan Savage, gay advice columnist for the *Seattle Stranger* newspaper, has various bits of his biography, philosophy and outright Things

He Made Up illustrated by various cartoonists. Hilarious, poignant, sarcastic and almost certainly libellous. The best pieces are 'Ken Comes Out To Barbie' in 1 and 'You're A Gay Man Danny Brown' in 2, but there isn't a dud in either issue.~HS
Recommended: 1, 2

SAVAGE SWORD OF CONAN
Marvel: *235 issues 1974–1995*

Marvel's longest-running black and white magazine owed its success to two things. Firstly, a series of stable creative teams, particularly the enthusiastic meeting of Roy Thomas, John Buscema and a number of talented inkers, most frequently Tony De Zuniga. Secondly, the magazine moved with the times, and spiced up the stories with extra sex and violence in the later years while sticking close to the spirit of Howard's original Conan stories, more so than the colour comic.

Conan is a barbarian warrior from freezing Cimmeria, the product of a savage and brutish tribe who live for killing and hope for nothing more than to die in battle. Created by Robert E. Howard, a depressive loner who eventually shot himself because he couldn't cope with his mother's death, Conan was everything an arrested personality wished to be: ruthless but honourable, deadly in battle, indomitable of will and a pussy magnet to boot. *Savage Sword*, like the original stories, covers his whole career from teenager to middle-aged king, mixing short, 'see-monster-kill-monster' stories with longer quests. Initially, like most 1970s black and white magazines, it used a wide range of artists. In the first ten issues you get several Neal Adams stories, Barry Windsor-Smith reprints, Howard Chaykin, Jim Starlin and Alex Nino even. However, once John Buscema settled in he made the world of Conan his own, giving the surly barbarian his familiar beetle-browed look and shaggy knickers, while Thomas adapted his way through pretty much the whole Robert E. Howard canon, introducing figures from other stories and filling in the bits Howard and his many editors had missed out. Since Howard's 'natural man vs the decadence of civilisation' philosophy was common to most of the genres he wrote in, not just the fantasy stories, Thomas was able to plunder widely.

Also worth reading, even if you aren't a particular fan of heroic fantasy, are Michael Fleisher's irreverent and politically incorrect scripts, starting with 88, which, when he took over from Thomas for a brief period, were a breath of fresh air, and rather funny with it. Despite its lengthy run, *Savage Sword Of Conan's* appeal didn't really waver. Sampling half a dozen issues will tell you whether it's for you or not. *Marvel Super Special* 9 was an all-Conan issue, most notable for Howard Chaykin's intelligent take on Red Sonja, Conan's occasional partner/girl-friend. Unfortunately it has some of the most hideous colouring you'll see in a comic, which all but obscures the art.~FJ
Recommended: 15–31, 88

SAVAGE TALES
Marvel: *Series one 11 issues, 1 Annual 1971–1975, series two 9 issues 1985–1987*

The flagship of Marvel's black and white magazine line, the first series of *Savage Tales* featured consistently fine strips starring Conan, Ka-Zar and a lot of lesser sword-and-sorcery characters. Its first issue boasted the first Man-Thing by Gerry Conway and Gray Morrow, and the début of Stan Lee and John Romita's Femizons as well as a rather brutal Ka-Zar tale by Lee and John Buscema. Its highspot, though, was the Conan strip 'The Forest Giant's Daughter', by Roy Thomas and the ever-improving Barry Windsor-Smith. In the eighteen months between 1 and 2, Smith had grown enormously in stature, and his art on the epic 'Red Nails' (fifty-eight pages spread between 2 and 3) was quite breathtaking. Writer Roy Thomas clearly relished the rather more mature audience afforded him by the magazine format, and the Conan tales in 4, drawn by Gil Kane, and 5, by Jim Starlin, were equally fine.

After five issues Conan graduated to his own magazine and Ka-Zar was promoted to the lead position. Gerry Conway's stories were efficient enough, but the feature lacked enough distinction from others of its kind, although 9's 'Dark Island Of Doom', with its emphasis on sabre-toothed sidekick Zabu, was excellent. The strip was unusually well blessed artistically, with John Buscema, inked by Tony De Zuniga in 6–8, and Steve Gan in 9 and 11, producing nice work, although the Russ Heath effort in 10 was clearly a rushed job.

The magazine's back-up strips drew widely from Marvel's roster of sword-and-sorcery characters, accompanied by the occasional article. Notable strips included Brak The Barbarian in 5 and 7–9, and Shanna The She-Devil in 9 and 10, while 2 and 11 contained a couple of nice shorts drawn by Gray Morrow and Russ Heath respectively. A couple of choice Joe Maneely Black Knight reprints in 2 and 4 rounded out a thoroughly satisfying package, with each issue having something of interest. The annual collected Barry Smith's Ka-Zar stories from *Astonishing Tales*, among other things.

The 1980s revival was quite a different proposition, eschewing more established characters, preferring instead short and contrived men's adventure stories (for want of a better phrase). The whole tone was disappointingly heartless and brutal, aiming

squarely at the Punisher's core audience, and not even the likes of John Severin, Gray Morrow and a surprisingly on-form Herb Trimpe could make it at all palatable. The sole exceptions to this were a pair of Vietnam shorts by Doug Murray, particularly well drawn by Michael Golden, very much a forerunner of their later 'Nam series.~DAR
Recommended: Series one 1–5, 9, 11

SAVIOUR
Trident: *5 issues 1989–1990*

Everyone thinks the superbeing known as Saviour is the new Messiah. Unfortunately for them the real Son of God has returned as a feckless down-and-out with a fat whore as a disciple, and Saviour is actually Satan. Or is he? Mark Millar churns guts in this unsubtle but powerful exploration of Christianity as superheroic myth. Although it tries to shock a bit too hard with scenes of child abuse and *Exorcist*-like priest-battering, blasphemy adds a certain sharpness to the story, excellently illustrated throughout, by Daniel Vallely (1) (a bit of a find who promptly disappeared off the face of the earth) and Nige Kitching (2–5). Sadly unconcluded.~FJ

SCARAB
Vertigo: *8-issue limited series 1993–1994*

This was previously announced as a *Dr Fate* miniseries. John Smith's premise has a former mystic hero of the 1940s rejuvenated and setting out to rescue his long-missing wife and former partner. DC had cold feet about the story and insisted on a taste-alike version being substituted for Fate. Just as well, since the ensuing *mélange* of Hippyshit 101 stream-of-consciousness drivel wouldn't have done Fate any credit. Best read under the influence of illegal substances.~HS

SCARE TACTICS
DC: *2 issues + 1996 to date*

Strangely likeable if simplistic comic about a bunch of ghouls (well, a vampiress, a werewolf, a shambling lump and a green, venom-spitting lizard boy) who end up forming a rock band to explain their strange appearance, and escape from a bunch of evil priests with madness in their hearts and stakes in their hands. Len Kaminski's script is lively, Anthony Williams and Andy Lanning's art suitably cartoony and bold. None of it stands up to much examination but it's perfectly harmless fun for younger readers.~FJ

SCARLET THUNDER
Amaze Ink: *3 issues + 1996 to date*

This could have been published in 1939 and not looked out of place. Set in that time, it's the story of the two fastest men alive and their quest for glory and the American dream. It focuses on the competition between the two men, with the winner taking the mantle of Scarlet Thunder, before detailing Scarlet Thunder's fight against the Nazis. Dan Vado's script is full of nostalgia and captures the period innocence, and Rick Forgus's art conveys the dynamism of the characters superbly.~SS
Recommended: 1–3

SCARLET WITCH
Marvel: *4-issue miniseries 1994*

Ostensibly an exploration of the former Avenger's status as a 'nexus being', this is in fact a tired exercise in shopworn demonic cliché-baiting. 'The end of the old Scarlet Witch', the conclusion boasts. So, is this gormless bint with her head stuck through a tablecloth supposed to be an improvement?~HS

SCARLETT
DC: *14 issues 1993–1994*

It seems the legends about vampires are true after all. They've been around since time immemorial, integrating with society, yet with their own hierarchy and several groups within it. Seventeen-year-old redhead Bly Pharis, the Scarlett of the title, becomes involved with these unsavoury creatures when her parents are murdered. She conveniently discovers abilities she was previously unaware of, and that she's mentioned in ancient prophesies. 1–4 have mystery, action, violence, an appealing lead character and adequate if not spectacular art, and are fun in a B-movie fashion. Gray Morrow's art in 5–9 improves matters, but the downside is massive and often unrequired exposition infodumps for new introductions, and too many characters whose sole reason for being part of the comic is wacky diversity for an issue or two. A brave failure, cancelled way before the ideas had expired, the final three issues are a premature and rushed conclusion.~FP

SCARY TALES
Charlton: *20 issues 1975–1979, 26 issues (21–46) 1980–1984*

Horror anthology that's entertaining in small doses, featuring the work of all of the usual 1970s Charlton suspects including Joe Staton, Don Newton, Steve Ditko, Tom Sutton, Nicholas Alascia and Wayne Howard. Of note are a Man-Thing rip-off in 4 and early work by Mike Zeck in 10. The stories, by Joe Gill and Nick Cuti amongst others, are usually sting-in-the-tail, randomly introduced by Countess Von Bludd. From 12, most issues are actually reprints from earlier Charlton horror series.~NF

SCAVENGERS
Quality: *26 issues 1987–1989*

Catchall title for more reprints from Britain's *2000AD*. Dinosaurs and giant animals are the theme, and it doesn't get better than the early issues, featuring 'Flesh'. When mankind has exterminated all animals, there's no longer any meat. The solution? Go back in time, farm dinosaurs and send the meat back to the future. Of course, the dinosaurs begin to take exception to the intrusion, particularly a battle-hardened tyrannosaur called Old One Eye. Gloriously and gruesomely violent, if your sense of humour extends that way it's a barrel of laughs, and the first two issues also have a good Judge Dredd dinosaur strip. The follow-up from 20 is basically the same plot, except it's sea-dwelling dinosaurs to be harvested. Beyond that, things go wrong. Once you've seen dinosaurs rampaging through 23rd-century factories you're not going to settle for the likes of the B-movie style 'Ant Wars', 'Shako' and 'Helltrekkers'. The former has giant ants rampaging through South America, Shako is a rampaging polar bear, and 'Helltrekkers' is a future version of the 19th-century wagon trails, beset by danger all the way, but pedestrian throughout.~FP

SCIMIDAR
Eternity: *4-issue miniseries 1988–1989, 4-issue miniseries (Scimidar II) 1989, 4-issue miniseries (Scimidar III) 1990, 4-issue miniseries (Scimidar IV Wild Thing) 1990, 4-issue miniseries (Scimidar V 'Living Color') 1991, 4-issue miniseries (Scimidar VI 'Slashdance') 1992–1993*
CFD: *1 issue 1995*

We've already wasted too much space just listing Scimidar miniseries. Suffice it to say that Scimidar is a violent badgirl, an 'intellectual' assassin who likes to understand who she's being asked to kill, but who also has a fondness for licking blood off her knives while showing you her crotch. Repulsive stuff that benefits from neither good writing nor art.~FJ

SCOOBY DOO
Gold Key: *30 issues 1970–1975*

Frankly excellent comic series, mostly written by Mark Evanier and drawn by Dan Spiegle. Evanier's scripts follow the cartoon formula but keep the jokes coming as Scooby, Shaggy, Velma, Daphne and Fred travel around America finding fraudulent ghosts and monsters practically anywhere. Spiegle doesn't overly define the main characters but his draughtsmanship is given full reign in the backgrounds and supporting cast. There are some short back-ups (including 'The Weird World of Dr. Strange' – a werewolf,

Jekyll-and-Hyde scientist – from 1966) until issue 17, after which most issues contain two Scooby adventures.~NF
Recommended: 12, 13, 17–22, 27, 28–30

SCOOBY DOO
Marvel: *9 issues 1977–1979*

Marvel's short-lived attempt to do Hanna Barbera's *Scooby Doo* at least keeps the talents of Mark Evanier and Dan Spiegle. The scripts are a little less fresh and Spiegle's artwork bears more of his own stamp, but overall these are still good comics that capture the spirit and flavour of the cartoon series. Dynomutt (1–6) is the back-up (by Evanier and Paul Norris) in short stories that preview the next month's *Dynomutt* issues.~NF
Recommended: 1–9

SCOOBY DOO
Archie: *21 issues 1995–1997*

It must be said that Archie have at least started to recognise that *Scooby Doo* comics have to be by Evanier and Spiegle. Quite apart from having Scrappy Doo in them, the tiresome stories by Vallely and Kirschenbaum make too many references to current culture or politics. The success of *Scooby Doo* has much to do with its universality: including comments about Mel Gibson erodes that. Fortunately, Evanier and Spiegle are on hand for 10 and 14 and, one trusts, many more to come.~NF

Swing With SCOOTER
DC: *36 issues 1966–1972*

Joe Orlando turns in some nice art in the first issues of this 1960s up-to-the-minute version of *Archie*. Considering it's basically a school and teen life strip there are transformations more bizarre than any superhero title as Scooter and crew are turned into vegetables in 7 and shrunk in 8. After Orlando's departure with 11 attempts to disguise the *Archie* style lapsed completely, with artists Goldberg, Mortimer, and Scarpelli obviously under instructions to copy. No better or worse than its inspiration, the concentration on being hip is always amusing in retrospect.~WJ

SCORCHED EARTH
Tundra: *4 issues 1991*

In a future Earth destroyed by pollution, scientist Elliot Godwin has the power to heal the environmental damage and is pursued by various factions, from the (predictably) evil government to Hopi Indians who want to make him the god of an ancient messiah prophecy. Michael Gaydos and John Gentile's tale is glossily presented, with shiny paper and painted artwork, but there's little original in here to make it worth the effort.~JC

THE SCORE
Piranha: *4-issue miniseries 1990*

Major rock star Philip Sand loses his memory while writing a movie soundtrack. As parts fall back into place he's caught between two moguls, each of whom believes he has information that would enable him to wrest control of the other's influence. The phrase 'The Score' keeps recurring, both as a motif and a possible threat. Unfortunately Sand has no idea what it refers to. This is a taut and surprisingly gritty mystery from Gerard Jones, ably illustrated by Mark Badger. There are plenty of surprises, not least the constant uncertainty of who's working with whom, but a major failing is that there's not a single likeable character, deadening any emotional impact. If you can live with that give *The Score* a try.~WJ

SCORPIO ROSE
Eclipse: *2 issues 1983*

With her leg-warmers, pink hair and leotard Scorpio Rose comes on like the Witch from *Fame*. Rushing to embrace the opportunities afforded by independent publishers, Steve Englehart reprised *Madame Xanadu* for Eclipse as a flame-haired gypsy whose mystic powers and immortality emerged when her lover, who was possessed by a demon during a knife fight, raped her. The story never really got going. Lots of people are after her Book of Fleshe, and the lover turns up after it along with the gypsy he killed in the original fight. Marshall Rogers provided shadowy, beautifully composed art, and also drew the back-up, Dr Orient, written by Frank Lauria.~FJ

THE SCORPION
Atlas: *3 issues 1975*

Howard Chaykin turns in pulp-style adventures of a 1930s mercenary in the first two issues, arguably the best comics published by Atlas. The third issue inexplicably concentrates on a contemporary costumed character with the same name, and is terrible. Chaykin later transferred his version of The Scorpion to Marvel, calling the character Dominic Fortune.~FP

SCOUT
Eclipse: *Series one 24 issues 1985–1987, series two ('War Shaman') 16 issues 1988–1989*

In Tim Truman's futuristic Western, Scout is an Apache summoned by the supernatural Gahn to defeat Four Monsters who are currently in positions of power in the USA (including the presidency). Forewarned by Scout's killing of the first monster, the President sends two of Scout's army-training friends (Rosanna Winter and Raymond Vaughan) to kill him. Operating in a world of ecological disaster and social disintegration, Scout has killed the monsters by the end of 6. He goes on to become a rallying point for the hungry and discontented people, accompanied by a spiritual leader, Doody, whose bible is *The Lord Of The Rings*. By 14 Doody is dead and Scout has been wounded and captured by Winter, but her allegiances have been shaken by contact with an Israeli secret agent who tells her about the real effects of the US policies she's supporting. Teamed up with Monday the Eliminator (after they've fought each other through the 3-D Special, issue 16), Scout winds up in the middle of a global war (20–24).

'War Shaman' picks up the story ten years later as Scout descends from a mountain retreat following the death of his wife. The America he returns to is still torn by civil war; the series depicts his search for a new home as he crosses paths with old acquaintances Vaughan and Winter. Arguably Truman's finest hour, *Scout* features mature scripts and artwork. Its main fault is a tendency to lose the plot and meander, but overall it's a very enjoyable read. Two further Scout series were discussed but haven't yet appeared. Notable back-ups include 'Fashion In Action' (1–8) and 'Monday The Eliminator' (11–14, before becoming part of the main story-line). There was also Beau Smith's 'Beau Le Duke' ('War Shaman' 13–16), centred around a supporting character from the first series.~NF
Collections: The Four Monsters (series one 1–7), *Mount Fire* (series one 8–14)

SCREEN PLAY
Slave Labor: *1 issue 1989*

A major movie is in production, reviving Major Nebula, an old space-hero TV series. The show underwent a complete transformation for its second run, progressing from pure corn to thoughtful terror under the hand of mysterious new writer I.M. Thorgon, except that all was not happy on set. Intriguing, well plotted and paced, and sadly incomplete, it's a very promising début from writer and artist Ashley Holt. Whatever happened to him?~FP

SCREWBALL SQUIRREL
Dark Horse: *3 issues 1995*

Yet another attempt to bring *Tom and Jerry*-style violent slapstick to comics. And yet another failure to capture the humour, energy and inventiveness of the cartoons. Written by Bob Fingerman and drawn by Greg Hyland, these Screwball Squirrel stories are madcap but terribly uninspired, with endlessly repeated jokes. Back-ups featuring other Tex Avery characters are not much better, with the Droopy story in 2 so knowing it's unbearable.~NF

SCROOGE McDUCK IN THE YUKON
Gladstone: *One-shot 1995*

For reasons best known to themselves, Gladstone published this Don Rosa Uncle Scrooge story as a special rather than allocating space in the regular *Uncle Scrooge* titles. It's good stuff, a continuity implant set in the Yukon before Scrooge hit the vein that made his fortune, with a fine supporting cast, good gags and the poignancy of Scrooge's failed romance with Glittering Goldie. As the lead features a Mountie the Three Little Pigs back-up concentrates on them as Mounties, but it's filler and you should be getting this for Scrooge and Rosa.~WJ
Recommended: 1

SEA DEVILS
DC: *35 issues 1961–1967*

Ahh… nostalgia. Why does no one produce undersea-adventure comics anymore? Graduating from *Showcase* 27–29, we have four Sea Devils, the cerebral leader, his blonde girlfriend, her kid brother and a loveable hunk of meat, surely the prototypes of the Fantastic Four. Elegantly illustrated by Russ Heath for the first ten issues, and featuring beautifully toned covers, the Sea Devils' stories are ephemeral light entertainment, as much a period piece as *I Love Lucy* and *Rock Around The Clock*.~FP

The SEARCHERS
Caliber: *4 issues + 1996 to date*

By virtue of mystical happenstance the characters from the most prominent turn-of-the-century science-fiction novels emerge from the books to procreate. In the present day their descendants are gathered to prevent another mystical event with potentially catastrophic consequences. Very enjoyable in the manner of the 1960s films made from the turn-of-the-century novels, although one might wish for more subtly inserted exposition dumps.~FP

SEBASTIAN O
Vertigo: *3-issue miniseries 1993*

Victorian England with 21st-century technology *à la* Captain Nemo is the setting for the exploits of a psychotic renegade dandy. Imprisoned for his bohemian behaviour, Sebastian O escapes to cause havoc among the somewhat seedy establishment. Surprisingly unpretentious writing from Grant Morrison and excellent period art from Steve Yeowell. 'One must commit acts of the highest treason only when dressed in the most resplendent finery…' How true. Marvellous.~HY
Recommended: 1–3

SECOND CITY
Harrier: *4-issue miniseries 1986–1987*

Confused mystery script from Paul Duncan throws in the kitchen sink and produces a story complicated but far from complex. With most other Phil Elliott artwork you at least get a story that's interesting, so there's little reason to seek this out.~FJ

Jack Kirby's SECRET CITY SAGA
Topps: *5 issues (0–4) 1993*

The prolific Jack Kirby's sketch pages were purchased by Topps, who developed *Secret City Saga* from his character designs. Since other Topps-initiated projects using Kirby-designed characters were a mess, it's surprising that this is an entertaining series, with an accompanying nostalgic glow that harks back to the early days of Marvel, not least by employing Roy Thomas and Steve Ditko to write and draw. That being so, the themes appear to be 100% Kirby. A millennia-old race has existed beneath the Earth, perpetuating themselves during times of disaster by suspended animation. Three warriors, mutated to give them extra abilities, awake in the 1990s and make their way to the surface. This is detailed in individual issues titled *Bombast*, *Captain Glory* and *Nightglider*, which introduce the cast. While also imbued with the spirit of early Marvel comics, they're not as skilfully written, although there is a small thrill to be had in seeing the always-odd art combination of Dick Ayers and John Severin once again. The ending of each solo issue leads into *Secret City Saga* 1. Some less reputable types have also survived the previous cataclysm and are bent on enforcing their will on Earth, and our heroes have to stop them. Naturally, this isn't easy. The zero issue is a largely superfluous trade promotion giving a little background to the series (explained in 1 anyway), but has some nice Walt Simonson art and also introduces *Satan's Six*. Ditko's not on top form throughout, but certainly adequate, and, denied previous continuity reference points, Roy Thomas remembers how to tell a story again. This thrilled few when originally published, but is deserving of another glance.~FP

THE SECRET DEFENDERS
Marvel: *25 issues 1993–1995*

The title apart, this has little to do with the first version of *The Defenders*, initially presenting off-beat combinations of Marvel superheroes pitted against mystical menaces they wouldn't usually encounter. The constant factor is Doctor Strange, who selects the necessary participants by consulting his tarot deck. It's all reasonable superhero stuff. Credit then to Ron Marz, Tom Grindberg and Don Hudson for experimenting with a team of villains under the direction of Thanos in 12–14, the best story in the run. With 15 the creative team changes and emphasis shifts to a regular team of Druid, Shadowoman and Cadaver plus guest stars. The resulting dull formula material lasts longer than any other period of the title, and cancellation was creative mercy killing.~WJ

SECRET HEARTS
DC: *153 issues, 1949–1973*

Second of the major DC romance launches, *Secret Hearts* was second to none in quality, with top-notch art (Toth, Sekowsky/Sachs, Morrow, Romita, Pike, Colan) and stories that, while every bit as silly as those in its sisters, at least showed some imagination. Covers, in keeping with the 'Secret' motif, frequently showed the heroine in some romantic dilemma, either self-inflicted (she'd made up a boy-friend so as not to be left out of girl talk... so what does she do when her girl-friends tell her 'new' boyfriend she's going steady?), or external (her declared-dead fiancé returns from the war... but what can she tell her new boy-friend?). Two serials ran in the book 'Search For Happiness', 110–138, a perfunctory and unsatisfactory saga of a young girl's quest for the perfect partner and her perpetual disappointments, and chapters 2 and 3 of the shorter but higher-voltage '20 Miles To Heartbreak', a drama of riches, deception and as much passion as the Comics Code would allow, which crossed over into *Young Love*.~HS

THE SECRET OF THE SALAMANDER
Dark Horse: *One-shot 1992*

The Secret of the Salamander, by Jacques Tardi, starring his female investigator Adele Blanc-Sec, is a particularly convoluted, self-referential mystery that starts out in World War I trenches and involves secret world organisations (a sort of Bildenberg Committee) and the Mafia. Humorous, cynical, toying with story-telling conventions, this is Tardi at his most disrespectful and intriguing.~NF
Recommended: 1

SECRET ORIGINS
DC: *Series one 7 issues 1973–1974, series two 50 issues, 3 Annuals, 1 Special 1986–1990*

The 1970s series reprints various superhero origin stories, ranging from 1938 (Superman in 1) to 1968 (Legion of Superheroes in 6). They're worth a look if any come your way, since the stories are usually entertaining, and each issue has a discussion of the way each character's origin story has changed over the years. Of course, they're also a cheap way of seeing now rather rare stories. 3's reprinting of Wonder Woman's origin from 1942 stands out above all the rest. Charles Moulton's story is fresh and

original, and the artwork from Harry G. Peter is utterly individual and charming. When you consider that people producing comics in 1942 thought that their work would be read once and thrown away, it is humbling to see how much care and effort Moulton and Peters still chose to pour into this story. Others covered are Batman and Flash (1), Supergirl, Atom and Green Lantern (2), Wildcat (3), Vigilante and Kid Eternity (4), The Spectre (5), Blackhawk (6) and Robin and Aquaman in 7.

The second series contains new stories (though most are based closely on older versions), and the characters covered become steadily more obscure as the series progresses. It was never a particularly strong series, though most issues have some entertainment value. The list of those worth tracking down is short: issue 10, for Alan Moore's take on the Phantom Stranger, with art by Joe Orlando, and useful comments on the problems faced by someone who refuses to pick a side on a particular issue; 24, for Gary Cohn and Dan Mishkin on the Blue Devil, with art by Ty Templeton and some hilarious moments, although it comes adrift at the end; 37 for Templeton again, on the Legion of Substitute Heroes (flawless, this one); and 46 for the origin of their clubhouse and an introduction to Arm-Fall-Off Boy, written by Gerard Jones with art by Curt Swan and Ty Templeton (again). Also of interest are Doll Man (8), Michael Gilbert's Spectre (15), the bizarre Creeper (18), the ludicrous Black Condor (21), Gil Kane's artwork on Midnight (28), Sheldon Mayer's short, humorous Red Tornado (29), Neil Gaiman on Poison Ivy (36), Detective Chimp (40) and Ambush Bug (48). The 1989 Special devoted itself to 'Gotham City's vilest villains', using a framing sequence featuring a TV crew making a documentary (writer Neil Gaiman, artists Mike Hoffman and Kevin Nowlan), and taking in the Penguin, the Riddler, and Two-Face – the Riddler story is particularly appealing, written by Neil Gaiman, with artwork by Bernie Mirault and Matt Wagner.~FC
Recommended: Series one 3, series two 10, 24, 37, 46, 1989 Special

SECRET SIX
DC: *7 issues 1968–1969*

Six people with different backgrounds and abilities were brought together by the mysterious Mockingbird to combat evil-doers beyond the reach of the law. Mockingbird had helped each of the six in the past and still controlled their fates. This was a fine espionage series written by the very versatile E. Nelson Bridwell, and would have made a great TV series. There was an intriguing twist: one of the six was Mockingbird, but who? Well, all was revealed almost twenty years on in *Action Comics* 601, when the feature was revived. Apparently the identity revealed wasn't who Bridwell intended the character to be.~HY

SECRET SOCIETY OF SUPER-VILLAINS
DC: *16 issues, 1 Special 1976–1978*

Despite the ludicrous title there's much to enjoy here in a light-hearted fashion. The title's plagued throughout by shoddy art, and the constantly shifting creative staff is a problem, with no one really having the time to settle until writer Gerry Conway takes control with 8. The best issues are 1–5, instituting the Society (complete with clubhouse) funded by a mysterious benefactor, and mixing in concepts from two classic DC runs, Jack Kirby's *New Gods* and the Manhunter strip from *Detective*. Publicist Funky Flashman (Kirby's thinly veiled Stan Lee jibe from *Mister Miracle*) is thrown into the mix to good effect from 4, but from 6 the title loses its way, with revived 1950s superhero Captain Comet teaming with assorted DC superheroes to bring the villains to justice. By the time Conway has begun to set matters right again, cancellation has struck, with plots being concluded in *JLA* 166–168.~FP

Marvel Super Heroes SECRET WARS
Marvel: *12 issues 1984–1985*

Marvel's grand event of 1984 materialised as a grand fiasco. The Beyonder, an omnipotent being who is the only denizen of his multiverse, discovers the Marvel Universe. His dubious method of investigation comprises transporting most major Marvel heroes and villains to an artificially constructed planet. Cue twelve issues of mindless mayhem. Even most sub-plots manifest as petty bickering amongst allies, unaided by Jim Shooter's artless dialogue and Mike Zeck's unusually lack-lustre pencils. The new Spider-Woman is introduced in 7, and Spider-Man's black costume makes its début in 8. Otherwise all developments, including character deaths, are reinstated to issue 1's *status quo* by the wish-fulfilment powers abounding in the final issues. What is the point?~APS
Collection: Secret Wars (1–12)

SECRET WARS II
Marvel: *9 issues 1985–1986*

Thus cometh Marvel's grand event of 1985, barely three months after the conclusion of the first series. The Beyonder somehow still considers the human race to be worthy of study, so manifests on earth as a white Michael Jackson lookalike in order to experience every facet of human existence. The inherent fatal flaw in this is that no human writer can convincingly portray utterly omnipotent characters, and Jim Shooter proceeds to demonstrate this. The resulting escapade depicts a spoilt two-year-old brat with limitless power flitting around the globe as multitudes of heroes chase mindlessly. That said, the diversity afforded by the premise results in a product which is an improvement on the first series, and the ending is creditable. Be warned that the relentless tie-ins to over thirty issues of other titles give an incomplete feel to this series if read in isolation.~APS

SECRET WEAPONS
Valiant: 21 issues 1993–1995

Built around a core of two characters introduced in *Harbinger*, Livewire and Stronghold, and the pre-pubescent Geomancer, *Secret Weapons* begins as Valiant's answer to *The Defenders*, with other superheroes augmenting the trio for each particular mission. Joe St Pierre writes and draws most of 1–10, and with the exception of 6 and 7 (involving the dull spider aliens that proliferate in Valiant titles) they're solid superhero stories. Power suits acquired by British intelligence services in 10 are distributed in 11, as the title changes direction to focus on a quartet of new characters. It transpires, though, that there are problems associated with the power suits, and most of the remaining issues are devoted to sorting them out. While okay, they don't match the earlier material, and 20 and 21, with Bloodshot on the rampage and crossing over into other titles, are very poor.~FP
Recommended: 1, 2, 8

SECRETS OF SINISTER HOUSE
DC: *14 issues (5–18) 1972–1974*

Continuing the numbering from Gothic romance comic *Sinister House Of Secret Love*, 5, nicely crafted by Michael Fleisher and Dick Giordano, was originally intended for that comic. From 6 it reverted to DC's more typical collections of twist-in-the-tale mysteries, and was a somewhat hit-or-miss affair. Writers like Robert Kanigher, Steve Skeates and Jack Oleck were at the very least competent, if often uninspired, but the occasional inventive story by Sheldon Mayer brightened things up a bit (particularly 7, which he wrote in its entirety). Artistically it was also a mixed bag, with the likes of Mike Sekowsky and Bill Draut rubbing shoulders with the rather more exciting likes of Sam Glanzman (7), and the team of Larry Hama and Neal Adams in 10. The title's most consistent quality was supplied by its Filipino contingent, notably Alfredo Alcala (6, 10, 12–14), Rico Rival (9), Gerry Talaoc (10) and the ever-reliable Nestor Redondo (7, 15). Alex Nino also produced some feverishly imaginative work (8, 11, 13), which occasionally approached psychedelic surreality.

What was really required was an individual identity, and towards the end of the run the

title experimented with a number of new directions. In one example E. Nelson Bridwell supplied a couple of nice literary adaptations of William Fryer Harvey (12) and Ambrose Bierce (14) short stories. The final few issues contained a number of inventory and reprint stories, most enjoyably a Johnny Peril story in 16, beautifully drawn by Frank Giacoia and Sy Barry, though it was Vincente Alcazar's moody drawing in 16 that most impressed. Overall, *Secrets Of Sinister House* is a comic for art fans or those after an unchallenging read.~DAR
Recommended: 7, 8, 11–13, 16

SECRETS OF THE HAUNTED HOUSE
DC: *48 issues, 1 Special 1975–1978*

Nothing here to give your spine a chill, but you can always find the occasional nicely drawn story. Mike Golden's effort in 10 comes to mind. A fairly interesting series starring the blind Mr E, who would later play a major role in the *Books of Magic* miniseries, appeared in 31–41.~HY

SECRETS OF THE LEGION OF SUPER-HEROES
DC: *3-issue miniseries 1981*

You know those sit-com episodes where time or money has clearly run out and the regulars gather round a set and say 'Remember when...' and flashbacks ensue? Well, this is like that. Legion father-figure R.J. Brande is fatally ill and being visited by all twenty-seven Legionnaires at once, which surely violates hospital regulations regarding maximum room occupancy. He can only be saved by genetic material from his hitherto unknown child, who is – gasp – one of the Legion. Cue the flashbacks, as every member has their origin reviewed. Ploddingly narrated by E. Nelson Bridwell and execrably illustrated by Jimmy Janes, this is probably the single most pointless LSH spin-off, and it's had stiff competition.~HS

SECRETS OF THE VALIANT UNIVERSE
Valiant: *3 issues 1994–1995*

Not a series, but three unconnected specials published sporadically several months apart. 1, a giveaway with the *Wizard* magazine's Valiant Special, showcased all of the Valiant heroes in two-page stories, a couple of which had major repercussions in their regular series. 2 featured Master Darque, and was part of the 'Chaos Effect' crossover, and 3 was an untold story of the Rai who perished in the 'Unity' crossover.~HS

SECTAURS, Warriors Of Symbion
Marvel: *8 issues 1985–1986*

'Somewhere in space spins a planet known to its insect-evolved inhabitants as... Symbion.' Well, who are we to judge what form insect evolution

would take on another planet, but it seems odd that it should produce an intelligent life-form exactly like *homo sapiens* apart from little antennae and compound eyes (which have a pupil-like dot in the middle so you can see where the characters are looking). What you have here is a standard sword-and-sorcery story with a few gimmicks such as giant insects instead of horses and the aforementioned eyes. The heroes are on a quest to find the centre of forbidden technology that dates from before the Great Cataclysm – a quest which is also a race against the baddies of the Dark Dominion. It's not painfully bad, but neither is it rewarding. Bill Mantlo's writing has minimal imagination, confused story-telling, a flat ending, and no signs of humour or characterisation. The artwork does keep a consistent alien feel, despite several changes of art team, but it's not an attractive feel. Don't bother.~FC

SEDUCTION OF THE INNOCENT
Eclipse: *6 issues 1985–1986*

Seduction of the Innocent reprints pre-Comics Code horror stories, mostly from Standard titles, but oh! what a collection of the great and the good. There's an Alex Toth strip in every issue which would, on its own, make this title worth buying, but over the six issues we also get work by Jerry Grandenetti, Jack Katz (of *First Kingdom* fame), Murphy Anderson, Ruben Moreira, Mort Meskin and Nick Cardy. These are not the stories that Fredric Wertham's infamous book used as examples, but by their nature they stood to be condemned along with the more disreputable stories then published. Two 3-D issues were also produced. The first contained the previously unpublished *Adventure Into Darkness* 15. Frankly, the 3-D process is a waste of time, obscuring the quality of the artwork.~NF
Recommended: 1–6

SEEKERS Into The Mystery
Vertigo: *15 issues 1996–1997*

J.M. DeMatteis is a writer attempting to transcend the mundanity clogging the shelves of the comic store, which is commendable. He tends, however, to retread the same ground in his 'serious' works, much in the manner of a dog following a scent. There'll be a few idiosyncratic foibles as diversions, some family trauma, and woolly symbolism, but short of a yank on the neck there's nothing that'll stop his pontifications meandering on to the same ineffable conclusion that there must be more to life. It's hardly a startling revelation, and DeMatteis has no insight which is unavailable to the remainder of humanity.

Given that the stated and titular premise of *Seekers* was once again to present a quest for enlightenment, the signs were dire. Which makes the quality of the early issues shocking. Instead of forcing superheroes into awkward plots or hiding behind twee counterparts, DeMatteis has largely dispensed with fantasy trappings to present real characters. Knowingly or otherwise, his initial lead, Lucas Hart, tormented, struggling writer, is autobiographically based to a degree, and other cast members also have a resonance beyond the dictates of plot. DeMatteis appears to have finally combined his undoubted and seemingly marginalised flair for humour with his preoccupations to produce a fully rounded story, referring to his past work in the first issue. He's also tapped into a growing fascination with all matters unexplained as the millennium approaches.

This is very much the writer's title, but artists Glenn Barr (1–4), Jon J. Muth (drawing, not smearing blobs of paint across a page, in 5 and 10), Jill Thompson (11 on), and particularly Michael Zulli (6–9) are sympathetic collaborators. Hart discovers why he's been plagued by an inner demon in 1–4 and takes a step on the road forward in 5. The best story arc is 6–9, in which Hart, accompanied by his daughter, meets two old ladies who've been conversing with angels since childhood, and Streiberesque aliens. It gave the series a greater purpose and hinges the mysteries with some possible answers. *Seekers* had some annoying aspects (and 10 is a horrendous lapse back, that almost serves as a catalogue of how bad DeMatteis can be), particularly the implicit call for a leap of faith, but it stood head and shoulders over DeMatteis' previous work. If you've found his other comics pretentious or irritating, give *Seekers* a try.~WJ

SELF-LOATHING COMICS
Fantagraphics: *2 issues + 1995 to date*

Autobiographical comic strips by Robert and Aline Kominsky-Crumb about life in France. Each takes one half of the comic to explore their daily routine with the usual rationalisations, daydreams and introspection. This is not comfortable reading and is barely story-telling in any conventional sense but both, in different ways, pull you in so that the centre-spread (and end of each story) comes as an unwelcome interruption.~NF

SEMPER FI'
Marvel: *9 issues, 1988–1989*

'Semper Fidelis' is the motto of the US Marine Corps; this series is one long tribute to the Marines. It appears that since its foundation in 1775, the Marine Corps has never been without a member of the Whittier family, and with two stories in each issue, we see the Whittiers in action across the globe and the centuries. The writing is pure propaganda, with almost no

imagination. There is the occasional hint that not every male Whittier is overjoyed at the anticipation or remembrance of war, but these hints are never allowed to develop. Andy Kubert and John Severin contribute some fine artwork, but it's not enough to bring any of the story up to 'good'.~FC

SENSATION COMICS
DC: *116 issues 1942–1953*

William Moulton Marston's creation, Wonder Woman, was so popular with readers (or at least with DC staff) following her début in *All-Star Comics* 8 that she was chosen to headline this new anthology book. Her proto-feminist adventures, illustrated in H.G.Peter's curiously blocky, woodcut style, gave the title a mood and atmosphere unlike everything else the industry had to offer. Unfortunately, Wonder Woman was the only star in *Sensation*'s early years. Her back-up strips were the most motley collection of costumed athletes and rip-offs of popular movies of the time ever assembled in a comic book. Mr. Terrific (1–63) was prodigy Terry Sloane. About to commit suicide because everything comes too easy, he discovers a new mission when he rescues a young boy from a life of crime. Throwing together a costume, the most remarkable aspect of which is a sweater with 'Fair Play' knitted on the belly, he sets out as the modestly named avenger of justice. Wildcat (1–90) was boxing champ Ted Grant, who became inspired by a *Green Lantern* comic book (!) to fight crime with his bare knuckles while dressed in black fur. Many fine artists worked on the strip in its later days, including Kurtzman, Krigstein (81, 84) and Kubert (65, 66). The Gay Ghost (1–42) was a deceased nobleman who, possessing the body of his dead descendant after the latter's criminal lifestyle has led to an untimely end, sets out to atone for the man's misdeeds – and score with the latter's girlfriend, handily the reincarnation of the Ghost's own dead love! And then there was Little Boy Blue and the Blue Boys (1–93), three tough slum kids who put on powder-blue long underwear and get laughed out of the neighbourhood... well, no, they should have been, but instead they wage war on crime. Towards the end of the series, they were occasionally joined by Little Miss Redhead, a crusading Lolita who clearly already knew more than she should about Life. Finally, The Black Pirate (1–51) was a Fairbanksesque period swashbuckler, later joined by his son on tame aquatic adventures. Art originally by Hawkman illustrator Sheldon Moldoff, tracing harder than ever. Despite the, to be polite, unoriginal nature of most of these strips, they all had respectable runs, the only significant addition after issue 1 being the visiting mystic gem wielder, Sargon the Sorcerer (34–36, 52–83).

By virtue of sheer longevity and persistence, most of these series improved as the years rolled on, but it almost didn't matter what was in the back of the book, as Wonder Woman's heady mix of sado-masochism and suffrage kept pulling in the readers anyway. By the late 1940s, however, sales were falling, and the DC editors decided to try a new tactic. Since Wonder Woman's presence gave *Sensation* a large female readership, they ditched all the, by then, tired-looking back-ups and relaunched *Sensation* as an all-girl comic. The first oestrogen-heavy issue was 94, and Wonder Woman received a makeover for the new look. Still the cover feature, she found herself being carried over stepping stones by her doll-like boy-friend, seated at a desk as 'Wonder Woman, Romance Editor' answering letters from the lovelorn, and modelling fashions, all on dismaying pink and lavender covers that must have made the old girl quite bewildered. New back-ups included Dr Pat, a young and, of course, beautiful female MD who struggled to be taken seriously; Valerie Vaughn, aka Lady Danger, dilettante débutante adventuress; and 'Astra, Girl of the Future', an outer-space telecaster. Unsurprisingly, the 'girlie' phase was a catastrophic failure. Despite some nice art (Infantino on Dr Pat, Oksner on Lady Danger), no more girls bought the title than had always done so, and male readers, unnerved by the pastel colours and soppy covers, deserted in droves. With 107, all the features – even Wonder Woman – were ousted, and the title reworked again with supernatural adventurer Johnny Peril as the lead, superbly illustrated by Alex Toth. Infantino, Sy Barry, and other top-line DC artists filled out the rest of the book with haunting and evocative tales of the uncanny. The new formula was a sufficient hit that the title was fleetingly rechristened *Sensation Mystery* from 110, but a lack of decisive sales figures, and the increasingly serious concern by parents and politicians about the – spurious – connections between comics and juvenile delinquency, caused DC to cancel the series with issue 116.~HS

SENSEI
First: *4-issue miniseries 1989*

Despising the complexity of modern society, Tadashi Natori uses a time machine to travel to the 19th-century. In the best tradition of time-travel stories, things go wrong. Half of him ends up in 19th-century USA, the other half is trapped in a post-World War III future, a future he himself determined in the nineteenth century. Wandering two strands of time, Tadashi discovers that the past holds its own

perils. Roger Salick and Val Mayerik's *Sensei* is better than most time-travel stories, and they leave you wanting to see more of the character.~FP

SERGIO ARAGONÉS
DC: *One-shot 1996*
Marvel: *One-shot 1996*

To give them their full titles, we have *Sergio Aragonés Destroys DC* and *Sergio Aragonés Massacres Marvel*. In each quixotic cartoon, genius Sergio Aragones delivers his interpretation of the company's major superheroes, with Mark Evanier supplying dialogue and additional jokes. There are plenty of wry smiles to be had as the foibles of both sets of characters are highlighted, but it's carried out in a loving fashion, and isn't really sustained beyond the initial pages. There's a joy in seeing Aragonés' individual interpretations of characters he wouldn't usually get to draw, with his smug Superman a treat, but neither of these is an essential purchase.~WJ

SEX WARRIOR
Dark Horse: *2-issue microseries 1993*

Meretricious pap, written by Pat Mills and stiffly drawn by Mike McKone, about a tantrist woman who assists guerrilla fighters by showing them how to go blue and become strong by having lots and lots of sex. Wankers away!~GK

SGT FURY and his HOWLING COMMANDOS
Marvel: *167 issues, 7 annuals 1963–1981*

The antithesis of realistic war comics and one of the most static of Marvel's long-run titles. Set in World War II, the plot for any issue picked at random involves Nick Fury and his team of crack soldiers parachuting into Nazi-occupied territory to rescue a captured Allied commander, destroy a missile base or free a town from Nazi domination. Once the fantasy premise has been swallowed, enjoy the jocular dialogue, initiated by Stan Lee and the well-established (if completely two-dimensional) personalities of Fury and his Howlers.

Roy Thomas took over as writer from 29 and Gary Friedrich from 42, but any changes in scripting style are barely noticeable. Dick Ayers deserves a mention for drawing almost every issue. From 80, every odd-numbered issue reprints earlier stories. Full reprint status is achieved in 121, with the last issue reprinting the first. Noteworthy issues are 13, guest-starring Captain America, the only superhero influence on the title, 18, with the death of Nick Fury's girl-friend, Pamela Hawley, 22's wonderfully humorous dialogue, 27, giving the origin of Fury's eyepatch, and 72, with an unusually thoughtful plot.~APS

SGT ROCK

DC: *Series one 120 issues (302–422), 4 Annuals, 1 Spectacular 1977–1988, series two 21 issues 1977 (1), 1988–1992 (2–21), 2-issue microseries 1992–1994*

In 1977 DC finally changed the title of *Our Army At War* to what it had been for almost twenty years in all but name, *Sgt Rock*, but otherwise it was largely business as usual. Joe Kubert was still editing, Robert Kanigher was still writing, Sgt Rock was still fighting World War II and various artists were still trying out to replace Russ Heath. The job eventually fell to Frank Redondo from 310, who proved a worthy successor. *Sgt Rock* opens with a three-parter, 302–304, locating Rock's platoon, Easy Co, in Italy. One of Easy's troop finds his fascist brother, now the town mayor and married to his sweetheart. Lots of personal rivalry and mixed loyalties here, and to compound things, the village is expecting a visit from Benito Mussolini himself. These sagas were a rarity for Kanigher, whose preference was for single-issue stories with an occasional twist. Take for instance 317, 'Comics Books Win A Purple Heart'. The cover has Rock standing in front of some classic 1940s DC comics. Inside we find that reading comics is good for the morale of the soldiers, and stuffed down your jacket they can help deflect that all-important bullet from your body.

Although scripting largely reality-based stories, Kanigher quite often introduced a fantasy theme, in two cases time travel. In 318 Rock pontificates on what war would've meant to humans in the Stone Age, and in 326 he imagines he's in the year 2994, battling robot Nazis. These aren't as corny as they may sound, but in a way quite poignant. The same could be said for 349, 'The Dummy', where Easy Co has a new ventriloquist recruit. The war is seen through the dummy's eye, which even sheds a tear at the end of the story when its owner is killed. He returns in 376, now with complete thought patterns. Of course Kanigher doesn't want us to believe the dummy is actually real, but through it makes us view war from all angles, showing how it affects all involved parties. He was also one for championing the rights of African-Americans. In 355 Easy comes across a group of black soldiers dressed in World War I uniforms. They were part of a large black battalion that fought in France during the 1914–1918 conflict, after which they stayed in Europe and were now offering their services to fight for the new cause. The black soldier theme is also taken up in 405–406, 'Angels With Black Wings'. The story begins in the 1960s, where a middle-aged black civil rights demonstrator recalls how he fought for the USA as a pilot during World War II; Kanigher uses the opportunity to spotlight real-life black American war heroes. These stories may seem a bit contrived, but Kanigher certainly had his heart in the right place and spotlighted the injustice of segregation between black and white soldiers during this era.

368 is a thirtieth-anniversary issue where Rock recalls the past through a number of dog-tags belonging to fallen soldiers. Rock in fact dreams of the dead Easy Co soldiers in 375, while 400 highlights the four hundred days that Easy Co have been involved in the war. There are a few issues of note around this time. 395 is an all-Kubert issue with art by Joe, Adam and Andy. 396 offers good reprints depicting children caught up in the conflict, and 404 features the once-regular nemesis of Rock, the Iron Major. The 1984 annual (4) depicts the realities a German major has to face, showing his side of the conflict, portraying a man of principle doing his job for his country. Everyone's a victim in war. 408 offers a tribute to artist Shelly Mayer. A soldier called Scribbly joins Easy Co and illustrates some of scenes he has witnessed. Mayer, of course, invented the 1940s character, the cartoonist called Scribbly.

412 has guest appearances by Mlle Marie and the Haunted Tank, while 413 is a Jews and Gentiles tale, where the Judaic and Christian faiths are explored in relationship to one another. 417 and 418 are illustrated by Andy Kubert and deal with a possible future featuring the offspring of the Easy Co soldiers. Sam Glanzman draws the lead story in 420, while the three Kuberts contribute to the final issue.

On the whole the series is extremely well produced, and it never glorifies war. Of course, there's the occasional bout of Ramboism, but that only serves to accentuate the day-to-day heroics performed by ordinary humans living under a pressure we can't comprehend. The constant high quality of Kanigher's scripts is amazing, and it extends to the back-ups, among which there are many gems. Alex Toth illustrates a tale set in Ancient Egypt in 385, but on the whole the back-ups were reserved as a training-ground for students of Joe Kubert's School Of Cartoon Art such as Tom Yeates, Jan Duursema, Tom Mandrake and Ron Randall. And look out for early work by Steve Bissette (323, 346), Rick Veitch (332–334) and Tim Truman (357, 363, 367, 371, 376). Sam Glanzman's 'USS Stevens' can be found in 304, 308 and 384.

Almost immediately after cancellation *Sgt Rock* returned for a reprint run, initially titled *Sgt Rock Special*; it later became plain *Sgt Rock*. It continued the numbering from the 1977 *Sgt Rock Special* and offered many choice items. Illustrators included the likes of Alex Toth (2, 8, 11), Wally Wood (4), Frank Miller (6), Krigstein (4, 8), Chaykin (9), Jack Kirby (7) and Neal

Adams (8); and of course there were many classics from Joe Kubert and Russ Heath. There were two more specials in 1992 and 1994. This time they feature new stories illustrated by a stellar line-up. Kubert, P. Craig Russell, Matt Wagner, George Pratt, Mike Golden and Tim Truman draw the first issue, and in 2 you have Eduardo Barreto, Howard Chaykin, Russ Heath and Graham Nolan. With the exception of a previously unused story in 1, none are by Kanigher, so the subtlety usually associated with Rock is missed, replaced by a more action-oriented scripts from the likes of Chuck Dixon. All in all, though, they're not bad efforts, and the Heath story in 2 was marvellous to look at.

For more classic Sgt Rock tales, plus many other DC war heroes, look no further than *Sgt Rock's Prize Battle Tales* in 1964 and the digest-sized 1979 edition, the early 1970s *100-Page Super Spectacular*, and a *Sgt Rock Spectacular* in 1978. Despite any views you may have on war and violence, they are a fact of history. In *Sgt Rock*, these experiences aren't glorified, and you might be surprised how much you enjoy them. The high standard of artwork throughout is undeniable.~HY
Recommended: 417, 418, 420

Savage Combat Tales Featuring
SGT STRYKER'S DEATH SQUAD
Atlas: *3 issues 1975*

It's a shame that ten years after writing one of the best war comics ever in *Blazing Combat*, Archie Goodwin was turning out this formula material, which took its cue from *The Dirty Dozen*. A bunch of convicts are welded into an élite strike force by Sgt Stryker, who isn't ranked at all, but has a strong personality. To Goodwin's credit he does also focus on the Germans, and there's decent art from Al McWilliams throughout, but the highlight is 2's back-up strip, drawn by Alex Toth.~WJ

SHADE THE CHANGING MAN
DC: *8 issues 1977–1978*
DC/Vertigo: *70 issues 1990–1996*

It's a rare comic that can be labelled 'unique', yet in both incarnations *Shade* earns the distinction. It began as a downright weird concept and became stranger. As introduced by Steve Ditko in particularly capricious mode, Rac Shade is an other-dimensional humanoid alien on the run for crimes he didn't commit, who manifests gruesome distortions of himself by means of his M-vest. It's technobabble, of course, but works surprisingly well, with Ditko's contorted figures having a memorably disturbing quality and his art in general at a 1970s peak. Ditko created a complex scenario with a fully realised background that unfolds in stages, and Michael Fleisher's scripts add to the complicated and subtle plots. At every

attempt to clear his name Shade is thwarted and manipulated into seeming ever more a criminal, and his former fiancée proves a merciless tracker. The origin of Shade's miraculous M-vest is detailed in 7 and 8, but regretfully the series is prematurely cancelled without conclusion. Shade reappears over a decade later in the pages of *Suicide Squad*, but even among the misfits of that title he's distinctly out of place.

The revived *Shade* is an altogether different experience. Whereas the first series was strictly superhero science fiction, the revived character is more reality-based. He's still Rac Shade, on the run from Meta, merged with his M-vest (rechristened the madness vest) and able to manipulate atoms to change reality, but not fully in control. He's also the vehicle for a distinctly skewed road-movie-style look at the USA through the eyes of imaginative British writer Peter Milligan. Although initially strained, and continued too long, Milligan's innovative approach, off-beat ideas and thoughtful prose more than compensate for weak plots and obvious pop-culture targets (Hollywood, psychedelia, Elvis Presley, serial killers etc). The better issues of *Shade* drag one through a unique and thought-provoking journey. As evinced by later issues, Milligan's ideas require an adaptable artist, and for 1–50 the work of Chris Bachalo, inked by Mark Pennington and then Rick Bryant, is astounding. Unsung for years until he moved to a higher-profile standard superhero title, Bachalo's layouts, characters and scenarios have an admirable fluid consistency, and he's able to switch from tenderness to horror with ease.

More than Shade's escapades, though, the appeal of the title concerns the excellently drawn cast and their interaction. The body Shade originally habits is that of the man who murdered Cathy George's parents, Shade having transferred at the moment of his execution. Disturbed and vulnerable, Cathy grows during the series, and certainly not in predictable fashion. This is due in no small part to the influence of the worldly-wise Lenny and her distinctly individual outlook, seemingly based on Madonna's character in *Desperately Seeking Susan*. She's a deliberate contrast to the self-absorbed and self-doubting Shade, plagued by aspects of his personality and unconsciously manifesting his abilities at awkward times.

Having purged America from his system, Milligan rather thrashes around for a while. After the disjointed character explorations of 'The Road' in 20–25, and the idea of Shade The Changing Woman, which isn't nearly as interesting as it sounds, there's the marvellous 26, giving further insight into Lenny. Everything pulls together again in the mid-30s, with *Shade* switching to the Vertigo imprint with 33. Therein Shade, Kathy and Lenny occupy a deserted hotel that's a magnet for weirdness, inheriting the odd inhabitants and off-beat problems. These include angels given human form, the reincarnation of Pandora, Milligan's self-parody, and a visit to the Salem witch trials accompanied by John Constantine in 42–44. Between 36 and 50 there's not a substandard issue, and the guest pencillers who help Bachalo maintain a monthly schedule, notably Philip Bond, Glyn Dillon and Steve Yeowell, merge seamlessly.

50 marks a turning point. It's Bachalo's final issue, and concludes the six-part 'A Season In Hell', the highlight of the run. Kathy is pregnant and determined to have the child, while Shade is being blackmailed into killing it. Lenny entertains two vastly different new guests while the hotel is collapsing around everyone. Reducing the plot to soap-opera précis does it no favours. Milligan has created a dense and squirming character study, putting his cast through the emotional wringer to a far greater degree than previously, leaving them shell-shocked and, to use the comic cliché, forever changed. It's a masterpiece. A selection of new characters is introduced in following issues, initially Shade's son George, growing at an accelerated rate until 57, a burning angel given human form, a nutty inventor and a single-minded and ambitious journalist investigating Shade. They're mixed, and swap bodies after an experiment gone wrong, in the most effective story arc for the remainder of the run, 'Nasty Infections' in 58–63, wherein five polaroid photographs lead into the most viscerally horrific tale in the whole of *Shade*. Mark Buckingham pencils most issues to 60 (with 51–53 by the underrated Sean Phillips), but 'Nasty Infections' introduces the pencils of Richard Case. He's dreadful here. His poor foreshortening, figurework and proportions are deficiencies that constantly draw attention away from otherwise excellent stories. Milligan sets up an effective plot leading to the final story arc in 68–70, in which Shade attempts to rectify the events of 50. By that point, though, the shoddy art is so at odds with the story it's no wonder the series was cancelled.

Overall both runs of *Shade* bring a stream of new ideas to comics, stretching conventions and toying with preconceptions. While not everything gels perfectly, and the series certainly won't be to everyone's tastes, the innovation and experimentation are a joy to see in a medium where adult content rarely refers to anything other than gratuitous nudity and violence.~FP

Recommended: Series one 3–8, series two 1, 5, 16–18, 26, 36–39, 42–50, 54, 58–61

SHADO: Song of the Dragon
DC: *4-issue miniseries 1991–1992*

Although not everyone's idea of a dream team, the creative forces behind *Shado* seem curiously suited to each other. Mike Grell writes an exceptionally terse script, which keeps the tension levels high, beginning with a well-handled, almost wordless attack on Shado and her child by a group of masked commandos. Michael Davis Lawrence is not the most detailed colourist, but his rough use of simple tones, without much concern for whether he's within the boundary of his own huge panels, and light pencils works, except where the whole page is drenched with a single colour for atmosphere. Gray Morrow inks his pencils with the lightest of touches, alternating between heavy blacks and spatter effects, and large panels bisected by a few, carefully weighted lines. There are few new ideas, but the prose is carefully modulated and the art striking.~FJ

THE SHADOW
Archie: *8 issues 1964–1965*

Imagine the Shadow – the 1930s, foggy nights, blazing 45's, one of the great pulp heroes. Well, the Archie Shadow runs around in blue and green underwear chasing panel borders and punching word balloons. Stories recycled the same plot, dialogue was abysmal, and the art wasn't too good either. One of the worst comics ever published: treat it like the bubonic plague.~DWC

THE SHADOW
DC: Series one 12 issues 1973–1975, 4-issue miniseries 1986, Series two 19 issues, 2 Annuals 1987–1988

For the 1970s series Denny O'Neil's writing apes the pulp style that introduced the Shadow in the 1930s, with basic mystery plots and terse dialogue. There's a galaxy of difference between the artists, but all offer a legitimate take on the 1930s setting. Mike Kaluta (1–4, 6) opts for moody and atmospheric scenes, while Frank Robbins (5, 7–12) has an all-action cinematic style. E.R. Cruz (10–12) manages a successful amalgam of the two approaches as another pulp hero, The Avenger, stops by in 11. O'Neil and Kaluta later reprised on a Marvel graphic novel.

As the 1986 miniseries opens it's been thirty-five years since the Shadow was last seen, yet someone's murdering his former agents. When the Shadow returns he's not aged since the 1940s, although he is a little more verbose. Howard Chaykin's mixture of sex and violence didn't sit well with older fans, but he clarifies the Shadow's origin, talents and longevity in issue 2 and successfully reworks the character for a contemporary audience while remaining faithful to the essence of the Shadow. The major supporting players from the novels are present, and Chaykin's new characters are engaging. Harry Vincent's daughter Mavis is a reluctant 1980s foil to the Shadow, deploring his methods, and the Shadow's two sons, Chang and Hsu, revel in New York after a lifetime spent in a remote Himalayan settlement.

The second ongoing title is a continuing series of individual stories (labelled as chapters on the cover). 'Shadows and Light' (1–6) is initially impenetrable, but rewards careful reading. Artist Bill Sienkiewicz is on top form, but Kyle Baker's simpler and more expressive artwork (8–19) better conveys the broad streak of humour underscoring the feature. It's well exemplified by the only single-issue story of the run (7), with Marshall Rogers illustrating the tale of a ghastly child on the loose in Washington.

Andy Helfer's scripts concentrate on the rich supporting cast and their varied eccentricities more than on the Shadow, who is a far from pleasant manipulative figure. The assorted villains also get their share of the spotlight in very dense scripts. 'Seven Deadly Finns' (8–13) is a masterpiece. The Finn brothers control New York's crime without having accumulated a criminal record. In addition to using all the Shadow's agents seen in the series to date and the well-characterised Finns, Helfer adds an Arab terrorist, five deadly lunatics, Dick Magnet and Private Eye; he even throws gorillas in the mix, without the story ever seeming crowded. The second annual is better than the first, bridging 13 and 14, taking its cue from *Citizen Kane* and revealing how the primary agents first met the Shadow.

For 'Body and Soul' (14–19) the Shadow is largely a background presence as the New York agents operate without him, and Chang and Hsu work their way back to Shamballa. Although not quite matching the previous story, it still contains more wit and entertainment than almost any other title you'd care to name. The tragic premature cancellation of *The Shadow* was apparently due to objections from the licensers, borne out by the rapid launch of the more conventional *The Shadow Strikes*. It's a shame, as the highlights of this series rank alongside the best comics of the 1980s.~FP
Recommended: Series one 3–6, 10, Miniseries 1–4, Series two 7–19, Annual 2
Collection: The Private Files Of The Shadow (Series one 1–4, 6 + new story), The Shadow (Miniseries 1–4)

The SHADOW
Dark Horse: 4-issue miniseries ('In The Coils Of The Leviathan') 1993–1994, 2-issue microseries 1994, 3-issue miniseries ('Hell's Heat Wave') 1995

This Shadow is very reminiscent of the 1970s DC version and the Marvel graphic novel, which isn't surprising, as Mike Kaluta has a heavy hand in the series for all publishers. He writes 'In The Coils Of The Leviathan' with Joel Goss and it's illustrated by Gary Gianni, which if Kaluta couldn't illustrate is the next best thing. He certainly does an excellent job setting up the mood and atmosphere required for these period pieces. The story is intricate, with the occasional twist, involving ritual slayings, strange rings, evangelists and a new war weapon. The second series adapts the Shadow movie. Again written by Kaluta and Goss, but this time illustrated by Kaluta himself. The result is, of course, beautiful. Shame about the story, which really didn't have that much going for it. Gianni once more joins Kaluta and Goss for 'Hell's Heat Wave'. This time there's a severed finger found in a dead man's mouth, gangland wars involving the Chinese and the Irish, and a strange spectre, to say the least. It's another good effort. If you like a mystery than look no further than the first and third series.~HY
Recommended: 'In The Coils Of The Leviathan' 1–4, 'Hell's Heat Wave' 1–4

THE SHADOW AND DOC SAVAGE
Dark Horse: 2-issue microseries 1995

Though the plot about Nazis kidnapping a scientist's daughter in order to persuade him to return to Germany and continue work on his supersoldier serum is rather predictable, there are enough twists and turns to keep the action coming. The comparison of Savage's humanitarian ideals with the Shadow's bloodthirsty attitude is nicely handled by writer Steve Vance. Artists Stan Manoukian and Vince Roucher use some odd angles that seem to be repeated more than necessary but overall it's not unattractive.~NF

SHADOW CABINET
Milestone: 18 issues (0–17) 1994–1995

Under the guidance of the mysterious Dharma, teams of superhuman operatives are sent out on missions to serve a political agenda, in a cross between *Mission Impossible* and the *Secret Six*. Needless to say, it's not long before several of the 'core team' – the agents we see most frequently – start questioning Dharma's actions, and striking out on their own initiative. Robert L. Washington and John Paul Leon start the comic, with Matt Wayne taking over the writing from 5. The action is kept brisk and entertaining enough that it takes a while for the obvious questions to occur. Questions like, 'Why haven't people as smart and conscientious as these folks asserted themselves before now?', or 'What sort of hold does Dharma have over them?' Unfortunately, the cancellation of the series meant none of these questions were adequately answered, but several of the more likeable protagonists – Iota, Donner and Blitzen – went on to form part of the Heroes team, in the miniseries of the same name. Despite the inevitable nagging questions, the series was generally enjoyable.~HS

SHADOW EMPIRES: Faith Conquers
Dark Horse: *4-issue miniseries 1994*

A complex saga mixing religious and political manoeuvring and space war. Christopher Moeller's plot hinges on alien worms that can possess humans, with the result that one is never sure of the allegiances of any of the cast members at any given time. He's also constructed a working theocratic empire and spent a long time laying out battle sequences. This would work magnificently in a film, but sadly the extraneous detail only serves to render an already difficult-to-follow story even more awkward. In some ways Moeller draws his inspiration from Masmune Shirow's similarly detailed works, and like Shirow he sometimes loses the wood for the trees. Overall, though it's an admirable effort.~FP

SHADOW RIDERS
Marvel UK: *4-issue miniseries 1993*

Astonishingly unappealing artwork and a plethora of macho men characterise this introduction of new forces combating the evil Mys-Tech corporation.~FP

SHADOW STATE
Broadway: *6 issues 1995–1996*

After the first two issues featured Fatale short stories, the title was give over entirely to co-feature *Till Death Us Do Part.* Troy and Wendi Hickenbottom, two none-too-bright, none-too-scrupulous people gain super powers and physiology courtesy of images taken from Troy's favourite comic. Troy is chuffed; Wendi is appalled. None of her clothes fit, and she feels like a freak! Troy attempts to teach Wendi 'proper' superheroic behaviour via his favourite comic *Team Blood S.C.R.E.A.M,* pages from which are wittily interpolated into the main story. Their wildly differing attitudes result in their previous domestic battles being escalated to the megaton level, with disastrous results for all around them. A gripping, if exasperating, read.~HS
Recommended: 1–6

THE SHADOW STRIKES
DC: *31 issues, 1 Annual 1989–1992*

This was DC's third and longest-running attempt at presenting the Shadow. Gerard Jones and Eduardo Barreto put together a coherent cast and authentic pulp atmosphere without making the whole thing seem dated. Jones quickly established the Shadow's best-known supporting cast members (Margo Lane, Harry Vincent, Shrevvie and Inspector Cardona) as central to the plot and used known Shadow history as a basis for adventures, without rewriting it. He sets the series firmly in the 1930s, and also does much to establish Margo and Harry as interesting and important parts of the story-lines, rather than just being foot-soldiers following orders. Barreto's artwork, though still developing, is suitably dark, reminiscent of Kubert or Toth, giving the scripts the period feel required.

The first story-line (1–4) involves Anastasia, Rasputin and a series of headless murders, hinting again at secrets in the Shadow's past. 5 and 6 were part of a Doc Savage crossover, the first time these two heroes had met, and 7 features a plot revolving around a Shadow radio show with a young entrepreneur not dissimilar to Orson Welles. 8–10 feature Shiwan Khan, the Shadow's arch enemy, followed by a four-parter involving butchers and Chicago's underworld. It provides a look both at the semi-mystical nature of the Shadow's powers and at the often dark and seedy side of his adversaries. Unfortunately, 15 was the last by Barreto, and though Rod Whigham worked hard to maintain the style already established, the artwork is too hard-edged.

16 and 17 'introduce' the real Lamont Cranston as guest penciller Mark Badger drew the Shadow involved in union activity. The epic seven-part 21–27 pits him against Shiwan Khan again, in China, preceding the series' final story-line, a retelling of the Shadow's origin. Jones tells a good story; in concentrating on the supporting cast, he enables the Shadow to be used effectively but mysteriously while hinting rather than coming right out with revelations about the character. The annual has the Shadow visiting Hollywood, written by Jones and drawn by Dan Spiegle (another artist with a good period feel), plus a short story about Margo Lane chunkily and unattractively drawn by Luke McDonnell.~NF

SHADOW WAR OF HAWKMAN
DC: *4-issue miniseries 1985*

As part of DC's 1980s revamping process, Hawkman returned to duty in this forerunner for his second series. Unfortunately, the revised Hawkman lacks the flair for science and weaponry that made the original character so interesting, although the supporting cast, including Hawkwoman, remains virtually unchanged. The plot centres on the Hawks fighting the armies of their home planet (Thanagar), who seek to destroy the Earth. The story-line progressed very little during this miniseries, as the writers needed a plot for the second series. Crisp dialogue from Tony Isabella, but dull artwork.~SS

SHADOWDRAGON
DC: *One-shot 1995*

Attempt to make a hi-tech martial artist, a supporting character from *Superman*, into a solo star. Lacklustre and predictable.~HS

SHADOWHAWK
Image: *4-issue miniseries 1992–1993, 3-issue miniseries 1993, 4-issue miniseries 1993–1994, 8 issues (0, 12–18) 1994–1995*

Shadowhawk is a dark vigilante of the night who breaks the spines of criminals, trapping them inside their own bodies. The series tries to conceal Shadowhawk's identity, but he's so dull that no one cared when it was revealed in the second issue of the second miniseries, and it wasn't much of a surprise to regular readers. In the third miniseries Shadowhawk contracts the HIV virus, which becomes the focus of the ongoing series as he travels back to 1963 to try to cure his illness. Jim Valentino writes dull scripts to match his terrible artwork, making this over-violent comic boring and forgettable.~SS
Collections: Out Of The Shadows (miniseries one), *The Secret Revealed* (miniseries two)

SHADOWLAND
Fantagraphics: *2 issues 1989*

Kim Deitch tells the story of Molly O'Dare from her upbringing in a convent and escape from a life of servitude in Lady Wyndham's whorehouse to her becoming an actress in the early days of cinema. Deitch creates his own skewed and distinctive fantasy world. His drawing may seem rather stiff but his characters are never static. A little cold in tone for some, and certainly not likely to provoke any debates on the meaning of life, Deitch's comics remain oddly compulsive.~NF
Recommended: 1–2

SHADOWMAN
Valiant: *44 issues (0–43), 1 yearbook 1992–1995*

Never try to pull a vampire is the lesson to be learned from the first issue. That's what New Orleans jazz saxophonist Jack Boniface does, and once the bite's been put on him he's compelled to go out and fight crime at night. There's a little more to it, but it's a slim and illogical premise that doesn't gel in the first few issues, despite some atmospheric art from David Lapham (1, 2, 4, 5). 4 and 5 are part of the 'Unity' crossover, and all-purpose Valiant evil tattooed mystic Master Darque is introduced in 8, and beefs things up considerably. Bob Hall writes from 6, and pencils from 10, and gradually develops *Shadowman* into a gloomy corner of the Valiant Universe. His plots are slim, but he manages to instil a mood through pacing and characterisation, and while Hall's no stylist his

story-telling is good and works with his plotting. Not every issue is a success, but by 12 *Shadowman* is a decent adventure title. Hall's other strength is the design skill he brings into play on the covers. Almost every one after 10 is striking and imaginative, with little repetition occurring. These wordless illustrations are excellent attention-grabbers, but Valiant's redesigned cover template from 30 reduces their effectiveness.

21–23 send Jack back in time to meet a previous incarnation, and lead into the zero issue, which clarifies once and for all what Shadowman is and who his predecessor was, and throws in the early days of Master Darque to boot. It's the best to that point and propels Hall to step up a gear and produce an excellent run. Several previously introduced characters return, along with a deadly new foe, the assassin Ishmael in 26, and Shadowman and Jack begin to diverge into two separate personalities. Sadly, the good run is brought to a halt by 'The Chaos Effect' crossover in 29. That crossover has the effect of powering up Shadowman to the point where he's a match for Master Darque, but from then on he's not nearly as interesting. The human-interest stories that had fired the book disappeared into a welter of less than absorbing fights, with Hall modifying his style to include more pin-up action pages. Anyone who finds Anne Rice's vampire writing tiresome should check out 40. The series ends with the police and crimelords uniting to bust Jack.~WJ
Recommended: 0, 17, 18, 24, 26–28
Collection: Shadowman (1–3, 6)

SHADOWMASTERS
Marvel: *4-issue miniseries 1989–1990*

The Shadowmasters were supporting characters in the *Punisher War Journal* and this spin-off book details their history. A dull story-line featuring an Americanised version of Japanese culture and a snail-paced plot.~SS

SHADOWMEN
Trident: *2 issues 1990*

Originally intended as a six-issue miniseries but never completed, this is early work from Mark Millar. Some men in black beat up a woman to prevent her repeating her story about a supernatural experience. The artwork by Andrew Hope is very atmospheric – lots and lots of black ink – but there's not a lot to get excited about.~NF

SHADOWS FALL
Vertigo: *6-issue miniseries 1994–1995*

Separated from his soul by instigating an act of violence costing an innocent life, Warren Gale wanders the world an empty shell while his soul is the cause of innumerable suicides.

Confronted by incidents from his past, Gale realises he must deal with his inhuman predator. Ludicrously pretentious twaddle, further compromised by ridiculous cut-and-paste art.~FP

SHADOWS FROM BEYOND
Charlton: *1 issue (50) 1966*

An anthology comic with horror and supernatural stories, usually involving the operation of cosmic justice. No masterpieces maybe, but they all make their point, and the artwork is usually very effective. Worth a look, if not a systematic hunt. In the peculiarly unique Charlton fashion, the numbering continued from *Unusual Tales*.~FC

SHADOWS FROM THE GRAVE
Renegade: *2 issues 1987–1988*

Horror series, written by Kevin McConnell and illustrated by David and Dan Day. Worth looking at for the detailed rendering, reminiscent of Steranko and Gulacy. The stories pale by comparison.~NF

SHAMAN
Continuity: *1 issue (0) 1994*

A by-the-numbers sword-and-sorcery title, intended as a comic-dealers-only incentive, and lifted from the mundane by quite extraordinary artwork by Alex Nino. A comic best read by not reading the dialogue or captions.~DAR

SHAMAN'S TEARS
Image: *13 issues (0–12) 1994–1996*

Joshua Brand is empowered to assume the attributes of the animal kingdom in a Native American ceremony. Stories take place over four issues, and Brand initially becomes involved with corporate, genetically engineered, human/animal hybrids, later to star in *Bar Sinister*. While never bad, Mike Grell's spartan story-telling and illustrative page composition disappoint in comparison with previous work, such as that of 5–8's guest star Jon Sable, and trivialities such as stupid names (Regus Patoff and Pat Pending) detract from what's occurring.~WJ

SHANNA the SHE-DEVIL
Marvel: *5 issues 1972–1973*

One of Marvel's several ill-fated attempts to produce Women's Lib comics written by women. Better than its counterparts. But not much. Shanna O'Hara, a normal American woman disillusioned with man's cruelty to man and beast, divorced herself from the trappings of civilisation (apart from make-up and an offstage hair salon) and did her Tarzan thing in the African jungle. Carole Seuling only lasted for three stereotyped issues. Steve

Gerber effected a partial rescue from 4, launching the Mandrill/Nekra story-line that blossomed into full glory in *Daredevil* 108–112. Shanna later became a major supporting character in *Ka-Zar*.~APS

SHATTER
First: *Special 1985, 14 issues, 1985–1988*

'The First Computerised Comic!' it says on the cover of the first issue. It looks so grainy you can count the pixels, especially in the lettering, and you think, 'Oh no, a gimmick.' Or 'Another sad case who wants to marry his Apple Mac. This is going to be hideous.' Well… no, and then yes for a while, and then no-ish. The special was written by Peter Gillis, with art by Michael Saenz, and they make magic with the story of an independent tough-guy (Shatter) on a freelance project for the police in a *Blade Runner* setting. It's a strong story with some truly clever plotting, and Saenz' story-telling is so effective that you're absorbed within pages, with no time to count pixels. After this, Shatter had eight pages in *Jon Sable, Freelance* 25–31, and when he came back with his own title, he no longer had Gillis as writer, and it certainly showed. It's yet another corporate conspiracy yarn, and it's hard for Saenz to demonstrate his story-telling skills when there is no story. By 3, Saenz had left, and any craftsmanship in the artwork left with him. Gillis returned as writer with 5, and the story instantly improved, although with perfunctory artwork there was never any danger of recapturing the excitement of that first special.~FC
Recommended: 1985 Special

SHATTERED IMAGE
Image: *4-issue miniseries 1996*

Image crossover that sees Savant (from *WildC.A.T.s*) trying to put together a cross-section of heroes to prevent the splitting of the Image Universe into six separate ones. Only Spawn seems content to let the crisis continue to its logical conclusion (on the basis that his murderer won't exist if the split takes place). In any case, the real world has made this whole plot redundant. Since it's written by Kurt Busiek and Barbara Kesel there's some good characterisation, but it's an utterly contrived crossover that barely holds the reader's interest. Michael Ryan's artwork is from the Manga-influenced school of big eyes and the Liefeld school of overly muscled anatomy but it's not that bad in context.~NF

SHAZAM!
DC: *35 issue 1973–1978, 4-issue miniseries 1987*

Captain Marvel's popularity rating rivalled Superman in the 1940s, but legal action instituted by DC, claiming too many similarities to Superman, forced him out of print. It's ironic, then, that firstly DC acquired the rights to the character, and then were unable to use his name as the title because it had fallen out of copyright and Marvel now had a comic titled *Captain Marvel*. The merits of the copyright infringement case are debatable. There's no doubt that Captain Marvel in heroic guise had similar attributes to Superman, but the remainder of the strip was completely different, being drawn in far cartoonier fashion for a start. Young newsboy Billy Batson called out 'Shazam!' in order to transform himself into the world's mightiest mortal by means of a lightning bolt from the heavens (ouch!) This endowed him with the wisdom of Solomon, the strength of Hercules, the stamina of Atlas, the power of Zeus, the courage of Achilles and the speed of Mercury. While in the process of driving Captain Marvel out of business DC (or the company they then were) appropriated several ideas for their Superman titles, most notably the introduction of Superboy, their answer to Captain Marvel Jr. Anyone wanting to sample the 1940s Captain Marvel can do so with a hardbound collection titled *Captain Marvel And The Monster Society Of Evil*, or with stories reprinted in the 100-page issues of the *Shazam!* series (8, 12–17).

The revival was very much in the simple, light-hearted vein of the original series, as written by Denny O'Neil and very cleanly drawn by original artist C.C. Beck. It's likely that the adherence to the original style prevented the character from catching on with the children of the original readers. Other characters had evolved over the years, but Captain Marvel was stuck in the 1940s, and his adventures were too unsophisticated for a 1970s audience. This shouldn't deter now from what were enjoyable and well produced stories. Another original artist, Kurt Schaffenberger, and the talented Bob Oksner also contributed artwork, with Elliott Maggin and E. Nelson Bridwell also writing. They all managed to capture the essence of Captain Marvel and his supporting cast, including Captain Marvel Jnr and Mary Marvel. The primary artist for 1–10, though, was Beck. As the visual designer of the character he obviously had a vested interest, but he also prevented any further development, being determined to keep gag-style humour. By all accounts his relationship with DC was turbulent, and the comic improved with his departure.

Editor Julius Schwartz had wisely kept Captain Marvel in a world separate from the integrated DC Universe where their other superheroes operate. You wouldn't see Superman fighting a cute little green worm, Mr Mind, as a would-be ruler of Earth, or with a talking tiger as friend. The point was emphasised in 15 when Superman's arch-foe Lex Luthor lands in Captain Marvel's reality, and believes he's entered a cartoon universe, but finds a soulmate in Mr Mind. Reduction in frequency to quarterly publication indicated that a change was required to save the title, and that came with 34, when Don Newton was appointed artist to give the entire feature an overhaul. The cartoony look was out, and Newton provided a more 1970s style superhero realism. It was too late, though, but the feature did continue, running in *World's Finest* from 253.

An even more realistic approach was taken for the 1987 miniseries, titled *Shazam! A New Beginning*. DC weren't going to make the same mistake twice. This Captain Marvel was firmly established in the DC Universe, and the miniseries trots through his origin and those of his major villains, mad scientist Sivana and Black Adam, an evil counterpart. Tom Mandrake pencilled scripts from Roy and Dann Thomas, and Captain Marvel has remained part of the DC pantheon ever since, now starring in *The Power Of Shazam*.~HY

SHE-HULK

Marvel: *Series one 25 issues 1980–1982, Graphic Novel 1985, series two 60 issues 1989–1994, 2-issue microseries ('Ceremony') 1990*

Mild-mannered lawyer Jennifer Walters, injured in an attack by criminals, is brought back from the brink of death by a transfusion of blood from her cousin, the only candidate on the scene at the time. Unfortunately, her cousin is Bruce Banner, aka the Incredible Hulk, and his gamma-irradiated blood causes her to swell up and turn green from time to time. No doubt to the disappointment of horny pubescent readers, she never quite burst out of her shirt the way her cousin was noted for doing. The first issue, written by Stan Lee and drawn by John Buscema, is competent, but after that, David Anthony Kraft and Mike Vosburg take over, and it becomes clear that nobody cares what they're doing on this. Our monosyllabic heroine fights villains like the Man-Elephant, meets Hellcat, Man-Thing and Morbius as her title rapidly becomes a halfway house for homeless heroes, and is romanced by the ludicrous Zapper. The series stumbled on for longer than logic and reason would have us believe, before finally collapsing. This series was titled *Savage She-Hulk*, as opposed to the second series, by which time she'd become 'Sensational'.

She-Hulk herself became a popular and established supporting player in *Avengers* and *Fantastic Four*, which led to a graphic novel, written and drawn by John Byrne. Lightweight, fun and cheesecakey (rather too much so in one offensive sequence that enables Byrne to explicitly condemn sexist attitudes while displaying them), it ushers in a significant development. It's confirmed that Jennifer Walters' physiology has adjusted to her gamma-irradiated state to the extent that she can no longer return to human form. Refreshingly, this isn't a cue for the usual overplayed angst. She enjoys the hell out of her seven-foot-tall green persona, and is happy to stay that way!

'Okay, this is your last chance. Buy my book this time, or I'll come round to your house and rip up all your copies of *X-Men*.' Writer/artist John Byrne thus establishes, on the cover of the second series' first issue, that the She-Hulk knows that she's in a comic book, and exploits that knowledge. She crosses panel borders to get around faster, uses the break between pictures to change outfits, and breaks the fourth wall to address the readers on the idiocy of her villains, and so on. This comedy routine is subverted to poignant effect when a supporting character, Louise Mason, is introduced in 4. As Louise Grant, she was the Blonde Phantom, a crimefighter of the 1940s, and possessed the same awareness as She-Hulk. Long retired, she discovers – at the cost of her husband's life, in a movingly told sequence – that the ageing process is suspended when you're in a currently published comic. This supporting-character gig is her way of fending off the ravages of time. 1–7 are quirky and imaginative, a highly enjoyable read, with She-Hulk triumphing in her own insouciant style over such insidious villains as the Terrible Toad Men, the Headmen, Stilt-Man and Dr Bong. The eighth issue, co-starring Father Christmas, is a bit over-sentimental, but still readable. Following 'creative disagreements', Byrne quit after 8, and fill-ins along the same lines, but less entertaining and imaginative, were the order of the day. Even though big names like Peter David and Steve Gerber worked on *She Hulk*, it never quite gelled. Better than the average was 21–23's 'Return Of The Blonde Phantom', involving a time-trip to the 1940s, a guest appearance by the All-Winners Squad, and a new second-generation superheroine.

Byrne returned with 31, on good form initially with the return of Spragg the Living Hill, leading into a confrontation with the Mole Man and the rejuvenation of Louise. A parade of third-rate bad guys swaggered through the pages, and were despatched with fine style, including the zombie master Black Talon, the Living Eraser and the malevolent Mahkizmo, excellent in 38–39. Sadly, Byrne's attention began to wander, and more space was given to gimmicks than to story. 40 had Shulkie spend seven pages purportedly nude rope-jumping, and 45 scattered the main story-telling in tiny panels around (admittedly well-executed) pin-up shots. 50 had several artists auditioning to replace Byrne. Dave Gibbons, Walt Simonson, Howard Chaykin, Terry Austin, Wendy Pini

and Adam Hughes drew their interpretations of the Emerald Amazon. Together with a coherent, if low-key, story, and a foil-enhanced cover that was actually attractive, this was an enjoyable and memorable send-off for Byrne. The 'regular' new artist, Todd Britton, lasted all of an issue and a half, but writer Michael Eury struggled on until the end of the run with a succession of less and less interested illustrators.~HS

Recommended: Series two 1–7, 31–33, 38, 39, 50
Collection: She-Hulk (Series two 1–8)

SHERLOCK HOLMES
DC: *1 issue 1975*

Denny O'Neil wrote this adaptation of fiction's best-known detective and managed a fair job, as did E.R. Cruz on art. It was seemingly only published to retain DC's copyright on the title, which resulted in a somewhat bland product.~DWC

SHERLOCK HOLMES In The Curious Case Of The Vanishing Villain
Tundra: *One-shot 1993*

Gordon Rennie and Woodrow Phoenix concoct an off-beat case for the classic detective and companion. He's approached by Dr Jekyll to locate the missing Mr Hyde; it transpires that he's escaped into the next book on the shelf, a decidedly rum affair. It's clever and stylish-looking, with Phoenix's sparing use of colour particularly effective.~FP

SHERLOCK JR
Eternity: *3-issue miniseries 1989*

In the 1930s Sidney Smith became the first cartoonist awarded a contract for $1,000,000, the price paid to retain the creator of *The Gumps*, then the most popular cartoon strip in the USA. In 1912, however, his feature was the appallingly inept and unlucky detective Sherlock Jr. Smith was neither a great cartoonist nor a great writer, but with *The Gumps* he hit on the then original idea of portraying life as it actually was for millions of Americans, thus creating the first soap opera. Devoid of that extra level, *Sherlock Jr.* has dated very badly, and one finds it difficult to conceive that it was ever riotous stuff. Filling six panels to the strip, Smith rarely departs from a formula that has Sherlock discovering a reward for criminals in the first panel, adopting a disguise or secreting himself in the second, and fluffing the capture by the sixth. So bland and predictable, *Sherlock Jr.* doesn't even qualify as a historical footnote.~FP

SHI: The Way Of The Warrior
Crusade: 8 issues + 1994 to date

Hugely popular 'bad girl' comic featuring an oriental avenging angel killing various low-lifes. Because she's tough and slaughters rapists, few people seem to worry that God-fearing creator William Tucci (who actually thanks Jehovah in the first issue for inspiration!) slavers over his heroine. Sensible creators do not come to the conclusion that skimpy leather knickers are the best outfit for crime-fighting. The book's a heady cocktail of blood-dripping swords, Eastern mysticism and crotch shots destined to delight adolescents of all ages for many years to come.~FJ

Collection: The Way Of The Warrior (1–4)

The Legend Of The SHIELD

!mpact: *16 issues, 1 Annual 1991–1992*

One of the few !mpact titles that sticks closely to the premise of the character as previously established, and none the worse for it. As the title implies, the series deals with more than one wearer of the army-developed superpowered force-field costume, and explores concepts of patriotism and duty. Writer/artist Grant Miehm handled similar topics in *The American*, and the culmination of these plots in 15 is truly shocking in displaying the moral redundancy of decision-makers; and it's unimpaired by the subtlety necessarily employed because this was a comic aimed at the younger end of the market. There's not a dud issue, with the best samplers being 7's teaming with the Fly or 14's surprisingly suspenseful attempt to waylay the detonation of nuclear warheads. The annual, though, is to be avoided, with stupid Shield and Web stories barely redeemed by an atmospheric Black Hood tale.~WJ

Recommended: 6, 7, 15

The Original SHIELD

Red Circle: *2 issues 1984*

The Shield was the first of the patriotic superheroes, débuting in 1940 and phased out in 1947 – transformed into an iron statue, which meant he could be revived at any time and still be as young as before! In this brief revival, he spends most of his time reminiscing about his 1940s origins. The stories are convoluted and weak, and the artwork variable, but as a character the Shield is refreshingly gentle, and full of melancholy for his former life. He was then usurped in his own title by Steel Sterling and not seen again until the !mpact title.~FC

SHILOH The Devil's Own Day

Heritage Collection: *One-shot 1996*

An admirable attempt to convey the intricacies of a decisive battle during the American Civil War. Wayne Vansant's research and art are excellent, but he's stymied by comics being a far from ideal medium for presenting the various facets of a battle. What should be action-packed and exciting is rendered dry. There are memorable moments, though,

particularly the Confederate soldier being showered by peach flower petals loosened by flying bullets. This is part of a series; the next is *Covered In Glory*.~FP

SHOCK SUSPENSTORIES

EC: *18 issues 1952–1954*

Originally a sort of sampler for EC's other titles – each issue to have a crime, horror, war and science-fiction suspenstory – with the second issue it started to earn its title. 'The Patriots', drawn by Jack Davis, combined two elements that at once raised the series above 'kiddie stories' and caused a controversy amongst its readers: relevance and violence. It tells the tale of a man who attends a parade but seems to sneer at the troops in the parade and doesn't lift his hat as the flag goes by. The crowd around him get angry and beat him to death before discovering that he was a blind veteran with a paralysed face. While the rest of the stories in each issue are of the generally high quality that continues to bring people back to EC's titles, the Shock SuspenStories in this series helped consolidate the publisher's reputation. These stories of mob violence and social relevance were hard-hitting, and if they seem tame or unnecessary today, at the time they could provoke such reader's reactions as '"Hate" is the worst example of a story I have ever read... I hope somebody does something about stories like that.'

Al Feldstein wrote all the scripts until the last four issues. 'The Patriots' was followed by other classics like 'The Guilty' (3), 'Confession' (4 – a policeman gets away with murder by beating a confession out of an innocent man), Hate (5, about anti-Semitism), 'The Assault' (8), '...So Shall Ye Reap!' (10 – parents and their lack of understanding of their children), 'In Gratitude' (11, a superb tale about a Korean veteran who tries to bury the dead friend who saved his life in his home town, only to find that the townspeople's racism prevents it) and the later cynicism of 'A Kind Of Justice' (16), as characters, more than before, are seen to be getting away with their crimes. Most of the Shock SuspenStories were drawn by Wally Wood (3–11, 13–15) and they brought out the best in him. '...So Shall Ye Reap!' and 'In Gratitude' in particular are finely controlled, emotionally telling pieces.

Other strips of note include: 'The Neat Job' (by Jack Kamen) in 1, a famous tale of obsessive neatness that results in a murderous wife bottling her dismembered husband; 'The October Game' (9, by Kamen), an adaptation of the Ray Bradbury story that ends 'Then... some idiot turned on the lights...'; 'The Monkey' (12, by Joe Orlando), another classic, detailing the disastrous (and supposedly inevitable) effects of drug-taking; 'The Small Assassin' (7, by George Evans), a Bradbury tale, like several others, that feeds on the idea that children are monsters (see also 'The Orphan' in 14); while 'Seep No More' (8, by Evans) and 'For Cryin' Out Loud!' (15, by Reed Crandall) both re-write Poe's *The Telltale Heart*. 'In The Bag' (18, by Bernie Krigstein) has seventy-seven panels in six pages, none of them wasted.

Jack Kamen is the only artist to be in every issue but Wood's in most (2–15) and others have good runs: Joe Orlando (1, 3–7, 9, 10, 12, 16, 17), mostly on science-fiction stories, George Evans (7, 8, 14–18) and Reed Crandall (9–13, 15–18), an excellent artist who set a high standard with his first story, 'Carrion Death', an atmospheric desert tale. Other artists drew odd stories. Al Williamson produced a funny-animal science-fiction story in 8, Johnny Craig worked on 'Tryst' in 11, Frank Frazetta on 'Squeeze Play' in 13 and Bernie Krigstein on 'You, Murderer' (14) and the aforementioned 'In The Bag'.

Just before the stringent terms of the Comics Code Authority were applied, new writers were introduced, including Jack Oleck, Carl Wessler and Gardner Fox. While not much is known about exactly who did what, Wessler definitely wrote some stories for this title, and in particular all of 18. The stories were a bit hit-and-miss but there are some notable high points, backed up by the customary high-quality artwork.~NF
Recommended: 1–5, 7–12, 14, 18

SHOGUN WARRIORS
Marvel: *20 issues 1979–1980*

Astoundingly, ahead of its time in featuring giant Japanese-style robots. It's pedestrian stuff, but if you must have them you'll want to know that the story concludes in *Fantastic Four* 226.~FP

SHORT ORDER Comix
Head Press/Family Feud: *2 issues 1973–1974*

The first anthology comic edited by Bill Griffith and Art Spiegelman, it was very much a dry run for the highly regarded *Arcade* and remains criminally overlooked. Griffiths contributes his usual incise dissections of culture and society, but it's Spiegelman who particularly shines with the autobiographical 'Prisoner On Hell Planet' in 1 and the cubist 'Ace Hole, Midget Detective' in 2. Strips by Joe Schenkman, Jay Kinney and Rory Hayes amongst others only serve to make this an even more impressive title.~DAR
Recommended: 1, 2

SHOWCASE
DC: *Series one 104 issues 1956–1970 (1–93), 1977–1978 (94–104), 12-issue limited series (Showcase 93) 1993, 12-issue limited series (Showcase 94) 1994, 12-issue limited series (Showcase 95) 1995, 12-issue limited series (Showcase 96) 1996*

This begins as adventure title with tales of firefighters and frogmen; however, the fourth issue is one of the most important comics ever in terms of what it spawned, being the origin and first appearance of the new look Flash. Editor Julie Schwartz and writer Robert Kanigher took the concept of the 1940s DC hero The Flash, applied it to a new character with a new costume, and relaunched the idea with only the name the same. The dynamic art of Carmine Infantino and Joe Giella completed a healthy package, and the comic was the starting-point for the revival of costumed superheroes. Flash reappeared in 8, 13 and 14, and superheroes have remained ever since.

Flash was the first to graduate from *Showcase* into his own title, but he began a run of similarly successful features. Next were Jack Kirby's adventurers The Challengers Of The Unknown (6, 7, 11, 12), Lois Lane, after years as a supporting character (9, 10), space adventurer Adam Strange (17–19), Rip Hunter, Time Master (20, 21, 23, 24). In fact it's not until Tommy Tomorrow in 41–42 that a *Showcase* presentation fails to graduate to lead strip status or their own title. Another 1940s character re-tooled for the new audience was Green Lantern (22–24), recreated by John Broome and Gil Kane, and the succeeding successes were underwater heroes the Sea Devils, beautifully drawn by Russ Heath in 27–29, with the underwater theme continued for Aquaman (30–33). The Atom, another 1940s name, was appropriated for a new character in 34–36, and the quirky Metal Men débuted in 37–40. Once the run stopped, though, the successes were few and far between, with only the Teen Titans (59), who'd already appeared in *The Brave And The Bold*, going on to anything approaching lasting success.

Still, despite the title's not generating any long-running new features, it did have short-term successes and plenty of worthwhile material. Russ Heath illustrates G. I. Joe in 51–53, and in 55 and 56 Gardner Fox and Murphy Anderson produced two nice stories teaming 1940s heroes Dr Fate and Hourman. Following that there was Enemy Ace, a World War I German fighter pilot, beautifully illustrated by Joe Kubert in 57 and 58. Another try at reviving a 1940s hero was in 60, 61 and 64, with the near-omnipotent supernatural Spectre, illustrated by Murphy Anderson. This did spawn a title, but it was a short run, as was the title of *Showcase*'s next characters, parody superhero group The Inferior Five in 62, 63 and 65, with the latter's X-Men parody a real treat. From 72, the Alex Toth-illustrated Western Top Gun, to 82, *Showcase* only gave new ideas a one-issue chance at stardom. Steve Ditko immediately launched two concepts destined for their own series, The Creeper (73) and The Hawk And The Dove (75), spliced by Howie Post's equally successful caveman Anthro, and followed by charming Western rogue Bat Lash

(76) and oddball detective duo Angel And The Ape (77). The mysterious Phantom Stranger in 80 was the last successful graduate of the first run, although there's other noteworthy material, including romance artist J. Scott Pike's silent and enigmatic underwater heroine Dolphin in 79.

82–84 introduced sword-and-sorcery to comics in the form of Nightmaster, written and illustrated by Jerry Grandenetti in 82, with new young artists Howard Chaykin, Jeff Jones and Mike Kaluta illustrating 83 and 84. 85–87 featured the adventures of Joe Kubert's Firehair, a white child raised by Native Americans. The first run came to a close with Manhunter 2070, ironically set in the future, when there was no future for the title. Until, that is, 1977, when it was revived with a reworking of The Doom Patrol, with only one of the old cast remaining; but it failed to pull in an audience until these stories were long forgotten. Power Girl, an alternate version of Supergirl, appeared in 97–99, cleavage very much to the fore, and 100 was an action-packed epic starring every character ever to have appeared in *Showcase*. Given the diversity, it wasn't too successful, and obviously didn't impress the audience, as the title was cancelled four issues afterwards. The final run was a Hawkman story guest-starring Adam Strange, and the final issue highlighted World War II US agents operating behind enemy lines. The overall percentage of features progressing from *Showcase* into their own titles is astonishingly high, with the quality rarely slipping below decent.

The series was revived in 1993 for an annual run. Rather than showcasing new features, these forty-eight-page issues concentrate on existing characters, and the showcase aspect is more likely to refer to new creative staff. Showcase 93 offers Catwoman, Blue Devil, The Creeper and The Huntress, but the highlight was in 7 and 8, as chapters of the *Batman* 'Knightfall' saga. These issues focus on old enemy Two-Face, written by Doug Moench and very nicely illustrated by Klaus Janson. *Showcase 94* was even more Batman-oriented, with every issue featuring solo appearances from his supporting cast or adversaries. Two-Face was back, along with The Joker and The Riddler, and 7 was again notable, spotlighting The Penguin, with Peter David writing and art by P. Craig Russell and Michael Gilbert. This run's highpoints are 8 and 9, with a solo for the best Batman villain to be created for many a year, the murderous ventriloquist's dummy Scarface. Scarface's creators Alan Grant and John Wagner chronicle his origin in the course of a gruesome tale, with art from Teddy Kristiansen.

1995 saw a new Supergirl strip, the Metal Men, continuing from their miniseries in 2, and the very welcome return of The Question in 3, by Denny O'Neil and Rick Burchett. 7 and 8 feature Mongul, catalyst for the downfall of Green Lantern, and *Showcase 96* kicks off with the new look Aqualad, while 8 is a prelude to the new Supergirl series. 11 and 12 are the most impressive issues, featuring 30th-century superteam The Legion Of Super-Heroes battling it out with Superman's old foe Brainiac. The revived series has featured a fine diversity, and there's something in most issues for any reader to enjoy, but the short-story formats often hinder development. Nevertheless, pick and choose at your leisure.~HY

Recommended: 6, 7, 11, 12, 55–58, 62, 63, 65, 73–76, 79

THE SHROUD

Marvel: *4-issue miniseries 1994*

Created as a surrogate Batman in *Super-Villain Team-Up*, the Shroud had a longevity that surpassed the pastiche, guest-starring in assorted titles over fifteen years before his own miniseries. Even then Marvel weren't confident enough not to plaster Spider-Man all over the covers. The Shroud fights gangsters by masquerading as one of them and using money obtained from defunct criminal organisations to finance further exploits. This time a heist has unforeseen complications tying into the Shroud's origins. No masterpiece, but a solid enough superhero adventure.~WJ

SIDNEY MELLON'S THUNDERSKULL

Slave Labor: *One-shot 1989*

Gerard Jones wrote a spoof column in *Amazing Heroes* using the persona of Sidney Mellon, a monumentally self-important 14-year-old. In the column, Mellon kept mentioning his own graphic novel 'Thunderskull' – naturally, the most important work in the history of the genre – and Jones was eventually persuaded to produce the beast. It stars Simon Medley, who appears to be a frail intellectual, with his time as a comics critic as his only experience of power, but see that retractable biro in his breast pocket? One click, and he transforms into Thunderskull, creature of myth. As a spoof, it gets steadily funnier. The fight scenes are classics: at least 50% speech-balloon, allowing room only for the odd glimpse of a heel or fist. The high-point, however, is Mellon's Afterword, where he frankly acknowledges his own genius and thanks his assistants, 'who helped me to the best of their abilities'. Hilarious.~FC

Recommended: 1

SILENCERS

Caliber: *4-issue miniseries 1991*

Canadian espionage title that's subtle, understated and stylised. The story sometimes slows to a plod, but there's a lot of thought behind *Silencers*, and careful reading pays off.~FP
Collection: Silencers (1–4)

THE SILENT INVASION

Renegade: *12-issue limited series 1986–1988*

Long before *X-Files*, Larry Hancock and Michael Cherkas had completed this complex tale of 50s paranoia. Matt Sinkage encounters a UFO and in his search for answers gets involved with the FBI, aliens, Communist agents and The Council, a secret government organisation. How much of this is in his head or is really happening is something you have to decide for yourself. It's well written by Hancock (plotted by both of them) and drawn in a European style by Cherkas (it owes much to the clear line of, for instance, Serge Clerc). 'Suburban Nightmares' (5, 7–9), with John Van Bruggen, is a back-up in much the same vein but concentrating on more domestic fears. It later spun off into its own series and collection.~NF
Recommended: 1–12
Collection: Silent Invasion Vol 1 (1–4), Vol 2 (5–8), Vol 3 (9–12)

SILENT MOBIUS

Viz: *Series one 6 issues 1991, Series two 5 issues 1992, Series three 5 issues 1992–1993, Series four 5 issues 1993–1994*

A squad of psychic policewomen protect 21st-century Tokyo from supernatural beings intent on destroying the city in this series by Kia Asamiya. The backgrounds of all but one of the squad members are revealed over three series as the entities remain a constant threat. The second series is the best. Katsumi Liquer discovers her mystical heritage and the youngest squad member, Yuki Saiko, is revealed to be something other than she assumed. The third series switches from colour to black and white, and in the fourth team leader Rally Cheyenne is revealed to have a past linked with the supernatural entities. Much championed by some as being among the best of Japanese girl-gang comics, it's not without charm, but not sufficient charm to have dragged the slim story over four series without concluding it. Neither is the peculiar title explained anywhere. *Silent Mobius* has continued for at least two further series in Japan, so perhaps the answers lie there, but as Viz appear to have ceased publishing the series you won't know unless you can read Japanese.~FP

SILVER SABLE & The Wild Pack

Marvel: *35 issues 1992–1995*

Operating from embassy premises, glamorous, lethal Silver Sable was introduced as a mercenary in *Amazing Spider-Man* 265. The Wild Pack, most prominently, consist of former villain Sandman, sadistic hard man Crippler, trainee flag-waver Battlestar, and the racist Powell, with Paladin an additional regular throughout. What makes the title work is that few are likeable, but all are strong characters that interact well. Fast-paced and inventive writing from Greg Wright and slick action-oriented art from Steven Butler (1–22, 25), often inked by James Sanders, and then Gordon Purcell and Pam Eklund, mean that most issues are better than average adventure fare. A bonus is few sub-plots, making it easy for new readers to pick up. Astute marketing sense ensures that the team are augmented with a cover-featured guest star for most issues, but these appearances are well considered and rarely detract from the title squad. Best samplers are 3, a rare issue with no guest star, and 30, with Silver Sable incarcerated.~WJ

SILVER STAR

Pacific: *6 issues 1983–1984*
Topps: *4-issue miniseries 1993–1994*

Call yourself a comic fan? If you're a serious one then you probably don't need to be told about this comic. Silver Star is Morgan Miller of the new breed of humans, Homo Geneticus, who were born of mothers implanted by a cowboy scientist determined to preserve life after atomic war. Homo Geneticus 'plays with atoms like we do with erector sets'. Silver Star, for instance, builds himself a chair ten times bigger than he would seem to need!

All this is told of with liberal use of Jack Kirby's trademark powerful high-contrast single and double-page spreads of exploding machinery and his equally distinctive, indeed unique dialogue. The structure is epic, dragging the reader from a lengthy prologue set in Vietnam (featuring a song written by Susan Kirby and sung by a little girl with an acoustic guitar reminiscent of the Dilly Sisters from *The Banana Splits Show*) to the disturbing climax, which features the Angel of Death and lakes of fire and evokes some of the racier passages in the Bible.

Beware the dismal formula back-up strips drawn by Kirby's regular late inkers D. Bruce Berry and Michael Thibodeaux, but make an exception for Steve Ditko's The Mocker (in 2), a suit-and-hat vigilante in the tradition of The Question and Mr A, drawn in 1981 and featuring some of Ditko's best late artwork, which rivals the standard of his classic *Spider-Man* stories. Old school madness all the way! There's no Jack anywhere near the Topps series. Stay away.~GK

The SILVER SURFER

Marvel: *Series one 18 issues 1968–1970, One-shot 1982, series two 123 issues +, 7 Annuals 1987 to date, 2-issue microseries 1988–1989*
Graphic Novels: The Silver Surfer 1978, 'Judgment Day' 1988, 'Parable' 1989, 'The Enslavers' 1990, 'Homecoming' 1991

Penciller and plotter Jack Kirby created the Silver Surfer, in *Fantastic Four* 48, but it was scripter and editor Stan Lee who wrote his comic. Kirby's Surfer was a powerful, almost emotionless alien being with impervious silver skin, flying the spaceways on his cosmic surfboard. He was the herald of the godlike alien Galactus, searching out suitable planets for his master to devour. On meeting humans the Surfer started to suffer pangs of conscience, and although he prevented Galactus from consuming Earth, he was imprisoned on the planet by an impenetrable barrier set up by his former master. The title originally offered forty-page stories at double the price of regular comics, and Lee used *Silver Surfer* to tell stories with relatively adult themes, a vehicle to carry Marvel further into its new college fanbase. Lee's choice of John Buscema as artist and co-plotter evidently shocked and angered Kirby.

Lee's origin story in 1 depicts the Surfer's former guise of Norrin Radd, a very human, very passionate rebel against the advanced but sterile civilisation of his homeworld, Zenn-La. When Galactus arrives to consume the planet, only Norrin has the courage to confront him, striking a bargain. He becomes Galactus' superpowered (and newly silver-plated) herald, Galactus swears never to harm Zenn-La, and Norrin can pursue a damage-limitation exercise by finding Galactus uninhabited planets to consume. He also gets to live a life of adventure that Zenn-La could never provide. Sadly, he had to leave behind his beloved, the beautiful Shalla Bal. With a recap of *FF* 48–50, the stage was set for the Surfer's adventures trapped on Earth, doomed never to see his love, and constantly attacked by humans who don't trust him. In 3 the Surfer meets Mephisto, a thinly disguised Satan, ruler of an underworld peopled by lost souls, who has kidnapped Shalla Bal from Zenn-La. He could physically destroy the Surfer, but it's Norrin Radd's immortal soul that Mephisto wants, and he tries mightily to tempt the noble Surfer from the path of righteousness. Both Lee and Buscema (inked by Joe Sinnott) excel themselves, and it ranks as one of the best Marvel comics of the 1960s.

Sadly, it's downhill from there. In 5 the Stranger, a mega-powerful alien, is trying to destroy all life on Earth because humanity's evil could poison the rest of the Universe. Lee makes some tentative points about racism as the Surfer befriends a black physicist, but he still received at least one letter warning him comics shouldn't tackle real-life issues! By 7 the giant-sized comic was clearly not selling well. For 8 and 9 a forty-page story (the return of Mephisto, plus pirate ghost the Flying Dutchman – pretty poor stuff) was chopped in two and the title became a regular-sized monthly. The abysmal back-up strip, 'Tales Of The Watcher', was dropped altogether. 10 and 11 are better. The Surfer joins a resistance movement against Communist invaders in an un-named South American nation. Shalla Bal, flown in from Zenn-La, is wounded and only a speedy return to her homeworld for advanced medical attention can save her life. By 12 the comic is not well either, with an exceedingly silly story in which a group of witches resurrect old Hulk baddie the Abomination. 16–17 have Mephisto back. The ailing series is really suffering from *déja vu* now, as Mephisto gets his evil paws on Shalla Bal again, and once more she is lost to Norrin. In 18 Marvel tried high-risk emergency surgery, giving the Surfer back to Jack Kirby to co-plot and pencil, while Lee remained as scripter. In what is little more than a prologue, the Surfer fights the Inhumans, more Fantastic Four supporting characters. The meat comes at the end, when he decides that he's been pushed around long enough by these crazy earthlings, and loses his temper big-time. 'Next issue: The Savagely Sensational New Silver Surfer!'…except there wasn't a next issue, which Kirby fans must consider a wasted opportunity on a cosmic scale. 18 went to print with the announcement that Kirby had left Marvel. Lee's miserable, neurotic Surfer had turned more readers off than on, in the final analysis.

Having recovered from his temper tantrum, the Surfer was a frequent guest star for twenty years, and Stan Lee said in 1971 that there would never be another solo Surfer strip unless he wrote it himself. In 1978, with Jack Kirby now back at Marvel, he made good his promise in the first Surfer graphic novel. Plotted by Lee and Kirby, drawn by Kirby and Sinnott, this 100-page book retells the story of Galactus' coming to earth, and the Surfer's rebellion against his master, this time without the Fantastic Four and their supporting cast. It seems likely that the book was intended as a springboard for a movie plot, hence it stands outside Marvel continuity. This revisionist version of the 'core myth' angered many, though it's powerful material. The Surfer is reclaimed by Galactus, and leaves Earth once again in his service, after a gruelling struggle of wills.

The 1982 one-shot is plotted and pencilled by John Byrne and scripted by Lee. It's 'Mephisto kidnaps Shalla Bal' again, but with new wrinkles. The Surfer returns to Zenn-La only to find it ravaged by Galactus, its people spared to live on the planet's barren, desert-like surface. At the end of the usual Mephisto/Surfer spat in Hell, Norrin is once more trapped on Earth and Shalla is whisked off to Zenn-La again. This time the Surfer imbues her with some of his cosmic power, so on her return she is able to bring new plant life, and new hope, to Zenn-La. Some old clichés, some new ideas, handled semi-well.

The Surfer's 1987 renaissance was due to Steve Englehart. Gone are the inconsistencies and sloppy plotting, and in the launch issue he's finally freed from his Earth exile, and embroiled in two complex and interlinked plots. A new war is looming between two rival races of Marvel's alien nasties, the Kree and the Skrulls, and a group of cosmic bad guys called the Elders Of The Universe have decided to kill Galactus, a plot that comes to fruition in 9–10. 1–10, 12 and 21 are pencilled by Marshall Rogers, whose art veers from the competent to the appalling, and these issues succeed only because of very strong scripts. Joe Staton brings the welcome gifts of dynamic anatomy and panel layouts, and clarity of story-telling, to 11, 13, 14 and the annual 1, before Ron Lim takes over for a long run, and falls somewhere between Rogers and Staton, with a strong George Perez influence. The Surfer is reunited with Shalla Bal in 2, but complications ensure she turns down his offer of marriage. He agrees to protect the neutrality of Zenn-La in the coming Kree–Skrull War, and they part, sadly, as friends. 8 is particularly good: the Surfer's soul, trapped in the mind of the Kree Supreme Intelligence, goes through a dreamlike psychodrama that partly satirises the 1960s comic. In 15–18, the FF's Reed and Sue Richards participate in an inventive Galactus story: he has indigestion on a cosmic scale. 20 is possibly a Marvel first, in that it has no fight scene at all! Mostly it's war-war and jaw-jaw this issue, but still an excellent read, and something of a break in the story-line.

Lee scripts both 1988 graphic novels, which are lacking in credibility and add nothing to the canon. 'Judgment Day' is plotted and drawn by John Buscema. Every page is one big panel, which at least makes the book look unique, but at key points Lee's script contradicts the story that Buscema's pictures are telling. Lee and Jean 'Moebius' Giraud's collaboration 'Parable' is barely better, published as a nice hardback edition and a two-issue newsprint comic. It's another retelling of the 'Galactus comes to Earth but the Surfer saves the world' story.

Back at the comic, 25 returns to the Kree-Skrull War with a vengeance as the Skrulls get their shape-changing powers back. Englehart wraps up the War in 31, at which point he was replaced. He'd sorted out some inconsistencies,

including the emotionless/emotional shifts in the Surfer's personality, how long he'd been Galactus' herald (centuries) and why Shalla Bal was still so young (Zenn-Lavians live a long time). Englehart's characters acted intelligently. They schemed and even negotiated, as well as fighting. Some of his cosmic explanations were a bit abstruse, and there is arguably too much musing and philosophising in an issue like 31, but overall he succeeded in making *Silver Surfer* into a superhero comic that didn't insult the reader's intelligence.

Marvel, however, thought this wouldn't sell enough toys, cartoons or company crossovers. From 34, Jim Starlin scripts, and returns Thanos, Drax the Destroyer and the rest of his *Captain Marvel/Warlock* supporting crew to repeat a tale told years before, in *Captain Marvel* and *Warlock*. From 1990 endlessly recycled spin-offs appeared, with numerous crossovers linked to such miniseries as *The Infinity Gauntlet*. The mobilising of cosmic forces is seen several times too often, and becomes just another firework display. The entire universe is devastated over and over again... all with the ultimate goal of selling more toys! And *Silver Surfer* 34 is where it all starts, leading up to 50 and *Infinity Gauntlet* 1. Starlin and Lim make a good team, though, and 35 is actually pretty strong stuff, as the formerly dead Thanos explains why he is going to kill half the universe. Also in 1990, the 'Enslavers' graphic novel, by Stan Lee and Keith Pollard, appeared. It's awful, and could have been a couple of poor fill-in issues. In 44–48 we find out that Thanos now has all six Soul Gems, now known as the Infinity Gems, giving him the power of a supreme deity. Mephisto reveals a silly origin in 45, and in 46 the Surfer meets Adam Warlock. In 48 he confronts Galactus, now knowing that Galactus had tampered with Norrin Radd's soul when he became the Silver Surfer, so he wouldn't feel guilty for helping him destroy planets. The Surfer just wouldn't be the Surfer without a bit of angst, and this adds something to the legend. In 50, Thanos forces more of the Surfer's buried memories to the surface. More angst, setting a pattern for issues to come. 51–59 are *Infinity Gauntlet* crossovers written by Ron Marz, as Thanos destroys half the universe, turning what's left into a madhouse dedicated to the worship of Death.

Starlin's major crime against the Surfer was the stupid 1991 graphic novel 'Homecoming', well drawn by Bill Reinhold. A giant alien brain kidnaps the whole planet of Zenn-La, reducing it to a mental construct. The Surfer can almost live out an idyllic existence with Shalla Bal in this mental world, but ultimately Zenn-La returns to reality, and Shalla apparently dies within the collapsing mind-universe. The sole purpose of this sadistic exercise appears to be to give the Surfer something else to grieve about, though Shalla Bal is resurrected in a later miniseries… otherwise, how could Marvel sell Shalla Bal toys?

61–64 is yet more psychobabble, as the Surfer contracts a nasty virus and visits the realm of the dead, confronting the victims of his days as Galactus' herald, and finally fights the dark side of his own soul. The worst aspect of this gratuitous nonsense is that the Surfer's 'heroic ideal' in this mental landscape is manifested as Jim Starlin's Captain Marvel! Ron Marz is now very much in the business of recycling old ideas, and not doing them great justice. In 70–75's 'Herald Ordeal', all the former Galactus heralds (Surfer, Airwalker, Firelord, Terrax and Nova) gang up on the new one, Morg, a vicious psychopath with no conscience. From 79, Lim provides increasingly sketchy layouts, before bowing out altogether. A high turnover of artists of varying quality follows. In 79–82 major new villain Tyrant returns from exile in the far reaches of the universe, and draws the attention of Galactus, an old adversary, leading into the *Cosmic Powers* miniseries.

83–85 cross over with *The Infinity Crusade*. Beta Ray Bill and Thor guest in 86, preceding Warlock and half the Marvel Universe in 87 as part of another crossover, 'Blood and Thunder' (more Infinity Gems nonsense). There are yet more guest stars in 93–99 (the FF, the Hulk, Thanos, Terrax, old uncle Tom Cobleigh), which see the Surfer tempted with sex, riches and other corrupting vices. It's all a plot by Mephisto, weakening the Surfer's soul for 100's big confrontation. Among other delights, Norrin's parents are suffering in Hell. The Surfer finally kills Mephisto (maybe!), which gives him something else to anguish over. From 101 Mike Lackey scripts, and Tom Grindberg draws in an Image-influenced style. 101 is Shalla Bal rejecting the Surfer again… he's never home! Always off with the cosmic-powered lads, getting into fights! What's a girl to do, but fall in love with Norrin Radd's long-lost (and previously unheard-of) bastard half-brother? This kind of cheap melodrama shows just how far the comic has fallen since Englehart's thoughtful Shalla Bal scenes in 2.

George Perez scripts from 111. The Surfer catches a giant wave in space in 112 (for the first time ever, the surfing idea is taken to its logical conclusion; it should have been the cover image, but the opportunity was missed). The wave is actually a time-space warp into another universe. Here the Surfer joins a rebellion against a galactic tyrant, and his body is broken up into a number of solid metallic pieces, whereas previously he believed he was basically silver-coated. Surviving this ordeal, he returns home to face further trauma in 122, as the planet of Zenn La (with its inhabitants, including Shalla Bal)

falls apart around him. Perez would have us believe that Zenn La died thousands of years ago, and only an illusion has been left in its place, no matter how much Marvel continuity this invalidates. This plot development should have been stopped by a conscientious editor as a Revision Too Far. New writer J.M. DeMatteis is left to pick up the pieces of a comic that has in the past been a star of the Marvel firmament.~GL

Recommended: Series one 1, 3, 18, Lee and Kirby Graphic Novel, series two 1–20, 22, 25–31 *Collections: Marvel Masterworks* Vol 15 (series one 1–5), vol 19 (Series one 6–18)

SILVERBACK
Comico: *3-issue miniseries 1989*

Plotted by Matt Wagner and based on his character Argent (the wolf) from the original *Grendel* series, *Silverback* sees William Messner-Loebs return to the genre in which he began with *Journey*. It's a very different frontier, however, as the spirit of death, Maslun, empowers an Algonquin brave with inhuman savagery, turning him into an immortal wolf.

It's not a tale for the squeamish, and Loebs creates a tragic, downbeat atmosphere that leaves little room for humour, while the artwork by Loebs and John Peck is minimalist but effective.~NF

SILVERBLADE
DC: *12-issue limited series 1987–1988*

Former silver screen heartthrob Jonathan Lord lives an embittered and reclusive life until rejuvenated and given the ability to transform himself into characters from his years of celluloid glory. One was Silverblade, hence the title. Lord's Hollywood mansion is populated with a former child star employed as a butler, the talking bird responsible for his new state and a fellow actor's ghost. Writer Cary Bates obviously enjoyed himself stringing everyone along with a romp resembling the 1930s action films he cheerfully parodies throughout, and the art team of Gene Colan and Steve Mitchell is also having a good time. A stunning, yet simple, revelation occurs well into the series, and once you've come to terms with it you can almost hear Bates chuckling in the background as everything's up-ended. The final issue rather falls to pieces, with unconvincing mystical mumbo-jumbo the order of the day. That shouldn't put you off sampling the remainder, but start with issue 1.~FP

SILVERHEELS
Pacific: *3 issues 1983–1984*

Introducing Scott Hampton's generally fine art, and Bruce Jones' hacked-out story about a Native American in a dystopian future challenging for the position of Earth's representative to a galactic council alongside his Aryan counterparts. Beyond the natural antipathy the leads have for each other, the story is complicated by a fawning female and Hampton's inability to keep to even a bi-monthly schedule. By the third issue there's only nine pages of the title feature, leaving Ken Steacy's whimsical transforming-robot back-up itself needing a back-up (provided by Jaime Hernandez). The *Silverheels* collection reprints the portions previously published and concludes the story.~WJ

Collection: Silverheels (1–3 + concluding material)

SIMPSONS COMICS

Welsh Publishing: *One-shot 1993*
Bongo Comics: *27 issues + 1994 to date*

In the event you're the one person on planet Earth who's never encountered *The Simpsons* on TV, you should be informed that it's a consistently vicious satire of all aspects of American life. It's admirably unsentimental in its presentation of the worst aspects of blue-collar families. Husband and father Homer is presented as a self-centred, under-educated boor with an unfailing propensity for making a bad situation worse. Bratty son Bart is Homer in the making, while wife Marge can see Homer for what he is, but loves him nonetheless. Daughter Lisa strives to overcome the family she's been dealt, and the series is populated with a magnificently considered platoon of supporting characters through which all aspects of America can be pointedly lampooned. The Welsh Publishing tryout and the first four issues by James and Cindy Vance and Bill Morrison are as close to the TV show as can be attained in comics. Well plotted and illustrated, they're laugh-a-panel stuff. Thereafter an army of writers is used, with Andrew Gottlieb best among a hit-and-miss bunch, although the art is consistently good in capturing the authentic look of the Simpsons, which isn't as easy it may seem. To 18 each issue also features a short back-up strip about one of the characters from the TV show, with standouts starring Police Chief Wiggum (6) and Barney Gumble (9). 19–22 feature Bill Morrison's 1950s movie pastiche *Roswell*. 26 (written by Rob Hammersley and Todd Greenwald) and 27 (written by Doug Tuber and Tim Maile) are the best issues since 1–4, with scripts consistently matching the TV show for gag ratio, characterisation and even the visual asides that add to already fully rounded stories.~FP

Recommended: Welsh Publishing 1, Bongo 1–4, 6, 7, 9, 16, 17, 20, 26, 27

Collections: The Simpsons Comics Extravaganza (1–4), *Simpsons Comics Simps-O-Rama* (11–14) *Simpsons Comics Spectacular* (6–9), , *Simpsons Comics Strike Back* (15–18), *Simpsons Comics Wingding* (19–23)

SIN

Tragedy Strikes: *4 issues 1992–1993*
Black Eye: *2 issues 1994*

Jason Stephens single-handedly produced a confusing but often amusing comic wherein many different kinds of characters read or dream about each other amid cranky cut-up old adverts and demented tributes to *Mad Magazine* tricks. There's Nod (from the land of Nod), who looks a bit like a devil-cat, the 'Young Violence' trio of Nice Kid, Knife Girl and Gun Boy, and the superhero-parodying Sinister Horde. It would probably hold most appeal for the habitual LSD user, but any switched-on reader should find something quirky to laugh at.~GK

SIN CITY

Cozmic: *1 issue 1973*

British underground whose most notable creator is Angus McKie. His early '2001 A Haze Odyssey' is an eco-warning in which London is an open sewer with the rich living at least two miles above the gas-masked majority. Wyndham Raine (!) has a similar style to *Zap's* Moscoso, while Bill Sanderson's woodcut effects enhance another tale from the grim city. Subtitled 'Tales of Urban Paranoia', the overall mix of satire and cruel humour doesn't quite give the title the coherence that it needs.~NF

SIN CITY

Dark Horse: *6-issue miniseries ('A Dame To Kill For') 1993–1994, One-shot ('The Babe Wore Red And Other Stories') 1994, 5-issue miniseries ('The Big Fat Kill') 1994–1995, One-shot ('Silent Night') 1995, 6-issue miniseries ('That Yellow Bastard') 1996, One-shot ('Lost, Lonely And Lethal') 1996*

Frank Miller's *Sin City* first appeared in *Dark Horse Presents* 51–62 before these stories. Each series is intended to stand alone, published when ready rather than on a strict schedule. Sin City itself is a setting for each story-line, unnamed but seemingly rotten to the core. The characters all converge on Old Town, a no-go area for cops where the law is the law of the fist, gun or, in some cases, sword. At the heart of Old Town is a bar where strippers dress as cowboys and money will buy you almost anything. The women of the bar are also the area's enforcers; if you cross them, you won't live to regret it. But underlying all of the tales is something like the Japanese code of Bushido, where honour means everything, especially if it's all you've got.

'A Dame To Kill For' is the story of Dwight and Ava, the latter an extremely manipulative woman who uses men to get what she wants and then dumps them, or at least tries to. Having set Dwight up for murder and seduced the investigating detective, it looks as though she's committed a perfect crime, but Dwight's still on the loose and determined to get revenge. 'The Babe Wore Red' sees Dwight investigating the death of a friend and running from a pair of hitmen with the lady of the title. It comes with two short stories, the first about a killer meeting his match in the Old Town 'girls', Miho and Gail, the second about a killer just doing his job. 'Lost, Lonely and Lethal' is a later collection of short stories, the longest tale in which introduces the colour blue to Miller's coded series with the deadly Blue Eyes.

'The Big Fat Kill' is the extremely violent story of a dead cop and the threat of a war in the Old Town if Dwight and the girls can't stop the cop's head from falling into the hands of a crime lord. 'Silent Night' is equally bloody, the story of a young girl's rescue from her kidnappers, told in single-page panels. The controversial 'That Yellow Bastard' features a senator's son whose perverted desire for young girls almost gets him killed by policeman John Hartigan. But Hartigan is betrayed and framed for the crimes. Only his correspondence with Nancy, the girl he rescued, keeps him alive in prison. When she's put in danger as the senator's son recovers from Hartigan's bullet all hell breaks loose.

Miller's hard-boiled prose is perfectly matched by his brutal black and white artwork, where everything is defined by the shadow it casts. Miller uses gimmicks sparingly but effectively, such as spot colour red for the 'Babe Wore Red' and yellow for 'That Yellow Bastard'. The series doesn't offer any great insights into the human condition but it's entertaining story-telling that's constantly daring.~NF

Recommended: 'The Big Fat Kill', 'A Dame To Kill For', 'That Yellow Bastard'

Collections: The Big Fat Kill (1–5), A Dame To Kill For (1–6), That Yellow Bastard (1–6)

SINISTER HOUSE OF SECRET LOVE
DC: 4 issues 1971–1972

Behind some of the finest covers ever to grace a comic, courtesy of Jeff Jones among others, this title offered up a number of lengthy Gothic-romance strips. The marriage of love and horror was an uneasy one, and despite the best attempts of Michael Fleisher and Len Wein, the attraction was its artwork. While Don Heck's efforts in 1 were far from inspired, Tony DeZuniga's 2 and 4 are quite gorgeous. The exception to the title's directionless feel was provided by 3's 'Bride Of The Falcon', written by Frank Robbins, which brilliantly concentrated on psychological tension rather than the half-hearted haunted-house milieu found elsewhere. Better yet, the thirty-six-page story

was drawn by Alex Toth, with inking from Doug Wildey and Frank Giacoia, who revelled in its Venetian setting and claustrophobic atmosphere.~DAR
Recommended: 3

SINISTER ROMANCE
Harrier: 4 issues 1988–1989

By turns poignant, amusing and just plain silly, but never boring, as B-movie stories of superheroines, mermaids, aliens and gangsters abound. The different art styles of the contributors work well, with Trevs (later to be Woodrow) Phoenix's graphic Infantino-style dynamism contrasting with the sketchy impressionism of Glenn Dakin and the solid black and white work of Warren Pleece. Bob Lynch brings a more traditional cartoon approach to the final two issues. The artists are having a good time, and so should you.~FP

SINNER
Fantagraphics: 6 issues 1988-1990

Depressing episodes from the life of Alack Sinner, an out-of-place P.I. in the slums of New York, created by Argentinian duo José Muñoz (artist) and Carlos Sampayo (writer). Over the years they've woven stories around all aspects of Sinner's life, using him as one of a cast of characters for their Joe's Bar series. This selects from the many Sinner stories, starting with some early pieces which, while you can see the seeds of greatness in them, stick quite firmly to a hard-boiled detective formula. 4 reprints a much later story, 'Viet Blues', an extraordinary piece of writing in which Alack keeps slipping into walking nightmares of his time in Vietnam, which are contrasted with the present. The shift from plot to characterisation is quite marked, as is the reduction of the Muñoz style from fine line to heavy black and white expressionism. 5 gives us the opportunity to read the first 'radical' Sinner story, created before 'Viet Blues', where the first breaks from noir tradition are being made. It's a great sadness that more Sinner strips have not been translated, as the sequence of stories adds up to a greater whole.~FJ
Recommended: 1–6

SIREN
Malibu: 4-issue miniseries (∞–3) 1995–1996, One-shot 1996

Pasty-faced cute female alleged assassin seeks guest stars for putative miniseries. Only second-stringers like War Machine, Diamondback and Whizzer showed up. Numbering the first issue with an infinity symbol was a joke so hilarious that hospitals are still regularly visited by Siren readers requiring their sides to be stitched back up. The one-shot guest starred Shuriken and was a parsimonious twenty-eight pages.~WJ

SISTERHOOD OF STEEL

Epic: *8 issues 1984–1986*
Eclipse: *Graphic Novel 1987*

The covers of 1 and 2 make it look like another babes-in-chainmail story, but they lie. Yes, it's the standard sword-and-fantasy setting, and yes, it's about a band of women warriors, but these women are startlingly different in that they fight with all their clothes on! The story centres on Boronwe, starting as she moves from Novice to Cadet, and following her through her first combat, her first night on the town, her first serious love affair... Not a babe-in-chainmail story at all, but a coming-of-age story about a young soldier who happens to be a woman. Christy Marx's writing gets more absorbing with each issue, and while Mike Vosburg's artwork is never appealing, it does differentiate the characters, and you soon get used to it. The story-line was cut short, to be concluded in the graphic novel. There should be more, though. Much more.~FC
Recommended: 1–8

SIX DEGREES

High Heels: *4 issues + 1996 to date*

Very sensitive territory is staked out by *Six degrees* (to use the correct lower case title), but thankfully it's responsibly handled. In 1994 the UK was shocked to hear the fate of missing toddler Jamie Bulger, abducted from a shopping mall and later found murdered. Tragic enough as it stood, it later transpired the killers were two pre-teenage boys. *Six degrees* examines a scarcely disguised version of the case, studying the circumstances of all involved parties, including the local police and journalists. The entire affair is then contrasted with similar events occurring in the nineteenth century. While writer Martin Shipp and artist Marc Laiming – working in a very traditional British black and white style – have produced a distinctive and worthwhile title, there's a distancing emotional detachment throughout, and at times it's a very dry piece. There's a need for intelligent comics tackling adult topics, and those who read Vertigo titles are likely to enjoy this as well.~WJ

SIX FROM SIRIUS

Epic: *4-issue miniseries 1984, 4-issue miniseries 1986*

In the future humanity has spread across the stars to encounter numerous alien races, most of which are biped humanoids. The first series requires a team of government-connected agents to stop an escalating inter-planetary war, and in the second an inter-dimensional gateway is cause for concern. *Six From Sirius* is old fashioned sci-fi adventure, ably handled by writer Doug Moench and artist Paul Gulacy.~FP
Collection: *Six From Sirius* (miniseries 1)

SIX MILLION DOLLAR MAN

Charlton: *9 issues 1976–1978*

Based on the TV series of the same name featuring Lee Majors as Steve Austin, the mechanically enhanced Bionic Man, the first two issues, by Joe Gill and Joe Staton, set the standard. They were awful, and from there things went downhill, resulting in some of the worst comics of the 1970s.~SW

SKATEMAN

Pacific: *1 issue 1983*

What was Neal Adams thinking? Roller Derby star Billy Moon's best chum and girl-friend are murdered, so after a bout of self-pity he ties a bandanna round his face and gets his skates on to avenge them as Skateman. Without a hint of irony, it's laughter on wheels, with Neal Adams throwing in fads like roller discos and halter-neck tops willy-nilly, all of which were five years past their sell-by date in 1983. In the back is an even sillier character (although knowingly so), Paul Power's Rock Warrior, who destroys spaceships with power chords.~WJ

SKIDMARKS

Tundra: *3-issue miniseries 1994*

Reprints Ed (Ilya) Hillyer's self-published title *Bic*. *Skidmarks* is a fluidly-drawn, downbeat tale of moral choices. Bike-obsessed Bic finds the loot dropped when his local shop is robbed. Should he give it back, or buy the bike of his dreams to impress the girls? Ilya writes sensitively about the wild enthusiasms of youth in this convincing slice-of-life tale.~FJ
Recommended: 1–3

SKIN GRAFT: The Adventures Of A Tattooed Man

Vertigo: *4-issue miniseries 1993*

John Oakes, petty criminal, falls in with Abel Tarrant, former supervillain The Tattooed Man, when in prison. The pair forge an unusual relationship, Tarrant using Oakes as a living canvas for his obsession, forgetting that Oakes might develop an agenda of his own. Striking art from Warren Pleece adds to the disturbing and off-balance feel of this miniseries, but ultimately Jerry Prosser's script fails to deliver what it promises.~HS

Voodoo & Zealot SKIN TRADE

Image: *One-shot 1995*

Underneath artwork which Michael Lopez has swiped too obviously from soft-porn mags is a half-decent story as *WildC.A.T.S.* heroines Voodoo and Zealot rescue orphans from an East European country which is Bosnia in all but name. One for the boys, but not as dismissible as the first glance would have you believe. ~JC

SKREEMER
DC: *6-issue miniseries 1989*

In the days before their Vertigo imprint DC issued adult-oriented series on better quality paper, but otherwise marketed alongside their standard titles. It meant the like of *Skreemer* was foisted on a superhero audience, who scratched their heads at this complex fusion of James Joyce with *The Godfather* and didn't bother with any further issues. It was their loss. Pete Milligan produces an appalling, cruel story the subtlety of which is belied by the simple blocky art of Brett Ewins and Steve Dillon. Spanning forty years, on one level it's the story of gang boss Vito Skreemer, a man cursed with a terrible ability, making a major power play. As he literally stands on the precipice he broods on his past and his rise to power. His career is contrasted with that of the tragic Finnegan family, permanently downtrodden residents in poverty, struggling to survive and live a more honest life. *Skreemer* has allegorical references to *Finnegans Wake*, both song and novel, and to the life of Jesus, alongside musings about the validity of predestination. It's a brutal masterpiece, long overdue for collection.~FP
Recommended: 1–6

SKROG
Comico: *1 issue 1984*

With hindsight *Skrog* is very much a prototype *Mask*, with the same mixture of madcap whimsy and parody, which makes the title sound far more interesting than it is.~WJ

SKULL Comics
Rip Off: *1 issue 1970*
Last Gasp: *5 issues (2–6) 1970 –1972*

This was one of several underground comics conceived very much in the tradition of EC's horror line, and after a slightly slippery start it grew into one of the best. Jack Jaxon, Dave Sheridan and Spain all contributed good material, but it was Richard Corben (2, 3, 5, 6) and Greg Irons (1–3, 6) who best captured the EC spirit in a series of astonishingly shocking strips. Irons' frequent collaborator Tom Veitch was responsible, with Irons and Corben, for the run's best (and most stomach-churning) tale, the full length *A Gothic Tale* in 6. The Veitch/Irons gore-a-thon The Clean-Up Crew from 3 was later turned into a notorious German underground film, albeit without their permission.~DAR
Recommended: 2, 3, 6

SKULL & BONES
DC: *3-issue miniseries 1992*

Excellently constructed thriller set in the disintegrating Soviet Union of the early 1990s. Ed Hannigan's plot takes advantage of how technology has outdistanced the state's ability to control it. Three loose cannons combat the resigned remnants of the Politburo, but one KGB controller has a grim agenda of his own. The focal point of the series is Andrian, a grim, single-minded and resourceful former special soldier, who began his anti-state activities by switching sides to join the rebels in Afghanistan. Returning to Moscow to begin a one-man war on the home front, he reluctantly accepts allies in order to actuate a grander plan. Rarely for a prestige-format title, this is actually a long read. Creator Ed Hannigan's art is admirably dark and his plotting dense and diligent, with not a page wasted. A true graphic novel.~FP
Recommended: 1–3

SKULL THE SLAYER
Marvel: *8 issues 1975–1976*

Bonkers example of Marvel at its hippy best. Marv 'equal opportunities' Wolfman starts off with a radical black physicist, a peace-loving young girl and an insecure teenager crash-landing while flying over the Bermuda Triangle, along with a ex-'Nam vet being taken home for trial for killing his brother. Cue 'Ideological Quarrels in the Land That Time Forgot'. But, even better, Skully and friends discover a sort of Time Ziggurat with a different age on each step. Steve Englehart has them fight aliens in ancient Egypt, then Bill Mantlo whisks them away to the time of Arthurian legend, whenever that is. The series, drawn initially by Steve Gan and then by Sal Buscema with help from Gan and Sonny Trinidad, ended with Skull the Slayer about to be sacrificed to an Aztec god, unless the readers made their voice heard. The best they could do was request a conclusion in *Marvel Two-In-One* 35–36.~FJ

SKRULL KILL KREW
Marvel: *5 issues 1995–1996*

Mad Cow Disease meets the *X-Files*, in this thinly disguised 'Reds under the bed' romp by Grant Morrison and Mark Millar, in the company of pencilling pal Steve Yeowell. Alien shape-shifting Skrulls have successfully infiltrated all levels of society. To redress the balance a psychotic shapeshifter, Ryder, assembles the Skrull Kill Krew to execute all Skrulls they come across. What an unpleasant bunch the SKK are. Besides Ryder, you have a English fascist skinhead, a pseudo-punk lesbian, a spoilt superstar model and a whimpering beach bum. Quite honestly you find yourself rooting for the aliens.

Originally intended as an ongoing title, the truncated run splits awkwardly into two parts. 1–3 have the SKK on a recruiting drive at an airport while Captain America is there to greet the president of a Baltic state. Putative world ruler Baron Strucker, head of evil organisation Hydra, and the Baltic president being a Skrull complicate matters further. This plot is

discarded for 4 and 5, in which the SKK stumble on a small town where everyone has been replaced by a Skrull. It's then gung-ho all the way as the aliens are slaughtered. This series didn't live up to expectations, being rather dry, considering the absurd scenario. Only 3 fulfils the humour quotient with an excellent over the top portrayal of Baron Strucker.~HY
Recommended: 3

SKY WOLF
Eclipse: 3-issue miniseries 1988

Spin-off from Airboy, where Sky Wolf had been a regular companion and back-up strip. Sky Wolf is a pilot (all right, no surprises there) whose brash attitude and recklessness involve him in various scrapes. In this case, having recently become estranged from his wife, in 1954, he goes treasure hunting with his friend Bald Eagle in Vietnam. It's forgettably told by Chuck Dixon and Tom Lyle.~NF

SLAINE The Berserker
Quality: 28 issues 1987–1989

Slaine, the barbarian warrior strip he created for UK weekly 2000AD, was undoubtedly Pat Mills finest hour. It's an ironic, knowing tale of a violent but enduringly cheeky warrior, which starts off as a simple poke at Conan, set in a mythical Britain before cataclysms separated it from Continental Europe. The story is told by Slaine's companion on his adventures, a malevolent and malodorous dwarf, Ukko. In his old age, when mankind have forgotten the magical events he witnessed, Ukko has retired to a mythical fastness where he is being alternatively cajoled and threatened into recording his memoirs.

Slaine is kicked out of his tribe at an early age despite being a prodigious warrior when gripped by a berserker-like fury, the Warp Spasm. Contrary to his best intentions to look out for himself, shag anything that moves and have fun, Slaine continually finds his destiny entwined with that of the decaying sorcerers who worship death and seek to destroy humanity. Many of the early episodes (written for a weekly comic and therefore requiring a climax every four or six pages) are little more than segments of protracted fights. But what fights. In the hands of Mike McMahon, one of the most underrated comic book artists ever, Slaine is the Straw Dogs of British comics, bloody, inventive, twisted. The artists who followed never captured the wildness of McMahon's drawing, until, in Simon Bisley, a maturer Mills found someone who could match the mellower, more humorous tone of the later stories and create a vibrant vision of his Celtic paradise which was packed with great visual characterisation. Before him, Glen Fabry made his name on Slaine with his ultra-detailed but relatively fluid artwork. It couldn't be more different from McMahon if it tried, but it was certainly value for money. David Pugh, on the other hand, compensated for a decided lack on the drawing front with even more detail, flooding his pages with ink until, as Slaine was elected king following the death of his enfeebled brother, he looked like a Mattel toy ascending the sacred mound. With 21 the title changes to Slaine The King, referring to his new-found status.

Throughout Mills draws upon his own interpretation of Celtic mythology and modern Goddess-worship. As the strip evolves Slaine goes from simple battle-lover to Sun King who unites the rival Celtic tribes through cunning and diplomacy rather than with three feet of steel in order to fight their greatest battle against the dread Slough Fegg. In phantasmagorical sequences he meets the Goddess herself and finds her a gurning, lusty maiden with whom he can happily flirt. Mills' humour evolves too, moving from straightforward contrast between the events depicted and Ukko's account of them to a broad parody of political and religious ineptitude. It's not subtle stuff, but the characters are rich and the plotting clever. The McMahon and Bisley issues are worth a look for the artwork alone, and the whole series is highly readable, but forget about the dull Blackhawk back-up strips.~FJ
Recommended: 1–4, 25–28
Collections: Slaine Book one (1–4), Slaine The Horned God (Slaine The King (21–23)

SLAPSTICK
Marvel: 4-issue miniseries 1992–1993

Good-hearted troublemaker Steve Harmon, out to spoil a carnival for a school rival, falls into Dimension X while wearing a clown outfit (it works in the story. Honestly). His choice of costume is fortuitous, as Dimension X is inhabited by evil clowns (okay, alien entities who coincidentally resemble clowns. Does that sound any better?), and he blends right in. Or he would, but interdimensional travel has taken its toll and reduced him to, well, a puddle of goo. Fortunately, a good clown scientist, trying to prevent the evil clowns' Invasion of Earth, reconstructs Steve in a spiffy new form, giving him the indestructible properties of an animated cartoon and sending him back to Earth to wreak havoc on the Marvel Universe. Oh, yes, this is supposed to be a superhero comic, and it's a very funny, likeable one too, written with flair and wit by Len Kaminski, and drawn by James Fry, who is unequalled among his contemporaries in his ability to fuse comedy and drama. Needless to say, Slapstick was relentlessly panned by the legions of humourless Marvelites who wanted to see their heroes suffer, goddammit!~HS
Recommended: 1–4

SLASH MARAUD
DC: *6-issue miniseries 1987–1988*

Doug Moench does his best to incorporate scenes from every film genre into this story about an Earth occupied by aliens who are five years from making the planet uninhabitable for humans. Hero Slash and a small group of survivors are aided by one alien who's begun to regret what his fellows are doing. It's an interesting idea and Moench packs a lot of action and character into the six issues. As drawn by Paul Gulacy, Slash looks remarkably like Clint Eastwood and behaves as inscrutably as the Man With No Name. Moench provides a good script and the artwork's good, but overall the series is a little too clinical to get passionate about it.~NF

SLAVE LABOR Stories
Slave Labor: *4 issues 1992*

A sampler for the idiosyncratic Slave Labor, one of the few comic publishing companies that's still one man's vision. If Dan Vado likes your work and can afford to publish it, you're in. Sadly, Slave Labor titles don't reach the audience they should, despite Vado's taste being generally excellent. He's also a pretty good writer, as displayed in 1's *Hero Sandwich* tale. It's an excellent first issue throughout, with a Dr Radium feature and a tale of Catholic childhood completing the mix. Succeeding issues don't match the first, but with Milk and Cheese, Bill the Clown and Samurai Penguin there's enough to make them worthy of a glance.~WJ
Recommended: 1

SLEAZE CASTLE
Gratuitous Bunny: *8 issues + 1989–1993 (1–6), 1996 to date (7 on), 4-issue miniseries (Tales From Sleaze Castle') 1992–1994*

Little or no actual sleaze in this comedy series operating in the territory between British humour great Leo Baxendale and *The Hitch Hiker's Guide To The Galaxy*. The name spoofs an old DC horror comic, and launching with the title *More Tales...* teasingly implied that there had been a previous comic called *Tales...* there hadn't: it followed later. If you find that amusing, you might enjoy these convoluted time-travel and alternate-world adventures, always rooted in the real-life England of university student Jocasta Dribble. Meticulous black and white artwork by Terry Wiley can turn its hand to parodies of album covers, *Peanuts* strips, *Love & Rockets...* anything that crops up in his own or main writer Dave McKinnon's fertile imagination. Enough to give the phrase 'wacky, zany English humour' a good name. The collections all include new material

and are therefore recommended above the original comics.~GL
Recommended: 7, 8, Directors Cut 1–3
Collections: *Directors Cut Zero (Tales of...1–4), Directors Cut 1 (More Tales... 1–3), Directors Cut 2 (More Tales... 4–6)*

SLEAZY SCANDALS Of The Silver Screen
Kitchen Sink: *One-shot 1974*

Hollywood Babylon comics by the cream of the underground cartoonists. Best is Art Spiegelman detailing the downfall of Fatty Arbuckle, with good art and inventive use of silent screen-style text captions. Kim Deitch, Bill Griffith and Spain are also on hand for a respectable package, and the obscure Jim Osbourne's Lupe Velez strip is also excellent.~FP

SLEEPWALKER
Marvel: *33 issues, 1 Special 1991–1994*

Laughably promoted as '*Sandman* done right', this pleasing series was ill-served by its advance publicity, which set most folks against it from the start. University student Rick Sheridan is troubled by dreams of a tall, grotesque creature whom he senses is trying to break into the waking world. This creature is one of a group called the Sleepwalkers, whose task it is to patrol the Mindscape, another dimension, and prevent any of its more evil denizens from preying on innocent minds. Having become accidentally 'lodged' in Sheridan's mind, it can only access the outside world and fight evil while Sheridan sleeps. It's a refreshing idea to have a heroic protagonist who is ugly, rather than fashionably 'exotic', and Bob Budiansky creates a group of likeable supporting characters for our teenage hero. Bret Blevins illustrates most of the first dozen issues with appealingly soft-focus lines, giving a natural look to the admittedly unrealistic characters. Sadly, after Blevins' departure the replacement artists weren't up to snuff, and Budiansky seemed to have lost heart, turning in rote scripts with obligatory guest appearances by Marvel heavy-hitters to try to pad the sales figures. Not a mega-hit series, but the first dozen issues have a certain charm.~HS

SLEEZE BROTHERS
Epic: *6 issues 1989–1990, 1 Special 1991*

The Blues Brothers are alive... and living in the future! With the music forgotten, the two stars are recast as penniless detectives causing disarray in the course of their inept investigations. Creators John Carnell and Andy Lanning bring a fine sense of slapstick humour to the title, but unfortunately repetition set in like rot and diluted the concept, which only just survived the published run. The highlight was the second issue's plot concerning virtual-

reality television. In this story the brothers are forced to become the stars of everything from *Tom and Jerry* to *Aliens*, hilarious.~SS
Collection: The Sleeze Brothers (1–6)

SLIDERS
Acclaim: *7 issues +, 1 Special 1996 to date*
This enjoyable series, based on the TV show in which three scientists and an R&B singer are flung from one dimension to another, through contemporary but differently distorted Earths, comes in three-issues-per-story chunks and in one-off specials. D.G. Chichester's scripts capture the flavour of the programme and the clear art by Dennis Calero, Kevin Kobasic and Val Mayerik makes it an easy read. The comics are able to cover subjects too expensive or risqué for television. The exciting *Sliders Special 1*, written by Jerry O'Connell, who plays Quinn Mallory, the show's youthful genius, is set on an Earth where the US government encourages citizens to take drugs.~GK

SLOW DEATH
Last Gasp: *11 issues 1970–1992*
Unlike most underground titles of the period, *Slow Death* has stories which are mostly grim or blackly humorous. Although the early creative line-up boasts Jaxon, Sheridan, Corben and Irons it's all rather primitive, derivative stuff. By issue 8, a Greenpeace special, the series had turned into a political and satirical title. The covers, by William Stout and Rand Holmes, encapsulate the militancy of the book's stance. Subsequent issues continued to mix didactic stories, documentary-style strips and inform-ation pages. Atomic power was the theme for 9, while 10 and 11 were cheery compilations of info on cancer and energy respectively. In 10 and 11 there's particularly good work from the late Greg Irons, one of the few creators who worked consistently on the title, including a *Donald Duck* strip based on the Kurtzman/ Elder Disney parody (from *Mad Magazine*). Otherwise most of the work in the later issues rarely rises above the preachiness of the scripts. The exceptions to this are Guy Colwell's 'Herpes Is A Virus' in 10 (don't read it if you're squeamish) and Alan Moore and Bryan Talbot's 'Cold Snap', reprinted in 11 from *Food For Thought*.~NF
Recommended: 8, 10

SLUDGE
Malibu: *13 issues, 1 special 1993–1994*
Despite occasional flashes of inspiration, *Sludge* isn't a patch on *Man-Thing*, Steve Gerber's previous series about a muck monster. In this one, corrupt copper Frank Hoag is transformed into a mass of gray gloop after his dying body interacts with a DNA-transforming chemical. Hoag retreats to the New York sewers, where he

either battles a series of bizarre mobsters (including the mysterious Lord Pumpkin), sits around working out ways to commit suicide or else talks to himself in irritating spoonerisms. Pedestrian artwork from Aaron Lopresti and Rob Phipps fails to enliven Gerber's dis-appointingly aimless story-line.~AL

Knight's SLUG'N'GINGER
Eros: *1 issue 1991*
Anthropomorphic sex comic by Milton Knight. Great cartooning, but feeble gags.~WJ

SLUTBURGER
Drawn & Quarterly: *6 issues 1993–1996*
Most of Mary Fleener's autobiographical strips revolve around music in some way, especially her adventures as a bass player over the years. She's a sharp, funny woman and her observations are diverting if not earth-shattering. Unlike many other female cartoonists her style is very polished, mixing in Cubism at every possibility. When people get stoned they start looking like black and white versions of Picasso paintings. When they get angry they start looking like Picasso paintings. And sometimes it's just because. This is a not entirely successful technique because Cubism is about more than drawing boxes, and the better strips are the short, surreal ones drawn entirely in a simplified style.~FJ

SMOOT
Fantagraphics: *1 issue 1995*
Skip Williamson's Snappy Sammy Smoot was a staple of late 1960s and early 1970s underground comics. He's an innocent who's that vital tinnie short of the barbie and used by Williamson as an obtuse commentator on all around him. This collection mixes one new strip with material culled over twenty years, some not previously seen in comics. As social commentary Smoot and his counterpart, the right-wing Radical Billy, are hardly subtle vehicles. While they raise a wry grin in small doses when they're part of anthologies, they haven't enough depth to sustain a solo run, so this only comes recommended to completists.~WJ

SNAKE EYES
Fantagraphics: *3 issues 1990–1993*
A short-lived attempt to find a successor to *Raw* and *Weirdo*, *Snake Eyes* maintained a feel for the underground while looking forward with a host of new talents. The best contributions to the first issue include David Mazzucchelli's inside-front-cover illo, Bob Sikoryak's 'Action Camus' (a series of redrawn covers from *Action Comics*), Chris Ware's short Clyde The Rat and Quimby Mouse strips, Julie Doucet's 'Alcoholic Romance', an untitled

two-pager by Alex Ross and 'Pixie Meat' by Tom De Haven, Gary Panter and Charles Burns. Glenn Head edited the first issue solo, but contributor Kaz co-edits 2 and 3, which are similarly varied issues featuring many of the same creators. Kaz's extended 'Sidetrack City' episode in 2 is a highlight but overall there's a feeling that all the energy went into issue 1. *Snake Eyes* attempts to experiment with the comic's page, using fold-outs and strange panel shapes, but only Ware really succeeds. If you like the creators, *Snake Eyes* will offer you solid examples of their work.~NF

SNARF
Kitchen Sink: *15 issues 1972–1981 (1–9), 1987–1990 (10–15)*
This underground anthology was initially a rather tepid collection of counterculture humour and knockabout funny-animal strips enlivened only by the beautiful art of publisher Denis Kitchen. 4, however, featured a short strip from Howard Cruse, who, from 5–9, would dominate the comic, growing in stature and sophistication from issue to issue. Other top-flight contributors attracted to the revitalised title included Justin Green (6–8) and Kim Deitch (7–9), although lesser-known talents like Robert Armstrong (6), Steve Stiles and Sharon Rudahl all contributed work of note.

Snarf's second run drew upon a different generation of cartoonists for its material, though again Howard Cruse weighed in with several superb strips in 10–12. To its credit, the comic admirably promoted then unknown creators like Chester Brown (10), Dennis Worden (11, 12) and Mary Fleener (10), along with the still undeservedly obscure Mark Landman (11, 12, 14, 15). Established cartoonists Rand Holmes (11) and Foolbert Sturgeon (12–14) also contributed fine work, but the real star of the comic was Joe Matt. Matt's hilarious, if tortured, autobiographical strips appeared in *Snarf*'s last five issues and still make riveting reading today. Some issues are inevitably a bit patchy, but there's at least some quality entertainment in every one.~DAR
Recommended: 6–8, 10–15
Collection: Peep Show (Joe Matt strips from 10–15)

SNOOKY FUDGE
Threshold: *One-shot 1993*
A compilation of newspaper-style strips by cartoonist Dave King. *Snooky Fudge* stars Hoo Hoo, the stupidest boy in the world, and his painfully intelligent cat Spap. The cat's disdainful thought balloons explain Hoo Hoo's mistaking of a cooker for a time-machine, for example ('Ouch! history hot!') and his scatological sense of humour. Very funny.~SW

SOJOURN
White Cliffs: *2 issues 1977*
Sojourn was an enormous tabloid-sized publication that featured a number of fine serials in three-page instalments, rather in the manner of British weekly comics. Publisher Joe Kubert revived his caveman feature Tor, and other contributors included Doug Wildey, Sergio Aragonés, Lee Elias and John Severin. The material was uniformly fine, but the format was obviously too different for readers of the time. While the bulk of the stories remained frustratingly unfinished, the Elias and Severin strips, respectively 'Kronos' and 'Eagle', were reprinted and concluded in Warren's *Rook*.~DAR
Recommended: 1, 2

SOLAR, MAN OF THE ATOM
Valiant: *60 issues, 1991–1996*
In the 1960s Gold Key published a comic called *Doctor Solar, Man of the Atom* about a physicist who was exposed to strange radiation and acquired powers over molecular structure along with a skintight red suit. It was all good clean fun. The Valiant story is rather more complicated. The protagonist is Doctor Philip Seleski, designer of a nuclear reactor about to start operating. A fault develops and in coming to the rescue, Seleski is exposed to radiation and develops powers over energy. As his abilities increase to god-like levels and he becomes distanced from humans, he makes an error of judgement that wipes out the planet. These are the events that take place in Timeline A, recounted in a gripping, vivid insert story called 'Alpha and Omega' in 1–10, written by Jim Shooter with artwork by Barry Windsor-Smith and Bob Layton.

Seleski survives the events in Timeline A and travels back in time to try to stop any of it happening. The events in the main comic, written by Jim Shooter and pencilled by Don Perlin, start with his arrival in Timeline B some time before the accident with the reactor. Soon after arrival he turns into Doctor Solar – or into his own idealised version of his hero from his favourite childhood comic – and he later switches between Seleski and Solar as appropriate. There's more to it than that, but strict accuracy would give too much away. However, no sooner is Timeline B saved from his error of judgement than he discovers that Earth is under threat from alien spiders. He leaves Earth for a year to fight them in space, then returns and attempts to live a normal life as a physicist. That pretty much exhausts the initial supply of plot, and from 16 onwards, with Jim Shooter gone, it's like almost any other superhero comic, shambling from issue to issue. Somehow, though, it keeps you turning the pages, even after the third crossover with other Valiant titles, where the final episode occurs in the other title, and ever after the seven-millionth (or so it seems) reappearance of the alien spiders. Why does it still work, at any level? It's probably the soap-opera aspects – will he and his girl-friend stay together? how will they get on in their new jobs? – and the fact that his power remains unsettling and distancing. The stories never follow through on any of the ideas, but at least the ideas are there.~FC

Recommended: 1–10

Collections: Alpha And Omega (Inserts from 1–10), *Solar, Man Of The Atom* (1–4)

SOLARMAN
Marvel: *2 issues 1990*

Light-hearted comics the way they used to be, written by Stan Lee the way they used to be. A flying hero whose power cuts out when clouds obscure the sun: it's as well he's located in California, not Washington State.~FP

SOLITAIRE
Malibu: *12 issues 1993–1994*

After failing to commit suicide, Nicholas Lone, son of evil businessman Anton Lone, is brought back to life with his father's nanotech engineering, microcomputers that 'rebuild and replace traumatized tissue'. Assuming the identity of Solitaire, a martial-arts expert able to survive shotgun blasts, Nicholas attempts to bring down Anton's corrupt empire. A late addition to the Ultraverse group of titles, *Solitaire* benefits from strong artwork by Jeffs Johnson and Parker. Writer Gerard Jones tries to spice things up with oddball villains (The Degenerate, Double Edge) and some purple prose. No amount of fancy rendering or garish computer colour, however, can disguise the fact that this is an extremely ordinary vigilante series. Nothing much is made of the potentially interesting father-and-son conflict, while towards the end the comic becomes unexpectedly hostile towards women.~AL

The Green Hornet SOLITARY SENTINEL
Now: *3-issue miniseries 1992–1993*

The 1990s Green Hornet combats City Hall corruption while all his allies are out of action. But wait, who's this mysterious Black Hornet fellow? There's a decent plot that isn't entirely diluted by slapdash artwork, although there's seemingly no reason it couldn't have been part of the regular series.~WJ

SOLO
Marvel: *4-issue miniseries 1994*

Described as a one-man anti-terrorist strike-force, Solo is heavily armed, has teleporting capabilities, and, for those that care, his past

unravels here. The early appearance of the acronymical A.R.E.S. (Assassination, Revolution, Extortion and Sabotage) organisation warns that intelligence and originality are going to be at a premium, and so it proves. As if in implicit acknowledgement of Solo being a poor premise and of poor quality, Spider-Man is an equal participant throughout.~FP

SOLO AVENGERS Starring HAWKEYE
Marvel: *20 issues 1987–1989*

Hawkeye's miniseries had proved him popular enough for a solo run, but for that extra oomph Marvel decided a title might sell better if a strip featuring another of the Avengers ran as a back-up. Since almost everyone not affiliated to the X-Men and Fantastic Four (and some who are) have been Avengers at one time or another, there's plenty of scope. The first issue sets the tone for this schizophrenic title, featuring some of Jim Lee's earliest Marvel art, inked by Al Williamson, on the Mockingbird back-up, and having Hawkeye fight a bunch of clowns at the circus in the lead. It's an introduction to his real origin and sequel thereto in 2–5, rectifying a twenty-year-old continuity conundrum that had Hawkeye brought up in a carnival and taught archery by the Swordsman.

Under Tom DeFalco and Mark Bright in 1–12 the Hawkeye feature is a decent, undemanding superhero strip. He fights villains, he cracks jokes, and he gets duffed up by the wife. The plots aren't spectacular, but there's more packed into ten pages than most of the back-ups can provide. 8 is a decent sample, with the introduction of a vigilante named Blind Justice. DeFalco loses the plot somewhat from 14, with a particularly stupid A.I.M. appearance in 16, but after he leaves things become rapidly worse.

While there's an ongoing continuity to the Hawkeye feature, the other ten pages are all one-shot stories, and a largely uninspirational bunch at that. It's the female characters who come in for the best treatment, with John Ridgway drawing a nice Scarlet Witch in places (5), in a silly tale returning Jon Kowalski from *War Is Hell*. Bob Layton produces a touching Black Widow story in 7, J.M. DeMatteis and June Brigman deliver the best back-up of the run, featuring Hellcat, in 9, and there's a fun Chris Claremont and Alan Davis She-Hulk in 14. That's under a stunning Sandy Plunkett cover, and Plunkett, with Scott Hampton, provides a Black Panther story in 19 that, while not entirely successful, is at least well considered and drawn. The other decent male solo outing is the Hercules effort (again by Layton) in 12. There's a break with formula in 16, 18 and 20, which have a continuing story returning Moondragon, but it's poor. And that's the problem with *Solo Avengers* throughout. Not stopping to consider that declining sales might equate with using the comic as a try-out title for substandard creators, the publishers deemed that the title might be the problem, so it became *Avengers Spotlight* with 21.~WJ

The Sword of SOLOMON KANE
Marvel: *6 issues 1985–1986*

Ralph Macchio's writing isn't particularly stupid, but it is in no way outstanding. Unless one's just read it, one generally has a problem recalling a single moment from one of his comics. Go on, give it try. There's never the nice crafting of a line, a clever plot twist, or even an anachronistic curse to stick in the memory. And *The Sword of Solomon Kane* is no exception. Robert E. Howard's globe-trotting Puritan is Marvel's least favourite Howard character because although he can protect the odd quavering maiden he can't rip her top off. Here he hunts an evil bandit from rural France to Africa, pops back for some werewolf action, has an Arabian nightmare (nicely drawn by Mike Mignola) in 4, and finishes up in Africa again for the series' unexciting conclusion.~FJ

SOLSTICE
Watermark: *2 issues 1995*

Russell Waterhouse is a man possessed by the idea of attaining eternal life, and follows any leads to the legendary fountain of youth, accompanied by his son Hugh, about whom he's particularly scathing. Riddled with cancer, Russell plans a final expedition to Chile, and it costs him his life. *Solstice* is Hugh's story, yet despite dying on the second page of the first issue Russell looms over the story, as Hugh recalls incidents from his past. Russell is brutal, arrogant and single-minded, dominating his son and inculcating feelings of inferiority. He's the equal of any costumed villain to be found in comics – a masterful creation from writer Stephen Seagle. The Grail aspect of the story is secondary to Hugh's development, free of his father and able to become master of his own destiny, yet there's enough incident and horror to ensure a compelling read. Justin Norman's art is oddly misproportioned and static, yet conveys the necessary emotion when called upon to do so. The third and concluding issue never appeared, but should the planned collected edition ever be published *Solstice* ought to be a compulsory purchase for anyone interested in adult comics.~FP
Recommended: 1, 2

THE SOLUTION
Malibu: *18 issues (0–17), 1993–1995*

The scripts for this were seemingly phoned in by James Hudnall to be drawn by such second-rate pencillers as Darick Robertson (1–4) and John

Statema (most issues thereafter until the series finally ground to a halt). Part of the Ultraverse, The Solution are a by-the-numbers superteam who undertake covert operations against all kinds of villainy. Their chief enemies are the evil Dragon Fang, the world's largest Triad, who have taken over the company that once belonged to Lela Cho, aka Tech, leader of The Solution. Most of the background to this dull feud is explained in 6, but only partially resolved by 17, making *The Solution* a painfully protracted read. If you do want to sample, 6 is the best place, detailing the origin of Tech. She pays $5 million for implanted enhancements which enable her to control electronic machinery, and discovers hitherto unrevealed unarmed-combat expertise when faced with a room full of gangsters. Yes, it's all that good.~AL

SOMERSET HOLMES
Pacific: *4 issues 1983–1984*
Eclipse: *2 issues (5–6) 1984*

Psychological thriller with more twists and turns than a rollercoaster, and a similar idea of pacing, co-plotted by Bruce Jones and April Campbell and gorgeously illustrated by Brent Anderson. A woman comes to on a quiet country road after a hit-and-run accident, unable to remember how she got there or who she is. Her only clue is the label sewn into her skirt, and a key. All she knows is that people keep trying to capture or kill her, and very few of those who befriend her can be trusted. Jones and Campbell unfold shock after shock – a real Hitchcockian puzzler. All six issues feature a Cliff Hanger back-up (by Jones alone). The plots, in homage to Republic-style serials, may be hoary but Al Williamson's artwork is excellent. The man was born to draw lean heroes, gutsy lady explorers and evil Nazis in lush jungle settings.~FJ
Recommended: 1–6
Collection: Somerset Holmes (1–6)

SON OF MUTANT WORLD
Fantagor: *5-issue miniseries 1990*

Originally in colour (1, 2) but forced into black and white for financial reasons, Jan Strnad and Richard Corben's sequel to *Mutant World* is much what you would expect: one girl and her grizzly bear, a man in a balloon with a bird, a father and son looking for food and a band of mutants out to destroy what little there is left of civilisation. It's good fun, told firmly tongue-in-cheek, but Corben's artwork suffers in 3–5, since it was clearly meant to be in colour and the printing is too dark or too light, obscuring the quality of line and removing much of the detail. There's a Bruce Jones back-up strip in each issue, the first four of which tell EC-style tales from a woman's perspective. Miscellaneous other Corben material fills out the rest of each issue.~NF

SON OF SATAN
Marvel: *8 issues 1975–1977*

Popular enough to graduate from *Marvel Spotlight* into his own series, the Son of Satan (honestly) was a curious fusion of superhero and horror elements that never quite mesh. He was later given some real wallop as *Hellstorm*.~WJ

SON OF VULCAN
Charlton: *2 issues (49, 50) 1965–1966*

Johnny Mann, reporter, is speaking aloud while contemplating a classical ruin on 'Cyprete': 'You, the gods of ancient Olympus – why do you permit man to wage stupid wars?' The gods are angry at being blamed for human faults, and transport him to their Council Hall for judgement. He stands up for himself, and Vulcan takes his side, and they end up giving him armour, superpowers, and a mission in the war against evil. It's an original start, but thereafter he behaves like any other superhero, and the only evil he seems to find is Dr Kong, the Meanest Man Alive (a Fu Manchu figure). On this level it's good, clean fun, with above-average humour and imagination. The series starts with 49, inheriting the numbering from *Mysteries Of Unexplored Worlds*, and that issue is the comics writing début of Roy Thomas.~FC

SONIC DISRUPTORS
DC: *7 issues 1988*

Destined to be a cult, but instead fizzled out. This concerns a future where rock music is banned in a puritan USA, and where musicians set up their own countries (the Republic of Rock); there are also orbiting radio stations, an Elvis Presley lookalike and a DJ called Sheik Rattle Enroll (you have to laugh). Plenty more interesting characters, both good and bad, come together for a convoluted plot. Just when things are starting to get interesting, the plug was pulled. Originally planned as a twelve-issue limited series, *Sonic Disruptors* was cancelled for 'production reasons'. Bit of a shame, really. Suggested for mature readers: sex, drugs and rock 'n' roll come to comics. Well, actually not much sex. Never mind, though, because this quirky series, written by Mike Baron and illustrated by Barry Crain and John Nyberg, still deserves some attention.~HY

Chilling Adventures In SORCERY
Red Circle: *5 issues 1972–1974*

After two issues bizarrely illustrated in the Archie house style this horror title featured some well drawn if overly wordy stories before changing title to *Red Circle Sorcery* with 6. Gray Morrow edited, wrote and drew all of issue 3, producing some of his finest work in the process. Morrow was also present in the final two issues, but they

were dominated by the excellent Vincente Alcazar, who brought a moody sophistication to the title. Dick Giordano's characteristically fine work in 4 only adds to a delightful package that comes highly recommended.~DAR
Recommended: 3–5

Red Circle SORCERY
Red Circle: *6 issues (6–11) 1974–1975*

Previously *Chilling Adventures In Sorcery*, this comic also contained a succession of beautifully drawn, if sometimes overwritten, short mystery tales. Editor Gray Morrow had art in almost every issue, as did the talented Spanish artists Vincente Alcazar and Carlos Pino. Other talents included Howard Chaykin (6, 10), Frank Thorne (8, 10) and the little-known Ed Davis in 8. 7's 'The Rival' was a nice prohibition-era story enlivened by Bruce Jones' art, in which he was aided by friends Berni Wrighton, Mike Kaluta and Jeff Jones. Alex Toth drew a story for 8, and 9's 'If I Were King' was a typically quirky role-reversal story, written by Marv Channing, and was the highpoint of the run. The mysterious Channing (possibly Morrow's pseudonym) wrote most of the stories, although there were contributions from Steve Skeates and Don Glut. This was never particularly challenging, or frightening, but the art elevates it beyond just a good read.~DAR
Recommended: 6–11

SOULSEARCHERS AND COMPANY
Claypool: *25 issues + 1993 to date*

In the sleepy Connecticut town of Mystic Grove a band of fearless supernatural investigators has arisen to do battle with lurking eldritch menaces. This courageous team consists of a failed Olympic athlete with an enchanted vaulting pole, a horny Arabic fire demon, a flaky teenage apprentice witch, a monstrously shapeshifting gypsy youth, an accountant with a bottomless carpet bag, and the firm's proprietor, currently a rodent, due to complications from a previous case. As you may have gathered, *Soulsearchers* isn't an entirely straight-faced series. Peter David's scripts, at least for the first ten issues, were both witty and articulate, and artists Amanda Conner and Jim Mooney perfectly complementary. Mooney's inks add depth to Conner's work while losing none of her trademark expression and vitality. Sadly, after 10 the title lost focus. Conner left and David seemed to flounder, going for cheap and easy parody rather than the charismatic blend of character-driven stories and atrocious puns that had graced the book. Things began to pick up when Dave Cockrum joined as regular penciller, and the outstanding 17 put it right back on top form with a genuinely shocking revelation for one of the team.~HS

Recommended: 1–10, 17
Collection: On The Case (1–6)

SOUTHERN KNIGHTS
Guild: *7 issues 1983–1985*
Comics Interview: *25 issues (8–33) 1985–1988*

Known for the first issue only as *The Crusaders*, Henry and Audrey Vogel's quartet of unlikely superbeings was slammed with a lawsuit from Archie, who had just revived their superheroic *Mighty Crusaders*. With Ms Vogel departing early on, Vogel retitled his comic more inventively *Southern Knights*, and wrote an amusing riposte to the lawsuit in 26, once *The Mighty Crusaders* had again ceased publication. Electrode (master of electricity), Dragon (a were-dragon who occasionally becomes human), Connie (wielder of a psychic sword) and Kristin, the strongest teenybopper in the world, had low-key but likeable adventures. Often the concerns were domestic rather than heroic, and the team would frequently explore and investigate, solving puzzles and mysteries rather than being content to break heads, though that they could do perfectly adequately. Beyond the core team there are odd supporting characters, such as a 17th-century teenage sorcerer attempting to adapt to life in the 1980s. There's a commendable variety to the stories, with Vogel throwing in other-dimensional fantasies, Cold War spy tales, straight superhero battles, aliens and parodies of how other companies would handle his heroes. Founding artist Jackson (then Butch) Guice left the series shortly after its début, leaving Henry to provide entertaining scripts with a variety of artists. The longest running was Mark Lamport, from 19 to the conclusion, but Chuck Wojtkiewicz (5–11, 26) and Mark Propst (12–18) also provided artwork very much in tune with the writing.~HS
Collections: Southern Knights vol 1 (1–4), vol 2 (5–8)

SOUTHERN SQUADRON
Aircel: *4-issue miniseries 1990*

Claimed to have outsold the *X-Men* in their original Australian incarnation, the Southern Squadron are a witty and irreverent superteam containing the ghastly, definitely non-PC Nightfighter. The first issue is little more than a set-up and elongated fight scene, albeit one with quite a few jokes, but beyond that writer David DeVries manages to turn in off-beat and unpredictable stories every time, and artists Glenn Lumsden and Gary Chaloner (with Paul Gulacy in 3) look to be enjoying the material as well. It's a great shame their American début was a small-circulation title, although one highly praised in introductions by pros in the know, and these are worth searching out.~WJ

Recommended: 2–4

SOVEREIGN SEVEN
DC: *17 issues +, 2 Annuals 1995–1997*

Chris Claremont made a quick return to superteams after leaving the *X-Men*. It's difficult not to draw comparisons when all the successful ingredients of that title have been transferred to this series. There's a group of disparate characters, thrown together for a common cause, with flashy powers and codenames (Cascade, Cruiser, Reflex, Indigo, Rampart, Network and Finale), lots of *angst* and self-doubt, aggressive attitudes, wicked parents and dark secrets. And, of course, every member of S7 has a tale to tell. The seven are refugees from a disaster that destroyed the societies of their home worlds, and the first issue firmly melds the series with DC's characters, as our feisty royals arrive from another dimension straight into a conflict with Darkseid's Female Furies. The S7 set up home in a bar in a strange place called Crossroads, which is a hive of interdimensional activity, and there's much amusement from the owners, two great female characters that steal many a scene.

It's a hectic and traumatic life for our displaced heroes, as one is possessed by a Greek god and becomes evil and they confront a superpowered serial killer, an international paramilitary organisation, and lots of villains such as Dystopia and Triage. The action never lets up, and the mix of Claremont's scripts and the dynamic art of co-creator Dwayne Turner makes for an appealing superhero package every month. Being a relatively new series, there's not years of back continuity to clog things up. More recent issues have just been titled *S7*, and there have been two annuals. The first is more entertaining as it guest-stars Lobo, and Big Barda of the New Gods.~HY

SOVIET SUPER SOLDIERS
Marvel: *One-shot 1992*

Here we have almost every one of Marvel's Soviet superpowered characters, with the notable exception of the Black Widow, who presumably had more sense than to involve herself. Assorted factions of Soviet superheroes bring their dispute to New York, while the Soviet mutants just want to be left in peace. This doesn't appear to be an option, as a baldy man with a big gun and cybernetic eye is killing them one by one. Curiously incomplete at the finish, this reads like a miniseries contracted to fill a one-shot. Don't bother unless Marvel's Soviet characters really push your buttons.~FP

SPACE: Above And Beyond
Topps: *3-issue miniseries 1996*

Well above average adaptation of the TV show pilot episode. The 21st-century equivalent of the Marines have to protect a planet colonised by Earth, but now under attack, and events develop from there. Roy Thomas has a good script to work with, and the art team of Yanick Paquette and Armando Gil convey a humanity whether dealing with battles or quieter moments.~WJ

SPACE ADVENTURES
Charlton: *Series one 60 issues 1952–1964 (1–59), 1967 (60), series two 13 issues 1968–1969 (1–8), 1978–1979 (9–13)*

Charlton's premier science-fiction anthology featured the first adventures of Steve Ditko's Captain Atom in 33–42. The stories ran five to seven pages, and all but the first were scripted by Joe Gill, with Pat Masulli scripting the Captain's origin. The forgettable Mercury Man, a benign alien made of mercury, appeared in 44–45, and the title was revived for a single issue in 1967, with *UFO* as the cover title and an excellent internal strip. 1968's revived *Space Adventures* featured the work of Charlton's late-1960s stable of artists such as Jim Aparo, Pat Boyette and Ditko, and they easily surpass the quality of the previous run. *UFO* returns in 1, starring Paul Mann and the saucers from the future, a little-known masterpiece. The late 1970s revival reprints Captain Atom stories from the first run.~SW

Recommended: Series one 60, series two 1, 9–13

SPACE FAMILY ROBINSON
Gold Key: *36 issues 1962–1969*

The comic, loosely based on the film *Lost In Space*, was retitled to capitalise on the successful TV series from 37, although the stories remain unrelated. This features the interplanetary escapades of the Robinson family – June and Craig (Mom and Dad), Tim, Tam and the pets – in their space-station home. Some imaginative plotting and reliable artwork from Dan Spiegle make most issues readable, but much of a muchness.~SW

SPACE GHOST
Comico: *1 issue 1987*

Space Ghost is a costumed hero in outer space. He was first seen in 1966, in a Saturday morning cartoon, which was one of the first to allow superhero cartoons to take their action seriously, rather than playing mainly for laughs. Steve Rude's artwork is very clean and dynamic, certainly captures the feel of a well-crafted cartoon, and is worth the price alone. Unfortunately the story starts to sprawl quite early on, and in a way that makes the action in the main fight sequence seem almost random. A shame, since the art is so good it could have been a gem.~FC

Recommended

SPACE MAN
Dell: *8 issues 1962–1964*
Gold Key: *2 issues (9–10) 1972*

Drawn by Jack Sparling with his left hand while piloting a bob-sled, the first issue of this now dated space-exploration series bears the cover blurb 'Man has broken the ties of Earth and is about to conquer space'. These days 'about' isn't good enough, although writer Ken Fitch's use of cyborgs must count as a comics first. 9 and 10 reprinted the first two issues.~SW

SPACE 1999
Charlton: *7 issues 1975–1976*

This followed the pattern of the TV series, with a new planet and a company in danger every issue, and was therefore somewhat predictable. Characterisation was sketchy, but most of the stories managed to catch the spirit of the TV show, particularly the John Byrne issues from 3. The companion black and white magazine title was exceedingly average.~DWC

SPACE USAGI
Mirage: *3-issue miniseries 1992, 3-issue miniseries 1993–1994*
Dark Horse: *3-issue miniseries 1996*

Though, as the title suggests, this is little more in some respects than *Usagi Yojimbo* in space, Stan Sakai's anthropomorphic Japanese characters translate easily into science fiction. Rather than a ronin, Space Usagi is a loyal bodyguard to Prince Kiyoshi, heir and then Lord of the Shirohoshi Clan, which is under attack by the Kajitori Empire. The first miniseries tells the story of the betrayal of the Shirohoshi by Matabe and his attempt to learn the clan secrets from Kiyoshi. The second, in colour, continues the story and sees Usagi and his friends, Tomoeh and Rhogen, break into the Shirohoshi castle, now in enemy hands, to prevent the Kajitori from gaining the clan's secrets from its computers. Sakai makes more of future technology than in the first series, with heat-seeking shuriken, robot dinosaurs and ninjas with mind probes and invisibility cloaks. The Dark Horse series sees Kiyoshi kidnapped in a race to retrieve the Shirohoshi treasures, the introduction of Kiyoshi's uncle and some very dangerous shapeshifters. Sakai's distinctive artwork owes much to Japanese comics and Moebius, but that's no bad thing and his characters and story-telling are compelling if a little naïve.~NF

SPACE WAR
Charlton: *34 issues 1959–1965*
Period science-fiction nonsense, with three or
four stories in each issue. The stories are
preposterous and the art unremarkable, but
most issues will provide a few chuckles, either
with bizarre origin stories for the moon (8), or
that old teeny-weeny invaders story (9), or giant
snails from Uranus (13), or a meteor-munching
space serpent (16). Issue 5 stands out, having
one story that seems intentionally funny,
'Objective Moon', and another with truly stylish
Ditko artwork, 'Exiled to Earth'.~FC
Recommended: 5

SPACEHAWK
Dark Horse: *4 issues 1992*
Spacehawk seems to equate Earth with America
and Uncle Sam when he's talking of his role as a
defender of the Solar System, but he's incredibly
strong and long-lived (in 4 he meets an old friend
after 600 years), and he does spend a lot of time
battling space pirates and preventing war on
various planets. By the end of the series he's even
got a girl-friend from Neptune (well, almost).
This reprint of Basil Wolverton's wonderfully
detailed but simplistic strip is a delight, full of
beautiful women, grotesque creatures and alien
landscapes.~NF
Recommended: 1–4

SPANNER'S GALAXY
DC: *6-issue miniseries 1984–1985*
Nicola Cuti, creator of the faddish 1970s
Charlton superhero *E-Man*, also overwrote this
tedious space opera, stuffed full of laughably
cosmic dialogue like 'Daddy, can I have a Droog
for a honey-pie?' On the run from the Space
Authorities, lead character Polaris Spanner
hops through the galaxy thanks to his ability to
'castle', which is matter transportation to you
and me. He also has a magic sword called a
Shek, a furry alien pal who speaks in a Southern
accent, and a sexy friend called Andromeda
Jones. Ugly artwork courtesy of Tom Mandrake
rounds off a miniseries best left to moulder in
every dealer's bargain box.~AL

SPARTAN: WARRIOR SPIRIT
Image: *4-issue miniseries 1995*
The WildC.A.T.S android leader wakes up to
find himself confronted by Dr Able, a scientist
who claims that Spartan is Zachary Kreiger,
imprinted with the memories of his dead son-
in-law. Before he has a chance to argue, Spartan
is under attack and lost in the battles he was
programmed to fight, with little time to reflect
on the memories Able and his daughter claim
he should have. Although he doesn't believe
what they tell him – that he's needed to
safeguard a remote Tibetan monastery, in which
his 'father-in-law' is conducting experiments,

from marauding Daemonites – he does what's
needed until the reasons behind the deceptions
become clear. Spartan doesn't have the history
on which writer Kurt Busiek usually hangs his
limited creativity, leaving a story which is
largely dull and not really worth the effort.~JC.

SPASM
Last Gasp: *1 issue 1973*
A collection of short pieces by Jeff Jones. A few
of them are horror stories and rather effective,
but most are pretentious or pointless or
documentation of Jones' sexual fantasies – and
some are all three. Worth a skim if it falls into
your lap, but worth searching out? Goodness,
no.~FC

SPAWN
Image: *53 issues + 1992 to date*
Always a dynamic and popular artist, Todd
McFarlane amazed everyone by creating a
character who was interesting and stories that
were readable. Al Simmons, after his
untimely death, signs a contract with the
Devil allowing him to return to his wife.
Naturally enough, Al is tricked by the Devil
and is forced to become his servant, so the
comic follows his battle to escape his new
circumstances and his life on Earth.
Early highlights are 2, which introduces the
Violator, who will become Spawn's arch-
nemesis (and returns in 14 and 15), and 5,
which tells the harrowing tale of a child
murderer and the way Spawn chooses to deal
with him. As part of Todd McFarlane's bid to
avoid the cheap gimmicks employed by other
Image titles, and as a response to comments
about his writing (which was actually
improving all the time), he enlisted the writing
talents of some of the best in the industry. Alan
Moore writes 8, while Neil Gaiman introduces
the popular Spawn hunter Angela in 9. The
best issue of the run is Dave Sim's brilliant 10,
guest-starring Sim's character Cerebus in a
well-conceived satire on the comics industry:
it's immensely funny. The Violator's return in
14–15 is fantastically over-the-top and very
entertaining. McFarlane stopped pencilling the
title after 26, but instead of bringing his own
style to *Spawn* new penciller Greg Capullo
delivers a diluted version of McFarlane's art.
Unfortunately, *Spawn* began to become stale
at issue 20, and far too many of the following
issues show Spawn moping about bemoaning
his being tricked by the Devil. 30–31 introduce
an anti-Spawn created by angels called the
Redeemer, a new recurring nemesis for Spawn.
This is good news, because once Spawn has
dealt with someone they remain dealt with, so
there are very few villains who ever reappear.
44 introduced Tiffany, who is another Spawn
hunter similar to the earlier Angela. Spawn

confronts the Devil in issue 50, which wraps up some of the earlier plot threads but fails to give a desperately needed new direction. *Spawn* is currently beginning to rest on its laurels.~SS
Recommended: 5, 10
Collection: Spawn (1–6)

SPAWN: BLOODFEUD
Image: *4-issue miniseries 1995*

In remarkably restrained fashion, this was the first spin-off from Image's top-selling title. Unfortunately, it was hardly worth the bother. It's a simple story about Spawn battling a group of Vampires in New York. Tony Daniels' art is good quality if very much in Todd McFarlane's style, but the real shame is writer Alan Moore, who fails to live up to the standard he set when he wrote *Spawn 8*.~SS

SPECIAL HUGGING
Slave Labor: *One-shot 1989*

A collection of stories about childhood, from various creators and with various themes: the near-impossibility of getting a sensible explanation of puberty and sex; the dilemma of how to act when you see someone mistreating their children; and memorable moments from a happy childhood. It sounds fairly promising but none of it really rings true, and you put the comic down wondering why they bothered.~FC

SPECIAL MARVEL EDITION
Marvel: *16 issues 1971–1974*

This started as a reprint title (Lee and Kirby's Thor in 1–4, Sgt Fury in 5–14) in which the only item of note is the début of Shang-Chi, Master of Kung-Fu, in 15. Although very different in tone from later strips, the Steve Englehart and Jim Starlin Shang-Chi stories are moody and interesting. Marvel realised they were on to a good thing, so the title became *Master of Kung-Fu* with 17.~FP

THE SPECTRE
DC: *Series one 10 issues 1967–1969, Series two 31 issues, 1 Annual 1987–1989, Series three 48 issues +, 1 Annual 1992 to date*

Introduced in the 1940s (in *More Fun* 52, reprinted in *Secret Origins* 5), and created by Jerry Siegel, the Spectre has evolved into the most powerful of DC's pantheon of super-heroes. God returns policeman Jim Corrigan to Earth after his murder, and he now hosts a ghostly *alter ego* in The Spectre. Operating as a ruthless agent of retribution and vengeful Angel of the Lord in the 1940s, he's in superhero mode to start the 1960s series, which followed try-outs in *Showcase* 60, 61 and 64. The standard DC gimmick plots of the time mean there's little of note in the early issues beyond art from a young Neal Adams in 2–5. The mid-period is more cosmic, but by the end of the series the

Spectre is little more than another horror host. When he resurfaced in *Adventure* 431, Michael Fleisher and Jim Aparo created a series of over-the-top, gruesome short strips prematurely cancelled due to their excessive violent content. Needless to say, they're great, and can be found along with stories that never saw print originally in the four issues of *Wrath Of The Spectre*.

It was twelve years before DC were confident enough to give the Spectre another solo run. This time, though, he's powered down to more human levels, and bonded with Corrigan, now a private investigator. Corrigan, returned from the dead, is not happy with his lot, and the mixture of detection and mystical menaces is an uneasy one, with each aspect intruding into the other's domain. The idea of Corrigan and the Spectre in danger of dying when separated for longer than forty-eight hours is overworked in the early issues. That's a problem solved in 19, in which writer Doug Moench has the Spectre transform from Corrigan rather than manifest from within him. 21 is as good as the run gets, with both elements investigating a death from differing angles and perspectives. An expanded cast from 20 beefs up a dull series, but not by much, and there can have been few sad to see the comic cancelled. Those few can check 7 of the next series for what became of the cast.

Given its lack-lustre predecessor, the comparatively rapid relaunch of *The Spectre* just over two years later was surprising, but it's a move that's worked, with the character currently more popular than in any previous incarnation. The startling glow-in-the-dark cover to the first issue (reprised on 8 and 13) surely enticed many people to sample it, but those responsible for the success are John Ostrander and Tom Mandrake, who've been on board since the revival. A powerful retelling of the Spectre's origin in 3 and 4 sets the tone for the series, affirming that the Spectre is the wrath of God fuelled by Corrigan, and assigning them the task of avenging the victims of murder until Corrigan comes to understand why evil exists. The Spectre is back to his nigh-omnipotent self, but Ostrander's aptitude at setting ethical dilemmas negates this at a stroke, while permitting effective and imaginative scenes of retribution. These sequences echo the vindictive Spectre of Fleisher and Aparo (who guests in the excellent 16), but constant questioning underscores the series. Mandrake's contribution is a succession of horrifically rendered nightmares blending effortlessly with modern urban settings. Mention must also be made of the startling selection of seductive covers, using a variety of top artists to produce a symbolic rendering of the Spectre, already a strikingly visual character. This series has lasted long enough for Ostrander to rectify most anomalies concerning the Spectre's history, generally in fine fashion even when dealing with the likes of his 1940s comedy-relief partner Percival Popp, Super Cop in 24. His plots remain unpredictable and don't shy from potentially uncomfortable topics such as the fragmentation of the American dream in issues from 38, and the constant questioning of celestial motivation. Continually thought-provoking, as much as anything *The Spectre* is about the many shades of grey. Best of all, though, for a title concerning the wrath of God manifested as man, there's an astounding humanity, personified by Father Cramer, introduced in *Suicide Squad*, but brought to fruition here as both conscience and adviser. Well worth sampling.~WJ

Recommended: Series three 3, 4, 6, 12, 16, 20, 23, 26–30, 38, 39

Collections: Crimes And Punishment (Series three 1–4)

SPEED RACER
Now: Series one 38 issues, 1 Annual 1987–1992, Series two 3 issues 1992

Based on a 1960s Japanese cartoon series, issue 1 answers many questions posed by regular viewers and provides an origin for Speed. Lamarr Waldron writes most issues to 30, and they're simple but well crafted, as Speed and his Mach 5 car take on other drivers in an ever-continuing circuit of races in exotic locations, having adventures wherever he goes. A good sample is 14, in which Speed's girl-friend Trixie is believed to be the reincarnation of an Egyptian princess. Later issues inject a greater dose of realism and continuity, but it's to the detriment of the strip. A darker and more violent tale occupies the second series, again at odds with the original spirit. The first issue is also available as an expanded fifth-anniversary special containing text features about Mach 5 and cover galleries.~WJ

SPEEDBALL The Masked Marvel
Marvel: *11 issues 1988–1989*

Steve Ditko returns to Marvel to create a teenage hero straight from the 1960s Marvel template – which, in essence, is the problem. Times have moved on, and despite Ditko's art topping anything else he's produced of late the entire project has a very dated feel (and a notoriously ill-advised title). The now traditional comics origin of an encounter with unknown energy bestowing powers transforms lab messenger Rob Baldwin into a costumed type able to bounce off any hard surface, an effect initially triggered by force,

and given a nifty design effect by Ditko. Speedball later frequently appeared in *Marvel Super-Heroes* and went on to join the New Warriors.~FP

SPELLBINDERS
Quality: *12 issues 1986–1987*

Initiated to showcase some of *2000AD*'s second-level strips for an American audience, it would be a quality package but for the unsympathetic application of colour. Each issue opens with Nemesis, continuing the run from the Eagle comics miniseries, with Kevin O'Neill's final story in the first issue, and the Bryan Talbot-drawn 'Gothic Empire' thereafter. It's an alien world with a society based on Edwardian Britain, but with a greater level of technology, and incorporates Hammerstein, Ro-Jaws and the ABC Warriors into the Nemesis saga for the first time. The Celtic warrior Slaine was introduced to American audiences with the first issue, and there's stunning Mike McMahon art from 4 to 9. The final strip opening the anthology was the rather dull Amadeus Wolf, fat demon-hunter, given an early departure to expand the other strips.~FP

Collections: Nemesis Book 3 (Nemesis in 1–8), Book 5 (9–12), *Slaine* Book One (Slaine in 4–9)

SPELLBOUND
Marvel: *6-issue limited series 1988*

Somewhere out there is a nasty spellbinder called Zxaxz who has two servants: Snugg, a fairy, and Snaarl, an ape. They are scared that Zxaxz is going to destroy the universe, so when they learn of another spellbinder in a different dimension, they pay a visit, attempting to recruit this spellbinder in the struggle against Zxaxz. The spellbinder is Erica Forture, an English teacher with no idea of her powers, and who overreacts at first after a lifetime of being ignored and taken for granted. It might have worked as a spin on the Cinderella theme if the writing had been better, but here it's doomed from the beginning. The writing has real problems with presenting information in a coherent way – the four pages that set the story up are impenetrable – and with making the characters believable or bearable. It does gradually improve, but the first issue is infuriating.~FC

SPELLJAMMERS
DC: *18 issues 1990–1991*

As part of the comic range created by the role-playing game company TSR, *Spelljammers* mixed a set of fantasy characters with a science-fiction plot. Barbara Kesel introduces the characters well during the first story arc, 'The Rogue Ship', and quickly creates strong links between them. Rising talent Joe Quesada takes over in issue 8 and demonstrates a real flair for action art. Towards the end of the run the stories falter and become less and less interesting.~SS

SPICY TALES

Eternity: *15 issues, 1 Special 1988–1991*

Subtitled 'A Naughty Anthology', *Spicy Tales* reprints strips that originally appeared in pulp magazines from the 1930s and 1940s. Publisher Frank Armer produced a series of disreputable pulps which dealt more blatantly with sex than was usual in that period. Alongside the prose stories they also ran two- to eight-page strips. *Spicy Detective's* Sally Sleuth's first appearance, from November 1934, is included in the first issue. She's an operative for an FBI-like organisation; her companion is a small boy called Peanuts; and she's usually rescued in the final panel by The Chief. Predictably, most of her clothes fall off in the course of these very short assignments, usually ripped off by a menacing foe. 'Dan Turner, Hollywood Detective' is more restrained sexually, but it's plenty hard-boiled, and the character's wonderfully colourful vocabulary, including neologisms like 'butched' and 'killery', is a wonder in itself. The series also includes reprints from *Spicy Western* and *Spicy Adventure*, such as 'Polly Of The Plains', which chiefly sees the naked cowgirl being tortured by Mexican bandits, and Diana Daw, globe-trotting adventuress.

Despite a predilection for bondage, torture and racism, these pre-Code stories are not entirely without merit so long as they are considered within their context. From number 9, 1950s characters Gail Ford and Roy Hale are reprinted, and the spicy nature of the strips is toned down. A *Spicy Tales Special* (1989) contains three 'Lucky Dale, Girl Detective' strips from *The Saint* and a Veiled Avenger story from *Authentic Police Cases*. Both strips' artwork is far superior to that in the ongoing title.~NF

THE SPIDER

Eclipse: *3-issue miniseries 1991, 3-issue miniseries ('Reign Of The Vampire King') 1992*

Millionaire businessman Richard Wentworth is a costumed scourge of the underworld at night, complete with gimmicks, hide-out and butler. Despite the similarities, The Spider pre-dates Batman, and the character's 1930s pulp-fiction origins are well served here. Tim Truman concocts an entertaining tale incorporating exotic cults, Nazi revivals and deadly yet glamorous women, and Alcatena's finishes add a fluidity and warmth often absent from Truman's art elsewhere. Unintentional humour is derived from The Spider's distinctive dentistry, with every tooth filed to a point,

rather a giveaway regarding his identity, you might think. Not so, as the civilian Wentworth communicates in the style of a ventriloquist, keeping his mouth tightly closed at all times. Sadly, the second series provides a prosaic explanation. Otherwise it's more of the same, this time with a supernatural feel.~ FP

SPIDER-MAN

Marvel: *75 issues +, 1 Super Special 1990 to date*

Launched in a blaze of variant cover colourings, states of baggedness and a hot creator, Marvel's astute marketing rocketed the first issue of Spider-Man's fourth concurrent regular series to the number-one-selling comic book ever to that date. Fresh from his acclaimed artistic run on *Amazing Spider-Man*, Todd McFarlane was joined by unknown, untried writer, Todd McFarlane. He was honest enough to admit in the first issue text-page that he did not profess to be a writer, and proceeded to prove it in the first fourteen issues. Lush artwork and thin stories evidence little development of McFarlane's plotting talents, and an over-use of staccato, monosyllabic scripting looks arty for half an issue and amateur over fourteen.

Déja vu struck as another hot *Amazing Spider-Man* artist, Erik Larsen, took over on plot and pencils in 18–23, with a hopelessly muddled Sinister Six story guest-starring superheroes galore who materialise and disappear without reason. It took fill-in creators Don McGregor and Marshall Rogers to produce this series' highlight: 'Something about a Gun' in 27 and 28. With research assistance from the police, this mature, heartfelt story of juvenile crime, school bullying and the danger of guns scores a perfect ten. Single-minded obsession with the major themes is avoided as original displays of Spider-Man's web tricks complement a portrayal of his heroism that has rarely been surpassed. Ann Nocenti's 'Return to the Mad Dog Ward' in 29–31 improves on the original (in *Amazing Spider-Man* 295, *Spectacular Spider-Man* 133 and *Web of Spider-Man* 33) with a sub-plot focusing on Peter's pathological lying running out of control during his never-ending quest to hide his secret identity. Mainly routine fill-ins, all of them three parts, follow to 43. Avoid 35–37, the fourteen-issue 'Maximum Carnage' fiasco of a bloodbath crossing into all the regular *Spider-Man* titles, and concentrate instead on DeMatteis' insightful Electro story in 38–40, with its amusing plot of a small-time crook who has been busted by Spider-Man countless times during his criminal career and is humiliated because the Web Man never recognises him.

Howard Mackie and Tom Lyle take charge from 44, and teasers for the 'Return Of The Clone' saga begin in 48, followed by the full event in 51–63. It crosses over into all the major Spider-Man titles and is reviewed under *Amazing*

Spider-Man. Publication halted whilst two issues of *Scarlet Spider* hit the stands, then 64 onwards concentrate on the Ben Reilly version, with John Romita Jr pencilling. Multi-part stories continue their weekly wrap around the four core Spider titles for six more months, and the clone thing still simmered until its culmination in the December 1996 cover-date titles with the double-size *Spider-Man* 75 dropping the final curtain. We can only hope.~APS

Recommended: 27, 28, 38–40

Collections: Chance Encounter (13, 14 plus *Amazing Spider-Man* 298, 299), *Masques* (6, 7), *Perceptions* (8–12), *Revenge Of The Sinister Six* (18–23), *Torment* (1–5)

Amazing SPIDER-MAN

Marvel: *418 issues +, 29 Annuals, 6 Giant-Size, 1 Super Special, 1963 to date*

'Bitten by a radioactive spider, student Peter Parker gained the proportionate strength and agility of an arachnid.' Thus has Stan Lee presented hundreds of issues of Marvel's flagship solo character. Response to Spider-Man's intended one-shot appearance in the dying issue of *Amazing Fantasy* was so favourable that his own series followed seven months later. By today's standards, all early 1960s titles recount naïve, simplistic tales, but after the first dozen issues *Amazing Spider-Man* stands up better than its contemporaries.

Weak and fallible by superhero standards, Spider-Man functions best in down-to-earth surroundings, often pitted against the New York underworld. Stan Lee and Steve Ditko quickly settled down to these perfectly pitched plots of the superhero plagued by mundane problems. How many other superheroes had to stay at home because their aunt had confiscated their costume? The banter and camaraderie between Peter and his peers is hard to better. Supervillain spats resulted in few clear-cut victories, and even these usually involved some pyrrhic element. Ditko never could draw a pretty girl, but his angular, gangling figures were right for Spider-Man, and his exquisite use of shadow suited the book perfectly. All these components created thirty-eight issues deserving of their classic status. Their appeal remains today, so much so that Marvel recently launched *Untold Tales of Spider-Man*, setting new stories in that era. It's proved popular and successful.

John Romita (Sr) launched his artistic stint with the revelation of the original Green Goblin's identity in 39–40, a tense story of the first villain to discover that Spider-Man is Peter Parker; his own identity had been a mystery since 14. After months of teasers, Mary Jane Watson finally shows her face in 42 and turns the dialogue seriously late sixties. Lee packs more soap opera and action in one issue than

can be found in half a dozen modern comics; 47 is the best example. But Ditko took part of Lee with him, and after issue 50 gaps between the landmarks stretch longer. By 1968, more complex social issues supplanted much of Lee's superficiality. The first black character, Joe Robertson, *Daily Bugle* City Editor, is introduced in 52 and opens the generation gap with his son Randy as student riots infiltrate 68–70. Peter goes steady with Gwen Stacy and sub-plots tire as they run the gamut of options: 'She digs Spider-Man but hates Peter Parker' and its permutations. 96–98 are a noteworthy drugs-use story as Marvel deliberately defied the Comics Code and published these issues without its stamp of approval – an event *de rigueur* nowadays, but sacrilegious in 1971.

By 110 Lee had outstayed his shelf-life and Gerry Conway warmed up for a year before killing off Gwen Stacy and the Green Goblin (allegedly) in 121–122. These issues acted as the catalyst for the superlative original Jackal War running intermittently through to 150. Conway introduces the Punisher in 129, eloquently portrays Peter's anguish, grief and guilt over Gwen's death and tantalisingly feeds the reader with scattered helpings of the Jackal's machinations rather than with a continuous bombardment. The resolution in 144–150 ushers in clones of Peter Parker and Gwen Stacy. The 'resurrection' of a non-superpowered supporting character was controversial at the time, but handling of the climax is first-rate, mainly because, as is evident, it's been properly planned. But little could Conway have guessed the terrible legacy this story would leave twenty years later. Despite the occasional absurd sub-plot and editing glitch, 121–150 is arguably Spider-Man's second finest hour after Lee and Ditko. Ross Andru's art is always adequate, never amazing, and a text page in 153 usefully ties up loose Jackal ends. 153 also holds its ground as a poignant one-shot, but Len Wein's stint (151–180) is generally mediocre. Marv Wolfman starts with a bang as Peter proposes to Mary Jane in his first issue, 182. Her rejection of him in the next issue effectively writes her out of the title for five years. The slide under Wolfman is slow, steady and inexorable. His only other mark is the first appearance of the Black Cat in 194–195, a supporting character developed more fully in *Spectacular Spider-Man.* Denny O'Neil effortlessly prolongs Wolfman's trend. His stories in 207–223 are not quite exciting enough to be described as poor.

Roger Stern's tenure from 224 coincided with the first period of artistic stability since Ross Andru's departure in 185, as John Romita Jr followed in his father's footsteps. The title was crying out for a scenario of tooth and intrigue, which Stern delivered courtesy of the

Hobgoblin in 238. A shadowy figure discovers the Green Goblin's hide-outs and adopts a similar persona. This move rescues all aspects of the book. Mary Jane's return in 242–243 is classic soap opera and 'The Kid Who Collects Spider-Man' half-issue tale in 248 is one of the most original and touching reappraisals of a superhero's origin you will see. Hobgoblin teasers permeate until Stern's grand finale in 251, with the mystery left unresolved.

Since her first appearance, Mary Jane had always been depicted as shallow, empty-headed and carefree: characterisation cleverly realised by a dearth of attached thought balloons. We learn the reason why in her origin issue, 259, following her stunner two issues earlier that she has known that Peter Parker is Spider-Man for a long time (see also the *Parallel Lives* graphic novel). It forms part of Tom DeFalco's best-ever work as 252–285 copiously feed the Hobgoblin enigma and integrate the *Secret Wars* black costume into mainstream Spider-Man mythology (from 252). The Rose, another mystery man in a mask, débuts in 253 and becomes Hobgoblin's conspirator. 269– 270 form a heroic two-parter as Spider-Man outthinks Firelord, an adversary who, on paper, he stands no chance of defeating. The run is littered with fill-ins and guest creators but all issues by the regular team of DeFalco and Ron Frenz shine. Although they both take an early bath, Jim Owsley admirably concludes the Gang War story (284–288, revealing the Rose), as does Peter David on the Hobgoblin exposition in 289. *Web of Spider-Man* 29, 30 and the *Spider-Man versus Wolverine* one-shot are essential reading to these plot-lines. Beware the slice of revisionist history, all the rave at Marvel nowadays, as the 1997 miniseries *Hobgoblin Lives!* overturns the identity of the face beneath the Hobgoblin's mask.

David Michelinie steals a leaf from Marv Wolfman's portfolio as Peter proposes to Mary Jane in his first issue. 290–292 recount a fine modern-day follow-up to her origin, which concludes with her acceptance. Formal proceedings unfold in Annual 21. Fill-in issues follow forthwith, but fill-ins as stunning as 293–294 are welcome any time, as Marc DeMatteis presents the newly-weds with a honeymoon to remember as Kraven buries Spider-Man alive for two weeks in *Amazing Spider-Man*'s two chapters of 'Kraven's Last Hunt'. Todd McFarlane joins as regular artist in 298 and Venom débuts in 300, but both of these two fine characters would later become victims of their own success as exploitation set in. McFarlane brings the best out of Michelinie as they paint another purple patch in the Webslinger's history. But after McFarlane's departure around 325, the art of Erik Larsen (to 350) and

Marvel Try-Out Contest winner Mark Bagley is unable to save the title from an excess of crossovers, superhero guest stars and inane plot-lines, such as the turbo-charged, superpowered Spider-Man in 327–329. The last worthwhile appearances of Venom and offspring Carnage grace 361–363. Subsequent outings reek of mass exploitation and gratuitous gore, exemplified by the egregious fourteen-part 'Maximum Carnage' bloodbath in 378–380 and other titles.

Spider-Man's recent past has been blighted by two appallingly ill-considered decisions by Marvel. To provide a blockbuster plot for Spider-Man's thirtieth anniversary (365), Peter Parker's parents are reintroduced, having been absent since 1968's Annual 5 recounted their deaths. Michelinie's absurdly shallow final issue (388) reveals them as androids, with no explanation as to how their mannerisms and personalities were created. DeMatteis' scripting stint overdoses on the psychoanalysis. But before long Marvel unveiled a second poke in the eye. Jumping on the fashion trend for major character revamps, Marvel unleashed the 'Return Of The Clone', a story-line they hoped no one would forget. In that respect they indisputably succeeded.

Peter Parker's clone and the Jackal did not die in 149. Adopting the name of Ben Reilly, the Parker clone returns after five years of self-imposed exile and confronts Spider-Man in *Spectacular Spider-Man* 216. Unable to beat the habit, Ben assumes a webslinging identity as the Scarlet Spider. The Jackal returns and we learn that he created multiple copies of clones of himself, Gwen Stacy and hundreds of Spider-Men, which all crawl out of the woodwork at a moment's whim. In the endgame (*Spectacular Spider-Man* 226) scientific tests 'prove' that Parker is the clone and Reilly the real McCoy. Parker packs his bags for Oregon with expectant wife in tow. This story is an unmitigated disaster. It weaves its weekly way through all the Spider-Man titles from October 1995 to October 1996, although each title keeps its own creative team. Once all the associated one-shots, limited series and follow-ups are counted, the story clocks up close to a hundred issues of drivel. Its most serious fault is that the reader cannot believe anything any character says. All the bad guys are lying and all the good guys don't have a clue what's going on. Its most infuriating fault is that most characters are unable to maintain consistent attitudes for more than five pages, exemplified by Reilly agonising that he must quit New York and leave it as Parker's territory, only to decide moments later that he can't. This questionable technique allows the same themes to be recycled endlessly and pads a hundred issues better than polystyrene ever could. The sorry saga smells of 'We'll make it up as we go along', as indeed they did.

Marketing Dept sticks its finger in the pie as all titles are suspended and replaced by Scarlet Spider versions, renumbered from issue 1, in November/ December 1995. But Reilly saves tradition with redesigned Spider-Man costume, lifestyle and hair colour as the established titles and numbering resume from January 1996, also featuring the return of DeFalco.

And thus could the clone story have ended. But it was so vilified from all quarters that Marvel finally realised They Had Made A Mistake. Further teasers culminated in the four-part 'Revelations' story-line in the December 1996 issues. We now learn that the original Green Goblin did not die in 122. He has been manipulating all the major players behind the scenes, and rigged the scientific clone tests to read a false result. Re-enter Peter Parker as the one, true and only Spider-Man as Reilly disintegrates before his eyes. This story and its companion, the 1997 one-shot *Osborn Journal*, inevitably heap hundreds of further inconsistencies on the not inconsiderable pile. Nevertheless, it does as much as is humanly possible to fix an irredeemable shambles. In the midst of the chaos, issue 400 shines brightly. Marvel's most senior citizen passes away in a beautifully sentimental gem from Marc DeMatteis, bereft of histrionics, melodrama or superfights.~APS

Recommended: 15, 17–21, 23, 25–27, 31–33, 38–40, 47, 50, 63–65, 121–125, 129–131, 134–137, 139–149, 153, 201, 202, 238, 239, 243, 248–251, 259, 269, 270, 275, 276, 278, 289–294, 300, 308, 309, 314–317, 361–363, 400, Annual 19, 20

Collections: *Assassin Nation Plot* (320–325), *Carnage* (361–363), *Chance Encounter* (298, 299, *Spider-Man* 13, 14), *Clone Genesis* (141–151), *Complete Frank Miller Spider-Man* (Annual 14, 15, *Marvel Team-Up* 100, *Marvel Team-Up* Annual 4, *Spectacular Spider-Man* 27, 28), *The Cosmic Adventures* (327–329, *Spectacular Spider-Man* 158–160, *Web of Spider-Man* 59–61), *Fox and Bug* (304–306), *Invasion of the Spider Slayers* (368–373), *Kraven's Last Hunt* (293, 294, *Spectacular Spider-Man* 131, 132, *Web of Spider-Man* 31, 32), *Marvel Masterworks* Vol 1 (1–10, *Amazing Fantasy* 15), *Marvel Masterworks* Vol 5 (11–20), *Marvel Masterworks* Vol 10 (21–30, Annual 1), *Marvel Masterworks* Vol 16 (31–40, Annual 2), *Marvel Masterworks* Vol 22 (41–50, Annual 3), *Maximum Carnage* (380–382, *Spider-Man Unlimited* 1, 2, *Spider-Man* 35–37, *Spectacular Spider-Man* 201–203, *Web of Spider-Man* 101–103), *Spider-Man Masterworks* (1–5, *Amazing Fantasy* 15), *Nothing Can Stop the Juggernaut* (229, 230), *Origin Of The Hobgoblin* (238, 239, 244, 245, 249–251), *Return of the Sinister Six* (334–339), *Round Robin* (353–358), *Saga Of The Alien Costume* (252–259), *Sensational*

Spider-Man (Annual 14, 15, *Amazing Spider-Man* 8), *Silver Sable* (301–303), *Spider-Man vs Doctor Doom* (349, 350), *Spider-Man vs Green Goblin* (17, 96–98, 121, 122, *Spectacular Spider-Man* 200), *Spider-Man vs Venom* (300, 315–317), *Spider-Man's Wedding* (290–292, Annual 21 plus newsstrips), *Venom Returns* (331–333, 344–347)

Peter Parker the Spectacular
SPIDER-MAN

Marvel: *Series one 2 issues 1968, Series two 241 issues +, 14 Annuals, 1 Super Special 1976 to date*

Series one was Marvel's first experiment with magazine publication, an election story by Stan Lee, John Romita and Jim Mooney later re-jigged in *Amazing Spider-Man* 116–118. The colour second issue by the same creative team is better, featuring a psychological set-to between Spider-Man and the Green Goblin in their civilian identities before developing into a standard Spider-Man battle.

Series two is the only Marvel comic introduced in the 1970s still published today, and initially intended to focus more on the complex social life of his *alter ego* Peter Parker, hence the title. There's minimal recognition of the intent inside the comic, but it wasn't until 134 that Parker's name disappeared from the masthead of Spider-Man's second ongoing solo comic.

For a title that eventually turned out well, the only spectacular things about 1–50 are their consistently dull content, and the amount of villains that attack Empire State University (five between 37 and 43 alone). There are cheap sniggers to be had from CB character Razorback in 11 and the disco Hypno-Hustler in 24, and the dozen die-hard *Champions* fans will require 17–18, featuring the team breaking up. Roger Stern shows the first glimmer of adequacy among writers and from 57, despite ever-changing artists, he's turning out reasonable stories.

It's the surprising team of Bill Mantlo and Ed Hannigan from 62 who begin the first run of good issues. Hitting form early with the moody introduction of Cloak and Dagger in 64, Hannigan's pencils are detailed, imaginative, occasionally live up to the titular adjective, and are enhanced by the inks of Al Milgrom. Mantlo's writing outshines his work elsewhere by light-years, deftly juggling Peter Parker's university supporting cast, and even the most ridiculous of returning foes (Boomerang in 67) is made interesting. Their finest issue is Hannigan's last, 72, in which Spider-Man encounters a very different Doctor Octopus. Al Milgrom and Jim Mooney are the artists by 74, pleasingly concluding a long-running sub-plot involving timid secretary Debra Whitman in the midst of a multi-issue war between Dr Octopus and the Owl, also involving the Black Cat. 80 is a fine solo run for *Daily Bugle* proprietor J. Jonah Jameson, and 84 an excellent tale about a kidnapped child. Mantlo's scripts remain above average until Spider-Man's ridiculous romance with the Black Cat pushes everything but supervillains out of the title.

The black-costume era starts with 90. Al Milgrom writes to 100, restoring Peter Parker and cast. Most issues between 103 and 136 are by Peter David, displaying his customary facility for witty dialogue and situations. The most acclaimed story of his run is 'The Death of Jean De Wolff' in 107–110, a detective story tracing the killer of the *Marvel Team-Up* supporting character, but the sequel in 134–136 is better. 103, 113 (in May Parker's old folks' home) and the *Rashomon* tribute in 121 are also good, and there's a clever surprise revelation in 129. By 130 there are three monthly Spider-Man titles, and stories begin to cross over, providing a shorter wait between instalments, but meaning that some long-running sub-plots are cleared up in the other titles, although usually referenced here. Chapters of J.M. DeMatteis and Mike Zeck's laudable Kraven six-part story occupy 131–132, and there's a very good sequel of sorts, founded on the repression of childhood abuse, in 178–183.

There'd been no regular penciller since Al Milgrom, but Sal Buscema returns with 134, and makes up for lost time by pencilling the comic ever since. In 137 Gerry Conway returns as writer, reuniting the team responsible for the first issue (original inker Mike Esposito is back with 154). Most of their issues are entertaining superhero comics with effective sub-plots and page-turning twists – second nature to Conway – and crisp, solid art – second nature to Buscema. In 139–143 the Punisher's back and *Bugle* Editor Joe Robertson faces the consequences of an early career mistake, a plot kept on the boil until 157, a good sampler of the Conway/Buscema style. There are two dumb villains, the hasty resolution to Joe Robertson's problems, and plenty of the supporting cast. In 158–160 Spider-Man is cosmically powered, making him, in effect, Superman, a stupid device predicating stupid stories, but from 161 it's business as usual. Conway's swansong sees the return of Dr Octopus in 173–175, and J.M. DeMatteis inherits the title from 178. His plots are slender, but he more than compensates with accomplished characterisation. Parker's Aunt May is transformed from the comic hindrance to Spider-Man's dual identity she'd been for twenty-five years to a sympathetic old lady; villains seen umpteen times previously are given believable motivation for their actions. A particular triumph is his unsettling depiction of the madness afflicting the Green Goblin (189,

200). While maintaining elements of continuity, DeMatteis' stories are generally complete in a set amount of issues. 'Funeral Arrangements' in 186–188 is a good sample of his style, as The Vulture has cancer and wants to tie up his life neatly before death. Sal Buscema, inking his own pencils, continues to be excellent throughout.

After DeMatteis concludes his tenure with the 'Maximum Carnage' chapters (201–203), there's a variety of writers filling time to the start of the infamous 'Spider-Clone' saga, none with particular distinction. Beginning in 216, the 'Spider-Clone' story runs as individual chapters through all Spider-Man titles until 229, and is dealt with in the review of *Amazing Spider-Man*. Sal Buscema remains as penciller but Bill Sienkiewicz's inks make for an uncomfortable mixture, much improved when he's replaced by John Stanisci. A dumb marketing move replaces the title for two months with *The Spectacular Scarlet Spider* (don't bother with it), and from the reinstatement with 230 Ben Reilly is Spider-Man for a short while, with an almost blank slate for writers – not that it seems to make a difference. With the mess of 'Spider-Clone' brought to a predictable conclusion everything is once again as it was, and there's some indication that the future may be a little brighter with 241. It's a decent stocktaking issue from regular writer J.M. DeMatteis, dynamically, if not always anatomically correctly, drawn by the team of Luke Ross and John Stanisci.

Best of the annuals are the John Byrne-drawn battle with Dr Octopus in 1, and Peter David and Mark Beachum's stories of the mysterious Ace in 5 and 6.~WJ

Recommended: 64, 66, 67, 69, 70, 72, 80, 84, 103, 131, 132, 139–142, 157, 173–175, 178–183, 186–189, 200

Collections: Spider-Man and Daredevil Special Edition (25–28) *The Death of Jean DeWolff* (107–110),

Sensational SPIDER-MAN

Marvel: *12 issues + (0–11), 1 Annual 1996 to date*

Seemingly replacing *Web Of Spider-Man* only to trumpet the signing of writer and penciller Dan Jurgens, the first seven issues exhibit the Jurgens trademarks of perfectly acceptable art and woefully uninspired script. In his defence it must be pointed out that he's not helped with the latter by having to cross the title over with all the other Spider-Man publications. Unfortunately, once an the editorial decision to dispense with this has been made, Jurgens has also gone. There are precisely three items of note in the series to date: a nice multi-pose Spider-Man reflector adorns the cover of the zero issue, Jurgens tinkers with Spider-Man's

costume (introducing a larger central spider motif), and there's the annual. Actually titled *Sensational Spider-Man* '96, it's a reworking of *Amazing Spider-Man* 15, by J.M. DeMatteis, the writer who's been most successful with the villain of the piece, Kraven. Unlike most reworkings of old stories, Kraven's début retreads familiar ground, but adds to the original in myriad subtle ways without either ruining or discounting it, and the art of Shawn McManus is delightful. A back-up strip returns the original Spider-Woman.~FP
Recommended: *Sensational Spider-Man* '96

Untold Tales of SPIDER-MAN
Marvel: *16 issues + 1995 to date*

By the 1990s keeping track of Spider-Man's life had become unenviably complex over the assorted titles he occupied, never mind factoring in specials and guest appearances. Those who yearned for the simpler self-contained stories of previous years found their solution here, with continuity implants set in the earliest days of Spider-Man's career. He'd already met a few of his regular foes, but they'd not yet become too familiar. Kurt Busiek manages a good impersonation of Stan Lee's original snappy dialogue for Spider-Man and Peter Parker's self-pity, and given that comics are now more character-driven than in Spider-Man's introductory years, he's able to provide a greater depth to the slimmer supporting cast, and he's also wise enough to refrain from an excess of knowing captions or dialogue. Penciller Pat Olliffe's wisdom is in not imitating the Steve Ditko artwork from the period portrayed, providing more modern layouts and style. All issues are self-contained, and *Untold Tales* is a consistently involving and satisfactory read. Any issue sampled will provide better than average superhero entertainment.~WJ
Collection: Untold Tales Of Spider-Man (1–8)

Web of SPIDER-MAN
Marvel: *129 issues, 10 Annuals, 1 Super Special, 1985–1996*

This replaced *Marvel Team-Up* after the latter's cancellation. The main periods of creative stability centre around Alex Saviuk, who pencilled 35–116 apart from about a dozen fill-ins, and writers Gerry Conway (47–70), Howard Mackie (84–96) and Terry Kavanagh (97–120). Paradoxically, however, better issues cluster amongst the early numbers, even though most read as routine fill-ins between Spider-Man's adventures in his other titles.

11–12, written by Fingeroth and David, confront Peter Parker with a tricky moral dilemma when he's tempted to adopt a vigilante role in his civilian identity. 29–30, by Jim Owsley, oversee the finale of the first Hobgoblin plot-line. Much more than just a

recap, these excellent issues adroitly tie up all loose ends of a complex story and capture the despair of the Kingpin's son. 31–32, along with *Amazing Spider-Man* 293–294 and *Spectacular Spider-Man* 131–132, print the outstanding 'Kraven's Last Hunt' by Marc DeMatteis and Mike Zeck. Peter David entraps Betty Brant in a religious cult in 40–43, which also feature Mary Jane contemplating nude modelling and Aunt May chancing across the glossies.

Conway brought consistency – unfortunately of a second-rate nature – but Saviuk's barren pencils supplied little nourishment. Their best effort has Chameleon kidnapping and replacing J.J. Jameson (50–54). Conway's long-running sub-plot of Mary Jane's young cousin Kristy's bout of anorexia provides needed substance. The book slid further downhill after Conway's departure. Mackie's 'Name of the Rose' (84–89) instils a brief surge as a new character adopts the Rose identity, but the original Rose sequence in *Amazing Spider-Man* is far superior. 100, 104–109 contain short solo back-up strips of Spider-Man supporting characters Nightwatch, Cardiac and Calypso. 'The Return of the Clone' story-line starts in earnest in 117 and wraps around all the Spider-Man titles. It is discussed in the review of *Amazing Spider-Man*.

Like the other Spider titles, *Web of Spider-Man* was cancelled in October 1995 and replaced by Scarlet issues: *Web of Scarlet Spider* 1–4. Unlike its counterparts, it did not reappear and was replaced by *Sensational Spider-Man*.~APS
Recommended: 11–13, 29–32, 37, 40–43, 49

SPIDER-MAN ADVENTURES
Marvel: *16 issues + 1994–1996*

Cashing in on the success of *Batman Adventures*, this series, based on Spidey's current cartoon series, is great fun, evoking a certain innocence and simplicity that the current ongoing series lacks. The art is refreshingly cartoony, with bold brush strokes. Worth a look.~TP
Recommended: 5, 6
Collection: Spider-Man Adventures (1–5)

SPIDER-MAN CLASSICS
Marvel: *16 issues 1993–1994*

Issue 1 reprints the origins of Spider-Man and Doctor Strange from *Amazing Fantasy* 15 and *Strange Tales* 115. Reprints of *Amazing Spider-Man* 1–15 follow.~APS

SPIDER-MAN DIGEST
Marvel: *13 issues 1987–1989*

Bumper-size title continuing reprints of *Amazing Spider-Man* from 51 on after *Marvel Tales* stopped its consecutive reprints in 190 and went hot. Three issues of *Amazing* are packed into each *Digest*. The title changed to *Spider-Man Comics Magazine* with 7.~APS

SPIDER-MAN Graphic Novels and One-Shots

The expansive variety of Spider-Man one-shots ranges from special projects deserving of graphic-novel status to mundane offerings amounting to little more than big, thick comic books. All are independently produced by unrelated creators and quality varies accordingly.

It's old boys' reunion day in *Fear Itself* as Lee, Conway and Andru concoct a routine tale of Spider-Man and Silver Sable sucked into a Baron Zemo scheme. When the plot involves a fear-provoking, hallucinogenic gas, you just know an overdose of padded pages will follow. The Holiday Special 1995 stuffs stockings with five tales of Spidey and his pals all baked to give you that cosy Yuletide feel. Spider-Man goes magical-dimension-hopping in *Hooky*, with Doctor Strange, unusually, nowhere in sight. With a child sorcerer in tow, this has all the ingredients of schmaltz overload. However, Susan Putney's charming story and Berni Wrightson's sumptuous, expansive artwork deliver one of Spider-Man's most off-beat adventures. *Legacy Of Evil* gives sophisticated treatment to the aftermath of the Green Goblin. It reads much like a Goblin biography but has enough substance to carry its own weight. *Maximum Clonage* Alpha and Omega are crap tie-ins to the clone saga, intertwining with Spider-Man's ongoing titles. Published two years after the wedding issue, *Parallel Lives'* history class compares and contrasts Peter and Mary Jane. All script and artwork is new, despite reprising many panels from past issues. Background details are retrospectively fleshed out; most significantly that Mary Jane discovered that Peter Parker is Spider-Man during the events of *Amazing Fantasy* 15. One for Spider-Man connoisseurs only. Like most sequels, *Soul Of The Hunter* is inferior to its ancestor, the really outstanding 'Kraven's Last Hunt' story-line in *Amazing Spider-Man* 293, 294, *Spectacular Spider-Man* 131, 132 and *Web of Spider-Man* 31, 32. Unlike most sequels, it is excellent. Peter Parker must lay Kraven's soul to rest in this palpable portrayal of his haunting. DeMatteis' cultured, if intense, script unfolds fine Mary Jane characterisation as she assuages Peter's agony. The pencil/ink team of Zeck/McLeod displays its customary synergy as their chaste artwork comes to life on the page. *Spider-Man And Batman* is a Marvel/DC co-production written by DeMatteis, who plays it dead safe as he trots out the heroes' familiar character traits. Twin lunatics Joker and Carnage contribute to adequate superheroics. *The Way To Dusty Death* has veterans Thomas and Conway recycling a veteran plot as Spider-Man and Doctor Strange team up to fight their perennial nemesis Xandu. A bountiful premise

is wasted by Terry Kavanagh in *Designer Genes* as he produces a slugfest from the uneasy alliance formed by Spider-Man, Punisher and Sabretooth. Roxxon Corporation, their common enemy, manufactures chimeras to pad out the page count. Ugly, misproportioned artwork from Scott McDaniel does not assist. Spider-Man versus Wolverine pairs the twosome in Berlin and it's not for sightseeing. The dialogue is first-rate, a major character dies and Jim Owsley's depiction of Spider-Man losing his bottle is highly convincing. Further ramifications continue in *Amazing Spider-Man* 289. Charles Vess indulges his love of the Scottish Highlands in *Spirits Of The Earth* as Peter and Mary Jane take a vacation. The beautiful, mellow art does justice to the location and the domestic aspects are warm as the New Yorkers interact with the locals. But the main plot reeks of habitual megalomaniacs and predictable holographic Scottish ghosts. The vignette of Spider-Man impeded by a herd of cows sitting in the road is risible. In *Trial Of Venom*, Spider-Man, Daredevil and Venom meet *L.A. Law* in the famous UNICEF donation special. Peter David injects just enough intrigue to rise above the gimmick.

Clone Journals, *Jackal Files*, *Spider-Man vs Dracula* and *Parker Years* are reprints. The first two feature edited reprints of clone-related matters, *Spider-Man vs Dracula* reprints *Giant-Size Spider-Man* 1 and in *Parker Years*, Spider-Man or his clone (who knows or cares?) grapples with the validity of his past years unknowingly spent in clone form and fills an enormous number of pages with flashbacks in doing so.~APS

Recommended: *Hooky, Soul of the Hunter, Spider-Man versus Wolverine*

SPIDER-MAN limited series

The Arachnis Project 6 issues 1994–1995, Deadly Foes Of Spider-Man 4 issues 1991, The Final Adventure 4 issues 1995–1996, Friends And Enemies 4 issues 1995, Funeral For An Octopus 3 issues 1995, Lethal Foes Of Spider-Man 4 issues 1993, The Lost Years 4 issues (0–3) 1995–1996, Mutant Agenda 4 issues (0–3) 1994, Power Of Terror 4 issues 1995, Redemption 4 issues 1996, Saga 4 issues 1991–1992, Spider-Man Megazine 6 issues 1994–1995, Spider-Man/Punisher: Family Affair 2 issues 1996, Spider-Man/X-Factor: Shadowgames 3 issues 1994, Web of Doom 3 issues 1994

There is scant story reason for any of these titles to merit their own series. Each could quite comfortably have been accommodated as a continuing story in an ongoing Spider-Man title. But as limited series became increasingly viable in direct-market outlets, marketing fads demanded their presence to capitalise on a popular character and to maximise the number of books on retailers' shelves having issue number 1 on the cover. These outings do afford irregular *Spider-Man* creators the opportunity to road-test the character, but results are generally below the standard of the continuing *Spider-Man* titles.

Arachnis Project serves up substandard superheroics as Spider-Man helps out an old college professor in time of need and excessive numbers of villains pile in. *Deadly Foes* looks at events from the point of view of six Spider-foes as Spider-Man grants little more than a token guest appearance. The villains are portrayed as bumbling incompetents in this verbose offering from Fingeroth and Milgrom. *Lethal Foes* serves as its sequel and mixes a somewhat more concrete effort. Nevertheless, it is still feeble, as villains appear from nowhere and play pass-the-parcel with a nuclear blaster. In *Final Adventure*, the one who thinks he is a clone leaves New York City to the other Spider-Man. His wife and unborn child move to Oregon with him. He works in a scientific research institution and vows never to don the costume again. She leaves him when he does. This touching, well-written and well-researched tale from Fabian Nicieza and Darick Robertson is the only silver lining on the dark, clouded clone saga. Darkhawk, Nova and Speedball team up in *Friends And Enemies* to save six newly empowered teenagers from a variety of evil clutches. Spider-Man's appearance is a mere courtesy. Danny Fingeroth sprouts plot events without reason in a story that should appeal to a very juvenile audience. *Funeral For An Octopus* is a clone-tied miniseries starring the Amazing and Scarlet Spider-Men as an undignified squabble breaks out over the Octopus arms following the Doctor's death in *Spectacular Spider-Man* 221. Tables are turned as Spider-Man wears the tentacles, but no events of consequence transpire.

The Lost Years is a clone spin-off in which a Parker body fills in his life during the five absent years between 1975 and 1995 (work that one out). DeMatteis' thoughtful script is somewhat overloaded with character introspection. Romita Jr/Janson turn out clean artwork, but the entire affair is incomprehensible without intimate knowledge of fifty other Spiderclone issues; it's also rendered meaningless by subsequent clone reversals. The posthumously released zero issue reprints clone stories barely a year old. *Redemption* is an inferior sequel in which clone scenarios already recycled a thousand times are brought out for yet another airing. In *Mutant Agenda*, Spider-Man and Beast confront Hobgoblin and Brand Corporation in an anti-mutant narrative. The zero issue is essentially a blank 'stamp album' to paste in the daily newspaper strips that simultaneously ran a version of the

same story. *Power Of Terror* clashes heroes with villains in a cast of thousands as the Maggia battles for control of New York City in Gregory Wright's messy plot. The emotional *angst* Peter Parker suffers from the bloodbath and Darick Robertson's pencils are the plus points. *Spider-Man/Punisher: Family Affair* has the co-stars thrashing out their usual stances on killing whilst up against the Mob in a standard story by Tom Lyle enhanced by a fine moral ending. *Shadowgames* pits Spider-Man and X-Factor against designer supervillains courtesy of a shady military research project. Kurt Busiek and Pat Broderick conjure a rare event: meaningful contributions from Spider-Man supporting characters in a limited series. In *Web Of Doom*, a civilian suffocates to death, cocooned by Spider-Man's webbing. Jack C. Harris fails to capitalise on a favourable premise.

Megazine weighs in at ninety-six pages an issue and reprints selected issues from Spider-Man's ongoing titles, predominantly guest-starring hot characters. *Saga* chronicles a biography of Spider-Man using pasted panels from old issues linked by a new textual framing sequence. Each issue covers approximately seventy-five issues of *Amazing Spider-Man*, ending with 300, shortly after his marriage to Mary Jane.~APS

Recommended: *Final Adventure* 1–4
Collections: *Deadly Foes Of Spider-Man* (1–4), *The Lost Years* (1–3)

SPIDER-MAN TEAM-UP
Marvel: *5 issues + 1995 to date*

Marvel Team-Up revived with a more obvious name in an oversize quarterly format. One wonders why. In the first four issues there's Spider-Man alongside the X-Men, Silver Surfer, the Fantastic Four and the Avengers. Despite the use of high-profile creators, they're all working on autopilot and there's nothing to justify the extended format or price. The best issue by a country mile is 5, containing a decent teaming with Gambit, and the far better Steve Gerber-written story reuniting both Gerber and Spider-Man with Howard The Duck. Gerber has a ball reviving the elf from his *Defenders* run and guest-starring the Savage Dragon (but hush, it's a secret), in the process subtly moving Howard to Image Comics. It's no classic, but far better than could be expected.~WJ

SPIDER-MAN 2099
Marvel: *46 issues, 1 Annual, 1 Special 1992–1996, One-shot 1995*

The most popular of the *2099* revampings of present-day favourites, highlighted by the longevity of the series. Peter Parker is long gone, and in his place there's Miguel O'Hara, a high flyer in the global corporation Alchemax. Spidey 2099's origin is very similar to that of his predecessor, but O'Hara's world is a very different place. In a society split down the middle between the rich corporate head honchos and the masses, he's an anomaly: a head honcho with a conscience who battles his employers when he dons his hi-tech costume. A nice extra ability which Miguel acquires is the bite of a spider, temporarily paralysing his victims.

While not up to the standard of his Hulk run, Peter David's scripts are amusing, and reminiscent of the first Spider-Man series, with Spider-Man quipping as he battles. The art by Rick Leonardi and Al Williamson makes the series worth a quick browse at the very least. As the series continues, though, David loses direction and resorts to reviving old Spider-Man villains, including the Goblin, the Vulture and Venom, updated for slugfests in 2099. After David left, Ben Raab and Terry Kavanagh wrote the remainder of the series, with 34–37 part of the 'One Nation Under Doom' story as Doom takes over America and offers Miguel a cushy job. 40's art is interesting, with Bill Sienkiewicz's inks looking a cross between Walt Simonson and Howard Chaykin, and the series concludes with a huge cataclysm for Miguel, his family and Alchemax. The one-shot has the inevitable meeting between Miguel and Peter Parker, his 20th-century counterpart.~TP

Recommended: 1–3

SPIDER-MAN UNLIMITED
Marvel: *14 issues + 1993 to date*

The formula's the same as Marvel's other quarterly *Unlimited* titles, either an extra long story or several shorter ones, all featuring Spider-Man and not having to fit the close continuity of the regular titles. Unless, of course, money can be made by launching an expensive new title with a protracted plot that runs through all *Spider-Man* titles before concluding in the second issue three months later, as was the case with 'Maximum Carnage' in the first two issues. 9 and 10 are also chapters of multi-part story-lines. Sadly, given the opportunity, space, and no continuity restrictions, there's little more than average material throughout, with plenty of it downright shoddy. Tom DeFalco and Ron Lim's biography of Dr Octopus in 3 has moments, as does James Felder's reuniting of Power Man and Iron Fist in 13. That's completely ruined by the appalling stylised pencils of Joe Bennett whenever there's a costume in sight, which is a shame as his office scenes are quite acceptable. Overall, stay well away.~WJ

SPIDER-WOMAN
Marvel: *50 issues 1978–1983*

With astonishing restraint, it took Marvel almost fifteen years to introduce a female counterpart to their most popular character, and then, rumour has it, only in order to copyright the name before anyone else did so. Having been introduced in *Marvel Spotlight* 32, she was either foolishly or admirably, depending on your point of view, designed to be as different as possible from Spider-Man. Initial issues, although featuring costumed villains, were set in a distinctly horror milieu, with stories emphasising Spider-Woman's macabre background. 9's 'Eye Of The Needle' features as demented and bizarre a villain as you're ever likely to see in comics, but the majority of issues by Mark Gruenwald and Carmine Infantino, although passable, didn't really thrill. Neither did much else. Chris Claremont and Steve Leialoha become the creative team that will see the title out with 34, improving it a little. There's some nice art, although it's muddied beyond belief by the appalling printing used by Marvel at the time, and their best issues are 42–44. Therein the Silver Samurai and the Viper, an incompatible pairing of villains for some reason very close to Claremont's heart, go through their paces. The best sampler of their run is the daft Impossible Man story in 46. If you like that try more. The Needle apart, the best portions of *Spider-Woman* rely on Claremont's ability to surprise. He does so first with a seemingly capricious revelation to end 44, and manages it again with an unpredictable conclusion to the series.~FP

SPIDER-WOMAN
Marvel: *4-issue miniseries 1993–1994*

This is new Spider-Woman, introduced in *Secret Wars*. She's strong and she psychically projects spider webs, prompting one to ask why she doesn't project psychic brick walls instead. Her other novelty is that she's bringing up a pre-teen daughter. This series tinkers with her origin while her parents come to visit, and while never less than competent it's never more than competent either. With the demise of *Force Works* she's been left in limbo, though she meets the original article in *Sensational Spider-Man* annual 1.~FP

THE SPIRAL PATH
Eclipse: *2 issues 1986*

Two-issue reprint of Steve Parkhouse's rather dull tale of shamanism and magical battles, originally printed in British anthology title *Warrior*. Parkhouse is a much more talented artist than he is a writer, but his artwork, while faultless in its detail, somehow bogged down the story. Overall the strip reads as though it belongs to a bygone age.~FJ

THE SPIRIT

Quality: *22 issues 1944–1950*
Fiction House: *5 issues 1952–1954*
Super: *2 issues 1964*
Harvey: *2 issues 1966–1967*
Warren: *16 issues 1974–1976*
Kitchen Sink: *Series one 2 issues 1973, series two 25 issues (17–41) 1977–1983, series three 87 issues 1983–1992*

Will Eisner's *Spirit* has a longevity almost unequalled in comics. With few exceptions (noted below), the content of all *Spirit* comics is material originally published as 7-page newspaper inserts between 1940 and 1952. Unless otherwise indicated, all issue numbers refer to the third Kitchen Sink series, which reprints the post-1945 work in chronological order, mainly four stories to an issue. The stories work perfectly well in isolation, but there is an element of continuity giving an added level of enjoyment if they're read sequentially.

The Spirit is a whimsically portrayed (barely) masked and trenchcoated crimefighter. Central City police Commissioner Dolan, to whom Eisner bore an uncanny resemblance in later years, becomes a confidant, and his daughter Ellen a paramour. He also has an assistant, Ebony, considered by some to be racist comedy relief, but generally written with dignity. Strengths of *The Spirit* are that the supporting cast and parameters are so well drawn that it's possible to tell any type of tale. Ostensibly a detective strip populated by *femmes fatales* and exotic criminals, the Spirit often plays no more than a cameo role in stories bearing his name. A striking example is 'Heat' (72), in which a battered Spirit lies barely conscious in an alleyway while life goes on in the streets and tenements around him. Eisner's not above resorting to gimmickry or re-working old material, but his brilliantly expressive cartooning compensates.

The first post-war tales see Eisner reclaiming his strip, instituting a quantum improvement over his successors (and predecessors) and eclipsing his previous work. He'd refined his art, and within nine months he'd introduced additional characters who would recur for years: Carrion (6) and his buzzard, the mysterious crimelord The Octopus (8, only ever recognisable by his distinctive gloves), and, back again, the Spirit's pre-war nemesis Silk Satin. P'Gell, best defined of a number of female criminals who are alternately drawn to the Spirit yet turned by profit, débuts in 10. Her introduction is eclipsed in that issue, however, by the strange story of Artemus Peap, who assembles Central City's largest-ever gang.

By 26 (stories from early 1948) Eisner had hit peak form as both writer and artist, and there's

at least one great story every issue: the inventive story-telling still inspires today. Poe and fairytales are adapted to modern settings, stories are written in rhyme, there are heart-shaped panels for a Valentine's Day tale, and increasingly imaginative ways of working a *Spirit* logo into the splash page. Above all, the amount packed into seven pages is a masterful lesson in economy. Eisner's broad streak of sentimentality underlies the feature, and many of the best have a little man caught in circumstances beyond his control. 'Gerhard Schnobble' in 35 is a typical example, often cited by Eisner as his favourite *Spirit* story. A night watchman recalls that he can fly, only to die in crossfire without anyone having noticed.

From 40 Jules Feiffer and Klaus Nordling contributed scripts, and from 47 Ebony disappears, replaced by the less controversial Sammy. Eisner turned to other projects with 73, leaving Feiffer as the main writer. His scripts match Eisner's but are invariably dragged down by a selection of inferior artists, with Eisner only returning for the final newspaper sections. This often-reprinted story sends the Spirit into space, and while Wally Wood's artwork is excellent, removing the Spirit from his environment doesn't really work.

Since 1952 there have been few new *Spirit* stories, although Eisner has drawn many new covers for reprinted material. The new stories can be found in the Harvey issues, giving the origins of the Spirit and the Octopus, and in the first Kitchen Sink series. The second Kitchen Sink series is magazine-format, continuing the numbering from Warren's magazines. 30 has many contemporary creators collaborating on a story featuring the Spirit, the result more a curiosity than anything else, and also features some inferior Spirit stories by wartime creators. Most issues between 31 and 40 contain chapters from what would become the *New York* graphic novel.~FP
Recommended: 5, 8, 12, 15, 16, 20, 24, 26, 29–32, 35, 36, 38–45, 48, 50, 52, 55–57, 59, 61–66, 69, 70, 72, 74, 78, 82
Collections: *The Christmas Spirit* (assorted Christmas stories), *The Outer Space Spirit* (85–87), *The Spirit Colour Album* vols 1–3 (assorted stories)

THE SPIRIT, The Origin Years
Kitchen Sink: *6 issues 1992–1993*

While *The Spirit* is justifiably lauded as a great comic strip, it was some while before the memorable stories appeared. From its introduction in 1940 it took creator Will Eisner almost two years to hit a groove on the feature, and even then his work was of a lesser standard than his post-war material. This series didn't last long enough to reach that point.~FP

SPIRIT OF WONDER
Dark Horse: *5-issue limited series 1996*

A beautifully drawn historical Manga series by Kenji Tsuratu in which a young woman, China, owner of a restaurant/rooming house, is host to a couple of very eccentric inventors. It's a love story, odd, humorous and touching.~NF
Recommended: 1–5

SPIRIT WORLD
DC: *1 issue 1971*

Jack Kirby's black and white companion magazine to *In The Days Of The Mob*, this time concentrating on the supernatural. As you would expect from Kirby at his creative peak everything was marvellously imaginative and beautifully illustrated. Stories for the unpublished second issue appeared in *Weird Mystery Tales* 1–3.~HY
Recommended: 1

Ghost Rider and Blaze SPIRITS OF VENGEANCE
Marvel: *23 issues, 1992–1994*

The 1970s Ghost Rider, Johnny Blaze, teams up with his skull-headed 1990s successor in a supernatural series that seems to serve little purpose other than to provide bridging chapters for crossovers into other titles. Of the twenty-three issues, no fewer than eight are direct crossovers with other titles, and several more are heavily referential to others in the 'Midnight Sons' series. This leaves little opportunity for developing characterisation for the leads, let alone any real supporting cast, and so the twosome lurch from one eldritch rumble to another, with little motivation or purpose.~HS

SPITFIRE AND THE TROUBLE-SHOOTERS
Marvel: *13 issues 1986–1987*

Despite the basic artwork (to say the least) this told an interesting tale about a group of MIT students who come across a superpowered suit of armour. Caught in a web of intrigue deadlier than they at first imagine, they find themselves pitted against foreign nationals and even their own government, who want the suit for themselves. Sadly, it moved to cancellationville, USA.~TP

SPLAT!
Mad Dog: *3 issues 1987*

Surely one of the best 'alternative' anthologies ever attempted. If each issue has its share of duff stories, each also has at least one strip that, on its own, is worth the price of admission. 1 has an early Peter Bagge strip from 1982, 'Just Like Pop', plus good stuff from Ron Wilber, J.R. Williams and Hunt Emerson, but is the weakest of the three issues overall. 2 has Eddie Campbell's 'Dead End Job', Marc Hempel's

'Cartoon Man's Best Friend', reprints of Alan Moore's Maxwell The Magic Cat and more Peter Bagge, J.R. Williams and Hunt Emerson. 3 has a sneak preview of Ted McKeever's *Eddy Current* and a *Calvin and Hobbes* parody by Scott Saavedra. In addition each issue had an interview with a humour cartoonist: S. Gross, P.S. Mueller and B. Kliban respectively.~NF
Recommended: 2, 3

SPLITTING IMAGE
Image: *2 issues 1993*

Spoof on the Image characters by Rob Liefeld and Jim Valentino, along the lines of Marvel's *What The?* and about as funny.~JC

SPOOF
Marvel: *5 issues, 1970–1973*

Satire of the TV, films and personalities of the day, very much in the style of *Mad* magazine. It's quite entertaining even if you haven't seen the originals, and the spoof of *The Birds* in issue 3 is a classic.~FC
Recommended: 3

SPOTLIGHT ON THE GENIUS THAT IS JOE SACCO
Fantagraphics: *1 issue, 1994*

An anthology of short pieces by Sacco, mostly on the weak side. Worth a look, though, for 'Zachary Mindbiscuit' (who nobly starves his cat in the name of his own principles), 'Johnny Sentence' (corporate power games), and Sacco's own scathing comments on each story.~FC

Hit Me With A SPUD
Spud Press: *1 issue + 1996 to date*

Catholic guilt and dream-driven strangeness merge in the work of Art Baxter, the disturbing subject-matter rendered all the more potent through the use of an appealing kids' cartoon style. Billy is a high-school kid terrorised by nuns, Sherry and Terry are teenage girls with secrets, and the silent Dominic DeSanto occupies a surreal and depressing world. An excellent début, and a cartoonist to watch out for.~FP
Recommended: 1

SPYKE
Epic: *4-issue miniseries 1993*

It could be taken as editorial comment when the lead character concedes three issues in that the concept of the series is so crazy 'Oliver Stone wouldn't touch it with a bargepole'. Having been transported to another dimension, Spyke Jones ('Just like the bandleader!') learns that one can travel between further dimensions by killing selected individuals. This distasteful concept sets the tone for a predictable plot about humanoid extra-dimensionals taking over the planet. But hey… there's one man able to stop them.~WJ

SPYMAN
Harvey: *3 issues 1967–1968*

Created by Jim Steranko, Spyman was fitted with a prosthetic hand on which each robotic digit contained a different gimmick (magnet, camera, blaster). Probably best ignored as the initial fumblings of precocious talent.~FP

Ultraverse Year Zero: The Death of THE SQUAD
Malibu: *4-issue miniseries 1995*

James Hudnall tells the story of the Squad, Hardcase's original team, which retrospectively inaugurated the Ultraverse. The Squad are four newly-superpowered beings who decide to try and help (what?) but are hindered by a lack of precedent for their kind (precedent of what? and in what way?) and by having unknowingly been targeted for destruction by the immortal Rex Mundi. The series offers some insights into Hardcase's character and Ultraverse history but doesn't make for particularly interesting reading.~NF

SQUADRON SUPREME
Marvel: *12-issue limited series 1985–1986, Graphic Novel 1989*

Introduced as alternate Earth allies in *Avengers* 85 as a homage to DC's Justice League Of America in the days when company team-ups were unthinkable, the similarities were far fewer as this series ends. When it opens, the Squadron Supreme's Earth is in considerable disarray after a period of totalitarian rule and the subsequent battle for freedom. The Squadron decide that, as the planet's most powerful individuals, they should impose, as the optimum solution, a twelve-month period of global authority to implement a 'Utopia Program' aimed at solving the world's ills, after which they will step down.

Mark Gruenwald's plot examines the ethics of a dictatorial system, however benign, through qualms being voiced by Nighthawk. He resigns from the team, and then actively opposes it on discovering that the Squadron are using mind-altering devices to rehabilitate criminals. Unusually for a superhero series, there's considerable change over twelve issues (each issue spanning a month). The characterisation of the team members is excellent, with the thrust of the series permitting most a turn in the spotlight, and events are rarely predictable. Pencillers Bob Hall and Paul Ryan are adequate without flash, but this is Gruenwald's comic and it's a rare treat to see twelve issues (or thirteen if the crossover into *Captain America* 314 is included) so well conceived and executed. The series stands alone and makes its point, so the graphic novel, although following up on the

characters, is adequate but superfluous to requirements. The team return in *Quasar* 13.~FP
Recommended: 1–12
Collection: Squadron Supreme (1-12)

SQUALOR
First: *4-issue miniseries 1989–1990*

Squalor is Harry Keller – gentle psychotic with two PhDs – who has stumbled on A-Time: 'not just another dimension, but your own neighbourhood bereft of linear time'. He meanders between A-Time and normal time, trying to help people and to save the world. In places, this works very well as a depiction of his psychosis, but the writer obviously thinks there's an actual story underway, and one that needs four issues to tell, and there isn't, there just isn't.~FC

SQUEAK THE MOUSE
NBM: *2 volumes 1988 and 1992*

Before *Itchy and Scratchy* there were Massimo Mattioli's ultra-violent cat-and-mouse 'goretoons' in which a dumb but cruel feline is constantly outwitted by a resourceful and equally nasty mouse. Mattioli's short strips are a hilarious wordless mix of old *Tom & Jerry* plots and zombie slasher movies. No matter how deranged and decaying the two characters become, they keep coming back for more. Mattioli's simplistic drawings reach a peak of hilarity in the second volume, when Squeak and a zombie cat begin cutting each other up on the beach using crabs and lobsters as weapons.~FJ
Recommended: 1–2

THE STAINLESS STEEL RAT
Eagle: *6-issue limited series 1985–1986*

Kelvin Gosnell adapts Harry Harrison's novels *The Stainless Steel Rat, The Stainless Steel Rat Saves The World* and *The Stainless Steel Rat For President*, each over two issues. Carlos Ezquerra uses James Coburn as his template for the character of Slippery Jim Di Griz, suave intergalactic rogue. The stories romp along in fine comic fashion, although those who've read the novels will note there's a fair amount of material excised in order to cram them into the necessary length. Otherwise these are perfectly acceptable.~WJ

STALKER
DC: *4 issues 1975–1976*

Exchanging his soul for combat skills leaves Stalker devoid of any human emotion. Well written by Paul Levitz, and with the art team of Steve Ditko and Wally Wood conveying the eldritch mood, this stands as a miniseries almost a decade ahead of their proliferation.~FP

STALKERS
Epic: *12 issues 1990–1991*

A series of mediocre covers and sketchy and uninspired interior artwork from – let's name the guilty – Mark Texeira and, primarily, Val Mayerik ruins consistently inventive plots from co-creators Mark Verheiden and Jan Strnad. Stalkers are a franchised private police force operating in the near future, and the series concentrates on both operatives and people whose lives are touched by them. Beginning with the nuclear destruction of Detroit, interesting characters abound, and the scripts continue to surprise and entertain. Most issues contain chapters of separate ongoing stories, one written by each co-creator. Issue 4 offers a good sample of the series.~WJ

STANLEY AND HIS MONSTER
DC: *4 issues (109–112) 1968, 4-issue miniseries 1993*

Arnold Drake's creation was introduced in 1965 as a back-up strip in *Fox And The Crow* 95. This feature introduced us to six-year-old Stanley and his parents, who won't allow Stanley to have a pet dog. Meanwhile, hiding in a local sewer is a monster, who desires only to live in peace and solitude, but who is constantly persecuted by unfeeling humans. Stanley, being a well-behaved brat, asks his parents if he can keep the twelve-foot shaggy red monster he found in the sewer. Laughing at Stanley's imagination, they say 'sure'. And that's your premise. It actually sounds a lot more fun than it was, since comics were firmly for children at this time: innocuous rather than entertaining was the order of the day. Artists on the strip included Bob Oksner and Winslow Mortimer. In 1993, Phil Foglio turned his attention to this strip, and ingeniously tied it in with the critically acclaimed *Sandman*, making the Monster a demon exiled from Hell for the crime of compassion. Hell, however, is under new management. And, not knowing the monster had been exiled, the new owners want him back. The Phantom Stranger and Ambrose Bierce get involved in the action, as does a voluptuous demoness named Nyx (closely modelled on a character from Foglio's *Xxxenophile*), a former lover of the monster. Bitingly funny, mildly salacious, and poking fun at the Vertigo line while plausibly meshing with it, this series is one to watch out for. A kind of prequel to the series, also by Foglio, is in *Secret Origins* 48.~HS
Recommended: Series two 1–4

STAR
Image: *4-issue miniseries 1995*

Spun off from Erik Larsen's *Savage Dragon*, this features rock-star-by-day, superhero-by-night Peter Klaptin (a cross between Peter Frampton

and Eric Clapton, according to Larsen – what a thought). Quite why 'the rogue prince of rock' should want to become wisecracking do-gooder Star is never fully explained, perhaps because scripters Tom and Mary Bierbaum spring a feeble 'surprise' in the final issue. The rest of the series is taken up with a series of plodding fight scenes between Star and sinister arms dealers Securitech, all quite slickly rendered by penciller Ben Herrera.~AL

STAR BRAND
Marvel: *19 issues, 1 annual 1986–1989*

The most successful of Marvel's New Universe titles, this told the story of the most powerful and seemingly only superhero in existence. Cold and calculating, the 'hero' feels totally alienated from his human origins after being given great cosmic powers (wouldn't we all?) After a shaky start, John Byrne was brought in as writer/artist on 10 and he soon made it his own, even giving himself a cameo in 12. The most interesting issues are where the new Star Brand, a baby, decides to destroy Pittsburgh (for the good of humanity?), with gruesome ramifications in 12–13. The Star Brand was later to re-appear in issues of *Quasar*.~TP
Recommended: 12, 13

S.T.A.R. CORPS
DC: *6-issue miniseries 1993–1994*

S.T.A.R. Labs are the all-purpose scientific research labs in the DC Universe, the acronym standing for Scientific and Technological Advanced Research. This takes a look at the people employed by S.T.A.R., and how they cope when an alien entity possesses the computers and some of the staff. The underlying message appears to be that folk shouldn't mess with what they don't know. It's a diverting read, worth hefting out of the cheap boxes where it now resides, but move no mountains to pick it up.~WJ

STAR HUNTERS
DC: *7 issues 1977–1978*

Infected with a disease that prevents them remaining on Earth, Donovan Flint and crew are charged with locating an artefact that apparently reveals the origin of mankind. Despite some distinctly slipshod art this is a better-than-average space opera that débuted in *DC Super Stars* 16, but unfortunately cancelled one chapter ahead of the conclusion.~FP

STAR MASTERS
Marvel: *3-issue miniseries 1995–1996*

Hideous would-be cosmic drivel starring The Silver Surfer, Beta Ray Bill (the horse-faced Thor) and Quasar, who is falsely accused of murdering three million characters, who are blatantly brought in so that they can be murdered and some over-powered and under-characterised moron accused of it.~GK

STAR*REACH
Star*Reach: *18 issues 1974–1979*

Groundbreaking anthology title that attempted to create a middle ground between the extreme excesses of the underground and the superhero-obsessed dullness of Marvel and DC in the mid-1970s. The title featured many of the brightest stars of that period. Some of them went on to greater things, although most have retained a cultish approach in their work that continues to set them apart from the mainstream. Having said that, the title itself has dated badly, with only a few stories showing long-term quality. Others are interesting, especially early work by people such as Dave Sim and Steve Leialoha. *Star*Reach* was also noticeable for the predominance of writer/artists who proved to have lasting appeal.

Of particular note: Howard Chaykin's grown-up space opera Cody Starbuck in 4; 'I'm God', by Dave Sim and Fabio Gasbarri in issue 7; P. Craig Russell's early attempt at opera adaptation with *Parsifal* (8 and 10); 'The Sacred And The Profane', by Dean Motter and Ken Steacy (9–13); Gene Day's 'Divine Wind' in 9; Gray Morrow producing an impeccably drawn but rather sixties-looking interpretation of Roger Zelazny's science-fiction story 'The Doors Of His Face', retitled 'The Lamps Of His Mouth', and 'Replay' by Michael T. Gilbert, both in 12.~NF
Collections: The Sacred And The Profane (9–13)

STAR*REACH CLASSICS
Eclipse: *6 issues 1984*

Reprints from various Star*Reach productions, including *Star*Reach* itself, *Quack* and *Imagine*. The colouring does the stories no favours, despite being reprinted on better paper with higher production values. The selection of strips does the company little credit either, offering Jim Starlin, Mike Vosburg and lesser works by Steve Leialoha, Frank Brunner and Lee Marrs. The better tales include Dave Sim's 'I'm God', drawn by Fabio Gasbarri, Howard Chaykin's Gideon Faust and 'Warlock At Large', both in 5, and P .Craig Russell's *Parsifal* in 6. There's a dated quality about the material as presented that doesn't show up in the originals. A taster, possibly, but the original anthologies, in context, are a better buy.~NF

STAR SEED
Broadway: *3 issues (7–9) 1996*

Continuing the numbering from *Powers That Be*, where Star Seed had been the lead feature, this continues the top-notch adventure as Cor searches for his father. You'll believe a comic produced by committee can be good.~FP
Recommended: 7–9

STAR SPANGLED WAR STORIES
DC: *205 issues (131–133, 3–204) 1952–1977*

Originally a superhero comic titled *Star Spangled Comics*, in its later days it featured Western and mystery stories, hence the peculiar numbering system. This was amongst DC's earliest war comics, and, as was the case with the others, early issues contained one-off short stories. Initially these were drawn by the likes of Curt Swan, Leonard Starr, Carmine Infantino and Bernie Krigstein (34), and written by Ed Herron, Bill Finger and Bob Haney among others. By the time of Joe Kubert's début in 33 the regular line-up of artists Jerry Grandenetti, Russ Heath, Irv Novick, and Ross Andru and Mike Esposito, with editor and chief writer Robert Kanigher, was in place. With a pedigree like that pretty well any issue is a decent read, although as with other 1950s DC war comics their most exceptional artist was Mort Drucker (25, 26, 28, 38, 41, 59, 61, 64, 66–68, 73, 74, 76, 78, 83, 84). Drucker is closely associated with the comic's first series, 'Mlle Marie', although he only drew the first four instalments in 86–89.

While the title was always inventive, the short-story format was inevitably limiting and was prone to gimmickry. The lengthier 'Mlle Marie' stories allowed Kanigher the scope to stretch out as a writer. Mademoiselle (not Millie as a generation of readers have assumed) Marie was a French resistance fighter in World War II, but, although the milieu was fresh and the execution good, readers simply didn't warm to the feature. Unlike its successor.

With the basic premise of US soldiers fighting dinosaurs, 'The War That Time Forgot' (90, 92–138) was never going to be exactly high art, but the fans loved it, and today it has a certain whacked-out appeal. Again created by Robert Kanigher, the feature was drawn for the most part by Ross Andru and Mike Esposito, with great vigour but little regard for prehistoric accuracy. Later stories were illustrated by Russ Heath (124–126, 131–133), Gene Colan (123, 128), Neal Adams (134) and Joe Kubert (124–126, 137, 138), amongst others. The team of Kanigher and Kubert were reunited for the comic's next feature, the far more memorable Enemy Ace. It started in 139, though the character had earlier appeared in *Our Army At War* and *Showcase*.

Rittmeister Hans Von Hammer was the 'Enemy Ace', a Von Richtofenesque German World War I pilot with a crimson Fokker Triplane. A troubled, brooding character, Von

Hammer's only friend was a wolf, and he was much given to calling himself 'a human killing machine'. Though occasionally marred by historical inaccuracy, particularly in the case of outlandish opponents like The Hangman and St George, the strip had an astonishing intensity, and its pensive, bleak tone was a far cry from the usual triumphalism of the era's war comics. With the exception of a couple of fill-ins (Adams in 144 and Heath in 152), the entire run was drawn by Joe Kubert, who excelled at the aerial battle scenes. 146 and 151 had already featured old material, and from 153 to the strip's demise it was all reprints, but by then Enemy Ace had long since lost the cover slot to its replacement. It was a strip both written and drawn by Kubert, The Unknown Soldier, which had débuted in 151 with an origin in 154.

The Unknown Soldier was both a skilful make-up artist and a consummate soldier, and each episode starred him in a different role, frequently behind enemy lines and often disguised as the enemy. Plagued by reprint stories introduced by Unknown and retroactively claimed to be previous missions (153, 157, 162), the feature's early episodes were a treat, and Kubert, joined by writer Bob Haney from 158, was on top form. Following a couple of fill-ins (Doug Wildey in 161 and Dan Spiegle in 163 and 164), Jack Sprang became the regular artist with 165, joined three issues later by new editor Archie Goodwin. Against all expectations, these, and later issues written by Frank Robbins (172–182), were every bit as good as Kubert's had been, and the strip remained both inventive and hard-hitting. Goodwin brought with him an adventurous approach to back-ups and utilised a wide variety of talent, including Howard Chaykin (167), Tom Sutton (168), Vincente Alcazar (178) and, most interestingly, a young Walt Simonson (170, 172, 180). The comic's finest back-up, though, and indeed its best-ever story, was Robert Kanigher's 'Yellow Devil', masterfully drawn by Alex Toth in 164. Frank Thorne also contributed a number of fine back-ups (173, 176, 178), including a lovely Enemy Ace three-parter in 181–183. Enemy Ace's last appearance here was to be in 200, by Kubert.

183 saw the installation of David Michelinie and Gerry Talaoc as the creative team, and their issues are, if anything, even more hard-hitting than those of their predecessors, particularly 183, in which we see the Unknown Soldier's hideously scarred face for the first time. Also notable during their tenure was a short back-up written by Archie Goodwin, with art from Steve Harper, and, surprisingly for a war comic, Mike Kaluta, in 197. With 205 the comics title changed to *Unknown Soldier*.~DAR

Recommended: 86–89, 138–152, 154–156, 158–160, 164, 170, 172, 180–183, 197, 200

STAR TREK
Gold Key: *61 issues 1967–1979*

Well, here we see Kirk and company boldly exploring new planets and such in exactly the same manner as portrayed in the TV series. This adaptation was doomed from the first issue (drawn by Nevio Zeccara, as was the second). The characters are so well established and defined in the TV series that there's no opportunity for any author to do anything interesting or innovative with them in a comic. Not that Paul S. Newman, writer of most early issues, tried. The situations the crew find themselves in are far less imaginative, and overall the run yields a very monotonous and wearisome read. Furthermore it seems that the main artist until 37, Alberto Giolitti, had never seen the TV show. (*2000AD* completists might be interested to know that Massimo Belardinelli assisted Giolitti.) Al McWilliams illustrated most issues from 37 on, and was a considerable improvement, but the plots he was given, largely from Arnold Drake and George Kashdan, were as uninspiring as those in previous issues.~APS

Collections: Enterprise Log 1 (1–8), Log 2 (9–17), Log 3 (18–26), Log 4 (27, 28, 30–34, 36, 38)

STAR TREK
Marvel: *18 issues 1980–1982*

Beginning with the Marv Wolfman-written adaptation of the first *Star Trek* film, Martin Pasko beamed on and managed to catch the style of *Star Trek* very well. Characterisation was good, but early issues suffered from some of Dave Cockrum's most uninspired art, and on the whole there was a certain predictability, due to the comic going where the TV series had been before. Matters improved to an extent in later issues, particularly those drawn by Walt Simonson.~DWC

STAR TREK
DC: *Series one 56 issues, 3 Annuals 1984–1988, series two 80 issues, 6 Annuals, 3 specials, 2 Graphic Novels 1989–1996*

Given the poor quality of the previous attempts at adapting *Star Trek* for comics, Mike Barr, Tom Sutton and Ricardo Villagran didn't really have to exert themselves to produce better material, and they certainly didn't. It seemed to be considered enough to get the likenesses right, ensure that the characteristic quirks of the crew remain intact, and reprise ideas from the TV series every now and then. The one departure from expectation is Saavik replacing the temporarily deceased Spock in the early issues as the comic followed the events of the second *Star Trek* movie. A return for the evil Enterprise crew from the TV episode in 9–16 was selected for collection, but it's no better than the rest of Barr's run. He left with 16, with 19 written by Walter Koenig (Ensign Chekov). It's badly written, although well drawn by Dan Spiegle, and was but one of a succession of one-shot stories written by a variety of folk, but usually all drawn by Sutton and Villagran (although Gray Morrow draws nice fillers in 28, 35 and 56). The best of them is by Diane Duane in 24 and 25, who adds some much needed light relief, although she pulls her plot from *The Mouse That Roared*.

Len Wein's short run as writer adds some much-needed continuity, but his plots are no better than Barr's. He celebrates his departure by running through almost every bridge-scene cliché in the first five pages of 39, yet another issue in which an internal surprise – in this case on the final page – is blown on the cover. Mike Carlin is a marginal improvement in 41–47, again taking his cue from old TV episodes. By simple virtue of a fine ear for dialogue, Peter David improves the scripting immensely from 48. If not exactly realistic dialogue, most people simply not being *that* witty off the cuff, and sometimes too glib, it combines well with the first really engaging plot for over twenty issues, to provide one of only two runs worth bothering with in the first series. Someone is attempting to engender war between The Federation and the Klingons, and counterpointing this in microcosm are the sudden doubts of Klingon Konom and his bride-to-be Nancy in 48–50. Thereafter 51 and 52 are merely average, and Kirk starts 53 by almost dying. That and the following two issues involve the mystery of who was trying to kill him. David's now confidently dealing with the characters, and while the ending is a little too contrived (although well set up) it's a decent story, with Gordon Purcell filling in as penciller for two issues.

Given his successful run on the previous series it's no surprise to see Peter David returning to write the new series, launched alongside the ongoing series starring the Next Generation crew. He starts well. 1 has the Klingons putting a price on Kirk's head, and issues to 10 see a gradual escalation in problems for Kirk until he eventually flouts one regulation too many, leading to a trial occupying 10–12. Of course, as with his 'death' in the previous series, there's not going to be any significant change to the *status quo*, but David is adept at keeping the interest up, and he introduces some intriguing new characters along the way. The bounty-hunting Sweeney in 7–9 is David's idea of the stiff-upper-lip Englishman, and R.J. Blaise, appointed by Starfleet to supervise Kirk, is surely based on Katherine Hepburn's movie characters. 1–12 in their entirety are a decent story arc that should be enjoyable to any *Star Trek* fan, the only real fault being their concentration on Kirk to the neglect of the remaining crew. Gordon Purcell

replaces James Fry as penciller on 11, and will be present for much of the series. Instead of relying on freehand drawing as he had during the first series, his lightbox works overtime in tracing likenesses, which gives his art a very static look overall.

David teams with Bill Mumy for 13–15, not his best work, and after a decent one-shot in 19 bids his farewells. His replacement is Howard Weinstein, who'd written *Star Trek* episodes and novels; he débuts with 17 to pen most of the rest of the run. His approach differs from David's, and isn't as appealing. Factors making David's scripts entertaining included his willingness to introduce new characters and incorporate them into an ongoing continuity interacting with the regulars, and short story arcs as part of a longer ongoing continuity. Weinstein is more focused on retaining the TV show formula, introducing new characters only for a particular story arc. The resulting familiarity dulls the comic to an extent, and Weinstein, although never less than professional, doesn't produce plots captivating enough to overcome this, although his stories are better than the majority of the first run. He also often runs plots over four to six issues at a time, providing fewer jumping-in points. 35–40, largely a fable about arms escalation, provide a decent sample of Weinstein's run, with four of the six chapters pencilled by Rod Whigham, who goes on to draw more of the series than anyone else. It returns Saavik and gives McCoy and particularly Sulu, now promoted to Captain and on his first mission, a turn in the spotlight.

Steve Wilson writes a nice character episode involving Spock and Captain Christopher Pike in 61, and another story returning a TV series favourite is Weinstein's 'The Peacekeeper' in 49 and 50, with the enigmatic Gary Seven, who's back again in the sixth annual. Harry Mudd, rogue by trade, is a popular choice of recurring character from the TV series, returning in 22–24 as well as 39 and 40 of the first series.

Later issues diverge from following the continuity of the movies to present untold stories from the 'five year mission', i.e. the TV series era. This has the benefit of locating all the popular members of the crew back on the Enterprise, although to Weinstein's credit his plots generally united them anyway in a subtler fashion. Many of these later issues are written by Kevin Ryan, who's welcome for an ability to cram a plot into less than four issues, and drawn by Rachel Ketchum. She seems to trace the faces of the cast from photographs and stick them onto already drawn bodies, for a very odd, distorted look.

Of the assorted annuals and specials accompanying both series, by far and away the best is the first annual from the second series (1990). Written by Peter David and George Takei, the story naturally enough focuses on Takei's *Star Trek* character Mr Sulu. A number of late-twentieth-century concerns are transferred to the twenty-third century and combined with a story about lost love, all expressively drawn by Gray Morrow. The sixth annual teams the Enterprise crew with their 24th-century counterparts, but keep your expectations low. DC also adapt the third, fourth, fifth and sixth *Star Trek* movies as one-shot specials. They're all workmanlike, without being spectacular, the quality depending largely on the film script, thus making *Star Trek IV* the best of the bunch.

The graphic novel 'Debt Of Honor' was much trumpeted. Writer Chris Claremont relates an unlikely incident from Kirk's past concerning a female Vulcan civilian named T'Cel (!) saving his life when they were attacked by *Alien*-like aliens. He was rescued, but she was captured by Romulans, eventually becoming one of their commanders. Their encounters since have all involved the mysterious aliens, who remain unknown except for rare attacks, and twenty years later, Kirk, T'Cel and a Klingon commander decide it's time to investigate. It's a decent plot, but Claremont undermines it by being unable to resist peppering the story with extraneous 'smart' references. It's not big, it's not that clever, and it's as distracting as hell. Artist Adam Hughes wore the freeze-frame button on his video remote down to nothing capturing those cast likenesses, and he's turned in some nice pages, but by and large they're swamped by excess verbiage. There's wads of expository dialogue, lacking any finesse where inserted, and several rambling character pieces, rendering this appallingly overwritten for a relatively simple plot. It's as if Claremont wanted to ensure that nothing he loves about *Star Trek* was omitted, which makes for an unsatisfying read. 'The Ashes Of Eden' adapts a *Star Trek* novel ostensibly authored by William Shatner, but which also credits Judith and Garfield Reeves-Stevens as writers. It's a decent romp that pushes the feelgood buttons throughout, with Kirk, now apparently surplus to Starfleet requirements, offered the promise of eternal life, but unknowingly labelled a traitor, which requires his old crew to hunt him down. Considering Kirk was played by Shatner, he's surprisingly and effectively harsh on the character. Steve Erwin's art isn't as decorative as Hughes's, but his story-telling is excellent, and of the two graphic novels this is the one *Star Trek* fans are more likely to enjoy.~FP
Recommended: Series one 49, 50, 53–55, Series two 4–12, Annual 1, *The Ashes Of Eden*
Collections: The Best Of Star Trek (Series one 24, 25, Annual 2, 3, series two 10–12), *The Mirror Universe* (series one 9–16), *Revisitations* (series two 22–24, 49, 50), *Tests Of Courage* (series two 35–40), *Who Killed Captain Kirk?* (series one 49–55)

STAR TREK: DEEP SPACE NINE

Malibu: *33 issues (0–32), 2 Annuals, 1 Special 1993–1996*

Malibu's first issue of *Deep Space Nine* comes in a bewildering array of covers, but what really matters is the story inside, about a stange toxic substance causing large areas of the space station to be evacuated. Written by Mike Barr, as are all issues to 6, and continued into the following issue, it's very average, as are all issues to 6. The art by Gordon Purcell and Terry Pallot is good, though, dynamic and lively. The team would later move to working on DC's *Star Trek* titles. 6 is the first of number of issues in the run with multiple short stories, and thereafter until 19 it seems as if everyone and their grandparents is given the chance to write an issue. The approach obviously varies wildly, from Charles Marshall's overly comedic tales in 11–13 to Mark Altman's character studies; and his two-part story in 8 and 9 is the best of this run.

The experienced Dan Mishkin, who'd supplied 10, writes from 19, and is... average, with nothing in his plots inspiring must-have, double-bag status, but he provides a baseline level of enjoyment each time. His epic's in 23–25, with the Bajoran sacred orb the subject of some to-ing and fro-ing. There are also three one-shots. 'Blood And Honor' is written by *Star Trek* actor Mark Lenard, and has a stupid twee twist to a story of the Romulan ambassador to Bejor and a mysterious artefact, while a more Ferengi-based story takes place in 'The Rules Of Diplomacy', in which Nog escorts a Klingon officer to his home planet. It's written by Aron Eisenberg, who plays Nog in the TV show, but there's no acting connection with the very ordinary 'Worf', which has two stories about the Klingon.

Overall, while there's nothing particularly outstanding in the comics, neither is the barrel dredged very often. *Deep Space Nine* fans with a cash surplus might want to try a few issues, because the characters are well treated, but there's better *Star Trek* material elsewhere.~WJ
Collections: Deep Space Nine (1–3), *Emancipation And Beyond* (4, 5), *Requiem* (8, 9), *Dax's Comet* (14, 15), *Shanghaied* (16–18), *Lightstorm/Terek Nor* (both specials)

STAR TREK: The Next Generation

DC: *6-issue miniseries 1988, 80 issues, 6 Annuals, 3 Specials 1989–1996*

The introductory miniseries is the work of Mike Carlin and Pablo Marcos, with inkers Carlos Garzon and Arne Starr, and there are certainly teething problems. It was obviously produced with Carlin having seen very few of the TV episodes, and there's a stiffness in the dialogue and situations and an over-reliance on scenarios from those early episodes. Marcos, never the most dynamic or anatomically correct of pencillers, is adequate, but no more.

Marcos remains to draw the ongoing series, now using more photo reference, and the new writer is Jan Michael Friedman, who's a wise choice. He's an adroit hand at maintaining the character interaction and the human-interest stories that were so much the driving force of the TV series, and also turns in good plots and mysteries. While rarely stunning, his issues, which comprise almost the entirety of the run, are largely enjoyable reads for anyone familiar with the TV show, and have an admirable consistency. Of his early material, 7–8 focus on Data being kidnapped by space pirates whose dying leader wants to transfer his consciousness into Data's body. They're good representative issues and have the bonus of being drawn by Gordon Purcell, whose art is less static than that of Marcos. 19's one-issue character study 'The Lesson' is also a decent sample, this pencilled by Peter Krause and inked by Marcos, a competent art team that lasts through most issues until 51.

Friedman's first outstanding multi-part story runs in 20–24. Worf, Riker and Will Crusher depart for a short mission in a shuttlecraft, but are sucked through a vortex that disables their star drive, in effect stranding them in a strange part of the galaxy. The story focuses both on their attempts to return home and on the emotions of those on the Enterprise who believe them dead; it also gives the Enterprise a mission diverting enough to be an effective counterplot, and to put everything to rights by the conclusion. 25–28 don't have quite the same emotional pull, but are still solid issues. After a poor Q appearance in the second annual, written by John DeLancie, the actor who portrays the character, Q returns under Friedman's pen in 33–35 for a more effective story, in which he transforms the Enterprise's crew into Klingons.

Those for whom a detailed time-scale slotting DC's comics and the novels into the TV continuity is necessary will find it on 37's editorial page (with an update in 69), the story being the middle chapter of a merely average piece starring the Next Generation's Harry Mudd counterpart Ardra. 39–44 appear to be in response to readers requesting more action, and stretch a slim plot that extra mile too far, but Friedman's right back on form with 47–50, a tale of a parallel dimension in which Riker captains the Enterprise this is that universe's last hope against the otherwise all-conquering Borg. Plot and counter-plot ensue, and, given that all the crew are duplicated, Friedman has the luxury of permanently changing the status quo. Excellent stuff, with Krause on top form for his penultimate issues.

Considering the opportunities afforded writers by virtue of the Holodeck's ability to recreate any period or setting, Friedman was remarkably restrained in his use of it. 52–54, though, see Picard there in P.I. Dixon Hill mode, desperately trying to solve a mystery when the lives of crew members are dependent on his doing so. It's not the best of the longer stories, due to yet another appearance from an overused adversary. By this point Deryl Skelton is the regular penciller until 70. His layouts are dull and his art less expressive than Krause's by some distance, with stiff figures, and faces too obviously copied, and thus distracting. Gordon Purcell, for most of the remaining issues, is far better. 66 is whimsical solution to the problem of dealing with nuclear stockpiles, and 71–75 return the Tholians in a story picking up after the final Next Generation TV episode. While not quite up to Friedman's best, there's still a well-constructed plot with plenty of twists and escapes and not one, but two decent revelations as to who's responsible for some attacks on lonely outposts.

The final two issues, as did the final TV show episode, concern further intervention by Q. Hearing a funeral eulogy in which Picard wishes that all his crew had Data's android immunity to many forms of danger, Q grants the wish. All start on the same level that Data did, logical, nearly emotionless and lacking basic human concern, while Friedman masterfully includes Data's reactions to the occurrence. He's grown immensely through interaction with humans and other species, and sees his friends failing as humans. The eventual message is obvious, but getting there is hugely entertaining.

The annuals and specials are a generally rum bunch, with Friedman not on form for those he writes. There's a nice Diane Duane-written short in the first special, and Chris Claremont follows up on the Star Trek 'Debt Of Honor' graphic novel in the second, but it's the third special that's the best of them all, with a quiet story about complex negotiations and new technology, yet nonetheless absorbing for all that, from Michael DeMerritt and Ricardo Villagran. The back-up has Scotty in the twenty-fourth century. There's also a one-shot special adapting the final TV episode, and the sixth annual continues a story from Star Trek annual 6 that mixes and matches the crews from both Enterprises, although it's hardly compelling.~FP

Recommended: 20–24, 47–50, 79, 80

Collections: Beginnings (miniseries 1–6), *The Best Of Star Trek The Next Generation* (5, 6, 19, Annual 1, 2), *The Star Lost* (20–24)

STAR TREK Miniseries

Oddly enough, there's only been a single miniseries featuring the original Star Trek characters, that being 'The Modala Imperative'. It actually comprises two separate four-issue series under the same title, the second dealing with the 24th-century Enterprise crew. In the four issues featuring the 'classic' crew, the Enterprise journeys to Modala on Ensign Chekov's first mission. The planet has applied for Federation membership, and Chekov accompanies Kirk on an assessment mission. What they find is a totalitarian regime possessing weapons far beyond the current level of technology. A century later the mysterious suppliers of those weapons to Modala come calling for payment just as the next Enterprise makes a check back to see whether or not Modala is ready for Federation membership. Michael Jan Friedman, regular *Next Generation* writer, handles the original crew just as well, while Peter David gets his first crack at Picard and company, and both provide stories with a high entertainment value. The only fly in the ointment is artist Pablo Marcos, who draws all eight comics unaided and is pedestrian throughout. Story-driven readers should take a look, art lovers should avoid.

The Enterprise, acting as security for the Solar Sailing Cup, begins the 'Ill Wind' miniseries. It's a curiously subdued piece from Diane Duane, as Picard and The Mestral, a head of state unable to resign yet with many enemies, each feels hemmed in, and each envies the other's freedoms. Sabotage during the race and an assassination attempt complicate matters, but the nice character touches don't disguise that this is stretched too long over four issues. Worf and Riker are the leads for 'Shadowheart', in which Worf learns that his human brother, believed recently dead, is leading a rebellion in a Klingon outpost. Again, it's stretched too far, although the creative team of Michael Jan Friedman and Steve Erwin pack in a little more conflict, both physical and emotional.

A teaming between the 24th-century crew of the Enterprise and those manning Deep Space Nine occurs over four issues, but as different companies have the comic rights to each series, each publishes two parts, both numbering them 1 and 2. DC publish the first and fourth chapters and Malibu the second and third. Mike Barr and Michael Jan Friedman construct a perfectly acceptable plot set as the Enterprise stops off at Deep Space Nine shortly after its recovery. The interaction between the two casts is well handled, and artists Gordon Purcell and Terry Pallot also do a fine job.

Malibu published two *Deep Space Nine* series, both written by Mark Altman and pencilled by Rob Davis. 'Hearts And Minds' starts with Sisko having to mediate in order to avoid full-scale hostilities between the Cardassians and the Klingons. Meanwhile Dax and Bashir find something very interesting. It's a suspenseful story, over four issues, that's

leagues better than any of the regular series, and should be a worthwhile purchase for any *Deep Space Nine* fan. The three-issue 'Maquis' story isn't quite as successful, with a weaker plot, and Davis's art not looking as good inked by Jack Snider as it did when inked by Terry Pallot for the previous miniseries. The Maquis are a group of former freedom fighters who chose to remain unaligned when peace broke out. First they capture Dr Bashir, and the entire group is then taken prisoner by some Cardassians, at which point Sisko takes a more direct hand.~FP

Collections: Hearts And Minds (1–4), *The Landmark Crossover* (*Next Generation/Deep Space Nine* 1–2, *Deep Space Nine/Next Generation* 1–2), *Maquis: Soldier Peace* (1–3), *The Modala Imperative* (*Star Trek* 1–4, *Star Trek The Next Generation* 1–4), *The Maquis* (1–3)

STAR TREK/X-MEN
Marvel: *One-shot 1996*

Stepping straight into the spirit of the original *Star Trek* series, writer Scott Lobdell has the crew of the Enterprise encounter a strange dimensional rift through which they're pulled. For maximum effect, shake the comic about a bit when reading this sequence. On the other side they encounter the X-Men. It's an unlikely forced team-up involving Gary Mitchell, seen in the 1960s TV series, under the influence of X-Men adversary Proteus. Lobdell throws in all sorts of other superfluous characters, but the title is saved by the deftly written interaction between the Enterprise crew and the X-Men. Fans of both should figure out the Dr McCoy joke, but the opportunity to have Kirk say to Cyclops 'Beam me up, Scotty' is sadly missed. A number of artists contribute, most notably Mark Silvestri.~HY

STAR WARS
Marvel: *107 issues, 3 Annuals, 1977–1986, 4-issue miniseries ('Return Of The Jedi') 1983–1984*

Star Wars merchandising branched out into every conceivable medium in the late 1970s, and comics were no exception. Marvel started with a competent adaptation of the film in 1–6, including some scenes from the original script that never made it to the screen, such as the sequence in the Tatooine workshop between Luke Skywalker and his friend Biggs. The adaptation was also released as an oversize Marvel Treasury edition, initially in two parts, then collected. *The Empire Strikes Back* adaptation was also issued in the Treasury format, and as a colour magazine. The gap between 6 and the next film was bridged with a series of stories which, while entertaining, were visibly unable to advance plot or character. The unresolved (and unresolvable) love triangle between the major characters was a particular albatross around the neck of many plots, with Han, Luke and Leia unable to have each other or, indeed, anyone else. Adventures instead focused on weird aliens and bizarre robots, interspersed with fights with storm-troopers and TIE fighters, which wasn't too far from the spirit of *Star Wars* in any case. 39–44 detail the events of *The Empire Strikes Back*, but, like the first film, leave the comic in limbo until the subsequent movie, this time without even the advantage of having all the main characters available for use, as the middle film of the trilogy had left Han Solo a captive of his old enemy Jabba the Hutt – a useful device in case Harrison Ford, by now a major Hollywood star, chose not to return for a third outing. This left the comic in the awkward position of not being able to have Solo's friends attempt to rescue him while trying, unsuccessfully, to make it seem like they hadn't got round to it yet because they had better things to do. *Return Of The Jedi* was adapted in a separate miniseries, written by Archie Goodwin with art by Al Williamson throughout. It came in two formats, regular comic-size and collected as a magazine, in a attempt to attract a non-comics audience. *Star Wars* itself survived for a few years after the end of the trilogy, basically running on until interest in the movies began to peter out.

During its near-ten-year run, *Star Wars* boasted some impressive creators, particularly on the art side. The first ten issues, written by Roy Thomas, were pencilled by Howard Chaykin. Archie Goodwin, with Carmine Infantino on pencilling duty, took over from issue 11, and, under a succession of inkers, steered the book to 37, during which period the stories took Luke Skywalker back to Tatooine, and dealt with both Han and Chewie's debts to Jabba the Hutt, and Ben Kenobi and Darth Vader's pasts. Many of the stories either noticeably skirt around actually revealing anything at all, or are simply inaccurate in the face of later developments. Goodwin stays on the writing through to issue 50, aided by Al Williamson on art, starting with the *Empire Strikes Back* adaptations and lasting through to Infantino's return with 45. After this, an unsettled creative team dooms the book to a succession of fill-in issues until David Micheline (writer) and Walt Simonson take over with 56, kicking off with a tale of Lando Calrissian on Bespin. The next regular team is Jo Duffy and Ron Frenz, inked by Tom Palmer, who take the book up to its unspectacular finish. Unlike the Death Star, the comic dies with a whimper rather than a bang. The final issue includes art by Whilce Portacio – some of his earliest published Marvel work. In general, however, while the series always remains around average, it is the interest in the films, rather than the comics for their own

sake, which keeps the back-issues prices ridiculously high.

To their credit, since Dark Horse have begun publishing *Star Wars* comics, they've also reprinted several of the Marvel comics, including all three movie adaptations, and 95. The latter, by Goodwin and Williamson, was released as *Classic Star Wars: The Vandelheim Mission*.~JC
Collections: The Empire Strikes Back (39–44), *A New Hope* (1–6), *Return Of The Jedi* (*Return* 1–4)

STAR WARS: Dark Empire
Dark Horse: *6-issue miniseries 1991–1992, 6-issue miniseries (Dark Empire II) 1994–1995*

The first *Dark Empire* series was the first Star Wars title that Dark Horse released and it set a standard so far unsurpassed. The story begins after the events of *Return of the Jedi* and focuses on the Emperor, who escaped death and plans to create a new body for himself. The job falls to Luke to beat this powerful adversary once again. The story is fast-paced and very detailed, with the best feature being Cam Kennedy's fantastic art, which is full of imaginative vehicles and mysterious figures. The sequel is unfortunately not as good. Tom Veitch's script is okay and Cam Kennedy's art is once again brilliant, but the problem is that the story is so similar to the first *Dark Empire* that this isn't worth reading.~SS
Recommended: *Dark Empire* 1–6
Collections: Dark Empire (*Dark Empire* 1–6), *Dark Empire II* (*Dark Empire II* 1–6)

STAR WARS: Empire's End
Dark Horse: *2-issue microseries 1995*

This begins after the *Dark Empire II* miniseries. The Emperor returns (again!), this time requiring a Jedi host body in order to live forever. His target is Leia's third-born, Anakin Solo. Tom Veitch's script cannot disguise the fact that the Emperor's resurrection is dull. Making matters worse is artist Jim Baikie being unable to capture likenesses of the characters, and seemingly rushing his art. The only redeeming feature is that the story concludes properly; there appears to be little chance of a sequel.~SS

STAR WARS: Heir To The Empire
Dark Horse: *6-issue miniseries 1995–1996*

Adapted from a novel by Timothy Zahn, chronologically this dates just before the *Dark Empire* miniseries. The plot concerns the efforts of an Imperial officer to reunite his defeated forces in order to destroy the rebels. To ensure success he strikes a bargain with a character called Joruus C'boath, who promises help in return for Luke and Leia, whom he wants to train as dark Jedis. Other interesting features include Leia's trip to

Kashyyk, home of the Wookies (the same race as Chewbecca), and that since they were last seen in *Return Of The Jedi* Leia has married Han and is pregnant. French artist Olivier Vatine is superb, equally adept at striking characters and battle in space.~SS

STAR WARS: River of Chaos
Dark Horse: *4-issue miniseries 1995*

Louise Simonson writes a great story about Princess Leia forced to go undercover behind enemy lines in order to stop an attack on the republic. It's fast-paced, Leia is well characterised and the art, by June Brigman, is ordinary but passable. It would be nice if Leia was as well handled in other Star Wars titles.~SS

STARBLAST
Marvel: *4-issue miniseries 1994*

Utterly stupid story making little sense to anyone who doesn't also read *Quasar*, particularly issues 54–57, with which it crosses over. Dozens of superheroes are embroiled in a plot to siphon off the Starbrand energy welded to Quasar's girl-friend and use it for nefarious purposes. The appalling dialogue – step forward, Mark Gruenwald – makes everyone sound like kids playing at being superheroes, and the ending is extremely rushed.~FP

STARFIRE
DC: *8 issues, 1976–1977*

A sword-and-science/sorcery series about a slave who attempted to free her world from alien invaders (she was a sort of love-child of Princess Leia and Attila the Hun), *Starfire* had potential, but lacked direction. And without wanting to sound sexist, Starfire (not to be confused with the *New Teen Titans* character) didn't seem to have enough strength to file her nails, let alone fight with a sword.~HY

Legends of the STARGRAZERS
Innovation: *5 issues 1989–1990*

An all-female space crew roams the galaxy in this distressingly exploitative series. There's not much to the plots other than ways of showing off skimpily dressed women in poses copied from glamour mags, making the entire concept a rather unsavoury substitute for pubescents unable to buy *Playboy*. The back-up strips and detours are usually better conceived, with Tom Yeates contributing to 3.~WJ

STARJAMMERS
Marvel: *4-issue miniseries 1995–1996*

Intelligent space opera in which the Starjammers and Shi'ar dance around each other in the face of a new, common menace: the Uncreated. Warren Ellis injects welcome background and

characterisation into Starjammer personnel. Breathtaking Carlos Pacheco pencils and beautiful, airbrush effect computer colouring make this series a very attractive package.~APS
Recommended: 1–4

X-Men Spotlight on STARJAMMERS
Marvel: *2 issues 1990*

Team of *X-Men* supporting characters embarks on a space-operatic quest in a race against its traditional enemies, the Shi'ar empire. Writer Terry Kavanagh lacks a clear direction. The plot features too many characters (Imperial Guard, Excalibur, X-Factor), too many token appearances and too many plagiarisms of *Star Trek* devices.~APS

STARLORD
Marvel: *One-shot 1982, 3-issue miniseries 1996–1997*

Always heavily promoted as science fiction, *Starlord* is little more than superheroics in outer space. None the worse for it though, as the sporadic tales of Peter Quill and his symbiotic relationship with a starship regularly surpass average. His bibliography reads: *Marvel Preview* 4, 11, 14, 15, 18, *Marvel Super Special* 10, *Marvel Premiere* 61 and the second series of *Marvel Spotlight* 6, 7 in addition to the eponymous entries. The 1982 one-shot is a colour reprint of *Marvel Preview* 11 by Chris Claremont and John Byrne, wrapped up in a cosy six-page framing sequence by Claremont and Michael Golden. Seven pages of Dr Who by Steve Moore and Dave Gibbons provide back-up.

In the miniseries, weakly telepathic Sinjin Quarrel faces a life of mundane obscurity as a justice administrator on a backwater planet until he stumbles across Starlord's abandoned and derelict ship. Science-fiction author Timothy Zahn shows his strengths as Quarrel struggles to come to terms with the Starlord identity, powers, gadgets and Ship's sentient persona. Substantial plotting weaves Quarrel through tangled political machinations of corrupt officials, and the non-explanation of Quill's disappearance whets the appetite for the future. Dan Lawliss' painted art is solid but unspectacular; the story just lacks sufficient fizz and sparkle to earn recommendation.~APS

STARMAN
DC: *46 issues 1988–1992*

Although DC published various Starmen over the decades a new character first occupied an eponymous title. It's light superheroics, aping the 1960s Marvel template. Will Payton wakes up in a morgue unable to account for six weeks of his life.

During that time he's somehow learned to fly and acquired superhuman strength and resilience along with being able to generate great heat. He can also morph his features and skin-tone. Roger Stern and Tom Lyle produce most of 1–30, during which Payton faces an assortment of villains, meets plenty of other DC characters and generally plays the superpowered boy scout. There's a nice mixture of action and introspection, with issue 10's face-off against Blockbuster a good sample of the former, and issue 24 of the latter. For an all-round sampler try 7, revealing what Payton is and featuring most of the supporting cast. Len Strazewski continues the formula from 30, but he's not as adept, and later issues, while competent, lack any spark.~FP

STARMAN

DC: *25 issues + 1994 to date, 1 annual*

This *Starman* series has greater depth that its predecessor, and at its best is an unusually satisfying read. Writer James Robinson introduces another new Starman, Jack Knight, son of the first DC character to adopt the name. Knight's brother wore his father's costume to battle the Starman above in 26 of his title, but was dispatched with little ceremony here only to make an annual return as a ghost in twee bonding issues. Generally, though, this series is excellent. Robinson enjoys switching styles of story-telling, his plotting is exceptional, foreshadowing events over a year in advance, his nostalgia for old DC superhero comics serves well, and his characters are finely tuned and memorable. Old villain The Shade is particularly well manifested as a literate *eminence grise*. A factor adding to the mood is the conception of Opal City, Starman's hometown. It's gloriously designed by pencil artist Tony Harris: a consistent and individual backdrop gives the series a mystique and history and at once sets it apart. Starting as a reluctant superhero, preferring to run his memorabilia store to following the family tradition, Knight eventually falls into line, and his awkward yet loving relationship with his father is particularly well presented. The career choice permits *Starman* to wash over the breadth of popular culture past and present, and superhero standbys such as the costume and the secret identity are discarded, to no detrimental effect. Although tying up loose ends of a multi-part story and hinting at the future, 17 sums up the mood of *Starman* in a single issue.~FP

Recommended: Series two 0–4, 6–8, 10, 12–17, 20–25

Collection: Night And Day (7–10, 12–16), *Starman* (0–5)

STARSLAMMERS

Marvel: *Graphic novel 1983*
Bravura: *4 issues 1994–1995*

The Starslammers are a race of mercenaries who're the best combat soldiers in history. They had a considerable incentive for learning to fight, once being hunted for sport by a race with superior technology. This is the story Walter Simonson tells in the graphic novel, but it's told in a needlessly convoluted manner that removes most of the impetus. The art is impressive, though, and Simonson's approach to depicting telepathic communication is particularly clever and effective. The Bravura series is set hundreds of years later, and is currently unfinished, as Simonson withdrew it from Bravura before publication of the final issue. It's still worth reading, however. In this story one of the Starslammers has been captured after an unsuccessful attack on the colony of a small and unlovely empire, and some strange things start happening on the ship transporting him to the emperor's planet. It's a lively, interesting read with solid characterisation and good dialogue. Take a look at it, if only for the scene where the mercenary asks Colonel Phaedra why she chooses a bikini as her military uniform, to which she gives a witty, intelligent answer!~FC

Recommended: 1–4

STARSLAYER

Pacific: *6 issues 1982*
First: *28 issues (7–34) 1983–1985*

After many years doing *The Warlord* for DC, Mike Grell moved to the fledgling independent company Pacific and produced a mirror-image title in *Starslayer*. Instead of a modern man in a barbaric land he gave us a barbarian in the far-flung future. He goes over old ground thematically – the lone warrior's quest for a honourable way to live, etc – and left as artist with 7 and scripter with 9 for *Jon Sable, Freelance*. Torin Mac Quillon, a half-Scythian somehow living with Celtic Britons, is seized at the moment of death by Tamara, an Earth super-agent on a mission to save our solar system. Why she needs a hairy, middle-aged swordsman is never really explained to anyone's satisfaction but she does, and they do, but not without chucking the Earth into the Sun to 'reignite' it, which pisses off the Earth's rulers, who promptly chase them across the universe for the rest of the series.

In John Ostrander's hands, Starslayer quickly became an adjunct of Grimjack, with the heroes based in Cynosure fighting Celtic goddesses, a Grimjack crossover in 18 (it had been the back-up strip from 10 onwards), and various characters, such as Kallibos, in common. Lenin Desol's art, 7 onwards, was very flat, and singularly unsuited to the continual fight-and-flight pages he was required to draw. Tim Truman, who took over from 16, depended on his inker (soon finisher) Hilary Barta excessively, ending up being credited with 'continuity'. By 19 the title was seriously losing its way. Ostrander's attempt to give it its own feel by introducing various deity/protectors for the characters and staging fights between life and death reads like a load of pseudo-religious hogwash, which indeed it is. Dave Stevens fans will find The Rocketeer's first appearance in 2 and 3, while Tom Sutton fans can enjoy his lush artwork on The Black Flame from 17 onwards (27 is all Black Flame). Unfortunately, the script is bilge by Peter Gillis. Starslayer was an okay idea, poorly executed, which soon descended into predictable pirates-in-space clichés. Early issues were reprinted, modified with some new dialogue and colouring by Valiant's Windjammer imprint in 1994 as Starslayer: The Director's Cut.~FJ

STARSTREAM
Whitman: 4 issues 1976

Conscientious, but ultimately unsuccessful attempt to adapt classic science-fiction stories to comics. Anderson, Asimov, Bloch, McCaffrey, Niven and Van Vogt, among others, supply rich source material, but the stories, though competently recounted, are cramped and stifled and suffer from largely unimaginative artwork.~HS

STARSTRUCK
Epic: Graphic Novel, 6 issues 1985–1986
Dark Horse: 4 issues 1990–1991

Starstruck began life as a stage play, written by Elaine Lee with sets and costumes by Mike Kaluta. Epic published a graphic novel and this six-part series in colour, while the Dark Horse series was intended to run for twelve issues, reprinting what had gone before with 320 pages of new material. It's a complicated story containing pleasure robots, the great houses of the multiverse, March Baptists (the wealthiest Christo-Zedian denomination in the inhabited universe), Andromedicones (a self-propagating race of androids), Galatia-9 (once Molly, now an Amazon), the Guernican art squad, the tranquil nunz and Brucilla The Muscle (not to mention the Galactic Girl Guides and their terrorist tendencies). Told in a variety of voices and not always in a linear timeline, Lee's script requires some effort to understand but it's worth it and Kaluta's artwork is gorgeous.~NF
Recommended: Dark Horse 1–4

STATIC
Milestone: 45 issues 1993–1997

Present at the massive gang war known as the Big Bang, Virgil Hawkins, geeky high-school student, gains electromagnetic powers from the chemicals unleashed by corrupt authorities on the rioting crowds. Calling himself Static, he sets out to improve his neighbourhood. Yawn, right? Heard it before. What that synopsis doesn't convey is the essence of Virgil's personality. He's tough, engaging, with a well-hidden sensitive side and a highly literate streak that wins you over, making you root for him during his days as a neophyte superhero. His cast of supporting characters is equally diverse and appealing, primary among them being Frieda Goren, his best friend (but refreshingly not a romantic interest), in whom he confides his secret; and Daisy Watkins, the insecure and troubled girl who wins his heart. R.L. Washington III and John Paul Leon carry him through his trials and tribulations with skill and panache, turning him over to Ivan Velez Jr and the unsurnamed Wilfred seamlessly in the middle of a story arc (19), after which the comic, against all odds, gets even better! The superheroics are well conceived, with Virgil using his head as much as his powers to defeat his enemies in a variety of surprising ways. Additionally, the creators tackle issues – bulimia, anorexia, drugs, sexual identity – faced by real teenagers, and present them intelligently, realistically, and without any of the preachy 'quick fixes' that usually plague comics with 'morals'. This policy caused the creators problems from time to time. 'What Are Little Boys Made Of?' (16–20), the story arc dealing with a gay supporting cast member, was rejected by the Comics Code Authority, and a safer-sex hint on the cover of 25 made distributors DC freak out completely and stick an extra cover on the issue! After 29, the creative team changed again, to less skilled hands, and it became routine superstunts, albeit with a beautifully drawn, but nonsensical, Gil Kane fill-in in 31. Some people will also want to get the Rod Ramos issue, 32, but frankly it's not great work. Eventually, sadly, it fizzled out in a flurry of inappropriate and short-run creators.~HS
Recommended: 1–29

STEED AND MRS. PEEL
Eclipse/Acme: 3-issue miniseries, 1990–1991

Scripters Grant Morrisson and Anne Caulfield with artist Ian Gibson reunite the title characters from the Avengers cult TV show, with Tara King and Mother thrown in for good measure. The two stories serialised over this series are intelligent, lively, and very true to the spirit of the show, with secret societies committing murder with impeccable manners, and mysterious goings-on in quaint country villages. Printing defects plague the print run, though, with many issues printed off-register, smeared or otherwise marred.~HS
Recommended: 1–3

STEEL
DC: *5 issues 1978*

Gerry Conway's attempt to merge the then current fads of bionics and World War II was one of the more deserving victims of DC's mass cancellation in 1978. Clichéd plots and Don Heck art made for an extremely vapid product best forgotten, although the character's son later turned up in the poorest incarnation of the Justice League.~DWC

STEEL
DC: *35 issues +, 3 Annuals 1994 to date*

One of the four successors to Superman introduced during his temporary demise, John Henry Irons, armour-clad weapons scientist, graduated into his own series under the *nom-de-guerre* of Steel. Louise Simonson's deft and empathic scripting, focusing closely on Irons' family circle and his own confusion as he struggles with his heroic role, stops the title from becoming 'Black Iron Man', as it so easily might have. It even distracts the reader from the appalling Bogdanove art, of the 'everyone looks like they've been hit in the face with a shovel' school. More competent artists Chris Batista, then Phil Gosier, take over, and the book becomes a pleasing, low-key study of the responsibilities of power and the duties of family, interspersed with the inevitable kicking of heads. That's until 30, when, presumably in light of the Shaquille O'Neal movie deal, Simonson and Gosier were abruptly yanked from the series, replaced by generic creators who pump up the action and downplay the emotion, hugely to the series' detriment.~HS

The STEEL CLAW
Quality: *4-issue miniseries*

The Steel Claw originally ran in the British weekly comic *Valiant*, and this miniseries collects its first episodes from the early 1960s. Louis Crandall, inexplicably renamed Randall here, was a conniving lab assistant with a steel hand, the result of an earlier accident. Caught in an explosion, he survived, but whenever his hand touched electricity he became invisible. He was a crook here, but later reformed, becoming a secret agent and even a superhero for a while. With scripts by science-fiction author Ken Bulmer, and exquisite art from Jesus Blasco, this should have been a great comic. Unfortunately, the printing is dire, and the colouring seemingly consists of nothing but pink and green. Nice Garry Leach covers, though.~DAR

STEEL STERLING
Red Circle/Archie: *4 issues (4–7) 1983–1984*

Steel Sterling is one of the craziest superhero titles around, especially considering when it was produced. Robert Kanigher's hero is an everyday kind of guy, superstrong and supermoral, but beset by ordinary doubts and fears. He drives around the USA in a van full of multicultural teenagers encouraging everyone to fulfil their potential and making inspirational feature films. Chiefly drawn by Luis Eduardo Barreto in a hurry, Steel's adventures bring him into contact with ghosts, mysteries, mercenaries and more prosaic dangers like drunk drivers. 4 is one of the most unintentionally funny comics ever written: Kanigher's script jumps effortlessly from the Four Horsemen of the Apocalypse to drink-driving statistics; after showing the perpetrator of a crash one of his victims' heads in a carrier bag Steel then starts in on a peculiar eulogy to macho women (which lumps tennis player Chris Evert in with Joan of Arc and the Amazons). It prompted responses from Robert Dole and Nancy Reagan! After becoming an Archie title the adventures of Steel's kid sidekicks, the Steelers, were emphasised, and the book padded out with other Kanigher material.~FJ

STEELGRIP STARKEY
And The All-Purpose Power Tool
Epic: *6-issue limited series 1986–1987*

Steelgrip is an extravagantly muscled young construction worker, and one day he's offered the chance to work with the new Power Tool, the invention of the mysterious Mr Pilgrim and the first use of 'Technalchemy'. At rest, it's a small box, but when Steelgrip pulls the handle it builds itself into whatever form will suit the current task. In the first issue, this has a certain clean-limbed charm, but even then it is already obvious what we're in for: a problem occurs, Steelgrip pulls the handle, the machine solves the problem, Steelgrip gets called a hero. Boring.~FC

STEELTOWN ROCKERS
Marvel: *6-issue limited series 1990*

Life has become tough in Steeltown since the steel mill closed, and Johnny dreams of leaving for California and becoming a rock star. Just as soon as he's finished paying for his guitar. In the meantime, he forms a band: the Steeltown Rockers. It's classic soap opera: the wildboy drummer, the problems at home, the jealousies… and it's written with great character- isation and pacing by Elaine Lee, and matched by Steve Leialoha's artwork. The six issues fly by and leave you wanting more, more, more, but that's good showmanship.~FC
Recommended: 1–6

STEVE CANYON
Kitchen Sink: *24 issues 1983–1989*

By the time *Steve Canyon* began, in January 1947, over two hundred newspapers had already signed up to take it, on the strength of its creator's name alone. Having left *Dickie Dare* to do *Terry and the Pirates* for the *Chicago Tribune* Syndicate, Milton Caniff had created an enormously popular strip but wanted more – ownership and editorial control. To get that he had to take the risk of creating a new strip and signing a contract with the *Chicago Sun*'s Marshall Field.

Steve Canyon is an adventure strip in the mould of *Terry and the Pirates* but for an older audience. The basic idea is that Canyon is a flyer whose small company, Horizons Unlimited, undertake any assignment as long as it's exciting and perilous (and legal, of course). Caniff himself described it as a picaresque novel. It's got thrills, adventure and romance, all wrapped up in complex narratives. The action is always fast-moving and can take place all over the world – the more exotic the better, to begin with. Artistically, Caniff's style didn't change but he continued to exhibit his mastery of the techniques of cinema (longshots, close-ups, odd angles etc).

Kitchen Sink's magazine reprints, in four-month batches, the first episode (including the Sunday strips, which could be read separately but which were part of the same story as the dailies). Each issue includes articles about Caniff and examples of his other work. Edited by Shel Dorf and including commentaries by Caniff himself, it's an excellent production.

The early adventures introduce Copper Calhoun, a rich, dangerous woman who wants to inspect properties overrun by the war; Happy Easter, an ornery old confederate who becomes a regular cast member, Madame Lynx, Dr Dean Wilderness (an attractive but very capable lady), Lady Nine and Convoy, who would eventually grow up to lead a group called The Black Widows. All of this took Canyon around Africa and the Middle East. 6 introduces Fancy and Cheetah in tropical-island and Hong Kong settings. With 8, the page count was increased and the magazine became square-bound. It features Canyon in a fighter plane group battling the Red Chinese, it introduced Summer Olsen, who would later become Mrs Steve Canyon. 9 has Canyon teamed with Doe Redwood for a dangerous undercover assignment, 10 brings back Madame Lynx (with Canyon pretending to be her husband), and in addition throws in the start of the serialisation of Noel Sickles' strip *Scorchy Smith*.

With 12 Canyon has rejoined the Air Force and has to track down a war profiteer with the aid of Cheetah. 13 has extra editorial pages; the first story features the death of Raven Sherman. 15 contains Canyon's proposal to Summer Olsen and 16 sees him fighting the Russians over the Aleutian

Islands. 17 and 19 are special issues, the latter celebrating the fortieth anniversary of the strip and containing a full year's worth of story-lines. With 'In Formosa's Dire Straits' (22), Kitchen Sink changed the format again, including the name of one of the adventures on the cover and increasing the size of the artwork. 'The Scarlet Princess' (23) features strips from 1955 and 1956, taking Canyon from the Cold War in the US back to the war in China. Unfortunately, the series ended with 24, with at least thirty-two years of Caniff's strip still waiting to be reprinted.

The influence Caniff would have is hard to underestimate – from Frank Robbins and Lee Elias to Hugo Pratt and many others. His story-telling is remarkable. Though the circumstances might now seem strange, these strips are also a kind of social, cultural and political history, firmly set in the world as it was then.~NF
Recommended: 1–24

STEVEN
Kitchen Sink: 7 issues 1989–1990, 1 issue + (8) 1997 to date

Doug Allen's Steven is the ultimate nihilist. The first time he says 'yes' in the strip is when his idiot friend hits him with a plank and reverses his personality. Allen's half-page gag strips (and I use the world 'gag' loosely) first appeared in a local Providence newspaper. Steven's world is full of nursery-rhyme characters shakily drawn against detailed settings. There's a cleverness to some of the work (which is reminiscent of Peter Blegvad's cartooning both in style and in humour) but the persistent negativity of it all soon becomes boring.~FJ

STIG'S INFERNO
Vortex: *5 issues 1984–1986*
Eclipse: *2 issues (6–7) 1987*

When Stig's piano lid falls on him he's ejected into hell, whereupon he comes across all kinds of demons and distressed souls. Excellently drawn by Ty Templeton, the amount of gags both visual and verbal packed into an issue is immense. Unfortunately, the effect is one long shaggy dog story. Full marks for inventiveness, but it won't be to everyone's taste.~WJ
Collection: Stig's Inferno (1–5)

STING of the Green Hornet
Now: *4-issue miniseries 1992*

A wartime adventure of the Green Hornet and Kato as they battle a slinky Nazi baroness and her tame supersoldier in an affectionate tribute to Captain America's origin. The Shadow cameos, amusingly, in issue 1. Perfectly competent, but by no means exceptional.~HS

STORM

British European Associated: 1 Graphic Novel ('The Deep World')1982
Titan Books: 2 Graphic Novels ('The Last Fighter', 'The Pirates Of Pandarve') 1987–1989

British artist Don Lawrence spent much of the 1960s painting chapters of The Trigan Empire, a magnificent futuristic adventure strip concerning two brothers ruling over an empire based on the Roman Empire of old. There have been several British collections, and all are worth searching out, particularly the Hawk Books Tales Of The Trigan Empire. Lawrence's sumptuously painted artwork was appreciated far more in Europe than at home, where graphic novels were still twenty years away, and he began illustrating strips never seen in the English language. His next major series, begun in 1976, was Storm.

Following Storm in English is a particularly frustrating exercise. Written initially by Paul Dunn, then from the second volume by Martin Lodewijk, there are now almost twenty volumes in plenty of European languages, but few have been translated. Storm is an astronaut who returns to Earth in a state of suspended animation, and emerges to discover plenty of changes. He's now in a world in which Conan The Barbarian would feel at home, with minimal technology, but plenty of cut-throats. Once the absence of oceans has been explained in 'The Deep World', there are few references to the planet ever having been known as Earth, as Storm encounters assorted alien scenarios wherever he travels. He's accompanied by a gorgeous redheaded woman named Ember (except in 'The Deep World', where she's Red).

The Titan volumes continue the story, with Storm proving himself extremely adaptable at coping with whatever and whoever is thrown at him, including escaping a gladiatorial arena in 'The Last Fighter'. By jumping to the 'The Pirates Of Pandarve' the Titan edition skips several volumes to the point where Storm and Ember are transported across the universe to Pandarve. Storm is of particular interest to the Theocrat of Pandarve as 'an anomaly'. Storm is high on fantasy and action, and low on character, dragging the reader along through fast-paced adventure, but the stories are very similar in plot and structure. As such they're almost old-fashioned, a feeling sometimes heightened by Lawrence's stunning but precise and illustrative painting, but it's the art that makes each volume worth a look. Lawrence has influenced plenty of British artists in his day, and more recently has himself taken on board the different styles of painted artwork in Britain and Europe. The January 1997 issue of Heavy Metal features another Storm volume, again jumping a few

since 'The Pirates Of Pandarve'. It's hoped that more will follow, as Lawrence's art for more recent Storm volumes is ever more stunning.~WJ

STORM

Marvel: 4-issue miniseries 1996

The X-Men's co-leader gets her own competent miniseries by Terry Dodson and Warren Ellis. Plagued by guilt that had she not neglected the Morlocks, the band of deformed mutants from the New York sewers she once led, she might have prevented them from becoming the terrorists Gene Nation, Storm searches for a way to say 'sorry', and finds herself transported into the other-worldly realm where her former followers now live. Okay, but by no means unmissable.~JC

STORMWATCH

Image: 43 issues +, 2 Specials 1993 to date

Stormwatch is a global anti-terrorist force operating from the orbiting Skywatch space station and controlled by Weatherman One, whose enhanced mental abilities allow him to keep an eye on what's happening globally. 1–3 introduce Battalion, leader of the main team, his brother (who later becomes Strafe) and baddies The Mercs and Regent. Backlash is introduced in 3 while 4 and 5 feature Daemonites attempting to take control of the bodies of the Warguard (a dangerous group in cryogenic storage on Skywatch for use as a doomsday weapon). In the next two issues, three members who've been held captive by Kaizen Gamorra and the Mercs pop up (Flashpoint, Nautika and Sunburst), and Rainmaker and Ripclaw turn up in issue 8 as a prelude to Rainmaker joining Gen13.

In a radical, if not entirely advisable, move Image released issue 25 immediately after issue 9, then returned to the regular schedule, thereby dropping hints as to the outcome of the various plots developed in the fourteen subsequent issues. The plots are very much standard superhero team fare: Battalion appears to be killed, Weatherman One gets replaced by Synergy and the team starts falling apart, they take part in the 'Wildstorm Rising' crossover (22), and the Warguard get wakened again for a final showdown (23–27) that results in various members' deaths and the destruction of Skywatch. The next issues concentrate on introducing a new line-up for a battle with Islamic terrorists in 30–34. 35 and 36 are 'Fire From Heaven' crossovers with more changes to the team's membership, as a result of which Weatherman One splits them into three units: Prime to deal with superhuman threats, Black for covert operations and Red for 'deterrent, display and retaliation'. As the team takes a political stand, the various members are showcased in darker story-lines – policing the world isn't fun anymore.

Co-created by Brandon Choi and Jim Lee, who provide the stories to begin with, the initial strength of *Stormwatch* is in the dynamic illustrative style of its artists, Scott Clark (1–3, 6–8, 25) and Brett Booth, both inked by Trevor Scott. Matt Broome's similar but less ornate work (11–20) is best when inked by Scott, while Renato Arlem's artwork (22–24, 26, 30–36) is looser but craggy. When Choi and Lee aren't plotting, H. K. Proger and Ron Marz keep things going with good intentions, but are constrained by various crossovers and Lee's masterplan for the Wildstorm universe. Lee's decision to hire Warren Ellis as scripter from 37 onward was a gamble. Ellis has taken *Stormwatch* to the edge of Lee's world and seems keen to keep them there. Coupled with the improved scripts, Tom Raney and Randy Elliott provide simple but effective artwork with plenty of cold, hard inking. Give them a try.~NF

Barry Windsor-Smith STORYTELLER
Dark Horse: *3 issues + 1996 to date*

Large-size, large-scale work from Barry Windsor-Smith, who, it seems, has taken to comedy. Each issue contains episodes of three ongoing stories, each alternately occupying half the magazine. 'The Freebooters' features a character much like Armstrong (of *Archer and Armstrong*) in that he's an old boozer who's not as good a fighter as he used to be but who is being sought by a dim-witted young man who wants him to help save the world. The difference is that it harkens back to Windsor-Smith's earliest triumph by taking place in a barbarian setting. 'The Paradoxman' is about a young man on a bike that travels through time and lands him in the hands of aliens at some point in Earth's past. 'Young Gods' (dedicated to Jack Kirby) begins with Heros about to be married to Celestra but going for one last drunken binge with her sister Adastra and his friend Strangehands. Only time will tell where these stories are taking us and whether Windsor-Smith can maintain a monthly schedule for his intricate and ornate style.~NF

STRANGE ADVENTURES
DC: *244 issues 1950–1973*

The comic opens with an adaptation of *Destination Moon*, but very soon settled into the formula of printing the generally imaginative and well drawn science-fiction short strips that saw DC very nicely through the 1950s in a number of titles. The first ongoing character was Captain Comet, introduced in 9. Adam

Blake was born on Earth; his future identity was selected by his father, who watched a passing comet and told his infant son that this signified he was destined to become a great man. Exhibiting powers and a supernormal intelligence, Adam discovered he was the man of the future, born with abilities that wouldn't be common on Earth for 100,000 years. Of course, this being the 1950s, Adam chose to adopt the identity of Captain Comet and protect the Earth. His adventures were hardly strange, though, more… mundane. He lasted until 49. Notable contributing artists include Alex Toth (17), Bernie Krigstein (32, 33), Murphy Anderson in almost any issue to 50, and Carmine Infantino in almost every issue to 150, and plenty of Gil Kane. The latter three characterised the look of the title, and, as they were also contributing to companion comic *Mystery In Space* (Kane less than the other two), the look of DC's science-fiction output as well.

104 saw the idea of ongoing series reintroduced, initially tentatively with the Mike Sekowsky, then Infantino-drawn Space Museum, in which father and son visit said museum, prompting a Gardner Fox story about one of the artefacts therein. The début of Star Hawkins in 114 (who appeared sporadically until 185) brought a more definite lead character in the shape of a permanently muddled detective of the future whose robot secretary Ilda usually pulled his fat out of the fire. There was a curious romantic subtext on her part also. 117 introduced the best-known ongoing feature to grace the title, John Broome and Gardner Fox's Atomic Knights, with lovely Murphy Andersom artwork. The story's again set in the future, this time after an atomic war; the knights brought law and order to lawless times wearing old-fashioned medieval armour that somehow also shielded them against the prevalent 'nuclear radiation'. Inventive and beautifully drawn, the series ran until 160, and ran as reprints in 217–231. Animal Man made his début in 180 and ran sporadically thereafter, in an attempt to woo the superhero audience. Able to adopt the characteristics of any animal, he never caught on here, and was destined for far better things in the 1980s. There's a case to made for 187's débutante the Enchantress being the original bad girl, as mild-mannered June Moon transformed into the unrestrained sorceress, but the stories were half-hearted, and, once again, she would be destined for better moments in the 1980s (in *Suicide Squad*).

The one feature for which *Strange Adventures* is still remembered more than any other is Deadman. It starred a murdered circus acrobat whose ghost was able to possess living humans as he searched for his killer, a mysterious man with a hook replacing one hand. It's a mixture of *The Fugitive* and *Quantum Leap* (which it preceded by two decades). Neal Adams brought his distinctive and dynamic illustrative style to the ghostly detective, although Carmine Infantino drew Deadman's début in 205. The story, incomplete when *Strange Adventures* ousted all originated strips, was concluded in *The Brave And The Bold* after several Deadman guest appearances elsewhere, and Deadman has since had several solo runs.

With 217 DC finally made the obvious decision and moved their best-known space adventurer Adam Strange into *Strange Adventures*. Sadly, it was all as reprints from 217, although they provide a cheap way of obtaining some classic old stories, along with one final new Adam Strange story by O'Neil, Kane and Anderson in 222. 226–236 are all giant-sized issues with plenty of choice reprint shorts. All in all, with the exception of Deadman and the charm of Star Hawkins, there's nothing remarkable about *Strange Adventures* other than its consistency. Throughout the run it offered competently crafted material, and any issue sampled at random is likely to provide a diverting read.~HY
Recommended: 117, 152, 155, 173, 176, 205–216

STRANGE ATTRACTORS
RetroGrafix: *14 issues + 1993 to date*

Charming SF saga by Mike Sherman and Michael Cohen. Sophie, curator of the Museum of Lost Things on Sisyphus, meets and falls in love with a diplomat, E-Meson, who becomes influenced by a magic amulet and leaves to marry her best friend, Widow. At the wedding, however, he kills Widow's father, H.R. Widower, the richest, most powerful man in the solar system. *Strange Attractors* is a lively, witty story worth trying out.~NF
Collection: *Strange Attractors* (1–7)

STRANGE COMBAT TALES
Epic: *4 issues 1992–1993*

Extremely dull series mixing war stories with anomalous elements. There are Zombies in World War One, aliens in the Civil War, Dragons menacing fighter pilots and Crusaders fighting the Hydra in Manhattan in issues 1–4 respectively.~FP

STRANGE DAYS
Eclipse: *3 issues 1984*

Billed as the first 'truly New Wave comic', *Strange Days*, a collection of stories by Pete Milligan illustrated by Brendan McCarthy and Bret Ewins, certainly looked radical compared to the rest of Eclipse's output. Apart from the surreal, drug-fuelled Shockwave, for which

McCarthy conjured up amazing watery landscapes above which floated huge vessels in the shape of famous people's heads, the other strips were firmly rooted in superhero tradition, but given enough of a spin to make them fun and 'cool'. Unfortunately, Johnny Nemo, stylish future P.I., and Paradax, the gaunt, gauche teen superhero, didn't catch on, although these characters survived the title's brief lifespan to appear in UK newsstand anthology *Deadline*, and the Paradax stories were collected as a one-shot.~FJ

STRANGE EMBRACE
Atomeka: *4-issue miniseries 1993*

A criminally neglected masterpiece that easily sits alongside the most highly regarded comics of the past decade. As a study in malevolence and truly horrific obsession there's nothing to match *Strange Embrace* in comics. Writer and artist David Hine begins with the psychic Alex Steadman, who murders his parents before becoming a tenant in a vast house owned by the reclusive, broken Anthony Corbeau. Probing his mind as he sleeps, Alex learns of Corbeau's youth, seemingly one of callous indifference to those around him in keeping to a solitary indulgence. As more of Corbeau's family history seeps through, a tragic story is revealed, fleshed out by the hidden diaries of Corbeau's long-deceased wife. Magnificently plotted and considered down to the smallest observations, this deeply disturbing story is ideally matched by Hine's art. Jagged and dark, his choice of African tribal carvings as a recurring motif provides profoundly unsettling primal imagery to counterpoint the preposterously formal turn-of-the-century domestic structure. In a truly graphic novel that's part Joseph Conrad, part E.M. Forster and part Edgar Allen Poe, the shocking events depicted have resonance that remains long after the story concludes. If you're interested in intelligent adult comics you should spare no effort in locating this series, and that it's yet to be collected in more durable format by any publisher is a woeful oversight.~FP
Recommended: 1–4

STRANGE SPORTS STORIES
DC: *6 issues 1973–1974*

This was editor Julie Schwartz's pet project: sports stories with a science-fiction base. While not up to the Olympic standards of the 1960s stories in *The Brave And The Bold*, this knockout comic sailed along quite well without needing a kick-start. It had lots of balls going for it, with stories and art down to a tee. A nice series to net, but even though it didn't dive in quality, it was just about worth racing or wrestling for. Any more sport puns for future editions will be most welcome.~HY

STRANGE TALES

Marvel: *Series one 188 issues, 2 Annuals 1951–1968 (1–168), 1973–1976 (169–188), series two 19 issues 1987–1988, One-shot 1994*

The oldest Marvel title to survive to the superhero era. The first hundred issues exhibit weird and fantasy short stories, with the most notable for the modern reader being the introduction of Fing Fang Foom in 89. Thereafter, two ten-page features share each issue through to 168.

Human Torch in 101–134 takes the biscuit in the corn and hackney departments. Chill to the thrills as jocular Johnny Storm and his doll, dizzy Dorrie Evans, swing through this sixties scene. Stan Lee and Larry Lieber pitched plots and dialogue far lower than their intended juvenile level as they tried to encourage younger readers to identify with the junior Fantastic Four hotshot. Many endearingly laughable villains premiered here, including Eel, Plantman and Paste-Pot Pete. 124–134 co-star the Thing; these inevitably degenerate into continuous wisecracking bouts, written as only Stan the Man can. Ridiculous tosh. Horribly dated. Wonderfully nostalgic.

Doctor Strange began as a weird/fantasy back-up feature in 110 and quickly proved sufficiently popular to win his own continuing series a few issues later. His outstanding early adventure is the epic encounter with the Dread Dormammu, which ran virtually uninterrupted from 126–146, although the latter few issues are essentially drawn-out epilogues. Lee's scripts are enhanced by Ditko's pencils; his eerie depiction of alien dimensions and his rendition of various spells are a major factor in the strip's success. Continued stories play a major role thereafter, but turn labyrinthine and turgid as writers and artists chopped and changed.

Nick Fury, Agent of S.H.I.E.L.D.. started in the pits in 135 but improved constantly throughout the course. Nick Fury, established World War II hero, became Marvel's answer to James Bond as the current-day CIA colonel was promoted to director of espionage agency S.H.I.E.L.D. Plots hinge on a countless abundance of preposterous high-tech gizmos whipped up out of thin air. These serve as an amusing foil for Fury's blunt, coarse and raucous personality. Jim Steranko took control of art from 151 and plot from 154, and the strip soon became identified with his inimitable artistic style. 146–155 are reprinted as *Nick Fury and His Agents of S.H.I.E.L.D.*

After 168, the title fissioned into two books: *Nick Fury, Agent of S.H.I.E.L.D.* and *Doctor Strange*, the latter inheriting the old *Strange Tales* numbering. However, in 1973 *Strange Tales* was revived as a showcase title with issue 169. First on stage was Brother Voodoo, aka Jericho Drumm, who for five issues mastered the voodoo arts to gain revenge on the Houngan who killed his brother. Plots are thinly disguised by voodoo decorations in one of Len Wein's poorer efforts. The story-line continued in *Tales of the Zombie* 6. 174, 176–177 spotlight the Golem, a legendary humanoid statue animated by a human spirit to serve the forces of good. He was finally laid to rest in *Marvel Two-In-One* 11. 178–181 feature Jim Starlin's first assignment on Warlock. Starlin immediately plunged him into a cosmic epic against the Magus, an *alter ego* of Warlock from five thousand years in the future. The strip shone with subtleties and hidden meanings, particularly as Starlin used it as a vehicle to express his dissatisfaction with the Marvel hierarchy. Spot the 'Cosmic Code' stamp of approval on 179's cover. The story continued in *Warlock* 9. *Doctor Strange* reprints from 130–141 serve as *Strange Tales'* swan song.

When sales on the second series of both *Cloak and Dagger* and *Doctor Strange* faltered, Marvel revived an old title with an old format in 1987. Both features ran ten-page strips in each issue. Writers Bill Mantlo and Terry Austin plus various artists recycled rites-of-passage dramas around the young teenage superheroes Cloak and Dagger. Forgettable, juvenile approach. Their story continued directly in *The Mutant Misadventures of Cloak and Dagger*.

Peter Gillis and a mixed bag of artists engaged Doctor Strange on a single story-line throughout this run. After a promising start, it descended into a routine pilgrimage which depended heavily on Gillis' final few issues of *Doctor Strange*. The Doctor's adventures continued directly in *Doctor Strange, Sorcerer Supreme*. The 1994 one-shot is a multi-flashback with the Torch, Thing, Nick Fury and Doctor Strange, composed in the early-1960s *Strange Tales'* style with a fittingly daft plot.~APS

Recommended: Series one 126, 127, 130–141, 146, 178–181

Collection: Marvel Masterworks Vol 23 (Dr Strange stories from 110, 111, 114–141)

STRANGEHAVEN

Abiogenesis Press: *5 issues + 1995 to date*

Gary Spencer Millidge is making quiet waves with this self-published black and white series. It reads like a cross between *Twin Peaks* and *The Prisoner*, written by someone on Valium. A man comes to a small, almost clichéd English village and finds himself trapped there. All roads lead back into the village, and he soon becomes enmeshed in the ritualistic lifestyle the villagers lead. It looks very like Richard Piers Raynor's first self-published effort, *The Solthenis*: heavy on detail, with very little attempt to distinguish foreground from background via the inking, and stiff with photo-referencing. Quirky but commercial.~FJ

THE STRANGERS
Malibu: *26 issues, 1 annual 1993–1995*

The Strangers are a team of superheroes who all acquired superpowers at the same time when the Jumpstart effect hit a cable car in San Francisco, which is incredibly convenient. They start by pursuing an alien woman, Yrial, who lives on an island in the sky and whose leader claims to know why they got their powers. He's not about to just tell them outright though, is he? Grenade, Atom-Bob, Zip-Zap, Spectral, Lady Killer and Electrocute aren't the greatest names in superhero history, but Steve Englehart's scripts concentrate more on the people inside the costumes, ensuring that the code names don't get overused.

The Strangers help Hardcase and Choice against Aladdin in 4 and are then involved in the *Break-Thru* crossover (7), which goes some way to explaining the origins of the Ultraverse. 8 begins the story-line that examines the mystery of Yrial and the island in the sky, concluding with 12. The introduction of villain Pilgrim, out to destroy the team, runs through to issue 18 and the first Night Man and Strangers annuals, wherein Atom-Bob betrays them and the Teknight (ancient warrior resurrected in futuristic armour) gets picked up before joining the team in 19. Taboo and TNTNT (a group of villains) feature in 23–24 and the final issues after Marvel acquired Malibu are part of the 'Godwheel' crossover – which effectively destroyed the credibility and quality of the entire Ultraverse.

Englehart's scripts and Rick Hoberg's artwork make this an enjoyable, different superhero series which quite effectively examines the problems and characters of people suddenly and inexplicably given strange powers. The personal relationships and family ties are well defined and Hoberg's tight pencils (fortunately in most, if not every issue) give *The Strangers* a distinctive feel. It didn't really have enough time to prove itself but might well have done so if Marvel hadn't put the boot in.~NF
Collection: Jumpstart (1–4)

STRANGERS IN PARADISE
Antarctic: *3-issue miniseries 1994*
Abstract: *12 issues 1994–1996*
Homage: *2 issues + 1996 to date*

The Antarctic Press series introduces Katchoo and Francine, two high-school friends who are now, ten years later, sharing an apartment. Francine has a boy-friend, Freddy, with whom she won't sleep because she's afraid that that's all he wants from her. Katchoo has a king-size crush on Francine but meets David, who starts to take her thoughts in another direction. Then Francine catches Freddy with another woman and sets in motion a series of events that

culminates in Katchoo getting arrested. The Abstract Studio series starts two months later. 1–9 is a complex story looking at Katchoo's past while exploring her continuing relationship with David and Francine. Hitherto played for laughs, the stories begin to take a more serious turn. After moving to Homage the series takes another leap in time, and starts up ten years later, with Francine and Katchoo now living separate lives.

Creator Terry Moore writes in a very naturalistic style. His simple linework is enhanced by rather florid inking. The title has been critically acclaimed for its realism, but there's none the less something not quite satisfying in the way he handles his central characters – there are too many lingerie shots and too much teasing in the way their sexuality is developed for the mostly male readership.~NF
Collection: The Collected Strangers In Paradise (Antarctic 1–3), *I Dream Of You* (Abstract 1–8)

STRATA
Renegade Press: *5 issues 1986–1987*

An ambitious fantasy tale combining various schools of writing, from Edgar Rice Burroughs to Stephen Donaldson. Inspector Flambeau is transported from England to the floating world of Strata, peopled by a number of secret societies, all of which are at war with each other. Accompanied by two Zen Buddhist otters, Flambeau meets the Air Pirates and finds himself switching between London and Strata whenever his life's threatened. Regrettably, the series was never finished. Written by Joe Judt and drawn by Ray Murtaugh and Jim Brozman, *Strata* was witty and deftly structured; it could have been a cult hit given the opportunity.~NF

STRAY BULLETS
El Capitan: *11 issues + 1995 to date*

With a past consisting of work on Valiant and Defiant comics, no one had any right to expect much from David Lapham's self-published *Stray Bullets*, but it's proved to be one of the finest titles of the 1990s. Each issue focuses on a different character, or set of characters, and is a complete story in itself, but each episode also relates to every other one, combining together to form a larger continuity. The comic also flits from year to year (1 was set in 1997, 2 in 1977, 3 in 1980 and so on). Early episodes were almost unbearably violent, but as the series progressed Lapham has allowed himself to concentrate far more on characterisation, which is a joy, since one of Lapham's greatest skills is an ear for dialogue.

Broadly speaking, *Stray Bullets* has three continuity strands. There's the violent, retarded Joey (1, 3), the troubled *ménage à trois* on the run from the Mob (Orson, Beth and Nina in 5, 8, 9 and 11), and, most impressively, the

dysfunctional childhood of Ginny (2, 4, 7), though elements from all three strands overlap. 6 and 10 featured the exaggerated and goofy adventures of Amy Racecar, apparently a grown-up or fantasy version of Ginny. On top of delightful plotting, cinematic story-telling and gripping dialogue, Lapham's art is a revelation. It's expressive, kinetic and totally unique, making the comics an essential purchase.~DAR
Recommended: 1–11
Collection: Innocence Of Nihilism (1–7)

STRAY TOASTERS
Epic: *4-issue miniseries 1988–1989*
Oddly compelling experiment by writer/artist Bill Sienkiewicz. A woman is killed by what may be a toaster. It mutilates her body as if trying to rewire a machine but gets a couple of wires crossed. A damaged psychologist, Egon Rustemagik, is called in by the police. He's been in a mental institution until recently and the trail leads him from the dead woman to her psychiatrist, an old lover of his called Abby. She, in turn, has taken in a small boy called Todd, who turned up on her doorstep and whose only words are 'toast and jam'. Sienkiewicz's artwork is nearly abstract in places; at other times he uses exaggeratedly cartoony images (like Ronald Searle), detailed brushwork or collage. It's frustrating reading but draws you in with its mystery.~NF
Collection: Stray Toasters (1–4)

STREET MUSIC
Fantagraphics: *6 issues 1988–1989*
Anthology title with day-to-day life as a theme that promises more than it delivers from a list of creators including Rick Taylor, Mark Martin and Richard Sala. The majority of the material is written by Mark Burbey, and the meat of each issue is the eponymous title strip about a mixed relationship in a working-class area. While combining triumph and tragedy, it does so in a detached fashion, never really inducing the care factor necessary to make the strip work. Consequently the best contributors are Angela Bocage and Carol Tyler. Tyler's strips of appalling jobs she's had, and appalling characters she's encountered in the workplace, are by turns hilarious and distressing. Justin Green's return to *Binky Brown* stories in 2 would be cause for celebration were it not illustrated text. Green's a top comic creator, but a merely average writer. Buy *The Job Thing*, collecting the Carol Tyler stories, and investigate better anthologies before sampling this.~WJ

STREET POET RAY
Epic: *5 issues 1990*
A series of 'hello trees! hello flowers!' poems illustrated with child-like drawings does not add up to an intelligent commentary on the state of the world. One wonders if it was a cynical joke, rather like the *Marvel Fumetti Book*, designed to test just how much crap we'd take if it came from the right company.~FJ

STREETS
DC: *3-issue miniseries 1993*
Turning-points in the life of hooker Jenny Masden are related in this *NYPD Blue*-style wannabe-*noir* miniseries. Writer James Hudnall's terse style evokes the grimy, hopeless environment admirably, and the three issues are cleverly constructed so each can be read as a stand-alone story. John Estes and Rob Ortaleza illustrate 1 and 2 well, but sadly John McCrea's tendency to make everyone look amiably loony makes him an inappropriate choice for the third issue.~HS

STRIKE
Eclipse: *6 issues 1987–1988*
Imaginative and brutal early Chuck Dixon and Tom Lyle strip for which they've concocted a past and previous owners for the force-field-emitting and strength-giving Strike harness. Fake 'reprints' accompany the main strip, and the story continues first in a one-shot *Strike Vs Sgt Strike*, and then into *Total Eclipse*.~WJ

STRIKE FORCE AMERICA
Comico: *5 issues 1992, One-shot ('Legacy') 1993*
A spin-off from *The Elementals* that isn't much to write home about. This governmental agency of superheroes has a rotating membership of characters such as Vortex, Ratman (puh-lease) and other not very interesting miscreants. An immediate indication of the quality level is provided by the first issue's story, where the gang have to stop a giant supernatural dog from running across the USA! And it's downhill from there. The 'Legacy' special panders to the worst form of patriotism, with the team going to kick Saddam Hussein's butt, only to end up fighting his superheroes. The art is amateurish at best and the stories plain embarrassing. These people should really know better.~TP

STRIKEBACK
Bravura: *3 issues 1994*
Image: *5-issue miniseries 1996*
Rascal and Nikita Dragonryder are lovers and very happy ones at that, until Nikita's father sends bounty-hunters Doberman and Rotweiler to kidnap her. Rascal and new friend Midnight Devil set out to rescue her but are impeded by the likes of Red Ferret and the Golden Armadillo. What follows is a madcap escapade with plenty of action and humour, as Rascal learns just why the family's called Dragonryder. Written by Jonathan Peterson and Kevin Maguire, and drawn by Maguire, this is a fun series that doesn't make any big demands on

the reader but which does have a lot of charm. The Bravura title remained unfinished, but the Image series contains the complete story.~NF
Recommended: Image 1–5

STRIKEFORCE: MORITURI
Marvel: *31 issues, 1986–1989*

In a not-too-distant future outside regular Marvel continuity, Earth was losing a battle against invading aliens. A formula was developed which could give humans the edge but which would kill its recipients within a year. The novelty of the series was that it was planned to move in 'real time', creating a constant stream of disposable heroes who burned brightly and gave their lives for their planet. Perhaps predictably, characters created to last for an average of twelve issues were never going to be much more than throwaway ideas, which made it difficult for the series to build up much of a following. 1 has three pages of early Whilce Portacio art and he also inks some later issues.~JC.

STRIKER
Viz: *4-issue miniseries ('The Armoured Warrior')* 1992, *4-issue miniseries ('Secret of the Berserker')* 1995

Yu Ominae is a member of a special team created to protect dangerous artefacts which come from ancient civilisations. Twelve multi-national corporations, united in a plan to rule the world, send powerful killers against Yu and his team (including a werewolf, Jean Jacquemonde). These artefacts include Noah's Ark, which is discovered to be the mechanism that created the flood. Hiroshi Takashige, writer, and Ryoji Minagawa, artist, move the whole thing on briskly enough but there's no great inspiration to the scripts or artwork.~NF

STRIPS
Rip Off: *9 issues, 1989–1991*

The adventures of Zack, a horny student, preoccupied with the usual monomania of heterosexual seventeen-year-old males: scoring with the shapely co-eds of his acquaintance, and filling in the gaps between encounters with frenzied masturbation. Predictable and obvious? Well, no. As written and drawn by Chuck Austen, the characters of Zack, his girl-friend Shari, and Lee and Kenna, two fantasy objects of his acquaintance, are complex, engaging, self-contradictory masses of hormones, and hugely appealing to look at, too. The assured, trenchant dialogue makes this a rare sex comic you can enjoy reading two-handed, and Austen's cartoony, Mangaesque art is zany, funny and sexy. Light years removed (and improved) from his painfully constipated early superhero artwork. Sadly, its appearance

coincided with the rise of the crazed Anti-Sex League in both the US and the UK, and the series was, as far as we can tell, bludgeoned into extinction by censorious cretins.~HS
Recommended: 1–9

STRONTIUM DOG
Eagle: *4 issues 1985–1986*
Quality: *One-shot 1986, 30 issues 1986–1989*

Johnny Alpha is a mutant in a time when mutants are despised throughout the galaxy. Largely normal-looking compared with some, it's his pupil-less eyes that give the game away, eyes that are able to see through walls. He's a bounty-hunter, one of the few professions open to mutants, known as a Search and Destroy agent. The SD on his badge is derisively considered to stand for Strontium Dog, hence the title. His constant companion is Viking warrior Wulf Sternhammer, and the only other major recurring character is Gronk, a furry alien that subsists on a diet of metal, and is so timid that he's liable to fall into shock-induced coma at the slightest excitement.

In the USA Strontium Dog débuted in *2000AD Monthly* before the miniseries. It's a biography of Johnny Alpha, intertwined with the political campaigning of Nelson Kreelman, who is calling for mutants to be outlawed. Of course, he has a secret… Thereafter in the Quality series Alpha and Sternhammer go on one job after another. Writer Alan Grant plays *Strontium Dog* as a relatively straightforward adventure strip, and, while never stunning, his plots are always functional. The humour that characterises his writing elsewhere is largely absent, and when present is in the form of tough-guy quips and irony. Carlos Ezquerra draws almost every issue. He's a dynamic and imaginative action artist, but his sometimes almost pointilliste style isn't to everyone's taste.

In the story told over 20–25 Wulf Sternhammer dies, and Alpha is framed for his murder by gangster Max Bubba. It was a brave move by Grant, and one that works. With the old buddy act no longer a feature he's forced to become more creative with plots, and introduces more interesting supporting characters. The previously seen Scottish Middenface McNulty grows into a sardonic and resourceful cast member, and Durham Red, introduced in 26, became the most popular of all the Strontium Dogs. She's a glamorous, red-headed female vampire, as likely to feast on her victims as turn them in. Her début has a plot involving the kidnapping of Ronald Reagan that leaves one in no doubt what Grant thought of the man. Start with the final issues, and if you like what you read sample further.~WJ

STUCK RUBBER BABY

Paradox: *Graphic Novel 1995*

Stuck Rubber Baby is cartoonist Howard Cruse's masterpiece, and it's no exaggeration to label it one of the finest comics ever published. Its 210 pages trace the coming of age and coming out of Toland Polk, a teenager growing up in the fictional Southern town of Clayfield. Much of the story has an autobiographical feel, so unsurprisingly Toland's gradual awareness of his homosexuality is extremely convincing. Cruse's masterstroke, however, is to link Toland's sexual awareness with both the progressive emergence of the gay movement throughout the 1960s and the fight for racial equality. Many of the book's most powerful scenes involve the constant, almost institutionalised, racism of the South, exemplified by clashes between black protesters and police. For all its length and weighty themes, Cruse never once forgets that this is all meant to be entertaining, and the book is a delight from cover to cover. The art's good, too.~DAR

Recommended

Peter Laird's STUPID HEROES

Next: *3 issues 1994*

Co-creator of the Teenage Mutant Ninja Turtles Peter Laird tries his hand at Kirbyesque superheroics. It's third-rate imitation, and you'd be far better off sampling the genuine article.~WJ

SUB-MARINER

Marvel: *72 issues 1968–1974, 4-issue miniseries ('Prince Namor, The Sub-Mariner') 1984*

Although rarely one of Marvel's top titles, *Sub-Mariner* was a well-crafted mainstream superhero comic with occasional bouts of inspiration. Continuing from the Sub-Mariner's feature in *Tales To Astonish* (after the one-shot stopover in *Iron Man And Sub-Mariner*), the series started well. Roy Thomas and John Buscema produced eight issues of solid entertainment that was almost proto-sword-and-sorcery due to its Atlantean setting. Subsequent issues never quite matched the momentum of the early run, though one notable feature was Thomas' excellent handling of guest stars, from the Thing (8) and Dr Strange (22) to the first, and unofficial, gathering of the Defenders. The first teaming of Sub-Mariner with the Hulk and Silver Surfer occurred in 34 and 35. Typically for Thomas, he occasionally used the comic to re-introduce Golden Age characters, notably the original Human Torch in 14 and the Red Raven in 26. The comic only regained a sense of direction, however, at the end of Thomas' tenure, with a nice run from 36–39, where Namor marries his sweetheart, the Lady Dorma, who is then killed. At the time that was a daring move which resulted in his

abdication and subsequent quest for his father, effectively relocating the strip to the surface world. Visually, Thomas was well served by Marie Severin (9, 12–19, 21–23, 44, 45), Sal Buscema (25–36) and Ross Andru (37–39), though the strip only really came alive again under Gene Colan (40, 43, 46–49). Thomas' successor Gerry Conway, though at the peak of his powers, was never able to do very much with the dangling quest plot, and eventually ended up killing Namor's father in 46.

With 50 the comic took a dramatic turn with the return of its creator (way back in 1939) Bill Everett, whose playful, perhaps simplistic, writing polarised the readers of the day. Artistically, however, he had never been better, and each issue is a finely detailed treat. Sadly, Everett was plagued with ill health, resulting in a number of fill-in artists (the superb Dan Adkins in 56, Sam Kweskin in 58–60): the partly finished 61 was to be the last comic he drew. Illness also led to the occasional back-up strip. There are 1950s reprints in 53 and 54, and a gorgeous little gem from Alan Weiss, again in 54.

Everett's successor, the normally excellent Steve Gerber, never really got to grips with the character, and he wasn't particularly helped by uninspired Don Heck art. More interesting was Gerber's 'Tales From Atlantis' back-up strip, drawn by Howard Chaykin (62–64) and Jim Mooney (65–66), but it came as no surprise when the comic was cancelled. The last issue, by Steve Skeates and Dan Adkins (hampered by Vince Colletta's inks), was notable for an early sympathetic portrayal of homosexuality, albeit somewhat disguised.

In an attempt to update *Sub-Mariner* the 1984 miniseries explored Atlantis in greater depth than before, and ultimately led to Namor being forced to abdicate the throne. Despite some quite interesting insights into Namor's rather haughty personality from writer J.M. DeMatteis, there's little outstanding here.~DAR

Recommended: 1–8, 50–58, 72

Saga Of The SUB-MARINER

Marvel: *12 issues 1988–1989*

Prior to their relaunch of the Sub-Mariner in the ongoing series *Namor* in 1990, Marvel issued this 'guidebook' to his career so far. It covers his début in 1939 and takes him up to the present day, but while continuity maven Roy Thomas certainly tied up the threads, his obsession for detail led to a rather leaden pace. Informative, but very dull.~HS

SUB-MARINER COMICS

Timely: *32 issues 1940–1949, 10 issues (33–42) 1954–1955*

Hybrid offspring of Atlantean Princess and American explorer, Namor the Sub-Mariner, belonging to both worlds but at home in neither, battles with his conscience. Will he join his father's people or conquer them? This intriguing dilemma occupied the first few years of the Namor stories, and even as late as the start of World War II he wasn't quite sure. Although he eventually joined the allies, one was left with the feeling that it was out of expediency, and his amorality remained fascinating. Sadly, after the war his creator Bill Everett had less to do with the strip and the tone changed noticeably. From the brooding figure of the past Namor became seemingly an American, the Atlantean heritage forgotten. His vast physical power stunted, he seemed to be just a muscleman in trunks, albeit one with a triangular head. Fighting petty crooks and murderers he and his cousin Namora, a Janice-come-lately addition to the strip in 1947, looked out of place. Eventually the Great Beach Bully kicked sand in his face and he retired in 1949.

Like his contemporaries Captain America and the Human Torch, Namor enjoyed a 50s revival, but unlike them he had the advantage of a revitalised Bill Everett, at perhaps the height of his creative powers, writing and drawing his adventures. Although a few stories pandered to the Commie-bashing mood of the day, they were still exquisitely rendered, and most of the tales dwelt on his role as protector of the oceans. Eerie monsters, beautiful women and frequent visits to his Atlantean homeland filled the strip. A flawed but lovely nine issues were released before he sank once more into the depths, later re-emerging as a supporting anti-hero in *Fantastic Four* 4.~HS
Recommended: 33–42

SUBVERT Comics
Rip Off: *3 issues 1970–1976*
The early work of Underground stalwart Spain Rodriguez is an acquired taste. The heavy-handed political moralising and basic humour of his 1960s and early 1970s work is wrapped in stories looking like nothing so much as poorly drawn Marvel material. His Trashman character, starring in all three issues, is a heavily armed avenger, espousing right-on 1960s politics as he encounters the minions of fascist America and blows them away. Twenty-five years on it's all very hackneyed, and issues of *The Punisher* have better confronted political issues.~FP

SUBURBAN NIGHTMARES
Renegade: *4-issue miniseries 1988*
Inventive retro look at the 50s, continuing themes explored by Larry Hancock, John Van Bruggen and Michael Cherkas in *Silent Invasion*. Each issue has a chapter of *The Science Experiment*, a cautionary tale about a purpose-built community near an atomic testing site, a new short strip and one reprinted from *Silent Invasion*. The moods and art styles are varied, but all stories deal excellently with disturbing occurrences on some level.~FP
Recommended: 1–4
Collection: The Science Experiment (1–4)

SUBURBAN NINJA SHE-DEVILS
Marvel: *One-shot 1992*
This Teenage Mutant Ninja Turtles parody by Steve Gerber is funny for about three pages and then trips up on its own Kantana.~TP

SUGAR AND SPIKE
DC: *99 issues 1956–1971 (1–98), 1992 (99)*
A marvellous long-running humour series created by Sheldon Mayer, a cartooning genius, who made a name for himself with Scribbly in the 1940s, a strip about a would-be cartoonist. Neighbours Sugar Plumm and Spike Wilson were two infants who could walk but not talk – but they communicated in baby talk, not understood by adults, of course. Though it was never a great seller, DC maintained *Sugar and Spike* to ensure a young entry-level readership to comics. The readers more often than not saw the world through the eyes of the youngsters, which is why adults are usually only seen as legs (though you do see what the tots' parents look like in 5). As you would expect, the lovable brats had amusing names for various objects, e.g., a mirror was a magic window. The supporting cast also played an important part, the most surreal being Sugar's 125-year-old great-great-great-grandfather, who first appears in 24. Some of the tots' friends included Little Arthur, a four-year-old pest, Bernie the Brain, a clever little brat, Zelda, a toy robot, and, in the early 1970s, a black child, Raymond Smith.

The series easily splits into two parts. The first 63 issues were collections of short pieces focusing on the many misadventures of the tots as they discovered the world around them. 64 ran the first full-length story, edging the series into slapstick, more in tune with Mayer's Scribbly series (Scribbly made his first appearance in many a year in 30). Mayer's failing eyesight along with falling sales led to cancellation in 1971, although he did revive the series for foreign markets a decade later. A previously unpublished final issue saw the light of day as one of DC's otherwise all-reprint *Silver Age Classics* in 1992.

Any issue comes recommended as a sample. All are of high quality, so you won't go wrong. Good-condition issues are very hard to find, though. Besides being thumbed by grubby young fingers, many have the paper doll cut-outs cut out. Don't be put off by the childish appeal of the series: as with today's *Rugrats* (for which this was very much a forerunner) Sugar and Spike works on two levels. Though it's ostensibly a children's comic, older readers will appreciate the very amusing situations our two antagonists got themselves into, and the finesse with which their characters are drawn. One thing will become quite obvious: as in real adult life, the bossy female, Sugar, was able to wrap the poor sap, Spike, around her little finger!~HY

SUGARVIRUS
Atomeka: *One-shot 1993*

The promise of art team Martin Chaplin and Garry Marshall shines through this gratuitously unsavoury vampire story, hampered by overwritten first-person narrative as a story-telling device. Writer Warren Ellis would progress to better ideas.~FP

SUICIDE SQUAD
DC: *66 issues 1987–1992*

A preposterous name belies an interesting concept and woefully underrated super-hero adventure series. The Suicide Squad offers supervillains imprisoned for life the opportunity to have the sentence commuted by undertaking a government mission. The catch is that the mission is likely to result in their death.

The first two issues are as good as any, setting out the premise and introducing those who carry a large portion of the run. They're largely flotsam and jetsam who'd been knocking around for years, but about whom no one really cared. Given almost blank slates, writers John Ostrander and Kim Yale transform the likes of Nightshade, Deadshot, Nemesis, Count Vertigo and Captain Boomerang into memorable characters. The costumeless supporting cast are also particularly well conceived and handled, and are integral to the Squad. The finest creation is Amanda Waller, the formidable squad leader who manipulates, coerces, blackmails and just plain stamps her authority all over everyone. She's a one-person lesson about the corruption inseparable from absolute control, yet alongside the powers-that-be as portrayed in the series she's almost virtuous. Ostrander and Yale have favourites, but generally remain true to the concept, resulting in a reasonable turnover that keeps the interaction, and therefore the title, fresh. There are also well-considered plots for the Squad's missions, and sympathetic artwork from pencillers Luke McDonnell, John K.Snyder and Geof Isherwood, all of whom can adapt to suit action scenes or quieter moments of introspection and interaction. In fact some issues (8, 19, 31) are little but. For the best early action issues see 5–7, in which a rescue mission to Russia goes catastrophically wrong.

39 wraps up the first portion of *Suicide Squad*

as official sanction is withdrawn. From that point the Squad work on a freelance basis. The *modus operandi* is much the same except there's no one pulling Waller's strings, resulting in her becoming even more forceful and a more active member of the team. From 52 the costumes are little in evidence, more in keeping with the covert overseas operations undertaken by the Squad (although you wouldn't know this from the covers). Representative of later missions, 'The Dragon's Hoard' (53–57) is a complex thriller with various parties interested in obtaining a cache of weapons hidden in Cambodia.~FP

Recommended: 1–8, 10, 13, 17–20, 24–26, 31–33, 38–43, 46–49, 51–57, 59–66

SUN DEVILS
DC: *12-issue limited series 1984–1985*

Intergalactic space opera with a war against sauroid tyrants who, oddly enough, seem to have purchased Nazi strategy plans. There are four three-issue story arcs in the series, the best of which is 7–9, as a traitor puts the entire group at risk, but chief writer Gerry Conway works similar ideas far more adroitly in *Atari Force*.~FP

SUN RUNNERS
Pacific: *3 issues 1984*
Eclipse: *4 issues (4–7) 1984–1985*
Sirius: *2 issues 1986*
Adventure: *1 issue (3), 1 Special 1987*

Why so many companies consider this science-fiction adventure with an energy-distribution team in the far future so compulsive is a question for the times. Damning with faint praise, 1–5 have the best Pat Broderick art you'll find, but are otherwise unremarkable. Better by far is Roger McKenzie and Paul Smith's back-up strip in 2–4, Mike Mahogany, a hard-boiled detective with a difference: he's a ventriloquist's dummy. This works better than it sounds. The Sirius and Adventure issues are black and white, and titled *Tales of the Sun Runners*.~WJ

SUPER COPS
Red Circle: *One-shot 1974*

Before Starsky and Hutch there was this police adventure TV pilot. This comic tie-in features several short strips starring police officers Dave Greenberg and Bob Hantz. Marv Channing wrote the material, and there was art from Gray Morrow, Frank Thorne, Carlos Pino and the presumably pseudonymous V. Hack.~SW

SUPER DC GIANT
DC: *15 issues (13–27): 1970–1971 (13–26), 1976 (27)*

These are large-format, sixty-four-page, largely reprint comics, each with a different theme: Western, mystery, UFOs or occasionally specific superheroes. There's little of note. 24 has four Supergirl stories from *Action* 295–298, and delightful nonsense they are. Challengers of the Unknown in 25 contains three Jack Kirby stories, of which 'Captives Of The Space Circus' has its moments, but the four heroes are, frankly, a dull lot. The Western titles (14, 15, 22) contain some nice Gil Kane stories, with some outstanding artwork in 'Stand Proud The Warrior Breed' (in 15), a rare new story. Also worth a look is the Metamorpho origin story in *The Best Of The Brave And The Bold* (16), with lovely artwork by Ramona Fradon.~FC

Recommended: 15, 16, 24

SUPER FRIENDS
DC: *47 issues 1976–1981*

Based on the popular animated TV series, this proved a hit with the older DC fans, although primarily aimed at a younger audience, with simple stories written by E. Nelson Bridwell and illustrated by Ramona Fradon. Although the title is seemingly set in a universe on its own, Bridwell constructed the stories to fit within mainstream DC continuity, and featured little-used characters such as Black Orchid, Wonder Woman's black sister Nubia, and, from the Golden Age, T.N.T. and Dynamite. In some ways it was more *JLA* than *JLA*. Bridwell also created the Global Guardians, an interesting range of international superheroes, who in later years would play major roles in the *Justice League* titles. Well worth sampling.~HY

Tod Holton SUPER GREEN BERET
Lightning: *2 issues 1967*

In this title, released during the peak of xenophobic fervour about the war in Vietnam, teenager Tod Holton dons his magic green beret to become a superpowered GI. The prevailing jingoism and offensive racial caricatures prevent this slipping into the 'so bad it's good' category.~FP

THE SUPER HEROES
Dell: *4 issues 1967*

In the days before Marvel and DC had copyrighted the term 'superhero', four kids visited a museum staging an exhibition of superhero statues. Coincidentally a set of four superpowered androids are also on show. An atomic mishap transfers the minds of the children into the bodies of the Fab Four: laser-powered El, Hypersonic Hy, freezer-powered Crispy and mini-skirted Polymer Polly. With villains like Mr Mod and the Coal Man (sentient coal!) plus some execrable art from Sal Trapani, you just know this is one to be avoided.~SW

SUPER POWERS
DC: *5-issue miniseries 1984, 6-issue miniseries 1985–1986, 4-issue miniseries 1986*

A tie-in with to promote a line of DC superhero toys. More superheroes than you could shake a stick at team up against Darkseid and his anti-social plans: the most fiendish (in the 1985 series) involving seeds whose roots are burrowing down towards the Earth's core, and which send you back in time if you try to attack them! Profoundly stupid, but at its best, in the first two series, by Jack Kirby, propelled by a narrative drive so raw and powerful that you haven't got time to care.~FC

Recommended: Miniseries two 1–6

SUPER SOLDIERS
Marvel UK: *10 issues 1993–1994*

It seems that the formula used to create Captain America was shipped to Britain, and applied there as well. The five tedious, fight-crammed issues uniting those who survived its application ought to have prompted any sensible reader to pack the title in, but from 6 matters improve. The soldiers start to act as a government-sanctioned response team, and there's an injection of humour, making for a readable title. 7's martial arts tournament is the best indicator.~FP

SUPER-TEAM FAMILY
DC: *15 issues 1975–1978*

Despite a silly name (trying to capitalise on the popular *Batman Family* and *Superman Family* titles), this giant-sized comic featured better-than-average and more unusual superhero team-ups. Issues 1, 4–7 were all reprint and all good stuff, the most notable being 4's reprint of the Justice Society of America tale from *All-Star Comics* 32. All-new material began in 8 with a well-produced revival of the Challengers of the Unknown. 11–14 have various team-ups connected with a central story-line involving the Atom, and 15 offered the Flash and the New Gods.~HY

SUPER-VILLAIN TEAM-UP
Marvel: *17 issues, 2 Giant-Size 1975–1980*

This featured Dr Doom and the Sub-Mariner in most issues, and was very erratic in quality. Some of the best pieces are by Steve Engelhart, including his tribute to Batman in 5–7, the début appearance and origin of The Shroud. 8–10 cross over with Avengers 154–156, with 9 having rarely-seen Jim Shooter artwork. Although cancelled with 14, the title was revived as an annual publication solely to retain copyright on the term 'super-villain', and the final issues feature Red Skull and the Hatemonger.~DWC

SUPERBOY

DC: *Series one 196 issues, 1 Annual 1949–1973, One-shot 1980, series two 54 issues 1980–1984, series three 22 issues, 1 Special 1990–1992, series four 34 issues +, 3 Annuals 1994 to date*

Superboy first appeared in *More Fun Comics* 101 in 1945, and although the popularity of superheroes had declined sharply by the end of the 1940s DC still had a hot property in Superman. How better, then, to expand the line than by allocating a comic specifically for the adventures of Superman as a youngster? The adventures of Superboy were set in his hometown of Smallville, somewhere in Kansas, and supporting characters included Ma and Pa Kent, who'd found the rocket containing Superman as a baby; 10 introduced Superboy's childhood sweetheart Lana Lang. Like a junior version of Superman's Lois Lane, she was always attempting to discover Superboy's identity, being convinced he was Clark Kent. Her snooping was the catalyst for many a story, but by the end of the tale Superboy always convinced her he wasn't Clark Kent, and she'd believe him. But not for long, and in the next issues she was up to her tricks again.

1–16 were fifty-two pages, but even when the comic shrank to thirty-two pages it still provided three intricately plotted stories. With hindsight there's an absurdity to the *Superboy* stories, but at the time they were charming and innovative, and can still be so in moderation. They were very tightly plotted, packing a lot of story and action into eight pages, with characterisation and continuity secondary concerns, exactly the reverse of today's material. There was also an innocence not likely today: those into the idea should check out 55 and 75 for covers featuring spanking!

The Superman legend was rapidly expanding throughout the 1950s, and many of its elements were introduced in this series. 5, for example, featured a character called Supergirl, not to be confused with his cousin, introduced later in the 1950s, and 8 offers us the first story of Superbaby! The cast of the Superman family grew tremendously in the 1950s, and a major addition came in 68, with the origin and first appearance of Bizarro, an imperfect duplicate of Superboy. A more minor addition was Beppo, the Super Monkey, in 76, while 78 featured the origin of the imp from the fifth dimension, Mr Mxyzptlk, and 80 has Superboy meeting his cousin Supergirl for the first time. 104 has the origin of The Phantom Zone, the strange dimension where Kryptonian villains were imprisoned. In 124 Lana Lang rescues a passing alien, and in gratitude she's given a ring which enables her to change into any insect she desires, letting her become Insect Queen.

The Legion Of Super-Heroes also make various appearances, and in 86 their guest spot also introduces us to Pete Ross, who in 90 actually discovers Superboy's secret identity, but keeps it to himself. 89 has the first appearance of Mon-El, originally thought to be Superboy's long-lost older brother from Krypton, but in fact he's revealed as coming from the planet Daxam. Similar to Superboy in all but costume, he would go on to be a mainstay of the Legion Of Super-Heroes, and have his own title as Valor in the 1990s. 98 has the first appearance of another Legion member, Ultra Boy, and in the same issue Pete Ross is accepted as an honorary member. Naturally enough, Insect Queen is also soon accepted.

Throughout the 1950s George Papp, Curt Swan and (primarily) John Sikella were the main pencillers for *Superboy*, with pleasing, open styles suitable for the audience. Lack of credits in the comics makes the identification of writers far more difficult, but Otto Binder was definitely a mainstay, writing the first Bizarro story.

As the years went by we learned more and more about Superboy's home planet Krypton. Even though he was supposed to have been the sole survivor, more and more Kryptonians popped up throughout the years, or assorted Kryptonian artefacts came to light, giving Superboy an idea of the history of his ancestors. Of course, there was another important character playing a part in Superboy's life: Krypto the Superdog. Krypto came to Earth hidden away in the same rocket that brought Superboy, and therefore had the same powers as Superboy, and, luckily, a strange sort of intelligence for a dog. He couldn't talk, but his thoughts were distinctly human at times! He even got to join his version of the Legion Of Super-Heroes. 131 introduced us to the Space Canine Patrol Agents, a superpowered group of dogs in space. There was Chameleon Collie, Tail Terrier, with a stretchy tail, Tusky Husky, who could transform one of his teeth into a long tusk for prying things open; and who could forget Hot Dog, able to heat himself up like a furnace? During the 1960s the page length of *Superboy* stories increased, with the comic now offering only two stories per issue, but they were still very plot-driven. The main artists during the early 1960s were George Papp and Al Plastino, who'd been working on *Superboy* for the past decade, and the great Curt Swan. Though none of the trio were recognised for dynamic art, they could all tell a story perfectly. The Legion Of Super-Heroes played an increasingly large part in Superboy, and fans should watch out for the giant-sized 147, reprinting many older tales. It also contained a new story recounting the previously untold origin of the Legion.

By the end of the 1960s DC's sales were obviously being affected by Marvel, and there was a conscious attempt to make their titles look more dramatic. Newcomer Neal Adams, with his realistic and graphic style, became the main cover artist, and this reflected a slight change of mood inside as well. In 145 Ma and Pa Kent shed twenty years, now looking the right age to be Superboy's parents rather than his grandparents. The next event with major ramifications was Murray Boltinoff becoming Superboy's editor with 149: from the following issue he stamped his personality on the title by replacing the long-serving artists with the far more dramatic style of Bob Brown (further improved by Wally Wood inking 152–155 and 157–161). The stories, while keeping their charm, also received an injection of adrenalin through the writing of Frank Robbins. Boltinoff was an effective editor, using many of the elements introduced by Weisinger, but wasn't quite as hot on continuity, running a story in 158 in which Superboy discovers his Kryptonian parents in suspended animation. This story tends to be ignored by Superman fans. Lana Lang matured under Boltinoff, though Krypto retained his human intellect, and the Superbaby stories were never more than a few issues away, for example 167, which introduced the inks of Murphy Anderson to Brown's pencilling for an excellent combination.

By now shrinking page-counts had reduced Superboy to a standard twenty-four-page title, usually featuring one long Superboy story and one shorter back-up; in 172 this was the Legion of Super-Heroes. It was an uneventful story, but revived interest in the group and proved very popular with the readers. The Superboy stories at the time weren't really going anywhere, even with the return of Weisinger-era mainstay Leo Dorfman to the writing, and it was the occasional Legion back-ups from Cary Bates and George Tuska that were getting the attention. After 177 they appeared regularly, with 184 introducing the art of Dave Cockrum, former assistant to Murphy Anderson, with the latter's style very apparent in his work, and joining his protégé in 188 and 190. Cockrum's flair and stylings transformed the Legion, bringing the strip up to date with a 1970s version of the future rather than the 1950s version that had featured before, and with 193's redesigned costumes the team finally looked as if they belonged in the 30th-century. 195 introduced Wildfire, who would become one of the most popular Legionnaires. 196 was an all-Superboy issue, but without warning 197 was titled Superboy And The Legion Of Super-Heroes, the Legion having almost usurped Superboy's comic, doing so completely with 259.

Although it's always imaginative, there is a repetitive quality to Superboy, and readers wanting to sample material from the 1940s to the mid-1960s are best advised to pick up one of the giant-size reprint collections. These are 129, 138, 147, 156, 165, 174 and the hundred-page 185. They could also try the 1980 one-shot, the first comic produced by a major company specifically for the comic-shop market.

The new Superboy series in 1980 was an attempt to emulate the fun stories of the 1960s, with writing by Cary Bates and art from the great Kurt Schaffenberger, both of whom had worked closely with longtime Superman-family editor Weisinger. Titled The New Adventures Of Superboy, the series was definitely set in the 1960s, and Superboy was given the age of sixteen, as there seemed to be a concerted policy of ageing Superman and Superboy together. This was a strange title for the times, looking back and recycling old scenarios when everything else was geared to moving forward. It was a pleasant enough attempt at preserving the old Superman legend, though, and you can never go wrong with Schaffenberger art. There were back-ups starring Krypto and Superbaby, and Superboy's Secret Diary, all indicating that DC intended this as a title for their younger readers. This was further indicated by the 'Dial H For Hero' moving from Adventure Comics to be, between 28 and 49, the longest-running back-up. Readers designed brand-new superheroes, into which the lead characters transformed, with the strip written by E. Nelson Bridwell or Bob Rozakis. The lead feature's creative team changes to Paul Kupperberg and Alex Saviuk with 36, but the style remains the same. The only issue of note was the giant-sized 50, featuring an entertaining story by Kupperberg, with art by Schaffenberger and framing sequence by Keith Giffen, starring Superboy and the Legion of Super-Heroes, and a young, bald, Lex Luthor. A must. Eventually the retrospective subject-matter and old-fashioned style doomed the comic for a 1980s audience.

The next Superboy comic was launched to tie-in with the TV series, and the continuity bears no relation to the regular title. Clark Kent, Lana Lang and T.J. are all starting a new course at Shuster University, in a nice homage to Superman's artistic creator. Superboy has more or less just discovered his powers and origin, and starts his career while at college. Clark is no longer a wimpy schoolboy, and Lana is no longer a snoop, and they are just good friends. Writer John Moore and artist Jim Mooney (later Curt Swan) produce an adequate if average title, restricted by the TV continuity, although Legion Of Super-Heroes fans might want to pick up 5, featuring three strange characters from the thirtieth century. The special ties up all loose ends from the series.

With continuity revisions at DC having dispensed with Superboy (having Clark Kent begin his career as an adult), the current

Superboy is a completely different character. It's a grittier and more violent, action-packed series, resolutely set in the 1990s. This Superboy isn't from Krypton, he's a clone created by the genial scientists at Project Cadmus as a replacement for Superman when the world believed him dead. Introduced in *Adventures of Superman* 50, he simulates Superman's abilities through 'tactile telekinesis'. Superboy has settled in Hawaii without a dual identity, seeing himself as a media star rather than a superhero. The primary members of Superboy's supporting cast are his manager Rex Leach, Rex's teenage daughter Roxy, and Dubillex, a telepathic and telekinetic alien and fellow escapee from Project Cadmus, who looks after a scruffy little dog named Krypto. Superboy is very popular with the girls, and dates TV reporter Tanya Moon in addition to Roxy, and has been given a conscientiously trendy look with shades, leather jacket and a kinky leather belt around his right thigh.

With occasional fill-ins from other creators, 1–30 were the work of Karl Kesel and Tom Grummett, inked by Doug Hazlewood, and form a thoroughly entertaining series. 2 has the introduction of Knockout, a red-headed Amazonian with great strength, and 8, as part of the *Zero Hour* crossover, has the current Superboy meeting his 1960s counterpart. It's a sad story that pulls the plug on the old Superboy once and for all. Fans of *Suicide Squad* might want to pick 13–15, with one of their members having a crush on Superboy. History repeats in 18 and 19, with the new Mon-El, now Valor, arriving. 25–30 feature 'Losing It', a major story involving Knockout and those Apokaliptian favourites the Female Furies, with even the new Supergirl looking in for 28. The turbulent relationship between Knockout and Superboy comes to a head in the final chapter. The new creative team are in place from 31, but neither seem completely comfortable, with Ron Marz taking a more serious approach to the writing, and Ramon Demado's more abstract style lacking Grummett's light touch. The best of the annuals is 1995's 'Year One' story dealing with his origin.~HY

Recommended: Series one 193, 195, series two 50, series four 8, 13–15, 25–30

SUPERBOY AND THE LEGION OF SUPER-HEROES

DC: *62 issues (197–258), 1 treasury edition 1973–1980*

1973 was a joyous year for long-time fans of the Legion Of Super-Heroes as their favourite strip usurped Superboy's feature from his own title. Short strips written by Cary Bates had been appearing on and off in the title for a while, gradually growing in popularity, particularly since the artist had been Dave Cockrum. With

197, and little warning, the cover-title became *Superboy Starring The Legion Of Super-Heroes*. With more pages at his disposal, Bates was able to incorporate a greater depth to the stories; when this was combined with Cockrum's excellent story-telling abilities, wonderful sense of design and bright, clear style, there was a renaissance for the Legion. Cockrum also redesigned the 30th-century world occupied by the Legion, giving it a real futuristic look for the first time. 200 was an early pinnacle, with the wedding of two characters, not that important in itself, but signifying that the Legionnaires were getting older and there was a progression to the strip. Sadly, Cockrum only lasted until 202, being lured away to jump-start a similar revival for *X-Men*.

His replacement, though, was nearly as good, another new artist, named Mike Grell, who made an effort to assimilate Cockrum's style at first before establishing his own look. Besides Grell's début, 203 was also significant for the death of one of the characters, an unpredictable move despite the large cast. The ties with the past remained, with the Legion still falling under the *Superman* editorial umbrella, and they regularly made trips back to the past to visit their 20th-century team-mate Superboy, still nominally the star of the comic. After a while, Bates began to lose interest in the series, and the feature lost some of its revived lustre. A shot in the arm was provided with 209, when the writer responsible for many of the Legion's previous glories in *Adventure Comics* returned. Initially, Jim Shooter didn't seem entirely at ease with the new format, hindered by editorial dictums that everything had to be explained to the reader, even when it was obvious. Human-interest stories had been his forte, and in 211 he turned in his best when Element Lad, the sole survivor of his planet's destruction, confronts and nearly executes the person responsible. Shooter seemed to have sparked Bates, and they alternate on scripts, which did produce the occasional clunker such as 217's introduction of an appallingly stereotyped black character with a huge chip on his shoulder. Luckily he wasn't around for too long, and future stories showed a racially integrated society, so perhaps the mistake was for the best. Shooter and Grell both left with 224, Shooter not having lived up to his previous work, and Grell clearly losing any interest.

225 introduced a new creative team of Paul Levitz and Jim Sherman, inked by Bob Wiacek. Sherman's graceful figurework suited the tone of the strip, and Levitz, formerly a notable fan of the feature, set about making changes. He too dispensed with old characters, and in 226 introduced Dawnstar, another character with a chip on her shoulder. One of the joys of the feature had been the way the weaker members

of the team interacted with their more powerful counterparts, and since the revival most of the less powerful members had slipped away. It's to Levitz's credit that he was able to provide decent scripts without this option available. He also developed individual personalities for each of the Legionnaires, which, considering there were over two dozen of them, was no mean feat. 231 is particularly good Levitz story, featuring the return of their deadliest foes The Fatal Five, and is a good issue to sample from the late 1970s. There's a new burst of creative energy in 230–240, inspired by Levitz and Sherman, but also from the unlikely team of Gerry Conway and Ric Estrada. Many noted creators dropped by for guest shots at the Legion, including Walt Simonson (237, not well inked by Jack Abel), Jim Starlin (239) and Howard Chaykin (240), but Mike Nasser's Adamsesque styling was also notable on 231 and 235. Also appearing at this time was the oversize treasury edition in which Lightning Lad and Saturn Girl are married. It's not one of Levitz's best scripts, and the art by Grell and Vince Colletta is abysmal. Don't be tempted.

Levitz had been building up to the 'Earth War' story in 241–245, the best Legion epic for years. The events had the Legion having to battle assorted intergalactic races, culminating in the reappearance of a major adversary, Mordru. It's a well-paced story packed with action and intrigue, showing Levitz at his best, although Sherman left with 242, to be replaced by Joe Staton. Perhaps not the ideal artist for the feature, he did at least start on a high note. Levitz left with 245, leaving Len Wein, then, from 248, Gerry Conway, to write. Conway marked his lack of imagination from the start with a dull story featuring a creature from the sewers. He did sharpen some of the characters, but this wasn't a golden era. His run was interrupted by the Jim Starlin-produced 250–251, although he chose to operate under the alias Steve Apollo, not being happy with what was produced. He needn't have been ashamed: it was a decent story, with nice artwork, as one of the Legionnaires becomes totally insane, leading to some interesting later plots. It was also an oasis of quality in a mediocre run. Staton was beginning to lose his touch, possibly distressed by a parade of unsuitable inkers, and a succession of inane plots from Conway. Despite the lack of quality the comic continued to be a success, so much so that it no longer required Superboy's presence, so from 259 the title became The Legion Of Super-Heroes.~HY

Recommended: 197–203, 230, 231, 233, 236, 239, 241–245

SUPERBOY AND THE RAVERS
DC: *8 issues + 1996 to date*

At the invitation of the mysterious Kindred Marx, Superboy becomes a regular attendee of The Event Horizon, a dimension-hopping party frequented by superpowered beings from all known planets. The winner of the 'Worst Name For A Comic Since *Speedball*' and 'Most Likely To Sound Creakingly Outdated Within A Year' Awards, this tragic attempt at a 'Youth Culture' comic has its heart in the right place. Any series that attempts to revive the career of Rex The Wonder Dog and Dial H For Hero can't be totally evil, but good intentions alone will not save it.~HS

SUPERCOPS
Now: *4 issues 1990*

In an attempt to eradicate crime the American government creates a team that will be able to take on the problem. The title makes them sound more interesting than they actually are. For a start the characters are not superpowered, but hey, they have undergone vigorous training. This drivel was written by Chuck Dixon, who would probably deny it were his name not on the splash page. Peter Grau draws in some mediocre figures to complement his bland backgrounds.~SS

SUPERGIRL
DC: *Series one 10 issues 1972–1974, series two 23 issues 1982–1984, 1 Special 1985, 1 Special 1993, 4-issue miniseries 1994, series three 4 issues, 1 Annual + 1996 to date*

After a relatively successful run in *Adventure Comics*, the Maid Of Steel was finally granted her own title, but you wonder why DC bothered, as they made hardly any effort. The run has neither the fun of the 1960s stories nor the sophistication of her *Adventure* run, which was ignored entirely. Linda Danvers was now back at college, and the entire affair was more of a romance title: Cary Bates forgot it was the 1970s. The story-telling abilities of artists Artie Saaf and John Rosenberger were never in doubt, but the heavy-handed inking of Vince Colletta has dated this series. The only redeeming feature was a guest appearance from Prez in 10. The fishnet-clad magician Zatanna is the back-up in 1–4, quite nicely drawn by Don Heck.

The second series was the work of Paul Kupperberg, Carmine Infantino and Bob Oksner, and has Supergirl, the eternal student, back in college in Chicago, where she's moved to find her humanity as Linda Danvers. There's a nice soap-opera feel to the series, but little of any great excitement. The new Doom Patrol dropped by in 8 and 9, there's a new Supergirl costume in 13, and the wacky Ambush Bug appears in 16. The new costume was supposed to pave the way for the new *Supergirl* movie, but for some strange reason the title was cancelled before the movie was released. Maybe they'd seen a preview of the movie! While it's always nice to see Infantino artwork, he was ill-placed here, and given little chance to use his talents as a design-oriented artist. Lois Lane was a regular back-up, drawn by Bob Oksner, in 2–12. There was a one-shot Supergirl movie adaptation in 1985 featuring some very nice artwork from Gray Morrow.

1980s continuity revisions at DC wiped out Supergirl as the universe was recreated without her. Realising that the character was far too good to ignore, DC reinvented her. A new Supergirl was introduced in *Action* 674. She was created by the Lex Luthor of an alternate reality as a homage to Superman, and then despatched to Earth to enlist Superman's aid. Injuries caused in the subsequent battle reveal her to be a mass of tissue, who calls herself Matrix. Her powers are very similar to those of Superman, but she has the additional talent of being able to change shape. Matrix is an innocent soul when she meets the villainous Lex Luthor, who reminds her of her creator, and she begins to fall for him. Lex being the vile heel he is leads her on and uses her for his own purposes. It's not too long before he's enrolled her as Supergirl in his personal task force, called Team Luthor. This is best illustrated in the 1993 special.

The relationship between Supergirl and Luthor is further explored in the miniseries by Roger Stern, June Brigman and Jackson Guice, who'd produced the one-shot. Lex is pretending to be a good guy, but actually trying to clone Supergirl to produce an army of superpowered beings. Naturally enough, when Supergirl finds out, she's not very happy about it. It's a decent enough filler. Another ongoing Supergirl title arrived in 1996, written by fan favourite Peter David, and very nicely illustrated by Gary Frank and Cam Smith. Paying homage to the old Supergirl, Matrix has now merged with a young woman called Linda Danvers through some satanic rites that went wrong, as they always do. For all intents and purposes Supergirl now inhabits Linda Danvers' body. Once away from the demons, Peter David, obviously an old-time fanboy, is gradually introducing now-little-seen DC villains into the series, such as Gorilla Grodd in 4 and Chemo in 5. The series has been widely acclaimed, and if we can't have the original Supergirl back this is the next best thing. Keep your eye on this.~HY

SUPERMAN

DC: *Series one 423 issues, 12 Annuals, 2 Specials, 1 Spectacular 1939–1986, series two 122 issues + (0–121), 8 Annuals, 1987 to date*

Created by Jerry Siegel and Joe Shuster, Superman was the first superpowered and costumed superhero, spawning generations of imitators. To this day he remains among the most recognisable global cultural icons. After a year's appearances in *Action Comics* had made the title a runaway bestseller, Superman was also given a quarterly title. It originally featured reprints from *Action*, but as the comic-reading public couldn't get enough of the Man Of Steel, *Superman* switched to all new material. There's an undeniable crudeness and simplicity about the early stories, but they had a presence seldom seen in the contemporary comics industry, with Shuster and his assistants producing some fluid work. Siegel never bored the reader, writing diligently plotted stories, often with a social slant and well defined characters.

By the time of this series the core Superman cast had been established, with *Daily Planet* (initially *Daily Star*) employees Lois Lane, Jimmy Olsen and Perry White (initially George Taylor) all having débuted in *Action*, along with primary villain Lex Luthor. If anyone was added to here, it was Luthor in 4, now bald and resembling the more familiar figure that we're used to. The Lois and Clark rivalry was an early element, with the very capable Lois often annoyed and puzzled at being scooped by the seemingly slow Clark Kent. Lois, of course, had no time for Clark, but loved his *alter ego*, although it wasn't too long before she began suspecting they might be the same person. She was featured in a back-up strip between 28 and 42: simple tales, but they clearly established Lois. The covers were very striking from the start, and the US entry into World War II brought a parade of symbolic patriotic illustrations. The best of them was 14's Superman standing in front of a Stars and Stripes shield with an eagle perched on his shoulder, drawn by Fred Ray. Inside Superman often showed the Axis powers what for.

30 was the first appearance of Mr Mxyztplk, a mischievous magical imp from the fifth dimension who would return to taunt Superman every ninety days or so. That was the length of time he had to remain in the fifth dimension after Superman tricked him into saying his name backwards, the only means by which he could be returned against his will. Superman became more powerful as the series progressed, kept in good shape by the artists from the Shuster studio, including Leo Nowak, Fred Ray and John Sikela as well as Paul Cassidy and Wayne Boring. The most important Superman artist at the time was Jack

Burnley, who gave Superman a chunkier look, and was the most professional of the bunch. In 45 Lois gained superpowers for the second time, the first being in *Action* 60, and this was an indication of the direction the *Superman* titles were taking, with whimsical fantasy gradually edging out more reality-based stories.

53 is a nice expansion of Superman's originally very short origin story. The infant Kal-El is rocketed to Earth by his parents in order that he survives the destruction of his home planet, Krypton, Earth's yellow sun endowing him with superpowers. Wayne Boring, now becoming the primary Superman artist, drew the story, and writer Jerry Siegel seemingly forgot Superman's career as Superboy, despite the character having run in *Adventure Comics* for two years by that point. Superman's Kryptonian heritage would come to play an increasing role in the stories, with 61 introducing the concept of green Kryptonite, a mineral fragment from Krypton that was deadly to Superman when he was exposed to it. 65 had a story featuring some villains who'd also survived the destruction of Krypton, and with the amount of Kryptonians who'd turn up throughout the 1950s you'd be forgiven for thinking those who died were in the minority. 76 was another landmark, featuring the first team-up between Superman and Batman, who within two years would be teaming regularly in *World's Finest* (where, at this point, they occupied separate strips).

Superman's hundredth issue was celebrated by our hero appearing in a full-length story rather than in three separate stories, which had previously been the norm. The stories may have been light on characterisation in today's terms, but the amount of plot and action packed into an eight-page story is a lesson in economy that many contemporary writers might benefit from learning. An odd feature of the *Superman* comics, only really apparent in retrospect, was the number of precursors to characters who were introduced later. Perhaps reader feedback played a part, or maybe the fact that so many one-off characters populated the strips made such coincidences inevitable. A good example is 123, featuring Supergirl, not Superman's cousin, but a temporary creation made possible through magic. There were a few more long-running supporting characters introduced in the late 1950s. They've not stood the test of time, but Lori Lemaris, the mermaid from Atlantis, and Titano the superape, both recurred for a good ten years. Time-travel stories had also become popular in *Superman*, and 141 is notable for a Jerry Siegel story in which Superman gets to visit Krypton before it exploded and romance a film star.

Issues from the early 1960s pioneered the 'imaginary' story, where the writers had free rein to put Superman into situations that might compromise continuity if run as regular tales. A great example is 149's 'The Death Of Superman', in which Lex Luthor actually succeeds in poisoning Superman with Kryptonite. It features some marvellous scenes, especially as Superman lies in state and the progression of mourners pass his body. It's considered a classic of its time, as is 162's 'The Amazing Story Of Superman Red And Superman Blue', in which Superman is split into two people. One wears a red costume, one has blue costume. One marries Lois Lane, and one marries Lana Lang, thus solving the problem of which of them he really loved. In 170 there's a story in which Luthor travels back in time before Krypton explodes, in order to wine and dine Superman's mother, but luckily the marriage is stopped just in time. That issue also contains a story featuring John Kennedy and intended for publication before his assassination, with Kennedy stressing the importance of physical fitness and exercise. The popularity of the imaginary stories was such that even the anniversary 200th issue featured one, with Superboy growing up with a brother whom he later battles to see who'll become Superman.

The imaginary stories weren't the only string to *Superman*'s bow in an era that produced a number of other classics, if you can tune in to the peculiar world that had evolved around Superman. 156's marvellous 'The Last Days Of Superman' has a Superman apparently dying of a Kryptonian plague, and is heart-tugging homage to the hero. 161 chronicles the death of Superman's adopted parents, Ma and Pa Kent, and 164 has a showdown between Superman and Luthor, introducing a world where Luthor would become a hero. By now Curt Swan was the major *Superman* artist, a perfect story-teller whose work was raised even further when inked by George Klein. Wayne Boring still has his moments, though. One of them is 'Krypton Lives Again' in 189, where Superman once more returns to Krypton before it's destroyed. 199 has the first race between Superman and the Flash, and 204's cover, by Neal Adams, heralds a new era as DC begin to combat the rise of Marvel Comics. Things were soon to change for Superman as long-serving editor Mort Weisinger quit, but before he did so he left one last landmark in 205, with a story in which the villain Black Zero claims responsibility for the destruction of Krypton. It's been disregarded by fans, but stands as a decent story. Weisinger bowed out with a two-part imaginary story in 230–231, with Clark Kent as a killer and Lex Luthor superpowered.

233 was the most dramatic turning-point since the inception of the *Superman* title. New

editor Julius Schwartz had decided that some drastic changes were in order, so he appointed Denny O'Neil as writer, and while retaining Swan as pencil artist formed an inspired team by introducing Murphy Anderson as inker. The story has the transformation of all green Kryptonite on Earth into iron, thus wiping out at a stroke a recurring corny old plot. Of course, this left Superman almost invulnerable to harm, but that was also dealt with as an other-dimensional-energy creature seeped off some of Superman's powers, thereby limiting his activities. Clark Kent was also modified and transferred to TV reporting. O'Neil wrote some decent stories about a Superman who now had to expend some effort, with Cary Bates, Len Wein and Elliot Maggin chipping in. It was Maggin who wrote the best story of the era, 247's 'Must There Be A Superman?', where Superman is taken to task for interfering too much with humanity's destiny. New characters from this era with a lasting appeal included Steve Lombard, Sports Correspondent and practical joker, and Terra Man, a Western-themed villain introduced in 249. 241–253 were forty-eight-page page comics, with back-up strips including 'The Private Life Of Clark Kent' and 'The World Of Krypton', and plenty of good 1940s reprints. This was a well-considered attempt by DC to shunt what was still their top-selling title into the 1970s, but eventually the quality slipped.

Writers Bates and Maggin, while providing acceptable plots, were rarely outstanding individually, although Bates' Star Sapphire story in 261 was a treat. Maggin's best was a return to the flavour of the 1960s with a story about Krypto the Super-Dog in 287, but the essence of the early 1970s restoration was lost by then. Superman was again all-powerful, with only magic able to affect him, and to make matters worse Murphy Anderson left with 270. When teamed, though, Bates and Maggin did produce excellent stories, each obviously sparking the other. 296–299 have Superman losing his abilities when in Clark Kent mode, leading to some interesting situations and a redefinition of Kent, and their 300 has a story of Superman in the 21st century. 'The Second Coming Of Superman' in a 1977 Spectacular has a teaming of the villainous Brainiac and Luthor and involves an alien race that regard Superman as a God. It's a well-paced story by Bates, assisted by Martin Pasko, who provided some very good stories in 310–335. Pasko's stories worked by treating the superheroics as secondary to the soap-opera content, with Lois having given up on Superman to start a relationship with Clark Kent. 314 has a story in which Clark proposes marriage, and Lois accepts on the condition he admits to being Superman, but he doesn't. Lana Lang also plays

a larger part, comp... more assertive now... a professional and... and Lois. If you... Superman marrie... titled 'Mr And M... 1940s Clark and L... designated as liv... also tackles the topic o... managed to disguise his Superman ident... these years with just a pair of glasses. It's to do with superhypnosis affecting the subconscious mind of all who encounter Kent. It's all mumbo-jumbo, and the fans refused to believe it.

There are assorted writers from 336, all maintaining a level of competence but hardly ever producing anything outstanding. The romantic situations between Clark/Superman and Lois and Lana run through most permutations, with the occasional surprise provided by Lana's alien would-be suitor Vartox, who's based on Sean Connery's *Zardoz* movie character. The Cary Bates-written 365–368, featuring The Superman Revenge Squad, stand out from the surrounding issues, as do 385–387, which continue from *Action* 554. Beginning with the retirement of Lex Luthor, it's a powerful story that eventually transforms him into an even more vengeful villain. 400 is an excellent anniversary issue, written by Elliot Maggin and featuring pin-ups and stories by some of the best comic creators then working, including Frank Miller, Al Williamson, Mike Kaluta and Jim Steranko. It's a worthy celebration. 411 is a personal tribute to editor Julius Schwartz on his seventieth birthday, illustrated by the old art team of Swan and Anderson, and 414 has Superman dealing with the death of Supergirl. Although the title continued for another ten issues, Supergirl's death was a symbolic end to an era, or would have been if not for the superb Alan Moore and Curt Swan story that concluded the run. 423's 'Whatever Happened To The Man Of Tomorrow?' was the ultimate imaginary story, which featured almost everyone in the Superman legend. It was written by Moore in nostalgic and reverential fashion. It ends with the apparent death of Superman. Or does it? The story continued in *Action* 583, and one couldn't ask for a better finale.

This wasn't the first Superman story written by Moore, though, as he and Dave Gibbons had produced *Superman* Annual 11, another imaginary story showing what might have happened had Krypton not exploded, leaving Kal-El to be brought up there by his family. Other specials of note are the first special in 1983, written and drawn by Gil Kane, who also drew annual 10. Anyone wanting a flavour of Superman through the decades can't do better than pick up the DC/Titan collection *The*

...perman Stories Ever Told. Once ...n had been overhauled, the numbering ...ed as *Adventures Of Superman*.

...llowing his revamping of Superman in ... *Man Of Steel* miniseries, and the consequent interest, it made sense to tempt the collecting instinct of readers still further by restarting the title with a first issue. John Byrne wrote and drew 1–22 of the new series, maintaining a high standard throughout. An early standout is 9, which pits Superman against the Joker, not in the normal way of things an even match. The highpoint is that the Kansas-raised hero is unable to understand the Joker's psychotic nature. A complete character refit having been provided for Superman, which discarded many of the previous, less realistic elements along the way, 11 is a brave issue, which returned the imp from the fifth dimension, Mr Mxyzptlk, who causes all kinds of mayhem, yet fits this new Superman's world as easily as he did the old. 18 is a touching story, in which Superman returns to Krypton and dreams of the world that he has lost. 22 features the new Supergirl and also caused outrage among older Superman readers because Byrne had Superman execute three Kryptonian villains from another dimension. Superman had never killed before (well, not since 1939), but when the villains threatened to destroy Earth (after decimating their own dimension) he saw no other option. His anguish at this deed, however played an important part of his development and reaffirmed the reasons why he'll never kill again.

Byrne's departure enables Jerry Ordway to take over the scripting. Already known for clean, clear art and exceptional story-telling, he proves far more adept than might have been imagined as a writer, although he takes a while to settle in. The inevitable clash demanded by fans between the old-style clean-cut superhero and the new rough, tough rabble-rouser occurs when Lobo drops by in 41, a poor issue with a long, over-indulgent fight sequence. There's a distinct upheaval in 49–50, when Clark, after waiting over fifty years, proposes to Lois Lane, and Lois says… 'Yes'.

From 51 editor Mike Carlin introduced the concept of the cover triangles, which led to tighter editorial continuity threading between all three, later four, ongoing Superman titles, the numbered cover triangle indicating the sequence to be followed each year. This occasionally just applied to plot threads, but often resulted in Superman stories continuing through the whole family of titles, meaning that the individual titles lost their own interpretations of the character in order to fit longer stories. The first of the longer stories is 'Time And Time Again' (54–55), in which Superman is bounced backwards and

forwards through time. The action is fast-paced and very well planned, and in this title there's a memorable World War II tale and a meeting with the Demon in Camelot. It's also the final Jerry Ordway tale, and from 58 Dan Jurgens takes over as writer and penciller, introducing Agent Liberty in 60. He becomes a solid supporting character and alternative Metropolis superhero.

'Doomsday' (73–75) has its effect on all the ongoing Superman titles, with its main impact here as the infamous 75 sees the death of the world's greatest hero. Drawn in one-panel pages, the action is gripping, but the ending's an anticlimax after months of preceding promotional hype. The following story, which runs through all Superman titles, has four characters who may or may not be Superman, each title concentrating on one of them. *Superman* 78–82 focus on the cyborg Superman, whose methods were not only harsh, but prompted by ulterior motives, which are revealed in 81. The climax features the return of a certain red-pants-wearing hero. From 90 to 100 Clark Kent is slowly hunted down by an old nemesis, leading up to 'The Death Of Clark Kent' in 100. After Superman resolves the situation he has to deal with another problem. Lois has left (113); the following issues show a man racked with grief and loneliness. If a Superman has trouble with women, what chance do we mere mortals have?~SS

Recommended: Series one 53, 141, 149, 156, 162, 164, 168, 170, 189, 205, 233, 247, 249, 261, 296–299, 385–387, 400, 423, 1977 Spectacular, annual 11, series two 9, 11, 18, 50, 54, 55, 75, 81 *Collections: Bizarro World (Superman* 87, 88, *Man Of Steel* 31, *Adventures Of Superman* 510, *Action* 696), *The Death Of Clark Kent* (100, 101, *Man Of Steel* 44–46, *Adventures Of Superman* 523–525, *Action* 709–711), *The Death Of Superman (Superman* 73–75, *Man Of Steel* 17–19, *Adventures Of Superman* 496–497, *Action* 683–684) *The Greatest Superman Stories Ever Told* (series one 4, 13, 30, 53, 123, 125, 129, 132, 145, 149, 162, 247, Annual 11, series two 2, *Action* 241, *Forever People* 1, *Superboy* 68), *Krisis Of The Krimson Kryptonite* (49, 50, *Adventures Of Superman* 472, 473, *Action* 659, 660, *Starman* 28), *Lois And Clark* (9, 11, Annual 1, *Adventures Of Superman* 445, 462, 466, *Action* 600, 655), *The Last Superman Story (Superman* 423, *Action* 586), *Panic In The Sky (Superman* 65, 66, *Man Of Steel* 9, 20, *Adventures Of Superman* 488, 489, *Action* 674, 675), *The Return Of Superman (Superman* 78–82, *Man Of Steel* 22–26, *Adventures Of Superman* 501–504, *Action* 687–691), *Superman Archives* vol 1 (series one 1–4), vol 2 (series one 5–8), vol 3 (series one 9–12), vol 4 (series one 13–16), *Time And Time Again (Superman* 54, 55, 61, *Adventures Of Superman* 476–478, *Action*

663–665), *World Without A Superman* (*Superman* 76, 77, *Man Of Steel* 20, 21, *Adventures Of Superman* 498–500, *Action* 685, 686), *The Death of Clark Kent* (*Superman* 99, *Man of Steel* 43, *Action* 709)

The Adventures Of SUPERMAN

DC: 118 issues + (424–541), 8 Annuals, 1987 to date

The *Superman* titles were relaunched in 1987 following a makeover and continuity-straightening miniseries called *Man Of Steel*. From this point Superman was as new, and all previous occurrences were deemed not to have happened in terms of the new continuity. In order to attract new readers, launching a new *Superman* comic with a first issue seemed sensible, so the title of the previous ongoing *Superman* comic was changed to *Adventures Of Superman*. The initial creative team is Marv Wolfman and Jerry Ordway, and after the reshuffling Superman is once again the sole survivor of Krypton and Clark Kent works at the *Daily Planet*, so we're back to basics.

Ordway's art is excellent, although his Superman is a little stockier than the then current John Byrne equivalent, perhaps deliberately so in tribute to the early 1940s version. The new reality introduces several new characters, including Perry White's son, a new Metropolis superhero Gangbuster, and Jimmy Olsen's mother (after fifty years). 1940s superhero The Guardian and teen gang The Newsboy Legion also have a major role in the series, as does The Cadmus Project, a scientific research organisation experimenting with clones. Superman's villains have also been reconceived, with Lex Luthor now no longer a blatant criminal genius but a respected industrialist with a secret shady background and plenty of covert shady activities on the go. These activities provide many of the sparking points for plots over the initial revived issues. 438 introduces a new look Brainiac. From 445 Ordway begins writing the title as well (having written 443), with his plotting every bit the equal of his underrated art, making this by far the most stylish of the revived *Superman* titles. By 450 plots were regularly continuing through all the *Superman* titles, so anyone wanting to sample just the one can forget it.

With 452 Dan Jurgens became regular writer and penciller. Even more imaginative than Ordway with his plots, the actual execution often never gelled, with odd pacing and too many extended fights slowing things down. His art, while dynamic and certainly more than capable, wasn't quite up to Ordway's standard either, but then few artists are. In 458 Jurgens has the inspiration to reintroduce the old 1960s plot of Jimmy Olsen becoming

Elastic Lad, but his twist is that it's not a very enjoyable experience at all, as the stretching of his limbs is painful. With 465 we have Lana Lang with rather a dilemma. In the revised continuity Lana isn't a glamorous TV reporter, she's an unglamorous small-town girl who's known that Clark Kent was Superman since they were teenagers, and has very strong feelings for him that remain unreciprocated. Clark's parents have been restored to the continuity, still alive in Smallville, and provide a decent contrast with the stories set in Metropolis. The stories still cross over between all Superman titles, but to make following them easier the sequence is indicated by the cover placement of small triangles. A notable crossover story is 'Time And Time Again', a time-travel epic that begins in 476 with guest slots from the Legion Of Super-Heroes and Booster Gold, as Superman begins to be tossed through time. The story concludes in 478; another tale beginning and ending here is 'Blackout', with chapters in 484–485, in which Superman develops amnesia.

Tom Grummett took over the art in 480, continuing the tradition of good story-telling with a nice clean image instituted by Ordway. Although the occasional good plot surfaces, and there's plenty of action, the real attraction of the title becomes the soap content, with the ups and downs of the main cast. Jimmy Olsen, for instance, loses his job due to cutbacks at the *Daily Planet*, and has to leave his flat and take an advertising job wearing a giant turtle costume, another 1960s homage. For a 1970s homage try 495, guest-starring The Forever People and other folk from Jack Kirby's 'Fourth World Saga'. 497 is part of the Doomsday story-line in which Superman is killed, the next issue opening with him dead in Lois Lane's arms. 500 is a special event centring on the near-death experience of Jonathan Kent, Superman's earthly father, who's suffered a heart attack and is slowly slipping away. There are some touching scenes as he hallucinates, and the issue also introduces the four people who assume Superman's role, each occupying one of the ongoing titles. From 501 this title is written by Karl Kesel and concentrates on the new Superboy character, who's calling himself Superman, despite being a teenager. He meets Supergirl in 502, and the issue also introduces the supporting characters that would transfer to the *Superboy* title with him.

Superman is back, alive and very healthy, in 505, and confronts his young counterpart. 507 sees a new penciller in Barry Kitson, who's replaced by Stuart Immonen in 520, and 513 and 514 have the destruction of Metropolis by a dying Lex Luthor. 'The Death Of Clark Kent' in 523 and 524, and crossing into the other titles, has a childhood enemy of Clark's returning to murder all his friends, causing them all to go on the run. To protect them, Superman must disguise himself as other characters. 532 has the return of the mermaid Lori Lemaris, who will subtly come between Clark and Lois. 540 introduces Ferro, during the 1996 crossover 'Final Night'. On the whole this has been a decent, entertaining comic since the start, but as it's crossing over with the other Superman titles the individuality it might otherwise have is lost. All of the annuals are decent, but the standouts are 2, featuring Brainiac's son Vril Dox, and 4's 'The Darkness Within' story, guest-starring Guy Gardner and Lobo.~HY

Recommended: 424, 500, Annual 2.
Collections: See *Superman*

Legacy Of SUPERMAN
DC: *One-shot 1993*

This is an anthology of short stories starring the heroes who tried to fill Superman's boots following his untimely death. There are three featured characters, each tackling problems that Superman managed on his own, with Waverider coping with the supercriminals and Gang Buster dealing with the more down-to-Earth muggers and gangsters. Bibbo is out pulling down cats from trees, inheriting the more humane side of Superman's career. The stories are limited, and Arthur Adams provides a good front cover to an otherwise mediocre cash-in on Superman's death.~SS

SUPERMAN ADVENTURES
DC: *2 issues + 1996 to date*

Batman Adventures produces simpler, more straightforward Batman stories as an antidote to the vast history that otherwise encompasses the character, and with its success DC have adopted the same policy for a Superman title. Also based on an animated series that's drawn in a highly stylised manner, *Superman Adventures* is set in Superman's early days in Metropolis, but not so early that people don't know he's an alien or that Kryptonite is known to kill him. He's also built up a rogues' gallery, already including Toyman, The Parasite and Metallo. After Paul Dini's first issue, Scott McCloud takes over the scripts and proves to have a light-hearted touch while still providing a good old-fashioned fight against Metallo. Rick Burchett and Terry Austin provide the required artistic style. The major problem with the series is that it's so obviously comics-by-numbers.~NF

SUPERMAN FAMILY
DC: *59 issues (164–222) 1974–1982*

This giant-sized comic continued the numbering from *Jimmy Olsen*. From 164–181 it was mostly reprint, with a new lead feature alternating between Jimmy Olsen, Lois Lane

and Supergirl. On becoming a dollar comic with 182, it was new material all the way, starring the three previous leads, with new ones such as the witty *Krypto* (182–192), *Nightwing* and *Flamebird* (182–194), set in the bottle city of Kandor, and the most impressive *Mr and Mrs Superman* (from 195), starring the Golden-Age Superman and Lois Lane, set in the 1950s.

The three main features were disappointing on the whole, lacking the charm of their 1960s tales, with the exception being a Supergirl/Doom Patrol team-up in 191–193. While the title used many of the elements which made the Superman mythos such a success, it didn't add anything.~HY

SUPERMAN Graphic Novels

Considering he's the oldest superhero, and one with a very high profile over the past few years, there have been surprisingly few graphic novels and one-shots featuring Superman. He did star in some of the first, though. In the days before graphic novels there were oversize editions in which Superman met Spider-Man, leading to *Superman vs Muhammed Ali*. It remains a piece of hugely enjoyable old claptrap from Denny O'Neil and Neal Adams. Ali and Superman trade punches to see who'll fight the representative of an alien fleet holding Earth to ransom. Adams also worked overtime on the cover, which depicted over 170 celebrities, DC staffers, comic creators and Ali's helpers. 1988's *Earth Stealers* is some average hokum, written by John Byrne, about some aliens who plan to… well, you get the idea. The art is surprisingly average for Jerry Ordway and Curt Swan, and all in all this could have been incorporated very easily into the regular series. *For Earth* was originally released for Earth Day 1991, has all the trappings of comics released for a good cause, and, like most, is worthy but dull. Superman hugs a tree, Superman warns about global warming. Let's move on. *Under A Yellow Sun* is presented as the first novel by Clark Kent, who is, of course, Superman's journalist *alter ego*, juxtaposed with his real-life struggles against Lex Luthor. All the regular supporting cast appear in the book – a hard-boiled thriller – thinly disguised. The two strands are drawn by very different artists: Kerry Gammill and Denis Janke for the 'real-life' material and the far more accomplished Eduardo Barreto handling the novel. It's the best of the Superman one-shots, although writer John Francis Moore can't resist tacking on a sickeningly moralistic ending. The book format was previously used by James Hudnall for *The Unauthorised Biography Of Lex Luthor*.

'Elseworlds' titles are the 1990s equivalent of that old Superman staple the imaginary story, or one that enables writers to play with the Superman legend without being constrained by any previously established element. Tom Veitch and Frank Gomez's *At Earth's End* is ridiculous. Set deep in the future, it reads like a bad version of Kamandi, with a young male protagonist crossing wastelands to discover a white-haired and bearded ancient Superman – a Supersanta if you will – with a big gun. High jinks ensue as the duo, wait for it, try to save the world! While Gomez's art is refreshingly scratchy, Veitch's script is unimaginative. *Speeding Bullets* is about as stupid as Elseworlds gets, with the entire premise hanging on Thomas and Martha Wayne finding baby Kal-El when he arrives on Earth, so he becomes Batman. The subsequent adventures are predictable (with Luthor as the Joker) and the ending utterly futile. *Kal* is a little better, with a Dave Gibbons script and Barreto back for the art as the Man of Tomorrow's ship arrives in medieval times. He's raised as a blacksmith's son, but ends up falling in love with a Lois Lane clone and fighting a Luthor clone. Can you spot a pattern here? What makes this story stand out is its overall aggressive and nasty nature. Finally, there's *Metropolis*, the best looking of the bunch, with gorgeous Ted McKeever art. It inserts the regular cast and crew into a reworking of the classic novel (and film), giving them all appropriate roles. While nothing is added to the story it ain't half pretty to look at.~TP

Recommended: *Superman vs Muhammed Ali*

SUPERMAN: The Man of Steel

DC: *6-issue miniseries 1988, 53 issues +, 5 Annuals 1991 to date*

When John Byrne was asked to revamp Superman he did so in the *Man Of Steel* miniseries. He revised Superman's origin, created closer links with his adoptive parents in Smallville, introduced a contemporary career woman, Lois Lane, and a business tycoon called Lex Luthor. The series is a vital springboard for anyone trying to understand the new Superman, and an exciting story to boot, no matter how familiar some plot elements may be.

When the fourth monthly Superman title was added, creating in effect a weekly *Superman* comic, the *Man Of Steel* title was revived, although *Superman* takes prominence on the logo. Unusually, the series has managed to keep the same critically acclaimed creative team since its inception, creating an admirable consistency. Louise Simonson handles the scripting and Jon Bogdanove draws the legendary hero. *Man Of Steel* débuted nearly a year after the triangle scheme had been introduced (see *Superman*), and although the first five issues are self-contained, later stories were limited by having to fit into whatever story-line is running through the other titles. The first intrusion is 6's 'Blackout', in which the denizens of Metropolis' underworld rise up and try to take over the city.

The 'Doomsday' chapters (18–19) leading up to Superman's 'death' are particularly good. Bogdanove draws the most impressive Doomsday seen in any of the *Superman* titles, and the pace of the issues is frenetic. The aftermath and funeral are also well handled here, focusing on the emotional reactions of Lois Lane and Clark's parents. After Superman's death the possible Superman appearing here between 22 and 26 is John Henry Irons, who created an armoured metal suit and fought crime as Steel. He proved popular enough to warrant his own comic shortly after the story's conclusion. 30–31 feature a fight between Superman and Lobo, which is without doubt the low point of the series, which reverts to its wholesome superhero roots thereafter, and 35 and 36 have the (to date) only crossover between an established DC hero and the separate Milestone-published characters. 45 begins a story with Clark Kent being stalked, displaying how important the concept of an *alter ego* is to Superman. 50–53 have a new wrinkle with 'The Trial Of Superman', in which an alien tribunal accuses Superman of killing a billion Kryptonians. He's powerful enough to escape, but unwilling to break the law by doing so; the story shows a Superman helpless against his accusers.~SS

Recommended: Miniseries 1–6, 18–22

Collections: Man Of Steel (miniseries 1–6), see also *Superman*

SUPERMAN: THE SECRET YEARS

DC: *4-issue miniseries 1984–1985*

Apart from a terrible sub-plot about the Bermuda Triangle, this is a thoughtful exploration of Clark Kent's college days after the death of Ma and Pa Kent, up to his graduation and first day at the *Daily Planet*. It charts the way Superboy learns to deal with his parents' deaths, with friendship, love and loss, until he's finally ready to become Superman. Written by Bob Rozakis, with artwork by Superman regulars Curt Swan and Kurt Schaffenberger, the whole thing became apocryphal when John Byrne reinvented Superman; but in four issues it's a good condensation of what Superman is, was and always ought to be.~NF

SUPERMAN VS ALIENS

DC/Dark Horse: *3-issue miniseries 1995*

This is a hopeless idea, seemingly with no purpose beyond making money by teaming two popular features. The story features Superman in space being forced to take on the Aliens in order to prevent them overrunning a city. Dan Jurgens provides the worst visuals he's ever done for Superman, while Kevin Nowlan's story fails to mask the fact that the idea is terrible.~SS

SUPERNATURAL THRILLERS
Marvel: *15 issues 1972–1975*

One of many 1970s mystery comics, this one differed from the norm by initially adapting classic horror stories. Theodore Sturgeon's *It*, H.G. Wells' *The Invisible Man*, *Dr Jekyll And Mr Hyde* and *The Headless Horseman* in 1, 2, 4, and 6 respectively were decent, if not thrilling. Far better was Robert E. Howard's lesser-known *Valley Of The Worm* in 3, an out-and-out sword-and-sorcery strip feeling somewhat out of place here, retold to great effect by Roy Thomas, Gerry Conway, Gil Kane and Ernie Chua. 5's original story, *The Living Mummy*, has a slave of noble origins who has been mummified by an oppressive pharaoh reawakening centuries later to track down his murderer's descendants. It proved popular enough to spawn a series beginning in 7. Originally by Steve Gerber and Rick Buckler, the writing was taken over by Tony Isabella, Len Wein and John Warner, while Val Mayerik and Tom Sutton (in 15) drew it. Never near Marvel's top strips, it was always entertaining, and remains worthy of a look.~DAR
Recommended: 3

SUPERPATRIOT
Image: *4-issue miniseries 1993–1995*

Opening with one of the most shocking scenes ever presented in a comic, *Superpatriot* could have been a contender. Instead, though, it's all downhill from there, and an incredibly slow publication schedule didn't help matters for the original fans.~WJ

SUPERSWINE
Fantagraphics: *One-shot ('Christmas With Superswine')* 1989
Caliber: *2 issues 1991*

Gary Fields' cartooning is excellent. His stories leave something to be desired. Superswine is an all-drinking, all-belching pig in a cape and mask, who, whisper it, isn't really heroic at all. Of these issues the first is marginally better, as Fields combines the origins of Batman, Spider-Man and Superman to give our hero an origin. It's nowhere near as funny as it thinks it is, although there are plenty worse comics out there. Anyone whose funny bone is tickled should also hunt down *Kaptain Keen*, which Superswine shares, and issues of *Critters*.~WJ

SUPREME
Image: *43 issues + 1993 to date*

Cast in the same mold as Superman, Supreme shares similar powers, appearance and even name. The comic is full of superhero action, with generally no plot or characterisation, but, unlike its label-mates at Image, Supreme's artwork fails to impress. Instead of working on the existing cast to make them interesting, the creators constantly introduce new ones. The superpowered team Heavy Mettle (yawn) appeared in 1 and became instantly stale. Then Supreme's arch-enemy arrives and a big fight follows (surprise, surprise), lasting from issue 3 until issue 6, when Khrome is forgotten and Thor becomes the villain for a… big fight! In 22–23 Gary Carlson shamelessly rewrites Walt Simonson's *Thor* 337–338. The multi-part 'Supreme Madness' is more interesting, with the idea of Supreme becoming too powerful. Unfortunately, the story ends with another fight. Issue 25 was published before issue 13, as part of the 'Images of Tomorrow' crossover, which was a good idea, but the issue made little sense and continuity was forsaken for a gimmick. The series degenerated further, reaching its lowest point in 33, which featured Lady Supreme in a story called 'Babewatch'. The introduction of a female counterpart did nothing for the comic so along came a Kid Supreme, so instead of one boring Superman clone we have three.

There is, however, a light at the end of the tunnel: Alan Moore takes over as writer from 41, and revitalises the comic totally. Openly acknowledging Supreme's debt to Superman, Moore has him exploring both his own past and the history of the superhero genre. In 41 he meets all the different versions of himself that have existed since his 1938 origin, now living in a pocket limbo universe. From 42 on, flashbacks drawn by Rick Veitch fill in Golden Age and 1950s backstory. It's amusing and affectionate, and it tries hard to restore some of that sense of wonder and naïvety that so many superhero strips of the mid-to-late 1990s are striving for, in a backlash against the 'grim and gritty' trend. Unlike most other contenders, Moore's Supreme does it within an intelligent framework, with masterly skill, and with some points to make. Remarkable, unique and not to be missed.~SS/GL
Recommended: 41–43

The Legend Of SUPREME
Image: *3-issue miniseries 1994–1995*

When Supreme was introduced to the Image universe in his own title in 1993, the back story was that he had been an all-powerful superhero who'd left Earth to wander the stars. Hey, if you're an all-powerful being why stick in one place? Keith Giffen and Robert Loren Fleming (as writers) and Jeff Johnson and Dan Panosian (as artists) now fill in the previously untold story of Supreme's origin. What makes this better than a straightforward flashback tale (and light years ahead of the ongoing *Supreme* title) is the counterplot in the present day of Supreme dealing with all those who participated in his creation. Supreme is, of course, invincible. Or is he?~FP

SURGE

Eclipse: *4-issue miniseries 1984–1985*

Among fans Mark Evanier has never had a particularly high reputation as a writer, perhaps because his non-humour work has chiefly been on lesser-known superhero titles. Yet *DNAgents* was a clever series, exploring the idea of humanity through a group of heroes grown in tanks by the evil Matrix corporation. In this spin-off series Surge hunts down his girl-friend's assassin and is put on trial for murder in the great superhero tradition. Only the man who captured him can provide the evidence that will prevent his execution. Utilising supporting characters from the main series, Evanier and co-scripter and artist Rick Hoberg examine the nature and function of revenge. Each issue also contains a back-up featuring one of the other DNAgents, all written by Evanier. 3's Sham story is drawn by Mike Sekowsky and in 4 Steve Rude draws the Rainbow short.~NF

SURVIVE

Apple: *1 issue 1992*

Seemingly very early work in five-page segments from Don Lomax, by 1992 well ensconced at Apple producing the decent *Vietnam Journal*. This extrapolates what might occur following World War III. 'Want to see more? Then write!' pleaded the concluding type. We obviously didn't.~WJ

SWAMP THING

DC: *24 issues 1972–1976*
DC/Vertigo: *171 issues, 7 Annuals 1982–1996*

Len Wein's creation of an intelligent bog monster unable to communicate with people who fear him on sight provided a pathos well served by Berni Wrightson's moody and evocative art, for which the initial run is remembered. 9's alien encounter is a good sample. Wrightson was replaced by Nestor Redondo with 11 and the title began a slow decline to cancellation. Redondo's style is a complete contrast to Wrightson, but it's also very accomplished, and there are notable moments after the departure of the original creative team. All the Wein and Wrightson issues were reprinted in four issues of *Original Swamp Thing Saga* and five issues of *Roots Of The Swamp Thing*, and there was a dry run for the feature in *House Of Secrets* 92 (reprinted in 33 of the second run).

Initially titled *Saga of the Swamp Thing*, the revival was to tie in with the release of the 1982 B-movie based on the character, and the team of Martin Pasko and Tom Yeates delivered a sprawling epic over the initial fifteen issues. Encompassing corporate greed, ex-Nazis, witchcraft and an assortment of stock horror characters, the story rambles in places, but only really suffers in comparison with what was to come. The art team of Steve Bissette and John Totleben arrived with issue 16, and their talent for genuinely gruesome creations was more suited to the tone of the title. When Alan Moore became writer with issue 20 he quickly concluded Pasko's plots and only kept the recently returned Abigail Arcane (Swamp Thing's tragic love from the original series) from the supporting cast.

Moore discarded the idea that Swamp Thing was in any way human in a startling story titled *The Anatomy Lesson* (21), and eventually developed him into an Earth elemental who could materialise anywhere there was vegetation. Under Moore *Swamp Thing* became a true horror comic, encompassing horror standbys as manifestations of human problems and cruelty. Almost every issue by Moore, Bissette and Totleben (and subsequent artists Rick Veitch and Alfredo Alcala) can be recommended, and the variety of stories and story-telling methods is astonishing. As samples try four very different stories: the tale of a toxic hobo in 35 and 36, the examination of menstrual pain in 40, Gotham held hostage by Swamp Thing in 52 and 53, or the horrific return of Martin Pasko's supporting characters in 54.

Succeeding Alan Moore as writer, artist Rick Veitch produced some memorable issues, and no writer since has been as consistent, although Mark Millar tops his peaks. His story of a doomed airliner in 70–71 is noteworthy, as were Swamp Thing's encounter with Superman (79) and a surprisingly good tie-in with the cross-company *Invasion* story (81). Having Abby and Swamp Thing conce:ve was an interesting idea, although standby stud John Constantine was required for the actual deed. Veitch then sent Swamp Thing travelling back through time, meeting various DC characters along the way. Sadly, editorial qualms about a scene involving the crucifixion of Christ led to Veitch's resignation with 87.

Doug Wheeler began in solid if unspectacular fashion, wrapping up Veitch's plot-lines. He wrote a good tale about a musician (94), garnished by Kelley Jones' Wrightsonesque art, but thereafter produced dull stories, mirrored for half his run by Mike Hoffman's dull illustration. From 110 horror novelist Nancy Collins returned Swamp Thing to the Louisiana swamps, and the art team of Scot Eaton and Kim DeMulder (from 117) was the best since Veitch and Alcala. Although the run isn't bad, any sense of horror is outweighed by cosy domesticity (except in Collins' final issues) and any social commentary is hammered home. For a flavour, 121–123 feature environmental protesters and the return of the Sunderland Corporation from early issues.

A revitalisation was heralded when Mark Millar and Philip Hester joined DeMulder with 140, but it's slow in coming. Their initial story (co-written by Grant Morrison) starts with a surprise but descends into muddy symbolism. Issues to 150 stretch credulity by having the invincible Swamp Thing manipulated and on the run. Where Millar scores is by returning emotional despair, horror and unpredictability to the title. His next effort, 'River Run', is much improved, a connected story in individual chapters sending Swamp Thing into an assortment of alternate worlds. The best is a Nazi-controlled USA, stunningly illustrated by Chris Weston, in 153, but 154's alternate Abby Arcane, 157's story of the woman who destroys a chain letter and the tale of a boy and his dog in 159 are also excellent. The art, though, never matches former heights, with the problem appearing to be DeMulder's inks not suiting Hester's angular pencils. Gradually obtaining mastery over all the elements, Swamp Thing becomes a challenge to God, and from 166 the final tale encompasses almost every character who's been influential during the course of the series. It tugs at and unwinds fixed conceptions of the cast and their alignments in masterful fashion, with arch-enemy Anton Arcane's unpredictable return for a philo-sophical debate in 168 typical of the story. Although not the best chapter, the conclusion to *Swamp Thing* is a natural progression, with an upbeat ending, which is what most would have wanted.

The eleven Titan Books reprint volumes contain the entirety of the Alan Moore-written issues from 21, but in black and white. If you'd prefer to read those stories as originally printed, they're currently being reprinted in black and white on a monthly basis under the 'Essential Vertigo' label.~FP

Recommended: Series one 9, series two 3, 21–32, 35–42, 44–55, 57, 58, 63, 64, 70–72, 79, 81–84, 153, 154, 157, 159, 165, 168, 169, Annual 2

Collections: Saga of the Swamp Thing (series two 21–27), *Love and Death* (series two 28–34, Annual 2), *Swamp Thing* Vols 1–11 (series two 21–64, Annual 2)

SWEET XVI
Marvel: *6 issues, 1 Special 1991–1992*

Writer/artist Barbara Slate attempts to recreate her *Angel Love* success, but comes badly unstuck with an overly cute, wilfully anachronistic attempt to set up a bunch of *Archie*-type teens in Roman days. Cutesy, cluttered and irritating rather than charming.~HS

SWEETMEATS
Atomeka: *One-shot 1992*

A John Bolton cover of a female vampire smearing blood across the wall is certainly an appropriate welcomer for the contents, which begin with a strip showing a callous twentysomething vampire paying money for sex with a young girl. Writer Steve Tanner and artist Pete Venters appear to feel the twist ending justifies the sordid premise, and, unbelievably, it's downhill from there. The longer second story is of an alluring sixteen-year-old high-security-hospital patient with a taste for blood, who captivates all who come in contact with her. It's an exploitative, voyeuristic piece offending on numerous levels, finishing off with a bit of lesbian fantasy canoodling for the lads. While there's absolutely nothing wrong with stories about sex, context is everything; these are appalling.~FP

SWIFTSURE
Harrier: *18 issues 1985–1987.*

A companion to *Conqueror*, early issues had a space-opera and fantasy line-up, usually with a curiously 1950s feel to them, with the solo stories of Conqueror's Lt Fl'ff, illustrated by Steve Yeowell, amongst the best of them. An anomaly, though a welcome one, was Lew Stringer's guest Brickman strip in 6, humorous Batman parody. With 15, new editor Rob Sharp attempted to revitalise the title with three new series, all of which had some potential. Night Porter was a teleporting nocturnal super-heroine, written by Sharp and drawn in a delightful cheesecake style by Art Wetherell; Lone Shark, also written by Sharp and drawn by Geoff Harrold, was an aquatic vigilante with a nasty misogynist streak; and Nigel Kitching's Morningstar was an imaginative and intelligent tale of a modern woman coming face to face with the old legends of Faerie, rather predating Neil Gaiman's explorations of that realm. Despite a suddenly improved line-up, *Swiftsure* had lost too many readers, and folded a couple of issues later.~HS

Batman: SWORD OF AZRAEL
DC: *4-issue miniseries 1992–1993*

The story that introduced Jean Paul Valley to his destiny as the avenging angel Azrael and set him on the path to taking on the mantle of the Batman. Azrael's father is killed trying to assassinate Lehah, ex-treasurer of the Order of St Dumas, who has set himself up as an arms dealer and is now out to destroy his old partners. When Batman investigates a gun battle he finds himself caught between Lehah and the Order in Switzerland where, as Bruce Wayne, his identity becomes known to Azrael. Apart from the reasoning behind Batman's

secret identity being blown (isn't it enough that practically everyone works it out in the films?) and the need to set Azrael up for 'Knightfall', this is a reasonable Batman adventure, full of intrigue and even some detection, as written by Denny O'Neil. What really pushes it above many of the contemporary Batman stories is the artwork by Joe Quesada. His cinematic layouts are given a boost by inker Kevin Nowlan, whose tight, smooth technique gives the whole a sharp, dynamic feel.~NF
Collection: Sword Of Azrael (1–4)

SWORD OF SORCERY
DC: *5 issues 1973*

Certainly one of the best sword-and-sorcery series produced for comics. It starred Fritz Leiber's Fafhrd the Barbarian and the Gray Mouser. The contrast of the two main characters inspires entertaining stories from Denny O'Neil. Fafhrd is a red-haired giant of a man, with more brawn than brain, while the Mouser is a wily character If you like sword-and-sorcery with a touch of humour, and want a change from Conan, then give this a go. With impressive early art from the likes of Howard Chaykin, Walt Simonson and Jim Starlin, you can't go wrong.~HY
Recommended: 1–5

SWORD of the ATOM
DC: *4-issue miniseries 1983, 3 specials 1984–1988*

Conceived by Gil Kane and Jan Strnad, who then respectively drew and scripted the series, this isn't such a radical reinvention of the Atom, more a change in direction. Discovering his wife Jean in the arms of another man, Ray Palmer (The Atom) takes a job in South America, crashes over the Amazon, is stuck at six inches tall and discovers a lost alien race that happens to be the same size as him. From then on the story is worthy of a *Conan* epic as the Atom aids a princess and some rebels against her father, contending with various jungle threats like soldier ants along the way. The series ends with the Atom back at regular size but determined to re-find the princess, Laethwen. The first special is the story of Ray and Jean splitting up. The gimmick is that the special is excerpts from Ray and Jean's book about their break-up. The second special is something of a retread of the miniseries, though there's some fun in the size-changing antics of Jean and her new lover Paul as they too get to visit the jungle. The final special is still by Strnad, but Kane is replaced by Pat Broderick, whose similarities to Kane merely highlight the fact that it's not Kane. This is more of a horror tale, as the Atom visits another of the aliens' cities, which is in the middle of a plague that causes the dead to return to life after burial. Strnad's scripts are fine as far as they go but it

hardly matters that it's Ray Palmer in these Burroughs/Howard-inspired tales. Kane's artwork is at its best on the miniseries, thought the first special contains some of his latter-day minimalism.~NF

SWORDS OF TEXAS
Eclipse: *4-issue miniseries 1987*

Scout spin-off as the Swords accept a contract to ship some arms to Mexico, but get more than they bargained for. There's also some good old boy roister-doistering with the 'Dogs Of Danger' back-up strip.~WJ

SWORDS OF THE SWASHBUCKLERS
Epic: *Graphic Novel 1984, 12-issue limited series 1985–1987*

Preposterous stuff. Space pirate Raader's mother was an 18th-century Earth pirate, so Raader speaks with a 'ho ho Jim m'lad accent'. You know it's proper space opera because characters have apostrophes in the middle of their names, and most aliens are biped humanoids, many based on earth animals. Raader's race has pointy flaps of skin extending from their temples. It's meant to be light-hearted and fun, but is dull and derivative.~FP

SWORDS OF VALOR
A+: *3 issues 1990*

Anthology reprinting often obscure short strips drawn by the good and famous for Charlton, ACG and 1970s Atlas titles. The muddy black and white reprinting of stories originally in colour is less than desirable, but for those wanting to search out the early work of John Buscema, Jim Aparo and Walt Simonson among others this is a cheap place to begin.~FP

THE SYSTEM
Vertigo: *3-issue miniseries 1996*

Peter Kuper is probably best known for his *Third World War* comics or his *New York* album. Both are intensely political works and though *The System* doesn't have the same focus, it too is about politics. Experimentally told without word balloons, its a series of vignettes, much like Robert Altman's film *Short Cuts*, as a number of individuals cross paths as they go about their daily business in the city. Though the characters have their own stories there's an underlying terrorist plot and a political scandal that threatens all their lives. Kuper's artwork is minimalist but carries the story along at a brisk pace, though careful reading is required because of the lack of dialogue.~NF
Recommended: 1–3
Collection: The System (1–3)

TABOO

SpiderBaby: *3 issues 1988–1989*
SpiderBaby/Tundra: *4 issues (4–7), 1 Special 1990–1992*
Kitchen Sink: *2 issues (8–9)1995*

Lavish, infrequently published horror anthology founded by Steve Bissette. Despite a tendency to indulge its creative team, *Taboo* stands head and shoulders above other horror titles since the demise of *Creepy* and *Eerie*. Bissette as editor explored the parameters of how and why things upset us and frequently triumphed by persuading creators not known for working in the horror genre to contribute. Notable for running major series such as Alan Moore and Eddie Campbell's 'From Hell' (from 2) and Moore and Melinda Gebbie's unfinished erotic what-if? 'Lost Girls' (5 onwards).

Stories range from schlock horror to disturbing mood pieces. Many of them are experimental in both form and content, challenging the reader. You may feel that much of the content ultimately fails, but they fail in an eye-opening way. Of particular note are Rick Grimes' stories, set in a sardonic world of tortured lines and sick humour, and Jeff Nicholson's downbeat stories of office life in a weird, inexplicably sinister corporation.~FJ
Recommended: 2–4

TAD MARTIN

Caliber: *5 issues 1991–1993*

Uncompromisingly brutal and utterly amoral, therefore compelling, all the more so for having the feel of autobiographical confession about it. Tad Martin is ironically subtitled 'Average American teenager' on the cover of the first issue, and the comic covers the twin teenage obsessions of sex and violence, with the crude drawing matching the crude text. 4 is text with a few illustrations. Creator Al Frank's apparent misogynism is disturbing, but don't let that put you off sampling the comic world's answer to punk music: loud, simple, and in and out in three minutes.~FP

TAILGUNNER JO

DC: *6-issue miniseries 1988–1989*

Thankfully absolutely nothing to do with Senator Joe McCarthy, but an extremely odd take on the idea of a cyborg vigilante. A renowned geneticist is made the subject of a test operation which gives him cybernetic implants and merges the personality of his dying daughter Jo into him. She spends most of her time in a convincingly portrayed fairytale cyber-reality while her father attempts to exact restitution from the corporation that transformed him and still holds his wife. The title stems from the fact that Jo operates her father's cybernetic implants while he's occupied with other matters. Peter Gillis turns in a stunningly bizarre concept that works extremely well, and sank almost without trace in the days when DC published adult material, but didn't quite have a handle on how to promote it. Successfully avoiding the twin traps of becoming either too twee or too testosterone-influenced, *Tailgunner Jo* both delights and excites, much of the credit being due to the art of Tom Artis. He switches from one locale to the next with aplomb, never short-changing the children's fantasy elements for the more popular action sequences. The series sags a little in the middle, which is odd as the ending might have been expanded, and prospective readers should be warned that the story really has to be read in sequence to make sense.~WJ
Recommended: 1, 2, 5, 6

TAKION

DC: *7 issues 1996*

It's not every superhero who drops an aircraft carrier on a skyscraper or three to deal with a problem. Then, not every superhero is a being of pure energy embodying the source of all life. Scientific mumbo-jumbo sees Earthman Josh Saunders transformed and able to instinctively manipulate the fundamental energy of the universe. For all that, he's rather a fuckwit, bumping through space and time into battle scenarios. Confusing, non-linear and with an irritating stream-of-consciousness narrative, *Takion* ties into Jack Kirby's *New Gods* concepts. Perhaps preferable to diluting those stories still further, *Takion* is nonetheless a mess.~WJ

THE TALE OF ONE BAD RAT

Dark Horse: *4-issue miniseries 1994–1995*

Rumour has it that when Dark Horse supremo Mike Richardson signed this Bryan Talbot miniseries he thought he was getting the second part of Talbot's *Luther Arkwright* epic. He can't but have been delighted by what he did get: a multi-award-winning story of Helen, a young runaway whose only friend on the street is her pet rat. Her love of Beatrix Potter takes her on a pilgrimage to the Lake District, where she finds the resources to come to terms with the paternal sexual abuse that drove her from home in the first place. In an astoundingly well written final scene she confronts her father, who's looking for forgiveness. Talbot avoids preaching or editorialising about this most difficult subject, producing a work more powerful for its lack of conclusions.

One Bad Rat is an excellent introduction to comics, and ought to be put before a much wider audience. The plot is intelligent, the writing sensitive and the art clear but detailed. Talbot produces an excellent Potter pastiche and uses other English illustrative techniques – most notably the simplified figures and detailed background style Alfred Bestall used to such effect on Rupert – to enrich his style, finally getting beyond the stiffness that characterises much of his earlier work.~FJ
Recommended: 1–4
Collection: The Tale Of One Bad Rat (1–4)

TALES FROM THE CRYPT
EC: *27 issues (20–46) 1950–1955*
Gladstone: *Series one 7 issues 1990–1991*
Russ Cochran/EC: *Series one 6 issues 1991–1992, series two 16 issues + 1992 to date*

Continuing its numbering from *Crypt of Terror*, *Tales From The Crypt* was the original horror comic, spawning hosts of imitators, outraging the parents of a generation, inspiring countless artists, and resulting in a TV series thirty years after publication. That the material is still reprinted today speaks volumes for the high editorial standards employed: EC horror titles stand head and shoulders above the many imitations they spawned over the decades.

Each issue contains four twist-ending stories, written for the most part by Al Feldstein and Bill Gaines. Early issues have interesting moments (Kurtzman's college initiation story in 21, though the usually excellent Wally Wood fails to draw convincing horror), but it's not until the arrival of Jack Davis with 24 that everything begins to gel as Gaines and Feldstein settle on their formula of strangely moralistic tales of evil thwarted in appropriately gruesome fashion or revenge somehow occurring from beyond the grave. Davis, Jack Kamen and Graham 'Ghastly' Ingels are the featured artists in almost every issue from the mid-20s, and are consistently excellent, with Ingels' story of a murdering shadow in 39 outstanding. A precociously competent Joe Orlando is most commonly the fourth contributor, although George Evans (who

illustrates a quiz show story in 43) and Bernie Krigstein (whose best is *Murder Dream* in 45) are also of note. The sheer volume of stories Gaines and Feldstein wrote for these and the other EC horror titles inevitably ensured a dip in quality, and the pair began substituting more explicit gore to cover predictable plots from about 34. Razor-sharp fire poles, a bigamist dismembered and used as sporting accessories by his wives, and butchers short of meat selling parts of corpses are typical of this era (although the title wasn't above self-parody, as evinced in 31's story about artist Jack Kamen). With Senate hearings on horror comics beckoning, the writers were forced to be less reliant on gore, and the final issues are a return to form. The quality of the art never dips. *Tales From The Crypt* is best read an issue at a time. *En masse*, the stories are formularised and predictable, although their over-the-top nature can still raise a chuckle.

These stories have been reprinted many times and in many different formats, few following the original numbering. If you can afford the boxed set, it's a complete reprinting, although not in colour. The Gladstone series couples reprints of *Tales From The Crypt* with *Crime SuspenStories*. The first Russ Cochran series combines two original issues every time, and some are also available as oversize editions. The second series is chronological facsimile editions of the originals and can also be found bound with five issues per collection.~FP
Recommended: 27–33, 43, 44, 46
Collection: Tales From The Crypt boxed set (20–46 and *Crypt Of Terror* 17–19)

TALES FROM THE FRIDGE
Kitchen Sink (US)/Cozmic (UK): *One-shot 1973*

Very funny EC pastiche also taking the time to lampoon the Dick Tracy and Flash Gordon newspaper strips along the way. Bob Stewart and Russ Jones introduce obese glutton Global McBlimp, whose hamburger recipe is parlayed into a chain of Globalburger franchises by his manipulative flatmate Rod Usher. When Global's gorging finally results in cardiac arrest and pauper's grave, the EC morality tale and horror elements come to the fore, complete with a totally over-the-top final panel. There's even room for some good one-pagers at the end. PC be damned, fatties are funny.~WJ
Recommended: 1

TALES FROM THE HEART
Entropy: *2 issues 1987*
Slave Labor: *9 issues + (3–11) 1988 to date*
Epic: *One-shot ('Temporary Natives') 1990, one-shot ('Bloodlines') 1992*

Witty, warm-hearted, endearing and educational in the best fashion, *Tales From The Heart* is a unique comic. It draws on the experiences of co-writer Cindy Goff and others of two years spent as Peace Corps volunteers in the Central African Republic, known as 'The Heart of Africa', hence the title. 1–3 detail the Peace Corps induction and composite lead character Cathy Grant's arrival and orientation in Boguila. She's naïve, but with an open mind, which is just as well, as her preconceptions are challenged as she gradually learns to adapt to a totally different reality and set of expectations. Goff and co-writer Rafael Nieves are adept at painlessly incorporating an immense amount of background detail and local custom into their stories, at the shorthand introduction of new characters, and of subtly progressing their cast. This would count for little were not pencil artists Seitu Hayden (1–6) and Aldin Baroza (7 on) not also first-rate at conveying mood through posture and expression, and at portraying the sparsity of the area in sympathetic fashion.

Each issue is complete in itself, with 8 being a good sample. With her room-mate departing for the capital, Cathy's anticipating a peaceful day, but it doesn't materialise that way. Issued with the added marketing clout of Epic, the colour one-shots were intended to direct a new audience back to the parent title. They're a contrasting pair. 'Bloodlines' reflects on the harrowing atrocities committed by former C.A.R. dictator Bokassa, and 'Temporary Natives' deals with a Peace Corps volunteer at an impasse. Both are excellent. Never patronising and always absorbing, *Tales From The Heart* is a neglected gem.~FP
Recommended: 1–11, 'Temporary Natives', 'Bloodlines'
Collection: Hearts Of Africa (1–3)

TALES FROM THE OUTER BOROUGHS
Fantagraphics: *5 issues 1991–1992*

Douglas Michael's off-beat humour is very similar to that of Rick Geary, unfolding often ridiculous stories in a wayward manner. His layouts and style are very similar to Geary as well, choosing to caption individual illustrations and using minimal dialogue. Where he differs is in extending his stories over an entire issue. This works well for the first issue's nicely meandering tale of a murder attempt that doesn't quite go as planned, but thereafter drags on stories way beyond any point of interest. When it comes to art Michael is certainly no Rick Geary. All things considered you're advised to sample the first issue and then plenty of Rick Geary.~WJ

TALES From The TUBE
Print Mint: *One-shot 1973*

To date probably the only comic devoted to surfing, this is superb collection of strips put together by Rick Griffin. Griffin's several

contributions include a mixture of travelogue pieces on surfing haunts and semi-mythical paeans to the sport, all drawn in his trademark psychedelic style. Robert Williams contributes a fantastically drawn strip, 'The Ties That Bind', and the little-known Jim Evans is also of note. Add work by S. Clay Wilson and Robert Crumb and you have an essential addition to anyone's collection, whether a surfing fan or not.~DAR
Recommended: 1

TALES OF ASGARD
Marvel: *One-shot 1968, One-shot 1984*

Reprints of the five-page back-up strips of the same name from *Journey into Mystery* 97–106 in the 1968 one-shot and *Thor* 129–136 in the 1984 volume.~APS

TALES OF EVIL
Atlas: *3 issues 1975*

Standard predictable horror notable only for the typically Atlas lashings of excess gore. Bog-Beast and Man-Monster starred in the third issue, and the paucity of imagination applied to their names reveals all you need to know about the content.~WJ

TALES OF ORDINARY MADNESS
Dark Horse: *4-issue miniseries 1992*

Writer Malcolm Bourne, a psychiatrist by trade, turns in a surprisingly naïve and simplistic view of mental illness. This slice-of-life look at a young doctor's reactions to other people's mental decay, and the tragic route his empathy leads him down, could have been much more powerful, but as it is, it comes across as stolid and patronising. Fans of Michael Allred's art might be interested, but leave your expectations at the door.~HS

TALES OF SUSPENSE
Marvel: *99 issues 1959–1968, one-shot 1995*

Weird/monster shorts populate 1–38 and also serve as back-ups until 48. 49–58 feature a Tales of the Watcher back-up strip, consisting of the Watcher narrating morality tales of himself and other alien races, but it's Iron Man who dominates from his introduction in 39. All but a few stories are written by Stan Lee; early tales in particular are very crude. There are three plot-lines: Iron Man fights Communists, Iron Man modifies armour, Iron Man nearly dies after forgetting to put life-supporting armour's battery on charge last night. Better examples are 57, 60, 64 (all Black Widow and Hawkeye) and 95–99, introducing Whitney Frost as Big M. This story-line continues in *Iron Man and Sub-Mariner* 1.

Also written by Stan Lee, Captain America's first Silver Age solo strip in 59–99 suffers from an abundance of World War II reminiscences, Bucky Barnes hallucinations, androids and general clichés. 64–71 consist entirely of Cap's narrations of his war exploits. Avoid most issues except 66 (origin of the Red Skull), 77, 79–81 (Red Skull and Cosmic Cube) and 92–94 (passable AIM story with Modok). Captain America becomes the book's title bearer from 100.

The one-shot is a posthumous slice of nostalgia, with Iron Man and Captain America pitted against a super-secret high-tech terrorist organisation as S.H.I.E.L.D. pulls the strings. A plot in the tradition of the 1960s series, narrated in a refreshingly modern style.~APS

Collections: *Marvel Masterworks* Vol 14 (Captain America stories from 59–81), *Marvel Masterworks* Vol 20 (Iron Man stories from 39–50)

TALES OF THE CLOSET
Hetrick-Martin: *9 issues + 1987 to date*

One day in 1986 eight youngsters discover they've something in common: they're gay, or think they might be. The series explores their feelings of shock, confusion, acceptance or rejection, and the reactions of those around them. Stated baldly it sounds obvious and schlocky, but writer/artist Ivan Velez Jr deftly captures the anguish and alienation of gay youth and, in ensuing issues, moves the cast through hilarious and cataclysmic events without missing a step. This isn't a stroke book, rather it's a moving and intelligently presented evocation of the perils and pitfalls any youngster can fall victim to when first exploiting their sexuality. The only gripe is the slower-than-molasses progress. Announced as ten issues, it's managed roughly an issue a year, and the finale has yet to appear.~HS
Recommended: 1–9

TALES OF THE GREEN LANTERN CORPS
DC: *3-issue miniseries 1981*

The first issue imparts a wealth of background information to anyone interested in the Green Lantern Corps, but the succeeding two could be any ordinary issues of *Green Lantern*.~FP

Star Wars: TALES OF THE JEDI
Dark Horse: *5-issue miniseries 1993–1994, 2-issue microseries ('Freedom Nadd Uprising') 1994, 6-issue miniseries ('Dark Lords Of Sith') 1994–1995, 6-issue miniseries ('The Sith War') 1995–1996*

This collection of miniseries stars characters created specifically for the comics, with no relation to the *Star Wars* films other than sharing their universe. They all occur in a period before the first film, at a time when the Jedi were more numerous and the galactic republic was growing. For those not familiar with the concept, the Jedi are superlatively

trained protectors of the galaxy, but must be on their guard not to be seduced by the dark side of the forces they wield.

The first miniseries introduces the trainee Jedi Ulric Qel-Droma, and details his first mission – to bring peace to the world of Onderon. Once on the war-ravaged world Ulric learns of a dark force at work. There's then an odd switch from 3 to concentrate on another new Jedi, Nomi Sunrider, forced to accept Jedi training after the death of her husband. She quickly shows she's a natural. The fully painted covers by Dave Dorman are spectacular, while the interior art is uneventful. Tom Veitch provides a good script, but the events at which the tale breaks are left unresolved and lead into 'The Freedom Nadd Uprising', which tells the story of a revolt on Onderon by followers of an old dark-side Jedi. Nomi is picked to help Ulric, and the conclusion reveals a dire prognostication concerning the return of the ancient Sith overlords. Cue another miniseries.

'The Dark Lords Of Sith' has the two Jedis battling the students of Freedom Nadd. Eventually even Ulric falls under his spell, so it's down to Nomi to save the day. Once again Veitch provides a fine story, but is let down by Art Wetherell's poor art. Thankfully, all loose ends and various plots are rounded up in the 'Sith Wars'. The followers of the Sith are attacked by the Jedis and after a great sacrifice by Ulric the villains are defeated. Kevin Anderson takes over the script and concludes the story-line well.~SS.

TALES OF THE MARVELS
Marvel: *One-shot ('Blockbuster') 1995, 2-issue microseries ('Wonder Years') 1995, One-shot ('Inner Demons') 1995*

Banner title for various independent one-shots and microseries thematically linked to *Marvels* and all similarly adorned with painted artwork. Each lead character is an ordinary man or woman whose life is changed by an encounter with a superbeing. 'Blockbuster' has private detective Ramon Stewart witness his parents' deaths in a free-for-all between the Silver Surfer, Fantastic Four, Doctor Doom and Tyros. This reappraisal of *Fantastic Four 260* focuses on the survivors' plight as their claims for compensation falter in a legal quagmire and Stewart's frustrations shift to a personal vendetta against the Surfer. Mike Baron's narrative is very creditable, although the suggestion that Stewart could actually kill the Silver Surfer is not entirely convincing.

'Wonder Years' tells a powerful tale of young, painfully shy Cindy Knutz (that's Knutz with a 'kay') and her obsession with a superhero, Wonder Man, who saved her life from Red Ronin's footprint at the time of

Avengers 198. Dan Abnett and Andy Lanning's portrayal of her tunnel vision is utterly believable. Sunglasses are advised for the colouring in this, the strongest *Marvels* spin-off to date. In 'Inner Demons', Bowery bum John Mahoney forms an uneasy friendship with a fellow pointy-eared, strong, silent, amnesiac down and out. Mahoney's battle with his inner demon (alcoholism) takes centre stage before the amnesiac's identity is revealed in the dénouement. Read *Fantastic Four* 4 for the answer. Mariano Nicieza pens marginally the weakest Tale of the Marvels, but only because the general standard is so high. There are some excellent painted pages from Bob Wakelin, who unfortunately didn't paint the entirety, and there are some substandard pages by others towards the end.~APS

Recommended: Blockbuster 1, Wonder Years 1, 2

TALES OF THE Teenage Mutant Ninja TURTLES
Mirage: *7 issues 1987–1989*

Jim Lawson, who would develop into the main Turtles man, cut his teeth here, alternating with Ryan Brown, both of them writing and drawing. There are robots, giant alligators and dinosaurs. Lawson's issues are better by virtue of his being a more talented artist, but there's nothing that isn't improved on in the main Mirage Turtles comic.~WJ

TALES OF TERROR
Eclipse: *13 issues 1985–986*

When Bruce Jones didn't want to continue *Twisted Tales*, Eclipse came up with this series, pretty much carrying on where that title had left off. There are some good stories here by writers like Chuck Dixon, Bill Pearson and even Jones himself. There's good artwork too, from John Bolton (7, 9, 12), Gray Morrow (3, 4), Carol Lay (6, 7, 11) and José Ortiz (10), and some really stand-out covers: Tim Conrad (5), John Bolton (9, 12) and John Begley (2).

The stand-out combinations, however, are: Mark Wheatley's 'Suzy Dreams' (1), about a battered wife's escape into fantasy; Eric Vincent and Anthony Smith's 'Live In Dead' (2), also drawn by Vincent, in which an over-tidy husband, returning as a zombie after being killed by his wife and her lover, finds time to do the dishes before remembering just why he came back from the dead; Dixon & Micheluzzi's 'A Fine Head On Her Shoulders' (2), in which a murderess expects to get away with it because she's been told that she can only die by being beheaded and so has no fear of the hangman; Tim Truman's 'Every Evening Billy Comes Home' (6), in which a dog dreams of protecting its dead master; Scott Hampton's 'The Revenant' (8), in which an artist helps a

ghost get revenge for her rape and murder; and Toren Smith and Lela Dowling's take on Cabbage Patch dolls in 4.~NF

Recommended: 2

TALES OF THE BEANWORLD
The Beanworld Press: *21 issues 1985–1993*

As the covers suggest, this is 'a most peculiar comic book experience'. Beanworld is a fantasy world where everything depends for its survival on its place within that world. The beans get a sprout-butt from Gran'Ma'Pa and give it to the Hoi Polloi, who turn it into chow, which the beans can then eat and thus live while they wait for the next sprout-butt to emerge. Larry Marder creates a huge cast of peculiar characters, from Mr Spook, leader of the bean army, to Beanish, an artist who has a strange, secret meeting with Dreamishness, a mysterious shining creature. Marder waits until issue 20 to reveal the origin of the Beanworld, while 21 explains how Professor Garbanzo, the beans' inventor and toolmaker, first discovered the Four Realities in which they live. Utterly charming, *Tales Of The Beanworld* can be read as an adventure story but it's also about the way things need to work for beings to live together. If this sounds odd, it is, and there's little by way of explanation in the series: you'll have to make of it what you will, but it's worth the effort. From 2 *Beanworld* was distributed by Eclipse, and the Eclipse logo appeared on the cover from 5.~NF

Recommended: 1–21

TALES OF THE JACKALOPE
Blackthorne: *8 issues 1996*

Taking the mythical Jackalope (part rabbit, part antelope) as his lead, R.L. Crabb turns in a series of funny-animal explorations of real-world issues. There's some nice cartooning, but it's often swamped in text, none of which really offers any new insight. Some diverting moments don't compensate for having to wade through the rest.~WJ

TALES TO ASTONISH
Marvel: *Series one 101 issues, 1959–1968, series two 14 issues 1979–1981, one-shot 1994*

Most of the early output of this title is science-fiction stories, often very well illustrated by the likes of Kirby, and Don Heck at his best, but, with very few exceptions, routinely scripted and relying on EC-style twist endings. Without EC's liberal use of gore, prohibited by the still-new Comics Code, or their A list artists, the content lacked bite. Stories by the Stan Lee/Steve Ditko pairing, each seeming to bring out the best qualities of the other, were honourable exceptions, imaginative and eerie. A one-shot tale in 27, 'The Man In The Ant Hill', wherein a scientist shrank himself to the size of an insect, scored unexpectedly heavily in sales, so the lead, Dr Henry Pym, was brought back as a series star, becostumed and dubbed 'Ant-Man', with 35. Given some thought, the Marvel staff might have realised that a tiny human up against full-size humans might make for less than dynamic conflicts; but then, they'd tried something unlikely with The Fantastic Four and that had worked, so what had they to lose? The early Ant-Man stories have a certain clunky charm, but the series badly needed a shake-up. It got two. Janet Van Dyne arrived in 44, as Ant-Man's partner, the Wasp. A refreshing character who gave the impression of having a keen mind behind a flighty façade, she livened up the stuffy Hank Pym no end. His early protests of romantic detachment notwithstanding, it wasn't long before they were a couple, and the only one of Marvel's early couples whom you could believe actually desired each other. The second major change came when Pym discovered how to grow as well as shrink, and ventured forth as Giant-Man from 49. Despite these changes, and many charming moments between the bantering lovers, the strips remained weakly plotted, and Hank & Jan's villains are third-rate. With 60, the Hulk, who had failed in his own title but been a success as a roaming villain, started a series backing-up, and soon eclipsing, the Giant-Man stories. Old Jade Jaws concentrated a bit more on the tragic-monster side than on his old rampaging routine, with the ragged and weary Bruce Banner waking up in strange locations all over the world, helpless to do anything but speculate what his *alter ego* had wrought. Giant-Man and the Wasp were pushed to the back of the comic, then ousted all together, as Prince Namor, the Sub-Mariner, another anti-hero from the beginnings of Marvel, took over their slot with 70. Hank and Jan became popular supporting characters, most prominently as part of the Avengers, and Namor and the Hulk vied with each other to see who could be most tragically misunderstood. This state of affairs continued until 101, when, a distribution restriction having been lifted, Marvel was able to split *Astonish* and its other shared titles, *Strange Tales* and *Tales Of Suspense*, into their component parts. The *Hulk* title continued *Tales To Astonish*'s numbering (to this day), while *The Sub-Mariner* restarted from 1. The title, though not the numbering, was revived for a short-lived series of reprints from *Sub-Mariner* in 1979, and the 1994 one-shot was a prestige-format painted story teaming Hank Pym, no longer Giant-Man, and the Wasp with the now intelligent and erudite Hulk. Peter David's script was adroit, especially in catching echoes of the old Hank and Jan banter, but John Estes' painted art merely looked vague and washed-out.~HS

TALK DIRTY
Eros: *3-issue miniseries 1992*

A woman, a man and a crane. Matthias Schultheiss' rumpathon is well drawn, but the distancing technique of printing dialogue alongside individual illustrations tends to highlight the banal nature of any talk during sex, although that could also be an unsympathetic translation. If the comic's working as intended you won't notice any of that. The couple manage to keep going for three issues, so you've got to admire their staying power.~FP
Collection: Talk Dirty (1–3)

TALOS of the Wilderness Sea
DC: *One-shot 1987*

Fantasy story that's not so much a boy and his dog, but a boy and his big cat. Sterling illustration from Gil Kane is marred by poor plotting from Gil Kane, and there's little here that hasn't been seen in countless fantasy novels and films.~FP

TANDRA
Hanthercraft: *14/15 issues (1–12 – see below) 1976–1993*

Tandra is a little-known masterpiece; a fantasy epic strong on plot and characterisation. Stylistically very much in the mould of *Prince Valiant*, being blocks of text accompanying individual illustrations, *Tandra* is a generational saga spanning twenty years of both the characters and the creator, Christopher Hanther (known only by his surname), who began work on the series in 1973. Hanther's art isn't up to Hal Foster's standard, but doesn't fall very far short by the later issues, and is already confident and composed by the conclusion of the first volume.

A striking opening sequence sets the tone for the series. On seeing a woman being attacked, David Galon leaps to her rescue. A relationship develops, but she's summoned away through an iron door in a brick wall. When he attempts to follow, the door peels off the wall like paper. Galon's persistence pays off, and he's transported to Tandra, a primitive world where he has to survive through his wits and strength. Although not always centre stage, Galon is the central figure throughout the series. His intelligence, engineering skills and adaptable nature ensure his success in a world almost unblemished by science, but whose inhabitants fear the occasional visits of wizards from the sky. From Galon's invention of a superior airship in *The Iron Cloud*, the series really takes off. It transpires that the wizards dwell in a ring surrounding the planet, and from that point revelations about the world and the relationships between various factions increase with each succeeding chapter, leading to an inevitable battle for supremacy between Galon and the brutish Kilthane.

The original chapters have been re-sequenced for more commonly available packages, numbered from 1 to 12 (including a 9A, 9B and 9C), with the most obvious reconstruction being the combination of two early collections, titled *The Golden Warrior* and *The Iron Cloud*, into a single volume. Although not all *Tandra* issues are numbered, each page is numbered in sequence (up to 718 as the final page of 12), enabling the saga to be followed in order. Those interested in a complete researched chronology will find it in issue 7 of the succeeding series, *Dragonrok Saga*. For someone so accomplished with pen and ink, Hanther's cover paintings are strangely poor, but this shouldn't put anyone off sampling a series that has a rightful place alongside the most highly regarded comics of recent years.~FP
Recommended: 3–12

TANK GIRL

Dark Horse: *4-issue miniseries 1991, 4-issue miniseries 1993*
Vertigo: *4-issue miniseries ('The Odyssey')1995, One-shot ('The Movie') 1995, 4-issue miniseries ('Apocalypse') 1995–1996*

Created in 1988 by Jamie Hewlett and Alan Martin for *Deadline*, the unwashed, violent, hard-drinking, chain-smoking, kangaroo-shagging Tank Girl became the magazine's strongest selling point, and idol of dykes and crusties the world over. Originally living in an unspecified near-future Australia as some form of agent, she quickly abandoned even that flimsy persona for life as an outlaw causing lots of explosions – for no very good reason – and indulging in everything imaginable that's bad for you. In a brain-dead way, her *Deadline* adventures, a selection of which were reprinted in two Dark Horse miniseries (and the first series of *Deadline USA*), are great fun.

When Tank Girl was optioned for a movie, DC's Vertigo imprint took an interest, and two new miniseries were commissioned. Suddenly, Tank Girl had to have 'meaning'. Sigh. Peter Milligan got away with it in 'Odyssey', an amusing, alleged commentary on James Joyce's *Ulysses* in which Tank Girl discovers secrets behind her parentage, but Alan Grant's take on 'Apocalypse' was crude and gross without being inventive or funny.   Both Vertigo miniseries had covers by Brian Bolland. The movie was made in 1995, starring Lori Petty and Ice T, and was an unmitigated disaster, featuring a sanitised, unrecognisable version of the character. The comics adaptation by Milligan and Andy Pritchett sported an inappropriate John Bolton cover, and succeeded in being more amusing than the movie which

spawned it. Despite the failure of her movie, she seems to have penetrated the public consciousness. A Tank Girl lookalike was the star of an advertising campaign for Wrangler Jeans in 1991, and that staid institution, the *Daily Telegraph*, used the heading 'Daughters of Tank Girl' (with a Hewlett illo) as a front-page tease for a rather limp appreciation of girls in computer games in its *Connected* supplement for 4/2/97.~HS
Collections: Book One (Dark Horse miniseries 1), Book Two (Dark Horse miniseries 2), Book Three (reprints from *Deadline*)

TANTALISING STORIES

Tundra: *One-shot 1992, 5 issues 1992–1993*

Tantalising Stories features the inspired pairing of Jim Woodring's Frank, frequently seen in *Jim*, and Mark Martin's Montgomery Wart. It manages to be very funny, but it makes you question the reassuring world of children's adventures. The juvenile presentation and subject-matter belie subtle narratives that play heavily and knowingly on our mature cynicism.

To call 'Frank' a funny-animal strip is to do it a disservice. Woodring has created a silent, surreal world inhabited by strange beasts. Although his dream-like milieu at first seems to make little sense, as the title progresses relationships and conflicts emerge. Frank goes about his everyday life, reading books, going to parties for the dead, on the alert for attacks from a warthog creature straight out of a Bosch painting. The conflict provides much-needed stability in a world of confusing symbolism. Frank is fundamentally nice, while the warthog is nasty but stupid. You'll either love the strip's quiet humour or wonder what all the fuss is about. Woodring is a consummate cartoonist, able to communicate complex emotions without words. For the black and white series he adopts a broad, brush-inked style reminiscent of Robert Crumb's bolder efforts. Whereas Woodring keeps to a single style, his companion Mark Martin rings changes, from explosive Bigfoot cartooning to sophisticated wash styles. His main characters (Montgomery Wart, a bullfrog who likes to think himself cynical and worldly-wise, Cicero Buck, a very naïve deer indeed, and Murgatroid, a thick but happy frog) get into boyish escapades, *à la Tom Sawyer*. Martin's jaundiced morals, appended to each story, reflect the true spirit of Twain's tales. The dialogue and approach to story-telling, which owe a lot of the classic US newspaper strip *Pogo*, are superb.

The series is good, and the colour one-shot, titled *Frank In 'The River'*, is superlative. Tundra didn't spare the pennies when producing it, and the thick, glossy paper is put to good use. Woodring's Frank story is among his best work. The painted pages glow with

primary colours as Frank becomes involved in a bizarre mystery while working for the bad warthog. Woodring reflects the reader's incomprehension as Frank presses further and further into a nightmare world. Montgomery Wart also benefits from colour treatment, painted in a rough watercolour style which adds a great deal of charm to Martin's fluid cartooning. After such an unsettling Frank story you're more than ready for a straight humour piece like this, where the grasping Wart is inspired by a magazine article to leave home. To get away he decides to train as a flight attendant but his attempts at a dry run involving Halloween lanterns are frustrated by his pal Murgatroid's stupidity. Matters are complicated when the insects inhabiting the jack 'o lanterns begin demanding extra peanuts, vegetarian meals and frequent flyer stamps. It's a quite fabulous package.~FJ
Recommended: One-shot, 1–5

Clive Barker's TAPPING THE VEIN
Eclipse/Titan: *5 issues 1990–1992*

It's arguable that Clive Barker's short stories are his best work, and these adaptations from *Books of Blood* are powerful even if you've read the originals. They have sympathic scripts and excellent art throughout from the likes of John Bolton, Tim Conrad, Bo and Scott Hampton and P. Craig Russell. Titan Books published UK editions of the first four issues.~WJ
Recommended: 1–5

Weird Suspense featuring the TARANTULA
Atlas: *3 issues 1975*

Gross and tasteless, even by Atlas' standards, The Tarantula is humanoid except for a giant spider's head. He traps his victims in a web, injects them with poison and eats them. Not to be read before meals.~FP

TARGITT
Atlas: *3 issues 1975*

In later years Targitt would have been designed as a testosterone-fuelled, heavily armed, pumped-up vigilante who'd have been the centrepiece of the Atlas line. Alas, in 1975 he was a blonde guy with a penchant for roll-neck jumpers and a pistol, whose adventures are as exciting as watching paint dry in Tedium, Nebraska. An unfortunate letters-page seer compares this with *The Spirit* and predicts popularity on a level with Spider-Man. Oops.~FP

TARZAN
Dell: *131 issues, 4 Annuals 1948–1962*

Edgar Rice Burroughs' noble savage had been a phenomenon in pulp magazines, consolidating his fame with films and top newspaper strips in the 1920s. With artwork by Hal Foster and later Burne Hogarth, the syndicated Tarzan strip was one of the seminal influences on the developing adventure strip. He featured in text stories in Dell's *Crackajack Comics* from 1939 to 1942, whilst his daily and Sunday strips were reprinted in *Tip Top* and *Sparkler Comics* from the beginning of the 1940s. In 1947 Dell experimented with originated Tarzan material in their *Four Color* series (137 and 161). The stories were written by clergyman Gaylord DuBois, who'd been writing newspaper strips since the 1930s, and the art was by Disney storyman Jesse Marsh. A regular title was promptly launched the following year, every issue of which was produced by the same team. Some may find Marsh's artwork crude, but his simplicity of style disguises a sophisticated knowledge of texture, animal anatomy and locale. His eighteen-year stay on the strip is only slightly overshadowed by DuBois managing a staggering twenty-five years between 1947 and 1972. His stories are rarely controversial, but effortlessly maintain the language and mythos founded by Burroughs.

Early issues feature a forgettable back-up strip, 'Two Against The Jungle', which gave way to Brothers Of The Spear with 25 in 1951. Dan-El and Natongo, one white, one black, are the adventuring princes who rule the jungle kingdom of Aba-Zulu. Although it had been initiated by DuBois and Marsh, the job of drawing the strip fell to Russ Manning in 1953 (*Tarzan* 39). These strips are a treasure trove worthy of collection, not only for Manning's gorgeous art, but for DuBois' gentle portrayal of his view of racial equality. This was long before it became a socially aware selling point in the 1960s.

When the comic covers weren't painted they featured photos of the film Tarzans Lex Barker (13–54) and Gordon Scott (80–110). Between 1952 and 1955 Dell also issued hundred-page annuals, some of which featured stories by Marsh, rather uncomfortably inked by Manning.~SW

TARZAN
Gold Key: *75 issues (132–206) 1962–1972*

Continuing the numbering from the Dell issues, this title was of merely average quality, which only took an upswing when long-time artist Jesse Marsh left the strip to Russ Manning with 154. Gaylord DuBois had written the strip since the 1940s, but such was Manning's flair that his run outshone the syndicated newspaper strip that he soon took over. On Manning's departure much of the life left the title, despite brave tries by Doug Wildey and Mel Keefer, among others. Brothers Of The Spear continued as a back-up until Manning began drawing the lead feature, and returned as reprints in 196–206. They were briefly replaced by Leopard Girl, which starred Meru, a teenage zoologist who could talk to the animals. DC purchasing the licence to produce *Tarzan* was the best possible tonic, even if they lost DuBois in the process.~SW

TARZAN of the Apes
DC: *52 issues (207–259) 1972–1977*

Gold Key, previous publishers of *Tarzan* comics, had rather let the feature fall into disrepute, with years of dull plots accompanied by merely acceptable Jesse Marsh art. A final spurt with Doug Wildey drawing the series didn't improve the plots, and DC really only had to be competent to succeed. That they produced some outstanding material was a bonus. Joe Kubert edited the comic, wrote most of the stories and seemed to have found the strip he was born to draw. He began by adapting *Tarzan Of The Apes* in spectacular fashion in 207–210, bringing both the jungle atmosphere and Tarzan's originally primal nature to vivid life. His adaptations of *The Return Of Tarzan* in 219–223 and *Tarzan And The Lion Man* in 231–234 are of an equally high standard, as are all his original stories until 235. Once he'd reached that point, though, he seemed to run out of inspiration, and although he continued writing and providing layouts for the likes of Franc Reyes, Rudy Florese and the Redondo Studio it was formulaic stuff. Gerry Conway and José Luis Garcia-Lopez take over from 250, but it's early Lopez and his pencils are unsympathetically inked throughout. Denny O'Neil writes the final two original issues, and 257–258 reprint Kubert stories.

230–235 are all one hundred pages, featuring some notable back-up strips, including a Mike Kaluta-drawn short in 230 and Alex Nino-illustrated Korak strips in 231–234. Besides standard Detective Chimp and Congo Bill reprints in those issues, there are also Russ Manning *Tarzan* newspaper strips, rejigged to resemble comic material. Given a trial run in 226, they were obviously popular enough to occupy 237 and 238 in their entirety. Other classic newspaper strips from an earlier era, by Hal Foster, can be found in 208, 209, 211, 215 and 221. There are also other Burroughs stories adapted, with John Carter in 207–209, and *Beyond The Furthest Star* in 213–218.~HY/DAR
Recommended: 207–210, 219–223, 230–235

TARZAN
Marvel: *Series one 29 issues, 3 Annuals 1977–1979, 2-issue microseries 1984*

Marvel's record with licensed material other than toys is appalling, and this is no different. There are unimaginative stories and dull art, mostly from John Buscema, whose Tarzan is almost indistinguishable from his Conan.

Leave well alone. The 1984 series is a two-part reprint of *Marvel Super Special* 29, with Dan Spiegle adapting the *Greystoke* film.~FP

TARZAN
Malibu: *5-issue miniseries ('The Warrior') 1992, 3-issue miniseries ('Love, Lies And The Lost City') 1992, 7-issue limited series ('The Beckoning') 1992–1993*

'The Warrior' introduces three men who might be Tarzan, but none of them ruling the jungle. The likeliest candidate lives in Baltimore, locates dimensional rifts in the company of his wife Jane, and takes over tribes of ape-men. The plot is slim, but the mystery drags it along to the final issue, which establishes Tarzan in 20th-century USA. The science-fiction elements in 'The Warrior' are intrusive, but it succeeds in retrieving Tarzan from cinema and TV clichés. 'Love, Lies And The Lost City' is better, a thrilling lost-civilisation story by the all-Danish team of Henning Kure, Teddy Kristiansen and Peter Snejbjerg, while Kure collaborates with Tom Yeates for 'The Beckoning'. It's the best Tarzan in comics since the DC issues, marred only by pages of issue 3 being printed out of order. While in San Francisco destroying an illegal ivory operation, Tarzan is mentally manipulated by an African witch doctor into experiencing flashbacks to jungle battles. The trails of poaching and the hallucinations lead back to Africa, where everything pulls together along, with an explanation of how Tarzan and Jane are now both over a century old. Kure and Yeates weave an enthralling adventure that slightly overextends itself with a convenient conclusion, and Yeates draws a Tarzan with both grace and power.~WJ
Recommended: 'The Beckoning' 1–7

TARZAN
Dark Horse: *6 issues + 1996 to date*

We're back with Tarzan in the grand tradition as Bruce Jones tells a tale involving a plant virus that Tarzan has brought back from Mars and which has revived the ancient races of the Kavell and the Ahrtan (1–6). The Ahrtan want to rule the world by creating a hybrid human/plant race and only Tarzan is immune to the virus. There are plenty of twists and turns to keep the plot moving, and if Christopher Schenck and Tom Yeates haven't really distinguished themselves as having their own artistic vision of Tarzan, it may yet come.~NF

TARZAN FAMILY
DC: *7 issues (60–66) 1975–1976*

Continuing the numbering from the cancelled *Korak* title, the Korak feature simply shifted into this new umbrella title, which also encompassed other Edgar Rice Burroughs creations. Robert Kanigher packs his stories with action – in twelve pages in 60 Korak fights a giant octopus, a horned ape and panther, enough material for a miniseries now – but they never really excite. They're mostly drawn by Rudy Florese or Noly Zamora, and it's interesting to see them attempt to imitate editor Joe Kubert's art style. Zamora also illustrates the new John Carter stories in 62–64, with the Carter tales in the final two issues being reprints. An early, but very welcome, reprint is Len Wein and Mike Kaluta's 'Carson Of Venus' adaptation, to be found in every issue, and there are also Tarzan newspaper strip reprints. The 1930s Hal Foster pages in 60, 62 and 63 are printed as single pages, but the 1960s Russ Manning illustrated strips are bizarrely cut and pasted to resemble a comic strip.~HY

TARZAN versus PREDATOR at the Earth's Core
Dark Horse: *4-issue miniseries 1996*

Competent but formulaic Tarzan scenario as Jane hangs about getting kidnapped, this time in fabulous Pellucidar, lost world at the Earth's core plucked from the Jurassic Era. Tarzan plus allies confront the humanoid, alien Predators who hunt for sport. Useful Tip For Alien Invaders: don't park your spaceship in the path of a stampeding herd of Triceratops.~APS

TEAM AMERICA
Marvel: *12 issues 1982–1983*

After their first appearance in *Captain America* 269, five mavericks grudgingly gang up to use motorbikes licensed from Ideal Toy Corporation for stunt exhibitions and competition racing. Jim Shooter's yarns (1–2, 8–9, 11–12), which concentrate on racing and character interaction, outstrip Bill Mantlo's weary stories of espionage and environmental disasters. The mysterious, unidentified Marauder and a weak psionic link between the five major stars maintain some intrigue. Latter issues are surprisingly better than the lame premise promises. 9 is noteworthy for a fight-free guest appearance by Iron Man. The admirable issue 12 kicks off with a wonderful cover caption: 'Because You Demanded It... The End Of Team America!', resolves all plot-lines and contains a forthright text page about the cancellation by Shooter, who points out that the title was more successful than *Daredevil* during Frank Miller's first year. How different it all could have been.~APS

TEAM 7
Image: *4-issue miniseries 1994, 3-issue miniseries 1995, 4-issue miniseries 1996*

When Image's WildStorm branch gave its comic universe a retroactive continuity dating back over several decades, the untold story most readers wanted to see was that of Team 7, the supersoldier unit of which many modern-day WildStorm heroes – including Backlash, Deathblow, WildCATs' Grifter, Wetworks' Dane and Gen13's Lynch – had been members. Almost everyone in Team 7 who didn't now have their own book was the father of at least one other major WildStorm character. After various hints and teasers, the real story was eventually told over three miniseries written by Chuck Dixon, and did not disappoint.

The Team 7 story tells of a unit of Navy SEALs set by the US government to be unwitting guinea-pigs for an experiment which gives them immense psychic powers and makes them the ultimate weapon. But the powers are more than many of them can – or should even be asked to – handle, and the stresses of dealing with what they've become, added to the more and more insidious manipulation and betrayal by a government they had previously trusted, drive the team apart. By the end of the first series many have defected. The following two series carry on the air of doom and inevitability as the Team gradually realise they can't escape the clutches of a government which has used and abused them, and eventually they resign themselves to hoping that if they can't save themselves then at least they can try to save their children. The hindsight of reading a story to which we already know the ending adds a tragedy to the unfolding action, which is both poignant and incredibly fast-paced. As stand-alone stories the series is good, as background to the WildStorm universe it is excellent – and essential for understanding the motivations of the characters in their present-day incarnations.~JC
Recommended: Miniseries one 1–4
Collection: Team 7 (Miniseries one)

TEAM TITANS
DC: *28 issues (5 x 1–24), 2 annuals 1992–1994*

Once fresh and exciting, by 1992 stale and ordinary, DC's idea to revive interest in the *New Teen Titans* was to have Marv Wolfman repeat what he used to do best and introduce another Titans title. It worked for the *X-Men*, right? Although there are only issues numbered 1 to 24, a cynical marketing ploy accounts for the release of five different first issues, each relating the origin of one member of the new team. Young and brash, just like the Titans, this gang come from ten years in the future and consist of a vampire called Nightrider and a brand-new version of popular former Titans traitor Terra, along with several other miscreants. Donna Troy eventually switched from the parent title to watch over them. The first major villains are Judge and Jury in 4–5, who look cool in their red leather bondage gear and skull masks, but are in fact crap. Wolfman's scripts are poor, and the art is downright amateurish. Fortunately, Wolfman left within the first year, but, unfortunately, his successor, Jeffrey Jensen, chose to continue with the forced humour, weak plots and predictable fight sequences. Representative of his issues is 16, a contrived punch-up in a shopping mall featuring all of DC's time-travelling villains in the sort of piece that might work if written by Grant Morrison, but falls flat here. Most of the remaining issues crossed over with *Teen Titans* or *Zero Hour*, and you don't really want to know about that, do you? When *Team Titans* was cancelled, it was a mercy killing.~TP

TEAMX/TEAM 7
Marvel: *One-shot 1996*

This cross-company pairing has the two teams independently sent into action by rival US secret services against a Middle-Eastern supersoldier factory. As things start to go wrong, they find themselves joining forces against Omega Red and a group of half-finished supersoldiers who've acquired a nuclear missile. There's no inventiveness in Larry Hama's script, which incorporates continuity mistakes, and the art by Steve Epting and Klaus Janson is very dull. Only if you must.~NF

TEAM YANKEE
First: *6-issue limited series 1989*

War is certainly hell in this fictitious Soviet invasion of the USA, but it's also bloody boring in the pages of *Team Yankee*. Whether that's down to the original novel or a poor adaptation is debatable. There's so much concern that the military terminology and soldier's shorthand conversation is correctly transcribed that large quantities of dialogue become so much babble to the average reader. One doesn't want to be referring constantly to the explanatory pages in the rear of the issue (1 and 4 only) to have an idea of what's going on. By concentrating on the activities of one battalion, war is presented in microcosm, but what might be an exciting against-the-odds war movie is dull and lifeless here.~WJ

TEAM YOUNGBLOOD
Image: *22 issues, 1993–1996*

Mega-proportioned babes falling out their costumes, ludicrously muscled guys, big, big, big guns and pin-up pages mid-story. Early issues, though, have an odd occurrence for Rob Liefeld titles: a modicum of plot, making *Team Youngblood* a veritable Sistine Chapel ceiling among Rob's product, but compared to most other superhero comics it reads like an enthusiastic fanzine. For later issues someone's realised a plot gets in the way of the fighting and pin-ups, and corrected the deficiency.~FP

TEEN TITANS
DC: *Series one 53 issues 1966–1973 (1–43), 1976–1978 (44–53), series two 91 issues, 4 Annuals 1980–1988, series three 131 issues (0–130), 7 Annuals (5–11) 1984–1996, series three 6 issues + 1996 to date*

Sparked by a team-up of three kid sidekicks – Robin the Boy Wonder, Kid Flash and Aqualad – in *The Brave And The Bold* 54, DC threw in a distaff member – Wonder Girl, whose existence as a separate entity from her adult self had not previously been suspected – and dubbed the quartet the Teen Titans. Two further try-outs (*The Brave And The Bold* 60, *Showcase* 59) established sufficient demand for the team to be awarded their own comic. In the annals of truly silly comics, there's little to beat your average issue of *Teen Titans* from the 1960s. Their early pledge to help 'Teens in trouble', their truly inane Rogue's Gallery – The Mad Mod? Captain Rumble? Ding-Dong Daddy Dowd? Aieee! – and the excruciating dialogue, product of how middle-aged to elderly men thought 'hip' teens actually spoke, made these issues a strange, almost hallucinogenic experience. For the best example of this, check out the numbing 'A Christmas Happening' (13), with a magnetic Christmas tree (and the Titans as ornaments!), a ray that turns junk back into new consumer goods, and Wonder Girl in a Santa Claus mini-skirt, in a tortuous mod retelling of *A Christmas Carol*. The series' regular artist, Nick Cardy, once he'd hit his stride in the first few issues, did beautiful, lush artwork that glowed from the page. The combination of this vital, almost tactile art and the outstandingly sappy stories resulted in some seriously trippy comics. From 16, the creators tried a more serious adventure angle, relying on interdimensional invaders to kick-start some long-term plot threads. This led to, among other things, the revelation of Wonder Girl's origin (and a spiffy new costume!), and the addition to the cast of Hawk and The Dove, a philosophically opposed pair of sibling superheroes from a cancelled title. With 25, another new direction, the Titans are inadvertently involved in the death of a great humanitarian figure, and swear off the use of their powers until they have made amends. Approached by the intermittently psychic go-go dancer Lilith, they team with the mysterious Mr Jupiter and undergo training as his agents, after Robin, too hot a property to nullify, has left the team. Mal Duncan, the first black Titan, joined in 26, a sadly stereotypical ghetto kid with a dream. The non-costumed aspect got old real fast, and by 30, except for Mal and Lilith, the group were mostly back in uniform, but occasionally ventured out in plain clothes to investigate matters, still under the auspices of Mr Jupiter. By now, desperation was setting in and the writers were stealing ideas from anywhere they could:

The Stepford Wives, Romeo And Juliet, even *Uncle Tom's Cabin,* all overlaid with an attempt at Gothic horror in which the brightly costumed Titans looked embarrassed and out of place. When the series saw its finale, in a truly cringe-making *Rosemary's Baby* swipe, it was a merciful end. Fleetingly revived in 1976, the new version was straightforward superheroics, but of a rather inferior sort, and lasted only long enough to introduce a whole bunch of second-string heroes. Along into the Titans canon came the original Bat-Girl, the Bumblebee, the Joker's Daughter (later the Harlequin) and junior Hawkman the Golden Eagle.

The 1980 *New Teen Titans,* when announced, was dismissed as unlikely to succeed, but surprised the critics by being a monster hit from day one. Wonder Girl, Kid Flash and Robin of the old team, plus part-time member Beast Boy, now named the Changeling, were teamed with brand-new characters Raven (half-demon empath), Starfire (energy-shooting alien princess) and Cyborg (what do you think?). Cosmic drama and high *angst* were the theme, writer Marv Wolfman and artist George Perez clearly taking their inspiration from Claremont and Byrne's *X-Men,* then still fondly remembered. The New Teen Titans fought the JLA, defeated Raven's demon daddy Trigon, battled Starfire's evil sister Blackfire, tracked down the killers of the Doom Patrol, and faced off against the Titans of Myth, stopping off at Paradise Island on the way. The pace was brisk, the characterisation deft, and the title a good solid read. Where it truly excelled, however, was in the stories that dealt as much with emotions as with action. The two part 'Runaways' (26–27), the haunting 'Who Is Donna Troy?' in 38, and the stunning 'Judas Contract' of 42–44, climaxing in the series' third annual, were moving and skilful stories emphasising the emotional frailty of the humans behind the masks. Unfortunately, 'The Judas Contract' was virtually the swan song for quality in this incarnation of the Titans.

The success of the *New Teen Titans* was such that DC issued a more expensive companion title, relaunching from issue 1, and Perez left the original comic to work on it. DC had pre-empted this by rechristening the original series *Tales Of The Teen Titans* from 40, and, with the launch of the new comic, this foundered in a year's worth of inferior material before becoming a reprint of the deluxe edition. The new series started off promisingly, with another match with Trigon, but that story never reached the heights of the previous series, and Perez left the Titans at its conclusion in 5, swiftly forcing upon the readers the realisation that he'd had more to do with the book's plotting than had been let on. Without Perez, Wolfman took the Titans through a series of drab fight scenes,

pointless exposition, clichéd character traits, and relentless attempts to introduce new characters while frequently ignoring the supposed stars of the book. DC's management was eventually bludgeoned into publishing *Deathstroke The Terminator,* a spin-off starring an unremarkable Titans villain, in an attempt to climb the then popular *Punisher* bandwagon, but that didn't stop Wolfman shoehorning him into the Titans at every opportunity, to the series' constant detriment. Perez was persuaded to return with 50, as the title changed again to *New Titans,* but his heart was no longer in it. The 'Who Is Wonder Girl?' tale, an attempted sequel to 38 of the first series, was a botched effort which raised more questions than it resolved about the Titan whose complete history had been unravelled by Crisis on Infinite Earths. Staying only long enough to bestow one of the ugliest new costumes ever on the hapless Ms Troy (54), Perez fled again. Other distinguished illustrators worked on the title – José Luis Garcia-Lopez, Tom Grummett, Eduardo Barreto – but all seemed ill at ease. By now, the Titans were looking desperate; relaunch followed 'New Beginning' and then followed 'Old Order Changeth', each new line-up of Titans barely getting time to become known to the readers before being reshuffled again. By 100, an aborted wedding between Nightwing and Starfire, the book had lost the compensation even of good artwork; the last thirty or so issues were drawn in a sub-professional manner that was simply an embarrassment to what had once been DC's finest title. Eventually, DC realised the harm this was doing to their reputation, and cancelled it; about eighty issues too late, but still.

Not wanting to lose the name, they promptly relaunched from number 1 again, with an entirely new group of Titans – Argent, Risk, Prysm, Joto and the Atom, a mainstay hero rejuvenated in *Zero Hour.* Perez is back, albeit only as an inker, and the writing and art are in the hands of Dan Jurgens. It's too early yet to tell whether the new Teen Titans will equal the heights of their predecessors, but so far, although not very good, the new series is at least a great deal better than anything else we've been offered under the *Titans* banner for a decade or so.~HS

Recommended: Series two 26, 27, 38, 42–44, Annual 3

Collection: The Judas Contract (series two 39–44, Annual 3)

Tales Of The New TEEN TITANS
DC: *4-issue miniseries 1982,*

This miniseries spotlights the new characters introduced to the then extremely successful *Teen Titans,* one per issue. Respectively it concentrates on Cyborg, Raven, Changeling and Starfire, all written by Marv Wolfman and lavishly illustrated by George Perez, the creative team who introduced the characters. Each of the characters has a tale to tell and a few secrets to reveal, and they're all well crafted and worthwhile supplements to the regular series.~HY

Recommended: 1–4

TEEN TITANS SPOTLIGHT
DC: *21 issues 1986–1988*

This spin-off title was released at the height of the Teen Titans' popularity, giving readers a chance to see their favourite characters in solo adventures. The series is, on the whole, mediocre, with only a handful of memorable issues. 7 has an *Asterix* parody with Jackson Guice drawing a reasonable Hawk story; 11 saw the same treatment for *Tintin*. Erik Larsen draws an Aqualad solo in 10 and the Omega Men in 15, and 14 stars Nightwing and shows a Batman removed from real emotion with a lack of understanding for his former partner. The best issue is 21, which has a nostalgia-drenched story of the original Teen Titans steeped in a 1960s psychedelic vibe.~SS

Eastman And Laird's TEENAGE MUTANT NINJA TURTLES
Mirage: *62 issues 1984–1993*
Image: *5 issues + 1996 to date*

This is the title that began an industry, in the process making its two creators, who'd self-published the first issues of their comic, multi-millionaires. It's a heartening tale, not least because the comics industry has a shabby history of ensuring that creators whose properties have earned their publishers fortunes rarely share in the proceeds. Kevin Eastman and Peter Laird's concept is decidedly off the wall, although owing a little to the ninja stories Frank Miller had been running in *Daredevil*. Raphael, Leonardo, Donatello and the incorrectly spelled Michaelangelo are our heroes, living in the sewers and trained as ninjas by the humanoid rat Splinter (all explained in the first issue). In addition to the ongoing series each stars in an Eastman and Laird-created solo issue, the best of which is Michaelangelo's Christmas story.

There's a grubbiness, grittiness and violence in the early issues which is certainly not apparent in later, sanitised versions. These turtles look as if they live in the sewers, and when their human companion April visits she does also. For all that, though, it's the idea and characters that carry the stories, as neither Eastman or Laird are great plotters and the best stories are after their departure. Most early issues contain extended choreographed fight sequences spliced with the odd quip or mission recap, and the joke soon wears very thin. A guest shot from Cerebus, along with his creator Dave Sim, in 8 is the best of them.

From 9 creators other than Eastman and Laird begin contributing to the comic with increasing frequency, Michael Dooney being the first. Eric Talbot and Mark Bodé also come aboard as semi-regular contributors, but it's Mark Martin's début in 16 that's the stand-out. His inventive story-telling, visual asides and ideas beyond fights make for an early treat. He returns in 22 and 23, the second part of which is all but a Gnat Rat tale, but this time his whimsy may prove off-putting, and the participation of the Turtles is minimal. Rick Veitch presents a three-parter in 24–26, but far better is his Ed Roth-influenced 30. Michael Zulli's art in 35–36 is nice and Rich Hedden and Tom McWeeney are also notable contributors in 34. With 38–40 their madcap script and art provides another highlight. By this time the comic has progressed far away from the ninja roots, and is open to all kinds of different interpretations. Those who enjoyed the earlier issues probably won't care much for Hedden and McWeeney, with a Raphael solo story featuring spectacularly inept, yet nonetheless deadly small aliens. Perhaps the most unlikely contributor of the entire run is Richard Corben in 33, a colour issue. It works surprisingly well, with Jan Strnad's story of alternate turtles in time stretching Corben beyond his usual vistas.

With 46 it's goodbye to the guest creators (with the exception of those contributing pin-ups to the strange, almost wordless 50), and welcome back Eastman and Laird, with artist Jim Lawson. From 50 the cover is redesigned with the word 'Turtles' eclipsing all else. The remaining issues of their run are almost all one continuing story, 'City At War', with preludes to 50 and the deal itself to 62. It's a back-to-basics approach and works far better than the earlier issues because by this point the turtles have individual characters, and there's more than just fights. If you prefer the ninja emphasis these issues are as good as it gets. Lawson's art has a nice European feel, and those who wish can see 62 as an ideal finishing point.

The second Mirage series is easily distinguished from the first by the lack of Eastman and Laird's names on the cover. Lawson writes and illustrates, and the warm colouring of Mary Woodring, then Eric Vincent, gives the comic a distinct look, although Eric Talbot inking Lawson isn't welcome. The first issue is very fragmented, foreshadowing what's to come: greater issue-to-issue continuity for one thing, and a feeling of the ninja issues without a return to them. Anyone who enjoyed the Eastman and Laird run ought to find something worthwhile

here also. Which probably won't be the case in the Image issues. Altogether more violent and unpleasant, they lack the contrasting wit previously characteristic of the title.~WJ
Recommended: 16, 38–40
Collections: Book one (1–3), Book two (4–6), Book three (7–9), Book four (10, 11, *Leonardo*), The Collected Book vol 1 (1–11, *Donatello, Leonardo, Michaelangelo, Raphael*), vol 2 (12–14), vol 3 (15, 17, 18), vol 4 (19–21), vol 5 (16, 22, 23), vol 6 (24–26)

TEENAGE MUTANT NINJA TURTLES ADVENTURES
Archie: *3-issue miniseries 1988, 74 issues, 1 Special 1988–1995*
The phenomenon that was the Teenage Mutant Ninja Turtles took off globally in the late 1980s to spawn three movies, a cartoon series, a multitude of comics imitators, and about three million toys. Simple art and basic plots conceal very funny writing at times, and although it's predictable it's worth switching off your brain and enjoying a few of these issues. The miniseries coincided with the TV show and retold the origin of four turtles exposed to highly toxic gook who grew to become intelligent biped pizza-munching ninjas. Locked in eternal battle with arch-villains Krang, Shredder, Bebop and Rocksteady, the turtles establish themselves in the New York sewers and learn the mystic arts from a rat named Splinter. The highlight of the regular series is 20, which shines out as a homage to the old Marvel monster Fing Fang Foom, with art from Bill Wray and Hilary Barta. Also worth a look is the special drawn by Steve Bissette and Don Simpson in which the Turtles meet Archie, the most bizarre team-up in comics until the Punisher visited Riverdale. It's as ridiculous as it all sounds, but Donatello, Raphael, Michaelangelo and Leonardo's personalities are extremely likeable and their banter should amuse all but the most jaded cynic. Cowabunga!~TP
Recommended: 20
Collections: *Teenage Mutant Ninja Turtles* Vol 1 (1–4), vol 2 (5–8), vol 3 (9–12), vol 4 (13–16)

TEENAGENTS
Topps: *4-issue miniseries 1993*
Based on characters and concepts created by Jack Kirby, this is a lousy tribute to The King's creative genius. Writer Kurt Busiek and artist Neil Vokes tell a stunningly average yarn about a group of young heroes – Seera, Kreech, Dijit and Aurik – who travel to earth from an underground city with the aid of their 'Omni-Bus', a cosmic coach that is one of the book's few authentically Kirbyesque touches.~AL

Neil Gaiman's TEKNOPHAGE
Tekno: *10 issues 1995–1996*
Rob Nichols, a real-estate salesman, is transported to Kalighoul, the home of Mr Henry Phage. By good luck he manages to work his way up through the ranks of the workers to threaten Phage, a reptilian monster who rules through fear, as seen in issues of *Mr Hero*. His subjects are so used to living in terror that when, as often happens, he decides to eat them, they don't put up much of a struggle. 1–6 tell the story of Rob Nichols and his attempt to strike a deal with or kill the Teknophage in order to attain power/wealth and/or rescue a missing earthwoman. Written by Rick Veitch, it's blackly humorous but not really that interesting. Brian Talbot's artwork, as ever excellent, and Angus McKie's colouring are points of interest but ultimately it's the characters and story that disappoint. The Paul Jenkins and Al Davison issues (7–10) present a more hopeful view of life on Kalighoul, but there's less humour involved, making the whole thing seem rather pretentious.~NF

William Shatner's TEKWORLD
Epic: *24 issues 1992– 1994*
Based on the books 'written' by William 'Captain Kirk' Shatner. This sad attempt at a science-fiction P.I. story tells of one Jake Cardigan, a dick (in every sense of the word) addicted to Tek, the world's most addictive drug. Virtual reality (yawn), boring stories, dull art, 'nuff said.~TP

TEMPEST
DC: *4-issue miniseries 1996–1997*
The editorial in the final issue best describes this series: '...a tale of love and hate, passion and vengeance, familial ties and the ties that bind. Garth, the kid everyone called Aqualad, is now the man called Tempest.' Yep, Aquaman's sidekick finally comes of age. Ignored for decades, Aqualad is given new powers with a snazzy new costume. Now able to control heat and cold, he takes on the new codename.
Tempest was a very pleasant surprise, written and beautifully pencilled by Phil Jimenez (who is heavily influenced by George Perez), with impressive colouring by Carla Feeny. The main plot deals with Tempest's inheritance, his dysfunctional family and the historical myths concerning the ancient cities and legend of Atlantis. The story evolves around Garth's emotions and the manner in which he deals with the return of his apparently dead lover, Tula, the Aquagirl. Longtime *Aquaman* readers may welcome the return of the beautiful Tula, but probably won't appreciate the emotional ending of the series. Many comic fans find it hard to accept the death of favourite characters, and always

expect them to return (as so often happens), but Jimenez handles Tempest's sense of loss quite excellently (drawing on his own personal experience) in concluding that life must go on, and the past doesn't return.~HY
Recommended: 1–4

TEMPUS FUGITIVE

DC: *4-issue miniseries 1990–1991*

Written and painted by Ken Steacy, this was very much a labour of love from a former US Air Force brat growing up with a fascination for all aircraft. Unfortunately, the story, about a pilot who escapes from the future to the past, is just an excuse for Steacy to draw lots of planes, and the plot is as transparent as clingfilm. Pretty artwork for a pretty penny.~TP
Collection: Tempus Fugitive (1–4)

TERMINAL CITY

Vertigo: **9-issue** *limited series 1996–1997*

This is rather slowly paced but that's no bad thing when there's a lot of territory to cover. In a massive city, four famous men, an adventurer, a boxer, a daredevil and an actor, are all publicly disgraced before their scheduled appearances at a major City Fair. One of them is Cosmo Quinn, human fly, now a window-cleaner crawling up the sides of very tall buildings. As the story progresses we find out what the others have been doing as they return to the city to seek revenge for their humiliations. It's fun and intriguing, though there are so many significant characters to keep up with that there's not much time given to characterisation. However, Michael Lark's artwork is suitably modernist to go with Deam Motter's retro city. Worth a look.~NF

TERMINAL POINT

Dark Horse: *3-issue miniseries 1993*

There's a conspiracy by an organisation called Terminus to assume control of time, and to this end an operative called Pilot has been sent to construct a beacon for their use. He turns renegade, though, and hides out in 1946, where he falls in love with a nightclub singer. Terminus, of course, come after him. It's all simple action stuff from Bruce Zick, still very much in Kirby-style story mode, but fails to involve.~FP

THE TERMINATOR

Now: *17 issues 1988–1990, 5-issue miniseries ('The Burning Earth') 1990, 2-issue microseries 1990*

If ever there was a film suited to comics where unlimited special effects cost nothing, it's *The Terminator*. Sadly, Now appoint shoddy amateur artists who consistently scupper decent scripts. The comic stays in 2031, a world controlled by machines, one in which the robotic Terminators are programmed to wipe out humanity. Initially there are separate story arcs to look in on assorted human communities and loners, the best of which is 7's story of a modified wolf. From 8 the community introduced in 1–3 is the central focus; John Connor, the hero mentioned in the *Terminator* film, returns in 12. Writer Ron Fortier must have wondered who he angered in a previous life, given the appalling artists who illustrate his always effective scripts. It seems, though, that he was storing credits for 'The Burning Earth' miniseries, illustrated by Alex Ross: a quantum leap in quality. Ross paints a dark and gloomy world to match the circumstances, and the story has a final assault on Skynet. This is the series to sample. Now's final fling before their licence was revoked was a two-part story, just titled *Terminator*, recounting events preceding the first film.~FP
Collection: Tempest (1–4)

TERMINATOR

Dark Horse: *4-issue miniseries 1990, One-shot ('One Shot') 1991, 4-issue miniseries ('Secondary Objectives') 1991, 4-issue miniseries ('The Enemy Within') 1992, 3-issue miniseries ('Hunters And Killers') 1992*

Essentially the four miniseries and the one-shot comprise one long story-line broken up into convenient bite-size parts. The first follows the original film's main premise. For those who haven't seen it, the plot is that an invulnerable android is sent back to the 1980s to kill one Sarah Connor, mother-to-be of the man who will lead the resistance against the Terminators in the future. Unfortunately for women named Sarah Connor, they're not too sure which one she is, but there is a solution… The writer of the first miniseries is John Arcudi, with art by Chris Warner and Paul Guinan, and they don't bring anything new to the genre. Their new twist is that a team of crack commandos led by Colonel Mary are sent back to kill the inventor of the said androids. Pretty ho-hum stuff, all things considered. Gunfights, car chases etc. The one-shot, amusingly titled 'One-Shot', involves another Terminator sent out to kill another Sarah Connor. Unknown to her, her husband is planning exactly the same so that he can claim her life insurance. James Robinson writes big explosions and more car chases in San Francisco, but Matt Wagner's wonderful painted art, using a gorgeously subtle palette, raises this above the norm. It also has a neat gimmick in the centre of the comic: a Terminator pops out at you on a motorbike.

'Secondary Objectives' has the survivors, Mary, Dr Hollister and a half-human, half-android Terminator aka Dudley, searching for Sarah Connor in Mexico when they are attacked by yet another Terminator. How many of these things are there anyway? James Robinson's

scripts are laughable at times, with over-long introspective monologues that Captain America would have been proud of. Paul Gulacy and Karl Kesel's art is pretty but desperately static in what is supposed to be an action comic. By 'The Enemy Within' the story's running thin and Ian Edginton is writing by numbers. More Terminators and commandos arrive from the future, leaving you to wonder if anyone is left back there, with even more explosions, shootings and general mayhem. Oh, and some vague plot about killing the inventor of the androids (again). With 'Endgame', Robinson returns with the final instalment of the saga. His writing has improved greatly, although Jackson Guice and John Beatty's art falls into the same traps that snagged Gulacy. Mary and her new partner, Detective Sloane, finally track down Sarah Connor just as she is about to give birth to mankind's saviour. The final episode has a nice angle that compensates for the wham-bam of earlier issues.~TP
Collections: Endgame (1–3), The Enemy Within (1–4), Secondary Objectives (1–4), The Terminator Collection (first miniseries 1–4), Tempest)

TERMINATOR 2
Marvel: *One-shot 1991*
Malibu: *6-issue miniseries ('Present War: Cybernetic Dawn') 1996, 6-issue miniseries ('Future War: Nuclear Twilight') 1996*
Marvel's adaptation of the *Terminator 2* movie is a pedestrian affair with hurried art from Klaus Janson, but has the bonus of being prepared from a shooting script, so it includes some scenes cut from the movie. In 'Future War: Nuclear Twilight' we see an adult John Connor, Sarah's son, leading the resistance movement against the Terminators and Skynet in the future. Mark Paniccia's script is slightly too wordy, but does tie up all loose ends about Kyle Reese, Sarah's protector in the 1984 movie, and the T-800 model from *Terminator 2*, and has some gorgeous artwork from Gary Erskine. 'Present War: Cybernetic Dawn' is a disappointment in comparison, with unimpressive art from Rod Whigham and Jack Snyder. It continues from the *Terminator 2* movie, and writer Dan Abnett throws up a similar story-line as an excuse for big fight sequences.~TP
Recommended: *Nuclear Twilight 1–6*
Collection: *Cybernetic Dawn (1–6)*

TERRARISTS
Epic: *4-issue miniseries 1993–1994*
As corporations continue to plunder the planet the Earth creates her own superpowered champions with a brief to save the planet. Subtlety isn't a consideration, but the story is solid enough and the painted art of John Erasmus shows promise until deadline pressures obviously cut in.~FP

TERROR Inc
Marvel: *13 issues, 1992–1993*
A very dark sense of humour is at work in the creation of a stylish and articulate inhuman mercenary able to dismember humans and demons alike. Having done so, Terror can replace his own bodily parts with them, absorbing all memories, sensations and abilities. Realising that his Schreck character from the Epic series *Doctor Zero* was too good to waste in a supporting role, Dan Chichester reincarnated him here. The execution, so to speak, doesn't match the concept, but if you want a look try the typically gruesome Christmas tale in 8.~FP

TEX BENSON
Metro: *4 issues 1987*
3-D Zone: *4 issues 1990–1991*
Tex Benson is an impossibly desirable space-jock in a light-hearted guns'n'girls strip. Creator Chuck Roblin's art is heavily influenced by the 1940s great Lou Fine, but his story-telling is very muddled and difficult to follow.~WJ

TEX DAWSON Gunslinger
Marvel: *3 issues 1973*
1950s reprints featuring Tex of the title who 'rode the Western range with his fighting pals Whirlwind and Lightning'. Whirlwind and Lightning were respectively a horse and a wolf, but this doesn't stop Tex chattering away to them both. These days he'd be in a Care In The Community programme; in the 1950s he had his own comic with predictable plots and dull art. Were kids really that naïve once?~FP

THANOS QUEST
Marvel: *2-issue microseries 1990*
Thanos quests for the six infinity gems in his never-ending bid for Mistress Death's approval. This inferior Jim Starlin plot regurgitates past classics, strips Thanos of his awe and majesty and portrays Marvel's cosmic entities as five-year-olds.~APS

THB
Horse Press: *5 issues + 1994 to date*
Paul Pope seemed to spring out of nowhere. In the time it took him to self-publish three thick black and white volumes of his futuristic teen adventure story *THB* he'd gone from small press unknown to one of the most fêted new comic artists. Although you can see his art developing over the first couple of issues (a delightful process in itself), he is obviously a talented artist from the start, drawing in several styles, using watercolour and washes for particularly atmospheric scenes, but returning frequently to an elongated brush style reminiscent of the Italian adventure tradition. His page design and pacing owe

something to Moebius and Jean Claude Forest, but he's also taken tricks and effects from the likes of Alex Toth: an excellent selection of influences that never overwhelm his natural drawing abilities.

THB is packed with the escapades of H.R. Watson, the precocious young daughter of an important scientist who, on the cusp of adulthood, is one minute the intrepid adventurer and the next an impulsive schoolgirl. To protect her from people who might want to attack her father through her she is given THB, a giant genie-like bioconstruct concealed in a tiny pill. Just add water and you have an instant body guard. Sometimes, however, water is hard to find, especially as the series is set on Mars. Pope, with all the enthusiasm of an science-fiction fan, has mapped out the minutest details of his extraordinary yet often anachronistic future, which helps create a thoroughly engrossing, if often mystifying, read.~FJ
Recommended: 1–5

THEY WERE 11
Viz Comics: 4-issue miniseries 1995

A science-fiction romance with the premise that teams of trainees from all over the galaxy have to face a final test before being allowed to enter the Galactic University. It's important to all of them to a greater or lesser extent. Though each team is supposed to have ten members, the story is about one that has eleven. That there is an extra member is kept secret from the rest of the teams but also remains mysterious to them. With a delicate but deft touch, Moto Hagio, who both writes and draws the story, has produced a fun but thoughtful tale.~NF
Collection: Four Shojo Stories (1–4)

THIEVES AND KINGS
I Box: *13 issues + 1994 to date*

A peculiar title, much prized by those who read it, yet little known generally. Unable to pack in enough material per issue to tell his broad fantasy story, creator Mark Oakley (M'Oak) opts to separate his comic pages with pages of text continuing the story. Certainly a valid story-telling device, it comes a cropper here because M'Oak is no more than a functional writer, although an ever-improving artist. The plot centres on Rubel, teenage thief under royal protection, having located a crown (which has been hidden to determine who would succeed to the throne) and having passed it on to the princess. Accompanied by an imp, Rubel manages to make enemies with ease, and in 5 learns that his royal patronage might not be the boon he assumed. In later issues the focus begins to shift a little from Rubel. *Thieves And Kings* is a frustrating title, with plenty of seemingly superfluous detours. If there really is

an extended story to tell why have most issues to date contained so many ultimately meaningless chases and battles? Reading as it does like a children's fairy-tale with the occasional adult intrusion, there's never any real sense of danger about the title, but those who enjoy fantasy material might be as charmed as the regular readership.~WJ
Collection: *Thieves And Kings* (1–6)

THE THING
Marvel: *36 issues 1983–86, Miniseries 4 issues 1992*

During his critically acclaimed run on the *Fantastic Four*, writer/artist John Byrne took The Thing – one of the team's founder-members – away from the group and gave him a solo title. The Byrne issues are excellent, using the extra space to explore the character intelligently. Later issues, written by Mike Carlin, aren't as good but are still worth picking up. Byrne returned for the final two issues, a story completed in *West Coast Avengers* 10. The second series reprinted selected Thing team-up adventures from *Marvel Two-In-One*.~JC
Recommended: Series one 3

THE THING FROM ANOTHER WORLD
Dark Horse: *2-issue microseries 1992, 4-issue miniseries ('Climate of Fear') 1992, 4-issue miniseries ('Eternal Vows') 1993–1994*

Continuing where John Carpenter's film ended, the first series has a team of Navy Seals massacred, giving the alien an opportunity to escape into the outside world, leaving hero MacReady adrift. Chuck Pfarrar's script seems rushed and rather cramped, while John Higgins' artwork is patchy. MacReady is rescued from the ice and some Argentinians encounter the alien in 'Climate Of Fear', by John Arcudi and Jim Somerville, but it's David deVries' 'Eternal Vows' that really moves the idea on, introducing two Things and keeping the suspense at high pitch throughout. In this he's greatly helped by the artwork of Paul Gulacy, who's not at his best but still sharp.~NF

THIRD WORLD WAR
Quality: *6 issues 1990–1991*

Reprints from the groundbreaking British comic *Crisis*. A crack team of conscripts are sent by a corporate-run fascist Britain to 'protect its concerns' in South America. This gives Pat Mills a chance to air his grievances about Third World poverty, destruction of the environment and global politics under the transparent guise of plot. At the time it was hard-hitting stuff, but in hindsight it now seems simplistic, naïve and a little contrived. An interesting antidote to the Thatcher years, with some nice artwork by Carlos Ezquerra.~TP

THRILL-O-RAMA
Harvey: *3 issues 1965–1966*

All three issues feature Bob Powell's 'Man In Black Called Fate' – a whimsical story-teller reprinted from the 1950s comic named after him. 2 and 3 cover-feature Pirana, an Aquaman clone, and his pets Bara and Cuda. The 1950s reprints win hands down.~SW

The Mighty THOR
Marvel: *377 issues (126–502), 19 annuals, 1 Giant-size 1966–1996*

Stan Lee and Jack Kirby's corny blending of *Norse Myths* 101 and pseudo-Shakespearian dialogue has enjoyed an astounding longevity considering its frequent and prolonged periods of mediocrity. Issues from 126 have at least dispensed with the over-reliance on the duplicity of Thor's half-brother Loki, the God of Mischief, that characterised Thor's *Journey Into Mystery* appearances; instead, they trot out another set of clichés: battles in the underworld, allegedly unknown menaces from beyond, constant arguments with his father Odin, with consequent reduction in his powers, and quests for all and sundry. While there's surprisingly little integration with the remainder of the Marvel Universe, the repeated plots lead one to believe that were it not for the increasing grandeur of Kirby's artwork *Thor* would surely have been cancelled thirty years ago. 136's transition in girl-friends is silly and misogynistic; featuring a lumpy creature for Thor to beat up is representative of the period. The often charming 'Tales Of Asgard' back-up ran between 126 and 145, to be replaced by a strip detailing the origins of The Inhumans until 152.

Lee finally runs out of variations on the standard plot around 160, and following issues see marginally more interesting encounters with Galactus (whose origin is in 168–169) and the introduction of the character who would later become Adam Warlock in 165 and 166. Kirby is replaced by John Buscema with 180, but there's little to highlight until Lee turns the comic over to Gerry Conway with 193. Often underrated as a writer, Conway's certainly been responsible for a considerable amount of hack work, but while he can be erratic, his new creative approach turned *Thor* around. Plots to come were foreshadowed and science-fiction elements added, providing more interesting stories over three years than the title had seen since its introduction. Sending Thor into space meant the old plots couldn't be used, and if the new ideas weren't all brilliant they were an improvement on the repetition. For an example of the Conway/Buscema style try 218–220, which use old science-fiction concepts well. Conway's peak, though, oddly enough, involved Loki, this time invading

Earth with the immortal forces of Asgard in 232–234. Len Wein turns in a passable story featuring an old enemy, the Tomorrow Man, in 242–245, but thereafter it's back to business as usual with all the familiar plots returning.

With 272 Roy Thomas began writing *Thor*, and, to his credit, attempted something different: reconciling Marvel's cut-and-paste version of Thor and his cast with the Norse myths, and conceiving an origin for Asgard, home of the Gods. Encompassing the Eternals and Wagner's *Siegfried* opera, the ambition is admirable, but it drags on far too long at thirty issues, and was continued by the team of Mark Gruenwald and Ralph Macchio. The best individual issues of the period were, strangely enough, the fill-ins in 280–282, and those following the conclusion of the story, 303–305. Doug Moench's story of a Catholic priest questioning his faith in 303 is a stand-out, but when given the title on a regular basis all inspiration deserts him, and Stan Lee's clichés are brought out for another airing.

Walt Simonson's arrival with 337 was a revelation, attaining the mix of myth and grandeur striven for by Lee and Kirby, and his run on *Thor* was never bettered. He restored the sense of awe and majestic splendour about the art which had been missing since John Buscema's departure, and his stories are romances in the classical sense, mixing myths with familiar elements and characters without ever dropping back into the familiar standby plots. A characteristic of his issues is treating the comic as a soap opera. Thor is always centre-stage, but the reader is continuously kept aware of the whereabouts of other major characters, particularly Loki, finally a considered threat and master of manipulation. Simonson's first issues hinged on the worthiness of an individual to possess the hammer of Thor; this resulted in the transformation of the daftly named alien Beta Ray Bill into Thor, and Simonson shortly thereafter dispenses with the Donald Blake *alter ego*. These are his best-recalled issues, possibly as they're collected, but they're not the best of his run. 345–348 return to the elves of legend and are a welcome antidote to the cuddly elves populating comics in the 1980s. After numerous false dawns 353 actually does change the series for the long term. The plot of having Thor besotted by bewitchment is well played as farce initially, and, despite lasting over a year and tying into another of Loki's machinations to rule Asgard, it's to Simonson's credit that it never seems tired. Simonson is even confident enough to take the preposterous idea of having Thor transformed into a frog, run with it and actually make it work for three issues in 364–366. Sal Buscema starts as artist in 368. 370's rushed fill-in and

Thor's return to Earth for a humourless *Judge Dredd* pastiche and meeting with X-Factor in the succeeding issues are the only dud issues during Simonson's tenure. He recovered in time to produce his best story as his finale in 379–382, and departed having transformed a once shoddy title into a beacon of splendour.

Almost inevitably, what follows falls short, although a desperate and courageous Thor facing off against a Celestial to save a world of cut-throats in 387–389 has its moments. Tom DeFalco doesn't return to all the familiar old plots, but does integrate Thor into Marvel's New York, reducing the title to another assembly-line superhero comic whenever Thor's on Earth. The first respite is another assault on Asgard by a seemingly invincible foe, a plot last trotted out to far better effect less than fifty issues previously, although the source of the invading Seth's power is a neat twist. From this point DeFalco seems determined to serve up Stan Lee-style plots, while Ron Frenz begins his wholesale and inferior imitation of Jack Kirby's art, an impression heightened by the inks of Joe Sinnott. *Tales Of Asgard* is revived as a back-up from 402 (interrupted by Beta Ray Bill flying solo in 411–414) and vacillates between displaying events leading to Thor's involvement in the main strip and solo stories for the supporting cast. Hercules returns to hang out in 407–425, and the only other items of note during a period of familiar scenarios are the lack-lustre introduction of the New Warriors in 412 and the merging of Thor with architect Eric Masterson to restore a human identity. Masterson is pivotal to the series, as with 433 he's the possessor of Thor's power, rather than a human host for a God. The substitution puts an end to Frenz's Kirby stylings, and a novice Thor is a plot springboard adding a necessary boost to what was becoming a moribund title. The Christmas story in 444 is representative of the later DeFalco and Frenz issues, which retain a predictability, but are perfectly acceptable superhero comics. With 459, DeFalco and Frenz complete a creative stretch beaten only by Lee and Kirby, leaving Masterson transformed into Thunderstrike, a surrogate Thor who moves into his own title.

460–471 have a mindless plot in which Thor goes mad and attacks all and sundry, crossing over with numerous other titles in order to accrue Marvel that fast buck. It's a duff period, continued by the returning Roy Thomas with 472 in the company of artist M.C. Wyman for the birth of a new race of Gods and the return of Don Blake, contrary to all previous stories and for no good reason. Warren Ellis and Mike Deodato take over with 491 for 'Worldengine'. The plot's slim, Deodato's surface style doesn't always compensate for his distorted figures and the smart-arsed British detective is irritating. In four issues, however, Ellis and Deodato manage to instil a long-absent mood, suspense and dynamism into a creatively redundant title. It's partially continued by Bill Messner-Loebs, although the inevitable battle for Asgard (and far from the best of them) occupies 500. The final issue is a low-key play-out with several in-jokes, and with 503 the title reverts once more to *Journey Into Mystery*.~WJ

Recommended: 234, 303, 305, 342–348, 353, 359, 367, 379–382

Collections: *Alone Against The Celestials* (387–389), *The Mighty Thor* (337–340), *Worldengine* (491–494)

THOR CORPS
Marvel: *4-issue miniseries 1992*

This series unites three different incarnations of the Thor character, Dargo, Beta Ray Bill and Eric Masterson. It would have been better to leave them separate. What follows is a dull traipse through time and space with little direction. Tom DeFalco adds some amazingly lifeless dialogue and the art looks static at best.~SS

THREAT
Fantagraphics: *10 issues 1985–1987*

The Holo Brothers, Enigma, Zone and occasionally Bob The Mercenary, occupy this anthology magazine. They're well designed characters, and the art is fine, but there's very little story for your money.~FP

THE 3-D ZONE
The 3-D Zone: *21 issues 1987–1989*

The brainchild of Ray Zone, this series contains artwork from many of the greatest names in comics, including Basil Wolverton (2), George Herriman (5), Joe Kubert (8), Bob Powell (10) and Harvey Kurtzman (15). Unfortunately the artwork has been doctored to be in 3-D. The original pencils and inks are in black, and red and green shadows have been added to create depth when the reader uses a pair of 3-D glasses. This process makes the pages difficult to read without the glasses, so if you can't see in 3-D (or indeed have no particular desire to experience the artwork in 3-D) then the title will have little interest for you. Zone's handling of the process is first-rate but ultimately rather pointless. Since most of these stories were never intended for 3-D, the individual benefits are minimal.~NF

THE THREE MOUSEKETEERS
DC: *7 issues 1970–1971*

Fatsy (aka The Captain), Patsy (the dumb one) and Minus (the cute, mischievous one) are members of a club with its own secret (tin can) headquarters. Together they have to deal with telephones, sticks of rock, moles and, of course, the occasional cat. Sheldon Mayer's mice are a

delight and their short tales are funny and entertaining. From 5, the page-count went up to sixty-four and more of DC's lost anthropomorphic characters reappeared: Dizzy Dog, the Dodo and the Frog, Doodles Duck and Bo Bunny. Mayer's genius is that his work is ageless. This is classic material.~NF
Recommended: 1–7

Blast Off Presents Fantastic New Worlds With THE 3 ROCKETEERS
Harvey: *One-shot 1965*
This little treasure collects five unpublished stories drawn for Harvey's anthology titles in 1956, with the first two drawn by the unforgettable team of Jack Kirby and Al Williamson. Williamson contributes two more stories in his late EC style, and the central two-pager, often incorrectly attributed to Harvey Kurtzman, looks more like the work of editor Joe Simon. The Rocketeer stories star dashing space Captain Rip McCoy, his gruff Sergeant 'Beefy' Brown and balding boffin Montrose 'Figures' Faraday, all members of Earth's military space force. There are marked similarities between this trio and Kirby's later *Challengers Of The Unknown*, and with the *Sky Masters* newspaper strip. It's all good, clean, enjoyable and extremely well drawn fun.~SW
Recommended: 1

THRILLER
DC: *12-issue limited series 1983–1984*
Thriller was the first major work by writer Robert Loren Fleming, who co-created this unusual team of superheroes with artist Trevor Von Eeden. Sadly, neither creator finished the twelve issues, and neither fulfilled the promise of such a radical yet engaging title. Angeline Thriller ('a cross between Jesus Christ and my mom', according to Fleming) is a bodiless, precognisant entity accidentally bonded to her scientist husband in an atomic explosion. He's terribly guilty about this, and most of the characters have terrific amounts of psychological baggage. Thriller picks on hopeless cases to be her physical emissaries, and the story follows a news cameraman whom she rescues after he's filmed the death of his brother at the hands of a religious maniac.

Thriller uses age-old devices like introducing a newcomer into the situation so you can have everyone introduce themselves, but manages to be at once more intense and more mythical than most superhero comics. Fleming writes about powerful human emotions and deals in mythical archetypes while retaining a subtle and humorous edge. As the series progresses, Trevor Von Eeden's artwork gets increasingly experimental (although he's obviously learnt a trick or two from Miller's early *Daredevil*). Sadly, Fleming left with 7 and Von Eeden

followed an issue later, for no very clear reasons; they were replaced by Bill Dubay and Alex Nino, who make an ugly hash of the epic conclusion.~FJ
Recommended: 1–7

THRILLING ADVENTURE STORIES
Atlas: *2 issues 1975*
Very good black and white magazine anthology that almost justifies the appalling colour comics published by Atlas. The second issue is an artistic feast, with Russ Heath, John Severin, Walt Simonson, and Alex Toth having decent stories to illustrate and all turning in superlative jobs. The first issue is patchier, but has Heath and Frank Thorne, and if you can't get enough of Tigerman he's also in here.~FP
Recommended: 2

THRILLING MURDER Comics
San Francisco Comics: *One-shot 1971*
It's thought that this was originally intended for the fourth issue of *Bogeyman*, although that comic's creator doesn't actually appear here. Like *Bogeyman*, *Thrilling Murder* was a horror comic, but one with a hard, uncomfortable edge. Its most notable story, Robert Crumb's 'Jumpin' Jack Flash', was a Mansonesque exercise in misogyny, though Jim Osbourne's semi-autobiographical 'Kid Kill' manages to surpass it in unpleasant content. With a stellar line-up also including Bill Griffith, Kim Deitch and S. Clay Wilson, *Thrilling Murder* promised much, but only Spain's 'In The Gloom Of Nite' is really up to par. Disappointing.~DAR

THRILLING PLANET TALES
Paragon: *1 issue 1991*
Eight sample stories from the 40s title, *Planet Comics*, originally published by Fiction House and featuring Flash Gordon-style space opera, often with strong, if scantily clad, female leads. If the stories seem rather dated and xenophobic, the real strength of the title is in its artwork. Fran Hopper, one of several female artists employed by Fiction House during the war, is represented by a Gale Allen strip. Lee Elias, better known for *The Black Cat*, draws a Space Rangers story, George Evans, who later made his mark at EC, illustrates 'The Lost World', and popular 'good girl' artist Matt Baker handles 'Mysta Of The Moon'.~NF

THRILLING SCIENCE TALES
AC: *2 issues 1989–1990*
Reprinting neglected (and indeed odd) stories from the 1950s, this is well worth searching out. Behind a Mike Kaluta cover the first issue includes 'The Invasion From The Abyss', a curious collaboration between Al Williamson, Wally Wood, Frank Frazetta, Roy Krenkel and Joe Orlando, plus a solo story by Wood, both

from Avon's *Strange Worlds*. The former's not five times as good as any of their individual efforts, but worth reading. Also included are a Fred Guardineer Space Ace story from *Manhunt* and a science-fiction Western (not many of those about) from Fawcett's *Bob Colt*. 2 featured Fawcett's Captain Video illustrated by George Evans, Mysta of the Moon by Ruben Moreira from *Planet Comics* and Avon's *Captain Science* by Orlando and Wood.~NF
Recommended: 1–2

THRILLING WONDER TALES
AC: *1 issue 1991*

Black and white reprints of four great 1950s creators: Kenton of the Star Patrol battles space sirens, beautifully drawn by Wally Wood, from Avon's *Strange Worlds*, from which there's also Joe Kubert's 'The Adventures Of Henry Twist', a humorous story of a nerd being fought over by thousands of alien women. Dick Ayers illustrates 'The Third Element', a story of mankind uniting against an alien enemy, originally printed in Fago Publications' *Atom-Age Combat*; and finally, just a little out of place, is Bob Powell's first episode of 'Thunda, King of the Congo' (originally drawn by Frank Frazetta), a frothy mix of half-naked babes, naughty natives trying to sacrifice them and brutal action as Thunda and his tiger sidekick come to the rescue.~NF

THRILLKILLER
DC: *3-issue miniseries 1997*

Howard Chaykin is in his element, writing this Batman miniseries set in a universe similar to the familiar DC one, but with some differences and a beatnik influence. Wayne Manor is owned by Barbara Gordon, estranged from her father after her mother's death. Discovering her mother's corpse in a bat-shaped pool of blood she becomes a vigilante, sucking in Dick Grayson, an ex-circus acrobat, with her womanly wiles. Dick loves her; she's afraid she's falling for one of her father's dour detectives, Bruce Wayne, penniless when his parents' paper fortune imploded on their deaths. He's one straight cop in a city on the make, where a green-haired woman with a big grin seeks to control the heroin trade via her nightclubs. What starts off for Barbara as a bit of a thrill soon becomes deadly as Dick's family are involved in a fatal 'accident'. Wayne's informer, stripper Selena Kyle, turns up dead, and her own feelings undergo a sea change. Dan Brereton's heavy-handed drawing style gives the story a solid, fleshy feel. It's seedy and it's muscular, full of rain-washed streets and smoky jazz clubs. A class act by all involved.~FJ
Recommended: 1–3

THRILLOGY
Pacific: *1 issue 1984*

This contains three stories written and drawn by Tim Conrad, one set in prehistoric times (pretentious), one in medieval times (long-winded and poorly told), and one in the future (derivative). However, the artwork is beautiful. The colouring has nice effects with firelight, but this really deserves to be seen in black and white.~FC

T.H.U.N.D.E.R. Agents
Tower: *20 issues 1965–1969*

The acronymically named T.H.U.N.D.E.R. Agents topped the TV vogue for spy organisations by additionally employing superheroes, and managed to innovate besides, not least by issuing giant-sized 25-cent comics when 12 cents was the industry norm. The most interesting concept was Noman, able to shift his consciousness between a host of android bodies in an instant. The brave but blundering Len Brown, named after one of the writers, wore a strength-enhancing belt as Dynamo, and had a sexual frisson with armoured villainess Iron Maiden. The mind-reading helmet of Menthor also showed a spark, which was, unfortunately, not present in the creation of standard superspeedster Lightning and flying hero Raven. The heroes appeared in separate but sometimes connected stories in each issue, and in an era when superheroes were rarely hurt, 7's death of one cast member was a major shock. Unusually, the non-powered supporting players were also fully characterised; they included Weed, a thinly disguised version of chief artist Wally Wood. Other top-notch artists working on the stories included Reed Crandall, Gil Kane, Ogden Whitney, Dan Adkins, Steve Ditko, an on-form Mike Sekowsky and the underrated and distinctive Manny Stallman, largely on the Raven solos. Mind you, there were also John Giunta and George Tuska. So with innovative ideas and several top-notch artists, why no recommended issues? Unfortunately, the step between concept and art was script, and they were generally little more than ordinary, and sometimes dreadful, particularly on Noman. This didn't prevent a Noman solo series, or one for Dynamo. The reprint collections were paperbacks issued by Tower (who were primarily paperback publishers anyway) in the 1960s; they're rarely seen today. There was also a short-lived 1980s reprint series from JC Productions. In case you're wondering, by the way, the T.H.U.N.D.E.R. stands for The United Nations Defense Enforcement Reserve. There. You can sleep easy now.~WJ
Collections: Dynamo (most of 1), *Menthor* (Menthor stories from 2–5), *Noman* (Noman stories from 2–5), *The Terrific Trio* (Dynamo stories from 2, 3, Menthor and Noman stories from 6)

T.H.U.N.D.E.R. AGENTS
JC Comics: *2 issues 1983–1984*

These are new T.H.U.N.D.E.R. Agents stories, featuring the characters from the 1960s stories reprinted in the Hall of Fame series, along with some new ones. There's some nice artwork by Lou Manna and Willie Blyberg, some nice dialogue… but the story-telling's so muddled it makes it hard to care what's happening or to whom.~FC

Wally Wood's T.H.U.N.D.E.R. AGENTS
Deluxe: *5 issues 1984–1986*

Believing the copyright on the *T.H.U.N.D.E.R. Agents* had expired, Deluxe collected an impressive roster of creative talent to produce new stories. Over five issues there are Dave Cockrum, on-form Steve Ditko, Steve Englehart, Jerry Ordway and George Perez, and, wisely sticking to the original formula of mixing team stories with those of individual agents, these are good superhero comics. The Lightning stories by Keith Giffen and Tom and Mary Bierbaum are the best of the bunch, setting off the light, glossy action nature of the rest of the comic with downbeat stories about a man who ages every time he uses his superspeed suit and who's being stalked by a murderous enemy. Unfortunately for fans, the copyright on the characters rested elsewhere, and the series came to a premature end.~FP

Peter Cannon THUNDERBOLT
Charlton: *11 issues (1, 51–60) 1966–1967*

A pacifist master of the martial arts was an unusual concept in the 1960s, and Pete Morisi's strange Thunderbolt strip probably couldn't have emerged at any other time. Signing his strips anonymously as 'PAM', Morisi's writing is deadpan and stilted, and his art is sparse and functional. Furthermore, in his two-tone swimming trunks Thunderbolt is cursed with an all-time stinker of a costume, yet somehow everything meshes into a halfway decent strip. Thunderbolt's pacifist attitude is fundamental, inculcated through his having grown up in a Tibetan monastery and preserved despite battles against weird pulp-style foes. 53's Gore is typical, a would-be world-beater whose left hand is an ape's paw. 57, 59 and 60, by more proficient creators, don't match Morisi's po-faced sincerity, and fail without his input. The bizarre numbering is a Charlton speciality, with the series continuing *Son of Vulcan*'s issue numbers for no apparent reason.

Thunderbolt's back-up features strips are every bit as off-beat as the lead. The Sentinels, a rock'n'roll trio bequeathed gimmicky devices by a dying scientist, are an interesting idea poorly executed in 54–59, but The Prankster in 60 is plain bizarre. It's set in the futuristic Ultraopolis where playing music is punishable by public execution; the Prankster is a garish foe of authority, using the arsenal of a clown to humiliate the regime. Script by Denny O'Neil (under his Sergius O'Shaughnessy alias) and early Jim Aparo art make for a rare original.~FP

THUNDERBOLT
DC: *12 issues 1992–1993*

Conscientious and tolerably entertaining revival of the 1960s action hero by Mike Collins, nevertheless lacking a certain spark to make it really take off.~HS

THUNDERBUNNY
Red Circle: *1 issue 1984*
WaRP: *6 issues 1985– 1986*
Apple: *6 issues (7–12) 1987–1989*

Continuing from the character's semi-pro début in *Charlton Bullseye* 6 and 10, the Red Circle issue retells how young Bobby Caswell finds an alien artefact, a gift from a dying race who sealed the power of their greatest hero therein. Bobby gains the power, but what he doesn't realise, until he looks in the mirror, is that the aliens in question were anthropomorphic animals, and the heroic form he changes into when he claps his hands is that of a giant, pink-furred bunny rabbit. Under the imprint of WaRP Graphics after Red Circle's collapse, creator Martin L.Greim and artists Brian Buniak and Gary Kato took this ingenious but flimsy premise surprisingly far. Thunderbunny discovered a group of 1940s superheroes being held in suspended animation, teamed fleetingly with the T.H.U.N.D.E.R. Agents, and had romantic problems with the fledgling superheroine Moon Miss, all written divertingly and (save for 9's atrocious fill-in) stylishly illustrated. When cancellation loomed, rather than leave the characters dangling, Greim wrote an 'Imaginary Story', set five years or so in the series' future, which serves quite satisfactorily as a farewell to the title, a thoughtful gesture to his readers.~HS

THUNDERSTRIKE
Marvel: *24 issues 1993–1995*

There are few original ideas in this substitute Thor's comic, but old concepts are endearingly recycled to provide a reasonable superhero title. You wouldn't know it from a truly wretched first issue, though, packed with leaden expository thought balloons. Once past that, Thunderstrike finds his destiny very much intertwined with the rampaging Bloodaxe. 13–16 were also issued as flip-books featuring New York police's superhero containment squad Code Blue, and Thunderstrike's page-count is halved by back-up strips in 17–21.~FP

THE TICK
New England: *Series one 12 issues, 2 Specials 1988–1993, series two 9 issues 1993–1995*

Ben Edlund's original low-budget black and white cult series ran for surprisingly few issues before being developed into an MTV animated feature. The first issue reprints the first special, in which the Tick is introduced, and the quality of writing and art is high. Having started the strip as a specific parody of Daredevil, Superman and Batman, Edlund went on to expand his universe, populating it with incompetent ninjas, killer cows and bread-wielding samurai. The Tick wanders from adventure to misadventure with the wide-eyed innocence of a child, blissfully unaware of the chaos often surrounding him. His portly bachelor sidekick Arthur, garbed as a hybrid moth/rabbit, is the brains of the operation, with the Tick taking an Obelix role, attacking ninjas with gay abandon instead of Roman soldiers. The first series is one of the best humorous looks at the superhero genre around, and is reprinted in colour as *The Chroma Tick*. Unfortunately, the second series starts to fall into the very traps which the first series had originally lampooned. *The Tick* also spawned two spin-off series, *Paul The Samurai* and *Man-Eating Cow*.~TP
Recommended: Series one 1–4
Collections: *Karma Tornado* (series two 1–5), *Sunday Through Wednesday* (series one 1–6)

TIGER GIRL
Gold Key: *1 issue 1968*

Lily Taylor, circus aerialist, dons a black and orange swimsuit, borrows the circus tiger and pops off downtown to fight crime as Tiger Girl. Realism not a priority, then.~FP

TIGERMAN
Atlas: *3 issues 1975*

As created by Ernie Colon, a scientist injects himself with tiger chromosomes. Rather than have him dying an undignified and agonising death, it gives him the strength and agility of a tiger. Having lucked out once, he really pushes the boat out by costuming himself in tiger-striped all-in-one vest-and-underpants outfit. Still, with tiger strength who'd laugh at him… to his face? It's all very ordinary.~WJ

TIMBER WOLF
DC: *5 issues 1992–1993*

The Legion of Super-Heroes' follically unchallenged member is zapped back to the 20th century. His companion, goddess in progress Aria, is, of course, immediately kidnapped, so Timber Wolf fights his way through all and sundry to rescue her. Lovely feral art by Joe Phillips, but inker turned writer Al Gordon doesn't have a clue as to story structure.~HS

TIME JUMP WAR
Apple: *3-issue miniseries 1989*

Taking the entire first issue of only three to set up the idea that our heroes Doyle and Ron have jumped back through time, and incorporating an *Alien* homage along the way, seems awfully extravagant. From there it's cavemen vs guns in 2 and guns vs aliens vs cavemen in 3. Chuck Dixon provides a decent enough, if undemanding, plot and Enrique Villagran's art is functional but decidedly old-fashioned. Anyone yearning for the type of story once occupying British boys' adventure comics will love *Time Jump War*.~FP

TIME KILLERS
Fleetway/Quality: *7 issues 1992–1993*

Science-fiction anthology reprinting early 1990s stories from Britain's *2000AD*. The lead strip, 'Killing Time', mixes Jack the Ripper and genteel Victorian etiquette with time-travellers and the early, but very promising, art of Chris Weston. Mark Millar and Pete Milligan are among those writing the back-up strips, but seemingly with little enthusiasm.~FP
Collection: *Killing Time* ('Killing Time' from 1–5)

TIME MASTERS
DC: *8-issue limited series 1990*

This is a revival of the time-travelling Rip Hunter from the 1960s. This version of Rip Hunter has discovered two methods of travelling through time, but also discovered on his first trip that an individual could use each method only once. This means that he must now discover a third method before he can go on another trip, and he'll also need a fourth method if he wants to come back. At the beginning of the story, his lab is destroyed and he suspects the Illuminati, the ultimate secret conspiracy group. He also suspects that the Illuminati are planning to start a nuclear war, so with each issue a member of Hunter's team goes into the past to try to bring down the Illuminati. The characters are paper-thin and the plots feeble, but it manages to generate just enough curiosity to keep you reading: will they succeed, and if so, how?~FC

TIME TWISTERS
Quality: *18 issues 1987–1989*

Britain's *2000AD* comic has frequently run three-to-five-page sting-in-the-tail science-fiction strips under assorted names. More often than not they were treated as try-outs for new writers and artists, and there's little imagination at work, except for a period in the early to mid-1980s, when the quality level was upped considerably by the use of established professionals. Alan Moore, for instance, wrote almost two dozen, and Grant Morrison about half that amount, and both were generally matched with decent artists. Although both writers would consider the strips little more than an intellectual exercise, and none rank with their major work, there's considerable enjoyment to be had from a sample issue. Unfortunately, the artists fare less well, with the pages originally drawn to reduce to *2000AD*'s page size being stretched and thinned to accommodate their reproduction at standard American comic page size. Most issues to 12 contain plenty of Alan Moore strips, and thereafter 18 is a decent sample, with early work from both Glenn Fabry and Neil Gaiman.~WJ

Collections: *Alan Moore's Shocking Futures*, *Alan Moore's Twisted Times* (all Alan Moore written strips)

TIME WARP
DC: *5 issues 1979–1980*

An attempt to revive the science-fiction anthology in a format similar to the horror titles, this dollar comic featured many good individual tales, but as whole far too many that suffered from clichéd and predictable endings. The best stories appeared in the earliest issues, particularly 2.~DWC

TIMESPIRITS
Epic: *8-issue limited series 1984–1986*

Cusick the Tuscarora is the one with experience, the teacher, while Doot of the Wawenoc is the student, struggling to come to terms with the shamanic, mystical powers he's discovered in himself. As the title suggests, they travel through time in search of knowledge, ever ready to sell what they already have if the price is right. Thus they become involved with the original floods (2, 3) while saving New Iberia from the Spurtyn Duyvel (a creature that can't go home until its grief and sadness are drained), or join Jimi Hendrix and an alien siren on a mission to change history in Central America (5, 6). Written by Steve Perry and drawn by Tom Yeates (guest creators in 4 include Steve Bissette, Al Williamson, Rick Veitch and John Totleben), it's an entertaining, visually evocative series that didn't get enough of a chance to develop. The political undercurrents of 5 and 6 probably did the series no favours but would seem less controversial now.~NF

TIMEWALKER
Valiant: *15 issues, 1 Yearbook 1994–1995*

Ivar is an immortal with great strength and healing powers, and he has an affinity for the 'time arcs' that appear periodically and catapult him backwards and forwards through time. OK. So he can't be hurt, he wins all his fights, and whenever he's in trouble there's a good chance an arc will appear and whisk him away. Have you guessed this is not a compelling read? Maybe you're not supposed to read it, but just soak up the sight of all those muscles in his arms – the quantity keeps changing, but at best he has about three times the human norm. The only issues with any merit are 10, 11 and 15, co-written by Debra Doyle and James MacDonald, which have actual plot and humour, and above-average artwork, too.~FC

Recommended: 10, 11, 15

TINTIN
Atlantic-Little Brown/Methuen/Magnet/ Mammoth: *21 graphic novels 1932–1976*
Sundancer: *Tintin in the Land of the Soviets*

Hergé's adventures of Tintin have been continually in print in the English language for over thirty-five years. The simple *ligne claire* art has been hugely influential throughout Europe, over 100 million *Tintin* albums have been sold, and the only European comic character to surpass Tintin's popularity is Asterix. Making the statistics all the more remarkable is that *Tintin* was among the earliest European comic strips. Whereas his American and British counterparts are nothing more than curiosities, Tintin is loved by each succeeding generation.

Conceived as an adventure strip for a Christian newspaper's insert for children, the earliest stories are little more than chases propped up by poor jokes and surprisingly slapdash artwork. *Tintin In The Land Of The Soviets* and *Tintin In The Congo* remain unavailable as mass-market English-language editions. They're largely unappealing, motivated more by each weekly deadline than by any plot consideration, and were later disowned by Hergé. Not that *Tintin In America* is any better, despite being redrawn for album publication.

Cigars of the Pharaoh is a big step forward, with well-timed comic sequences, a lack of Christian or colonialist propaganda, and a well observed cast. It introduces recurring villain Rastapopoulos and, if one doesn't count Tintin's constant canine companion Snowy, the first regular supporting characters, inept detectives Thompson and Thomson. *The Blue Lotus* continues the improvement with a structure to the story, effective sub-plots, and researched and detailed artwork. It's almost the best of the early Tintin stories. In comparison *The Broken Ear* and *The Black Island* are disappointing, the latter having been largely redrawn in the 60s by Hergé's chief assistant Bob de Moor. It's worth noting, though, that both were originally produced in the late 1930s, and are streets ahead of most contemporary American product.

King Ottokar's Sceptre is the final fling for

Tintin as a solo character, and the best. By this point Hergé has graduated from adventure-reel stories to political satire, taking a swipe at the covetous foreign policy of 1930s Germany. Forever armed with a thundering torrent of inventive invective, irascible seadog Captain Haddock débuts in *The Crab With The Golden Claws*, is featured in all succeeding Tintin stories and transforms the series. His short fuse and frequent inebriation, allied with the silent-film comedy of Thompson and Thomson, provide all the slapstick sequences required. The later introduction of deaf and absent-minded Professor Calculus and irritating insurance salesman Jolyon Wagg rounds off an eccentric supporting cast.

With the exception of the muddled *Land Of Black Gold* (which nevertheless has its moments) all albums from *Secret Of The Unicorn* until the strangely lack-lustre *Flight 917* are Hergé and assistants on top form. The running gags have been established, the comedy is masterful, the plots are almost mathematically constructed, the characters resonate, there's a great attention to detail and the deceptive simplicity of the art appears almost effortless. The best album is *The Castafiore Emerald*, with Haddock a masterful study in repressed rage. Initially it recalls nothing so much as Georgian farce, but becomes a classic locked-room mystery starring imposing opera singer Bianca Castafiore, who was previously restricted to memorable cameos.

After this masterpiece, *Flight 917* is a grave disappointment. Whereas previous potentially incongruous elements have been seamlessly fused to *Tintin* plots, a rescue by extraterrestrials (although not shown) to conclude a thriller as ordinary as any produced by Hergé since the 1930s just doesn't work. Thankfully, *Tintin And The Picaros*, the final *Tintin* story, is a partial return to form. Purists have been known to carp over superficial attempts to modernise Tintin (particularly losing his plus fours), but it's funny, Hergé has a point to make about South American dictatorships, and there are interesting new characters. From anyone else it would be considered excellent.

Oddly for such an enduring character, Tintin actually lacks charisma, never being developed beyond the earnest, plucky and wholesome adventurer introduced in the earliest books. It's the engaging supporting cast and their fully realised comic potential that elevates the title to greatness and to the level where *Tintin* is appreciated by adults as well as their offspring. Forget the substandard animated versions of the novels and the embarrassing film: every true comics fan ought to own at least half a dozen *Tintin* books.~WJ

Recommended: *King Ottokar's Sceptre, The Crab With The Golden Claws, The Shooting Star, The Secret Of The Unicorn, Red Rackham's Treasure, The Seven Crystal Balls, Prisoners Of The Sun, Destination Moon, Explorers On The Moon, The Calculus Affair, The Red Sea Sharks, Tintin In Tibet, The Castafiore Emerald, Tintin And The Picaros*

TINY TOON ADVENTURES
DC: *4 issues 1990–1991*

The Tiny Toons are junior versions of Bugs Bunny, Daffy Duck and the other Warner Bros cartoon characters. These magazine-size issues are aimed at a very young audience and consist mostly of puzzle pages, jokes, games and mazes, with one short, undistinguished comic strip in each issue.~NF

TITAN
Dark Horse: *One-shot 1994*

One long-drawn-out fight between Titan and his old sidekick Golden Boy. There is practically no story and the art is feeble. Why was this ever published?~SS

TITS AND CLITS
Last Gasp: *8 issues 1972–1980*

Originally created by Joyce Farmer and Chyn Lyvely as a backlash against the misogynistic violence depicted in most undergrounds, *Tits and Clits* wisely refrained from male-bashing and instead concentrated on sex-positive strips for women. Not a porno book *per se*, *Tits and Clits* focuses on the wry and amusing side of sexual relationships, including the difficulty of having any at all. Originally written and drawn solely by its originators, other contributors were soon invited in. Roberta Gregory, Mary Fleener and several others have livened up its pages. As usual with anthologies, the variety of contributors means that an unqualified recommendation is impossible, but open-minded readers will find something to amuse them in most issues.~HS

TOKA, Jungle King
Dell: *10 issues 1964–1967*

You can bet this 'Jungle King' didn't set too many people on fire back when Gold Key's *Tarzan* comic was being drawn by Russ Manning. Completely forgettable.~SW

TOM MIX WESTERN
AC: *2 issues 1988–1989*

Do-gooder Tom starred in over 350 films between 1910 and 1930 and then appeared on a radio show until 1950, despite his death in 1940. The strips reprinted here are from Fawcett's *Master Comics*, illustrated by Carl Pfuefer and John Jordan. In 2 Tom finds himself buried alive in a coffin full of substandard cement, which explains why he escapes to catch the men responsible, but that's as exciting as it gets. Mix is another Western hero who prefers shooting guns out of the baddies' hands rather than risking killing them. Good job he's such a spectacular shot. The *Tom Mix Holiday Album* (1990) is just more of the same.~NF

TOMAHAWK
DC: *130 issues 1950–1970*

The adventures of a rebel band of Rangers from the American War of Independence. It hails from the very start of the 1950s, after running in *Star Spangled Comics* from the late 1940s. If you open any issue up until the late 1960s you'd think time had stood still as you look at Fred Ray's art and read Bill Finger and Ray's scripts. Progress finally came with a new look for *Tomahawk*, with Neal Adams covers, stories by Robert Kanigher and interior art by Frank Thorne, all of which led to a drop in sales. Further experimentation led to retitling the comic *Son Of Tomahawk*. Any issue after 116 is worth a glance; before that, don't bother.~SW

Son of TOMAHAWK
DC: *10 issues (131–140) 1970–1972*

Having failed to spark interest in the dynamic new *Tomahawk* from 116, DC switched tactics, moving the series forward twenty years and spotlighting Hawk, Tomahawk's son by Moon Fawn, a Native American woman. Glorious Joe Kubert covers grace every issue, while inside Bob Kanigher and Frank Thorne provide dynamic and thrilling stories, largely with a moral point, taking on racism (133) and slavery (136) among other topics. Tomahawk sneaks back in from the first issue, older, but still in full possession of his skills and faculties, acting as a counterpart to the headstrong Hawk. The best issue of the run is 138's Christmas story (despite Kanigher somehow having Christ crucified at Christmas), in which Moon Fawn and Small Eagle, Hawk's brother, are taken hostage by renegade tribe members. Giant-sized from 136, well selected reprints (including Frank Frazetta-illustrated strips in 131 and 139) and Joe Kubert's 'Firehair' strip in 132, 134 and 136 round out an excellent package.~FP
Recommended: 133, 135, 136, 138, 139

TOMATO
Starhead: *2 issues + 1994 to date*

A smorgasbord of fictional tales and autobiographical items, *Tomato* is underscored throughout by a wicked sense of humour. Whether it's the first issue's previously unseen use for a bottle of ketchup, or the problems of arranging to meet Camille Paglia, or issue 2's tale of Grandma Forney's games of scrabble, or the over-the-top-costume-party reminiscences, the common thread is laughter. There's little else linking the mainly short strips, drawn in wildly differing styles by Ellen Forney, some more successfully than others. The unsatisfying content in both issues is the 'Birdie and Spike' strips, about two female friends larking about. Their stories just peter out, serving little purpose other than titillation, which, presumably, isn't the intention. Admirably diverse, *Tomato* lacks pretensions and is generally entertaining, and one only wishes publication was more frequent.~WJ

TOMB of DARKNESS
Marvel: *15 issues (9–23) issues 1974–1976*

1–8 are titled *Beware*. This title reprints weird/horror shorts from the 1950s to the early 1960s. The only story of interest is 22's 'I Created Grutan' from *Strange Tales* 75, which features a mad scientist who attempts to create a growth serum. In this reprint, his assistant's name is crudely relettered as 'Pym'. This is considered the first chronological story about Hank Pym.~APS

THE TOMB OF DRACULA
Marvel: *Series one 70 issues, 4 Giant-Size (2–5) 1972–1979, series two 6 issues 1979–1980*
Epic: *4-issue miniseries 1991–1992*

That a Dracula comic written by a man named Wolfman exists at all is preposterous. That it's among the best supernatural titles ever stretches credulity beyond breaking point, but so it is. Although introducing key members of the supporting cast – Dracula's descendant Frank Drake, his partner Rachel Van Helsing and the mute Indian Taj – 1–6 don't develop Dracula beyond cinema cliché. 1–2 were reprinted in 1992 as *The Savage Return of Dracula*.

Gene Colan pencils from the off, Marv Wolfman arrives with 7, and inker Tom Palmer rejoins with 12, cementing the creative team for series one. While the Colan/Palmer art is always atmospheric and excellent, it took some initial fumbling before Wolfman began mining gold. It came as the fascinating supporting cast gelled. In addition to the insecure Drake, confident Van Helsing and Taj, there are Quincy Harker, old and wheelchair-bound from a lifetime fighting Dracula, and Blade débuting in 10, a hip 1970s vampire-hunter in search of a vampire who killed his mother. The first signs of greatness are apparent with 12–14, in which Dracula is cornered and killed, although not without cost, and then resurrected by a misguided priest. These were reprinted as the *Halloween Megazine* in 1996. Hannibal King makes his début in a great twist-ending story in 25, losing little of its effect through King's later familiarity. 32–33 have Dracula confronting the infirm Harker; it relates their previous confrontations and Harker's losses in a moving story. At this point Dracula realises that his vampiric abilities are being sapped, and he relocates to Boston to confront the cause of this. 37 introduces two further regular cast members – hack writer Harold H. Harold and the woman of his dreams, Aurora Rabinowitz – in a tale running until 42, in which Harker and company discover that there are worse threats than Dracula.

Wolfman and Colan's Dracula retains a nobility and seductive attraction despite revelling in his status as Lord of the Undead and murdering with ease, Wolfman making each kill more resonant by presenting a brief biography of the victim before death. Dracula retains a sense of honour, though, and is capable of affection, as is seen in later issues with his wife Domini. Beyond the cast a positive factor is that *Tomb of Dracula* is largely self-contained. When this relative insularity is breached by reminders of the Marvel Universe beyond, the guest appearances of Dr Strange and Silver Surfer (44 and 50) produce lack-lustre reading, although the Dr Strange story was reprinted as a one-shot in 1994. The supernatural guest stars, the ridiculously named Brother Voodoo and Son of Satan (35 and 52), mesh more comfortably. Dracula marries in 46 (reprinted out of context and rendered meaningless in the 1992 *The Wedding of Dracula*) and the marriage is consummated in 47, with Janus born in 54. Janus' destiny is hinted at in 51, while 59–61 deal with his transformation. That story told, the series, though it's never actually bad, meanders as Dracula becomes human, and must then face his successor as Lord of the Undead. The final story, reprinted in edited form as *Requiem For Dracula* in 1992, has the death of two regular cast members, but the lack of emotional impact typifies later issues.

Series two is a black and white magazine, better displaying Colan's art, which makes it a shame that he only illustrates the first and third issues. With Wolfman, Colan and the majority of the supporting cast gone it's an average title, on a par with the *Giant-Size Dracula* series, but failing the inevitable comparison with the previous series. The Epic series reunites Wolfman, Colan and Dracula for 'Day Of Blood, Night Of Redemption', picking up in 1991 and the resurrection of Dracula as if he'd been buried since *Tomb of Dracula* 70. The intervening years have seen the death of Rachel Van Helsing, and Frank Drake referred for depression. Blade's also on hand, and this Dracula is more savage and brutal than his previous incarnation. Despite the introduction of the fascinating Inspector Golem it's an unwise return for Wolfman (and, eventually, Dracula), who seems to be going through the motions with no real structure to the story.~FP
Recommended: Series one 12–14, 17, 20, 24–29, 32, 33, 37–42, 45–49, 54–57, 59–61

TOMORROW KNIGHTS
Epic: *6-issue miniseries 1990–1991*

In a future scenario where multi-national corporations are the real powers and elected governments merely puppets, the Tomorrow Knights are a freelance team recruited by the US President to break the corporate control. Written and drawn by Rod Whigham and Roy Richardson, *Tomorrow Knights* overcomes the contrived title to develop into a sound adventure series.~WJ

TONGUE LASH
Dark Horse: *2-issue microseries 1996*

Inspired by Moebius, Randy and Jean-Marc L'Officier have created an alien world of animal-headed slaves, constantly masked men and under-dressed women. The plot involves political intrigue and an attempt by the Begetters (who create the animal-headed creatures) to gain access to the secrets of 'metatime'. Unfortunately, it's all rather derivative, including the artwork of Dave Taylor, which, while not entirely following Moebius (there are also touches of Mañara), can't escape the comparison. Perhaps if more space had been available for background information and characterisation, the title would have succeeded in creating more of its own identity.~NF

TOO MUCH COFFEE MAN
Adhesive: *5 issues +, 1 Special 1993 to date*

Possibly the first existentialist superhero, Too Much Coffee Man is gloriously designed by creator Shannon Wheeler as a paunchy guy with a massive coffee-cup helmet on his head and that permanently caffeinated bug-eyed look. Despite the costume, this is no superhero comic, and when superhero-style fights occur, they've a greater purpose than the parody of superheroes. Continuing from his début in *Jab*, he sits around contemplating his dull life and reasons for living it, with caffeine-stimulated rushes the major highlight of his day. The lead strip is also backed up by a strange, possibly autobiographical, strip about a relationship, punctuated by bizarre interludes when a curiously Neanderthal-style Wheeler contemplates his work. Also appearing in *Dark Horse Presents* 92–95, *Too Much Coffee Man* won't be to everyone's taste. Try the ludicrous death issue (5) and work back. The special is colour reprints of strips Wheeler produced for a newspaper. Restricted to a page at a time, there's a repetitive quality when they're read one after the other.~FP

TOR
DC: *6 issues 1975–1976*
Epic: *4 issues 1993*

Rarely can a story have taken forty years in the telling, yet Joe Kubert's tales of the caveman Tor began in 1953, and the DC series reprints the original issues in 2–6. 1 was a new story explaining how Tor came to be. The Epic series continues and expands the story of a man fighting alone in a hostile world. It's to Kubert's credit that although more fantasy-style creatures appear, Tor's existence remains credible. The art on the early stories is primitive compared with the splendour of the magazine-size Epic issues. Tor also appeared in the difficult-to-find tabloid-size *Sojourn*.~FP

TORCH OF LIBERTY Special
Dark Horse: *One-shot 1995*

Seemingly striving for authenticity while simultaneously being a pastiche of the Commie-bashing comics of the 1950s, John Byrne's script is altogether too knowing to succeed, and Kieron Dwyer's art too 1960s. That's not to say it isn't fun, though, but largely pointless.~WJ

TORPEDO
Hard Boiled: *4 issues 1993–1994*

The Spanish creative team of Abuli and Bernet have obviously studied their Humphrey Bogart, Jimmy Cagney and George Raft movies. Torpedo is a truly ghastly and compulsive creation, a relentlessly brutal 1930s hitman without a hint of conscience for whom humanity is merely a tool to serve his needs. The only redeeming factor is that his victims are equally distressing specimens. His grim world is expounded in three short stories per issue, with his first kill being detailed in 2. Bernet's art is a curious amalgam – part Frank Robbins, part Alex Toth and part Milton Caniff – but very effective in creating the necessary grimy locations and characters, and Gil Jordan's excellent translations of Abuli's scripts are better than those in the Catalan paperback collections. There are six volumes of the latter, containing most of these stories and many more. Issue 4, though, has material previously untranslated into English. Torpedo also appeared, in ill-advised colour, in issues of *Echo Of Futurepast*.~WJ
Recommended: 1–4

TOTAL ECLIPSE
Eclipse: *5-issue limited series 1988–1989*

At a time when every comic company was issuing crossovers involving every character they'd ever published, this Eclipse team-up fest proved to be one of the most bizarre of the bunch. Eclipse had a wide variety of publications at the time, from relatively straightforward superheroes to surreal nonsense such as *Tales of the Beanworld*, and, though throwing them all together might have seemed crazy, it also, remarkably, worked. In fact, it works precisely because it's so ludicrous. As Valkyrie puts it in 5: 'At last

we're evening up the odds, even if our side is composed of talking ducks, beans, and Ninja hamsters.' It's rubbish really, but it's mad enough to be fun.~JC

TOWER OF SHADOWS
Marvel: *9 issues, 1 special 1969–1971*

The type of horror story that saw Marvel through the 1950s is produced by the contemporary freelancers with surprisingly good results, especially on the part of artists like Neal Adams, Gene Colan, Jim Steranko and Wally Wood. Unfortunately, the mixture is diluted with duff reprints from 6; the title changes to *Creatures On The Loose* with 10.~FP

THE TOWERS OF BOIS MAURY
Titan: *2 Graphic Novels*

Belgian artist Hermann is revered throughout Europe, and it's easy to see why, looking at these masterpieces. They're set in the Middle Ages. Bois Maury is a dispossessed knight with a sense of honour and justice lacking in many of his contemporaries, who view the peasants as little better than animals. The first volume, 'Babette', depicts the tragic events set in motion when a knight attempts to force himself on a peasant girl, and the second, 'Eloise de Montgri', tells of an attempt to restore a castle to the rightful owner. Both are named after the female lead. In both cases Hermann's plotting is meticulous, and his art is astonishing, seemingly effortless in evoking the Middle Ages in a simple *ligne claire* style and in conveying a wealth of emotion and exposition in a single panel. Sadly, these volumes weren't successful enough to merit further translations, and later volumes are only available in Europe.~FP
Recommended: 1, 2

TOXIC AVENGER
Marvel: *11 issues 1991–1992*

Moronic drivel inspired by the allegedly cult film.~HS

TOXIC CRUSADERS
Marvel: *8 issues 1992*

Originating from the deliberately bad taste *Toxic Avenger*, *Toxic Crusaders* must have been the unlikeliest kiddies' cartoon show ever, yet the comic works. It's the same story as its originator up to a point, with a nerdy janitor transformed into a hideous but superstrong monster on contact with toxic waste. He's the only deformed inhabitant of Tromaville, but mutation is a common condition elsewhere in New Jersey, and there are enough comrades to protect the one unpolluted city from the designs of a malign alien cockroach. Never intended as anything more than a companion to the TV show, *Toxic Crusaders* is better than many of Marvel's contemporary mainstream

titles. There's a wealth of bad puns, stupid henchmen and knowing asides, and the anti-pollution messages are painlessly passed on. Don't expect anything deep and there'll be a lot to enjoy here. The best sample is 5, with the excellent art of Derek Yaniger, and a funny Steve Gerber script incorporating an *Archie* parody sequence amid the usual mess. Full marks also to the team of Jeremy Banx and David Leach in 8 for the first man-on-toilet-with-trousers-round-his-ankles scene ever in a Marvel comic. A second series was widely solicited and advertised, but never actually published.~FP
Recommended: 5

TOYBOY
Continuity: *7 issues 1986–1989*
Oh, this is so tedious. Toyboy is Jason Kriter, whose father is probably the richest man in the world. Twelve-year-old Jason has everything, and he's also an electronics genius who makes his own toys – exo-skeletons, etc – which function in the plots on the level of magic, effectively removing any logic or tension. Avoid.~FC

TRAGG AND THE SKY GODS
Gold Key: *8 issues 1975–1977*
Taking their cue from the Von Danekin books popular at the time of publication, humanity is given a giant step forward when aliens endow two foetuses with intelligence way above your average caveman. Just as well, because twenty years later more aliens arrive, and they aren't as benign. A modicum of plot is stretched to breaking point. Don't bother.~FP

TRAILER TRASH
Tundra: *6 issues 1992–1993*
Fantagraphics: *2 issues + (7–8) 1996 to date*
Homing in on Middle America, Roy Tompkins delivers the zany goings-on of Harvey The Hillbilly Bastard and his colourful pals, such as Tony, the alien-obsessed schizophrenic who's receiving hidden messages in re-runs of *C.H.I.P.S.*, and Davy the drug dealer. Without question one of the most disturbed, repellent and unremittingly offensive comics ever published, *Trailer Trash* comes with the highest recommendation. Tompkins' Wolvertonesque art delights in detailing almost unimaginable scenes of degeneracy, reaching its apogee in 3 and 4's back-up strip 'The Lousy Bad Kid In Very Bad Times'. From 6 on the title has concentrated on equally appalling *über*-brat Billy Dalton, and has had a greater sense of continuity. Recommended only for the very strongest of stomachs.~DAR
Recommended: 1–8

TRANSIT
Vortex: *5 issues 1987–1988*
Extraordinary début comic by Ted McKeever, reportedly written and drawn in a fortnight while the fledgeling artist was under house arrest recovering from a contagious illness. Crooked Boss Traun is trying to use tele-evangelist Reverend Grisn as a puppet mayor, and graffiti artist Spud is the only witness to Grisn committing a murder. *Transit* is a confusing mix of metaphor and chase sequences, centred around a city's transport system, with wasted characters drifting through a nightmare urban landscape. Ideas spark off the pages, and if it is a little muddled in places it's worth the extra thought required to work out what McKeever's getting at. Unfinished, the last issue ends with Boss Traun ranting about the new order as flames sweep through the city. Characters from *Transit* turn up in *Metropol*, where their story is resolved.~FJ
Recommended: 5

THE TRANSMUTATION OF IKE GARUDA
Epic: *2 issues, 1991–1992*
It's the future and we have the technology for teleporting people, but Transit Authority has a monopoly on this technology, with all the opportunities for corporate conspiracy plots that this implies. Ike Garuda is a private detective who gets drawn into the plotting. It starts well, with a scene of Garuda going through the teleportation process to get to his first meeting with the client – very effective writing and artwork. The goodwill from this beginning may last you through the first issue, keeping you happily trying to guess what's really going on. But pages into the second issue it's clear that the plot is hopelessly convoluted, and you suspect that it's going to be a lot of running around and, 'Ah, but X was really working for Y.' And so it proves. Most disappointing.~FC

Bart Simpson's TREEHOUSE OF HORROR
Bongo: *2 issues + 1995 to date*
A sort of comics equivalent to the annual *Simpsons Halloween Special*, this doubles as a chance for known comic creators to dabble with the Simpsons. It's odd to note that they almost all come up short, most surprisingly of all Peter Bagge in 2, whose own comics obviously influenced *The Simpsons*. Bill Morrison has a hand in drawing all the strips in both issues; the most successful of them is Mike Allred's opening strip in 1, 'Little Shop Of Homers'. Allred captures the humour and offhand comments of the TV show perfectly, with a tale of Springfield

being plagued by a man-eating plant. James Robinson and Jeff Smith also contribute to 1, and animator Paul Dini writes the other tale in 2.~FP

TREKKER
Dark Horse: *6 issues, 1 special 1987–1989*

Spun off from *Dark Horse Presents* (4–6), *Trekker* follows the adventures of Mercy St Clair, a licensed bounty hunter in a far future world, where hunters augment the work of the police force. Underlying the stories of tracking smugglers and mad-dog killers writer/artist Ron Randall creates an atmosphere of paranoia around the government's mysterious actions. The story in issues 4–6 encapsulates both the appeal of the series and its recurrent themes: Mercy's on-off relationship with a police officer and her tendency to take risks due to inexperience. Randall's writing is roughly crafted and his artwork's a little too stiff and illustrative but the character's well thought out, and if the setting's not particularly original, it's well delineated. The special fills in most of Mercy's past – her father's murder, her own first killing, her training – with a framing sequence dealing with a past lover trying to kill her old mentor.~NF

TRENCHER
Image: *4 issues 1994*

Keith Giffen's *Trencher* is best described as over the top. The main character is brought back from the dead to hunt down and kill superpowered villains. Giffen draws brightly coloured, elaborate panels to match his zany mercenary, and the style is very similar to DC's *Lobo*. The plot would fit on the back of a postage stamp but the cartoon violence makes it readable… just.~SS

TRIBE
Image: *1 issue 1994*
Axis: *2 issues (2–3) 1994*

The fashionable concept of being politically correct comes to Image Comics in this Afro-American title. Todd Johnson contributes a poor story so confusing and cluttered it's difficult to understand what the comic is about. A guess at a government conspiracy and a breakthrough in technology can be hazarded, but this could be wrong. To make things worse, Larry Stroman's artwork is weak and appears rushed. The title's main flaw is that in its desire to appeal to ethnic minorities it excludes white people, therefore endorsing the very problem it is trying to remedy: segregation.~SS

TRIDENT
Trident: *8 issues 1989–1990*

Ambitious UK anthology that tried to offer something for everyone, from Neil Gaiman and Nige Kitching's 'cyberpunk' superheroes,

The Light Brigade, to Grant Morrison and Paul Grist's downbeat 1980s fable 'St Swithin's Day' (1–4), in which an *angst*-ridden teenager sets out to assassinate Margaret Thatcher. Morrison has rarely matched the perfectly observed, *faux*-cynical voice of his young narrator in 'St Swithin's Day', and the strip is undoubtedly the highpoint of the title. The central ideas of many of the other contributions were often too ambitious for the space allotted, and many of the creators involved were not really ready for professional publication, but any title that featured Eddie Campbell's Bacchus, plus early efforts by the likes of Mark Millar, D'Israeli and Mark Buckingham, is worth a look.~FJ

The TRIGGER TWINS
DC: *1 issue 1973*

Western reprints featuring the twins from *All Star Western* and a great Pow Wow Smith story by Fox and Infantino make for an interesting one-shot.~SW

TRIUMPH
DC: *4-issue miniseries 1995*

One of DC's perennial revamps, this time a retroactive continuity implant concerning a founder member of the Justice League who then vanished for decades without anyone noticing. So far we have something that's silly, but no sillier than many other superhero comics. Our bog-standard blond jock type must have motivation, though, so, inspired by his father's inglorious criminal career, he's determined to become a superhero. And whaddya know, after some intense training latent superpowers just happen to manifest themselves. Unbelievably, that's the good stuff, and it slides downhill from here. The daft and nonsensical plot is passed off with the explanation that the villain of the piece is a nutcase. *Triumph* is an all-time turkey – no TR7, rather a battered and rusting old Herald at the bottom of the junkyard.~WJ

TROLL
Image: *6 issues (all number 1's!) 1993–1994*

Bartholomew J. Troll is a member of Rob Liefeld's Youngblood who happens to look a bit like a troll. The first number one, by Liefeld himself with Jeff Matsuda pencilling, sees Troll fighting Evangeliste for possession of a Daemonite orb, concepts borrowed from Jim Lee. *Troll II*, by Robert Napton and Karl Alstaether, has a Nazi plot that involves Shaft and Badrock from Youngblood plus a bonus British superheroine called The Jack, which may or may not have anything to do with a costume made out of the British flag. A Halloween special has the Maxx playing

Leather Apron in a Victorian setting. A Thanksgiving special and a 'stocking stuffer' help bulk out the number ones, along with a story set in World War II. Occasionally funny but rarely rising above its clichéd origins.~NF

TROLLORDS
Tru Studios: *13 issues, 1 special 1986–1987*
Comico: *4 issues 1988–1989*
Apple: *6 issues 1989–1990*

An odd, and strangely compelling for some, series, presumably an attempt to teach responsible behaviour to young readers, about Three Stooges-like playful monsters who live with a realistic suicidal female character and learn lessons about decent human interaction. It can be pious, though it's usually funny, but hanging around on the off-chance of the arrival of amusing little green chaps is a dubious hope for a cure for depression. Story and art, by Scott Beaderstadt and Paul Fricke, improve fairly consistently throughout the run but the late Tru Studios issues, in black and white, are the best representatives.~GK

TROMBONE
Knockabout: *1 issue 1989*

Given that Europe is awash with fine humorous cartoonists and there are precious few in Britain and the USA, this anthology was a sensible attempt to bring the best of them to an English-speaking audience. *Quel dommage!* It transpires that while the drawings are as funny as ever, the text is far from hilarious, struggling to raise even a smile on most occasions. There is the redeeming aspect of Hunt Emerson pages, but even he's not enough to make this a worthwhile purchase.~FP

THE TROUBLE WITH GIRLS
Eternity: *Series one 14 issues, 1 Annual 1987–1989, series two 23 issues, 1 Special 1989–1991*
Comico: *4 issues 1989*
Eternity: *19 issues (5–23) 1989–1991*
Epic: *4-issue miniseries 1993*

Will Jacobs and Gerard Jones' secret agent spoof follows the adventures of reluctant international playboy/spy Lester Girls, who would much rather have been living a quiet life in the suburbs, with 2.4 children, a friendly dog and Sunday mornings washing the car. Fate has other plans for poor old Les: he can never escape the glamorous women, fast cars, big guns, international agents and would-be world conquerors who are constantly on his trail. His friend Apache Dick is usually happy to relive him of the burdens of unwanted wealth and half-naked nymphomaniacs. The basic joke is a funny one and almost all issues are well done, but it does wear thin quickly and seems a little too formulaic after an extended run. The only differences between the publishers are that the Comico and Epic issues are in colour, the others aren't. Pick up a few issues and re-read them when you've forgotten the plot.

The series is nonetheless popular enough to have spawned several spin-offs starring both Les himself (*Lester Girls* 3 issues, Eternity, 1990–1991) and other members of the regular supporting cast such as the *Lizard Lady* (Arciel one-shot 1991) and *Apache Dick* (Eternity, 4-issue miniseries 1990). During the short spell with Epic, a Lester Girls story appeared in the *Heavy Hitters* anthology.~JC
Collections: My Name Is Girls (Eternity series one 4–6), The Trouble With Girls (Eternity series one 1–3)

TROUBLEMAN
Image: *4-issue miniseries 1996*

Plotted by Charles Drost and Michael Davis, scripted by Davis and John Hervey, pencilled by Drost – Extreme Studios certainly knows how to create work for themselves, though this is a collaboration with Motown Machineworks – suddenly every man's a corporation, complete unto himself. Anyway, with heavy-handed references like 'Giraud Spaceport', Troubleman-5 and Troubleman-36 exist in a world of homage-ridden, scantily-clad sci-fi. It's not completely without interest, but far too dependent on superhero action rather than story.~NF

TRUE CONFESSIONS
Fox Comics/Fantagraphics: *1 issue 1991*

Autobiographical story with odd digressions into space-opera parody from Dave Hodson. Primarily dealing with the death at birth of one of his twin children, Hodson's sketchy work neatly avoids dragging the reader down into depression, and, while it's visually inventive, there's a raw, minimalist feel to it.~NF

TRUE CRIME
Eclipse: *1 issue 1993*

A companion to Eclipse's series of *True Crime Trading Cards*, there was obviously little market for a continuing series. There are two stories, both drawn impeccably by Dan Spiegle. Jenny Proctor and Dave Robinson relate John Gotti's induction into the ranks of the Cosa Nostra, while Valerie Jones outlines the case against Aileen Wuornos, 'the first female serial killer'. The former works quite well as a story but the latter's really just a lot of exposition that, though nicely illustrated, doesn't really work as comics.~NF

TRUE LOVE
Eclipse: *2 issues 1986*

Selected reprints from 1950s romance comics, mainly from the defunct Standard line. Lovingly represented art from Alex Toth and others, and some imaginative scripts. Great stuff.~HS

TRUE SWAMP
Peristaltic Press: *3 issues 1994*
Slave Labor: *2 issues (4–5) 1994–1995*

A refreshing variation on anthropomorphic themes, in which Lenny the frog endures the dangerous world of the swamp. There are encounters with humans and fairies and many references to 'folktales' amongst the various inhabitants of the swamp. Jon Lewis has an unpolished drawing style but his unsentimental stories are clever and (blackly) humorous.~NF
Recommended: 1–5
Collection: True Swamp (1–5)

TRYPTO The Acid Dog
Renegade: *one issue 1988*

Given the title one might assume this is a joke that came up in the bar one night, then got out of hand. It's an oddly affectionate homage to the old Krypto stories in *Superboy*, throwing in some exaggerated ecological villains along the way. Nicely drawn by Steve Leialoha and charmingly written by Bill Mumy and Miguel Ferrer, Trypto is fun, but hardly essential. He reappears in early 1997 issues of *Dark Horse Presents*.~FP

TUG AND BUSTER
Art & Soul: *4 issues + 1996 to date*

Mark Hempel's 'lusty, zesty, four-fisted he-man misadventure', *Tug And Buster* is the adventures of a pair of misbegotten losers, one a big, quiet lump, the other a gibbering idiot. Most of the humour comes not from situations but from Buster's incessant chatter, full of sexual innuendo and scatological humour, and that wears thin after a while. Hempel works hard to give it a different visual look to *Gregory* and *Sandman* (he's obviously been studying O'Neill or Muñoz, probably both, and has roughed things up considerably). Like *Gregory*, *Tug And Buster* is initially engaging, features repeated jokes and catchphrases that soon become tiresome, suffers from a limited set of scenarios, but contains some brilliant cartooning and visual jokes to offset this.~FJ

TUROK Son Of Stone
Dell: *29 issues 1954–1962*
Gold Key: *96 issues (30–125) 1962–1980*
Whitman: *39 issues (92–130) 1974–1982*

Turok and his younger companion Andar are two 19th-century Native Americans who chance on a tunnel while out hunting. It leads them to a region populated by both humans and, more pertinently, dinosaurs. Unfortunately, there's no return trip, since the land is surrounded by sheer cliff walls, and Turok has to adapt to a unfamiliar new world. As written by Paul S. Newman, *Turok* is a basic lost-land scenario, and, while individually fine, the stories tend to become repetitive with more thorough immersion. What raises the 1960s material above the remainder is the excellent artwork of Alberto Giolitti, replacing the pedestrian Rex Maxon from 24. Largely predictable, Newman occasionally surprises, and in 58 aliens in a crashed UFO are thrown into the mix. In testing the repairs Andar actually surmounts the cliffs to view his tribe. It came to nothing, though, and it wouldn't be until the Valiant series that Turok and Andar returned home. As with other Dell titles, Turok was introduced in trial issues of *Four Color* (596 and 656 respectively) before starting his own title from 3. Rather confusingly, Turok was published under both Gold Key's imprint and that of affiliated company Whitman from 92, with Whitman being the sole publisher of the very ordinary final issues. This incarnation of Turok is best (and cheaply) sampled through Valiant's 1994 four-issue series *The Original Turok Son Of Stone*.~FP

TUROK, Dinosaur Hunter
Valiant: *48 issues (0–47), 1 Yearbook 1993–1995*

After Valiant's *Unity* crossover, Turok is returned from the now named Lost Land into contemporary South America. Along with him come the bionically enhanced dinosaurs named in the title, thus hanging a millstone the size of Mount Rushmore round the comic's metaphorical neck. The dinosaurs are boring. Boring, boring, boring. A couple turning up every now and then would be okay, but Turok comes across so many in the first twenty issues you'd lay odds on them being mass-produced by General Dinosaurs. Beyond that they're more sparingly used.

This Turok bears little relation to his predecessor, being more action-oriented and seeing it as his mission to slaughter all the dinosaurs now on Earth. A selection of writers and artists are mixed and matched on the title, producing one story arc at a time. Tim Truman turns in the best scripts, recognising that Turok is a 19th-century Kiowa Indian, whereas other writers treat him as little more than the Punisher with a bow and arrow. Truman's is the best story so far, in 20–23, set in an equivalent of Jurassic Park as a couple of old adversaries return and a pair of unconventional bounty-hunters are introduced. Rags Morales is consistently tops of a respectable selection of pencil artists used, depicting a powerful and dynamic Turok.

Turok makes frequent trips back to the Lost Land, and Truman introduces the idea that Turok wasn't the only person to wander there and not find his way out, leading to some interesting stories. Among the stranded is a group of demented Nazi women in 37–38. Truman and Morales cobble the plot together from old cinema adventure reels as the Nazis attempt to transfer Hitler's brain into Elvis Presley's corpse. It's very silly, but in the right frame of mind it's also very enjoyable. It's followed by a good Paul Gulacy illustrated story in 39–40, with a far more serious approach. The series ends on a high, but very abruptly.~WJ
Recommended: 0, 20–23, 37–40, 47

2099 World of Tomorrow
Marvel: *6-issue miniseries 1996–1997*

With the cancellation of the remaining 2099 titles there was still a story to be told. Earth is in a bad way. A flood has sunk most of the world, and the only habitable portions seem to be Latveria, ruled with an iron fist by Doctor Doom, and The Savage Land in the Antarctic. There's also an alien race called the Phalanx, who have infected much of what remains of humanity with a techno virus that gradually transforms them into machines. The entire 2099 cast (and the Fantastic Four in 1–2) battle to save the world. If you're familiar with the characters then there's fun to be had from the interaction between a usually unrelated cast. If you're not familiar with the characters this sprawls and isn't the place to begin investigating the world of tomorrow.~FP

2099 UNLIMITED
Marvel: *10 issues 1993–1996*

This anthology of the revamped, futuristic Marvel Universe has some pleasant surprises. Concentrating mostly on Spiderman 2099 (the most successful of the new generation) and Hulk 2099, the writing is intriguing. Gerard Jones' scripts on Hulk are enjoyable as he takes the character back to his roots and recreates a far more feral 'Hulk smash' than of late. Kyle Baker pops up and lends a professional hand to the inks on 2. All this is backed up by some bizarre one-off strips by Bob Fingerman, Kyle Baker, Ned Sontag, Warren Ellis and D'Israeli. Don't be put off by the covers, take a look.~TP

20 NUDE DANCERS 20
Tundra: *2 issues 1990–1991*

Collection of one-page strips originally published in *Comic Buyer's Guide*. With few limits on content and a great artistic talent, Mark Martin's imagination and invention is astounding, with the pages including ridiculous cartoon characters, fake Mexican comics, fake Marvel ads, full-page posters,

brilliant autobiographical pieces, and lots more. And it's almost all very funny. That's just the first issue, by the way, which measures about 15 inches by 12 (and is called the *Year One Posterbook*). The second is conventional magazine size; it has more strips, which, although still magnificent, require a little knowledge of comics for the full effect.~FP
Recommended: 1–2

21
Image: *3-issue miniseries 1996*

Scrap Freeman is accidentally transported to the future, where a resistance force is trying to combat the tyranny of the Internex. 21 is a robot, the twenty-first in the series, whose creator is now a part of the resistance and who acts as guide and protector to Scrap while he tries to recover the vehicle in which he travelled to the future. A clichéd science-fiction series from Mark Silvestri and Len Wein with pencils by Billy Tan Mung Khoy. It's not unappealing but needs much more work to create a decent atmosphere.~NF

22 BRIDES
Event: *4-issue miniseries 1996–1997*

Snappy, sassy and fearless, the 22 Brides are a girl gang living a precarious existence involving them with mobsters. Artist Scott Lee has an appealing anime big-eye style and creates commendably grimy and realistic locations. He also knows which parts of girls he likes, and manages to emphasise them throughout. Let's hope he sees some real ones some day. Fabian Nicieza writes up a storm. There's wit and imagination and some very funny dialogue, especially from an erudite enforcer who quotes from Bertrand Russell, and a gangster who takes Huggy Bear as his inspiration. Don't expect much beyond girls and guns and you'll be pleasantly surprised, but come expecting anything more and you'll be disappointed.~FP
Recommended: 1–4

TWILIGHT
DC: *3-issue miniseries 1991*

The innocent and bland characters who populated DC's 1950s science-fiction titles are the focus of *Twilight*. There's no real nostalgic glow around them, so writer Howard Chaykin is able to play fast and loose to good effect. Everything necessary to the plot is explained along the way, while readers familiar with the featured cast can have a wry smile or rage at their progression. Thankfully there's little resemblance to the unsophisticated characters of old. Chaykin uses the worldly-wise and amusing Homer Glint of The Star Rovers to narrate events in hindsight. As the story begins, Tommy Tomorrow has become an Oliver North figure, popularised as a war hero and becoming

powerful on the basis of his standing. By the end of 1 humanity is immortal, which proves to be both blessing and curse, and their religious conflicts spread throughout the galaxy. In the end *Twilight* is a simple story, very well told; the excellent art of José Luis Garcia-Lopez raises this well above average.~WJ
Recommended: 1–3

TWILIGHT MAN
First: *4 issue miniseries 1989*

The old tyrant gods want to reclaim Earth, but there's one man with the ability to prevent them, because the knowledge has been passed from father to son for 10,000 years. Half-baked tosh.~FP

THE TWILIGHT ZONE
Gold Key: *91 issues 1962–1979*

The pattern was unwavering from start to finish: either three or four sting-in-the-tail stories featuring a generally high standard of script and art. Many top-notch artists are featured alongside creators who went on to better things but started here, with Howard Chaykin in 54 your starter for ten. Frank Miller allegedly contributed to 83 and 89, although you'd be hard pressed to recognise it.~WJ

THE TWILIGHT ZONE
Now: *One-shot 1990, series one 16 issues, 4 Specials 1991–1993, series two 6 issues 1993*

Given the generally inventive quality of the TV shows from which this comic is derived, this is a real let-down, failing to spark the imagination. 'As ye sow, so shall ye reap' is an all-too-common plot device, closely followed by the last-panel twist-ending mined by comics for decades. In the first series TV writer J. Michael Straczynski turns the formula on its head in 2, a story diluted by duff art, and Steven Dorfman writes two unpredictable surprise-ending stories in 10. Gimmicks and variant editions are commonplace. The 1990 one-shot is available in a bewildering array of formats, all containing a decent Harlan Ellison and Neal Adams story, 9 has a long 3-D section and series three 2 is totally computer-generated, although not very well, which is indicative of the remainder of the series.~FP

TWIST
Kitchen Sink: *3 issues 1987–1988*

The only common thread among the strips in these comics is that they deal with things that aren't quite acceptable, whether it be Daniel Clowes' dangerous child Freddy Brown The Squirt, J.D. King's forthright 'Sammy' or Peter Bagge's 'Geniuses'. With short contributions from Robert Crumb, Richard Sala, Basil Wolverton and the Friedman brothers it certainly is an eclectic collection. As a bonus, 3

reprints Harvey Kurtzman and David Levine's 'Return Of A Christmas Carol' from *Esquire*. As with most anthologies of this kind the stories are a little hit-and-miss but editor J.D. King tried hard to provide something a little bit different.~NF

THE TWIST
Dell: *1 issue 1962*

That's right, folks, a comic devoted to Chubby Checker's dance. In a 'Why don't we do the show right here?' plot two rival establishments compete for the custom of young and old mad keen to twist wherever they can, even in the police station. Very much a daft timepiece: read and believe.~FP
Recommended: 1

TWISTED SISTERS Comics
Kitchen Sink: *1 volume 1993, 4 issues 1994*

The aim of promoting female cartoonists in a male-dominated industry is admirable, not least because the topics of interest to women have a broader appeal beyond the comics ghetto. The diversity of approach here is such, though, that there's little to connect the material other than the premise. Perennial underground stalwart Diane Noomin edits both the introductory 256-page volume and the subsequent magazine-size series, and provides a career highlight with her strip for 4 about miscarriages.

Humour is a priority for most contributors, and Carol Lay and Carol Tyler come up trumps. One would seriously question, however, if the contributions from Fiona Smyth and the tedious Dame Darcy would be published anywhere outside such a display-of-solidarity project, with story-telling not a priority for either; yet the equally off-putting art of Aline Kominsky-Crumb is used to provide some of the most moving stories of the run in 4. There's something to enjoy in each issue, and no two readers will agree on which those stories are.~FP
Recommended: 4
Collection: Drawing The Line (1–4)

TWISTED TALES
Pacific: *7 issues 1982–1984*
Eclipse: *3 issues (8–10) 1984, Graphic Album 1987*

Horror anthology title edited by Bruce Jones (who also wrote just about every story in it) and April Campbell. Modelled on the EC anthologies of the 1950s, as the series progressed the stories became longer. In some cases this allowed Jones room to do something a bit more penetrating than an eight-page shocker, but in other cases it encouraged him to stretch thin suspense tales by wasting space on unnecessary characterisation.

Twisted Tales benefited from some superb

realistic artists, John Bolton and Richard Corben among them, maintaining a high artistic standard throughout its run. Probably the most notable story is 'Banjo Lessons' in 5, which Jones and Campbell managed to turn into a *cause célèbre* by writing an editorial about it to pre-empt any charges of racism that might arise from misunderstanding on the part of readers. Since stories of this type hammer you over the head with their morality their worries are particularly hard to swallow. The story itself has a very dull structure and the editorial completely ruins any element of surprise.~FJ

TWISTER
Harris: *4-issue miniseries 1992*

Twister is a murderer of serial killers, earning his name from the distinctive way he twists their necks. Always a step ahead of the authorities in tracking the killers, he himself becomes a target of the FBI and an acupuncture adept, using the vicious Animal as bait for his trap. The latter earns his name by preferring to eat his victims. James Hudnall explores a singularly unpleasant, yet riveting, mindset while Bill Koeb's art varies between great beauty on the panels he likes to dashed-off on those he doesn't care about, thus diluting the tale. In any case, it's not for the fainthearted.~FP

Batman: TWO FACE STRIKES TWICE
DC: *2-issue microseries 1993*

Being in two parts and telling two stories each issue, this is a play on the duality of the Batman villain, of course also heavily featuring the Dark Knight himself. Mike Barr and Joe Staton do the Batman 1940s-style, complete with giant props and a proper detective story. Barr returns with Daerick Gross for the other half of the title, but few stories would be good enough to overcome the awfulness of the painted artwork, especially not this slight tale.~NF

TWO-FISTED TALES
EC: *24 issues (18–41) 1950–1955*
Russ Cochran: *18 issues + 1992 to date*

Odd as it may seem, before *Two-Fisted Tales* war stories in comics had never developed beyond the 'Eat leaden death you Ratzi goosestepper' school. Harvey Kurtzman changed that forever as editor, chief writer and often illustrator of stories of ordinary people involved in conflicts through the ages. Continuing its numbering from *Haunt of Fear*, *Two-Fisted Tales* was conceived as an adventure title, but after a dreary first issue, and two stronger follow-ups, Kurtzman took full editorial control and war became the focus. By 21 the artists most associated with the series, Jack Davis, Wally Wood and the John Severin

and Will Elder team, had arrived, with Kurtzman initially illustrating the fourth tale in each issue. Other artists worked on *Two-Fisted Tales*, but few matched the consistently high quality of the regulars.

The initial publication period coincided with the Korean War, and while using the conflict for stories Kurtzman was careful never to glamorise the action; indeed his stories often plotted the downfall of characters too eager to participate. He also wrote stories detailing the effect of war on innocent Koreans, a poignant example being the story of the Chun family house in 24. Detailed research and historical accuracy characterise the title, particularly in stories concerning the day-to-day lives of those occupying submarines (32) or the biographical tales featuring Custer, Grant, Washington and others. It's also apparent in the Civil War issues (31 and 35), which depart from the template to encompass wider themes. 22–32 can be ranked among the best comics ever published, each containing four superbly written and illustrated stories. The often reprinted 'Corpse on the Imjin' (25) is a masterpiece and typifies Kurtzman's editorial approach to war stories. During the Korean War a GI sitting on the riverbank notices a corpse floating down the Imjin and, as he begins his lunch, begins to speculate on how the person died. The soldier is then ambushed by a Korean, and, having laid his rifle to one side, becomes involved in desperate hand-to-hand combat. Emerging victorious, the GI staggers away as the story comes full circle with his assailant now floating down the river.

Initially successful enough to spawn a companion title, *Frontline Combat*, sales eventually didn't match the quality. With 36 the format revived the original concept of an adventure comic under the editorial aegis of John Severin, switching the title to *The New Two-Fisted Tales* in recognition of the change. The attention to detail characterising earlier issues was absent under chief writer Colin Dawkins, who preferred a rollicking good yarn. 36–39 certainly aren't bad, in fact 36 is very good, but neither do they match the war era. Kurtzman was back for the final two issues, which stuck to the adventure theme and contain some great artwork, but, again, don't match the earlier material, though they provide a template for the later EC title *Valor*.

All numbering refers to the original EC publications, which are being sequentially reprinted by Russ Cochran. As any issue of *Two-Fisted Tales* stands alone, you're encouraged to sample affordable reproductions of what are among the best regular comics ever produced.~WJ
Recommended: 22–36
Collection: Two Fisted Tales (18–41)

The New TWO-FISTED TALES
EC/Dark Horse: *1 issue 1993*

It was a worthwhile idea to create a new version of what was arguably Harvey Kurtzman's finest achievement. Sadly, he seems to have had little to do with the day-to-day editorial duties, and he died before the comic was published. While the stories are fine, the artwork for the new material would never have been acceptable to Kurtzman in the 1950s.~FP

TWO GUN KID
Marvel: *10 issues 1948–1949, 49 issues (11–59) 1953–1961, 33 issues (60–92) 1962–1968, 44 issues (93–136) 1970–1977, 2-issue microseries ('The Sunset Riders') 1995*

Lawyer Matt Hawk secretly keeps law and order in the Wild West of the 1870s as the Two Gun Kid. While notable artists such as Jack Davis, Jack Kirby, John Severin and Al Williamson worked on the title during the 1940s and 1950s, only Kirby gave anything resembling his best, and the stories are identikit Westerns with little resonance once the comics are closed. Stan Lee and Kirby revamped the masked man in 1962, giving him a revised origin in 60 and an extraordinary sidekick named Boom Boom four issues later. The secret-identity twist and humorous touches made this entertaining reading throughout the 1960s, with the mid-period team of Steve Skeates and Dick Ayers producing the most noteworthy stories. From 99 onwards it's reprints all the way.

There'd been significant changes to Two Gun Kid between the last original story in his title and the 1995 tale. In *Avengers* 142, Two Gun met the superheroes from the future, initially teaming with Hawkeye in the 1870s and then spending some time in the present day before eventually returning back where he belonged. The microseries takes the interesting idea of Matt Hawk being his own murderer as Two Gun Kid, effectively destroying both his identities. Teaming with a Native American, a Canadian spy and a samurai, Two Gun has to stop a potential international incident sparking a global war in the 1890s. Nicely designed and decently created, it's a shame the cover price was extortionate.~SW/WJ

2000AD
Eagle: *6-issue miniseries 1985, 4 issues 1986*
Quality: *22 issues (5–26 2000AD Presents) 1986–1988, 28 issues (27–54 2000AD Showcase) 1988–1990*
Fleetway/Quality: *15 issues 1991–1992*

With their reprints of British weekly *2000AD*, Eagle got off to a good start, testing the waters with a 'mega-series' that featured Judge Dredd, D.R. and Quinch and Strontium Dog. The Dredd tales are by John Wagner and Ron Smith, who manages some of Brian Bolland's detail while retaining the looseness of Mike McMahon, though overall his layouts are too static. Wagner includes the usual mix of humour and action in 'The Black Plague' (1, 2) (mutant spiders in the Cursed Earth) and Pirates of the Black Atlantic (5, 6). Alan Grant and Carlos Ezquerra send Johnny Alpha, Strontium Dog on a mission to bring back Adolf Hitler for trial (3–6), which about sums up the sophistication on show here. Fun, but neither of the creators are at their best. 1–5 feature Alan Moore and Alan Davis' bad boys D.R. and Quinch. These hooligans seem to ruin pretty much everything around them in their quest for fame and fortune, but it's very pretty and very funny.

The regular series, keeping the same title initially, dropped Dredd and Strontium Dog, who had their own titles, and added Judge Anderson of Psi Division, beginning with a rematch against her old nemesis, Judge Death (1–6), and Skizz, Alan Moore's ET in Birmingham (1–8). Anderson gives writers Wagner and Grant more room for characterisation and she's a good, strong lead. Jim Baikie draws a scratchy Skizz and does a good job but it's not Moore at his best. The transposition to England allows some satirical digs at Thatcher's government, but it doesn't come across as a fresh approach to the subject. D.R. and Quinch last a couple of issues (and return briefly for 12) but the title is otherwise reliant on Tharg's Future Shocks for light relief (this does, however, include an early Grant Morrison piece in 13). With 7, the page-count increased. The next big mistake was adding Dan Dare. Written by Gerry Finlay-Day and drawn by Dave Gibbons, it's not good. Finlay-Day also wrote Harry Twenty on the High Rock, drawn by Davis, which is an unconvincing escape-from-prison plot, set in space. Judge Anderson appears again for a run-of-the-mill story of demonic possession (9–12), with art again by Brett Ewins, which has its moments. Strontium Dog is recalled for an extended story-line while Dan Dare and Harry Twenty lumber on, until by the time Zenith begins (31) we're left with a number of long-running strips of little merit: Return To Armageddon is about the discovery of a frozen planet that was once Hell; Inferno, featuring Harlem's Heroes, is a Rollerball rip-off; Meltdown Man features an ex-SAS sergeant blown by a nuclear explosion into an alternate universe in which animals have been engineered into human forms. They all suffer from poor pacing and quickly become tedious.

Zenith, by Grant Morrison and Steve Yeowell, is a post-*Watchmen*, post-*Miracleman* attempt to do serious superheroes and is okay as these things go, but it's highly overrated and doesn't impress. The Quality issues are poorly printed on cheap paper. After S.Q.P. Inc. starts to appear in the credits there are no dates (bearing in mind that issue 5 is dated 1985 according to the indicia) on any of the issues and very little by way of editorial content. In the final issue, which concludes Meltdown Man, the Mean Arena story ends without explanation, apparently mid-episode.

The final attempt to reprint from *2000AD* in a regular series is on expensive paper and in colour to show off the painted artwork. Rather than cover several characters it concentrates on one main story with various one-off back-ups. It begins with 'Below Zero', by John Brosnan and Kev Hopgood, and features Zero City's bionic taxi-driver, Tanner, in a case involving frozen bodies but wandering minds. It ends with the ABC Warriors' Khronicles of Khaos, in which Kevin Walker's painted artwork is surprisingly effective. However, there's still no editorial content or dates.~NF

Recommended: Miniseries 1–6, 1–4
Collections: D.R. and Quinch's Guide To Life (miniseries 1–5, 1–4), *Zenith* Vol 1 (31–38), Vol 2 (39–45)

2001: A Space Odyssey

Marvel: *Treasury Edition 1976, 10 issues 1976–1977*

Stanley Kubrick and Arthur C. Clarke's 1968 film brought sophisticated musings on the space race, alien encounters, and the meaning of life itself to science-fiction cinema. Jack Kirby's Treasury Special film adaptation (eight years late!) was, in its writing, a satisfying blend of the movie and Clarke's novelisation. On the visual side, Kirby let *2001* down badly. His dynamic art did not adapt well to the cool, detached story, and the legendary 'trip' sequence is particularly badly rendered. Crude inking and big Treasury-size pages didn't help.

In the film a mysterious, black, alien monolith guides evolution from man's ape-like ancestor to spacefaring astronaut, and beyond, as one man is evolved into a super-being resembling a foetus. At the end, this god-like creature apparently hovers above Earth, ready to judge humanity. Kirby has the New Seed, as he called it, orbiting some other planet, ready to colonise it and start a new race. In 1–4 he shows several more New Seeds being created, robbing the notion of its impact. The spear, shamanic religion, the wheel etc., are given to prehistoric humans by the Monolith, while in parallel stories their astronaut descendants become New Seeds. With good Kirby/Royer art, and action-packed stories well suited to his style, Kirby is however open to accusations that he trivialised the film's themes. One might equally say he exposed them for the tosh they were. 7 actually shows a New Seed travelling

the universe and creating new life, though all it does is finish off any dignity the idea had left in it. 8–10 are worse, launching a new robotic Marvel superhero, Machine Man, here called Mister Machine. Can a machine have a soul? You bet he can, especially if he's touched by that ol' black Monolith magic.~GL

2001 NIGHTS

Viz: *10-issue limited series 1990–1991*

A comic deserving the term 'epic' as mankind journeys to the furthest reaches of the universe to gradually colonise the stars. The title harks back to both *2001: A Space Odyssey* and the *Arabian Nights* format of vignettes: together they're used to tell the story of how mankind pushed further into space. It's a wide-reaching and complex science-fiction saga that initially seems disjointed and somewhat ethereal, but it rewards careful reading when the pieces start falling together with 3. The stories thereafter show glimpses of continuing progress. Yukinobu Hoshino's art is astounding, but his tendency to dwell on the technical aspects denies the warmth that's definitely there. 6 is probably the best sample, as humanity discovers there are forces of nature it can't control, but 8's heart-wrenching tale of love's longevity is the best single chapter.~FP

Recommended: 8

TYPHOID

Marvel: *4-issue miniseries 1995–1996*

Daredevil's foe Typhoid Mary manifests multiple personalities. While Mary Walker, detective, investigates the murder of prostitutes, Typhoid has a more direct manner of looking into the situation. Simultaneously the third personality is a shy artist. Complicating the plot are two film students who want her to star in a movie investigating what turns people into killers. That Ann Nocenti and John Van Fleet are attempting something out of the ordinary is to be commended. This aspires to be more than a simple punch-'em-up, but peel away the affectation and obfuscation and there's a very little left. A triumph of style over content.~WJ

TYRANT

Spiderbaby Graphix: *4 issues + 1994 to date*

Steve Bissette's beautifully detailed but extremely slow-moving dinosaur adventure. Every fern, every twig, every drop of moisture is beautifully delineated as Bissette recreates antediluvian landscapes. As the second-best living dinosaur artist (Bill Stout still holds the crown), Bissette is the best person to tackle this epic history, but the real question is, can anyone tackle it entertainingly?~FJ

ULTRAFORCE

Malibu: *11 issues (0–10) 1994–1995*
Malibu/Marvel: *16 issues (Infinity–15) 1995–1996*

The zero issue reprints a two-part preview that ran in *Wizard* magazine. Written by Gerard Jones and drawn by George Perez, it ought to have been a promising team comic, but the selection of members and the first villain, Atalon (from an underground kingdom), didn't bode well. Ghoul, Prototype, Topaz and Hardcase might have worked but Contrary, Pixx and Prime, with the continual arguments that they brought and Contrary's hidden agenda, were just so dull that readers were more likely to be asleep than paying attention to the action. It didn't help either that it took six issues to be resolved, by which time Pixx was dead and Atalon, plan awry, still droning on.

7 was a Ghoul solo story by guest creators Kanalz, Ulm and Erwin, while 8–10 were part of the countdown to 'Black September', which merged the Marvel universe with the Ultraverse and was pretty much the death knell for the latter as its writers, attracted by independence and a new world with which to work, mostly found themselves in the event with no further control of the characters. However much nostalgia there might be in seeing Perez back on the Avengers (8), *Ultraforce* struggled for over a year before finding a settled creative team. 10 isn't even the end of a story, continuing as it does into *Ultraforce/Avengers* Prelude, *Avengers/Ultraforce* and *Ultraforce/Avengers*.

The Infinity issue preceding the second series is a 'Black September' tie-in with an alternate version of the Avengers; it is otherwise forgettable. The new series proper was started by Warren Ellis and drawn by Steve Butler (1–3). After a fill-in fourth issue, Ellis and Edginton (5–7), then Abnett and Edginton (8, 9), paved the way for Len Wein (10 on). Now led by the Black Knight and government-sanctioned, the team gained a headquarters but, as far as characterisation went, nobody seemed to know who was going to be in the team anymore. The Black Knight himself kicked most of them out for not being nice enough and then managed to

find a way back to the Marvel Universe just as Hardcase found his own way back, only to sacrifice himself to save the lives of his team-mates in the final issue.

If the writers weren't really putting their best into it, it was a minor miracle to get the same artist one issue after another until those journeymen the Deodato Studios came on board with Wein. Two back-up strips, though short, are worth mentioning: 'A Lonely Place' (10), featuring Lament, drawn by the Kelley Jones-influenced Kyle Hotz, and a Ghoul story, drawn by The Pander Brothers (11) – but don't go out of your way for them. All in all, a terrible waste of effort that serves as a damning indictment of Marvel's misuse of the Ultraverse.~NF

ULTRAFORCE/SPIDER-MAN

Malibu: *1 issue (1A) 1996*

Written by Marv Wolfman but drawn by committee. Spider-Man and the Green Goblin team with Ultraforce to try to prevent their two worlds declaring war on each other as events are manipulated by a mysterious, pointy-fingered alien. Oh dear.~NF

ULTRAGIRL

Marvel: *3-issue miniseries 1996–1997*

It's finally Marvel's turn to join the grim-and-gritty backlash with this cross between *Gen13* and *Impulse*. Suzy Sherman, trying to get a modelling job in Los Angeles, is attacked by a Sentinel that claims she's both mutant and alien (specifically Kree). In a nice touch, Suzy beats the robot and then dismantles everything but the head so that she has someone to talk to about what's happening. Written by Barbara Kesel, with artwork by Leonard Kirk and Bob Almond, it could become a cult comic.~NF

UNCANNY ORIGINS

Marvel: *4 issues + 1996 to date*

An interesting approach is taken in representing the origins of Marvel's superheroes by having them drawn in appealing cartoony fashion by Dave Hoover, in a low-priced package. For those who care, it's useful to have the entire origins of Cyclops (1), Quicksilver (2) and Angel (3), previously detailed in bite-size chunks over several years, presented in their entirety. With Firelord in 4, thus far, commendably, more obscure characters have been spotlighted in the early issues. All in all a worthwhile title for continuity completists.~WJ

UNCANNY TALES
Marvel: *12 issues 1973–1975*

Yet another title recirculating Marvel's 1950s horror short stories. During the period when this was being published bi-monthly Marvel had another seven similar titles on the go. That they all sold defies belief.~FP

THE UNCENSORED MOUSE
Eternity: *2 issues*

Early 1930s Mickey Mouse daily newspaper strips by Floyd Gottfriedson portraying a character yet to metamorphose into the wholesome corporate symbol, and therefore never previously reprinted.~FP

UNCLE SCROOGE
Dell: *39 issues 1952–1962*
Gold Key: *134 issues (40–173) 1962–1980*
Whitman: *36 issues (174–209) 1980–1983*
Gladstone: *33 issues (210–242) 1986–1989*
Disney: *38 issues (243–280) 1990–1993*
Gladstone: *21 issues + (281–301) 1993 to date*

In terms of quality Carl Barks's *Uncle Scrooge* stories stand alongside *Asterix* and *Tintin* as the greatest children's comics. In common with the European strips, Scrooge stories work almost instinctively on two levels, appealing to children with stories opening the imagination and by the simplicity and humour of the artwork, and additionally to adults with impeccable plotting, research and a repertoire of fine comic touches. Unlike *Tintin* and *Asterix*, there's a wealth of material, but as Scrooge is corporate property he's therefore been sullied by lesser hands until more recently being rescued by the more than capable Don Rosa.

Scrooge is fabulously wealthy, yet resents spending a dime more than he has to unless his status as the world's richest duck is challenged. He keeps his money in a giant structure known as the money bin, through which he dives like a porpoise and burrows like a gopher in a memorable sequence of creative inspiration which opened *Scrooge*'s first issue. Underneath the miserly front, though, Scrooge has a better nature, and one that's readily appealed to. Despite the often-repeated work ethic, materialism is a central theme to Barks's Scrooge, yet the most fondly recalled aspects of his stories are the exotic locations. Scrooge, often accompanied by Donald Duck and nephews Huey, Dewey and Louie, travels the globe, if not in search of some fabulous treasure, then for a way of increasing his fortune by a business opportunity or other means.

Scrooge débuted in 1947's *Four Color* 178, a Donald Duck Christmas tale, and proved popular enough to return again and again. His first solo outing was 1952's *Only A Poor Old Man'* in *Four Color* 386 (reprinted in 1965 as *Uncle Scrooge and Donald Duck*), followed by *Four Color* 456 and 495. The series title *Four Color* only appears in the indicia, and it's an *Uncle Scrooge* logo on the cover, so these issues are commonly referred to as *Uncle Scrooge* 1–3. Scrooge's own title picks up the numbering with 4. Barks writes and draws every issue to 70 (although 67 is the first reprint, of 10), and writes 71, and they're a great run. A 1995 comic titled *Uncle Scrooge In Arabia* reprints 'The Mines Of King Solomon' from 19, as good an example as any of how Barks excels. Scrooge decides to inspect his properties throughout the world, accompanied by Donald and by Huey, Dewey and Louie, who've recently been practising their bird and animal calls for the Junior Woodchucks. The combined tickets stack up to Donald's shoulders. Assorted attempts at attracting wildlife go comically wrong, and Scrooge learns the possible location of the legendary lost diamond mines of King Solomon. Unfortunately local gangsters have arrived first, and Scrooge and Co. must outwit them, eventually succeeding by surrendering portions of the tickets to Arab ruffians who've always wanted to travel. Comedy, action, adventure, excellent art and an unexpected ending add up to a great story, and Barks pulled this off almost every issue. The assorted schemes of the criminal Beagle Boys to separate Scrooge from his wealth, and of the sorceress Magica De Spell to acquire the first dime Scrooge ever earned, occupy a great portion of later Barks issues. Magica believes possession of the dime will spark her good fortunes, and the Beagle Boys are just out to steal.

Barks retired in 1966, and his replacements were unable to capture the spirit or scope of his stories. Between 1970 and 1979 *Uncle Scrooge* consisted almost entirely of Barks reprints before Gold Key and later Whitman began running stories originally prepared for the European market, along with the occasional reprint. The European stories are technically adept, but concentrate more on Scrooge's wealth than any other facet of his character or the exotic adventure tales that continue to thrill, although Romano Scarpa occasionally manages to surprise. The Barks stories have now all been reprinted in later issues, most in several. Dell marked the splash page of each story with the original issue number, so it's easy to piece together a run without having to pay premium prices. Issue 16's 'Back To Long Ago', for instance, has been reprinted in 103, 177 and 279.

Gladstone, who'd had some success producing expensive hardbound editions of

Barks's work, inherited the Disney licence in 1986. They immediately dispensed with five decades of anonymity by running credits. More significantly, they began commissioning new material from American creators, a practice continued for Disney's short run. William Van Horn is good, but Don Rosa is the spiritual heir of Carl Barks. Rosa fashions his stories to the Barks template, but isn't a mere copyist. Even when drawing heavily on Barks's work for his excellent 'Life and Times of Scrooge McDuck' (285–297) Rosa throws in his own touches. There are plenty of background visual gags, his new characters are memorable, and he's confident enough to show a developing Scrooge rather then presenting the familiar character from day one. Rosa's other stories, here and in the other Disney duck titles, are all worth finding. The only sadness is that he's not as prolific as Barks.~FP

Recommended: 1–13, 15–17, 19–23, 25–30, 32–40, 42–52, 54–57, 59, 62–66, 69–71, 219, 220, 224, 235, 261, 262, 276, 285–297.

Collections: Carl Barks Library Vol 4 & 5 (1–71), *Disney Comics Album* 2, 6 (6, 45), *Gladstone Albums* 1(19), 4 (2), 6 (13), 11 (4), 14 (21), 20 (*Four Color* 386), 24 (17, 31), 28 (224, 226, + *Uncle Scrooge Adventures* 5), *Gladstone Giant Special* 2 (5), 4 (15, 27, 61, 219), 6 (36, 38, 43, 48, 50), *The Life and Times of Scrooge McDuck* 1 (285–287), 2 (288–290), 3 (291–293), 4 (294–296), *Uncle Scrooge Adventures* (proposed fifty-six-volume set reprinting all Carl Barks's *Uncle Scrooge* stories in chronological order), *Uncle Scrooge His Life & Times* (2, 3, 6, 7, 9, 13, 15, 18, 29, 48, 65)

UNCLE SCROOGE ADVENTURES
Gladstone: *40 issues + 1987–1990 (1–21), 1993 to date*

Vintage Carl Barks *Uncle Scrooge* stories occupy the majority of issues, with European reprints filling most of the rest. That alone would make for a quality package, but the occasional new stories by Don Rosa are the highlights. In 5 he follows up on Barks's story of how Scrooge made his fortune ('Back To The Klondike' from *Uncle Scrooge* 2), dropping back in on the characters from that story, and also contributing stories to 12 and 27. An even bigger coup, though, is 'Horsing Around With History', a new Carl Barks script illustrated by William Van Horn in 33. Containing all the elements of the classic Barks, that issue also reprints *Uncle Scrooge* 1.~FP
Recommended: 5, 12, 27, 33

Walt Disney's UNCLE SCROOGE GOES TO DISNEYLAND
Dell: *1 issue 1957*
Gladstone: *1 issue 1985*

Two years after Disneyland opened Dell published this one-shot anthology featuring some odd teamings of Disney characters. Mickey Mouse and Goofy, and Donald Duck with Huey, Dewey and Louie are straightforward, but how about Daisy Duck alongside Alice from Wonderland, or Pinocchio with Pluto and Mickey's nephews Morty and Ferdy? Carl Barks drew a fine twenty-pager pairing Uncle Scrooge with Gyro Gearloose, but this is more a curiosity than a must-have. The Gladstone issue reprints the Dell comic.~FP

Andrew Vacchss' UNDERGROUND
Dark Horse: *4-issue miniseries 1993–1994*

In common with the other Dark Horse / Andrew Vacchss series *Hard Looks*, to call this anthology bleak would be an understatement. Reading just a few of the stories will cause all but the sturdiest to reach for the paracetamol. The premise evolves around an undefined future where society exists in a warren-like system of tunnels, and we're given glimpses into the dystopian life below. Each chapter contributes to a profile, never rushing expectations, and there's a high proportion of illustrated text. It's often grim and deeply depressing: morbid curiosity is a prime factor in dragging the reader in. Highlights include Al Davison's story of physical and emotional cripples banding together to survive and help a violent criminal escape his own fears (3), and 4's 'Phreak'. It's by John Weeks and Ted Naifeh in full Barry Windsor-Smith mode. Worth a gander.~TP
Recommended: 3

UNDERSEA AGENT
Tower: *6 issues 1966–1967*

The adventures of Davy Jones (!) Undersea Agent weren't the highspot of Tower's short life. Most of the plots were idiotic, and they weren't helped by Ray Bailey's art, which was, with few exceptions, dull. The bright spots were the Gil Kane-drawn stories in 3–6.~SW

UNDERWATER
Drawn and Quarterly: *6 issues + 1994 to date*

Underwater doesn't immediately appear to make sense. By following the pictures, the reader can tell that a woman is giving birth, but any language that appears is gobbledy-gook, a mixture of nonsense words and odd sounds. As the story progresses it becomes clear that you're experiencing the world through the eyes and ears of the woman's new-born twins, and nothing makes sense because they don't yet understand it. The dialogue starts to become clearer as the babies start to recognise more words, one or two to start with, more as the series goes on, and the twins understand each other more than they do the adults, who don't always understand them either. Chester Brown's idea is interesting and nicely presented, but it's really only a one-issue joke and the continued package isn't all satisfying, especially in such small doses. All but issue 1 also contains Brown's adaptations of Bible stories; 4 has a short piece on his thoughts regarding the nature of schizophrenia.~JC

UNDERWORLD
DC: *4-issue miniseries 1987–1988*
Each issue is a separate story in the lives of a group of New York cops. The stories are simple – chasing pickpockets, talking a potential suicide off a ledge – but Robert Loren Fleming's writing makes them rich, and Ernie Colon's artwork does them justice and more. This deserves another series or seven.~FC
Recommended: 1–4

UNDERWORLD Unleashed
DC: *3-issue miniseries 1995*
The devil, Neron, tempts DC's supervillains in 1 and sends them off, powers enhanced, to battle throughout DC's titles. 2 sees the Trickster, a longtime Flash villain, engineer the defeat of Lex Luthor, The Joker, Polaris, Circe and Abra Kadabra, whom Neron has sidetracked into thinking that they will be his lieutenants in his new world. Meanwhile, Neron himself is off trying to tempt the superheroes – with some success. The final issue reveals Neron's real plan, which is only thwarted by a group of heroes invading Neron's Hell. Mark Waid has actually produced a clever story that, though contrived (and rather unappealing), at least makes better use of a large number of heroes than most of these crossovers. The artwork by Howard Porter and Dan Green is, unfortunately, rather stiff and gimmicky.~NF

UNEARTHLY SPECTACULARS
Harvey: *3 issues 1965–1967*
The editorial staff appear to have been thrashing around in the dark to produce this very strange anthology, which mixes the truly inane with some excellent material. Cover stars Jack Quick Frost (a gimmicky Iceman) and Tiger Boy are both dreadful. The latter has to be seen to be believed, having a human head on a tiger's body, but that's not all: he's also the robot Steelman and stretchy Rubberman. It's hard to believe the erudite Gil Kane was involved with this fiasco. 'Clawfang', drawn by Al Williamson, is better, but the highlights are Wally Wood, again proving he's without peer when it comes to science-fiction adventure in 2's excellent 'Earthman' and then turning his hand to superhero spoof with Miracles Inc. Joe Orlando takes on a longer Miracles Inc story in 3, which also has a nice Archie Goodwin and Reed Crandall story and the preposterous 'Never Say "no" To Dr Yes'.~WJ
Recommended: 2, 3

UNEEDA Comix
Print Mint: *One-shot 1970*
Coming at the end of R. Crumb's hippie period, *Uneeda* reflects his growing lack of interest in the counterculture. The centrepiece, 'Honeybunch Kominsky, The Drug Crazed Runaway', is a very unconvincing procession of counterculture clichés that even seems to have bored Crumb. Rounding out the comic are a short Mr Natural strip and a few Bo Bo Bolinsky shorts that have far more power (even poetry) than the lead strip. Middling Crumb.~DAR

Tales Of The UNEXPECTED
DC: *104 issues 1955–1968*
The 1955 introduction of The Comics Code Authority, whose stringent guidelines had to be observed in order to obtain the parent-assuaging stamp of approval, resulted in the collapse or disembowelling of many early 1950s horror titles. DC stepped into the gap with several Comics Code-approved anthologies. The predominantly science-fiction-flavoured stories here were by editor Jack Schiff's crew of writers, including Ed Herron, Otto Binder, Jack Miller and Ed Hamilton, with fine if conservative artwork from the likes of Ruben Moreira, Bill Ely, Mort Meskin, Nick Cardy, Bernard Bailey and, in some early issues, Jack Kirby.

With August 1959's 40 the title became home to Herron and artist Bob Brown's 'Guardian of the Space Lanes' – the Space Ranger who had débuted in *Showcase* 15–16 the previous year. The Ranger was Rick Starr, who patrolled in his rocket ship The Solar King in a yellow and red outfit complete with salad-bowl helmet. He operated out of a secret asteroid base with the assistance of his blonde 'Girl Friday', Myra Mason, and a little pink shapeshifter called Cryll, who resembled nothing more than a walking pair of testicles. The stories managed a drab mix of private eye and Western lawman in outer space. The Ranger ran until 88 in 1964, when the title was shaken up by Schiff, with the story content becoming more farcical, typified by the new feature, a wish-fulfilling cloud known as 'The Green Glob'. One of DC's obscurest heroes, Automan, a sentient bop-talking robot, also appeared in 91, 94 and 97, drawn by Bill Ely. In 1968 the title continued as simply *Unexpected*.~SW

UNEXPECTED
DC: *118 issues (105–222) 1968–1982*
Originally titled *Tales of the Unexpected*, this continued the numbering and, initially, the somewhat half-baked mystery stories. The very uninspired Johnny Peril (106–117) and the very odd Mad Mod Witch occupied the comic, but the first items of any note were a few early Berni Wrightson strips (116, 119, 121, 128). By 120 the title had become a typical DC horror

comic, but with far fewer contributors than others, relying on George Kashdan, Carl Wessler and editor Murray Boltinoff for almost all its stories, and George Tuska and Jerry Grandinetti for most of its art. Consequently, though never less than professional, *Unexpected* never lived up to its name.

Packed with Filipino artists, 140–165 are the best of the run, with the hundred-pagers (157–162) the ideal jumping-on point. Along with Alfredo Alcala and Rico Rival, Nestor Redondo drew some nice strips (133, 155, 195), as did token non-Filipinos Lee Elias and Ralph Reese (145). The single best story was a swamp-based Michael Fleisher/Alex Nino tale in 152, and Nino had other strips in 159 and 162.

The last few years were a very mixed bag, with the occasional delight (such as lovely Noly Panaligan jobs in 186, 187, 189 and 214) surfacing among much grade Z hackery. 189–195 were dollar comics and amongst the eighty pages of new strips were a few nice surprises from Vincente Alcazar (189, 191), Marshall Rogers (191) and Doug Wildey (193). They also featured material commissioned for the cancelled *House of Secrets*, and *Witching Hour* and *Doorway To Nightmare* stories in 190, 192, 194 and 195, the last of which, *Deadly Homecoming*, by Denny O'Neil and Johnny Craig, was actually quite good. With 200 Mike Barr and original artist Jack Sparling revived Johnny Peril, though only the very brave are advised to sample it. Far more exciting was some lovely artwork by the hopelessly obscure Arthur Geroche in 202. In retrospect the most unexpected thing about this comic was how it managed to outlive most of its competition.~DAR

Recommended: 152, 157–162, 186, 187, 189, 191, 195, 202, 214

UNICORN ISLE

WaRP: *4 issues, 1986–1987*
Apple: *1 issue (5) 1987*

It was supposed to run to twelve issues so didn't even get halfway, but is still worth a look if you like lively, imaginative fantasy. The people of Unicorn Isle have custody of the two sacred unicorns, the last of their kind. But some baddies want the power of the unicorns, manage to abduct one, and the young twins Nils and Nola are sent on the rescue mission. Your standard soft-fantasy quest, but Lee Marrs brings a fresh touch to the writing, making the unicorns distant and strange and the other characters thoroughly human. The black and white artwork is suitably otherworldly (and particularly strong on costume), though the story-telling tends to fall apart during the action sequences. Not perfect, but a story that deserves to be finished.~FC

Recommended: 1–5

UNION

Image: *4-issue miniseries 1993, 9 issues (0–8) 1995–1996*

Written by Mike Heisler and drawn by Mark Texeira, the Union miniseries establishes the character on Earth after he's accidentally passed through a dimensional gate during a battle with the Directorate. As a Protectorate soldier, and therefore at war with the Directorate, Union confronts a group of his enemies, which results in the destruction of a whole town and his acceptance as a hero by Stormwatch. Aided by a woman called Jill, he then clashes with a few villains before learning from his old girl-friend that he may have ended the war. Believing himself responsible for the loss of a town, he decides to stay on Earth. *Union* 0, published as a precursor to the first regular series, provided a background to the war between the Protectorate and the Directorate and explained Union's appearance on Earth. Texeira's style was perhaps too influenced by Neal Adams, and for the regular series Ryan Benjamin (1–3) and Pop Mhan (4–8) were brought on board. Easier on the eye and more attuned to the Homage Studio house style, it's rather uninspired but in keeping with the superheroic direction the title took. Of note, Union meets Savage Dragon in issue 3 of the second series and Majestic in 4 (as part of the 'Wildstorm Rising' crossover). 5 and 6 are the best of the series, as Union is kidnapped into a parallel world to be its champion and meets an alternate Fairchild (from *Gen13*).~NF

UNITY

Valiant: *2 issues (0–1) 1992*

These issues bookended the first big crossover story involving all Valiant's then fledgeling line of titles. Each title contained two chapters of an eighteen-chapter ongoing crossover. Read in its entirety it's a well plotted, if sometimes meandering, story of every major Valiant character involved in the machinations of The Mother God. She originated in the Solar series, and here unites past, present and future in a land out of time. Barry Windsor-Smith illustrates, and although these issues won't make much sense on their own the larger picture is worth a look. Not all company crossover sagas are bad.~WJ

Collection: Unity vol 1 (*Unity* 0, *Eternal Warrior* 1, *Archer And Armstrong* 1, *Magnus* 15, *X-O* 6), vol 2 (*Shadowman* 4, *Rai* 5, *Harbinger* 8, *Solar* 12), vol 3 (*Eternal Warrior* 2, *Archer And Armstrong* 2, *Magnus* 16, *X-O* 7), vol 4 (*Shadowman* 4, *Rai* 6, *Harbinger* 9, *Solar* 13, *Unity* 1)

UNKNOWN SOLDIER

DC: *Series one 64 issues (205–268) 1977–1982, series two 12 issues 1988–1989*

This anonymous allied agent with the bandaged head finally inherited his own title when *Star-Spangled War Stories* was renamed in 1977, having starred there since 151. A watered-down World War II version of G8, the famous pulp master of disguise and espionage, the Soldier had been facially disfigured in the Philippines by a hand grenade that also killed his brother, Harry. Thereafter, the 'Immortal GI' pledged to stay officially dead, operating on the principle that 'one man in a pivotal position can exert an influence on hundreds, even thousands, of others'. His wartime impersonations had settled into something of a rut by the late 1970s. Filipino artist Gerry Talaoc, aided by veteran war artist Dick Ayers for much of the title's run, reduced the Soldier to a hackneyed cartoon character, and scripter Bob Haney's stories were definitely off the boil. The title also featured other DC war series, including Robert Kanigher's 'Enemy Ace', drawn here by John Severin, (251–253, 260, 261, 265–267), and an elegant interpretation of 'Captain Fear' by David Michelinie and Walt Simonson in 254–256, as well as many single stories by young artists, including Frank Miller in 219.

After an absence of six years, our redefined bandaged hero returns for a twelve-issue series in 1988, courtesy of Jim Owsley and artist Phil Gascoine. The first two issues contain, in flashbacks, the Soldier's childhood and the story of how he virtually became immortal. The series begins in the 1970s and ends in the late 1980s, with each issue involving the Soldier in an international conflict of the time. Cambodia 1970 is the setting for 1, the US Embassy in Iran in 1977 is featured in 2, and for 3 in 1982 it's off to Afghanistan, and so on. It misses the Gulf War by two years, or you can be certain that would've featured too. It's a very well produced series with entertaining period pieces, which sadly highlights how little peace there's been in the world for the past few decades. It's interesting to see the Soldier's supporting cast grow older, while he remains young. We even apparently meet his grown-up daughter in 10. His first assignment is recalled in 6, which particularly stands out as it delves deeper into his origin. A worthy action and espionage successor to the earlier series. The title was revived again in early 1997 under the Vertigo imprint.~SW/HY
Recommended: 6

UNKNOWN WORLDS
ACG: *57 issues 1960–1967*

What can one say about a comic whose cover for 28 boasted '4329 Gasps'? *Unknown Worlds* was ACG's third mystery anthology of the 1960s and as such resembled all their others content-wise. No one wrote stories quite like Richard E. Hughes (some might add 'thank goodness'). The hokey 'O. Henry on medication' flavour of

Hughes' science fiction and mystery is, admittedly, an acquired taste. Nevertheless, his work does have an undeniable old-fashioned charm. By the early 1960s ACG had evolved a functional mythos for its fantasy tales, centred on an all-green afterlife called The Unknown. Familiar to regular readers of *Adventures Into The Unknown* and *Forbidden Worlds*, this realm was inhabited by various light green ghosts, objects and supernatural entities. The ACG milieu is, in essence, a mixture of these verdant idiosyncrasies with the sentimental and the downright wacky.

Despite authors such as Shane O'Shea, Zev Zimmer, Ace Aquila, Lafcadio Lee and Kurato Osaki getting story bylines, everything was in fact written by Hughes. Once you know this, the mini author/artist portraits that preface many of the early 1960s stories are particularly amusing. Highlights of the distinctly conservative artwork came courtesy of Ed Ashe, John Rosenberger, Pete Costanza, Paul Reinman, John Forte, Chic Stone and the incomparable Ogden Whitney. Later in the 1960s occasional stories by Johnny Craig (Jay Taycey) and Steve Ditko also cropped up. Several classic ACG stories appeared here, the most famous being 'The People Versus Hendricks' in 36, a courtroom drama involving artificial humans, romance, jealousy and murder. '1000 Years Ago... In 1962', in 20, was an alien invasion story with a difference and featured a guest appearance by ACG's oddest protagonist, Herbie Popnecker. Other well-received stories include 'Witch Boy' in 38, '100 Year Witch' in 43 and 'Goodbye Johnny' in 48. The further, less than inspiring, adventures of ACG's supernatural superspy John Force, Magic Agent, appeared in 35, 36, 48, 50, 52 and 54.~SW
Recommended: 20, 36, 38, 48

THE UNKNOWN WORLDS OF FRANK BRUNNER
Eclipse: *2 issues 1985*

Horror and sword-and-sorcery tales drawn by Frank Brunner during his Berni Wrightson phase. The stories are written by Brunner himself plus Nicola Cuti, Gerry Conway, Jan Strnad, Phil Seuling and Buddy Saunders, but none of them offer any surprises.~NF

UNKNOWN WORLDS OF SCIENCE FICTION
Marvel: *6 issues, 1 special 1975–1976*

One has to assume the marketing department vetoed the title *Largely Familiar Or Predictable Worlds Of Science Fiction*. In their attempt to carve a slice of the black and white anthology magazine market mined so well by Warren in the early 1970s, Marvel hired away Warren contributor Bruce Jones, who's responsible for writing approximately a third of the run, although the adaptations were cover-featured. In selecting and commissioning largely twist-ending stories the editors (and there are four credited by the final issue) resisted the opportunity to move on from an anthology formula which had been in place since the 1950s. There's nothing bad here, but there's nothing very good either. Artists of the calibre of Howard Chaykin, Neal Adams, Mike Kaluta and Gray Morrow are used among the more formularised selection of Filipino draughtsmen. The best issue is the first, which could pass for a Warren comic, with Wood, Torres, Williamson and even a Frazetta reprint.~WJ

THE UNSEEN HAND
Vertigo: *4-issue miniseries 1996*

Maybe this is too familiar territory, but Terry LaBan's script for a secret-society-who-run-the-world thriller is a let down. There's too little scepticism at work, as our student hero, Mike, accepts in a flash that his dying father isn't his 'real' father, and that the Bildenberg-like group of superfinanciers are out to get him, never considering that just because someone's shooting at him it doesn't mean they're automatically part of a worldwide conspiracy. LaBan writes like we can't handle anything very complicated, although there are some deft touches of student dialogue. Mike sets out to find his lost sister in Russia and, after falling foul of some rock'n'roll-obsessed militia crossing Serbia, stumbles upon a cult of White Russians who've built a new city under Moscow, where they're growing the foetus of Czar Nicholas III with the help of the midget, Siamese-twin descendant of Rasputin. When you put it all down on paper it sounds like a ridiculous piss-take. It's rather like that when you read it, too. Ilya illustrates this ludicrousness with aplomb, turning in clean, cartoony artwork and concentrating on getting expressions right. He is surprisingly well-suited to drawing panoramic scenes of urban life and destruction, although he falls back on a 1960s cliché for Mike's drug experience. Overall, very unsatisfying.~FJ

UNSUPERVISED EXISTENCE
Fantagraphics: *6 issues 1990–1992*

An infuriatingly inconsistent slice of bohemian life, with consistently excellent underground style cartooning from Terry LaBan. The primary cast are cab-driver Danny, who dreams of a writing career, his partner Suzy, who makes a career of indolence and staring into the middle distance, overweight performance artist Bob and the bisexual object of his unrequited love, Annadette. Intertwined stories of their lives switch back and forth, soap-opera style, over the first two issues, and while passing the time they're hardly compelling. A leap forward is achieved by cleaving Bob off from the remaining cast and sending him on a world tour. His naïvety and depression lead to some very funny moments, primarily 3's arrival in Greece and 5's Bob solo, the highlight of the run. Danny and Suzy also benefit from the extra attention, with some fine farcical concepts thrown into the Danny stories, particularly the idea of the cab-drivers' writing collective. Overall, though, the cast is too flawed and irritating to retain long-term interest, and freed from the shackles of continuity with *Cud* LaBan blossoms. The final two issues were conventional comic-size, while 1–4 were magazine-sized.~FP

Collections: International Bob (Bob stories from 1–6), *Love's Not A Three Dollar Fare* (remainder of 1–6)

UNTAMED LOVE
Fantagraphics: *One-shot 1987*

Collects several 1950s romance stories illustrated by Frank Frazetta at the height of his power. Outstandingly stupid stories, but lovely, glorious artwork.~HS

UNTOLD LEGEND OF BATMAN
DC: *3-issue miniseries 1980*

John Byrne drew the first issues, with Jim Aparo concluding the series. This is a collection of scenes from earlier Batman comics, and despite highlighting the amazing number of coincidences in the Batman legend it's a nice romp down memory lane, though it has an unconvincing framing plot from Len Wein.~DWC

URBAN LEGENDS
Dark Horse: *One-shot 1993*

This has since been superseded by *The Big Book Of Urban Legends*, containing most of the material plus plenty more besides, but it's nonetheless entertaining for all that. Plenty of artists who don't contribute to the Big Books are to be found here, including Peter Bagge, Matt Wagner and Art Adams. This was intended as a two-issue series, but only the first issue ever saw publication.~FP

URTH 4
Continuity: *4 issues 1989–1990*

An elemental supergroup consisting of, yes, you've guessed it, Urth, Ayre, Fyre and Watr, Urth 4 specialised in righting environmental wrongs. Beyond this quirk, though, it was a typical superhero title. The writing is absolute tosh, but the comic looks nice enough, courtesy of Trevor Von Eeden (1–3) and, amazingly, Ron Wilson in 4, with the inevitable visual tinkering from Neal Adams.~DAR

USAGENT

Marvel: *4-issue miniseries 1993*

Hoary superheroics from Mark Gruenwald, who once again tries to tie up loose threads in the Marvel universe. This time he pits the one-time successor to Captain America, USAgent, against a group of vigilantes calling themselves Scourge of the Underworld. Along the way he retells USAgent's origin, brings back an old hero and tries to make the title character seem a little more innovative. There has been no call for a second series.~NF

USAGI YOJIMBO

Fantagraphics: *1 Special 1986, 38 issues, 3 Specials 1987–1993*
Mirage: *16 issues (1–16) 1993–1995*
Dark Horse: *7 issues + 1996 to date*

Stan Sakai's rabbit bodyguard was first introduced in *Albedo* 2 and then had some adventures in *Critters* before a one-shot collected the early stories as a prelude to the regular series. Sakai's lettering on *Groo*, much praised by Mark Evanier in an introduction, would not, however, have prepared anyone for the quality of his story-telling.

Usagi is a ronin (masterless samurai), allowing Sakai the freedom of having his character wander through an anthropomorphic Japanese landscape that's full of mystery, intrigue and the occasional supernatural demon. There's obviously a heavy debt to Japanese Manga like *Lone Wolf And Cub*, both in the choreography of the sword fights and in the way that the background to many stories is based on specific Japanese traditions or professions. Sakai uses an underlying humour to lessen the brutality of death (of which there is a great deal), much as Kurosawa did in *Yojimbo*; he has an emotional awareness that allows the characters to be more than just stereotypes in another adventure strip. In a similar fashion, his artwork is composed of simple lines but never seems short of detail.

The story of Usagi's early life and the death of Lord Mifune, which led to his becoming a ronin, is told in flashback to the bounty-hunter Gennosuke (1–4). 'The Dragon Bellow Conspiracy' runs through 13–18, featuring all of the major characters so far. Tamakuro plots to seize the Shogunate and rival clans are drawn together to help prevent civil war. Tomoe, Lord Noriyuki's retainer, is an old friend of Usagi's and the romantic potential between them is one of the constants of the series. 'Blood Wings' (21–22) features the Komori Ninja, bat-like, flying and very dangerous, and 24 is called 'Lone Goat And Kid', a tribute, of course, as the Lone Goat is deceived into accepting the job of killing Usagi. 'Circles' (28–31) harks back to Usagi's youth and then switches to the present as Usagi helps an old friend, now married to the mother of his son. The colour specials feature

Tomoe's story (1), Tomoe and Usagi fighting a supernatural attempt on Lord Noriyuki's life (2), and have Tomoe rescuing Usagi from the spell of a fox-woman (3). Most of the Fantagraphics issues also had back-up strips by alumni of *Critters* and *Albedo*.

The Mirage series picks up where Fantagraphics left off, with Usagi and Gen still wandering together, but now in colour (by Tom Luth). 1–3 co-star the Teenage Mutant Ninja Turtles as Usagi meets Chizu, a devious woman who has plans to become leader of the Neko Ninja, old sparring partners of Usagi's. 'Slavers' (9–12) is the story of a renegade general, Fujii, whose outlaw band has enslaved a whole village. In freeing the villagers, Usagi has his swords stolen and sets out to track down Fujii. In 'Runaways' (13–14), a tale of Usagi's past, he has to escort Princess Kinuko to her wedding but political intrigues mean that the Neko Ninja have been hired to kill her. Left for dead, Usagi and Kinuko have to make their own way to safety on foot. It's a classic tale of impossible love. At this point, Mirage stopped publishing and Sakai, as had many others before him, found a new home at Dark Horse, though it meant a return to black and white. Chizu returns in 4 as the Komori and Neko Ninja vie for possession of a scroll that contains the secrets of gunpowder, and Usagi seems to have met his match in Nakamura Koji (7), who is really looking for a fight with Usagi's old teacher.

This is an intelligent adventure series, drawing heavily on Japanese and comic traditions but always individual and never short on ideas.~NF

Recommended: Fantagraphics 13–18, 28–31, 38, Colour Special 3, Mirage 4, 5, 13, 14, 16, Dark Horse 4, 6

Collections: *Usagi Yojimbo* vol 1 (*Albedo* & *Critters* stories), vol 2 (Fantagraphics 1–6), vol 3 (Fantagraphics 7–12), vol 4 (Fantagraphics 13–18), vol 5 (Fantagraphics 19–24), vol 6 (Fantagraphics 25–31)

U.S.1

Marvel: *12-issue limited series 1983–1984*

Universally derided at the time of publication, it now seems the last time anyone at Marvel apart from Peter David had any fun. Writer Al Milgrom packs in aliens, ghostly truckers, highwaymen, Germans with Zeppelins and down-to-earth redneck folk. His tongue is planted firmly in the vicinity of his cheek, and lead Ulysses Solomon Archer is so wholesome, Peter Parker is Richard Nixon in comparison. You're not getting Dostoevsky here, but it's nowhere near as bad as you've heard.~FP

V
DC: *18 issues 1985–1986*

V the TV series was a none too subtle Nazi analogy that had nice friendly humanoid aliens arriving on Earth offering technological advances in exchange for a few minerals, all the while plotting to take over. Furthermore, they were really grim, lizard-like creatures. Budget restrictions on the show made the latter aspect a surprise revelation, but lacking those restrictions and able to supply armies of lizards, the comic is surprisingly dull. Initially concentrating on the resistance movement, particularly the resilient Diana, *V* might appeal to those who enjoyed the TV show as kids on the basis that it can now be found in almost everyone's discount boxes.~FP

V FOR VENDETTA
DC: *10-issue limited series 1988–1989*

Arguably Alan Moore's greatest work, *V For Vendetta* had a long and troubled history, originally appearing in *Warrior* with stark artwork by David Lloyd. This was a radical departure for British comics at the time, telling a dark, disturbing tale set in the dystopian future of 1997's Britain.

Fascism has become the new state. Everyone is under constant supervision, and society lives in fear. Evey is a young destitute forced to prostitution to survive, but unfortunately her first customer is an undercover policeman. She is about to be gang-raped, but is rescued by an enigmatic figure dressed as Guy Fawkes and only known as V. His next action is to blow up the Houses of Parliament, succeeding where his counterpart failed, after which he takes Evey under his wing. We are introduced to various characters who are drawn into the investigations, most prominently Almond, a young, embittered detective, and his partner, the older, more jaded Finch. In the background there's the unstable Leader, and all have secret pasts, dark and terrible, which they are slowly forced to confront due to the actions of V as he assassinates them one by one.

The series ended dramatically in 1984 (ironically) when *Warrior* ceased publication, with Evey in jail and the security forces closing in on V. It was four years before DC completed the story, with purists outraged at the decision

to publish in colour. *V For Vendetta* had always been intended as a black and white strip, the monochrome adding to the bleak Orwellian feel, but Lloyd, along with colourists Siobhan Dodds and Steve Whitaker, created a tasteful, muted palate that nicely complemented the original art without detracting from the essential grimness. The conclusion was equally controversial, with many readers feeling cheated, but that's an unfair reaction. The whole series works on so many levels that anyone expecting a neat little ending has surely missed the point. Success relied heavily on some of the best characterisation ever seen in comics, mixed with a bizarre mood akin to the 1960s TV series *The Prisoner*. *V For Vendetta* is a study of British society, a biting political satire, a rollicking mystery and a great adventure. Sadly, the media interest that had bombarded comics a year or two earlier passed by *V For Vendetta*, and the series never gained the full attention it deserved. Any intelligent fan of the graphic medium should read this series. A true classic.~TP
Recommended: 1–10
Collection: V For Vendetta (1–10)

VALENTINO
Aardvark-Vanaheim: *1 issue 1985*
Renegade: *2 issues (2–3) 1986–1988*

On the basis of his mediocre superhero comics one could be forgiven for thinking that Jim Valentino is almost bereft of talent, which isn't the case. These autobiographical vignettes offer a breadth of topics with far more life and commitment than anything Valentino's done since. They encompass a range of emotions, and the honesty and humanity are quite endearing. The third issue is a little lighter than the previous two.~FP
Collection: Vignettes (1–3)

VALERIA THE SHE-BAT
Continuity: *2 issues (1 & 5) 1993*
Windjammer: *2 issues 1995*

Another beautifully drawn Continuity title whose publishing complexity is ultimately more interesting than its content. Briefly: Issue 1 was a dealers' only incentive to persuade them to order more copies of the 'Deathwatch 2000' story-line, of which it's a chapter, and 5 is material originally intended to appear in a Valeria and Spawn team-up, substituting Knighthawk for Todd McFarlane's character. The Windjammer run reprinted the first issue, and printed for the first time what would have been the second issue. Neal Adams did most of the writing and drawing himself, but typically it's absolutely unreadable.~DAR

VALERIAN
Hodder/Dargaud: *4 volumes 1984–1985*
Much-loved French science-fiction strip that débuted in the pages of *Pilote* during 1967. Valerian and his companion Laureline are spatiotemporal agents operating in the year 2070, by which time humans have occupied the entire galaxy. Pierre Christin's scripts seem very much based on the thrill-a-minute adventure reels of 1940s cinema, with exotic locations, inventive ideas and last-gasp escapes, well suited to children's fiction. The strength of J.C. Mézières' art lies in his imaginative, other-worldly landscapes and creatures, but beyond that his work is adequate without ever being distinguished. Overall *Valerian* is ill served by uninspired translations and shoddy colouring. The best of the four translated volumes is *Heroes Of The Equinox*, in which Valerian must compete with heroes from other civilisations to become the father of a new generation for a humanoid race that undergoes a mass reproduction only once each generation. If you enjoy that, sample *Ambassador Of The Shadows, Welcome to Alflolol* and *World Without Stars*.~FP

VALKYRIE
Eclipse: *3-issue miniseries 1987*
Airboy's reformed Nazi girl-friend has her past return to haunt her under Chuck Dixon, Paul Gulacy and Willie Blyberg. Valkyrie is captured by Steelfox, a Soviet villain seeking revenge for the Nazi bombing raid on his home village during World War II, which he believes she led. While Val is put up before a Russian war crimes tribunal, her flatmate Marlene sets about tracking down her former Airmaidens comrades to help clear her name. The unexpected resolution leads to the formation of a modern-day Airmaidens. The joys of this series are the constant surprises: even once you're expecting them they are still well enough plotted to shock and keep the pages turning.~JC
Recommended: 1–3
Collection: Prisoners of the Past (1–3)

VALOR
EC: *5 issues 1955*
This wonderful series offered historical 'Tales of Mortal Combat' and 'Deeds of... Valor'. Considering that *Valor* only ran five issues, maximum mileage was eked out of ancient Rome, used in 1–3, usually illustrated by Al Williamson (1, 2, 3). Other recurring themes were the Crusades, with gorgeous art by Reed Crandall (3, 4), and the Arthurian legend, illustrated by Wally Wood (1, 2). France was also a popular setting, with stories concerning the French Revolution (1, 5) and the Napoleonic era (2), expertly rendered by Graham Ingels, while Bernie Krigstein and Joe Orlando chipped in other beautiful period pieces, making the entire comic a visual delight. None of the stories, many of them written by Carl Wessler, are bad, but on occasion they tend to be heavy on the narrative in order to set everything out for the reader. This does sometimes restrict the art, and the twist at the end of stories isn't always that surprising. On the whole, though, *Valor* is a fine comic throughout, and the diversity of material presented provides a flattering contrast with the superhero-dominated market of today. It's a great pity that distribution problems ended the series.~HY
Recommended: 1–5
Collection: Valor (1–5)

VALOR
DC: *23 issues 1992–1994*
Once upon a time in the 20th-century, there was a hero named Valor, destined to live a thousand years and play a pivotal role in future history, including helping to settle the homeworlds of many of the Legion of Super-Heroes. Sadly, things didn't work out that way. This started out, courtesy of Robert Loren Fleming and sundry artists, as an attempt to establish the former Mon-El as a 'Johnny Appleseed of the Cosmos', wandering the universe and helping new cultures flourish and develop. Unfortunately, both stories and art were lack-lustre and uninspired, until Mark Waid had the brainwave of tying in with *Legion Of Super-Heroes* and *Legionnaires*, two titles, which, like *Valor*, were going to have their reasons for existing undermined by the time-rewriting *Zero Hour* series. The series begins with the 'D.O.A.' story-line (12–17), in which Valor, suffering from a nameless malaise, consults his colleague Vril Dox of *L.E.G.I.O.N.*, who informs him that he's suffering from a form of poisoning. It's untreatable and terminal. Meanwhile, in the 30th-century, the Legionnaires discover that Valor's name has been erased from history, including his role in their founding. And Lori, Valor's companion and lover, turns out to have a secret plan of her own. These strands are deftly tied together (aided by the striking art of Colleen Doran from 14) into a heady mix of romance, drama and tragedy, which ends, at the conclusion of 17, with the Legionnaires looking on awestruck as Valor dies. Who steps in to fulfil his role in history, and how the fabric of time is

prevented from unravelling... well, unless you're familiar with about thirty years of *Legion Of Super-Heroes* history, it'll make rather a less enjoyable read, but they're still nice to look at.~HS
Recommended: 12–17

THE VAMPIRE LESTAT
Innovation: *12-issue limited series 1990–1991*
Apart from the John Bolton covers, this adaptation of Anne Rice's cult vampire novels has little to recommend it. Sub-professional painted artwork and uninspired scripting make it unlikely that the elevated prices back-issues command are due to anything more than fans of the books or the film buying it for the name.~JC
Collection: The Vampire Lestat (1–12)

VAMPIRE TALES
Marvel: *11 issues, 1 Annual 1973–1975*
Marvel's black and white magazines usually have something to keep your interest even if, overall, they lack the consistency that makes for a must-buy title. In the case of *Vampire Tales* it's Don McGregor and Doug Moench's scripts that save the day. McGregor writes the Morbius series (1–5, 7, 8), while Moench is responsible for some short stories and the two final Morbius episodes (10, 11). Morbius is a self-made, scientific vampire from the pages of Spider-Man, but McGregor, while flinging him into supernatural action, uses wit and humanity to guide Morbius' search for salvation. Moench's stories have clever twists in the tail. His anti-heroic 'Shards Of The Crystal Rainbow' (9), drawn by Tony DeZuniga, marks him out as an expert story-teller. The quality of the artwork is variable, with many of the artists coming from Filipino studios. Yong Montano, Virgilio Redondo and Vincente Alcazar compare unfavourably with Pablo Marcos, Tom Sutton, DeZuniga, Alfredo Alcala and Sonny Trinidad. Other occasional artists of note include Russ Heath (9), Joe Staton (8), Paul Gulacy (5) and Howard Chaykin (5). Apart from Morbius, Blade The Vampire Hunter (8–10), Satano (2–3) and Lilith (6) were all featured. The annual contains reprints from the early issues and is a good place to start.~NF

VAMPIRELLA
Warren: *112 issues, 1 Annual, 1 Special 1969–1983*
Harris: *1 issue (113) 1988*
Another black and white anthology title, though uniquely it featured a regular strip starring the comic's eponymous heroine. Conceived by Forrest J. Ackerman as a camp *Barbarella*-style science-fiction strip, it almost immediately lost direction, something that was to plague the strip for much of its life, and disappeared after 2. She was back in 8 along

with original artist Tom Sutton and new writer Archie Goodwin, who wrote unquestionably the best stories in the strip's run. He placed Vampirella very much in the horror milieu and introduced the supporting cast of the vampire hunters, Conrad and Adam Van Helsing, and the drunk magician Pendragon. With 12 Goodwin was joined by Spanish artist José Gonzalez, whose beautiful draughtsmanship came to define the look of the strip. Goodwin's successor, T. Casey Brennan (17–21), concentrated on a romantic tryst between Vampirella and Dracula, to little effect, and following a number of fill-ins British writer Mike Butterworth (under the pen-name of Flaxman Loew) took over. All notions of continuity and characterisation were discarded, but visually it was getting better and better. Initially very inconsistent, Gonzalez really hit his peak from 31 on, though the increase in quality was matched by a decrease in productivity, and consequently other artists pitched in. The best of these were José Ortiz (35, 36) and Leopoldo Sanchez (39–41), although it was Gonzalez Mayo who eventually took over the strip. With 43 editor Bill Dubay became the character's principal writer, and for a while proved as clueless as his predecessor. One bright spot was a sequence in 61–66 which returned Vampirella to her homeworld of Draculon, but this brush with decent writing was short-lived, and subsequent Hollywood-based tales were utterly risible. 82 was Gonzalez's final issue, and it wasn't until the arrival of the excellent Rudy Nebres (88–96) that *Vampirella* became noteworthy again. 100 contained a nice one-off story by Goodwin, with terrific art from Anton Caravana, but all other issues after 90 were written by Rich Margopoulos, and it's a brave man who claims they're any better. Gonzalez returned better than ever with 103, and it's a real shame the comic was cancelled when it was.

The strength of *Vampirella* was the accompanying stories. Following a period of substandard material typical of late 60s Warren titles, the first works of note were a number of fantasy strips by Wally Wood (9, 10, 12) that sparked off a lengthy period of quality. Other fine artists contributing included Barry Smith (9), Frank Brunner (10), Neal Adams (1,10), Ralph Reese (10) and Mike Ploog (14), but Spanish artists dominated the comic from 15. Unusually, it developed its own roster of artists, who rarely drew for other Warren titles. Foremost were Felix Mas, José Bea, Esteban Maroto, Ramon Torrents and the exceptionally gifted Fernando Fernandez (28–32, 35, 36 and 40–43). 30–33 featured Steve Skeates' seedy *Pantha*, a ghetto variation on the werewolf legend, drawn by another regular, Raphael Auraleon. The best of the occasional American artists featured were Richard Corben (30, 31,

33, 54) and Jeff Jones (5, 12, 32), who drew Berni Wrightson's chilling masterpiece Cold Cuts in 34. Towering above everyone else, however, was the nowadays obscure Spanish artist Luis Garcia, whose ultra-realistic art has yet to be bettered in the comics medium. While all his strips are excellent , of particular note is 'Wolves At Wars End' in 43, which contains possibly comics' finest-ever artwork.

20–60 are a cornucopia of quality not matched by later issues, though *Vampirella* never plumbed the depths of other late Warren comics. Notable later strips were a pair by the comic's best writer, Bruce Jones: 'Yellow Heart' in 58, the story of a young tribesman's rite of passage, exquisitely drawn by Russ Heath (also in 61, 67, 76–78), and 89's 'Sight Unseen', about a blind girl, drawn by José Ortiz. Alex Nino's Fishbait in 67 was a treat, as was a nice Anton Caravana strip in 90, but from 93 a change of direction replaced the short stories with regular continuing strips. Cassandra Saint Knight and the revived Pantha were joined by The Fox with 101, an unusual series about a shapeshifter, by Nicola Cuti and Luis Bermejo, set in turn-of-the-century China. Even better were a pair of European strips, Jeremy Of The Isles (104, 106, 108, 110) and Torpedo, by Sanchez Abuli and Alex Toth (108, 110, 112), though the title's final year was bedevilled by reprints. Warren regularly produced entirely or part reprint issues of its best material (18, 27, 37, 46, 55, 63, 74, 81, 83, 87, 91, 100, 105, 107, 109, 111) and these may be the best jumping-on points for new readers. There's also a five-issue Harris reprint series titled *Vampirella Classic*. The 1972 annual contained a new origin story among choice reprints, and a 1977 special reprinted some of Gonzalez's early Vampirella stories in colour. In 1988 Harris published a one-off small-print-run issue that was largely reprint, and is now almost impossible to find. Finally, it's worth mentioning the superbly iconic covers by the Spanish painter Enrich, whose sultry depiction of Vampirella for much of the run was as much a selling point as any of the strips inside.~DAR
Recommended: 9, 10, 12, 15, 17, 18, 20–63, 65–67, 76, 85, 89, 100, 103, 104, 106, 108, 110, 112
Collections: Queen Of Hearts, The Cult Of Chaos, Transcending Time And Space (17–23)

VAMPIRELLA
Harris: *4-issue miniseries 1991–1992*

Distributed through Dark Horse, hence their logo on the covers, and tying in to the Warren Vampirella stories, this story occurs ten years since Vampirella was last seen. It's a decent effort, capturing the spirit of the original stories, but the best portions of the package are the gorgeous Mike Kaluta covers.~FP
Collection: Mourning In America (1–4)

Vengeance of VAMPIRELLA
Harris: *22 issues + 1994 to date*

The Harris Vampirella is a far more active succubus than her Warren predecessor. It having been wisely decided that the passive character wouldn't really work in the 1990s, all-out action was the order of the day. Unfortunately, there was very little else for the early issues, and the downside of the more aggressive Vampirella was discarding the subtle sexuality of the original (in as much as anyone wearing *that* costume can claim subtlety). The six-part 'Mystery Walk' (14–19) is the highlight of the run so far. It modifies Vampirella's origin, introduces several interesting characters and explains the bizarre costume. All in all, though, there's very little substance. Come to leer, by all means, but you'll grow out of it one day.~FP

VAMPIRELLA Strikes
Harris: *7 issues +, 1 Annual, 1995 to date*

This was designed for different creators to present one-off tales of the scantily clad bloodsucker without impinging on the continuity of the regular Vampirella title. It's just as insipid and bland as that title, though, and anyone seeking more than rather pricey thrills should look elsewhere. The best of a ropey bunch is Mark Millar and Louis Small's story in 6, with Vampirella infiltrating a community of vampires based in the Arctic and threatening to detonate nuclear missiles to create more favourable conditions for vampires. There's some wit about the story, but it's also the issue pandering most flagrantly to the jumping hormones of teenage boys.~FP

VAMPS
Vertigo: *6-issue miniseries 1994–1995, 6-issue miniseries ('Hollywood and Vein') 1995-1996*

Hot babe book with an attitude starring five vampire tarts. Our bike-riding sirens wreak a carnage-littered, blood-splattered, semen-drained trail of mutilation across America. Unlike the blood, plot and character background are thin, yet it is hard to label the book gratuitous since it sets out to provide sensationalist titillation, and Elaine Lee and William Simpson achieve this aim admirably. The slightly inferior sequel by the same creative team is more wet-dream stuff as the biker vampires relocate to Hollywood to star in… a biker vampire movie. Pity vampires don't photograph.~APS
Collection: Vamps (series one 1–6)

VANGUARD Illustrated
Pacific: *7 issues 1983–1984*

As an anthology, *Vanguard* succeeds in allying generally very good art with generally average or below-average stories. Tom Yeates provided some nice Al Williamson stylings in

1–3, also featuring Peter Milligan and Brendan McCarthy's imaginative 'Freakwave', which preceded *Waterworld* by a good decade, but Baron and Rude's plain daft encyclopedia-salesman story was very tiresome by its conclusion in 4. Rude's art, while acceptable, hadn't yet totally developed. Michael Gilbert's Mr Monster débuts in 7, but is for completists only, and there's nice Rick Geary pontification on his early career in 5, but on the whole the covers are the best thing about *Vanguard Illustrated*, with a Mike Kaluta beauty on 5.~FP

VANITY
Pacific: *2 issues 1984*

Vanity is a cave-girl who finds a spaceship and ends up fighting aliens on the moon. Will Meugniot's attempt to recreate the light-hearted 'good girl' strip is only partly successful. The artwork's fine if a little flat, but the humour is very forced and the story not particularly thrilling.~NF

VAULT OF EVIL
Marvel: *23 issues 1973–1975*

Another title reprinting Marvel's seemingly inexhaustible supply of horror, mystery and monster shorts from the 1950s. There's the usual mixture of Ditko and lesser artists, and only a muddy reprint of a Bernie Krigstein-illustrated story in 20 is of any note.~FP

The VAULT OF HORROR
EC: *29 issues (12–40) 1950–1955*
Gladstone: *6 issues 1990–1991*
Russ Cochran: *Series one 5 issues 1991–1992, series two 18 issues + 1992 to date*

The Vault Of Horror was one of the three horror anthologies, along with *Tales From The Crypt* and *The Haunt Of Fear*, that generated so much heat for EC publisher William M. Gaines. The immediate popularity of the 'gore books' allowed Gaines to underwrite less popular titles like *Weird Fantasy* or *Two-Fisted Tales*. At the same time their violence and Gothic melodrama outraged parents, politicians and psychologists like Fredric Wertham. EC comics, totally forbidden in post-war England, were the 'video nasties' of the 1950s, killed off by moral panic, jittery distributors and the pusillanimous Comics Code Authority.

After taking over the numbering from *War Against Crime*, a routine cop comic that gradually became *Vault* in all but name, *Vault*'s first issue proper (12) finds the title's host, The Crypt Keeper, and main contributors pretty much locked in place, although such early artists as Harvey Kurtzman (12, 13) and the Wood/Harrison team (12–14) soon gave way to the regular quartet of Jack Davis, Graham Ingels, Jack Kamen and Johnny Craig.

Johnny Craig drew all the covers and many of the lead strips, most of which he also wrote (and he even edited the last five issues of the title). He returned to his favoured scenes and themes again and again, helping to define *Vault Of Horror*'s identity through numerous stories about 'voodoo, zombies, personality transference and above all the psychological aspects of fear', as John Benson puts it in his notes for the boxed set. Although many of his covers were among the most gruesome images EC ever published, Craig's strips were comparatively restrained, emphasising internal terror over the violent retributions doled out by Feldstein in *Haunt* and *Crypt*. 32's 'Whirlpool' is both typical and exceptional. Over eight brilliantly designed pages, Craig plunges an unnamed woman into a terrifying nervous breakdown, where she is haunted by demons and then (another recurring horror) buried alive. There is no twist ending. The nightmare is circular, as reality and fantasy have become indistinguishable. However, Craig's best-drawn strip is 35's Christmas story 'And All Through The House', another psychological masterpiece adapted for the 1971 movie *Tales From The Crypt*, where Joan Collins is menaced by a mad Santa. Craig's version is blacker, wittier, and much more scary.

The large size and crisp black and white reproduction of the Russ Cochran boxed sets do wonders for the artwork of modernists like Craig and Bernie Krigstein, a late contributor, with stunning stories in 36 ('Pipe Dream', an opium-drenched horror much admired by Gaines), 38 ('The Catacombs'), 39 ('The Purge') and 40 (a savage strip entitled 'The Pit'). Of course, Krigstein was something of a rare treat, unpopular with the many readers used to the more full-blooded work of an Ingels or a Davis. Graham Ingels was the master of ugliness and putrefaction, his style perfect for scripts about rotting zombies, creepy carnivals (see the truly vile 'Out Of Sight' in 38), witches, and all things Gothic. Jack Davis was, like Craig and Jack Kamen, an extremely versatile artist, equally adept at horror, crime or humour. His frantic, cartoony style undercut the scripters' more ponderous moments, and emphasised the absurdity and black humour hiding under the surface of most EC comics. It's also worth noting how consistent all these artists were. It's rare to see a below-par job from any of the regulars, and Craig and Davis actually improved with every issue, both reaching an absolute pinnacle around issues 35–40. It's inspiring to see these artists giving their all at a time when the horror comic was considered indistinguishable from pornography. At the same time, prolonged exposure to the often overwritten scripts makes clear the limitations of EC's beloved revenge formula. Still, when read in small doses *Vault Of Horror* remains

one of the most varied and blackly entertaining horror comics ever published. All 1990s issues are reprints, with the current series representing each issue in original format on a quarterly publication schedule.~AL
Recommended: 18, 32, 36, 38–40
Collection: The Vault Of Horror (12–40)

THE VC'S
Fleetway/Quality: *5 issues 1990*

This science-fiction series from the British anthology title *2000AD* was repackaged for the American market by the original publishers. Told through the first-person narrative of a new recruit sent to replace a dead member of the VC's, a platoon in an intergalactic conflict, the story focused as much on the horror and futility of war as on the glory and action one might expect. The saga's ending was particularly downbeat and far from happy, rounding off one of the stronger of *2000AD*'s long-running series.~JC

VELOCITY
Pleece Brothers: *5 issues 1988–1989*
Eclipse: *2 issues (4, 5) 1991*
Pleece Brothers: *1 issue + (6) 1996 to date*

This self-published comic marked the way forward for the British small press. Written and drawn by brothers Gary and Warren Pleece, it displayed work of unparalleled quality for the time. Warren's stark black and white artwork and Gary's witty and acerbic scripts melded perfectly. Most stories are self-contained, although there are a few ongoing strips with bizarre and ludicrous characters like '70's Cop', a parody of American police TV shows. A move to Eclipse occurred just in time for that company to fold, but both brothers worked elsewhere on the strengths of the magazine, most notably Warren for Vertigo titles. A return to self-publishing in 1996 was excellent news, and although the older issues, particularly the pocket-sized issue 1, are very hard to track down they reward your diligence.~TP
Recommended: 1–6

VENGEANCE SQUAD
Charlton: *6 issues 1975–1976*

Poor title featuring a group of crimefighters running through a series of nondescript adventures. The book is only interesting for its back-up feature, which starred Mauser, the seedy detective from *E-Man*, by the same team of Nic Cuti and Joe Staton. The stories have a great whimsical humour and compensate for the awful lead feature.~DWC

VENGER ROBO
Viz: *7-issue limited series 1993–1994*

Crazily fast-paced Manga by Go Nagai and Ken Ishikawa. The distorted faces are funny but the

frantic robot action sequences are really quite abstract and almost impossible to follow. This one really is for psychotic speed freaks only.~GK

VENOM
Marvel: *6-issue miniseries ('Lethal Protector') 1993, 3-issue miniseries ('Funeral Pyre') 1993, 3-issue miniseries ('The Madness') 1993–1994, 3-issue miniseries ('The Enemy Within') 1994, 4-issue miniseries ('Nights of Vengeance') 1994, 4-issue miniseries ('Separation Anxiety') 1994–1995, 4-issue miniseries ('Carnage Unleashed') 1995, One-shot ('Venom Special') 1995, 5-issue miniseries ('Sinner Takes All') 1995, 4-issue miniseries ('Along Came A Spider') 1996, 4-issue miniseries ('The Hunger') 1996, 3-issue miniseries ('Tooth And Claw') 1996–1997*

To all intents and purposes a monthly publication since it began, *Venom* is split into miniseries, thus avoiding having to employ permanent creative staff. And, of course, there's a new number one issue every few months, usually with a glow-in-the-dark/sparkly/embossed cover. Venom is the unity of a symbiotic alien and the human Eddie Brock, with the resulting character resembling Spider-Man because the symbiote first attached itself to Peter Parker in years gone by. Formerly decidedly the villain, for his own series, if not quite transformed to benevolence, Venom works from the best of intentions, seeing himself as protector of the weak. There's little inspiration over the first six series, as fight scenes and guest stars substitute for plot, although the art is competent enough. 'Nights of Vengeance' is the best of a mediocre bunch. Larry Hama's appointment as writer for three stories with 'Carnage Unleashed' improves matters to the point of including a story each month, but Venom remains way short of top-notch superhero material.~FP
Collections: Carnage Unleashed, Lethal Protector, Separation Anxiety

VENUS WARS
Dark Horse: *14-issue limited series 1991–1992, 15-issue limited series 1992–1993*

In stories set towards the end of the twenty-first century, Venus is an Earth colony where two large countries exist uneasily together. When Ishtar attacks Aphrodia, dirt-bike rider Ken Sano joins the élite bike corps which seems to be their only hope against superior forces. That's about the story for around 400 pages of the first series. Creator Yoshikazu Yasuhiko nods towards political and ecological allegory, but his pacing is too expansive, with long, silent action sequences that, no matter how spectacular, are no substitute for a plot.

The second series is immeasurably better. It switches from battle action to political intrigue,

from Aphrodia to Ishtar, and contains more story in the first two issues than there is in the entire first series without sacrificing the action. Solider Matthew Radom is a pawn in a power struggle, but his manipulators have reckoned without his depth of resolve, and the series is his quest for revenge and justice. Having set up an action thriller, Yasuhiko diverts into astonishing farce with a cartoon scientist, in issues 9 and 10, but the final chapter is extremely powerful (owing more than a little to *All Quiet On The Western Front*).~FP
Recommended: Series two 1–7, 15

The VERDICT
Eternity: *4-issue miniseries 1988*

The idea of a city vigilante was being worked to death by the major companies when *The Verdict* was published, yet despite inconsistent and sometimes poor art it succeeds. The primary reason for this is the work put in by writer Martin Powell in evolving a background and a history for his feature. For twenty years a serial killer has been operating in Thermo City, and for twenty years the Verdict has been attempting to put an end to his killing. Along the way he's prevented many crimes, but has only recently come close to achieving his aim. Matters are complicated by the FBI turning ruthless in an attempt to capture the Verdict. The verdict? Okay.~WJ

VERMILLION
Helix: *12 issues 1996–1997*

Science-fiction writer Lucien Shepard brings his talents to the comic field with an epic concerning the city of Vermillion, which is a living entity so large it occupies the entire universe. How it became that way is explained in the story of Jonathan Cave, the only man with the memory of how things were previously. There's also a mysterious religious sect with a strange agenda. The story centres on a spaceship called the Marcus Garvey (nice touch), and is a complex plot still unfolding from the early issues: anyone wanting to sample should start at the beginning. It's certainly well conceived, and Al Davison's intricate art brings out the weirdness that is Vermillion.~HY
Recommended: 1

VERSION
Dark Horse: *15 issues (1.1–1.8 and 2.1–2.7) 1993–1994*

Version consists of two parts. Firstly, a search for Dr Higure, the inventor of a living biochip named EGOS. On the trail are his daughter Eiko, Hap Happo, a private detective, and Black Echo, the head of a secret organisation with a hidden interest in the chip's development. By the end they've realised that EGOS is a new 'version' of life which might supersede humanity. In part two Black Echo kidnaps the others and takes them to an undersea lab, Black Tokyo, where he is transformed into a monster by communicating with EGOS. Hisashi Sakaguchi has created a somewhat worthy strip examining artificial intelligence and the threats posed to our current ecosystem by man. Despite lots of explanations that bog the plot down, the visual story-telling is excellent, and there's enough adventure to make you wish the planned third part had been published.~NF

VERTIGO One-shots

Vertigo is the mature readers' line of color comics launched by DC in 1993, publishing long one-shot comics as well as serial works. *Mercy*, written by J.M. DeMatteis, appeared in 1993. Paul Johnson evidently put heart and soul into the artwork, with generally agreeable results. A fifty-something businessman, after a near-fatal stroke, lies on a hospital life-support system. His spirit – looking just like his bed-ridden body, right down to the pyjamas – floats into limbo, where he meets a Hinduesque blue lady who descends to Earth to bring peace to troubled souls. Predictably, this includes our hero, who's been a cynical swine all his life, but is redeemed by this encounter. It ends with the admirable idea that we ought to be nice to one another while we're here on Earth, but the clumsy mysticism of the story is a terrible vehicle for the concept.

Doctor Occult is DC's oldest magic'n'mystery character, and his Vertigo title (1994) sports a lovely cover by Kent Williams. Do not be fooled. Dan Sweetman's interior art is appalling, and so is Dave Louapre's story. He attempts to use the Doctor's two (male and female) identities to spin a yarn about human sexuality. It is (a) not a bit sexy, (b) incoherent and (c) insulting to both genders. Avoid. *Dhampire: Stillborn* (1996), by horror novelist Nancy A. Collins and artist Paul Lee, is all too coherently told, but almost as bad. This is just another in the long list of morbid post-Anne Rice vampire tales, full of gore and carnage, with teenage *angst*, incest and patricide supposedly giving it some depth or relevance. Depressed teens, or those of all ages who affect the style, will love it. Evidently a series is to follow this one-shot. Oh joy.

In 1995 UK-based editor Art Young tried to lead Vertigo away from fantasy and towards real-life drama with the Vertigo Voices series. In *Face*, Peter Milligan scripts a chilling tale of a plastic surgeon who's invited to an isolated private island by a millionaire modern artist. The mysterious purpose behind his visit appears more and more sinister as the story progresses. There is a brilliant twist at the end of the tale, and Duncan Fegredo's classy art helps give the comic a filmic feel, reminiscent of the 1960s movie version of John Fowles' *The Magus*.

Tainted, by Jamie Delano and Al Davison, is a compelling story of a lonely voyeur victimised by a couple of low-life neighbours, who try to exploit his sexual frustrations for blackmail purposes. The reader really gets under the skin of two characters in particular; so much so that one longs for the apparently inevitable tragic ending to be averted. Truly affecting, then, when Delano leaves no room for redemption of any of the three sinners. *Kill Your Boyfriend* is a disappointing effort from writer Grant Morrison, with some funny and effective moments in a generally hackneyed tale of young lovers on the run from an oppressive society etc. etc. It reads like a rejected Radio Four afternoon play, a failed attempt to do a light-hearted but subversive English version of *Bonnie and Clyde* or *Badlands.* Artist Philip Bond isn't really trying either, but it's still better than 99 percent of the stuff on the shelves. *The Eaters* is a blackly funny story of a decent, God-fearing all-American family who just happen to be cannibals. Hey, it's a life-style choice, OK? It doesn't make them bad people. In fact, it's the corrupt, wasteful society of the USA itself which is really under the moral microscope here. Peter Milligan and artist Dean Ormston cooked this one up, and of the four Vertigo Voices titles it's the most irreverent and humorous, and the one which makes its points most tellingly. There's a lesson there somewhere.

Vertigo also picked up some creator-owned titles from elsewhere for US editions. *Rogan Gosh,* by Peter Milligan and Brendan McCarthy, first appeared in UK monthly *Revolver.* Two young Englishmen, one Caucasian and one of Indian race, get caught up in a spiral of Eastern magic, demonic plots, reincarnation and bisexual love. It's a loosely plotted, at times incomprehensible, tale, but that's partly the point: relax and go with the flow, life doesn't always have to make sense. It's influenced by gaudy Indian comics based on Hindu legends, Lee and Ditko's *Dr. Strange,* and the menu at the local curry house. A potent mix, and a tasty dish. *Mr Punch,* by Neil Gaiman and Dave McKean, follows *Violent Cases* as the second in Gaiman's semi-autobiographical tales of childhood. McKean's artwork is somewhat experimental. Sometimes the juxtaposition of photographs with painted colour or line-drawn work comes off beautifully, but it can jar too. The story once again revolves around a young boy's experience of the mysterious adult world. This time the family's tangled and not entirely wholesome lives reflect the story of Punch and Judy, but the vague parallels are not easily grasped from the narrative. Many felt the effort required was not repaid.

Likewise, Grant Morrison and Jon J.Muth's *The Mystery Play,* a Vertigo original, left most readers feeling they had missed the point, if there was one, and it was the creative team's fault. In an English town, the annual folk event of the religious Mystery Play, with its ancient roots, is disrupted by the murder of the actor playing God. How does this relate to the previous rape and murder of a young girl in the town, the detective and reporter trying to solve both cases, and life in a post-religious world? God knows. The best thing about this book was the slogan Vertigo used in the ads, 'God is dead... whodunnit?' Too bad the comic itself leaves you thinking 'Who cares?'

Don't expect logical sense from Grateful Dead lyricist Robert Hunter and artist Timothy Truman's *Dog Moon* (1996) either, as the story is based closely on a fever-dream of Hunter's. The driver of a truck which transports dead souls on their journey picks up a dead woman different from the rest, whose story emerges as closely linked to his own fate. He both gets the girl and loses her at the end, while finding some kind of significance for his own previously meaningless life. Makes good use of words (all mono-syllables!), pictures and their conjunction, to achieve something like a comics poetry. The cover blurb's comparison with Coleridge actually holds water, for once.~GL

Recommended: *Dog Moon, The Eaters, Face, Tainted*

VIC AND BLOOD
Mad Dog: *2 issues 1987*

Adaptation by Richard Corben of Harlan Ellison's famous story about a boy and his telepathic dog struggling to survive in a post-holocaust wasteland. It's a good story, which plays to Corben's strengths, and the artwork is more restrained than his usual pneumatic stuff.~NF

VICKI
Atlas: *4 issues 1975*

Desperate and peculiar attempt by short-lived publisher to muscle in on the *Archie* market by reprinting slightly changed stories from *Tippy Teen,* a 1960s humour comic.~HS

VICTIMS
Eternity: *5 issues 1988–1989*

Two female college teens progress from being menaced in one B-movie horror scenario to being menaced in the next, all the time questioning what's going on in almost existentialist fashion. Created for the horror film magazine *Scream* in the 1970s, *Victims* hasn't aged well. Utter drivel.~FP

VICTORY

Topps: *1 issue 1994*

Stillborn attempt to unite the Jack Kirby characters published by Topps, with Kurt Busiek and Keith Giffen providing an intriguing opening chapter, but that's all there was.~WJ

VIDEO JACK

Epic: *6-issue limited series 1987–1988*

Very underrated as a writer, Cary Bates spent most of the 1970s turning in consistently imaginative short-story plots for *Superman* and *Flash*. Keith Giffen is given more credit for imagination, so the combination of the two, with art by Giffen, should be worthwhile. Well, yes and no. Jack's a bit of a sad case, obsessed with television to the extent of repelling reality. His fixation precludes attempts at a relationship and most social intercourse. Some old hocus-pocus transforms him, though, enabling him and his more outgoing pal Damon to interact with any currently broadcasting TV reality at the touch of a remote button. The wilful wackiness can be off-putting. Giffen enjoys drawing the snippets of assorted TV programmes, but this seems to be the total *raison d'être* of *Video Jack*. It's a novel trick, but it's trick that wears as thin as the thread connecting it to a murder plot. 4 presents some contrasting scenarios if you'd prefer not to work your way through the first issue's extended set-up.~WJ

VIETNAM JOURNAL

Apple: *16 issues 1987–1989, 6-issue miniseries ('Tet '68') 1991–1993, 4-issue miniseries ('Bloodbath At Khe Sanh') 1993, 2-issue microseries ('Valley of Death') 1994*

Picking up with the escalation of hostilities in 1967, these are well researched and detailed stories about the Vietnam war, written and drawn by Don Lomax. His focal point and narrator is a war correspondent cornily referred to as 'Journal', whose occupation allows attachment to different combat units. Set against an admirably passionate depiction of the ordinary soldier's missions in hell, there's little questioning of the rights or wrongs of US involvement in Vietnam, and the portrayal of the Vietnamese is rarely more than silent gook killers. If this doesn't bother you, *Vietnam Journal* comes highly recommended, although the abundance of expository dialogue sometimes bogs it down. Every issue is complete in itself, and packs a lot of detail, with 3's story of a manipulative TV journalist, or 10's raid on a NVA outpost, good examples of the style and content. Other commitments prevented Lomax from maintaining a bi-monthly publication schedule beyond 16, so future stories were released as self-contained miniseries. 'Tet '68' effectively relates the story of the New Year offensive, but the best story in this series is the first issue, concerning a rogue CIA agent previously seen in 4 and 10. The historical-reportage tone of the story-telling renders the remainder of 'Tet '68' and 'Bloodbath At Khe Sanh' far drier and wordier than the more anecdotal and personal-experience-based parent title, although matters marginally improve with 'Valley of Death'.~FP

Recommended: 3, 4, 10, 11, 14

Collection: Indian Country (1–4), The Iron Triangle (5–8)

VIGILANTE

DC: *50 issues, 2 Annuals 1983–1988*

Introduced in *New Teen Titans Annual* 2, Vigilante begins as DC's answer to the Punisher. Former District Attorney Adrian Chase feels that the system enables too many criminals escape punishment, so he costumes himself to dispense a little extra-curricular justice. To his credit, creator Marv Wolfman doesn't sidestep the complex issues raised by the character, and 2 partially explores his justifications. Oddly enough, considering the character was his creation, the series doesn't really go anywhere until Wolfman's departure. The Alan Moore-written story in 17–18 is only a little better than average, after which Paul Kupperberg and Tod Smith develop Wolfman's plots rather better than he had. Chase becomes a judge, but a psychopath adopts his costumed identity. When this plot concludes in 27 there's immediately a third Vigilante, also taking his cue from Chase, but with a more reasoned approach. 28, despite little costumed action, offers a good feel of this period. With 37 Chase is back in costume, now officially sanctioned, but by this time he's a man balanced precariously on the edge of sanity. This leads to a surprising and brave conclusion in 50. By and large the second half of the run is better than the first.~WJ

VIGILANTE City Lights, Prairie Justice

DC: *4-issue miniseries 1995–1996*

Although only making his solo début years after the 1980s Vigilante, this is, in fact, the original holder of the name, who'd waited over fifty years for his own title since debuting in *Action* 42. When he's crimefighting the Vigilante disguises his identity as Greg Saunders, country singer, by wrapping a red scarf over the lower portion of his face. Writer James Robinson wisely sets the story in the 1940s, having the Vigilante confront both his traditional nemesis, the Dummy, and powerful gangster Bugsy Siegel, then attempting to set the foundations for what would become Las Vegas. Robinson's pacing is very jumpy: he often chooses to depict the prelude to violence, and then leaps to the consequences, with the action occurring off-panel. This leaves plenty of talking heads for Tony Salmons to draw, and he's already having to produce too many abstract montages and illustrate captions updating events rather than a story. Too detached to engage any emotion, this is nonetheless an improvement on many superhero titles, but one of Robinson's lesser works.~FP

Phil Elliott's VIGNETTE COMICS
Harrier New Wave: *1 issue 1988*

Rather a hotchpotch collection, with Phil Elliott in largely wistful or whimsical mode, and lacking his 1980s crowd-pleaser Gimbley. While they're all drawn in Elliott's appealing *ligne claire* style (apart from those by guest artists Ed Pinsent and Paul Grist), there's little bite, and in the end one is left feeling the time spent reading *Vignette* could have been better occupied doing something else.~FP

The Last of the VIKING HEROES
Genesis West: *12 issues, 3 Specials 1987–1992*

Any pretence at historical accuracy disappeared long ago during this strip's début as a back-up in *Silver Star* 1, 5, 6. Four friends – a barbarian, a swordsman, a prince and a bumbling sorcerer's apprentice – indulge in light-hearted romps through wine, women, song and brawl, not to mention a few monsters, wizards and demons thrown in to flesh out the pot. The medieval setting is clearly located in some tropical Nordic land, judging by the number of scantily clad lovelies frolicking about. Michael Thibodeaux composes most of the creative aspects and delivers some dynamic fight sequences; on rare occasions the gentle touches of humour actually work. 4–12 form a continued story. Improbably, those Mutant Turtles show up in Summer Special 3 and sort of muscle-in on Special 2 as well. Overall verdict: undemanding.~APS
Collections: The Last of the Viking Heroes (1–3), *Nidhogger Lives* (4–12), *The Teenage Mutant Ninja Turtles Visit the Last of the Viking Heroes* (Specials 1–3)

VIOLATOR
Image: *3-issue miniseries 1994*

In this *Spawn* spin-off, Violator, a demon from Hell, has been banished for his failure to kill Spawn. Not only is his own family after his head, a Mafia boss he's annoyed along the way has set hitmen on his trail too. Violator is fast, wicked, violent and, as written by Alan Moore, as black a comedy as you'll find in comics.~NF

VIOLATOR VS BADROCK
Image: *4-issue miniseries 1995*

Alan Moore returns to take Violator back to Hell in the company of Youngblood team-member Badrock, a scientist intent on tapping

the power of Hell, and the angel Celestine. Again, a fast, furious and funny read, if not exactly taxing. Moore certainly shows how to craft a good book out of unpromising material.~NF

VIRUS
Dark Horse: *4-issue miniseries 1993*

A rescue barge comes across a deserted Chinese research ship, but once it's been boarded the machinery begins to operate independently and strange robotic creatures attack crew members. Even more disturbingly, Chinese jets attempt to bomb the ship, despite having seen that it's inhabited. *Virus* is *Alien* at sea: classic horror material, predictable all the way, but fun with it.~FP
Collection: Virus (1–4)

The VISION
Marvel: *4-issue miniseries 1994–1995*

Plenty had happened to the Vision since his last outing away from the Avengers in the company of the Scarlet Witch. Their marriage had broken up, he'd been dismantled, reconstituted devoid of all capacity for emotion, blanched, then had his consciousness switched into the body of a Vision from an alternate world, restoring him (more or less) to his previous appearance. Writer Bob Harras, at the time writing the Vision in *The Avengers*, holds his end up with an initially intriguing plot concerning a few of Marvel's sentient machines which suddenly display odd personality traits. The robotic Ultron as good ol' Texas boy is a laugh, for a start, as is the Vision as Sam Spade, given his distinctive red appearance. There is, naturally, a reason for the uncharacteristic behaviour, but it's not revealed until the final issue, by which point it's been dragged on too long, with 3 an obvious filler. Manny Clark's art is a triumph of design over technique, and he's a particular exponent of the everyone-speaking-through-gritted-teeth-or-pouting lips style of art. Miss out 3 and pick up the rest for a quick, fun read.~WJ

VISION and the SCARLET WITCH
Marvel: *4-issue miniseries 1982–1983, 12-issue limited series 1985–1986*

Controversial married superheroes take a leave of absence from the Avengers and go domestic in the suburbs. Naturally, supervillains follow, and normal service is quickly resumed, with Avengers and other guest stars galore. The four issues are only loosely related, improve as the series progresses and feature revelations about the stars' origins. The final issue confirms the identity of Wanda and Pietro's father.

Back to the suburbs for take two at the domesticity routine. Although Steve Englehart expends plenty of effort at turning in a fully-fledged soap opera, the end-product is cloying and twee, and Richard Howell's pencils are monstrously pedestrian. The second series centres around Wanda's pregnancy and the eventual birth of her and Vision's twins in the final issue. All their kinsmen drop in throughout the series to reasonable effect, but the new supporting characters are duff and the choice of villains lamentable (are three issues of the Toad really necessary?). The series starts with a crossover to *West Coast Avengers* 1 and 2 and has its epilogue in *West Coast Avengers* Annual 1. By a short head, issue 6 is the pick of the bunch, featuring Wanda, Pietro and their father's first steps down the rocky road to reconciliation.~APS

The VISITOR
Valiant: *13 issues 1995*

The hook for this series was that the true identity of the Visitor was a character who had previously appeared in the Valiant Universe, but the secret was kept until the final issue, by which time this lacklustre story had long since run out of steam.~HS

The VISITOR VS. THE VALIANT UNIVERSE
Valiant: *2-issue microseries 1995*

This introduces the Visitor, who is allegedly a non-human alien would-be superhero, in what boils down to a slugfest against all the Valiant heroes. The Visitor span off into his own series thereafter.~HS

Dracula:VLAD THE IMPALER
Topps: *3-issue miniseries 1993*

Once again, the secret origin of the vampires, but handled with unexpected flair and panache by Thomas and Maroto.~HS

VOGUE
Image: *3-issue miniseries 1995*

Another multi-creator title from Rob Liefeld's Extreme Studios, as Brian Witten and Cy Voris (writers), Marat Mychaels (layouts) and Andy Park (penciller) tell the tale of Nicola Voganova, model by day, superheroine by night. Vogue's a member of Youngblood, on a mission that takes her back to Russia to fight Stroika and his superterrorist team, Redblood. Lots of shots of scantily-clad women in action poses ensue.~NF

VOID INDIGO
Epic: *Graphic Novel, 2 issues 1984–1985*

Marvel pulled the plug on this Steve Gerber fantasy series shortly after the second issue appeared, apparently in a dispute over the strong nature of the material. These days Vertigo publish far 'harder' comics without much fuss. Certainly, *Void Indigo* takes an unremittingly bleak view of life in the late 20th century – as one character puts it, 'Nobody makes anybody happy anymore. Why should they? What's to be gained?' The series is full of gruesome torture scenes, ritual murders and polymorphous perversity, but this isn't gore for gore's sake, some chic attempt to be shocking, this is Gerber's fully rounded vision of millennial collapse, as downright loopy, cosmic and funny as his best 1970s work (Howard The Duck, or his run on The Defenders). Also like much of his 1970s output, the comic suffers only from inadequate artwork. Val Mayerik's decision to paint the graphic novel reveals his limitations with a brush, and he appears to have coloured the Epic comics with a couple of old felt-tip pens.

Gerber packs these three instalments with enough ideas and plot threads to sustain a hundred lesser comics. The graphic novel begins with the cruel murder of barbarian Ath'agaar by evil sorcerers The Dark Lords of Kur. This routine barbarian opening segues into a long psychedelic sequence, where Ath'agaar enters the void indigo ('blue emptiness') and merges with an alien called Jhagur, from the planet Gebura. Got all that? Jhagur lands in present-day LA, where he assumes the human identity of Michael Jagger (!) and shacks up with a tart with a heart, Linnette Cumpston. By 2 Jhagar has begun to seek out his reincarnated enemies, in order to avenge his terrible demise, and to prevent humanity descending into 'barbarism and cataclysm'.

The abrupt cancellation of *Void Indigo* makes it impossible to tell if the comic could have sustained its initial intensity, but what remains still deserves rescuing from the blue emptiness of critical neglect. Sadly, but understandably, Gerber hasn't written anything half as stimulating since.~AL
Recommended: Graphic Novel, 1, 2

Magic Carpet 1 VOLTAR
Comics & Comix: *1 issue 1977*

Alfredo Alcala's brainchild *Voltar* originally appeared in Alcala's native Philippines. Much like Conan, whom he predated in the comic format, Voltar was an all-conquering warrior, and the scripting, by Manuel Avad, is, not surprisingly, rather typical sword-and-sorcery. The story, though, is merely an excuse for Alcala to show off his incredible art, and the intricately etched linework here is absolutely bewitching. The wash-delineated 'Buccaneers Of The Skull Planet' rounds out a lovely showcase of top-quality artwork.~DAR
Recommended: 1

VORTEX
Vortex: *15 issues 1982–1988*

Amateurish anthology that, despite its good intentions and willingness to include a broad range of material, never really managed to produce anything of real note. Occasional work by Ken Steacy, Ty Templeton and Dan Day may have raised the quality of individual issues to an acceptable level but the lack of clear editorial vision actually works against the series. Of note, however, are the contributions of the Hernandez Brothers, Gilbert in 7 with 'Return of ZZIK' and Jaime in 11 with 'The He That Walks'. They're both early works but stand head and shoulders above anything else here.~NF

VORTEX
Comico: *4-issue miniseries 1991–1993*
A member of the Elementals superteam, Vortex is a superhero with amazing flying powers, gifted to him by Aer, Lord of the Air. This spin-off miniseries begins on the environmental moral high ground – greedy corporation threaten to destroy sacred Native American reservation – before quickly descending into bog-standard superhero clichés, ineptly served up by Writer Roland Mann and Artist Steven Butler.~AL

VOX
Apple: *6 issues 1989–1990*
This is a pleasantly deceptive series, beginning as a good-natured buddy science-fiction comic before opening up into a tense story of intergalactic espionage and possible war. The heart of the plot concerns a matter transporter being tested by the transportation of living beings to remote worlds. It's a human invention, but coveted by two other races, the Borodok and the Zetaceans. Escalating tensions lead to unpredictable situations, and the whole is very nicely conceived.~FP

VOYAGE TO THE DEEP
Dell: *4 issues, 1962–1964*
The Proteus is an experimental 'telescopic' submarine that can change its length by a factor of eight (I can hear your gasps of wonder from here). The Enemy keeps trying to use the Earth's natural forces to destroy the US and the Proteus keeps coming to the rescue, pausing midway through the issue to escape the clutches of a giant sea creature, with the lobster in 4 my favourite. The stories are technobabble taken to genius level: in 1 The Enemy has injected helium into the Earth's core and this has tilted the planet out of orbit, tipping the Atlantic so it's flooding the US; Proteus draws out the helium using 'a gas possessing a molecular structure exactly opposite that of helium', to which the helium is, of course, irresistibly attracted, and the world is saved. Inspired! You will laugh yourself sick.~FC
Recommended: 1–4

Children Of The VOYAGER
Marvel UK: *4-issue miniseries 1993*
Noted science-fiction writer Sam Wantling is increasingly plagued by terrifying nightmares of being consumed by an all-powerful being. His work suffers and his relationship collapses, as he becomes convinced that the dreams have a basis in reality. Indeed they do, and it's a shame that editorial page teasers give the entire game away when writer Nick Abadzis has constructed a slow-release plot. The full implications of the nightmares aren't revealed until the third issue, by which time Sam has found some help. Paul Johnson's scratchy style of art is effective in conveying Wantling's uncertainty and terror, and while both creators would progress to better things, this is a worthwhile read.~FP

WACKY SQUIRREL
Dark Horse: *4 issues, 2 Specials 1987–1988*

Cartoon comedy transferred to comics rarely succeeds in print. Perception of animation's manic action is slowed by the printed page and without the speed the gags fall flat. Mike Richardson and Jim Bradrick make a brave attempt, though: their best is 4, in which Wacky and Kal-El's spaceships each arrive at the wrong planet. Wacky ends up pushing cream pies in Lois Lane's face, and Superman can't understand why every time he feels angry an oversized mallet appears. Some readers caught similarities between this and Tex Avery's *Screwball Squirrel*, and ironically Dark Horse eventually published the original.~WJ

THE WANDERERS
DC: *13 issues 1988–1989*

Old time *Legion Of Super-Heroes* fans were delighted to hear that the little-used group created by Jim Shooter in the 1960s was to be revived twenty years later. DC, in their infinite wisdom, decided to take these 30th-century characters, kill them, clone them and give them new appearances and powers. You wonder why they bothered. Doug Moench's scripts were as dull as dishwater (he had to write something in his tea-break) and the artwork and story-telling were abysmal (the penciller had to practise on something). There was one saving grace – after thirteen issues it was cancelled, unlucky for it, lucky for us.~HY

WANDERING STAR
Pen & Ink: *11 issues 1993–1996*
Sirius: *10 issues (12–21) 1996–1997*

Two hundred years in the future, Earth is part of a Galactic community, but its peoples are despised for their warlike heritage and the environmental disasters that almost destroyed the planet. Now the daughter of the President of the United Nations of Earth, Cassandra Andrews, has been accepted to the Galactic Academy, alongside the children of the leaders of other worlds. Struggling to find acceptance, she is befriended by psychic Madison, furry Graikor and energy-being Elli. When the Academy is attacked by the Bono Kiro, Cassandra and the others escape in an experimental ship, the Wandering Star, and join the Alliance forces, only to find that the Earth has already fallen and that the Alliance is losing, badly. Things get even worse as friends start to die and Cassandra's father decides that Earth would be better off destroyed than in enemy hands (16).

Teri S. Wood's science-fiction series builds slowly, reaching through Cassandra's narration for an emotional resonance that attempts to lift an otherwise unexceptional story-line. That it's partially successful is due to the strip's charm and her pretty artwork. It's not challenging or profound enough for greatness but deserves attention for its story-telling.~NF

WANDERING STARS
Fantagraphics: *1 issue 1987*

Projected science-fiction series that never had the chance to reach the audience it deserved. A strange woman, Magen, is injured in battle with government forces and is aided by the wealthy Amelia. An assassin is despatched to kill Magen, while Amelia tries to understand what drives her to rebel. Written by Stuart Hooper and drawn by Sam Kieth, it's a promising début but was never finished, and on its own it can't really be considered more than a curiosity.~NF

WANTED
DC: *9 issues 1972–1973*

Having published two issues of *DC Special* (8, 14) using the *Wanted* cover design to obviously good response, DC followed up with a series. The covers resembled old-style Wanted posters, but inside the stories were largely standard superhero reprints. The attraction was that it was a cheap way of obtaining very old stories. Issue 2, for example, contained the first teaming of the Joker and the Penguin from *Batman* 25 along with an early 1960s Flash story. It's the 1940s material that seemed to press the right buttons with the readership, and from 3 there's only one story (a Gil Kane Green Lantern) dating from later than 1949. There's an undeniable spirit to the earlier material, but most of it is crudely drawn by today's standards, with even the more renowned artists (Bernard Bailey on Starman in 6, for instance) not wearing well. Oddly, the most interestingly plotted stories of the run originate from companies DC later took over, with Kid Eternity in 4 and Doll Man in 5. The Sandman, by Simon and Kirby, in 9 is the best of the 1940s DC material.~FP

THE WAR
Marvel: *4-issue miniseries 1989*
The conclusion to Marvel's well-considered but unsuccessful 'New Universe' titles, set on an Earth as close to ours as possible, the only incongruous elements being a restrained selection of superheroes introduced at the inception. Or that, at least, was the original concept. With sales never high, more superpowered characters were introduced, even to the point of revealing that the Ronald Reagan of that Earth had been affected in *The War*'s predecessor, *The Draft*. That showed assorted new heroes being inducted into the military services to be prepared for some vague threat. Most of the remaining New Universe characters are involved in Doug Murray's plot about one superhuman doing his best to engineer World War III. Does he succeed? Do you really care? It's a perfunctory series dragged on too long and published in an unnecessarily expensive format in the hope of parting the last dollars out of the few remaining New Universe fans.~WJ

WAR DANCER
Defiant: *7 issues 1994*
Co-created by the erratic Alan Weiss and the ubiquitous Jim Shooter, *War Dancer* is a frankly baffling mixture of standard superhero antics, pseudo-Eastern mysticism and tongue-in-cheek humour. Our hero is a time-travelling superbeing who defeats his many enemies by dancing on them, or as he puts it in issue 1, in a typically flowery monologue, 'I dance to the rhythms of the universe, one with the energy.' Pompous and overblown, *War Dancer* contains only two redeeming features – the constant use of the phrase 'Org's Phlegm', and a scene in issue three where a villain grows and grows until he literally bursts!~AL

WAR IS HELL
Marvel: *15 issues 1973–1975*
The first eight issues reprint 1950s war stories and a couple of tales from *Sgt Fury and his Howling Commandos*. With 9, Chris Claremont was handed the scripting chores for his first regular series. John Kowalski, the cursed spirit of a dead soldier, was forced by Death to temporarily animate the bodies of the recently dead. Destined to repeatedly relive the horrors of World War II, he served as a perfect focus to depict the grisly nature of war. One of the better war comics, the strip avoids the glorifications and clichés that are usually so prominent.~APS

WAR MACHINE
Marvel: *25 issues 1994–1996*
Previously a substitute Iron Man whenever required, a tiff with his former employer left James Rhodes at a loose end, but with an amazingly powerful armoured flying suit. In keeping with his name, he decides his mission in life is to steam in where political angels fear to tread, sometimes manipulated into acting as in 1–4. As a civilian Rhodes heads WorldWatch, an organisation that exposes injustice and abuse of power the world over. It's all competently set up, but it's not until the final issues that a major problem is addressed. It's that once the armour's on there's little to differentiate War Machine from Iron Man, and even out of armour both run companies with far-reaching, enormous influence. Dan Abnett's plotting from 11 is a little more imaginative than the original creative team, and he solves the Iron Man clone problem by having Rhodes bond with a more organic armoured suit from 18. By that time the art has degenerated beyond all redemption. All in all there are plenty more interesting comics to occupy your time.~FP

WAR MAN
Epic: *2-issue miniseries 1993*
An arms dealer has to lead a politician through the Amazon after a plane crash and fight off mercenary troops while doing so. Could be any two issues of *The Punisher*.~FP

WAR OF THE GODS
DC: *4-issue miniseries 1991–1992*
1991 was the fiftieth anniversary of Wonder Woman's début, and all we got was this sprawling, incoherent series crossing over into other titles, with chapters misnumbered, unidentified or appearing in the wrong order. The Greek and Roman pantheons declare war on each other, and Earth's superheroes, led by Wonder Woman, are caught in the crossfire. Good luck following the chapter order.~HS

WARBLADE: Endangered Species
Image: *4-issue miniseries 1995*
Another well-thought-out crossover between the Jim Lee Wildstorm and Mark Silvestri Top Cow universes, as Cyberforce's Ripclaw joins forces with old comrade Warblade (now in WildC.A.T.s) to prevent a daemonite conspiracy from taking over Brazil, using a new armoured suit. Cleverly interpolating background information on both characters and setting the stage for future stories, the series has plenty of action, and Steven T. Seagle's script is a cut above the average, as both Ripclaw and Warblade confront an old friend who may or may not be their enemy. Scott Clark's artwork has some rough edges and appears rushed in places, particularly in 4, but otherwise shows promise.~NF

WARFRONT
Harvey: *35 issues 1951–1958, 4 issues (36–39) 1965–1967*

An anthology comic of war stories, all pretty much identical: much rushing around and shooting and standing up to interrogation and cursing of Commies. Towards the end of the series regular characters started appearing ('Dynamite Joe, the blast-crazy marine'), and the stories become more far-fetched (we have 'Half Mask', a disfigured Nazi with 'death ray lenses'). Most of each issue is unreadable, but there are occasional treasures, such as the following speech from Issue 36: 'Thank you for saving me from losing my confidence in us Americans! If a dope like me can bamboozle a Commie officer, our scientists can out-think their eggheads!' There's notable artwork from Bob Powell in most of the 1950s issues, and 36–39 have Wally Wood. And, of course, there are the adverts: the 3-Way Hurricane Lantern, the Electronic Computer Brain, the Automatic Firing Tripod Machine Gun, the Glamorous Dress for your Barbie Doll, and Rupture-Easer Hernia Belt. Makes you wonder what picture they had of their typical reader.~FC

WARHEADS
Marvel UK: *14 issues 1992–1993, 2-issue microseries ('Black Dawn') 1993*

The tagline 'Mercenaries across time and space' had potential largely unexplored as the time-travelling protagonists mainly get lost in limbo and fight Marvel US guest stars rather than doing much in the way of time-travelling. Listlessly written, formlessly illustrated, it seems no one involved could be bothered to fake it. The microseries had a new creative team, but the same old ennui.~HS

WARLOCK
Marvel: *15 issues 1972–1973 (1–8), 1975–1976 (9–15)*

It all started with the creation of the High Evolutionary (*Thor* 134–135), a human become god who sets out to create a new race of evolved animals, the Knights of Wundagore. Then in *Fantastic Four* 66 and 67 four scientists, in attempting to create a new race with which to conquer mankind, unleash from a cocoon the gold-skinned being known as Him. Awakened only once more (*Thor* 165–166), Him is then reborn in *Marvel Premiere* 1 and 2 when the High Evolutionary creates the Counter Earth, a perfect world hidden from our view by the simple expedient of being on the other side of the sun. Unfortunately the High Evolutionary falls asleep and the Man-Beast subverts his plan by introducing the killer instinct to the creatures on Counter Earth, precipitating war. On the verge of destroying the planet as a failed experiment, the High Evolutionary is stopped

by Him, who emerges from his cocoon once more and offers to rid the Counter Earth of the Man-Beast. The High Evolutionary gives him a powerful gem and Him, now calling himself Adam Warlock, gathers some teenage disciples and sets off to fulfil his promise.

The first run starts from this point, introducing various characters with counterparts in the regular Marvel Universe (Reed Richards, Doctor Doom). However, up until this point there have been no superheroes on the Counter Earth. Despite several changes of writer (Roy Thomas, Mike Friedrich, Ron Goulart and then Friedrich again) the parallels with the story of Jesus remained apparent, although they became more subtle as the series progressed until the story-line was concluded in *The Incredible Hulk* 176–178, with Warlock being crucified and resurrected! Originally drawn by Gil Kane (1–5), *Warlock* looked good until Bob Brown took over.

After the Hulk, Warlock put in an appearance in *Strange Tales* (178–181) as part of Jim Starlin's Thanos saga, which Starlin continued into the revived *Warlock* series. Warlock must face his evil future self, The Magus, in 9–11. Thereafter a story concentrating on one of the supporting cast, Pip the Troll, is followed by a two-parter in which Warlock fights the Star-Thief, a being who is literally stealing the stars. In the final issue before cancellation Warlock struggles to retain his power over the gem he's been using, which contains the souls of all those he's killed with it. Starlin concludes the story elsewhere, this time in *Marvel Team-Up* 55, *Avengers* Annual 7 and then *Marvel Two-In-One* Annual 2, with Warlock's third death and the end of Thanos.

Starlin's version of Warlock is powerful and mysterious, with intelligent scripts and dynamic, detailed artwork, tightly inked. Much of his work since has been over-indulgent, but don't let that put you off seeking this out. All of the Starlin issues were reprinted as *Warlock* 1–6 (1982–1983).~NF
Recommended: 9–15

WARLOCK And The Infinity Watch
Marvel: *42 issues 1992–1995*

Carrying on from where the Infinity Gauntlet series leaves off, Warlock and friends (Pip the Troll, Gamora, Moondragon, The Destroyer) are made guardians of the six Infinity Gems. To ensure that no one can use them again the team relocates to Mole Man's Monster Island. You just know that that's not the end of it, and the series is dominated by tie-ins (to *Infinity War* (8–10), *Infinity Crusade* (19–22), 'Blood And Thunder' (23–25) and 'Atlantis Rising' (41–42). The whole thing's written by Jim Starlin, but he's lost the inspiration that made the original *Warlock* series worth reading, and is just going through the motions here.~NF

THE WARLOCK CHRONICLES
Marvel: *8 issues 1993–1994*

Yet more Warlock-related nonsense from Jim Starlin. Issues 2–5 cross over with the *Infinity Crusade* and 6–8 with the 'Blood And Thunder' story in which Thor goes mad.~NF

WARLOCK 5
Aircel: *Series one 22 issues 1986–1989, series two 7 issues 1989–1990*
Nightwynd: *2 issues 1994*

Savashtar (the dragon), Zania Nervana (the psychotic), Tanith (the sorceress), Doomidor (the knight) and Argon (a Terminator-type) are the five warlocks who guard the gates of the Grid, a nexus of alternate realities. Each strives either to maintain a balance or usurp the power of the Grid for themselves. 1–13 are by creators Gordon Derry and Denis Beauvais, whose airbrush and watercolour effects make this a visually impressive series. It's violent and sexy but there is some thought behind it all and, as science-fiction fantasy goes, this is a reasonable attempt at something different. Barry Blair's Warlock 5, which is a completely different series, begins with 14. Blair's simpler cartooning came as a shock after the sophistication of Beauvais, although replacement penciller Dale Keown on 16 and 17 was already showing promise. Unfortunately Blair's more straightforward adventure/fantasy scripts weren't a patch on Derry's.~NF
Collections: Warlock 5 vol 1 (1–5), Vol 2 (6–10)

WARLORD
DC: *133 issues, 6 annuals 1976–1988*

The introductory issue carries on the story from Warlord's début in *First Issue Special* 8, written and illustrated by Mike Grell. Adventurer Travis Morgan finds himself in a strange world beneath the Earth called Skartaris, populated by various beasts; it's a place where sorcery still exists. Grell was in his element here. His artwork suited a sword-and-sorcery feature far better than it did his superhero series, and he was able to come up with, if not original, certainly entertaining ideas to keep the action flowing. Skartaris is a well conceived place, eventually revealed to be in another dimension accessed through Earth. There's permanent daylight, and time passes at a considerably slower rate, as Morgan discovers each time he returns home. Grell also merges Earth science with the fantasy elements, giving the series that unique touch, an example being chief villain Deimos, whose mystical scrolls of power are actually computer manuals.

Morgan adapts well to the new world, and to a skimpy furry jock-strap. Grell creates an interesting cast, including companion Machiste, met when they were sold as gladiators together in 2, Morgan leading a

subsequent revolt which earned him the title Warlord. Partner Tara is rescued from a voracious dinosaur in true sword-and-sorcery fashion in *First Issue Special* 8, but her frailty disguised her being quite a dab hand with the sword. Shakira, introduced in 32, is a warrior woman who can transform herself into a cat, yet retain her human intellect.

It actually doesn't take Warlord long to make his way back to the world he knows, but he chooses to return to Skartaris in order to free the entire land from occupation by Deimos and his Theran forces. He's accompanied back by a former lover, Mariah, conveniently also a former fencing champion, and he manages to defeat Deimos. He's a hardy old mystic though, and returns from the dead. Several times. Each time he's nastier, culminating in a plot where he makes Warlord believe he's killed someone very dear to him. Morgan is actually knocking on a bit, old enough to have served in Vietnam, and has an adult daughter, Jennifer, who comes looking for her father in 38. Intending a once-only visit, through circumstances beyond her control Jennifer stays, progressing to become Skataris' premier sorceress. Fantasy fans should find most of the Grell issues enjoyable. A decent sample is 28, in which Warlord has to defeat an alluring cobra woman.

Other commitments mean that Grell stops drawing *Warlord* after 52, and 71 is his final issue as writer. Mark Texeira is an acceptable temporary artist between 53 and 58, after which Dan Jurgens begins a long run from 63, but the series slides once it completely loses Grell's creative vision. Cary Burkett initially keeps everything rolling, but doesn't have the necessary imagination for the long run. Michael Fleisher, from 100, certainly has the imagination, but is on autopilot. What is obviously an attempt to boost sales by having assorted DC heroes pop in and out (from 116) rather destroys the unique aspects of *Warlord*. It all ends in tears, with DeSaad and the forces of Apokalips attempting to take control of Skartaris, the Atlanteans having had a good try in the issues leading up to 100. Along the way there are a few notable artists: Art Thibert (121–122, guest-starring Power Girl), Rob Liefeld's first DC work in 131's insert, Ron Randall from 104–118, Andy Kubert (100) and Adam Kubert (95, 99). Father Joe obviously took a hand as well, since many successful graduates from his School Of Cartoon Art ended up working on back-up features.

The most successful was Arion, Lord of Atlantis, which ran from 55 to 62, drawn by Jan Duursema, before moving into his own title, and Ron Randall's Conquerors Of The Barren Earth has a lengthy run from 63. Saga Of Dragonsword in 51–54 by Paul Levitz and

Tom Yeates, is a nice series with a talking ape, long a DC tradition, and 48 has an insert previewing *Arak*, and the first of two Claw the Unconquered stories, returning a character introduced at the same time as Warlord, but not as successful. The light-hearted Wizardworld can be found in 28, 29, 40 and 41, and Omac is the back-up in 37–39 and 42–47, the first by Jim Starlin, the second by Mishkin, Cohn and LaRoque, with the first run better all round.

Creator Mike Grell returned for the miniseries, illustrated by Damon Willich and Rick Hoberg. A wandering minstrel tries to discover the legend that was Warlord, and in doing so seeks out various people who've shared Travis Morgan's adventures, eventually meeting Morgan himself. Warlord, however, is disillusioned with the myth that's grown around him, but with old enemy Deimos resurrected once again he's forced into action. The story is almost a tribute, and those who enjoy the Grell issues from the ongoing series will find much to their liking here.~HY

WARP
First: *19 issues, 3 specials 1983–1985*

Warp began life as a 1971 stage play parodying fantasy and superhero clichés. First's version, by Peter B. Gillis and 1970s fan favourite artist Frank Brunner, eradicated all trace of satire, making this adaptation simply another third-rate cosmic dust-up. The first issue begins when mild-mannered bank clerk David Carson discovers that he's the host body for potential universe saviour Lord Cumulus. Cumulus' mortal enemy Lord Chaos intends to steal a magical crystal that will allow him to rule the galaxy. By 2 it's revealed that Chaos and Cumulus are brothers, and by 6 they've put aside their differences to fight side by side in a series of interminable battles. Brunner's sub-Neal Adams artwork on 1–9 is at least vaguely appropriate, as Adams designed the costumes for the stage production, but the poor finishing of Bob Smith, Bruce Patterson and Mike Gustovich (who also slaughtered Jerry Bingham's pencils on 10–18) makes this a chore to look at as well as to read. The specials are no better, featuring Lord Chaos in 1 and 3, and the daft Sargon, Mistress Of War in 2, drawn early in his career by Marc Silvestri.~AL

WaRP GRAPHICS ANNUAL
WaRP: *One-shot 1986*

In 1986 WaRP was beginning to expand beyond publishing just their immensely successful *Elfquest* material, and this acts as a showcase for their newer titles. There's inevitably an *Elfquest* chapter, and *Myth Adventures* and *A Distant Soil* fans might consider it worth sampling, otherwise it's a selection of competently produced but long-forgotten fantasy strips.~WJ

WARRIOR
Quality Communications: *26 issues 1982–1985*

This black and white monthly magazine represented a renaissance in English comics. People who read it are liable to go misty-eyed when remembering its riches, chiefly offering the young Alan Moore to an audience unprepared for anything so intelligent but effortlessly entertaining in a mainstream comic.

Editor Dez Skinn pulled in old friends and found strong new talent, and was therefore able to give Moore's scripts to the likes of Garry Leach, Alan Davis, Steve Parkhouse and, most significantly, David Lloyd. Moore and Lloyd's 'V For Vendetta', the only strip that ran in every issue, was the backbone of the magazine, a unique, harrowing and creatively successful attempt at a political story. The politics of the strip were not tokenistic ornamentations for the superheroics. They were intrinsic and they were dealt with in a balanced manner. Lloyd's moody, shadowed art suited the story of a near-future Fascist Britain to a 't'. Moore's other great contribution was a revamping of the 50s bargain-basement Man of Steel, Marvelman. In Moore's hands Marvelman behaved just like you imagined someone who'd just realised they had almost unlimited power, increased sensitivity and the ability to fly would: buzz a few planes until the novelty wore off and go home for some fabulous sex. Garry Leach's ultra-detailed art helped convince until episode 6, where Alan Davis took over with his cleaner, elegant pencils (though you wouldn't know it from many of his recent efforts, Davis can draught beautifully). Marvelman appeared in every issue except 12, which had a Young Marvelman story, 19, 20, and 22 onwards, and the episodes in 9 and 10 have never been reprinted. Moore also contributed the perplexing Warpsmiths, indescribably alien aliens doing peculiar things to keep the universe in check (illustrated with great verve by Garry Leach in 9–10) and 'The Bojeffries Saga', a nutty English take on The Addams Family, with Steve Parkhouse (11–12, 19–20).

The diverting Laser Eraser and Pressbutton, far future assassins, by Steve Moore and a variety of artists, most notably Steve Dillon, appeared in the majority of issues, as did 'Father Shandor', by Steve Moore with art by John Bolton or John Ridgway, an interminable and rather old-fashioned fantasy story about a monk fighting demons. Magical fantasy 'The Spiral Path', written and drawn by Parkhouse, appeared in the first 12 issues. Very good art, very dull story.

Once Marvelman had finished, *Warrior* went downhill as Skinn introduced reprint material and filled out the magazine with features and self-penned strips such as Big Ben. Although this 'Man With No Time For Crime' notionally existed in the Marvelman universe his sub-Avengers-TV-show high jinks, badly drawn by Will Simpson, were no substitute. Nor was Bogey, the old hard-boiled detective in a far future routine. The last couple of issues were truly dismal, including such forgettable nonsense as Cyril Tompkins, Chartered Accountant by Trillo and Altuna (who should have known better) and The Black Currant, a barbarian parody so limp Julian Clary would ask for a refund. Most of the good material (and quite a lot of the bad) was reprinted in America, including 'V For Vendetta' (coloured but thankfully concluded), Marvelman (as Miracleman, but also continued), 'The Spiral Path', 'Laser Eraser and Pressbutton' (leading into a series of new stories) and 'The Bojeffries Saga' (reprinted in Flesh & Bones and continued in A1 series 2).~FJ

Recommended: 9, 10

Collection: The Bojeffries Saga (all Bojeffries stories from Warrior and elsewhere)

WARRIOR NUN AREALA

Antarctic: *3-issue miniseries 1994–1995, 6-issue miniseries ('Rituals') 1995–1996*

The first series introduces a world where the Vatican (like other religions) has an élite fighting force of warrior Nuns, whose job is to aid the Magic Priests in defending Earth against demon attack. Sister Shannon, recently assigned to New York, meets up with former nun Shotgun Mary and together they thwart the latest Hell-born invasion (with a little help from the spirit of the original Warrior Nun, Areala, and a wayward demon princess, Lillith). 'Rituals' introduces more characters and builds up the background to the series, including warriors from other religions. Ben Dunn's creation isn't quite as bad as it sounds, though the artwork's rough in places and there's no real depth to the scripts. Still, if you like plenty of action featuring beautiful women with superpowers, swords and guns, then this might be to your liking. Issue 3 of the first series has an alternative version that came with a CD soundtrack.~NF

WARRIORS OF PLASM

Defiant: *15 issues, 1993–1994*

Every now and again a comic comes along that's so appallingly bad you have to see it to believe it. *Warriors Of Plasm* is one of these. What really ruins any chance of redemption is the hackneyed dialogue. Meant to emphasise the other-worldliness of the title, it instead just sounds ridiculous. On a world composed mostly of what looks like snot, the Holy Inquisitor Lorca decides the best way to man a rebellion against the High Gore Lord Sueraceen is to kidnap some dweebs from Earth and give them snot-powers. Dweebs

escape, get back to Earth, get chased by more aliens, go back to snot-world, fight rebellion... but the dialogue doesn't improve any. Incredibly, there was later a spin-off series, *Prudence and Caution*, which was almost as bad. Jim Shooter, what were you thinking?~JC

WARSTRIKE

Malibu: *7 issues 1994*

Brandon Tark is a successful businessman but also a superpowered private detective who has superhealing powers. This is fortunate, since he gets beaten up a lot. In fact, in 6 he gets murdered by Rafferty, a killer who's after all superpowered beings. Fortunately for him it doesn't take. Dan Danko tries hard to make this more than 'big man, big gun, lots of mayhem' and manages some creditable characterisation, but, apart from the first story-line (1–3), the series doesn't have enough plot to go round. A giant-size issue (1994) sees the return of the villain Blind Faith, previously seen in 4, and serves as a prelude to the Ultraverse's *Godwheel* crossover.~NF

WARWORLD

Dark Horse: *One-shot 1989*

Slim science fiction from Gary Davis, a man who would be Moebius. Unfortunately he's not there yet, and this is an empty imitation.~FP

WASTELAND

DC: *18 issues 1987–1989*

DC's last, pre-Vertigo attempt to produce a horror title that was both adult and genuinely scary. Frankly, the latter was never likely but, written by Del Close and John Ostrander, *Wasteland* does approach the downright twisted. With the sound idea that readers would prefer to have a known, if rotating, group of artists, Don Simpson, William Messner-Loebs, David Lloyd and George Freeman were hired. One would do the cover and then one of the three stories in each issue. Although comparatively unknown at the time, this eclectic collection of styles proved very effective in giving the book a consistency (readers knew which artists to expect), variety and, given the quality of the contributors involved, a diversity of effective story-telling techniques.

Del Close's pseudo-autobiographical stories and Ostrander's more traditional, but still thoughtful and rarely obvious takes on the genre are always entertaining and often funny, and they're both willing to look for the horrific in the mundane, so you won't find many real monsters, aliens or supernatural beings. Of particular note is Close's parody of *American Splendor* in 3, drawn in the style of Robert Crumb by Simpson, and Ostrander's three-part 'Dead Detective' (8, 12, 17), in which a detective proves to be more successful dead than alive.

From 10 George Freeman dropped out and guest artists Tim Truman (10), Ty Templeton (11), Joe Orlando (12, 13, 15) and Rick Magyar (16 on) replaced him. Bill Wray replaced Lloyd in the regular contributor's circle from 13. The final issue is a retrospective of sorts which features elements from most of the previous issues. Playful and well worth reading, *Wasteland* was perhaps a little ahead of its time.~NF
Recommended: 8, 12, 16, 17

WATCHMEN
DC: *12-issue limited series 1986–1987*

It's several years since costumed adventurers had their heyday. An Act of Congress outlawing vigilantes has put a stop to their role as enforcers and moral avengers. Some, like the shy, retiring Nightowl, and Ozymandias, the smartest man in the world, have mothballed their cowls and gone quietly. Some, like the Comedian, a wisecracking warmonger, and Dr Manhattan, a scientist irradiated in a freak accident, have returned to the warren of counter-intelligence agencies and government projects whence they came. Others, like the sociopathic Rorschach, have carried on a one-man crusade against crime. When the Comedian is killed Rorschach is the only one who senses that time is running out for his old team-mates; in fact, time is running out for everyone.

Watchmen looks long and hard into the dark corners of the superhero psyche. It asks what kind of people want to dress up in funny costumes and beat the shit out of villains. It examines the practical ramifications of a traditional superhero story dynamic, where a character like Dr Manhattan, who can control matter and exists in serial time, where past, present and future are laid out in front of him like frames in a film, brush up against cheerful boy-scout vigilantes who just want to help people and guys who get a kick out of dressing up and doing violence. And it looks at why society might condone and support this behaviour, and how the presence of such people, from ordinary thrill-seekers to god-like beings, affects that society. Writer Alan Moore examines each character one by one, peeling back the layers slowly, turning over the familiar elements of the superhero team until all their glitter has rubbed off. Each one becomes a real person (or a real demi-god) as they slowly reveal their deepest anxieties. At the same time he writes an intriguing murder mystery that works on multiple levels and leads into a massive conspiracy, as the Comedian's old comrades (many of whom hated his guts) begin to wonder if there's something going on behind the scenes. There's also a counter-plot in which a young boy is reading a strange pirate comic whose psychological story points up the horrors

being faced by the 'heroes', and additional information in the form of memoranda, features and newspaper reports at the back of each issue.

The telling of much of the story is left to the pictures. Not only does Dave Gibbons create a cohesive world, subtly different from our own, he also builds up a web of symbols and icons around which the story is built. His clean, detailed style is perfectly suited to a story that shakes up how we look at superheroes forever, because it's exactly what we expect a good superhero comic to look like. Nothing is taken for granted in *Watchmen*. The view down a street behind a character's head is there for a reason, and is consistent with a view from the other end of the street shown eight issues previously. If only all comics were crafted and polished like this.

Originally supposed to be a reworking of old Charlton characters whose rights had just been bought by DC, *Watchmen* had a huge impact when it was published, and although it didn't generate many direct imitations (too much like hard work, one suspects, more's the pity) it altered the whole approach to superhero comics taken by many writers, encouraging them to deconstruct the myth of superbeings. It remains a superb read that will keep you on the edge of your seat, while enriching your understanding of humanity.~FJ
Recommended: 1–12
Collection: Watchmen (1–12)

WAY OUT STRIPS
Tragedy Strikes: *4 issues 1992*
Fantagraphics: *4 issues 1994*

Carol Swain's artwork is very simple, and her characters all look like pit-bull terriers. The stories are anything but simplistic, though. There's a crooked antique dealer who says she sold her soul to the devil, but the devil's name is Brian and he lives in a bedsit, and he's disconcertingly tentative when he asks if he can see her again. There's a woman who returns to her home town and makes some disturbing discoveries about her friend Sam. There are days, and gigs, in the life of a stand-up comic. Driving narrative, no, but she records states of mind that most writers seem unaware of, and brings a haunting clarity to every scene. Possibly an acquired taste, but worth the effort.~FC
Recommended: Fantagraphics 1–4

WCW World Championship Wrestling
Marvel: *12 issues 1992–1993*

It would be a reasonable assumption that having prodded costumed superheroes from battle to battle so successfully Marvel would have no trouble with costumed wrestlers. This was the 1990s Marvel, though, where dull, safe and uninspired was a way of life.~WJ

WEAPON ZERO
Image: *5-issue limited series (T4-0) 1995, 10 issues + 1996 to date*

In a miniseries running chronologically back from issue 4 to issue 0 Colonel Tyson Stone lands on the Moon. There he's infected by T'srri bio-technology, discovers that his wife, Lorelei, has been preparing him for the war between the Batai and the evil T'srri, and then watches her being killed by N'Golth, the T'srri leader. N'Golth has been taking people from different time periods and creating an army of T'srri/human hybrids. With three of them – an English boy about to be press-ganged, a Japanese Princess Kikuyo and a Roman child spared from Vesuvius – their human side has retained control. Now all four of them are ready to take on the T'srri in their Moon-base (T4–0). The ongoing series sees the time-lost team trying to adjust to a new world while they come to the attention of the Arsenal of Democracy, a secret US agency that believes they're aliens and therefore a threat to security (1–3). In the search for a means of living they visit Japan (4, 5) and the former home of Kikuyo before returning to the US to battle armoured insects and Lorelei's father, who then takes them out into space to begin the war against the T'srri. Walt Simonson and Joe Benitez have created an entertaining cross between science fiction and superheroes that obviously owes much to Japanese robot comics with their love of high-tech weapons and armour. Simonson keeps the whole reasonably light-hearted but has not so far shown much interest in developing character, later issues being mostly just battles.~NF

WEAVEWORLD
Epic: *3-issue miniseries 1991–1992*

Despite a generous 192-page allocation this adaptation of Clive Barker's doorstop suffers from contraction. Threats that may terrify as prose are reduced to comedy by the soundbites required for comics, and the pace is very forced, particularly in the first issue. A Barker completist might enjoy this; otherwise the original novel is probably better and cheaper.~FP

The WEB
!mpact: *14 issues, 1 annual 1991–1992*

One of the !mpact imprints' relaunches of the old Archie/MLJ concept, this Web, unlike previous versions, is an organisation rather than a person, an U.N.C.L.E.-like network of agents and operatives, several of whom wear armour and have weapons giving them virtual superpowers. In the 1960s, the Web agents used one identity, deceiving the public into thinking there was only one hero called the Web. Covert for twenty years, the organisation responds to a new flood of superhuman activity by surveying a new group of agents in training to determine who will now assume the public persona of the Web. Len Strazeswski handles the set-up engagingly, but Tom Artis' artwork looks skimpy and inattentive, and a rapid succession of 'guest artists' and fill-in writers blurs the appeal that the rather clever concept had.~HS

THE WEIRD
DC: *4-issue miniseries 1988*

Bernie Wrightson burst back on the comic scene after a long bout of illness to illustrate this more-than-average superhero tosh. The intermittent years had not been kind: this is a shadow of his former work. The JLA investigate a strange alien presence and spend four issues not really doing much. Jim Starlin's script has far too many talking heads and he never seems to quite get to grips with his own story.~TP

WEIRD FANTASY
EC: *22 issues (13–17, then 6–22) 1950–1953*

Continuing its numbering from *A Girl, A Moon, Romance*, the first story in *Weird Fantasy* ('Am I Man Or Machine', stiffly illustrated by Al Feldstein) was a romance, sort of. A seemingly normal man looks up his old girl-friend, two years after he's been declared dead in a car crash. His brain has been saved by two scientists, who've built a robot body to house it. The script goes into a lot of detail about what it's like to be isolated in a glass jar for months, and how various receptors can replace senses. When the man realises his sweetheart has married another he pretends it was all a joke, and leaves. This story immediately sets the agenda for the early issues, which concentrate on weird science more than fantasy. Later issues concentrate more on a 'don't meddle with nature' message, but early ones are packed with time-travel conundrums (although none really bettered Harry Harrison's 'Only Time Will Tell' from 1, with art assists from Wally Wood).

A regular line-up of artists was soon established, with editor Feldstein producing the slick, rather mechanical covers on the early issues, often concentrating on hardware rather than people, plus the lead story. Other regular contributors included Wally Wood, in his element, and Jack Kamen, whose fine-lined, reliable artwork appeared in most issues. Harvey Kurtzman wrote and drew a handful of wry, twist-in-the-tale stories that concentrated on character during the first year. They stand out a mile from the rest of the comic's largely Feldstein-plotted efforts, not just because they only have half as many words and panels. 'Atom Bomb Thief', from 2, is a typical Kurtzman tale of a janitor who smuggles plans for an atom bomb, is double-crossed, murders his buyer and ends up, after a plane crash, being shipwrecked on Bikini Atoll. It's not a particularly clever tale but it's economically done, emphasising human emotion rather than scientific discovery, drawn in a style halfway between his humour work and the tighter line he used for his war stories. More inventive is 'The Dimension Translator' from 6.

Apart from slight shifts in tone, one issue of *Weird Fantasy* doesn't really differ from another in story content. There's usually something about a matter transmitter, time machine or duplicator going terribly wrong, something about aliens (either they walk among us or I've discovered they're about to attack and no one will believe me) and something about space exploration (they're our lost comrades we've come to this planet to rescue and, oops, we just shot 'em because they looked like dangerous aliens). One of the funniest alien tales is 'The Thing in the Jar', from 11. Illustrated by Joe Orlando, who was a semi-regular from 9 onwards, it starts ingeniously with a strange pond which turns out to be a living creature. A sample from the pond starts talking to some researchers, suggesting it's part of a group mind and that it has come to help mankind. Naturally mistrusting it (this is the Cold War, after all), the researchers hit upon the novel idea of pouring a bottle of gin into the sample, so that, in a pissed state, it will reveal its hidden agenda, which is indeed the invasion and domination of the world. After a while this persistent paranoia can get boring for the modern reader.

Issue 14 featured the first Al Williamson art on the title and he fitted right in alongside Wally Wood. Together Wood, Williamson and Frazetta created the busty space-babe-in-a-bubble-helmet image that came to typify the magazine, but was in fact entirely untypical of the first half of its run. Later issues featured one or two more menacing space monsters and sexy girls, as the popularity of the horror titles encouraged it to become more gruesome. There remained a feeling, however, that *Weird Fantasy* didn't quite know where it fitted in the EC line.~FJ

Recommended: 1, 2, 6, 11, 20, 21
Collection: Weird Fantasy (1–22)

WEIRD MYSTERY Tales
DC: *24 issues 1972–1975*

Oh good, another average mystery title offering a few stories with nice art (Kaluta in 24) among the mundane majority. The first three issues do, however, stand out as they contain Jack Kirby stories originally planned for his cancelled black and white magazine, *Spirit World*. *Sandman* completists might also want to know that Destiny hosted the title in enigmatic fashion.~HY
Recommended: 1–3

WEIRD ROMANCE
Eclipse: *1 issue 1988*

Oddball collection of 1950s horror stories dealing with boy/girl relationships in which one or another partner is a vampire, ghost, merperson, etc. Sadly, the execrable standard of story and art makes it much less fun than it sounds.~HS

WEIRD SCIENCE
EC: *4 issues (12–15) 1950, 18 issues (5–22) 1951–1953*
Gladstone: *4 issues 1990–1991*
Russ Cochran: *20 issues + 1992 to date*

For various complex reasons concerning postal regulations applying to subscription copies, the first four issues of *Weird Science* are numbered 12–15, continuing the numbering of the cancelled *Saddle Romances*. They're easily distinguished from the later 12–15, which always open with a Wally Wood-drawn story. There's one issue with no cover number, and the succeeding issue is numbered 6, which had been the total number of issues to that point.

Long fondly recalled as *the* classic science-fiction comic, time hasn't been kind to *Weird Science*. While the art is still of a high standard, and outstanding in places, the vast majority of stories are distinctly of their period, science fiction having moved on considerably since the 1950s. Typical early plots have a nutty scientist making a great breakthrough, but not living to pass on the knowledge, using it for petty revenge, or, for some reason, the world never knows what they've discovered. Another wrinkle is that the cast, whom the reader is led to believe are human, turn out to be aliens or other-dimensional beings, often invading Earth. William Gaines and Al Feldstein wrote most of the stories, and other favourite plots concern the then topical effects of the atom and hydrogen bombs, flogged to death in early issues. Feldstein did prove before his time in relating the alleged events of Roswell wholesale in the first issue 13, and also adapted Orson Welles' famous *War Of The Worlds* broadcast in 15 (which also contained the only EC science-fiction story drawn by horror maestro Graham 'Ghastly' Ingels). Harvey Kurtzman both wrote and drew his contributions, and it shows. They're the highlights of the early issues, with Kurtzman either eschewing the shock ending altogether or being far more imaginative in getting there with stories that stand the test of time. 'Man Or Superman' in 6 is an amusing tale of a bodybuilder and his scientist brother-in-law, while 7's charming 'Gregory Had A Model T' predates *Herbie* by over a decade with its tale of a sentient car.

The artist most associated with EC science-fiction stories is Wally Wood, and while some argue his war stories were slightly superior, there's no doubt of a master at work here. Oddly enough, Wood himself would later cite *T.H.U.N.D.E.R. Agents* as his personal best, claiming his earlier EC work was 'compulsively and neurotically overdetailed'. That may have been the case, but for the 1950s no one was more convincing when it came to the nuts and bolts of spacecraft, or, indeed, capable of depicting more alluring humans. 'Gray Cloud Of Death' in 9 features the most amazing spacesuits, and the issue also has a second Wood-drawn story, 'Invaders', sadly a rather dated script. Possibly his best known science-fiction strip was 'My World' in 22, an absorbing narrative detailing the vistas and possibilities of science fiction. Since it's become so personally associated with Wood (and, indeed, was parodied by him in *Mad*), it's ironic to note that the story was written by Feldstein, and the narrative voice is his. Wood also illustrated some of the more audacious material to appear in 1950s comics with a trans-gender special in 10, and a tale of hermaphrodites in 14. 20's stunning tearjerker 'The Loathsome', distressingly based on a true story of an ugly young girl tormented and rejected by everyone, should raise a lump in all but the most cynical of throats, and 'He Walks Among Us' in 13 (an issue also containing the astonishingly downbeat 'A Weighty Decision') is blatantly 'the story of Christ transposed to another planet', according to Feldstein. It received surprisingly little critical attention at a time when the entire EC line was under fire for its content. 20's 'The Reformers' takes an obvious sideswipe at their critics, with crusading zealots attempting to reform heaven.

Having been pulled up for lifting plots from other sources, EC began cover-crediting adaptations of stories by known science-fiction writers, most notably Ray Bradbury (although future science-fiction favourite Harry Harrison actually drew stories in the first two issues). Al Williamson débuted in 16, and quickly became an artist only surpassed by Wood, his peak being 19's ambiguous and ethereal 'One Who Waits'. *Weird Science* hits its stride with the second issue 12, by which time the content is less predictable, and from there all issues are worth at least a glance. With 23 the title is merged with EC's other science-fiction comic to become *Weird Science-Fantasy*. The Gladstone reprints are random (containing 9, 16 and 22), while the Russ Cochran-published series reprints every issue sequentially in the original format.~WJ
Recommended: 13, 19, 20, 22
Collection: *Weird Science* (12–15, 5–22)

WEIRD SCIENCE FANTASY
EC: *7 issues (23–29) 1954–1955*

Continuing from *Weird Fantasy*, the celebrated writers and artists of EC went on weaving their magic here until the Comics Code Authority emasculated the line and finally drove EC out of business.

Behind fantastic covers by Wally Wood (23, 27), Al Feldstein (24, 26, 28) and Frank Frazetta (29), the stories concentrate on ideas about what makes society work and the relationship of man to his environment, rather than the grotesque endings for which EC is perhaps best known. Wood has a story in every issue, all good examples of his style, but none that leap out. Joe Orlando is also in every issue, but, strangely for EC, draws a continuing character. Otto Binder's Adam Link, a robot with human feelings who survives a trial to establish his right to citizenship, features in three strips (27–29). Orlando would later redraw the series for Warren Publishing.

26, written by Feldstein and drawing on notes from Major Donald E. Keyhoe, a leading popular writer on the subject, is a special issue given over to the 'actual facts' about flying saucers. It's drawn alternately by Wood and Orlando but is the least interesting issue, simply because there's no room to tell stories, just present the 'facts'. Al Williamson's exotic artwork (backgrounds reputedly by such diverse hands as Angelo Torres and Roy Krenkel) graces 'Fish Story' (23), the famous 'A Sound Of Thunder' (25), adapted from Ray Bradbury's tale of dinosaur hunters tampering with time, 'Upheaval!' (24), written by a young Harlan Ellison, 'Lost In Space' (28) and 'Vicious Circle' (29). The latter is one of several stories in which mankind has degenerated and some evidence of past technology provides the focus for the plot – see also Orlando's 'Fair Trade' about aliens buying Manhattan Island in 23.

Jack Kamen (27, 28) and Reed Crandall (27, 29) both produce some fine work but the title's other major artist is Bernie Krigstein. 'The Flying Machine' (23) is another Bradbury story, illustrated in a highly stylised manner, drawing on Chinese art for inspiration. 'The Pioneer' (24) is a grim tale, comparing and contrasting a space trip with a man's journey to the electric chair. His final story for the title was 'Bellyful' in 25. 27 came out at the height of the controversy over Wertham's *Seduction Of The Innocent* and, even more than the other issues, contains stories that plead the cause of tolerance and fair-mindedness. Far from corrupting the youth of America, EC comics strove for enlightenment; if one were cynical that would be enough to explain why they had to be stopped.~NF
Recommended: 23–25, 27–29
Collection: *Weird Science Fantasy* boxed set (23–29)

WEIRD WAR Tales
DC: *124 issues 1971–1983*

Largely featuring stories about World War II, new sequences by editor Joe Kubert (1–4, 7) and Alex Toth (5 and 6) framed fine reprints from the likes of Kubert and Mort Drucker, and occasional new strips from Reed Crandall (2), Russ Heath (3 and 5) and Frank Thorne (6), making a really nice package. Joe Orlando became editor with 8 and the title became a more typical horror comic, with all-new material. Scripts from veterans Robert Kanigher, Sheldon Mayer and Arnold Drake, while always competent, were never exceptional. Artistically, for much of its life *Weird War* featured fine material, almost exclusively from Filipino artists like Tony DeZuniga and Alfredo Alcala, with brief appearances from Nestor Redondo (13) and Noly Panaligan (45) for good measure. Notable other artists included Neal Adams (8), Alex Toth (10), Walt Simonson (10) and an inspired Frank Robbins (21, 27, 35, 36). The comic's artistic highspots, however, were provided by Alex Nino, whose unfettered imagination was at its peak here, with mostly science-fiction-themed stories in 11, 13, 16, 23–25, 31, 36, 55, 61, 69 and 70.

José Luis Garcia-Lopez made an early DC appearance in 41 and 44, as did Marshall Rogers and Terry Austin on Jack C. Harris' 'Canterbury Tail', originally intended for *Kamandi* and somewhat incongruous here. By 50 *Weird War* had passed its peak, and the remainder of the run is extremely patchy, though a Russ Heath strip in 59 is worth looking out for. Howard Chaykin (61, 62, 76) and Frank Miller (64, 68) both crop up, though none of their efforts were the least bit inspired. In an attempt to stem the title's malaise J.M. DeMatteis' *Creature Commandos* débuted in 93, pitting Frankenstein, Wolfman, Medusa *et al.* against the Third Reich. The series never lived up to its (unintentional?) comic potential, and the Pat Broderick artwork was no help. Robert Kanigher's GI Robot was introduced in 101 to little acclaim, though Kanigher's other series, 'The War That Time Forgot' (revived from *Star Spangled War Stories* in 94, 99, 100 and 103), at least boasted fine artwork from Dave Cockrum and Jerry Ordway. More interesting was Mike Barr's Jasper Pepperdyne (108), notable for some lovely Garcia-Lopez art and for being a breathtakingly blatant *Dr Who* swipe. For those wanting an introduction to *Weird War Tales*, 36 was a sixty-eight-page giant that reprinted a lot of the best early material.~DAR

Recommended: 1–10, 13, 16, 23–25, 36, 51, 52, 55, 59, 61, 69, 70, 108

WEIRD WESTERN
DC: *59 issues (12–70) 1972–1980*

Inheriting the numbering from *All Star Western* with 12, there was initially little difference. Bounty-hunter Jonah Hex was the cover star and lead feature, backed up by El Diablo, reprint strips, and the occasional other new strip (Alex Toth's in 16 is a beauty), but by 21 Hex had seen off all the back-ups and was occupying all twenty-four pages.

Writer John Albano cast Hex as an enigmatic stranger universally feared unless a gunfighter was required, vindictive and mean, although with a fine sense of justice. Artist Tony DeZuniga rendered grubby realistic locales and well-worn people. Their run was good, but basically standard Western plots with a propensity for crooks to be dealt poetic justice in the form of their own iniquities. For their best story see 'The Hanging Woman' in 17. Michael Fleisher from 22, though, honed Hex, transforming him into a fully rounded character. His largely single-issue plots were inventive and he fleshed out Jonah's character and past, revealing life-long enemies made during the Civil War (plot temporarily resolved in 29–30). De Zuniga left with 24, with Noly Panaligan and George Moliterni handling most remaining Hex stories here in equally suitable fashion. The entire Fleisher *oeuvre* is good, but for the best try the Doug Wildey-drawn 26, which shows the depth of resentment against the incursive railroad, an early take on feminism (27) or Jonah in a town where hanging is a public festival (35).

Jonah Hex was promoted to his own title after 38 and *Weird Western* was inherited by Brian Savage, Scalphunter, a white man raised by Indians. Strong social concerns permeate the stories, but he's dull, and the only weird thing is how he lasted thirty-one issues. If you're desperate to see them again, El Diablo turned up in *Jonah Hex* 32, 48, 56–60 and 73–75 and Scalphunter was in 41,42 and 45–47.~FP

Recommended: 17,19, 24, 25–27, 29–31, 34, 35, 37, 38

WEIRD WONDER TALES
Marvel: *22 issues 1973–1977*

Another round of 1950s reprints. 7 featured the individual stories of the characters who were to comprise the Headmen in Steve Gerber's *Defenders* stories, Bill Everett's Venus occupies 16–18 and Doctor Druid 19–22. Be warned, though, it's mundane stuff. This outlived the other Marvel horror reprint titles, and perhaps the occasional diversity provided by maverick artists helped. There are Doug Wildey (2), Angelo Torres (7), Bernie Krigstein (19) and Joe Kubert (22), in addition to the usual suspects.~FP

WEIRD WORLDS

DC: *10 issues 1972–1974*

An artistic treasure trove produced during DC's early-70s experimental phase. 1–7 had skilful adaptations of Edgar Rice Burroughs' *John Carter* and *Pellucidar* stories (previously seen in DC's *Tarzan* and *Korak* comics) by the likes of Denny O'Neil, Len Wein and Marv Wolfman, with art from the great Murphy Anderson, Mike Kaluta, Sal Amedola and Al Weiss, to name a few.

8–10 featured *Ironwulf*, a Howard Chaykin creation (scripted by Denny O'Neil). It was a wonderful sword-and-sorcery saga with all the ingredients of great space opera: an empire headed by a beautiful evil empress, vampire warriors, family feuding, a wooden spaceship and lots of marvellous-looking characters. A shame we had to wait twenty years for the continuation of the series in the *Ironwulf* graphic novel.~HY

Recommended: 1–10

WEIRDO

Last Gasp: *28 issues 1981–1993*

Weirdo is an anthology that kept the spirit of the underground alive through lean years until it was absorbed by a new generation. As such its importance is both vast and unquantifiable. Editorially, though, it's a mixture of the inspired and downright unreadable, but tipping the scales in its favour is that there's a vast quantity of Robert Crumb work here.

1 is almost entirely untempered Crumb – not a pretty sight. His editorial stamp dominates that and succeeding issues. They're populated by dull illustrated articles, weak one-panel cartoons and bizarre photostrips acting out Crumb's pitiful sexual obsessions. They're nonetheless saved by one good (often great) Crumb strip every time (except 2). A particularly poor issue, 4, is redeemed by five pages of Crumb waxing nostalgic about the 1960s (and two Drew Friedman one-pagers). Crumb's *Weirdo* strips have a broad sweep. Underground whimsy is set off by startling adaptations of Boswell (3) and the arcane psychological imperatives of Krafft-Ebbing (13, possibly an ironic response to reactions about his own predilections). He turns in engaging and passionate diatribes, plain silliness and one lapse into bizarre racist conspiracy theory in 28, inexcusable even if intended as ridicule. If his tirades on the superficial nature of fashion and society in Mode O'Day (9, 10, 12, 18 and 26) became overworked and repetitive, they're balanced by his outstanding autobiographical strips. 'Uncle Bob's Mid-Life Crisis' in 7 and the complementary 'I'm Grateful, I'm Grateful' in 25 are the work of a major talent on top form, as Crumb analyses his circumstances in

typically introspective fashion. Also surprisingly effective are strips about domestic bliss drawn by Crumb and his wife Aline Kominsky-Crumb (16, 23), with the material ensuring that the wildly contrasting artistic abilities don't jar.

Crumb quickly published new cartoonists, and, although he wasn't faultless in his selection, the fact that Drew Friedman, Kaz, J.D. King, Dori Seda, Dennis Worden and Peter Bagge all débuted here is sufficient to overlook some poorer judgements. Also in the Crumb-edited issues are Terry Boyce's forgotten (which is apparently how she now wants it) but oddly charming 'Peter The Penis' strips, satirising the male attitude to life. They were dropped by Peter Bagge when he took over with 10. He also discontinues the puerile photostrips, uses more Kaz and King, and publishes J.R. Williams, Mark Zingarelli and classic underground artists like S.Clay Wilson and Bill Griffith. Bagge's own strips are high spots, introducing the Bradleys (14) and Ken Weiner (13), but his best is 'The Reject ' (10), alienation and childhood torment presented without apologies. It's a theme also explored in the truly bizarre 'Fishlips' stories in 15 and 16.

Outside the editors, Kim Deitch and Spain are the most frequently published creators. Deitch mainly submits his strange strips of the Ledecker Carnival (15, 16, 19, 23). Despite an open, if static, clear style, his art disturbs on an almost primal level, prompting those unknown fears lying within us all. Spain is an acquired taste. While capable of brilliant work, his *Weirdo* strips generally feature the tiresome Big Bitch. Begun as a joke (one hopes), it's a one-note joke worked to death after a single appearance yet returns again and again, with plots that would seem slim to an anorexic.

Aline Kominsky-Crumb becomes editor with 18, and again broadens the contributor base, returning Spain and operating a positive-discrimination policy with regard to women. Carol Lay, Julie Doucet, Mary Fleener, Phoebe Glockner, Penny Moran, Leslie Sternbergh and Carol Tyler all contribute top-notch material to what is the best editorial selection of the run. The amazing Lindsay Arnold and Michael Dougan hold up the male end. Kominsky-Crumb's own autobiographical strips, appearing from 2, work well, presenting a generally positive and coping attitude towards a strange childhood, and always raising a laugh.

Weirdo may yet return. There was a three-year gap between 27 and 28, titled *Verre D'Eau* to reflect the large contingent of French contributors. Although cover-blurbed 'The last issue ever' the editorial takes a softer line.~WJ

Recommended: 3, 4, 7, 10, 12–14, 18–20, 22–28

WELCOME BACK KOTTER
DC: *10 issues 1976–1978*
A nice humorous title based on the TV series about a teacher, Kotter, and his misfit pupils. Not as good as 'The Bash Street Kids' in the UKs *The Beano*, but then what is?~HY

WEREWOLF
Dell: *3 issues 1966–1967*
Of the trio of Dell heroes named after screen monsters this is the most pathetic. Major Wiley Wolf of Secret Defence Unit One's adventures are the worst-drawn comics of the 1960s. Tony Tallarico, take a bow.~SW

WEREWOLF by NIGHT
Marvel: *43 issues, 5 Giant-Size 1972–1977*
This series' greatest achievement was to survive for forty-three issues. Owing to an ancient, hereditary curse, Jack Russell (yes, really) turned into a werewolf during the three nights closest to the full moon every month after attaining his eighteenth birthday. Marvel decided that the strip was most suited to the supernatural/fantasy vein. It wasn't actually suited to anything. As the entire series is related by the hirsute star, a cynical American teenager, his narration produces a grating contrast to the mood of the stories. Gerry Conway was the only scripter to display any feel for the strip. He wrote the first three appearances in *Marvel Spotlight* (first series) 2–4 and the first four issues of this series, but all his successors contrived utterly ridiculous plot coincidences and a sense of pacing that would shame a legless corpse. The first Giant-Size issue, titled *Giant-Size Creatures*, guest-stars Tigra and scrapes a pass. Mike Ploog contributes acceptable pencils in some of the first sixteen issues, and 31–33 (the latter two introducing Moon Knight) by Doug Moench achieve mediocrity. Further compliments are impossible.~APS
Recommended: 1

WEST COAST AVENGERS
Marvel: *4-issue miniseries 1984, 102 issues, 8 Annuals 1985–1994*
Hawkeye is given the task of setting up a West Coast franchise of the Avengers with a maximum of six members, and the initial miniseries describes the formation of a five-person team and the team's first action. It's an entertaining piece of superhero soap opera, with some decent ideas in the plotting, from Roger Stern, and perfunctory art from Bob Hall and Brett Breeding.
1–41 of the main series were written almost entirely by Steve Englehart, with uninspired layouts from Al Milgrom, usually finished by Joe Sinnott. Although he was responsible for a golden era on *The Avengers*, Englehart's plotting here starts out silly and gets sillier – and the dialogue is no better (e.g. from 14: 'It's the one thing that's made the loss of his robotic son bearable'). 1–10 still work as soap opera: who will be the sixth member? when will Tigra accept that she's good enough for the team? After that the characterisations collapse under the weight of the daft story-lines. The most preposterous has the team time-travelling in 17–23, which at its peak (if 'peak' is the word) splits the action across seven timelines, and involves love potions and a spectacular string of coincidences to deliver a message from those stranded in the past. Read it, and recalibrate your definition of chutzpah. From 42–57, John Byrne took over as writer and penciller, bringing some discipline and imagination to the plotting, and producing some striking images and changes, not least of the title, which became *Avengers West Coast* from 50. It's an enormous improvement, but it still only brings the comic up to the level of 'forgettable superhero yarn'. After Byrne, the main writers were Roy and Dann Thomas, artwork mostly by Paul Ryan and Danny Bulanadi (63–69) and David Ross and Tim Dzon (76–100). The only glimmerings of interest centre around USAgent, who was foisted on the team by the government and whose failure to fit in comes to a peak in 69. It's a huge relief when we stagger to 102 and all those giant robots can go back to the lab for an overhaul.
The annuals are both frustrating and surprisingly rewarding. In most of them, at least half of the comic is occupied by one episode of a story spread over several other Marvel annuals, so will be incomprehensible unless you have the four or fourteen others. However, the remainder of these issues was occupied by three or four short stories, some quite strong. The 1989 annual has an interesting stream-of-consciousness treatment of USAgent, the 1991 annual has Wasp discussing her *Avengers* screenplay with a Hollywood producer (amusing) and Living Lightning paying a visit to his old gangland neighbourhood, and the 1992 annual has a similar encounter with the past for Spiderwoman and a humorous piece where the team argue the Top Ten rankings for supervillains.~FC

WESTERN GUNFIGHTERS
Marvel: *33 issues 1970–1975*
The giant-sized 1–7 each ran a lead story featuring the original Western Ghost Rider by the inevitable and very ordinary combination of Gary Friedrich and Dick Ayers. The back-up strips and the last twenty-six issues reprinted a variety of 1950s Western stories, including Apache Kid, Wyatt Earp, Tex Dawson and Kid Colt. Some notable artists feature: Angelo Torres (26), Joe Kubert (4), Jack Kirby (1, 10, 11),

Doug Wildey (8, 9) and Al Williamson (18), but only Kirby and Williamson are anywhere near on form. 4 also has a curiosity in the form of the first story which Barry Windsor-Smith, or plain Barry Smith as he was then, drew for Marvel. Don't waste time looking for it.~APS

THE WESTERN KID
Marvel: *5 issues 1971–1972*

The Western Kid was Tex Dawson, and these 1950s reprints are illustrated with no particular distinction by the likes of John Romita and Al Williamson. Someone must have liked them, though, because Tex was promoted into his own title.~WJ

WESTERN TEAM-UP
Marvel: *1 issue 1973*

Seemingly pointless reprint title, with only Jack Davis' Gunsmoke Kid of any interest.~FP

WET SATIN
Kitchen Sink: *1 issue 1976*

Published in the wake of *My Secret Garden*, the standard text on the topic, and subtitled 'Women's erotic fantasies', this is a strangely subdued and unarousing collection of stories from assorted underground cartoonists. The whole affair is rescued, though, by Joyce Farmer's absolutely delightful 'A Mature Relationship', showing that sex doesn't stop once you're collecting your pension.~FP

WETWORKS
Image: *24 issues + 1994 to date*

Created by Whilce Portacio and Brandon Choi, scripted by Francis Takenaga with pencils by Portacio for 1–9, *Wetworks* is a superhero team led by Jackson Dane, one of the original members of the militaristic Team 7. At the start the team consists of Dane, Dozer, Pilgrim, Mother One, Claymore, Jester, Grail, Crossbones and Flattop. The fledgeling team are sent on a suicide mission by Miles Craven, and in order to survive have to don symbiotic suits owned by Prince Drakken of the Vampire nation, who wants them as protection from the sun. Both the vampiric Blood Queen and Armand Waering of the Were-Nation have been plotting to create just such a team, subverting the plans of Craven and Drakken. Wetworks agree to help Waering in his fight against the Vampires in return for a chance to pay Craven back for his treachery.

1–3 set the scene and introduce the major players, while 4–11 see the symbiotes causing changes in the bodies of the team members, as Drakken overthrows the Blood Queen and seeks to unite the Night Tribes for his war. 12–15 provide more background information on Waering and the symbiotes, as the team search for a cure for a virus that is killing

Claymore, and 16 and 17 are part of the 'Fire From Heaven' crossover. In later issues Pilgrim, missing since 6, returns and her brother, Blackbird, is introduced to the team. There's a battle between Dane and the Blood Queen which leads into the return of team members who're apparently dead.

After Portacio left, the series suffered from a rota of different artists, few lasting more than an issue, until Jason Johnson took over with 20. Although completely different in style, Johnson's Manga-influenced artwork is proving well suited to the book and is still improving. What has kept the series going, however, is Takenaga's story-telling. It's sometimes frustratingly slow, but the steady pacing adds a great deal to the atmosphere. The Night Tribes are an excellent device and the characterisation of the team members has been subtly handled. The series bears investigation if you like team books. A *Wetworks Sourcebook* (1994) appeared between issues 3 and 4.~NF

WHA..!?
Bruce Henderson: *1 issue 1975*

One of Steve Ditko's mid-1970s solo comics, *Wha..!?* contained a number of short strips, all of them suffused with his philosophy of rampant individualism. It was a mixture of superheroes (The Void, Masquerade), science fiction ('Premise To Consequence') and crime stories (Sgt Kage), all drawn with great vigour and enthusiasm. None of the strips are exactly memorable, though, and Ditko's obsessed invective manages to get in the way of the stories without there being enough of it to make it interesting. Too much action, not enough ranting.~DAR

WHAT IF...?
Marvel: *Series one 47 issues 1977–1985, one-shot 1988, series two 92 issues + 1989 to date*

When initially launched, *What If* had the potential to be an inventive and entertaining series for readers familiar with pivotal events in Marvel's by then already convoluted superhero universe. Unfortunately, writers Roy Thomas (who did have his moments), and particularly Don Glut, in the company of assorted hack artists, ensured that inspiration was minimal when it came to conceiving new outcomes from generally known events. The most off-the-wall concept of the entire run was series one's 11, in which Jack Kirby had a ball bestowing the Fantastic Four's abilities on the early Marvel office staff. That story, though, typified the idea being generally far better than the execution, a common flaw, never more apparent than in 14's dire 'What If Sgt Fury Fought World War II In Space?' A less pertinent, but equally annoying flaw of most early stories was the formula decreeing that something occurred to ensure that the alternate Earth which was glimpsed ended up much the same as the regular version. The series did find a home for the Watcher, perennial Marvel guest star, who didn't actually do much except, er, watch. Here he was given a purpose as mine host opening the curtain on the alternate universes where significant differences occurred in familiar scenarios.

The best of the first ten issues, oddly, was a story later accepted as part of Marvel's official canon. Thomas and Frank Robbins' issue 4 explained how Captain America continued to appear in post-1945 tales when his 1960s re-emergence at Marvel had had him frozen in a block of ice since the dying days of World War II. Thomas triumphed again in 13, with regular Conan collaborator John Buscema illustrating 'What If Conan The Barbarian Walked The Earth Today?' For once the actuality matched the novel concept, although a reprise in 43 stretched the idea too thin. Remarkably, there were even stories that went on to occur in the 'real' Marvel universe, notably 2's 'What If The Hulk Had Bruce Banner's Brain?' (although Thomas and Herb Trimpe provided a less satisfactory sequence than Peter David would years later), and 30's 'What If Spider-Man's Clone Had Lived' (handled with considerably more economy in 1979).

Content of note during the latter half of the first series included Frank Miller reworking his Daredevil and Elektra concepts in 28 and 35, although both are slim in content, a spirited alternative to *Uncanny X-Men* 137 in 27 and a humour special, 34, packed with still funny shorts. Highlights included 'What If Cyclops' Energy Beams Came Out Of His Ears?', 'What If Daredevil Were Deaf Instead Of Blind?' and the *Blondie* and *Spidey Super Stories* pastiches. Beyond that the best issue is John Byrne's glimpse of a universe where the Fantastic Four never gained superpowers in 36, which drew heavily on *Fantastic Four* 1, with some fine extrapolation on how their lives and humanity progressed. Peter Gillis writes many of the later issues, and while never stunning, he does manage to add a semblance of originality. His best tale, though, concerned Spider-Man parlaying his abilities into a showbiz career in 19. By the time the first series concluded, inevitably, the alternatives worth covering had decreased issue by issue, and the series had just about run out of steam by cancellation. The 1988 one-shot is an unprinted leftover from the first series, twisting Iron Man's origin by having him work with the Vietcong.

The problem of redundancy affects the second series from the start. By 1989 Marvel had begun a policy of multi-part stories crossing over between various titles, and

continuing blockbuster plots in most titles. The result in *What If* was alternative presentations of more recent events that didn't have the freshness which a few years' distance would have provided, and that were handled by lesser talents than those who'd created the original stories. Additionally, the premises of some issues are so slim that they could easily have been part of a regular title. 7's 'What If Wolverine Were An Agent Of S.H.I.E.L.D.?' (by Valentino, Liefeld and Williams) is a prime example, although far from the worst story. The malaise of complacency afflicting Marvel throughout the late 1980s and early 1990s is woefully highlighted by *What If*. If much of the first run was poor, this largely standard-comic-length series is worse. There was seemingly little, if any, editing, resulting in bland stories – step forward, Danny Fingeroth, Roy Thomas and Jim Valentino – with poor characterisation and marked concentration on characters already well exposed elsewhere. A further fault was the proliferation of tales reversing a superhero battle's result ('What If The Marvel Superheroes Had Lost Atlantis Attacks?' in 25, for instance), then merely holding round two with different characters. If anything, though, it sold better than the first series.

On the plus side, from the earliest issues the second series had one or two pages of humorous suggestions for *What Ifs*, and the all-humour issue (once again 34, with Galactus as Elvis) is a highlight, although not up to the standard of its predecessor. Amid the pile of mediocrity that comprised the second series, though, there's little of note until the final issues. Greg Capullo drew 2's Daredevil issue and the Iron Man story in 8; the two-part Captain America story in 28 and 29 at least shows some inspiration and twists from writer George Caragone, even if Ron Wilson's art is the usual bland fare and it's padded with too many fights. The loosely connected 'Timequake' stories ran through 35–39, as Roy Thomas returned to a few previously glimpsed realities, Ann Nocenti, along with artists Steve Carr and Deryl Skelton, turned in a decent Storm story in 40, and Daredevil as ally of the Kingpin in 73 had its moments. 87 marked a change in editorial policy away from lighter material and provided a desperately need stab of inspiration. Most issues since that point have been readable: 87 itself is the single best issue of the run. Again, it was a story that might easily have occurred in the regular titles (were the X-Men not such cash cows), as Sabretooth decimated the X-Men. Dan Abnett and Andy Lanning delivered a tense script that was illustrated by Frank Teran in powerful and disturbing fashion, although it's not for the squeamish. Also very good is 92, investigating the possibility of a teenager in control of a giant robot. Rather dangerously, though, it's a Sentinel.

So What If Marvel had decided to let their better creators loose, or employed some of the more imaginative creators who didn't regularly work for Marvel? No, that's just too preposterous an alternate reality.~WJ
Recommended: Series one 4, 13, 19, 34, 36, series two 87
Collection: X-Men: Alternative Visions (Series two 40, 59, 62, 66, 69)

WHAT THE... ?!
Marvel: *24 issues 1988–1992*

A latter-day successor to *Not Brand Ecch*, this. As you would expect from a parody series, for every story that hits the target a couple fall short, but many creators seemed to rush in at the chance to make fun of their favourite characters. John Byrne has Superbman battling the Fantastical Four in 2, rather a gem of an issue, also containing Knick Furey, ex-agent of S.H.E.E.L.D., by Fred Hembeck and John Severin, featuring the Hydra Ladies Auxiliary. Also featured are Phil Foglio's Dr Deranged, and Mike Mignola and Al Williamson illustrating an Al Milgrom story lampooning Wolverine. There are plenty of other choice items scattered throughout the run, but no other single issue matches 2 laugh for laugh. Some of the more amusing include Don McGregor's Black 'n' Blue Panther in 9, and, also in that issue, 'Hotel Galactus', featuring the Imperial Guard, by Scott Lobdell, and a special Goon Knight story illustrated by veteran humour artist Win Mortimer. Doc Samson and Homer Simpson merge to form Doc Simpson in 18, while 7 offered one of the most eagerly awaited battles of all time, the Revengers vs Just-a-League. Who needs Amalgam Comics? This series may not make you giggle throughout, but pick and choose, and expect the occasional smile.~HY
Recommended: 2

Neil Gaiman's WHEEL of WORLDS
Tekno: *2 issues (0–1) 1995–1996*

Two disparate issues. 0 is a pivotal anthology in the Tekno Universe featuring all the Neil Gaiman characters – Lady Justice, Mr Hero, Teknophage – and passably chronicles the history of the latter. A year later, Bruce Jones' issue 1 is essentially a Lady Justice story of mad scientists creating the perfect woman by pick 'n' mixing body, mind and soul from three unwilling contenders. 'Nuff said.~APS

WHEELIE And The CHOPPER BUNCH
Charlton: *7 issues 1975–1976*

Earlier in his career John Byrne was known to have cited this as among his favourite work. The reason may have been that it's among the

first he had published. Based on a Hanna Barbera cartoon show, Wheelie and his sentient car mates have the usual kiddie cartoon adventures.~SW

WHERE CREATURES ROAM
Marvel: *8 issues 1970–1971*

Yet another title tapping into Marvel's seemingly endless reservoir of 1950s horror tales. There's plenty of Jack Kirby and Steve Ditko, but little inspiration.~FP

WHERE MONSTERS DWELL
Marvel: *38 issues 1970–1975*

Admittedly reprinting 1950s horror material meant a comic with reduced overheads, but just who bought this lack-lustre stuff? This was the longest running of Marvel's reprint horror titles, 12 is giant-sized, there's a Reed Crandall strip in 4 and the usual quota of Ditko is peppered throughout.~FP

WHISPER
Capital: *2 issues 1983*
First: *Special 1985, 37 issues 1986–1990*

The Capital issues begin the Whisper story-line in distinctly unpromising fashion. Rich Larson's artwork is truly ugly, making it hard to find any merit in Steven Grant's story of Alexis Devlin, the reluctant ninja. On a visit to Japan and her Japanese stepfather, she is thrown into the middle of a yakuza power struggle, and takes to a masked costume for her plan of rescue and revenge. Nothing in these issues makes her convincing as a character. Many of her heroic stunts break the laws of physics, and the background that we're given on her screams 'gimmick', the flatmate who's a model, the flatmate's senator lover, the childhood polio... You can skip these, quite happily. The 1985 one-shot completes the story started with Capital. The artwork is just as ugly, and the plot not improved by the introduction of the CIA. Again, feel free to avoid.

Whisper next appeared in the *First Adventures* anthology, and when she returned to her own title, it was transformed. Steven Grant's writing had really started to work: the plotting was tight – always complex and demanding, but you soon learn that your effort as a reader will be rewarded eventually – and the characters are suddenly real people, reacting as real people would to the eruption of violence in their lives. Most impressive is the way that aspects of Alexis that at first seemed only gimmicks become more and more convincing, not just lines on a resumé, but burdens she still carries. The story still concentrates on organised crime, the CIA and international conspiracies, which can make for lazy and boring plotting in the wrong hands, but Grant manages it all beautifully. He keeps

the focus on the human level throughout, yet still faces up to the chilling implications of covert operations. Although the entire series is well above average, the peak occurs around 23. Thereafter, there are signs of exhaustion in the writing, with more effort being put into reviving old characters than in introducing us to new ones, and with conspiracy sub-plots becoming ever more convoluted. The artwork in the new title was transformed as well, and worked with Grant's writing to produce a dramatic, inventive, and intelligent read through several changes of artist: Dell Barras (1–2), Norm Breyfogle (3–11), a much improved Rich Larson (12, 25), Spyder (13–24), Vince Giarrano (26–28), and Steve Epting (29–31).~FC
Recommended: 1–23

WHITE LIKE SHE
Dark Horse: *4-issue miniseries 1994*

Luther Albert Joyce, janitor at a nuclear facility, is disfigured during one of those pesky leaks, and, after an unsuccessful sojourn as a radioactive panhandler, seeks help from one Dr Flounder, pioneer in brain transplants. Simultaneously, Louella Schwartz, belligerent twentysomething rebel, decides that she deplores Dr Flounder's work, and goes armed to end it. The two meet, and after the shootout, Dr Flounder is killed, Luther is dying, and Louella is in a coma. Luckily, Dr Flounder's assistant is nearby, and so Luther's brain ends up in Louella's body. Black man into white woman, in the most intimate of bonds. Bob Fingerman uses the Mad Doctor clichés to make intelligent and perceptive points about the nature of sexual and racial politics, as Luther comes to terms with his/her new body (his reaction to menstruation is hilarious, but disturbing!), and the way it changes his and other people's perceptions. Meanwhile, Louella's brain is still hanging around in a jar in Dr Flounder's lab, when a young man meets with a fatal accident… Insightful, disquieting, amusing, and with some of the most inventive covers seen in a while.~HS
Recommended: 1–4

WHITE TRASH
Tundra: *4-issue miniseries 1992–1993*

Teenage metalhead Dean is picked up by a barely disguised Elvis Presley (pseudonymously named The King) in a pink Cadillac, and four issues of glorious cartoon violence follow. The King intends to make a Las Vegas comeback to show folk what being a real American is all about, but continuous mayhem means that an ever-growing band of assorted distressing examples of humanity are on his trail. There's no little irony that it's taken a Scottish writer and an artist from New Zealand to produce comics' first road movie, a distinctly American proposition. Martin Emond's grotesquely exaggerated painted artwork and facility for throwaway visual gags propel Gordon Rennie's observational script, the pair taking their chance to lampoon American culture and stereotypes with rapier accuracy.~FP
Recommended: 1–4
Collection: White Trash (1–4 + preview strip from *Heavy Metal*)

WHOA, NELLIE!
Fantagraphics: *3-issue miniseries 1996*

Jaime Hernandez' first series since discontinuing *Love And Rockets* concentrates on lady wrestlers Xochitl Nava (Vicki Glori's niece) and Gina Bravo, who wants nothing more than to be Xochitl's tag-team partner. With lots of wrestling action there's not much by way of story or characterisation but it's entertaining enough.~NF

WHODUNNIT?
Eclipse: *3 issues 1986–1987*

Bail bondsman Jay Endicott investigates murder mysteries, each left unsolved until the following issue in order for readers to make their guesses and for one correct entry to win a cash prize. It's an engaging idea, smoothly assembled by Mark Evanier and Dan Spiegle. They also worked on *Crossfire* (Endicott's other identity), and 24 of that title is where you'll find the solution to the third issue's puzzler.~HS

WHOTNOT
Fantagraphics: *4 issues 1993–1994*

A collection of satirical, philosophical and scatological strips from the mind of Jeremy Eaton. Eaton works in a number of forms, from single-page gags like 'The Rose-Coloured Man' to a pseudo-documentary about the Giant Hitler TV series to Walt Whitman's superhero daydreams (censored!). Then there's the serial, 'Americaville', a tour of the darker side of America's landscape and the horrors it all too often contains. Not for the squeamish.~NF

WILD ANIMALS
Pacific: *One-shot 1982*

Though this was meant to be a showcase for Scott Shaw's You-All-Gibbon (The Junk-Food Monkey), the funny-animal genre is better served here by Larry Gonick's Bronty, Sergio Aragonés' prequel to King Kong and Jim Engel's *Krazy Kat* homage, Bungalow Bill Bunny. Worth a look.~NF

WILD CARDS
Epic: *4-issue miniseries 1990*

Wild Cards is an enormously popular series of books where science-fiction and fantasy novelists can handle the topic of superheroes.

This comic ties in, but can be read on its own. The stories are set in a world which was struck by a strange virus in 1946: of those infected, 90% died, 9% were horribly deformed, and 1% (the Aces) gained a superpower. The main writer is Lewis Shiner, who contributed to the prose stories from the start, and the better artists include Barry Kitson (providing framing sequences), Gray Morrow, David Roach and Tom Yeates. The comic concentrates on a detective as he investigates a series of bomb attacks related to the virus and the Aces, which is really just a way of giving a history lesson and an introduction to the main Aces. It's entertaining while it lasts, but an hour later you'll struggle to remember the first thing about the characters or the plot-line.~FC

WILD DOG
DC: *4 issues 1987, 1 Special 1989*

Writer Max Collins and artist Terry Beatty tried their hands at real-life superheroics with this series, which went from the miniseries to a run in *Action Comics*, then to the special. The 'real life' tag stems from the fact that all of Wild Dog's crimefighting equipment is available over the counter, with no science-fiction technology or supernatural elements involved. The original series offered several candidates for the hockey-masked, taser-wielding vigilante's real identity. By the time of the special, Wild Dog's ID is known to the readers, but still a keen source of interest to investigative reporter Susan King, a hard-nosed manipulator who makes Lois Lane look like Tessie the Typist. This fast-moving series doesn't have the emotional involvement of *Ms Tree*, but it's readable, and worth picking up if you find it cheap.~HS

WILD LIFE
Fantagraphics: *2 issues 1994*

'My Life Is An Open Comic Book!' says writer/artist Peter Kuper, in this more-engaging-than-most entry in the overworked autobiographical genre. His desperate attempts to lose his virginity and score drugs may or may not push your buttons, depending on whether you shared those experiences, but his eccentric art style, reminiscent of old linocut prints, holds the attention.~HS

Nikki Doyle: WILD THING
Marvel UK: *9 issues 1993*

Able to infiltrate computer systems, Nikki Doyle encounters virtual-reality versions of Marvel's mainstream heroes and villains. It's a clever way of using popular characters while avoiding continuity problems, but the comic's average. Best issues are fill-ins 7 and 8.~WJ

WILDC.A.T.S.
Image: *31 issues + 1992 to date*

Fresh from a revitalising run on *X-Men*, Jim Lee arrived at Image with this superhero team, which just follows the trend of bland Image superheroes begun by Rob Liefeld. Events are set in motion with a meeting between Void and Lord Emp that establishes the purpose of the team: they are brought together to fight the evil daemonites. 5–7 feature the 'Killer Instinct' crossover, which co-stars Cyberforce. 8 has all the heroes taking a break and going on a cruise, which at least spares readers sitting through another fight sequence. 10–11 feature a collaboration between Chris Claremont and Jim Lee, introducing the Huntsman. There were high expectations of the former X-Men team, and the result was disappointingly average even by *WildC.A.T.S* standards. The team are a seminal part of the 'WildStorm Rising' crossover in 19–20, which features a vast array of heroes from Jim Lee's corner of the Image universe battling the evil daemonites. 24 features the origin of Maul, which is duller than an attempt on the watching-paint-dry world record.

There is no escaping the fact that *WildC.A.T.S.* is a very weak title. The stories are dull, and they overemphasise the violence. The only positive aspect was Jim Lee's visuals, which lasted up until 11, at which point a host of clones took over, all of whom draw a diluted version of Lee's style.~SS
Collection: *WildC.A.T.S. Covert Action Team* (1–4)

WILDC.A.T.S ADVENTURES
Image: *10 issues 1994–1995*

A cartoon series was spun-off from Jim Lee's successful *WildC.A.T.S* comic and this is the comic version of the cartoon. It simplified the characters' backgrounds, keeping the team's *raison d'être* (namely to defend Earth from the alien Daemonites) but limited the stories to battles involving this purpose. The first issue sees Warblade join the team in a skirmish with Helspont and during the series many of the other concepts (the Kherubim, noble enemies of the Daemonites, Coda, quasi-religious amazons and daemonite possession) introduced by the original comic are reintroduced. Written by Jeff Mariotte from the cartoon series scripts, the stories work hard to create a sense of character rather than concentrate wholly on action, but the changing rota of artists undermines their appeal from issue to issue.~NF

WILDSTAR
Image: *4-issue miniseries 1993, 3 issues 1995–1996*

A nice little tale of superheroes of the future given their powers by symbiotic aliens, who

attach themselves to humans and prove almost impossible to remove, providing some gruesome scenes in the first issue. Michael, aka Wildstar, is blasted back to the past to meet himself before his merging with the alien, only to discover he's been followed through time by his enemies. There's a surprise twist to end the miniseries, which has a fast story and art provided by co-creators Al Gordon and Jerry Ordway. It was far superior to the intended ongoing series, cancelled after three issues.~TP
Recommended: Miniseries 1–4
Collection: Sky Zero (miniseries 1–4)

WILDSTORM
Image: *4-issue miniseries 1995*

Short-lived WildStorm inventory title containing six- to eight-page short stories. As you might expect, the quality varies somewhat, but there's usually at least one goodie per issue. Some issues have unrelated stories, others focus on solo-stories featuring characters from the same team. The latter tend to be more worthwhile. The *Union* story in 3, by Mike Heisler and Randy Green, is the best of the bunch.~JC

WILDSTORM RISING
Image: *2 issues, 1995*

The two issues top and tail a ten-part story running through the WildStorm titles cover-dated May and June 1995. When one of the keys to a spaceship believed to belong to the evil alien daemonites is discovered it's up to the good alien Kherubim and their friends to stop two other keys, needed to power the vessel, from falling into the wrong hands. Well-structured for a multi-part team-up, the story set up events for both Alan Moore's take-over of *WildC.A.T.S* from issue 21 and the first Grifter solo-series.~JC

WILL EISNER'S Quarterly
Kitchen Sink: *8 issues 1983–1986*

Predominantly black and white magazine showcasing Will Eisner's work. The major presentation is the serialisation of his graphic novel *A Life Force* in the first five issues prior to its publication in a single volume. This thematic sequel to *A Contract with God* depicts urban decay in the 1930s Bronx shortly after the Great Depression, focusing on a tenement building inhabited by deprived immigrants and undeprived cockroaches. Eisner's great gift shines in the depth of imagery and story-telling conveyed by his minimalist artwork, yet great excitement is rarely generated and much of the social satire is heavy-handed. Long-underwear characters and Pamela Anderson clones refuse to be spotted, no matter how hard you look. Anyone who believes that superheroes are a requirement for good comics should take note of this eye-opener.

From 6 onwards, stand-alone Eisner stories take centre-stage. Irregular back-ups include 1940s newspaper reprints of the Spirit, Mr Mystic and Lady Luck, the latter two not by Eisner. Irritating partial colour and format changes detract from the overall package, which is rounded off with several interviews and articles concerning Eisner.~APS
Collection: A Life Force (1–5)

WILL TO POWER
Dark Horse: *12-issue limited series 1994*

Now a government representative, Titan takes a tour of the *Comics Greatest World* venues, meeting the local cast. Manipulated at every turn, but with his power increasing, Titan is finally pushed over the edge. Decent story and decent art.~FP

WIMMEN'S COMIX
Last Gasp: *10 issues 1972–1984*
Renegade: *3 issues (11–13) 1987–1988*
Rip Off: *5 issues + (14–18) 1989 to date*

Created by the San Francisco Women's Comics Collective, this was a follow-up to *It Ain't Me Babe*, the first women's underground comic; it was designed as an ongoing anthology title to help women get published in the often violently misogynistic world of underground comix. The initial run of *Wimmen's* often featured immature and amateurish work, but also gave folks like Trina Robbins, Lee Marrs, Roberta Gregory, Melinda Gebbie and Sharon Rudahl greater exposure, in some cases their début, and consolidated their progress. When *Wimmen's Comix* returned in 1982 several former mainstays were still present, but new contributors appeared – Lee Binswanger, Leslie Ewing, Mary Fleener, Leslie Sternbergh, Julie Hollings – and the standard was higher. Theme issues appeared, international contributors were invited... even the occasional male was allowed to be an ancillary contributor, provided a woman was doing most of the work! On average, since 1982, *Wimmen's* (*Wimmin's* since 17) has averaged an issue about every eighteen months. The Supernatural issue 13, 'Disastrous Relationships' issue 14, and 'Men' theme issue 16, are probably the best overall to date, the latter including an outrageously horny 'Desert Peach' vignette by Donna Barr.~HS
Collections: *The Best of Wimmen's Comix* (selected stories from 1–7)

WINTER WORLD
Eclipse: *3-issue miniseries 1987–1988*

Combines the American writing talents of Chuck Dixon and the Argentinian artwork of Jorge Zaffino to produce a European-style adventure comic that wouldn't be out of place in *Heavy Metal*. In a cold, bleak post-holocaust world a trader and his pet badger meet a young woman, only for them all to be captured and enslaved on a jealously-guarded enclosed farm, where it's still possible to grow food. The series chronicles the trader's escape from the farm and subsequent attempts to rescue the woman. The script's as bleak as the landscape and as violent as you'd expect. Zaffino's artwork, influenced by Caniff and Toth, never quite reaches those heights but is pleasurable, although the third issue looks rushed.~NF

WITCHBLADE
Image: *10 issues + 1995 to date*

The titular witchblade is a gauntlet of incredible power passed through the ages, which affixes itself to ridiculously proportioned attractive policewoman Sara Pezzini. Able to transform into very scanty body armour (wouldn't want to omit any tits or ass shots!), it guides its novice owner against a ruthless businessman who also desires the gauntlet's power. If one can overlook frequent 'homages', Michael Turner's art is decent titillation, and there's more plot and characterisation between the pin-ups than is usual for Image titles. 1–8 comprise the initial story and are being collected two issues to a book. The next story has been well foreshadowed over the first ten issues.~WJ

WITCHCRAFT
Vertigo: *3-issue miniseries 1994*

The former hosts of DC's Witching Hour are the traditional three aspects of womanhood, the Maiden, Mother and Crone. Here each is involved in a cyclical story that begins with a Welsh barbarian and his horde devastating a Goddess-worshipping women's coven. Each issue has the coven's leader reincarnated with the opportunity for revenge on the reincarnated barbarian, although there's a richness to the plots extending beyond that simple theme. Peter Snejbjerg draws a tale of revenge in the Dark Ages for the first issue, while the explorer and adventurer Richard Burton's diaries provide the inspiration for Michael Zulli's second issue. A modern-day tale of an old woman distrusting her son-in-law, with good reason, is illustrated by Steve Yeowell and completes the story and cycle. The package is rounded out with framing sequences drawn by Teddy Christiansen and fine Mike Kaluta covers. The artwork throughout is excellent, but James Robinson's plots vary considerably in the course of three issues, with the third being particularly daft. The thematic unity never really convinces, and only the second issue really stands up, as Burton recounts a shaping experience of his early life.~FP

Collection: Witchcraft (1–3)

WITCHING HOUR
DC: *84 issues 1969–1978*

As with other DC horror comics, *Witching Hour* was a mixture of the excellent and the bland, although its horror hosts, the three witches, gave it a character of its own. Up until 12 most of the witches' intro pages were drawn by Alex Toth, who provided many of the comic's artistic highlights. His strips in 1, 3, 8, 11 and 12 were typically fine, but he excelled himself on Gerry Conway's haunting script for 'Hold Softly, Haunting Death' in 10. The stories were typical DC horror material, rarely outstanding, almost always competent, and rarely appalling, and as such it's largely the contributions of the artists that raise them occasionally to greatness. Other early artistic contributors of note included Berni Wrightson (3, 5), Neal Adams (8), Gray Morrow (10, 13, 15, 16) and Gil Kane (12). This early period's best issue was 14, with lovely art from Jeff Jones, Stanley Pitt and Al Williamson, although it was the following issue that contained the best story, 'Freddy Is Another Name For Fear', by George Kashdan and Wally Wood.

16–21 were fifty-two pages long and featured a number of 1950s reprints by Jack Kirby, Nick Cardy and Ruben Moreira amongst others. From this period on the comic was increasingly drawn by Filipino artists, and consequently from 20 to 50 most issues have at least one nice job. Artists to look out for include Alex Nino (31, 40, 45, 47), Alfredo Alcala (24, 27, 33, 41, 43), Nestor Redondo (20, 21, 23, 34), and the little-known but highly talented Romy Gamboa (32, 36, 49). The Canadian Bill Payne provided this period's finest hour, though, with 'Happy Death Sweet Sixteen' in 25, a deliciously rendered story in Graham Ingels mould. Art enthusiasts should also look out for a lovely Ralph Reese strip in 23.

Adding to the feeling of consistency, each cover from 15 to 52 was by the excellent Nick Cardy, and it's no coincidence that his departure coincided with a general downturn in *Witching Hour*'s quality. Since 14, when Murray Boltinoff had become editor, almost every story had been written by Carl Wessler, George Kashdan or Boltinoff himself, and, not surprisingly, later issues are rather lacking in inspiration. Artistically, the highspot was 83's five-page strip by the woefully obscure Nords Cruz, but in general issues after 50 contain little of note. 38 was a hundred-page collection reprinting some choice early material.~DAR

Recommended: 1, 3, 5, 8, 10–15, 20, 21, 23, 25, 31, 32, 34, 36, 40, 45, 47, 49, 83

WITHIN OUR REACH
Star*Reach: *One-shot 1991*

Although Star*Reach stopped producing comics in 1979 the company continued to represent comics creators' rights. This one-off

Christmas special was a charitable project in aid of an AIDS and an environment charity. Most of the stories are worthy rather than interesting, but there are some gems to be found, including a *Concrete* Christmas tale by Paul Chadwick and an adaptation of O. Henry's *The Gift Of The Magi* by P.Craig Russell. The Spider-Man story about evil landlords and poor tenants is execrable, even if it is for a good cause.~NF

WITZEND

Wally Wood: *4 issues 1966–1968*
Wonderful: *5 issues (5–9) 1968–1976*
CPL: *1 issue (10) 1976*
William Pearson: *3 issues (11–13) 1978–1985*

As the first significant example of self-publishing and distribution directly to comic shops, Wally Wood's *Witzend* is of enormous historical importance. It was the first time mainstream artists produced work for a primarily adult audience and sold it directly to the fan market. In this it even predates the underground comics. However, as both the market and the concept were so new, the creators involved had seemingly little idea of what actually constituted adult material, and much of the content was inconsequential. 1–8 contained work from several different directions: mainstream professionals, unpublished strips from Wood's circle of artist friends, early strips by underground artists and work by new discoveries.

Of the mainstream cartoonists, Wood, not surprisingly, was the most prolific, and his contributions varied from straight adventure (Animan in 1 and 2) through winsome cod psychology ('Pipsqueak Papers' in 3–5) to Tolkienesque fantasy ('The Wizard King' in 4, 5, 8). While Wood's idea of artistic freedom didn't extend much beyond drawing naked women, for Steve Ditko it meant an opportunity to have a good old rant. His notorious right-wing strips Mr A (3, 4) and 'Avenging World' (6, 7) must have come as a shock to unsuspecting Spider-Man fans. Gray Morrow's work in 2 and 7 was also high on the tits-and-ass count, and it was left to Archie Goodwin's affecting tale of religious intolerance, 'Sinner', in 1, to produce the title's intellectual content.

The previously unpublished material included strips by Al Williamson (1), Frank Frazetta (3, 8) and Wood (6) that had been lying around for a while, and a series of Edgar Rice Burroughs illustrations by Reed Crandall in 2–5. Art Spiegelman (2, 3), Roger Brand (3–5, 7) and Vaughn Bodé (5, 7) were soon to become stars of the underground scene, but only Bodé's work had much to offer at this point. His 'Cobalt 60' (later reprinted in *Epic Illustrated*) was one of Witzend's more thought-provoking stories. New mainstream discoveries Jeff Jones (6),

Berni Wrightson (7) and Ralph Reese (8) were to go on to better things.

9 was, bizarrely, all text about W.C. Fields, and readers had to wait five years for Witzend's best issue. It was far less ambitious, favouring more straightforward fare by the likes of Dick Giordano, Mike Zeck, Joe Staton and Wood, in this case an episode of his Sally Forth. Howard Chaykin's three-page 'March 17, 1969' was intriguing, but the issue's real substance was provided by Alex Toth's '39/74', a majestic piece set on a 1930s cruise liner. By comparison 11 and 12 were a sorry collection of mostly semi-pro material, with Wood himself clearly past his best (he was to die soon after). 13, actually titled *Good Girls* on the cover, was a collection of illustrations from editor Bill Pearson's collection, including art by Roy Krenkel, Mike Zeck, Stan Drake and, inevitably, Wood. Despite its shortcomings, there's much to enjoy here for most readers, but *Witzend* is something of a missed opportunity.~DAR
Recommended: 10

The WIZARD OF 4th STREET

Dark Horse: *6-issue miniseries 1987–1988*

This adapts the comedy-fantasy novels of Simon Hawke, starring Wyndrune, 23rd-century thief by trade. By this time science has all but been forgotten, and the ancient arts of magic have been rediscovered. Wyndrune's plans for heisting some ancient gems attract a spanner by the name of Kira. Finding the gems a little too hot to handle, the pair decide to offload them quickly. Unfortunately, the gems won't stay offloaded, leading to farce, fun and frolic. *Wizard Of 4th Street* is a sprightly enough read, but Phil Normand's art is still developing, and his vision of the 23rd century is remarkably similar to 1988, so one can't help but feel the original novel might be a better read.~WJ

WOLF AND RED

Dark Horse: *3-issue miniseries 1995*

Henry Gilroy's scripts make this the most successful of Dark Horse's Tex Avery titles. Sparsely written, with just enough plot to keep things moving, the Wolf And Red strips are actually quite droll, avoiding comparison with the frenetic pace of the cartoons by playing to the strengths of the comic page. Bob Fingerman's overwritten Screwball Squirrel is the poorest of the back-ups (2), while, fittingly, the Droopy story in 3 is practically another Wolf And Red adventure.~NF

WOLFF & BYRD, Counsellors of the Macabre

Exhibit A: *12 issues + 1994 to date*

'Beware the creatures of the night!' screams the cover, 'They have lawyers.' Wolff and Byrd, paranormal solicitors, began life as a newspaper strip, and their early comic-length adventures suffer from jerky pacing and low-rent jokes that might be excusable on a daily strip. Later the writing improves as writer/artist Batton Lash has to work harder to find unusual supernatural plots for them to become involved in, such as defending a guardian angel when his client accuses him of not being watchful enough. The strip's concept is almost a one-joke idea but the quality of the later scripting and artwork carries it through. Lash's angular, elegant-lined artwork suits the quirky nature of the stories.~FJ

WOLFPACK

Marvel: *12-issue limited series, Graphic Novel, 1988–1989*

In the midst of their usually colourful superhero comics, Marvel attempted to do a take on 'normal' streetwise kids with this series following the adventures of a gang of interracial tough-but-well-meaning teenagers from the wrong side of town. Perhaps predictably, the formula is not a complete success, and comes over far more as a picture of how Marvel writers think streetwise kids behave than the kind of social comment it sometimes tries to be. Early issues, written by Larry Hama (later to become a fan favourite on *Wolverine*), are better than the later ones by John Figueroa, but none are really worth the trouble, although Ron Wilson's pencils (especially under Kyle Baker's inks in earlier issues) deserve an honourable mention and at least suit the subject-matter, which is more than can be said for any other aspect of the series.~JC

WOLVERINE

Marvel: *4-issue miniseries 1982, 108 issues +, 2 Specials 1988 to date*

Wolverine is one of Marvel's most successful second-generation characters. Débuting in *Hulk* 181, he graduated to star status as part of the new X-Men as an ultra-violent character with adamantium skeleton and claws, and a mutant healing factor. His past is shrouded in secrecy, although it's known he used to work for the Canadian Secret Service, and he was always cast as the beer-swilling, cigar-smoking loner in the *X-Men*. Given his instant popularity, it took a surprisingly long time before he was given a miniseries. That miniseries was, however, a landmark. Written by *X-Men* writer Chris Claremont and pencilled by an up-and-coming Frank Miller, it took the anti-hero to Japan, where he becomes involved in a feud between Yakuza clans and falls in love. Miller's art is sublime, drawing on obscure-at-the-time influences like the Japanese comic *Lone Wolf And Cub*. Claremont's scripts, surprisingly sparse for a change, match the art.

Wolverine mania finally hit big time in 1988,

when he was awarded a regular solo slot in *Marvel Comics Presents* and an ongoing solo series. The early issues, with art by John Buscema, aren't much to write home about as he goes to the Far East to mix with beautiful spies and nefarious secret organisations. When Peter David became writer, his sardonic wit, coupled with art by *X-Men* stalwart John Byrne raised the title, above the norm. Revelations were dropped every now and then as to Logan's past, particularly in 'The Lazarus Project' (27–30), in which an android Wolverine appears, and the over-hyped 40–42. Those issues revealed that Wolverine's arch-nemesis and ex-partner Sabretooth was, in fact, his father. It prompted a massive jump in sales, but turned out to be a bunch of lies. Further clues as to his past included a sequel to Barry Windsor-Smith's 'Weapon X' story (*Marvel Comics Presents* 72–84) in 48–49, with his true origin revealed in 50, but as anybody who follows these things knows, nothing is for certain. Notable artists at the time included Adam Kubert, Marc Silvestri and Mark Pennington. Logan's sweetheart from the miniseries is killed in 57, and the next big issue is 75, in which Wolverine loses his adamantium skeleton as it's extracted by magnetic-powered supervillain Magneto. Still able to use his retractable claws despite the pain they cause, he quits cigars (!) and sets off an a quest to discover his true origins and peace of mind.

The stripping of his adamantium skeleton is a worthwhile plot device beyond the shock value. Previously overly reliant on all-shredding claws, they're now bone claws and not invulnerable. Attempts to set things right take him to Canada (76–78), Scotland (79–81) and Japan, meeting old colleagues in each location. 82 is particularly good, as Logan checks back on the daughter of his dead love Mariko. To further compound Wolverine's problems, he's reverting to a more primal and feral nature, as exemplified by a stunningly brutal battle with Sabretooth in 90. Hama drags this plot on way too long, though, obviously treading water until 100, but with that issue Hama confounds all expectations as to the resolution. Along the way there's plenty of decent art from an assortment of creators, with 82 again being worth a look to see Adam Kubert's art, inked by his father Joe as well as by regular inker Mark Farmer. Post-100 there's been an involvement with ninja warrior Elektra; 107 and 108 are the best of the run since 82; and, coincidentally, have Wolverine back in Japan.~TP/WJ

Recommended: Miniseries 1–4, 41, 42, 50, 75, 82
Collections: The Essential Wolverine (1–23), vol 2 (24–47), *Triumphs And Tragedies* (41, 42, 75, miniseries 4, *Uncanny X-Men* 109, 172, 173), *Wolverine* (miniseries 1–4), see also *Marvel Comics Presents*

WOLVERINE AND GAMBIT: Victims
Marvel: *4-issue miniseries 1995*

What's going on 'ere then? Two of the most popular X-Men star in this effort, with lovely art from Tim Sale and a 'whaffer thin' story by Jeph Loeb. A very silly plot has Jack The Ripper roaming the streets of London again, cor blimey, Guv! The fifth victim is a friend of Gambit's so he goes to investigate. Strewth! It only looks like it might be old Wolvie what done 'er in. More misunderstandings than a Brian Rix farce ensue, with the good old British bobbies in hot pursuit. It's a right old pea-souper of a mystery, but it transpires that everyone is being manipulated by the new female version of Mastermind and a completely bonkers version of another old X-Men villain. Strike a light! There's a big fight at the end. Hurrah! No real conclusion. *Exeunt omnes*. Curtain. Lord luv a duck, an' no mistake.~TP

WOLVERINE One-Shots

Given Wolverine's status as most popular Marvel mutant, it's not surprising that several one-off specials have been published. Many have weak story-lines accompanied by some top-notch art, foremost among them the Bill Sienkiewicz illustrated *Inner Fury*. It's beautiful to look at, but the story, about Wolverine infected with nano-machines wreaking havoc with his body, is as see-through as a window. *Bloody Choices* has Alan Davis pencilling a sixty-four-page fight between Wolverine and Sabretooth. There are no real revelations or plot, just a lot of fur'n'fangs. *The Killing*, by John Ney Rieber and Kent Williams, is a pompous look inward at the man/beast conflict of our hero. Pretty, but ultimately pointless. *Evilution* starts with a lot of eco-babble and hunted mutants and goes downhill from there. *Rahne Of Terra, Rahne Fall* and *Knight Of Terra* are three very silly tales set in an alternate universe populated by knights and faeries. Absolute tosh, although the first has the benefit of decent Adam Kubert art. Slightly better is *Logan: Shadow Society*, which is reminiscent of an *X-Files* episode. It's a tale from the past when Logan was employed by the Canadian Secret Service and before mutants were known to the population at large. Full of espionage and paranoia, it also (retroactively) includes the first meeting of Wolverine and Sabretooth. There are, however, a pair worth looking at. *Bloodlust* is by Alan Davis and Paul Neary, and has the Canadian superhero heading into the wilds of Alaska to discover misunderstanding and fear over a lost tribe of alien creatures. *The Jungle Adventure*, by Walt Simonson and Mike Mignola, has Wolverine entering a jungle and having to revert to his most primal instincts to survive. As for any others, don't bother.~TP

WOLVERINE SAGA
Marvel: *4-issue miniseries 1989*

The title suggests the complete history of Wolverine, but unfortunately Marvel have other ideas. This collects all the available material about the character and explains very little or nothing new. The format departs from the norm, being text-based, with reprinted comic panels and quotes from old Wolverine stories.~SS

WONDER MAN
Marvel: *One-shot 1986, 29 issues, 2 Annuals 1991–1994*

Introduced as a one-shot character in Avengers 9 (1964), the superstrong Wonder Man died and was forgotten. Except that his brain patterns were used as a template for the Vision when introduced in *Avengers* 58. Given that was the case, his resurrection in *Avengers* 152 was a surprise to all concerned. Now healthy apart from red eyes lacking pupils, he was a part-time member of the team. The one-shot was merely a schedule filler to test Marvel's ownership of the name, since DC had long contested Marvel's right to publish a Wonder Man, stating it infringed upon their *Wonder Woman*. Featuring the safari-suited geek incarnation, it was a throwaway slugfest. In 1991, following moderately favourable responses to his presence in *West Coast Avengers*, Marvel gave the bionic-powered hero another try. Simon Williams' thespian aspirations were brought to the fore, and he moved to Hollywood to pursue an acting career. Scripter Gerard Jones deftly introduces the cast of phonies, eccentrics and hangers-on that Simon accumulates, and Jeff Johnson's pleasing, clean line was a refreshing change from the hyper-distorted illustration prominent at the time. The emphasis on characterisation, humour and intelligence was sadly lost on the readers, and the series changed direction after a three-part introspective story which culminated in 25. Purists should disregard the last four issues, cynical team-ups with the Hulk and Spider-Man in an attempt to turn the title around. Both annuals should also be dismissed. The first was an interminable crossover with other series, and the second introduced one of the most embarrassing new 'heroes' ever to hit the pages of comics in the form of Hitmaker. Make these culls, and you're left with twenty-five issues of definitely B+ entertainment.~HS

WONDER WARTHOG
Rip Off: *3 issues 1973, graphic novel 1980*

First appearing during Gilbert Shelton's student days in 1961, Wonder Warthog began as a humour-packed parody of Superman, even down to his human identity as mild-mannered reporter Philbert Desanex. Although the issues were obviously not published in chronological order, one can still trace the development of Shelton's cartooning, with strips in 3 being refined and polished in terms of both script and art. The material has recently been republished as Hog Of Steel, collecting even more obscure strips. The paperback *Wonder Warthog And The Nurds Of November* is a full thirteen chapters, although there's little in the way of connecting threads between chapters. Indeed, the twelfth chapter, 'Philbert Desanex's 100,000th Dream', has been issued as a separate comic. It's one of three dream sequences punctuating the book, which is by a fully-formed Shelton casting his net wide. Not quite matching the belly laughs of Shelton's Freak Brothers strips, there's still plenty of worthwhile material and the cartooning is great.~WJ

WONDER WOMAN

DC: *Series one 329 issues 1941–1986, series two 120 issues +, 6 Annuals, 1987 to date*

In the late 1930s, William Moulton Marston, psychologist and inventor of the polygraph lie detector, was concerned about the comics medium, then in its infancy in the USA. He deplored the violence, the emphasis on criminal activity, but primarily what he termed 'the blood-curdling masculinity' of the stories, where women, if present at all, were decorations, mere trophies to be fought over by the men. Marston was a popular psychologist. In addition to several books, one tellingly titled *The Natural Superiority Of Women*, he was a frequent writer of articles for national magazines. DC's executives cynically, but accurately, reasoned that Marston's qualms might be set aside if he was invited to join the 'Advisory Board' of psychologists and educators who nominally supervised DC's output. From this position, Marston lobbied to create a series that would encapsulate his views on the relationship between the sexes, offering a counterpoint to the often brutal heroes of comics' formative years. Together with artist Harry G. Peter, an illustrator who cut his teeth in sophisticated humour magazines, Marston created Wonder Woman, who débuted in *All-Star Comics* 8.

On the island hideaway of the legendary Amazons, Princess Diana and her friend Mala see a plane crash. The pilot, a man on the brink of death, is swiftly restored to health by Amazon science. This presents Diana's mother, Queen Hippolyta, with a dilemma. The Goddesses of ancient Greece, whom the Amazons still worship, have commanded her to send an Amazon champion to warring Man's World, to fight for freedom. A contest is to be held to determine who is the mightiest Amazon, and she will accompany the pilot,

Steve Trevor, back to the United States. Hippolyta knows that Diana is the Amazon champion, and fears that she is already half in love with Trevor. Does she allow Diana to win, and leave Paradise Island?

Well, this would be a pretty short review if she didn't, wouldn't it? Diana wins through, and, after being awarded a costume bearing the stars and eagle of her new nation, flies to the USA as Wonder Woman. From her one-off première to the lead story in *Sensation Comics*, her own title, stories in *Comics Cavalcade*, and membership of the Justice Society of America back in *All-Star Comics*, within a year of her début Wonder Woman was one of the most popular and recognisable characters in comics.

Perhaps one reason for this is that Marston and Peter – operating under the pseudonym of Charles Moulton – were both mature men when they began work on *Wonder Woman*, as opposed to the youngsters who comprised the bulk of comics workers, lending the series a gravity and authority its contemporaries often lacked. Furthermore, Peter's distinctive, organic, woodcut style gave it a look unlike anything else on offer, an incalculable advantage by the mid-1940s, when there were hundreds of titles from dozens of publishers on the market. Under their guidance, the Amazing Amazon fought some of the most bizarre villains in comics history: the misogynistic Dr Psycho, the schizophrenic Cheetah, Zara, Priestess of the Crimson Flame, Dr Poison and Hypnota. Then there was the Duke of Deception, pawn of the war god Mars, the psychotic Mask, in reality an abused wife pushed over the edge of sanity, and Villainy Inc., the first alliance of female villains in comics, with several of the Amazons' most noted foes teamed to destroy her.

Many critics and comics historians, dismissive of female heroes in general, have reserved their harshest criticism for Wonder Woman. She has been accused of encouraging lesbianism and sadomasochistic practices, and of appealing to male fantasies of sexual domination. The last charge may have some validity. Marston's own comment, in response to the unpopularity of heroines in comics, that men, 'given an alluring and powerful woman to submit to… will become her willing slaves', is certainly open to interpretation. Loaded language such as the Amazons' credo of 'Submission to loving authority' has been seized upon by detractors, but the submission in question relates to rehabilitation. Unlike most heroes of the time, who were content to either kill or imprison their opponents, Wonder Woman made strenuous and frequently successful attempts to reform her enemies. Paula Von Gunther, an implacable foe in 1941, becomes one of Diana's closest friends and allies, and in the strip's first ten years numerous other women are shown as having turned away from crime thanks to the intercession of Diana and her Amazon sisters.

The female solidarity of the stories is a bond of empowerment and mutual support, not of sexual allure; far from the aloof and unattainable feats of Superman, Wonder Woman is adamant on many occasions that any woman can achieve power such as hers if she can overcome the mental shackles placed upon her by Man's World. Samples of her dialogue to other women from the middle 1940s include 'You saved yourselves. I only showed you that you could!'; 'All you have to do is have confidence in your own strength'; 'Make yourself strong! Don't be dependent on a man – earn your own living!'; and, from a woman who has been betrayed by her lover; 'I've learned my lesson – I'll rely on myself, not on a man!' Contrary to many critics' beliefs, Wonder Woman's stories do not centre on hatred of men, but on righteous indignation towards bullies and abusers of all kinds. True, she is shown saying that romantic love is often (not always) a trick men use to make women give up their independence, and that marriage is often (not always) a mind-numbing trap for women, but to true love between equals she's the first to give her blessing.

And yes, Wonder Woman tied people up a lot; this was because her main weapon was a magic lasso, which she used to restrain her captives harmlessly, as opposed to punching them out. Get a grip, folks. People didn't bitch about the number of times Robin the Boy Wonder got his tight little buns tied up over in *Batman*! Not that socio-political or putatively quasi-sexual themes were all that *Wonder Woman* had to offer. Rooted in mythology and magic rather than the pseudo-science of the majority of superheroes, she ranged freely between historical, extraterrestrial and contemporary adventures, presenting a rich and dazzling canvas to her readers. If the stories were sometimes a little inaccurate (as when she travelled back in time to help Boadicea overthrow the Romans and drive them from Britain!), then what the heck, they were more fun that way.

In 1947 Marston died, though he was so far ahead that his scripts continued to be published for at least two years. Without his patronage, Wonder Woman's star began to fall. The empowerment ethos faded, the villains (with the exception of the limp Angle Man and a toned-down Duke of Deception) were gone, and she became just another adventuress. Even H.G. Peter's art, through the bulk of the 1950s, altered in tone, looking cluttered and badly dated. Whenever Wonder Woman did use her powers, the action was shown in tiny panels in extreme longshot, as if she was doing something vaguely indecent.

When Peter died in 1958, a radical new look was introduced courtesy of artists Ross Andru and Mike Esposito, who gave Wonder Woman a slick European makeover with wild, windblown, tousled hair. Unfortunately, DC decided Wonder Woman looked too 'loose', and ordered a return to the curly permed look by 110. Under writer/editor Robert Kanigher, Wonder Woman's powers were revealed to be the gifts of the Gods, making her in effect a super-Amazon. Wonder Girl and Wonder Tot flashback stories, showing that even at an early age Diana had been capable of feats her sisters could not hope to equal, left the original concept of any woman being a potential Wonder Woman trailing in the dust. As her powers expanded, her aspirations narrowed, becoming domesticated. She daydreamed about marrying Steve Trevor, but these fantasies inevitably went awry, usually because her Amazon education hadn't covered cookery or housekeeping. Things went from bad to worse. Wonder Girl and Wonder Tot were written into contemporary stories, firstly as 'Impossible Tales', narrated by Hippolyta (who got a blonde rinse and started calling herself Wonder Queen, trying to muscle in on her daughter's act!), then, without explanation as to how these characters could exist alongside Wonder Woman, as *bona fide* members of Amazon society. The comic was haemorrhaging readers, but because of her long history, and her involvement in the *Justice League Of America*, it would have been too embarrassing to cancel her. A silly attempt to restore her to her 1940s glory was initiated in 159, but it came across as a camp parody of the old tales.

A more radical revamp was needed, and occurred in 178, where, under the new team of Denny O'Neil, Mike Sekowsky and Dick Giordano, Diana quit her job at military intelligence, ditched the female Clark Kent frump look, and went undercover to help Steve Trevor when her Amazon *alter ego* could not. In the next issue, a still greater change occurred as her sister Amazons retreated to another dimension to replenish their magical energies. Left behind because she couldn't leave Steve Trevor, Wonder Woman was suddenly bereft of all her Amazon powers and weapons, and forced to face the world as a mortal, fragile human. Several feminist critics, including Gloria Steinem, look down upon these stories as a negation of the liberated Wonder Woman, dismissing these adventures as those of a 'female James Bond, but even more boring because she was denied his sexual freedom'. These folks have missed a couple of important points. Firstly, that the true Wonder Woman, who insisted that any woman could achieve her feats and believed that even enemies could be rehabilitated, hadn't actually been published for decades at this point. The silly, fluffy stories of an addlepated Amazon whose powers were a christening gift from the Gods was the true violation of the character, and had been the *status quo* since about 1949. Secondly, the non-powered Wonder Woman was a symbol of empowerment and self-determination. She was a woman of vast power and wealth, who has all that stripped from her in a moment, and, completely unprepared and untrained, re-invents herself and takes charge of her life again. Okay, she had help from her friends (including, yes, a rather embarrassing blind Oriental mentor who handily teaches her self-defence skills), but she still had to do the work. And it was quite a workload. Reeling from major losses in her life, she's caught up in the machinations of one Dr Cyber, who earns Diana's enmity by killing someone close to her. In rapid succession, Diana and her allies faced off against an international crime cartel; urban sadists who prey on runaways; the War God Mars, who has followed the Amazons to their dimensional hideaway; a stroppy carousing witch; assassins, ghosts, cross-dressing pickpockets and more.

After Denny O'Neil's initial script assistance, artist Mike Sekowsky wrote the stories, deftly alternating espionage, supernatural and slice-of-life stories and establishing Diana as a warm, vivacious character with a previously unsuspected sense of irony. The illustrations were stylish and engrossing, Sekowsky's kinetic approach lending a sense of movement even to the talking-heads scenes, and Giordano's inking finishing off the package with slick sophistication. These stories may not be 'real' Wonder Woman to the purists, but they were closer to the original concept than most people acknowledge.

Sadly, health problems made editor/writer/artist Sekowsky later and later. There were fill-in issues, reprinting material that was barely two years old, and some of Sekowsky's last issues were uninspired. By 199, the series was back in the hands of Denny O'Neil, who tried to turn Diana into a toned-down Modesty Blaise. These issues were not without merit, even the notorious 'Women's Lib Issue' (203), which, though justifiably hootered, er, hooted at for its chick-in-bondage cover, raised some intelligent concerns inside.

In the early 1970s, Diana was optioned for a TV movie, so she was back in the star-spangled panties, but with the hallmarks of a rush job. Steve Trevor was alive again; no, he wasn't, it was an illusion of Amazon scientists; yes, he was; whoops, he's dead again; now he's back. Wonder Woman has to be tested by the JLA to prove she's fit to rejoin; she's a member in good standing; she's on probation; now she's back; Wonder Woman has a black sister called Nubia; no, she doesn't, she never existed. For the next, Gods help us, eighty issues, creative teams changed faster than most people's underwear, barely getting one set of parameters established before the next, equally mediocre, team altered it all again. The TV show starring Lynda Carter was the only reason the comic continued publication at all for several years. And for a couple of years, the title focused on World War II adventures to tie in with it, the contemporary Wonder Woman being unseen in her own comic.

With 288, a relaunch that stood a chance took effect. Roy Thomas and Gene Colan assumed control, and while the spooky, moody art of Colan was regarded as ill-suited for a creature of sunlight like Wonder Woman, the track record of both creators stood them in good stead. Unfortunately, within six issues of the takeover, it seemed both had lost interest, and the series was barely less mediocre than it had been before. Following 300, which had a semi-intelligent story about different perceptions of the Amazon, and several interesting guest artists, *Wonder Woman* fell into the hands of the Mishkin and Cohn writing team, and DC workhorse Don Heck. All parties, unexpectedly, produced some decent work, Heck, in particular, having shaken off his 1970s hack mantle to draw his nicest art in twenty years. Tragically, it was too late to help: Wonder Woman's fate was already sealed, and the new team were just marking time until the *Crisis On Infinite Earths* crossover, which was to end the old Wonder Woman and make way for the new. In the final issue of the series, pleasingly, Diana did get to marry Steve Trevor, who was handily alive at the time, before going off to meet her final fate. It could be argued that the comic should have been cancelled long before, but, to those with memories of her finer hours, it's hard to read the last issue without a pang or two.

Following the events of *Crisis On Infinite Earths*, it was retroactively declared that Wonder Woman's career 'never happened', and she was to be reintroduced to the DC Universe as a new character, starting over from a new issue 1. New writer Greg Potter was teamed with superstar artist George Perez to produce the Amazing Amazon's new adventures, but for reasons that remain unknown, Potter's name vanished from the credits, and from comics, after 3, leaving Perez illustrating and plotting the series, with Len Wein helping with the scripts until issue 16, after which Perez flew solo.

The new incarnation of Wonder Woman, like the old, was the daughter of Queen

Hippolyta of the Amazons, sculpted from clay and given life by the Goddesses. When US pilot Steve Trevor crashes on Paradise Island, now named Themyscira, in keeping with a greater emphasis on Diana's Greek background, he is once again taken back by an Amazon champion, who becomes a heroine in the United States. This Steve Trevor is older, and becomes a friend and ally of Diana's, rather than an insipid romantic interest. The new version is closer to her predecessor's original philosophy, too. Once more the first among equals, she outstrips her sisters only in skill, not power, and strives to deliver a message of peace and forbearance – though, Man's World being what it is, she often has to kick in a few heads to do so. Settling in Boston, Massachusetts, she develops a circle of friends: Julia Kapatelis, Professor of Archaeology at Harvard University, and her daughter Vanessa; Etta Candy, in the original series treated as comic relief, here given a dignified role and a romantic involvement with Steve Trevor; Ed Indelicato of the Boston Police Department, who may or may not be in love with our heroine; and Myndi Mayer, a gloriously synthetic publicist who seizes upon Diana, whom she names 'Wonder Woman', as her meal ticket. Most importantly, Wonder Woman is given intelligent, well-crafted stories, thoughtfully paced and full of interesting characters who, one feels, are around to do more than just advance the plot or be kidnap fodder of the month. These stories are slower paced than those in many comics, and there is, particularly in the early issues, a grandeur, an epic feel, suiting the characters' ties to mythology. And Perez's art, sumptuous and detailed, has never been finer.

Forced by Myndi Meyer's machinations into the role of a superheroine, something for which she is completely unprepared, Diana faces some of the classic menaces – Mars (now Ares) and the Cheetah – and entirely new opponents, such as the tragic Silver Swan. All the time she's still trying to understand her mission in this strange new world, her new human friends, and her relationship with her Gods, several of whom, particularly the pushy Hermes, become significant supporting characters. A high point of this run was issue 20, with the death of a major character, and the impact of her demise on the rest of the cast, being subtly and movingly portrayed.

With 25, financial hardship ('It sold better than any other version of Wonder Woman had done for years, but that still wasn't enough to make royalties') forced Perez to withdraw from the art, though he continued to write, and new artist Chris Marrinan proved inappropriate. Muddy art and less imaginative stories, as Perez devoted the bulk of his time to other projects,

led Wonder Woman into the doldrums. Mindy Newell came aboard as co-plotter with 36, but made little impact. DC seemed to realise a change was needed, and tried different artists on the title: Colleen Doran, Jill Thompson and Cindy Martin all filled in on the odd chapter and issue, with Thompson appointed the new regular artist. 46's powerful and moving tale of teenage suicide and its repercussions, Mindy Newell's last issue and Jill Thompson's first entire issue, featured the strongest work either of them would do on the series. The fiftieth issue featured guest contributions from Chris Bachalo, Brian Bolland, Adam Hughes, Kevin Nowlan, P. Craig Russell and Marie Severin, among others, after which Thompson's etiolated version of Wonder Woman was seen in most issues until 65. Perez left the title after 62, passing it into the hands of Bill Messner-Loebs, who promptly took Diana into outer space for an ill-advised story in 65–71, which rambled endlessly and served no purpose. Despite lovely cover illustrations from Brian Bolland between 63 and 100, these issues are disposable.

When Diana returned to earth, Loebs made a consistent and conscientious attempt to reintroduce the character-driven stories that had been the series' trademark. New supporting characters were introduced, and with the addition of artist Lee Moder (from 72) things were looking promising. Unfortunately, with 90, Mike Deodato took over the artwork, and it all went horribly wrong. Suddenly, Diana was ten feet tall, with a six-inch waist and enormous hooters. So was Queen Hippolyta, her regal robes replaced by three (small) handkerchiefs and a string of pearls. So were both the fifty-something Julia Kapatelis and her fifteen-year-old daughter Vanessa! In came a new supporting character, a rival Amazon named Artemis, who fought Diana for the right to be Wonder Woman. Guess what she looked like? Yup. Deodato just wasn't capable of drawing any other kind of physique. The stories took a noticeable nose-dive at this point. One is forced to the conclusion that either Messner-Loebs saw the art, thought 'Oh my God' and gave up trying, or, more sadly, that he continued to write in all that plot and characterisation and stuff, and the editor excised it all in favour of more boob-and-butt shots. Sales shot up and Wonder Woman was suddenly a big hit with the retarded adolescent market.

Thankfully it was a temporary phenomenon, and, from 101, John Byrne took over the writing and art. Disappointingly, though superior to the issues that immediately preceded it – what wouldn't be? – his rendition of the Princess of Paradise Island has turned her into a generic, hatchet-faced superwoman, stripping her of everything distinctive and unique to the character. Now in his second year on the series, there are some marginal signs of improvement. Let's hope they're maintained.~HS

Recommended: Series one 1–6, 10, 11, 21, 24, 28, 178–190, 192, 193, series two 1–23, 46, Annual 2.

Collections: The Challenge of Artemis (series two 94–100), *The Contest* (series two 90–93 & 0), *Second Genesis* (series two 101–105)

Legend of WONDER WOMAN
DC: *4-issue miniseries 1986*

Published as a bridge between the old Wonder Woman title and her reworking, this story opens with Queen Hippolyta of the Amazons in mourning for her daughter, Princess Diana, Wonder Woman. Trying to ease her grief, she uses the Magic Sphere to look upon happier times, and takes courage from one of Diana's triumphs against Atomia. Kurt Busiek's script and Trina Robbins' art mesh well in this intriguing hybrid of old and new, and Robbins' homage to 1940s Wonder Woman illustrator H.G. Peter is skilful and enjoyable. A respectful and affectionate farewell to the old girl.~HS

Rick Geary's WONDERS AND ODDITIES
Dark Horse: *1 issue 1988*

Collection of short strips by the magnificently offbeat Rick Geary. Possessed of a talent similar to Gary Larson in being able to view the mundane with a unique perspective and transform it into something strange and magical.~FP

Recommended: 1

WORDSMITH
Renegade: *12 issues 1985–1988*
Caliber: *4 issues + 1996 to date*

It's the 1930s and Clay Washburn is a writer, making his living working for pulp magazines. Detective stories, gangster stories, Westerns, jungle adventures... he'll produce almost anything for his penny-a-word, but none of it under his own name. The comic deals with his searches for a good plot-twist and the right words, and with more abstract issues: how much should he analyse his stories? how much reality should he try to put into them? when should he say no to publishers and editors? and how much can you talk about politics without alienating your friends? For the first six issues or so, it's an entertaining read, with his small, real-life dilemmas mixed to good effect with extracts from the raw, dramatic escapism he's producing. But it starts to flag as he becomes more successful in the business: the extracts are longer, but Rick Taylor's stories are weaker, and by now it's obvious that the tone of the comic will remain abstract

throughout, without a hint of humour and with characters who are mere mouthpieces. The Caliber issues reprint the previous material.~FC

Recommended: 1–6

THE WORLD OF KRYPTON
DC: *3-issue miniseries 1979, 4-issue miniseries 1988*

The original *World of Krypton* was the first miniseries produced by DC, and is the biography of Superman's father Jor-El. Paul Kupperberg's writing is minimal, resulting in a weak story, but Howard Chaykin and Murphy Anderson's artwork compensates, with exemplary panel layout. The second series is a revised version of the original in the wake of changes instigated by the revamping of Superman. This version of Krypton is a troubled paradise, and creator John Byrne depicts a cold, harsh and generally emotionless world, examining the moral implications of such a place, while Mike Mignola's art portrays the barren technological Krypton superbly.~SS

THE WORLD OF METROPOLIS
DC: *4-issue miniseries 1988*

Released as part of Superman's fiftieth birthday celebrations (along with *World Of Smallville* and *World Of Krypton*), this features Superman's supporting cast Perry White, Jimmy Olsen, Lois Lane and Lex Luthor, explaining their relationships and dealings. The script is intelligently written by John Byrne, but the artwork is unimaginative and appears rushed.~SS.

WORLD OF SMALLVILLE
DC: *4-issue miniseries 1988*

The first two issues feature the history of Superman's foster parents, the Kents. After an awkward start with Martha Kent's out-of-place confession of a lost spouse and a troubled past, the story-line gets off the ground. The third and final issues are the biography of Lana Lang, including her role in the *Millennium* crossover in which it is revealed that she is an alien spy who has been waiting to betray the human race for a thousand years. Don't you just hate it when that happens? Badly drawn, poorly scripted and an embarrassment to read.~SS

WORLD OF WOOD
Eclipse: *4-issue miniseries 1986*

A collection of black and white stories drawn by Wally Wood between the late 1960s and early 1970s, but coloured, often very poorly, to suit a comic audience. Writers include Archie Goodwin, Bill DuBay, Nick Cuti, Gerry Boudreau and Wood himself. Both episodes of Wood's superhero team 'The Misfits'

(originally from *Heroes Inc*) are reprinted in the first two issues, alongside choice examples of the work Wood drew for *Creepy* and *Eerie*. There are also two war stories from *Blazing Combat*, and, mercifully in monotone, the superb 'To Kill A God', which traces vampirism back to Ancient Egypt. As a sampler of a magnificent artist you can't go wrong, but don't blame him for the colour.~SW
Recommended: 4

WORLD WITHOUT END
DC: *6-issue limited series 1990–1991*

Sumptuously illustrated by John Higgins, this is a convoluted science-fiction parable set on a devastated Earth. There's ongoing war between the sexes, who are divided into two separate camps, and Jamie Delano's bleak story matches the bleak planet as the aptly named Rumour moves ever further towards a showdown with the brutal and megalomaniac Brother Bones. Not one to be read for comfort and relaxation, Delano's script pulls no punches regarding gender relations or, by implication, a need for greater ecological awareness. Any messages, though, are couched in the unrelenting and off-putting stylised language Delano's created for Brother Bones and his acolytes. It can be understood, but it takes time, and doesn't really repay the effort. Delano would later address similar concerns in far more satisfying fashion in *Animal Man*.~FP

WORLD'S FINEST Comics
DC: *323 issues 1941–1986, 3-issue miniseries 1990, 3-issue miniseries 1994, 2-issue microseries 1996*

For one issue only titled *World's Best Comics*, when introduced this was a quarterly title, with 1–9 a hundred pages long. Superman and Batman shared the early covers, often in patriotic style once the USA entered World War II, but never met inside. The earliest issues featured a variety of strips to contrast the superheroics of the cover stars. Hop Harrigan was an adventurous pilot, Young Dr Davis is self-explanatory, and Red, White And Blue were three young soldiers battling Nazis and saboteurs. There were also the Crimson Avenger (until 5) and offbeat superhero strips Johnny Thunder and his humorous Thunderbolt, and Zatara the magician, who would run to 51. Gradually, though, other superheroes edged out the supporting features. T.N.T. and Dan the Dyna-Mite, two heroes with explosive punches, were only in 5, But Sandman (by Simon and Kirby in 6 and 7) and Star Spangled Kid (from 6) lasted longer. So did Green Arrow, who made an impressive début in 7, not surrendering his slot until 140. The Boy Commandos joined the line-up from 8. A shrinking page-count and fall in

the popularity of superheroes meant they in turn were replaced, initially by a succession of short-run features. War Of Independence and frontier hero Tomahawk managed a long run, though, from 65 to 101 before moving into his own title.

In 1954 71 was an important issue. Another reduction in pages led to the decision to combine the Superman and Batman strips, thus introducing the idea that would see the title through the next fifteen years. The danger that these two heroes might be incompatible never arose, because at the time Batman was no longer dark and foreboding, but was encountering aliens and travelling through time in his own titles. Much like Superman in fact. The way the stories were plotted meant that Superman was the brawn while Batman used his acrobatic and detective skills. Editor Jack Schiff also edited the Batman titles, so visually Batman tended to predominate, with his artist Dick Sprang being a regular here, sometimes inking Curt Swan's pencils. At the time, however, Superman was by far the more popular of the pair. The stories were gimmick-driven, with plots very similar to those in the Superman titles, but more likely to use the Batman supporting cast. In 90, for instance, Batwoman takes the Lois Lane role of acquiring superpowers for a single story.

In the back-up strips Green Arrow was still going strong, largely drawn by George Papp, but in 96–99 Jack Kirby took over, with Lee Elias thereafter. Tommy Tomorrow replaced Tomahawk in 102, and you couldn't ask for a greater contrast than a historical strip giving way to stories of intergalactic policemen of the future (in purple shorts with yellow boots). It was a charming strip, illustrated by Jim Mooney, who would progress to the Superman and Batman lead strip, alternating with Dick Sprang. In 125 Aquaman, beautifully illustrated by Nick Cardy, then Ramona Fradon, displaces Tommy Tomorrow, and runs until 139. With these issues *World's Finest* collected the only superheroes that had survived since their 1940s introduction (with the exception of Wonder Woman).

There was a drastic change with 141, as Mort Weisinger became editor, planting *World's Finest* firmly in the Superman stable of titles. The lead strip is the Olsen/Robin team facing the Superman/Batman team, with art by Curt Swan and George Klein. There was a greater flair to the stories from this point, some of them being very good indeed, and far better than those appearing in the other *Superman* and *Batman* titles, although elements from both were used here. Jim Shooter wrote some of the best: his peak came with 164's 'Brainiac's Super Brainchild', in which the evil android creates a female computer called Genia to battle the *World's Finest* team. One feature similar to the *Superman* series was the introduction of 'imaginary' stories that gave the writers a greater freedom by not tying them to established continuity. An early example is 154, with the sons of Superman and Batman, who make an early return in 157. These children were kids, as opposed to another series using the same idea in the 1970s, where the sons were teenagers. A nice variation on the regular theme came with the teaming of Supergirl and Batgirl in 169, plotting to usurp their male counterparts. The best of the 'imaginary' stories is 172, positing that Bruce Wayne might have also been adopted by the Kents, making Superman and Batman brothers.

Change was in the air at DC in 1968, with a definite effort to make their titles more exciting to compete with Marvel comics. There's a Neal Adams cover on 174, and he draws the stories inside the following two issues. While his art is lovely, the style of story hadn't changed, and Adams' strength is pseudo-realism, not goofy superheroes. Swan is back for the following two issues, but it's Ross Andru and Mike Esposito art from 180, with the writing handled by Cary Bates, Robert Kanigher and Bob Haney. The strength of Bates' writing was always his ingenious plotting, so he was in his element here, but the art still wasn't quite up to par. By 1970 there was a certain predictability to *World's Finest*, with the title failing to live up to its name. Drastic surgery came with 199, as Batman was evicted, giving Superman the chance to team with other characters. Denny O'Neil began with a crowd-pleaser as Superman raced against The Flash, ostensibly the fastest man alive, with art regularly by Dick Dillin and Joe Giella. The Superman team-ups lasted to 214, with 210's script by Elliott Maggin picking up on a plot last seen in Green Lantern, in which the socially aware Green Arrow planned to run for mayor. The best of a generally decent bunch, though, is 212's return of The Martian Manhunter. When last seen in *JLA* 71 he'd gone into space to locate other survivors from his race, and this story followed on. 207–212 were forty-eight-page comics with reprinted 1940s back-ups, the best being a very nice-looking Black Pirate from Sheldon Moldoff in 210.

Batman was back in 215, although only by proxy as one of the teenage Super Sons, which seemed popular with the readers for some inexplicable reason. Bob Haney was now writing. Always a good plotter, and packing a lot into his stories, these weren't his most exciting work, and he didn't improve when the real Batman returned in 220. Salvation was at hand with 223–228, each one hundred pages, with the reprint strips more than compensating

for the lack-lustre lead feature. The Super Sons continued to appear every now and then when the magazine reverted to normal size; the less said about them the better, of course.

It's ironic to note that what eventually breathed new life into *World's Finest* again was its reversion to the original idea of an oversize comic with a selection of all-new features. From 244 Green Arrow, Black Canary, Martian Manhunter and Wonder Woman all ran in solo strips after the Superman and Batman team. The best of the early runs was the Gray Morrow-illustrated Vigilante in 244–248, although the Gerry Conway and Sal Amendola Black Canary strip in 247 looks very nice. Steve Ditko returned to his creation The Creeper in 249–255, and the E. Nelson Bridwell and Don Newton Captain Marvel strip modernised the classic old hero without destroying the innocent feel of the character in 253–282. It continued from the cancelled *Shazam* title. 283 returns the title to a standard twenty-four pages, though it retains a back-up strip, in this case a Green Arrow strip nicely drawn by Gil Kane. Throughout the changes in format the Superman and Batman team-ups remained, and remained uninspired. Even an overlong story in 300, drawn by George Perez and guest-starring the Justice League, Outsiders and Teen Titans, only temporarily livened up a moribund title. Writer Joey Cavaleiri institutes a marginal rise in quality as the title limps to its demise, but there's nothing of real note.

Did the comic ever live up to its name? No, to be honest. There were some decent strips, but very little that can be ranked above acceptable, with the stories from the mid-1960s the best. When the title was cancelled to make way for the new look Superman it was unmourned.

When DC revived the comic there was a little more effort to ensure that the contents matched the title, with Dave Gibbons writing, Steve Rude and Karl Kesel illustrating and colourist Steve Oliff contributing considerably to the package. Gibbons delivers a plot that mixes and matches Superman and Batman's supporting cast, cities and villains, contrasting and playing them off each other. Lex Luthor turns up in Gotham for a business deal, and the Joker decides to take a vacation in Metropolis, each well characterised. There's a nice touch in that all of Luthor's henchmen are bald, and the Joker is more manic than maniac: the exchanges between the two make good reading. Steve Rude's city designs are excellent, and he also captures Superman and Batman very well, with an original take on the latter. It's taken a long time, but this is finally a series that lives up to the title, with the best Batman and Superman teaming since the 1960s.

In the 1994 series, titled *Legends Of The*

World's Finest, writer Walt Simonson takes a different slant on the Superman/Batman team, including supernatural elements. The plot is based on a little-used Superman villainess The Silver Banshee and her partner, the evil spirit Tuallas, who're trying to escape the wrath of the demoness Blaze. In doing so Superman and Batman are used as their pawns, and their dreams and nightmares blend, with deadly consequences. Superman becomes ever more brutal, and Batman begins to question his sanity after dreaming constantly of Krypton's destruction. It's a well-paced story, lavishly illustrated by Dan Brereton.

World's Finest 3 is very much a departure from the norm, teaming Superboy and Robin. There's nothing dark and gloomy about this series, as the pair take on Metallo, now able to morph into any robotic shape, and the sexy Poison Ivy, able to control any man she's kissed. In this story it happens to be Superboy, whose help she wants in transforming Hawaii into a Garden of Eden. Metallo's abilities may be far-fetched, but they're imaginatively employed, as he transforms into an express train and an escalator among other items, and he has the best dialogue of the story. Chuck Dixon and Karl Kesel deliver an action-packed story that's very nicely illustrated by Tom Grummett and Scott Hanna.~HY

Recommended: 162, 164, 169, 172, 212 , miniseries 1, miniseies 2
Collection: World's Finest (miniseries one 1–3), *World's Finest* (miniseries two 1–3)

WORLDS COLLIDE
DC/Milestone: *One-shot 1994*

In an attempt to boost Milestone's profile this crossover had Superman, amongst others, visiting the black-superhero-populated universe. In a time when gimmick covers were *de rigueur* this had one of the best: vinyl stickers of all the heroes so you could create your own fight sequence.~TP

WORLDS UNKNOWN
Marvel: *8 issues 1973–1974*

1–6 contain adaptations of science-fiction stories that mostly suffer from being contracted to fit the comics' page-count, but with some notable art, particularly Ralph Reese in the first issue. The final issues adapt *The Golden Voyage of Sinbad*.~FP

WORLD'S WORST COMICS AWARDS
Kitchen Sink: *2-issue miniseries 1990*

A leisurely trawl through comics' lowlights presented as an awards ceremony. Categories such as Worst Costume (male and female), Worst Team, Worst Name and Worst Series are interspersed with other less than shining

moments, leading to a top ten rundown of the Worst Comics. The choices are good and the linking material amusing. To be avoided by those without a sense of humour about their funnybooks.~WJ

WRATH
Malibu: *9 issues, 1 Giant Size 1994*

It's rumoured that Marvel bought out Malibu Comics chiefly to get hold of their impressive computer-colouring process. Certainly the colouring on *Wrath* is the most impressive thing about this superhero series... and even that ain't so hot. Although the series is credited to Plotter/Penciller David Ammerman and Scripter Mike W. Barr, *Wrath* might as well've been produced by another of Malibu's fancy computers, so generic are their efforts. Wrath works for the shadowy organisation Aladdin, seeking out other superpowerful 'Primes' and teaming up with fellow Ultraverse heroes Mantra, Freex and Prime in a series of dull escapades that never justify the high cover price or deluxe packaging. ~AL

WULF The Barbarian
Atlas: *4 issues 1975*

Of the many sword-and-sorcery books produced in the 1970s this, although not particularly original, was one of the best. 1 and 2 are handsomely drawn by Larry Hama, who also wrote the title, and inked by Klaus Janson (and a cast of thousands in 2). 3 and 4 are respectively bizarre and banal and need only trouble completists.~DAR
Recommended: 1, 2

WWF World Wrestling Federation
Valiant: *4 issues 1991*

Considering that in its heyday the World Wrestling Federation was the nearest thing to live-action superhero fights, their transfer to comics is surprisingly feeble. The central idea is that the wrestlers carry their grudges out of the ring into social situations. For hard-core WWF fans only.~FP

WYATT EARP
Marvel: *34 issues 1955–1960 (1–29), 1972–1973 (30–34)*

Exploits of the frontier marshal by Stan Lee and Dick Ayers. They're all flaccid Western fare, as are the accompanying strips by Lee, with such talents as Williamson, Crandall and Torres on art. The 1970s reprint series was deservedly short-lived.~SW

X

Dark Horse: *24 issues, 1 Special 1994–1996*

Part of Dark Horse's *Comics Greatest World* series of superhero titles, *X* concerns a masked vigilante in the city of Arcadia. X warns his victims once only with an X mark. The next time they're marked he kills them. Initially his targets are the corrupt controllers, police, politicians and gangsters of Arcadia. With 15 the war is over and X is unofficial ruler of the city, but now he has to face forces from outside that seek either to exploit the lack of government or simply to take revenge on X. 18 sees X fighting a Predator, while the remainder of the series concerns his visit to Washington to warn off any federal interference and the subsequent invasion of Arcadia by every psycho looking for a home.

Full of early promise, Steven Grant has some good ideas but doesn't really develop them, hinting at a moral debate over X's actions but never stopping the action long enough to have it. The artwork was originally by Doug Mahnke and Jimmy Palmiotti (1–5). Ron Wagner and then Chris Warner took over for a while until, with 13, Javier Saltares became the regular artist. Although he provided a consistency to the series his compositions are rather rigid and, frankly, dull.

The X Special, 'One Shot To The Head', by Jerry Prosser and Chris Warner, is actually a prequel to *Comics Greatest World: X*, which is X's first appearance. There is also a two-part giveaway series from *Heroes Illustrated* (1994) by Grant and Vince Giarrano. Other elements of note: there's a Ghost guest appearance in 8 and Frank Miller provides covers for 18–22 and the *X Special*.~NF

XENOBROOD

DC: *7 issues (0–6) 1994–1995*

A couple of anthropologists find some crystals that hatch four superpowered aliens made of superdense protoplasm. Unfortunately, while they have to learn all about their new environment, other aliens want them back. Doug Moench can't do much with this slim premise, even with Superman guest-starring in 3 and 4. Changes in artist after only the second issue suggest that DC didn't have any confidence in the strip either.~NF

XENOZOIC TALES

Kitchen Sink: *14 issues + 1987 to date*

Although it's the 26th century, post-cataclysm, Mark Schultz's world of dinosaurs and ruined cities owes more to the 1950s. In the Xenozoic Age small pockets of humanity, who've spent the last four and a half centuries underground, emerge and set up tribal societies in the ruins of the old world. Jack 'Cadillac' Tenrec is a mechanic who spends his spare time fixing up old cars until he meets Hannah Dundee, an ambassador from the neighbouring Wassoon tribe, who's really on a mission to find the stash of books Jack's people are reputed to hold in their ruined City In The Sea, but who seems perfectly happy to hang out, have adventures and ride around in his cars.

There are usually two or three interconnected stories in each issue, with plenty of action, but *Xenozoic Tales* is actually a slowly developing love story between the two leads, drawn in mock Wally Wood style with just a hint of Williamson for good measure. Schultz fixes it so he can have all the things he likes in one comic book (shapely women, guys in safari suits, dinosaurs and classic cars), and while the exercise is diverting and pretty to look at, it's ultimately a load of very pretty fluff.~FJ

Recommended: *1–3, 13*

X-FACTOR

Marvel: *132 issues +, 9 Annuals, 1986 to date*

X-Factor's long run has been somewhat schizophrenic since the first issue débuted, amid much hype, after a lead-in story in *Avengers* 263 and *Fantastic Four* 286. Initially written by Bob Layton and drawn by Jackson Guice, the comic reunited the five original X-Men. Disillusioned by the growing bigotry against mutants and angered by Professor X's decision to hand the running of the main team over to their former enemy Magneto, Cyclops, The Beast, Angel, Iceman and Jean Grey set up their own team to combat the problems. Posing as mutant hunters who could be hired to 'remove' mutant problems, the team gathered frightened young mutants – including many who would later become major characters in *X-Force* and other X-books – with the aim of training them in the way they themselves had been trained, in line with

Xavier's dream. There's a heavy soap-opera feel to early issues, along with a sub-plot that leads into the introduction of Apocalypse as a major new X-villain.

Louise Simonson takes over the writing from 6, and is joined by husband Walt on the art chores from 10. Walt's arrival coincides with events leading to the loss of the Angel's original wings and his transformation into one of Apocalypse's horsemen – a sub-plot still developing a decade later. He remains regular penciller until 40, and his entire run, during which the team sensibly drop the mutant hunters charade, is eminently readable. Louise Simonson then works with a series of artists (including Art Adams on 41–42) until Jim Lee (with occasional assists from Chris Claremont) and Whilce Portacio take over on 61. They bring a welcome vitality to the comic on their short but nonetheless impressive run, and 68 sets into motion the events that will one day lead Cyclops' young son to become the futuristic warrior Cable, complicating X-Men continuity for evermore.

There's a complete change of direction from 71. The original members go back to the X-Men, to be replaced by Havok, Polaris, Strong Guy, Wolfsbane and Madrox the Multiple Man. Under the wing of government liaison Val Cooper the team become, effectively, the US government's pet mutants during a run by Larry Stroman and fan favourite Peter David. The new look received an appreciable amount of critical acclaim, relying as usual on David's tricks with in-jokes and one-liners to carry along plots which are generally weaker than the scripts.

After David's departure with 92, X-Factor suffers from frequently changing creative teams until John Francis Moore and Steve Epting arrive with 114. Immediately bringing the criminal Mystique into the team, a move forced by Cooper, who aims to make Mystique pay for her crimes by helping the group, the new creative team sets off in a new direction as the heroes begin to question the amount of government control over their operation. The sub-plot continues when Howard Mackie seamlessly takes over the writing from Moore, and is still a major feature when Jeff Matsuda replaces Epting on the art. Recent issues, in which more and more 'reforming' criminals have been forced on the increasingly unhappy team, have continued the thread.

Throughout its ten-plus years X-Factor has never been an outstanding comic but has always been a solid read, with some of fandom's favourite creators and generally above-average story-telling. If you can get the entire run, you could do worse than sit down and read them in one go... ~JC.
Collections: see Uncanny X-MEN

X-FACTOR - Prisoner Of Love
Marvel: One-shot 1990

A dire X-Factor spin-off that has the usually cheery Beast moaning about being a monster. What is most interesting about this otherwise forgettable comic by Jackson Guice and Jim Starlin is how obviously it was written to be a Fantastic Four story, and how out of character the X-Factor heroes are made to act in a quick reworking which has done nothing but change the names.~JC

THE X-FILES
Topps: 24 issues, 1 Annual + 1995 to date

Topps underestimated the building appeal of cult TV series The X-Files when they released the first issue of the comic. The first twelve original stories are linked by a common theme (memory), and subsequent issues investigate computer programs (13), survivalists (15–16) and ball lightning (18–19), the fascinating phenomenon scientists had refused to believe in for years, until a big ball of it passed through the wall of a laboratory and killed several research scientists, at which point they sat up and took note. Stefan Petrucha writes 1–19 in the same vein as the TV series but his interest in the subject-matter shows in the wordiness of the scripts. Characterising Mulder and Scully remains secondary to whatever strange phenomenon is being investigated. Charles Adlard works hard to capture the FBI agents' likenesses in his heavy-lined, blocky style and, given the nature of the stories, can't avoid drawing a lot of pages of talking heads.

'Family Portrait' (20–21), by Kevin J. Anderson and Gordon Purcell, is less satisfying, despite previous comments, because it moves nearer to a traditional supernatural plot about vampirism rather than looking at things scientifically. An annual (1995) and two issues of X-Files Comics Digest are also by Petrucha and Adlard. There's also a highly-sought-after 'half' issue published as a freebie with Wizard from 1995, and a special edition reprinting the first three issues.~NF
Collections: Firebird (1–6), The Haunting (Annual 1, 13, 14), Project Aquarius (7–12)

X-FORCE
Marvel: 57 issues +, 3 Annuals 1991 to date

Rob Liefeld transformed the flagging New Mutants title into this new series, with the main difference being that the team are now led by the enigmatic Cable instead of Professor X. The series begins with an insight into the workings of the new team, and there's the introduction of Deadpool in 2. He quickly became a fan favourite with some witty dialogue and a mysterious past, associated with the new Weapon X character Kane (Wolverine was the first Weapon X). There's little excitement until 8,

which features part of Cable's origin. Unfortunately the origin presented here is far from complete, and the story drags on forever. Shortly after this, in 10, Cable departs, giving more space to concentrate on the rest of the team, and in his absence Cannonball does his best to lead the team. After Liefeld's departure with 14 Fabian Nicieza writes the title, while Greg Capullo from 15–27 is a very good replacement artist. Following issues have a greater emphasis on characterisation and allow each team member some individual attention as X-Force battle a mutant named Gideon. The title often foreshadows events in other mutant titles, with Magneto's return in 24 a prime example. 'Child's Play', in 30–34, concerns a rich businessman capturing Boomer and Cannonball to appease an evil sense of adventure. 38 leads into the *Generation X* series and is the début of new artist Tony Daniels, while 41 has a reasonable exploration of Feral's character. As *X-Force* becomes caught in the mutant crossover 'Age of Apocalypse' the title is transformed into an alternate reality where Gambit leads the team (see *Gambit and the X-ternals*). Issues 46, 52 and 56 all see appearances by the evil Onslaught, the character who later goes on to battle all the mutant teams and pretty well destroy the Marvel Universe. As things stand, *X-Force* has become too closely linked to the other mutant books. The characters are strong and imaginative, but for any progression they should be omitted from multi-title crossovers.~SS
Collections: see Uncanny X-MEN

X-MAN
Marvel: *25 issues + 1995 to date*

Starting in Marvel's *Age of Apocalypse* alternate timeline experiment, *X-Man* is the alternate version of *Cable*, and was the only book to continue on into the regular Marvel Universe after the other series finished. Adolescent Nate Grey was bred by Mister Sinister from the genetic material of Scott Summers and Jean Grey (Cyclops and Phoenix) to be a weapon against the evil Apocalypse, but was freed by Summers and brought up by a troupe of mutants disguised as travelling actors. When 'reality' was restored the immensely powerful Grey survived into the regular Marvel Universe, further complicating an already ridiculously convoluted alternate world/time-travel continuity. In amongst numerous fights with the X-Men, Cable and the Hellfire club, the series is competently written by the reliable Jeph Loeb but never escapes the fact that the Marvel Universe doesn't need yet another X-book, even one where the main character is having a relationship with his alternate-world father's ex-wife – who also happens to be a clone of an alternate-world version of his mother. If you're confused already, the title is best avoided.~JC

X-MEN
Marvel: *60 issues + 1991 to date*

Following a period during which the X-Men had been bi-weekly, Marvel launched a new series on the back of the popularity of both the team itself and co-plotter/artist Jim Lee. Lee's input had revitalised the parent title, and his enthusiasm carried over well into the new one. 1–3, which credit Chris Claremont as co-plotter, deal mainly with Magneto, the X-Men's sometime enemy, sometime ally, who is trying his best to mind his own business on the moon, pestered by those who would see him brought to justice for past crimes. Claremont's final issue, ending a fifteen-year involvement with the book, sets in motion events which will have far-reaching consequences for both Magneto and the heroes over the next few years. Jim Lee's issues are above average until 11; then Fabian Nicieza took over until 45, a run mostly drawn by Andy Kubert. Nicieza takes until 20 to get into his stride, when Psylocke turns up claiming she's been replaced with an impostor and the woman who has been fighting alongside the X-Men in recent issues is a fake named Revanche. 20–23 offer some answers, and are followed, in 24, by a piece of pure soap as Gambit and Rogue head for a night on the town and the rest of the X-Men relax in and around the mansion. Afterwards, the Psylocke/Revanche plot starts up again, interrupted only by the wedding of Cyclops and Phoenix in 30, which is the usual mix of nostalgia and soap but nothing special. The issues leading up to it in other X-books are much better than the wedding itself. 34 brings a new major plot to the books: the introduction of Sabretooth to the team. One of the team's most savage enemies, Professor X is convinced he can reform him. Sabretooth is not so sure, and the conclusion of the plot-line brings tragedy. There's then a three-part confrontation between the team and Magneto's followers, the Acolytes, dealing with some interesting themes on mutant hatred in the Marvel Universe and the best way to combat it. Nicieza leaves with the character-driven double-sized 45. Long-time X-fan favourite Scott Lobdell takes over, bringing a slightly soapier feel to the comic which leads up to the Onslaught multi-part crossover. This starts to gear up from the excellent 50 and ties up with 57 (via several issues of every other Marvel comic). Issues since have stayed away from playing on the increased mutant hatred as much as *Uncanny X-Men* did, instead focusing on the effect the events have had on the team personally. 59 is particularly touching. Long may Lobdell and Kubert continue.~JC
Recommended: 1–3, 24, 34, 42–44, 50, 59–60
Collections: X-Men/Ghost Rider (9, 10, *Ghost Rider* 27, 28), see also *Uncanny X-MEN*

The Amazing X-MEN
Marvel: *4 issues 1996*

The X-Men's brief excursion into the alternate Earth ruled by their arch-enemy Apocalypse offered a new take on relationships within the group. The X-Men here are Quicksilver, Storm (a couple, in this universe), Dazzler, Iceman, Banshee and the real Marvel Universe villain Exodus – not the most dynamic team, but overall more cynical than this world's other X-group in *Astonishing X-Men*, led by the more optimistic Rogue. It's the darker of the two comics; while they fight on because they have to, this team no longer believes it can win. Their main efforts are channelled into helping humans escape to the relatively unscathed Eurasia.~JC

The Astonishing X-MEN
Marvel: *4 issues 1996*

A limited run during the period when the world of all X-titles was altered by Apocalypse. *Astonishing* is more upbeat than *Amazing X-Men*, in as much as the X-Men are ever upbeat. Faced with what Bishop tells them of the way the world should be, the X-Men are determined to do what they can to put things right. These X-Men are Magneto, Rogue, Sabretooth, Wild Child, Blink, Sunfire and Morph, a hardened bunch who nonetheless can still just about dream of a better world. Focusing more on the relationship between Rogue and Magneto than the other title does, and touching on the complicated relationship between Rogue and Quicksilver, it's more character-driven and truer to the spirit of the 'real' X-Men: heroes who are prepared to fight to the death for what they believe to be right, no matter what the cost.~JC

The Uncanny X-MEN
Marvel: *340+ issues, 18 Annuals, 2 Giant-Size, 1 Graphic Novel 1963 to date*

One of the final titles introducing the first flush of Marvel Comics (only *Daredevil* would follow), the X-Men were the flip side to the Fantastic Four. Also a closely knit team, instead of being loved and admired by the public at large, their inherent extra abilities, designating them as mutants, made them figures to be feared. The slim reasoning that endemic superpowers somehow make their possessor a threat, whereas accidentally conferred abilities are okay with the public at large, has seen the X-Men through three decades of plots. This stood up a little better in the less populated Marvel Universe of 1963, and a début issue that introduced Professor X, Angel, Beast, Cyclops, Iceman, Marvel Girl and Magneto, all still going strong 33 years later, wasn't a bad week's work from Stan Lee and Jack Kirby. The adjective 'uncanny' was sparingly appended in the early

issues, and only a permanent addition to the logo from 141.

The teenage heroes were theoretically honing their powers at Professor Xavier's School For Gifted Youngsters, yet emerged almost every issue to confront new mutant threats. 2's Vanisher was always a second-stringer, but 3's introduction of The Blob (a corpulent, immovable mutant) was more permanent, and further perennials arrived in 4, with Scarlet Witch and Quicksilver introduced as Magneto's henchmen. This is the most memorable of the early issues, packing a lot into twenty-two pages under a fabulous cover of Magneto and Co. looming over the X-Men. The Mastermind, another second-stringer, also débuted that issue and would later prompt one of the most powerful stories of the 1970s revived team. Lee and Kirby were having a lot of fun here, and even the unsympathetic inking of Paul Reinman (1–5) couldn't dull the edge. Chic Stone, from 6, was a superior inker and remained until Kirby's final fling at full pencils in 11. 12 has the bizarre art combination of Alex Toth pencilling Kirby layouts, and Werner Roth did the same between 13 and 18 (under the alias of Jay Gavin) before drawing the comic himself until 49.

The Juggernaut was introduced in 12, and has since battled almost every Marvel superhero, but a daft moment of plotting established him as Professor X's brother, a fact generally forgotten these days. The X-Men's other great recurring foes, the Sentinels, arrived in 14–16. Fearing mutant supremacy (after all, there were over a dozen of them at Marvel by that time), giant robots were constructed to protect humanity, but they proved a little too zealous in deciding that the best way to do so would be to subjugate humanity. Roy Thomas supplanted Stan Lee as writer with 20, one issue after Lee had created The Mimic in a memorable finale.

Thomas moved the plot on a little with less reliance on Magneto (eight villainous appearances in the previous nineteen issues), moved the team out of the school more often, and generally produced a good run of comics until 39. Memorable issues included a battle with an endearing set of loser villains in 22 and 23, the début of the Banshee in 28, and the very silly Mekano in 36. Thomas' ongoing plot concerned the foreboding Factor Three. Despite sounding like a toothpaste, they were a threat, and in 39's disappointing conclusion Professor X dies. Don't worry, he doesn't really, it's all explained away in 65, but at the time this was a daring move and the issue retains a certain poignancy today. Without the Professor the X-Men were aimless, and without Roy Thomas *X-Men* became gormless, as Gary Friedrich, then Arnold Drake, turned in what remain among the most dreadful *X-Men* comics to date. 50 and 51 have noteworthy Jim Steranko art on a stupid story; Barry Smith's first comic is 52, and boy, does it show. Between 39 and 56 the only items of note are the back-up strips detailing the origins of the individual X-Men, but they're certainly not worth the price of admission alone.

Thomas returned with 56, in the company of Neal Adams, whose illustrative style and dynamic layouts resulted in a startlingly drawn run, on which Tom Palmer's smooth inking was a factor. Cyclops' brother Havok had been introduced in 54, also a mutant and unsure of how to cope with his blossoming power. Thomas and Adams showed the way in 57–59, with the frightening return of the Sentinels, this time looking invincible, and the desperate conclusion is excellent. It's truncated for republication in *Giant-Size X-Men* 2. 60–61 introduce Sauron, a villain who transforms himself into a pterodactyl and who's proved surprisingly long-lasting. It runs into 62's adventure in Ka-Zar's Savage Land, and the début of a new group of mutants genetically engineered by an old foe in 63. Sunfire arrives in 64, drawn by Don Heck, and 65 is the last Adams *X-Men*, and even he can't save a daft Denny O'Neil story returning Professor X. The first-run finale is a surprisingly low-key battle with the Hulk, after which the title reprinted 12–45 until 93, two stories per issue until 72 permitting the otherwise impossible mathematics. In the meantime the X-Men were kept alive with odd guest slots (*Marvel Team-Up* 4, *Captain America* 172–175), while the Beast was transformed in *Amazing Adventures* 11–16.

The X-Men re-emerged in 1975, eventually becoming comics' most successful makeover. *Giant-Size X-Men* 1, written by Len Wein with art by Dave Cockrum, told the story of the original team's disappearance and the efforts of a new team gathered to rescue them. Like the original Lee and Kirby series, the new X-Men had the feel of a group of outsiders who found friendship and understanding with each other. The originals had been teenagers struggling to understand their mutant powers; the new team added a multiracial, multinational tilt to remind us even more that, at its core, *X-Men* has always been about intolerance towards those who are different. Of the newcomers, Wolverine (introduced in *Hulk* 181) went on to become one of Marvel's most popular characters, and Storm and Nightcrawler still appear regularly.

After Giant-Size 1, the *X-Men* title switches back to new material with 94, and Wein and Cockrum guide it through the next two issues, with Chris Claremont coming aboard as co-plotter from 95 and writer from 96 through to, incredibly, 279 – an unbroken run of over sixteen years. The early part of 94 deals with the

departure of three original X-Men, reducing the cast from battalion levels, although everyone returns sooner or later. Claremont's first solo story, which deals with Cyclops' remorse at the death of his team-mate Thunderbird in the previous issue, starts as Claremont means to go on, with an emphasis on *angst* and soul-searching that was to become his trademark. The Cockrum and Claremont issues are good, solid superhero fare, better than average, and a little overlooked in the wake of what followed. In the landmark 100, returning from a mission on the moon, Jean Grey (then still called Marvel Girl) apparently sacrifices her life to save her friends, piloting their crippled shuttle back to Earth through terrible radiation. In 101, though, she's revived as Phoenix, a being with phenomenal psychic powers, signalling the beginning of 'The Phoenix Saga', unarguably the greatest period in the *X-Men*'s run, if not the best superhero comics ever produced. Over the next ten or so issues, as the team battle the alien Imperial Guard and then Magneto, it becomes apparent that, whatever other effect the resurrection has had on Jean, it has turned her into something more godlike than human. The addition of John Byrne on art from 107 completes the *X-Men*'s creative team supreme, and for the next thirty issues there's hardly time to pause to catch your breath. After defeating Magneto, the team head to the Savage Land for a run-in with Sauron and Ka-Zar, then take on Moses Magnum (119 – the only forgettable issue of this period), Alpha Flight, Arcade and, in 125, Mastermind. By now, Jean's powers are so advanced she is effortlessly rearranging molecules of her costume to street clothes, holding back the forces of volcanoes, and wiping the floor with the best any villain has to throw at her. Mastermind, like Jean a telepath, starts playing with her mind. Unfortunately, it's at the same time that she's beginning to become overwhelmed by her powers, and the combination unbalances her completely. 129–137, 'The Dark Phoenix Saga', are the peak of an incredible run. Jean fights to control her sanity but is gradually more addicted to the destructive nature of her powers until, having destroyed whole solar systems for thrills, she takes the only way out – suicide, while she still has enough lucidity to do it. The power of these issues, intermixed with the soap-opera aspects that were also sending the popularity sky high, is incredible.

After this, you might think that Claremont and Byrne would give their heroes a break, but instead the story-line leads almost immediately into the 'Days Of Future Past' tale (141–142), in which the body of the team's youngest member, Kitty Pryde, is taken over by the mind of her adult self from a nightmarish future which, despite all their best efforts since, the X-Men are no closer to preventing now than they were then. Although this was the start of the convoluted time-travel that still dogs the *X-Men*'s continuity today, the story is excellent. Byrne leaves with 143, and Cockrum returns for what is again a more than creditable run. The team continue to face a constant stream of foes, including returns from old enemies Arcade, Magneto, and the Brotherhood of Evil Mutants, but it's already apparent that John Byrne's influence on the plots is going to be sorely missed.

The next regular artist is Paul Smith. The tempo relaxes slightly from the frantic pace of Byrne and Cockrum's all-action adventures, as Claremont focuses more on the characters. There's an adventure with the Morlocks, deformed mutants who live in the New York sewers, the addition of former villain Rogue to the team, and the introduction of Madelyne Prior, Cyclops' amnesiac lover, who looks remarkably like the late Ms Grey. The is-she-isn't-she-Jean plot becomes the focus of the next few issues, leading to a well-executed conclusion and wedding issue in 175. Claremont then teams up with John Romita Jr from 176 to 212. Although *X-Men* remains considerably above average, it never quite reaches the heights of the Claremont/Byrne days except for a few fill-in issues by Barry Windsor-Smith, in 186 and 198. The major sub-plot at this time is the introduction of Rachel Summers, the 'Days Of Future Past' timeline's daughter of Scott Summers, and her efforts to prevent her world coming about. 201, in which Cyclops fights Storm for the leadership of the X-Men, is also a classic.

By the time Romita leaves, however, it's clear that Claremont is growing bored. The art is handled by a succession of big-name, but irregular, pencillers, inducing a feeling of fill-in issues until Marc Silvestri comes on board with 220, at which point *X-Men* regains a sense of direction. Claremont's story-lines start to ramble too much, though, and although some good new ideas are introduced during this period, including the anti-mutant island of Genosha and the emergence of Mr Sinister as a major villain, the stories aren't great. At this period the book was bi-weekly: this publication frequency may have overstretched the creative team. The comic picks up again with the introduction of penciller Jim Lee, once again suggesting that Claremont works better with an artist who is prepared to make major contributions to the plot. Lee handles the art irregularly from 248 and regularly from 267, at which point his contribution is most easily noticeable, as the Lee issues brim with an enthusiasm lacking from those by Silvestri. By 274, a superb tale of Rogue and Magneto in the Savage Land, Lee is taking the plotting credits,

with Claremont relegated to scripter. The title's buoyed up by Lee's success, but his run is unfortunately short as, following 277, he switched to the sister book, *X-Men*, leaving Claremont to briefly reunite with Paul Smith, then Fabian Nicieza and Andy Kubert, for a mere two issues before leaving the book after nearly two hundred issues.

Writer/artist Whilce Portacio takes over from 280, sometimes assisted on the plots by Lee and the scripts by John Byrne. The comic moves back towards all-out action after Claremont's soap, gaining a reputation for big guns and violence not welcomed by long-term fans but enough to keep the book at the top of the bestseller lists. Trevor Fitzroy and Shinobi Shaw are developed as new major villains, and the time-travelling Bishop is introduced to the team in 283. Around the mid-280s, Scott Lobdell joined the creative team, initially as scripter on Portacio's plots, then as writer, and soon became a fan favourite by taking the comic back towards a more soap-opera feel. When Portacio left with 292, Lobdell continued, initially with Dan Petersen on art chores, then John Romita Jr for 308–310. The issues around the wedding of Cyclops and (the long since resurrected) Phoenix are particularly good. Joe Madureira, later a fan favourite, first pencils issue 313 in the middle of a run of fill-in artists before becoming regular penciller with 325. Lobdell and Madureira continue to be the creative team, and this continues to be the more character-driven of the *X-Men* titles, offering a downbeat alternative to its more action-driven sister title.

Oddly for what's been the most popular American comic for roughly the past ten years, there's only been a single graphic novel starring the *X-Men*, although with the plethora of related titles and associated miniseries perhaps there's not a need for more. And it was issued in both large and comic-size formats. Christopher (!) Claremont and Brent Eric (!) Anderson combined for 'God Loves, Man Kills', in which a charismatic televangelist covertly runs a paramilitary group that's executing mutants. To stop him the X-Men must work with Magneto, their deadliest enemy – the first time this plot was used. If a little verbose in places, it's still very good, a story saying in a single volume everything required about the humans-hating-mutants plot-line that's run through the *X-Men* since day one. Several of the collections are only available in British editions from Boxtree.~WJ/JC

Recommended: 4, 14–16, 28, 58, 59, 62, 63, 97–101, 109, 111–114, 120, 121, 129–137, 141, 142, 175, 179, 186, 198, 201, 268, 274, *God Loves, Man Kills*

Collections: *The Coming Of Bishop* (281–284), *Danger Room Battle Archives* (Annual 3, 10, 17, *New Mutants* annual 2), *Days of Future Past*

(141–142), *Days Of Future Present* (annual 14, *Fantastic Four* annual 23, *New Mutants* annual 6, *X-Factor* annual 5), *Essential X-Men* (Giant-Size 1, 94–119), *Fatal Attractions* (304, *Excalibur* 71, *X-Factor* 92, *X-Force* 25, *X-Men* 25), *From The Ashes* (168–176), *Inferno* (240–242, *New Mutants* 71–73, *X-Factor* 76–78), *Legion Quest* (320, 321, *X-Factor* 109, *X-Men* 40–41), *Marvel Masterworks* vol 3 (1–10), vol 7 (11–20), vol 11 (Giant-Size 1, 94–100), vol 12 (101–110), vol 24 (111–120), *Mutant Massacre* (210–213, *X-Factor* 9–11, *New Mutants* 27, *Power Pack* 46, *Thor* 373–374),*The Phoenix Saga* (129–137), *The X-Cutioner's Song* (294–296, *X-Factor* 84–86, *X-Force* 16–18, *X-Men* 14–16), *X-Men Visionaries* 1, *X-Men Visionaries* 2 (56–63, 65), *X-Tinction Agenda* (270–272, *X-Factor* 60–62, *New Mutants* 95–97)

Marvel and DC Present the Uncanny X-MEN and the New Teen TITANS
Marvel/DC: *One-shot 1982*

This first teaming of teams by the two industry giants fielded the most popular supergroups of the era in a one-shot which crammed in a massive sixty-four pages of story. This page-count is fortunate, as Chris Claremont is obliged to develop a snail-pace story over the first twenty pages as a cast of thousands is introduced to readers who might be familiar with only half the players. Yet after the aperitifs, he constructs a demanding tale that refuses to spoon-feed the reader, delivers smooth cross-company character interplay and, remarkably, never feels cluttered. Claremont courageously defies tradition by filling an unbalanced basket of guest stars (Dark Phoenix from Marvel; Darkseid, Terminator and Metron from DC), and Walt Simonson's first-rate pencils contribute to the finest Marvel/DC co-production. It was reprinted in 1996.~APS
Recommended: 1

Heroes For Hope Starring THE X-MEN
Marvel: *One-shot 1985*

A stellar line-up of creators contribute a page or two to this collective story produced with the intention of raising money for famine relief. As with all such endeavours, the good intentions mightily outweigh the quality, and unless you're a completist the novelty in seeing Neal Adams draw the new X-Men or pages by Richard Corben and Frank Miller will be entirely transient. Besides which, no money will now go to charity through your purchase.~FP

X-MEN Chronicles
Marvel: *2 issues 1995*

These two issues bookend the 'Age Of Apocalypse' story that occupied many of the X-Men-related titles in 1995. The past is altered, resulting in alternative groupings of Marvel's mutant teams. The first issue has Magneto leading a team of X-Men on their first mission, and the second has the same, now far more experienced, team of X-Men in an altogether better tale of love and superhero fights. That's not saying much, mind.~FP

X-MEN Miniseries
Marvel: *X-Men and the Micronauts 4 issues 1984, X-Men/Alpha Flight 2 issues 1985, X-Men vs Avengers 4 issues 1987, X-Men vs Brood: Day of Wrath 2 issues 1996, X-Men/Clandestine 2 issues 1996*

Most of the X-Men miniseries stand alone outside the regular continuity and are not essential to following the regular book. The best are *Fantastic Four vs X-Men* (see under F) and *X-Men/Alpha Flight* by Chris Claremont and Paul Smith, which finds the two teams in a mystical realm where their dreams appear to come true. On the other end of the scale, *X-Men vs the Micronauts* is entirely dismissible. Most of the others fall somewhere in between, with *X-Men vs Brood* deserving an honourable mention if only because it manages to be more interesting than any of the previous, generally tedious, Brood stories, reintroducing the evangelical preacher and his Brood-possessed wife from the regular series.

One-shots include team-ups with everyone from Star Trek to DC's Teen Titans, while almost every member of the merry mutant band has had at least one miniseries under their own name, including Archangel, Bishop, Cyclops and Phoenix, Dazzler, Gambit, Kitty Pryde, Magneto, Nightcrawler, Rogue, Storm and Wolverine. Being an X-Men completist is an expensive business.~JC
Recommended: *X-Men/Alpha Flight*
Collection: The Asgardian Wars (*X-Men/Alpha Flight* 1–2)

X-MEN The Animated Series
Marvel: *Series one 15 issues 1992–1994, series two 13 issues 1994–1995, series three 13 issues 1995–1996, series four 13 issues 1996–1997*

Given the success of the simpler version of the X-Men appearing on animated TV programmes, it made sense to have a comic version. As was the case with the TV series, this largely retold old adventures, adapting them to fit the core team of heroes featured on the show. Arch-enemies The Sentinels (1, 2) and Magneto (4) are introduced early, as is Cable (7). The second series features big dust-ups with Cable and Bishop, while the third re-runs the eternally confusing 'Dark Phoenix' saga in 10–13. Although technically an ongoing title, the numbering is restarted every year to coincide with the numbering of the series being screened that year, and with the second series the title changed to *X-Men Adventures*. The fourth series has brought another change of title to *Adventures Of The X-Men*, and a greater percentage of stories not based on earlier comic stories. It introduced Mojo to the roster of villains, and in 10 and 11 he has Storm forced to act in bizarre re-runs of Sheena, Queen Of The Jungle. Overall, this is of a standard, and worth a look if you've not read the original material; otherwise it's a safe bet to skip these.~TP

Collections: X-Men Adventures vol 1 (series one 1–4), vol 2 (5–8), vol 3 (9–12), vol 4 (13–15)

X-MEN: THE EARLY YEARS
Marvel: *17 issues 1994–1995*

Reprints the early issues of the 1960s *X-Men* , thoughtfully repackaged with often very lovely new covers, several by Adam Hughes. Cancelled, not because of poor sales, but solely to clear a schedule space for the trashy updating, *Professor X And The X-Men*. Philistines.~HS

X-MEN 2099
Marvel: *31 issues, 2 Specials 1993–1996*

In the far future of the Marvel Universe, a man named X'Ian dreams of a 'Mutant Nation', a place where the genetically enhanced can live in peace, free from prosecution. He holds 'Gatherings', at which mutants congregate, hoping to mobilise them, but when the Gathering is broken up by the ruling élite, he and a select few of his followers become fugitives, searching for their Mutant Nation. Written by John Francis Moore, illustrated by the lacklustre Ron Lim, this series patches together a bunch of post-Apocalyptic science-fiction movie clichés competently, but without vitality. Early on, the series becomes diverted into endless fight scenes with various other groups – the Freakshow, genetic barrel-scrapings; the Chosen, a twisted version of Xavier's original X-Men – and X'Ian's dream of a mutant nation fades further into the background, to be replaced by slugfest-of-the-month. Even the use of the hijacked X-Men name didn't prevent this title from sliding into deserved obscurity with the rest of the 2099 line.~HS

X-MEN UNLIMITED
Marvel: *13 issues + 1993 to date*

In an effort to sidestep some problems of the regular X-series – namely that the plotting and overlong story-lines are woefully convoluted – Marvel, in their wisdom, decided that what the readers needed was an over-priced, slick-paper giant-size comic in which they could find single-issue stories that concentrated on just a few characters at a time.

Cyclops, Storm and Xavier battle Sienna Blaze while lost in the Antarctic (1), Magneto gets some psychological profiling (2), Sabretooth is invited to tea with the X-Men (well, near as damnit, 3), Nightcrawler discovers that his mother is Mystique (years after everyone else guessed as much, 4), Storm gets some psychological profiling in Cairo (7), it's good Beast versus bad Beast in 10, Rogue's road-trip unearths Joseph (Magneto post-lobotomisation), giving the writers two options on the profiling (11), and Juggernaut gets a psychological profile while getting his powers back from Cyttorak (12). In the midst of all of this Freudian shit there are straightforward action-and-adventure stories featuring the X-Men in Space (5, 13) or against pirates and wizards (Bloodscream and Belasco respectively, but together in 9). The best story so far is the one about a young mutant having to come to terms with his powers when they manifest at school and then having the X-Men tell him he's got the Legacy Virus (8), though even this is stretched way too thin by the format. Fabian Nicieza, Scott Lobdell, John Francis Moore, Howard Mackie, Larry Hama, Mark Waid and Terry Kavanagh write to formula and you're lucky if there isn't a committee drawing the results. The worst example is John Francis Moore's tale of Sauron in 6, which not only has Paul Smith credited with storyboards but also lists four pencillers and seven inkers. Artistically, the best issues are by Liam Sharp (5), and Val Semeiks inked by Bob McLeod (9).

The first issue of 1997 is another psychological profile, this time of Franklin Richards, traumatised by the loss of his parents and family. Surprisingly, this is actually not a bad issue (by Terry Kavanagh and Jim Cheung).~NF

X-NATION 2099
Marvel: *6 issues 1996*

Despite its protagonists having little connection with their modern-day counterparts, the magic 'X' designation made *X-Men 2099* the most popular of the 2099 titles, and this spin-off was inevitable. *X-Nation* is Halo City, a haven for mutants. One of its more recent younger arrivals is prophesied to be the Mutant Messiah, who will alter the known world for good or bad, and to this end former X-Men (2099 variety, natch) member Cerebra bands a selection of teens to train them right and proper. This is the 2099 version of *Generation X*, and written for an audience with a minimal attention span. There are plenty of scraps, lots of arguing between the cast and a big fight each issue, but behind it all there's hardly a plot to be located. In the end all comes down to a battle between youth and the eternally old. Nice art from Humberto Ramos in the first three issues, though.~WJ

X 1999

Viz: *6-issue limited series 1995*

Kamui Shiro has returned to Tokyo after an absence of six years. His childhood girl-friend is having strange dreams about the end of the world and Kamui's strange powers seem to mark him out for some as-yet-unknowable destiny. Clamp's artwork is, unfortunately, rather unexceptional and the six issues don't contain enough by way of characterisation or explanation to involve the reader. The story was continued in anime magazine *Animerica* but it might be worth waiting for a collection.~NF

X-O Manowar

Valiant: *69 issues (0–67 – two number 50), 1 Yearbook 1992–1996*

X-O is the armoured hero of the Valiant Universe, but the inventive twist characterising the initial Valiant cast has him as a Goth barbarian who inherits a 20th-century corporation, Orb Industries. Early issues had Aric adapting to his new existence, aided and manipulated by Ken Clarkson, and the best of them were 9 and 10, as Aric returned to 400 AD and Ken had his chance to take over the X-O armour. Assorted other factions were also interested in the armour: the Harbinger Foundation (4), the government (18–20), the Armorines (25) and the spider aliens who created it. The initial planning behind the concept serves the series well. Aric was a sympathetic character in an interesting situation and the interplay between him, Clarkson and Orb's security chief Randy Cartier could carry a mundane plot. Jorge Gonzalez wrote most issues between 14 and 44, and they're almost all better-than-average superhero adventure despite artists generally lasting no more than five issues. The team of Rik Levins and Katherine Bollinger in 26–40 was the exception: their best issue was 30, with Aric requiring new armour.

Complications pertaining to that new armour arose in the two issue 50s, in which X-O underwent wholesale changes. Most of the supporting cast departed, and Orb Industries was wiped out, leaving Aric to wander in space. This new direction from 51 was dull, with issues to 57 particularly slim on plot, particularly big on large panels, and readable in three minutes. Character interaction was replaced by extended fight sequences, and the grimly distorted art of Bart Sears and, to a lesser extent, Andy Smith was ugly and unappealing. Keith Giffen's arrival with 60 to write all but the final issue was welcome. Plot and humanity once again come to the fore, and there were more surprises and horror than at any previous time during the run. Sadly, by then it was too late.~WJ

Collection: Retribution (1–4)

XOMBI

Milestone: *22 issues (0–21) 1993–1995*

First introduced during the convoluted Milestone crossover 'Shadow War', Xombi is David Kim, a research scientist working on 'the application of nanotechnology to biological regeneration'. When David is fatally wounded by 'The Rustling Husks' – weird monsters created by jealous rival boffin Dr Sugarman – his assistant saves his life by injecting him with nanomachines, advanced technology that continually renews Kim's limbs and organs. Unable to die, our hero finds himself becoming a weirdness magnet for such villains as 4's 'four stable boys of the apocalypse', Manuel Dexterity, a psychotic killer with a giant hand for a lower torso (7), a bizarre cult called the Beli Mah (issues 7–10, in a story-line entitled 'School Of Anguish'), and a race of subterranean man-eating monsters called the Kinderessen. As David learns more about his new immortality he seeks advice from such off-beat supporting characters as superheroine Catholic Girl and paranormal investigator Rabbi Sinnowitz.

The early issues of *Xombi* are rather uncertain, but by 4 writer John Rozum and artist J.J. Birch had begun to strike the right balance between absurdist humour, occult intrigue and superhero conflict. Birch's scratchy, stylised artwork takes some getting used to, but nicely accentuates the title's mysterious, menacing atmosphere. Although the story-telling is occasionally obscure for obscurity's sake, this rather neglected series easily compares with the best Vertigo titles, and should appeal to fans of Grant Morrison's run on *Doom Patrol*, a clear influence on *Xombi*'s surreal story-lines.~AL

Recommended: 7–10

X.S.E. Xavier's Security Enforcers

Marvel: *4-issue miniseries 1996–1997*

Introduced in *Uncanny X-Men* 282, Bishop arrived from the future as an X-Man with knowledge of a traitor in the 1990s team. His future, or past, so to speak, is explored for the first time as X.S.E. Given that the full name sounds like a disreputable squad of bouncers, inspiration was obviously in short supply when the title was conceived, and so it is for the content. There's reams of expository dialogue as Bishop and Shard discuss their history, and the revelations surely aren't worth wading through the morass from the usually reliable John Ostrander. The art begins badly and becomes worse, as, from 2, the Deodato Studios proceed to produce their regular crimes against human anatomy.~FP

X-TERMINATORS

Marvel: *4-issue miniseries 1988–1989*

This acts as the prelude to the mutant title crossover *Inferno*. Louise Simonson writes a fast-paced story in which the youngest mutants fight to save two of their own kind from a host of goblins and demons. The highlight is a hilarious sequence between Taki and a demon, in which Taki barters for fresh food and clothing. The series does, however, end prematurely and the rest of the crossover is required reading to gain a full grasp of the story.~SS

Star Wars: X-WING ROGUE SQUADRON
Dark Horse: *10 issues + 1995 to date*

Luke's friend Wedge, one of the few fighter pilots to survive the battle with the Empire, stars in this spin-off. With the major battle won Wedge and his team are freelance operatives using their admittedly impressive planes, and their skill in using them for combat, to lend a hand where required. This plot is, however, becoming tired already and the characters are beginning to look flat. Perhaps a miniseries would have been more sensible.~SS

X X X Triple X
Dark Horse: *7 issues 1994–1995*

Forty years from now multi-national industries control countries, and Hans Nobel has escaped martial law in the USA. Relocating to Amsterdam to discover how his grandfather died, and living with a bunch of squatters threatened by totalitarian police, he finds himself the prime suspect in a series of assassinations of leading corporate figures. Arnold and Jacob Pander craft a complex and depressing saga owing more to the European tradition of adventure strips than to traditional US comics. It moves at its own pace, encompassing over a dozen major characters, and by the climax the body-count is high. Mention should also be made of the excellent black and white tones of colourist Pamela Rambo, which serve the nature of the story far better than any other colours. The title has very little to do with the story, and salacious content is minimal, but you could do far worse looking for a thriller.~FP
Recommended: 1–7
Collection: XXX Triple X (1–7)

XXX WOMEN
Eros: *4 issues 1993–1994*

The logical extension of comics' largely misogynistic attitude to female superheroes. The XXX Women are big-breasted superheroes wearing next to nothing who bang like the outhouse door. It's all presented in graphic detail, with artist José Fonteriz having such an appealing style that he later went on to work for Marvel.~WJ
Collection: XXX Women (1–4)

XXXENOPHILE
Palliard: *10 issues +, 1989 to date*

The most accurate description of this series is the paradoxical phrase 'wholesome pornography'. Yes, it's a hard-core nomping comic, replete with dangly, wobbly and sticky-out bits, but mercifully free of the appalling artwork, repetitive story-lines and blatant misogyny that infests most 'erotic' comics. It's also clever, inventive, charming, funny, appealing, and, yes, sexy – regardless of your gender, or gender preference. Each self-contained story (there are two or three per issue) has different characters and settings, exotic, alien and mundane, and writer/artist Phil Foglio (with a tap-dancing chorus of celebrity guest inkers) shows no sign of flagging yet. Unlike most porno comics, this is a series you can actually read, and enjoy the hell out of. A spin-off, *Xxxenophile Presents*, was launched in 1993, with full-length stories by Foglio's friends, but, so far, it's not been as inventive or entertaining as the original.~HS
Recommended: 1–10
Collection: Xxxenophile Big Book O'Fun (1–6)

YAHOO
Fantagraphics: *6 issues 1988–1992*

This début series from acclaimed cartoonist Joe Sacco began rather shakily, with a competent but undistinguished collection of humour strips, such as 1's 'Cartoon Genius'. In 2 Sacco offered his disillusioned look at the music business from a roadie's perspective, and *Yahoo* began to profit from increasingly unusual story-telling and acute first-hand observation. 5 contains some of Sacco's most scathing, troubled musings on the Gulf War. Strangely, the collection chooses to omit this issue, while finding time for 2's largely unconnected story. 6 is a very effective change of pace. Written by cartoonist Susan Catherine, 'Take It Off' is a fascinating, coolly objective account of Catherine's career as a stripper, meticulously illustrated by Sacco.~AL
Recommended: 6
Collection: War Junkie (2–4)

YANG
Charlton: *13 issues 1973–1976, 4 issues (14–17) 1985–1986*

Tedious kung-fu, not even bothering to hide the fact it borrows heavily from the David Carradine TV series that mined the same old Western ideas so much better. Dull scripts from Joe Gill combined with dull art from Warren Sattler make it amazing that anybody would buy the series in the first place, never mind four reprint issues ten years on.~FP

YARN MAN
Kitchen Sink: *One-shot 1989*

A sneaky attempt to gain sales by publishing another first issue, this is actually part of Don Simpson's continuing *Megaton Man*. It follows *Megaton Man Meets The Uncategorizable X+ Thems* one-shot with a tale that includes Yarn Man (Ms Megaton Man's boy-friend) rather than stars him. There are some good laughs with the Origin Legion, who meet to retell their origins (though they save the best stories for the Secret Origin Legion), and Pammy's novel that's really about Megaton Man but no one notices. Fun but not essential.~NF

YELLOW DOG
Print Mint: *22 issues (1–8, 9/10, 11/12, 13/14, 15–25) 1968–1973*

One of the oldest and longest-running underground titles (bettered only by *Weirdo*), *Yellow Dog* started life as an underground newspaper before becoming a regular-sized publication with the combination issue 13/14. Despite some nice Robert Crumb art, the earliest issues were very insubstantial, consisting largely of dope-oriented vignettes and scatological humour. Issues from 7 up were considerably better, although still with a fair proportion of filler material each issue. Highlights included Gilbert Shelton's Freak Brothers (7–10), Crumb's Mr Natural (8) and some great art from Robert Williams (7, 9/10), Kim Deitch (9/10) and Skip Williamson (11/12).

The first comic-sized issue was the best of the run, containing substantial strips by Crumb and S. Clay Wilson, and a nice Nard'n'Pat story from Jay Lynch. After this the title increasingly came to be seen as a showcase for new talent, and again, most issues were patchy, although there was still a lot to admire. Greg Irons developed from a psychedelic artist into a cartoonist with some bite, and this is reflected in his fine strips in 13/14 and 17–20. Other notable contributors were Justin Green (15, 19, 21, 22), Trina Robbins (19, 20, 23, 25) and Bill Griffiths (18–20). Young cartoonists Bob Armstrong (23) and Howard Cruse (24) also got their breaks in *Yellow Dog*, though both were to progress to greater things.~DAR
Recommended: 13/14

YIKES
Steve Weissman: *4 issues 1994–1995*

Yikes is lots of stories about kids, whether they be Li'l Bloody, Kid Medusa, The Pullapart Boy or Dead Boy (who gets eaten by a dinosaur). Parodying *Caspar* and *Peanuts*, amongst others, the humour's sharp and black. The pencils owe much to Daniel Clowes and the inking style is a mixture of old (Eisner, Wood) and new (Burns, Ware), but the combination is distinctive and makes Steven Weissman a figure to watch.~NF
Recommended: 1–4

YOUNG ALL STARS
DC: *31 issues 1987–1989*

With *Crisis On Infinite Earths* rewriting DC's entire character continuity, the meticulous work that Roy Thomas had been doing patching up the history of DC's heroes in *All-Star Squadron* came to an abrupt end as radical changes were made across the DC Universe. Thomas, however, managed to persuade DC to let him create a new team with adventures set in World War II that wouldn't clash with their 'new' history. With his wife, Dann, he scripted the whole series, frequently including members of the All-Star Squadron but keeping the focus on his new heroes. This team consisted of Arn 'Iron' Munro, Tsunami, Flying Fox, Neptune Perkins, Fury and Dyno-Mite. From the start they were the junior All-Stars, propaganda vehicles whose exploits would, in their own time, have been meant to appeal to the hearts of Americans during the war. The first story-line in 1–6 establishing the team is actually quite condemnatory of the camps set up to house Japanese Americans during World War II (Tsunami included).

8 and 9 are *Millennium* crossovers, but 10 and 11 feature a retelling of Philip Wylie's 1930 novel *Gladiator*, which is the story of 'Superman' Hugo Danner and is widely credited with establishing the concept of superhumans. It turns out that Danner is Arn Munro's father. Thomas only puts a foot wrong when he attempts to bring in stranded aliens (being used by evil Nazis in the long 'Dzyan Inheritance' plot line in 16–19). The 1940s Atom turns up in 'Atom And Evil' in 21–25 in preparation for an all-hero slugfest (28–31) in which the whole of the All-Star Squadron join the Young All-Stars to battle the Nazis.

Artistically the series started badly, with Michael Bair, Brian Murray and Howard Simpson taking it in turns on 1–14. Until 19 there was no regular penciller, then Ron Harris turned up. Inker Malcolm Jones III did his best to deal with a number of disparate styles but the book suffered from a lack of visual coherency. *Young All-Stars* is full of good characters, but it's overwritten, looks rushed and uncared-for, and is, ultimately, too much like hard work.~NF

YOUNG CYNICS CLUB
Dark Horse: *1 issue 1993*

Cold story of a group of teenagers facing up to leaving home, getting jobs and generally living in the real world, the one in which they'll become insurance clerks, not famous writers. Glenn Wong's script is fluid and his art is clean and confident, but somehow it fails to engage your emotions. It's just too drab and realistic, with no peaks and troughs to the story.~FJ

YOUNG DEATH The Boyhood Of A Superfiend
Fleetway/Quality: *3 issues 1991*

As seen in several battles with Judge Dredd, Judge Death is an other-dimensional undead fiend whose solution to the problem of crime on Earth is to wipe out humanity. No humans = no crime = perfect world. This warped agenda is extrapolated as Death relates his childhood, youth and transformation to crass tabloid journalist Brian Skuter, along the way also explaining his acolytes and companions. It's both terrifying and thrilling, and writer John Wagner also has the black-humour button pushed to the max, particularly with a great dentist scene in 2. After an unsuccessful campaign, Death is in hiding, lodging with a half-blind old landlady ('If you don't eat you'll shrivel away to nothing'), and there's suitably dark and gloomy art from a débuting Peter Doherty.~FP
Recommended: 1–3

THE YOUNG INDIANA JONES CHRONICLES
Dark Horse: *12 issues 1992–1993*

Dan Barry adapts episodes of the *Young Indiana Jones* TV series, writing each issue and pencilling most of them. Indy encounters plenty of significant historical figures during World War 1. Stories intended for TV don't always transfer well to the comic, and the best are 9 and 10, showing both the eight-year-old and the sixteen-year-old Indy meeting the crowned heads of Europe. Each issue also has a text piece by Kurt Busiek giving a background perspective on the events or people of the issue.~WJ

YOUNG LOVE
Prize: *Series one 73 issues 1949–1957, series two 21 issues 1960–1963*
DC: *88 issues (39–126) 1963–1976*

Following the enormous success of their pioneering romance comic *Young Romance* in 1947, Joe Simon and Jack Kirby provided a sibling two years later. Assembled by the same skilful artists (Meskin, Powell, Starr, Brewster, etc.) with Simon and Kirby providing layouts and plot-lines, *Young Love* settled into the mixture of sophistication and melodrama that characterised its older sister. Stories focused on insane jealousy, romantic duplicity, and the dangers a young girl faced on the road to, she hoped, matrimony, but also, unlike the many competitors that sprang up from other companies, emphasised the need for fairness, honesty and responsibility, not only on the part of the young protagonists but on that of their parents too, who had the duty to deal fairly and openly with their children. A strong, but not preachy, morality was at the core of most of the stories. *Young Love* never reached quite the dramatic heights of its big sis, but the title featured strong and mature, but never lurid, stories until its final issue in 1957. The title was revived in 1960 for a continuation of another Prize romance title, *All For Love*, but had little in common with its predecessor. Now firmly in the grip of the Comics Code, the revived *Young Love* featured simpering stories with no conflict and little entertainment. Nevertheless, as one of the big names in the field, it accompanied *Young Romance* as the two titles were assimilated into DC's romance line when Prize closed its doors in 1963. The second Prize run was issued as an annual series of volumes numbered 1–6, beginning with volume 3, issue 3, and ending with volume 7, issue 1.

The DC *Young Love*, beginning inexplicably with 39, gained a semi-regular character in 'Mary Robin, Registered Nurse', whose one-chapter crushes and flings always ended in disappointment. Illustrated by John Romita, 'Mary Robin' epitomised the sleek, machine-tooled style of DC's romance titles at the time. In the mid 1960s, a slightly racier serial replaced Mary: 'The Lives and Loves of Lisa St Clare', the saga of a rich girl looking for someone to love her and not her money, ran for several issues, but never really caught on. If she really wanted true love, Lisa should have tried to look a bit less overdressed and slutty, but maybe it was just the way Dick Giordano drew her. In the late 1960s and early 1970s *Young Love* fell victim to the same problems as every other romance comic. Still conforming to the Comics Code Authority, they just couldn't compete with the more salacious TV soap operas and Confessions magazines that were soaking up the female consumers. Not that the romance books didn't try to tackle stronger subjects; 'That Strange Girl' was the first comics story to tackle the subject of lesbianism – albeit very, very obliquely, and only so that our heroine could turn out to be just a tomboy after all, much to everyone's relief. Other stories promised much in their titles – 'Daughter of Women's Lib!', 'Bad Trip!' and, God help us, 'Horoscope, Don't Fool With My Heart!' – but fizzled out. The loopy desperation of the 1970s romance titles is something to see. Nevertheless, *Young Love* did have the last laugh: while not the first romance comic, it was one of the last, outliving its big sister, *Young Romance*, by nearly two years.~HS

YOUNG LUST
Company And Sons: *1 issue 1970*
Print Mint: *1 issue (2) 1971*
Last Gasp: *1 issue (3) 1972*
Print Mint: *1 issue (4) 1974*
Kitchen Sink: *4 issues (5–8) 1977–1993*

Conceived as a hard-core spoof of romance comics, editors Bill Griffith and Jay Kinney

gradually transformed *Young Lust* into a rather more interesting satire on contemporary society and its sexual mores. With 2 Justin Green was added to the creative line-up, and by 4 it was successful enough to add colour. The comic's highlights include Art Spiegelman's formalist 'Little Signs Of Passion' in 4, Bill Griffith's jaded 'Too Much Fun' in 5 and Greg Irons' despairingly autobiographical 'Monkey Lust' in 6. Other noted contributors, like Spain Rodriguez (2–8), Kim Deitch (4, 6), Paul Mavrides (6, 7) and Daniel Clowes (7), helped make later issues far more essential purchases than the comic's original premise ever suggested.~DAR
Recommended: 4–6
Collection: *The Young Lust Reader* (selection from 1–4)

YOUNG ROMANCE
Prize: *124 issues 1947–1963*
DC: *84 issues (125–208) 1963–1975*

Launched by Joe Simon and Jack Kirby, this title was inspired in part by a humour title, *My Date*, that the two had worked on a year previously for another publisher. Although *My Date* was short-lived, its romantic-comedy tone inspired the duo to try something that hadn't been attempted before, a straight romance comic. Although romance pulps and magazines sold well, no one had previously attempted to translate the genre to comics .The first issue was a huge success, and made waves in the industry. Martin Goodman, publisher of Timely Comics, attacked *Young Romance*, with its emphasis on adult protagonists and situations, as 'virtual pornography'. He presumably had some sort of epiphany on seeing the sales figures, because within three years of *Young Romance*'s release, Timely was publishing thirteen romance comics! Altogether, *Young Romance* had no fewer then fifty imitators, including its own sibling, *Young Love*, within three years of its début. A new genre had been brought to comics.

No imitator could compete with *Young Romance* for quality and value. Simon and Kirby did the bulk of the work in the early years themselves, but when they had to start farming it out, they hired the finest artists in the business: Robinson, Meskin, Starr, Brewster, Premiani, Draut, Powell, Andru and dozens more filled the pages with vitality and emotion. Nor were they afraid to tackle contentious subjects. 'Different' dealt maturely with anti-Semitism, 'The Town and Toni Turner' had a young woman facing down her delinquent criminal past, and 'My Old Flame' neatly exposed the futility of romantic ideals and unrequited love, a controversial plot, in a comic where those commodities were a stock-in-trade. The Simon and Kirby romances were also much more vigorous than the average romance comic; love affairs took place at roller derbies, at sea, in the middle of teenage gang fights; the heroes and heroines were caught in hurricanes, involved in car crashes, arrested – anything to get some action in the story! But occasionally such tricks weren't necessary. The best Simon and Kirby romance story, 'The Girl Who Tempted Me' (17, 1950), has a rural farm setting and only four characters. There's an elderly woman, her two sons, and the fiancée of the younger son, a 'townie' with 'loose ways' who decides to seduce the older, religious brother, but finds that her game gets out of control. In a rare story inked by Kirby himself, her mounting passion is virtually a palpable presence in the story, and the irresistible attraction between two people who know they're bad for each other is superbly portrayed. Oh, it's melodramatic schlock, sure, but of the very finest quality.

Following Prize's closure in 1963, DC grabbed *Young Romance* and *Young Love* for its own romance line, but having secured them, did nothing to make them exceptional. 'Bonnie Taylor, Stewardess' had semi-regular self-contained flings in exotic foreign parts, but apart from that, it was very much by-the-book DC romance, illustrated by all the thoroughbred workhorses of the era – Romita, Rosenberger, Colan, *et al*. This state of affairs persisted until the late 1960s, when romance comics, haemorrhaging readers as the more lurid TV soaps grabbed their attention, resorted to ever more desperate come-on titles: 'Make Love to Me!', 'Greaser's Girl', 'Lily Martin – the Swinger!'. But because they had to abide by the wholesome Comics Code, the stories couldn't deliver the goods. Hitchhikers, hippies, rock stars and motorcycle gangs became the new staples, but in amongst the dross, there were some well-meaning, if clunky, attempts to innovate. 194's 'Full Hands, Empty Heart', by Bob Kanigher and John Rosenberger, showed, in a sympathetic way, the love affair between a white doctor and a black nurse (of opposite sexes: things hadn't loosened up that much. And needless to say, the guy got to be the doctor!)

Unfortunately, such efforts were lost in the frantic scramble for readers, and in an attempt to titillate, plots became ever more risible. A favourite is 'I Won't Kiss That Evil Way!' – written by a fledgeling Tom DeFalco! – in which we not only don't ever find out what evil way our heroine won't kiss, but we're also not told how evil it is. Is it the osculatory equivalent of shoplifting? Grand theft auto? Napalming a busload of nuns? Enquiring minds want to know... Sadly, the craziness couldn't be sustained forever, and in 1975 *Young Romance*, mother of a genre, breathed its last. *Young Love* trundled on for two years, but the last nails were already being pounded into the coffin of the romance genre, which, apart from sporadic nostalgia specials, seems well and truly dead.~HS

The YOUNG WITCHES
Eros: *4-issue miniseries 1991, 6-issue miniseries 1995–1996*

The first series is an atypical Eros comic as the sexual content isn't explicit, and there's a story, albeit a slim one, with gorgeous artwork from F. Solano Lopez. Lilian Cunningham is orphaned at birth, but sent to a college with feminist teachings dating back to the Amazons. Her latent powers of witchcraft emerge and it all ends very messily. Series two, as if by deliberate contrast, is so graphic the publishers feel obliged to print an editorial requesting readers not to judge individual episodes, but the series as a whole, since it concerns the hypocrisy of the Victorian attitude to sex (and, presumably by extension, the present-day attitude). This is a load of tosh, as there's little purpose to the story beyond hard-core sex. Lilian and her companion Agatha reach Victorian London to encounter many out-of- copyright fictional characters in the company of historical figures and all kinds of sexual activity. It's still beautifully drawn, but the sexual variations involved are potentially repugnant.~FP
Collection: The Young Witches (series one)

YOUNGBLOOD
Image: *Series one 11 issues (0–10) 1992–1994, series two 10 issues + 1995 to date*

Rob Liefeld released this as one of the first Image comics, a poor choice for a flagship title. *Youngblood* is a blatant *X-Force* clone with the strong theme of corporate heroes very reminiscent of DC's *Justice League*. There are too many characters to make any of them seem more than one-dimensional, and an appearance by Spawn in the final issues of the first series fails to inject even a flicker of interest. The second series has seen a great deal of improvement, with tighter scripting, greater concentration on the main characters and something more interesting than the repetitive fight sequences. The art has also evolved into a cartoon/Manga style through Roger Cruz and Fabio Laguna.~SS
Collection: Youngblood (Series one 1–5)

YOUNGBLOOD STRIKEFILE
Image: *11 issues 1993–1995*

Youngblood Strikefile was set up to approach the problem of poor characterisation in the parent book. This didn't happen due to an obsession with prolonged fight sequences and action-orientated stories. A succession of new characters is introduced, each one more clichéd than the last, and the only half decent effort was Jae Lee's Chapel story in 1–3. Although the series hasn't officially been cancelled we can all live in hope.~SS

YOU'RE UNDER ARREST
Dark Horse: *8-issue limited series 1995–1996*
Fast and furious comedy adventure about young police officers – either female or in drag – catching panty-thieves and paintball vandals. They also try to apprehend a vigilante who punishes people for petty antisocial behaviour and who calls himself alternately Strikeman and Santa Claus Man. Sexy and highly detailed when it comes to bikes or cars, Kosuke Fujishima's work isn't exactly PC but then it isn't meant to be more than high-speed fun. Beautifully drawn but slight.~NF

YUMMY FUR
Vortex: *24 issues 1986–1991*
Drawn and Quarterly: *8 issues (25–32) 1991–1994*
Chester Brown has never been afraid of telling difficult stories, as anyone who has tried *Underwater* will know. His work revolves as much around repetition of image, iconography and mythology as it does around plot and structure, making *Yummy Fur* a difficult but rewarding read. The first three issues reprint material from mini-comics, from which the recurring character, Ed The Happy Clown, emerges as star of the book as Brown settles down to telling a more complex and distinctly lateral tale involving the trappings of B-movies but the intensity of myth. It's a great tragedy wrapped up in ridiculous notions, including the infamous Ronald-Reagan's-head-on-the-end-of-a-penis sequence. This amazing tale of vampires, aliens and disappearances was backed up with a re-telling of the gospels intended to emphasise the differences between the versions in the Bible. Unfortunately, when the series ended (with an all-Matthew special issue 32) only two had been completed.

After the obtuse nature of the Ed stories Brown then went on to autobiographical material, including an examination of his relationship with *Playboy*, which struck a huge chord with the readership (21–23), and 'Fuck' (26–30), which traces his adolescent unwillingness to swear, and leads neatly into the story of his first love. Brown enunciates the shy and playful gropings of adolescents, the sudden silences, the retreats into childhood behaviour to cover your sudden and perplexing lusts, beautifully, but the work is nowhere near as stimulating as either Ed or the Gospels.~FJ
Recommended: 4–18, 32

YUPPIES FROM HELL
Epic: *3 issues 1989–1992*
Black and white prestige-format comics by Barbara Slate satirising yuppie manners, morals and standards. An obvious target, but still scathingly funny.~HS
Recommended: 1–3

ZAP Comix
Last Gasp: *13 issues (0–12) 1967–1989*

Zap Comix is the quintessential underground title, put together by a collective of cartoonists whose names have become synonymous with the movement: S. Clay Wilson, Robert Crumb, Victor Moscoso, Gilbert Shelton, Spain and Robert Williams. The unique mix of sexual abuse, drug-fuelled narratives, biting satire and crazy graphics in the early issues is still powerful today, and still shocking. The title was lionised for freeing comics from the grip of simplistic adventure stories, but many readers seem to have forgotten quite how nasty some of these creators' imaginations were. Anyone who worries about the depiction of women in Crumb's widely-known work should take a look at S. Clay Wilson's amazing vistas of degradation, the 1960s equivalent to Hogarth (the English allegorical painter, not the Tarzan artist). And predictably the title has its share of failed experiments, strips you can only understand when the wallpaper explains them to you, and unfunny parodies.

All the famous underground characters appeared here: Shelton's comic Fat Freddy's Cat and Wonder Warthog, Crumb's Mr Natural, Spain's impenetrable Trashman, Williams' Coochy Cooty and Wilson's The Chequered Demon. Although the drawing was often rough and scratchy the strips got their points across admirably. Many are achingly funny, although by the end of the 1980s the liberal agenda espoused by *Zap* was starting to look a little careworn. *Zap* was a huge liberating force in comics, and still rewards careful study (with laughter, if nothing else). All issues have been kept in print since original publication.~FJ
Recommended: 1, 3, 12

ZATANNA
DC: *One-shot 1987, 4-issue miniseries 1993*

Zatanna is DC's resident Mistress of Magic. The story of her quest to make peace with the spirit of her dead father Zatara was planned as a miniseries. Ill-judged economics resulted in drastic cuts, to the extent that the writer requested his name be removed from the credits, and the one-shot was all that remained. It's a shame, as the Gray Morrow artwork is deeply gorgeous. The later miniseries is profoundly ill-advised in its attempt to remove Zatanna from all that makes her distinctive and original and reduce her to a practitioner of the Generic Art Of Mystic Handwaving. Fortunately, it's subsequently been ignored editorially.~HS

ZEALOT
Image: *3-issue miniseries 1995*

Ron Marz and Terry Shoemaker span the centuries with historical tales from the past of the near-immortal *WildC.A.T.S* heroine Zealot. Taking in ancient Greece, classical Japan and Nazi Europe, the series presents three self-contained stories which mix established myths and WildStorm history. A framing sequence makes them all part of team-mate Voodoo's training to be a Coda Warrior, and a running theme of Zealot's continued battle against an evil nemesis from the same long-lived alien race.~JC

ZERO HOUR Crisis in Time
DC: *5-issue miniseries (4–0) 1994*

Parallax (formerly Green Lantern – the Hal Jordan one) decides the DC multiverse is too confusing. He embarks on a scheme to obliterate it and restart space-time from the Big Bang without all those messy alternate worlds. Every superhero and his brother objects to this self-appointed godhood. They thwart Jordan, but as a side-effect of the mêlée, space-time restarts from the Big Bang without all those messy alternate worlds. In the new squashed timeline Superman made his début ten years ago, thus solving all DC's generation-gap problems.

The five issues were published weekly in reverse number order with a September 1994 cover-date. As a prelude to this series, about forty mainstream DC titles carried tie-ins featuring characters and locales from different timelines coexisting. All these titles had their October 1994 issues numbered 0, and most zero issues retold origins according to the new timeline.

Zero Hour fails as a story because every event, action and assertion is built on a foundation of cloud, candyfloss and thin air. Nevertheless, *Zero Hour* would still have been creditable if it had simplified DC continuity. It didn't.~APS
Collection: *Zero Hour (0–4)*

ZERO PATROL

Continuity: *5 issues 1984–1985 (1–2), 1988–1989 (3–5)*

Zero Patrol reprinted Esteban Maroto's classic 1960s Spanish strip 'Ginco Por Infinito', rewritten, and to a large degree redrawn, by publisher Neal Adams. Despite the glorious art the story rarely rises above standard space-opera fare. It's a daft idea: five humans are selected for their various abilities, including capacity for forward thinking and understanding of emotions. They're then costumed and sent out to fight robots! Those after a good read are better directed elsewhere. To round out the package Adams provided a number of back-up strips. There's the début of Megalith in 1, an Adams high-school-era project also titled 'Zero Patrol' in 2, and the first appearance of Shaman in 3.~DAR

ZERO TOLERANCE

First: *4-issue miniseries 1990–1991*

Zero Tolerance is an organisation founded to investigate government corruption in 2017. Populated by caricatures like the tough-guy agent, the feisty female agent and the cartoon villainy of the President, this could be adapted as an episode of *Scooby Doo* with few changes.~WJ

ZERO ZERO

Fantagraphics: *13 issues + 1995 to date*

Editor Kim Thompson wants *Zero Zero* to be considered the worthy successor to *Raw* and *Weirdo*. There's a little way to go yet, but he manages to collate good contributions from a wide range of creators. Avoiding autobiographical work is a good move, but there's perhaps too much emphasis on the off-beat for its own sake here. That said, there's some startling material. Ted Stearn provides surreal tales of 'Fuzz and Pluck', a chicken and a bear trying to escape from slavery (1, 3, 6, 9, 11, 13), and Frank Stack's 'New Adventures of Jesus' (1–3) is fascinating. Spain (12), Skip Williamson (3, 9), and Bill Griffith (7) from the old guard are joined by Jeff Johnson (4), Carol Tyler (4), Chris Ware (5), Archer Prewitt (8) and the controversial Mike Diana (1, 8), a man subject to regular house searches in his home state after the county court declared his self-published comics obscene! Nice one, Florida. So much for free expression.

However, the best short stories are provided by more seasoned creators, including David Mazzucchelli (2, 11), David Collier (1–6, 8 ,9, 11) and Max Andersson (1, 3, 7, 11), who contributes 'Car-Boy' to 2, 5 and 8 and for issue 12 produces 'Death', the strangest 'road movie' you'll ever read. There are also several longer series, most notably Kim Deitch's 'Molly O'Dare' (6–8), a sequel of sorts to his *Shadowland*

series, and Mack White's 'Homunculus', the life story of a very small person set in Roman times. The title's also home to Rick Sala's twisted *magnum opus* 'The Chuckling Whatsit' (from 2 onwards), a convoluted horror tale about the Gull Street Ghoul, a notorious serial killer who starts killing again after years of inactivity.~NF
Recommended: 2–13

ZIPPY Quarterly

Fantagraphics: *13 issues + 1993 to date*

A magazine-sized compilation of underground legend Bill Griffith's daily newspaper strip *Zippy The Pinhead*. Griffith is one of the medium's finest creators and he's at his peak here, casting his scabrously critical eye over contemporary America. *Zippy* is a unique mixture of intellectualism, pop culture, knockabout humour and Dada that deserves a place in any collection. Griffith has been using Zippy in comics for years, and there are several collected editions of previous comic-format Zippy material, most prominently the Fantagraphics-published *Zippy Stories*.~DAR
Recommended: 1–13
Collections: Nation Of Pinheads, Pindemonium, Zippy's House Of Fun (Sunday colour strips)

Tales of the ZOMBIE

Marvel: *10 issues 1973–1975*

Much like *Vampire Tales*, with its main feature and themed back-up strips, *Zombie* (as its original credits ran) is similar in its lack of consistency. Steve Gerber tackles the Zombie's own story (1–9) as Simon Garth, once a wealthy New Orleans plantation owner, is turned into a zombie by the loyal Layla to avenge his death. As well as the tale of Garth's vengeance, Gerber uses the character much as he did Man-Thing, to comment on others, the Zombie being the *deus ex machina* that concludes the story. Pablo Marcos is very effective as artist, drawing in a style that's halfway between Maroto and Wrightson. Apart from Gerber, Doug Moench and Alfredo Alcala's fill-in issue (7) is a good *Cat And The Canary*-type story with very little zombie action at all. Brother Voodoo's appearances (6, 10) are best forgotten, even drawn by Gene Colan, and only the short stories, drawn by Alcala, really have anything to recommend them. The exception is Tom Sutton's 'Grave Business' in 10, a wonderfully drawn tale with hints of Kubert and Toth in the artwork, as Sutton's normally intricate pencils give way to a loose, freer style.~NF

ZONE

Dark Horse: *One-shot 1990*

By Michael Kraiger and collected from *Dark Horse Presents* 28 and 31–34. Two artists have stumbled across a seven-foot alien in the landfill sites of New Jersey and are deciding how to handle the situation. It's about dumping and pollution, but it seems a very indirect way of tackling the issue.~FC

ZONE CONTINUUM

Caliber: *4-issue miniseries 1992, 2-issue microseries 1994*

Zone Continuum is the story of a world that exists above the streets, where the search is on for the owner of the zone goggles. The goggles have the ability to open the portal to The Other World. The owner of the goggles is found and he relates the story of their origin and the world of the zones. He also relates the battle that caused the goggles to be lost in the normal world. Despite an interesting idea and some occasionally nice Bruce Zick panels, overall the whole affair is as dull and over-technical as a short-wave radio manual. In Welsh.~SS

ZOONIVERSE

Eclipse: *6 issues 1986–1987*

'Zoon' is the general term for any intelligent being in this part of the galaxy, where countless species meet to trade and intrigue and try to have sex. The three-Zoon Kren patrol is caught up in the intrigue when they are given the job of escorting a courier and things go wrong within minutes. The story is fine, but it's the travelogue aspects that make the comic special. Fil Barlow had been working out the details of these worlds and these species for years, and it shows. He's got quantities of imagination, most of it grotesque and quirky, and a sense of humour that's generally surreal but always grounded in a good understanding of human (zoonan?) nature. Any quibbles? The ending is decidedly abrupt, as if Barlow, in full flow, suddenly got a fax ordering him to wrap it up within three pages. This doesn't ruin the comic as it stands, but is cruelly tantalising. One could cope with a lot more of *Zooniverse*.~FC
Recommended: 1–6

ZORRO

Marvel: *6 issues 1990–991*

Like the TV series on which it's based, the 1990s comic ditches any sense of rebellion or suspense and tells moralistic tales in which no one dies, swords aren't really dangerous and the soldiers are good guys at heart. Gag me with a spoon.~NF

ZORRO

Topps: *12 issues (0–11) 1993–1994*

Well-thought-out series written by Don McGregor, which plays heavily on the political, racial and sexual problems of early-19th-century California. He creates a new supporting cast that includes Machete, an ex-slaver, Moonstalker, an Indian freedom fighter, and Lady Rawhide, a mysterious adventuress. Mike Mayhew (1–8) and Hearn Cho (9–12) provide rather stiff artwork but it's not unattractive, and there are some excellent covers from the likes of Paul Gulacy (7), Mike Mignola (6) and Adam Hughes (3). McGregor's skill with words keeps the scripts interesting, but there are always going to be plenty of them to get through in a McGregor opus, and this sometimes slows the pace.~NF

ZOT!

Eclipse: *36 issues 1984–1985 (1–10), 1987–1991 (11–36)*

Zachary T. Paleozogt, otherwise known as Zot, seems to have come from the far future, battling robots, carrying a blaster and talking about a lost key to the Doorway at the Edge of the Universe which a neighbouring planet, Sirius IV, wants back at any cost. In fact he's from an alternative Earth circa 1965 which is a paradise compared to our reality. Jenny Weaver and her brother Butch follow Zot back to his world and Butch is promptly devolved into a chimp by a crazy representative of the Church of De-Evolution. As the story of the key unfolds we meet 9-Jack-9, an electrical assassin, Dekko, a robotic world-conqueror, and Zot's Uncle Max, an inventor who represents Jenny and Butch's best chance of getting back to their own world. The colour series was cancelled due to poor sales at this point, but revived two years later in black and white.

From 11 Jenny has to adjust to being back on her own, flawed world, while Zot tries to fight crime and discovers just how difficult that can be in New York, when his only 'superpower' is flight. With 28 writer/artist Scott McCloud took a new direction. Zot becomes part of a love triangle with Jenny and a friend, Woody. Each issue is told from a different person's point of view. Thus McCloud explores the world-views of a variety of adults and teenagers as well as that of Zot himself, contrasting their hopes and fears with the beauty and perfection of his lost homeworld. The story reaches a peak in 33, one of the most beautifully crafted, humane single issues ever written. Read it.

With *Zot!*, McCloud created an exuberant, fun book that can still deal with important matters, that's more about feelings than adventures despite the science-fiction trappings of the early issues and the fantastic basis for its premise. *Zot!* 10½ (Not Available Comics, 1986) is a minicomic by McCloud and Matt Feazell, whose stick-figure character Cynicalman co-stars. 14½ is a regular sized comic entirely by Feazell which continues the off-beat but funny 'Zot in Dimension 10½' back-up strip that runs in issues 12–36.~NF
Recommended: 28–36

NON-SERIES TITLES

Some of these features may have appeared only for a single issue of an umbrella title, and unless particularly noteworthy may not be mentioned in the text piece on the title referenced.

AGE OF INNOCENCE see IRON MAN
A*K*Q*J see the Adventures of CAPTAIN JACK
ALBERTO see THE CRUSADERS
AMAZON see AMALGAM Comics
AMBASSADOR OF THE SUBURBS see VALERIAN
ANGEL OF LIGHT see THE CRUSADERS
ANT-MAN see MARVEL FEATURE, MARVEL PREMIERE, TALES TO ASTONISH
THE ARK see THE CRUSADERS
ASSASSINS see AMALGAM Comics
AVENGERS WEST COAST see WEST COAST AVENGERS
B-MAN see DOUBLE DARE ADVENTURES
BAREFOOT GEN see I SAW IT
The BEAST see AMAZING ADVENTURES
THE BEATLES see MARVEL SUPER SPECIAL
Tales from BEYOND see 1963
BLOODLINES see TALES FROM THE HEART
BLOODSTONE see MARVEL PRESENTS, Rampaging HULK
BOMBAST see SECRET CITY SAGA
THE BROKEN CROSS see THE CRUSADERS
BRUCE WAYNE AGENT OF S.H.I.E.L.D. see AMALGAM Comics
B'WANA BEAST see SHOWCASE
CALEB HAMMER see MARVEL PREMIERE
CAPTAIN GLORY see SECRET CITY SAGA
CAPTAIN UNIVERSE see MARVEL SPOTLIGHT
CAVE CARSON see SHOWCASE
CEASEFIRE see FANNY
CHAOS see THE CRUSADERS
CHAOS Prince Of Madness see WARP
DARK HORSE CLASSICS see CLASSICS ILLUSTRATED
DARK SHADE see The SCARLET SCORPION
DARKLON THE MYSTIC see EERIE
DEATH DREAMS OF DRACULA see BLOOD OF DRACULA
Sergio Aragonés DESTROYS DC see SERGIO ARAGONÉS
DHP see DARK HORSE PRESENTS
DISSENTING WOMEN see FANNY
DOCTOR DOOM see ASTONISHING TALES
DR RADIUM see IT'S SCIENCE with Dr Radium
DOCTOR STRANGEFATE see AMALGAM Comics
DOLPHIN see SHOWCASE
DOMINIC FORTUNE see BIZARRE ADVENTURES, MARVEL PREMIERE, Rampaging HULK
DOUBLE-CROSS see THE CRUSADERS
DRAGONLORD see MARVEL SPOTLIGHT
EXORCISTS see THE CRUSADERS
FACTOR X see X-FACTOR
FAMILY see FAST FORWARD
Ghost Rider, Captain America FEAR see GHOST RIDER
FIREHAIR see SHOWCASE
THE FORCE see THE CRUSADERS
FOUR HORSEMEN see THE CRUSADERS
FRANK IN THE RIVER see TANTALISING STORIES
No-One Escapes FURY see 1963
GIANT-SIZE SUPER-STARS see FANTASTIC FOUR
THE GIFT see THE CRUSADERS
THE GODFATHERS see THE CRUSADERS
GREEN LANTERN/SILVER SURFER see DC VS MARVEL
HALLOWEEN MEGAZINE see TOMB OF DRACULA
HALLS OF HORROR see HOUSE OF HAMMER
HEARTS OF DARKNESS see GHOST RIDER
HECTIC PLANET see PIRATE CORP$!
HEROES OF THE EQUINOX see VALERIAN
HORUS Lord of Light see 1963
I-SPY see SHOWCASE
INNER DEMONS see TALES OF THE MARVES
IT, the Living Colossus see ASTONISHING TALES
JACK Q FROST see UNEARTHLY SPECTACULARS
JASON'S QUEST see SHOWCASE
JIHAD see NIGHTBREED
JIMMY CORRIGAN see ACME NOVELTY LIBRARY
JLX see AMALGAM Comics
JOHNNY DOUBLE see SHOWCASE
JUDGE ANDERSON see PSI JUDGE ANDERSON
Bloodbath At KHE SANH see VIETNAM JOURNAL
KILLRAVEN see AMAZING ADVENTURES
KING CONAN see CONAN THE KING
KING TIGER see COMICS GREATEST WORLD
KISS see MARVEL SUPER SPECIAL
The LAST KISS see KISS OF DEATH
LEGENDS OF THE DARK CLAW see AMALGAM Comics
The LEGION OF CHARLIES see The Legion Of CHARLIES

LIBERTY LEGION see MARVEL PREMIERE
LONDON'S DARK see ESCAPE
THE LOST GODS see JOURNEY INTO MYSTERY
MAGNETO AND THE MAGNETIC MEN see AMALGAM Comics
MAN-GODS see MARVEL PREVIEW
MAN-WOLF see CREATURES ON THE LOOSE, MARVEL PREMIERE
MANIAKS see SHOWCASE
MANIMAL see HOT STUFF
MARVEL VS DC see DC VS MARVEL
Serigo Aragonés MASSACRES MARVEL see SERGIO ARAGONÉS
MONARK MOONSTALKER see MARVEL PREMIERE
MONSTER see COMICS GREATEST WORLD
MORBIUS Revisited see Adventure Into FEAR
MYSTERY INCORPORATED see 1963
NECROMANTRA see LORD PUMPKINHEAD
NICK FURY and his AGENTS OF S.H.I.E.L.D. see STRANGE TALES
NIGHT FRUITS see FANNY
NIGHTMASTER see SHOWCASE
1994 see 1984
100% TRUE see BIG BOOKS
ORLAK see CALIBER PRESENTS
OSBORN JOURNAL see Amazing Spider-Man
OUR CANCER YEAR see AMERICAN SPLENDOR
OUTLAW see ALL-STAR WESTERN
PALADIN see MARVEL PREMIERE
PANTHA see VAMPIRELLA, WARREN PRESENTS
PARADOX see STRANGE DAYS
PENGUIN TRIUMPHANT see BATMAN GRAPHIC NOVELS
PHILBERT DESANEX'S 10,000th DREAM see WONDER WARTHOG
PIT BULLS see COMICS GREATEST WORLD
PRIMAL MAN? see THE CRUSADERS
THE PROPHET see THE CRUSADERS
THE PUNISHER MAGAZINE see THE PUNISHER
REAL SCHMUCK see REAL STUFF
REAL SMUT see REAL STUFF
REBEL see COMICS GREATEST WORLD
REQUIEM FOR DRACULA see TOMB OF DRACULA
REX HAVOC see EERIE, WARREN PRESENTS
ROG 2000 see E-MAN
SABOTAGE? see THE CRUSADERS
SATANA see MARVEL PREMIERE, MARVEL PREVIEW
THE SAVAGE RETURN OF DRACULA see TOMB OF DRACULA
The Spectacular SCARLET SPIDER see Spectacular SPIDER-MAN
SCAR FACE see THE CRUSADERS
SCARECROW see MARVEL SPOTLIGHT
SECRET AGENT see SARGE STEEL
SEEKER 3000 see MARVEL PREMIERE
SHI/CYBLADE see CYBLADE/SHI
SHINING KNIGHT see ADVENTURE Comics
Talent SHOWCASE see NEW TALENT SHOWCASE
SPEED DEMON see AMALGAM Comics
SPELLBOUND? see THE CRUSADERS
SPIDER-BOY see AMALGAM Comics
STORYTELLERS see FAST FORWARD
SUPER SOLDIER see AMALGAM Comics
THE SURVIVORS see JEREMIAH
TAKEN UNDER see CALIBER PRESENTS
The TARANTULA see WEIRD SUSPENSE
TEMPORARY NATIVES see TALES FROM THE HEART
Captain Marvel Presents THE TERRIBLE 5 see CAPTAIN MARVEL (MF)
TET '68 see VIETNAM JOURNAL
3-D MAN see MARVEL PREMIERE
TIGER BOY see UNEARTHLY SPECTACULARS
TOM, DICK AND HARRIET see GOLD KEY SPOTLIGHT
TOMMY TOMORROW see SHOWCASE
The TOMORROW SYNDICATE see 1963
TORPEDO see MARVEL PREMIERE
TOTAL WAR see M.A.R.S. PATROL
Tales of the UNCANNY see 1963
VALLEY OF DEATH see VIETNAM JOURNAL
VIOLENT CASES see ESCAPE
VOYEUSE see FANNY
WACKY ADVENTURES OF CRACKY see GOLD KEY SPOTLIGHT
WACKY WITCH see GOLD KEY SPOTLIGHT
WAR OF THE WORLDS see AMAZING ADVENTURES
WARDRUMS see JOURNEY
WARRIOR (DC) see GUY GARDNER
WARRIORS THREE see MARVEL SPOTLIGHT
THE WEDDING OF DRACULA see TOMB OF DRACULA
WEIRDWORLD see MARVEL FANFARE, MARVEL PREMIERE, MARVEL SUPER SPECIAL
WELCOME TO ALFLOFOL see VALERIAN
WOLF PACK see COMICS GREATEST WORLD
WOODGOD see MARVEL PREMIERE
WORLD WITHOUT STARS see VALERIAN
X-MEN CLASSICS see CLASSIC X-MEN
X-PATROL see AMALGAM Comics
X-THIEVES see Aristocratic Xtraterrestrial Time-Travelling Thieves

INDEX OF CREATORS

The first number listed refers to the page number, and the bracketed number refers to the number of entries on that page mentioning the creator, if more than one. Please note that where one review covers an entire page a creator may be mentioned in connection with several strips, but will only be noted once for that page in this index. Where an entry runs over onto the following page creators are indexed under both pages by means of a hyphen. A further entry on the second page will then be noted separately.

Please note that index references contain mentions of a creator's name in an entry that they may not have contributed to as well as those to which they have contributed. This is particularly the case with regard to influential artists such as Adams, Caniff, Eisner and Toth. Authors whose works have been adapted are not listed unless they've had a direct input into the adaptation. Some European creators are known only by their first name or surname. We've supplied their full name wherever possible.

Pratt, George 147, 256, 358, 475, 488
Pratt, Hugo 102–103, 123–124, 263, 395
Preiss, Byron 464
Premiani, Bruno 173–174, 388, 670
Prewett, Archer 674
Priest, Christopher (*see also* Jack C. Harris) 312, 455
Pritchett, Andy 576
Proctor, Jenny 600
Proger, H.K. 545
Propst, Mark 34, 514
Prosser, Jerry 17, 28, 132, 505, 658
Pruett, Joe 397
Puckett, Kelley 52
Pugh, David 340, 507
Pugh, Steve 28, 470
Pulido, Brian 197, 327, 448
Purcell, Gordon 499, 534, 535, 536, 537, 659
Purcell, Steve 130, 207, 252, 471
Purves, Jeff 279
Putney, Susan 525
Pyman, James 408
Quagmire, Joshua 130, 134
Quesada, Joe 35, 132, 392, 410, 455, 519, 569
Quinlan, Charles 239
Quinn, David 100, 169, 207, 408
Quitely, Frank 63, 143, 217
Raab, Ben 205, 527
Raboy, Mac 239
Raine, Wyndham 503
Rall, Ted 396
Rambo, Pamela 667
Ramos, Humberto 35, 181, 230, 280, 285, 665
Ramos, Rodney 241, 541
Rancourt, Sylvie 370
Randall, Ron 18, 155, 178, 438, 459, 487, 599, 630
Raney, Tom 545
Rankin, Rich 456
Ranson, Arthur 144, 321, 443–444
Rausch, Barb 316, 398, 459
Ray, Fred 4, 559, 595
Raymond, Alex 217, 307, 355
Rayner, Richard Piers 331, 547
Rebner, Jeff 136
Redondo, Frank 417
Redondo, Jesus 398
Redondo, Nestor 61, 220, 233, 276, 277, 357, 452, 461, 467, 483, 567, 611, 637, 646
Reed, David 50, 53
Reed, Gary 46
Reese, Ralph 62, 126, 258, 276, 331, 385 (2), 458, 611, 617, 646, 647, 657
Reeves-Stevens, Garfield 535
Reeves-Stevens, Judith 535
Reiche, Volker 172
Reid, Ken 323
Reinhold, Bill 45, 443, 447, 501
Reinman, Paul 218, 220, 350, 376, 377, 612, 661
Rennie, Gordon 495, 643
Reyes, Franc 34, 578
Reynolds, Randy 11
Ribera, Julio 262
Rice, Rich 143, 194
Richards, Ted 119, 176, 236, 323, 330, 355

Richardson, Mike 17, 570, 627
Richardson, Roy 596
Ridgway, John 12, 23, 44, 169, 272, 274, 359, 389, 441, 511, 631
Ridsdale, Caroline 8
Rigg, Pete 323 (2)
Riplinski, Stephen 464
Rival, Rico 233, 430, 483, 611
Rivers, Daniel 237
Rivoche, Paul 16, 383
Roach, David 56, 142, 193, 398, 443, 644
Robbins, Frank 50, 159, 289–290, 354, 432, 489, 504, 533, 556, 597, 637, 641
Robbins, Trina 47–48, 92, 184, 194, 262, 293, 383, 396, 459, 463, 645, 654, 668
Roberts, Mike 64, 467
Roberts, Tom 241
Robertson, Darick 402, 463, 512, 525
Robinson, Andrew 397
Robinson, Cliff 306
Robinson, Dave 600
Robinson, James 80, 145, 193, 195, 211, 238, 248, 321, 330, 540, 584–585, 599, 623, 646
Robinson, Jerry 49, 144, 158, 239 (2), 670
Robinson, Roger 195, 442
Roblin, Chuck 585
Rodia, Debra 92
Rodier, Dennis 274
Rogers, Marshall 53, 93, 125, 160, 161, 168, 184, 205, 262, 276, 284, 349, 381, 489, 501, 519, 611, 637
Romero, César 258
Romita, John 60, 96, 139, 201, 236, 482, 520, 522, 640, 670, 671
Romita, John Jr 56, 141, 292, 355, 358, 446, 447, 520, 525, 663
Rosa, Don 171, 172 (2)–173, 374, 481, 608–609 (2)
Rose, Joel 62, 327
Rosenberger, John 201, 218, 220, 296, 558, 612, 671
Ross, Alex 37, 192, 256, 268, 319, 365–366, 475, 510, 584
Ross, David 639
Ross, Luke 400, 523
Rossi, Christian 203
Rota, Marco 172
Roth, Ed 257, 582
Roth, Werner 339, 661
Rothweiler, Kyle 131, 214
Rouchier, Vince 490
Roulet, Avril 179
Roulet, Petit 179
Rovin, Jeff 428
Royer, Mike 272, 300, 351, 380–381, 399, 473, 475
Royle, John 153, 424
Rozakis, Bob 6, 106, 207, 223, 369, 459, 556, 565
Rozum, John 324, 666
Rubi, Melvin 169, 249
Rubinstein, Joe 109, 276, 309, 407
Rudahl, Sharon 27, 119, 510, 645
Rude, Steve 46, 101, 118, 132, 155, 302, 351, 381, 388, 404, 567, 619, 656
Ruffner, Sean 318

Russell, P. Craig 22–23, 34, 54, 144, 191, 194, 284 (2), 290, 293, 350, 382, 397, 398, 406, 422, 425, 427, 457, 464, 466, 474, 488, 498, 532 (2), 577, 647, 653
Russo, Scott 300
Ryan, Kevin 534
Ryan, Matt 205
Ryan, Michael 493
Ryan, Paul 177, 196, 205, 292, 530, 639
Ryan, Tim 183
Saaf, Art 558
Saavedra, Scott 194, 294, 390, 529
Saba, Arn 130, 398
Sabljic, John 396
Sachs, Bernard 62, 482
Sacco, Joe 106, 143, 162, 421, 529, 668
Saenz, Mike 493
St Aubin, Jean-Claude 90
St Pierre, Joe 483
Saito, Takao 441
Sakaguchi, Hisashi 621
Sakai, Stan 14, 130, 251, 515, 614
Sala, Richard 66–67, 84, 89, 150, 223, 439, 549, 603, 674
Sale, Tim 23, 57, 58, 65, 109, 118, 144, 154, 247–248, 390
Salick, Roger 131, 486
Salinas, José Luis 371
Salmons, Tony 624
Saltares, Javier 18, 60, 232, 401, 658
Salter, Ellie 453
Sampayo, Carlos 101, 203, 455, 504
Samura, Hirokai 74
Sanchez, Leopoldo 185–186, 617
Sanders, James 499
Sanderson, Bill 503
Sanderson, Peter 362
Sanford, Jay Allen 465
Santiago, Ernie 220
Santos, Jesse 87
Sattler, Warren 668
Saudelli, Franco 76
Saunders, Buddy 612
Savage Pencil 223, 322
Saviuk, Alex 245, 524, 556
Scarpa, Romano 172, 374, 608
Scarpelli, Henry 479
Schaffenberger, Kurt 5, 6, 10, 299–300, 338–339, 366, 494, 556, 565
Schenk, Christopher 578
Schenkman, Joe 497
Schiff, Jack 49, 275, 390, 610, 655
Schiller, Fred 468
Schoenefeld, Klaus 317
Schomburg, Alex 290, 360
Schorr, Bill 430
Schreck, Bob 143
Schreck, Dean Allen 78
Schrier, Fred 282
Schuiten, Francois 262, 395
Schuiten, Luc 112, 262
Shultheiss, Matthias 102, 125, 263, 442, 575
Schultz, Mark 90, 153, 217, 658
Schwartz, Julie 38, 39, 50, 244, 259, 310, 494, 497, 546, 561
Seagle, Steven T. 20, 23, 248, 249, 277, 314, 438, 475, 512, 628

Sears, Bart 123, 290, 309–310, 350, 666
Seda, Dori 92, 203, 340, 439, 463, 638
Segar, E.C. 433–434
Segrelles, Vincente 262, 396
Segura, Antonio 104, 263–264, 265
Sekikawa, Natsuo 275
Sekowsky, Mike 10, 62, 184, 201, 210, 224, 239 (2), 310–311, 372–373, 389, 427, 432, 482, 545, 567, 590, 651–652
Semeiks, Val 121, 156, 337 (2), 665
Sendlebach, Brian 241, 341
Senior, Geoff 178
Serpieri, Eleuteri 104, 194, 263, 264
Seth 421
Setzer, Buzz 105
Seuling, Carol 493
Seuling, Phil 612
Severin, John 18, 58, 76, 81, 99, 112, 128, 199, 225, 272, 417 (2), 418, 462, 467, 478, 481, 485, 510, 589, 604, 605, 612, 642
Severin, Marie 64, 101, 109, 126, 201, 222, 411, 551, 653
Seyfried, Gerd 27
Shanklin, Ricky 77
Shanower, Eric 26, 113, 191, 256, 401, 404, 438
Sharp, Liam 78, 153, 163, 279, 665
Sharp, Rob 568
Shatner, William 535
Shaw, Scott 92, 97, 118, 449, 643
Shaw, Stan 60
Shelton, Gilbert 27, 32, 200, 209, 236, 272, 282, 322–323, 411–412, 451, 462–463, 649–650, 668, 673
Shepherd, Lucien 621
Sheridan, Dave 282, 323, 329, 462, 506, 509
Sherm 92
Sherman, James 218, 276, 332, 557
Sherman, Mike 546
Shetterley, Will 97
Shick, Lawrence 208
Shiki, Satoshi 462
Shiner, Lewis 254, 644
Shintani, Kaori 33
Shipp, Martin 505
Shirato, Sanpei 315
Shirow, Masamune 29–30, 70, 155, 171, 231, 416, 491
Shoemaker, Terry 401, 673
Shooter, Jim 5, 10, 40, 93, 140, 170, 240, 255, 351, 428, 437, 483 (2), 510, 554, 557, 579, 627, 628, 632, 655
Shores, Syd 140, 362
Showman, Galen 454
Shuster, Joe 3, 4, 8, 159, 559
Siegel, Jerry 3, 4, 8, 10, 159, 218 (2), 377, 559–560
Sienkiewicz, Bill 1, 51, 56, 60, 63, 66, 69, 115, 118, 142, 176, 183, 188, 205, 237, 280, 326, 340, 364, 385, 401, 413, 424, 457, 490, 523, 527, 548, 649
Siergey, Jim 241
Sifakis, Carl 62
Sikela, John 4, 555, 559
Sikoryak, Bob 509
Silkie, Jim 454
Silvestri, Eric 135